Written by
GRANT MORRISON

Art by
IVAN REIS JOE PRADO CHRIS SPROUSE KARL STORY
WALDEN WONG BEN OLIVER FRANK QUITELY CAMERON STEWART
MARCUS TO PAULO SIQUEIRA JIM LEE SCOTT WILLIAMS
SANDRA HOPE MARK IRWIN JONATHAN GLAPION DOUG MAHNKE
CHRISTIAN ALAMY KEITH CHAMPAGNE JAIME MENDOZA EBER FERREIRA

Colors by
NEI RUFFINO DAVE McCAIG BEN OLIVER DAN BROWN
NATHAN FAIRBAIRN HI-FI ALEX SINCLAIR JEROMY COX
GABE ELTAEB DAVID BARON JASON WRIGHT BLOND

Letters by
TODD KLEIN CARLOS M. MANGUAL CLEM ROBINS ROB LEIGH STEVE WANDS

Dustjacket and Case Art by
RIAN HUGHES, IVAN REIS and JOE PRADO

Original Series Covers by
IVAN REIS and JOE PRADO with NEI RUFFINO and DAN BROWN
CHRIS SPROUSE with DAVE McCAIG FRANK QUITELY with NATHAN FAIRBAIRN
BEN OLIVER CAMERON STEWART RIAN HUGHES
JIM LEE with RIAN HUGHES DOUG MAHNKE with DAVID BARON

SUPERMAN created by Jerry Siegel and Joe Shuster
By Special Arrangement with the Jerry Siegel Family

THE MULTIVERSITY

THE MULTIVERSITY

Published by DC Comics. All new material Copyright © 2016 DC Comics. All Rights Reserved.

Original compilation published as THE MULTIVERSITY: THE DELUXE EDITION. Copyright © 2015. Originally published in single magazine form as THE MULTIVERSITY 1-2, THE MULTIVERSITY: THE SOCIETY OF SUPER-HEROES 1, THE MULTIVERSITY: THE JUST 1, THE MULTIVERSITY: PAX AMERICANA 1, THE MULTIVERSITY: THUNDERWORLD ADVENTURES 1, THE MULTIVERSITY GUIDEBOOK 1, THE MULTIVERSITY: MASTERMEN 1 and THE MULTIVERSITY: ULTRA COMICS 1. Copyright © 2014, 2015 DC Comics. All Rights Reserved. All characters, their distinctive likenesses and related elements featured in this publication are trademarks of DC Comics. The stories, characters and incidents featured in this publication are entirely fictional. DC Comics does not read or accept unsolicited submissions of ideas, stories or artwork.

DC Comics, 2900 West Alameda Avenue, Burbank, CA 91505
Printed by Solisco Printers, Scott, QC, Canada. 10/14/16. First Printing.
ISBN: 978-1-4012-6525-0
Library of Congress Cataloging-in-Publication Data is available.

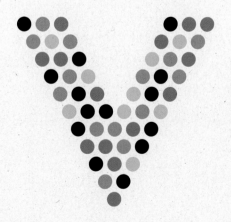

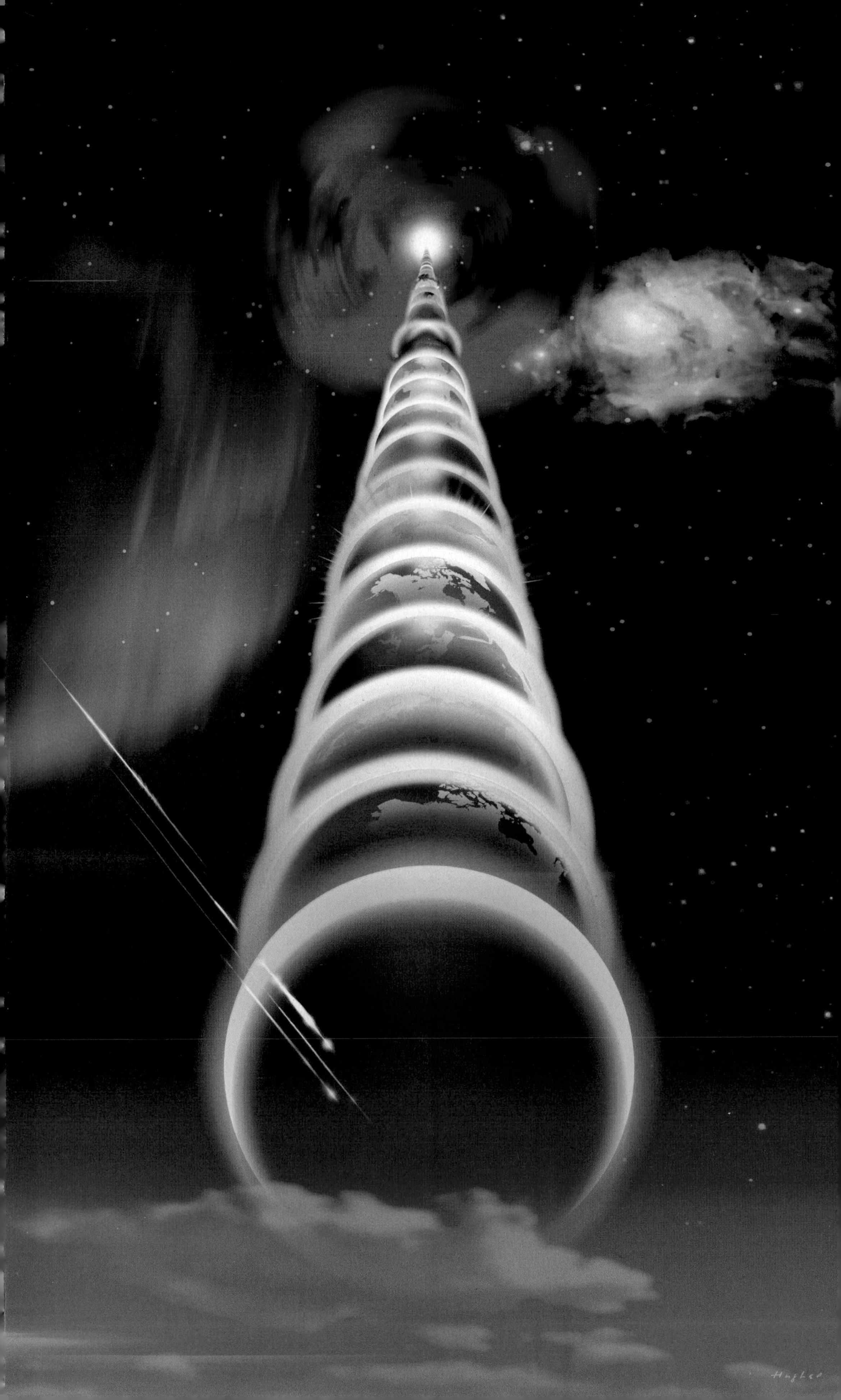
Hughes

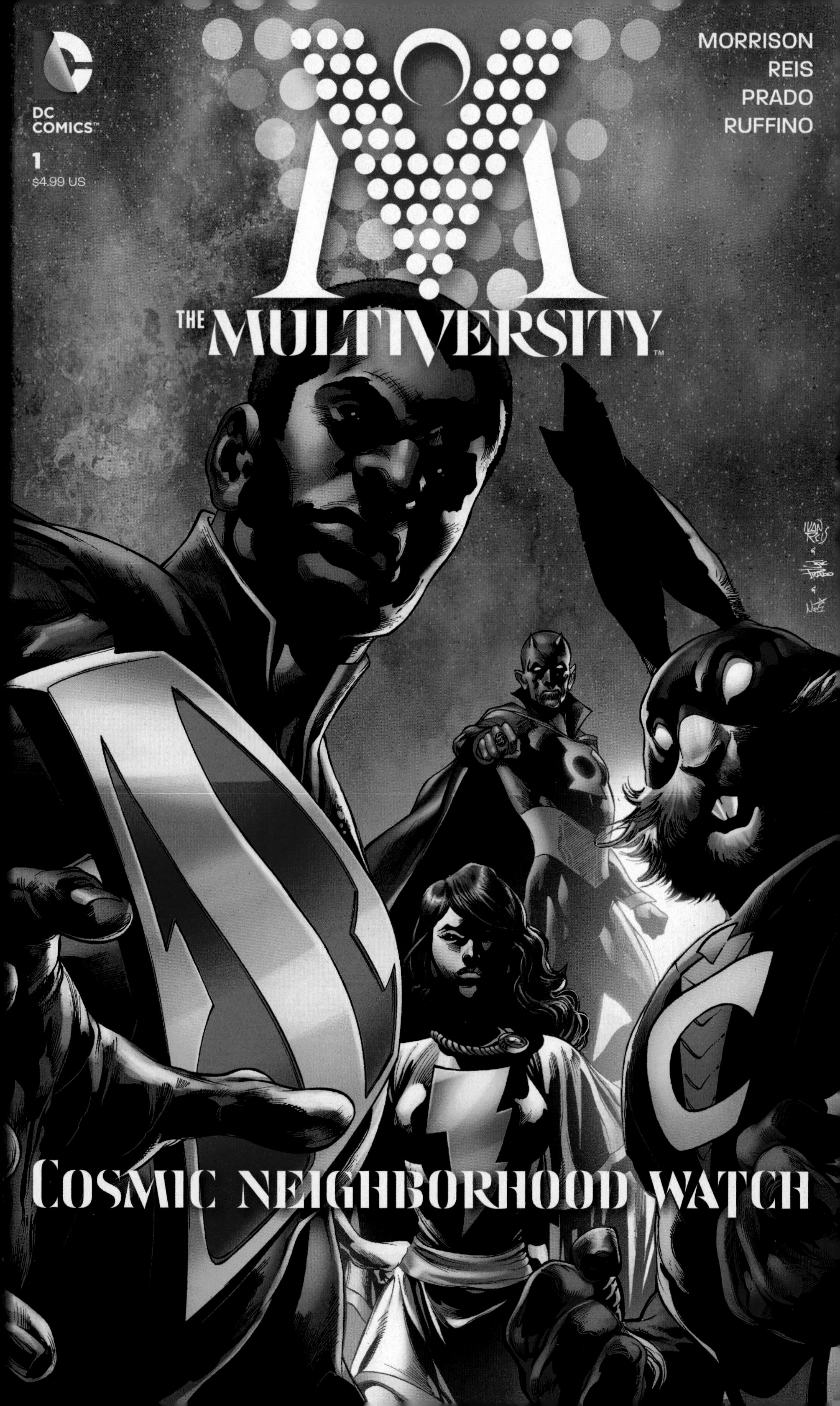

DC COMICS
1
$4.99 US
MORRISON
REIS
PRADO
RUFFINO
THE MULTIVERSITY
COSMIC NEIGHBORHOOD WATCH

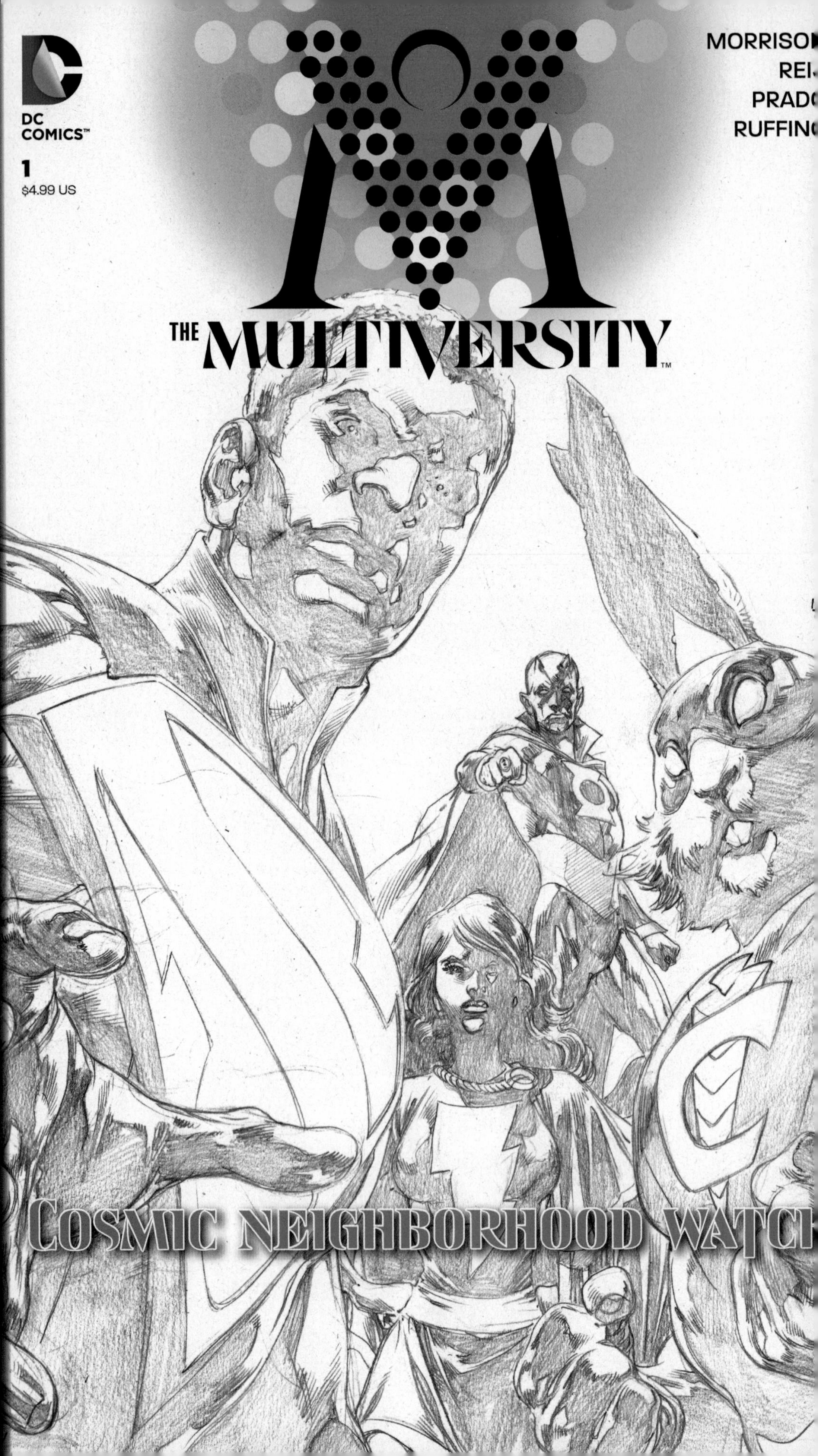

DC COMICS™
1
$4.99 US
MORRISO
REI
PRAD
RUFFIN
THE MULTIVERSITY™
COSMIC NEIGHBORHOOD WATC

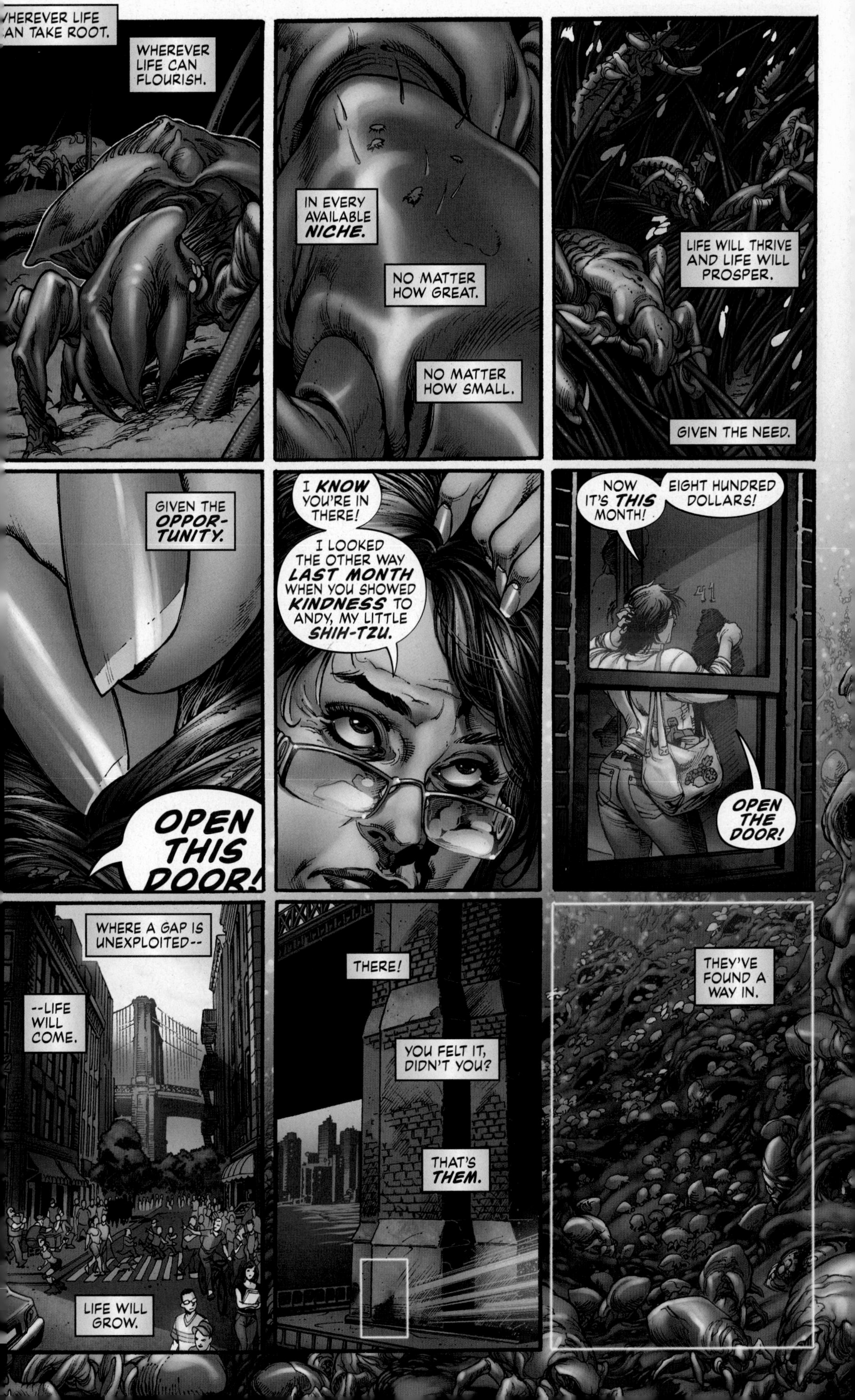

WHEREVER LIFE CAN TAKE ROOT.
WHEREVER LIFE CAN FLOURISH.
IN EVERY AVAILABLE NICHE.
NO MATTER HOW GREAT.
NO MATTER HOW SMALL.
LIFE WILL THRIVE AND LIFE WILL PROSPER.
GIVEN THE NEED.
GIVEN THE OPPORTUNITY.
OPEN THIS DOOR!
I KNOW YOU'RE IN THERE!
I LOOKED THE OTHER WAY LAST MONTH WHEN YOU SHOWED KINDNESS TO ANDY, MY LITTLE SHIH-TZU.
NOW IT'S THIS MONTH!
EIGHT HUNDRED DOLLARS!
OPEN THE DOOR!
WHERE A GAP IS UNEXPLOITED--
--LIFE WILL COME.
LIFE WILL GROW.
THERE!
YOU FELT IT, DIDN'T YOU?
THAT'S THEM.
THEY'VE FOUND A WAY IN.

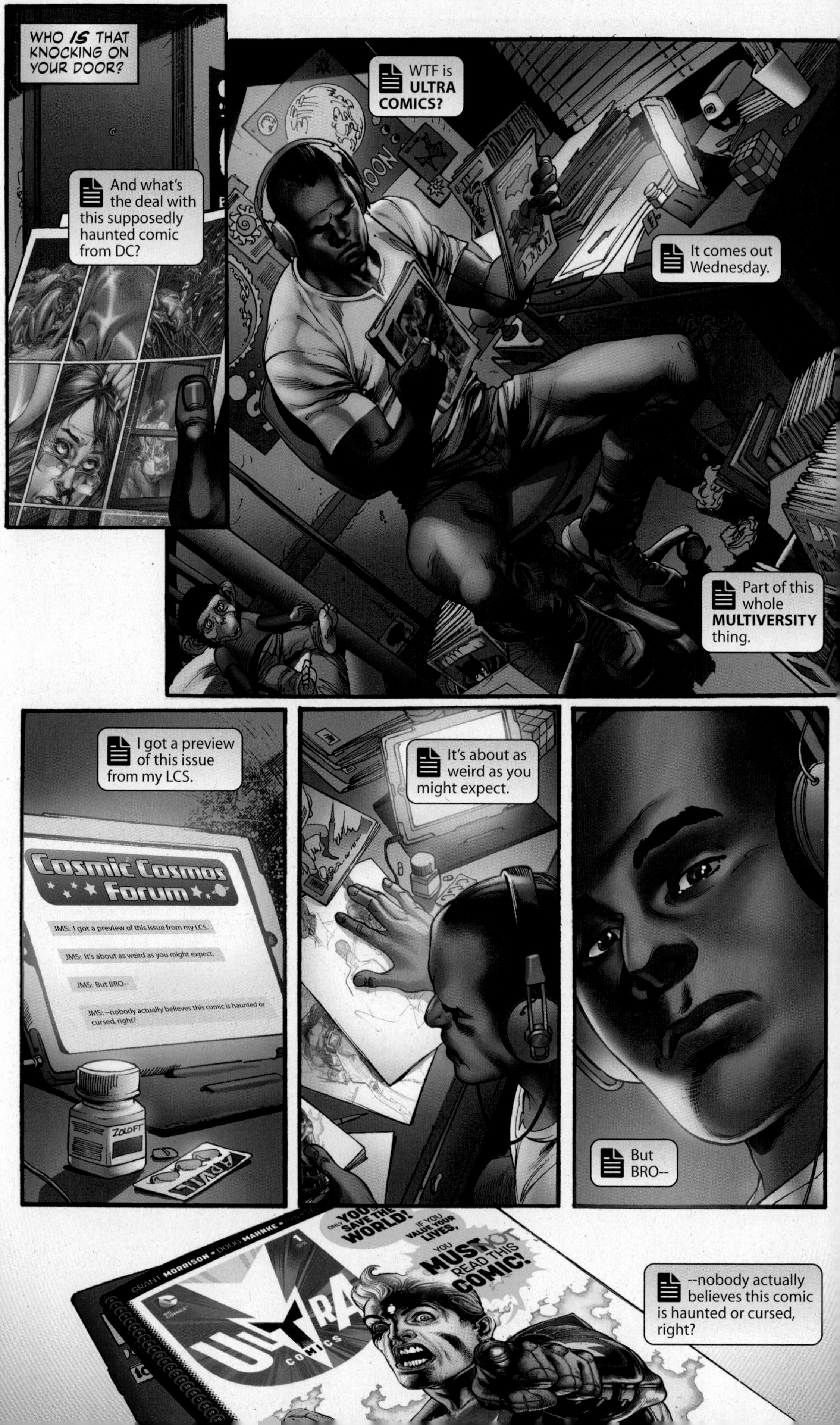

WHO IS THAT KNOCKING ON YOUR DOOR?
And what's the deal with this supposedly haunted comic from DC?
WTF is ULTRA COMICS?
It comes out Wednesday.
Part of this whole MULTIVERSITY thing.
I got a preview of this issue from my LCS.
Cosmic Cosmos Forum
JMS: I got a preview of this issue from my LCS.
JMS: It's about as weird as you might expect.
JMS: But BRO--
JMS: --nobody actually believes this comic is haunted or cursed, right?
ZOLOFT
ADVIL
It's about as weird as you might expect.
But BRO--
IF YOU VALUE YOUR LIVES, YOU MUST NOT READ THIS COMIC!
GRANT MORRISON • DOUG MAHNKE
ULTRA COMICS
--nobody actually believes this comic is haunted or cursed, right?

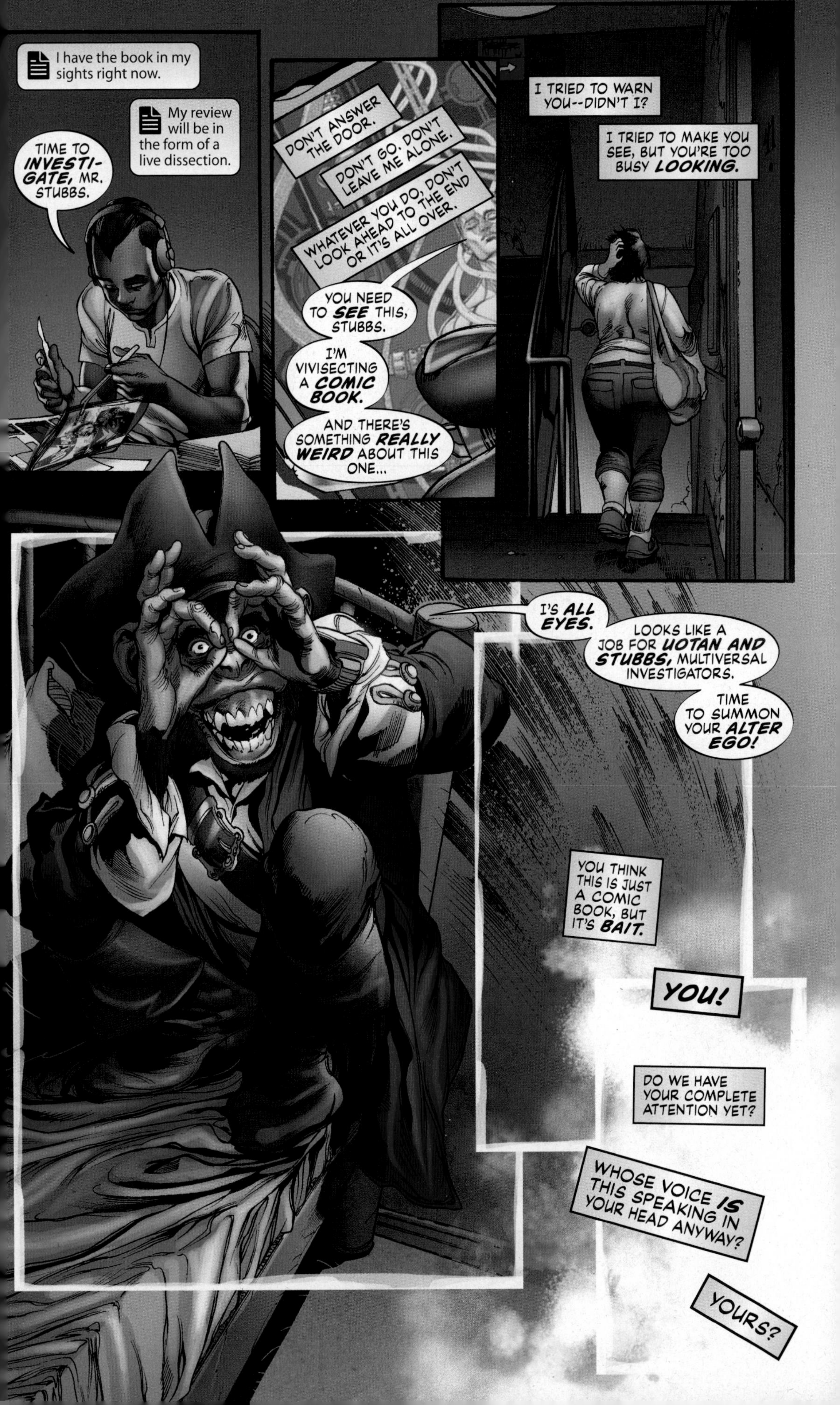

I have the book in my sights right now.
My review will be in the form of a live dissection.
TIME TO INVESTI-GATE, MR. STUBBS.
DON'T ANSWER THE DOOR.
DON'T GO. DON'T LEAVE ME ALONE.
WHATEVER YOU DO, DON'T LOOK AHEAD TO THE END OR IT'S ALL OVER.
YOU NEED TO SEE THIS, STUBBS.
I'M VIVISECTING A COMIC BOOK.
AND THERE'S SOMETHING REALLY WEIRD ABOUT THIS ONE...
I TRIED TO WARN YOU--DIDN'T I?
I TRIED TO MAKE YOU SEE, BUT YOU'RE TOO BUSY LOOKING.
I'S ALL EYES.
LOOKS LIKE A JOB FOR UOTAN AND STUBBS, MULTIVERSAL INVESTIGATORS.
TIME TO SUMMON YOUR ALTER EGO!
YOU THINK THIS IS JUST A COMIC BOOK, BUT IT'S BAIT.
YOU!
DO WE HAVE YOUR COMPLETE ATTENTION YET?
WHOSE VOICE IS THIS SPEAKING IN YOUR HEAD ANYWAY?
YOURS?

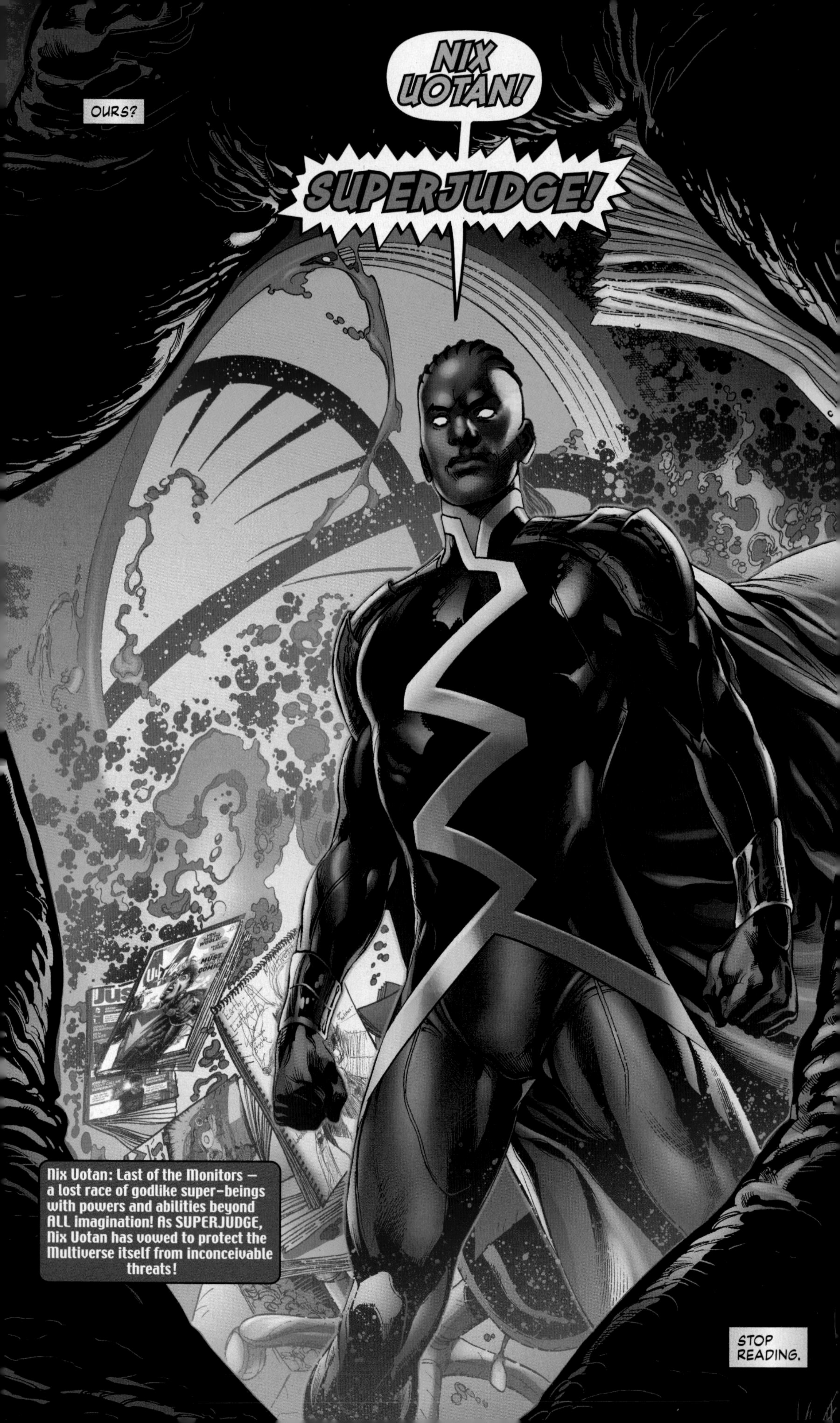
OURS?
NIX UOTAN!
SUPERJUDGE!
Nix Uotan: Last of the Monitors — a lost race of godlike super-beings with powers and abilities beyond ALL imagination! As SUPERJUDGE, Nix Uotan has vowed to protect the Multiverse itself from inconceivable threats!
STOP READING.

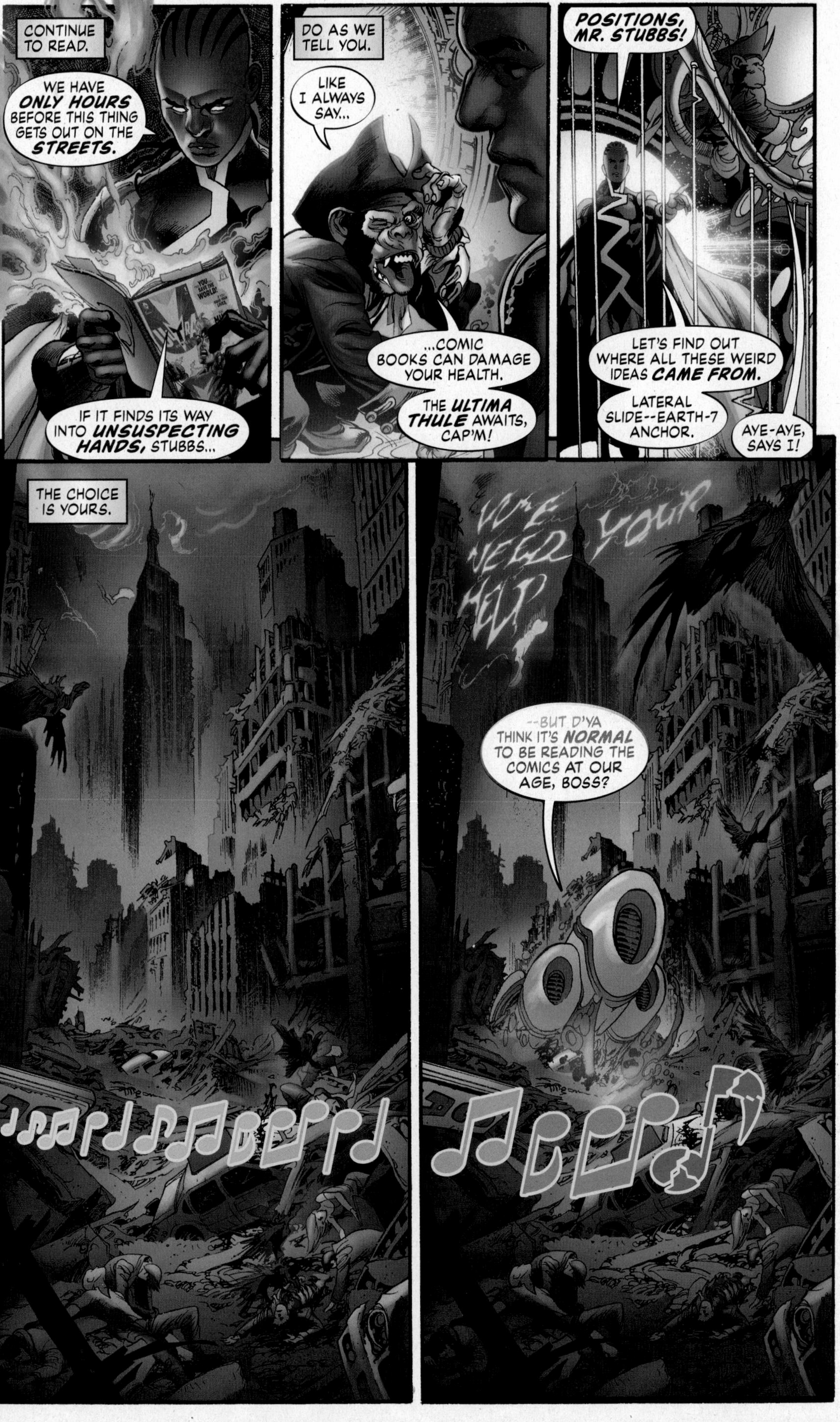
CONTINUE TO READ.
WE HAVE ONLY HOURS BEFORE THIS THING GETS OUT ON THE STREETS.
IF IT FINDS ITS WAY INTO UNSUSPECTING HANDS, STUBBS...
DO AS WE TELL YOU.
LIKE I ALWAYS SAY...
...COMIC BOOKS CAN DAMAGE YOUR HEALTH.
THE ULTIMA THULE AWAITS, CAP'M!
POSITIONS, MR. STUBBS!
LET'S FIND OUT WHERE ALL THESE WEIRD IDEAS CAME FROM.
LATERAL SLIDE--EARTH-7 ANCHOR.
AYE-AYE, SAYS I!
THE CHOICE IS YOURS.
WE NEED YOUR HELP
--BUT D'YA THINK IT'S NORMAL TO BE READING THE COMICS AT OUR AGE, BOSS?

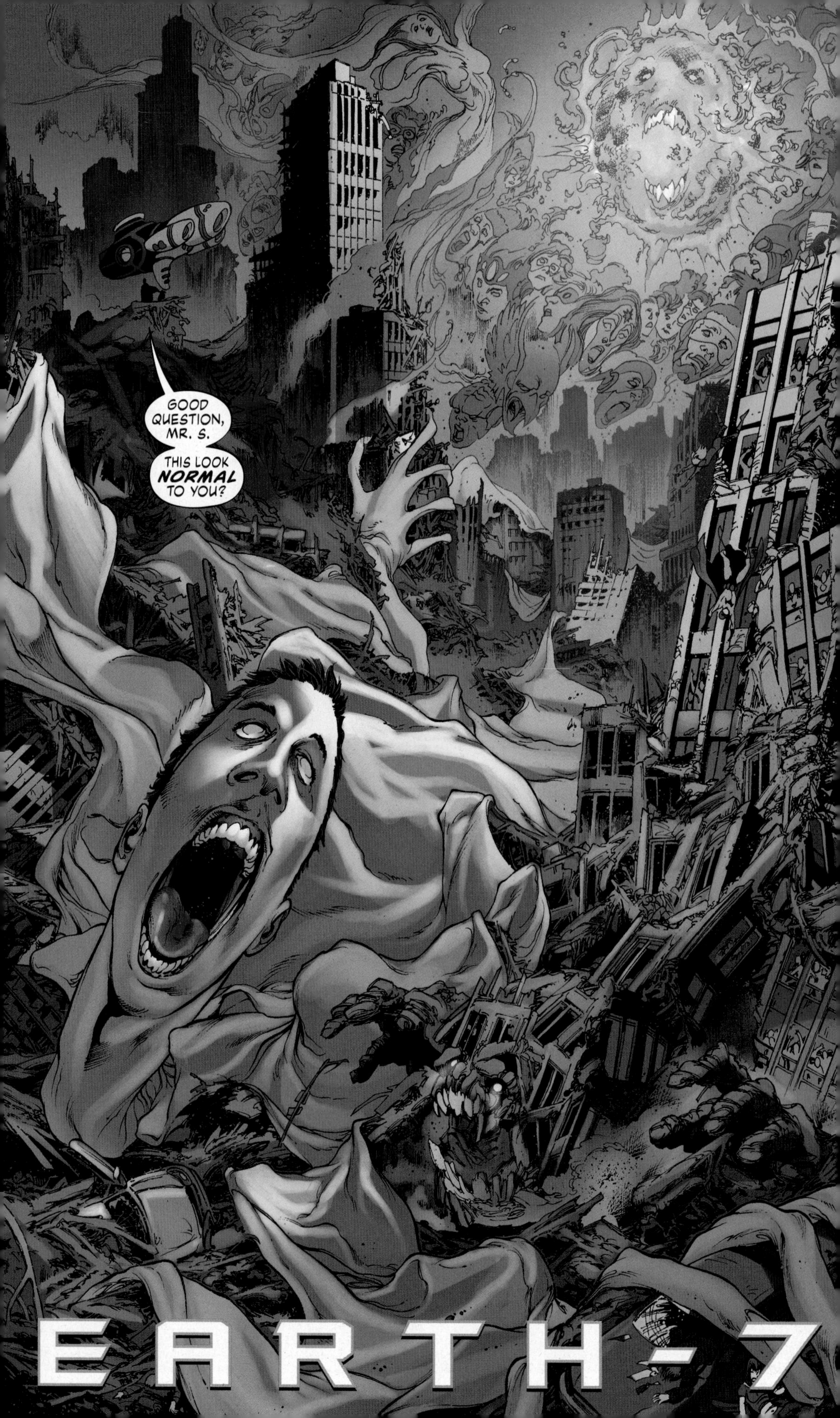
GOOD QUESTION, MR. S.
THIS LOOK **NORMAL** TO YOU?
EARTH-7

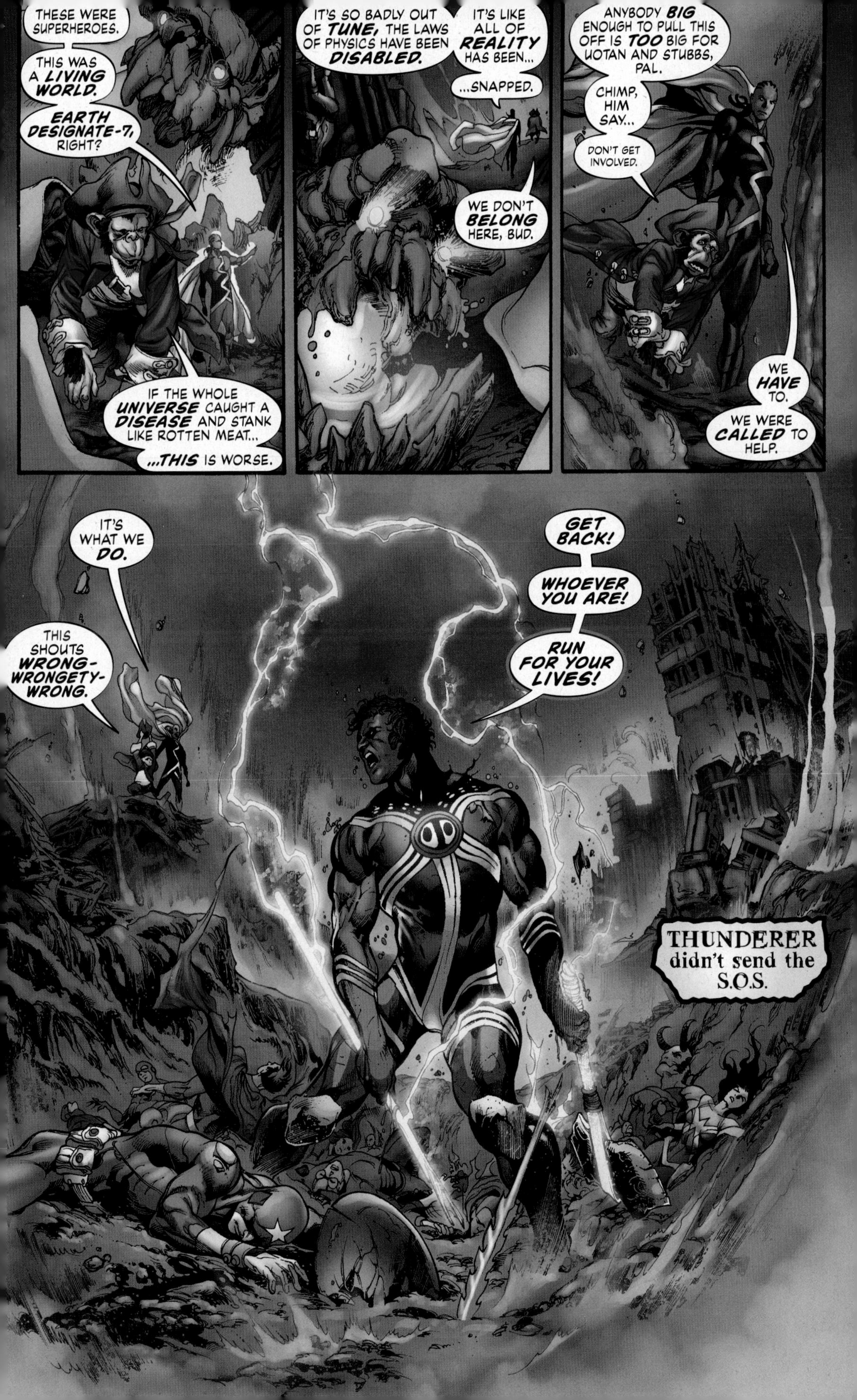
THESE WERE SUPERHEROES.
THIS WAS A LIVING WORLD.
EARTH DESIGNATE-7, RIGHT?
IF THE WHOLE UNIVERSE CAUGHT A DISEASE AND STANK LIKE ROTTEN MEAT...
...THIS IS WORSE.
IT'S SO BADLY OUT OF TUNE, THE LAWS OF PHYSICS HAVE BEEN DISABLED.
IT'S LIKE ALL OF REALITY HAS BEEN...
...SNAPPED.
WE DON'T BELONG HERE, BUD.
ANYBODY BIG ENOUGH TO PULL THIS OFF IS TOO BIG FOR UOTAN AND STUBBS, PAL.
CHIMP, HIM SAY...
DON'T GET INVOLVED.
WE HAVE TO.
WE WERE CALLED TO HELP.
IT'S WHAT WE DO.
THIS SHOUTS WRONG-WRONGETY-WRONG.
GET BACK!
WHOEVER YOU ARE!
RUN FOR YOUR LIVES!
THUNDERER didn't send the S.O.S.

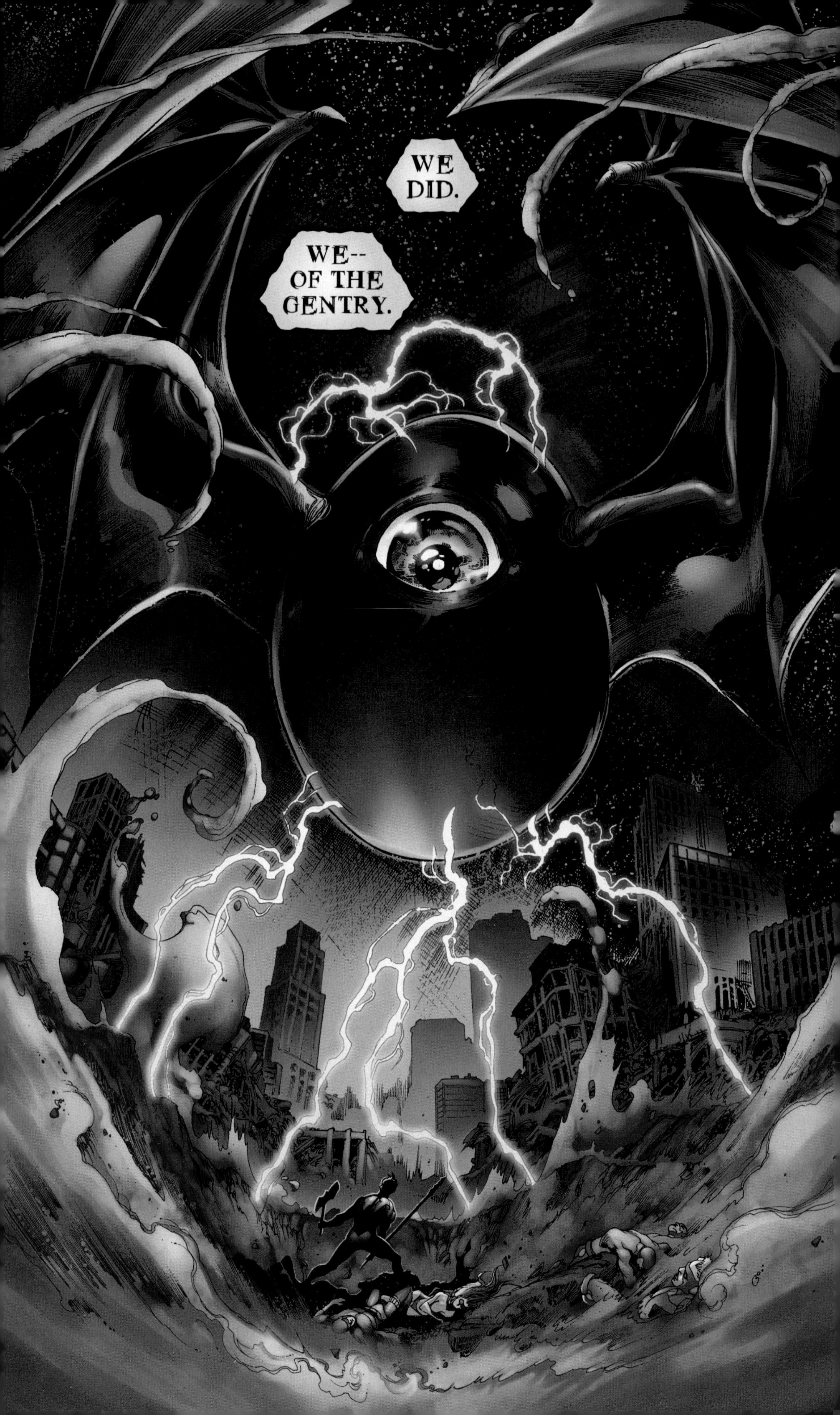
WE DID.
WE-- OF THE GENTRY.

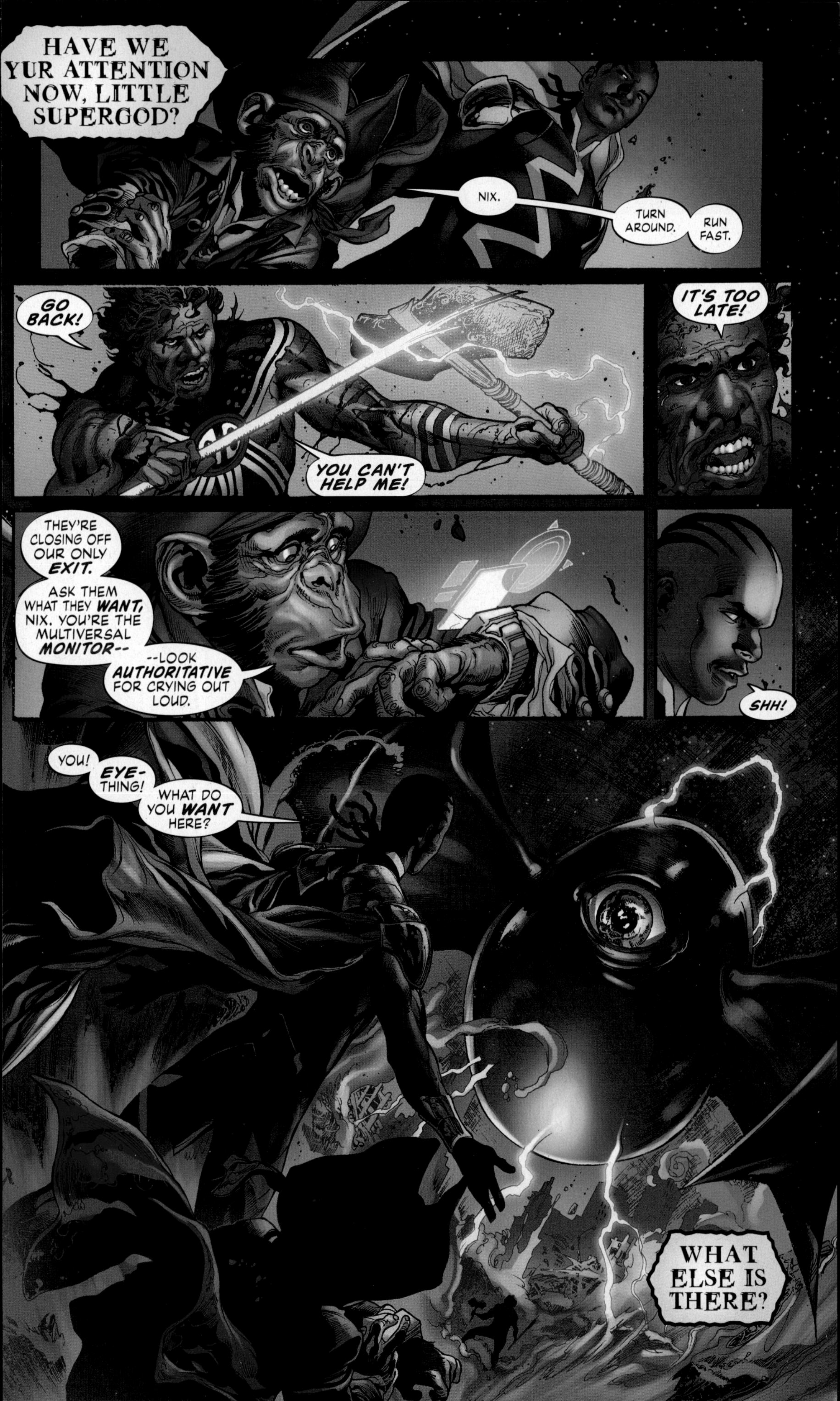
HAVE WE YUR ATTENTION NOW, LITTLE SUPERGOD?
NIX.
TURN AROUND.
RUN FAST.
GO BACK!
YOU CAN'T HELP ME!
IT'S TOO LATE!
THEY'RE CLOSING OFF OUR ONLY EXIT.
ASK THEM WHAT THEY WANT, NIX. YOU'RE THE MULTIVERSAL MONITOR--
--LOOK AUTHORITATIVE FOR CRYING OUT LOUD.
SHH!
YOU!
EYE-THING!
WHAT DO YOU WANT HERE?
WHAT ELSE IS THERE?

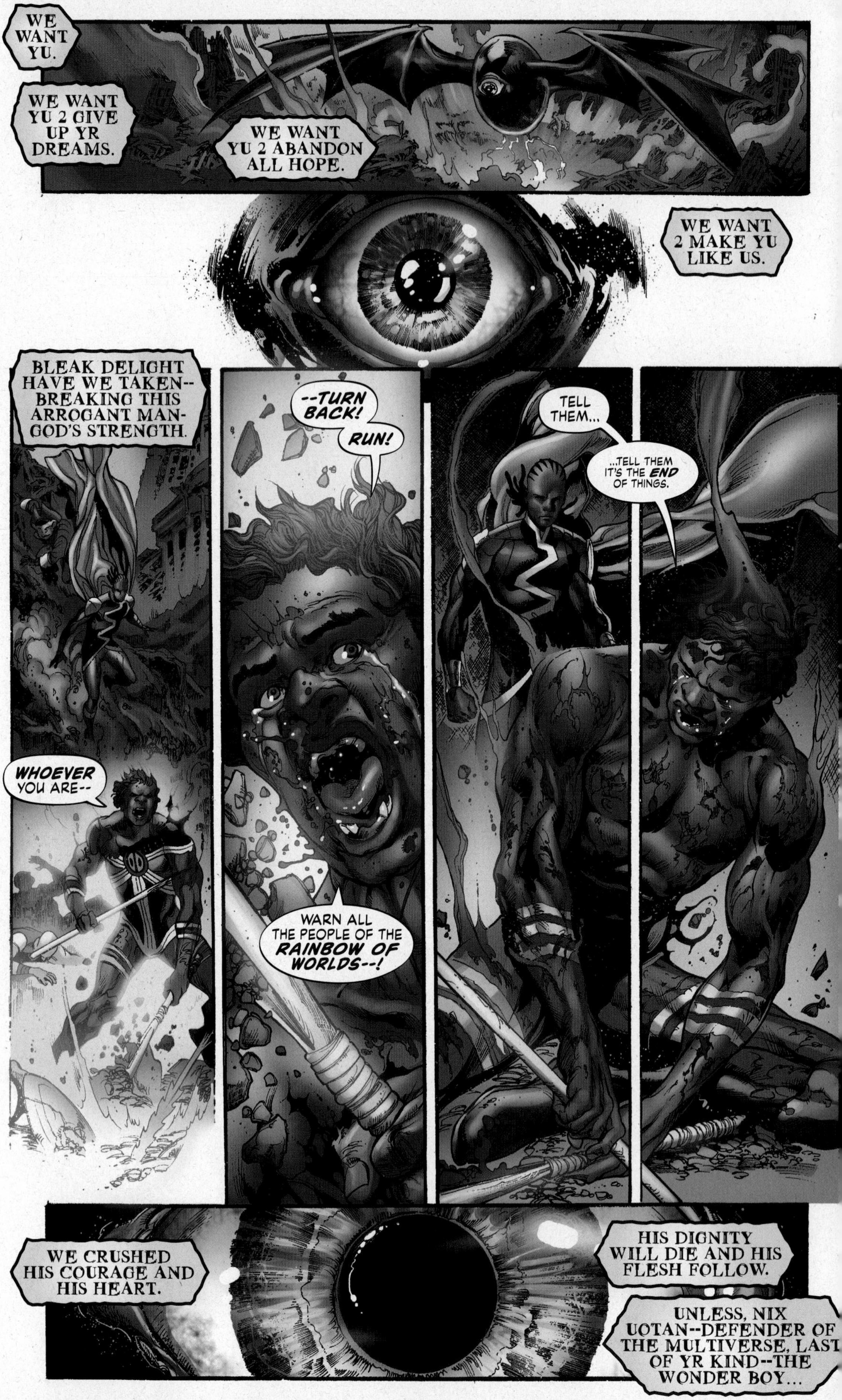

WE WANT YU.
WE WANT YU 2 GIVE UP YR DREAMS.
WE WANT YU 2 ABANDON ALL HOPE.
WE WANT 2 MAKE YU LIKE US.
BLEAK DELIGHT HAVE WE TAKEN--BREAKING THIS ARROGANT MAN-GOD'S STRENGTH.
WHOEVER YOU ARE--
--TURN BACK!
RUN!
WARN ALL THE PEOPLE OF THE RAINBOW OF WORLDS--!
TELL THEM...
...TELL THEM IT'S THE END OF THINGS.
WE CRUSHED HIS COURAGE AND HIS HEART.
HIS DIGNITY WILL DIE AND HIS FLESH FOLLOW.
UNLESS, NIX UOTAN--DEFENDER OF THE MULTIVERSE, LAST OF YR KIND--THE WONDER BOY...

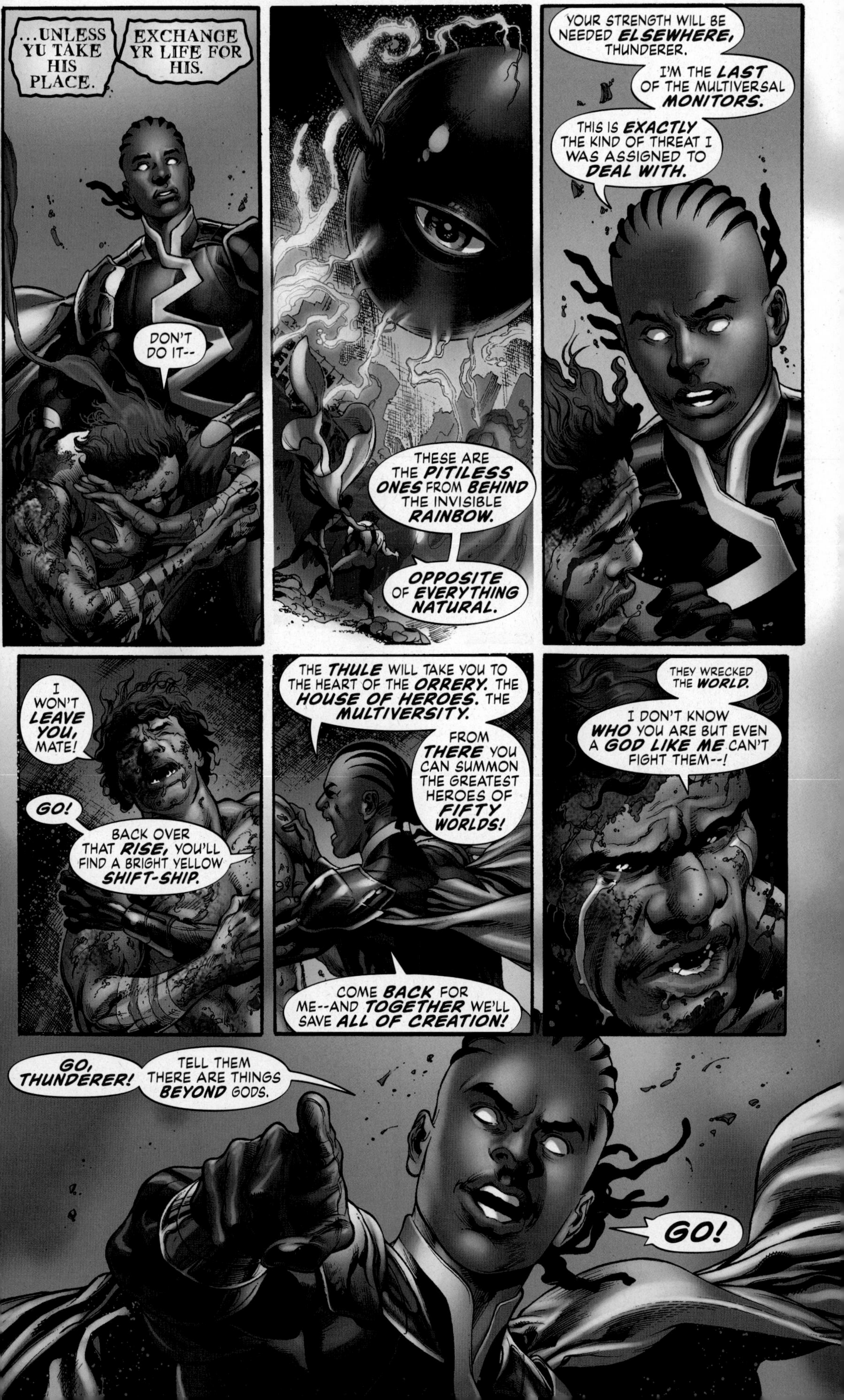

...UNLESS YU TAKE HIS PLACE.
EXCHANGE YR LIFE FOR HIS.
DON'T DO IT--
THESE ARE THE PITILESS ONES FROM BEHIND THE INVISIBLE RAINBOW.
OPPOSITE OF EVERYTHING NATURAL.
YOUR STRENGTH WILL BE NEEDED ELSEWHERE, THUNDERER.
I'M THE LAST OF THE MULTIVERSAL MONITORS.
THIS IS EXACTLY THE KIND OF THREAT I WAS ASSIGNED TO DEAL WITH.
I WON'T LEAVE YOU, MATE!
GO!
BACK OVER THAT RISE, YOU'LL FIND A BRIGHT YELLOW SHIFT-SHIP.
THE THULE WILL TAKE YOU TO THE HEART OF THE ORRERY. THE HOUSE OF HEROES. THE MULTIVERSITY.
FROM THERE YOU CAN SUMMON THE GREATEST HEROES OF FIFTY WORLDS!
COME BACK FOR ME--AND TOGETHER WE'LL SAVE ALL OF CREATION!
THEY WRECKED THE WORLD.
I DON'T KNOW WHO YOU ARE BUT EVEN A GOD LIKE ME CAN'T FIGHT THEM--!
GO, THUNDERER!
TELL THEM THERE ARE THINGS BEYOND GODS.
GO!

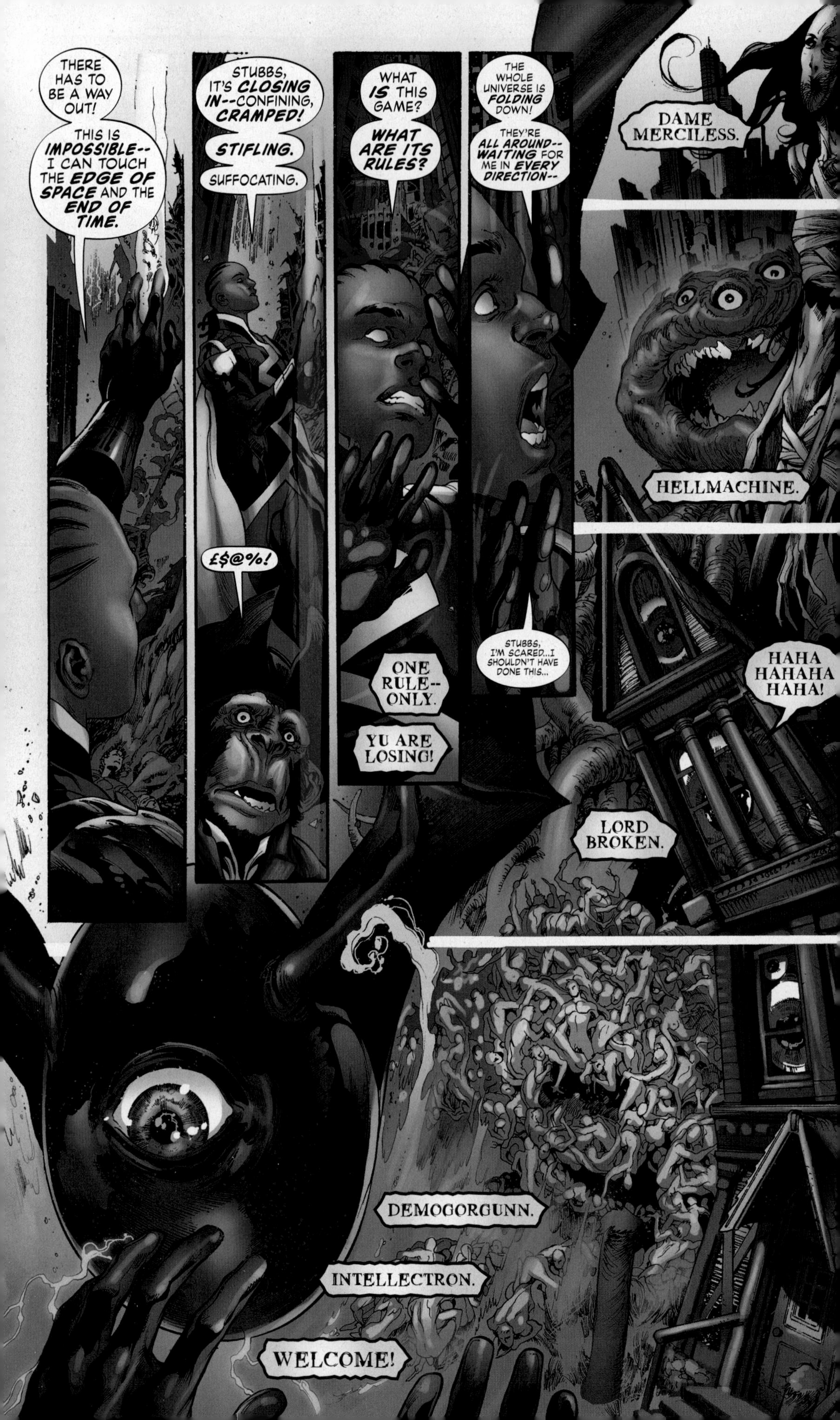
THERE HAS TO BE A WAY OUT!
THIS IS IMPOSSIBLE-- I CAN TOUCH THE EDGE OF SPACE AND THE END OF TIME.
STUBBS, IT'S CLOSING IN--CONFINING, CRAMPED!
STIFLING.
SUFFOCATING.
£$@%!
WHAT IS THIS GAME?
WHAT ARE ITS RULES?
ONE RULE-- ONLY.
YU ARE LOSING!
THE WHOLE UNIVERSE IS FOLDING DOWN!
THEY'RE ALL AROUND-- WAITING FOR ME IN EVERY DIRECTION--
STUBBS, I'M SCARED...I SHOULDN'T HAVE DONE THIS...
DAME MERCILESS.
HELLMACHINE.
HAHA HAHAHA HAHA!
LORD BROKEN.
DEMOGORGUNN.
INTELLECTRON.
WELCOME!

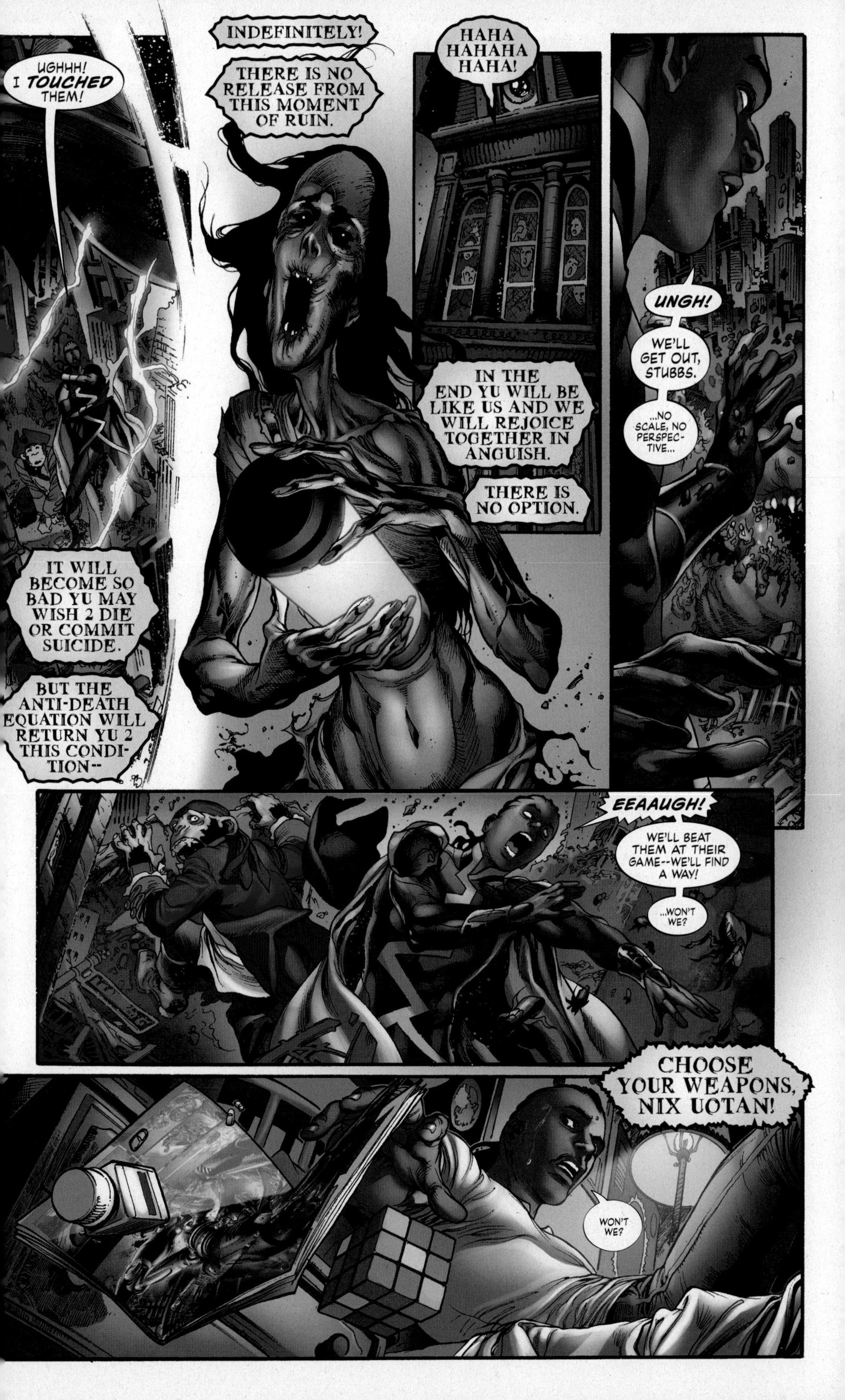
UGHHH! I TOUCHED THEM!
INDEFINITELY!
THERE IS NO RELEASE FROM THIS MOMENT OF RUIN.
HAHA HAHAHA HAHA!
IN THE END YU WILL BE LIKE US AND WE WILL REJOICE TOGETHER IN ANGUISH.
THERE IS NO OPTION.
UNGH!
WE'LL GET OUT, STUBBS.
...NO SCALE, NO PERSPEC-TIVE...
IT WILL BECOME SO BAD YU MAY WISH 2 DIE OR COMMIT SUICIDE.
BUT THE ANTI-DEATH EQUATION WILL RETURN YU 2 THIS CONDI-TION--
EEAAUGH!
WE'LL BEAT THEM AT THEIR GAME--WE'LL FIND A WAY!
...WON'T WE?
CHOOSE YOUR WEAPONS, NIX UOTAN!
WON'T WE?

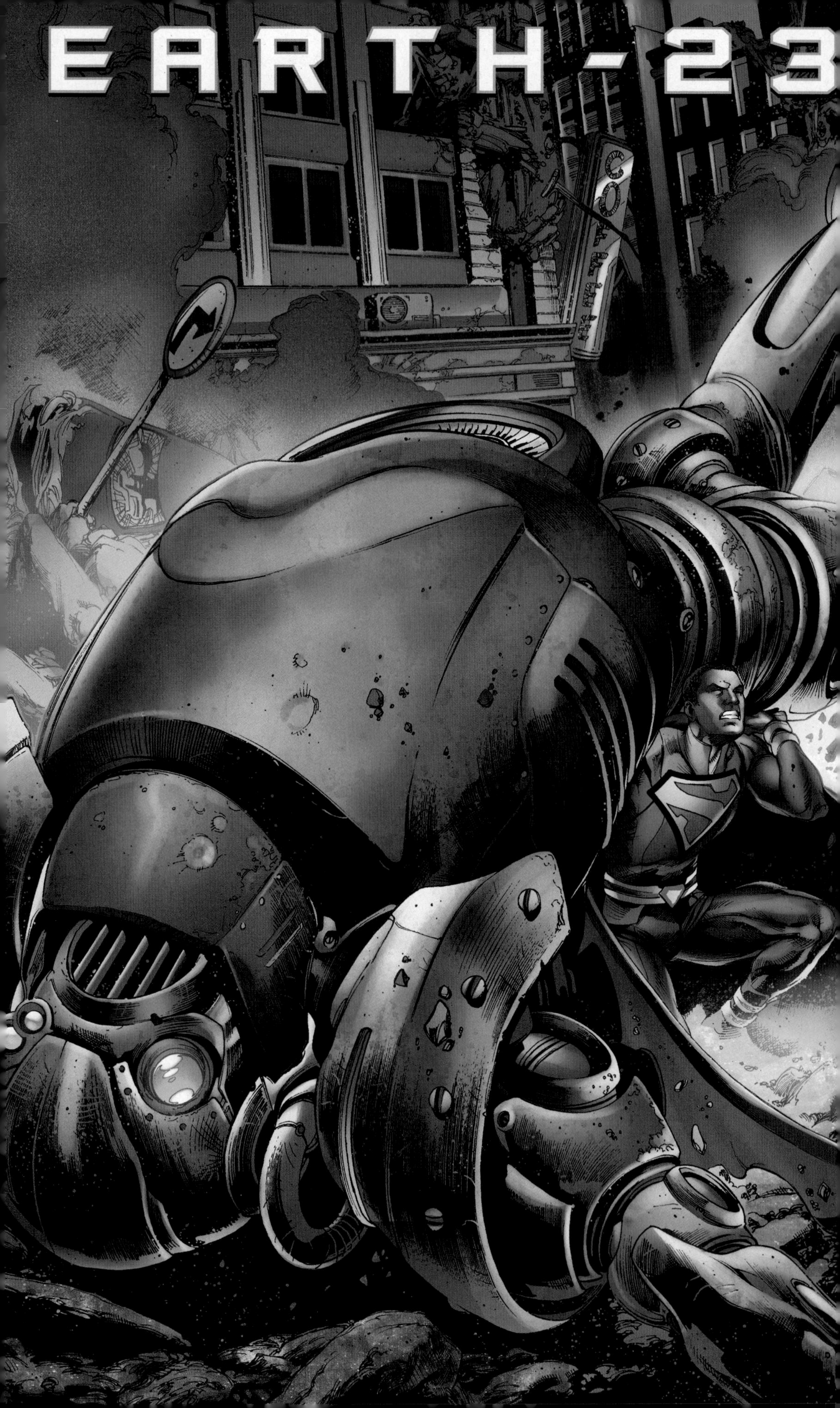
EARTH-23

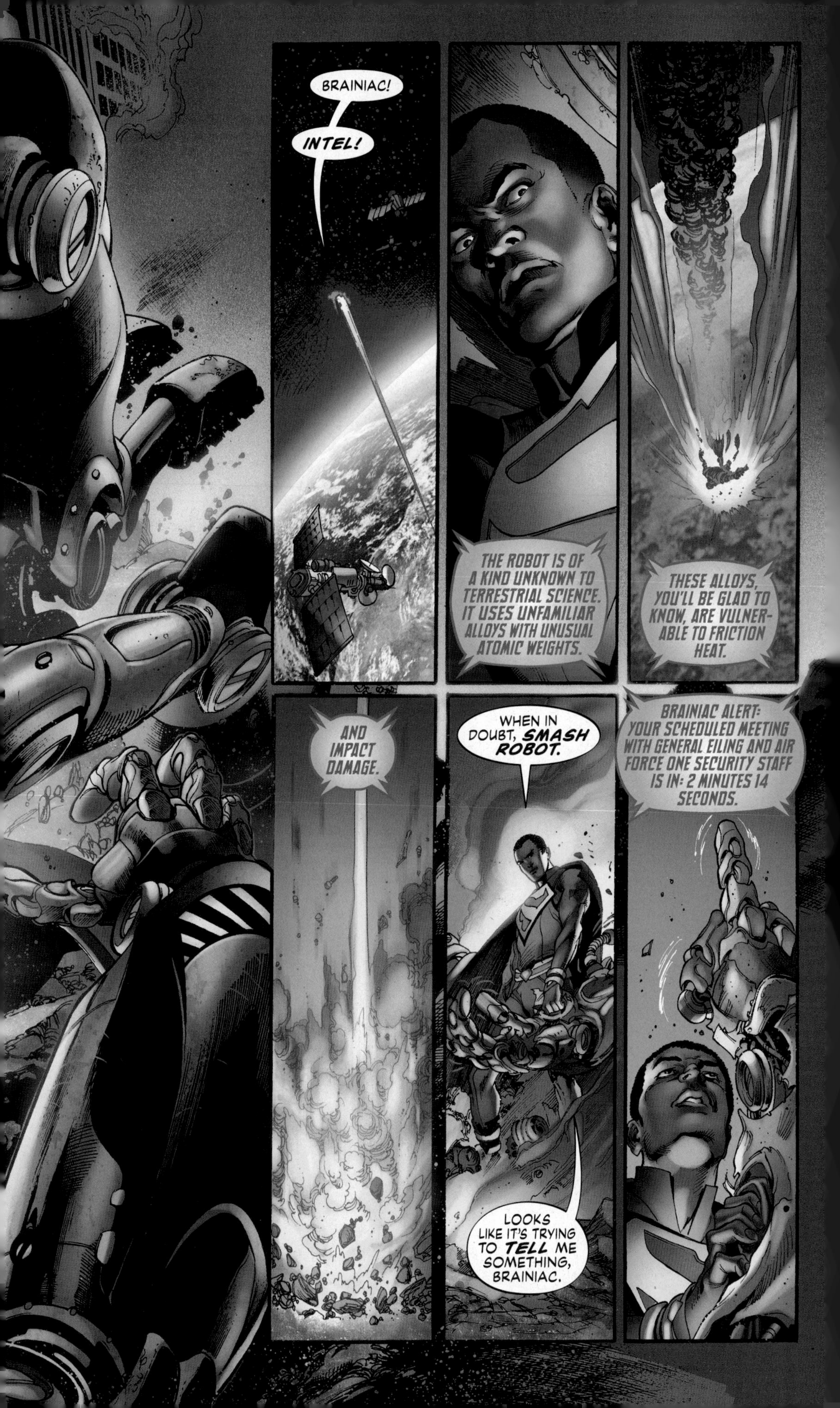
BRAINIAC!
INTEL!
THE ROBOT IS OF A KIND UNKNOWN TO TERRESTRIAL SCIENCE. IT USES UNFAMILIAR ALLOYS WITH UNUSUAL ATOMIC WEIGHTS.
THESE ALLOYS, YOU'LL BE GLAD TO KNOW, ARE VULNERABLE TO FRICTION HEAT.
AND IMPACT DAMAGE.
WHEN IN DOUBT, SMASH ROBOT.
LOOKS LIKE IT'S TRYING TO TELL ME SOMETHING, BRAINIAC.
BRAINIAC ALERT: YOUR SCHEDULED MEETING WITH GENERAL EILING AND AIR FORCE ONE SECURITY STAFF IS IN: 2 MINUTES 14 SECONDS.

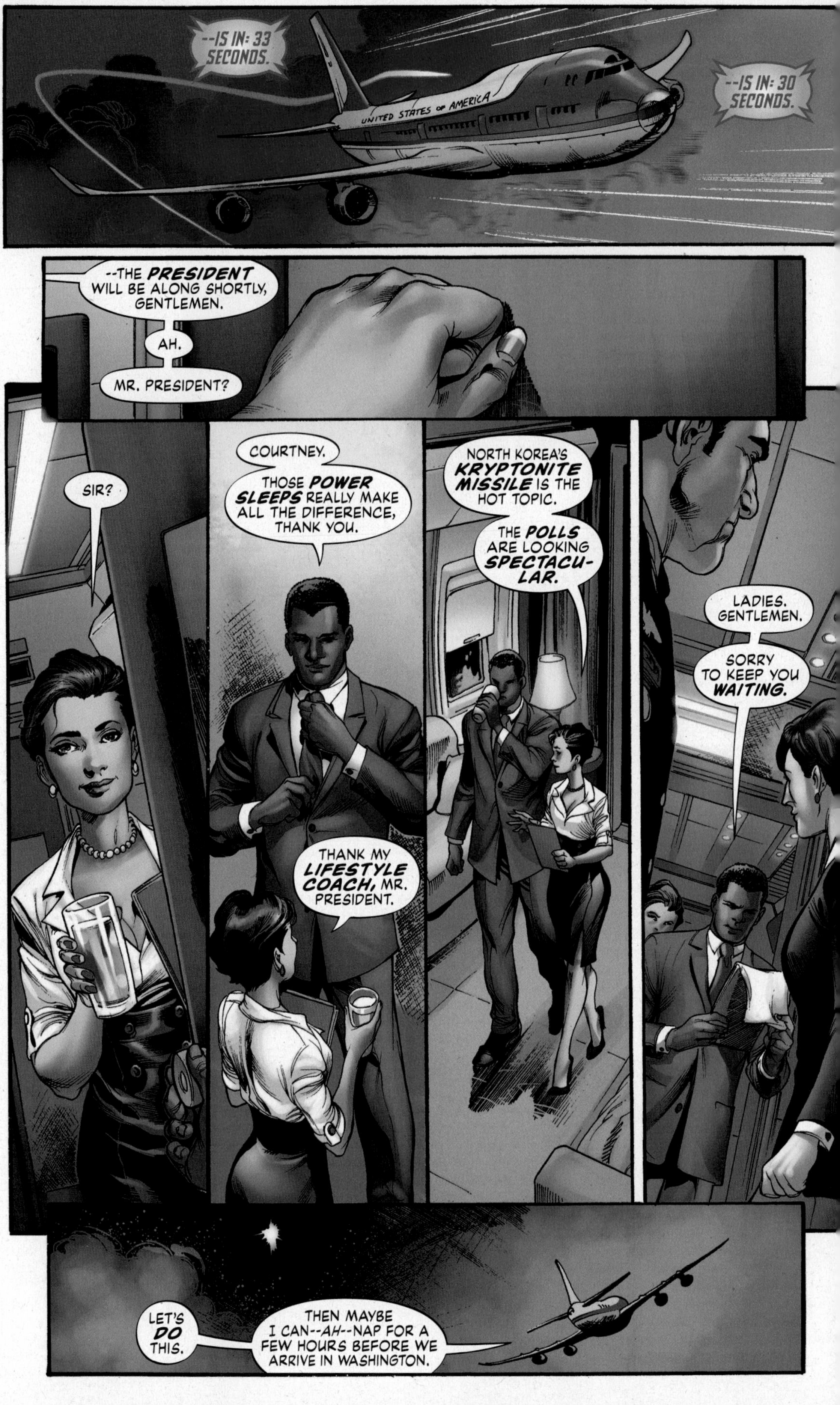
--IS IN: 33 SECONDS.
UNITED STATES OF AMERICA
--IS IN: 30 SECONDS.
--THE PRESIDENT WILL BE ALONG SHORTLY, GENTLEMEN.
AH.
MR. PRESIDENT?
SIR?
COURTNEY.
THOSE POWER SLEEPS REALLY MAKE ALL THE DIFFERENCE, THANK YOU.
THANK MY LIFESTYLE COACH, MR. PRESIDENT.
NORTH KOREA'S KRYPTONITE MISSILE IS THE HOT TOPIC.
THE POLLS ARE LOOKING SPECTACU- LAR.
LADIES. GENTLEMEN.
SORRY TO KEEP YOU WAITING.
LET'S DO THIS.
THEN MAYBE I CAN--AH--NAP FOR A FEW HOURS BEFORE WE ARRIVE IN WASHINGTON.

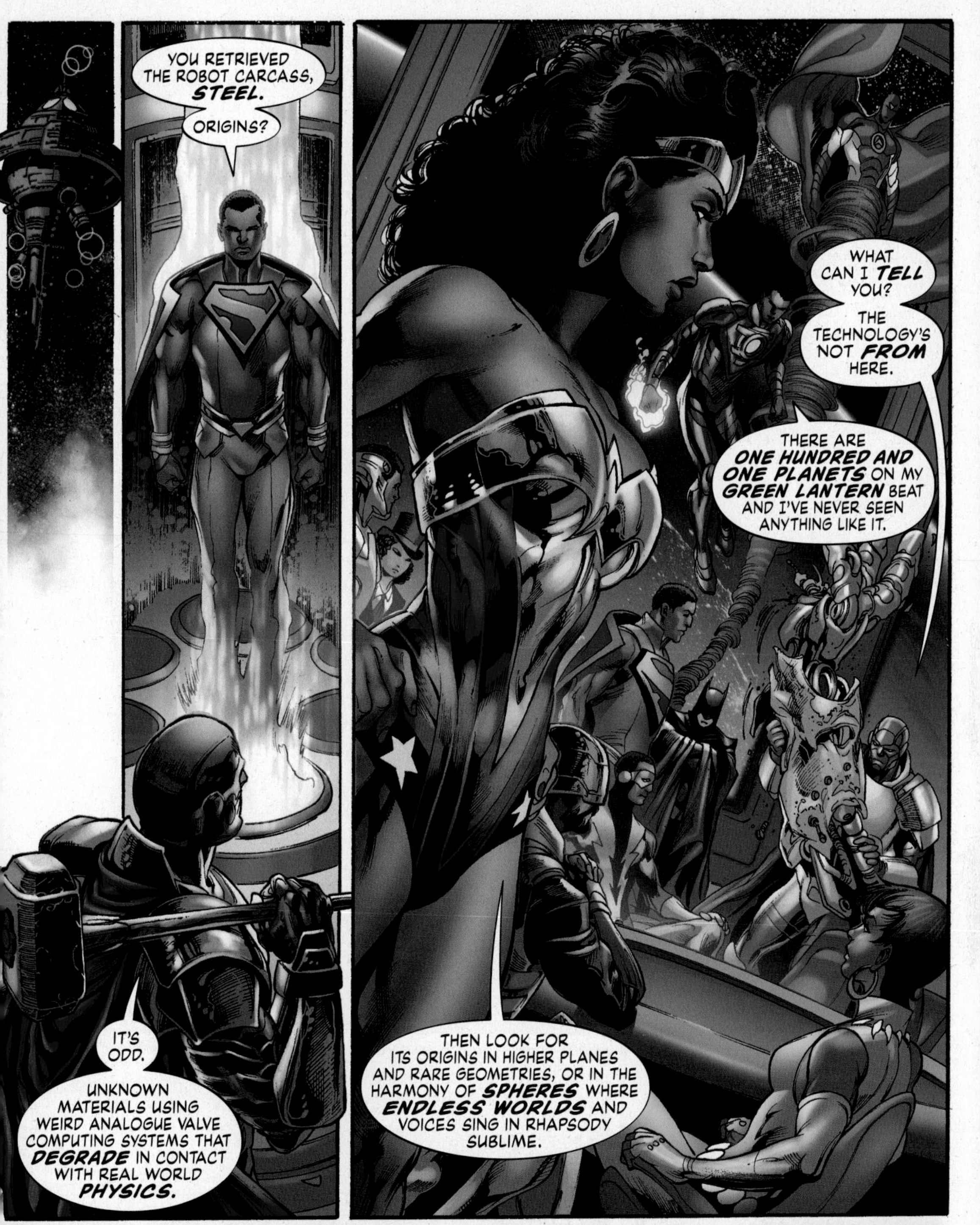

YOU RETRIEVED THE ROBOT CARCASS, STEEL.
ORIGINS?
IT'S ODD.
UNKNOWN MATERIALS USING WEIRD ANALOGUE VALVE COMPUTING SYSTEMS THAT DEGRADE IN CONTACT WITH REAL WORLD PHYSICS.
WHAT CAN I TELL YOU?
THE TECHNOLOGY'S NOT FROM HERE.
THERE ARE ONE HUNDRED AND ONE PLANETS ON MY GREEN LANTERN BEAT AND I'VE NEVER SEEN ANYTHING LIKE IT.
THEN LOOK FOR ITS ORIGINS IN HIGHER PLANES AND RARE GEOMETRIES, OR IN THE HARMONY OF SPHERES WHERE ENDLESS WORLDS AND VOICES SING IN RHAPSODY SUBLIME.
IT'S A MIRACLE IT EVEN WORKS AT ALL.
BUT IT WORKS IN SPITE OF ITSELF.
IF I HAD TO GUESS, I'D SAY IT'S A PROBE FROM A PARALLEL UNIVERSE.
ITS DRAWN TO THE CUBE--
--LEX LUTHOR'S DRUG-FUELED ATTEMPT TO BUILD A GATEWAY TO ALTERNATE WORLDS.

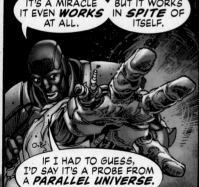

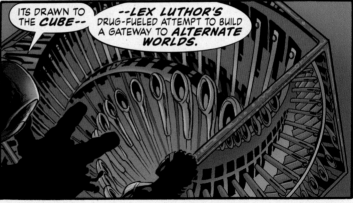

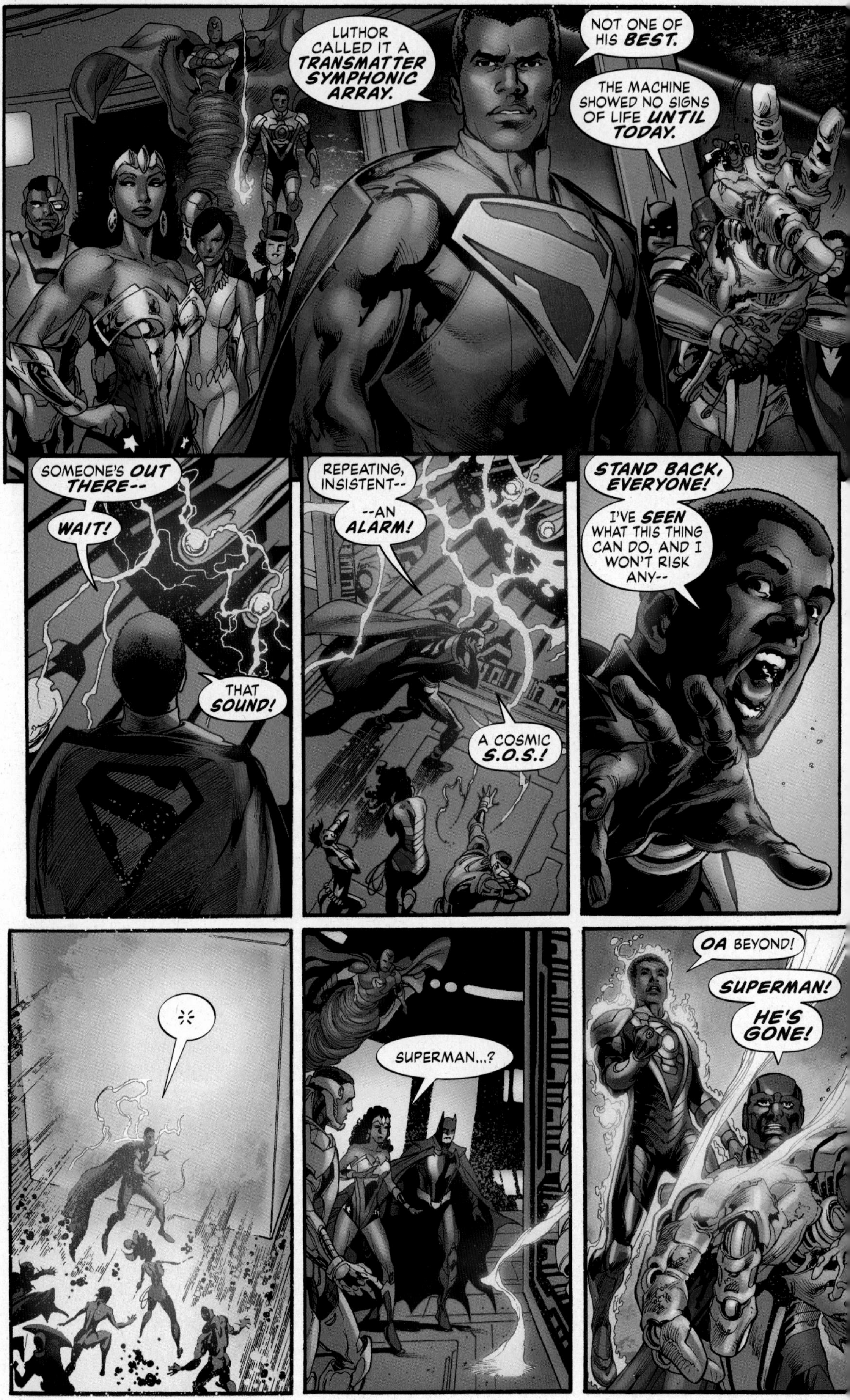
LUTHOR CALLED IT A TRANSMATTER SYMPHONIC ARRAY.
NOT ONE OF HIS BEST.
THE MACHINE SHOWED NO SIGNS OF LIFE UNTIL TODAY.
SOMEONE'S OUT THERE--
WAIT!
THAT SOUND!
REPEATING, INSISTENT--
--AN ALARM!
A COSMIC S.O.S.!
STAND BACK, EVERYONE!
I'VE SEEN WHAT THIS THING CAN DO, AND I WON'T RISK ANY--
SUPERMAN...?
OA BEYOND!
SUPERMAN!
HE'S GONE!

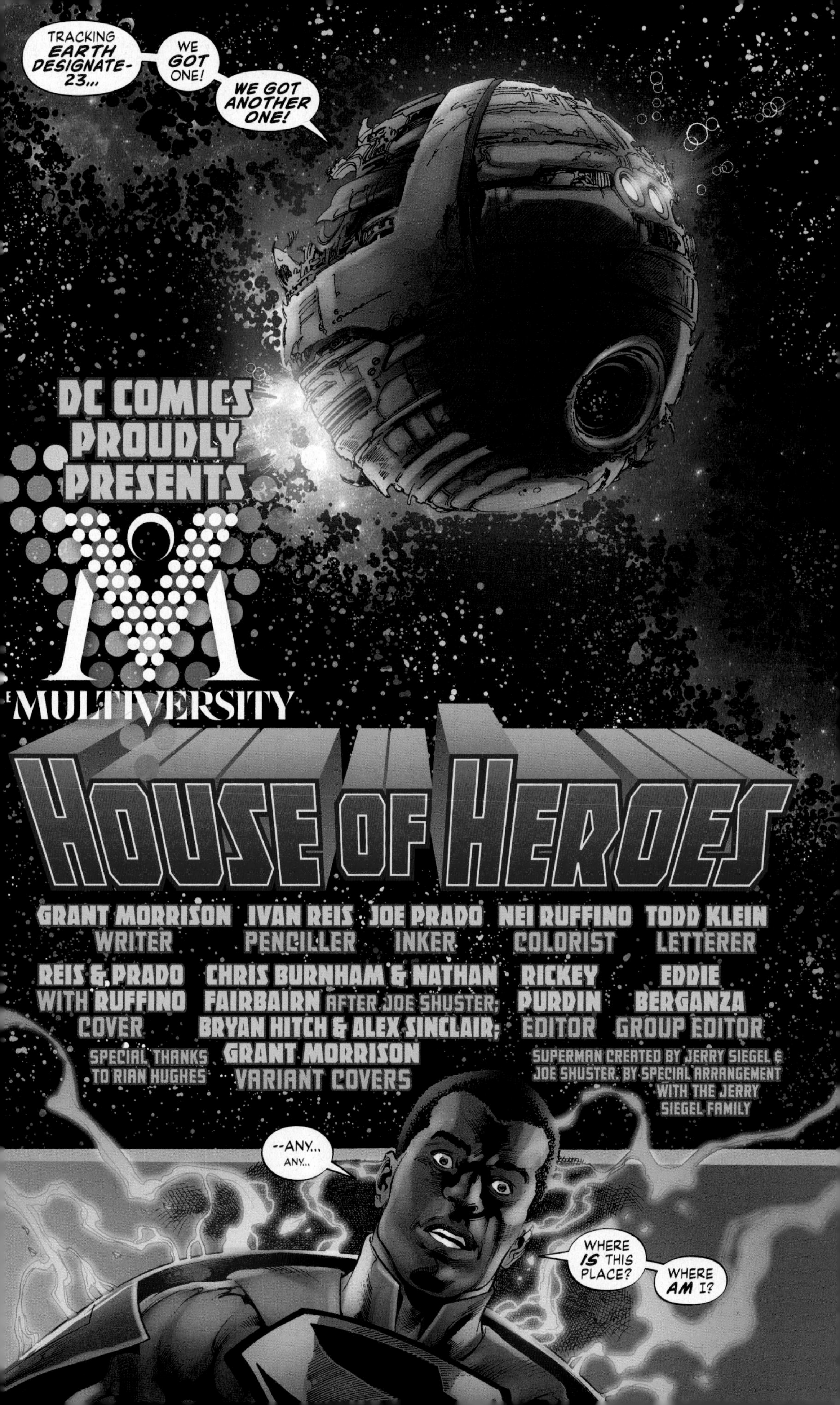

TRACKING EARTH DESIGNATE-23...
WE GOT ONE!
WE GOT ANOTHER ONE!
DC COMICS PROUDLY PRESENTS
MULTIVERSITY
HOUSE OF HEROES
GRANT MORRISON WRITER
IVAN REIS PENCILLER
JOE PRADO INKER
NEI RUFFINO COLORIST
TODD KLEIN LETTERER
REIS & PRADO WITH RUFFINO COVER
CHRIS BURNHAM & NATHAN FAIRBAIRN AFTER JOE SHUSTER; BRYAN HITCH & ALEX SINCLAIR; GRANT MORRISON VARIANT COVERS
RICKEY PURDIN EDITOR
EDDIE BERGANZA GROUP EDITOR
SPECIAL THANKS TO RIAN HUGHES
SUPERMAN CREATED BY JERRY SIEGEL & JOE SHUSTER. BY SPECIAL ARRANGEMENT WITH THE JERRY SIEGEL FAMILY
--ANY... ANY...
WHERE IS THIS PLACE?
WHERE AM I?

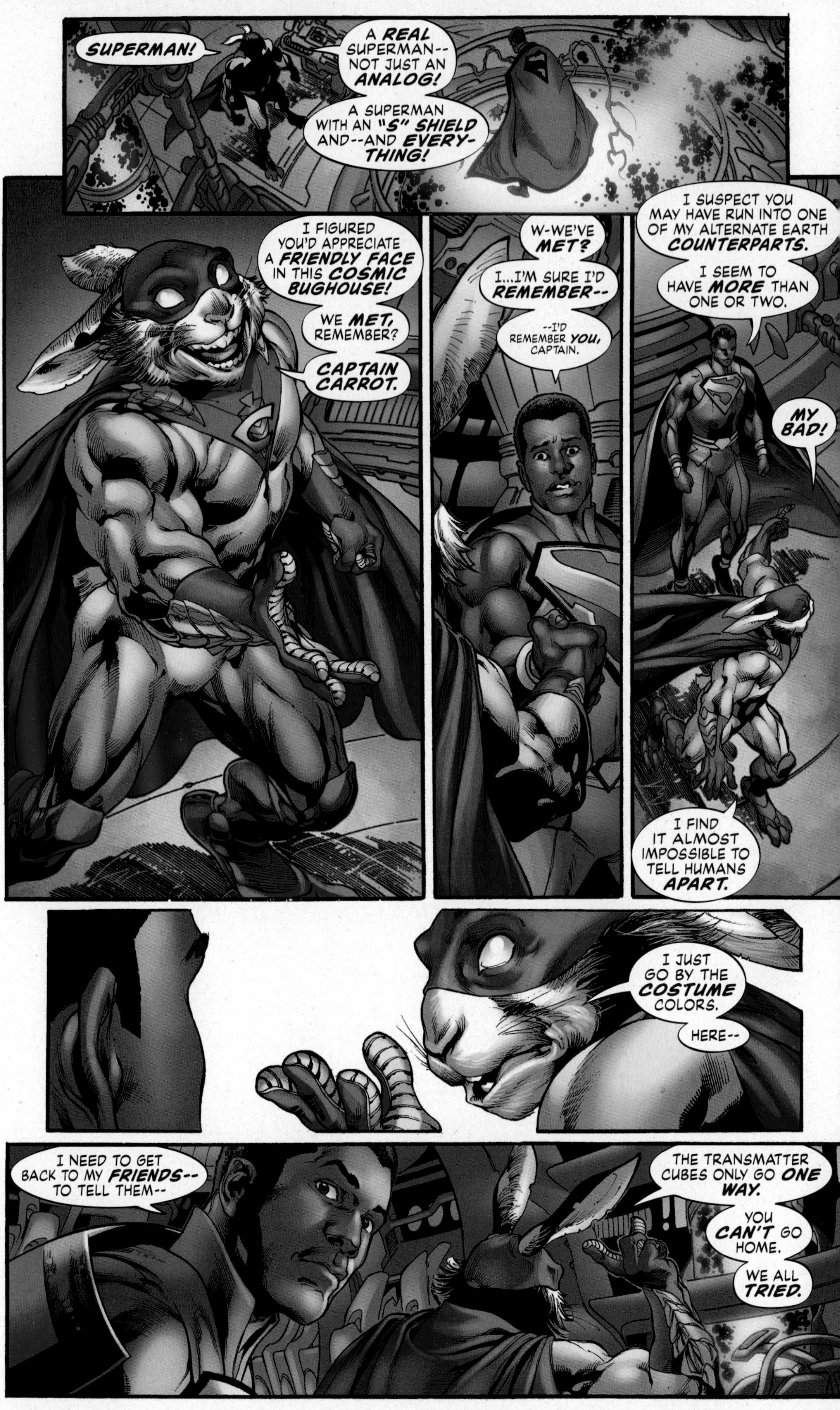
SUPERMAN!
A REAL SUPERMAN-- NOT JUST AN ANALOG!
A SUPERMAN WITH AN "S" SHIELD AND--AND EVERY-THING!
I FIGURED YOU'D APPRECIATE A FRIENDLY FACE IN THIS COSMIC BUGHOUSE!
WE MET, REMEMBER?
CAPTAIN CARROT.
W-WE'VE MET?
I...I'M SURE I'D REMEMBER--
--I'D REMEMBER YOU, CAPTAIN.
I SUSPECT YOU MAY HAVE RUN INTO ONE OF MY ALTERNATE EARTH COUNTERPARTS.
I SEEM TO HAVE MORE THAN ONE OR TWO.
MY BAD!
I FIND IT ALMOST IMPOSSIBLE TO TELL HUMANS APART.
I JUST GO BY THE COSTUME COLORS.
HERE--
I NEED TO GET BACK TO MY FRIENDS-- TO TELL THEM--
THE TRANSMATTER CUBES ONLY GO ONE WAY.
YOU CAN'T GO HOME.
WE ALL TRIED.

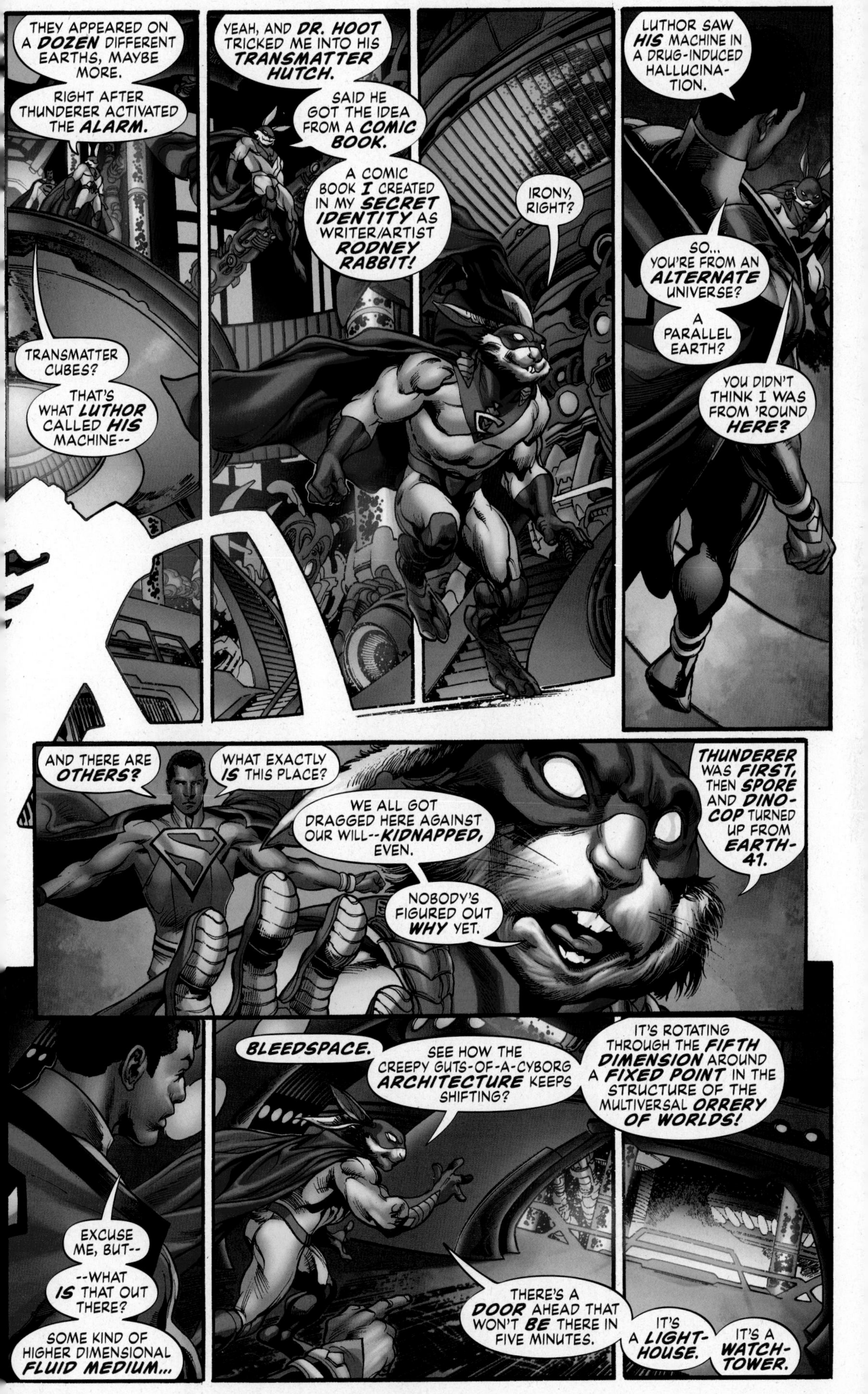
THEY APPEARED ON A DOZEN DIFFERENT EARTHS, MAYBE MORE.
RIGHT AFTER THUNDERER ACTIVATED THE ALARM.
TRANSMATTER CUBES?
THAT'S WHAT LUTHOR CALLED HIS MACHINE--
YEAH, AND DR. HOOT TRICKED ME INTO HIS TRANSMATTER HUTCH.
SAID HE GOT THE IDEA FROM A COMIC BOOK.
A COMIC BOOK I CREATED IN MY SECRET IDENTITY AS WRITER/ARTIST RODNEY RABBIT!
IRONY, RIGHT?
LUTHOR SAW HIS MACHINE IN A DRUG-INDUCED HALLUCINA-TION.
SO... YOU'RE FROM AN ALTERNATE UNIVERSE?
A PARALLEL EARTH?
YOU DIDN'T THINK I WAS FROM 'ROUND HERE?
AND THERE ARE OTHERS?
WHAT EXACTLY IS THIS PLACE?
WE ALL GOT DRAGGED HERE AGAINST OUR WILL--KIDNAPPED, EVEN.
NOBODY'S FIGURED OUT WHY YET.
THUNDERER WAS FIRST, THEN SPORE AND DINO-COP TURNED UP FROM EARTH-41.
EXCUSE ME, BUT--
--WHAT IS THAT OUT THERE?
SOME KIND OF HIGHER DIMENSIONAL FLUID MEDIUM...
BLEEDSPACE.
SEE HOW THE CREEPY GUTS-OF-A-CYBORG ARCHITECTURE KEEPS SHIFTING?
IT'S ROTATING THROUGH THE FIFTH DIMENSION AROUND A FIXED POINT IN THE STRUCTURE OF THE MULTIVERSAL ORRERY OF WORLDS!
THERE'S A DOOR AHEAD THAT WON'T BE THERE IN FIVE MINUTES.
IT'S A LIGHT-HOUSE.
IT'S A WATCH-TOWER.

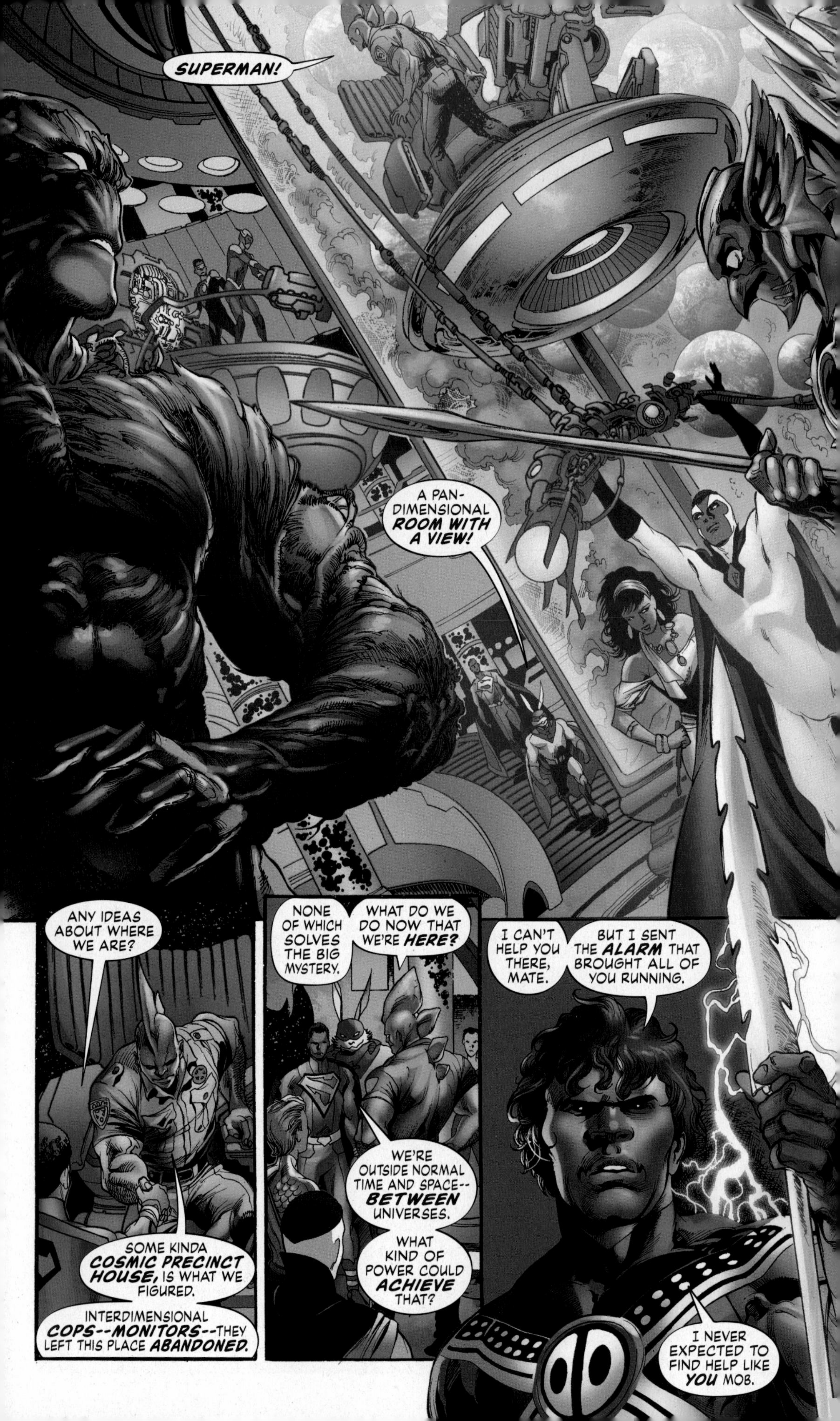
SUPERMAN!
A PAN-DIMENSIONAL ROOM WITH A VIEW!
ANY IDEAS ABOUT WHERE WE ARE?
SOME KINDA COSMIC PRECINCT HOUSE, IS WHAT WE FIGURED.
INTERDIMENSIONAL COPS--MONITORS--THEY LEFT THIS PLACE ABANDONED.
NONE OF WHICH SOLVES THE BIG MYSTERY.
WHAT DO WE DO NOW THAT WE'RE HERE?
WE'RE OUTSIDE NORMAL TIME AND SPACE--BETWEEN UNIVERSES.
WHAT KIND OF POWER COULD ACHIEVE THAT?
I CAN'T HELP YOU THERE, MATE.
BUT I SENT THE ALARM THAT BROUGHT ALL OF YOU RUNNING.
I NEVER EXPECTED TO FIND HELP LIKE YOU MOB.

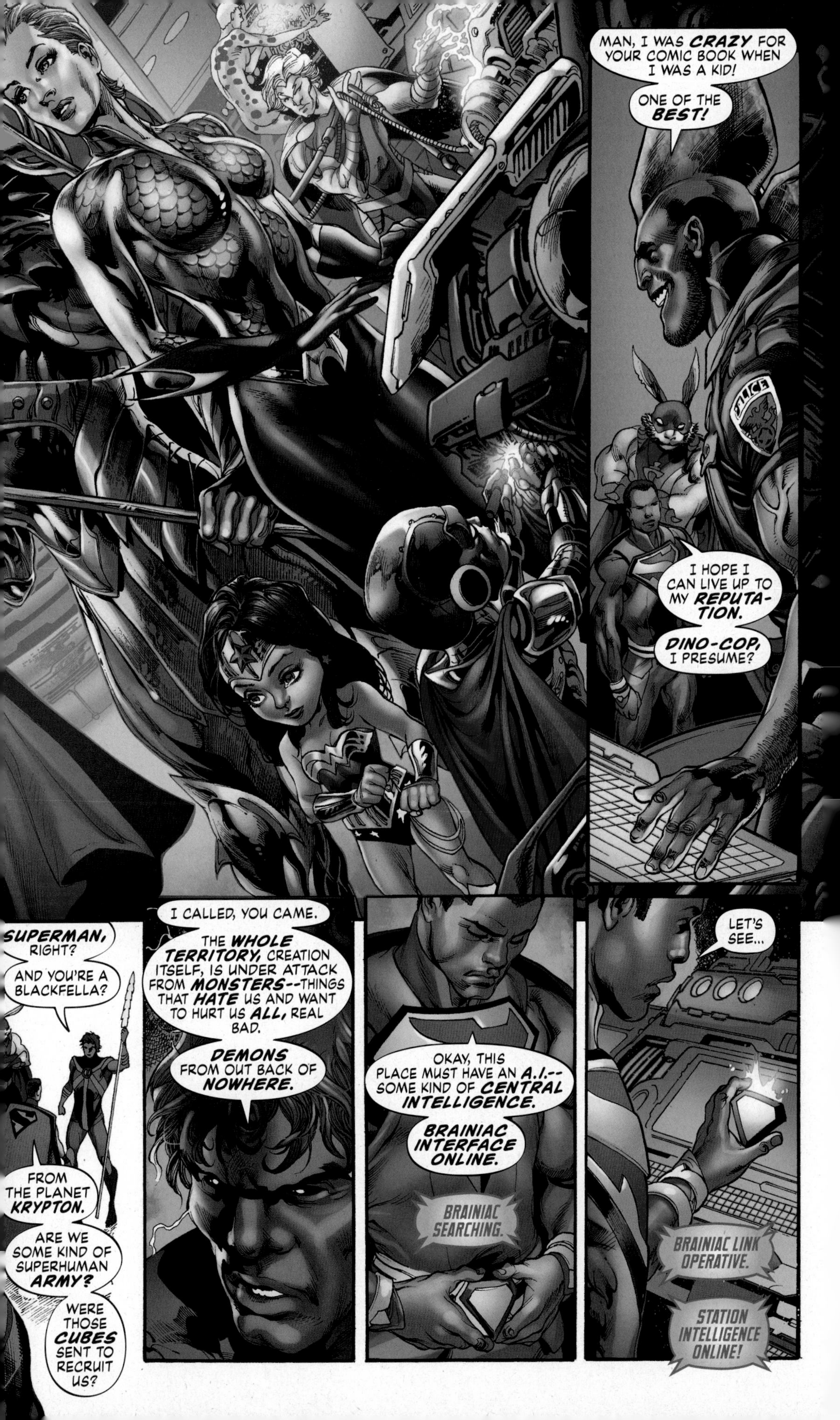

MAN, I WAS CRAZY FOR YOUR COMIC BOOK WHEN I WAS A KID!
ONE OF THE BEST!
I HOPE I CAN LIVE UP TO MY REPUTATION.
DINO-COP, I PRESUME?
SUPERMAN, RIGHT?
AND YOU'RE A BLACKFELLA?
FROM THE PLANET KRYPTON.
ARE WE SOME KIND OF SUPERHUMAN ARMY?
WERE THOSE CUBES SENT TO RECRUIT US?
I CALLED, YOU CAME.
THE WHOLE TERRITORY, CREATION ITSELF, IS UNDER ATTACK FROM MONSTERS--THINGS THAT HATE US AND WANT TO HURT US ALL, REAL BAD.
DEMONS FROM OUT BACK OF NOWHERE.
OKAY, THIS PLACE MUST HAVE AN A.I.--SOME KIND OF CENTRAL INTELLIGENCE.
BRAINIAC INTERFACE ONLINE.
BRAINIAC SEARCHING.
LET'S SEE...
BRAINIAC LINK OPERATIVE.
STATION INTELLIGENCE ONLINE!

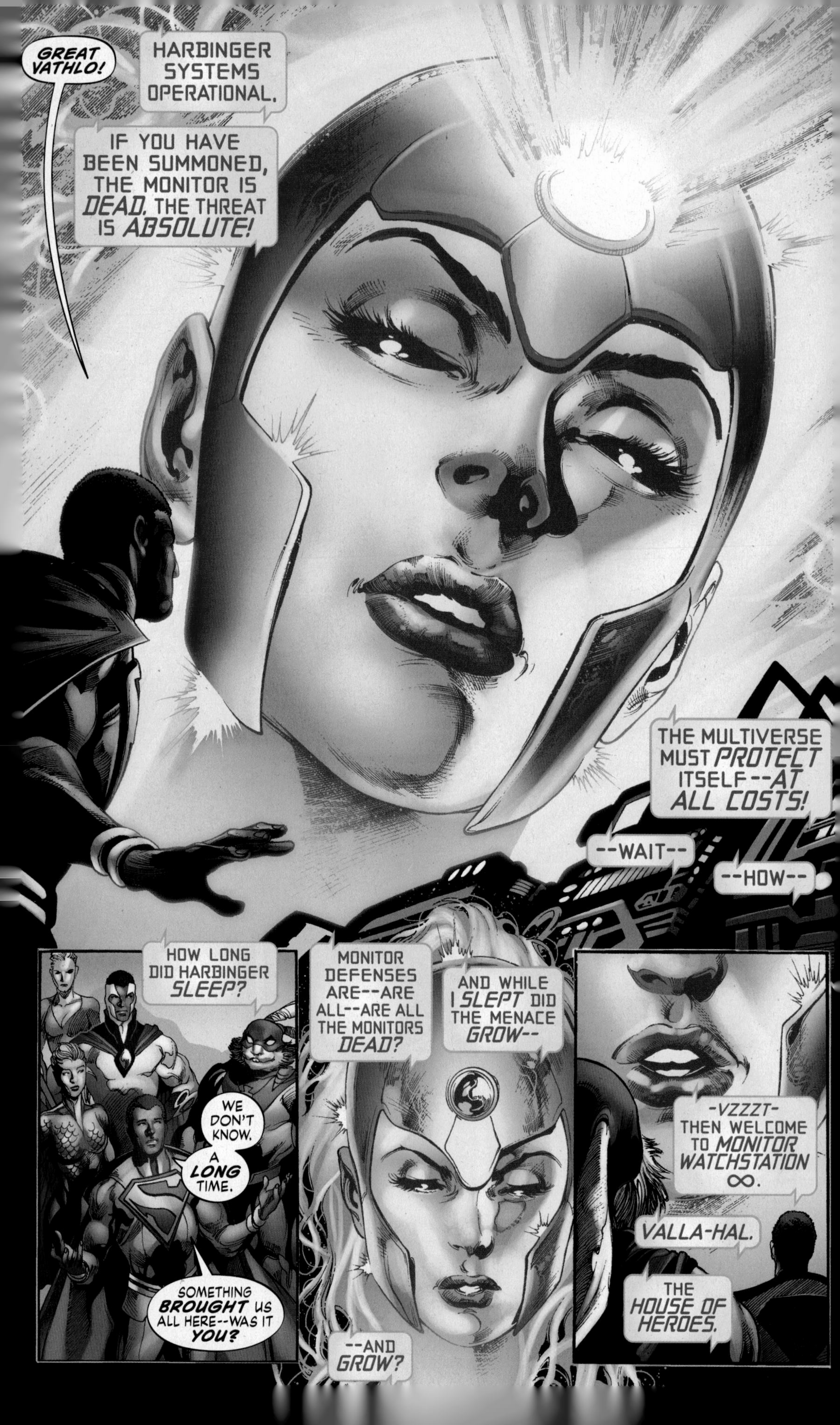
GREAT VATHLO!
HARBINGER SYSTEMS OPERATIONAL.
IF YOU HAVE BEEN SUMMONED, THE MONITOR IS DEAD. THE THREAT IS ABSOLUTE!
THE MULTIVERSE MUST PROTECT ITSELF--AT ALL COSTS!
--WAIT--
--HOW--
HOW LONG DID HARBINGER SLEEP?
WE DON'T KNOW.
A LONG TIME.
SOMETHING BROUGHT US ALL HERE--WAS IT YOU?
MONITOR DEFENSES ARE--ARE ALL--ARE ALL THE MONITORS DEAD?
AND WHILE I SLEPT DID THE MENACE GROW--
--AND GROW?
-VZZZT- THEN WELCOME TO MONITOR WATCHSTATION ∞.
VALLA-HAL.
THE HOUSE OF HEROES.

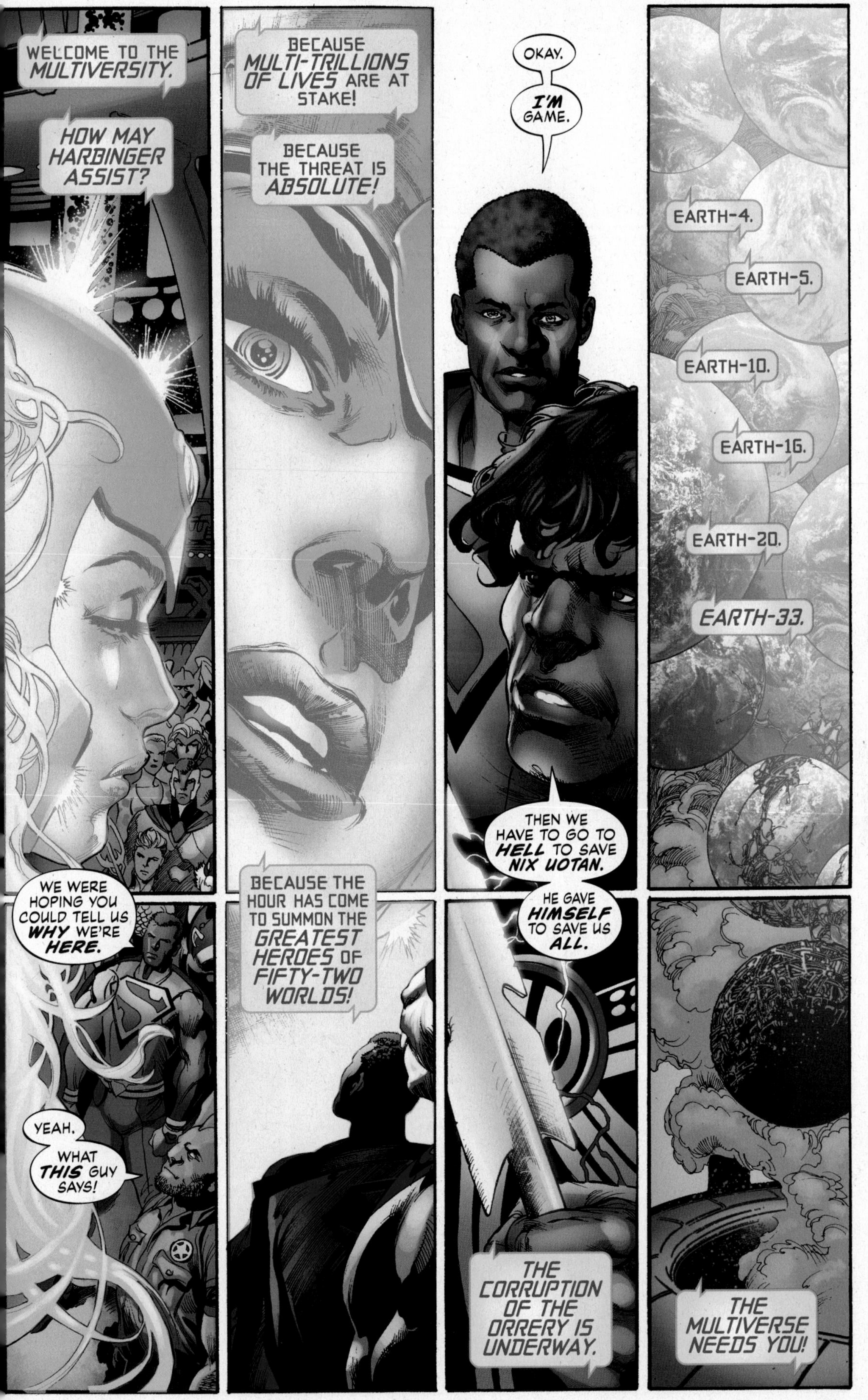

WELCOME TO THE MULTIVERSITY.
HOW MAY HARBINGER ASSIST?
BECAUSE MULTI-TRILLIONS OF LIVES ARE AT STAKE!
BECAUSE THE THREAT IS ABSOLUTE!
OKAY.
I'M GAME.
THEN WE HAVE TO GO TO HELL TO SAVE NIX UOTAN.
EARTH-4.
EARTH-5.
EARTH-10.
EARTH-16.
EARTH-20.
EARTH-33.
WE WERE HOPING YOU COULD TELL US WHY WE'RE HERE.
YEAH.
WHAT THIS GUY SAYS!
BECAUSE THE HOUR HAS COME TO SUMMON THE GREATEST HEROES OF FIFTY-TWO WORLDS!
HE GAVE HIMSELF TO SAVE US ALL.
THE CORRUPTION OF THE ORRERY IS UNDERWAY.
THE MULTIVERSE NEEDS YOU!

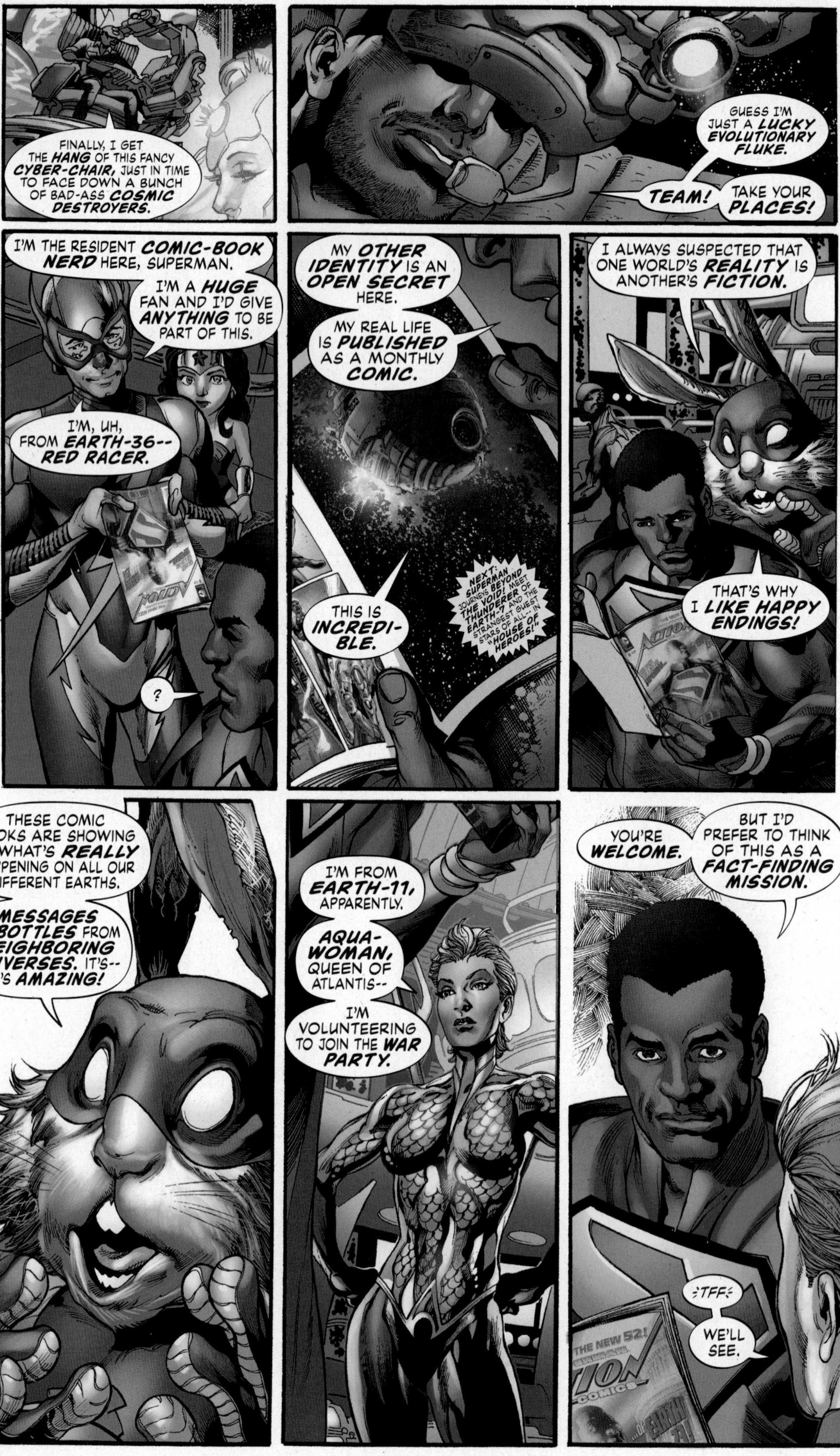

FINALLY, I GET THE HANG OF THIS FANCY CYBER-CHAIR, JUST IN TIME TO FACE DOWN A BUNCH OF BAD-ASS COSMIC DESTROYERS.
GUESS I'M JUST A LUCKY EVOLUTIONARY FLUKE.
TEAM!
TAKE YOUR PLACES!
I'M THE RESIDENT COMIC-BOOK NERD HERE, SUPERMAN.
I'M A HUGE FAN AND I'D GIVE ANYTHING TO BE PART OF THIS.
I'M, UH, FROM EARTH-36-- RED RACER.
?
MY OTHER IDENTITY IS AN OPEN SECRET HERE.
MY REAL LIFE IS PUBLISHED AS A MONTHLY COMIC.
THIS IS INCREDIBLE.
NEXT: SUPERMAN JOURNEYS BEYOND THE VOID! MEET THUNDERER OF EARTH-7 AND THE STRANGEST GUEST STARS OF ALL-- IN "HOUSE OF HEROES!"
I ALWAYS SUSPECTED THAT ONE WORLD'S REALITY IS ANOTHER'S FICTION.
THAT'S WHY I LIKE HAPPY ENDINGS!
THESE COMIC BOOKS ARE SHOWING US WHAT'S REALLY HAPPENING ON ALL OUR DIFFERENT EARTHS.
MESSAGES IN BOTTLES FROM NEIGHBORING UNIVERSES. IT'S-- IT'S AMAZING!
I'M FROM EARTH-11, APPARENTLY.
AQUA-WOMAN, QUEEN OF ATLANTIS--
I'M VOLUNTEERING TO JOIN THE WAR PARTY.
YOU'RE WELCOME.
BUT I'D PREFER TO THINK OF THIS AS A FACT-FINDING MISSION.
TFF
WE'LL SEE.

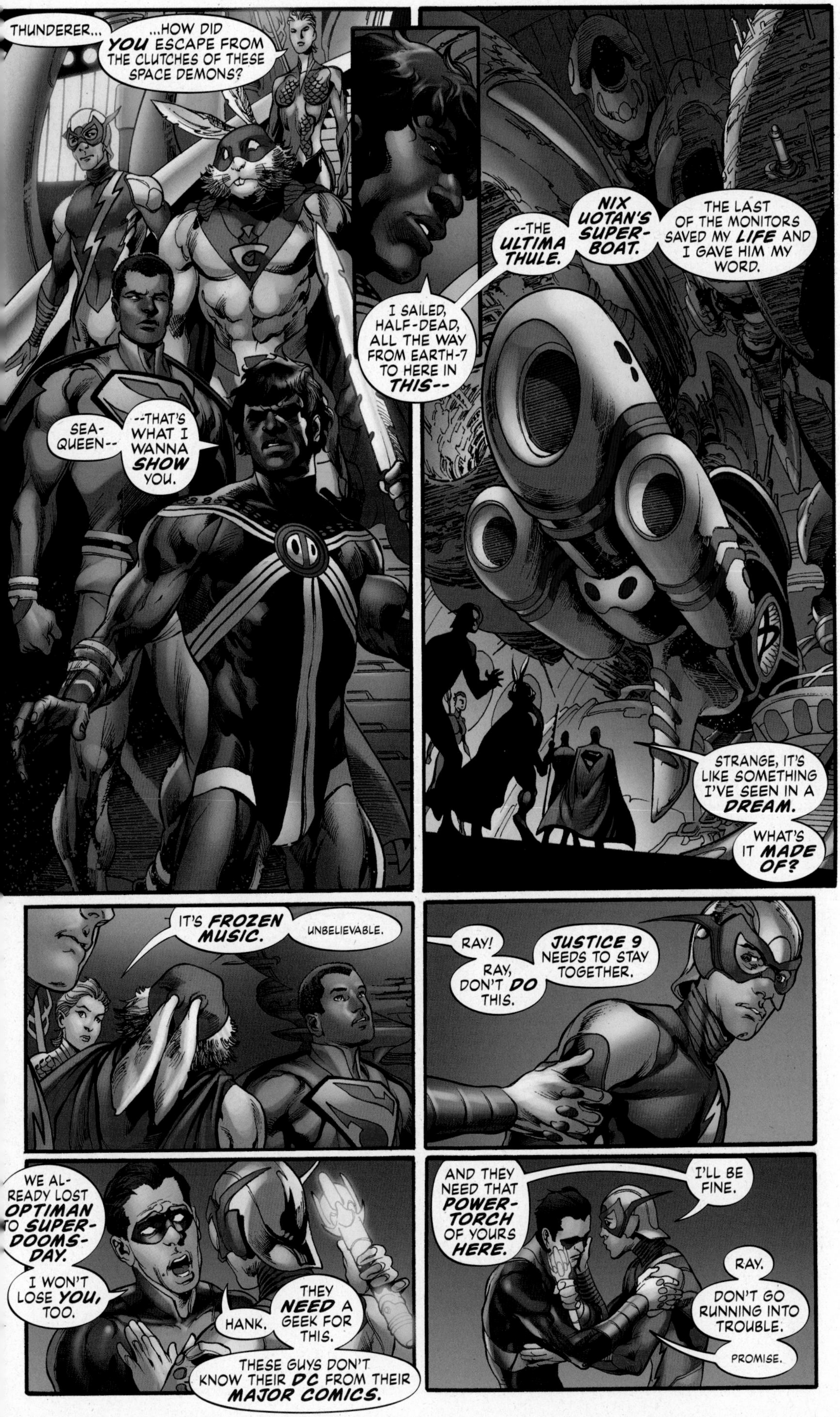
THUNDERER...
...HOW DID YOU ESCAPE FROM THE CLUTCHES OF THESE SPACE DEMONS?
SEA-QUEEN--
--THAT'S WHAT I WANNA SHOW YOU.
I SAILED, HALF-DEAD, ALL THE WAY FROM EARTH-7 TO HERE IN THIS--
--THE ULTIMA THULE.
NIX UOTAN'S SUPER-BOAT.
THE LAST OF THE MONITORS SAVED MY LIFE AND I GAVE HIM MY WORD.
STRANGE, IT'S LIKE SOMETHING I'VE SEEN IN A DREAM.
WHAT'S IT MADE OF?
IT'S FROZEN MUSIC.
UNBELIEVABLE.
RAY!
RAY, DON'T DO THIS.
JUSTICE 9 NEEDS TO STAY TOGETHER.
WE ALREADY LOST OPTIMAN TO SUPER-DOOMSDAY.
I WON'T LOSE YOU, TOO.
HANK.
THEY NEED A GEEK FOR THIS.
THESE GUYS DON'T KNOW THEIR DC FROM THEIR MAJOR COMICS.
AND THEY NEED THAT POWER-TORCH OF YOURS HERE.
I'LL BE FINE.
RAY.
DON'T GO RUNNING INTO TROUBLE.
PROMISE.

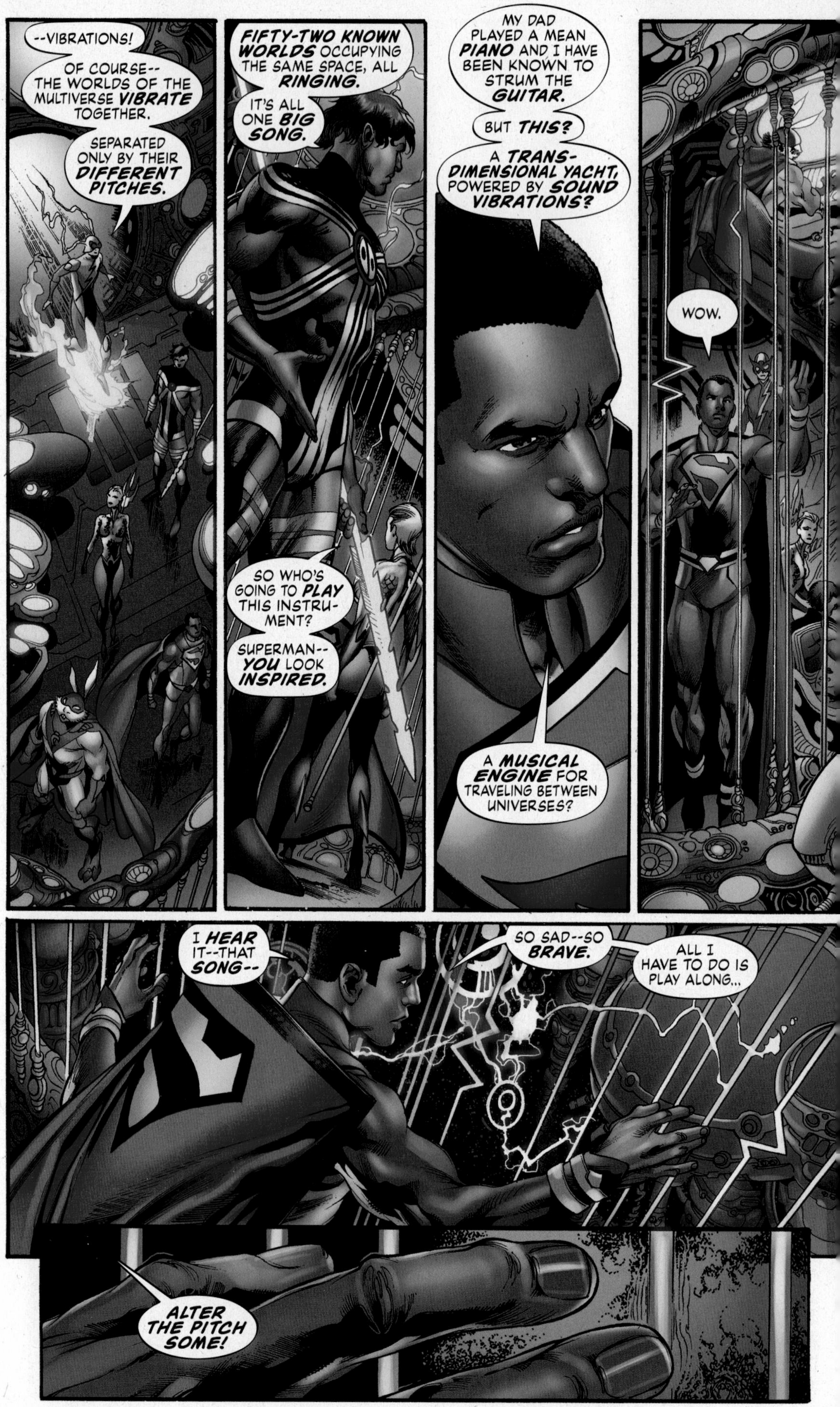
--VIBRATIONS!
OF COURSE-- THE WORLDS OF THE MULTIVERSE VIBRATE TOGETHER.
SEPARATED ONLY BY THEIR DIFFERENT PITCHES.
FIFTY-TWO KNOWN WORLDS OCCUPYING THE SAME SPACE, ALL RINGING.
IT'S ALL ONE BIG SONG.
SO WHO'S GOING TO PLAY THIS INSTRU-MENT?
SUPERMAN-- YOU LOOK INSPIRED.
MY DAD PLAYED A MEAN PIANO AND I HAVE BEEN KNOWN TO STRUM THE GUITAR.
BUT THIS?
A TRANS-DIMENSIONAL YACHT, POWERED BY SOUND VIBRATIONS?
A MUSICAL ENGINE FOR TRAVELING BETWEEN UNIVERSES?
WOW.
I HEAR IT--THAT SONG--
SO SAD--SO BRAVE.
ALL I HAVE TO DO IS PLAY ALONG...
ALTER THE PITCH SOME!

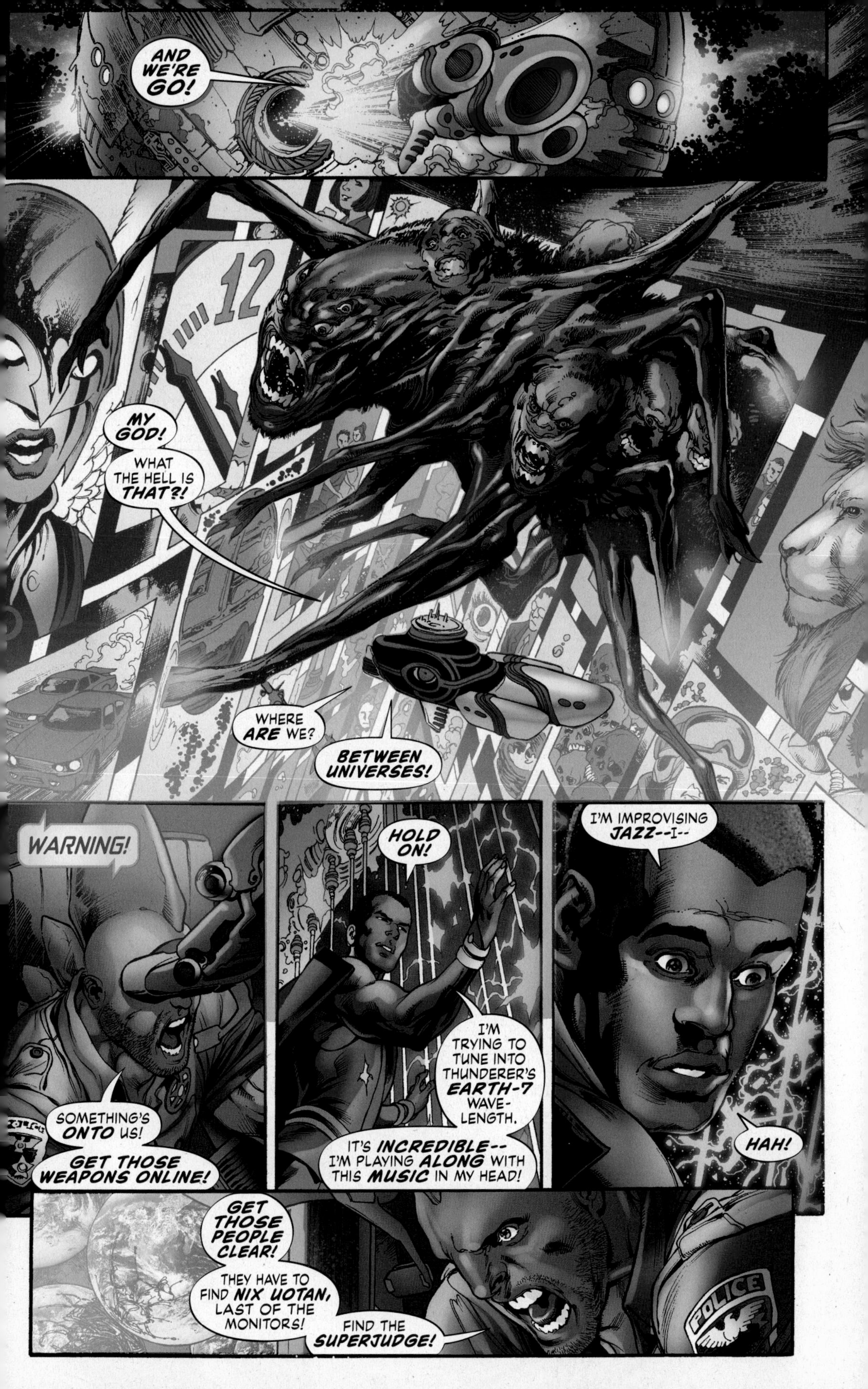
AND WE'RE GO!
MY GOD! WHAT THE HELL IS THAT?!
WHERE ARE WE?
BETWEEN UNIVERSES!
WARNING!
SOMETHING'S ONTO US!
GET THOSE WEAPONS ONLINE!
HOLD ON!
I'M TRYING TO TUNE INTO THUNDERER'S EARTH-7 WAVE-LENGTH.
IT'S INCREDIBLE-- I'M PLAYING ALONG WITH THIS MUSIC IN MY HEAD!
I'M IMPROVISING JAZZ--I--
HAH!
GET THOSE PEOPLE CLEAR!
THEY HAVE TO FIND NIX UOTAN, LAST OF THE MONITORS!
FIND THE SUPERJUDGE!
POLICE

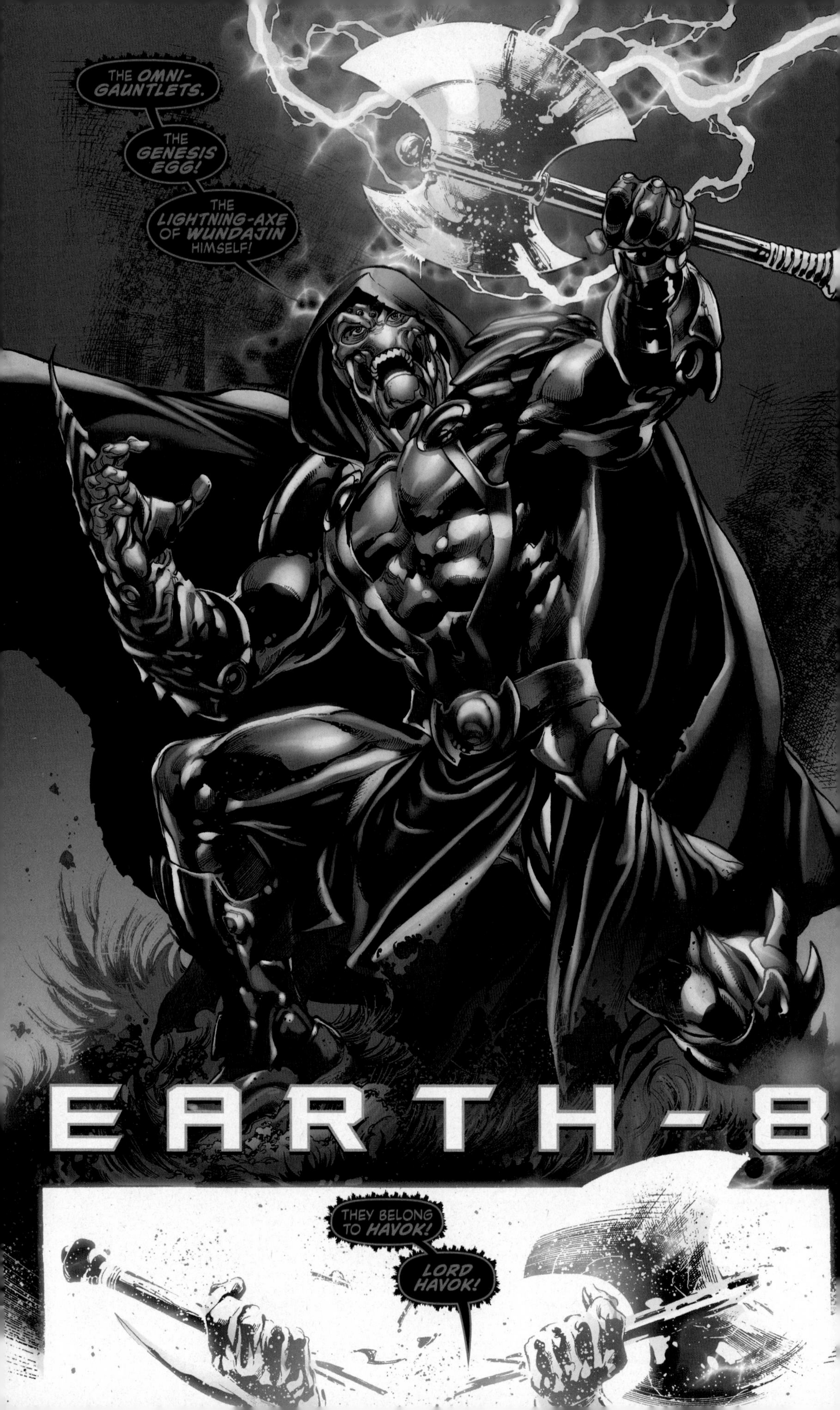
THE OMNI-GAUNTLETS.
THE GENESIS EGG!
THE LIGHTNING-AXE OF WUNDAJIN HIMSELF!
EARTH-8
THEY BELONG TO HAVOK!
LORD HAVOK!

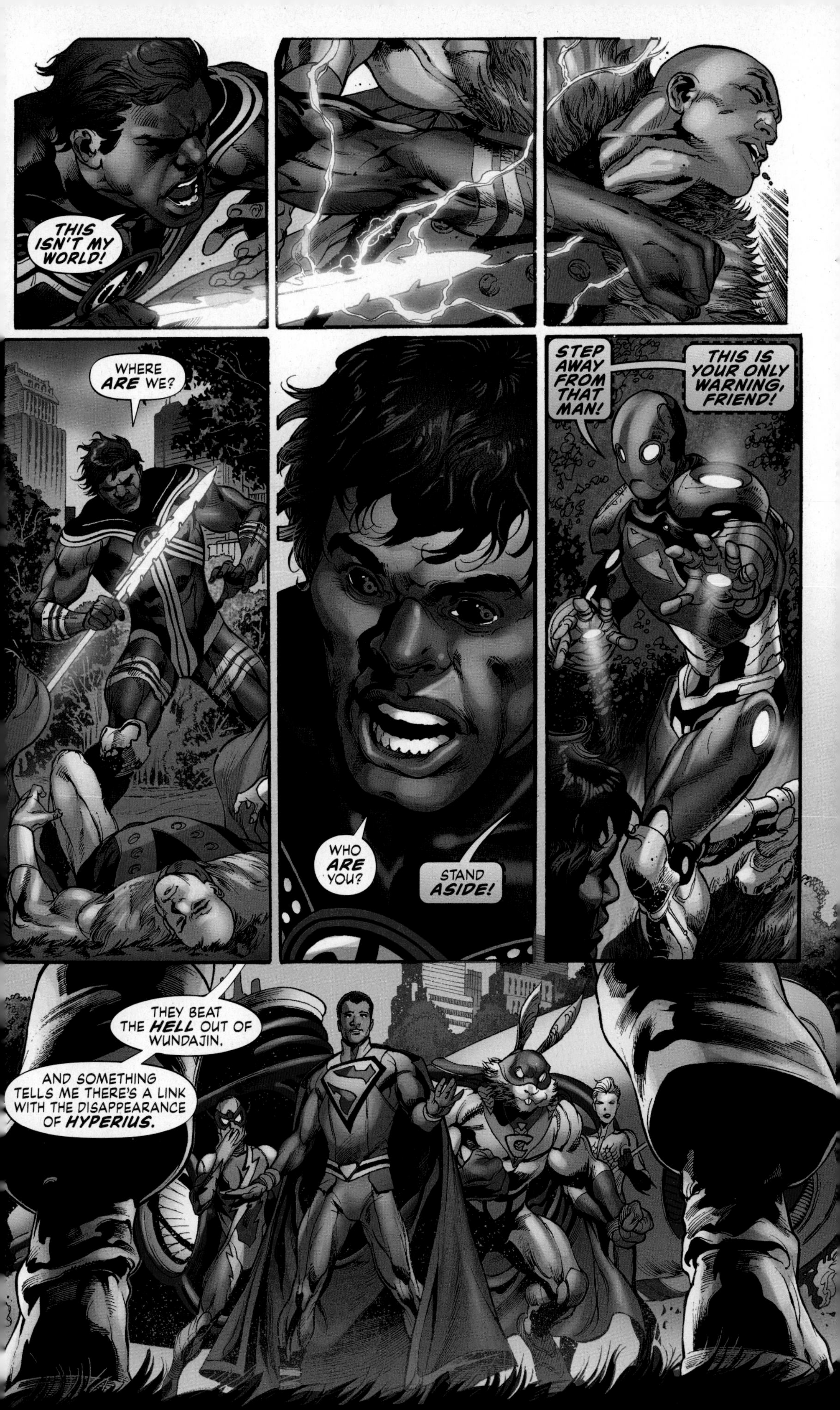
THIS ISN'T MY WORLD!
WHERE ARE WE?
WHO ARE YOU?
STAND ASIDE!
STEP AWAY FROM THAT MAN!
THIS IS YOUR ONLY WARNING, FRIEND!
THEY BEAT THE HELL OUT OF WUNDAJIN.
AND SOMETHING TELLS ME THERE'S A LINK WITH THE DISAPPEARANCE OF HYPERIUS.

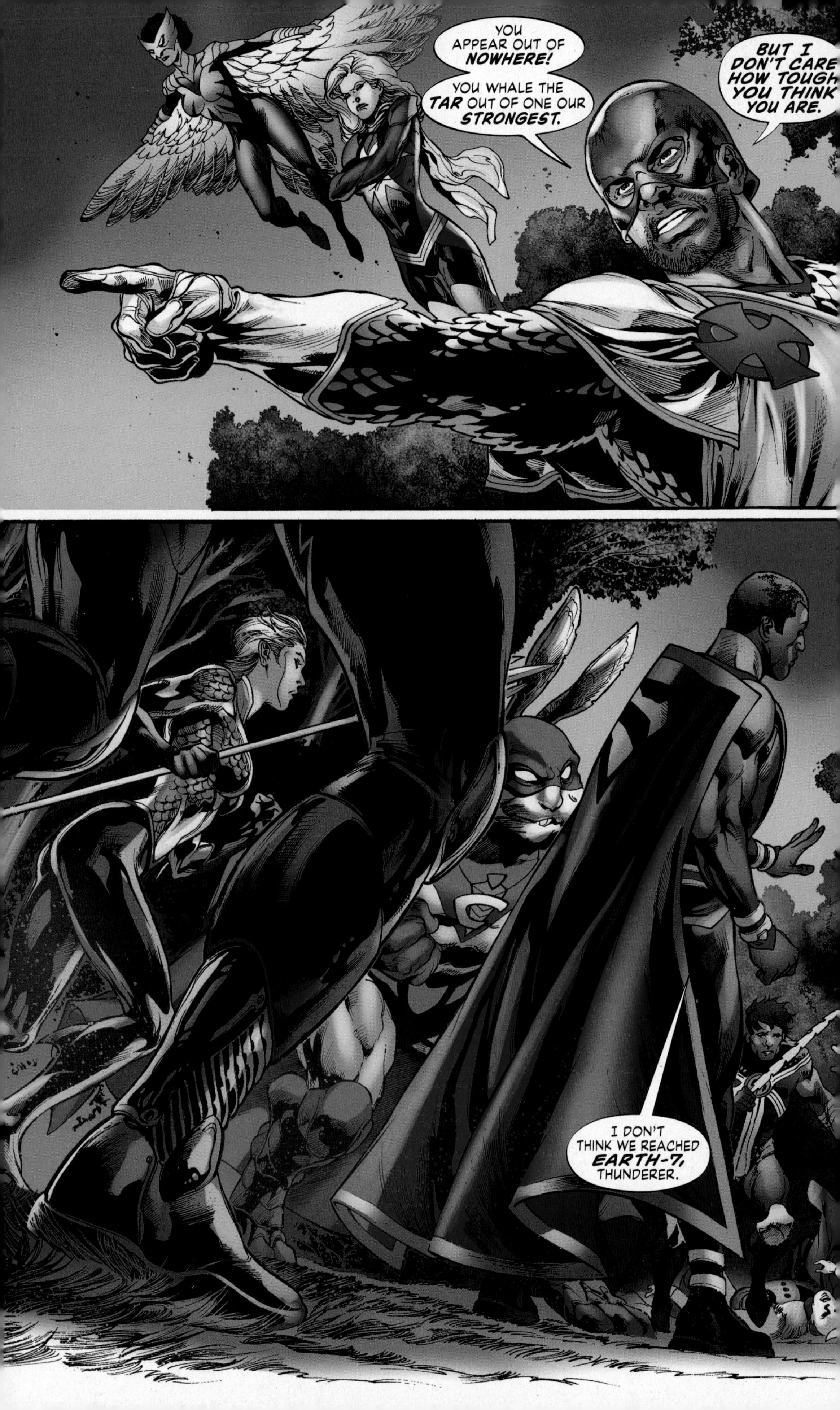
YOU APPEAR OUT OF NOWHERE!
YOU WHALE THE TAR OUT OF ONE OUR STRONGEST.
BUT I DON'T CARE HOW TOUGH YOU THINK YOU ARE.
I DON'T THINK WE REACHED EARTH-7, THUNDERER.

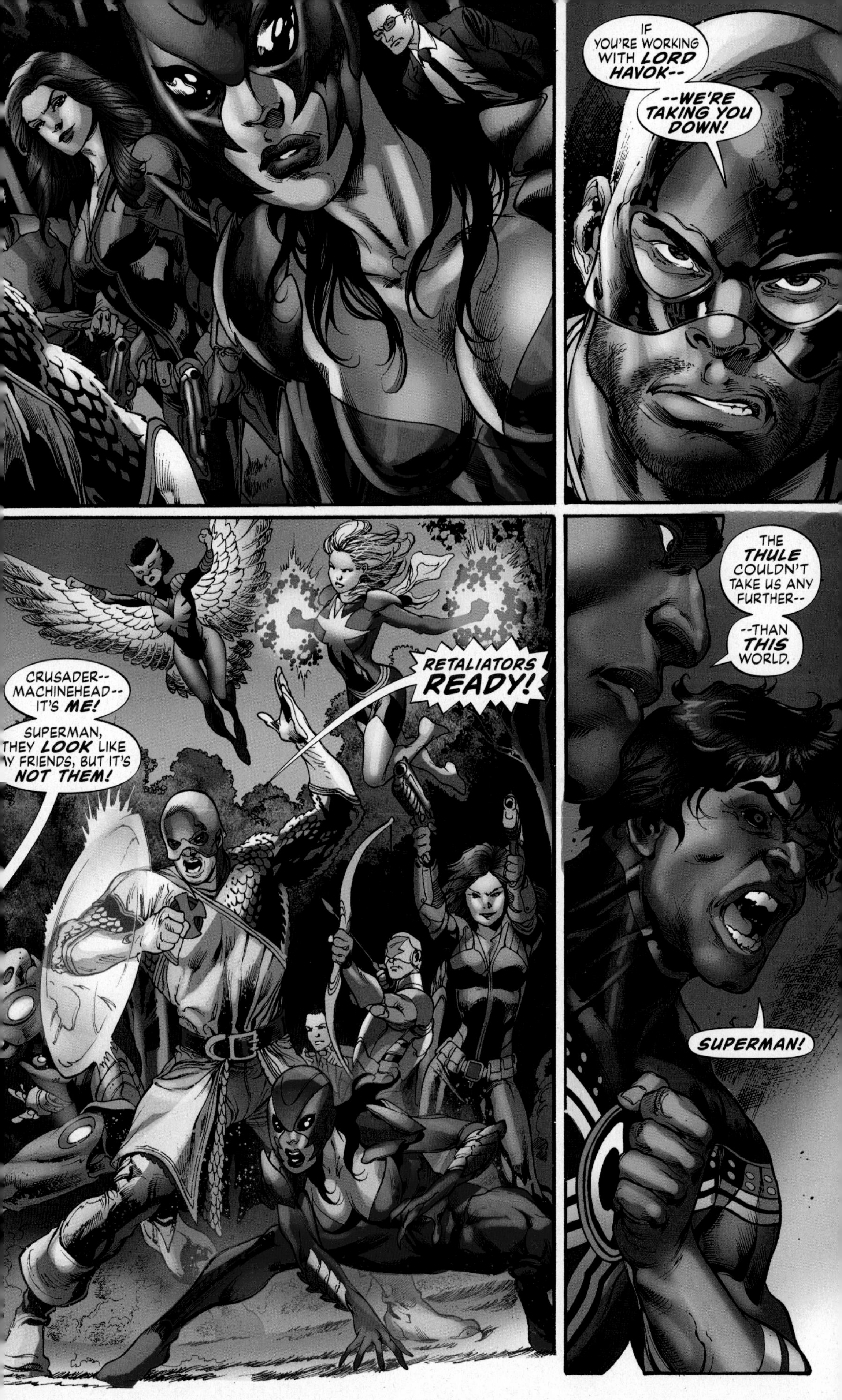

IF YOU'RE WORKING WITH LORD HAVOK--
--WE'RE TAKING YOU DOWN!
RETALIATORS READY!
CRUSADER-- MACHINEHEAD-- IT'S ME!
SUPERMAN, THEY LOOK LIKE MY FRIENDS, BUT IT'S NOT THEM!
THE THULE COULDN'T TAKE US ANY FURTHER--
--THAN THIS WORLD.
SUPERMAN!

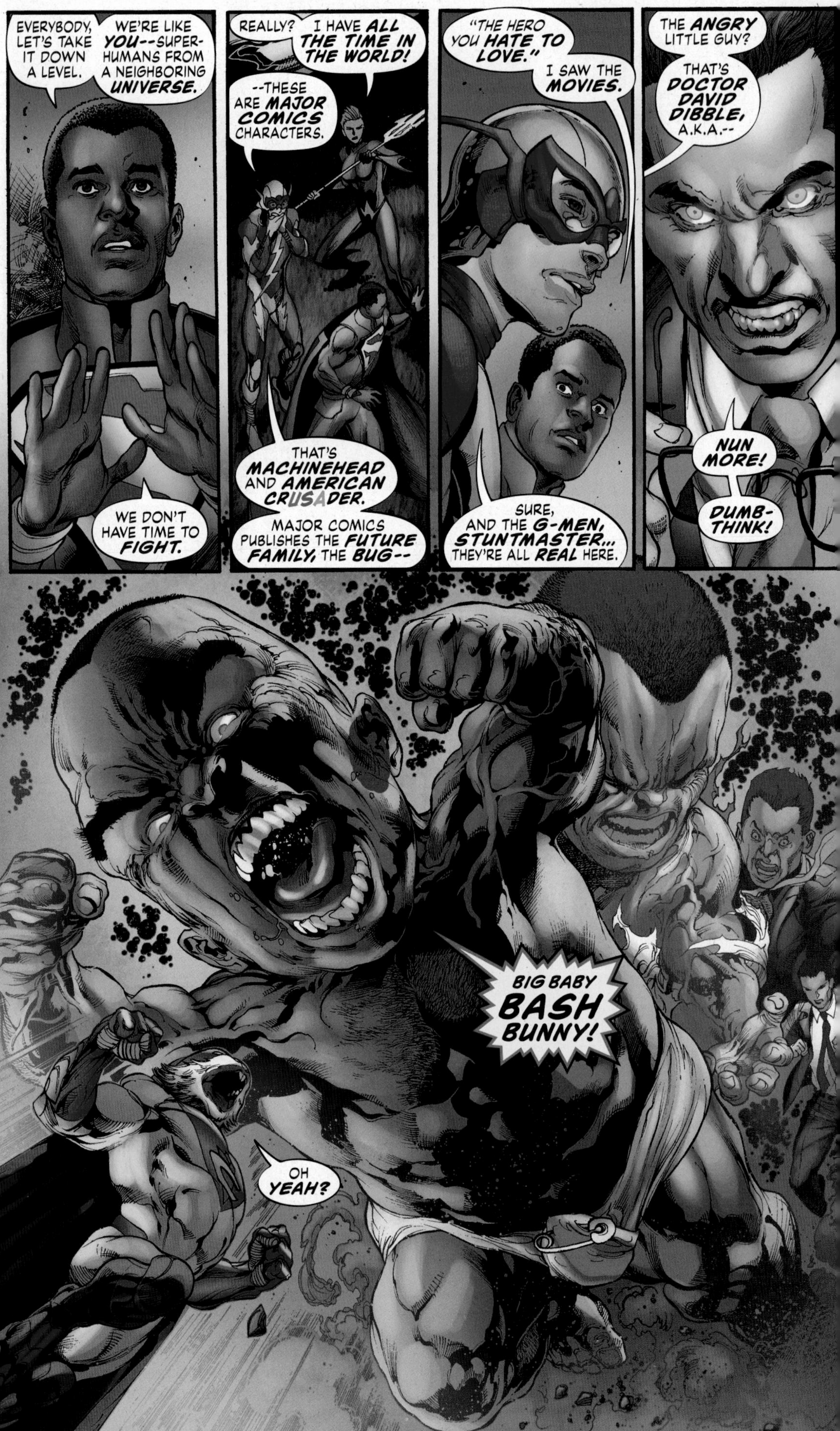
EVERYBODY, LET'S TAKE IT DOWN A LEVEL.
WE'RE LIKE YOU--SUPER-HUMANS FROM A NEIGHBORING UNIVERSE.
WE DON'T HAVE TIME TO FIGHT.
REALLY?
I HAVE ALL THE TIME IN THE WORLD!
--THESE ARE MAJOR COMICS CHARACTERS.
THAT'S MACHINEHEAD AND AMERICAN CRUSADER.
MAJOR COMICS PUBLISHES THE FUTURE FAMILY, THE BUG--
"THE HERO YOU HATE TO LOVE."
I SAW THE MOVIES.
SURE, AND THE G-MEN, STUNTMASTER... THEY'RE ALL REAL HERE.
THE ANGRY LITTLE GUY?
THAT'S DOCTOR DAVID DIBBLE, A.K.A.--
NUN MORE!
DUMB-THINK!
BIG BABY BASH BUNNY!
OH YEAH?

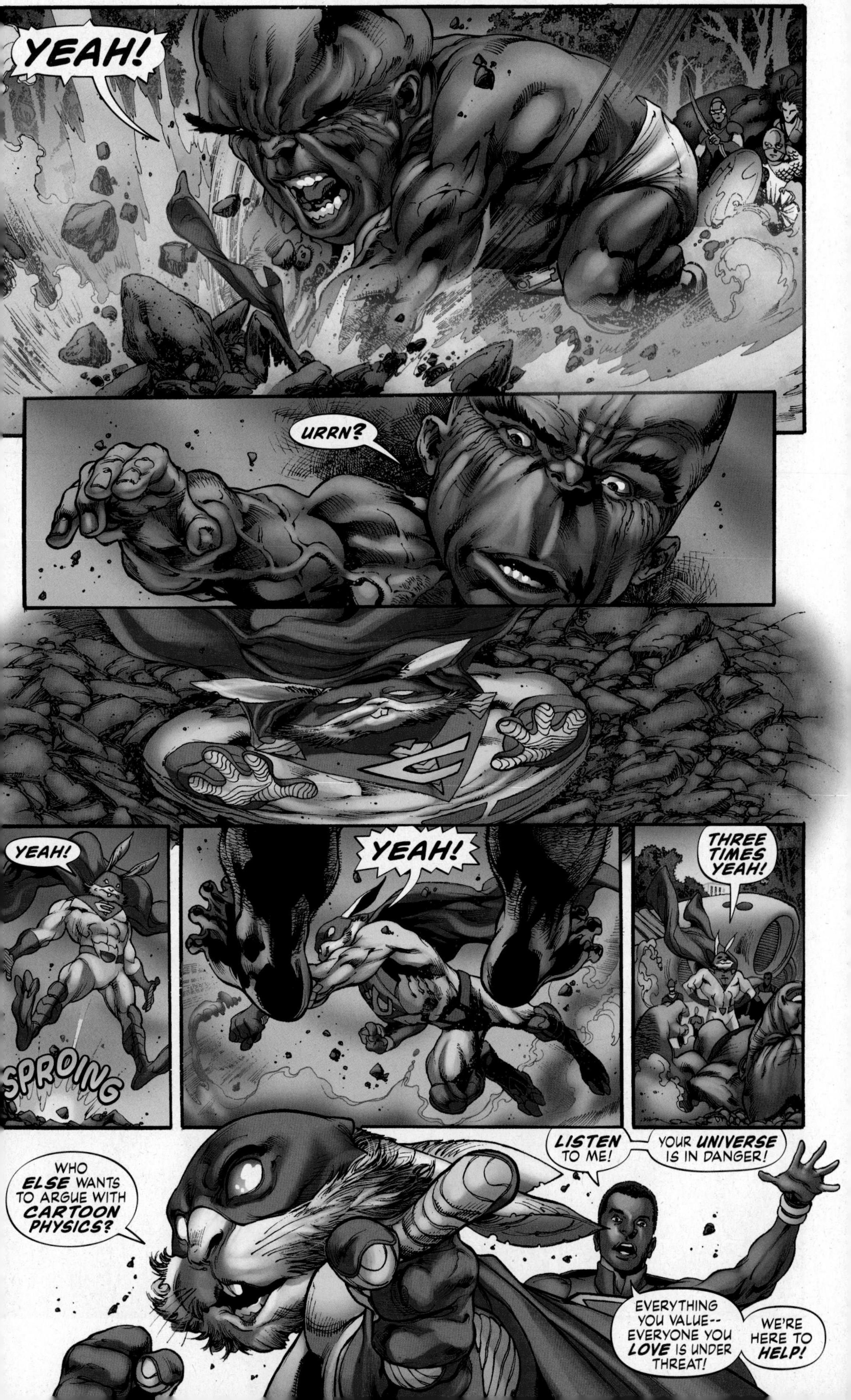
YEAH!
URRN?
YEAH!
SPROING
YEAH!
THREE TIMES YEAH!
WHO ELSE WANTS TO ARGUE WITH CARTOON PHYSICS?
LISTEN TO ME!
YOUR UNIVERSE IS IN DANGER!
EVERYTHING YOU VALUE-- EVERYONE YOU LOVE IS UNDER THREAT!
WE'RE HERE TO HELP!

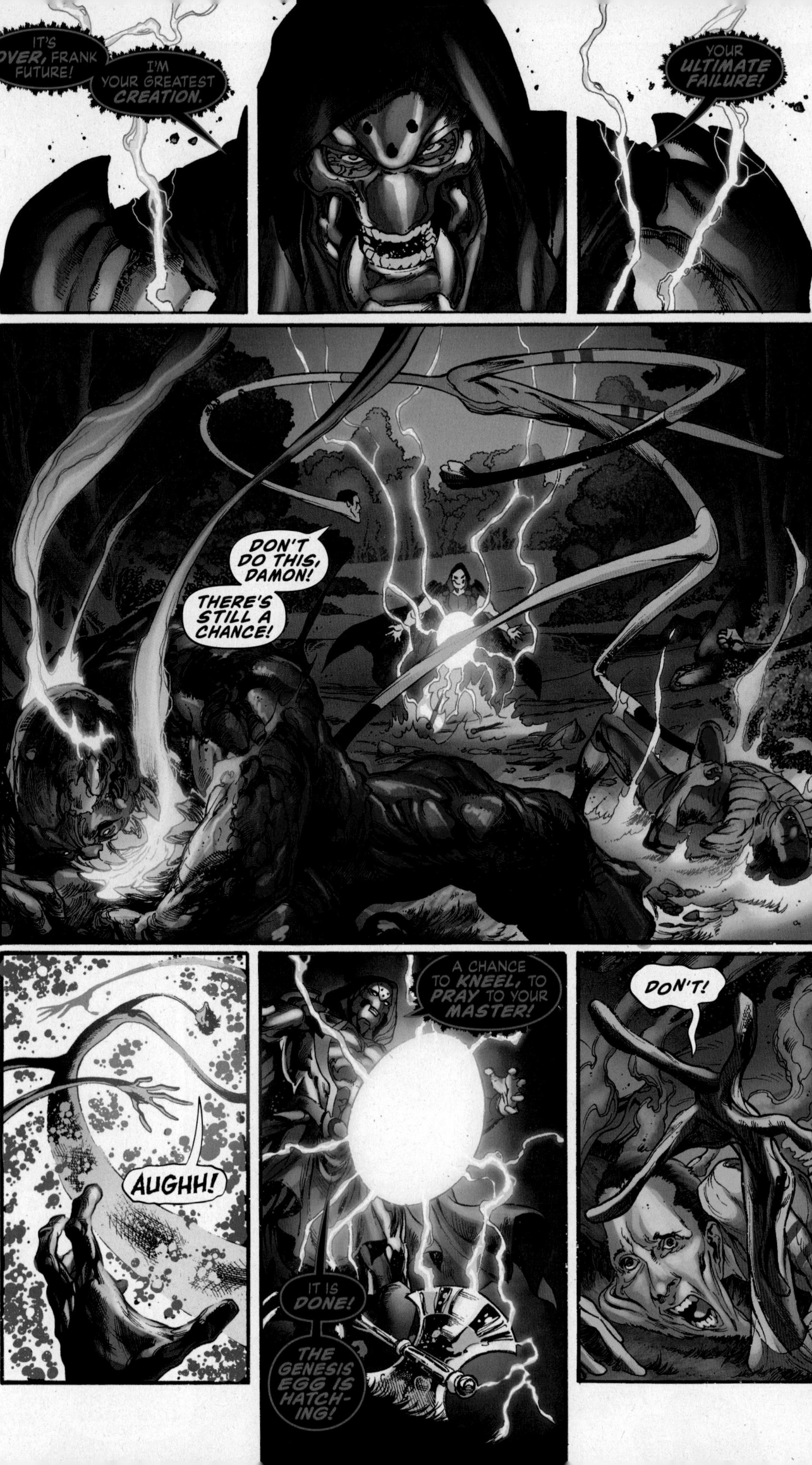
IT'S OVER, FRANK FUTURE!
I'M YOUR GREATEST CREATION.
YOUR ULTIMATE FAILURE!
DON'T DO THIS, DAMON!
THERE'S STILL A CHANCE!
AUGHH!
A CHANCE TO KNEEL, TO PRAY TO YOUR MASTER!
IT IS DONE!
THE GENESIS EGG IS HATCH-ING!
DON'T!

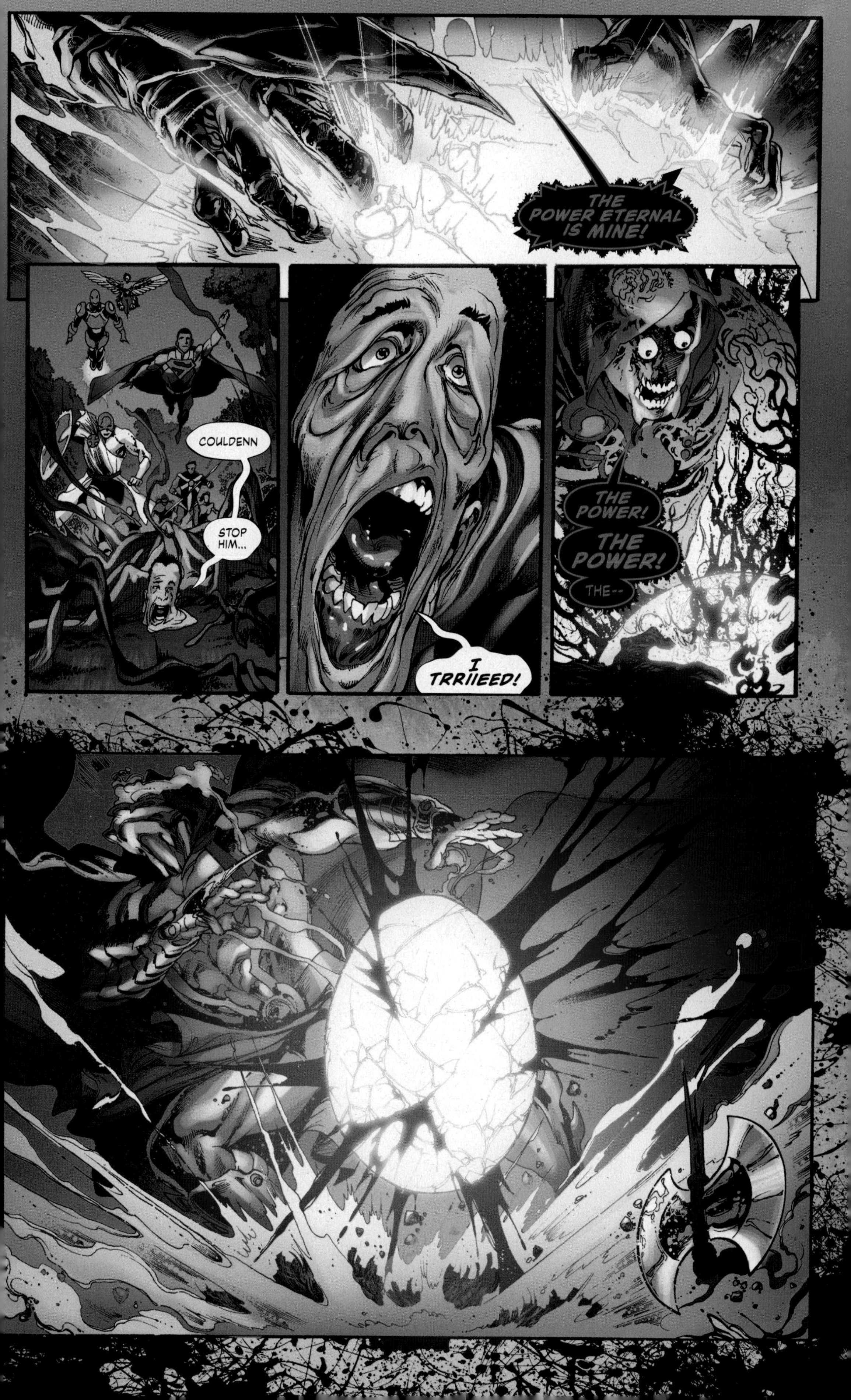
THE POWER ETERNAL IS MINE!
COULDENN
STOP HIM...
I TRRIIEED!
THE POWER!
THE POWER!
THE--

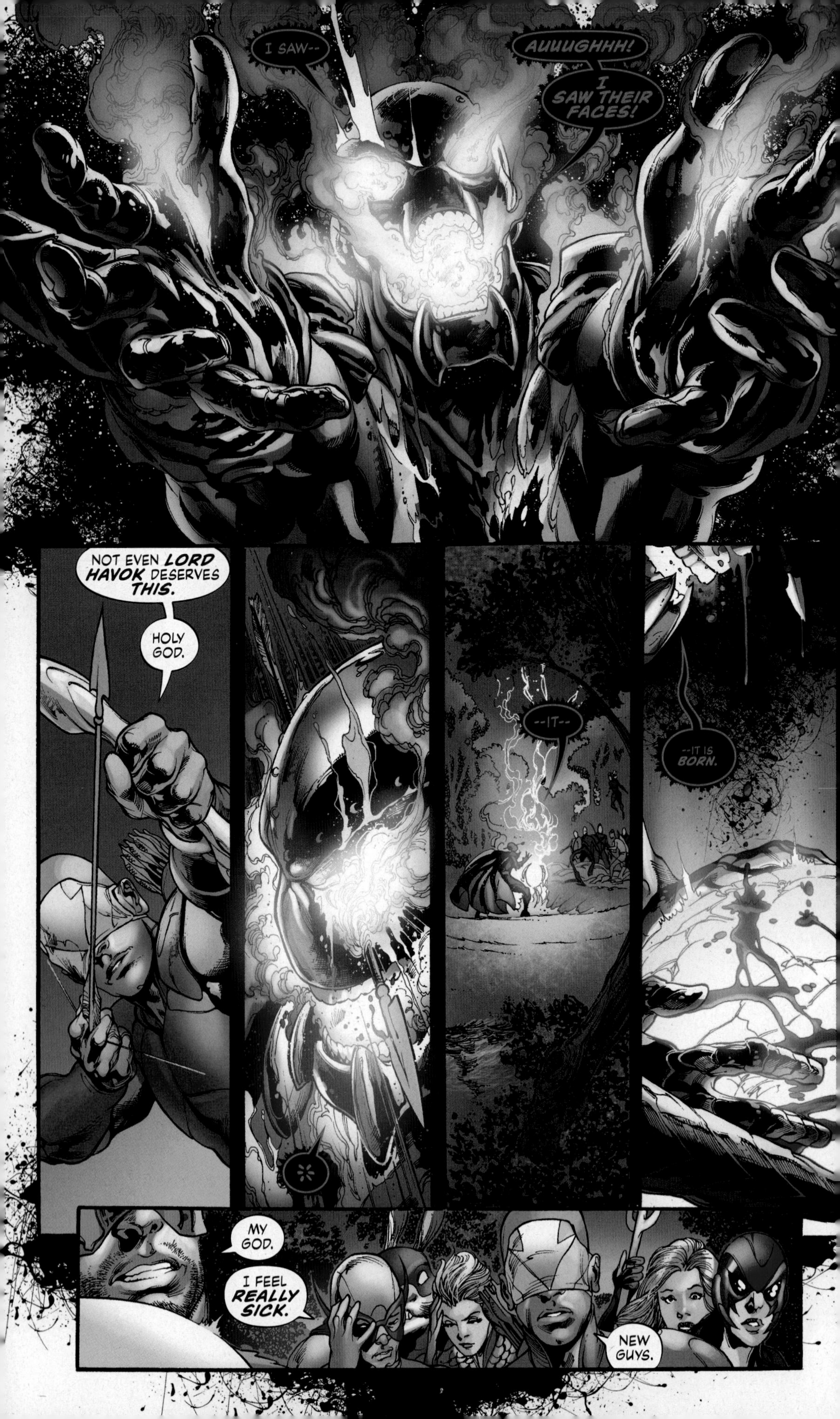
I SAW--
AUUUGHHH!
I SAW THEIR FACES!
NOT EVEN LORD HAVOK DESERVES THIS.
HOLY GOD.
--IT--
--IT IS BORN.
MY GOD.
I FEEL REALLY SICK.
NEW GUYS.

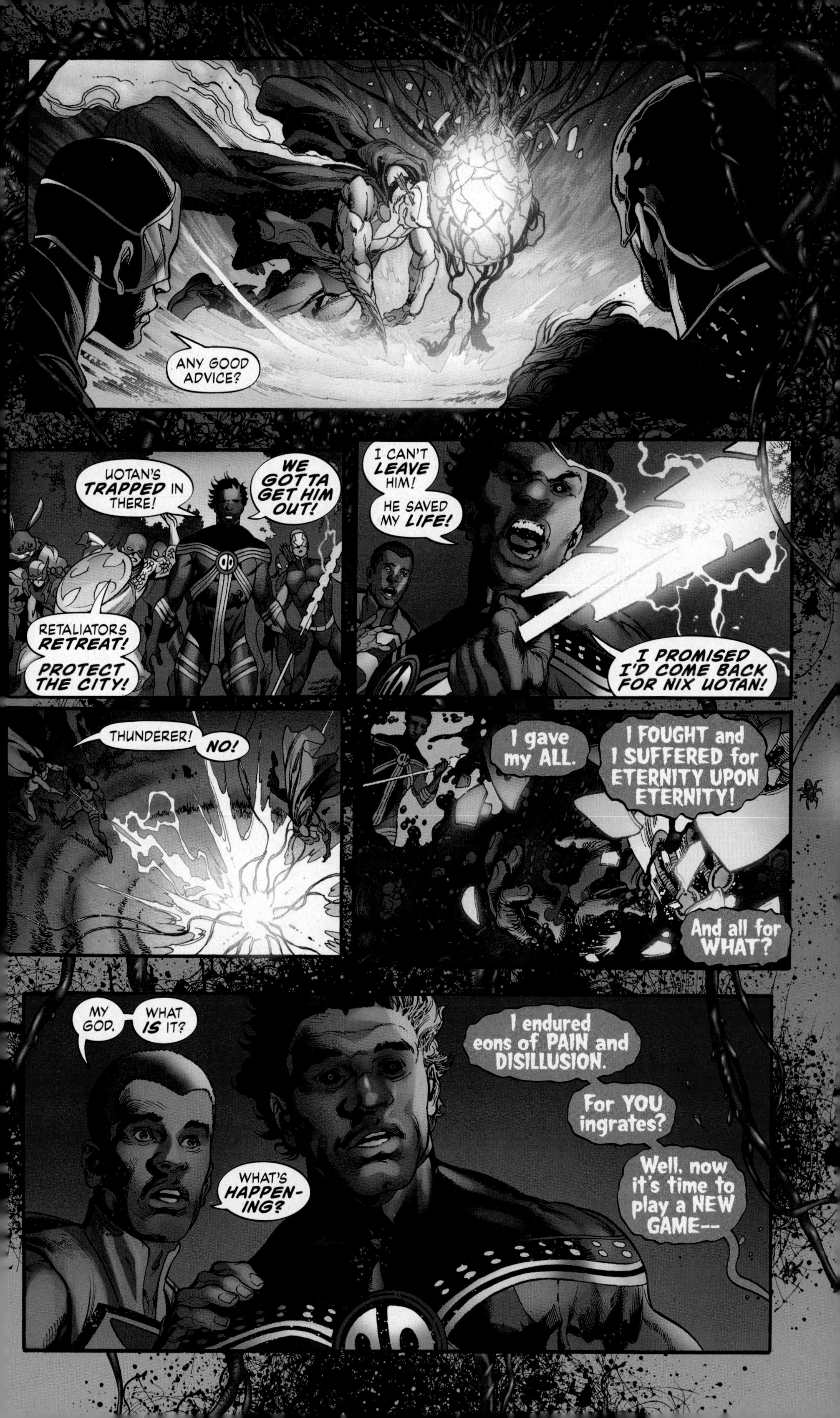
ANY GOOD ADVICE?
UOTAN'S *TRAPPED* IN THERE!
WE GOTTA GET HIM OUT!
RETALIATORS *RETREAT!*
PROTECT THE CITY!
I CAN'T *LEAVE* HIM!
HE SAVED MY *LIFE!*
I PROMISED I'D COME BACK FOR NIX UOTAN!
THUNDERER!
NO!
I gave my ALL.
I FOUGHT and I SUFFERED for ETERNITY UPON ETERNITY!
And all for WHAT?
MY GOD.
WHAT *IS* IT?
WHAT'S *HAPPEN-ING?*
I endured eons of PAIN and DISILLUSION.
For YOU ingrates?
Well, now it's time to play a NEW GAME--

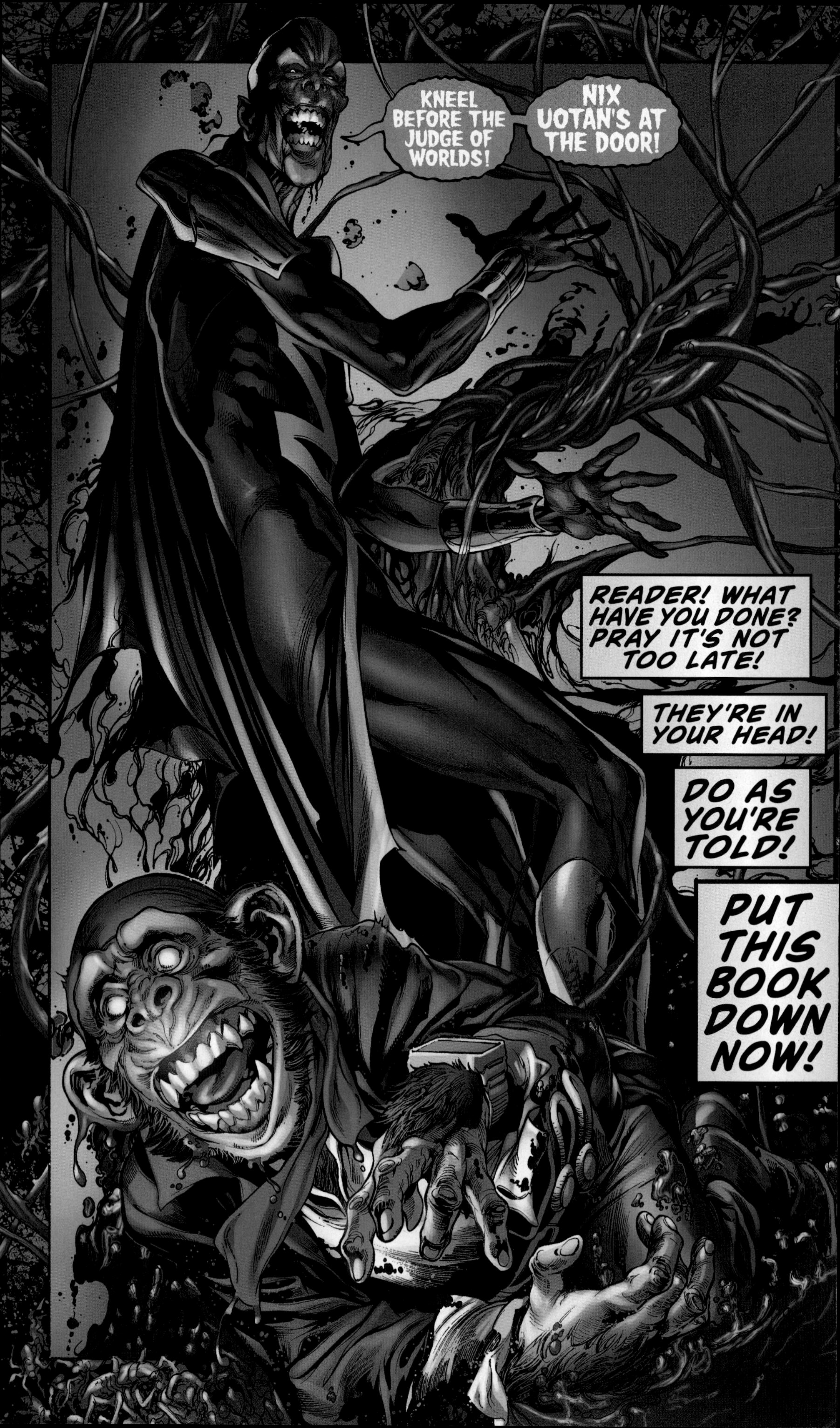
KNEEL BEFORE THE JUDGE OF WORLDS!
NIX UOTAN'S AT THE DOOR!
READER! WHAT HAVE YOU DONE? PRAY IT'S NOT TOO LATE!
THEY'RE IN YOUR HEAD!
DO AS YOU'RE TOLD!
PUT THIS BOOK DOWN NOW!

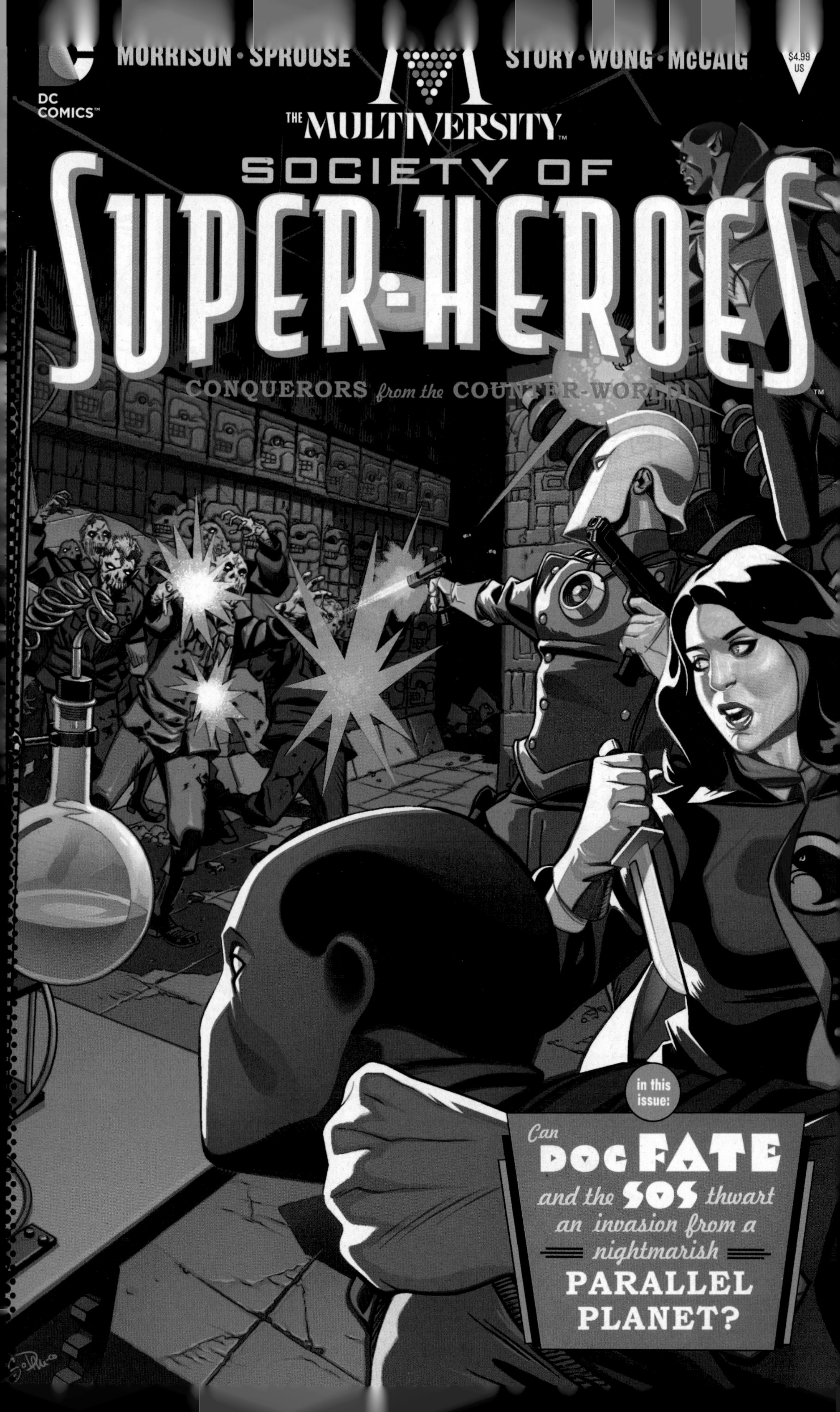
DC COMICS™
MORRISON · SPROUSE
STORY · WONG · McCAIG
$4.99 US
THE MULTIVERSITY™
SOCIETY OF
SUPER-HEROES™
CONQUERORS from the COUNTER-WORLD!
in this issue:
Can DOC FATE and the SOS thwart an invasion from a nightmarish PARALLEL PLANET?

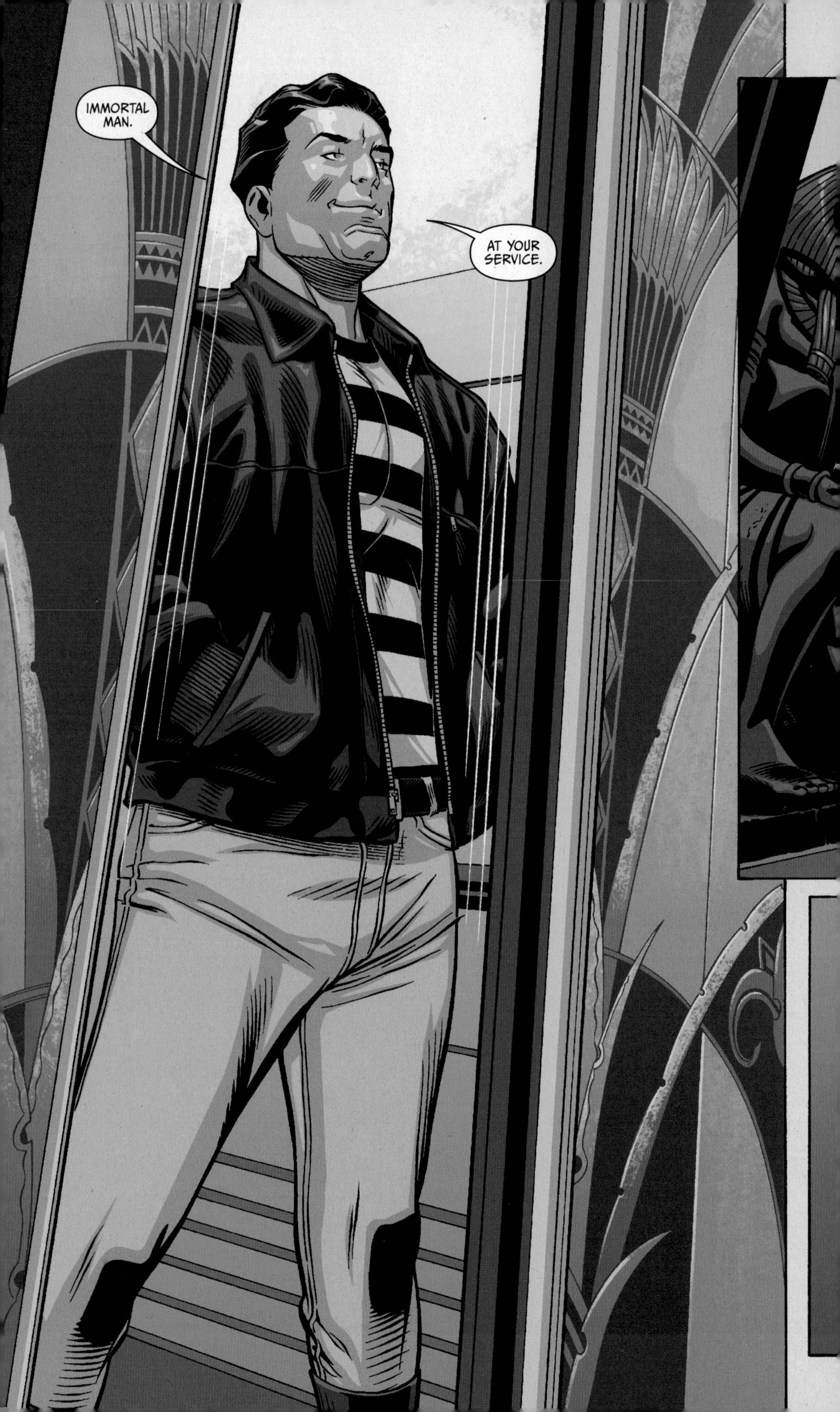
IMMORTAL MAN.
AT YOUR SERVICE.

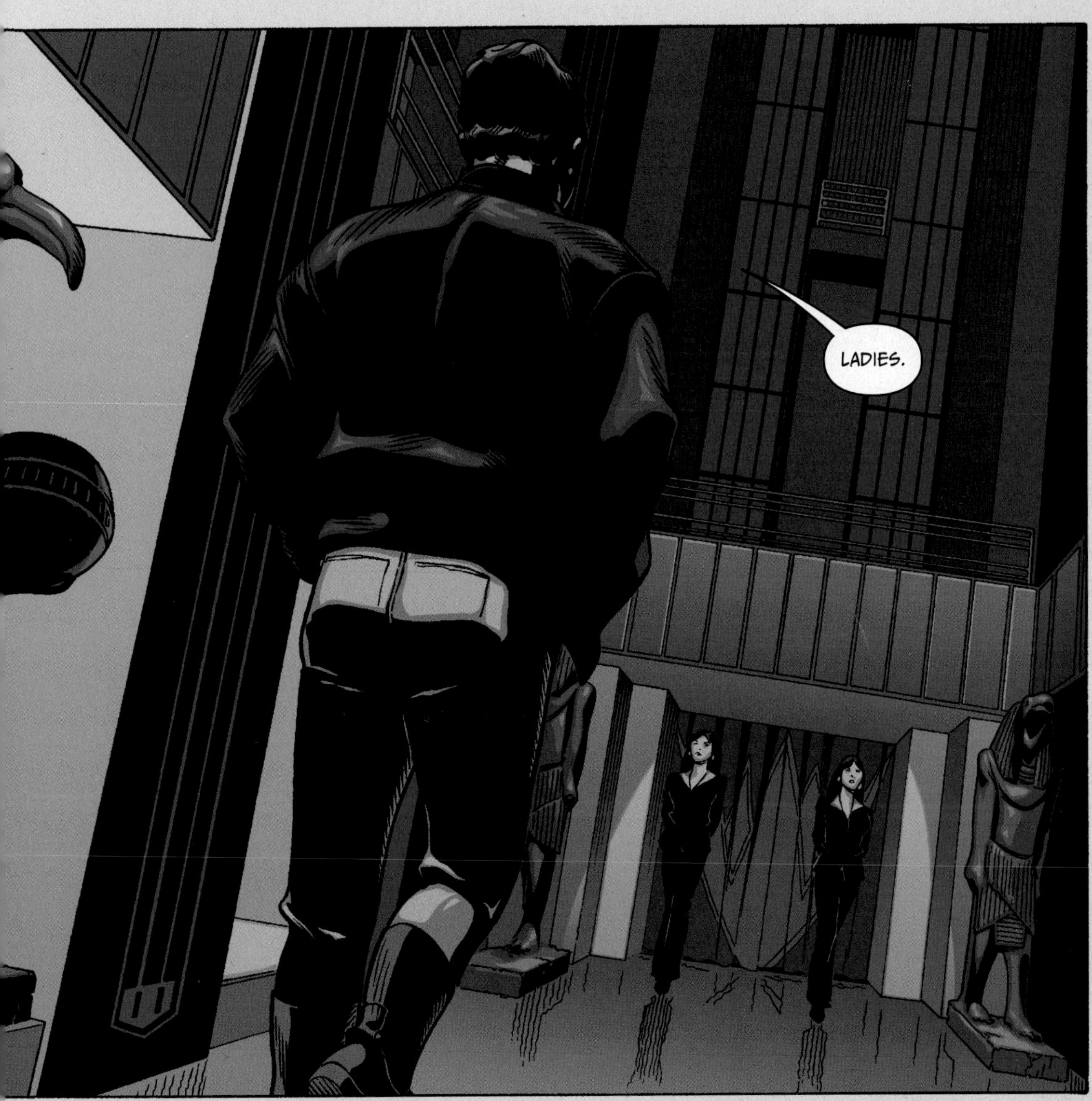
LADIES.

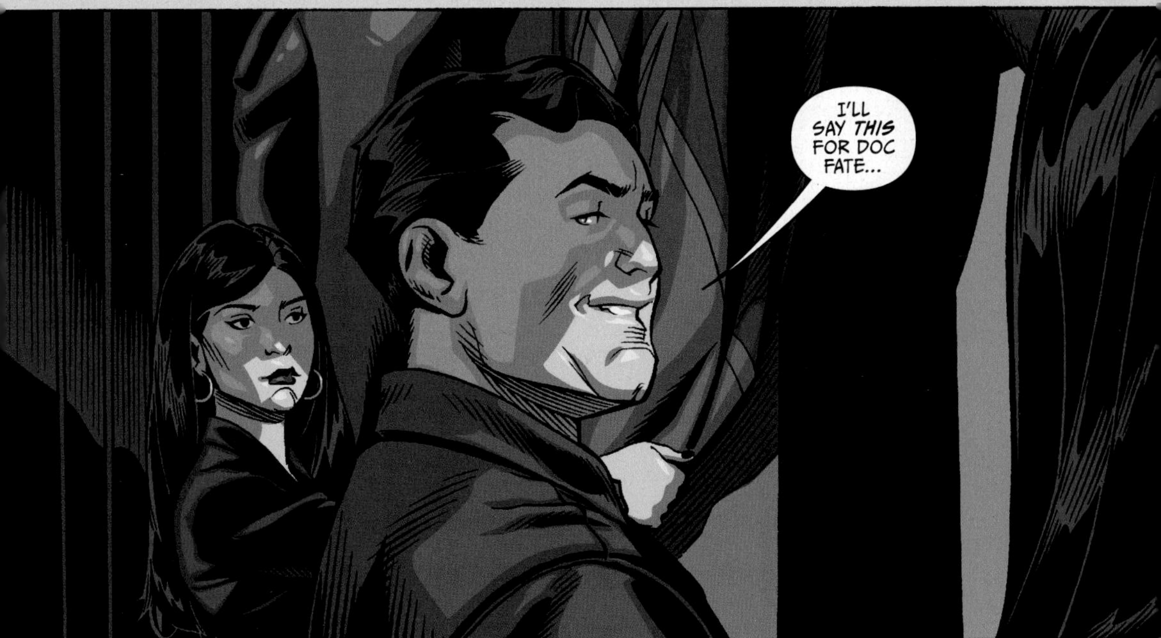
I'LL SAY *THIS* FOR DOC FATE...

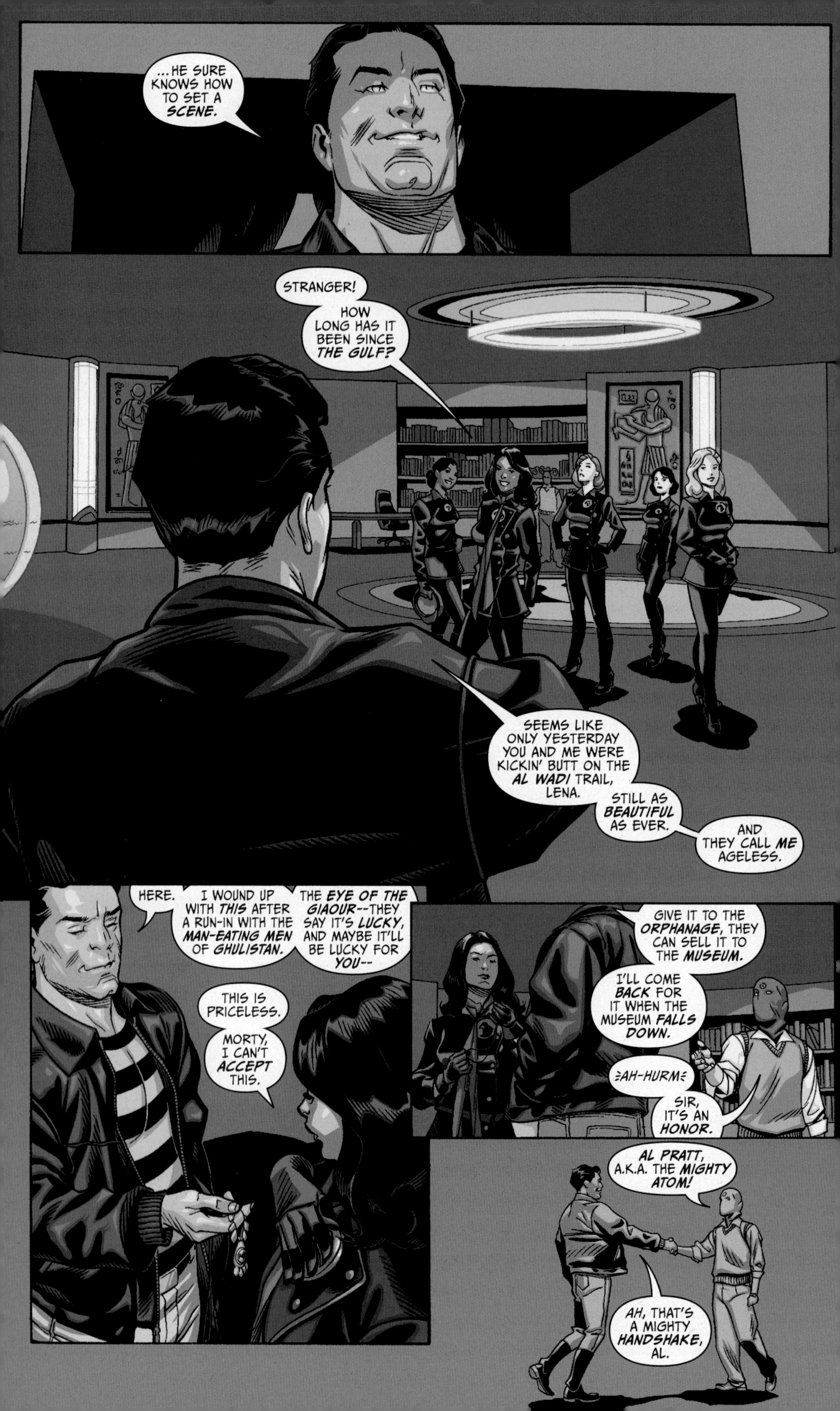
...HE SURE KNOWS HOW TO SET A SCENE.
STRANGER!
HOW LONG HAS IT BEEN SINCE THE GULF?
SEEMS LIKE ONLY YESTERDAY YOU AND ME WERE KICKIN' BUTT ON THE AL WADI TRAIL, LENA.
STILL AS BEAUTIFUL AS EVER.
AND THEY CALL ME AGELESS.
HERE.
I WOUND UP WITH THIS AFTER A RUN-IN WITH THE MAN-EATING MEN OF GHULISTAN.
THE EYE OF THE GIAOUR--THEY SAY IT'S LUCKY, AND MAYBE IT'LL BE LUCKY FOR YOU--
THIS IS PRICELESS.
MORTY, I CAN'T ACCEPT THIS.
GIVE IT TO THE ORPHANAGE, THEY CAN SELL IT TO THE MUSEUM.
I'LL COME BACK FOR IT WHEN THE MUSEUM FALLS DOWN.
AH-HURM
SIR, IT'S AN HONOR.
AL PRATT, A.K.A. THE MIGHTY ATOM!
AH, THAT'S A MIGHTY HANDSHAKE, AL.

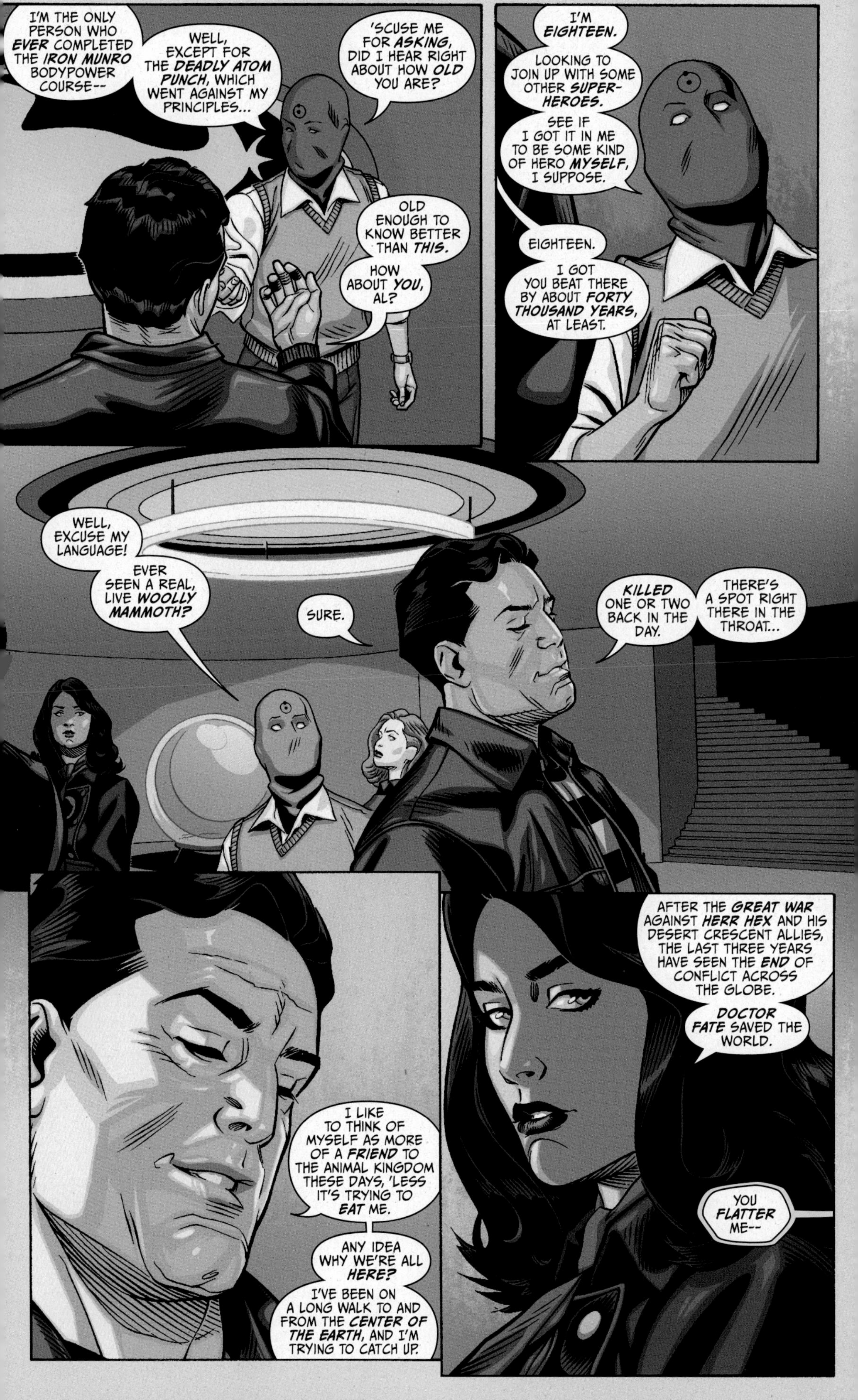

I'M THE ONLY PERSON WHO EVER COMPLETED THE IRON MUNRO BODYPOWER COURSE--
WELL, EXCEPT FOR THE DEADLY ATOM PUNCH, WHICH WENT AGAINST MY PRINCIPLES...
'SCUSE ME FOR ASKING, DID I HEAR RIGHT ABOUT HOW OLD YOU ARE?
OLD ENOUGH TO KNOW BETTER THAN THIS.
HOW ABOUT YOU, AL?
I'M EIGHTEEN.
LOOKING TO JOIN UP WITH SOME OTHER SUPER-HEROES.
SEE IF I GOT IT IN ME TO BE SOME KIND OF HERO MYSELF, I SUPPOSE.
EIGHTEEN.
I GOT YOU BEAT THERE BY ABOUT FORTY THOUSAND YEARS, AT LEAST.
WELL, EXCUSE MY LANGUAGE!
EVER SEEN A REAL, LIVE WOOLLY MAMMOTH?
SURE.
KILLED ONE OR TWO BACK IN THE DAY.
THERE'S A SPOT RIGHT THERE IN THE THROAT...
I LIKE TO THINK OF MYSELF AS MORE OF A FRIEND TO THE ANIMAL KINGDOM THESE DAYS, 'LESS IT'S TRYING TO EAT ME.
ANY IDEA WHY WE'RE ALL HERE?
I'VE BEEN ON A LONG WALK TO AND FROM THE CENTER OF THE EARTH, AND I'M TRYING TO CATCH UP.
AFTER THE GREAT WAR AGAINST HERR HEX AND HIS DESERT CRESCENT ALLIES, THE LAST THREE YEARS HAVE SEEN THE END OF CONFLICT ACROSS THE GLOBE.
DOCTOR FATE SAVED THE WORLD.
YOU FLATTER ME--

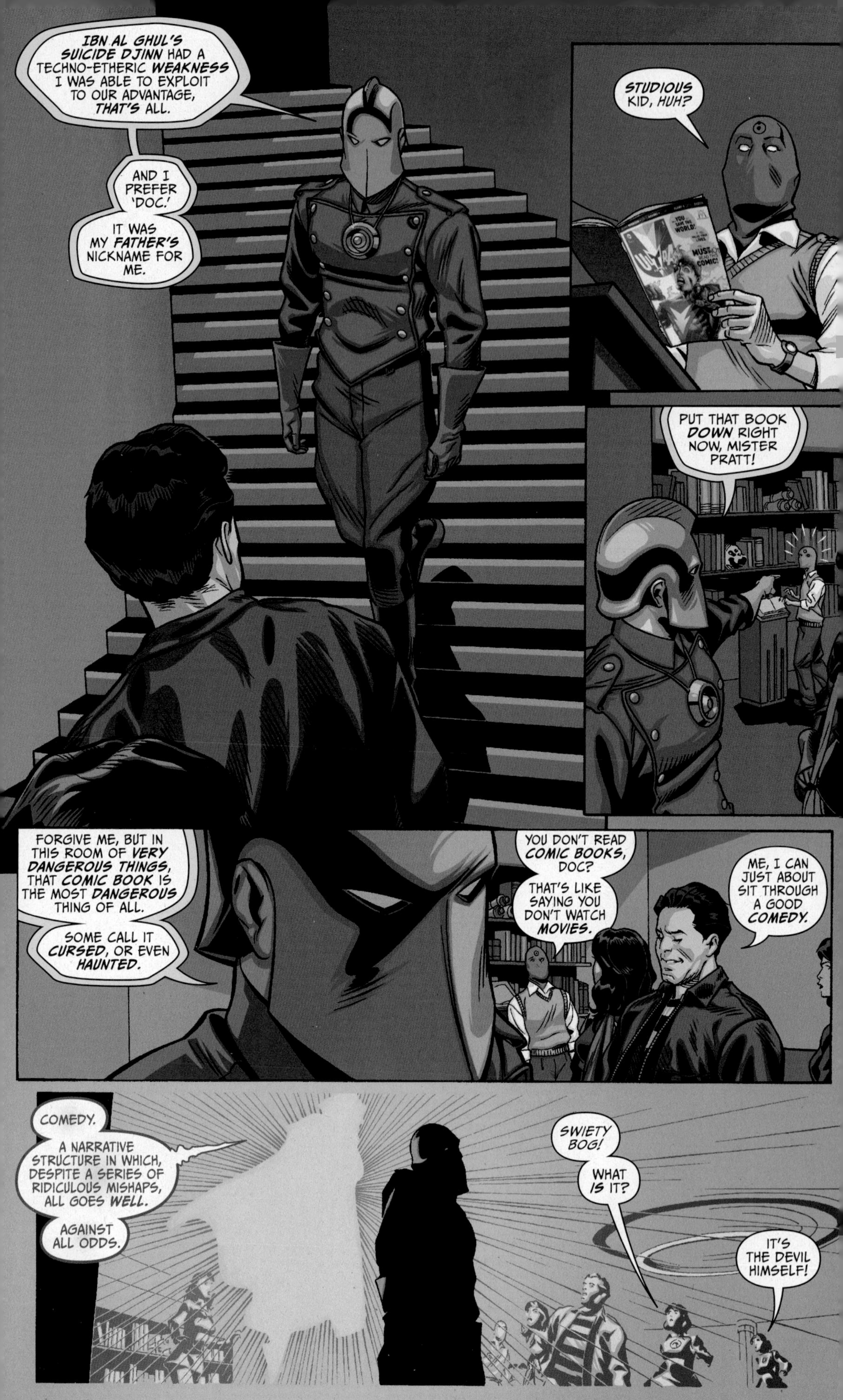
IBN AL GHUL'S SUICIDE DJINN HAD A TECHNO-ETHERIC WEAKNESS I WAS ABLE TO EXPLOIT TO OUR ADVANTAGE, THAT'S ALL.
AND I PREFER 'DOC.'
IT WAS MY FATHER'S NICKNAME FOR ME.
STUDIOUS KID, HUH?
PUT THAT BOOK DOWN RIGHT NOW, MISTER PRATT!
FORGIVE ME, BUT IN THIS ROOM OF VERY DANGEROUS THINGS, THAT COMIC BOOK IS THE MOST DANGEROUS THING OF ALL.
SOME CALL IT CURSED, OR EVEN HAUNTED.
YOU DON'T READ COMIC BOOKS, DOC?
THAT'S LIKE SAYING YOU DON'T WATCH MOVIES.
ME, I CAN JUST ABOUT SIT THROUGH A GOOD COMEDY.
COMEDY.
A NARRATIVE STRUCTURE IN WHICH, DESPITE A SERIES OF RIDICULOUS MISHAPS, ALL GOES WELL.
AGAINST ALL ODDS.
SWIETY BOG!
WHAT IS IT?
IT'S THE DEVIL HIMSELF!

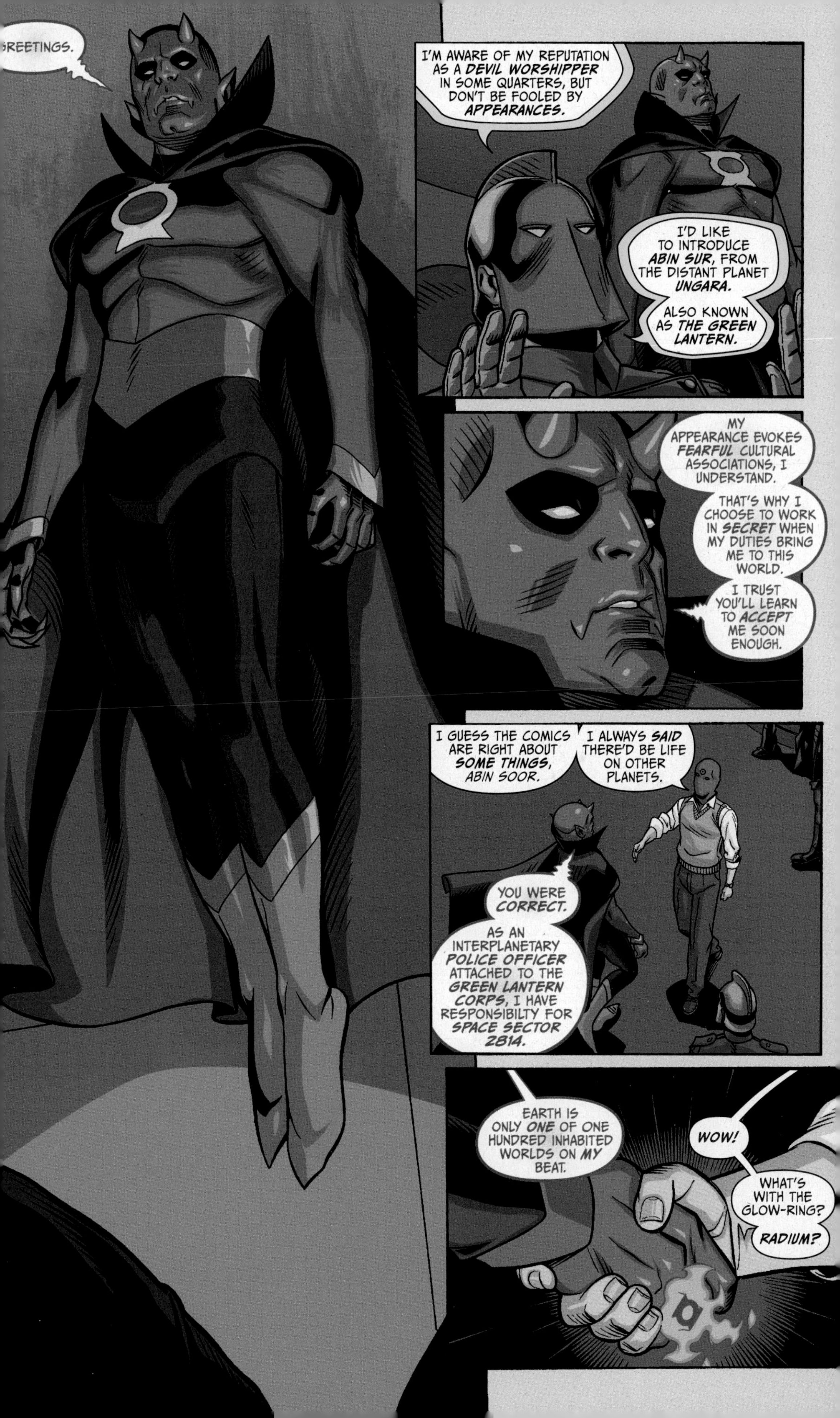
GREETINGS.
I'M AWARE OF MY REPUTATION AS A DEVIL WORSHIPPER IN SOME QUARTERS, BUT DON'T BE FOOLED BY APPEARANCES.
I'D LIKE TO INTRODUCE ABIN SUR, FROM THE DISTANT PLANET UNGARA.
ALSO KNOWN AS THE GREEN LANTERN.
MY APPEARANCE EVOKES FEARFUL CULTURAL ASSOCIATIONS, I UNDERSTAND.
THAT'S WHY I CHOOSE TO WORK IN SECRET WHEN MY DUTIES BRING ME TO THIS WORLD.
I TRUST YOU'LL LEARN TO ACCEPT ME SOON ENOUGH.
I GUESS THE COMICS ARE RIGHT ABOUT SOME THINGS, ABIN SOOR.
I ALWAYS SAID THERE'D BE LIFE ON OTHER PLANETS.
YOU WERE CORRECT.
AS AN INTERPLANETARY POLICE OFFICER ATTACHED TO THE GREEN LANTERN CORPS, I HAVE RESPONSIBILTY FOR SPACE SECTOR 2814.
EARTH IS ONLY ONE OF ONE HUNDRED INHABITED WORLDS ON MY BEAT.
WOW!
WHAT'S WITH THE GLOW-RING?
RADIUM?

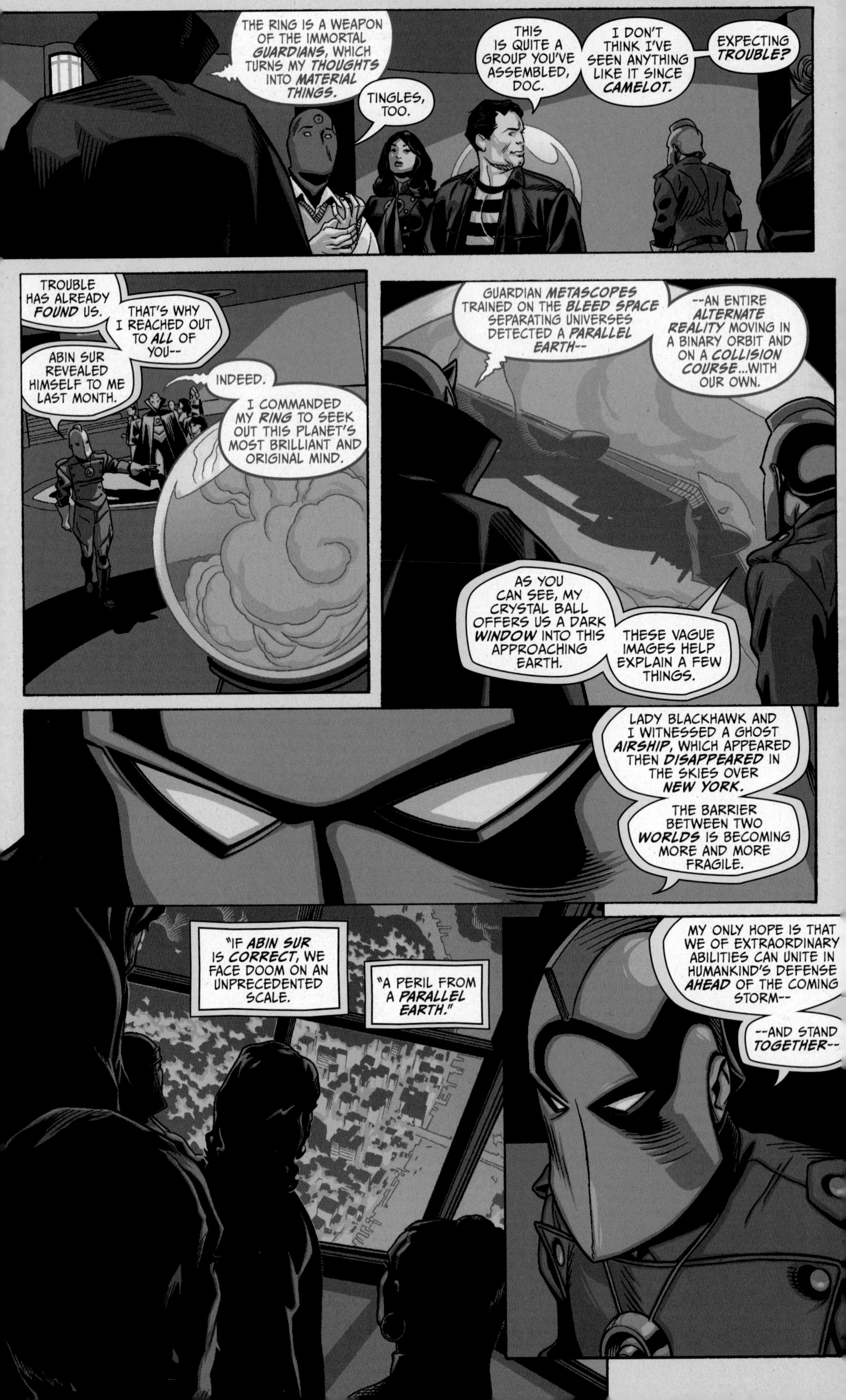
THE RING IS A WEAPON OF THE IMMORTAL GUARDIANS, WHICH TURNS MY THOUGHTS INTO MATERIAL THINGS.
TINGLES, TOO.
THIS IS QUITE A GROUP YOU'VE ASSEMBLED, DOC.
I DON'T THINK I'VE SEEN ANYTHING LIKE IT SINCE CAMELOT.
EXPECTING TROUBLE?
TROUBLE HAS ALREADY FOUND US.
THAT'S WHY I REACHED OUT TO ALL OF YOU--
ABIN SUR REVEALED HIMSELF TO ME LAST MONTH.
INDEED.
I COMMANDED MY RING TO SEEK OUT THIS PLANET'S MOST BRILLIANT AND ORIGINAL MIND.
GUARDIAN METASCOPES TRAINED ON THE BLEED SPACE SEPARATING UNIVERSES DETECTED A PARALLEL EARTH--
--AN ENTIRE ALTERNATE REALITY MOVING IN A BINARY ORBIT AND ON A COLLISION COURSE...WITH OUR OWN.
AS YOU CAN SEE, MY CRYSTAL BALL OFFERS US A DARK WINDOW INTO THIS APPROACHING EARTH.
THESE VAGUE IMAGES HELP EXPLAIN A FEW THINGS.
LADY BLACKHAWK AND I WITNESSED A GHOST AIRSHIP, WHICH APPEARED THEN DISAPPEARED IN THE SKIES OVER NEW YORK.
THE BARRIER BETWEEN TWO WORLDS IS BECOMING MORE AND MORE FRAGILE.
"IF ABIN SUR IS CORRECT, WE FACE DOOM ON AN UNPRECEDENTED SCALE.
"A PERIL FROM A PARALLEL EARTH."
MY ONLY HOPE IS THAT WE OF EXTRAORDINARY ABILITIES CAN UNITE IN HUMANKIND'S DEFENSE AHEAD OF THE COMING STORM--
--AND STAND TOGETHER--

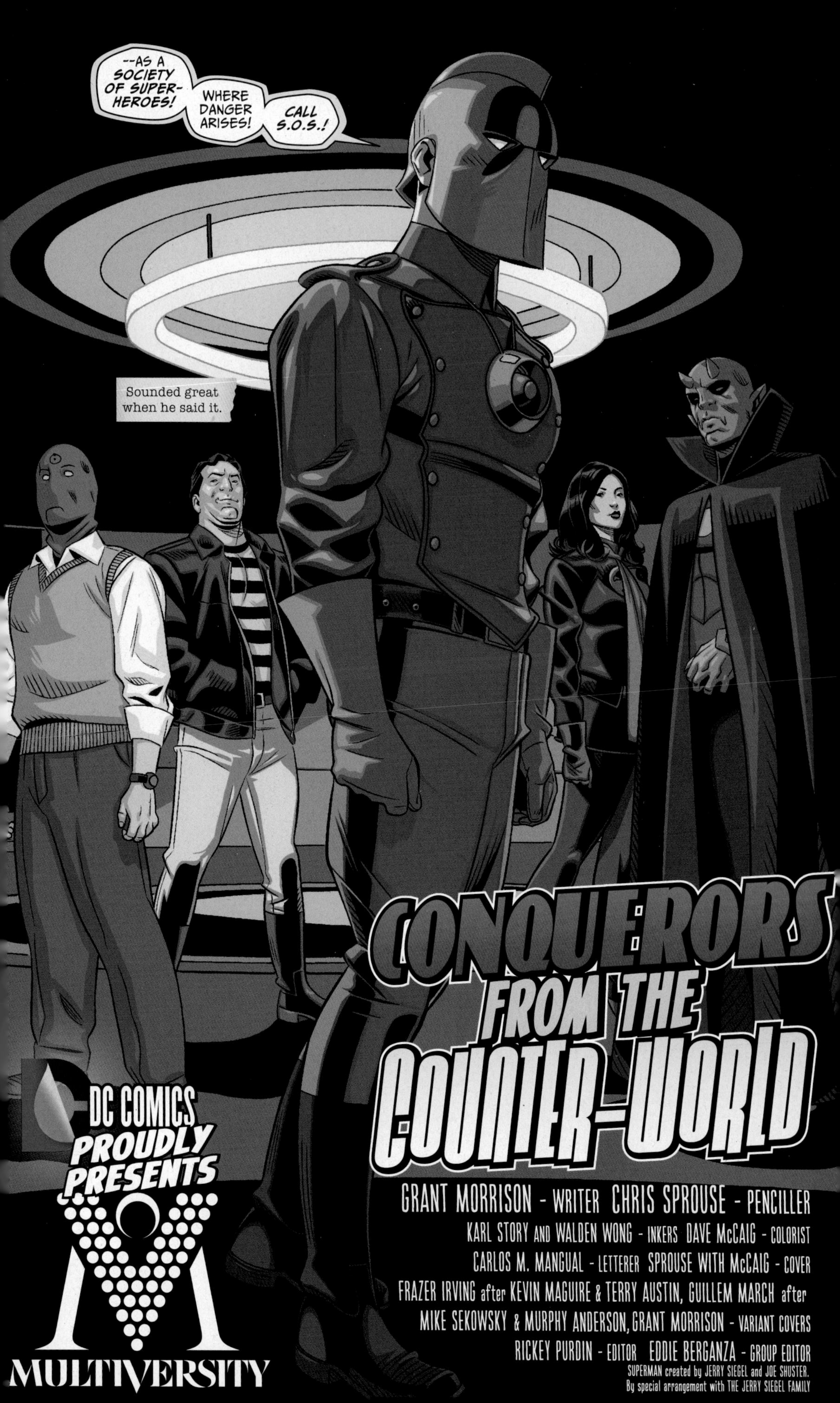

--AS A SOCIETY OF SUPER-HEROES!
WHERE DANGER ARISES!
CALL S.O.S.!
Sounded great when he said it.
CONQUERORS FROM THE COUNTER-WORLD
DC COMICS PROUDLY PRESENTS
MULTIVERSITY
GRANT MORRISON - WRITER CHRIS SPROUSE - PENCILLER
KARL STORY AND WALDEN WONG - INKERS DAVE McCAIG - COLORIST
CARLOS M. MANGUAL - LETTERER SPROUSE WITH McCAIG - COVER
FRAZER IRVING after KEVIN MAGUIRE & TERRY AUSTIN, GUILLEM MARCH after
MIKE SEKOWSKY & MURPHY ANDERSON, GRANT MORRISON - VARIANT COVERS
RICKEY PURDIN - EDITOR EDDIE BERGANZA - GROUP EDITOR
SUPERMAN created by JERRY SIEGEL and JOE SHUSTER.
By special arrangement with THE JERRY SIEGEL FAMILY

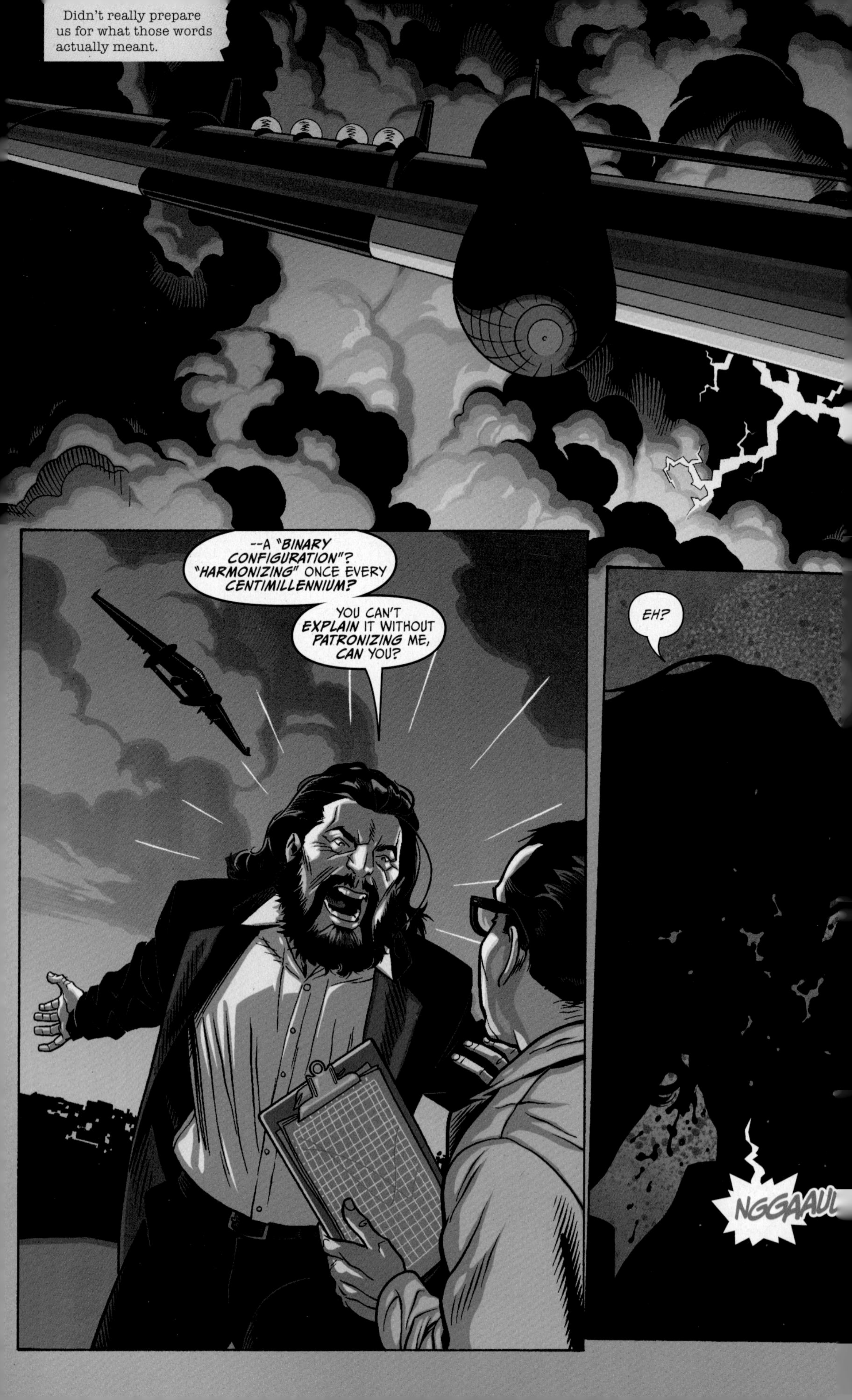
Didn't really prepare us for what those words actually meant.
--A "BINARY CONFIGURATION"? "HARMONIZING" ONCE EVERY CENTIMILLENNIUM?
YOU CAN'T EXPLAIN IT WITHOUT PATRONIZING ME, CAN YOU?
EH?
NGGAAUL

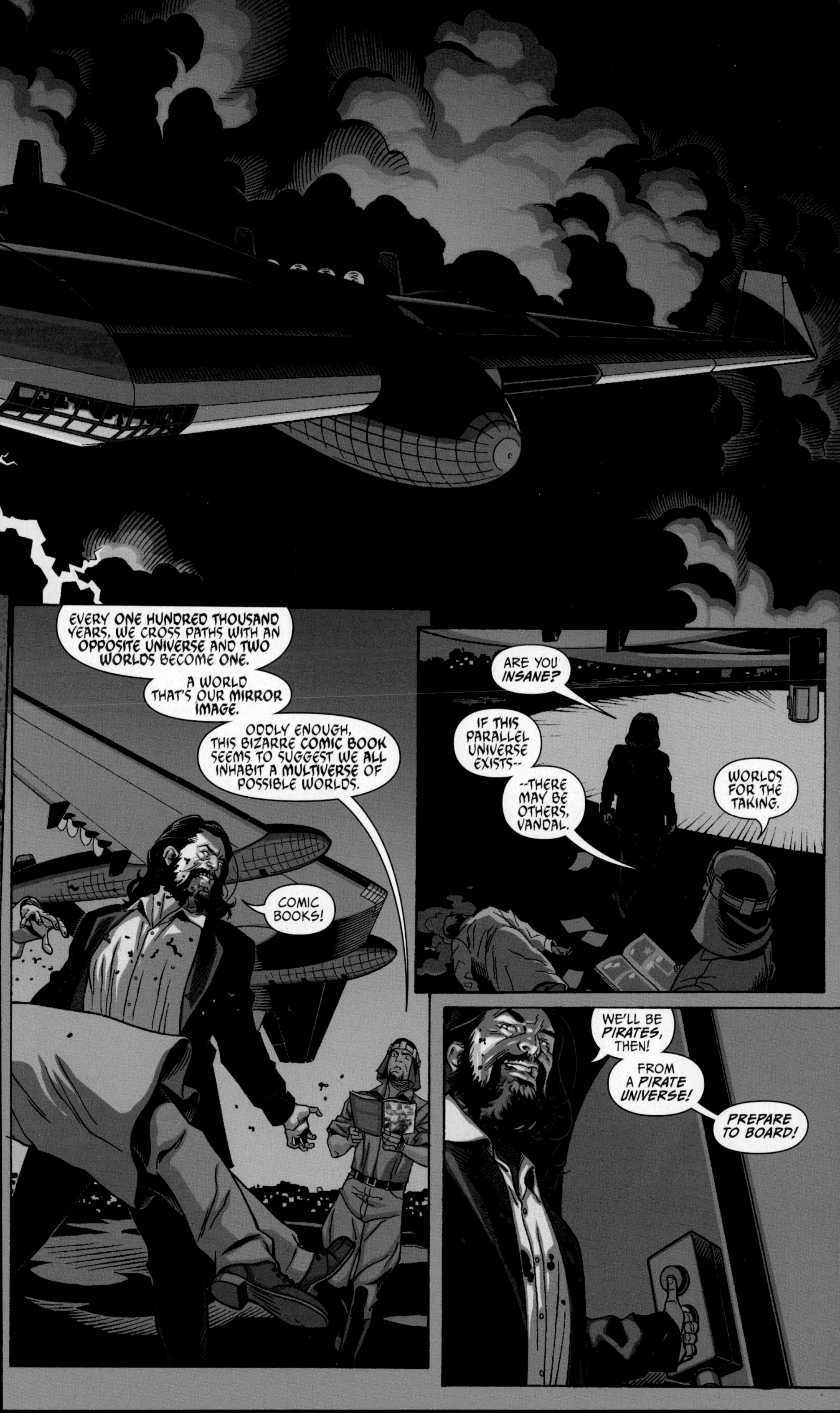
EVERY ONE HUNDRED THOUSAND YEARS, WE CROSS PATHS WITH AN OPPOSITE UNIVERSE AND TWO WORLDS BECOME ONE.
A WORLD THAT'S OUR MIRROR IMAGE.
ODDLY ENOUGH, THIS BIZARRE COMIC BOOK SEEMS TO SUGGEST WE ALL INHABIT A MULTIVERSE OF POSSIBLE WORLDS.
COMIC BOOKS!
ARE YOU INSANE?
IF THIS PARALLEL UNIVERSE EXISTS--
--THERE MAY BE OTHERS, VANDAL.
WORLDS FOR THE TAKING.
WE'LL BE PIRATES, THEN!
FROM A PIRATE UNIVERSE!
PREPARE TO BOARD!

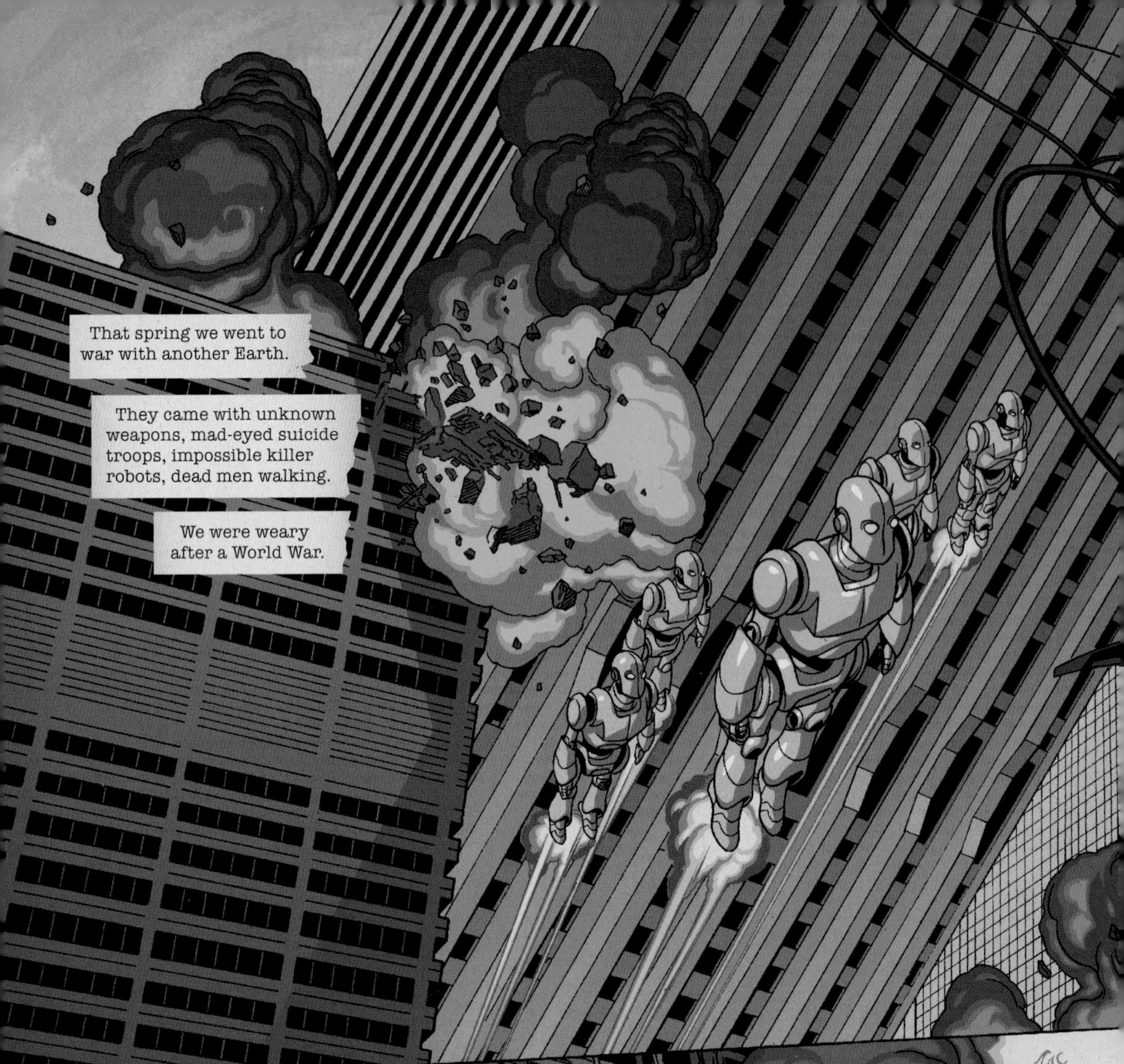
That spring we went to war with another Earth.
They came with unknown weapons, mad-eyed suicide troops, impossible killer robots, dead men walking.
We were weary after a World War.

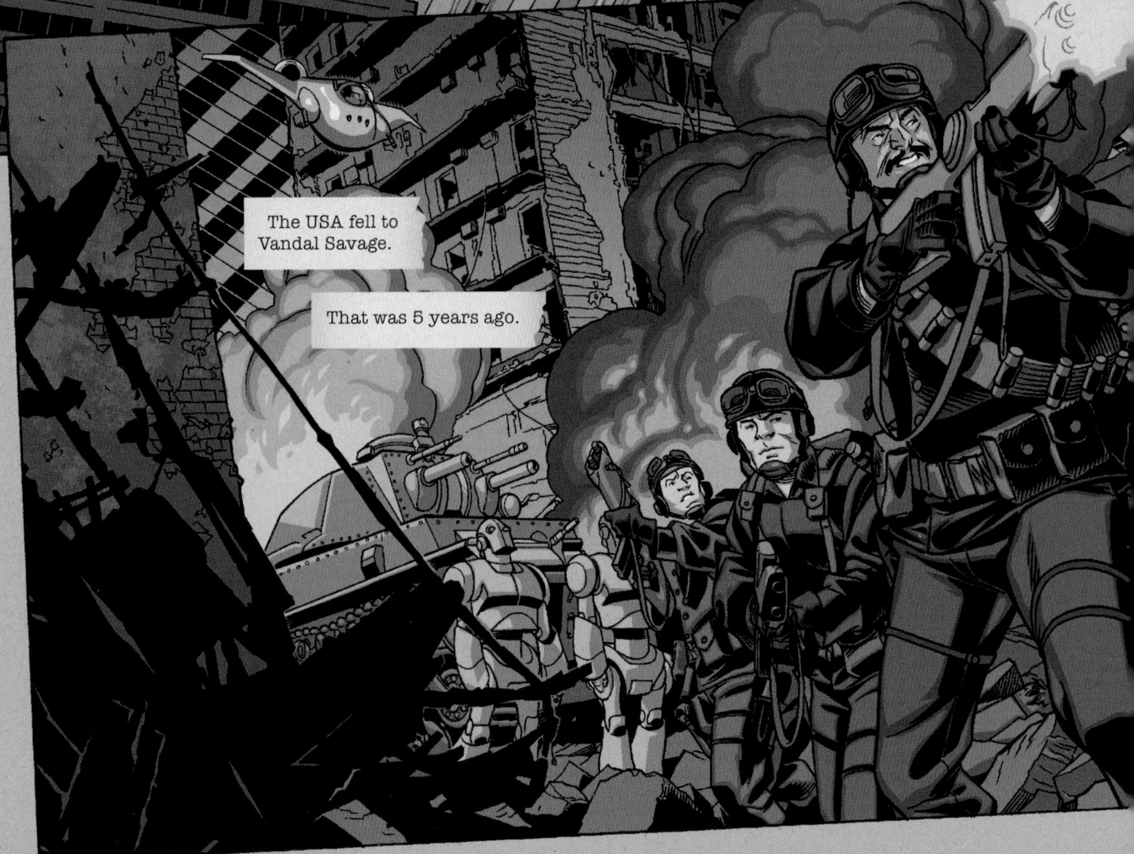
The USA fell to Vandal Savage.
That was 5 years ago.

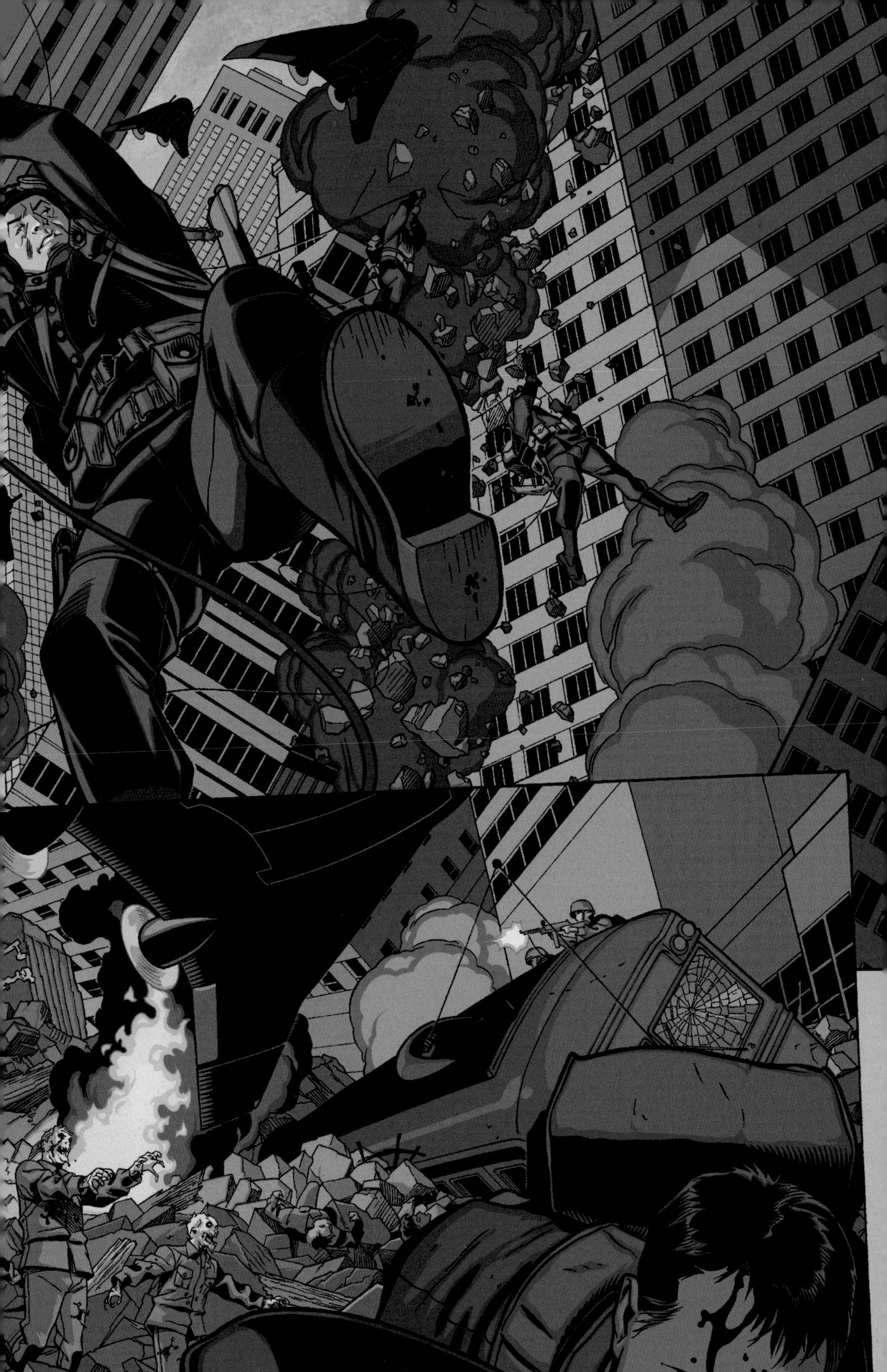

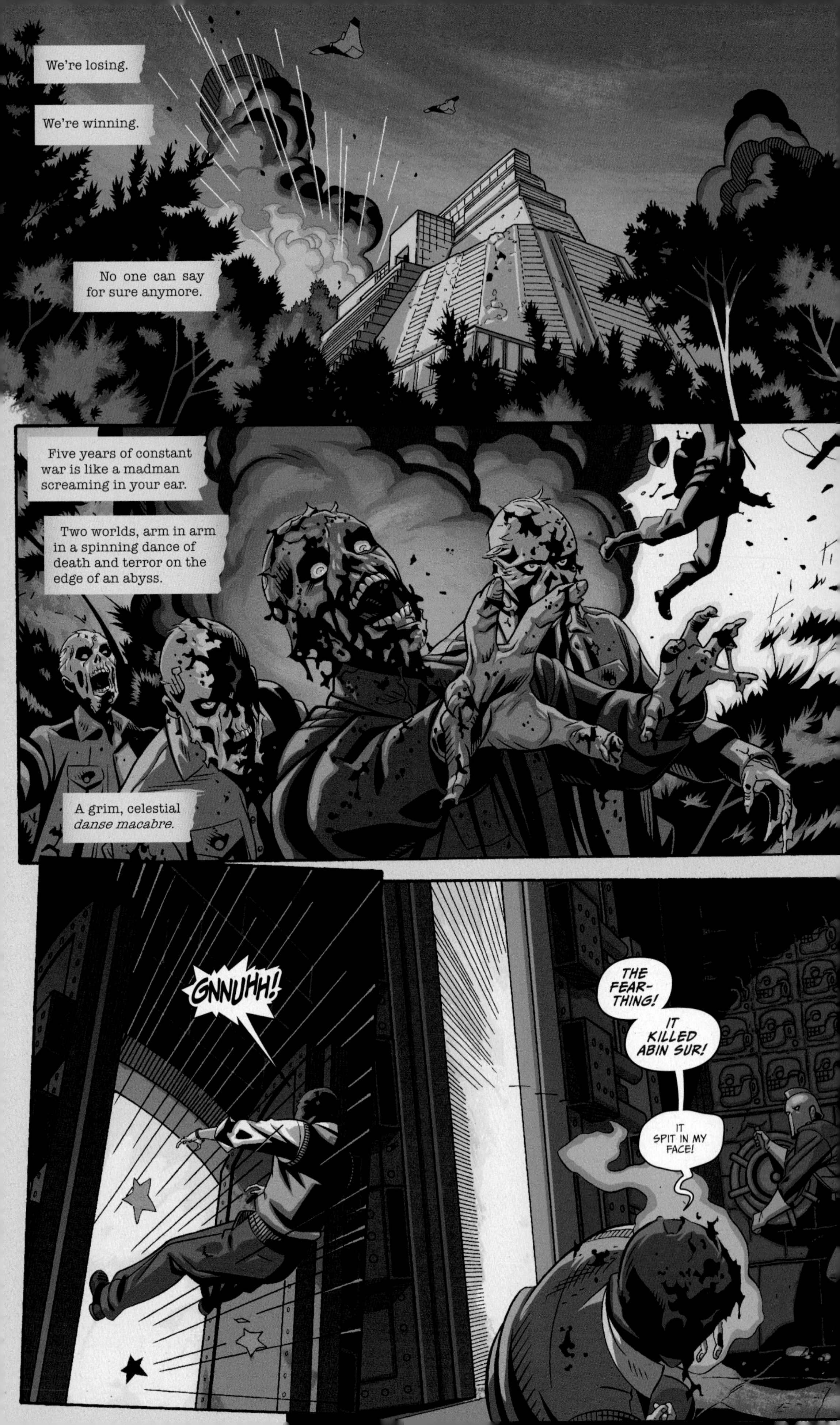
We're losing.
We're winning.
No one can say for sure anymore.
Five years of constant war is like a madman screaming in your ear.
Two worlds, arm in arm in a spinning dance of death and terror on the edge of an abyss.
A grim, celestial *danse macabre.*
GNNUHH!
THE FEAR-THING!
IT KILLED ABIN SUR!
IT SPIT IN MY FACE!

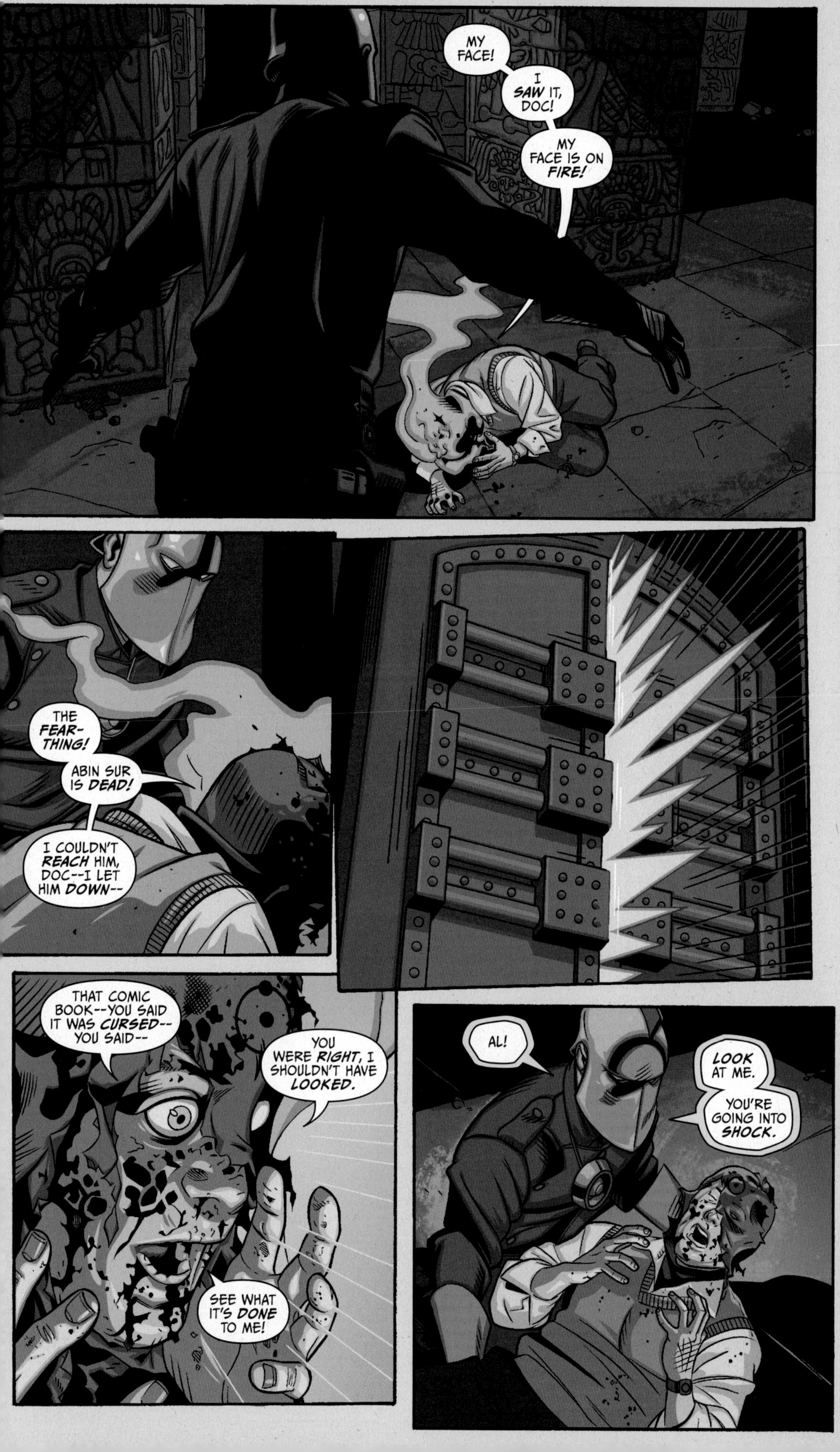
MY FACE!
I SAW IT, DOC!
MY FACE IS ON FIRE!
THE FEAR-THING!
ABIN SUR IS DEAD!
I COULDN'T REACH HIM, DOC--I LET HIM DOWN--
THAT COMIC BOOK--YOU SAID IT WAS CURSED--YOU SAID--
YOU WERE RIGHT, I SHOULDN'T HAVE LOOKED.
SEE WHAT IT'S DONE TO ME!
AL!
LOOK AT ME.
YOU'RE GOING INTO SHOCK.

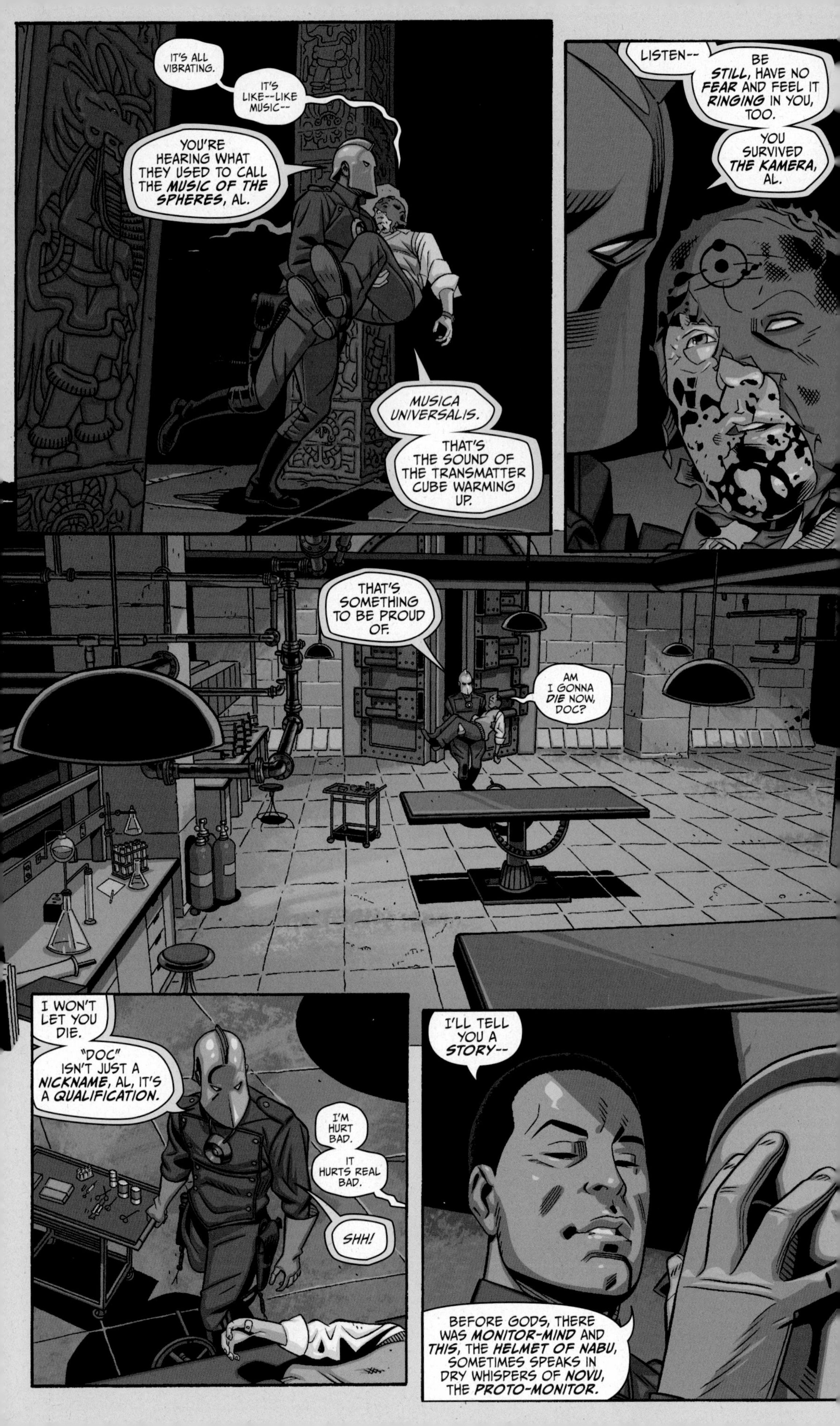

IT'S ALL VIBRATING.
IT'S LIKE--LIKE MUSIC--
YOU'RE HEARING WHAT THEY USED TO CALL THE *MUSIC OF THE SPHERES*, AL.
MUSICA UNIVERSALIS.
THAT'S THE SOUND OF THE TRANSMATTER CUBE WARMING UP.
LISTEN--
BE *STILL*, HAVE NO *FEAR* AND FEEL IT *RINGING* IN YOU, TOO.
YOU SURVIVED *THE KAMERA*, AL.
THAT'S SOMETHING TO BE PROUD OF.
AM I GONNA *DIE* NOW, DOC?
I WON'T LET YOU DIE.
"DOC" ISN'T JUST A *NICKNAME*, AL, IT'S A *QUALIFICATION*.
I'M HURT BAD.
IT HURTS REAL BAD.
SHH!
I'LL TELL YOU A *STORY*--
BEFORE GODS, THERE WAS *MONITOR-MIND* AND *THIS*, THE *HELMET OF NABU*, SOMETIMES SPEAKS IN DRY WHISPERS OF *NOVU*, THE *PROTO-MONITOR*.

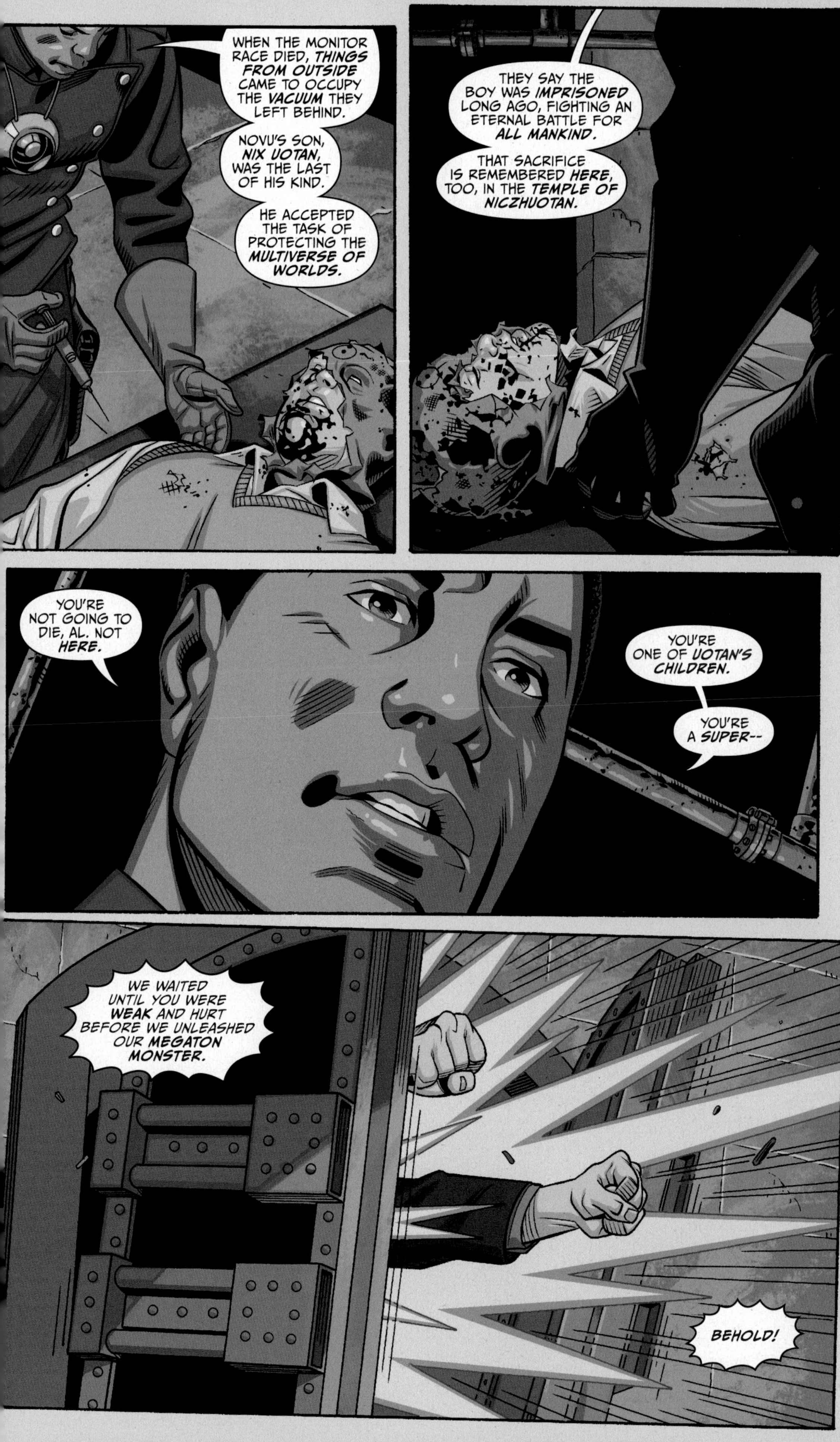

WHEN THE MONITOR RACE DIED, THINGS FROM OUTSIDE CAME TO OCCUPY THE VACUUM THEY LEFT BEHIND.
NOVU'S SON, NIX UOTAN, WAS THE LAST OF HIS KIND.
HE ACCEPTED THE TASK OF PROTECTING THE MULTIVERSE OF WORLDS.
THEY SAY THE BOY WAS IMPRISONED LONG AGO, FIGHTING AN ETERNAL BATTLE FOR ALL MANKIND.
THAT SACRIFICE IS REMEMBERED HERE, TOO, IN THE TEMPLE OF NICZHUOTAN.
YOU'RE NOT GOING TO DIE, AL. NOT HERE.
YOU'RE ONE OF UOTAN'S CHILDREN.
YOU'RE A SUPER--
WE WAITED UNTIL YOU WERE WEAK AND HURT BEFORE WE UNLEASHED OUR MEGATON MONSTER.
BEHOLD!

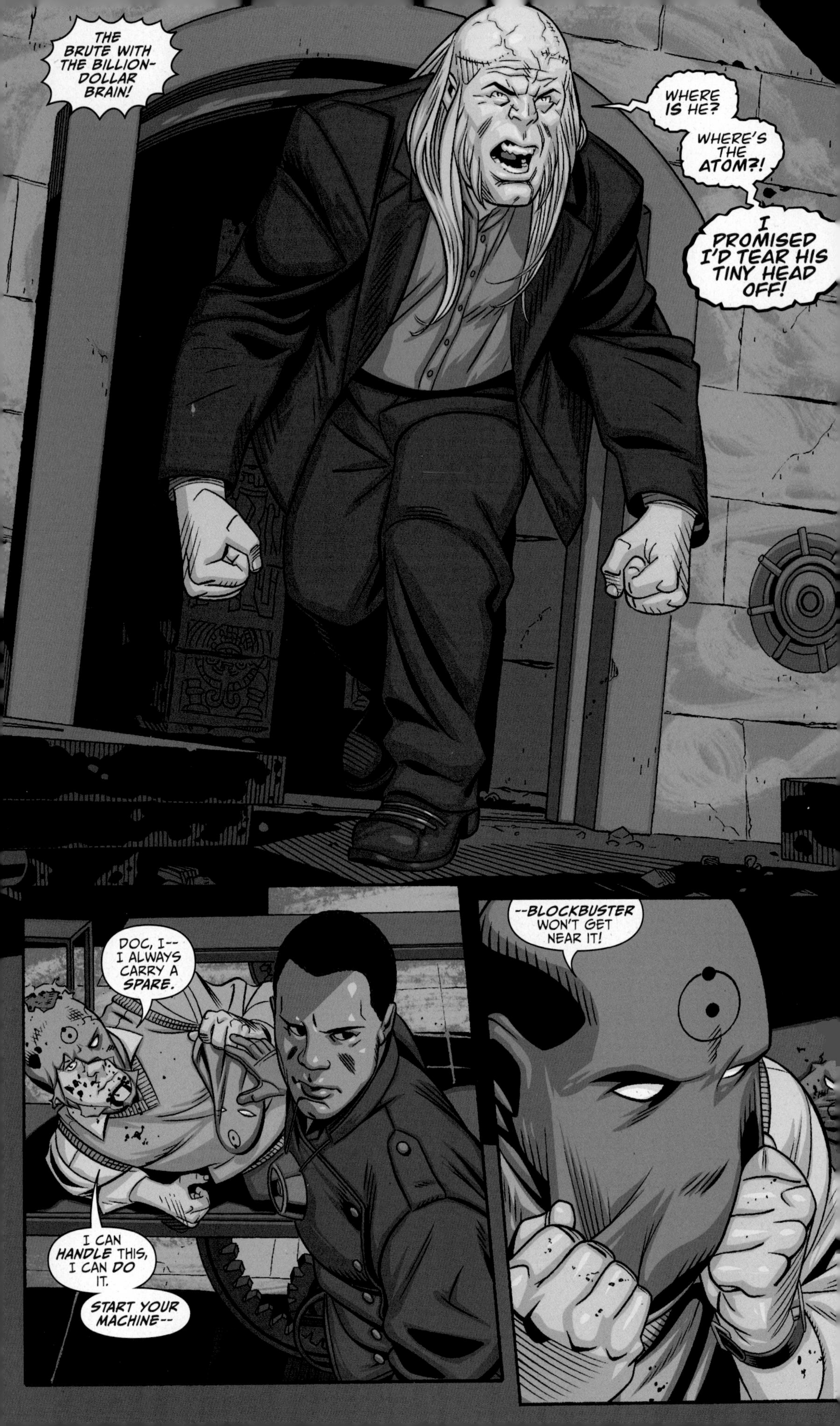
THE BRUTE WITH THE BILLION-DOLLAR BRAIN!
WHERE IS HE?
WHERE'S THE ATOM?!
I PROMISED I'D TEAR HIS TINY HEAD OFF!
DOC, I-- I ALWAYS CARRY A SPARE.
I CAN HANDLE THIS, I CAN DO IT.
START YOUR MACHINE--
--BLOCKBUSTER WON'T GET NEAR IT!

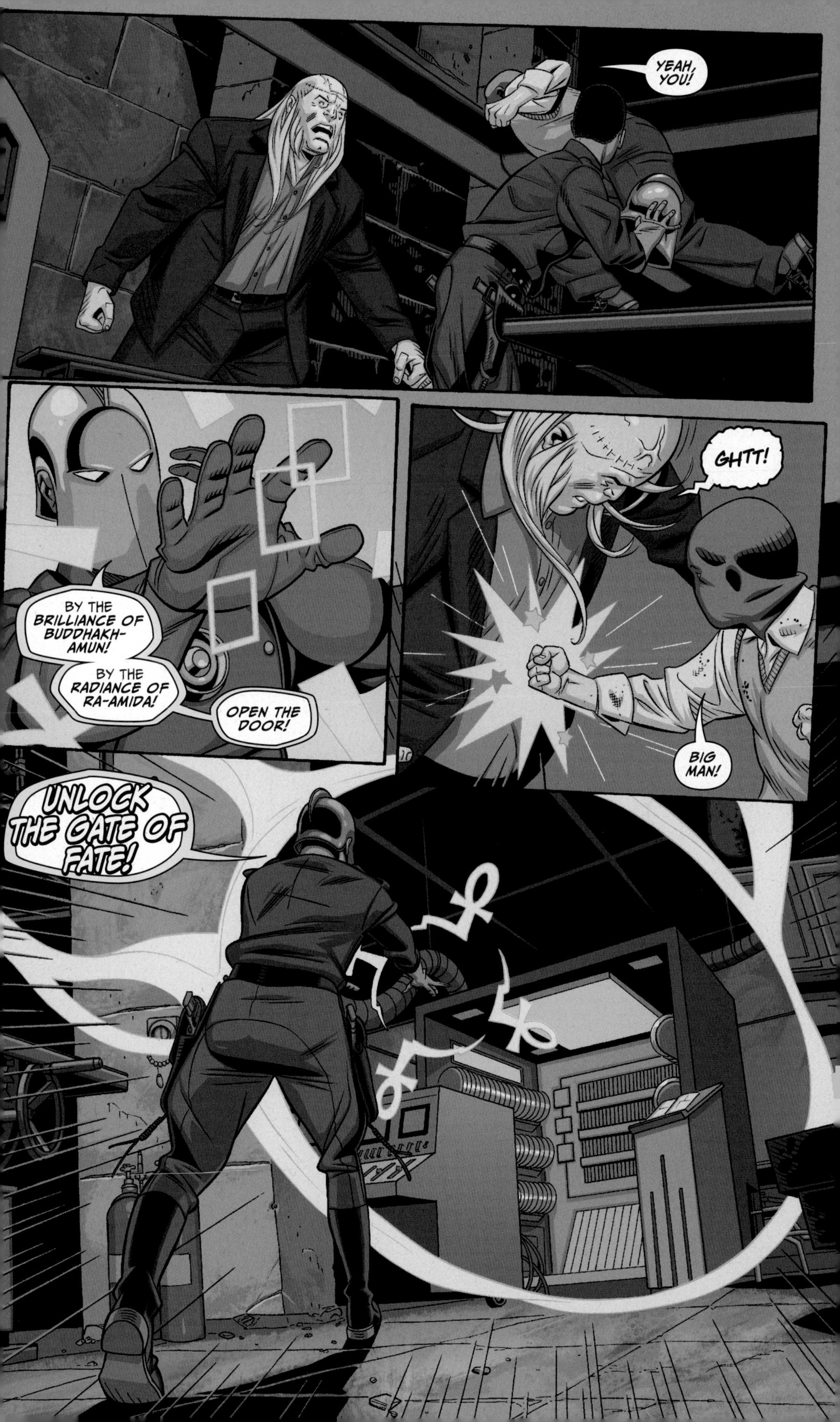
YEAH, YOU!
BY THE BRILLIANCE OF BUDDHAKH-AMUN!
BY THE RADIANCE OF RA-AMIDA!
OPEN THE DOOR!
GHTT!
BIG MAN!
UNLOCK THE GATE OF FATE!

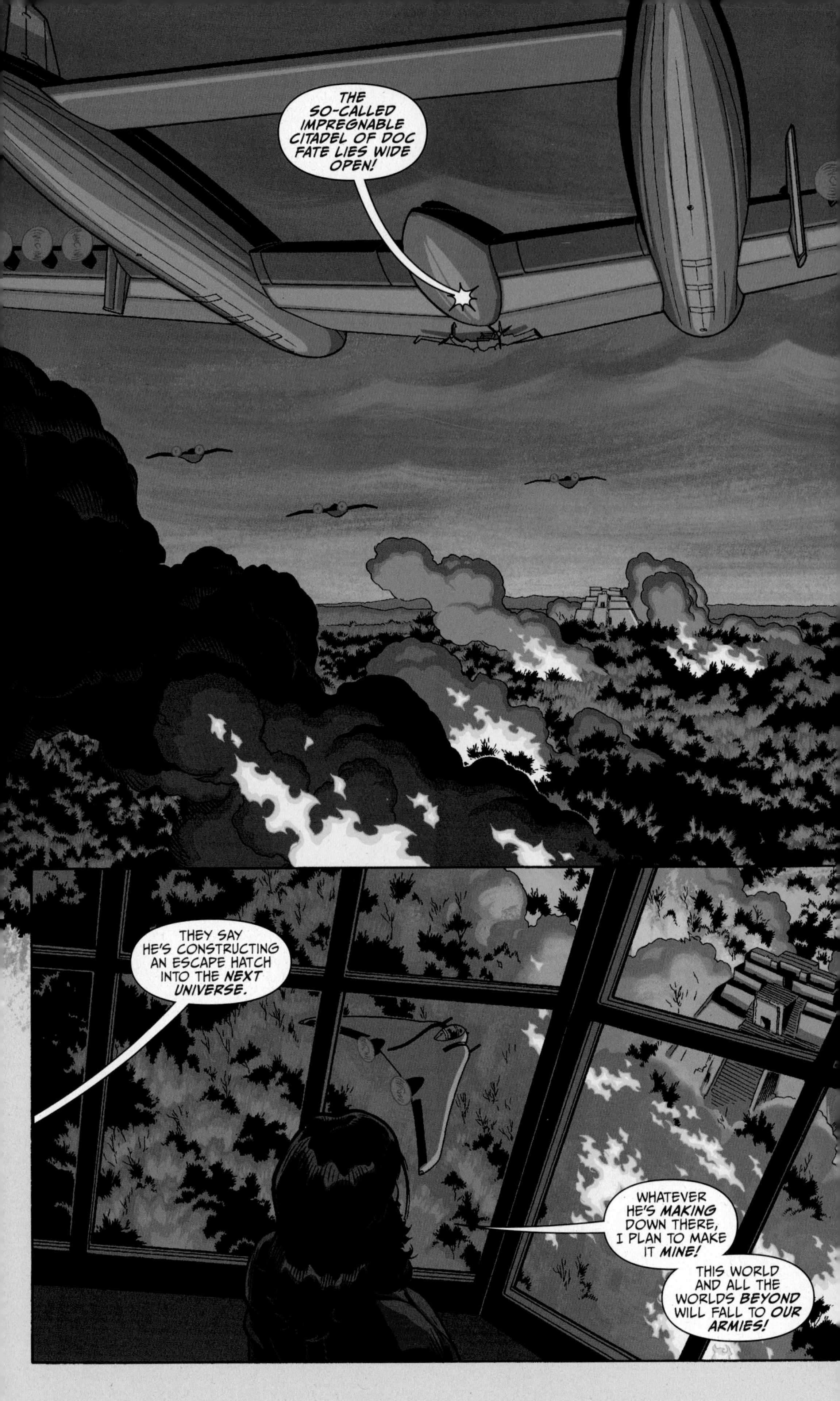
THE SO-CALLED IMPREGNABLE CITADEL OF DOC FATE LIES WIDE OPEN!
THEY SAY HE'S CONSTRUCTING AN ESCAPE HATCH INTO THE NEXT UNIVERSE.
WHATEVER HE'S MAKING DOWN THERE, I PLAN TO MAKE IT MINE!
THIS WORLD AND ALL THE WORLDS BEYOND WILL FALL TO OUR ARMIES!

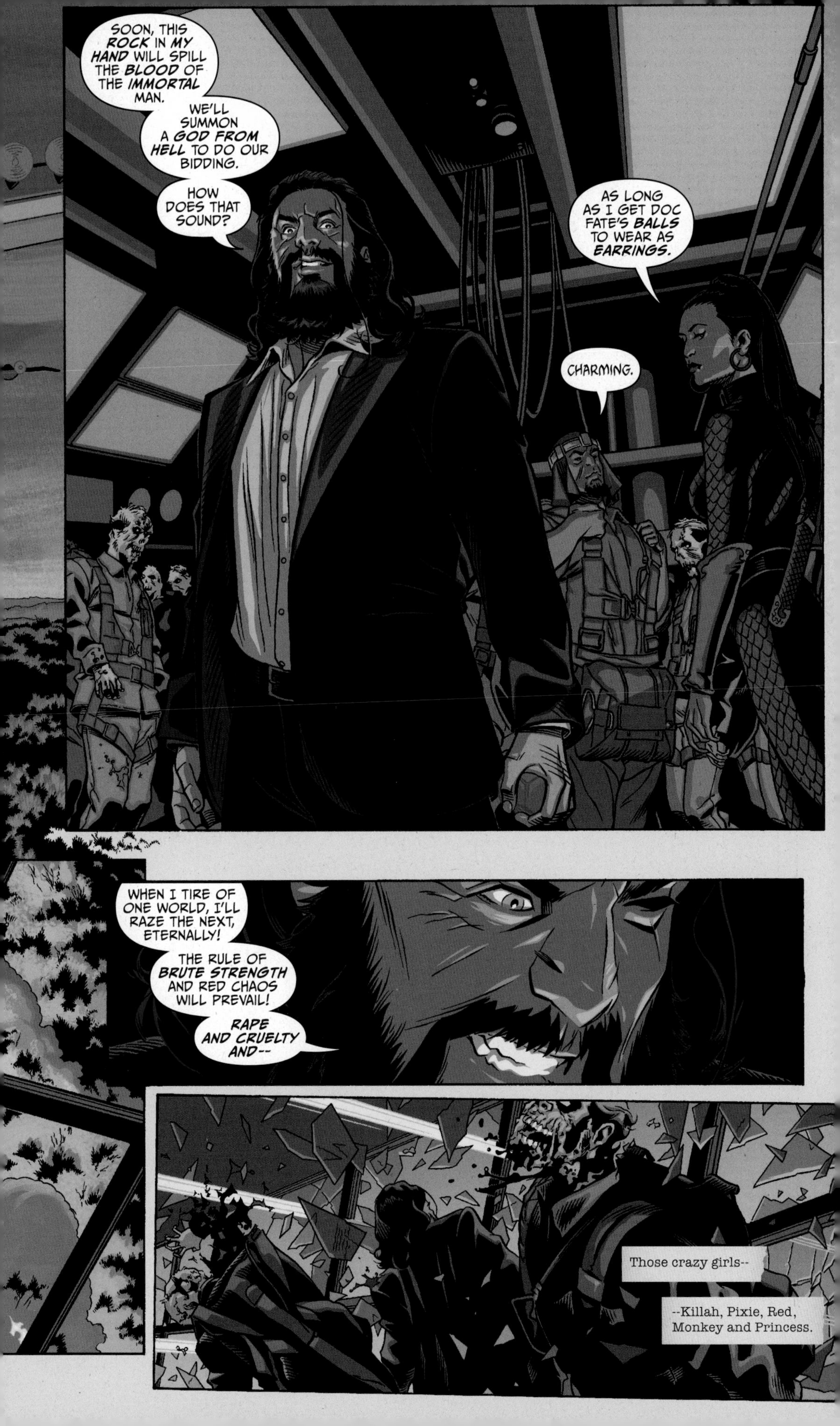
SOON, THIS ROCK IN MY HAND WILL SPILL THE BLOOD OF THE IMMORTAL MAN.
WE'LL SUMMON A GOD FROM HELL TO DO OUR BIDDING.
HOW DOES THAT SOUND?
AS LONG AS I GET DOC FATE'S BALLS TO WEAR AS EARRINGS.
CHARMING.
WHEN I TIRE OF ONE WORLD, I'LL RAZE THE NEXT, ETERNALLY!
THE RULE OF BRUTE STRENGTH AND RED CHAOS WILL PREVAIL!
RAPE AND CRUELTY AND--
Those crazy girls--
--Killah, Pixie, Red, Monkey and Princess.

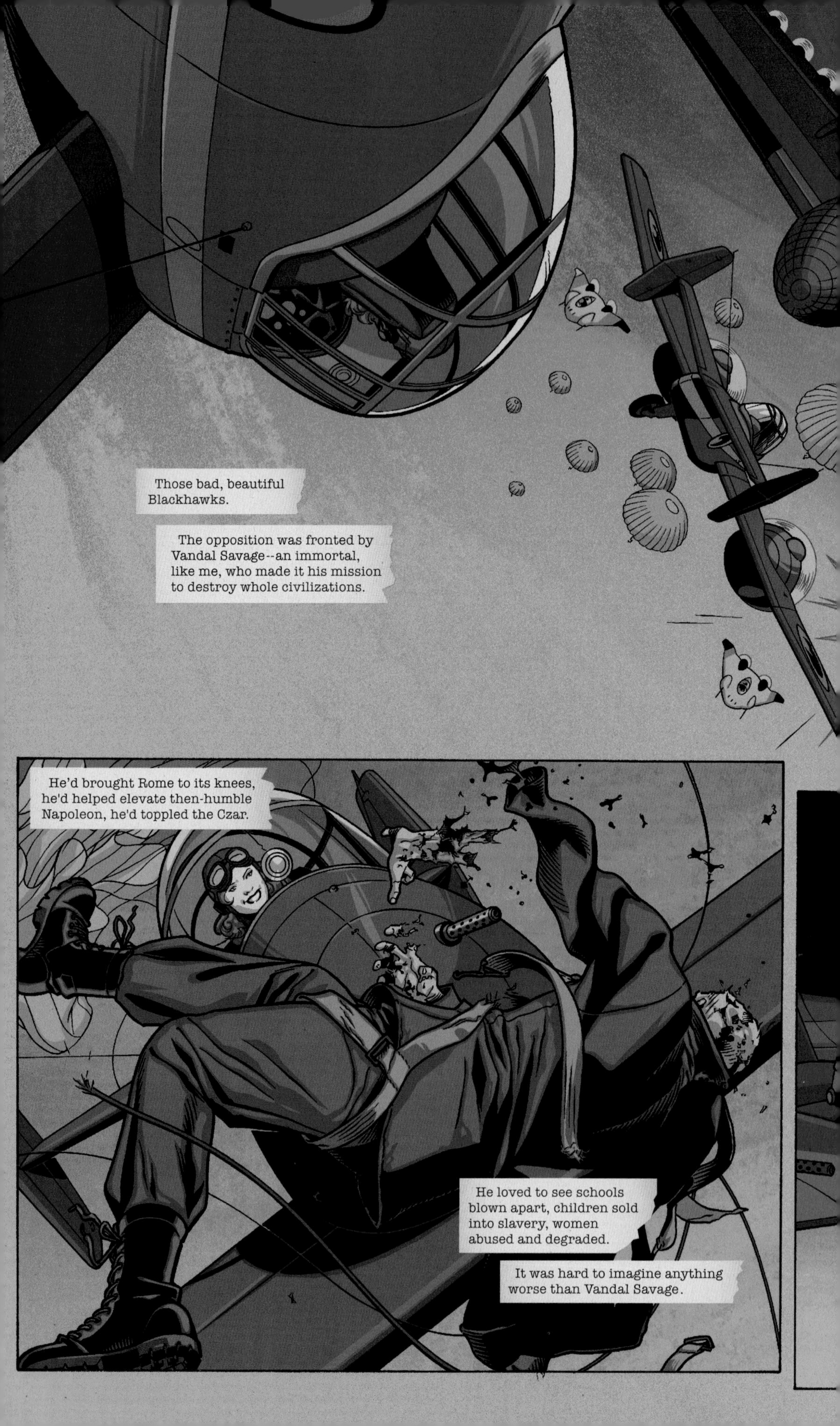
Those bad, beautiful Blackhawks.
The opposition was fronted by Vandal Savage--an immortal, like me, who made it his mission to destroy whole civilizations.
He'd brought Rome to its knees, he'd helped elevate then-humble Napoleon, he'd toppled the Czar.
He loved to see schools blown apart, children sold into slavery, women abused and degraded.
It was hard to imagine anything worse than Vandal Savage.

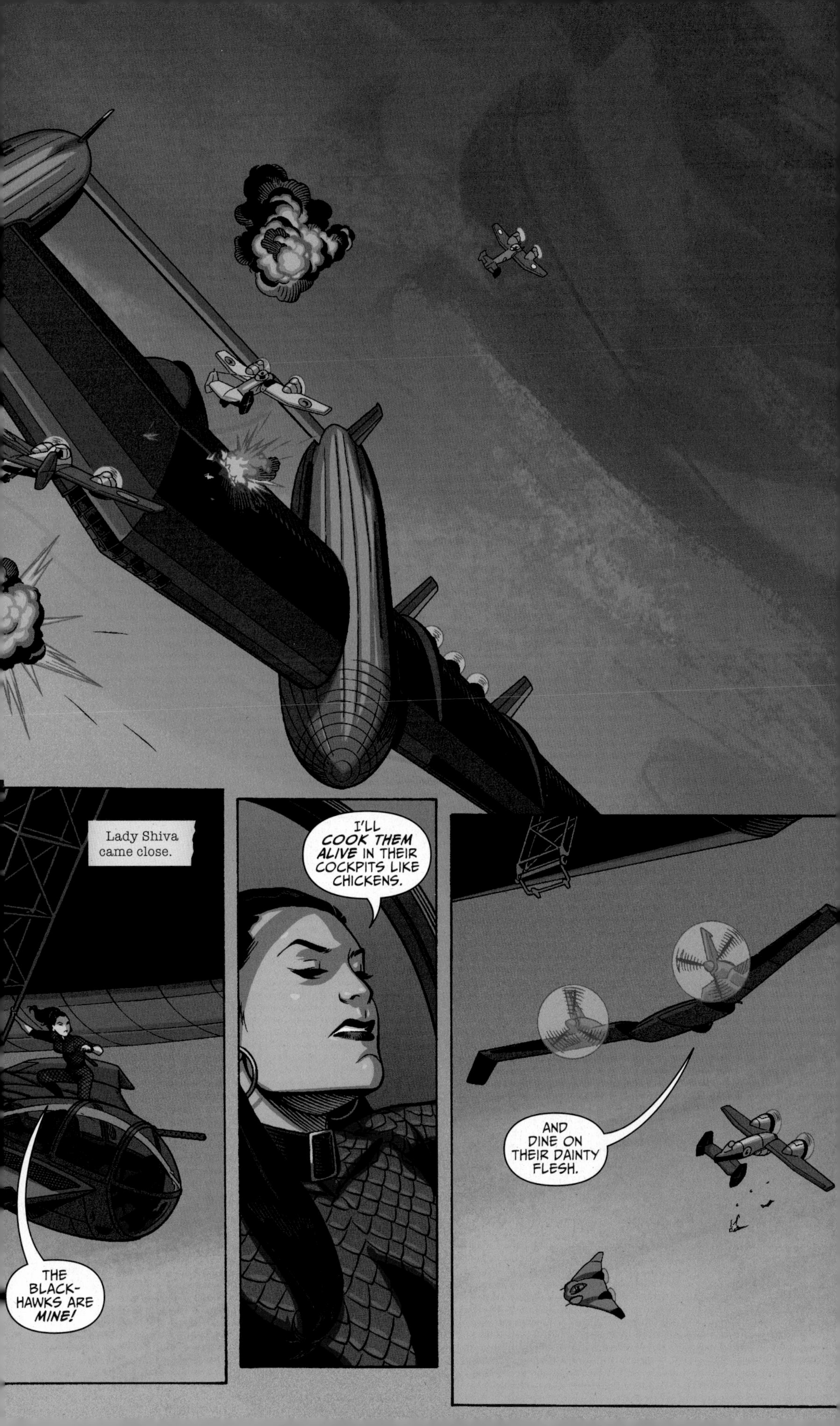
Lady Shiva came close.
THE BLACK-HAWKS ARE *MINE!*
I'LL *COOK THEM ALIVE* IN THEIR COCKPITS LIKE CHICKENS.
AND DINE ON THEIR DAINTY FLESH.

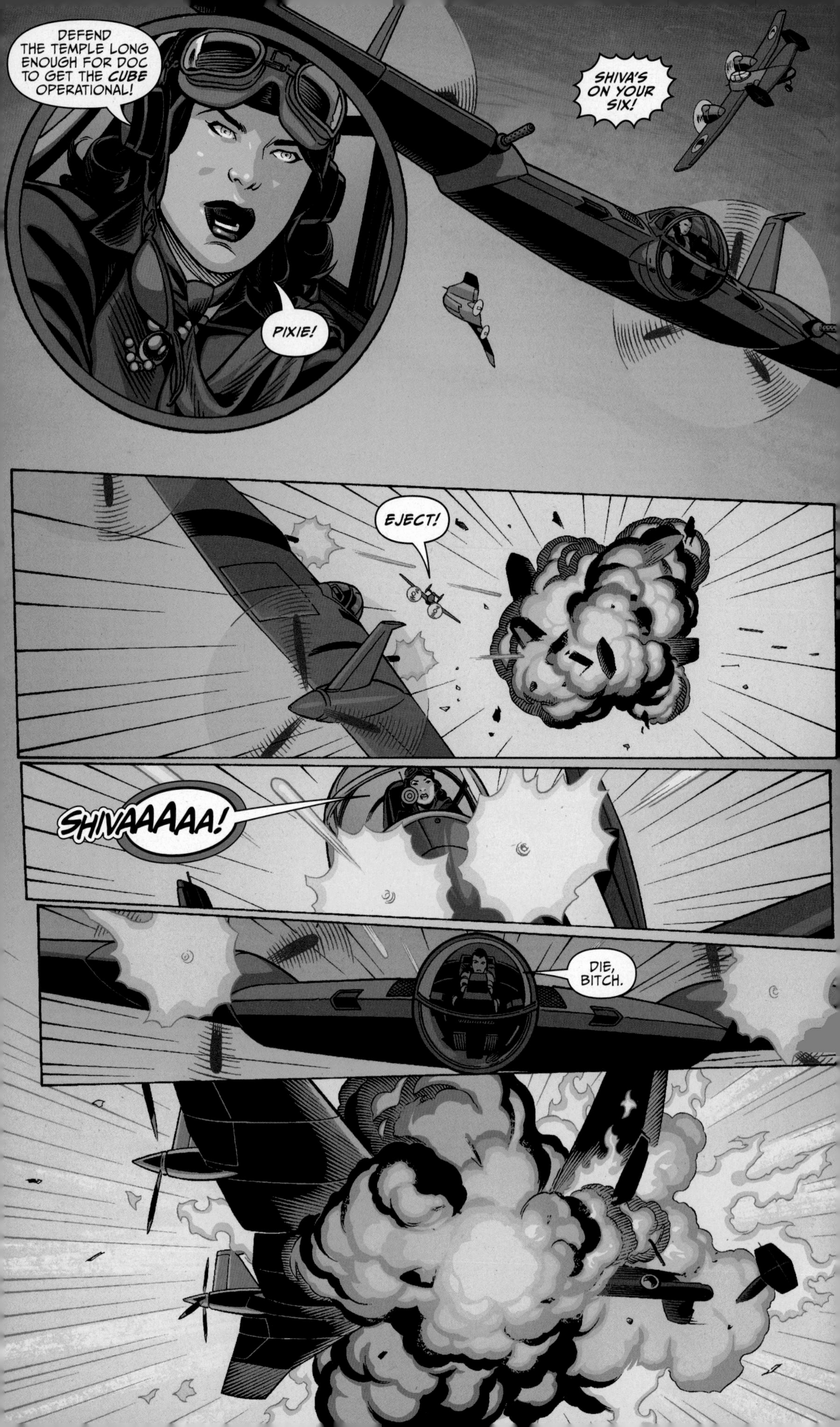
DEFEND THE TEMPLE LONG ENOUGH FOR DOC TO GET THE *CUBE* OPERATIONAL!
PIXIE!
SHIVA'S ON YOUR SIX!
EJECT!
SHIVAAAAA!
DIE, BITCH.

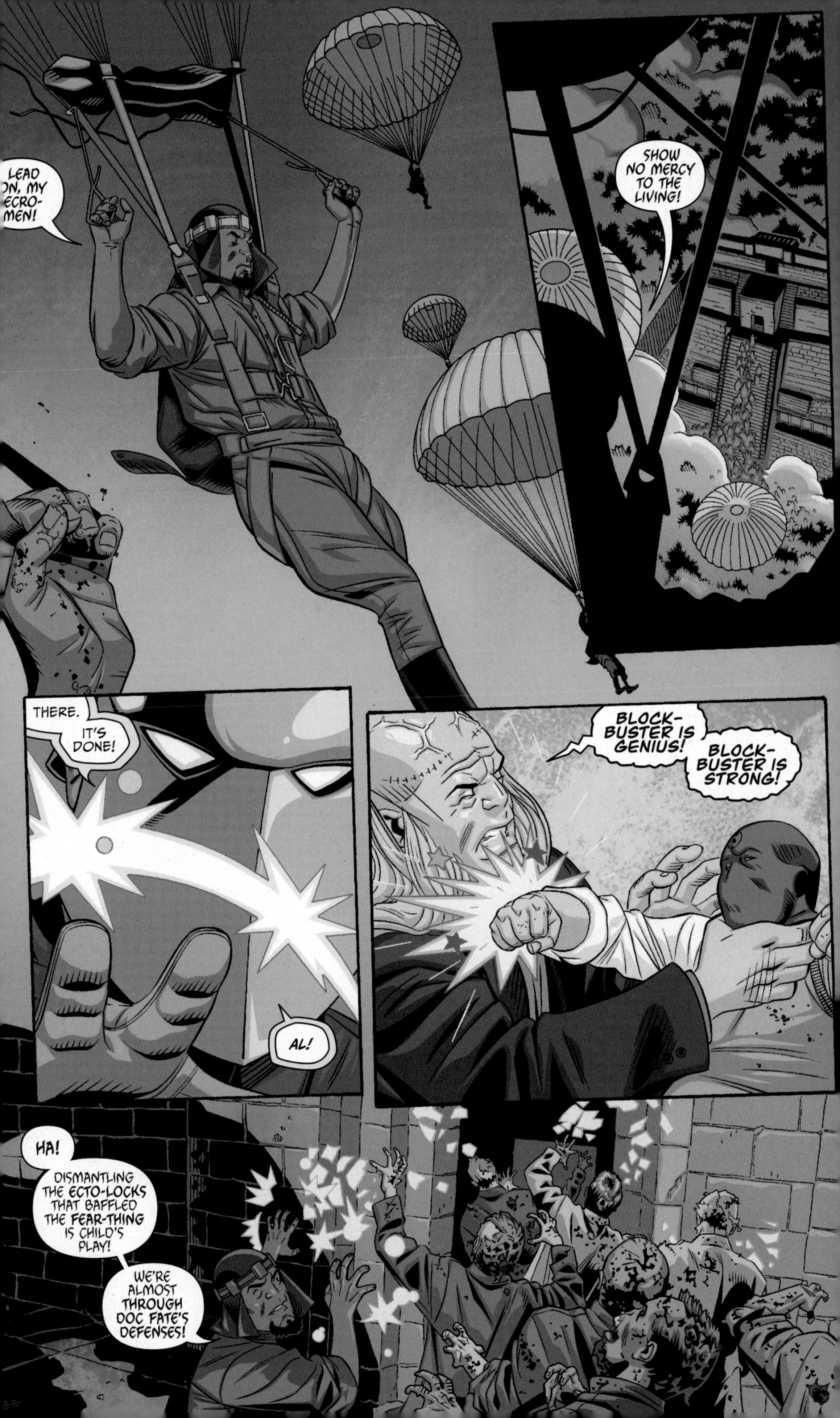
LEAD ON, MY NECRO-MEN!
SHOW NO MERCY TO THE LIVING!
THERE.
IT'S DONE!
AL!
BLOCK-BUSTER IS GENIUS!
BLOCK-BUSTER IS STRONG!
HA!
DISMANTLING THE ECTO-LOCKS THAT BAFFLED THE FEAR-THING IS CHILD'S PLAY!
WE'RE ALMOST THROUGH DOC FATE'S DEFENSES!

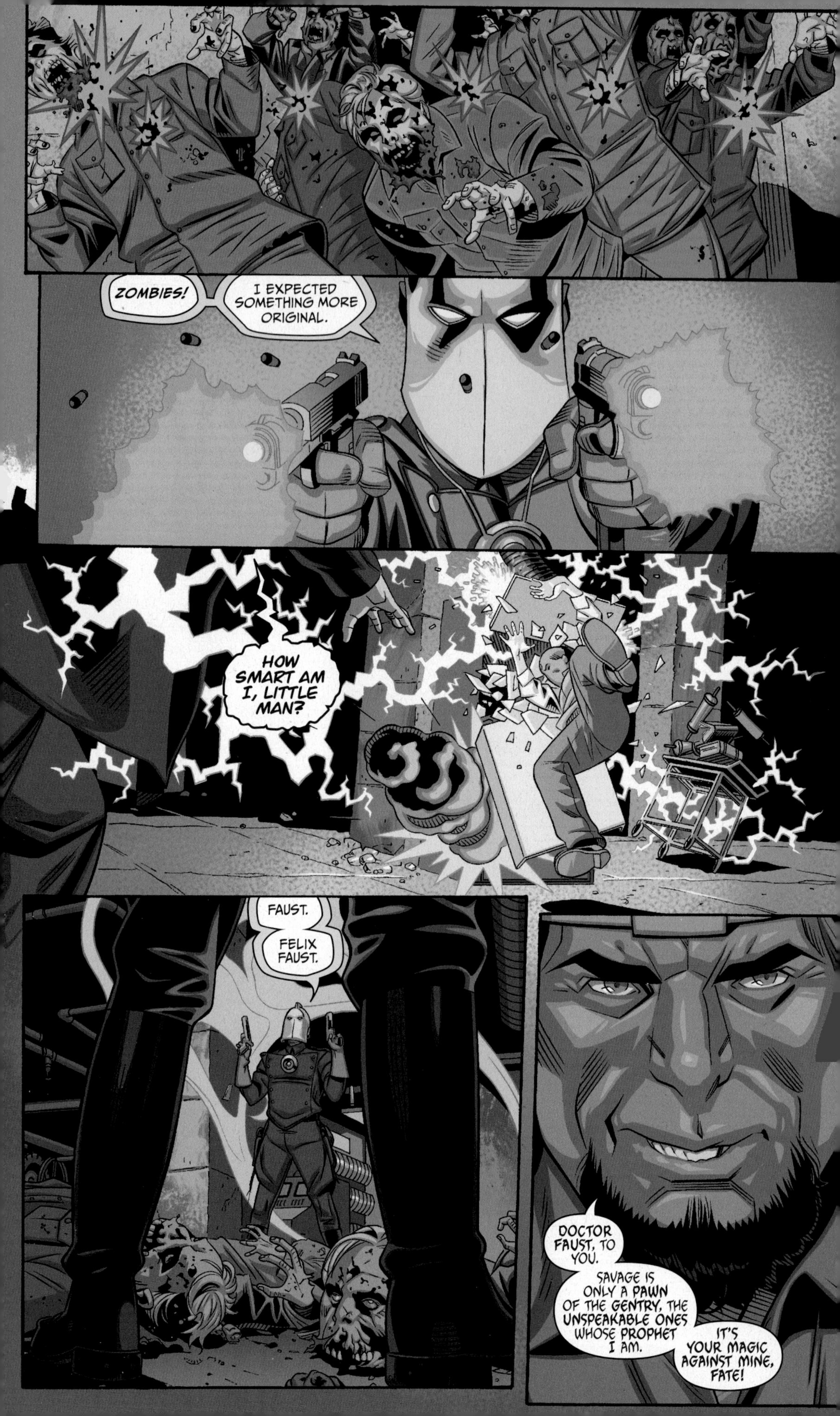

ZOMBIES!
I EXPECTED SOMETHING MORE ORIGINAL.
HOW SMART AM I, LITTLE MAN?
FAUST.
FELIX FAUST.
DOCTOR FAUST, TO YOU.
SAVAGE IS ONLY A PAWN OF THE GENTRY, THE UNSPEAKABLE ONES WHOSE PROPHET I AM.
IT'S YOUR MAGIC AGAINST MINE, FATE!

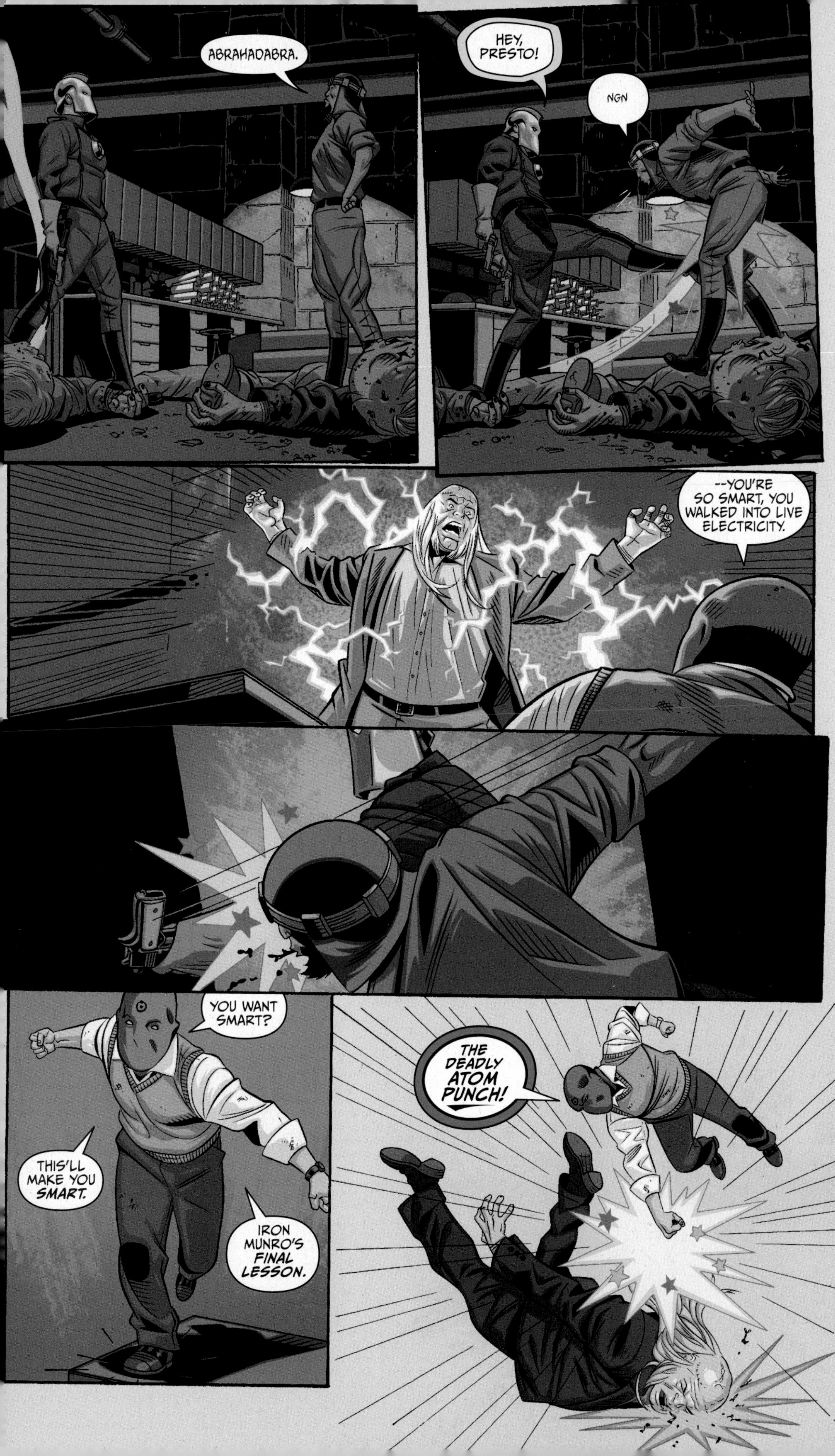
ABRAHADABRA.
HEY, PRESTO!
NGN
--YOU'RE SO SMART, YOU WALKED INTO LIVE ELECTRICITY.
YOU WANT SMART?
THIS'LL MAKE YOU SMART.
IRON MUNRO'S FINAL LESSON.
THE DEADLY ATOM PUNCH!

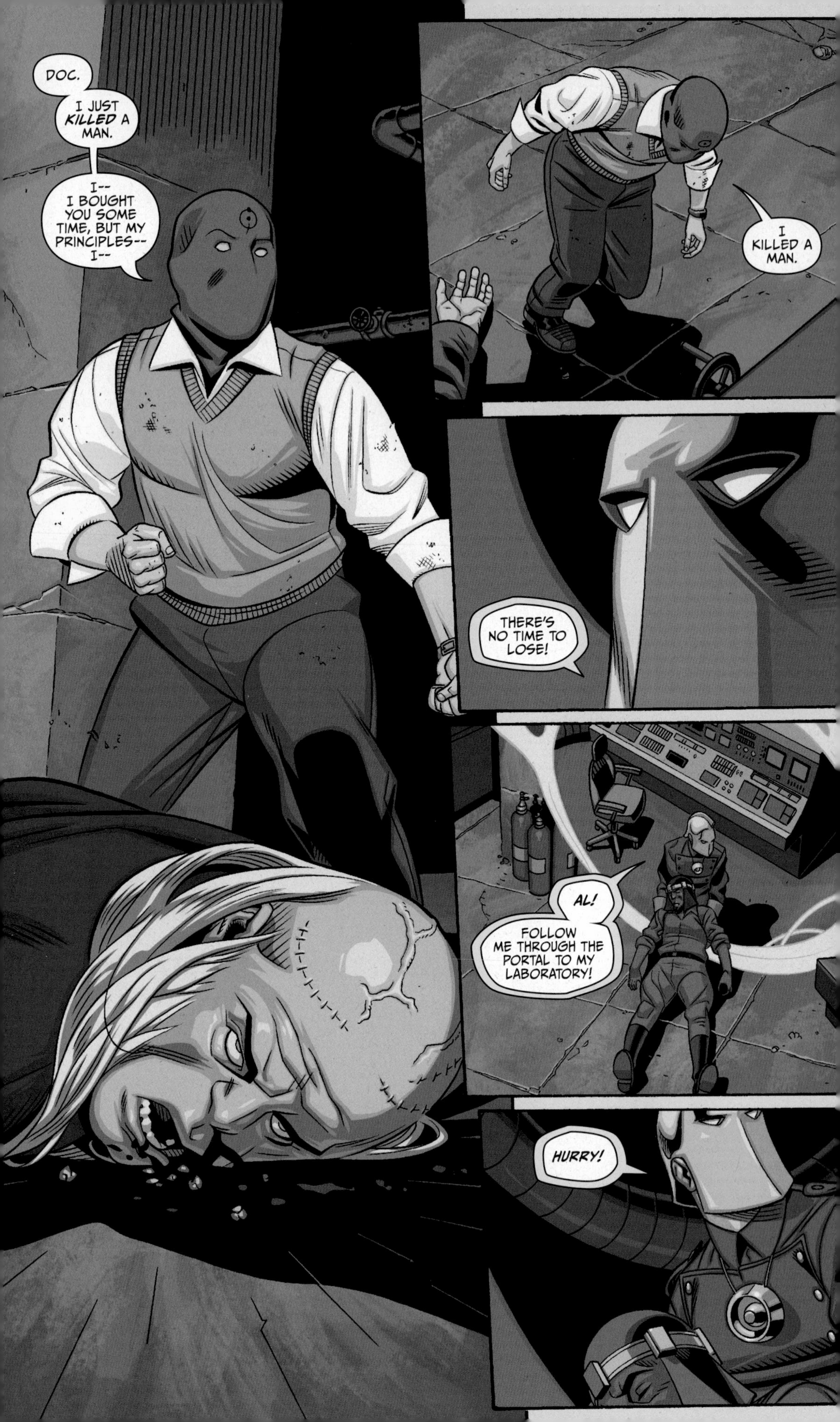
DOC.
I JUST *KILLED* A MAN.
I-- I BOUGHT YOU SOME TIME, BUT MY PRINCIPLES-- I--
I KILLED A MAN.
THERE'S NO TIME TO LOSE!
AL!
FOLLOW ME THROUGH THE PORTAL TO MY LABORATORY!
HURRY!

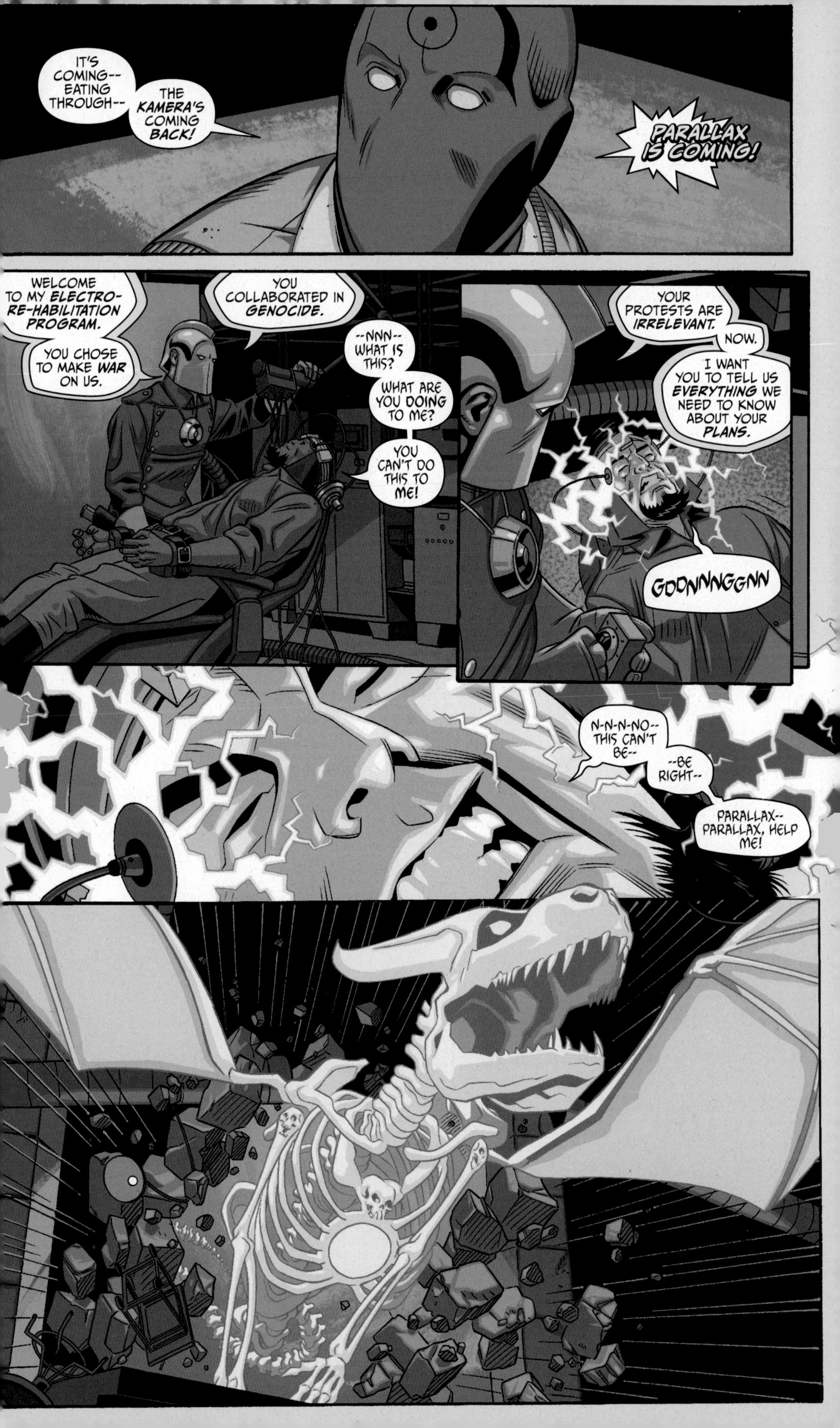
IT'S COMING-- EATING THROUGH--
THE KAMERA'S COMING BACK!
PARALLAX IS COMING!
WELCOME TO MY ELECTRO-RE-HABILITATION PROGRAM.
YOU CHOSE TO MAKE WAR ON US.
YOU COLLABORATED IN GENOCIDE.
--NNN-- WHAT IS THIS?
WHAT ARE YOU DOING TO ME?
YOU CAN'T DO THIS TO ME!
YOUR PROTESTS ARE IRRELEVANT.
NOW.
I WANT YOU TO TELL US EVERYTHING WE NEED TO KNOW ABOUT YOUR PLANS.
GOONNNGGNN
N-N-N-NO-- THIS CAN'T BE--
--BE RIGHT--
PARALLAX-- PARALLAX, HELP ME!

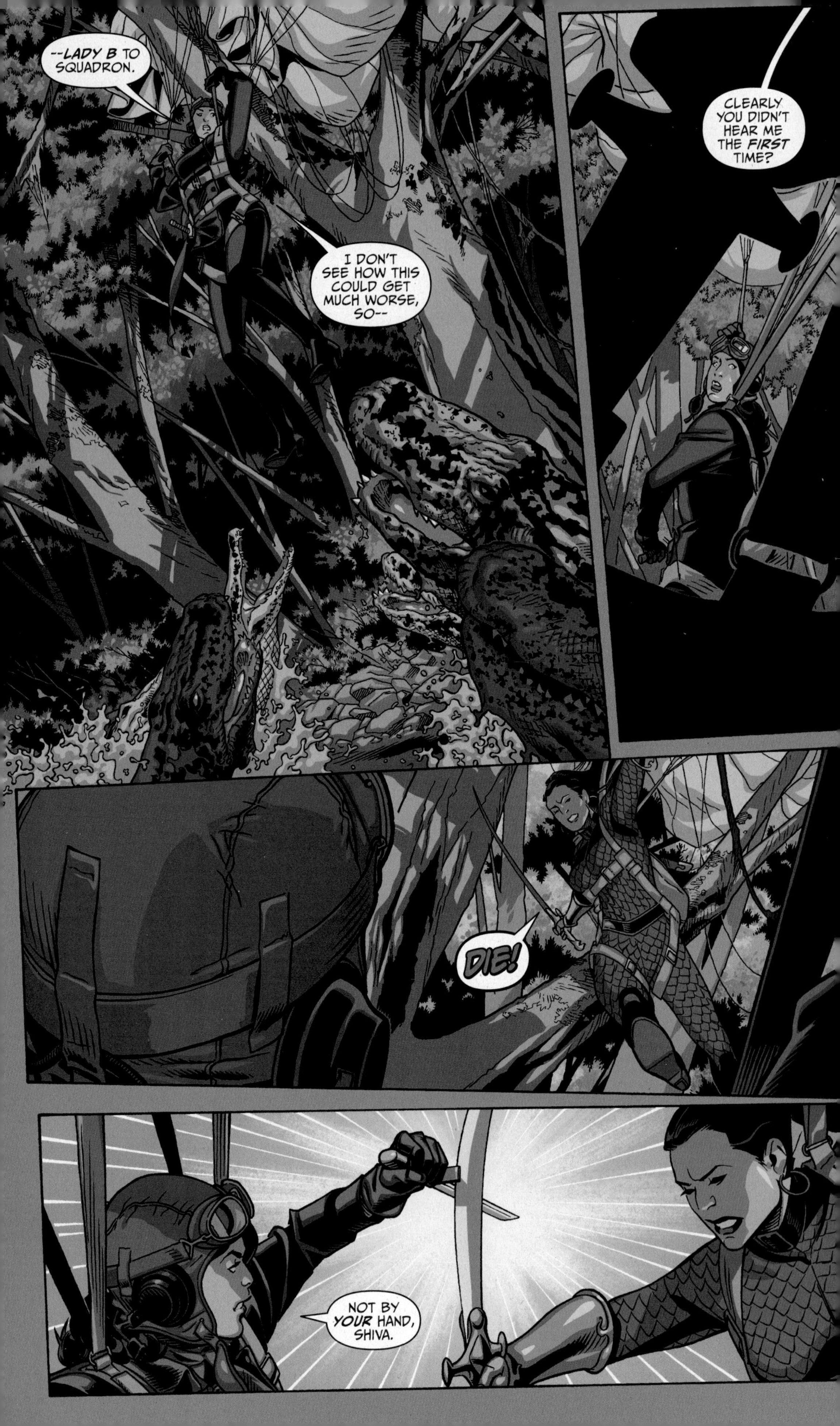
--*LADY B* TO SQUADRON.
I DON'T SEE HOW THIS COULD GET MUCH WORSE, SO--
CLEARLY YOU DIDN'T HEAR ME THE *FIRST* TIME?
DIE!
NOT BY *YOUR* HAND, SHIVA.

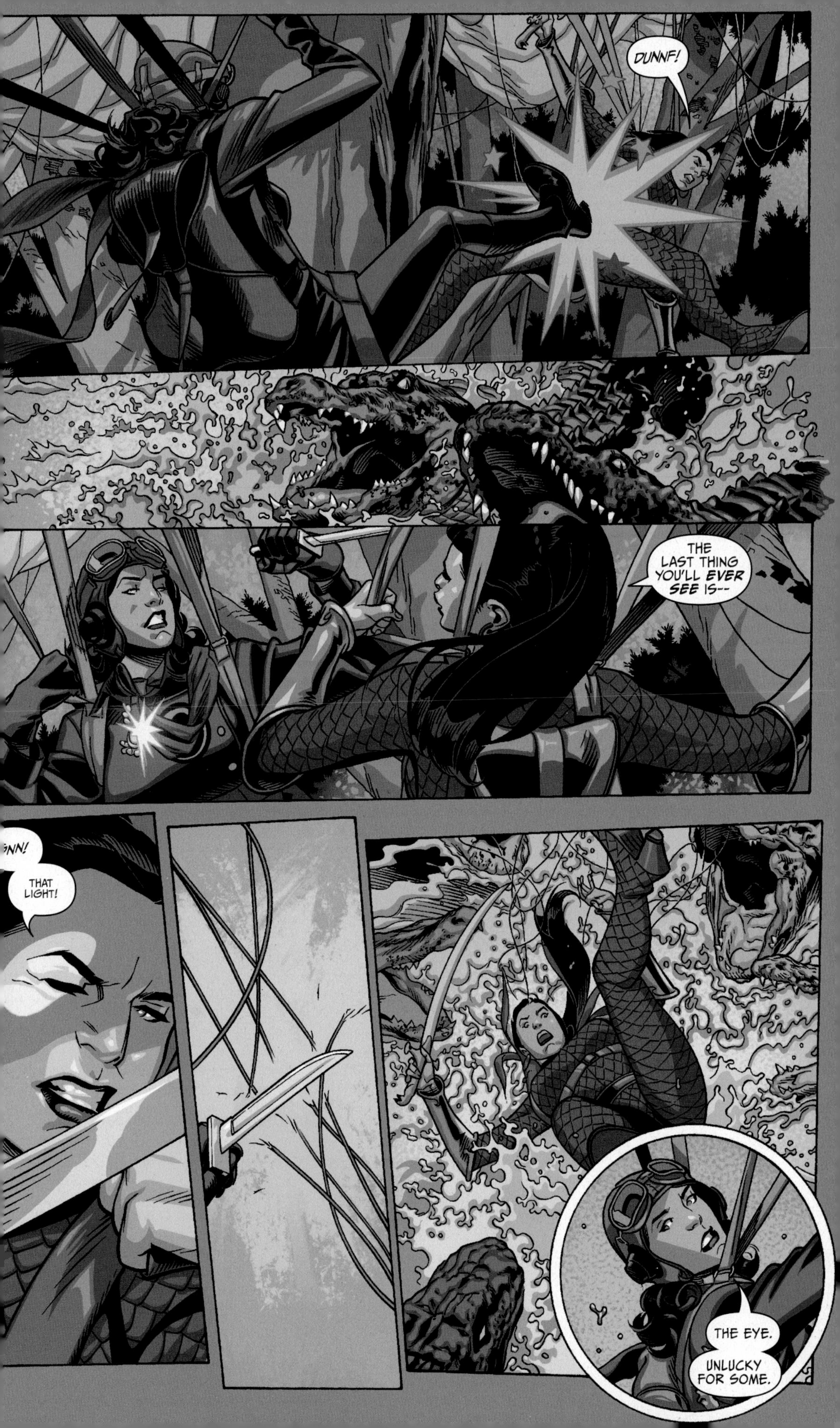
DUNNF!
THE LAST THING YOU'LL EVER SEE IS--
GNN!
THAT LIGHT!
THE EYE.
UNLUCKY FOR SOME.

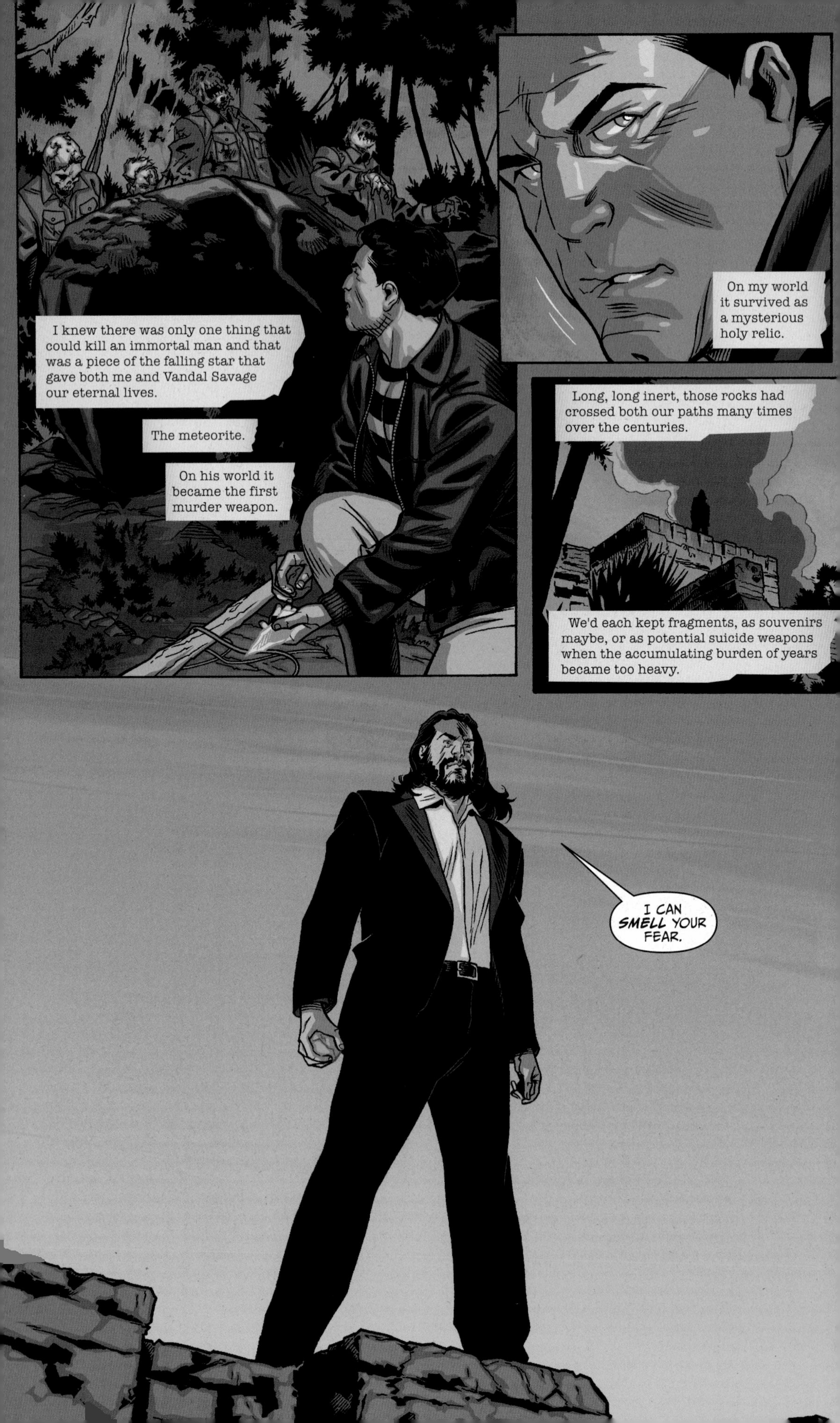
I knew there was only one thing that could kill an immortal man and that was a piece of the falling star that gave both me and Vandal Savage our eternal lives.
The meteorite.
On his world it became the first murder weapon.
On my world it survived as a mysterious holy relic.
Long, long inert, those rocks had crossed both our paths many times over the centuries.
We'd each kept fragments, as souvenirs maybe, or as potential suicide weapons when the accumulating burden of years became too heavy.
I CAN SMELL YOUR FEAR.

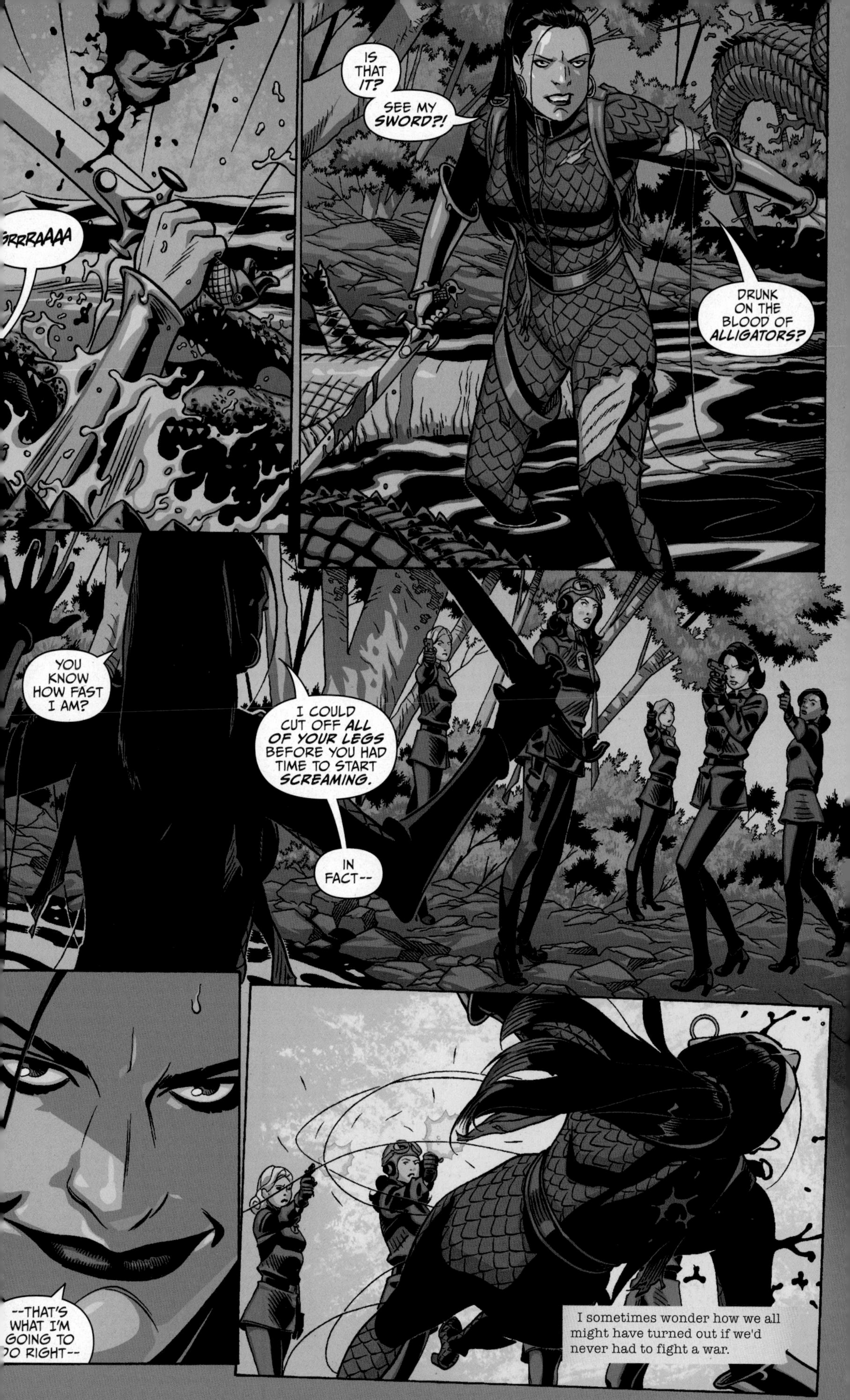

GRRRAAAA
IS THAT IT?
SEE MY SWORD?!
DRUNK ON THE BLOOD OF ALLIGATORS?
YOU KNOW HOW FAST I AM?
I COULD CUT OFF ALL OF YOUR LEGS BEFORE YOU HAD TIME TO START SCREAMING.
IN FACT--
--THAT'S WHAT I'M GOING TO DO RIGHT--
I sometimes wonder how we all might have turned out if we'd never had to fight a war.

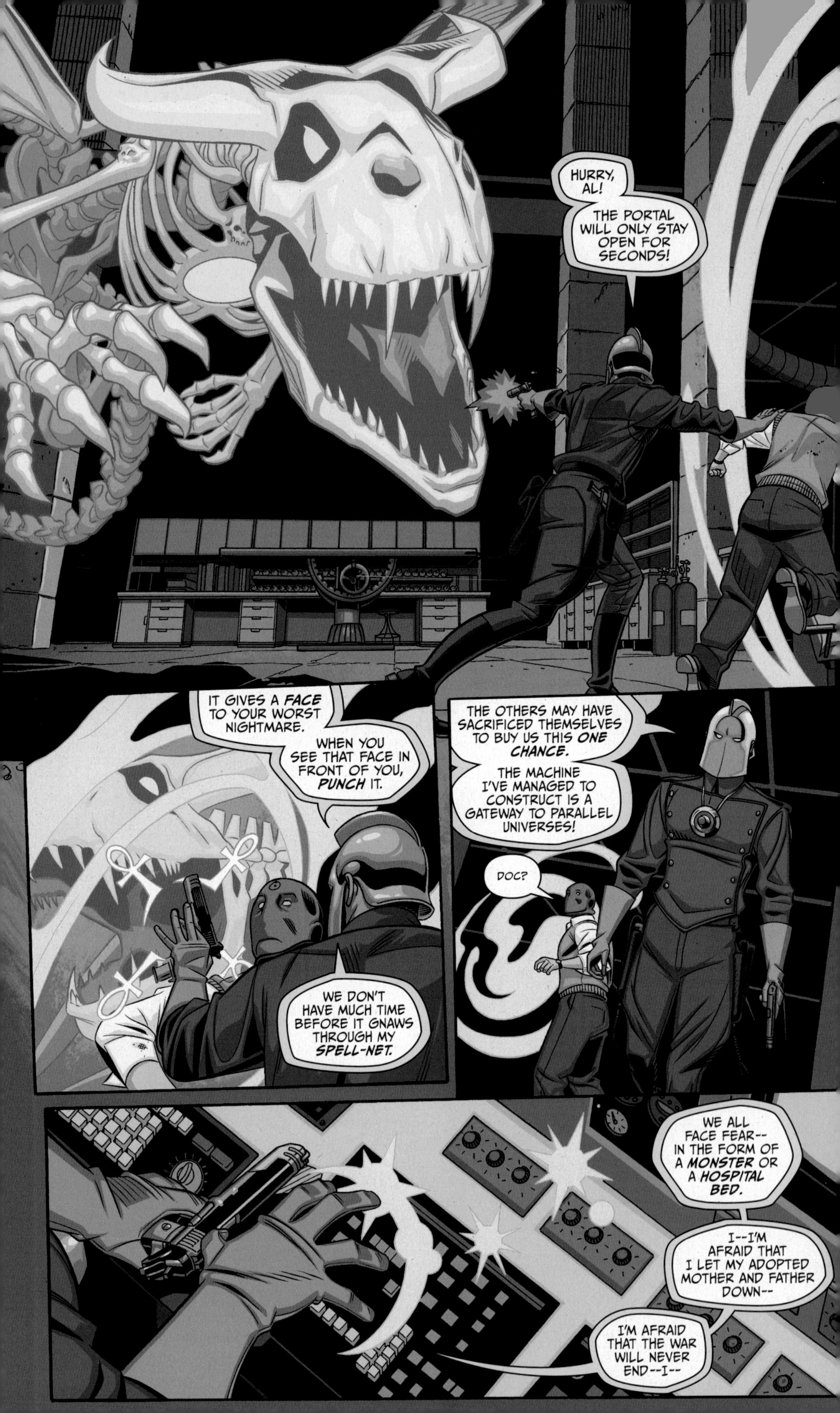
HURRY, AL!
THE PORTAL WILL ONLY STAY OPEN FOR SECONDS!
IT GIVES A FACE TO YOUR WORST NIGHTMARE.
WHEN YOU SEE THAT FACE IN FRONT OF YOU, PUNCH IT.
WE DON'T HAVE MUCH TIME BEFORE IT GNAWS THROUGH MY SPELL-NET.
THE OTHERS MAY HAVE SACRIFICED THEMSELVES TO BUY US THIS ONE CHANCE.
THE MACHINE I'VE MANAGED TO CONSTRUCT IS A GATEWAY TO PARALLEL UNIVERSES!
DOC?
WE ALL FACE FEAR-- IN THE FORM OF A MONSTER OR A HOSPITAL BED.
I--I'M AFRAID THAT I LET MY ADOPTED MOTHER AND FATHER DOWN--
I'M AFRAID THAT THE WAR WILL NEVER END--I--

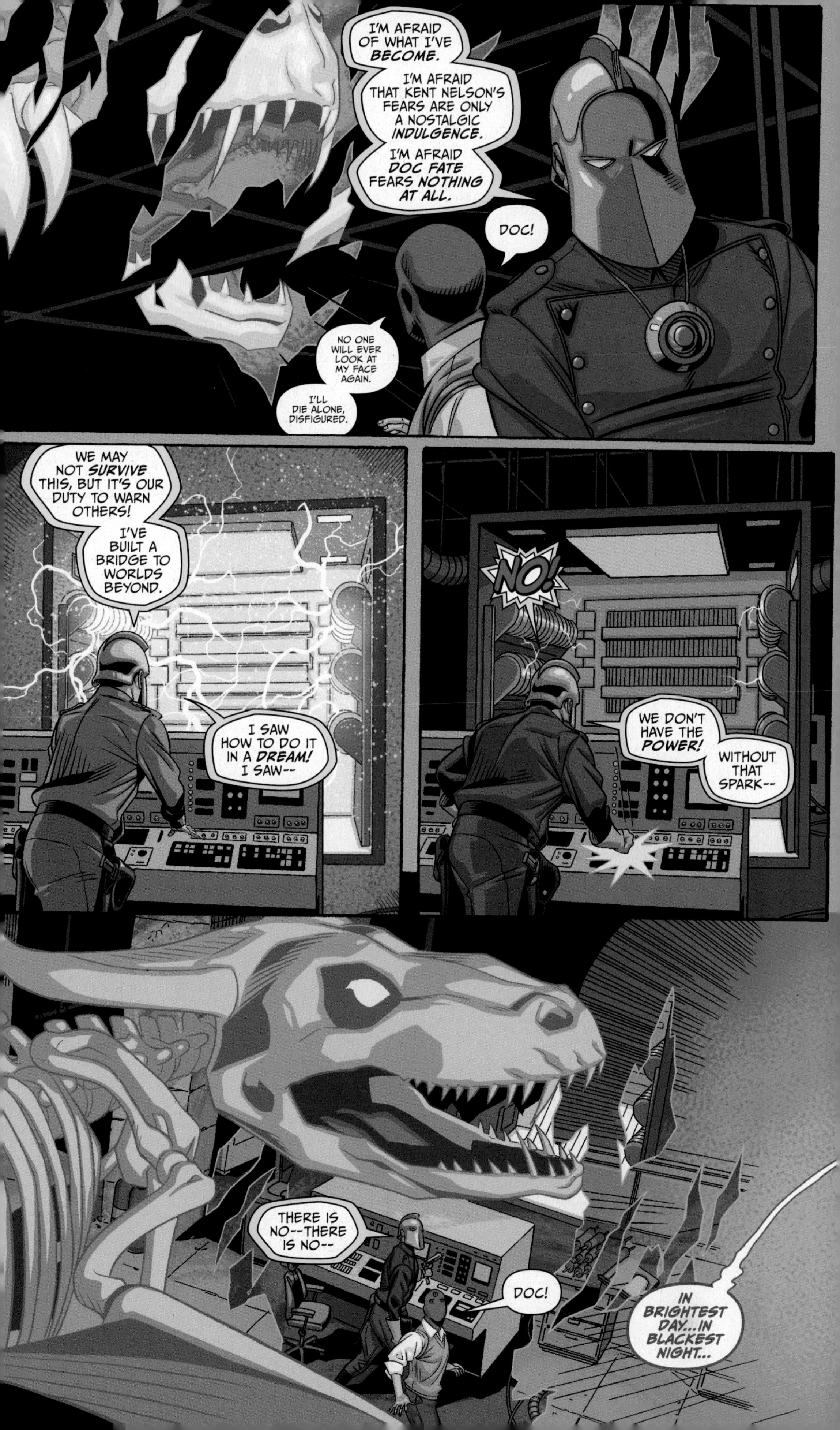

I'M AFRAID OF WHAT I'VE BECOME.
I'M AFRAID THAT KENT NELSON'S FEARS ARE ONLY A NOSTALGIC INDULGENCE.
I'M AFRAID DOC FATE FEARS NOTHING AT ALL.
DOC!
NO ONE WILL EVER LOOK AT MY FACE AGAIN.
I'LL DIE ALONE, DISFIGURED.
WE MAY NOT SURVIVE THIS, BUT IT'S OUR DUTY TO WARN OTHERS!
I'VE BUILT A BRIDGE TO WORLDS BEYOND.
I SAW HOW TO DO IT IN A DREAM! I SAW--
NO!
WE DON'T HAVE THE POWER!
WITHOUT THAT SPARK--
THERE IS NO--THERE IS NO--
DOC!
IN BRIGHTEST DAY...IN BLACKEST NIGHT...

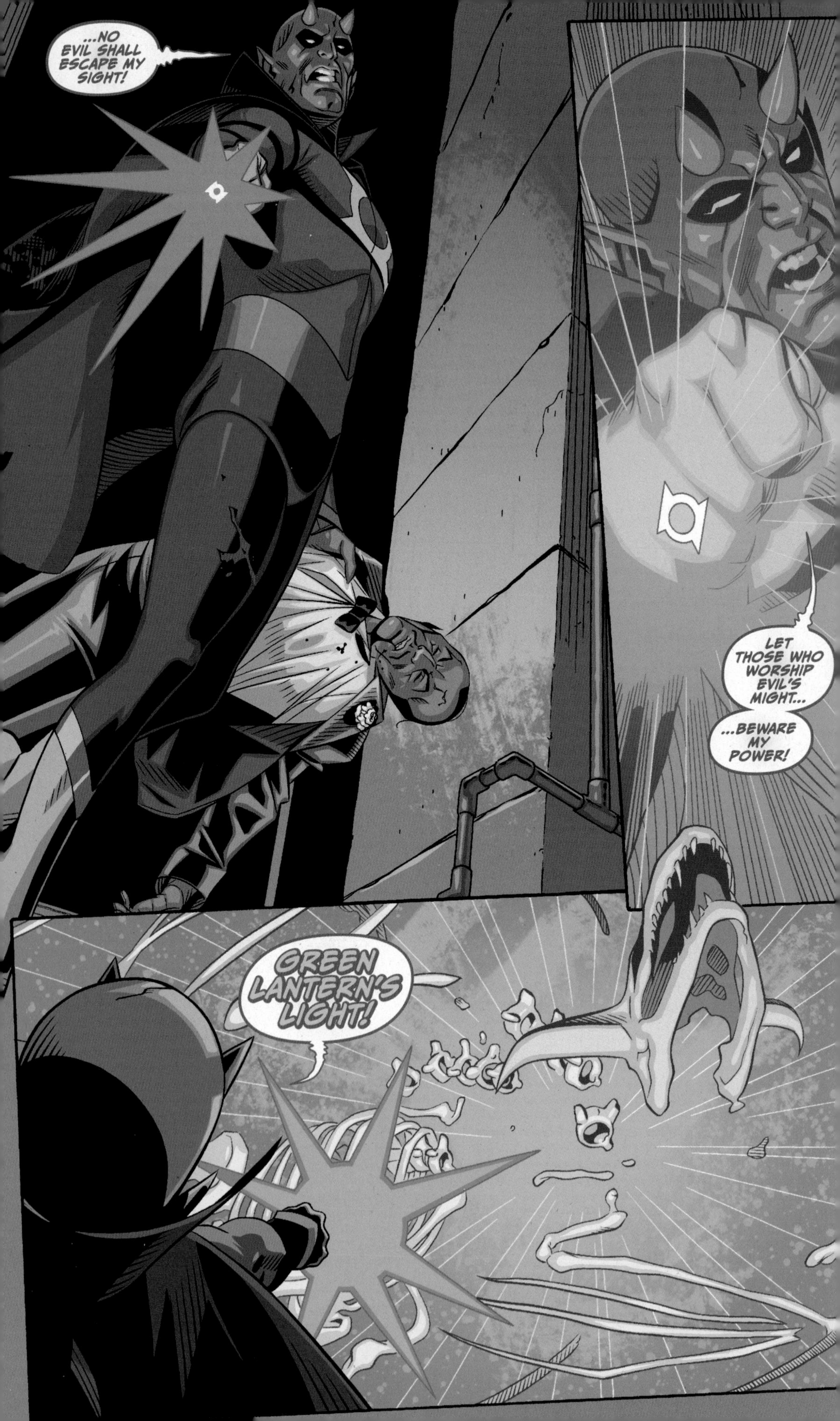
...NO EVIL SHALL ESCAPE MY SIGHT!
LET THOSE WHO WORSHIP EVIL'S MIGHT...
...BEWARE MY POWER!
GREEN LANTERN'S LIGHT!

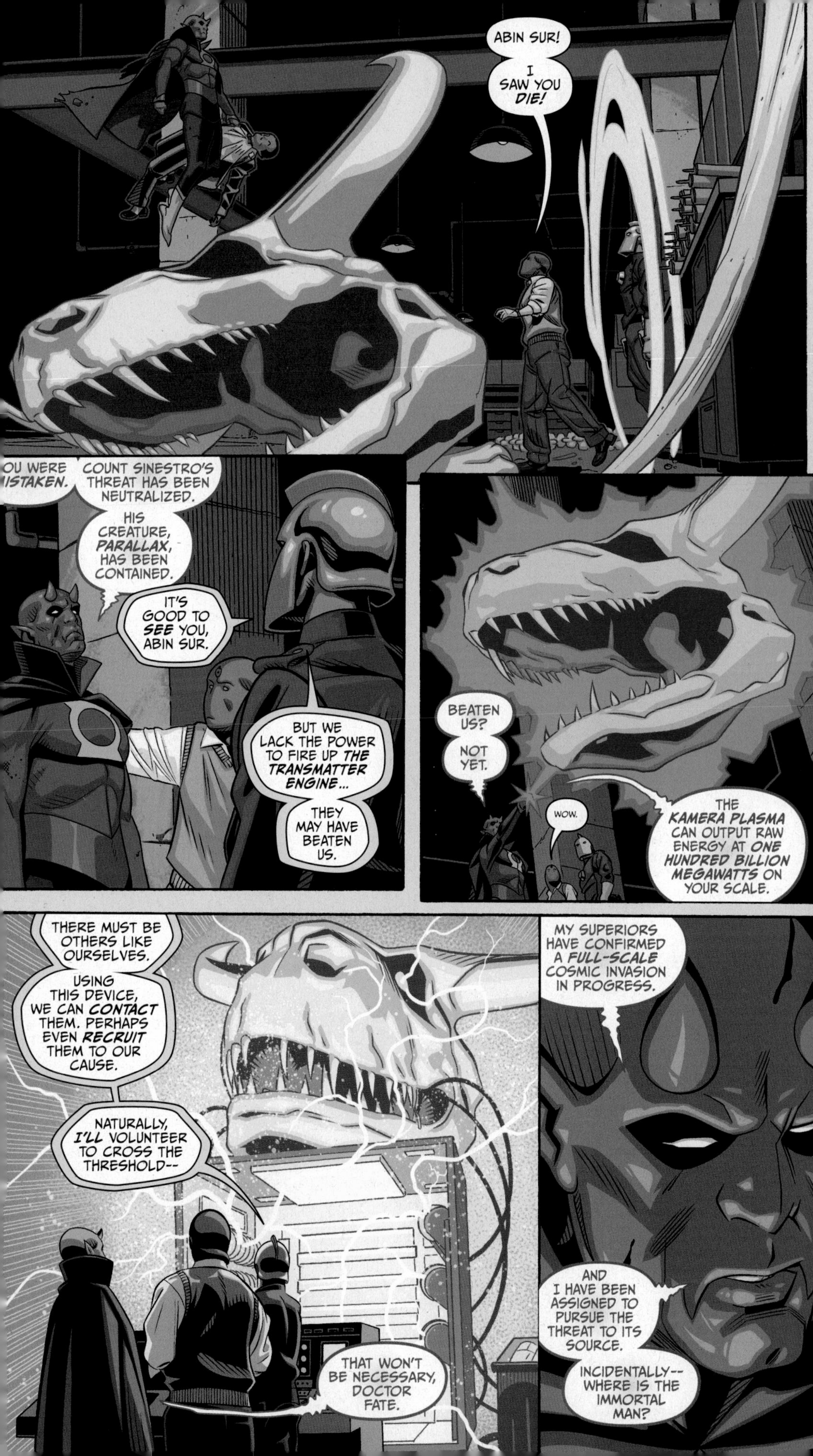

ABIN SUR!
I SAW YOU DIE!
OU WERE ISTAKEN.
COUNT SINESTRO'S THREAT HAS BEEN NEUTRALIZED.
HIS CREATURE, PARALLAX, HAS BEEN CONTAINED.
IT'S GOOD TO SEE YOU, ABIN SUR.
BUT WE LACK THE POWER TO FIRE UP THE TRANSMATTER ENGINE...
THEY MAY HAVE BEATEN US.
BEATEN US?
NOT YET.
WOW.
THE KAMERA PLASMA CAN OUTPUT RAW ENERGY AT ONE HUNDRED BILLION MEGAWATTS ON YOUR SCALE.
THERE MUST BE OTHERS LIKE OURSELVES.
USING THIS DEVICE, WE CAN CONTACT THEM. PERHAPS EVEN RECRUIT THEM TO OUR CAUSE.
NATURALLY, I'LL VOLUNTEER TO CROSS THE THRESHOLD--
THAT WON'T BE NECESSARY, DOCTOR FATE.
MY SUPERIORS HAVE CONFIRMED A FULL-SCALE COSMIC INVASION IN PROGRESS.
AND I HAVE BEEN ASSIGNED TO PURSUE THE THREAT TO ITS SOURCE.
INCIDENTALLY-- WHERE IS THE IMMORTAL MAN?

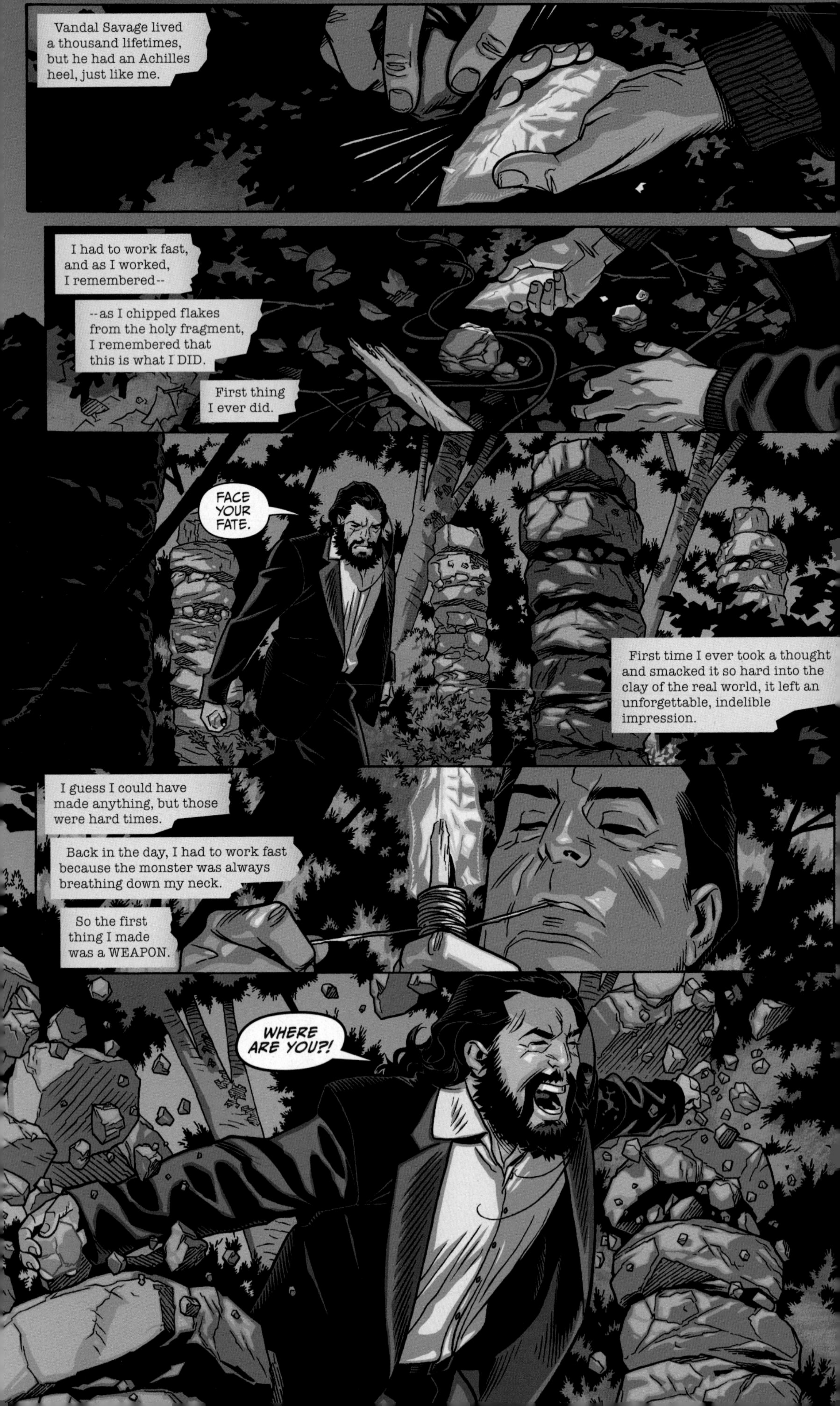
Vandal Savage lived a thousand lifetimes, but he had an Achilles heel, just like me.
I had to work fast, and as I worked, I remembered--
--as I chipped flakes from the holy fragment, I remembered that this is what I DID.
First thing I ever did.
FACE YOUR FATE.
First time I ever took a thought and smacked it so hard into the clay of the real world, it left an unforgettable, indelible impression.
I guess I could have made anything, but those were hard times.
Back in the day, I had to work fast because the monster was always breathing down my neck.
So the first thing I made was a WEAPON.
WHERE ARE YOU?!

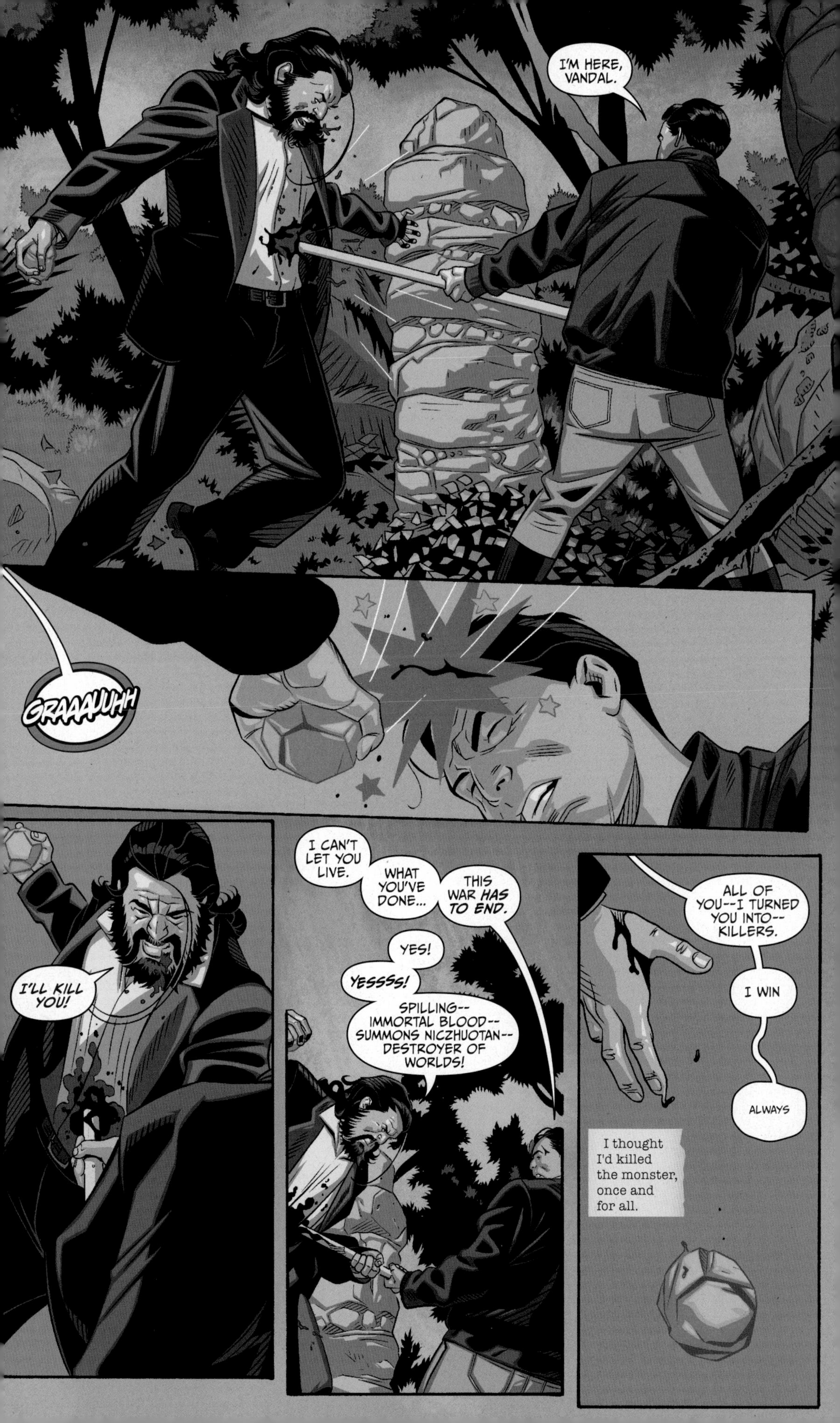
I'M HERE, VANDAL.
GRAAAUUHH
I'LL KILL YOU!
I CAN'T LET YOU LIVE.
WHAT YOU'VE DONE...
THIS WAR HAS TO END.
YES!
YESSSS!
SPILLING-- IMMORTAL BLOOD-- SUMMONS NICZHUOTAN-- DESTROYER OF WORLDS!
ALL OF YOU--I TURNED YOU INTO-- KILLERS.
I WIN
ALWAYS
I thought I'd killed the monster, once and for all.

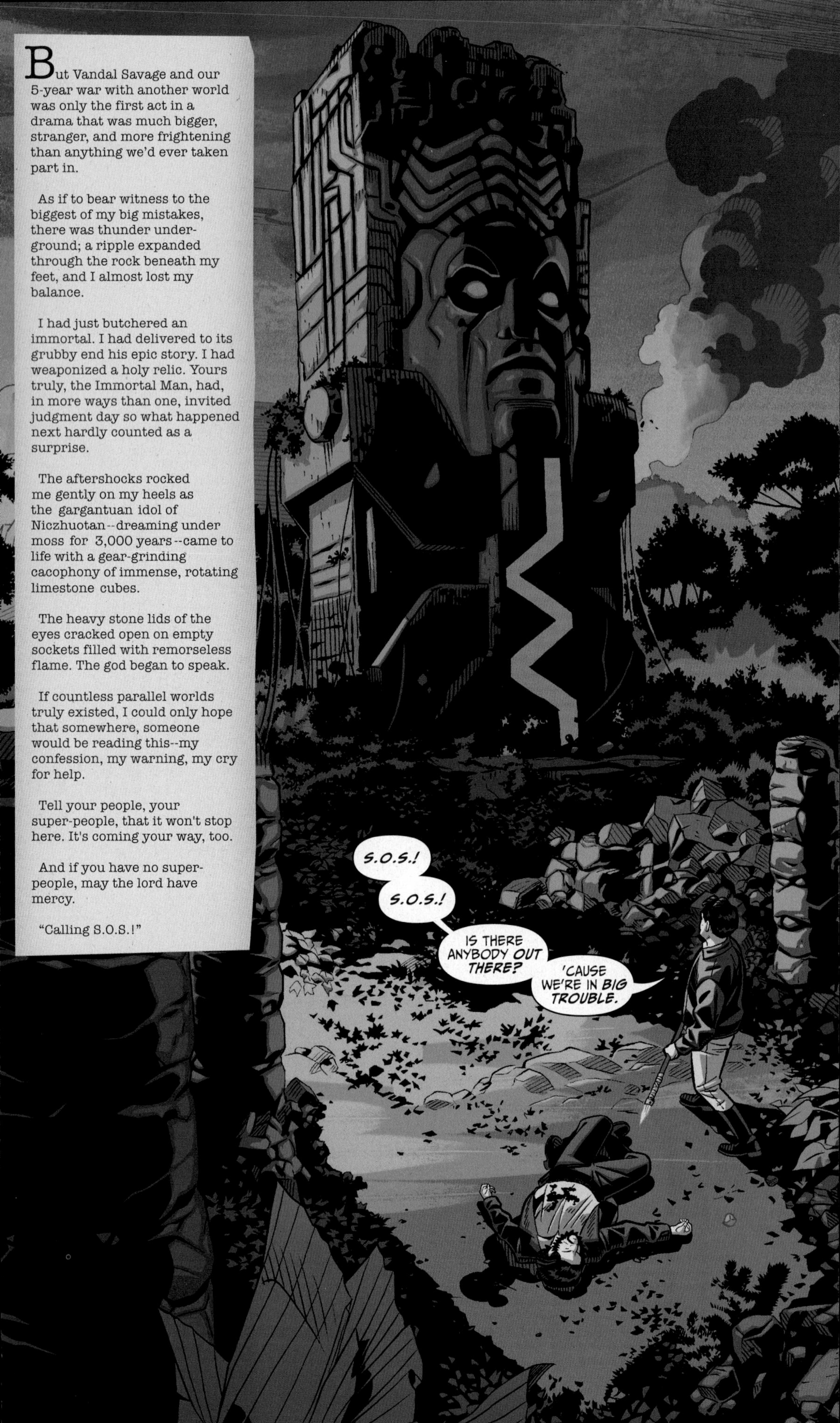
But Vandal Savage and our 5-year war with another world was only the first act in a drama that was much bigger, stranger, and more frightening than anything we'd ever taken part in.

As if to bear witness to the biggest of my big mistakes, there was thunder underground; a ripple expanded through the rock beneath my feet, and I almost lost my balance.

I had just butchered an immortal. I had delivered to its grubby end his epic story. I had weaponized a holy relic. Yours truly, the Immortal Man, had, in more ways than one, invited judgment day so what happened next hardly counted as a surprise.

The aftershocks rocked me gently on my heels as the gargantuan idol of Niczhuotan--dreaming under moss for 3,000 years--came to life with a gear-grinding cacophony of immense, rotating limestone cubes.

The heavy stone lids of the eyes cracked open on empty sockets filled with remorseless flame. The god began to speak.

If countless parallel worlds truly existed, I could only hope that somewhere, someone would be reading this--my confession, my warning, my cry for help.

Tell your people, your super-people, that it won't stop here. It's coming your way, too.

And if you have no super-people, may the lord have mercy.

"Calling S.O.S.!"
S.O.S.!
S.O.S.!
IS THERE ANYBODY OUT THERE?
'CAUSE WE'RE IN BIG TROUBLE.

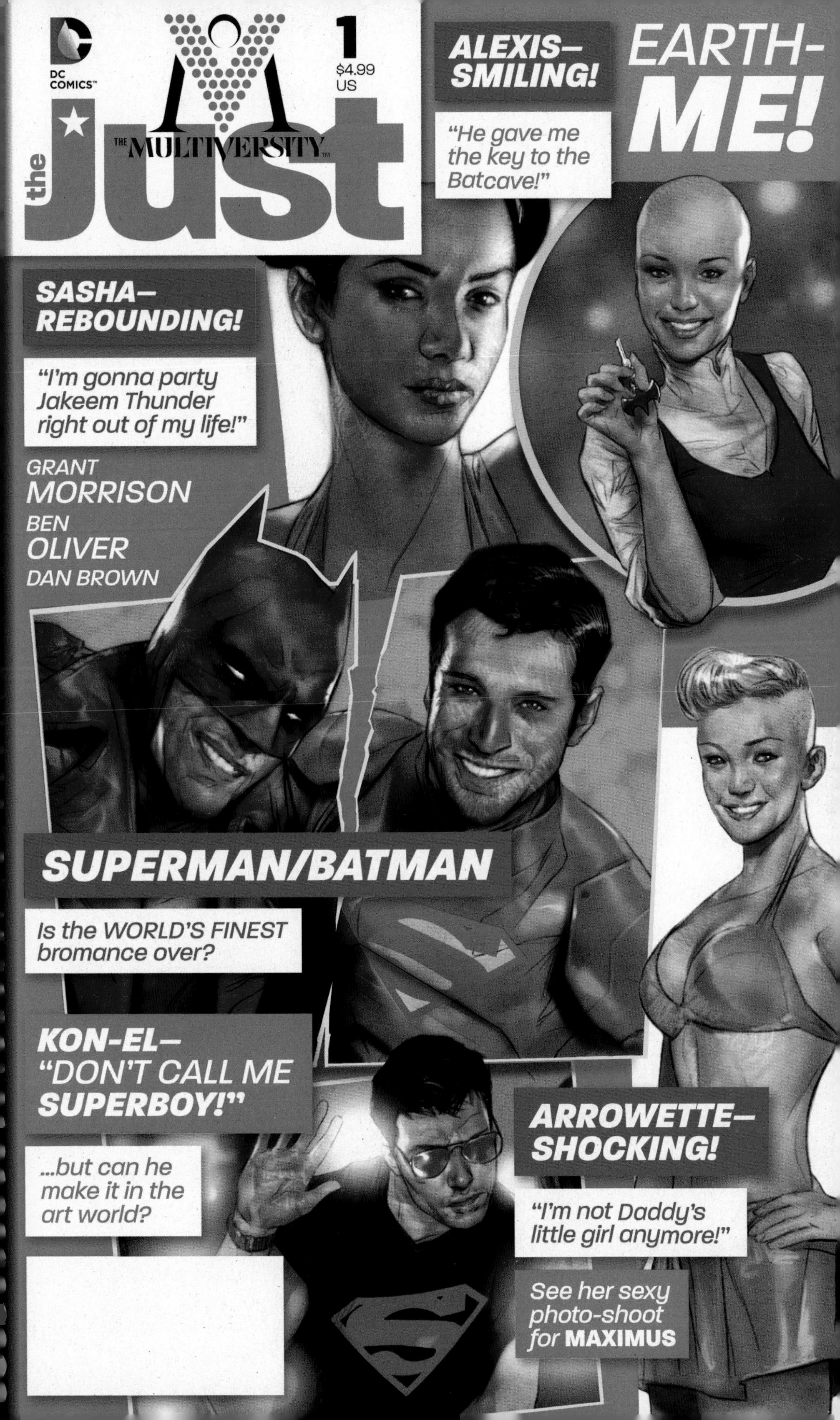
DC COMICS
1
$4.99 US
THE MULTIVERSITY
the Just
ALEXIS–
SMILING!
"He gave me the key to the Batcave!"
EARTH-
ME!
SASHA–
REBOUNDING!
"I'm gonna party Jakeem Thunder right out of my life!"
GRANT MORRISON
BEN OLIVER
DAN BROWN
SUPERMAN/BATMAN
Is the WORLD'S FINEST bromance over?
KON-EL–
"DON'T CALL ME SUPERBOY!"
...but can he make it in the art world?
ARROWETTE–
SHOCKING!
"I'm not Daddy's little girl anymore!"
See her sexy photo-shoot for MAXIMUS

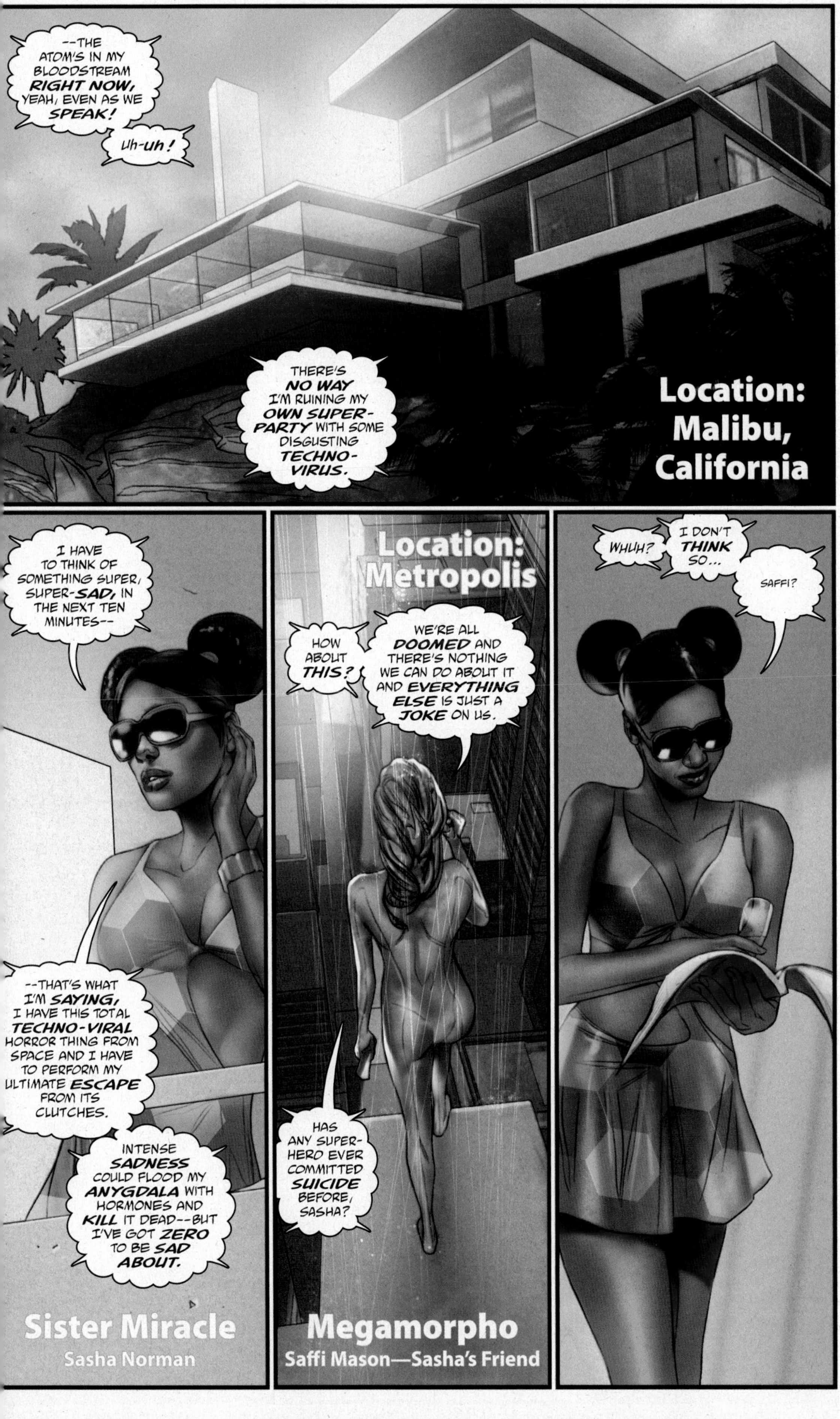
--THE ATOM'S IN MY BLOODSTREAM RIGHT NOW, YEAH, EVEN AS WE SPEAK!
Uh-uh!
THERE'S NO WAY I'M RUINING MY OWN SUPER-PARTY WITH SOME DISGUSTING TECHNO-VIRUS.
Location: Malibu, California
I HAVE TO THINK OF SOMETHING SUPER, SUPER-SAD, IN THE NEXT TEN MINUTES--
--THAT'S WHAT I'M SAYING, I HAVE THIS TOTAL TECHNO-VIRAL HORROR THING FROM SPACE AND I HAVE TO PERFORM MY ULTIMATE ESCAPE FROM ITS CLUTCHES.
INTENSE SADNESS COULD FLOOD MY ANYGDALA WITH HORMONES AND KILL IT DEAD--BUT I'VE GOT ZERO TO BE SAD ABOUT.
Sister Miracle
Sasha Norman
Location: Metropolis
HOW ABOUT THIS?
WE'RE ALL DOOMED AND THERE'S NOTHING WE CAN DO ABOUT IT AND EVERYTHING ELSE IS JUST A JOKE ON US.
HAS ANY SUPER-HERO EVER COMMITTED SUICIDE BEFORE, SASHA?
Megamorpho
Saffi Mason—Sasha's Friend
WHUH?
I DON'T THINK SO...
SAFFI?

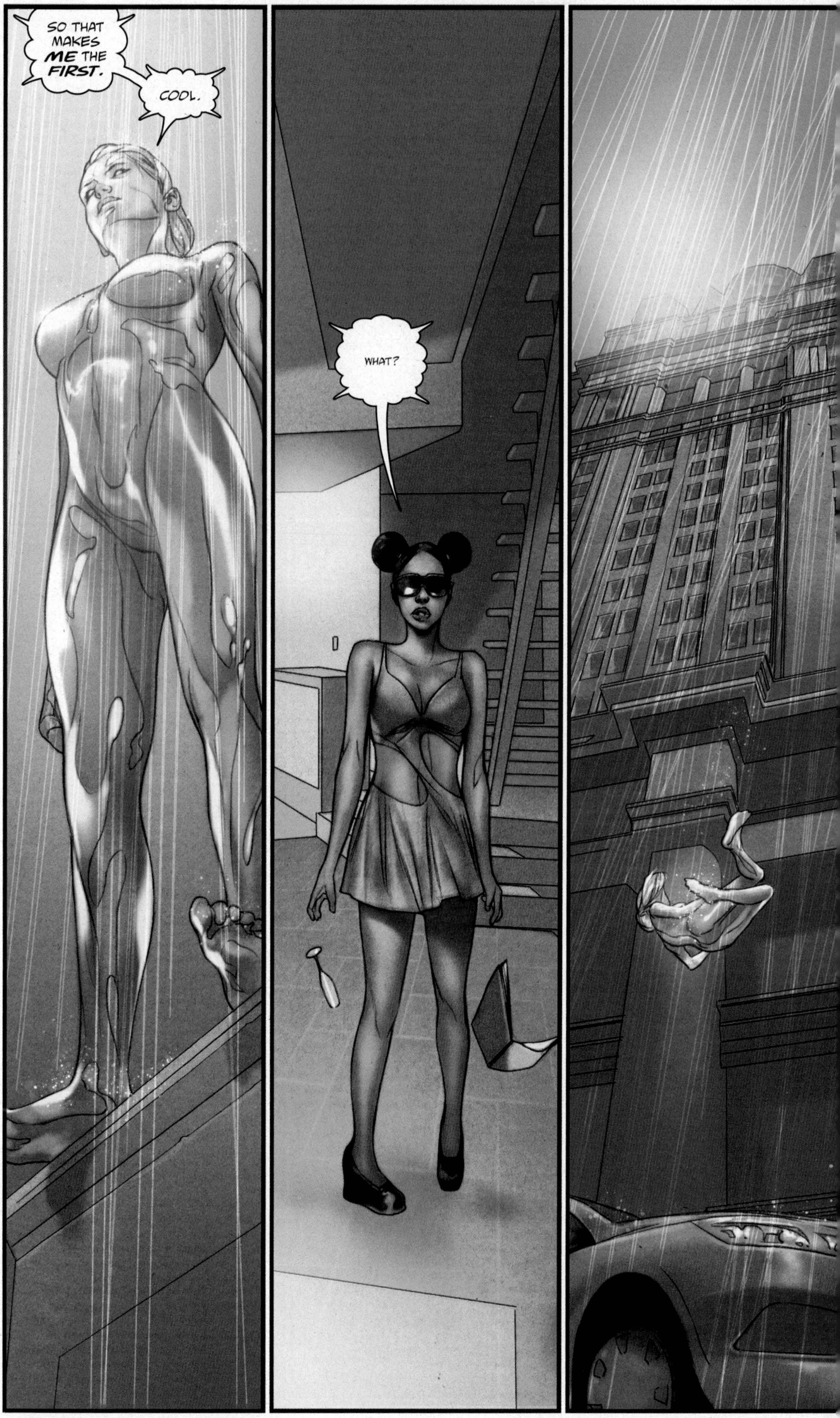
SO THAT MAKES ME THE FIRST.
COOL.
WHAT?

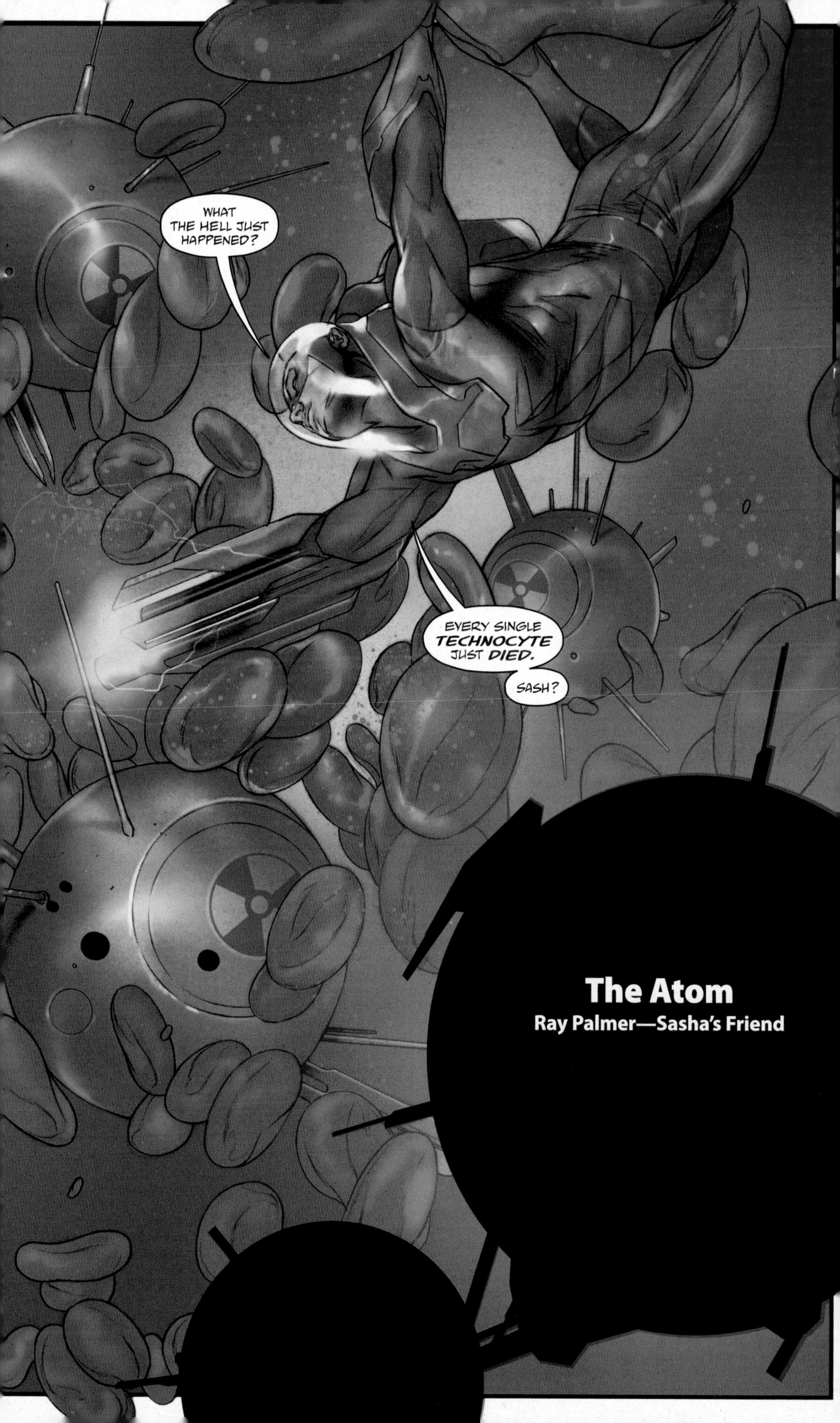
WHAT THE HELL JUST HAPPENED?
EVERY SINGLE TECHNOCYTE JUST DIED.
SASH?

The Atom

Ray Palmer—Sasha's Friend

Location:
Gotham City

WHAT'S *YOUR* TAKE ON THE WHOLE *COMIC BOOKS MMM-MIGHT BE ART* THING, DAMIAN?

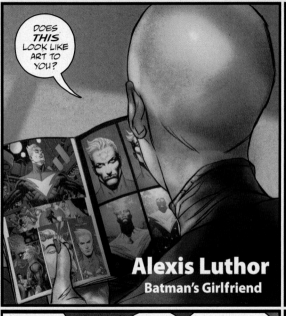

DOES *THIS* LOOK LIKE ART TO YOU?

Alexis Luthor
Batman's Girlfriend

WHAT ARE YOU *TALKING* ABOUT?

WHAT TAKE?

I DON'T *HAVE* A TAKE.

Batman
Damian Wayne

I'M *THE BATMAN.*

YOU SHOULD *SEE* THIS.

I SAW IT ONLINE.

THEY'RE FROM *ANOTHER* BORING *UNIVERSE* AND THEY'VE DECIDED TO --: YAWN:--

--TO INVADE REALITY ET CETERA ET CETERA ET CETERA...

MEANWHILE, I'M RIGHT HERE AND YOU'RE DELIBERATELY IGNORING MY OBVIOUS PHYSICAL AND INTELLECTUAL CHARMS.

IS BATMAN *GAY?*

TWO THOUSAND WORDS BY WEDNESDAY, STUDENTS.

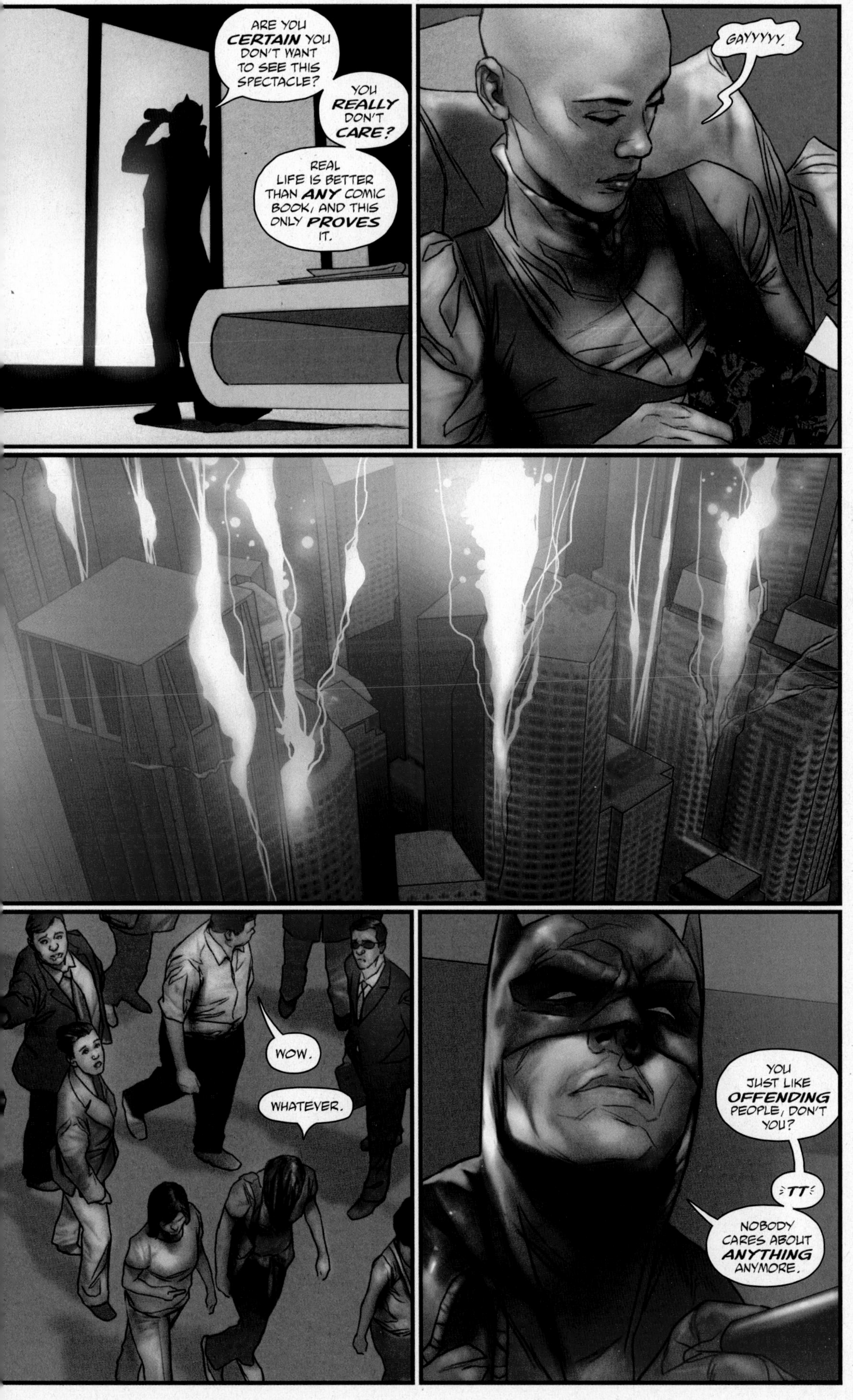
ARE YOU CERTAIN YOU DON'T WANT TO SEE THIS SPECTACLE?
YOU REALLY DON'T CARE?
REAL LIFE IS BETTER THAN ANY COMIC BOOK, AND THIS ONLY PROVES IT.
GAYYYYY.
WOW.
WHATEVER.
YOU JUST LIKE OFFENDING PEOPLE, DON'T YOU?
TT
NOBODY CARES ABOUT ANYTHING ANYMORE.

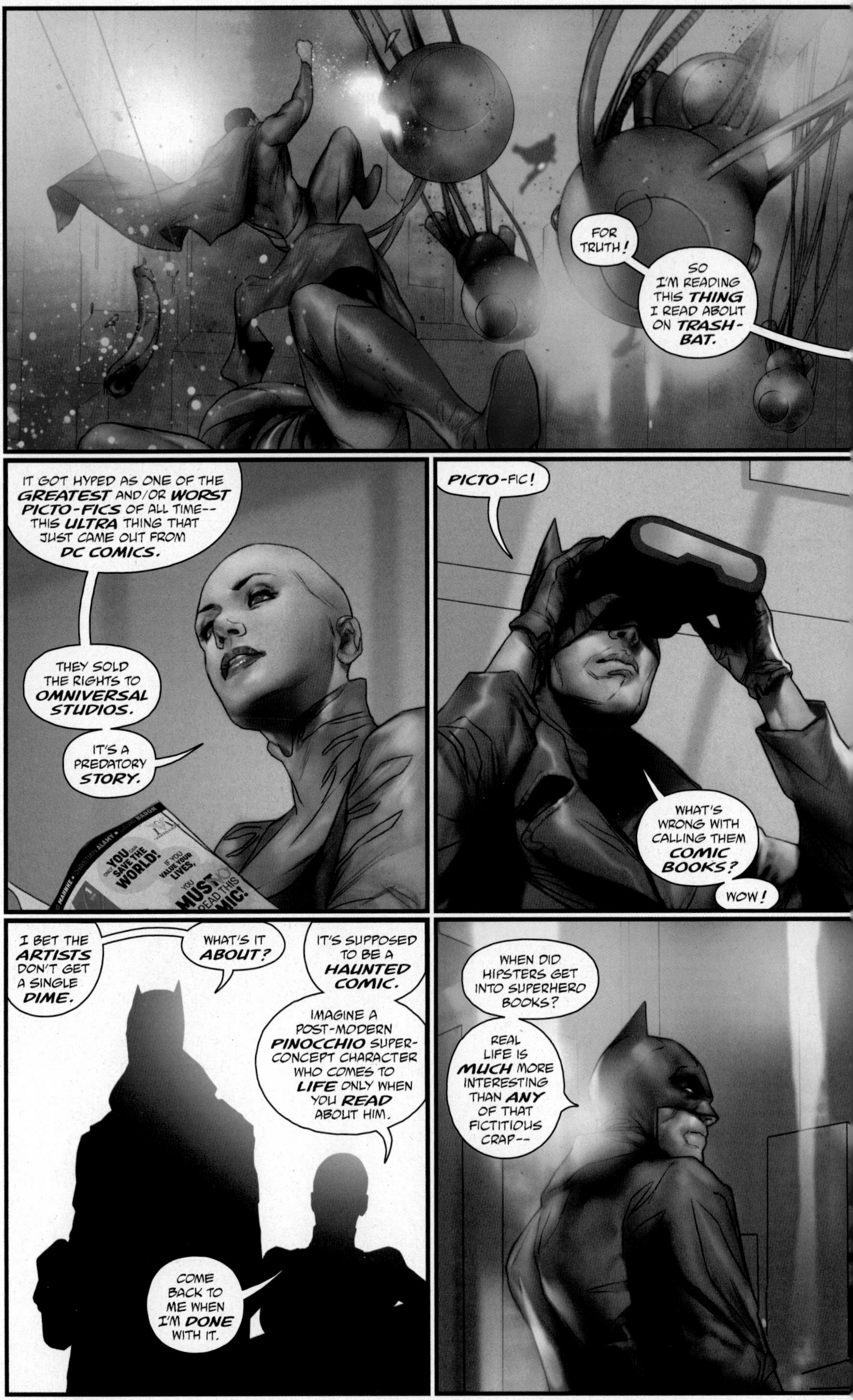
FOR TRUTH!
SO I'M READING THIS THING I READ ABOUT ON TRASH-BAT.
IT GOT HYPED AS ONE OF THE GREATEST AND/OR WORST PICTO-FICS OF ALL TIME-- THIS ULTRA THING THAT JUST CAME OUT FROM DC COMICS.
THEY SOLD THE RIGHTS TO OMNIVERSAL STUDIOS.
IT'S A PREDATORY STORY.
PICTO-FIC!
WHAT'S WRONG WITH CALLING THEM COMIC BOOKS?
WOW!
I BET THE ARTISTS DON'T GET A SINGLE DIME.
WHAT'S IT ABOUT?
IT'S SUPPOSED TO BE A HAUNTED COMIC.
IMAGINE A POST-MODERN PINOCCHIO SUPER-CONCEPT CHARACTER WHO COMES TO LIFE ONLY WHEN YOU READ ABOUT HIM.
COME BACK TO ME WHEN I'M DONE WITH IT.
WHEN DID HIPSTERS GET INTO SUPERHERO BOOKS?
REAL LIFE IS MUCH MORE INTERESTING THAN ANY OF THAT FICTITIOUS CRAP--

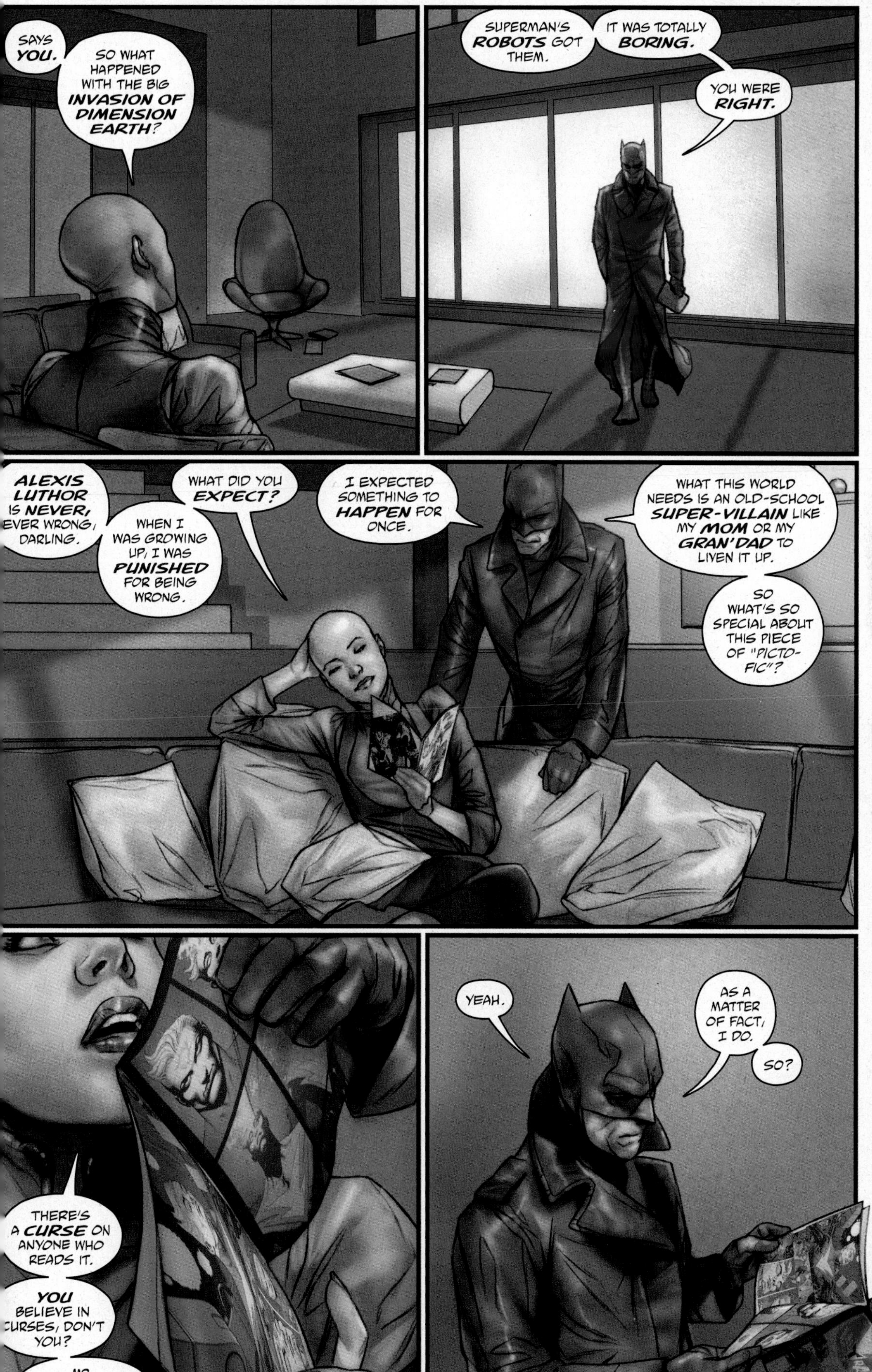
SAYS YOU.
SO WHAT HAPPENED WITH THE BIG INVASION OF DIMENSION EARTH?
SUPERMAN'S ROBOTS GOT THEM.
IT WAS TOTALLY BORING.
YOU WERE RIGHT.
ALEXIS LUTHOR IS NEVER, EVER WRONG, DARLING.
WHAT DID YOU EXPECT?
WHEN I WAS GROWING UP, I WAS PUNISHED FOR BEING WRONG.
I EXPECTED SOMETHING TO HAPPEN FOR ONCE.
WHAT THIS WORLD NEEDS IS AN OLD-SCHOOL SUPER-VILLAIN LIKE MY MOM OR MY GRAN'DAD TO LIVEN IT UP.
SO WHAT'S SO SPECIAL ABOUT THIS PIECE OF "PICTO-FIC"?
THERE'S A CURSE ON ANYONE WHO READS IT.
YOU BELIEVE IN CURSES, DON'T YOU?
MR. "SUPERSTITIOUS COWARDLY LOT."
YEAH.
AS A MATTER OF FACT, I DO.
SO?

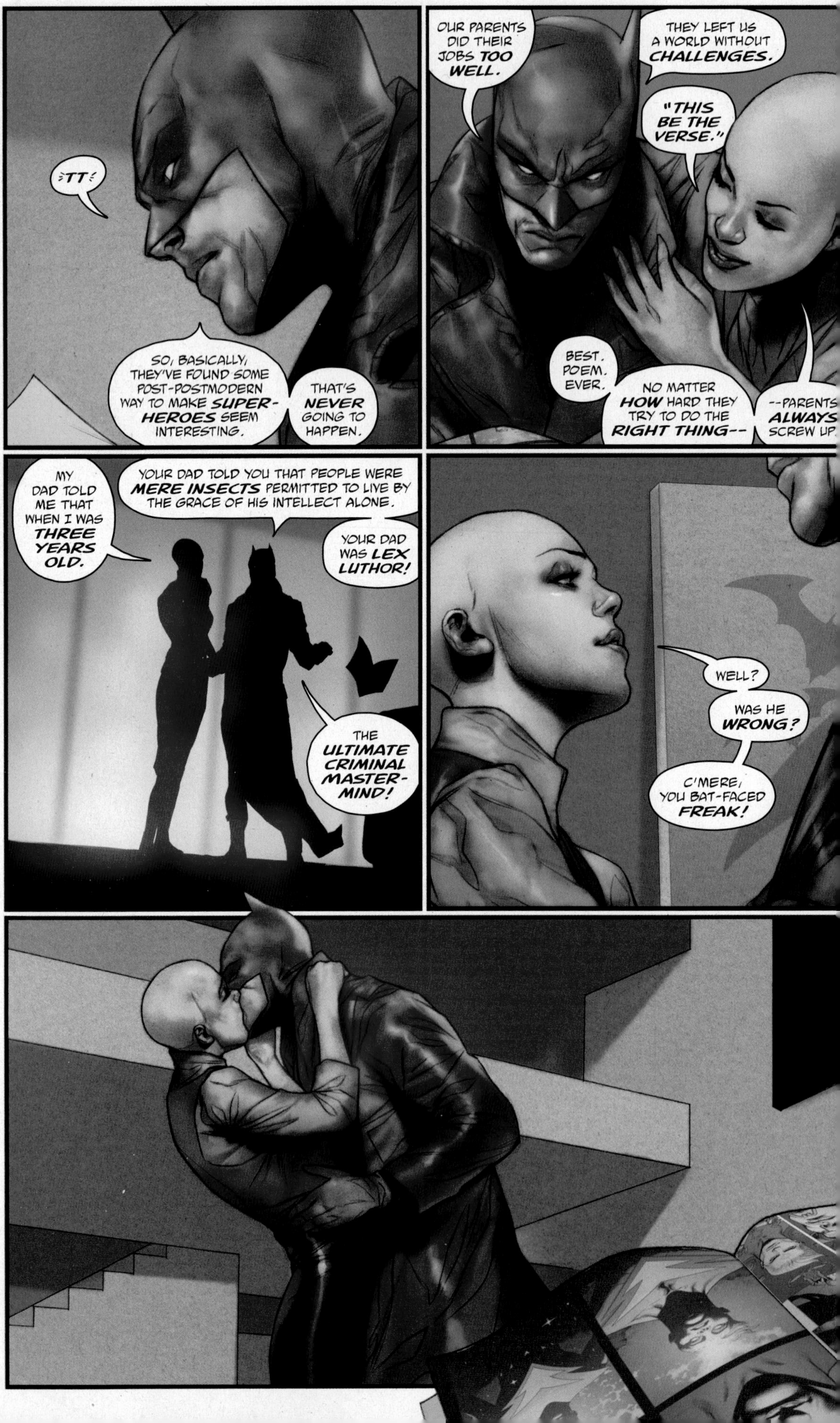
TT!
SO, BASICALLY, THEY'VE FOUND SOME POST-POSTMODERN WAY TO MAKE SUPER-HEROES SEEM INTERESTING.
THAT'S NEVER GOING TO HAPPEN.
OUR PARENTS DID THEIR JOBS TOO WELL.
THEY LEFT US A WORLD WITHOUT CHALLENGES.
"THIS BE THE VERSE."
BEST. POEM. EVER.
NO MATTER HOW HARD THEY TRY TO DO THE RIGHT THING--
--PARENTS ALWAYS SCREW UP.
MY DAD TOLD ME THAT WHEN I WAS THREE YEARS OLD.
YOUR DAD TOLD YOU THAT PEOPLE WERE MERE INSECTS PERMITTED TO LIVE BY THE GRACE OF HIS INTELLECT ALONE.
YOUR DAD WAS LEX LUTHOR!
THE ULTIMATE CRIMINAL MASTER-MIND!
WELL?
WAS HE WRONG?
C'MERE, YOU BAT-FACED FREAK!

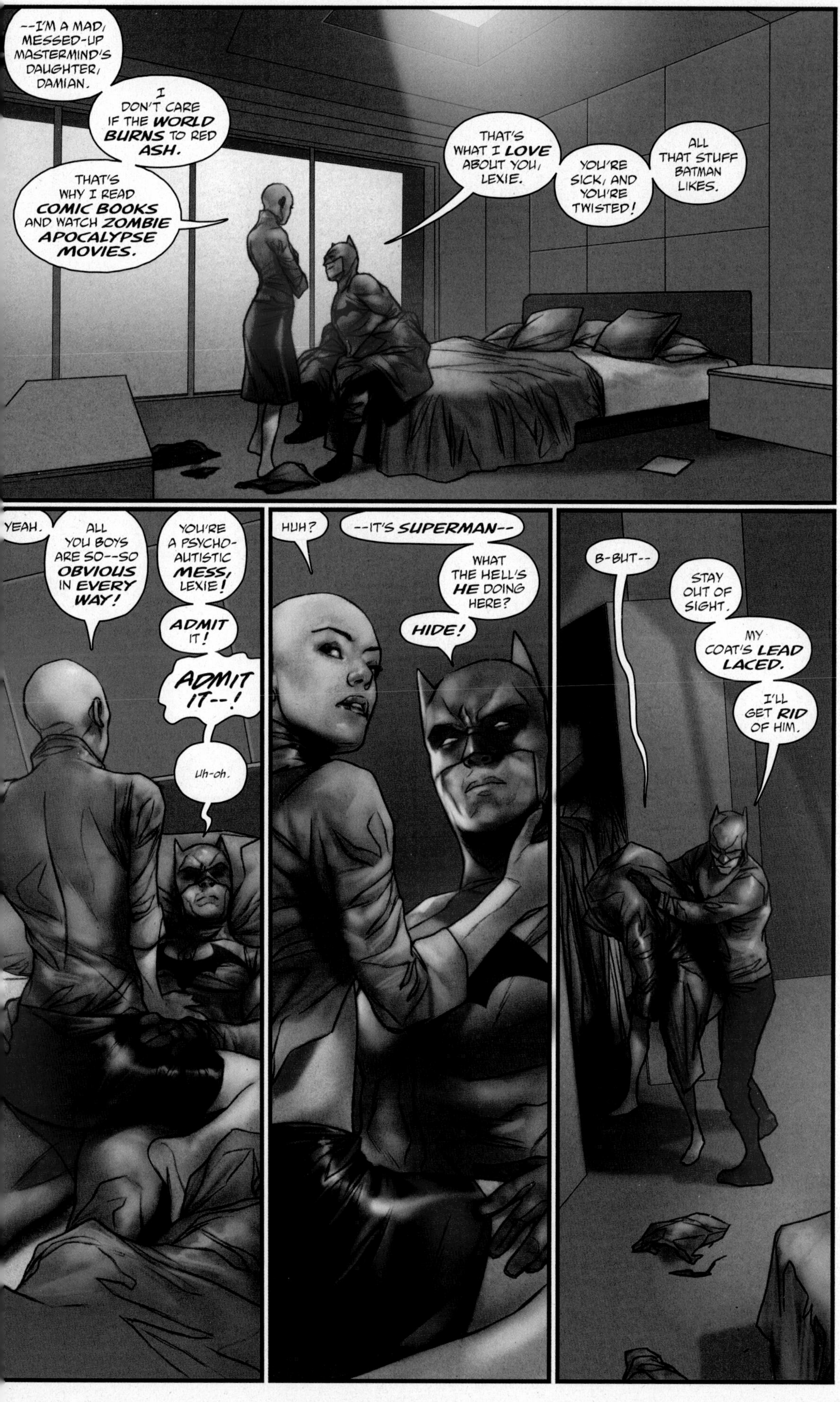

--I'M A MAD, MESSED-UP MASTERMIND'S DAUGHTER, DAMIAN.
I DON'T CARE IF THE WORLD BURNS TO RED ASH.
THAT'S WHY I READ COMIC BOOKS AND WATCH ZOMBIE APOCALYPSE MOVIES.
THAT'S WHAT I LOVE ABOUT YOU, LEXIE.
YOU'RE SICK, AND YOU'RE TWISTED!
ALL THAT STUFF BATMAN LIKES.
YEAH.
ALL YOU BOYS ARE SO--SO OBVIOUS IN EVERY WAY!
YOU'RE A PSYCHO-AUTISTIC MESS, LEXIE!
ADMIT IT!
ADMIT IT--!
Uh-oh.
HUH?
--IT'S SUPERMAN--
WHAT THE HELL'S HE DOING HERE?
HIDE!
B-BUT--
STAY OUT OF SIGHT.
MY COAT'S LEAD LACED.
I'LL GET RID OF HIM.

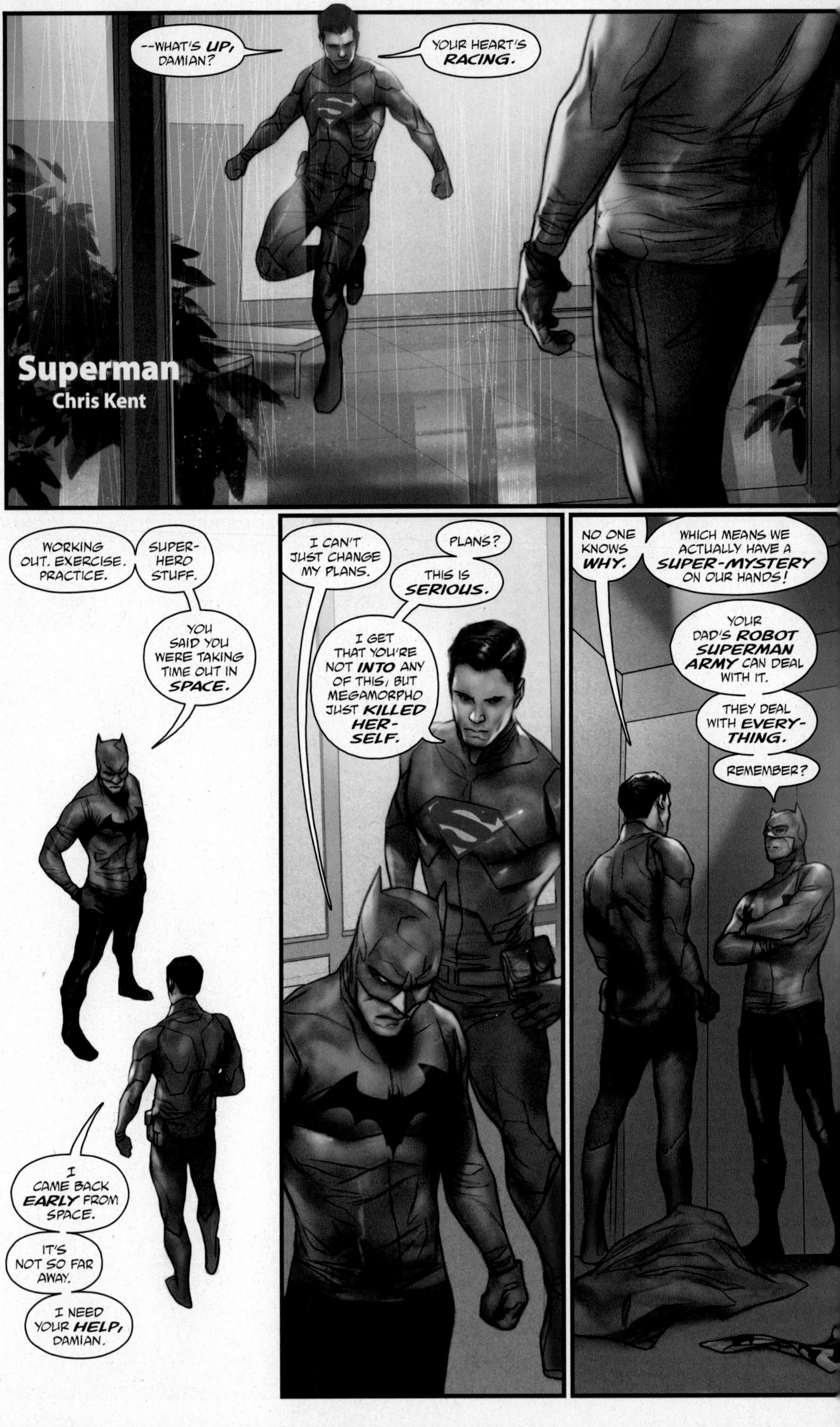
--WHAT'S UP, DAMIAN?
YOUR HEART'S RACING.
Superman
Chris Kent
WORKING OUT. EXERCISE. PRACTICE.
SUPER-HERO STUFF.
YOU SAID YOU WERE TAKING TIME OUT IN SPACE.
I CAME BACK EARLY FROM SPACE.
IT'S NOT SO FAR AWAY.
I NEED YOUR HELP, DAMIAN.
I CAN'T JUST CHANGE MY PLANS.
PLANS?
THIS IS SERIOUS.
I GET THAT YOU'RE NOT INTO ANY OF THIS, BUT MEGAMORPHO JUST KILLED HER-SELF.
NO ONE KNOWS WHY.
WHICH MEANS WE ACTUALLY HAVE A SUPER-MYSTERY ON OUR HANDS!
YOUR DAD'S ROBOT SUPERMAN ARMY CAN DEAL WITH IT.
THEY DEAL WITH EVERY-THING.
REMEMBER?

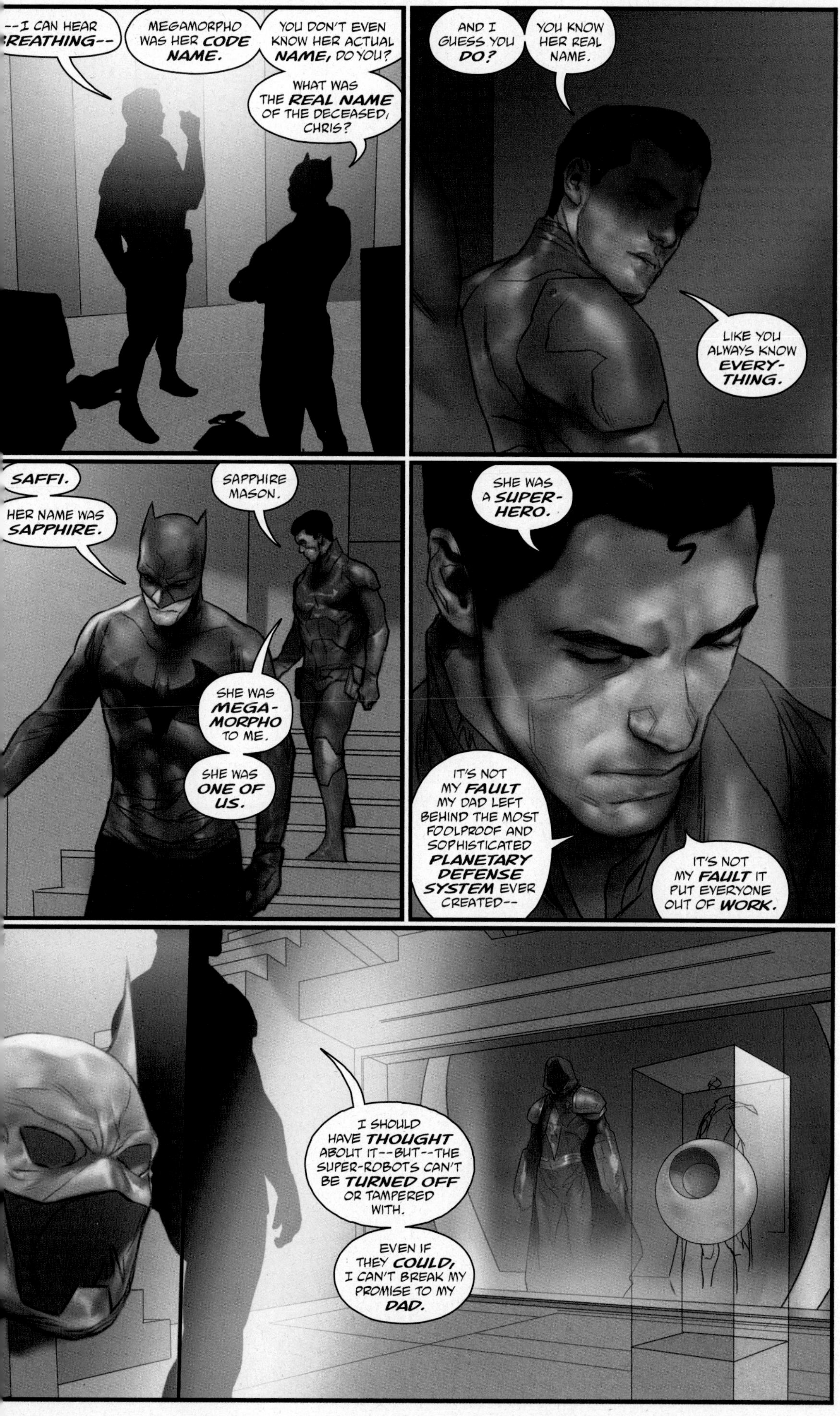
--I CAN HEAR BREATHING--
MEGAMORPHO WAS HER CODE NAME.
YOU DON'T EVEN KNOW HER ACTUAL NAME, DO YOU?
WHAT WAS THE REAL NAME OF THE DECEASED, CHRIS?
AND I GUESS YOU DO?
YOU KNOW HER REAL NAME.
LIKE YOU ALWAYS KNOW EVERY-THING.
SAFFI.
HER NAME WAS SAPPHIRE.
SAPPHIRE MASON.
SHE WAS MEGA-MORPHO TO ME.
SHE WAS ONE OF US.
SHE WAS A SUPER-HERO.
IT'S NOT MY FAULT MY DAD LEFT BEHIND THE MOST FOOLPROOF AND SOPHISTICATED PLANETARY DEFENSE SYSTEM EVER CREATED--
IT'S NOT MY FAULT IT PUT EVERYONE OUT OF WORK.
I SHOULD HAVE THOUGHT ABOUT IT--BUT--THE SUPER-ROBOTS CAN'T BE TURNED OFF OR TAMPERED WITH.
EVEN IF THEY COULD, I CAN'T BREAK MY PROMISE TO MY DAD.

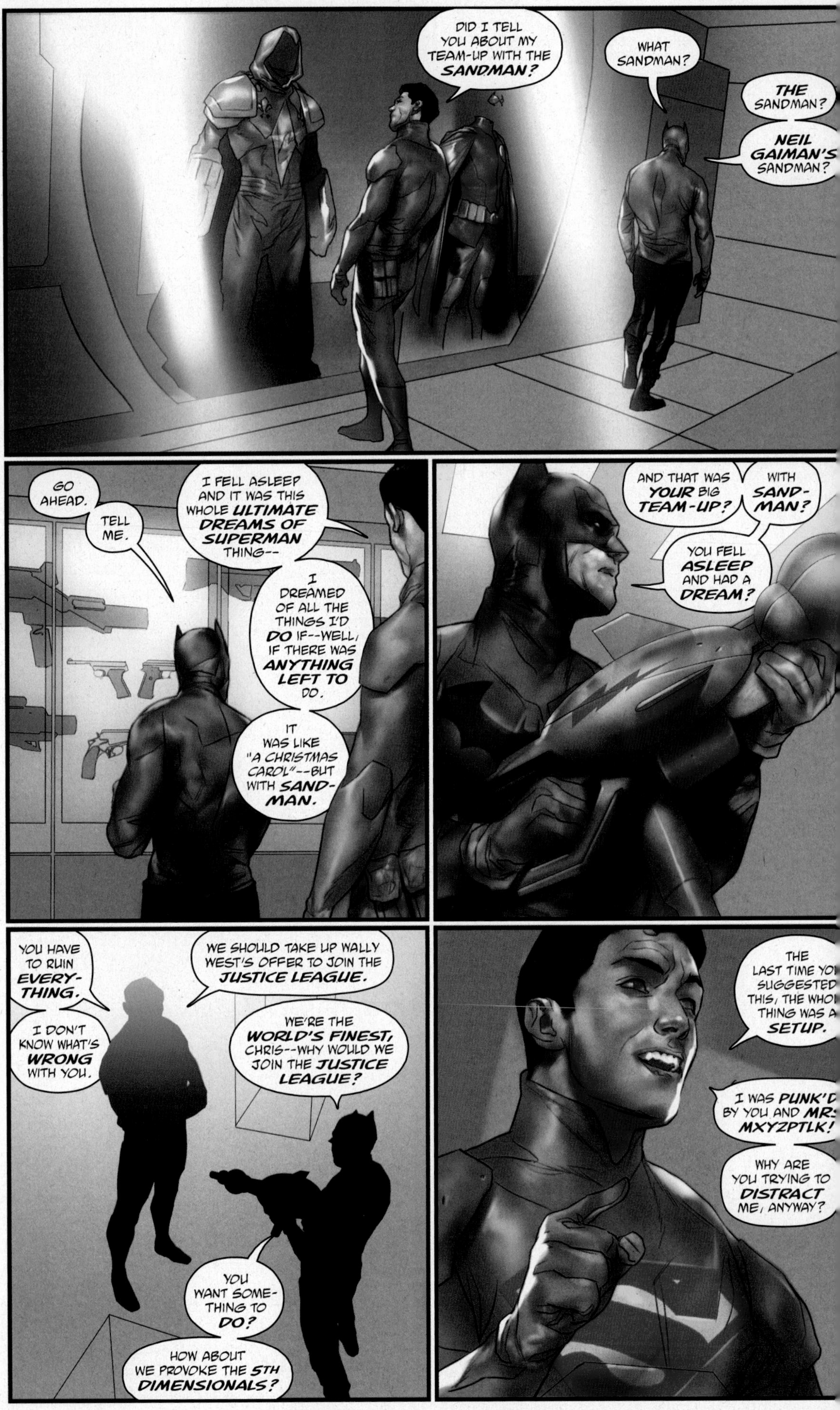
DID I TELL YOU ABOUT MY TEAM-UP WITH THE SANDMAN?
WHAT SANDMAN?
THE SANDMAN?
NEIL GAIMAN'S SANDMAN?
GO AHEAD.
TELL ME.
I FELL ASLEEP AND IT WAS THIS WHOLE ULTIMATE DREAMS OF SUPERMAN THING--
I DREAMED OF ALL THE THINGS I'D DO IF--WELL, IF THERE WAS ANYTHING LEFT TO DO.
IT WAS LIKE "A CHRISTMAS CAROL"--BUT WITH SANDMAN.
AND THAT WAS YOUR BIG TEAM-UP?
WITH SANDMAN?
YOU FELL ASLEEP AND HAD A DREAM?
YOU HAVE TO RUIN EVERYTHING.
I DON'T KNOW WHAT'S WRONG WITH YOU.
WE SHOULD TAKE UP WALLY WEST'S OFFER TO JOIN THE JUSTICE LEAGUE.
WE'RE THE WORLD'S FINEST, CHRIS--WHY WOULD WE JOIN THE JUSTICE LEAGUE?
YOU WANT SOMETHING TO DO?
HOW ABOUT WE PROVOKE THE 5TH DIMENSIONALS?
THE LAST TIME YO SUGGESTED THIS, THE WHO THING WAS A SETUP.
I WAS PUNK'D BY YOU AND MR MXYZPTLK!
WHY ARE YOU TRYING TO DISTRACT ME, ANYWAY?

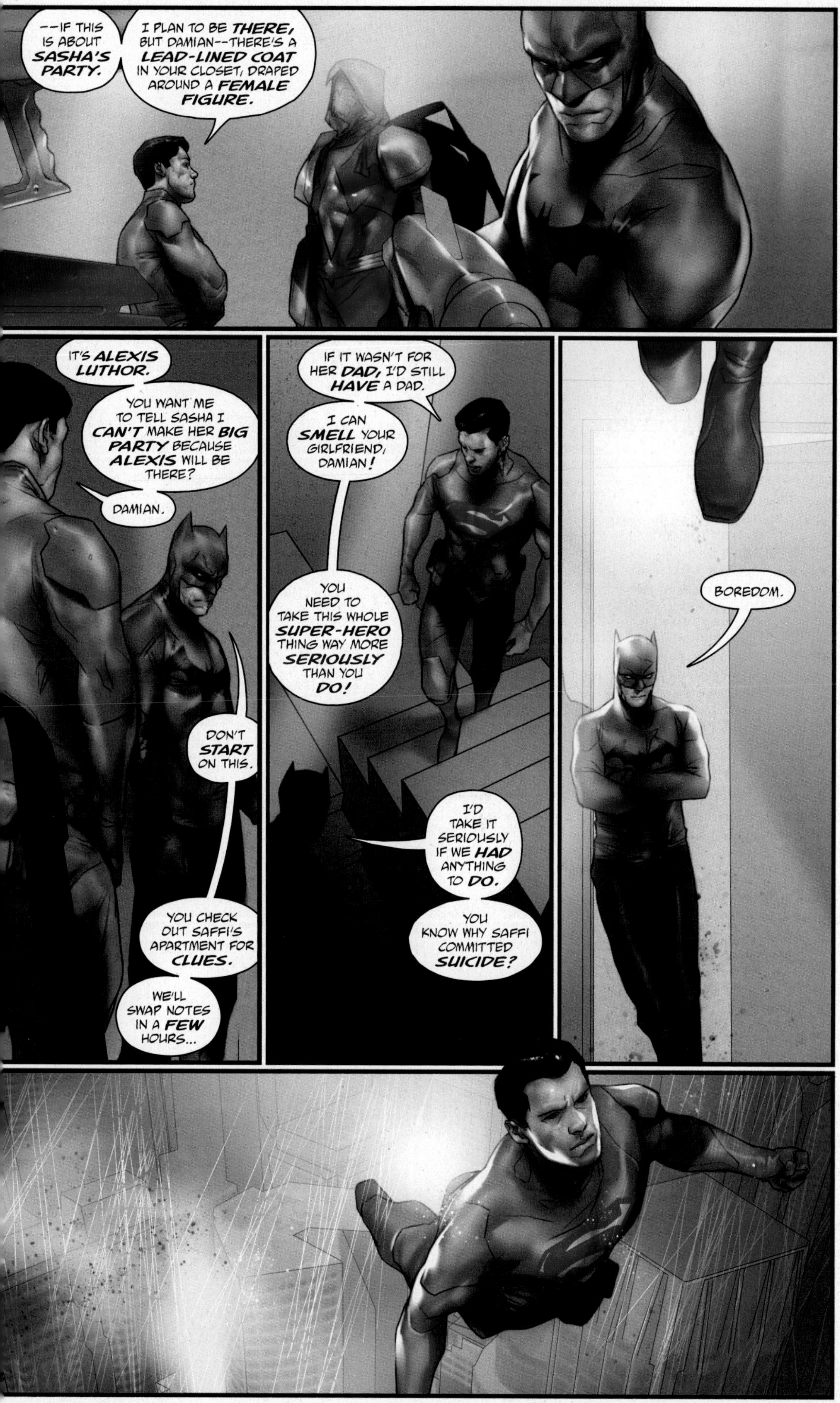
--IF THIS IS ABOUT SASHA'S PARTY.
I PLAN TO BE THERE, BUT DAMIAN--THERE'S A LEAD-LINED COAT IN YOUR CLOSET, DRAPED AROUND A FEMALE FIGURE.
IT'S ALEXIS LUTHOR.
YOU WANT ME TO TELL SASHA I CAN'T MAKE HER BIG PARTY BECAUSE ALEXIS WILL BE THERE?
DAMIAN.
DON'T START ON THIS.
YOU CHECK OUT SAFFI'S APARTMENT FOR CLUES.
WE'LL SWAP NOTES IN A FEW HOURS...
IF IT WASN'T FOR HER DAD, I'D STILL HAVE A DAD.
I CAN SMELL YOUR GIRLFRIEND, DAMIAN!
YOU NEED TO TAKE THIS WHOLE SUPER-HERO THING WAY MORE SERIOUSLY THAN YOU DO!
I'D TAKE IT SERIOUSLY IF WE HAD ANYTHING TO DO.
YOU KNOW WHY SAFFI COMMITTED SUICIDE?
BOREDOM.

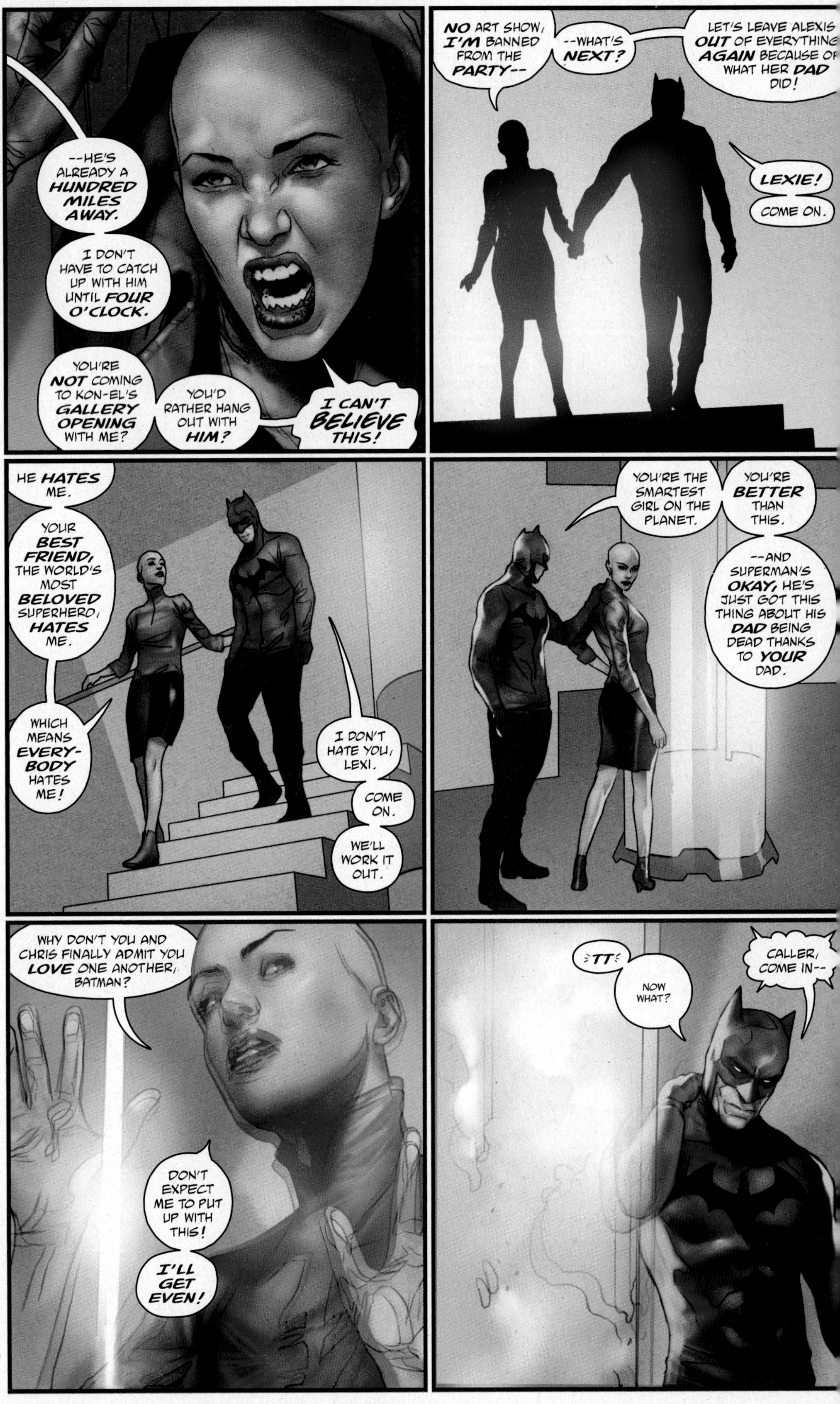
--HE'S ALREADY A HUNDRED MILES AWAY.
I DON'T HAVE TO CATCH UP WITH HIM UNTIL FOUR O'CLOCK.
YOU'RE NOT COMING TO KON-EL'S GALLERY OPENING WITH ME?
YOU'D RATHER HANG OUT WITH HIM?
I CAN'T BELIEVE THIS!
NO ART SHOW, I'M BANNED FROM THE PARTY--
--WHAT'S NEXT?
LET'S LEAVE ALEXIS OUT OF EVERYTHING AGAIN BECAUSE OF WHAT HER DAD DID!
LEXIE!
COME ON.
HE HATES ME.
YOUR BEST FRIEND, THE WORLD'S MOST BELOVED SUPERHERO, HATES ME.
WHICH MEANS EVERY-BODY HATES ME!
I DON'T HATE YOU, LEXI.
COME ON.
WE'LL WORK IT OUT.
YOU'RE THE SMARTEST GIRL ON THE PLANET.
YOU'RE BETTER THAN THIS.
--AND SUPERMAN'S OKAY, HE'S JUST GOT THIS THING ABOUT HIS DAD BEING DEAD THANKS TO YOUR DAD.
WHY DON'T YOU AND CHRIS FINALLY ADMIT YOU LOVE ONE ANOTHER, BATMAN?
DON'T EXPECT ME TO PUT UP WITH THIS!
I'LL GET EVEN!
TT
NOW WHAT?
CALLER, COME IN--

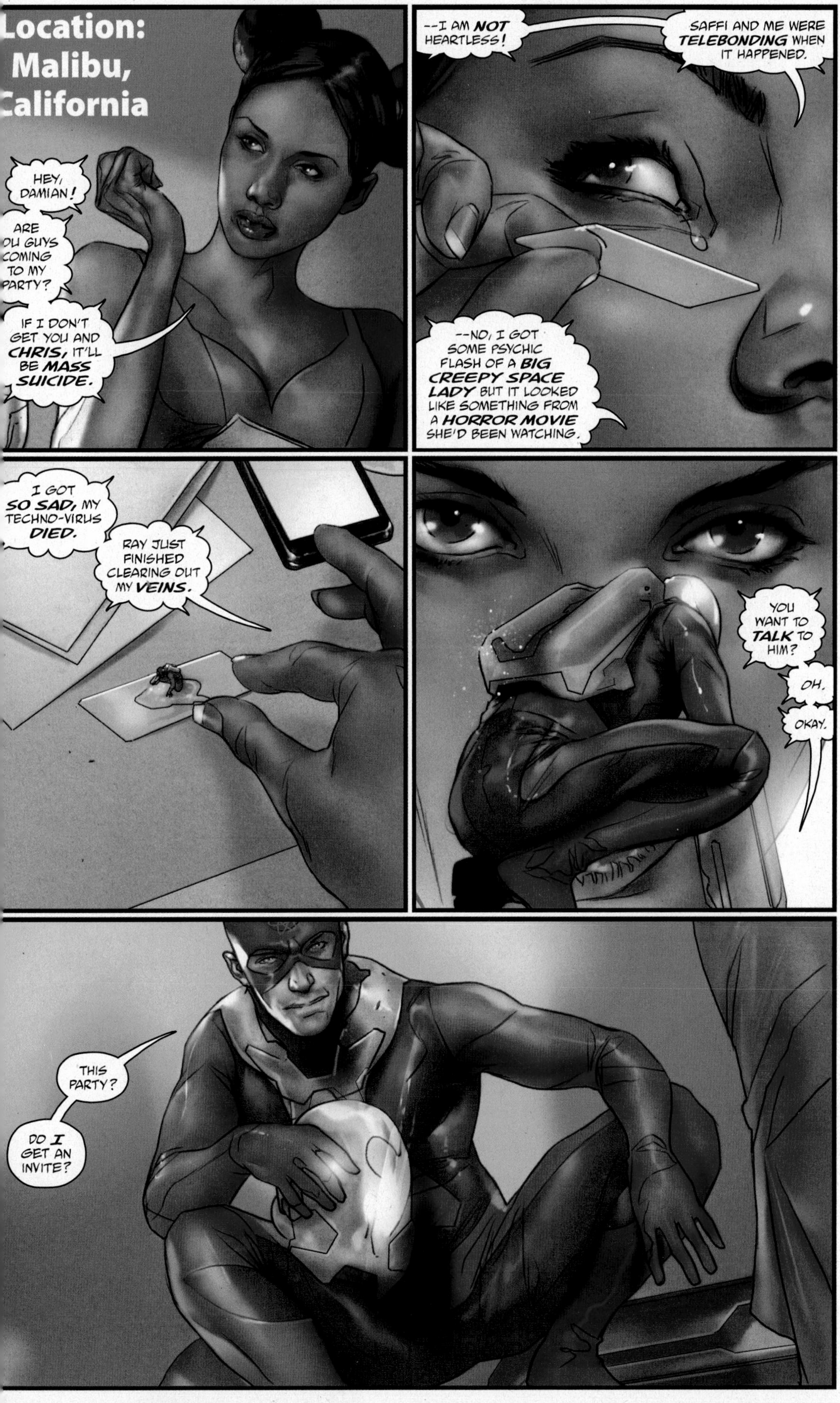
Location: Malibu, California
HEY, DAMIAN!
ARE OU GUYS COMING TO MY PARTY?
IF I DON'T GET YOU AND CHRIS, IT'LL BE MASS SUICIDE.
--I AM NOT HEARTLESS!
SAFFI AND ME WERE TELEBONDING WHEN IT HAPPENED.
--NO, I GOT SOME PSYCHIC FLASH OF A BIG CREEPY SPACE LADY BUT IT LOOKED LIKE SOMETHING FROM A HORROR MOVIE SHE'D BEEN WATCHING.
I GOT SO SAD, MY TECHNO-VIRUS DIED.
RAY JUST FINISHED CLEARING OUT MY VEINS.
YOU WANT TO TALK TO HIM?
OH.
OKAY.
THIS PARTY?
DO I GET AN INVITE?

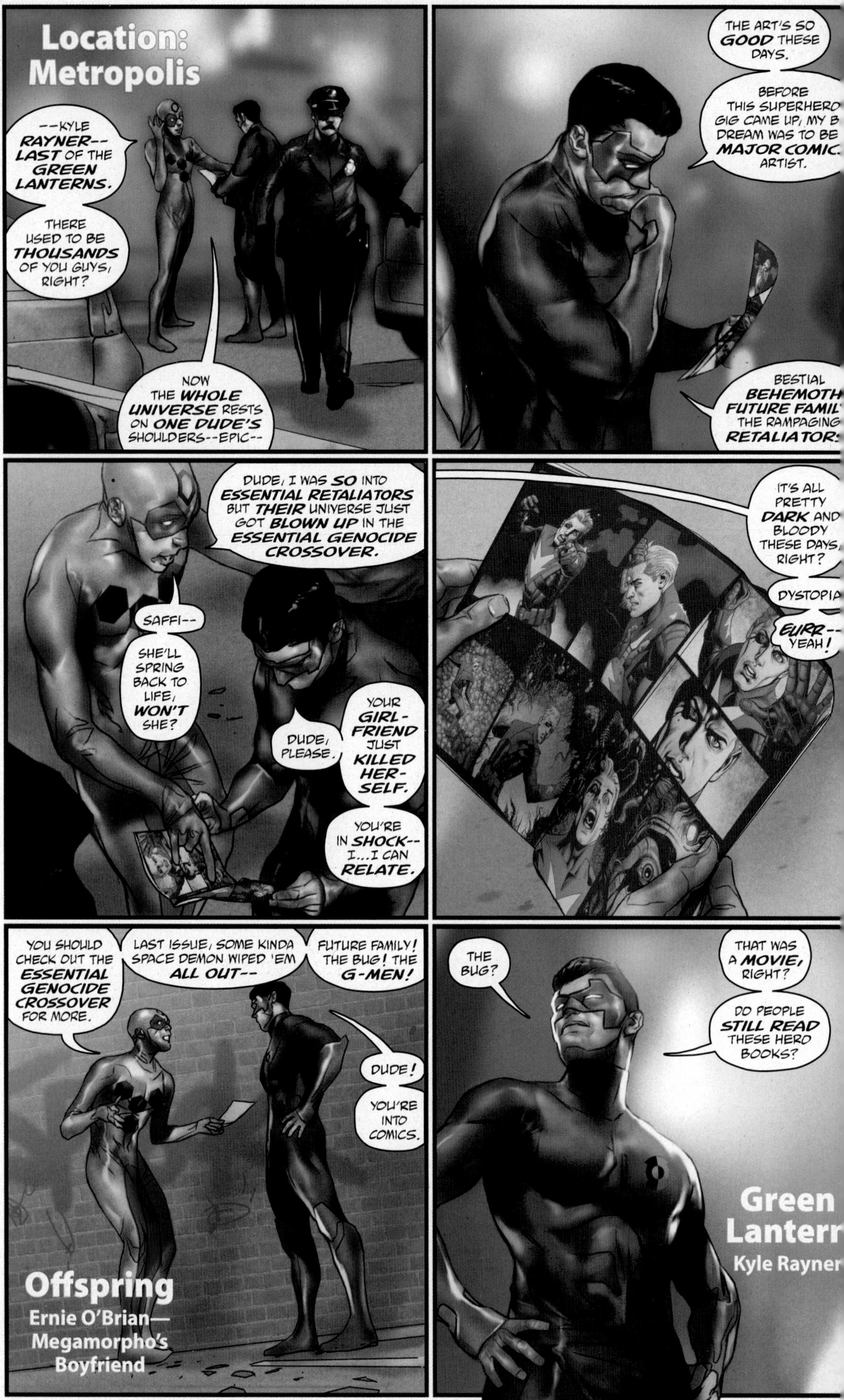
Location: Metropolis
--KYLE RAYNER--LAST OF THE GREEN LANTERNS.
THERE USED TO BE THOUSANDS OF YOU GUYS, RIGHT?
NOW THE WHOLE UNIVERSE RESTS ON ONE DUDE'S SHOULDERS--EPIC--
THE ART'S SO GOOD THESE DAYS.
BEFORE THIS SUPERHERO GIG CAME UP, MY B DREAM WAS TO BE MAJOR COMIC ARTIST.
BESTIAL BEHEMOTH FUTURE FAMIL THE RAMPAGING RETALIATOR:
DUDE, I WAS SO INTO ESSENTIAL RETALIATORS BUT THEIR UNIVERSE JUST GOT BLOWN UP IN THE ESSENTIAL GENOCIDE CROSSOVER.
SAFFI--
SHE'LL SPRING BACK TO LIFE, WON'T SHE?
DUDE, PLEASE.
YOUR GIRL-FRIEND JUST KILLED HER-SELF.
YOU'RE IN SHOCK--I...I CAN RELATE.
IT'S ALL PRETTY DARK AND BLOODY THESE DAYS, RIGHT?
DYSTOPIA
EURR--YEAH!
YOU SHOULD CHECK OUT THE ESSENTIAL GENOCIDE CROSSOVER FOR MORE.
LAST ISSUE, SOME KINDA SPACE DEMON WIPED 'EM ALL OUT--
FUTURE FAMILY! THE BUG! THE G-MEN!
DUDE!
YOU'RE INTO COMICS.
Offspring
Ernie O'Brian—Megamorpho's Boyfriend
THE BUG?
THAT WAS A MOVIE, RIGHT?
DO PEOPLE STILL READ THESE HERO BOOKS?
Green Lanterr
Kyle Rayner

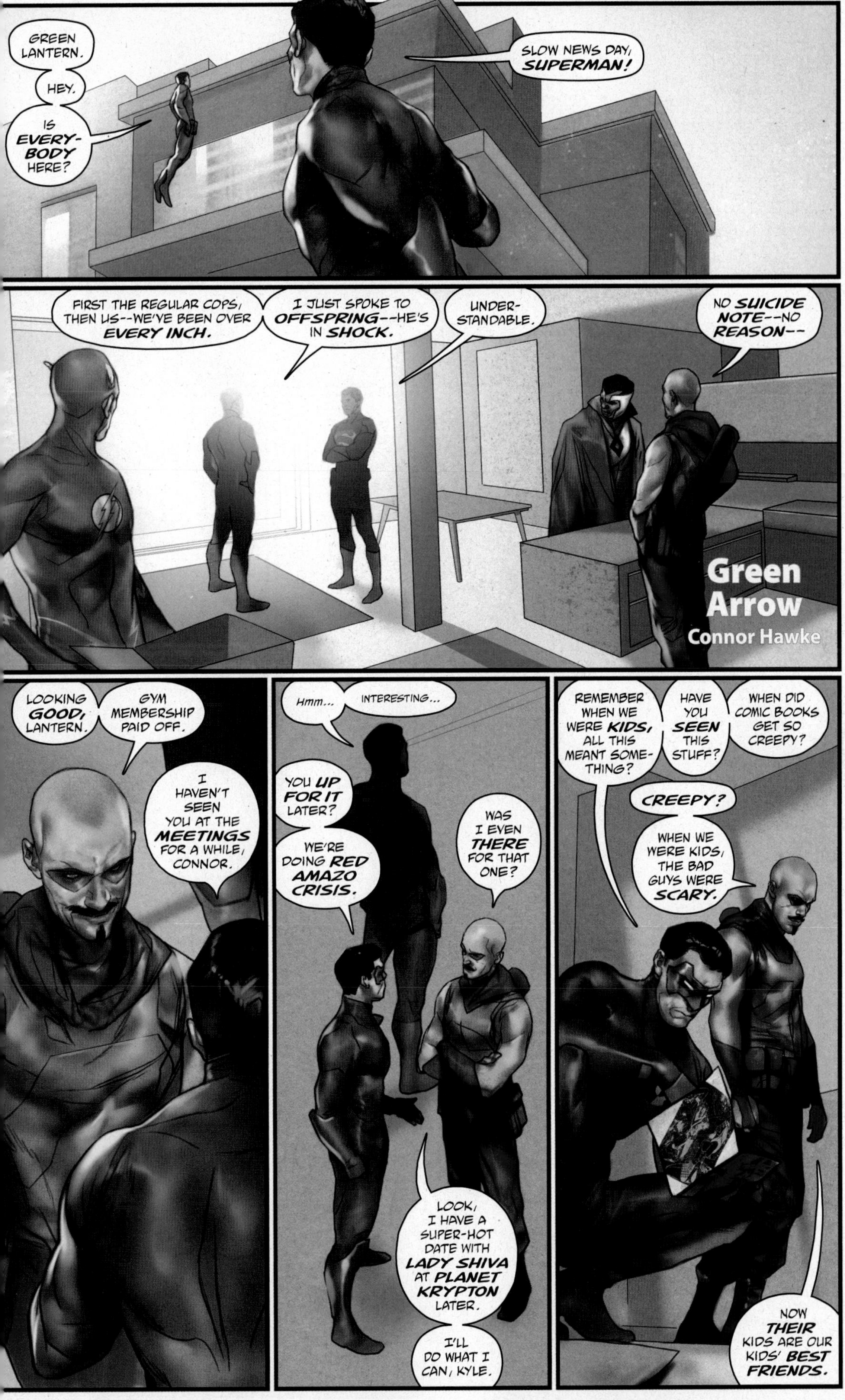
GREEN LANTERN.
HEY.
IS EVERYBODY HERE?
SLOW NEWS DAY, SUPERMAN!
FIRST THE REGULAR COPS, THEN US--WE'VE BEEN OVER EVERY INCH.
I JUST SPOKE TO OFFSPRING--HE'S IN SHOCK.
UNDERSTANDABLE.
NO SUICIDE NOTE--NO REASON--
Green Arrow
Connor Hawke
LOOKING GOOD, LANTERN.
GYM MEMBERSHIP PAID OFF.
I HAVEN'T SEEN YOU AT THE MEETINGS FOR A WHILE, CONNOR.
Hmm...
INTERESTING...
YOU UP FOR IT LATER?
WE'RE DOING RED AMAZO CRISIS.
WAS I EVEN THERE FOR THAT ONE?
LOOK, I HAVE A SUPER-HOT DATE WITH LADY SHIVA AT PLANET KRYPTON LATER.
I'LL DO WHAT I CAN, KYLE.
REMEMBER WHEN WE WERE KIDS, ALL THIS MEANT SOMETHING?
HAVE YOU SEEN THIS STUFF?
WHEN DID COMIC BOOKS GET SO CREEPY?
CREEPY?
WHEN WE WERE KIDS, THE BAD GUYS WERE SCARY.
NOW THEIR KIDS ARE OUR KIDS' BEST FRIENDS.

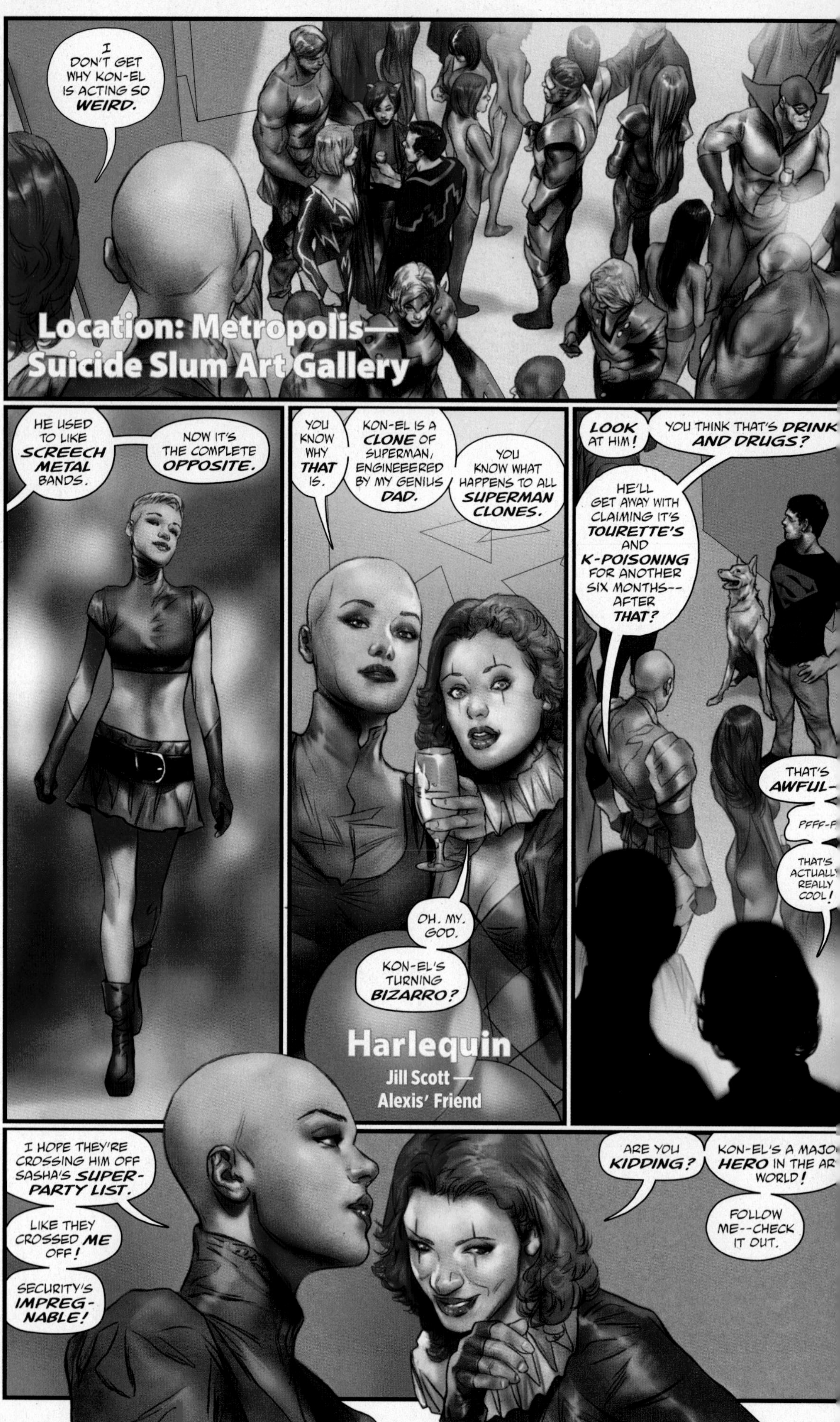
I DON'T GET WHY KON-EL IS ACTING SO WEIRD.
Location: Metropolis—Suicide Slum Art Gallery
HE USED TO LIKE SCREECH METAL BANDS.
NOW IT'S THE COMPLETE OPPOSITE.
YOU KNOW WHY THAT IS.
KON-EL IS A CLONE OF SUPERMAN, ENGINEEERED BY MY GENIUS DAD.
YOU KNOW WHAT HAPPENS TO ALL SUPERMAN CLONES.
OH. MY. GOD.
KON-EL'S TURNING BIZARRO?
Harlequin
Jill Scott—Alexis' Friend
LOOK AT HIM!
YOU THINK THAT'S DRINK AND DRUGS?
HE'LL GET AWAY WITH CLAIMING IT'S TOURETTE'S AND K-POISONING FOR ANOTHER SIX MONTHS--AFTER THAT?
THAT'S AWFUL-
PFFF-F
THAT'S ACTUALLY REALLY COOL!
I HOPE THEY'RE CROSSING HIM OFF SASHA'S SUPER-PARTY LIST.
LIKE THEY CROSSED ME OFF!
SECURITY'S IMPREG-NABLE!
ARE YOU KIDDING?
KON-EL'S A MAJO HERO IN THE AR WORLD!
FOLLOW ME--CHECK IT OUT.

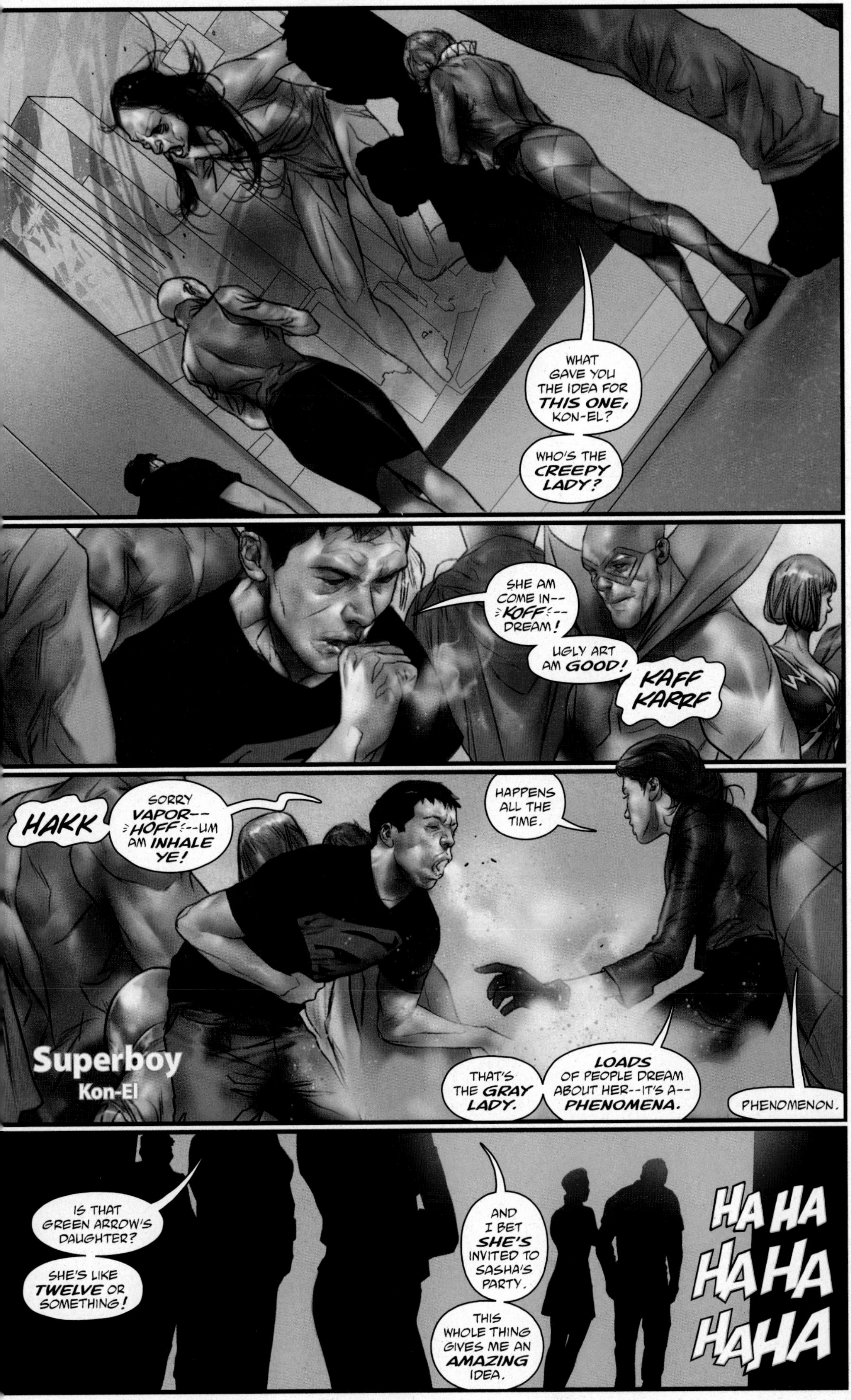
WHAT GAVE YOU THE IDEA FOR THIS ONE, KON-EL?
WHO'S THE CREEPY LADY?
SHE AM COME IN-- KOFF-- DREAM!
UGLY ART AM GOOD!
KAFF KARRF
HAKK
SORRY VAPOR-- HOFF--UM AM INHALE YE!
HAPPENS ALL THE TIME.
Superboy
Kon-El
THAT'S THE GRAY LADY.
LOADS OF PEOPLE DREAM ABOUT HER--IT'S A-- PHENOMENA.
PHENOMENON.
IS THAT GREEN ARROW'S DAUGHTER?
SHE'S LIKE TWELVE OR SOMETHING!
AND I BET SHE'S INVITED TO SASHA'S PARTY.
THIS WHOLE THING GIVES ME AN AMAZING IDEA.
HA HA HA HA HA HA

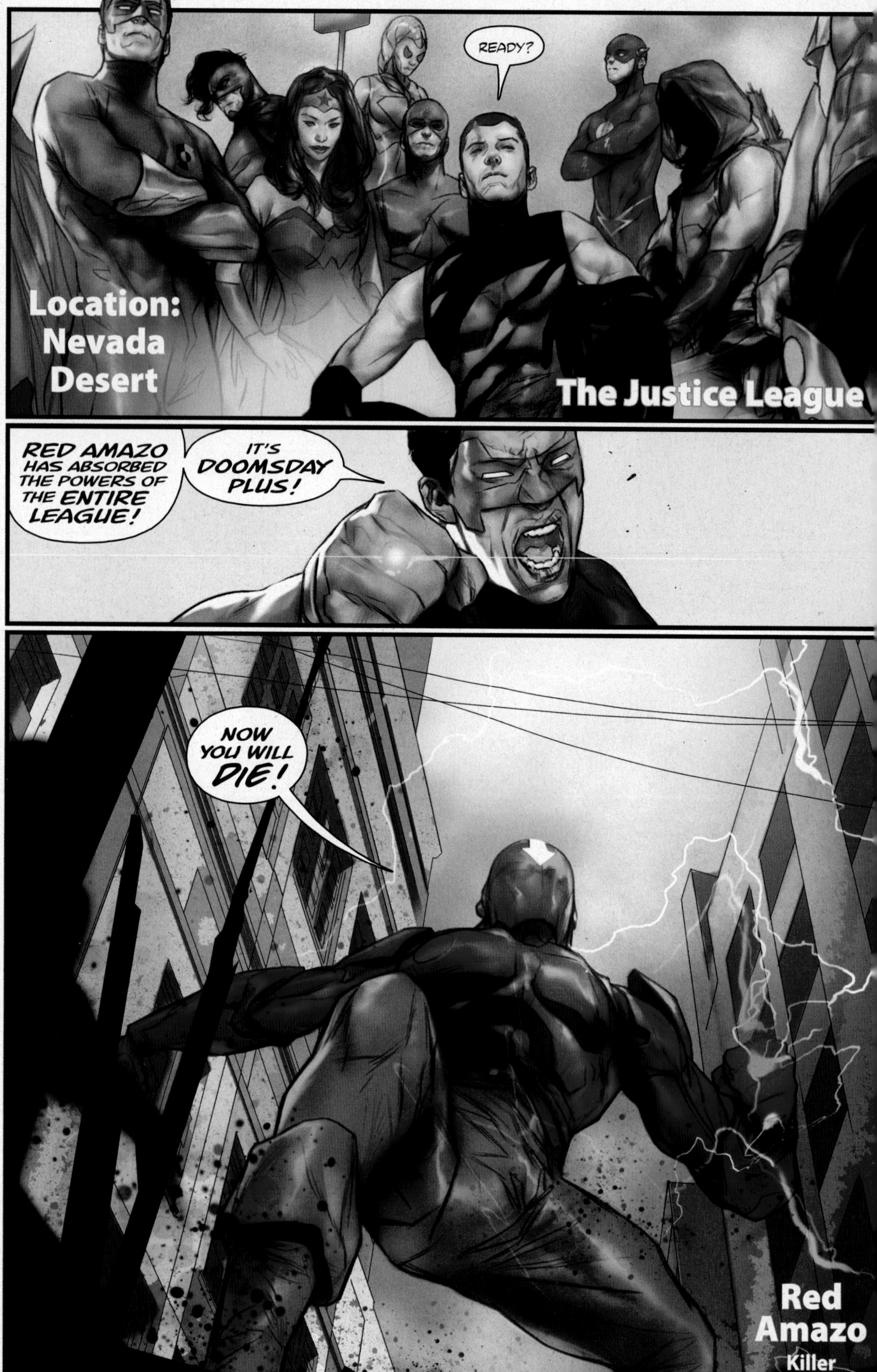
READY?
Location: Nevada Desert
The Justice League
RED AMAZO HAS ABSORBED THE POWERS OF THE ENTIRE LEAGUE!
IT'S DOOMSDAY PLUS!
NOW YOU WILL DIE!
Red Amazo
Killer Android Bastard

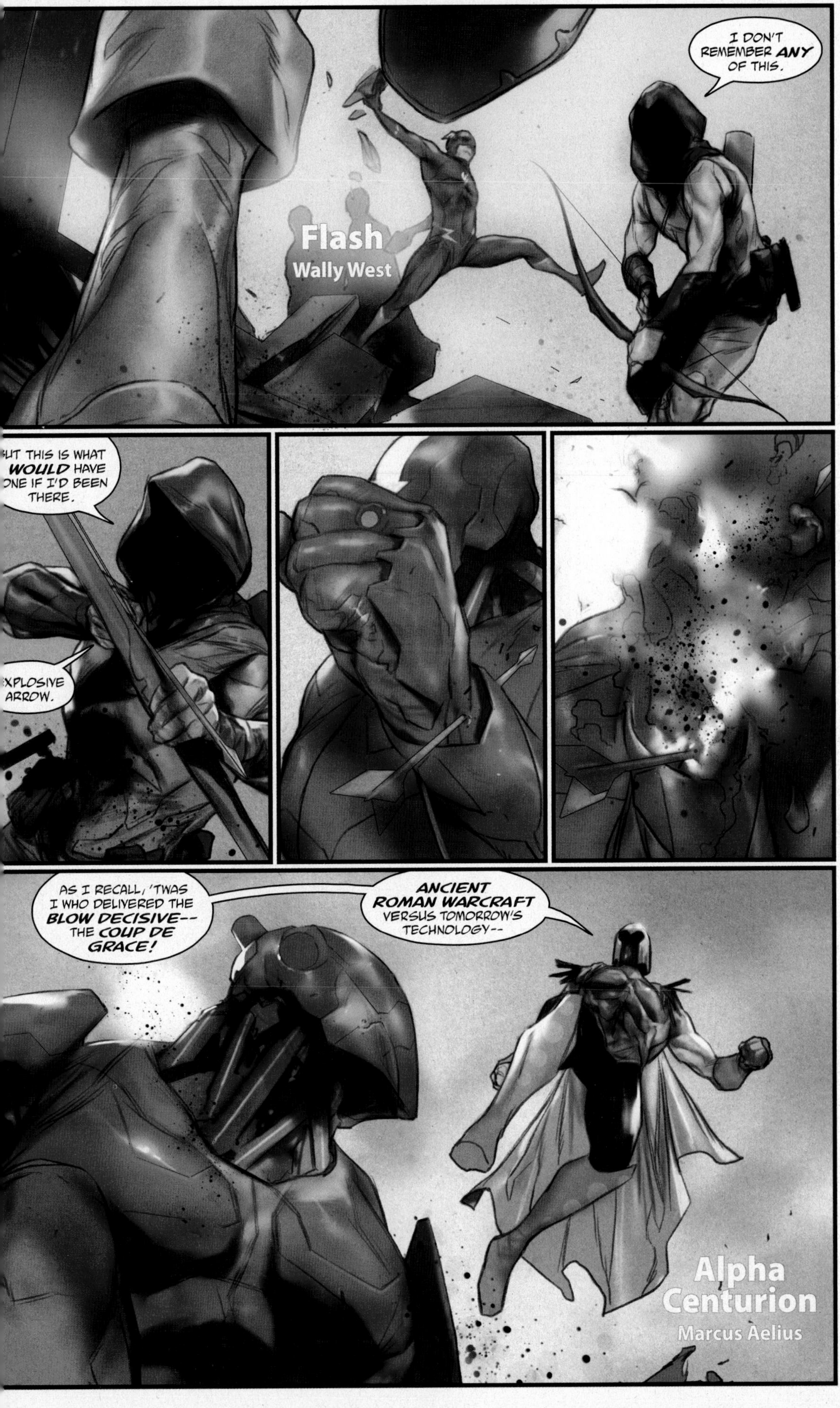

I DON'T REMEMBER ANY OF THIS.
Flash
Wally West
UT THIS IS WHAT WOULD HAVE ONE IF I'D BEEN THERE.
XPLOSIVE ARROW.
AS I RECALL, 'TWAS I WHO DELIVERED THE BLOW DECISIVE-- THE COUP DE GRACE!
ANCIENT ROMAN WARCRAFT VERSUS TOMORROW'S TECHNOLOGY--
Alpha Centurion
Marcus Aelius

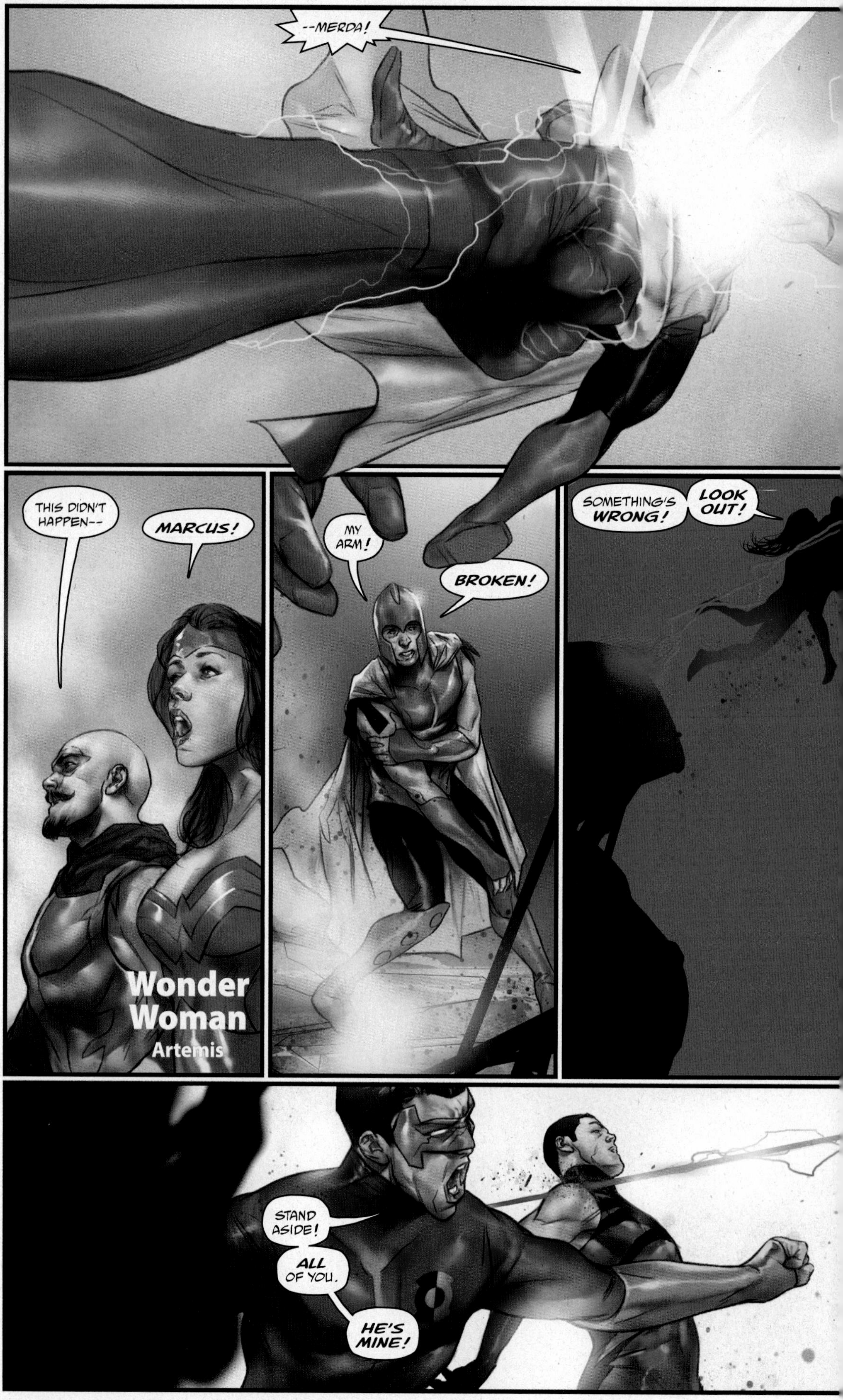

--MERDA!
THIS DIDN'T HAPPEN--
MARCUS!
Wonder Woman
Artemis
MY ARM!
BROKEN!
SOMETHING'S WRONG!
LOOK OUT!
STAND ASIDE!
ALL OF YOU.
HE'S MINE!

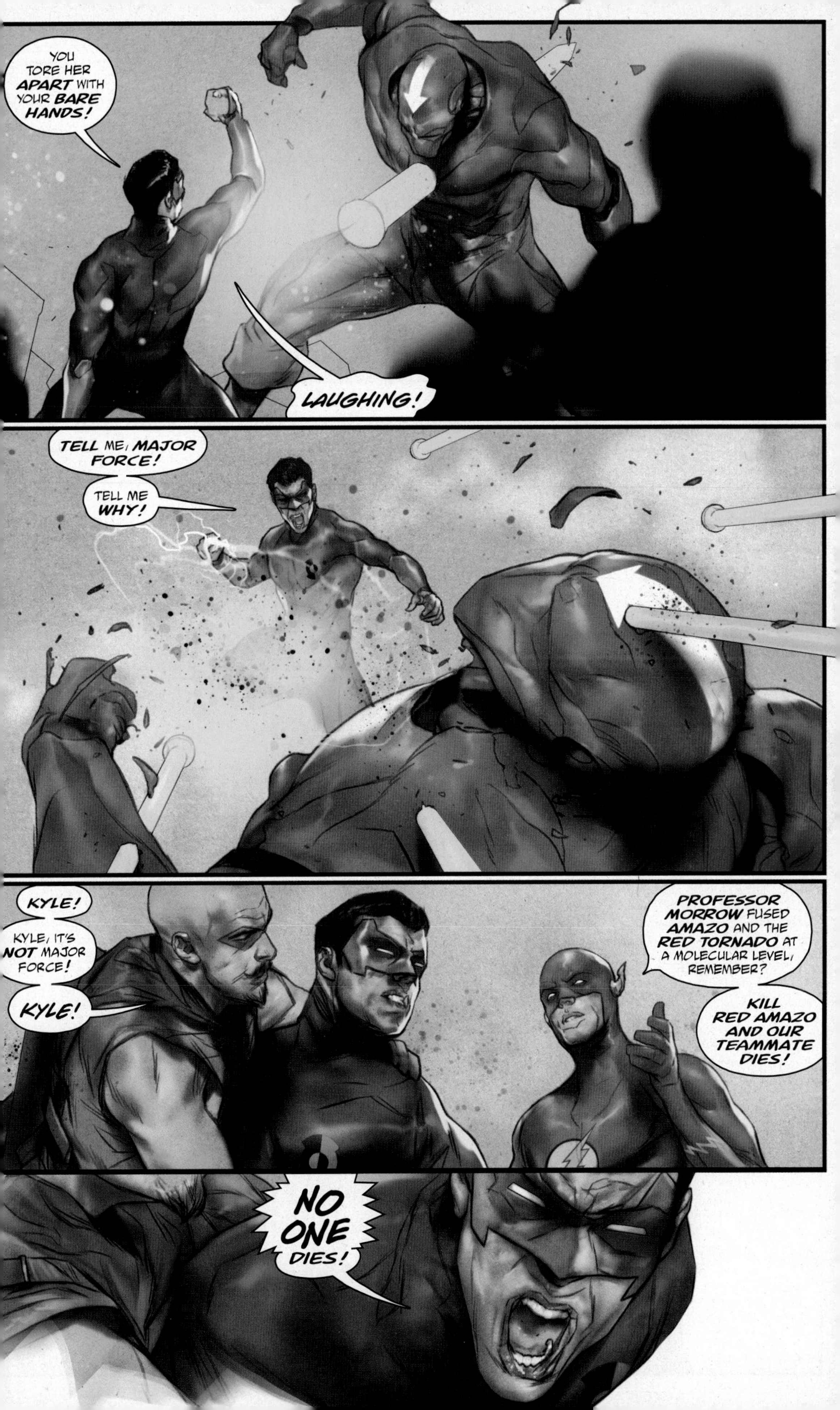

YOU TORE HER APART WITH YOUR BARE HANDS!
LAUGHING!
TELL ME, MAJOR FORCE!
TELL ME WHY!
KYLE!
KYLE, IT'S NOT MAJOR FORCE!
KYLE!
PROFESSOR MORROW FUSED AMAZO AND THE RED TORNADO AT A MOLECULAR LEVEL, REMEMBER?
KILL RED AMAZO AND OUR TEAMMATE DIES!
NO ONE DIES!

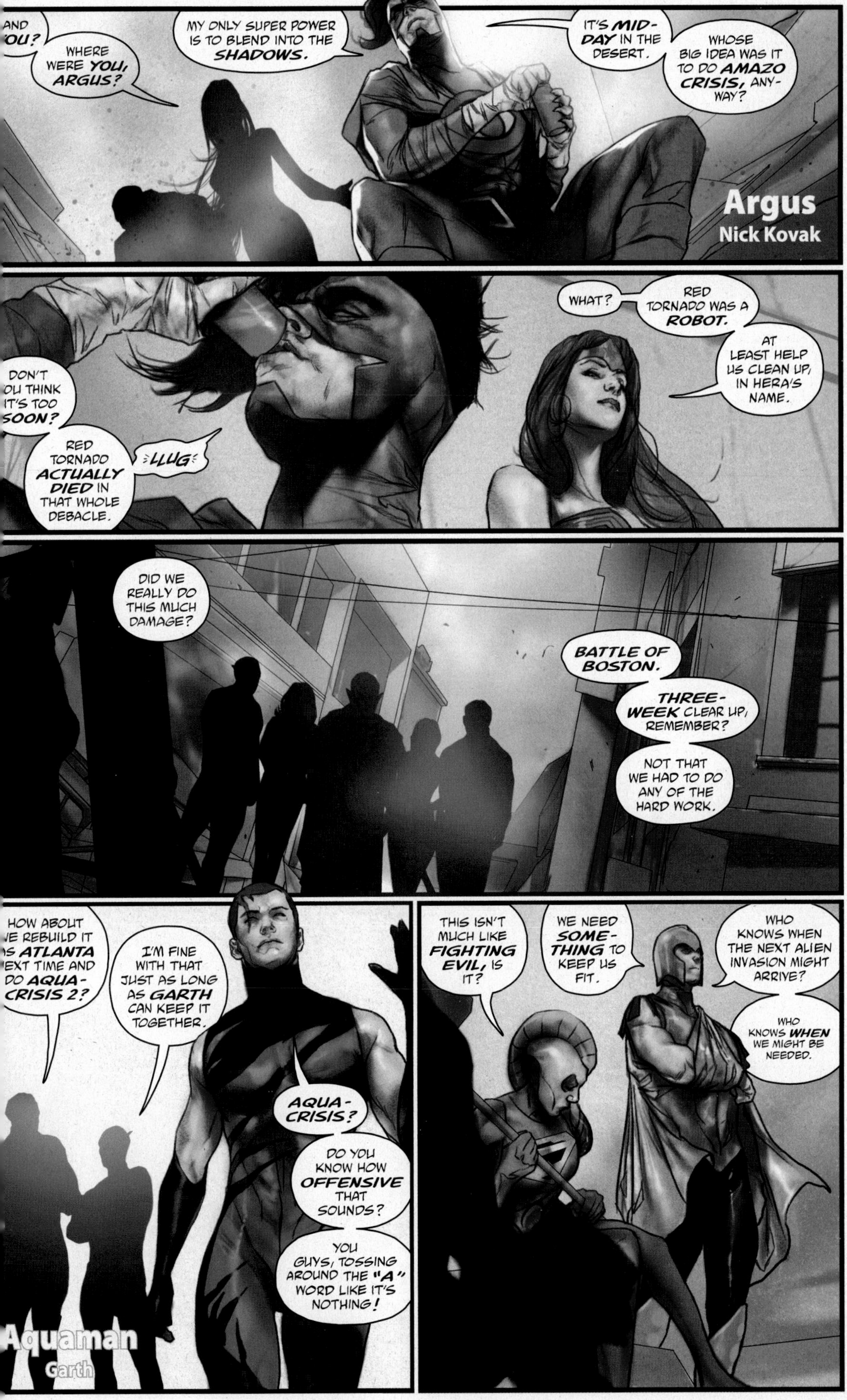
AND YOU?
WHERE WERE YOU, ARGUS?
MY ONLY SUPER POWER IS TO BLEND INTO THE SHADOWS.
IT'S MID-DAY IN THE DESERT.
WHOSE BIG IDEA WAS IT TO DO AMAZO CRISIS, ANY-WAY?
Argus
Nick Kovak
DON'T YOU THINK IT'S TOO SOON?
RED TORNADO ACTUALLY DIED IN THAT WHOLE DEBACLE.
LLUG
WHAT?
RED TORNADO WAS A ROBOT.
AT LEAST HELP US CLEAN UP, IN HERA'S NAME.
DID WE REALLY DO THIS MUCH DAMAGE?
BATTLE OF BOSTON.
THREE-WEEK CLEAR UP, REMEMBER?
NOT THAT WE HAD TO DO ANY OF THE HARD WORK.
HOW ABOUT WE REBUILD IT AS ATLANTA NEXT TIME AND DO AQUA-CRISIS 2?
I'M FINE WITH THAT JUST AS LONG AS GARTH CAN KEEP IT TOGETHER.
AQUA-CRISIS?
DO YOU KNOW HOW OFFENSIVE THAT SOUNDS?
YOU GUYS, TOSSING AROUND THE "A" WORD LIKE IT'S NOTHING!
Aquaman
Garth
THIS ISN'T MUCH LIKE FIGHTING EVIL, IS IT?
WE NEED SOME-THING TO KEEP US FIT.
WHO KNOWS WHEN THE NEXT ALIEN INVASION MIGHT ARRIVE?
WHO KNOWS WHEN WE MIGHT BE NEEDED.

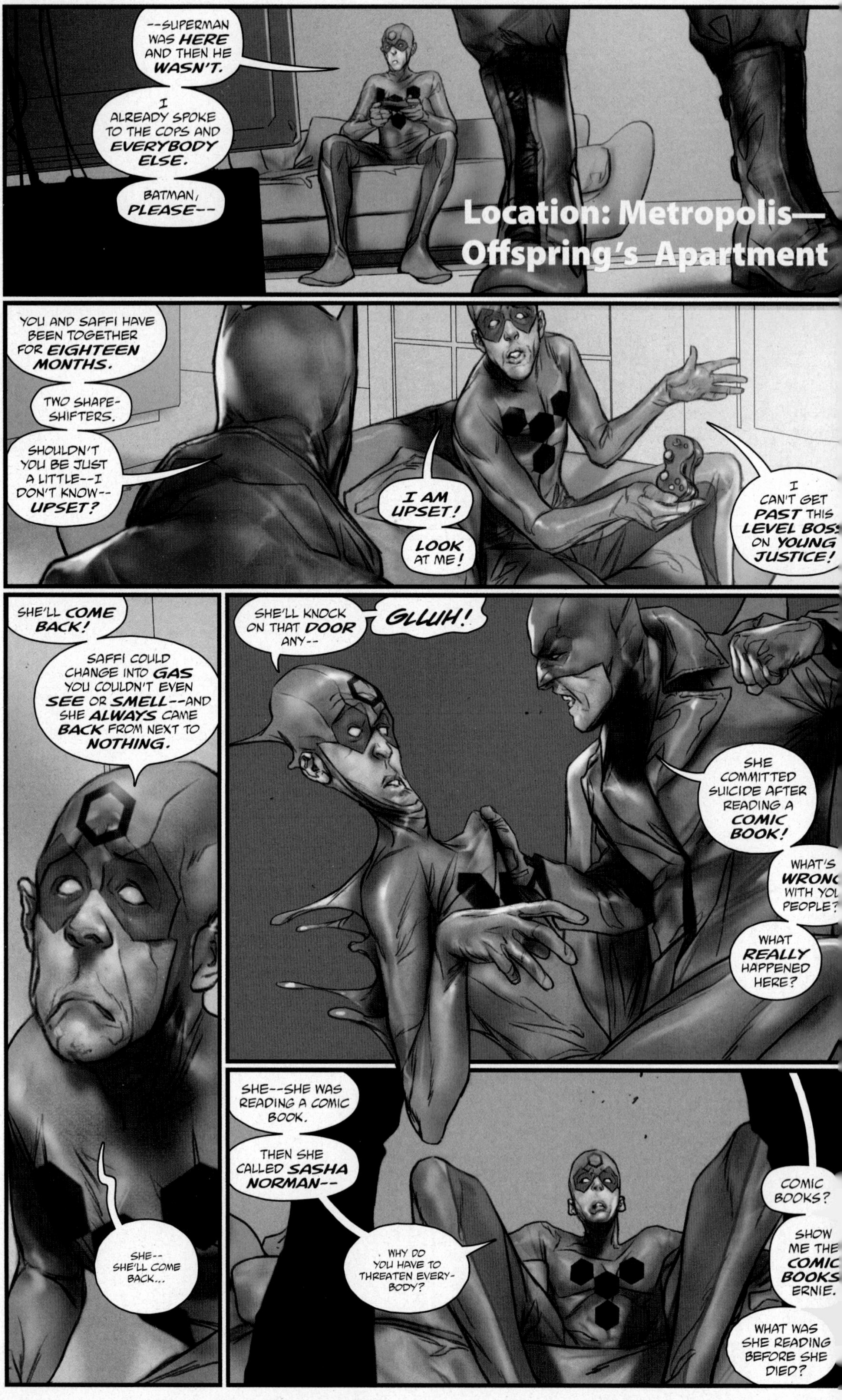
--SUPERMAN WAS HERE AND THEN HE WASN'T.
I ALREADY SPOKE TO THE COPS AND EVERYBODY ELSE.
BATMAN, PLEASE--
Location: Metropolis— Offspring's Apartment
YOU AND SAFFI HAVE BEEN TOGETHER FOR EIGHTEEN MONTHS.
TWO SHAPE-SHIFTERS.
SHOULDN'T YOU BE JUST A LITTLE--I DON'T KNOW--UPSET?
I AM UPSET!
LOOK AT ME!
I CAN'T GET PAST THIS LEVEL BOS ON YOUNG JUSTICE!
SHE'LL COME BACK!
SAFFI COULD CHANGE INTO GAS YOU COULDN'T EVEN SEE OR SMELL--AND SHE ALWAYS CAME BACK FROM NEXT TO NOTHING.
SHE'LL KNOCK ON THAT DOOR ANY--
GLUH!
SHE COMMITTED SUICIDE AFTER READING A COMIC BOOK!
WHAT'S WRON WITH YO PEOPLE?
WHAT REALLY HAPPENED HERE?
SHE--SHE'LL COME BACK...
SHE--SHE WAS READING A COMIC BOOK.
THEN SHE CALLED SASHA NORMAN--
WHY DO YOU HAVE TO THREATEN EVERY-BODY?
COMIC BOOKS?
SHOW ME THE COMIC BOOKS, ERNIE.
WHAT WAS SHE READING BEFORE SHE DIED?

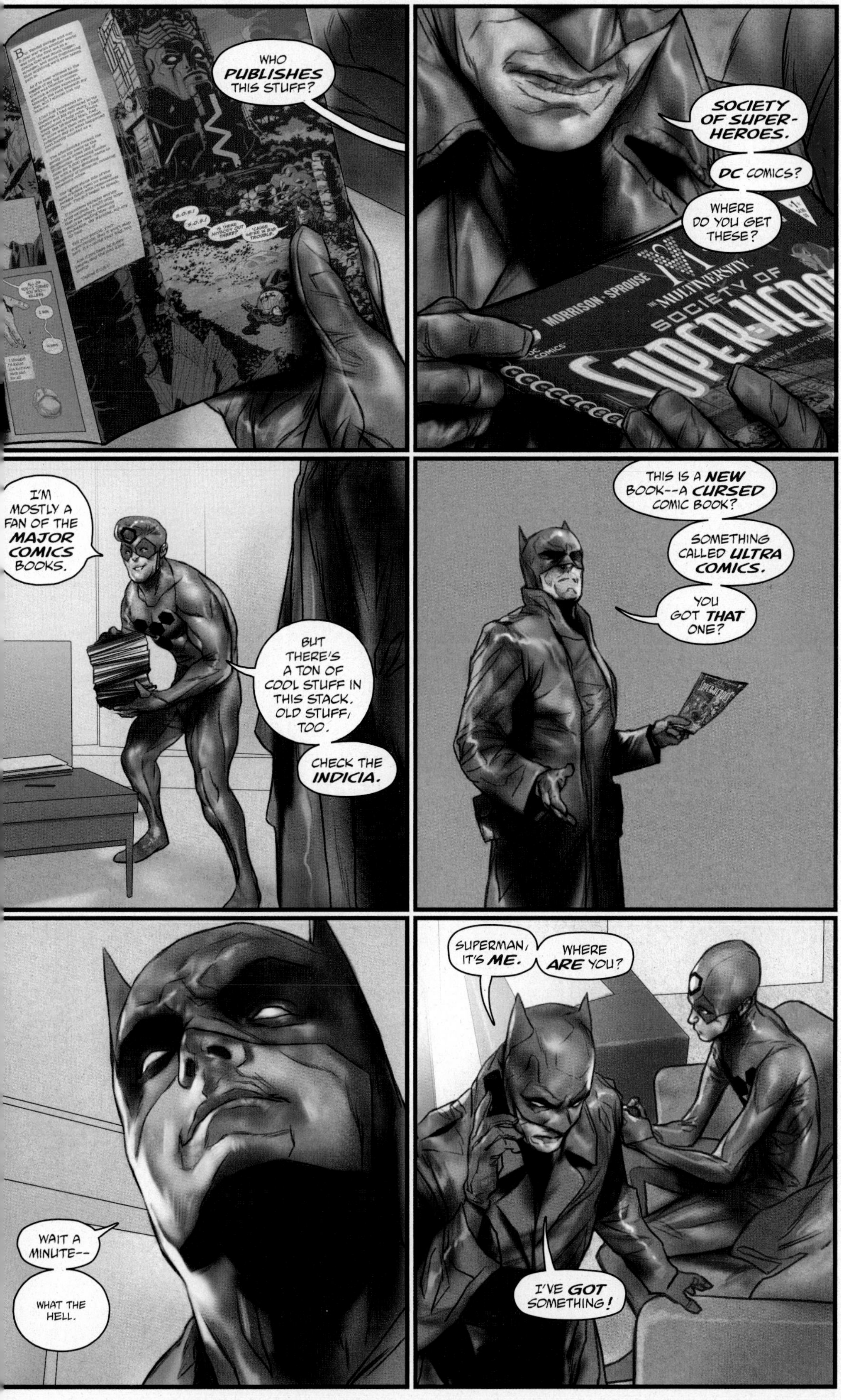
WHO PUBLISHES THIS STUFF?
SOCIETY OF SUPER-HEROES.
DC COMICS?
WHERE DO YOU GET THESE?
MORRISON · SPROUSE
THE MULTIVERSITY
SOCIETY OF SUPER-HERO
I'M MOSTLY A FAN OF THE MAJOR COMICS BOOKS.
BUT THERE'S A TON OF COOL STUFF IN THIS STACK. OLD STUFF, TOO.
CHECK THE INDICIA.
THIS IS A NEW BOOK--A CURSED COMIC BOOK?
SOMETHING CALLED ULTRA COMICS.
YOU GOT THAT ONE?
WAIT A MINUTE--
WHAT THE HELL.
SUPERMAN, IT'S ME.
WHERE ARE YOU?
I'VE GOT SOMETHING!

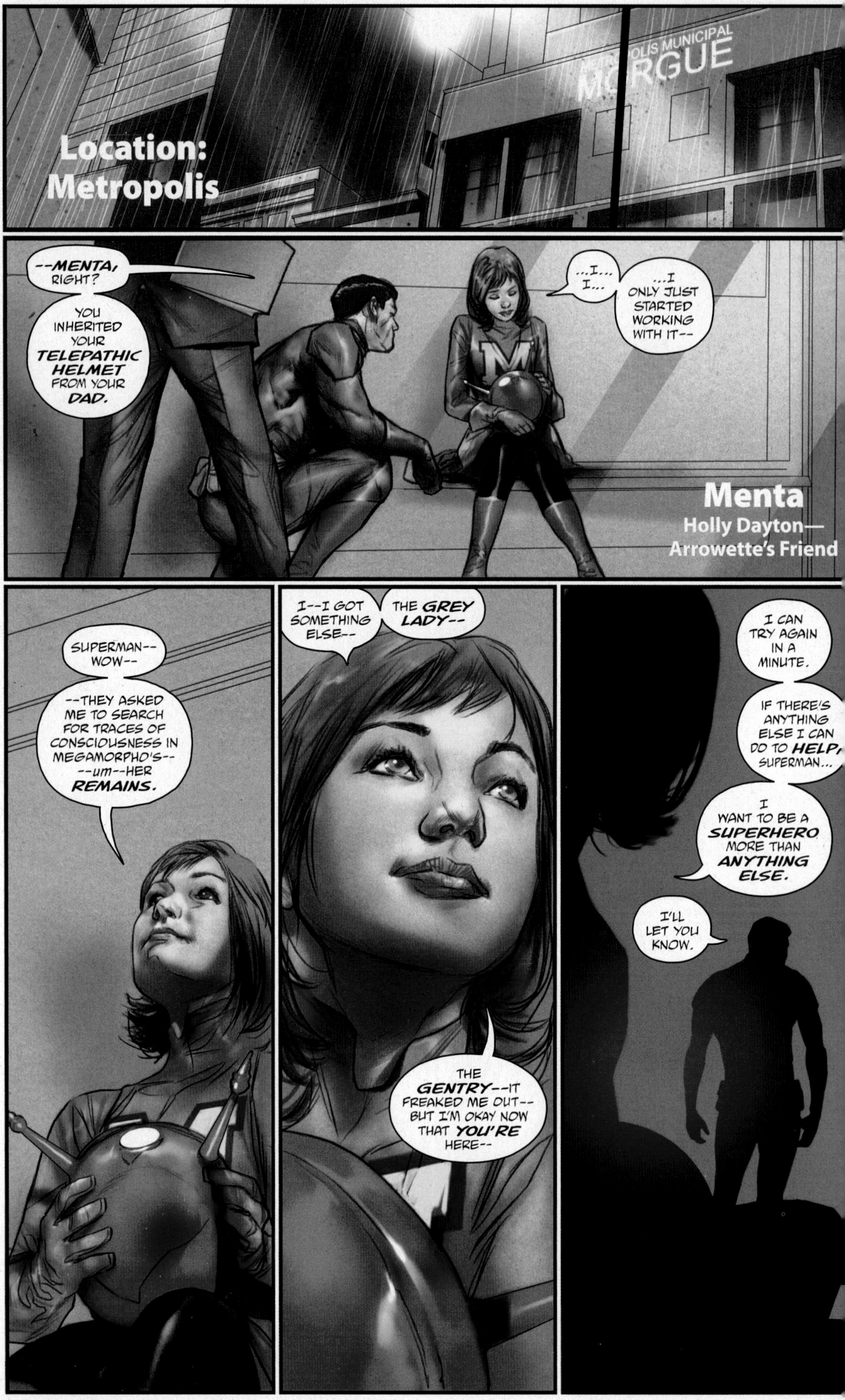
METROPOLIS MUNICIPAL MORGUE
Location: Metropolis
--MENTA, RIGHT?
YOU INHERITED YOUR TELEPATHIC HELMET FROM YOUR DAD.
...I... I...
...I ONLY JUST STARTED WORKING WITH IT--
Menta
Holly Dayton—Arrowette's Friend
SUPERMAN--WOW--
--THEY ASKED ME TO SEARCH FOR TRACES OF CONSCIOUSNESS IN MEGAMORPHO'S--
--um--HER REMAINS.
I--I GOT SOMETHING ELSE--
THE GREY LADY--
THE GENTRY--IT FREAKED ME OUT--BUT I'M OKAY NOW THAT YOU'RE HERE--
I CAN TRY AGAIN IN A MINUTE.
IF THERE'S ANYTHING ELSE I CAN DO TO HELP, SUPERMAN...
I WANT TO BE A SUPERHERO MORE THAN ANYTHING ELSE.
I'LL LET YOU KNOW.

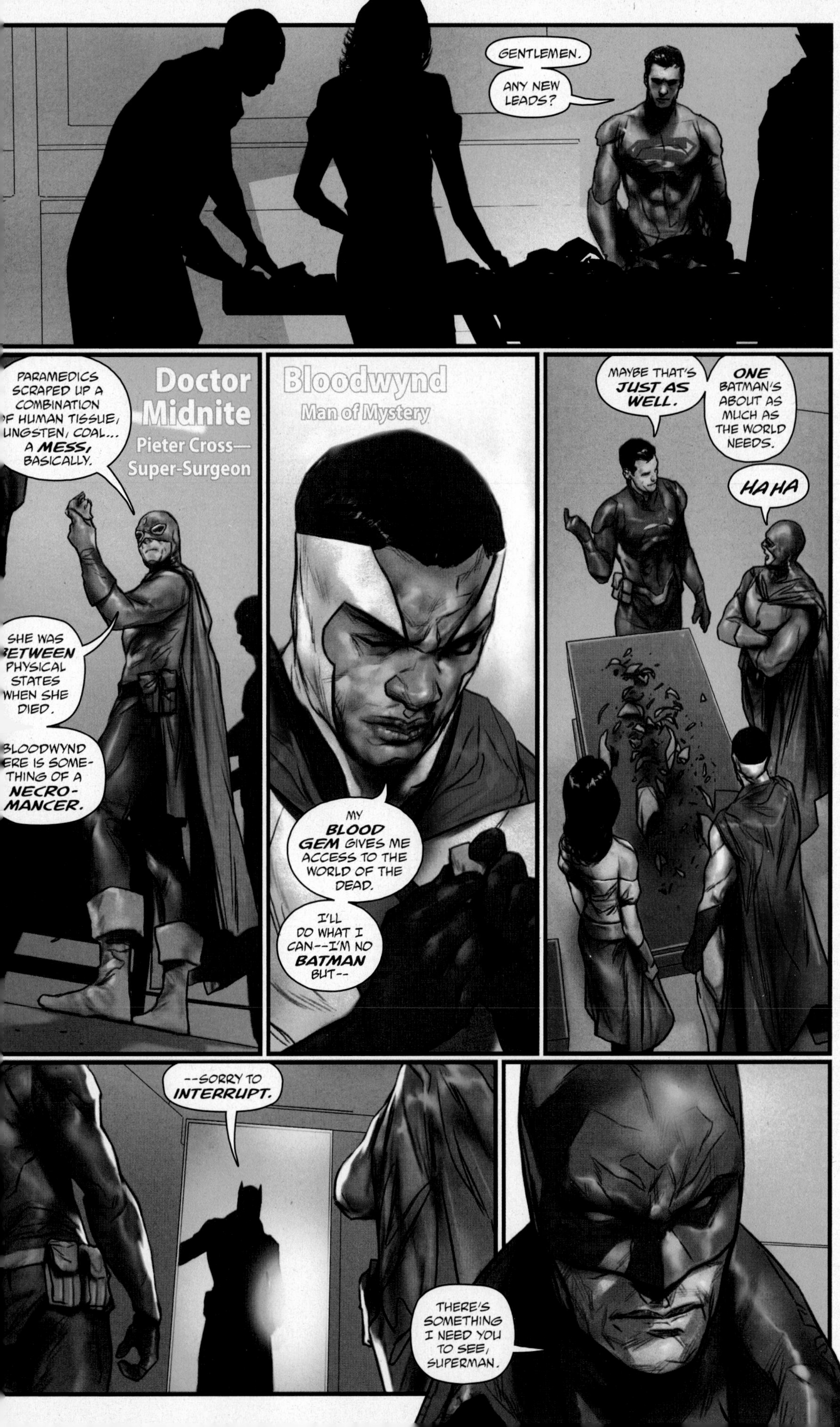
GENTLEMEN.
ANY NEW LEADS?
PARAMEDICS SCRAPED UP A COMBINATION OF HUMAN TISSUE, TUNGSTEN, COAL... A MESS, BASICALLY.
Doctor Midnite
Pieter Cross—Super-Surgeon
SHE WAS BETWEEN PHYSICAL STATES WHEN SHE DIED.
BLOODWYND HERE IS SOMETHING OF A NECROMANCER.
Bloodwynd
Man of Mystery
MY BLOOD GEM GIVES ME ACCESS TO THE WORLD OF THE DEAD.
I'LL DO WHAT I CAN--I'M NO BATMAN BUT--
MAYBE THAT'S JUST AS WELL.
ONE BATMAN'S ABOUT AS MUCH AS THE WORLD NEEDS.
HA HA
--SORRY TO INTERRUPT.
THERE'S SOMETHING I NEED YOU TO SEE, SUPERMAN.

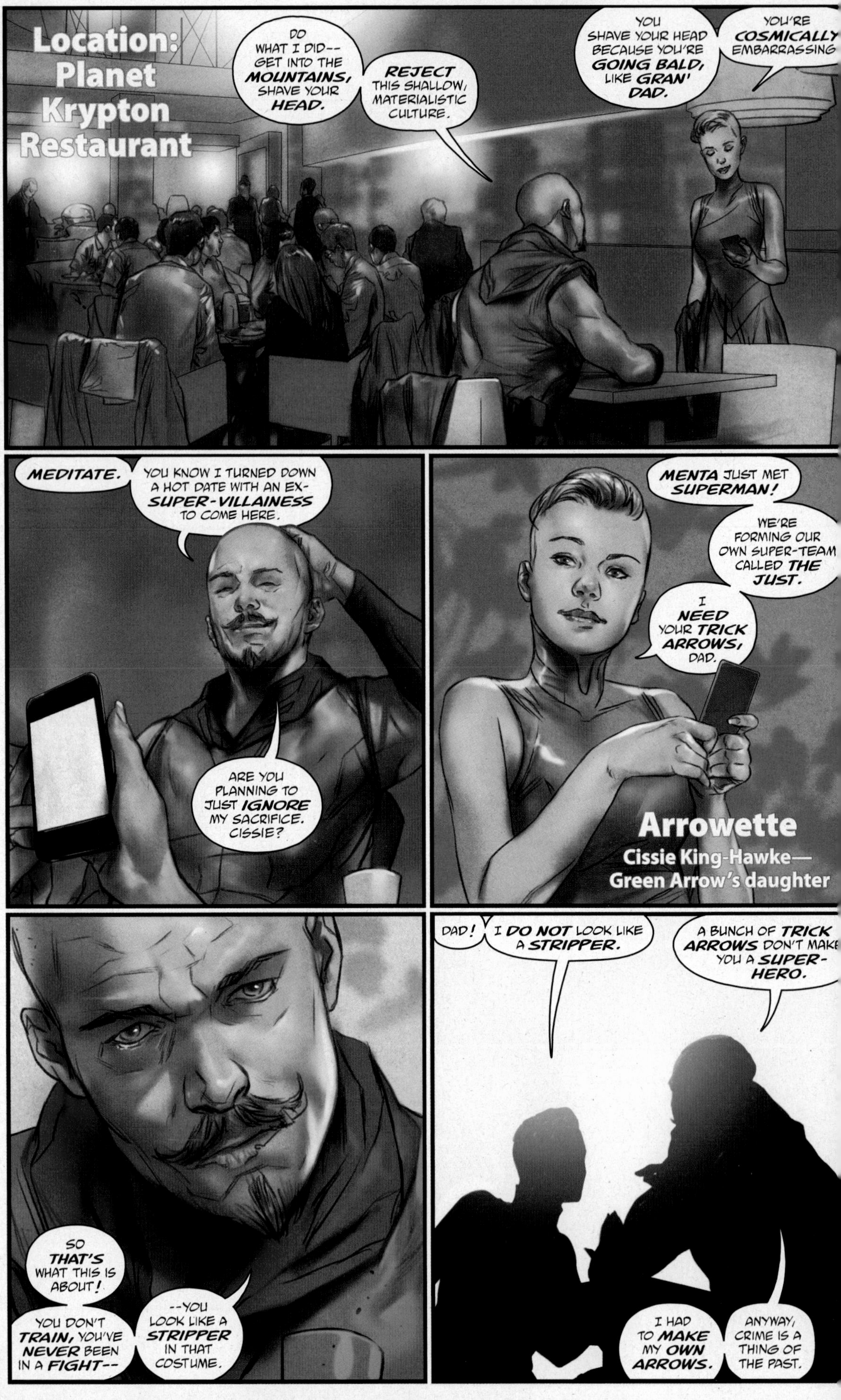
Location: Planet Krypton Restaurant
DO WHAT I DID-- GET INTO THE MOUNTAINS, SHAVE YOUR HEAD.
REJECT THIS SHALLOW, MATERIALISTIC CULTURE.
YOU SHAVE YOUR HEAD BECAUSE YOU'RE GOING BALD, LIKE GRAN' DAD.
YOU'RE COSMICALLY EMBARRASSING
MEDITATE.
YOU KNOW I TURNED DOWN A HOT DATE WITH AN EX-SUPER-VILLAINESS TO COME HERE.
ARE YOU PLANNING TO JUST IGNORE MY SACRIFICE. CISSIE?
MENTA JUST MET SUPERMAN!
WE'RE FORMING OUR OWN SUPER-TEAM CALLED THE JUST.
I NEED YOUR TRICK ARROWS, DAD.
Arrowette
Cissie King-Hawke— Green Arrow's daughter
SO THAT'S WHAT THIS IS ABOUT!
YOU DON'T TRAIN, YOU'VE NEVER BEEN IN A FIGHT--
--YOU LOOK LIKE A STRIPPER IN THAT COSTUME.
DAD!
I DO NOT LOOK LIKE A STRIPPER.
A BUNCH OF TRICK ARROWS DON'T MAKE YOU A SUPER-HERO.
I HAD TO MAKE MY OWN ARROWS.
ANYWAY, CRIME IS A THING OF THE PAST.

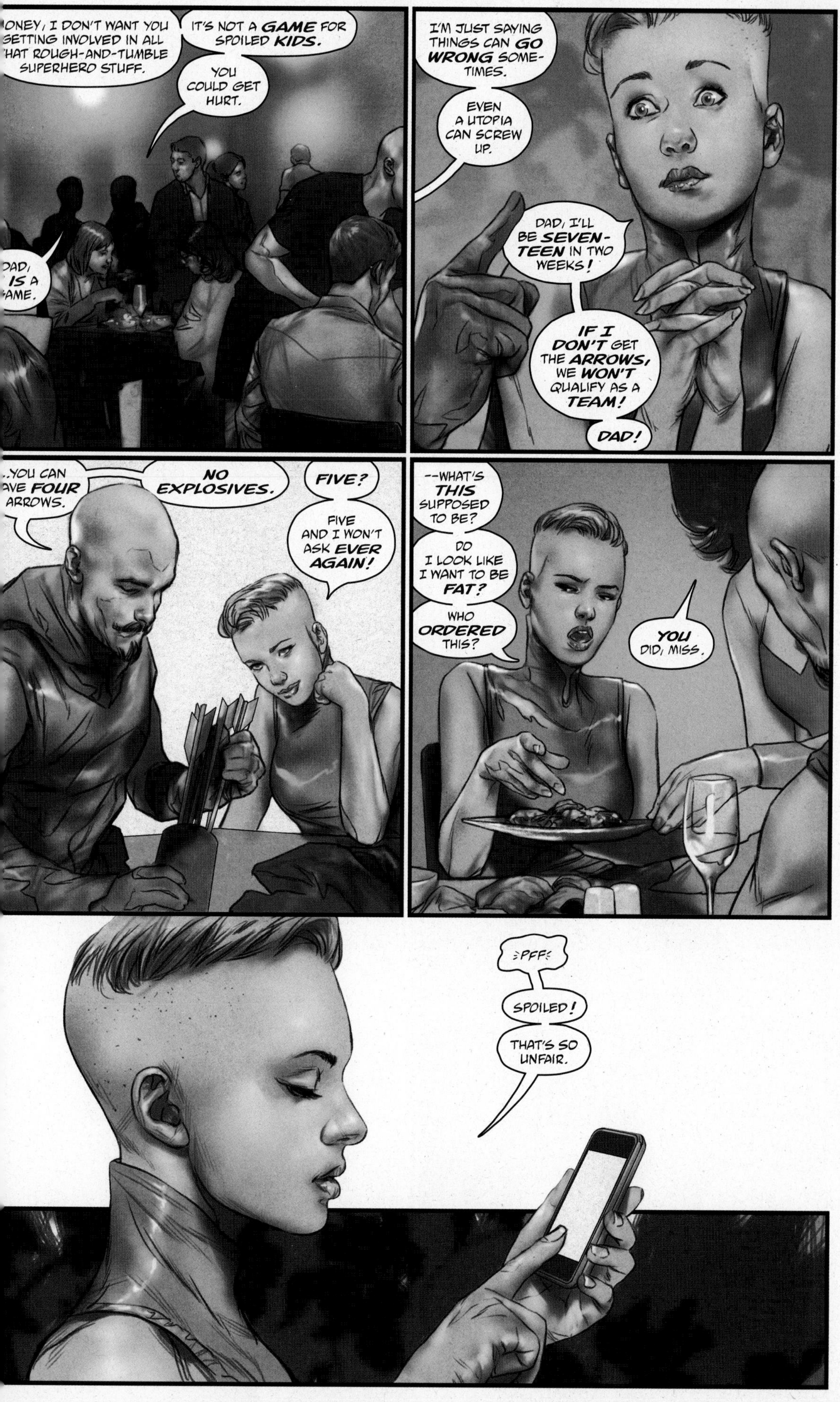
ONEY, I DON'T WANT YOU GETTING INVOLVED IN ALL THAT ROUGH-AND-TUMBLE SUPERHERO STUFF.
IT'S NOT A GAME FOR SPOILED KIDS.
YOU COULD GET HURT.
DAD, IS A AME.
I'M JUST SAYING THINGS CAN GO WRONG SOME-TIMES.
EVEN A UTOPIA CAN SCREW UP.
DAD, I'LL BE SEVEN-TEEN IN TWO WEEKS!
IF I DON'T GET THE ARROWS, WE WON'T QUALIFY AS A TEAM!
DAD!
..YOU CAN AVE FOUR ARROWS.
NO EXPLOSIVES.
FIVE?
FIVE AND I WON'T ASK EVER AGAIN!
--WHAT'S THIS SUPPOSED TO BE?
DO I LOOK LIKE I WANT TO BE FAT?
WHO ORDERED THIS?
YOU DID, MISS.
PFF
SPOILED!
THAT'S SO UNFAIR.

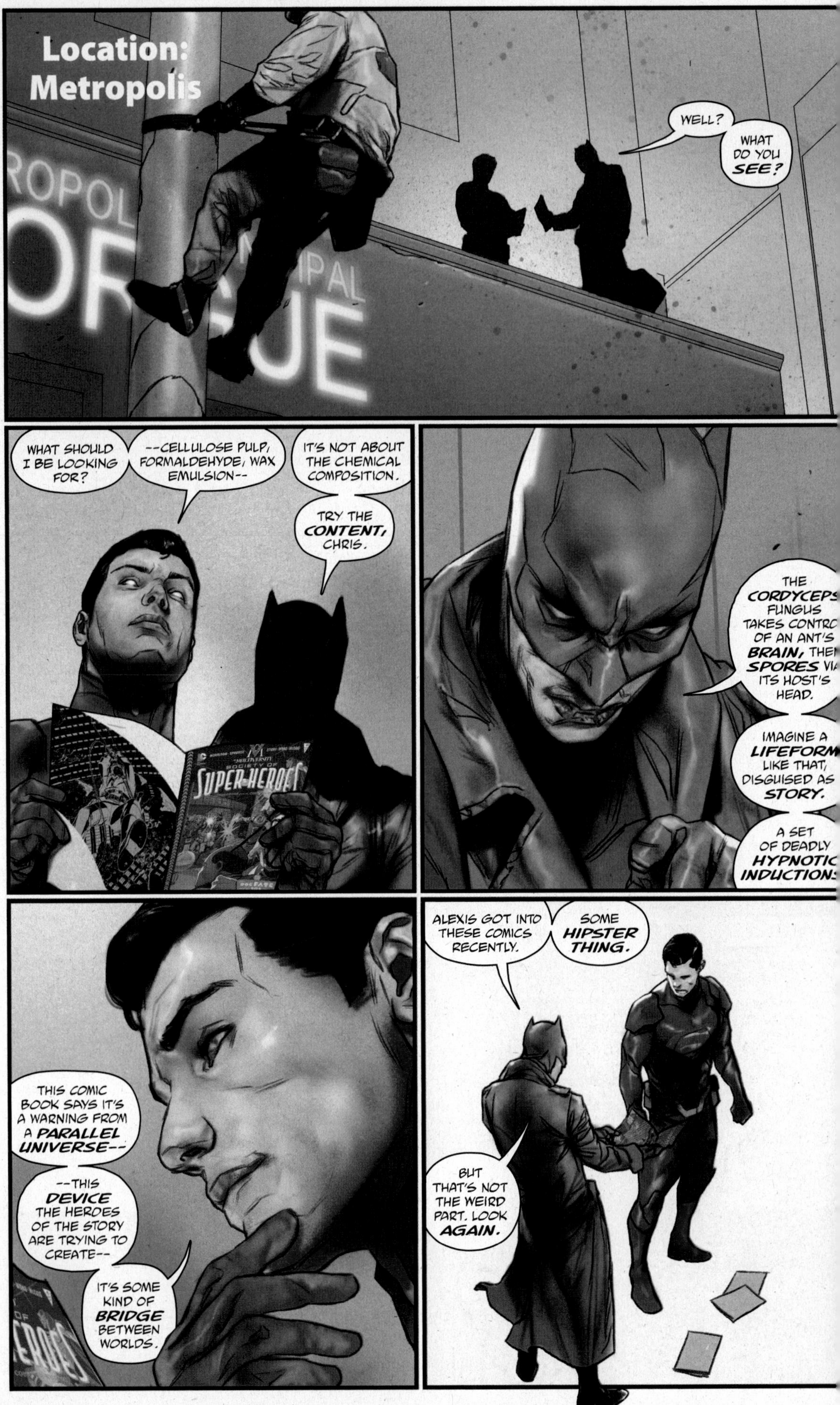
Location: Metropolis
WELL? WHAT DO YOU SEE?
WHAT SHOULD I BE LOOKING FOR?
--CELLULOSE PULP, FORMALDEHYDE, WAX EMULSION--
IT'S NOT ABOUT THE CHEMICAL COMPOSITION.
TRY THE CONTENT, CHRIS.
SUPER-HEROES
THE CORDYCEPS FUNGUS TAKES CONTRO OF AN ANT'S BRAIN, THEN SPORES VIA ITS HOST'S HEAD.
IMAGINE A LIFEFORM LIKE THAT, DISGUISED AS STORY.
A SET OF DEADLY HYPNOTIC INDUCTIONS
THIS COMIC BOOK SAYS IT'S A WARNING FROM A PARALLEL UNIVERSE--
--THIS DEVICE THE HEROES OF THE STORY ARE TRYING TO CREATE--
IT'S SOME KIND OF BRIDGE BETWEEN WORLDS.
ALEXIS GOT INTO THESE COMICS RECENTLY.
SOME HIPSTER THING.
BUT THAT'S NOT THE WEIRD PART. LOOK AGAIN.

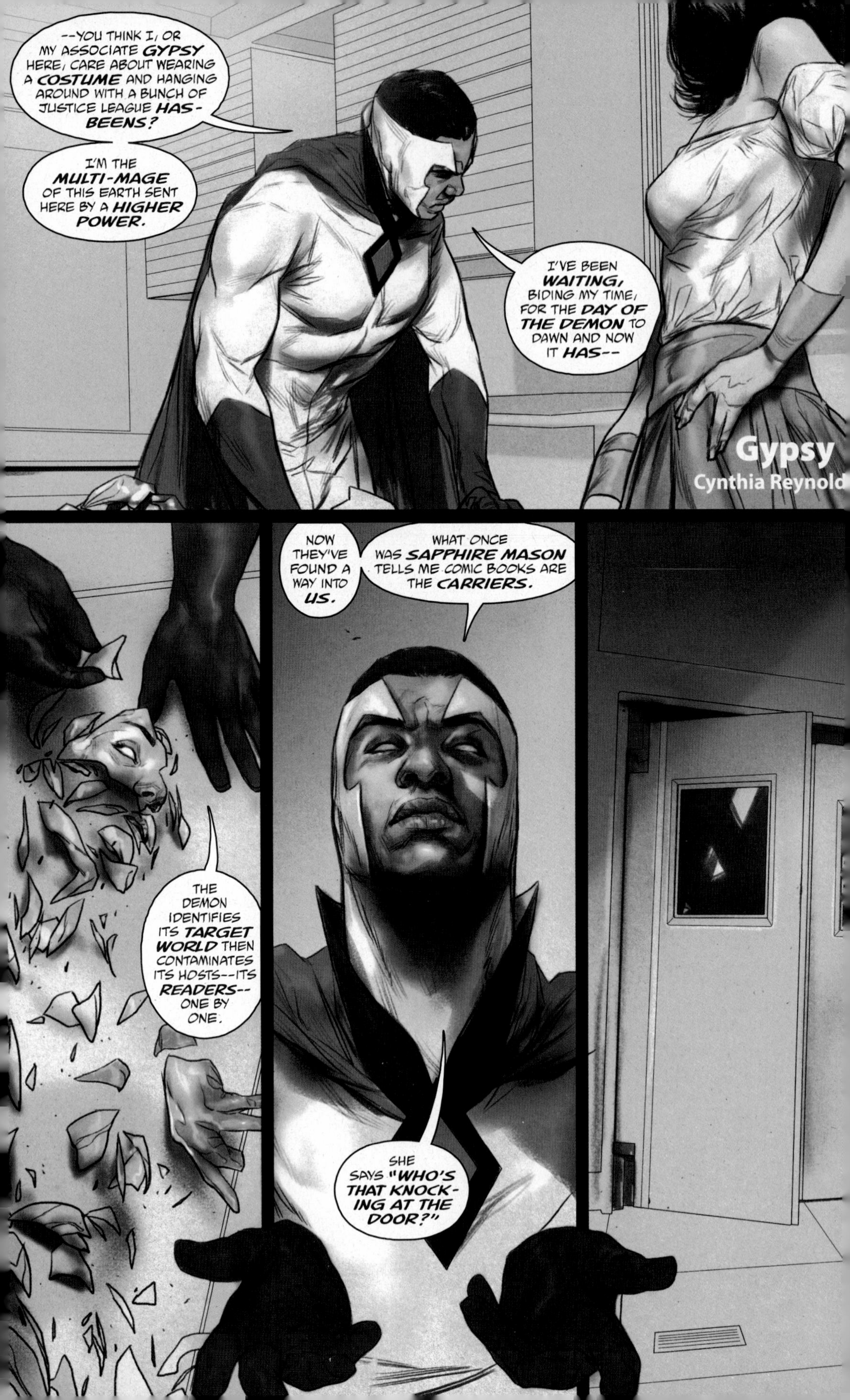
--YOU THINK I, OR MY ASSOCIATE GYPSY HERE, CARE ABOUT WEARING A COSTUME AND HANGING AROUND WITH A BUNCH OF JUSTICE LEAGUE HAS-BEENS?
I'M THE MULTI-MAGE OF THIS EARTH SENT HERE BY A HIGHER POWER.
I'VE BEEN WAITING, BIDING MY TIME, FOR THE DAY OF THE DEMON TO DAWN AND NOW IT HAS--
Gypsy
Cynthia Reynold
THE DEMON IDENTIFIES ITS TARGET WORLD THEN CONTAMINATES ITS HOSTS--ITS READERS--ONE BY ONE.
NOW THEY'VE FOUND A WAY INTO US.
WHAT ONCE WAS SAPPHIRE MASON TELLS ME COMIC BOOKS ARE THE CARRIERS.
SHE SAYS "WHO'S THAT KNOCKING AT THE DOOR?"

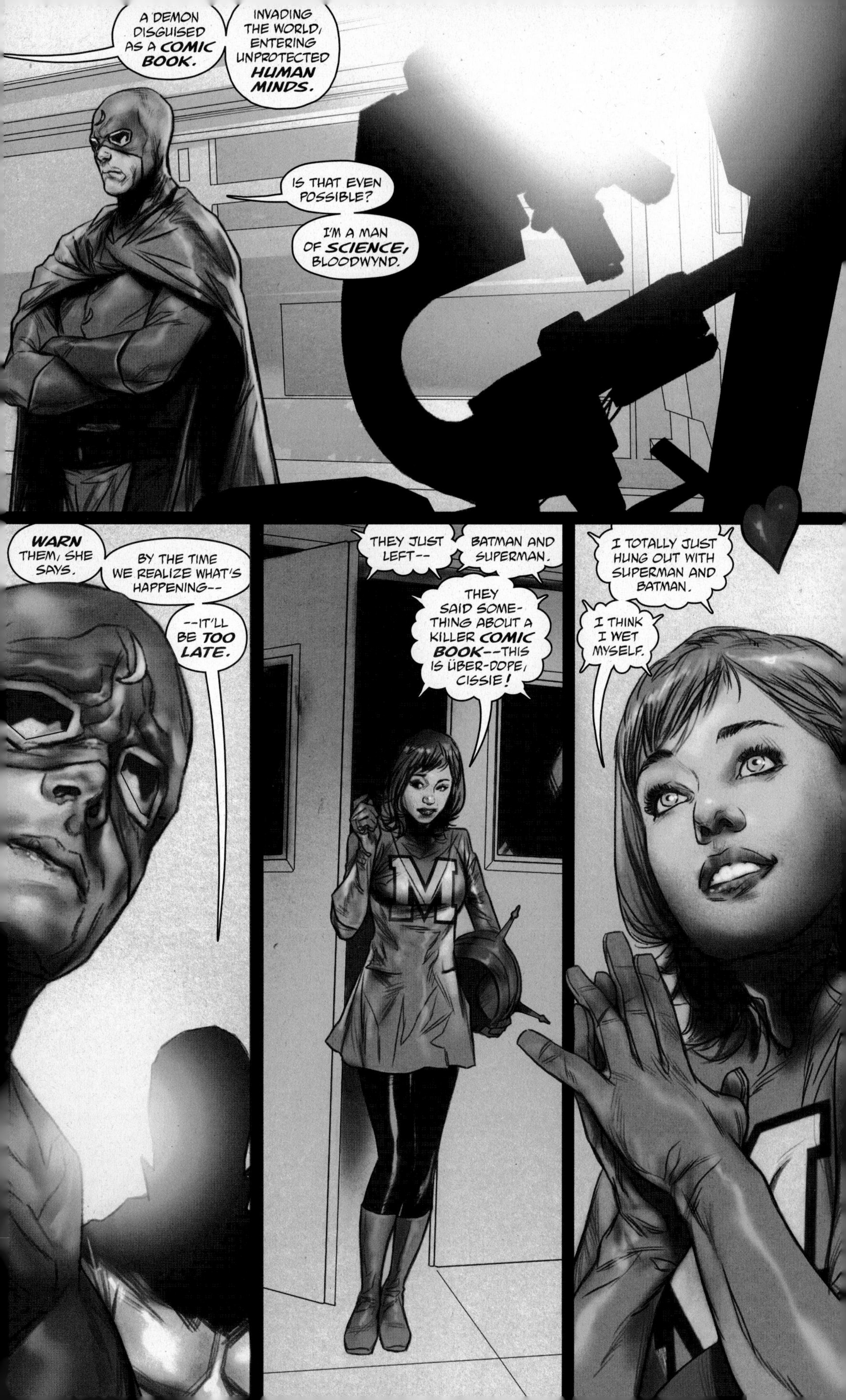

A DEMON DISGUISED AS A COMIC BOOK.
INVADING THE WORLD, ENTERING UNPROTECTED HUMAN MINDS.
IS THAT EVEN POSSIBLE?
I'M A MAN OF SCIENCE, BLOODWYND.
WARN THEM, SHE SAYS.
BY THE TIME WE REALIZE WHAT'S HAPPENING--
--IT'LL BE TOO LATE.
THEY JUST LEFT--
BATMAN AND SUPERMAN.
THEY SAID SOME-THING ABOUT A KILLER COMIC BOOK--THIS IS ÜBER-DOPE, CISSIE!
I TOTALLY JUST HUNG OUT WITH SUPERMAN AND BATMAN.
I THINK I WET MYSELF.

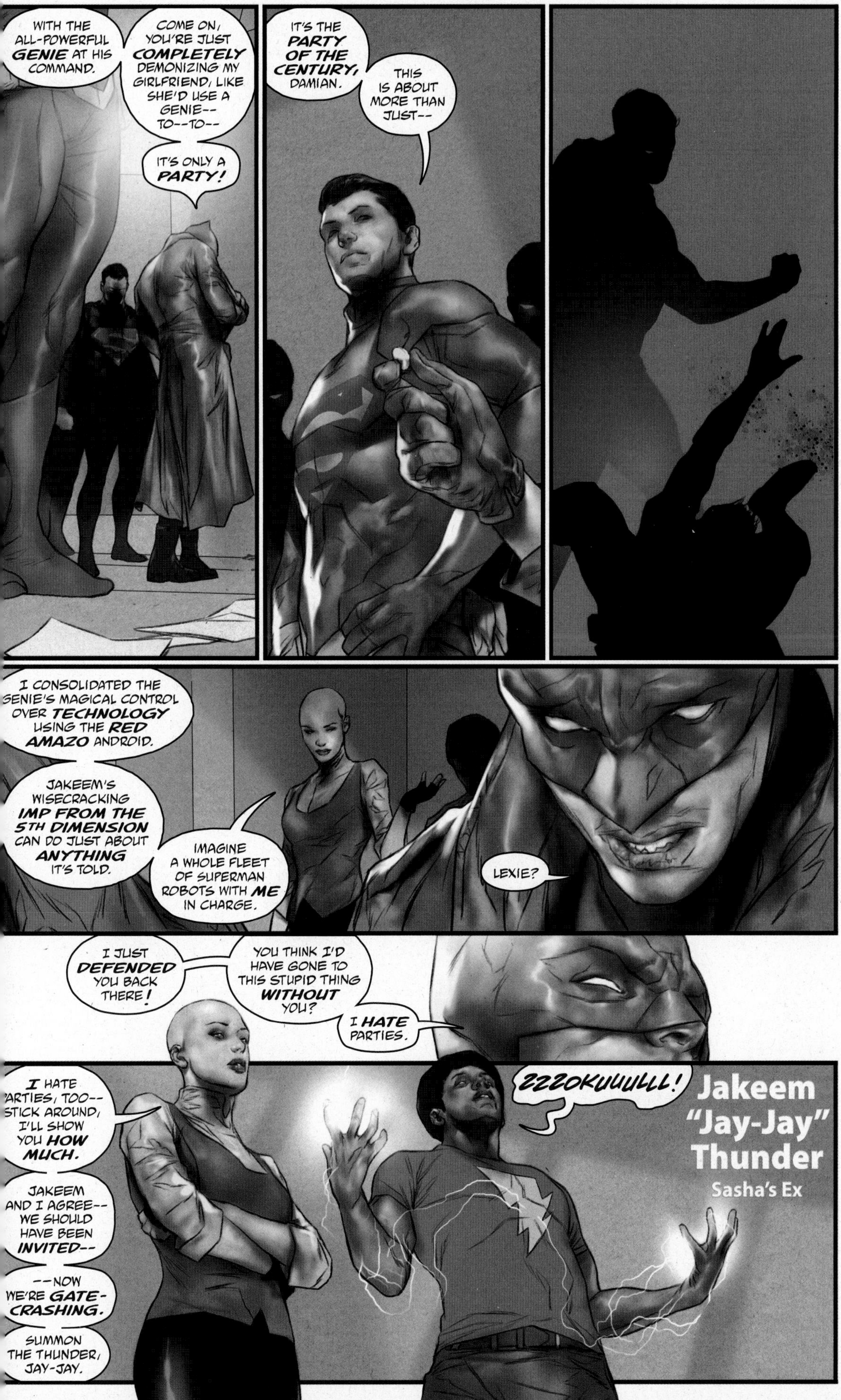

WITH THE ALL-POWERFUL GENIE AT HIS COMMAND.
COME ON, YOU'RE JUST COMPLETELY DEMONIZING MY GIRLFRIEND, LIKE SHE'D USE A GENIE-- TO--TO--
IT'S ONLY A PARTY!
IT'S THE PARTY OF THE CENTURY, DAMIAN.
THIS IS ABOUT MORE THAN JUST--
I CONSOLIDATED THE GENIE'S MAGICAL CONTROL OVER TECHNOLOGY USING THE RED AMAZO ANDROID.
JAKEEM'S WISECRACKING IMP FROM THE 5TH DIMENSION CAN DO JUST ABOUT ANYTHING IT'S TOLD.
IMAGINE A WHOLE FLEET OF SUPERMAN ROBOTS WITH ME IN CHARGE.
LEXIE?
I JUST DEFENDED YOU BACK THERE!
YOU THINK I'D HAVE GONE TO THIS STUPID THING WITHOUT YOU?
I HATE PARTIES.
I HATE PARTIES, TOO-- STICK AROUND, I'LL SHOW YOU HOW MUCH.
JAKEEM AND I AGREE-- WE SHOULD HAVE BEEN INVITED--
--NOW WE'RE GATE-CRASHING.
SUMMON THE THUNDER, JAY-JAY.
ZZZOKUUULLL!
Jakeem "Jay-Jay" Thunder
Sasha's Ex

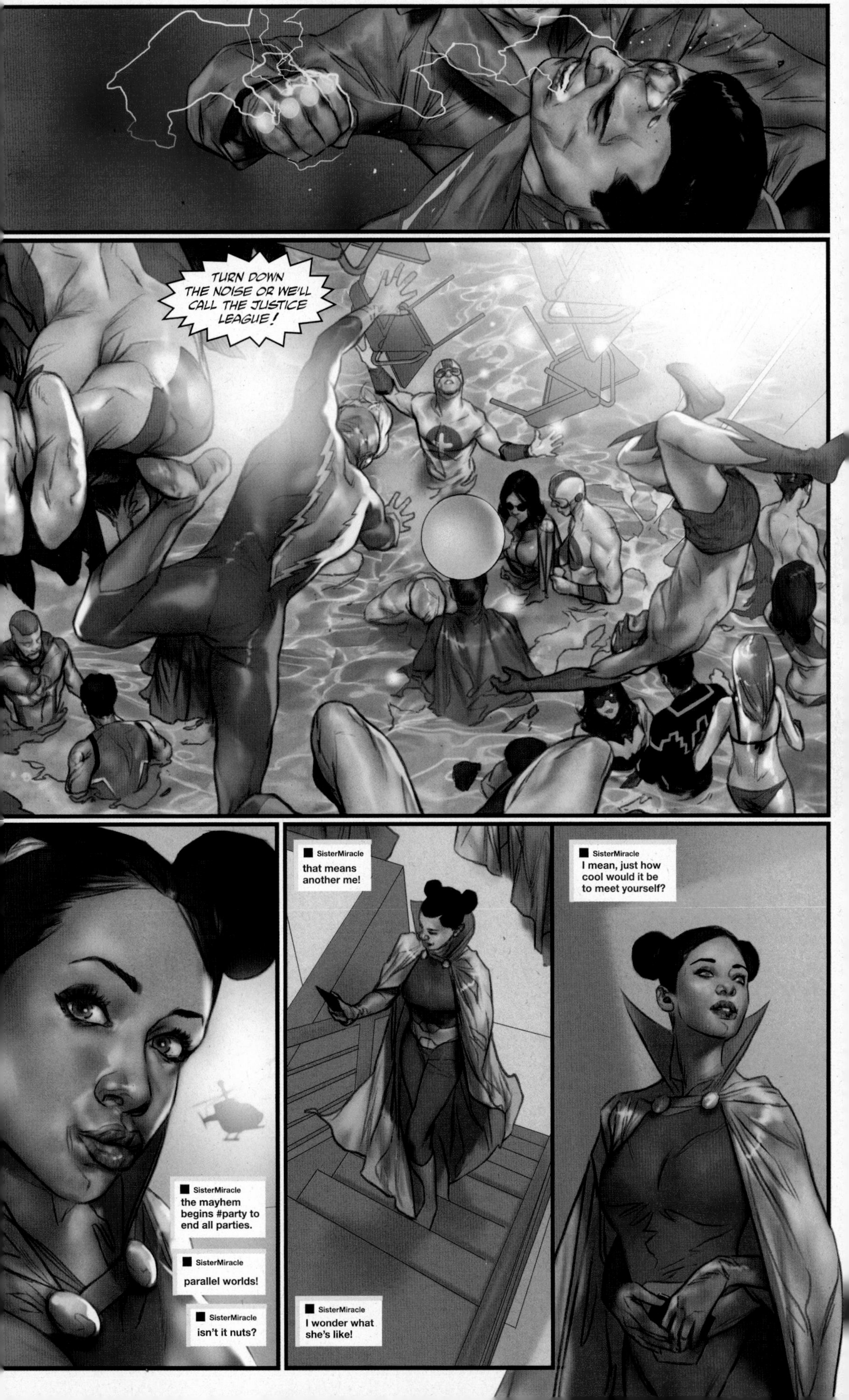
TURN DOWN THE NOISE OR WE'LL CALL THE JUSTICE LEAGUE!
SisterMiracle
the mayhem begins #party to end all parties.
SisterMiracle
parallel worlds!
SisterMiracle
isn't it nuts?
SisterMiracle
that means another me!
SisterMiracle
I wonder what she's like!
SisterMiracle
I mean, just how cool would it be to meet yourself?

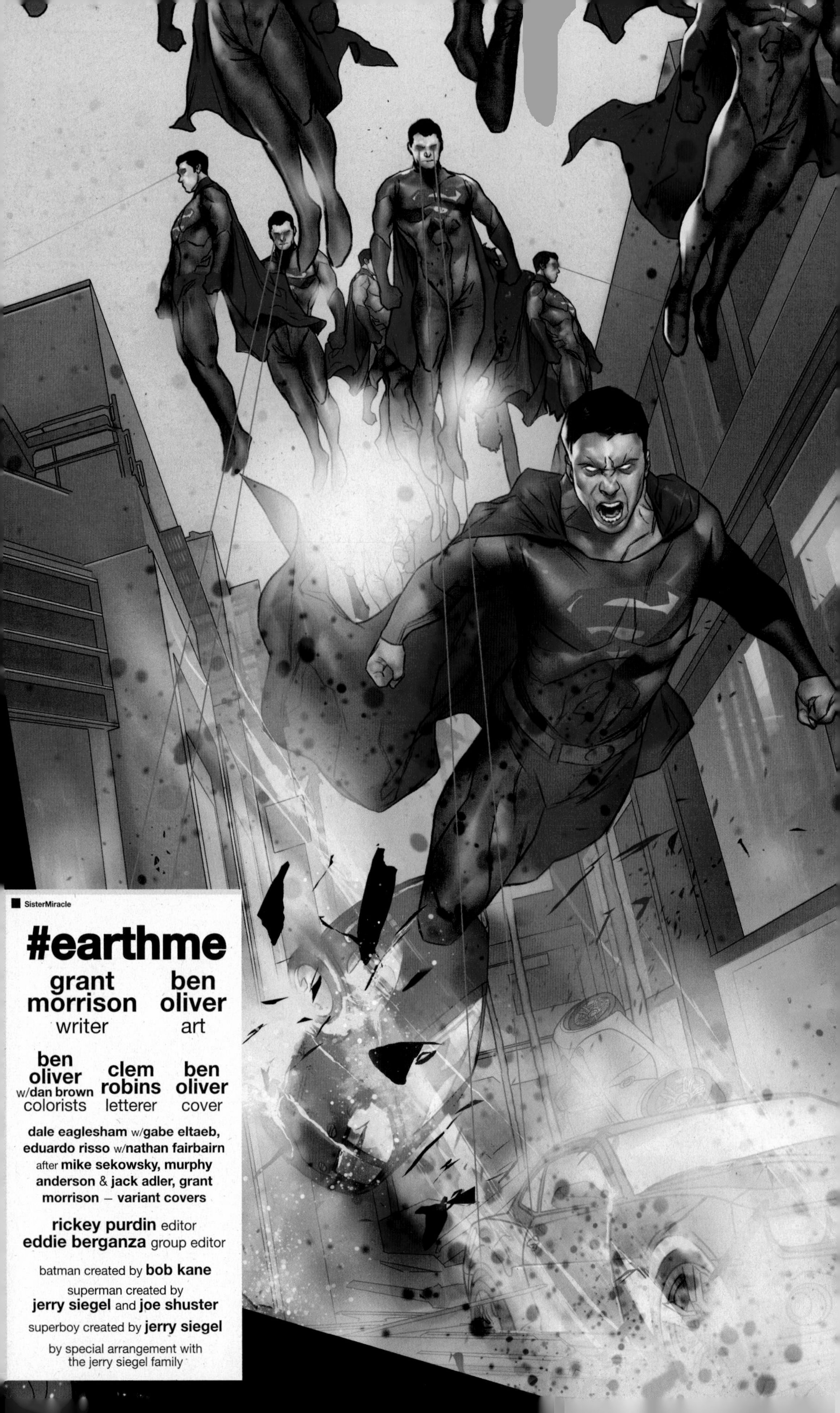
SisterMiracle
#earthme
grant morrison writer
ben oliver art
ben oliver w/dan brown colorists
clem robins letterer
ben oliver cover
dale eaglesham w/gabe eltaeb, eduardo risso w/nathan fairbairn after mike sekowsky, murphy anderson & jack adler, grant morrison – variant covers
rickey purdin editor
eddie berganza group editor
batman created by bob kane
superman created by jerry siegel and joe shuster
superboy created by jerry siegel
by special arrangement with the jerry siegel family

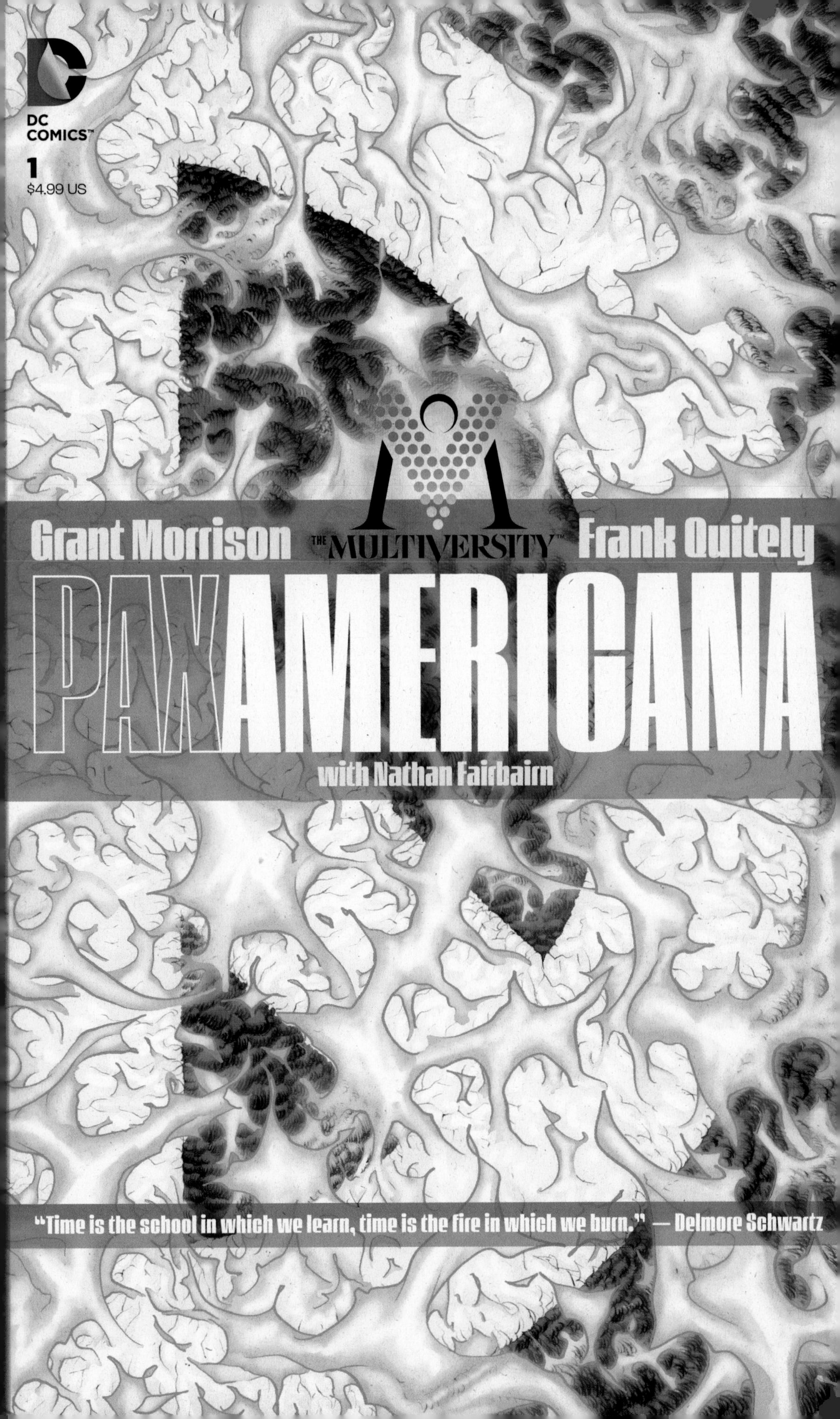
DC
COMICS™
1
$4.99 US
Grant Morrison
THE MULTIVERSITY™
Frank Quitely
PAX AMERICANA
with Nathan Fairbairn
"Time is the school in which we learn, time is the fire in which we burn." — Delmore Schwartz

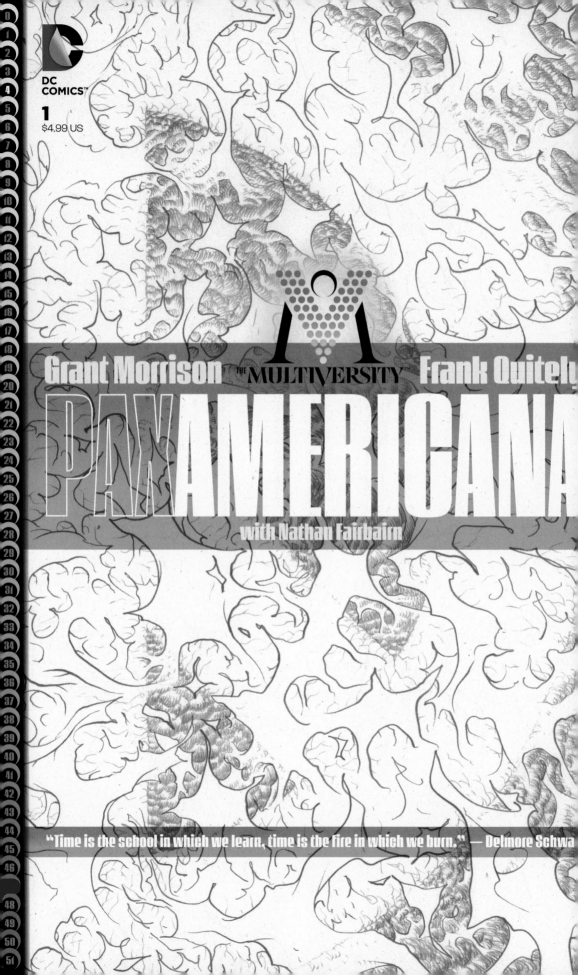

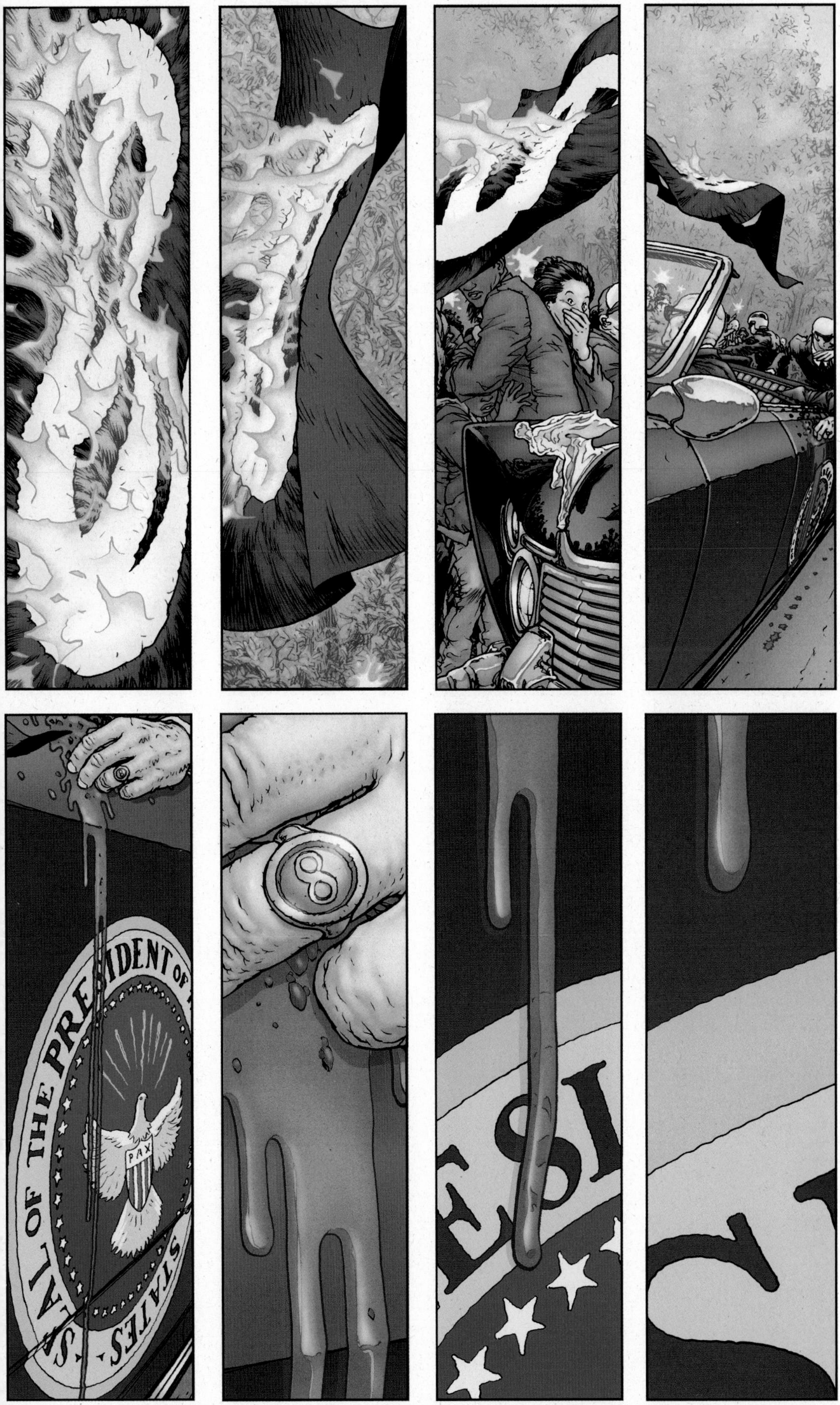
OF THE PRESIDENT OF
PAX
STATES

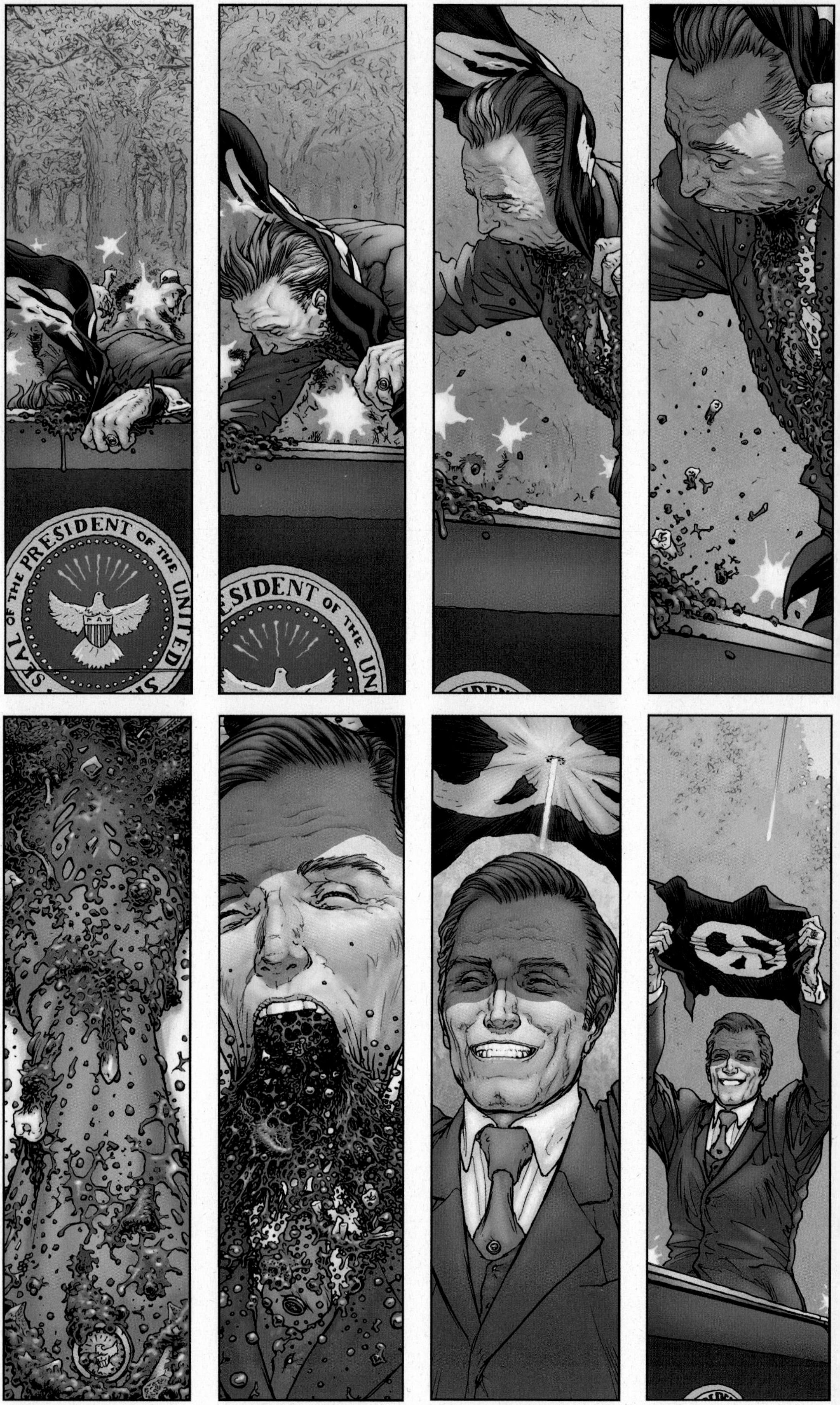
SEAL OF THE PRESIDENT OF THE UNITED
ESIDENT OF THE UN

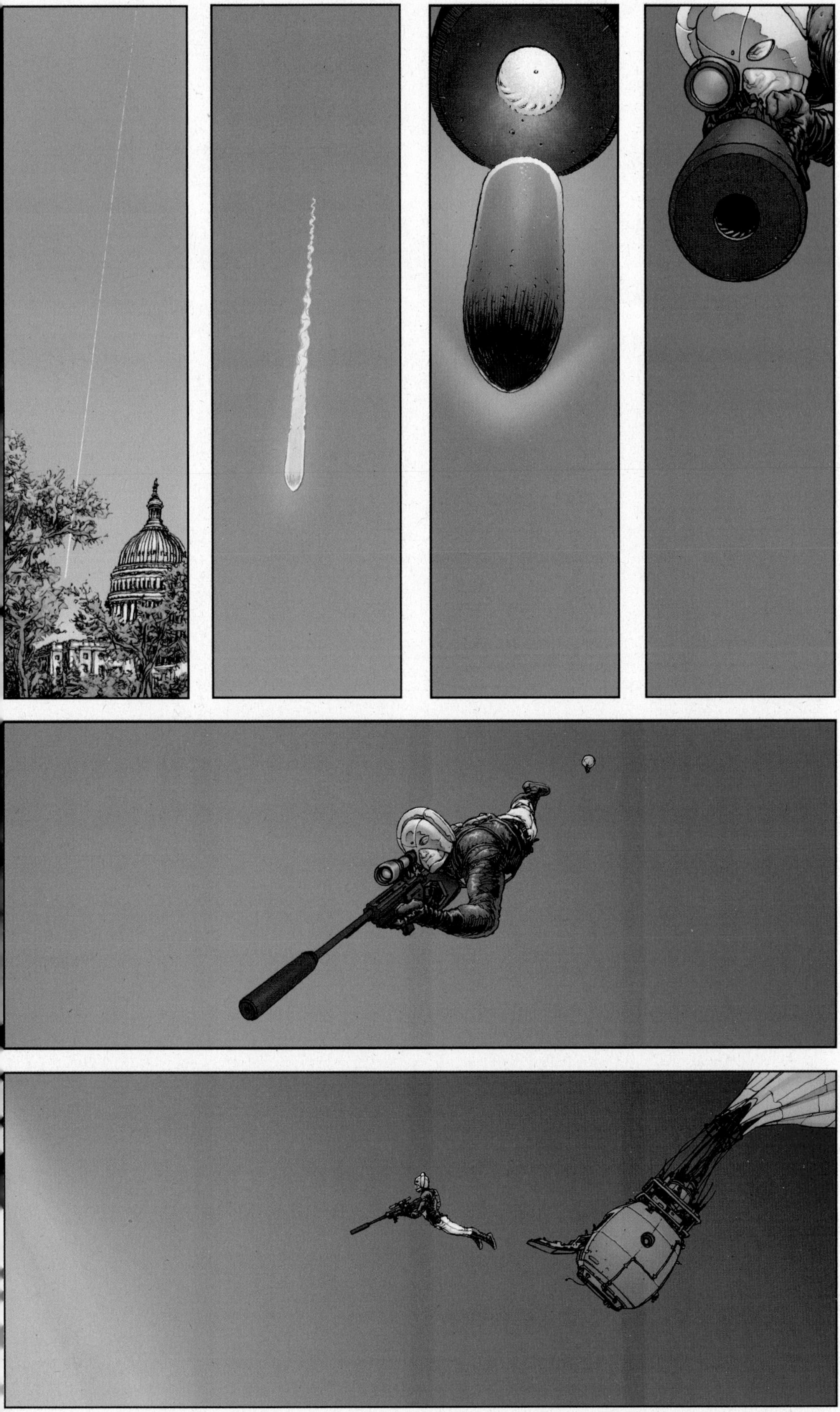

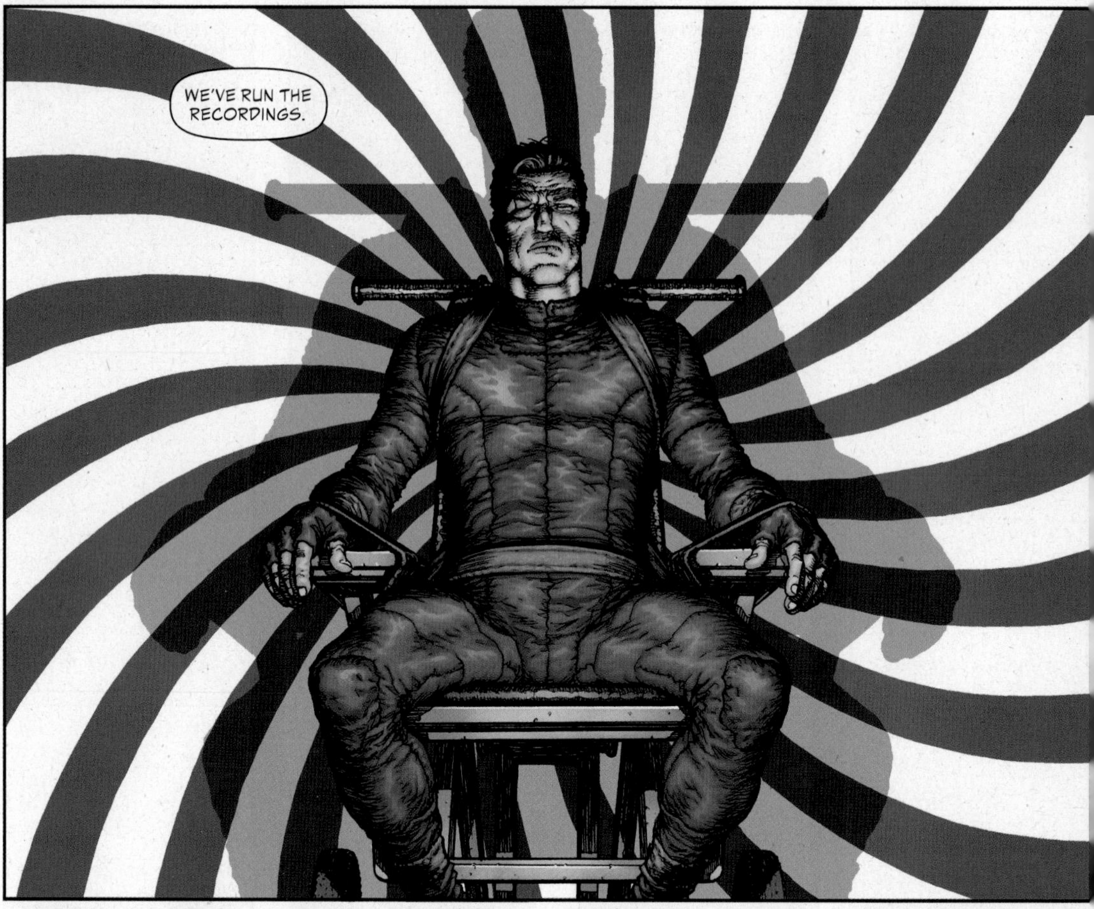
WE'VE RUN THE RECORDINGS.

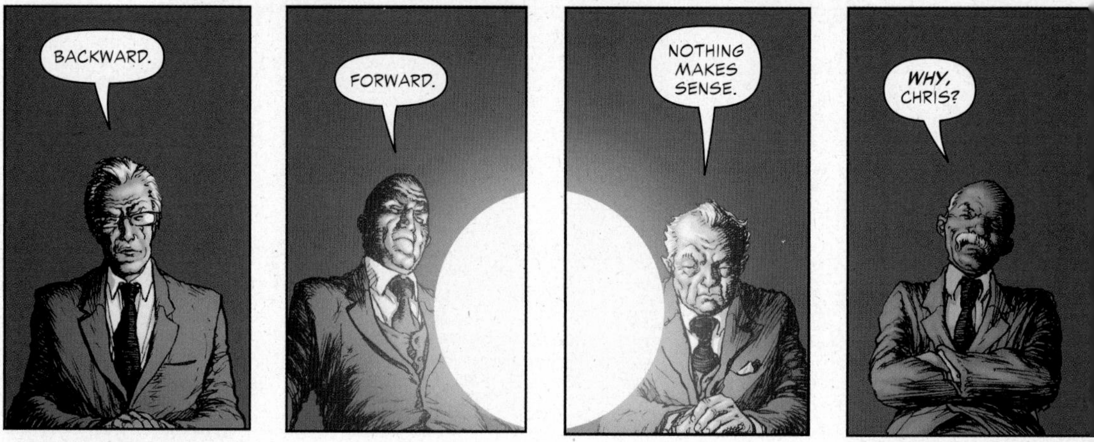
BACKWARD.
FORWARD.
NOTHING MAKES SENSE.
WHY, CHRIS?

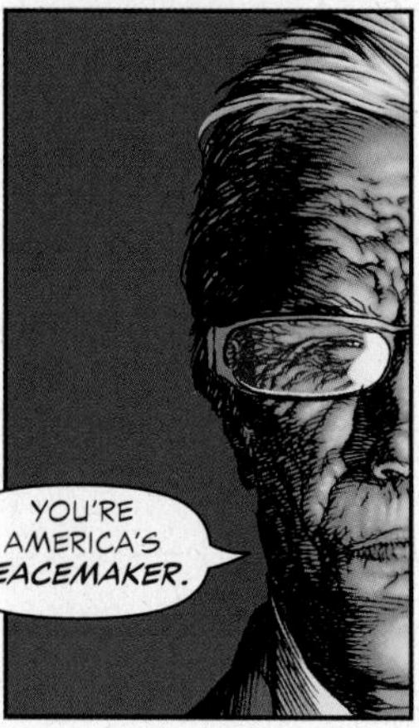
YOU'RE AMERICA'S *PEACEMAKER.*

morrison • quitely

In Which We Burn

fairbairn • leigh • purdin • berganza
special thanks to rob miller

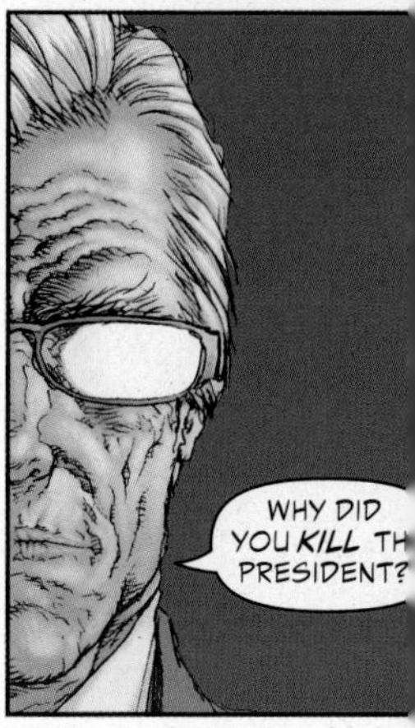
WHY DID YOU *KILL* TH PRESIDENT?

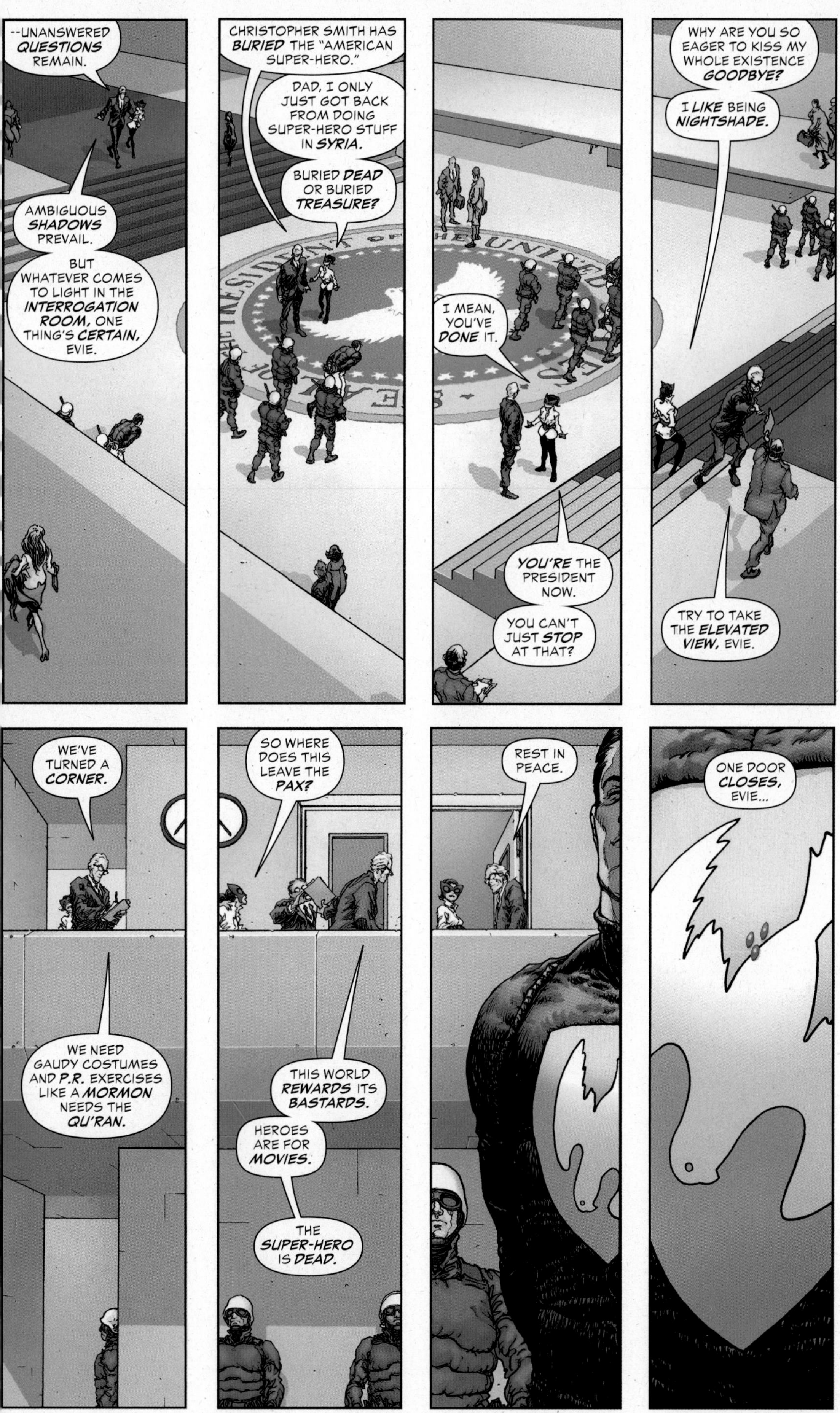
--UNANSWERED QUESTIONS REMAIN.
AMBIGUOUS SHADOWS PREVAIL.
BUT WHATEVER COMES TO LIGHT IN THE INTERROGATION ROOM, ONE THING'S CERTAIN, EVIE.
CHRISTOPHER SMITH HAS BURIED THE "AMERICAN SUPER-HERO."
DAD, I ONLY JUST GOT BACK FROM DOING SUPER-HERO STUFF IN SYRIA.
BURIED DEAD OR BURIED TREASURE?
I MEAN, YOU'VE DONE IT.
YOU'RE THE PRESIDENT NOW.
YOU CAN'T JUST STOP AT THAT?
WHY ARE YOU SO EAGER TO KISS MY WHOLE EXISTENCE GOODBYE?
I LIKE BEING NIGHTSHADE.
TRY TO TAKE THE ELEVATED VIEW, EVIE.
WE'VE TURNED A CORNER.
WE NEED GAUDY COSTUMES AND P.R. EXERCISES LIKE A MORMON NEEDS THE QU'RAN.
SO WHERE DOES THIS LEAVE THE PAX?
THIS WORLD REWARDS ITS BASTARDS.
HEROES ARE FOR MOVIES.
THE SUPER-HERO IS DEAD.
REST IN PEACE.
ONE DOOR CLOSES, EVIE...

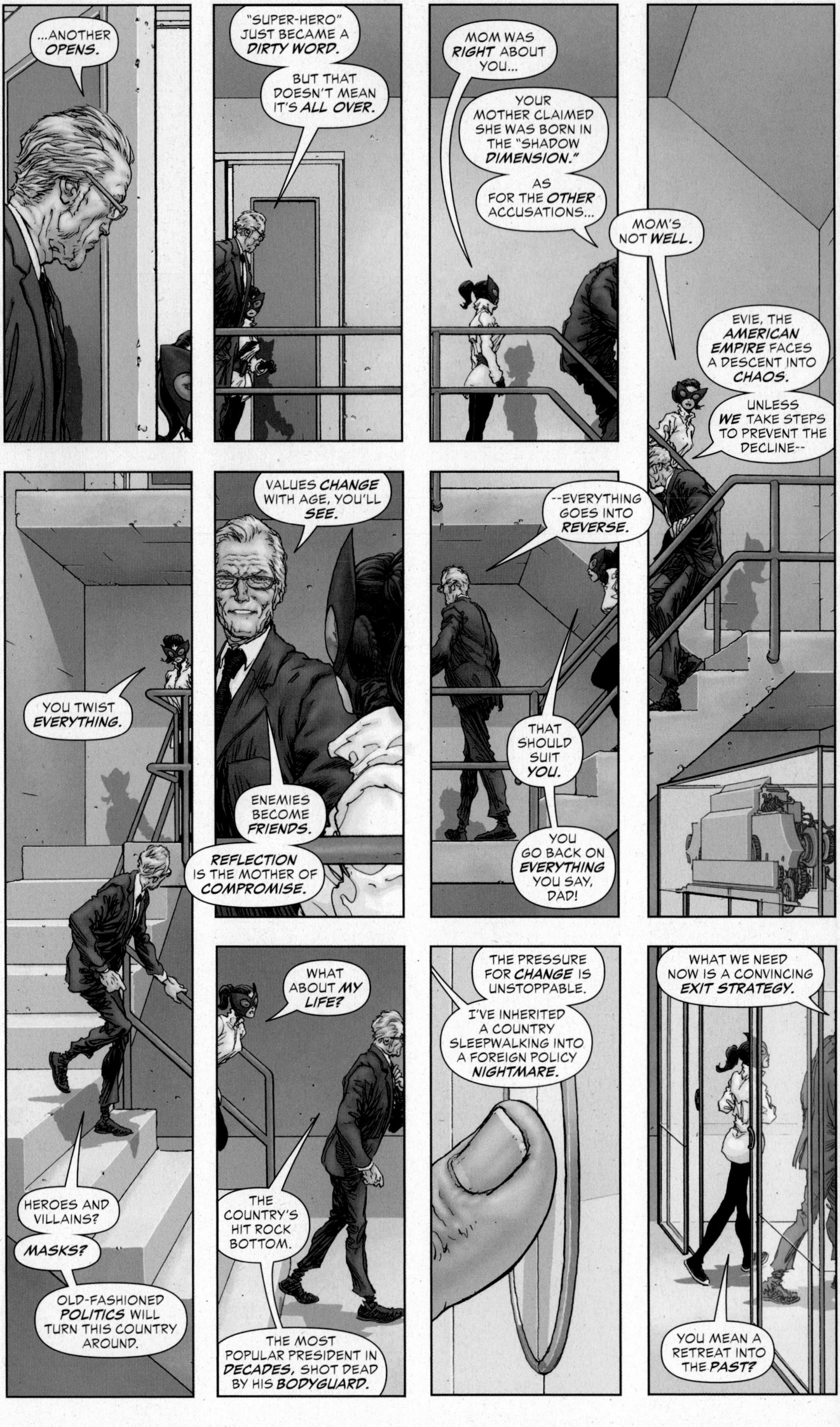

...ANOTHER OPENS.
"SUPER-HERO" JUST BECAME A DIRTY WORD.
BUT THAT DOESN'T MEAN IT'S ALL OVER.
MOM WAS RIGHT ABOUT YOU...
YOUR MOTHER CLAIMED SHE WAS BORN IN THE "SHADOW DIMENSION."
AS FOR THE OTHER ACCUSATIONS...
MOM'S NOT WELL.
EVIE, THE AMERICAN EMPIRE FACES A DESCENT INTO CHAOS.
UNLESS WE TAKE STEPS TO PREVENT THE DECLINE--
--EVERYTHING GOES INTO REVERSE.
THAT SHOULD SUIT YOU.
YOU GO BACK ON EVERYTHING YOU SAY, DAD!
YOU TWIST EVERYTHING.
VALUES CHANGE WITH AGE, YOU'LL SEE.
ENEMIES BECOME FRIENDS.
REFLECTION IS THE MOTHER OF COMPROMISE.
HEROES AND VILLAINS?
MASKS?
OLD-FASHIONED POLITICS WILL TURN THIS COUNTRY AROUND.
WHAT ABOUT MY LIFE?
THE COUNTRY'S HIT ROCK BOTTOM.
THE MOST POPULAR PRESIDENT IN DECADES, SHOT DEAD BY HIS BODYGUARD.
THE PRESSURE FOR CHANGE IS UNSTOPPABLE.
I'VE INHERITED A COUNTRY SLEEPWALKING INTO A FOREIGN POLICY NIGHTMARE.
WHAT WE NEED NOW IS A CONVINCING EXIT STRATEGY.
YOU MEAN A RETREAT INTO THE PAST?

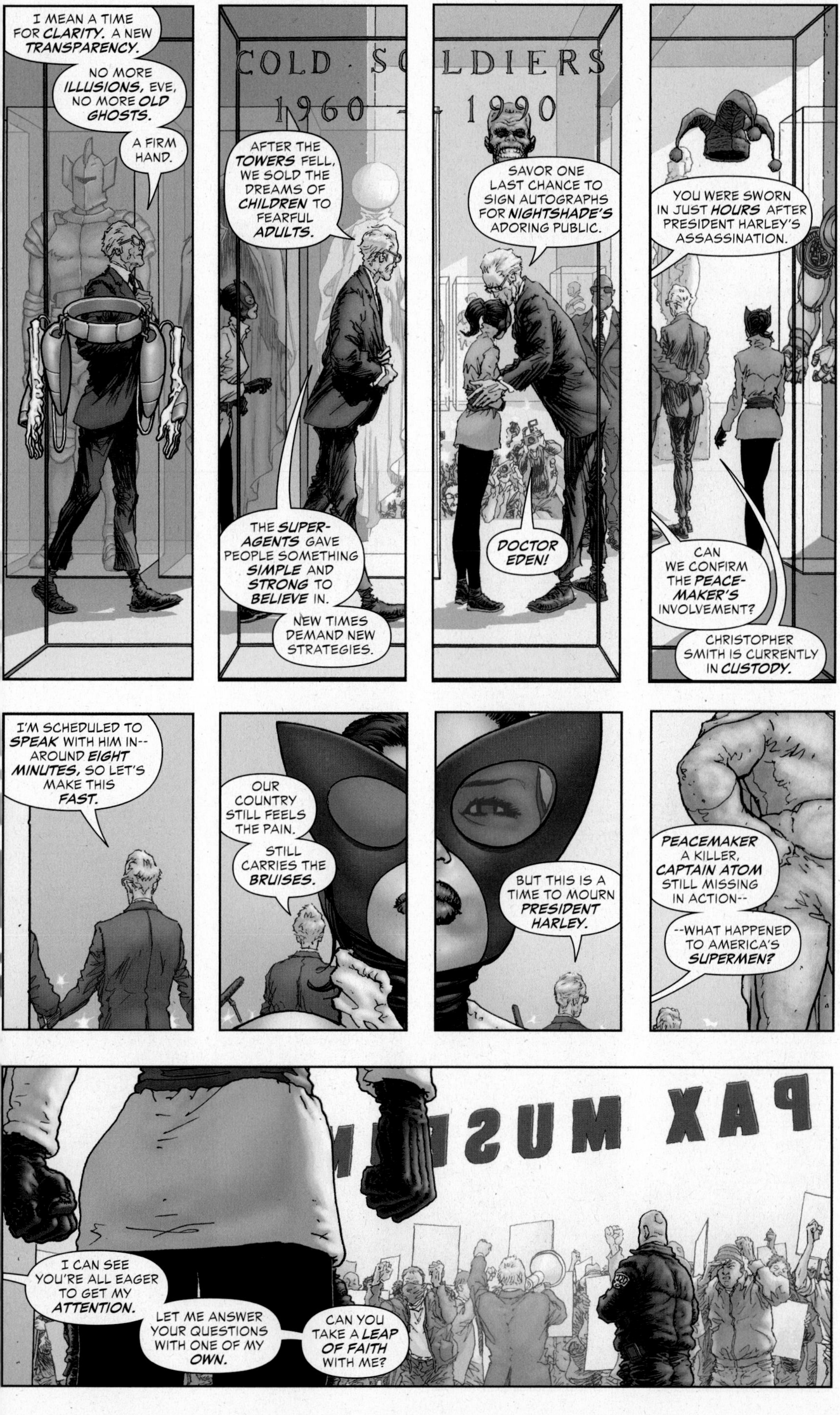
I MEAN A TIME FOR CLARITY. A NEW TRANSPARENCY.
NO MORE ILLUSIONS, EVE, NO MORE OLD GHOSTS.
A FIRM HAND.
COLD SOLDIERS 1960 – 1990
AFTER THE TOWERS FELL, WE SOLD THE DREAMS OF CHILDREN TO FEARFUL ADULTS.
THE SUPER-AGENTS GAVE PEOPLE SOMETHING SIMPLE AND STRONG TO BELIEVE IN.
NEW TIMES DEMAND NEW STRATEGIES.
SAVOR ONE LAST CHANCE TO SIGN AUTOGRAPHS FOR NIGHTSHADE'S ADORING PUBLIC.
DOCTOR EDEN!
YOU WERE SWORN IN JUST HOURS AFTER PRESIDENT HARLEY'S ASSASSINATION.
CAN WE CONFIRM THE PEACE-MAKER'S INVOLVEMENT?
CHRISTOPHER SMITH IS CURRENTLY IN CUSTODY.
I'M SCHEDULED TO SPEAK WITH HIM IN-- AROUND EIGHT MINUTES, SO LET'S MAKE THIS FAST.
OUR COUNTRY STILL FEELS THE PAIN.
STILL CARRIES THE BRUISES.
BUT THIS IS A TIME TO MOURN PRESIDENT HARLEY.
PEACEMAKER A KILLER, CAPTAIN ATOM STILL MISSING IN ACTION--
--WHAT HAPPENED TO AMERICA'S SUPERMEN?
I CAN SEE YOU'RE ALL EAGER TO GET MY ATTENTION.
LET ME ANSWER YOUR QUESTIONS WITH ONE OF MY OWN.
CAN YOU TAKE A LEAP OF FAITH WITH ME?

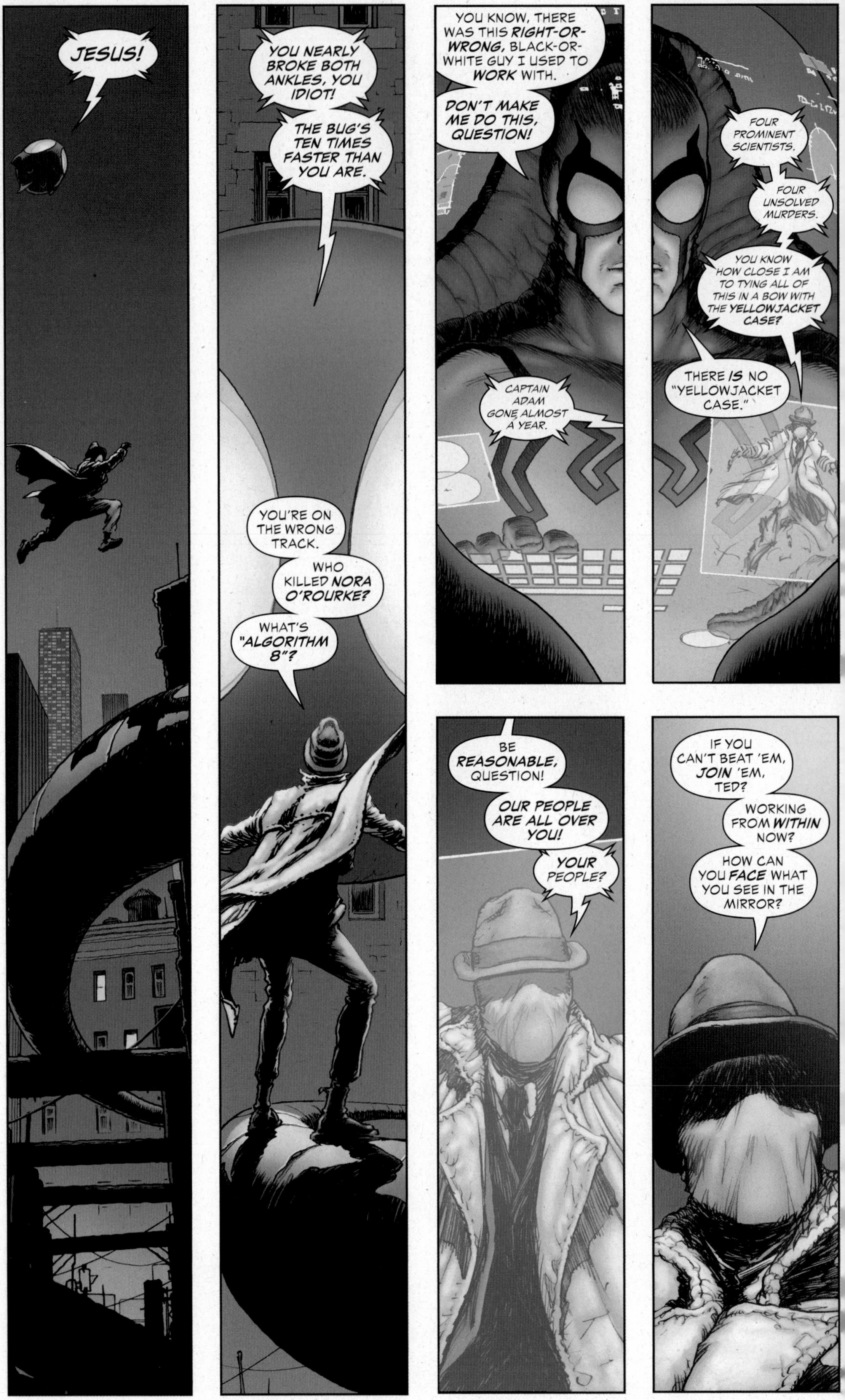
JESUS!
YOU NEARLY BROKE BOTH ANKLES, YOU IDIOT!
THE BUG'S TEN TIMES FASTER THAN YOU ARE.
YOU'RE ON THE WRONG TRACK.
WHO KILLED NORA O'ROURKE?
WHAT'S "ALGORITHM 8"?
YOU KNOW, THERE WAS THIS RIGHT-OR-WRONG, BLACK-OR-WHITE GUY I USED TO WORK WITH.
DON'T MAKE ME DO THIS, QUESTION!
CAPTAIN ADAM GONE ALMOST A YEAR.
FOUR PROMINENT SCIENTISTS.
FOUR UNSOLVED MURDERS.
YOU KNOW HOW CLOSE I AM TO TYING ALL OF THIS IN A BOW WITH THE YELLOWJACKET CASE?
THERE IS NO "YELLOWJACKET CASE."
BE REASONABLE, QUESTION!
OUR PEOPLE ARE ALL OVER YOU!
YOUR PEOPLE?
IF YOU CAN'T BEAT 'EM, JOIN 'EM, TED?
WORKING FROM WITHIN NOW?
HOW CAN YOU FACE WHAT YOU SEE IN THE MIRROR?

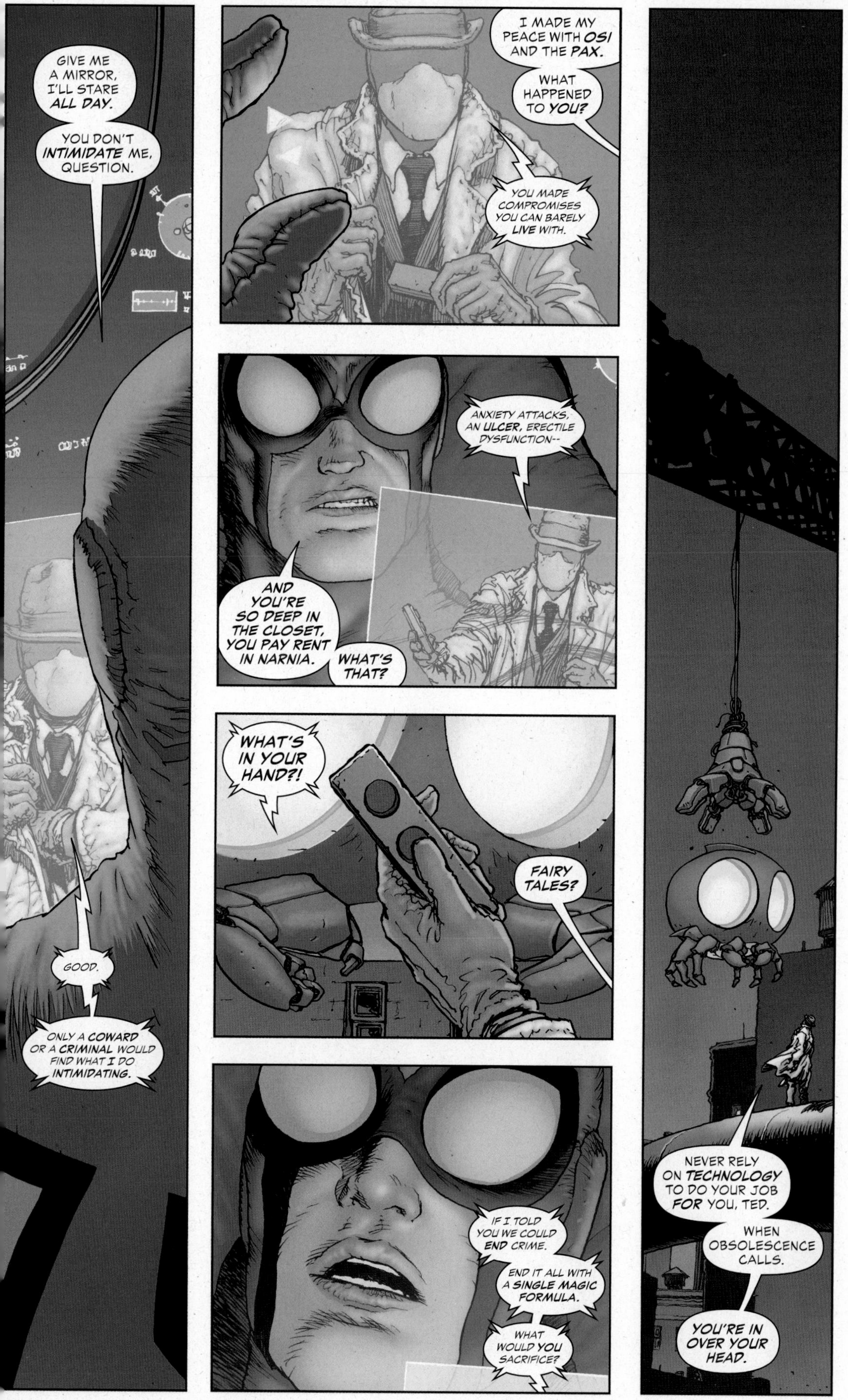
GIVE ME A MIRROR, I'LL STARE ALL DAY.
YOU DON'T INTIMIDATE ME, QUESTION.
GOOD.
ONLY A COWARD OR A CRIMINAL WOULD FIND WHAT I DO INTIMIDATING.
I MADE MY PEACE WITH OSI AND THE PAX.
WHAT HAPPENED TO YOU?
YOU MADE COMPROMISES YOU CAN BARELY LIVE WITH.
ANXIETY ATTACKS, AN ULCER, ERECTILE DYSFUNCTION--
AND YOU'RE SO DEEP IN THE CLOSET, YOU PAY RENT IN NARNIA.
WHAT'S THAT?
WHAT'S IN YOUR HAND?!
FAIRY TALES?
IF I TOLD YOU WE COULD END CRIME.
END IT ALL WITH A SINGLE MAGIC FORMULA.
WHAT WOULD YOU SACRIFICE?
NEVER RELY ON TECHNOLOGY TO DO YOUR JOB FOR YOU, TED.
WHEN OBSOLESCENCE CALLS.
YOU'RE IN OVER YOUR HEAD.

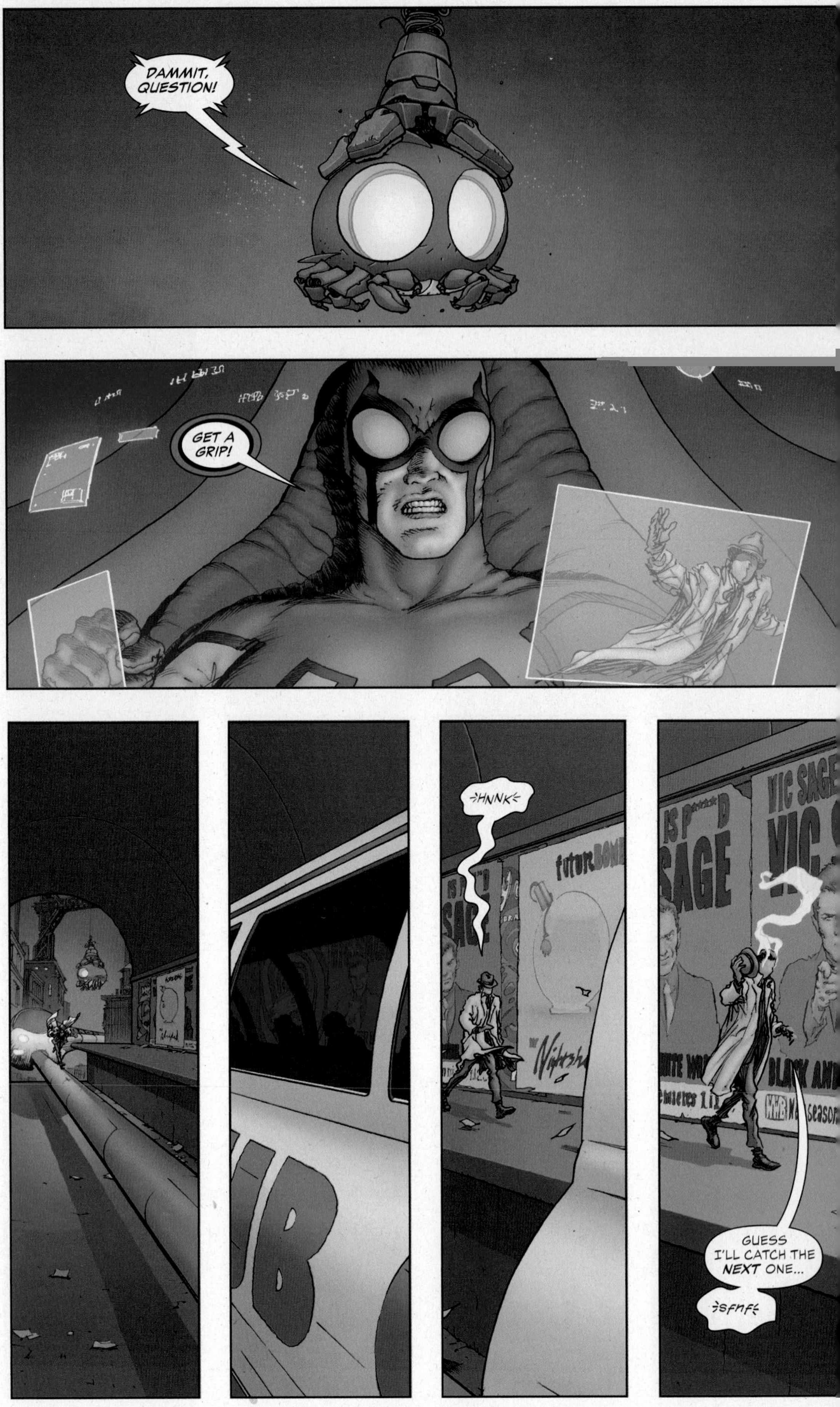
DAMMIT, QUESTION!
GET A GRIP!
HNNK
VIC SAGE
SAGE
GUESS I'LL CATCH THE **NEXT** ONE...
SFNF

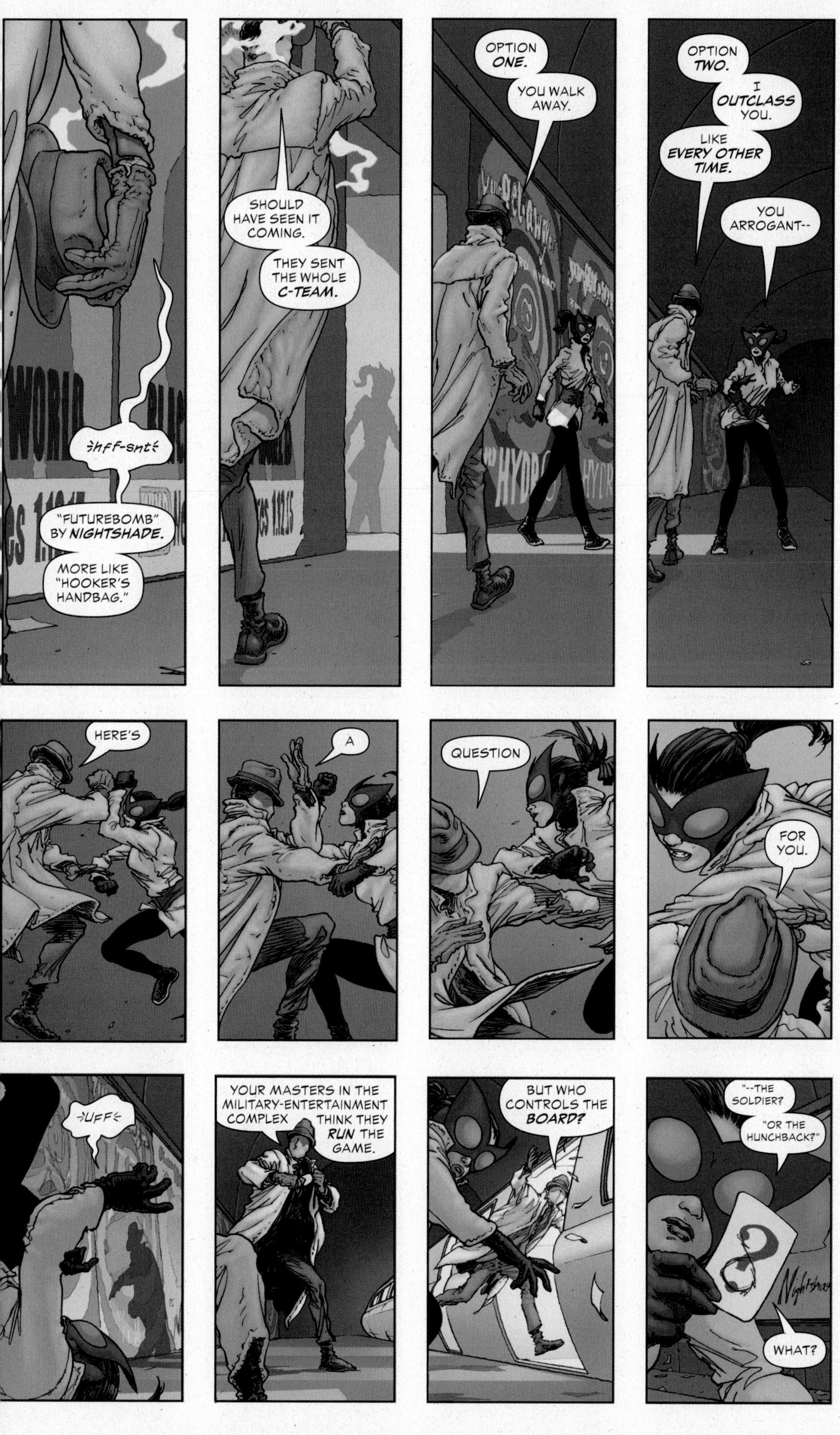
≈hff-snt≈
"FUTUREBOMB" BY NIGHTSHADE.
MORE LIKE "HOOKER'S HANDBAG."
SHOULD HAVE SEEN IT COMING.
THEY SENT THE WHOLE C-TEAM.
OPTION ONE.
YOU WALK AWAY.
OPTION TWO.
I OUTCLASS YOU.
LIKE EVERY OTHER TIME.
YOU ARROGANT--
HERE'S
A
QUESTION
FOR YOU.
≈UFF≈
YOUR MASTERS IN THE MILITARY-ENTERTAINMENT COMPLEX
THINK THEY RUN THE GAME.
BUT WHO CONTROLS THE BOARD?
"--THE SOLDIER?
"OR THE HUNCHBACK?"
WHAT?

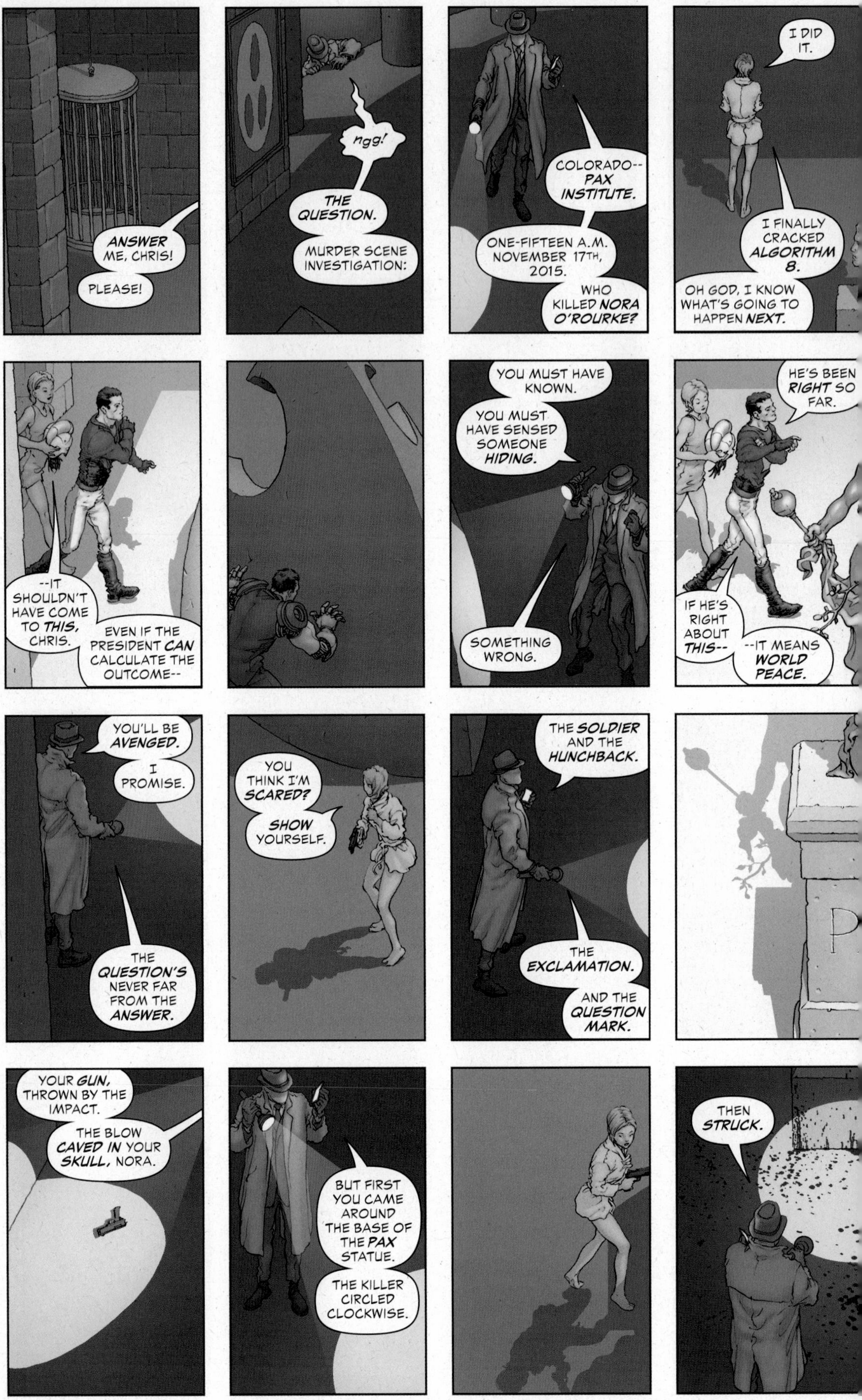
ANSWER ME, CHRIS!
PLEASE!
ngg!
THE QUESTION.
MURDER SCENE INVESTIGATION:
COLORADO-- PAX INSTITUTE.
ONE-FIFTEEN A.M. NOVEMBER 17TH, 2015.
WHO KILLED NORA O'ROURKE?
I DID IT.
I FINALLY CRACKED ALGORITHM 8.
OH GOD, I KNOW WHAT'S GOING TO HAPPEN NEXT.
--IT SHOULDN'T HAVE COME TO THIS, CHRIS.
EVEN IF THE PRESIDENT CAN CALCULATE THE OUTCOME--
YOU MUST HAVE KNOWN.
YOU MUST HAVE SENSED SOMEONE HIDING.
SOMETHING WRONG.
HE'S BEEN RIGHT SO FAR.
IF HE'S RIGHT ABOUT THIS--
--IT MEANS WORLD PEACE.
YOU'LL BE AVENGED.
I PROMISE.
THE QUESTION'S NEVER FAR FROM THE ANSWER.
YOU THINK I'M SCARED?
SHOW YOURSELF.
THE SOLDIER AND THE HUNCHBACK.
THE EXCLAMATION.
AND THE QUESTION MARK.
YOUR GUN, THROWN BY THE IMPACT.
THE BLOW CAVED IN YOUR SKULL, NORA.
BUT FIRST YOU CAME AROUND THE BASE OF THE PAX STATUE.
THE KILLER CIRCLED CLOCKWISE.
THEN STRUCK.

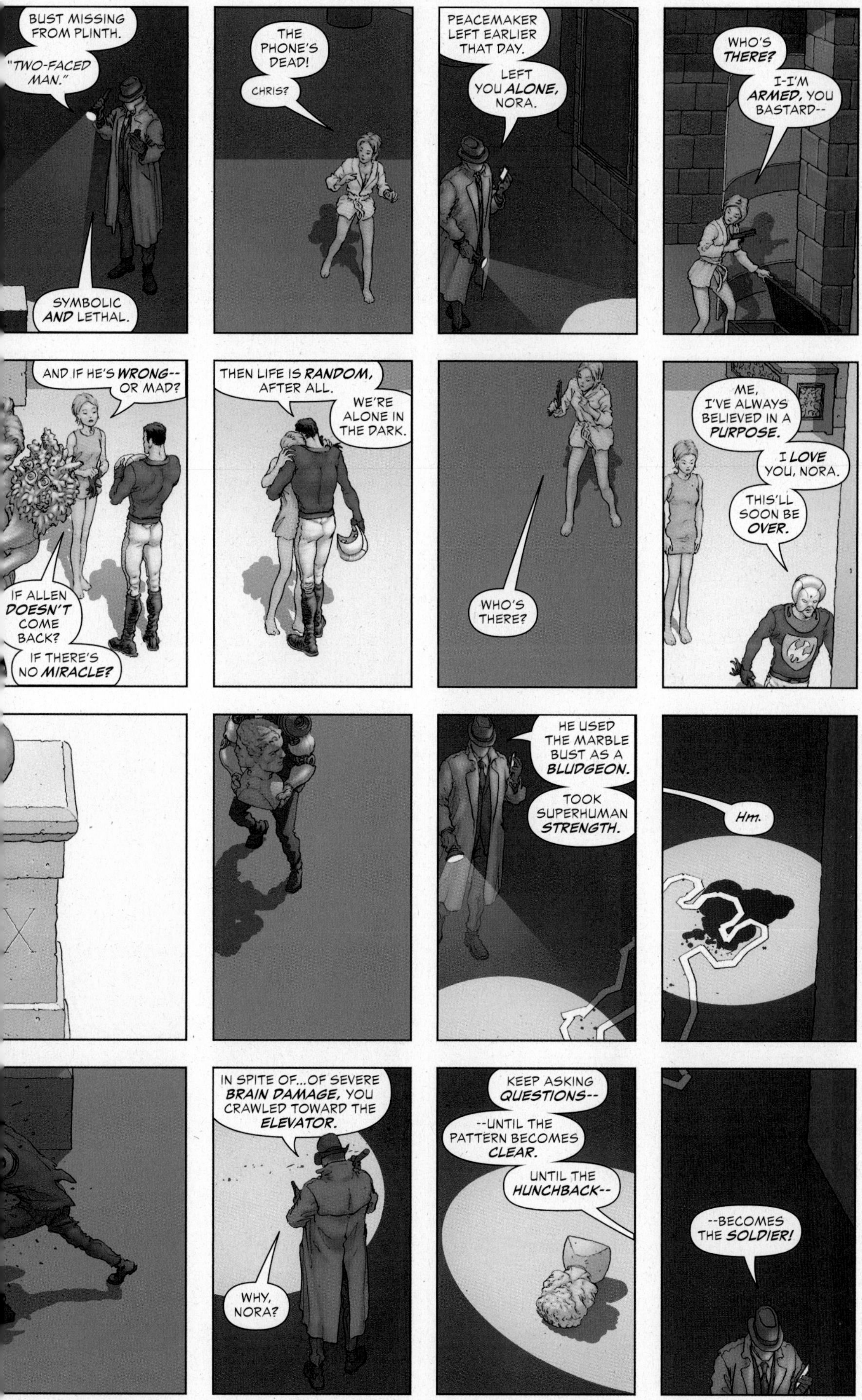
BUST MISSING FROM PLINTH.
"TWO-FACED MAN."
SYMBOLIC AND LETHAL.
THE PHONE'S DEAD!
CHRIS?
PEACEMAKER LEFT EARLIER THAT DAY.
LEFT YOU ALONE, NORA.
WHO'S THERE?
I-I'M ARMED, YOU BASTARD--
AND IF HE'S WRONG-- OR MAD?
IF ALLEN DOESN'T COME BACK?
IF THERE'S NO MIRACLE?
THEN LIFE IS RANDOM, AFTER ALL.
WE'RE ALONE IN THE DARK.
WHO'S THERE?
ME, I'VE ALWAYS BELIEVED IN A PURPOSE.
I LOVE YOU, NORA.
THIS'LL SOON BE OVER.
HE USED THE MARBLE BUST AS A BLUDGEON.
TOOK SUPERHUMAN STRENGTH.
Hm.
IN SPITE OF...OF SEVERE BRAIN DAMAGE, YOU CRAWLED TOWARD THE ELEVATOR.
WHY, NORA?
KEEP ASKING QUESTIONS--
--UNTIL THE PATTERN BECOMES CLEAR.
UNTIL THE HUNCHBACK--
--BECOMES THE SOLDIER!

--ON PAGES *12 AND 13*, I CAUGHT SIGHT OF A MASSLESS TIME-SYMMETRICAL *BOSON*.

A *MÖBIUS LOOP* CURVING THROUGH *EIGHT DIMENSIONS*.

I HEARD SOMETHING KNOCKING ON THE *DOOR* TO *GET IN*--

Um, ah, CAPTAIN, THIS IS *DOCTOR McDOUGALL* IN THE *CONTROL ROOM*.

CAN WE PUT AWAY THE COMIC BOOK, PLEASE?

I'M THINKING HOW *OUR* UNIVERSE APPEARS FROM A *HIGHER DIMENSIONAL* PERSPECTIVE.

FLAT.

CAPTAIN--PLEASE *CONCENTRATE*. THIS IS PROFESSOR LYONS.

COMMENCING *PARTICLE ACCELERATION*, ARE YOU READY?

COMPLETE YET ALWAYS BEGINNING AND ENDING.

ALWAYS *DIFFERENT*.

THE STORY'S *LINEAR*, BUT I CAN FLIP THROUGH THE PAGES IN *ANY* ORDER, ANY DIRECTION.

FORWARD IN TIME TO THE *CONCLUSION*.

BACK TO THE *OPENING* SCENE.

THE CHARACTERS REMAIN *UNAWARE* OF MY SCRUTINY, BUT *THEIR* THOUGHTS ARE *TRANSPARENT*, WEIGHTLESS IN LITTLE CLOUDS.

THIS IS HOW A *2-DIMENSIONAL CONTINUUM* LOOKS TO *YOU*.

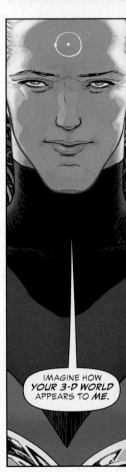

IMAGINE HOW *YOUR 3-D WORLD* APPEARS TO *ME*.

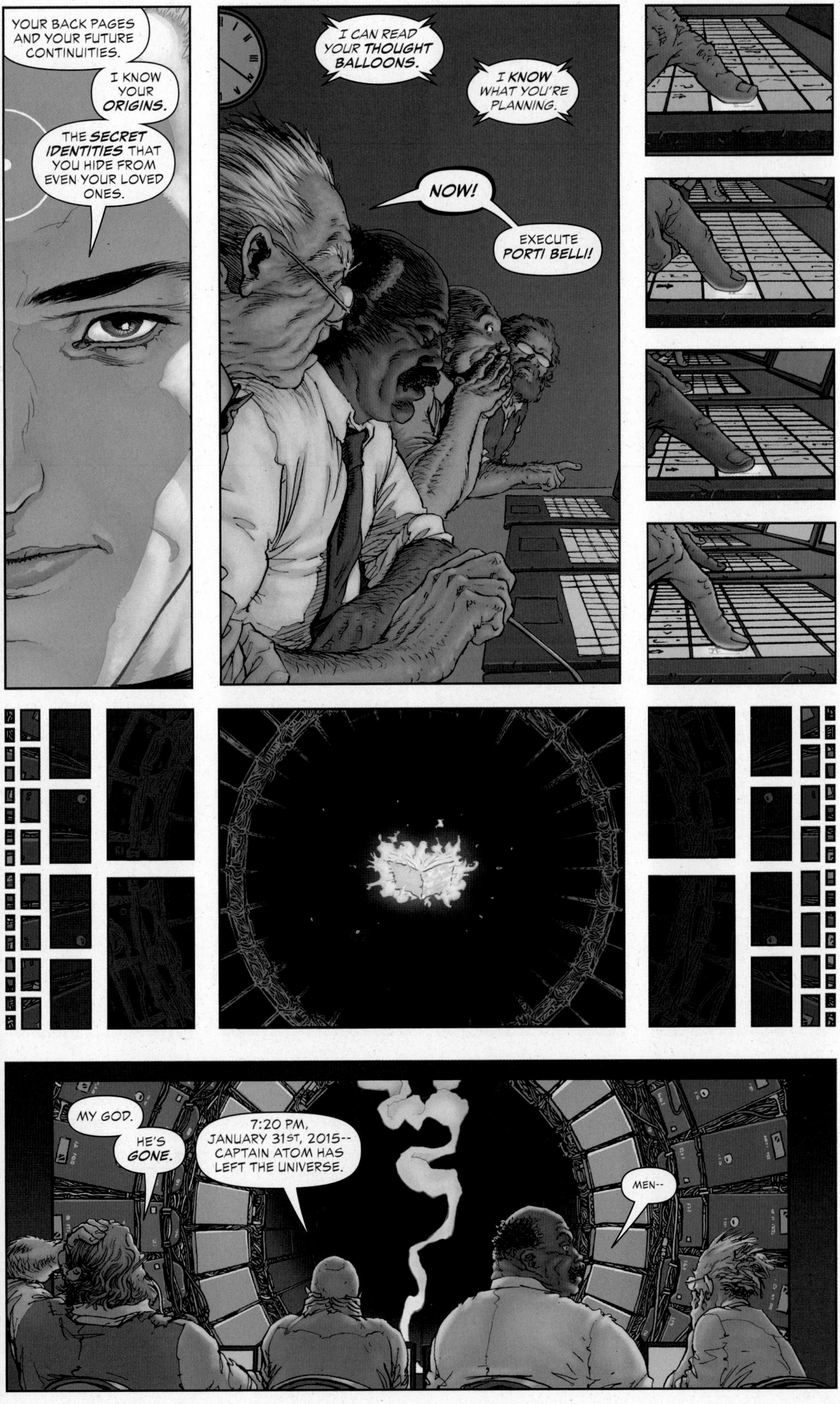
YOUR BACK PAGES AND YOUR FUTURE CONTINUITIES.
I KNOW YOUR ORIGINS.
THE SECRET IDENTITIES THAT YOU HIDE FROM EVEN YOUR LOVED ONES.
I CAN READ YOUR THOUGHT BALLOONS.
I KNOW WHAT YOU'RE PLANNING.
NOW!
EXECUTE PORTI BELLI!
MY GOD.
HE'S GONE.
7:20 PM, JANUARY 31ST, 2015-- CAPTAIN ATOM HAS LEFT THE UNIVERSE.
MEN--

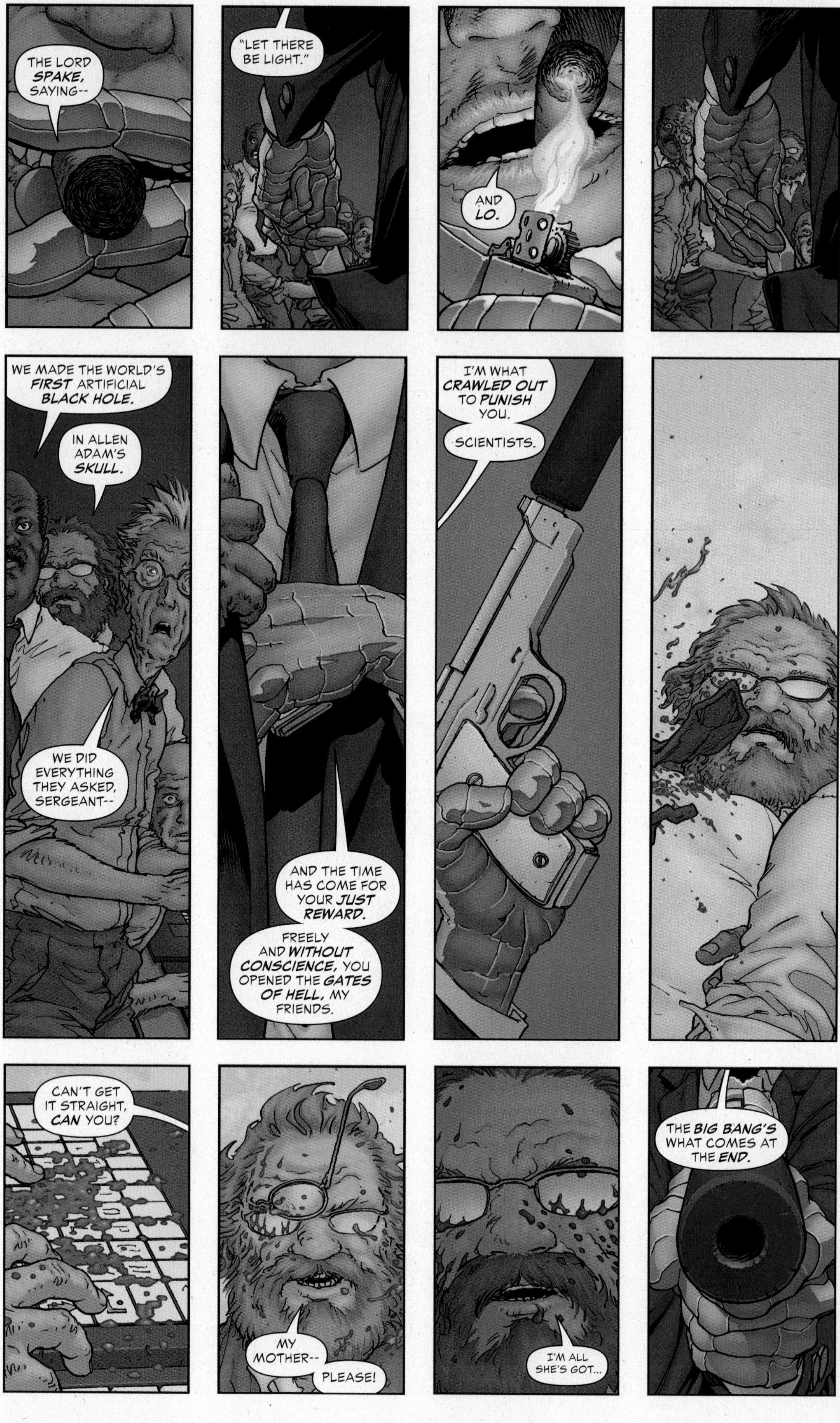
THE LORD SPAKE, SAYING--
"LET THERE BE LIGHT."
AND LO.
WE MADE THE WORLD'S FIRST ARTIFICIAL BLACK HOLE.
IN ALLEN ADAM'S SKULL.
WE DID EVERYTHING THEY ASKED, SERGEANT--
AND THE TIME HAS COME FOR YOUR JUST REWARD.
FREELY AND WITHOUT CONSCIENCE, YOU OPENED THE GATES OF HELL, MY FRIENDS.
I'M WHAT CRAWLED OUT TO PUNISH YOU.
SCIENTISTS.
CAN'T GET IT STRAIGHT, CAN YOU?
MY MOTHER--
PLEASE!
I'M ALL SHE'S GOT...
THE BIG BANG'S WHAT COMES AT THE END.

BOOM! AND THERE YOU *WERE*.

IT SAYS HERE YOU HAVE *JET BLACK* HAIR.

I REMEMBER YOU WERE *BLONDE*.

I AM BLONDE.

AS *NIGHTSHADE*, I WEAR A *BLACK WIG*.

THAT *i-SCENE* IS FIVE YEARS OLD, MOM.

WHAT HAPPENED TO "EVE OF SHADOWS-- QUEEN OF THE NIGHT"?

NIGHTSHADE IS AWFUL!

YOU PROMISED YOU'D GET ME A *FRAME*.

AND A *CIGARETTE*.

YOU'VE BEEN *CHAIN-SMOKING*!

YOUR CALENDAR'S OUT BY *MONTHS*.

IT'S *2014*. DAD SAYS--

MY BRAIN'S *DEFUNCT* AND THAT BASTARD'S *RESPONSIBLE*.

SO NOW YOUR HAIR'S DYED *BLONDE*?

THERE *WERE* NO BLONDES IN THE WORLD *BEHIND* SHADOWS.

YOU REMEMBER *ALLEN ADAM*?

ALLEN'S HELPING DAD HARNESS *BLACK HOLE ENERGY* SO WE DON'T HAVE TO RELY ON *OIL*.

IT'S LIKE *SCIENCE FICTION*.

IT'S ALL THE STUFF YOU USED TO *TALK* ABOUT.

THE DOCTORS ARE ALL FROM *SLOBOVIA* IN HERE...

THE PLACE IS *OVERRUN* BY SLOBOVIANS.

SCIENCE WILL NEVER UNDERSTAND THE MYSTERIES OF MOTHERHOOD.

I HAD A *PIANO*.

MOM-- I *LOVE* YOU.

EVE, I COULD FILL A *CONCERT HALL*.

BUT I HAVE TO GO SAVE THE *WORLD*.

I NEED A RAPID EXTRACTION AT THIS LOCATION.

--I'M WITH MY *MOM*.

SO YOU'RE DYING YOUR HAIR BLONDE?

SAY AGAIN?

IF THERE'S A *PATTERN*, I CAN'T SEE IT.

SHE JUST GOES ROUND AND AROUND.

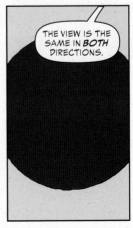

THE VIEW IS THE SAME IN *BOTH* DIRECTIONS.

JANUS WAS THE GUARDIAN OF *DOORS AND GATES* IN ANCIENT ROME.

THEN THERE'S THE LAST COMIC BOOK STORY HARLEY'S *DAD* WROTE.

"JANUS THE EVERYWAY MAN."

ALL THIS BLUE SKY THINKING, I'VE COME UP *EMPTY-HANDED.*

I WONDERED ABOUT YOUR LATEST *ART PROJECT.*

TWO HEADS ARE BETTER THAN ONE?

SO FORGET THE PAST.

YOUR PAST RECORD IS SPOTLESS.

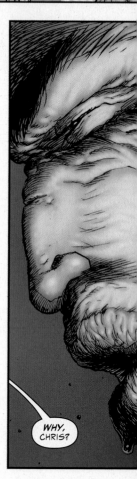

WHY, CHRIS?

TWO YEARS TO *VERIFY* THE EXISTENCE OF *ALGORITHM 8.*

THE *PAX INSTITUTE* WILL HAVE TRAINED THE *NEXT GENERATION* OF *PEACEMAKER* AGENTS BY THEN.

AFTER HE *WINS* THE 2015 ELECTION.

WHEN I'VE *DONE* WHAT HAS TO BE DONE, WE'LL GO WHERE THEY'LL NEVER FIND US.

JUST *YOU AND ME,* NORA.

SURE, IF I HAD YOUR *ULTIMATE ALGORITHM,* I'D BE SEARCHING THE *FUTURE* FOR INSPIRATION.

LET THAT *SUPER-BRAIN* OF YOURS LOOSE ON THE MATH.

IF HARLEY WON'T LET US INTO HIS SECRET, IT'S DOWN TO *YOU.*

AN *INTRUDER* KILLED HIS FATHER.

OPEN AND SHUT CASE, APPARENTLY.

HOW LONG DO I GET?

≥KMFF≤

IN GOD'S NAME, WHY?

YOUR FUTURE SAFETY CANNOT BE GUARANTEED.

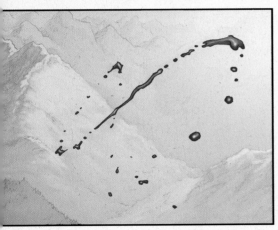

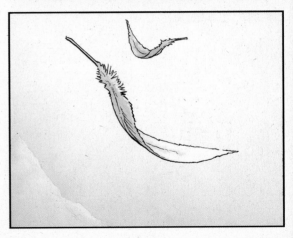

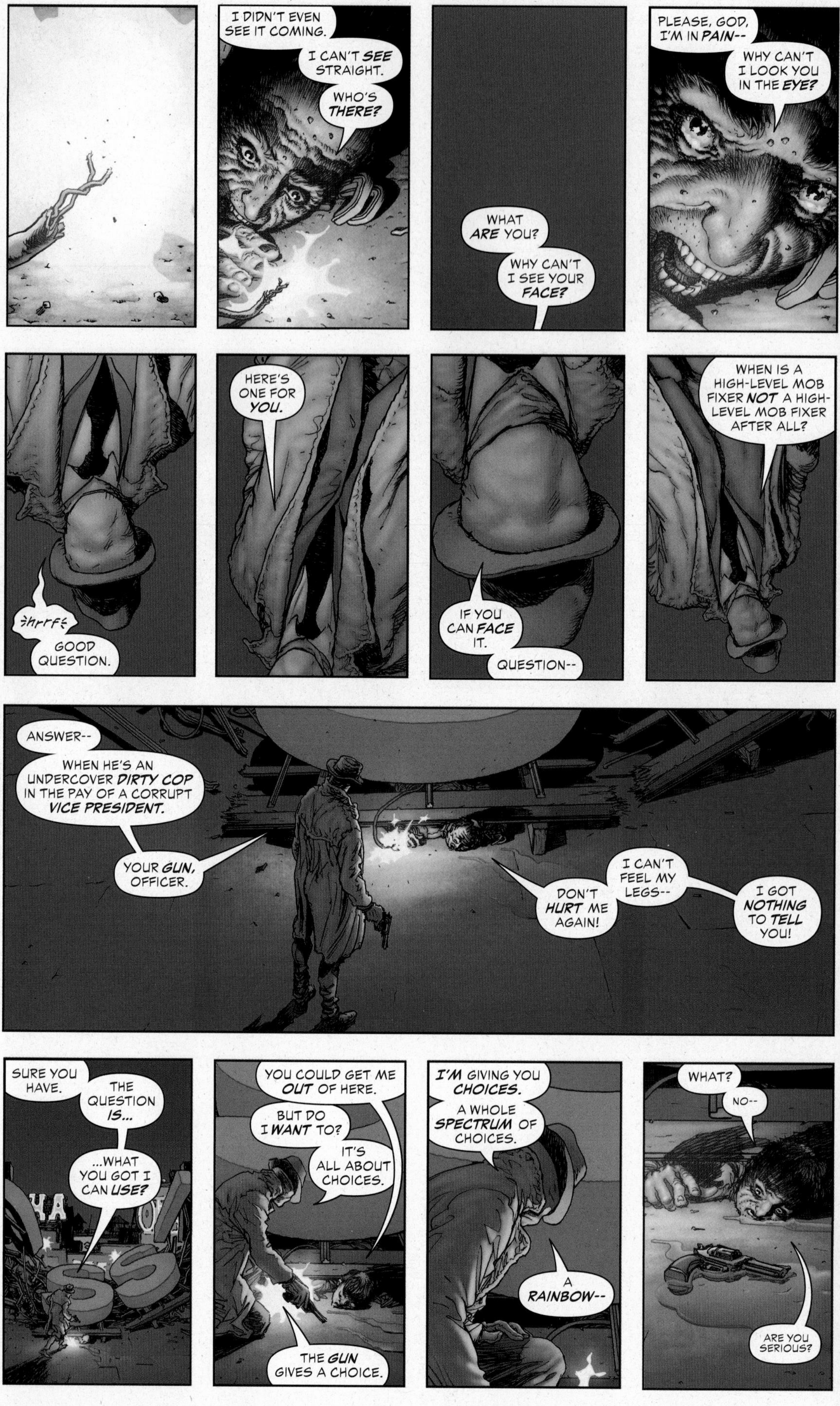
I DIDN'T EVEN SEE IT COMING.
I CAN'T SEE STRAIGHT.
WHO'S THERE?
WHAT ARE YOU?
WHY CAN'T I SEE YOUR FACE?
PLEASE, GOD, I'M IN PAIN--
WHY CAN'T I LOOK YOU IN THE EYE?
hrrf
GOOD QUESTION.
HERE'S ONE FOR YOU.
IF YOU CAN FACE IT.
QUESTION--
WHEN IS A HIGH-LEVEL MOB FIXER NOT A HIGH-LEVEL MOB FIXER AFTER ALL?
ANSWER--
WHEN HE'S AN UNDERCOVER DIRTY COP IN THE PAY OF A CORRUPT VICE PRESIDENT.
YOUR GUN, OFFICER.
DON'T HURT ME AGAIN!
I CAN'T FEEL MY LEGS--
I GOT NOTHING TO TELL YOU!
SURE YOU HAVE.
THE QUESTION IS...
...WHAT YOU GOT I CAN USE?
YOU COULD GET ME OUT OF HERE.
BUT DO I WANT TO?
IT'S ALL ABOUT CHOICES.
THE GUN GIVES A CHOICE.
I'M GIVING YOU CHOICES.
A WHOLE SPECTRUM OF CHOICES.
A RAINBOW--
WHAT?
NO--
ARE YOU SERIOUS?

AS THEY *GROW*, SOCIETIES, LIKE INDIVIDUALS, PASS THROUGH IDENTICAL STAGES OF *DEVELOPMENT.*

IT BREAKS DOWN INTO AN *EIGHT-STAGE COLOR-CODED* SYSTEM, WHERE THE FIRST LEVEL IS *BEIGE,* CORRESPONDING TO INFANCY.

TH___ ___ OF PRIM___ ___OLOGICAL SU___ ___S ARE PA___ ___UNT.

THIS IS WHY THEY KICKED YOU OUTTA THE PAX!

NEXT COMES *PURPLE*, EQUIVALENT TO *MAGICAL THINKING* AND THE STAGE AT WHICH HUNTER/ GATHERER SUBSISTENCE SOCIETIES EX___

RED IS ___ *POWER POLIT___* ___ET GANGS, WAR___ ___ETIES-- THE ___ ___WOS.

BLUE ___ ___ENTALIST RE___ ___*NGE* IS THE S___ ___*TIONAL* ___ET THE ___EA.

WESTERN SOCETY'S AT PLURALISTIC *GREEN* RIGHT NOW, BUT *YELLOW* COMES NEXT.

IF WE *MAKE* IT THAT FAR.

YELLOW ___ INTEGRA___ PLURAL___

A *TURQUOISE* SOCIETY WOULD RUN ON HOLISTIC, SYNERGISTIC ___PLES.

ME?

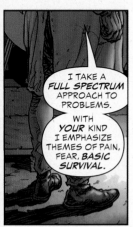

I TAKE A *FULL SPECTRUM* APPROACH TO PROBLEMS.

WITH *YOUR* KIND I EMPHASIZE THEMES OF PAIN, FEAR, *BASIC SURVIVAL.*

--PLEASE CALL AN *AMBULANCE*--

MY ORDERS COME FROM THE *SARGE...*

I CAN'T REACH--

THOSE ARE THE GUYS YOU *WANT!*

I'M *DEAD* WHEN THE SPARKS HIT THE WATER!

THAT'S A *DIRTY, ROTTEN* WAY TO GO!

I--I GOT *RUMORS* IS ALL--

--ABOUT KILLING *CAPTAIN ATOM.*

A SECRET *FORMULA...*

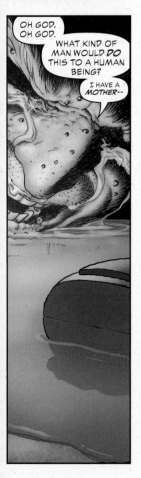

OH GOD, OH GOD.

WHAT KIND OF MAN WOULD *DO* THIS TO A HUMAN BEING?

I HAVE A *MOTHER*--

I'LL LET HER KNOW HER SON DIED *YELLOW.*

AS FOR *ME*--

--I'M A REGISTERED, CARD-CARRYING *SUPER-HERO.*

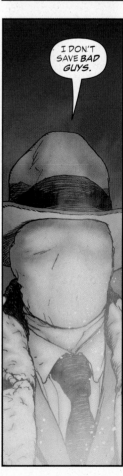

I DON'T SAVE *BAD GUYS.*

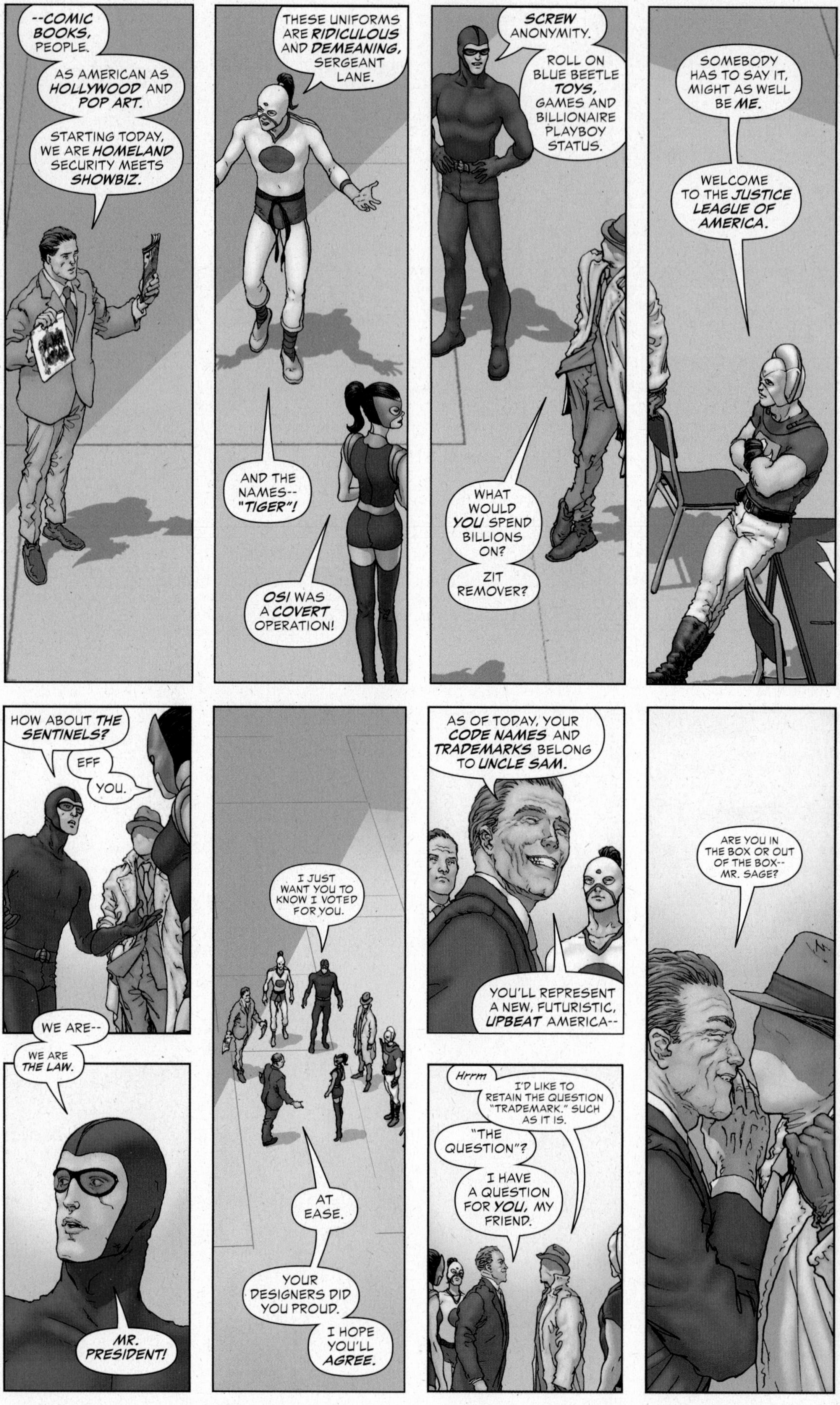

--COMIC BOOKS, PEOPLE.
AS AMERICAN AS HOLLYWOOD AND POP ART.
STARTING TODAY, WE ARE HOMELAND SECURITY MEETS SHOWBIZ.
THESE UNIFORMS ARE RIDICULOUS AND DEMEANING, SERGEANT LANE.
AND THE NAMES-- "TIGER"!
OSI WAS A COVERT OPERATION!
SCREW ANONYMITY.
ROLL ON BLUE BEETLE TOYS, GAMES AND BILLIONAIRE PLAYBOY STATUS.
WHAT WOULD YOU SPEND BILLIONS ON?
ZIT REMOVER?
SOMEBODY HAS TO SAY IT, MIGHT AS WELL BE ME.
WELCOME TO THE JUSTICE LEAGUE OF AMERICA.
HOW ABOUT THE SENTINELS?
EFF
YOU.
WE ARE--
WE ARE THE LAW.
MR. PRESIDENT!
I JUST WANT YOU TO KNOW I VOTED FOR YOU.
AT EASE.
YOUR DESIGNERS DID YOU PROUD.
I HOPE YOU'LL AGREE.
AS OF TODAY, YOUR CODE NAMES AND TRADEMARKS BELONG TO UNCLE SAM.
YOU'LL REPRESENT A NEW, FUTURISTIC, UPBEAT AMERICA--
Hrrm
I'D LIKE TO RETAIN THE QUESTION "TRADEMARK." SUCH AS IT IS.
"THE QUESTION"?
I HAVE A QUESTION FOR YOU, MY FRIEND.
ARE YOU IN THE BOX OR OUT OF THE BOX-- MR. SAGE?

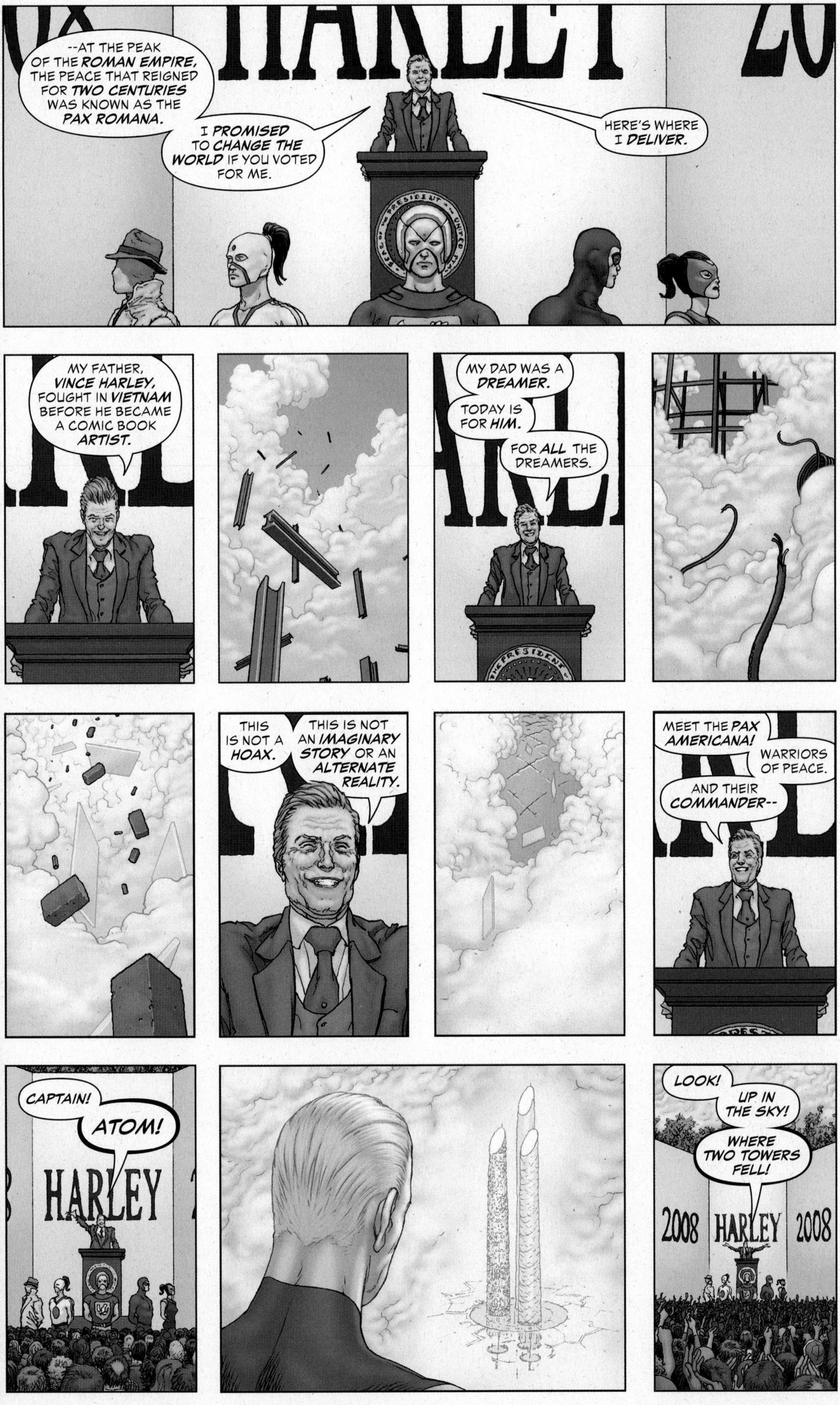
--AT THE PEAK OF THE ROMAN EMPIRE, THE PEACE THAT REIGNED FOR TWO CENTURIES WAS KNOWN AS THE PAX ROMANA.
I PROMISED TO CHANGE THE WORLD IF YOU VOTED FOR ME.
HERE'S WHERE I DELIVER.
MY FATHER, VINCE HARLEY, FOUGHT IN VIETNAM BEFORE HE BECAME A COMIC BOOK ARTIST.
MY DAD WAS A DREAMER.
TODAY IS FOR HIM.
FOR ALL THE DREAMERS.
THIS IS NOT A HOAX.
THIS IS NOT AN IMAGINARY STORY OR AN ALTERNATE REALITY.
MEET THE PAX AMERICANA!
WARRIORS OF PEACE.
AND THEIR COMMANDER--
CAPTAIN!
ATOM!
HARLEY
LOOK!
UP IN THE SKY!
WHERE TWO TOWERS FELL!
2008 HARLEY 2008

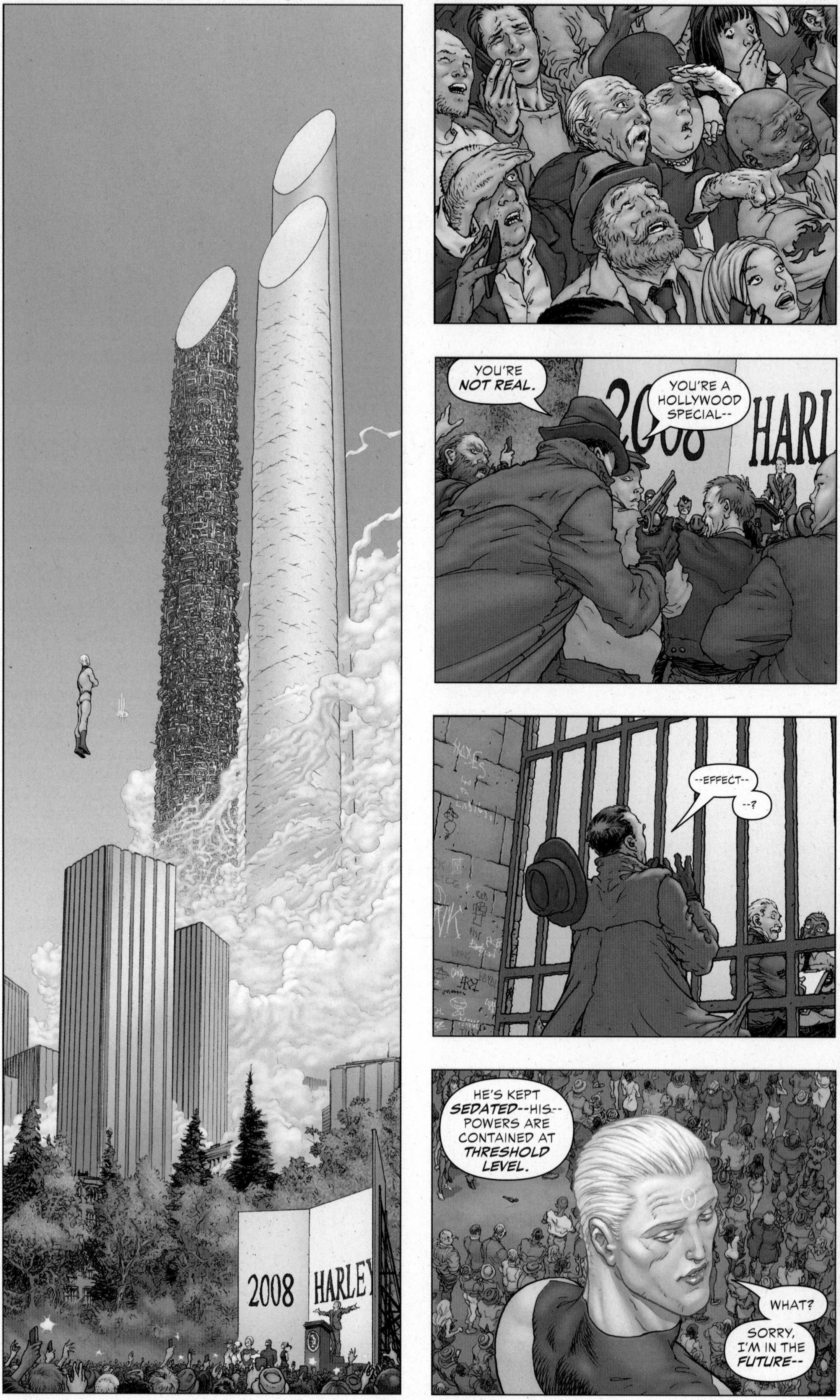
2008
HARLEY
YOU'RE NOT REAL.
YOU'RE A HOLLYWOOD SPECIAL--
2008
HARL
--EFFECT--
--?
HE'S KEPT SEDATED--HIS--POWERS ARE CONTAINED AT THRESHOLD LEVEL.
WHAT?
SORRY, I'M IN THE FUTURE--

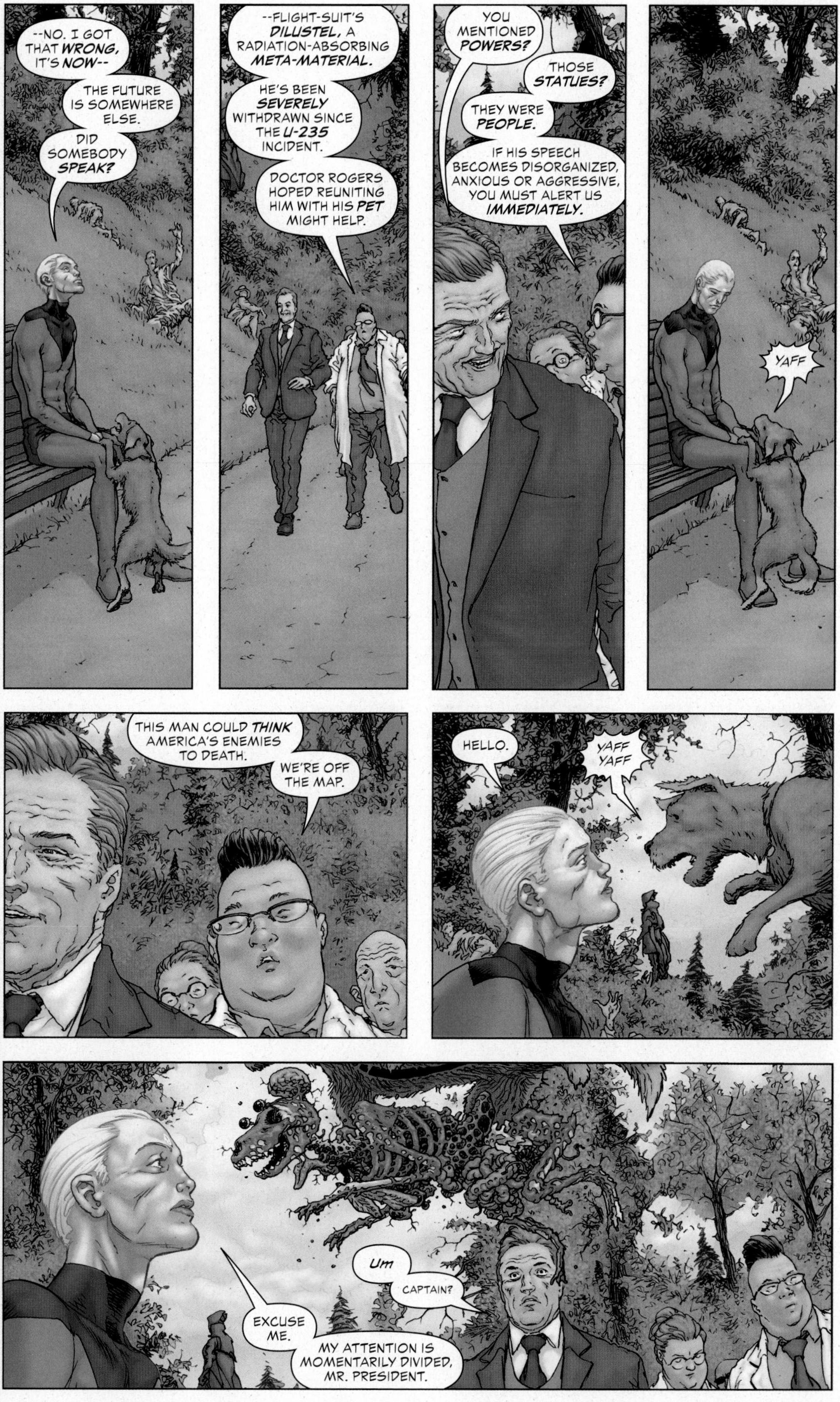
--NO. I GOT THAT WRONG, IT'S NOW--
THE FUTURE IS SOMEWHERE ELSE.
DID SOMEBODY SPEAK?
--FLIGHT-SUIT'S DILUSTEL, A RADIATION-ABSORBING META-MATERIAL.
HE'S BEEN SEVERELY WITHDRAWN SINCE THE U-235 INCIDENT.
DOCTOR ROGERS HOPED REUNITING HIM WITH HIS PET MIGHT HELP.
YOU MENTIONED POWERS?
THOSE STATUES?
THEY WERE PEOPLE.
IF HIS SPEECH BECOMES DISORGANIZED, ANXIOUS OR AGGRESSIVE, YOU MUST ALERT US IMMEDIATELY.
YAFF
THIS MAN COULD THINK AMERICA'S ENEMIES TO DEATH.
WE'RE OFF THE MAP.
HELLO.
YAFF YAFF
Um
CAPTAIN?
EXCUSE ME.
MY ATTENTION IS MOMENTARILY DIVIDED, MR. PRESIDENT.

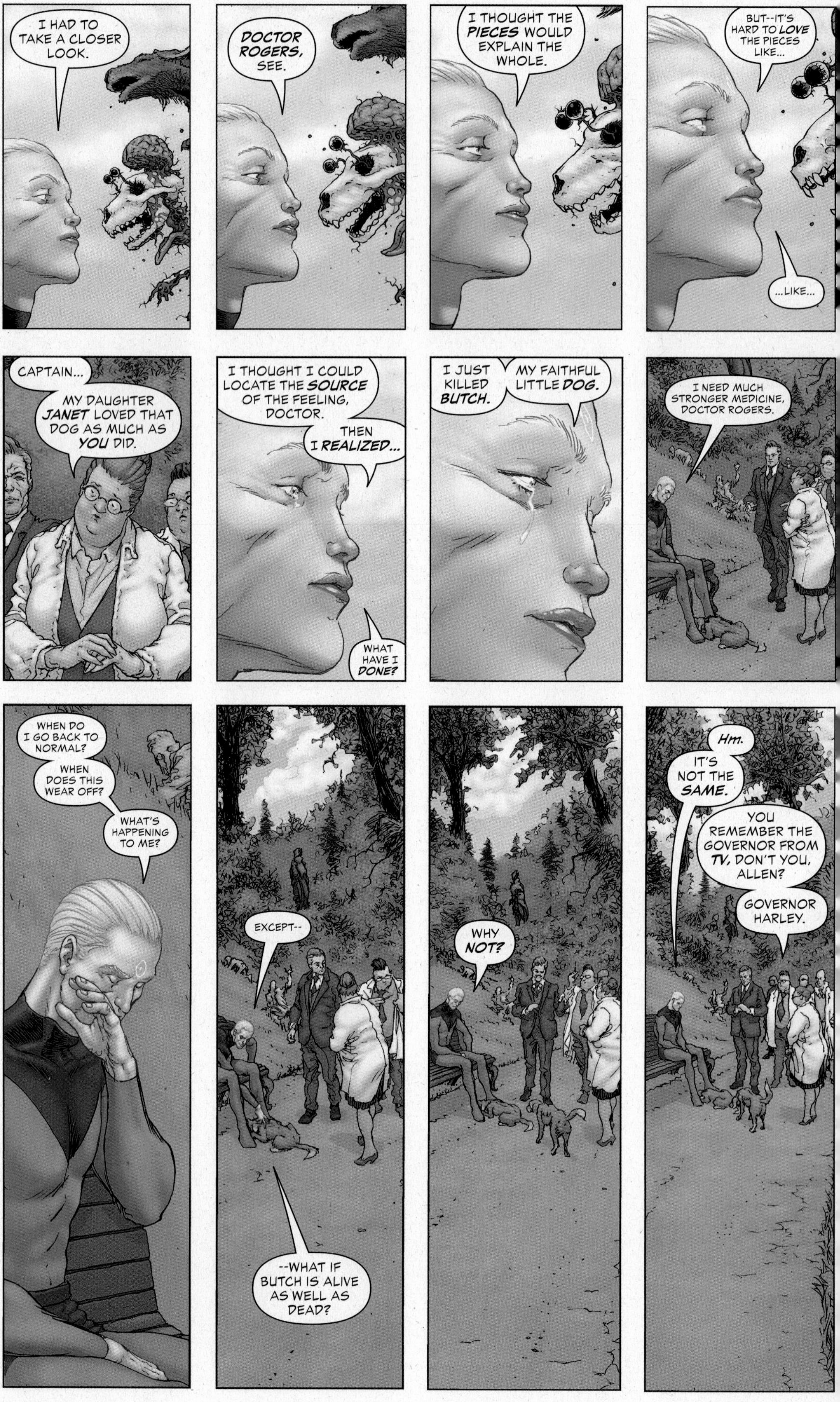

I HAD TO TAKE A CLOSER LOOK.
DOCTOR ROGERS, SEE.
I THOUGHT THE PIECES WOULD EXPLAIN THE WHOLE.
BUT--IT'S HARD TO LOVE THE PIECES LIKE...
...LIKE...
CAPTAIN...
MY DAUGHTER JANET LOVED THAT DOG AS MUCH AS YOU DID.
I THOUGHT I COULD LOCATE THE SOURCE OF THE FEELING, DOCTOR.
THEN I REALIZED...
WHAT HAVE I DONE?
I JUST KILLED BUTCH.
MY FAITHFUL LITTLE DOG.
I NEED MUCH STRONGER MEDICINE, DOCTOR ROGERS.
WHEN DO I GO BACK TO NORMAL?
WHEN DOES THIS WEAR OFF?
WHAT'S HAPPENING TO ME?
EXCEPT--
--WHAT IF BUTCH IS ALIVE AS WELL AS DEAD?
WHY NOT?
Hm.
IT'S NOT THE SAME.
YOU REMEMBER THE GOVERNOR FROM TV, DON'T YOU, ALLEN?
GOVERNOR HARLEY.

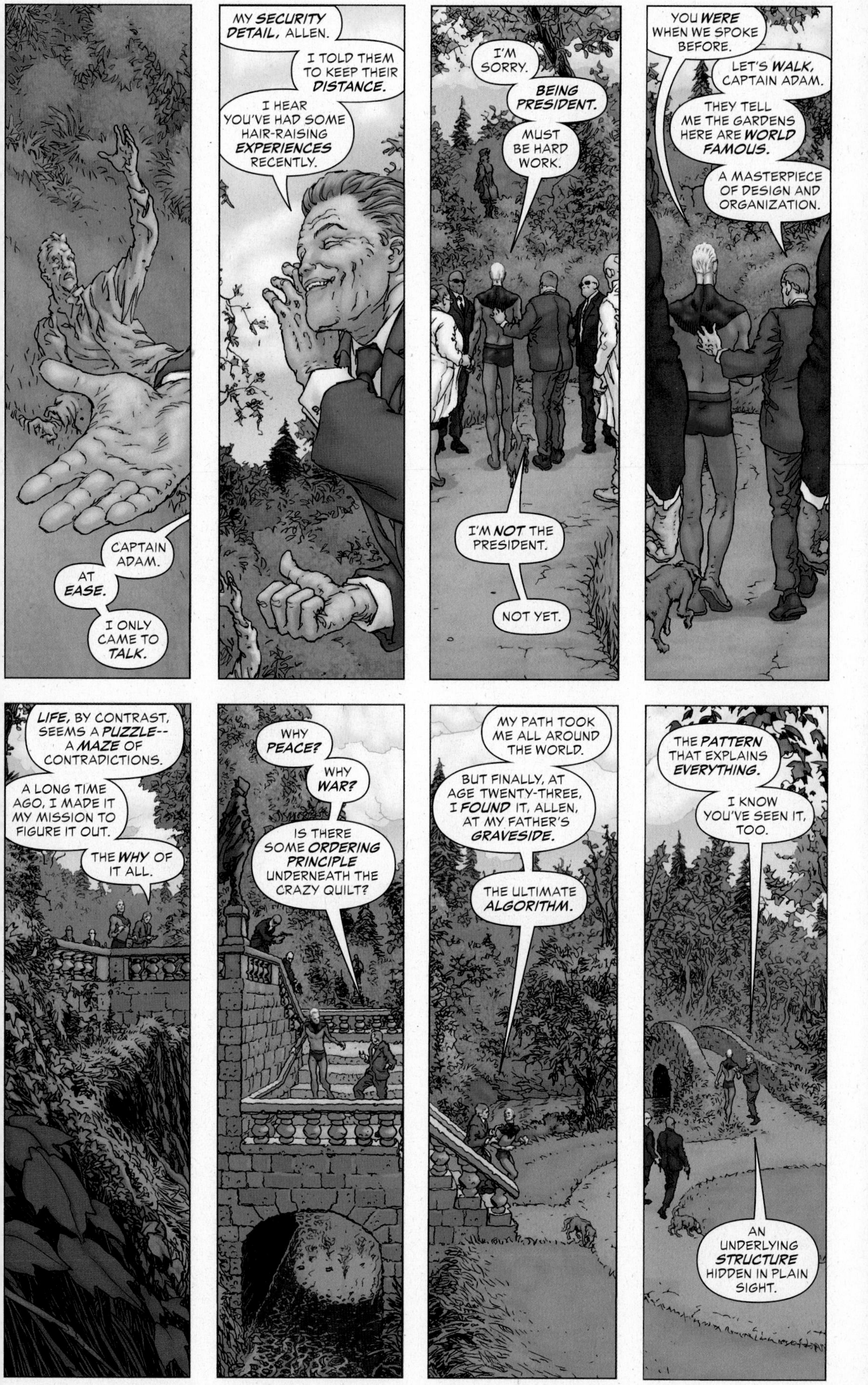
CAPTAIN ADAM.
AT EASE.
I ONLY CAME TO TALK.
MY SECURITY DETAIL, ALLEN.
I TOLD THEM TO KEEP THEIR DISTANCE.
I HEAR YOU'VE HAD SOME HAIR-RAISING EXPERIENCES RECENTLY.
I'M SORRY.
BEING PRESIDENT.
MUST BE HARD WORK.
I'M NOT THE PRESIDENT.
NOT YET.
YOU WERE WHEN WE SPOKE BEFORE.
LET'S WALK, CAPTAIN ADAM.
THEY TELL ME THE GARDENS HERE ARE WORLD FAMOUS.
A MASTERPIECE OF DESIGN AND ORGANIZATION.
LIFE, BY CONTRAST, SEEMS A PUZZLE-- A MAZE OF CONTRADICTIONS.
A LONG TIME AGO, I MADE IT MY MISSION TO FIGURE IT OUT.
THE WHY OF IT ALL.
WHY PEACE?
WHY WAR?
IS THERE SOME ORDERING PRINCIPLE UNDERNEATH THE CRAZY QUILT?
MY PATH TOOK ME ALL AROUND THE WORLD.
BUT FINALLY, AT AGE TWENTY-THREE, I FOUND IT, ALLEN, AT MY FATHER'S GRAVESIDE.
THE ULTIMATE ALGORITHM.
THE PATTERN THAT EXPLAINS EVERYTHING.
I KNOW YOU'VE SEEN IT, TOO.
AN UNDERLYING STRUCTURE HIDDEN IN PLAIN SIGHT.

WELL, I FOUND I COULD *APPLY* THE ALGORITHM TO *PREDICT* EVENTS-- LONG-TERM BEHAVIOR IN THE *STOCK MARKET.*

THE RISE AND FALL OF STYLES IN *FASHION.*

POLITICS.

AS AN *EXPLODING POPULATION* ROSE TO MEET DWINDLING *RESOURCES,* CIVILIZATION WOULD FRAGMENT INTO *NEO-BARBARISM.*

A NEW *DARK AGES.*

YOU'VE *SEEN* THOSE DEATH CAMP GATES AT HISTORY'S END.

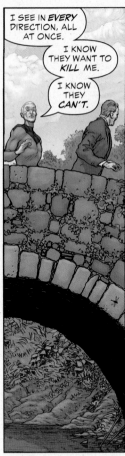

I SEE IN *EVERY* DIRECTION, ALL AT ONCE.

I KNOW THEY WANT TO *KILL* ME.

I KNOW THEY *CAN'T.*

I KNOW HOW TO *SAVE* US.

THEY TELL ME THE *PAST* IS JUST ANOTHER *PLACE* TO YOU, ALLEN.

THE PAST AND FUTURE ARE *PLACES* YOU CAN *WALK* TO.

I'M TRYING TO STAY ON THE STRAIGHT AND NARROW, SIR.

I SHOULD GO *BACK.*

FORWARD IS THE WAY FOR YOU AND ME, ALLEN.

BEAR WITH ME.

SEE, ON REFLECTION, MY PLAN WAS *IMPOSSIBLE.*

UNTIL *YOU* CAME ALONG.

TO SECURE WORLD PEACE, THE PRESIDENT HAS TO BE *SACRIFICED.*

I WANT TO GIVE YOU THE PURPOSE YOU'RE SEARCHING FOR.

I NEED A *SUPER-HERO,* CAPTAIN ATOM.

ADAM.

ATOM.

PERHAPS *THIS* WILL HELP EXPLAIN...

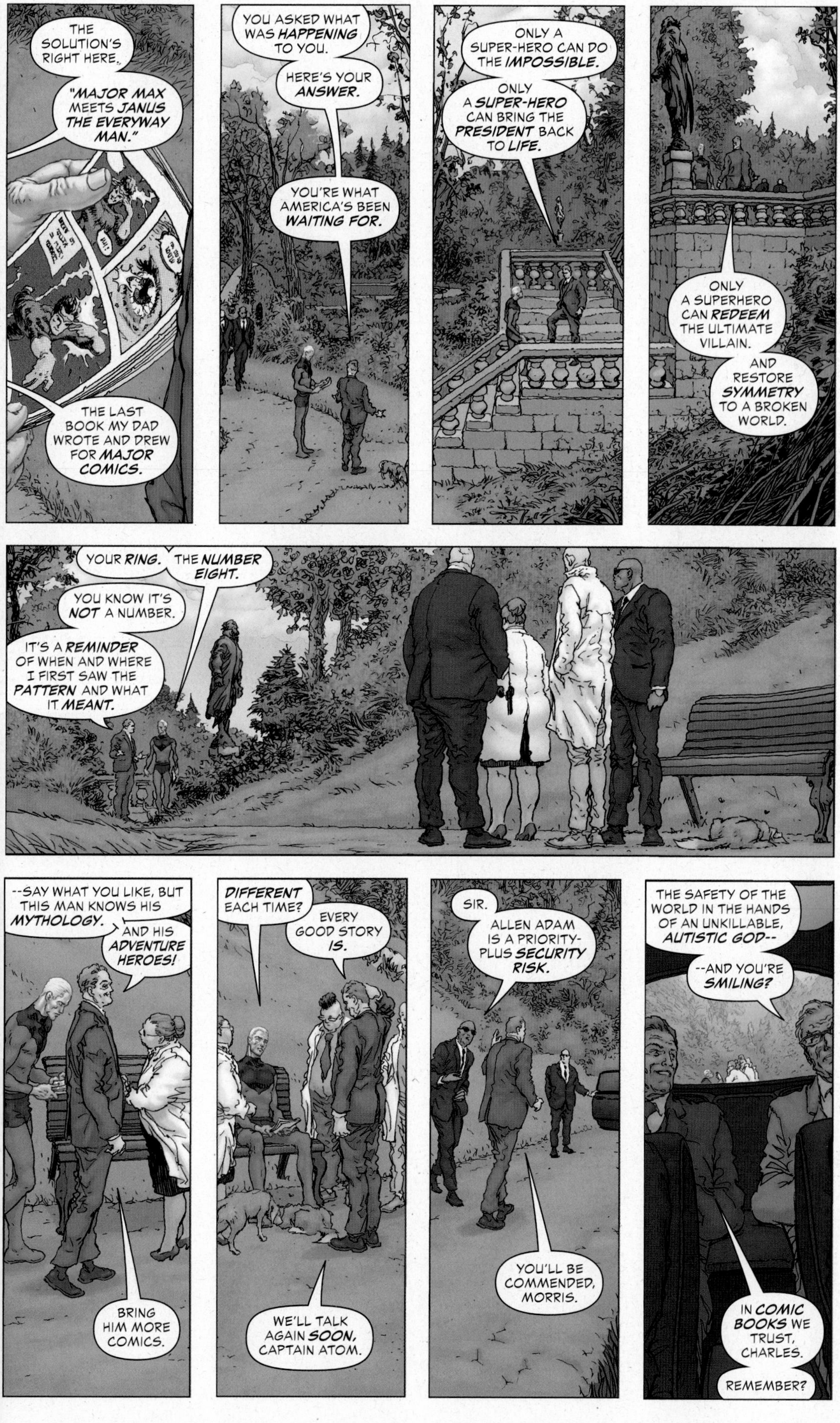
THE SOLUTION'S RIGHT HERE.
"MAJOR MAX MEETS JANUS THE EVERYWAY MAN."
THE LAST BOOK MY DAD WROTE AND DREW FOR MAJOR COMICS.
YOU ASKED WHAT WAS HAPPENING TO YOU.
HERE'S YOUR ANSWER.
YOU'RE WHAT AMERICA'S BEEN WAITING FOR.
ONLY A SUPER-HERO CAN DO THE IMPOSSIBLE.
ONLY A SUPER-HERO CAN BRING THE PRESIDENT BACK TO LIFE.
ONLY A SUPERHERO CAN REDEEM THE ULTIMATE VILLAIN.
AND RESTORE SYMMETRY TO A BROKEN WORLD.
YOUR RING.
THE NUMBER EIGHT.
YOU KNOW IT'S NOT A NUMBER.
IT'S A REMINDER OF WHEN AND WHERE I FIRST SAW THE PATTERN AND WHAT IT MEANT.
--SAY WHAT YOU LIKE, BUT THIS MAN KNOWS HIS MYTHOLOGY.
AND HIS ADVENTURE HEROES!
BRING HIM MORE COMICS.
DIFFERENT EACH TIME?
EVERY GOOD STORY IS.
WE'LL TALK AGAIN SOON, CAPTAIN ATOM.
SIR.
ALLEN ADAM IS A PRIORITY-PLUS SECURITY RISK.
YOU'LL BE COMMENDED, MORRIS.
THE SAFETY OF THE WORLD IN THE HANDS OF AN UNKILLABLE, AUTISTIC GOD--
--AND YOU'RE SMILING?
IN COMIC BOOKS WE TRUST, CHARLES.
REMEMBER?

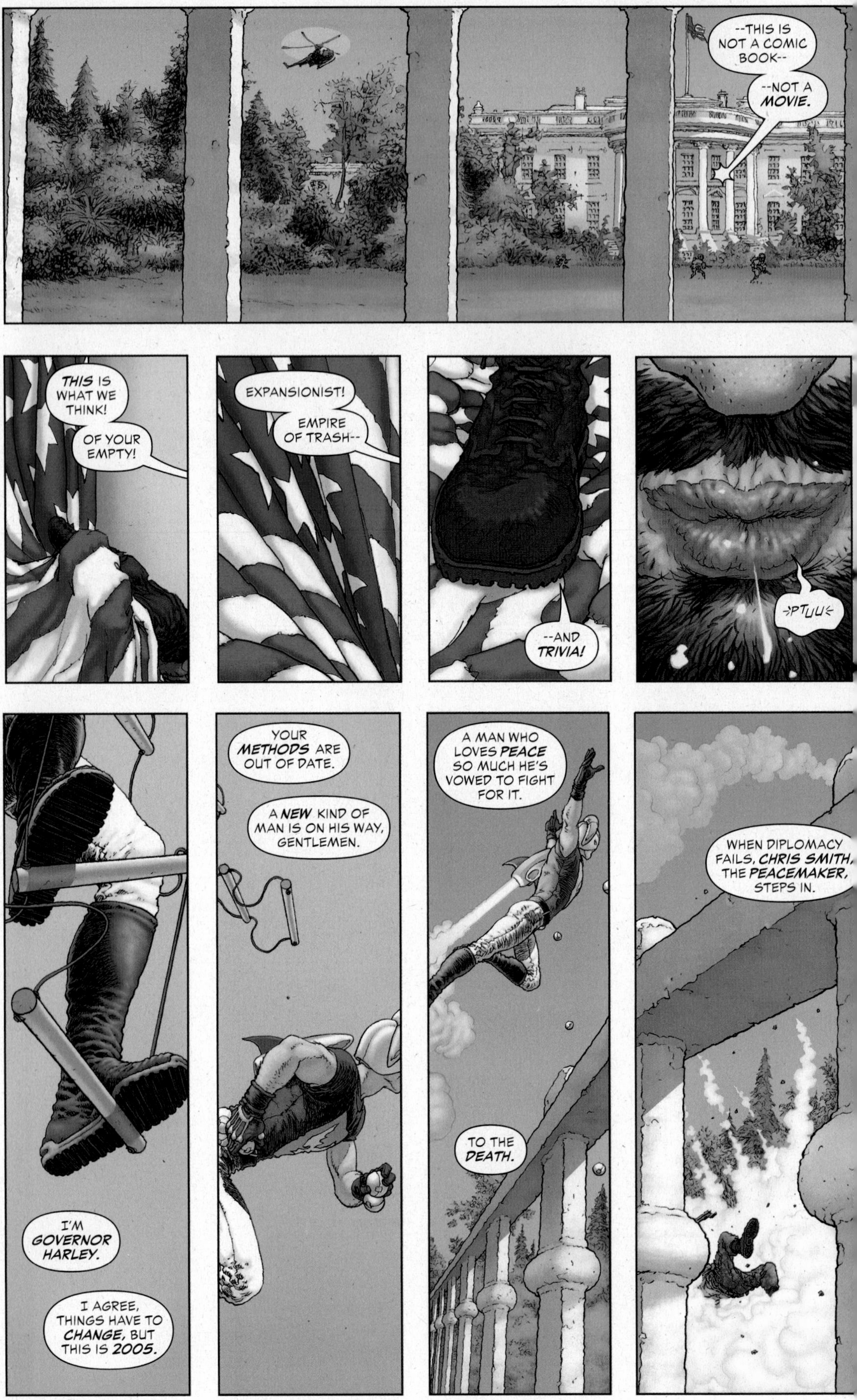
--THIS IS NOT A COMIC BOOK--
--NOT A MOVIE.
THIS IS WHAT WE THINK!
OF YOUR EMPTY!
EXPANSIONIST!
EMPIRE OF TRASH--
--AND TRIVIA!
PTUU
I'M GOVERNOR HARLEY.
I AGREE, THINGS HAVE TO CHANGE, BUT THIS IS 2005.
YOUR METHODS ARE OUT OF DATE.
A NEW KIND OF MAN IS ON HIS WAY, GENTLEMEN.
A MAN WHO LOVES PEACE SO MUCH HE'S VOWED TO FIGHT FOR IT.
TO THE DEATH.
WHEN DIPLOMACY FAILS, CHRIS SMITH, THE PEACEMAKER, STEPS IN.

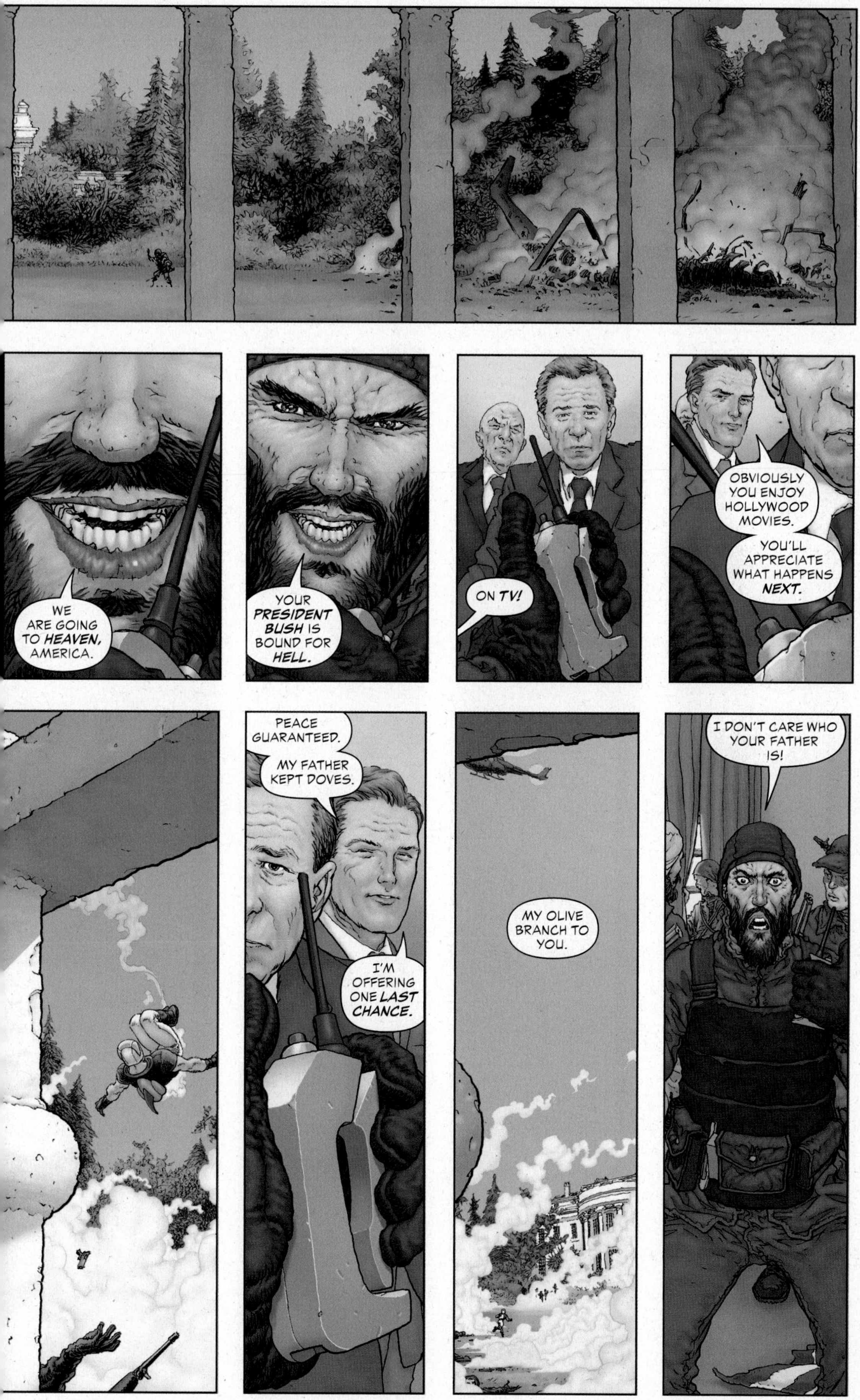
WE ARE GOING TO HEAVEN, AMERICA.
YOUR PRESIDENT BUSH IS BOUND FOR HELL.
ON TV!
OBVIOUSLY YOU ENJOY HOLLYWOOD MOVIES.
YOU'LL APPRECIATE WHAT HAPPENS NEXT.
PEACE GUARANTEED.
MY FATHER KEPT DOVES.
I'M OFFERING ONE LAST CHANCE.
MY OLIVE BRANCH TO YOU.
I DON'T CARE WHO YOUR FATHER IS!

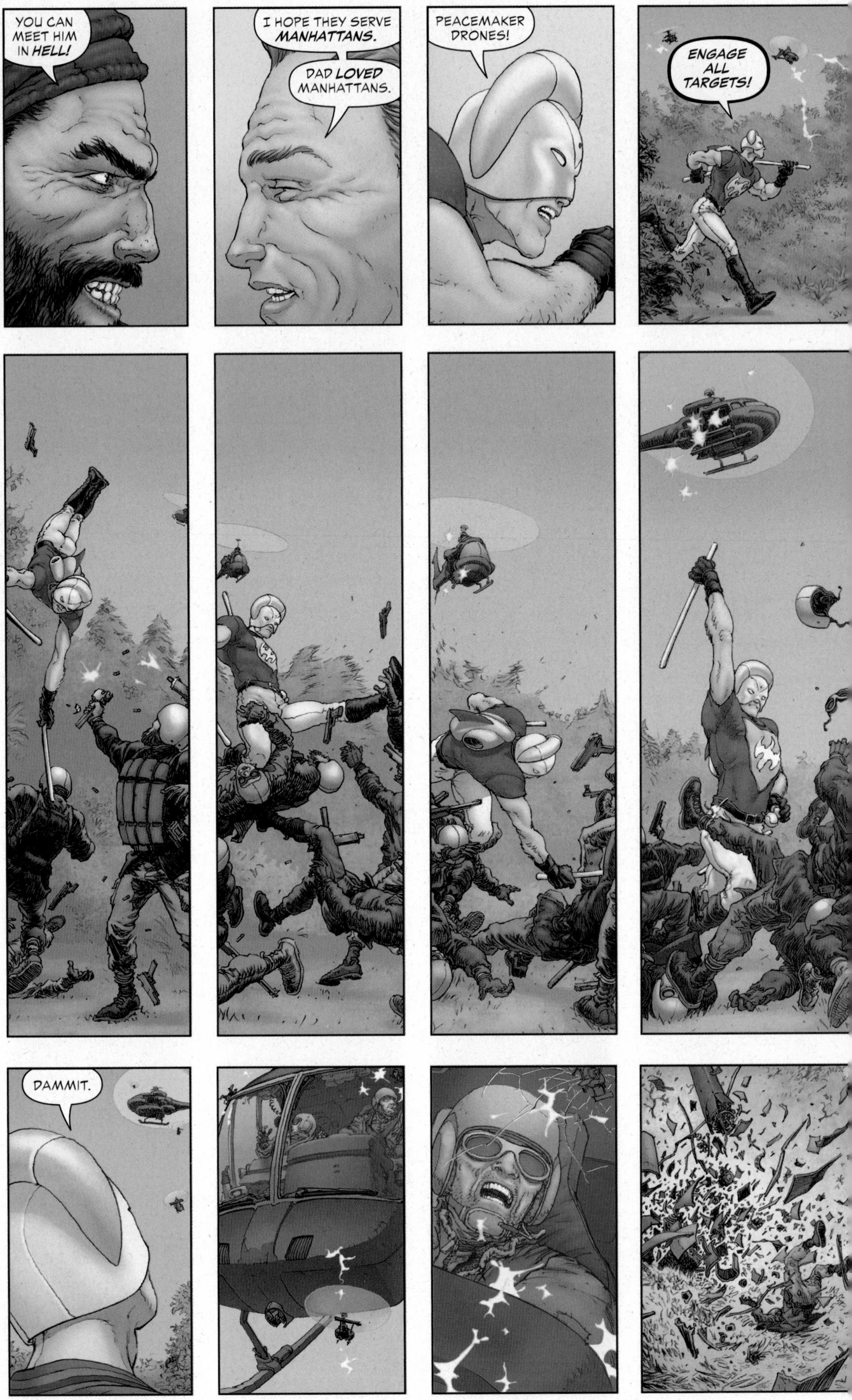
YOU CAN MEET HIM IN HELL!
I HOPE THEY SERVE MANHATTANS.
DAD LOVED MANHATTANS.
PEACEMAKER DRONES!
ENGAGE ALL TARGETS!
DAMMIT.

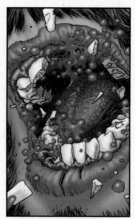

CASUALTIES?

MUST TRY *HARDER* NEXT TIME.

PEACEMAKER?

SOON THERE WILL BE MORE *JUST LIKE HIM.*

YOUR WORLD HAS COME TO AN END TODAY.

YOU AND YOUR KIND ARE *FINISHED.*

DONE WITH.

THANKS TO *YOU.*

YOU'RE A STRONG MAN, CHRIS.

THE DRUG IS *MUCH STRONGER.*

IT *DESTROYS* YOUR RESISTANCE.

IT CREEPS UP ON YOU.

I'LL ASK THE QUESTION *AGAIN.*

WHY?

SUVV

SUVVA WORLL

FROM WHOM?

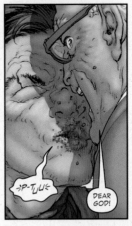

⇒P-T∪∪⇐

DEAR GOD!

HE'S *LOOSE!*

HE--

BANG!

GT

--I ASKED HIM THE *REAL* REASON HE'D CHOSEN TO *BECOME* THE SACRIFICIAL VICTIM.

"I DESERVE IT," HE SAID.

"LET THE PUNISHMENT FIT THE CRIME."

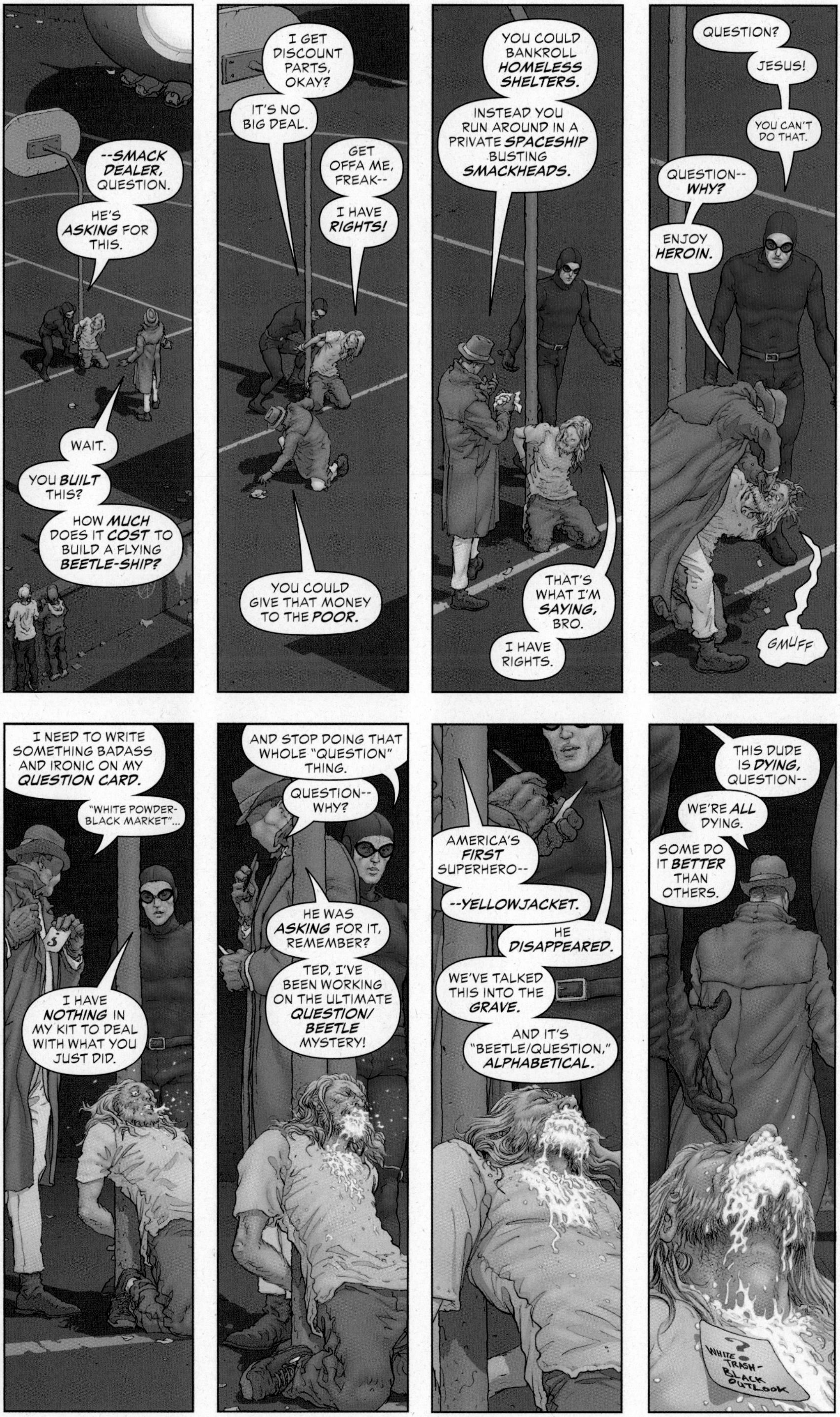
--SMACK DEALER, QUESTION.
HE'S ASKING FOR THIS.
WAIT.
YOU BUILT THIS?
HOW MUCH DOES IT COST TO BUILD A FLYING BEETLE-SHIP?
I GET DISCOUNT PARTS, OKAY?
IT'S NO BIG DEAL.
GET OFFA ME, FREAK--
I HAVE RIGHTS!
YOU COULD GIVE THAT MONEY TO THE POOR.
YOU COULD BANKROLL HOMELESS SHELTERS.
INSTEAD YOU RUN AROUND IN A PRIVATE SPACESHIP BUSTING SMACKHEADS.
THAT'S WHAT I'M SAYING, BRO.
I HAVE RIGHTS.
QUESTION?
JESUS!
YOU CAN'T DO THAT.
QUESTION-- WHY?
ENJOY HEROIN.
GMUFF
I NEED TO WRITE SOMETHING BADASS AND IRONIC ON MY QUESTION CARD.
"WHITE POWDER- BLACK MARKET"...
I HAVE NOTHING IN MY KIT TO DEAL WITH WHAT YOU JUST DID.
AND STOP DOING THAT WHOLE "QUESTION" THING.
QUESTION-- WHY?
HE WAS ASKING FOR IT, REMEMBER?
TED, I'VE BEEN WORKING ON THE ULTIMATE QUESTION/ BEETLE MYSTERY!
AMERICA'S FIRST SUPERHERO--
--YELLOWJACKET.
HE DISAPPEARED.
WE'VE TALKED THIS INTO THE GRAVE.
AND IT'S "BEETLE/QUESTION," ALPHABETICAL.
THIS DUDE IS DYING, QUESTION--
WE'RE ALL DYING.
SOME DO IT BETTER THAN OTHERS.
? WHITE TRASH- BLACK OUTLOOK

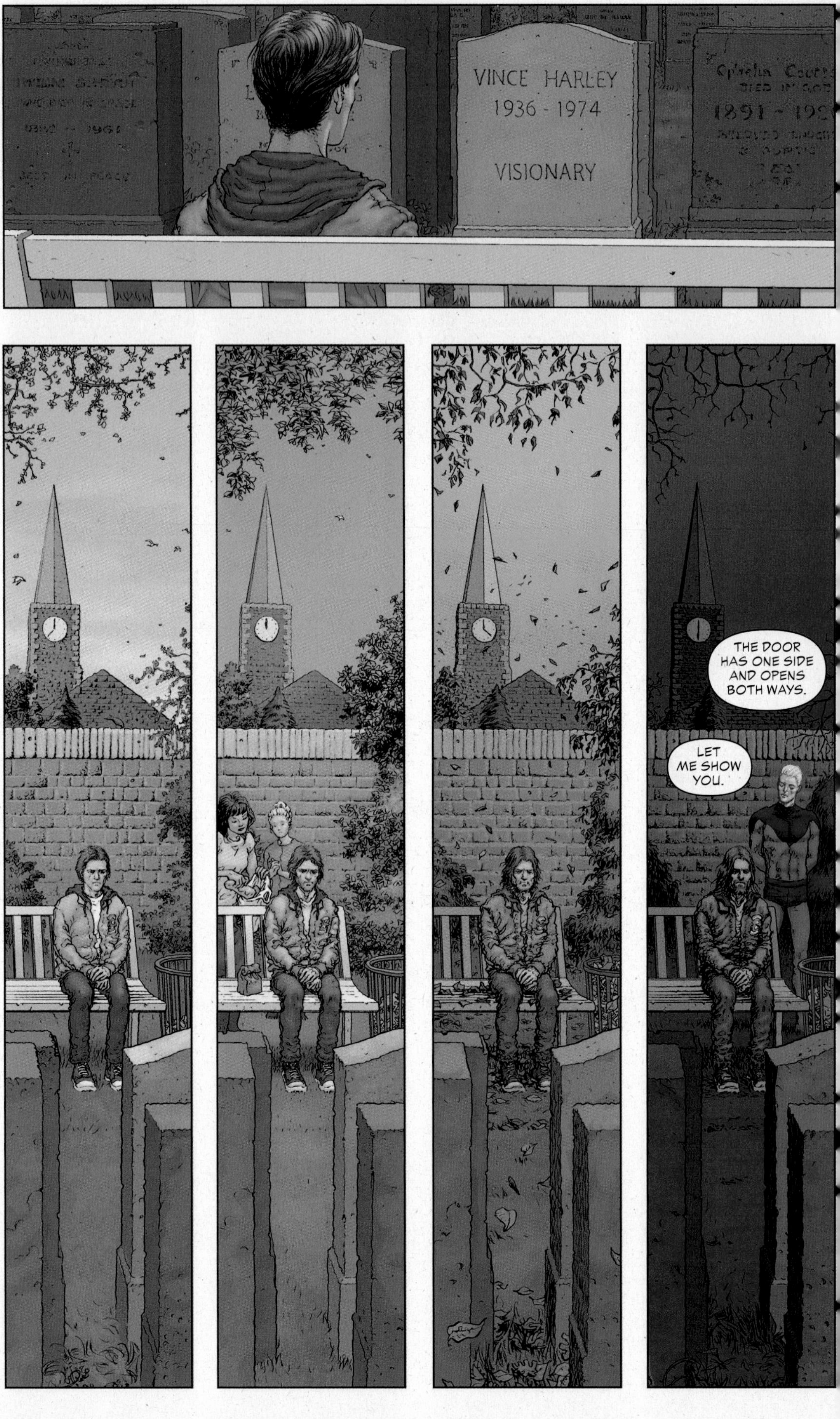
VINCE HARLEY
1936 - 1974
VISIONARY
THE DOOR HAS ONE SIDE AND OPENS BOTH WAYS.
LET ME SHOW YOU.

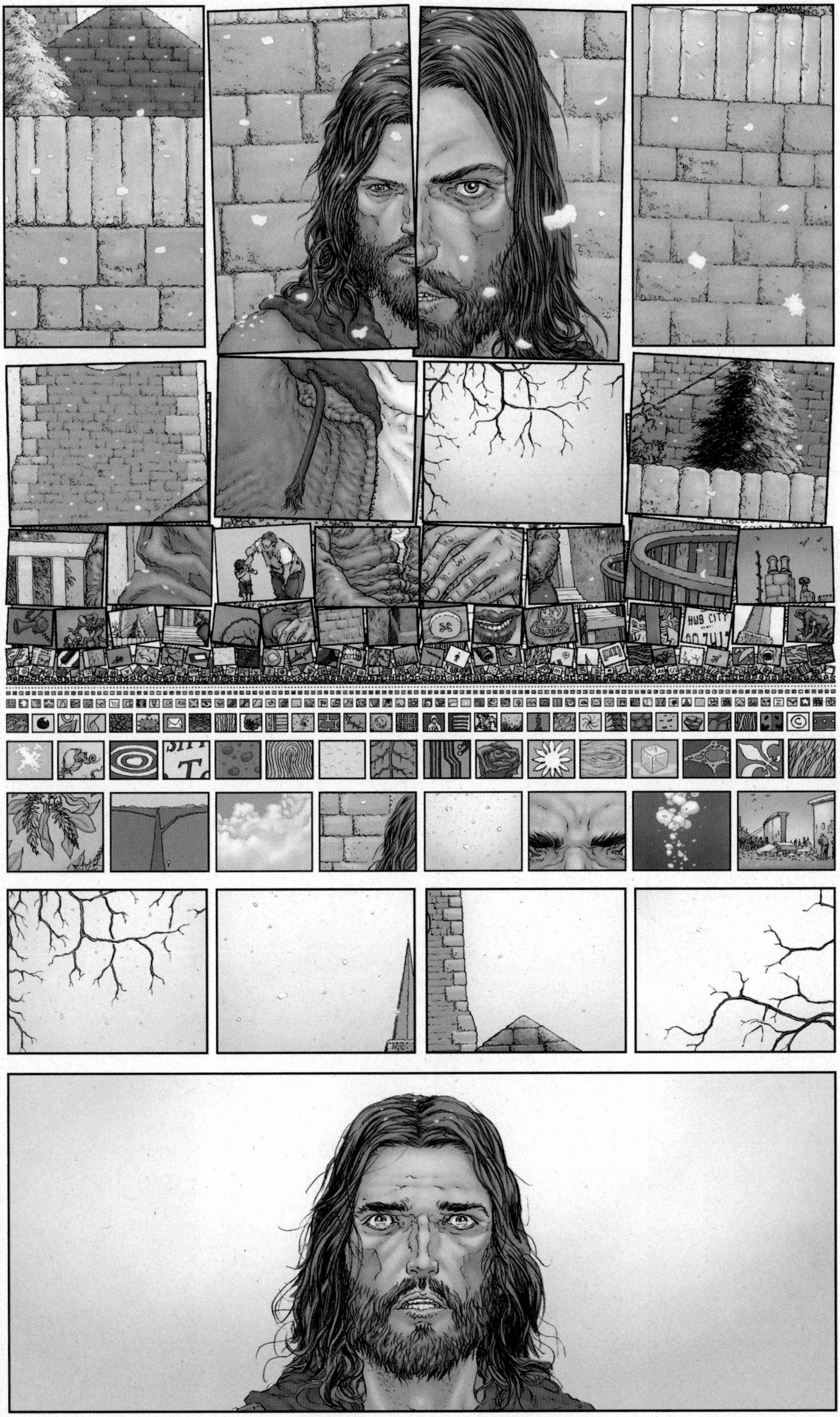
HUB CITY

IT'S SO OBVIOUS.

THE ANSWER IS STARING US IN THE FACE.

YELLOWJACKET IS NO OSI-SPONSORED COLD WAR SUPER-AGENT LIKE DAN GARRETT--

--HE'S ONE OF US!

AN ORDINARY CITIZEN, SICKENED BY TOP-DOWN HYPOCRISY FROM NIXON TO CITY HALL!

THEY CALL HIM DANGEROUS AND DERANGED!

I CALL HIM MR. 1970s AMERICA.

A NEW BREED IS ON ITS WAY, AND THEY'RE MAD AS HELL.

THEY SEE THINGS DIFFERENTLY.

THEY'VE HAD ENOUGH OF ANARCHY ON OUR STREETS.

THEY'RE PREPARED TO TAKE RESPONSIBILITY FOR THEIR COMMUNITIES.

MYSTERY MAN SMASHES DRUG RING

MYSTERY MAN WHO IS

MASKED HERO

HERO IS YELLOWJA

WHO IS YELLOW

AND GOD HELP US ALL.

THEY DON'T MIND TAKING THE LAW INTO THEIR OWN HANDS, EITHER.

I'M WALTER WYLIE, WWB.

I LEAVE YOU WITH THE DREAM OF A COUNTRY THAT MIGHT HAVE BEEN, IN THE WORDS OF JOHN F. KENNEDY.

HE SAID, "WHAT KIND OF PEACE DO I MEAN AND WHAT KIND OF PEACE DO WE SEEK?"

"NOT A PAX AMERICANA ENFORCED ON THE WORLD BY AMERICAN WEAPONS OF WAR.

"NOT THE PEACE OF THE GRAVE OR THE SECURITY OF THE SLAVE."

"I AM TALKING ABOUT GENUINE PEACE."

FORGOT MY KEY, KID.

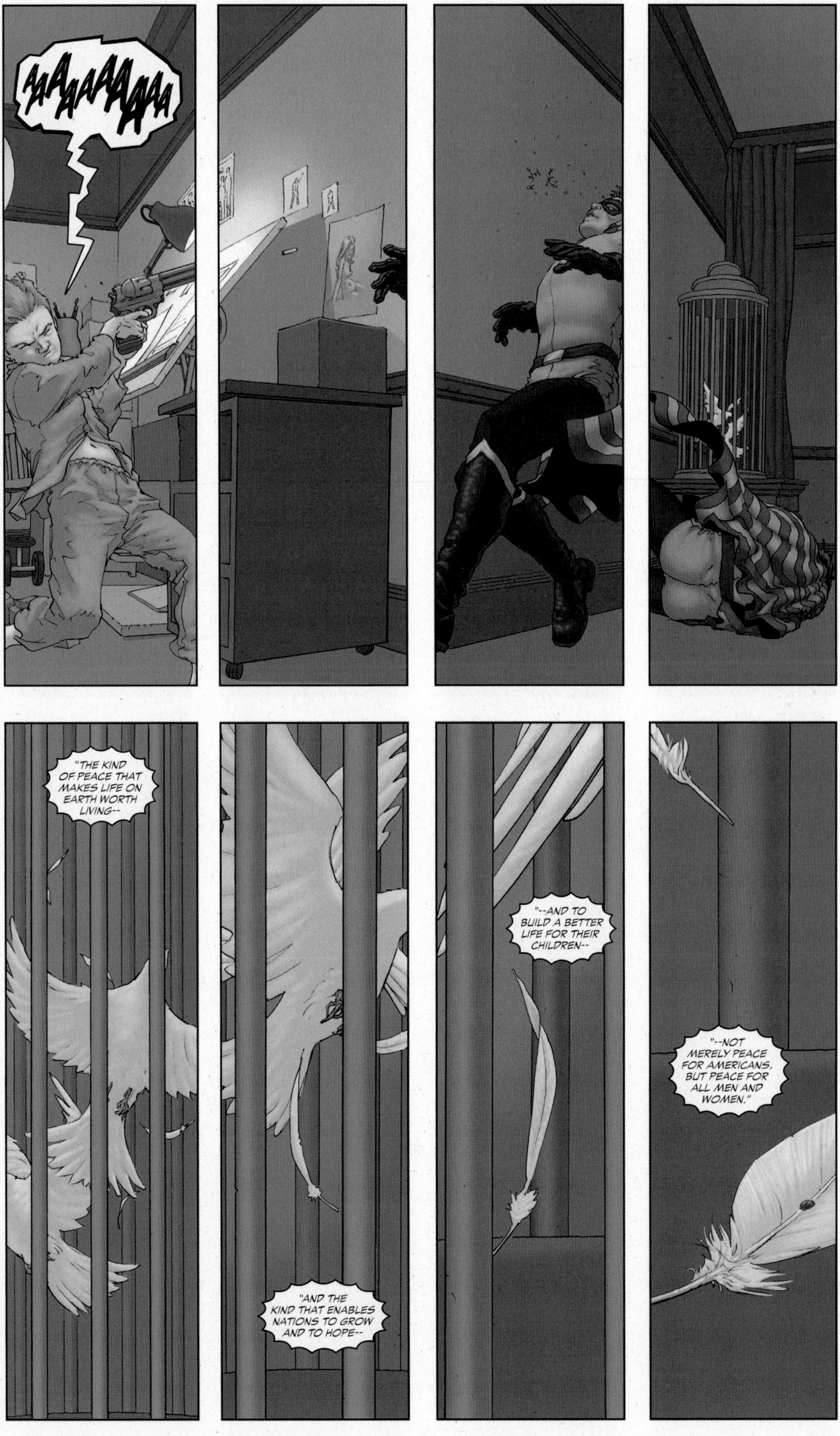
AAAAAAAAAAAA
"THE KIND OF PEACE THAT MAKES LIFE ON EARTH WORTH LIVING--
"AND THE KIND THAT ENABLES NATIONS TO GROW AND TO HOPE--
"--AND TO BUILD A BETTER LIFE FOR THEIR CHILDREN--
"--NOT MERELY PEACE FOR AMERICANS, BUT PEACE FOR ALL MEN AND WOMEN."

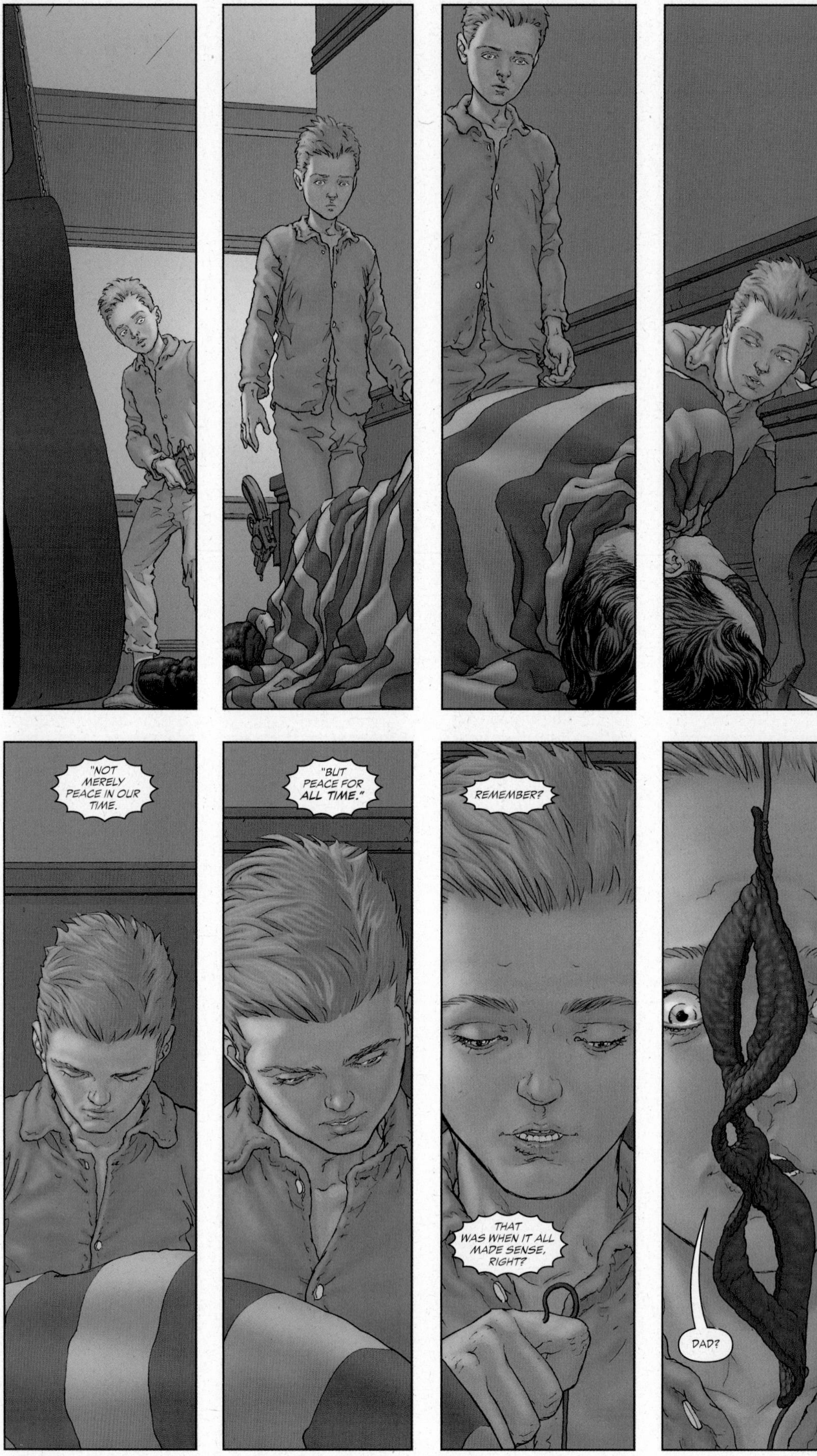
"NOT MERELY PEACE IN OUR TIME.
"BUT PEACE FOR ALL TIME."
REMEMBER?
THAT WAS WHEN IT ALL MADE SENSE, RIGHT?
DAD?

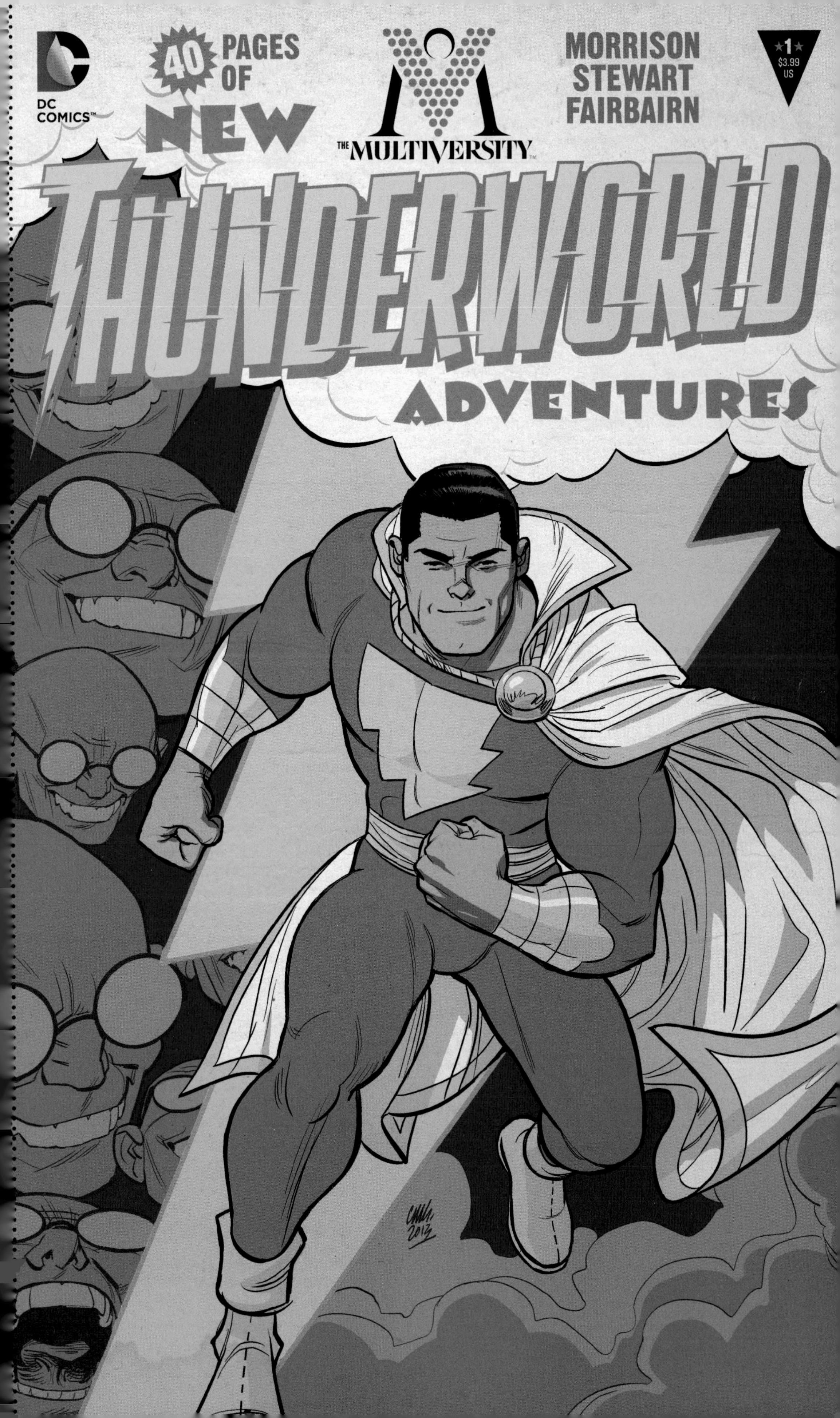
DC COMICS
40 PAGES OF NEW
THE MULTIVERSITY
MORRISON
STEWART
FAIRBAIRN
1
$3.99
US
THUNDERWORLD ADVENTURES

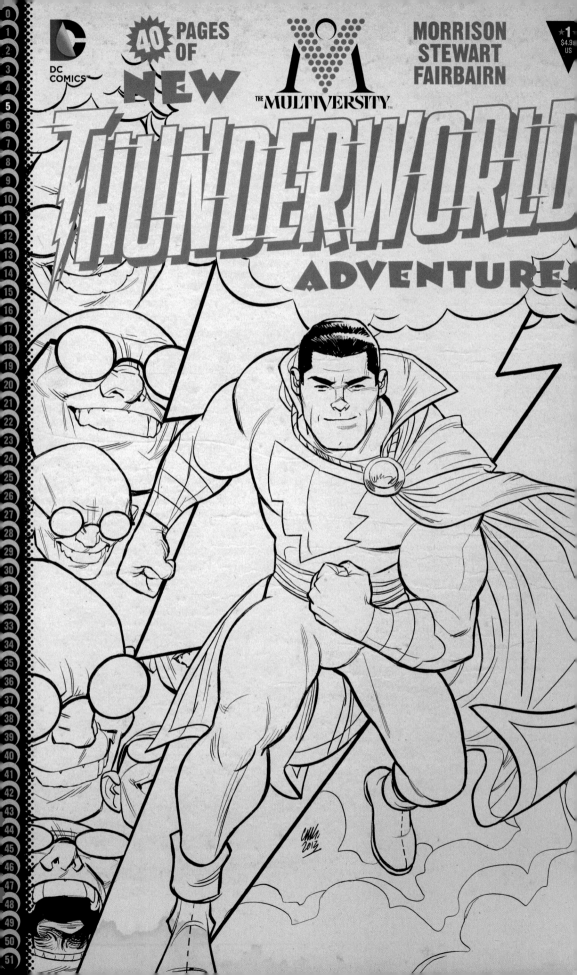

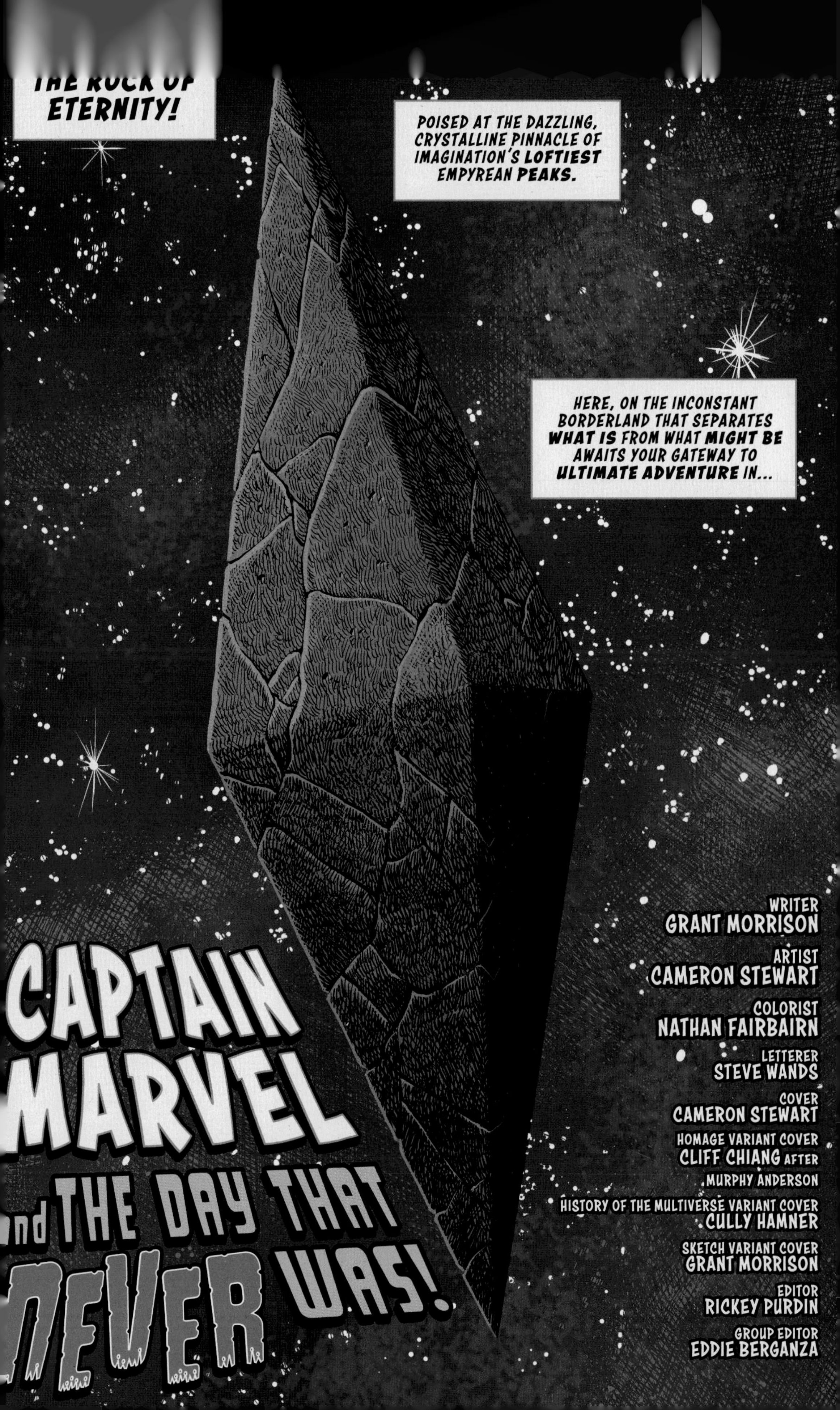
THE ROCK OF ETERNITY!
POISED AT THE DAZZLING, CRYSTALLINE PINNACLE OF IMAGINATION'S LOFTIEST EMPYREAN PEAKS.
HERE, ON THE INCONSTANT BORDERLAND THAT SEPARATES WHAT IS FROM WHAT MIGHT BE AWAITS YOUR GATEWAY TO ULTIMATE ADVENTURE IN...
CAPTAIN MARVEL and THE DAY THAT NEVER WAS!
WRITER GRANT MORRISON
ARTIST CAMERON STEWART
COLORIST NATHAN FAIRBAIRN
LETTERER STEVE WANDS
COVER CAMERON STEWART
HOMAGE VARIANT COVER CLIFF CHIANG AFTER MURPHY ANDERSON
HISTORY OF THE MULTIVERSE VARIANT COVER CULLY HAMNER
SKETCH VARIANT COVER GRANT MORRISON
EDITOR RICKEY PURDIN
GROUP EDITOR EDDIE BERGANZA

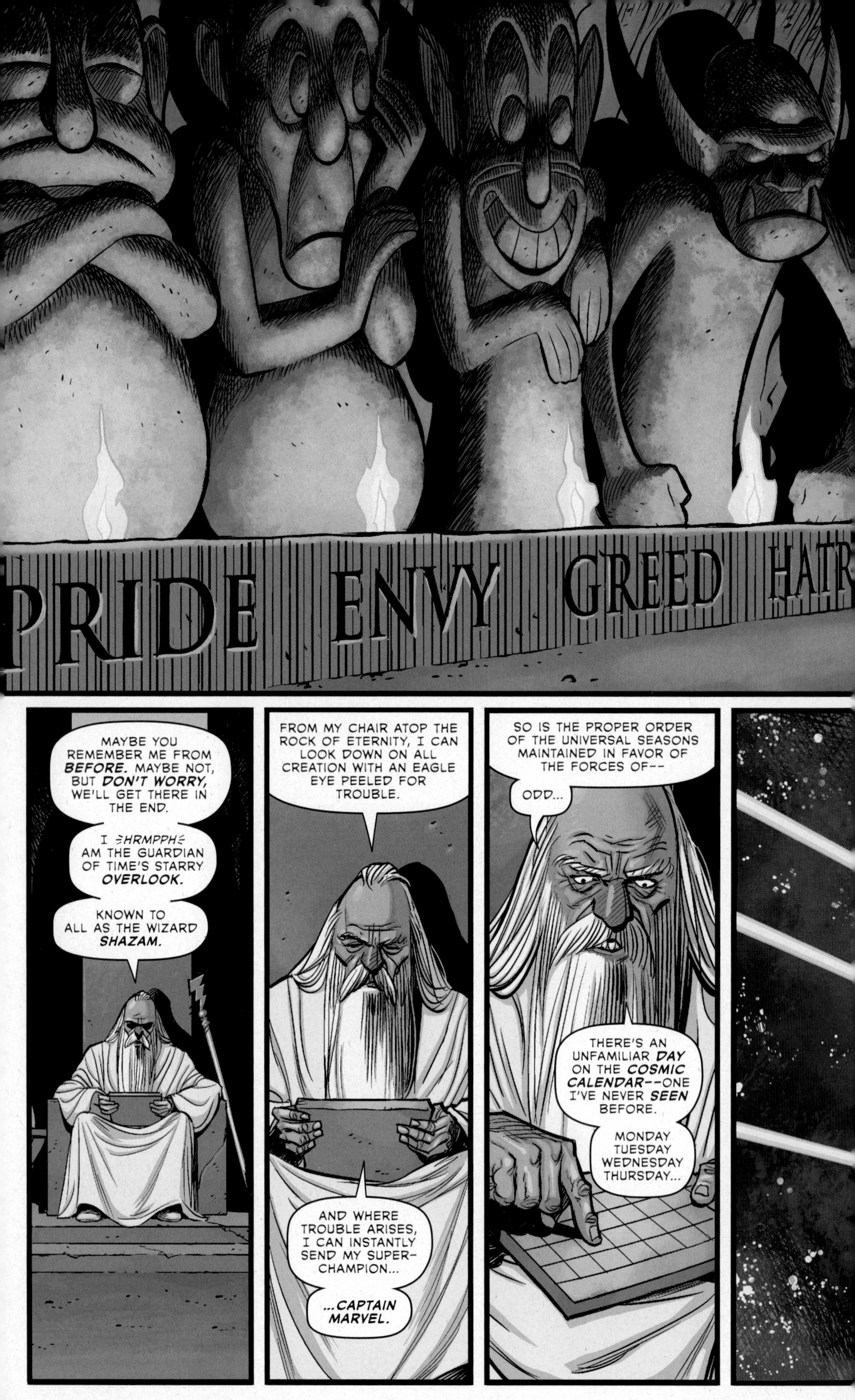
PRIDE
ENVY
GREED
HATR
MAYBE YOU REMEMBER ME FROM BEFORE. MAYBE NOT, BUT DON'T WORRY, WE'LL GET THERE IN THE END.
I ≑HRMPPH≑ AM THE GUARDIAN OF TIME'S STARRY OVERLOOK.
KNOWN TO ALL AS THE WIZARD SHAZAM.
FROM MY CHAIR ATOP THE ROCK OF ETERNITY, I CAN LOOK DOWN ON ALL CREATION WITH AN EAGLE EYE PEELED FOR TROUBLE.
AND WHERE TROUBLE ARISES, I CAN INSTANTLY SEND MY SUPER-CHAMPION...
...CAPTAIN MARVEL.
SO IS THE PROPER ORDER OF THE UNIVERSAL SEASONS MAINTAINED IN FAVOR OF THE FORCES OF--
ODD...
THERE'S AN UNFAMILIAR DAY ON THE COSMIC CALENDAR--ONE I'VE NEVER SEEN BEFORE.
MONDAY TUESDAY WEDNESDAY THURSDAY...

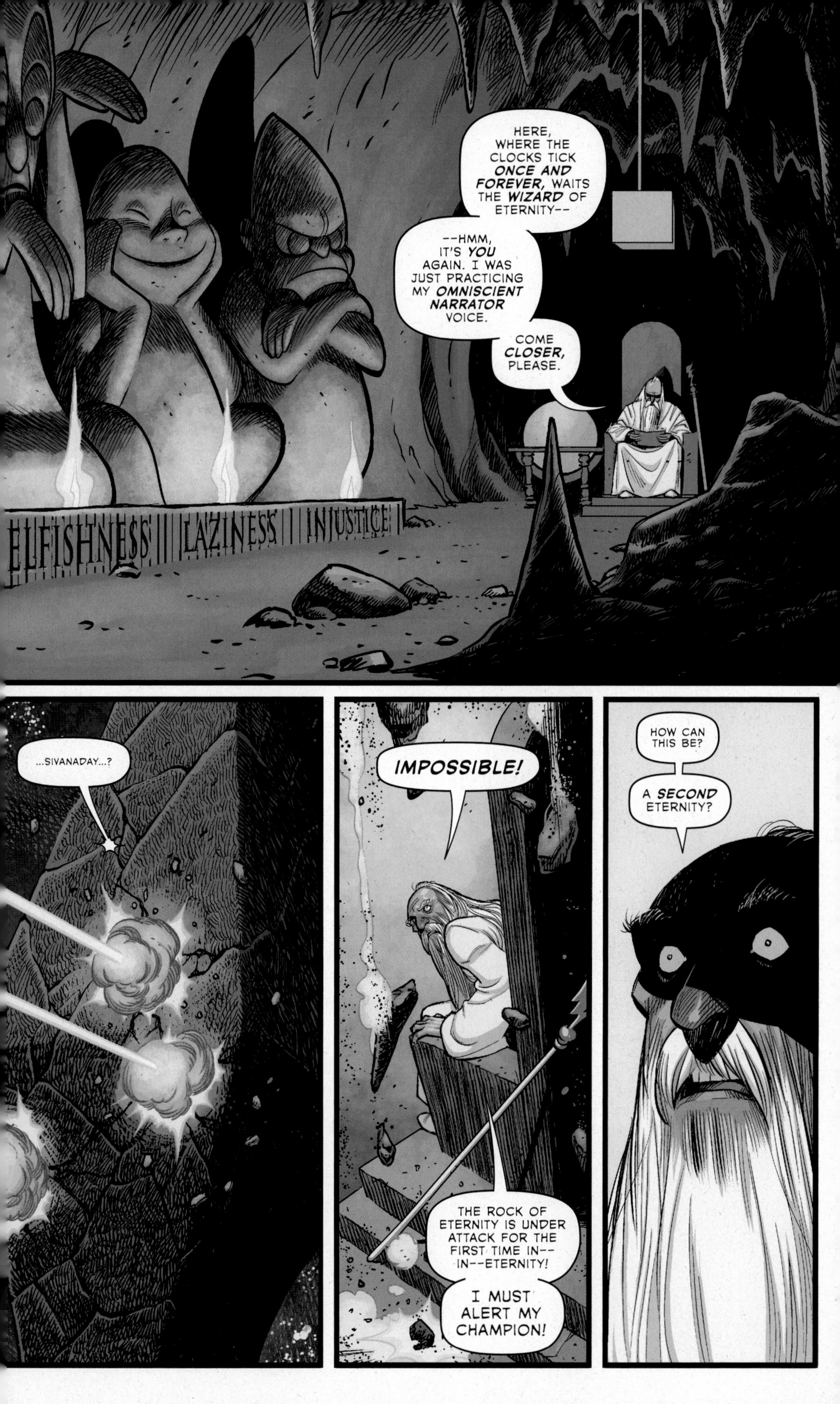
HERE, WHERE THE CLOCKS TICK ONCE AND FOREVER, WAITS THE WIZARD OF ETERNITY--
--HMM, IT'S YOU AGAIN. I WAS JUST PRACTICING MY OMNISCIENT NARRATOR VOICE.
COME CLOSER, PLEASE.
ELFISHNESS
LAZINESS
INJUSTICE
...SIVANADAY...?
IMPOSSIBLE!
THE ROCK OF ETERNITY IS UNDER ATTACK FOR THE FIRST TIME IN--IN--ETERNITY!
I MUST ALERT MY CHAMPION!
HOW CAN THIS BE?
A SECOND ETERNITY?

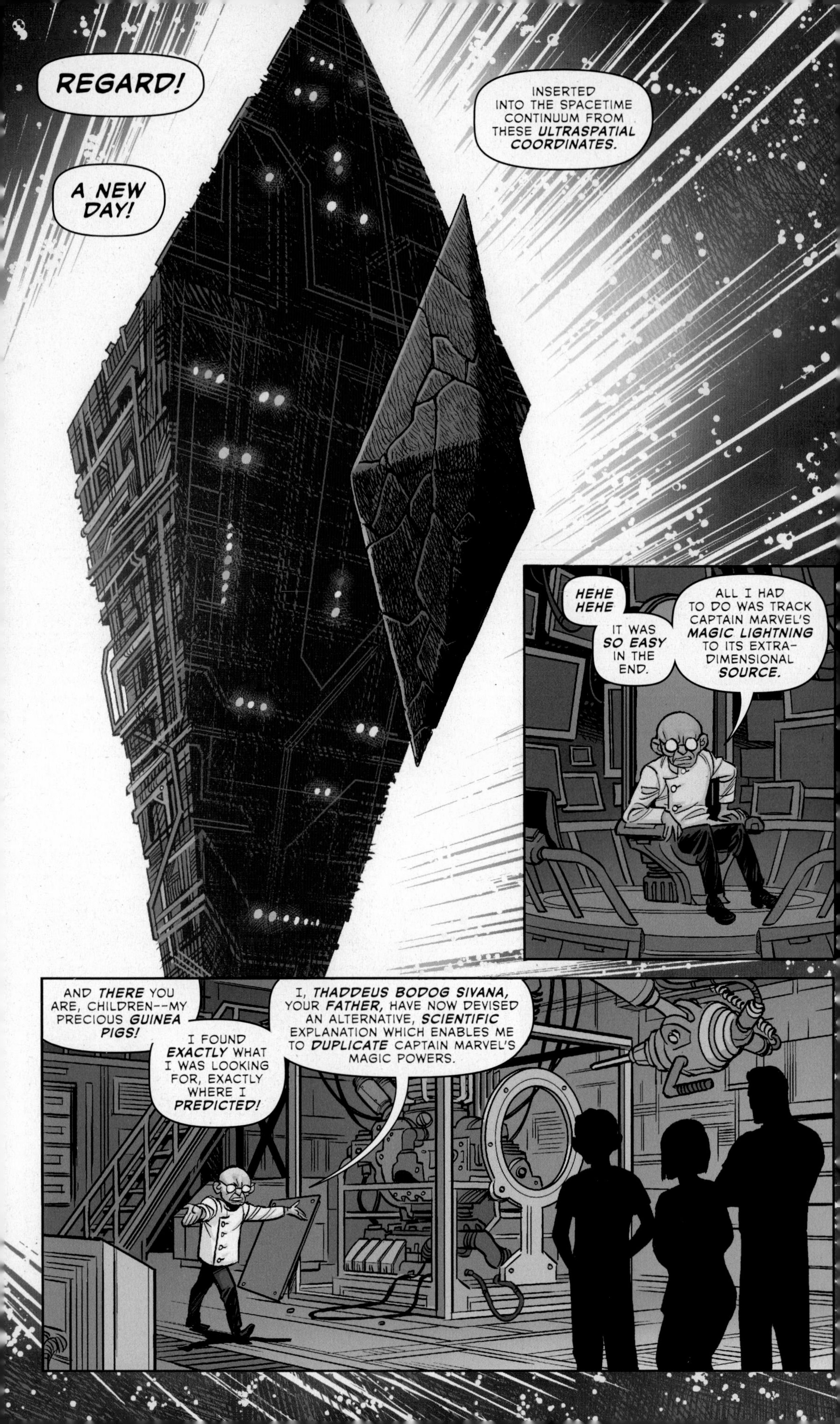
REGARD!
A NEW DAY!
INSERTED INTO THE SPACETIME CONTINUUM FROM THESE ULTRASPATIAL COORDINATES.
HEHE HEHE
IT WAS SO EASY IN THE END.
ALL I HAD TO DO WAS TRACK CAPTAIN MARVEL'S MAGIC LIGHTNING TO ITS EXTRA-DIMENSIONAL SOURCE.
AND THERE YOU ARE, CHILDREN--MY PRECIOUS GUINEA PIGS!
I FOUND EXACTLY WHAT I WAS LOOKING FOR, EXACTLY WHERE I PREDICTED!
I, THADDEUS BODOG SIVANA, YOUR FATHER, HAVE NOW DEVISED AN ALTERNATIVE, SCIENTIFIC EXPLANATION WHICH ENABLES ME TO DUPLICATE CAPTAIN MARVEL'S MAGIC POWERS.

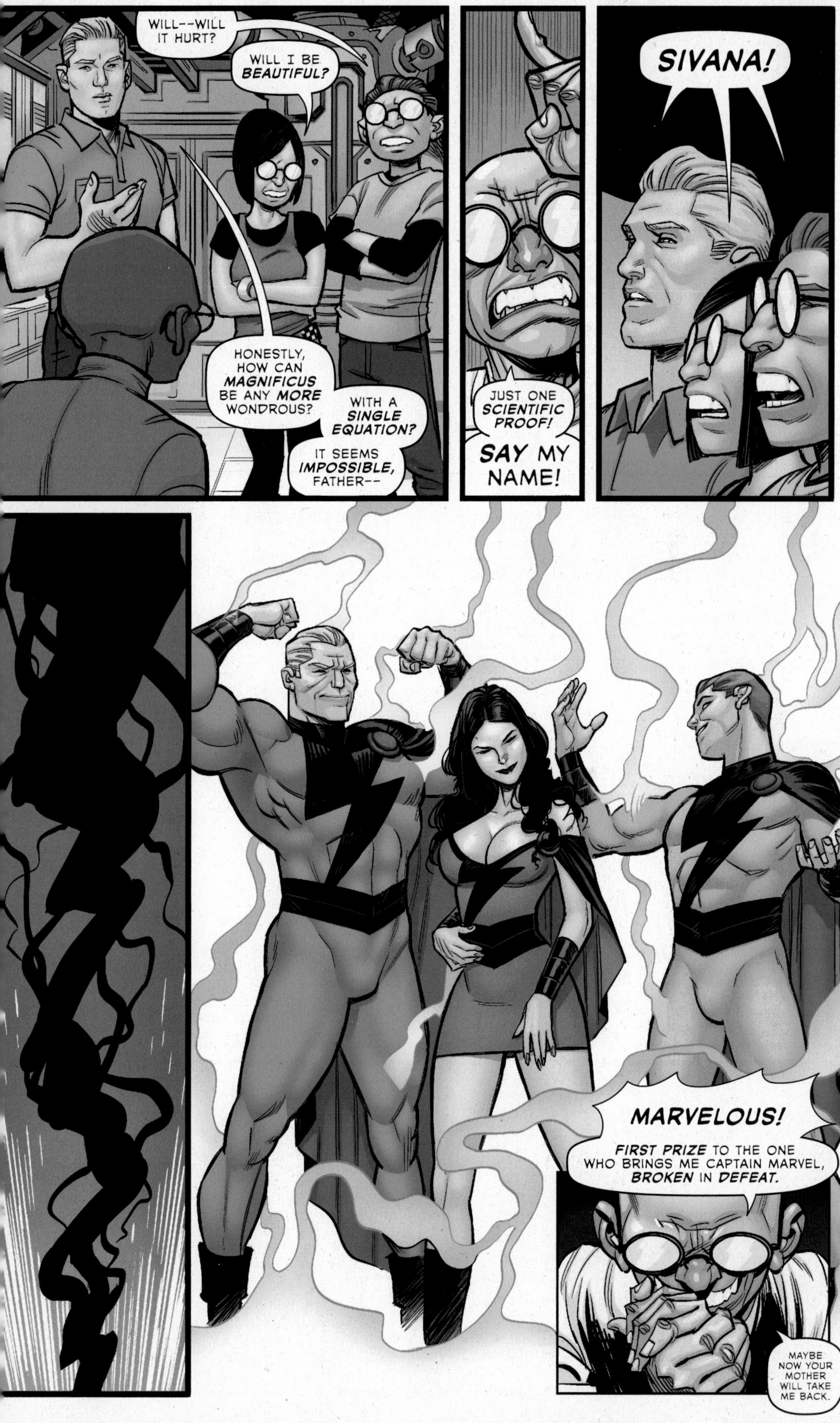

WILL--WILL IT HURT?
WILL I BE BEAUTIFUL?
HONESTLY, HOW CAN MAGNIFICUS BE ANY MORE WONDROUS?
WITH A SINGLE EQUATION?
IT SEEMS IMPOSSIBLE, FATHER--
JUST ONE SCIENTIFIC PROOF!
SAY MY NAME!
SIVANA!
MARVELOUS!
FIRST PRIZE TO THE ONE WHO BRINGS ME CAPTAIN MARVEL, BROKEN IN DEFEAT.
MAYBE NOW YOUR MOTHER WILL TAKE ME BACK.

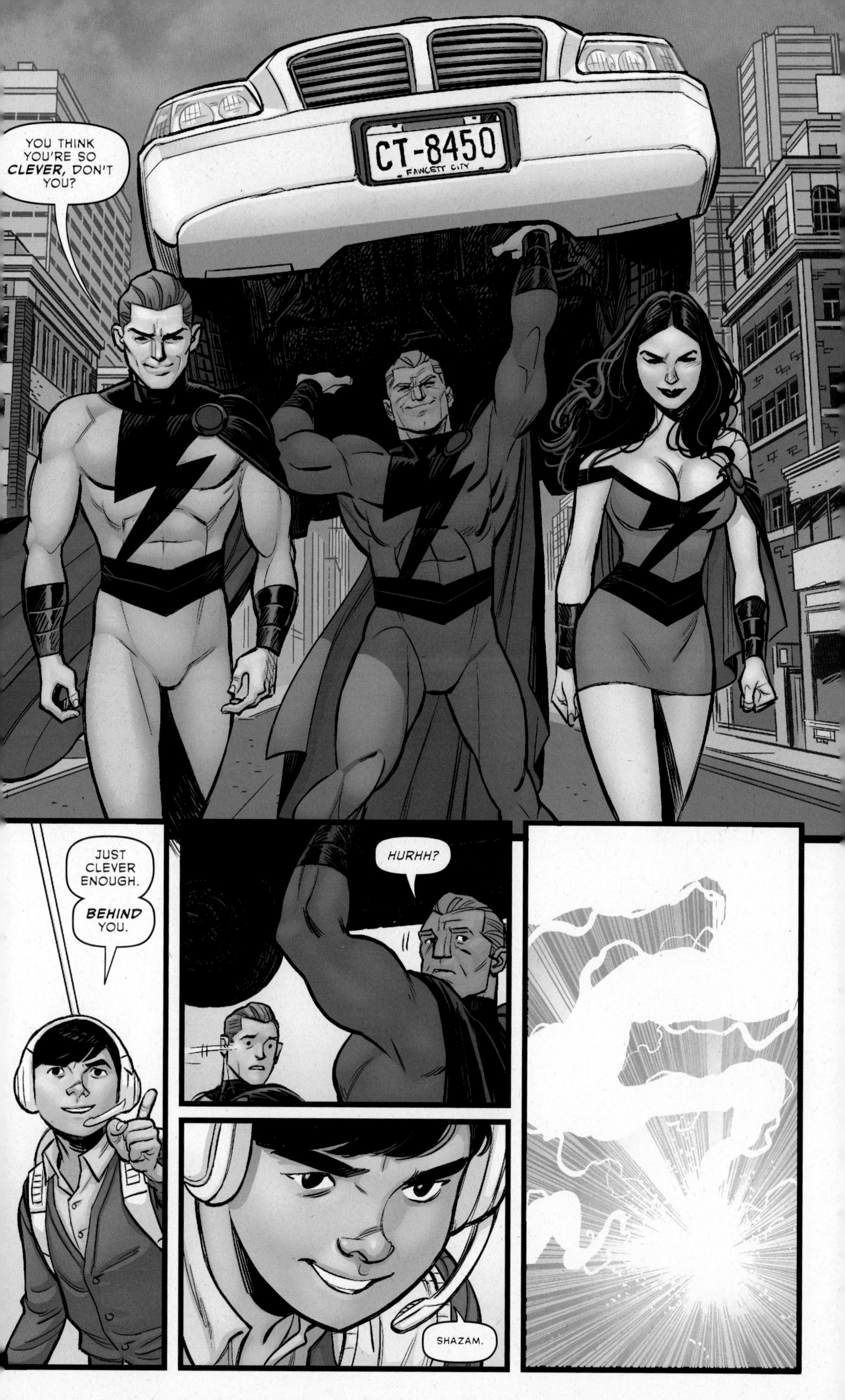
YOU THINK YOU'RE SO CLEVER, DON'T YOU?
CT-8450
FAWCETT CITY
JUST CLEVER ENOUGH.
BEHIND YOU.
HURHH?
SHAZAM.

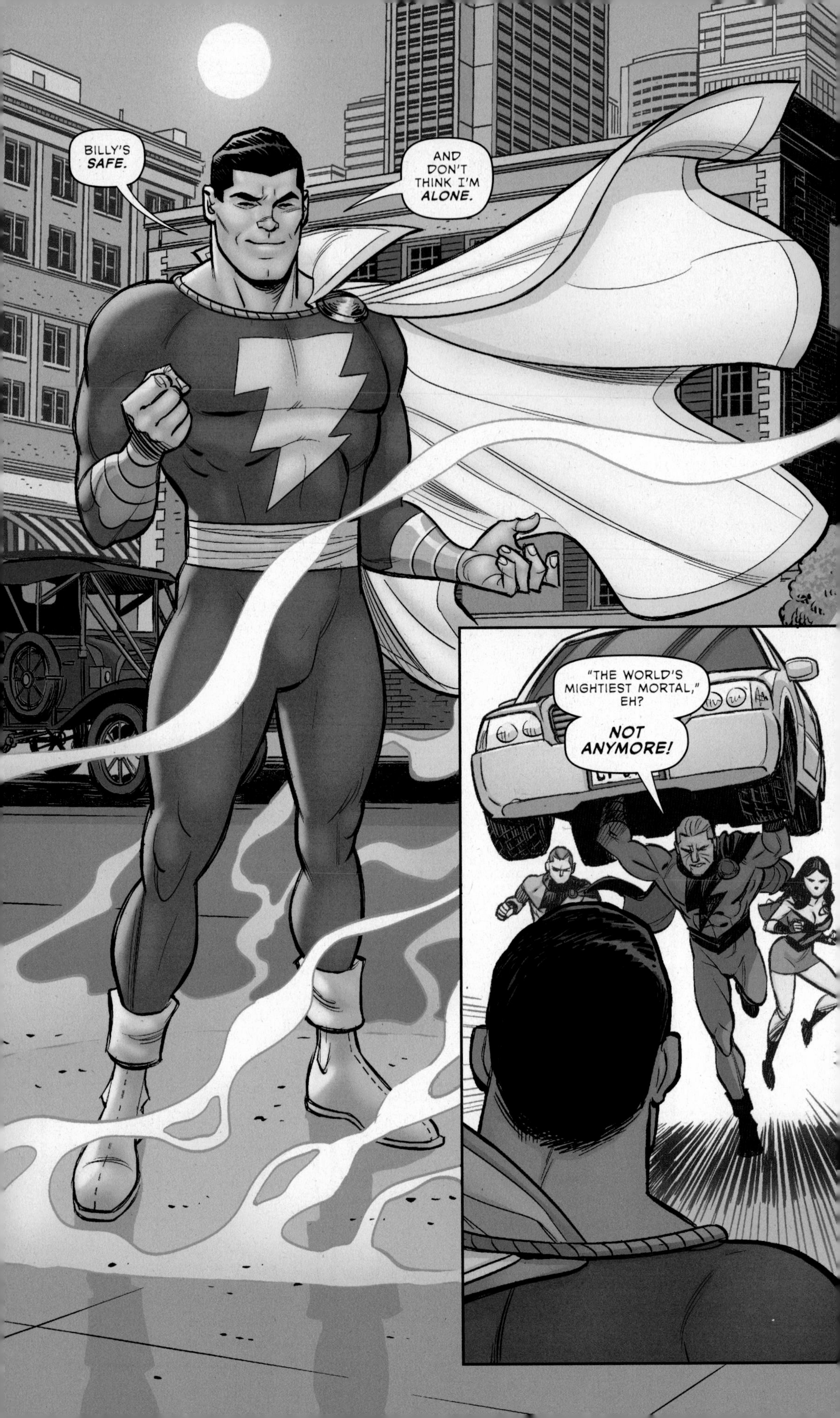
BILLY'S SAFE.
AND DON'T THINK I'M ALONE.
"THE WORLD'S MIGHTIEST MORTAL," EH?
NOT ANYMORE!

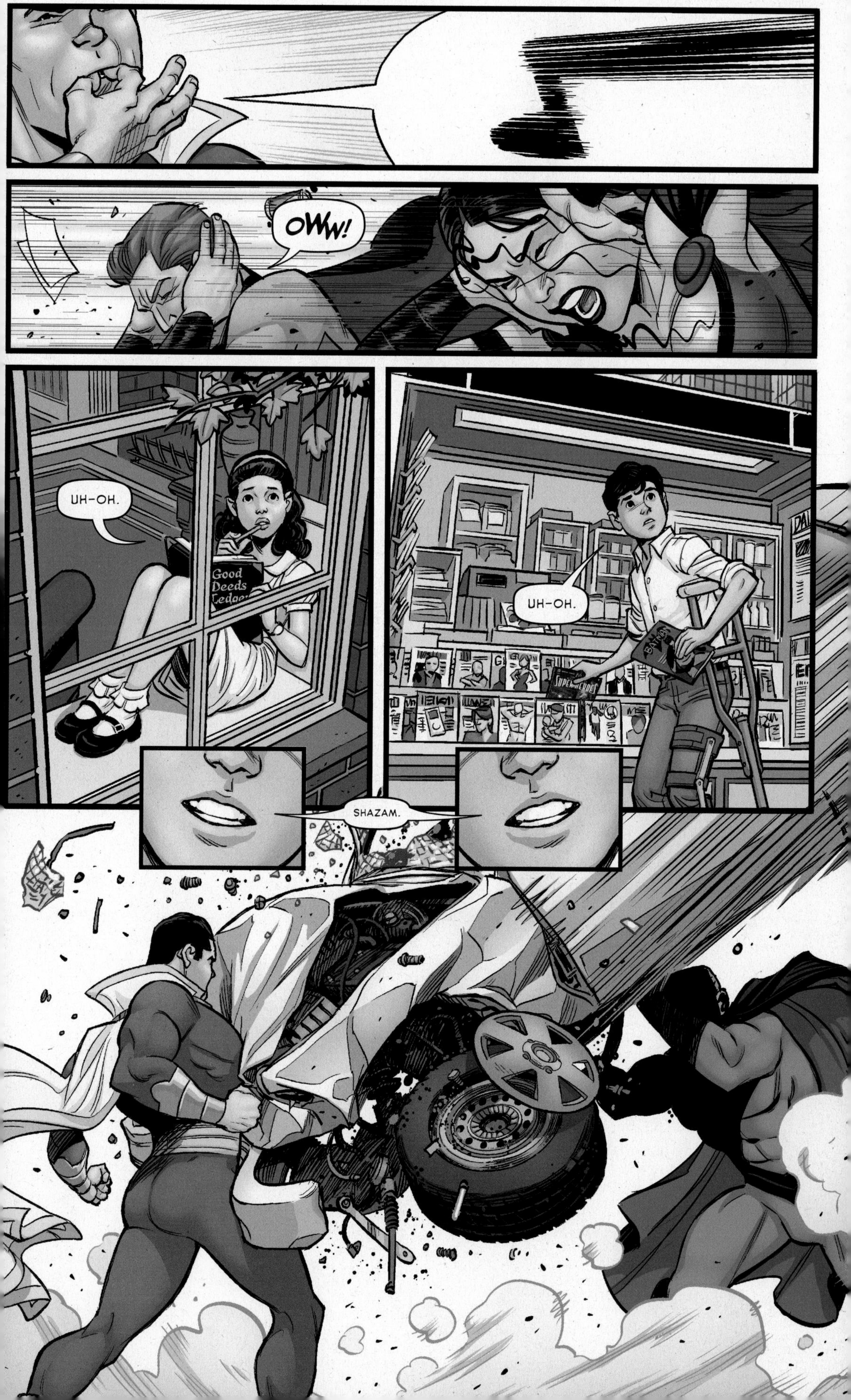
OWW!
UH-OH.
Good Deeds Ledger
UH-OH.
SHAZAM.

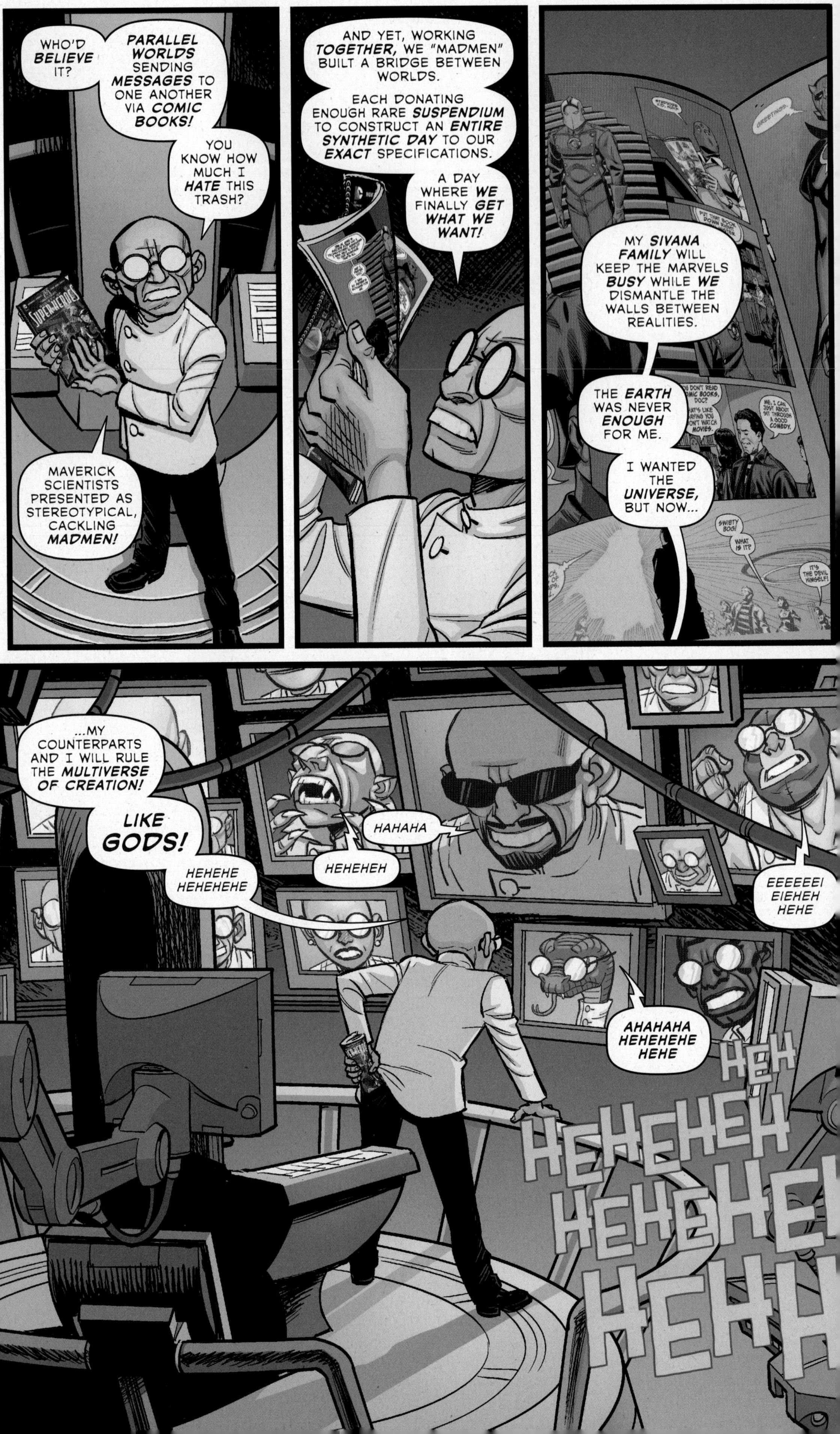

WHO'D BELIEVE IT?
PARALLEL WORLDS SENDING MESSAGES TO ONE ANOTHER VIA COMIC BOOKS!
YOU KNOW HOW MUCH I HATE THIS TRASH?
MAVERICK SCIENTISTS PRESENTED AS STEREOTYPICAL, CACKLING MADMEN!
AND YET, WORKING TOGETHER, WE "MADMEN" BUILT A BRIDGE BETWEEN WORLDS.
EACH DONATING ENOUGH RARE SUSPENDIUM TO CONSTRUCT AN ENTIRE SYNTHETIC DAY TO OUR EXACT SPECIFICATIONS.
A DAY WHERE WE FINALLY GET WHAT WE WANT!
MY SIVANA FAMILY WILL KEEP THE MARVELS BUSY WHILE WE DISMANTLE THE WALLS BETWEEN REALITIES.
THE EARTH WAS NEVER ENOUGH FOR ME.
I WANTED THE UNIVERSE, BUT NOW...
ME, I CAN JUST ABOUT SIT THROUGH A GOOD COMEDY.
IT'S THE DEVIL HIMSELF!
...MY COUNTERPARTS AND I WILL RULE THE MULTIVERSE OF CREATION!
LIKE GODS!
HAHAHA
HEHEHEH
HEHEHE HEHEHEHE
EEEEEEI EIEHEH HEHE
AHAHAHA HEHEHEHE HEHE
HEH
HEHEHEH
HEHEHEH
HEHH

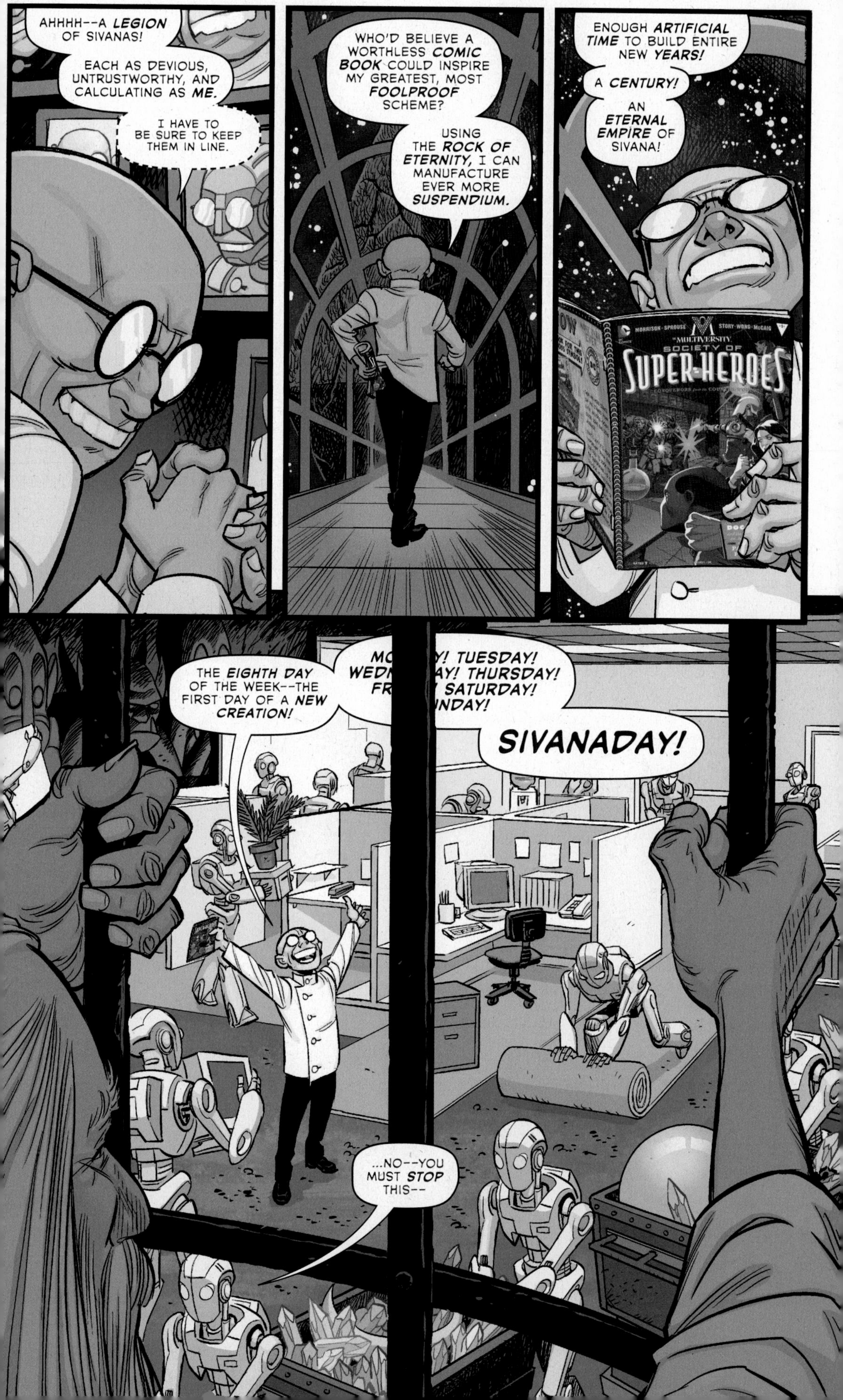
AHHHH--A *LEGION* OF SIVANAS!
EACH AS DEVIOUS, UNTRUSTWORTHY, AND CALCULATING AS *ME.*
I HAVE TO BE SURE TO KEEP THEM IN LINE.
WHO'D BELIEVE A WORTHLESS *COMIC BOOK* COULD INSPIRE MY GREATEST, MOST *FOOLPROOF* SCHEME?
USING THE *ROCK OF ETERNITY,* I CAN MANUFACTURE EVER MORE *SUSPENDIUM.*
ENOUGH *ARTIFICIAL TIME* TO BUILD ENTIRE NEW *YEARS!*
A *CENTURY!*
AN *ETERNAL EMPIRE* OF SIVANA!
MORRISON · SPROUSE
STORY · WONG · McCAIG
THE MULTIVERSITY
SOCIETY OF
SUPER-HEROES
THE *EIGHTH DAY* OF THE WEEK--THE FIRST DAY OF A *NEW CREATION!*
MO Y! TUESDAY! WEDN AY! THURSDAY! FR SATURDAY! NDAY!
SIVANADAY!
...NO--YOU MUST *STOP* THIS--

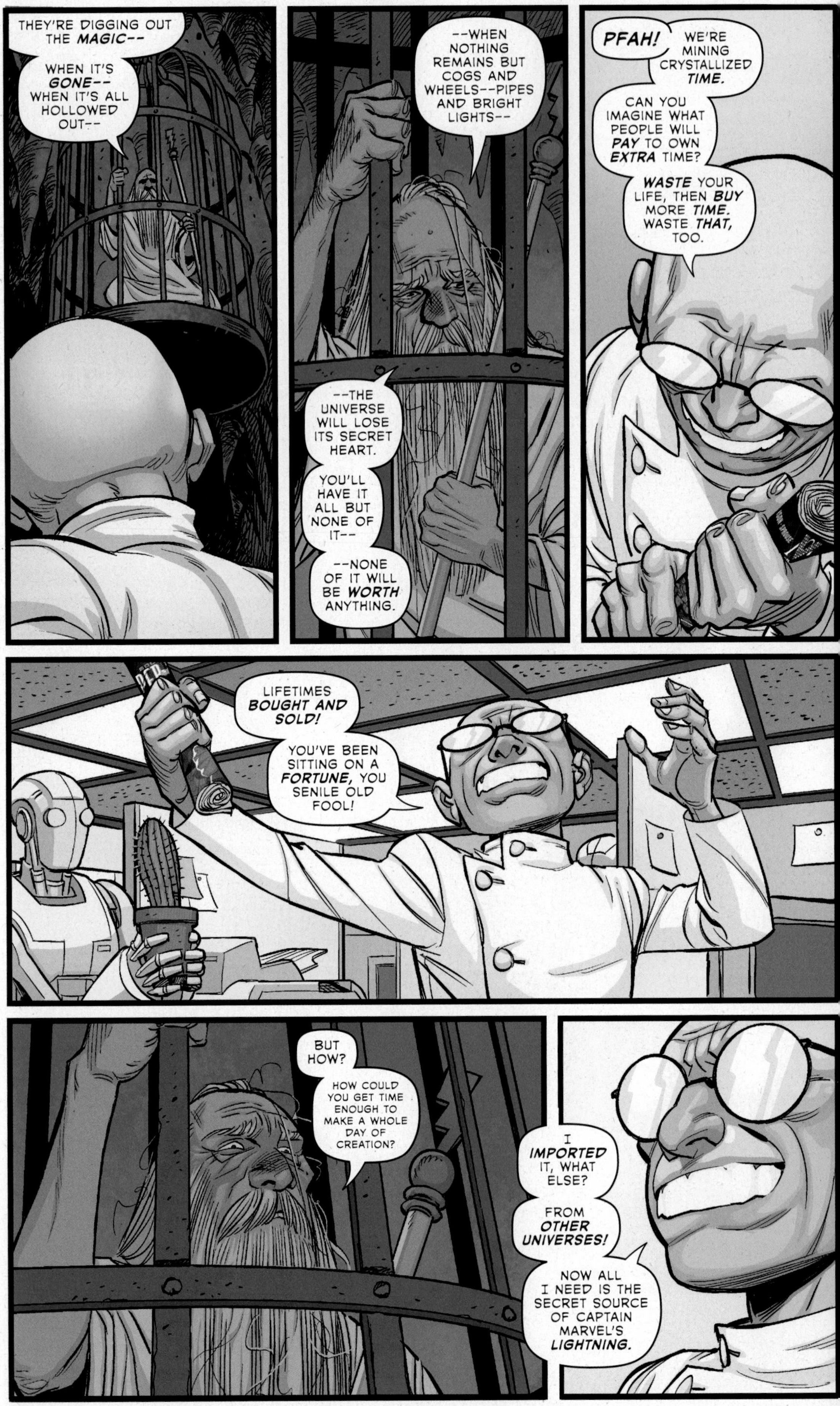
THEY'RE DIGGING OUT THE MAGIC--
WHEN IT'S GONE-- WHEN IT'S ALL HOLLOWED OUT--
--WHEN NOTHING REMAINS BUT COGS AND WHEELS--PIPES AND BRIGHT LIGHTS--
--THE UNIVERSE WILL LOSE ITS SECRET HEART.
YOU'LL HAVE IT ALL BUT NONE OF IT--
--NONE OF IT WILL BE WORTH ANYTHING.
PFAH!
WE'RE MINING CRYSTALLIZED TIME.
CAN YOU IMAGINE WHAT PEOPLE WILL PAY TO OWN EXTRA TIME?
WASTE YOUR LIFE, THEN BUY MORE TIME. WASTE THAT, TOO.
LIFETIMES BOUGHT AND SOLD!
YOU'VE BEEN SITTING ON A FORTUNE, YOU SENILE OLD FOOL!
BUT HOW?
HOW COULD YOU GET TIME ENOUGH TO MAKE A WHOLE DAY OF CREATION?
I IMPORTED IT, WHAT ELSE?
FROM OTHER UNIVERSES!
NOW ALL I NEED IS THE SECRET SOURCE OF CAPTAIN MARVEL'S LIGHTNING.

THE WELLSPRING OF THE POWER THAT *MADE* MY GREATEST ENEMY!

THE *SOURCE* OF ALL THIS ENERGY!

THE *FUEL ROD!*

THE FOUNTAINHEAD!

AS THE MAGIC DIES, I'M GETTING WEAKER, TOO...

...BECOMING FORGETFUL...

...ONLY MY CHAMPION...

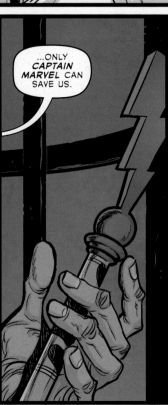

...ONLY *CAPTAIN MARVEL* CAN SAVE US.

I *THOUGHT* SO.

THE *LIGHTNING-STAFF.*

GIVE.

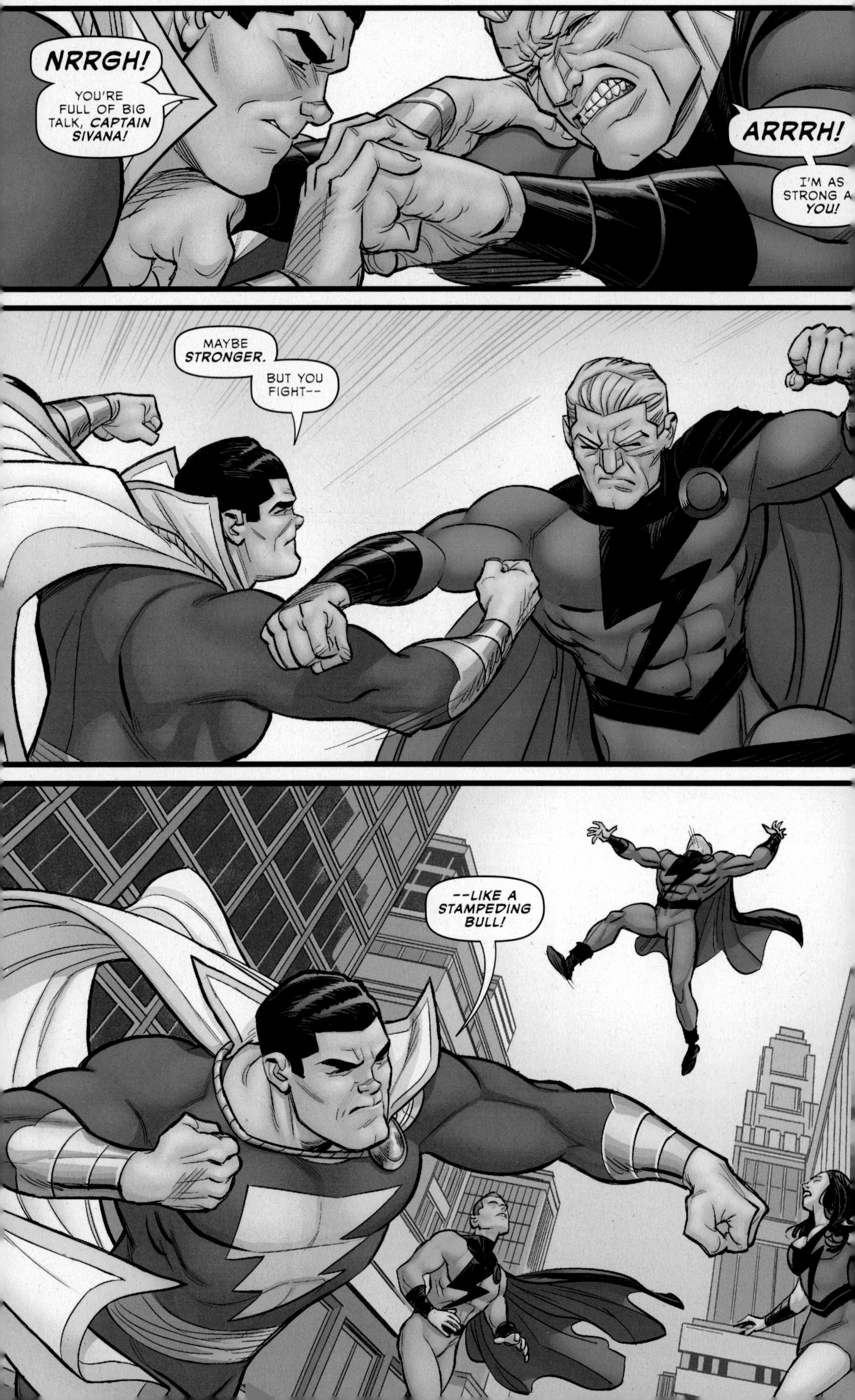
NRRGH!
YOU'RE FULL OF BIG TALK, CAPTAIN SIVANA!
ARRRH!
I'M AS STRONG A YOU!
MAYBE STRONGER.
BUT YOU FIGHT--
--LIKE A STAMPEDING BULL!

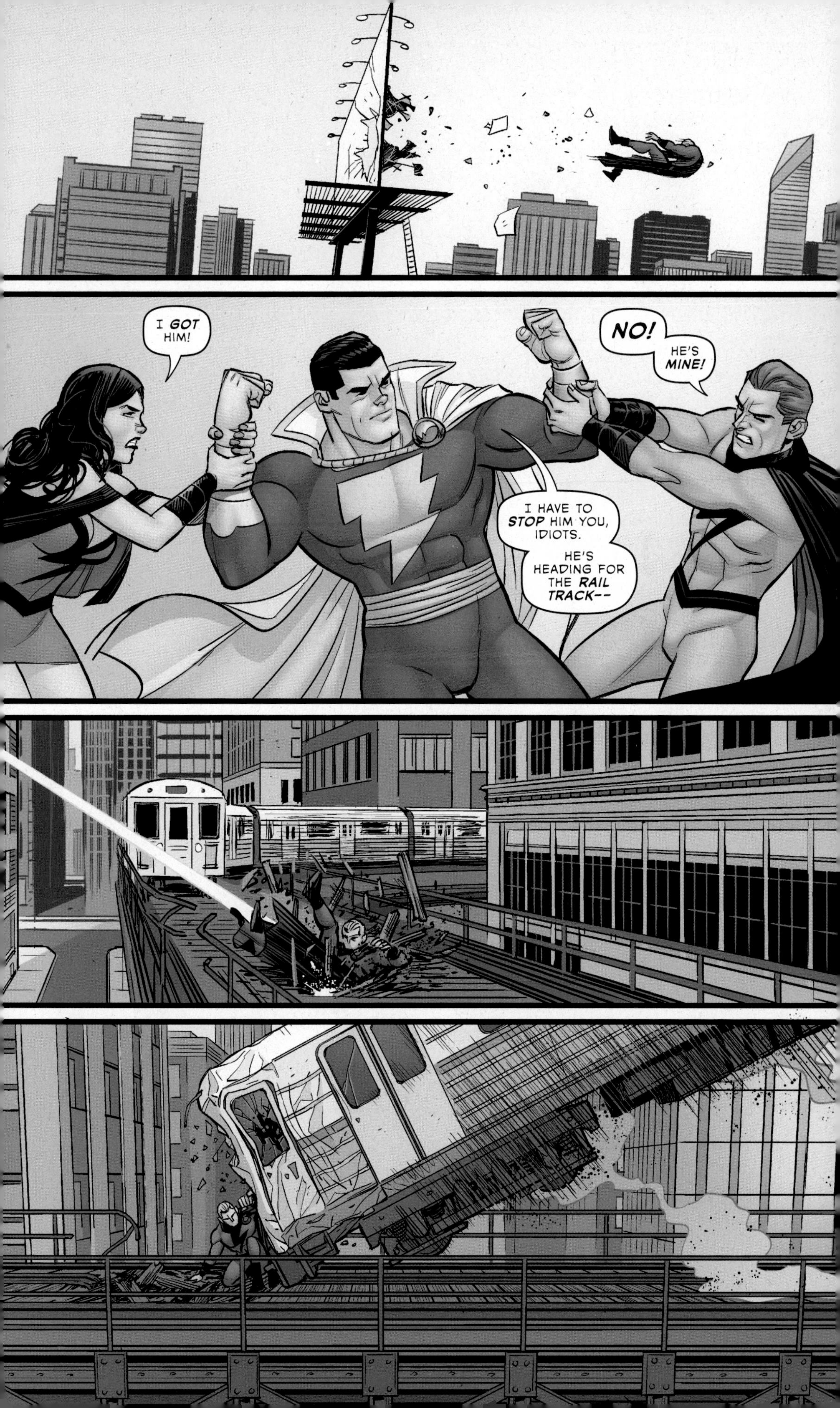
I GOT HIM!
NO! HE'S MINE!
I HAVE TO STOP HIM YOU, IDIOTS.
HE'S HEADING FOR THE RAIL TRACK--

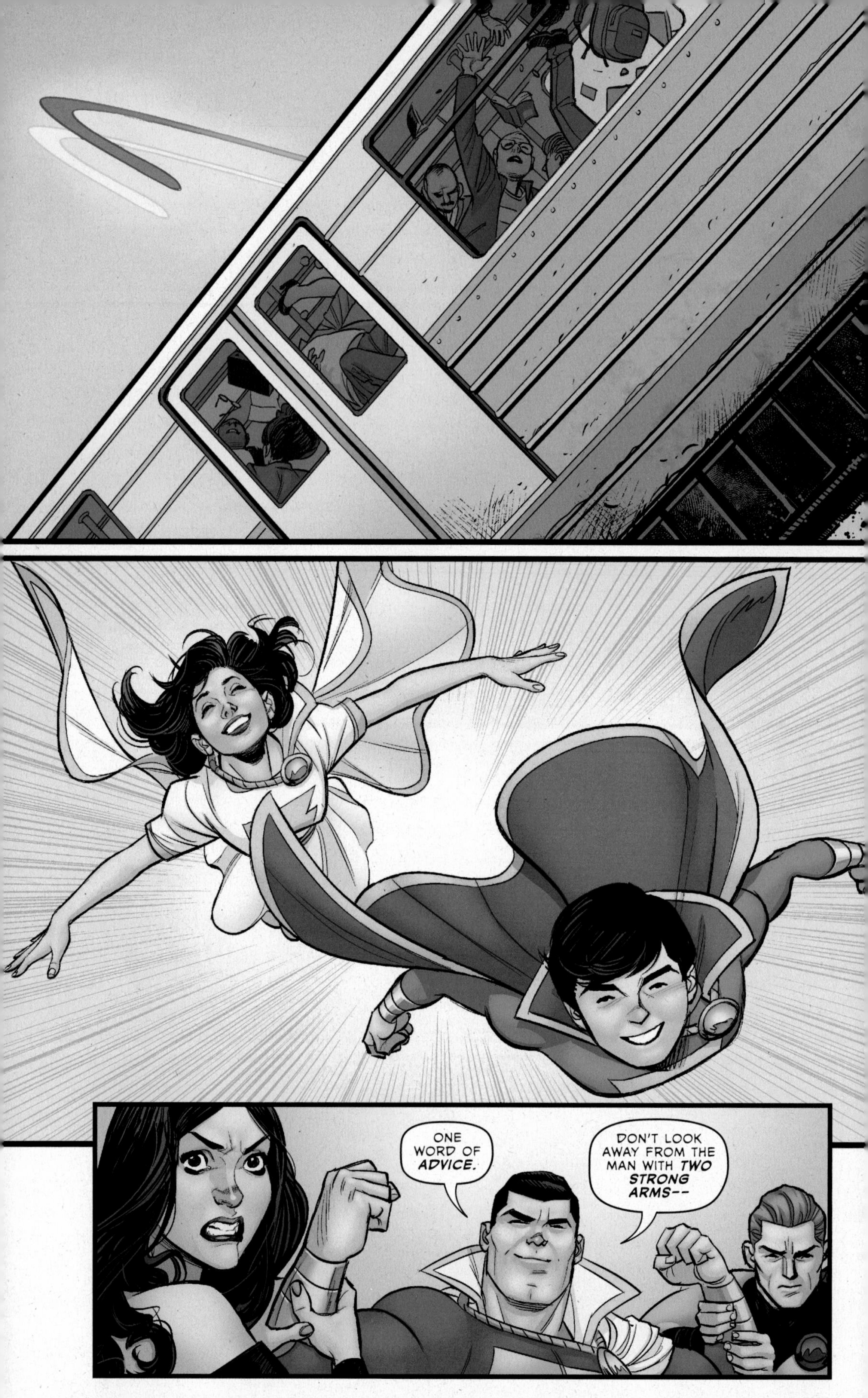
ONE WORD OF ADVICE.
DON'T LOOK AWAY FROM THE MAN WITH TWO STRONG ARMS--

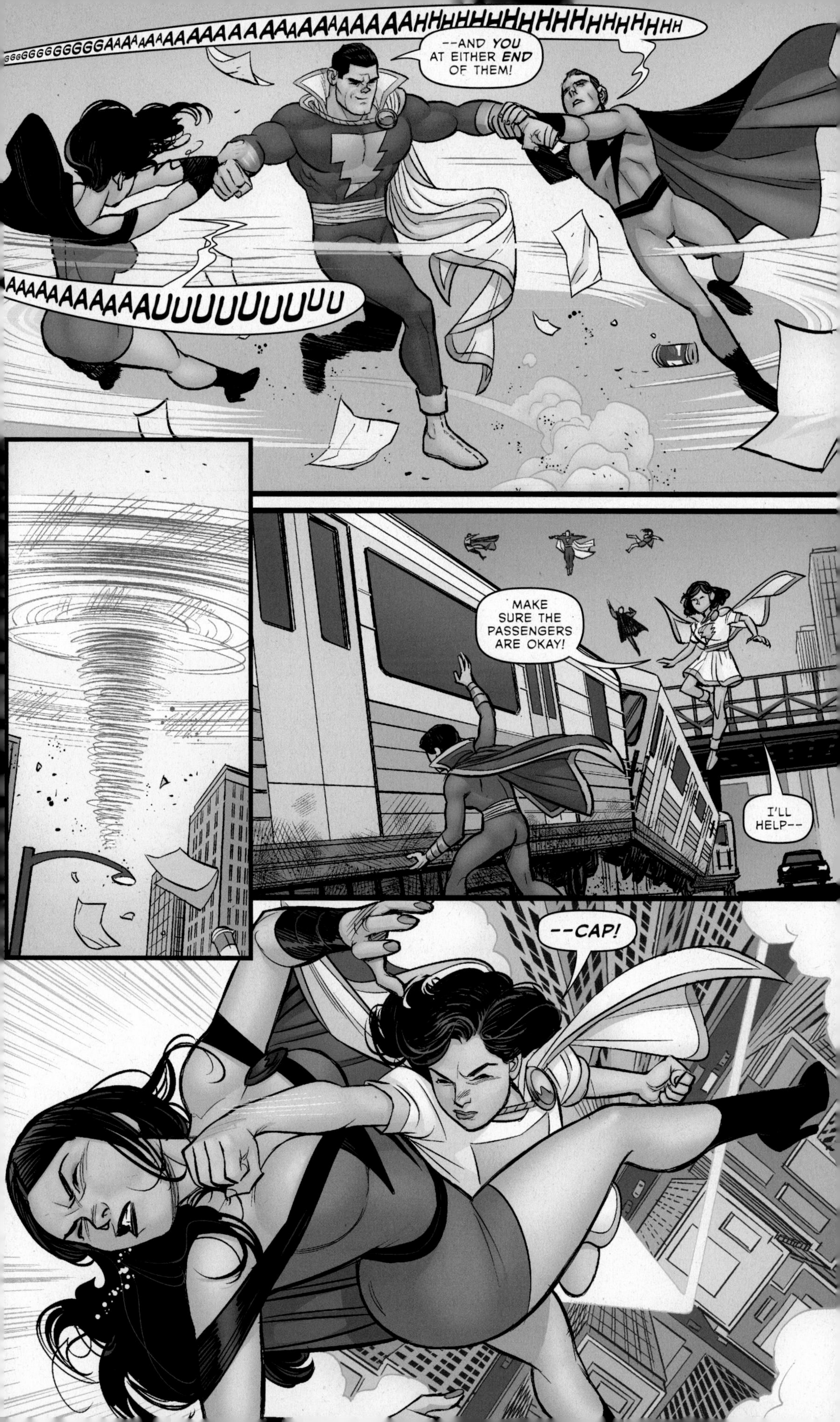

GGGGGGGGGGGGAAAAAAAAAAAAAAAAAAAAAAAAAAAAAHHHHHHHHHHHHHHHHH
--AND *YOU* AT EITHER *END* OF THEM!
AAAAAAAAAAAAAUUUUUUUUUU
MAKE SURE THE PASSENGERS ARE OKAY!
I'LL HELP--
--CAP!

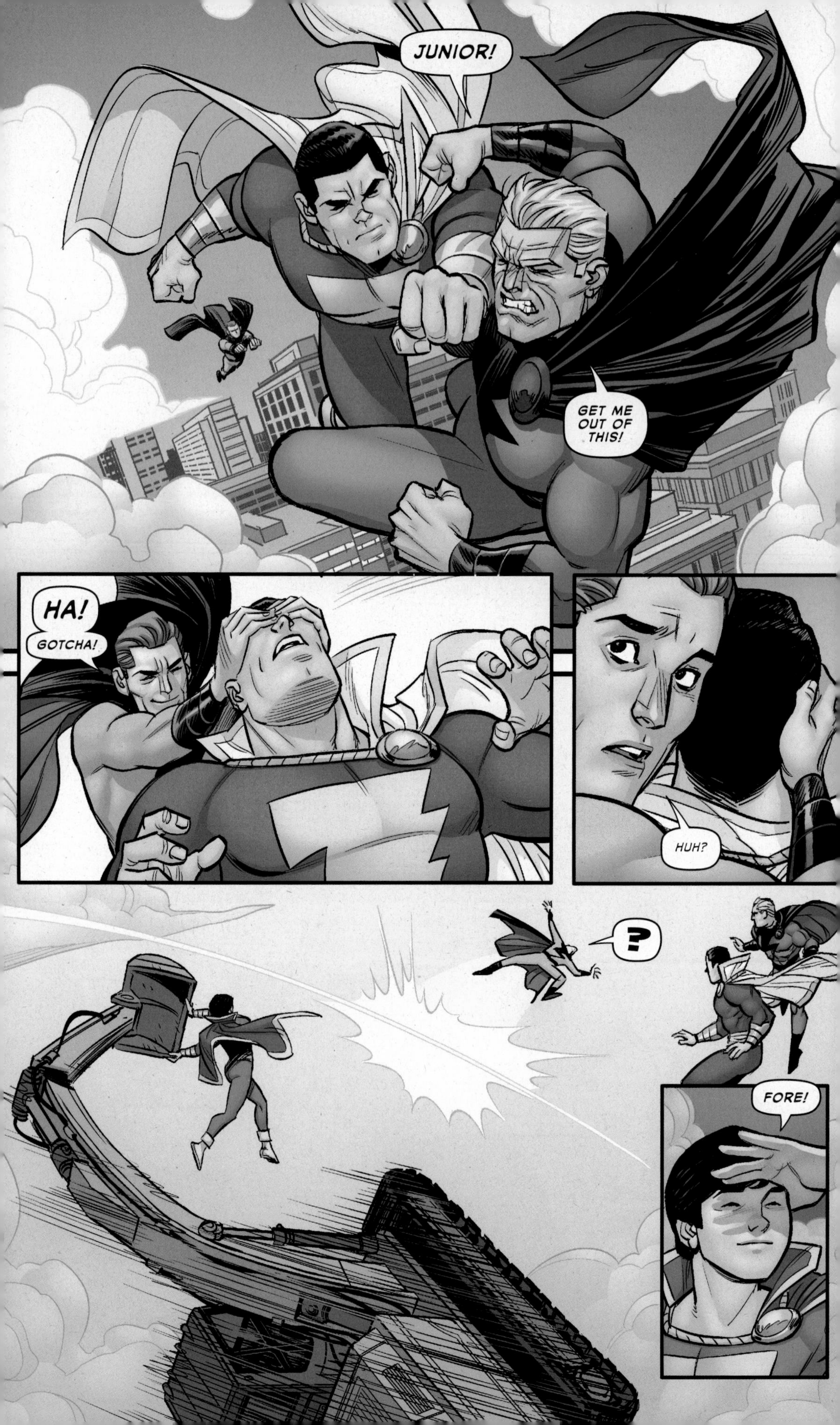
JUNIOR!
GET ME OUT OF THIS!
HA!
GOTCHA!
HUH?
?
FORE!

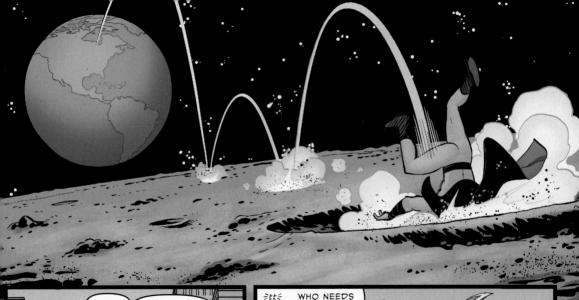

ADMIT IT!

I'M *WAY* PRETTIER THAN YOU NOW.

IF YOU SAY SO.

THERE'S MORE TO ME THAN JUST HOW I *LOOK*.

tt WHO NEEDS *BRAINS* WITH A BODY LIKE *THIS*?

JUNIOR.

BACK ME UP.

IT DOESN'T MATTER *WHAT* THEY SAY.

BOYS ONLY GO FOR GIRLS WHO *LOOK HOT*, RIGHT?

I-- WELL-- I--UH...

I *GUESS.*

YOU PRESENT SOME PRETTY GOOD EVIDENCE, THAT'S FOR SURE.

WOW.

WHAT?

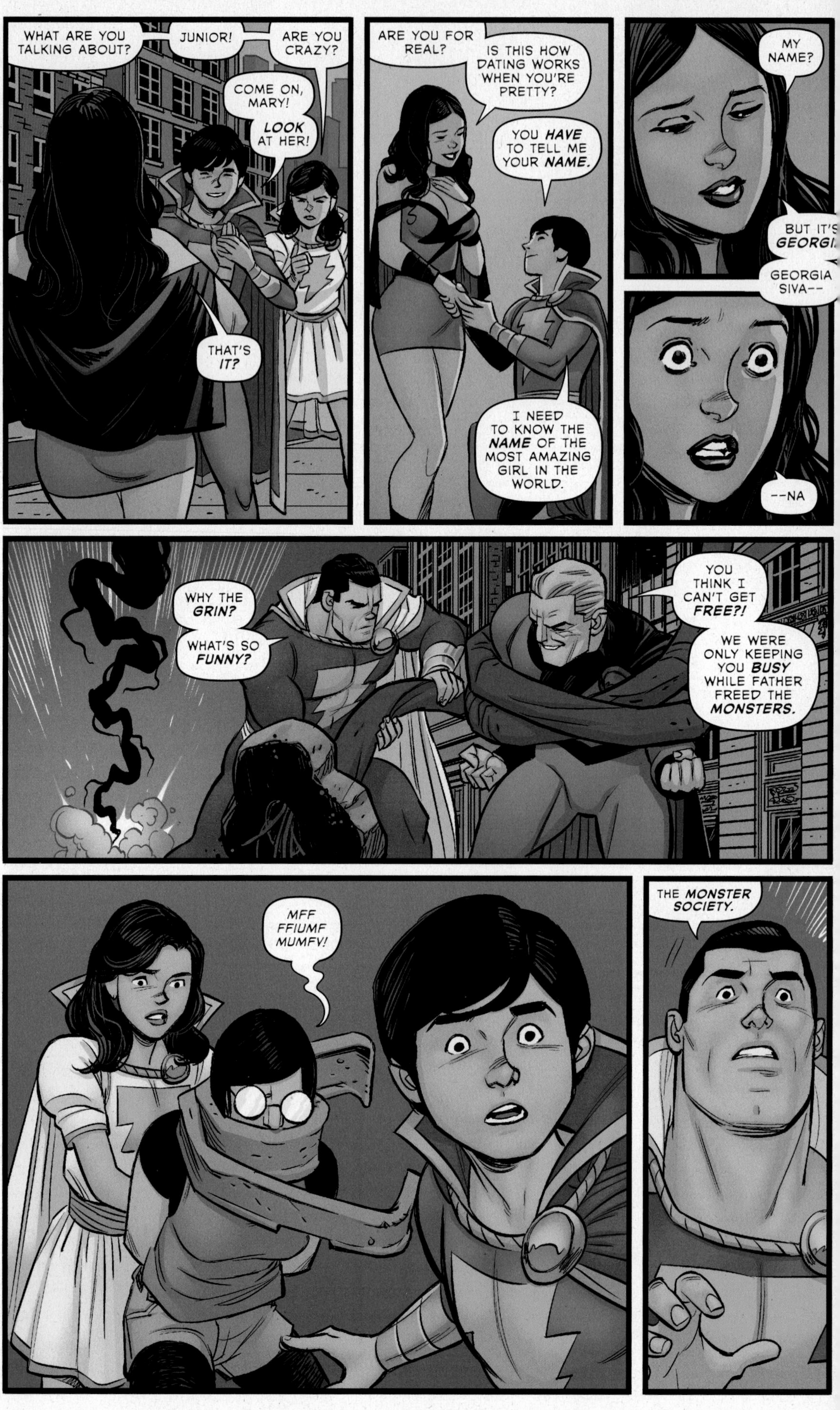
WHAT ARE YOU TALKING ABOUT?
JUNIOR!
ARE YOU CRAZY?
COME ON, MARY! LOOK AT HER!
THAT'S IT?
ARE YOU FOR REAL?
IS THIS HOW DATING WORKS WHEN YOU'RE PRETTY?
YOU HAVE TO TELL ME YOUR NAME.
I NEED TO KNOW THE NAME OF THE MOST AMAZING GIRL IN THE WORLD.
MY NAME?
BUT IT'S GEORGI
GEORGIA SIVA--
--NA
WHY THE GRIN?
WHAT'S SO FUNNY?
YOU THINK I CAN'T GET FREE?!
WE WERE ONLY KEEPING YOU BUSY WHILE FATHER FREED THE MONSTERS.
MFF FFIUMF MUMFV!
THE MONSTER SOCIETY.

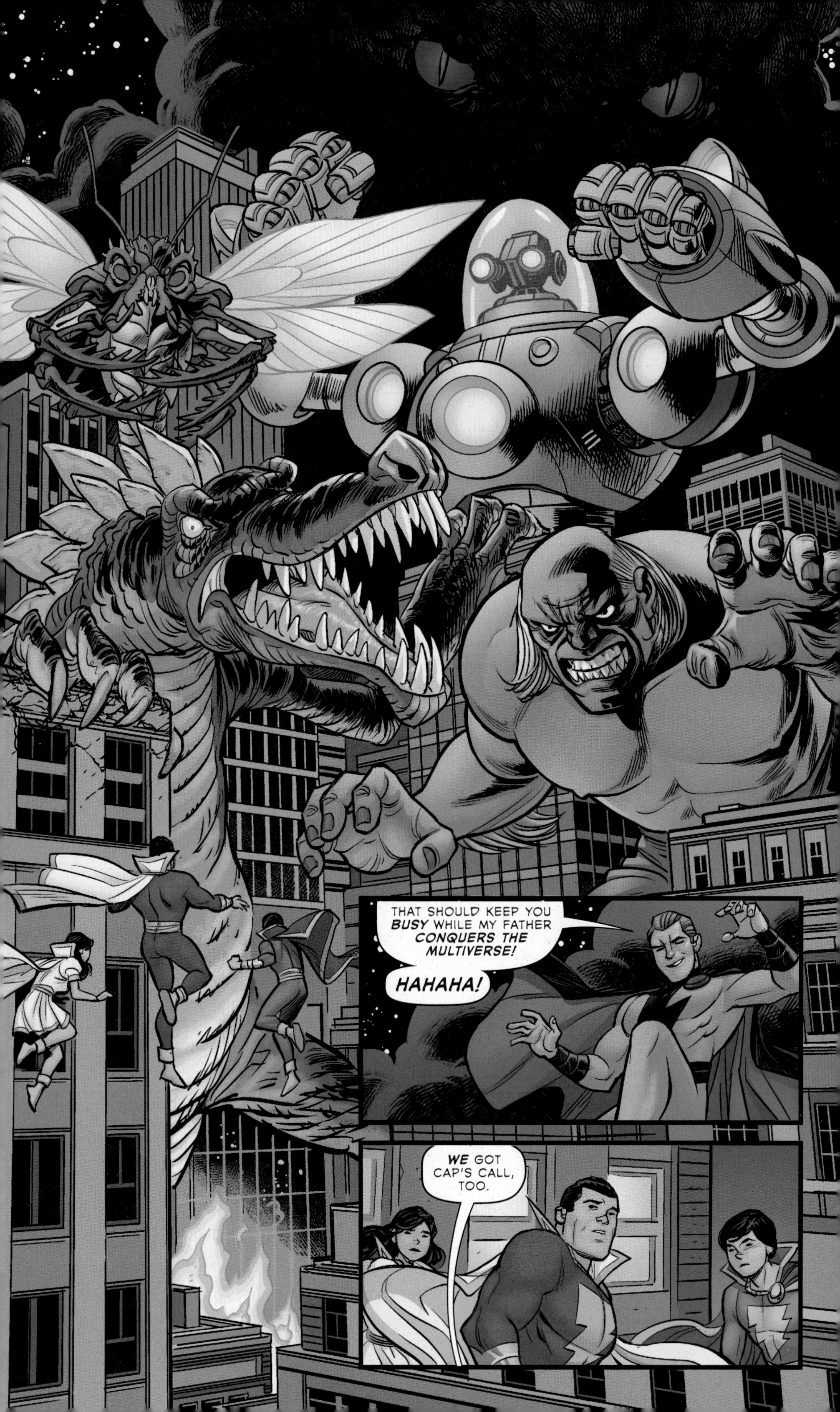
THAT SHOULD KEEP YOU BUSY WHILE MY FATHER CONQUERS THE MULTIVERSE!
HAHAHA!
WE GOT CAP'S CALL, TOO.

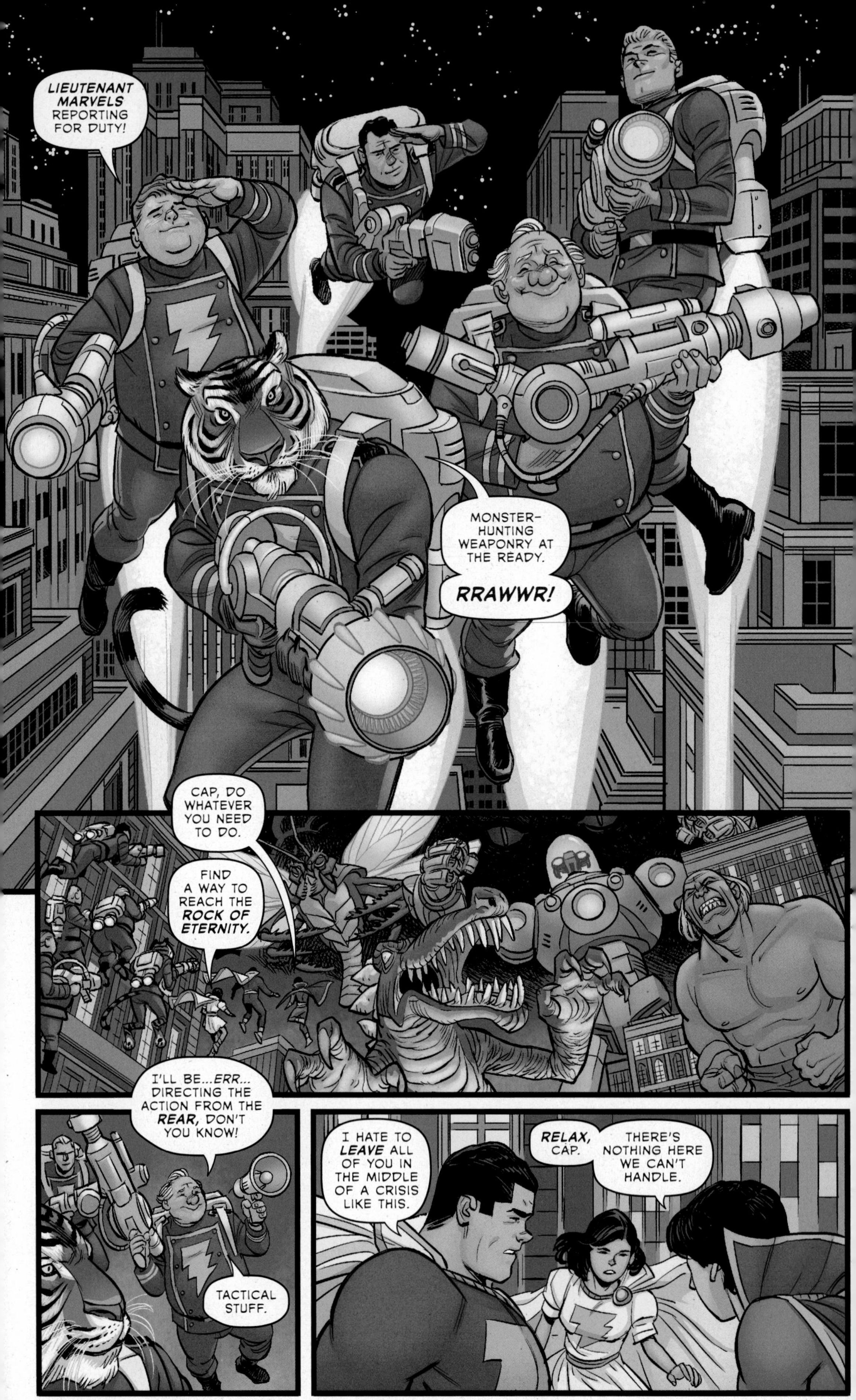
LIEUTENANT MARVELS REPORTING FOR DUTY!
MONSTER-HUNTING WEAPONRY AT THE READY.
RRAWWR!
CAP, DO WHATEVER YOU NEED TO DO.
FIND A WAY TO REACH THE ROCK OF ETERNITY.
I'LL BE...ERR... DIRECTING THE ACTION FROM THE REAR, DON'T YOU KNOW!
TACTICAL STUFF.
I HATE TO LEAVE ALL OF YOU IN THE MIDDLE OF A CRISIS LIKE THIS.
RELAX, CAP.
THERE'S NOTHING HERE WE CAN'T HANDLE.

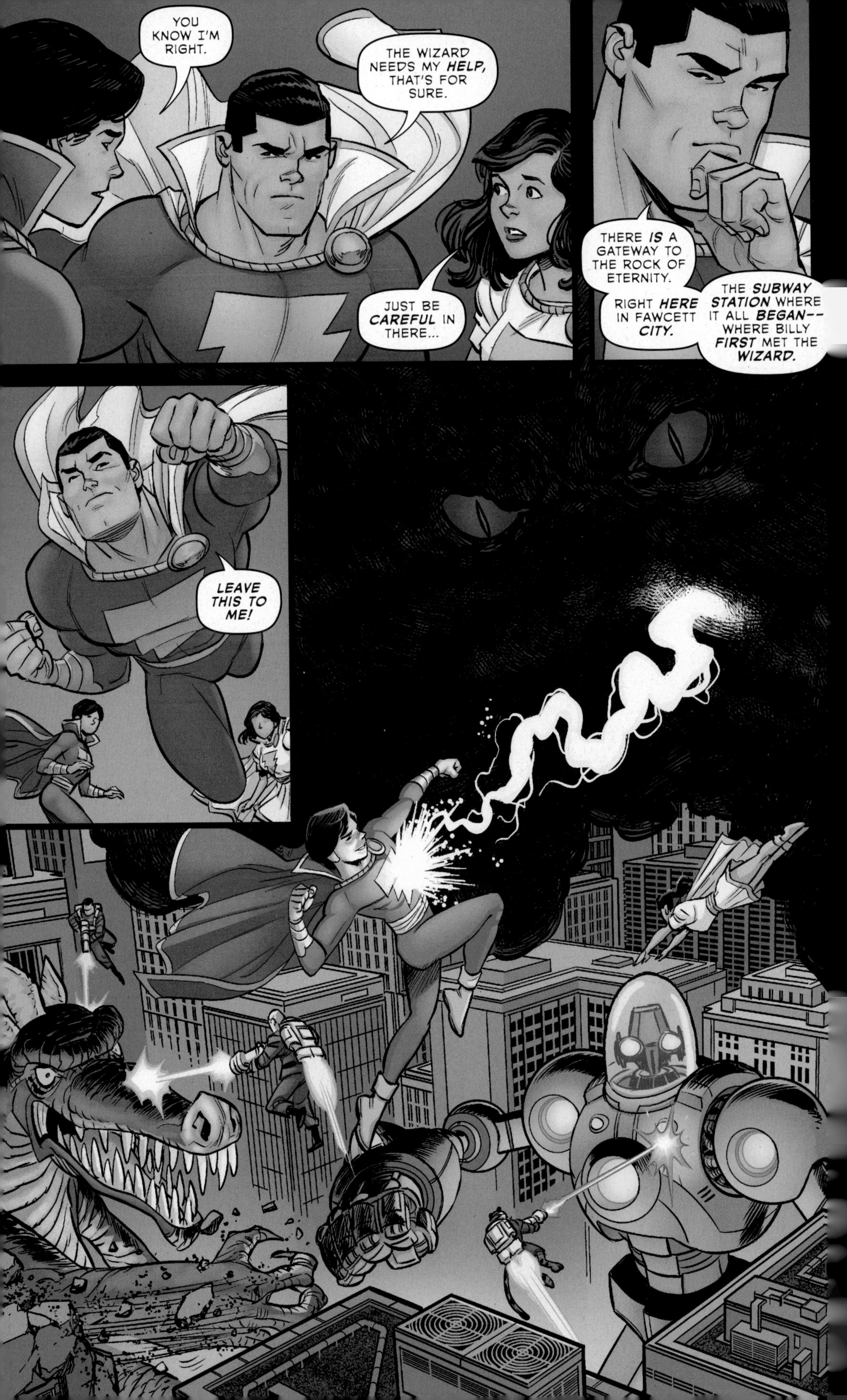
YOU KNOW I'M RIGHT.
THE WIZARD NEEDS MY HELP, THAT'S FOR SURE.
JUST BE CAREFUL IN THERE...
THERE IS A GATEWAY TO THE ROCK OF ETERNITY.
RIGHT HERE IN FAWCETT CITY.
THE SUBWAY STATION WHERE IT ALL BEGAN-- WHERE BILLY FIRST MET THE WIZARD.
LEAVE THIS TO ME!

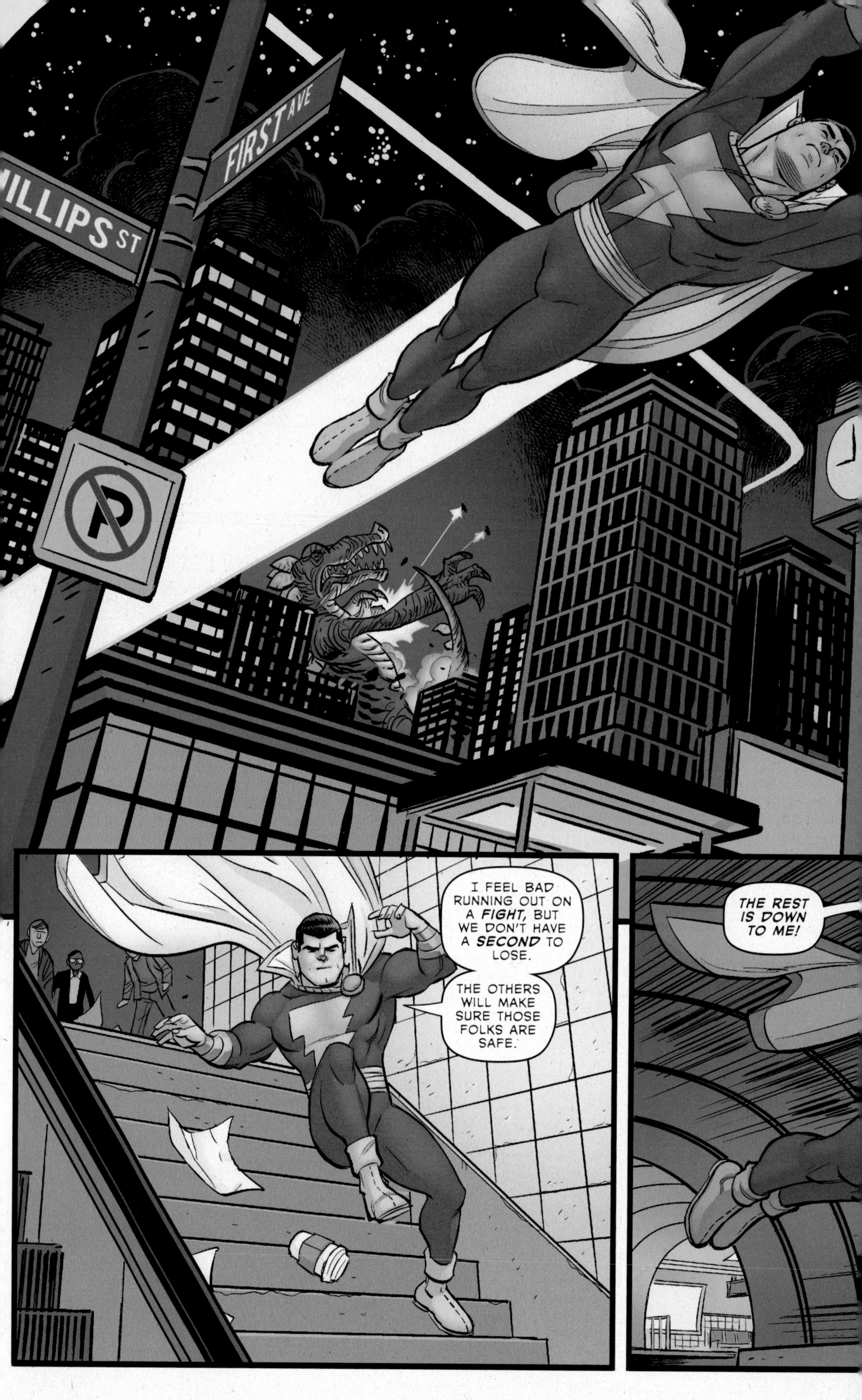
FIRST AVE
ILLIPS ST
I FEEL BAD RUNNING OUT ON A FIGHT, BUT WE DON'T HAVE A SECOND TO LOSE.
THE OTHERS WILL MAKE SURE THOSE FOLKS ARE SAFE.
THE REST IS DOWN TO ME!

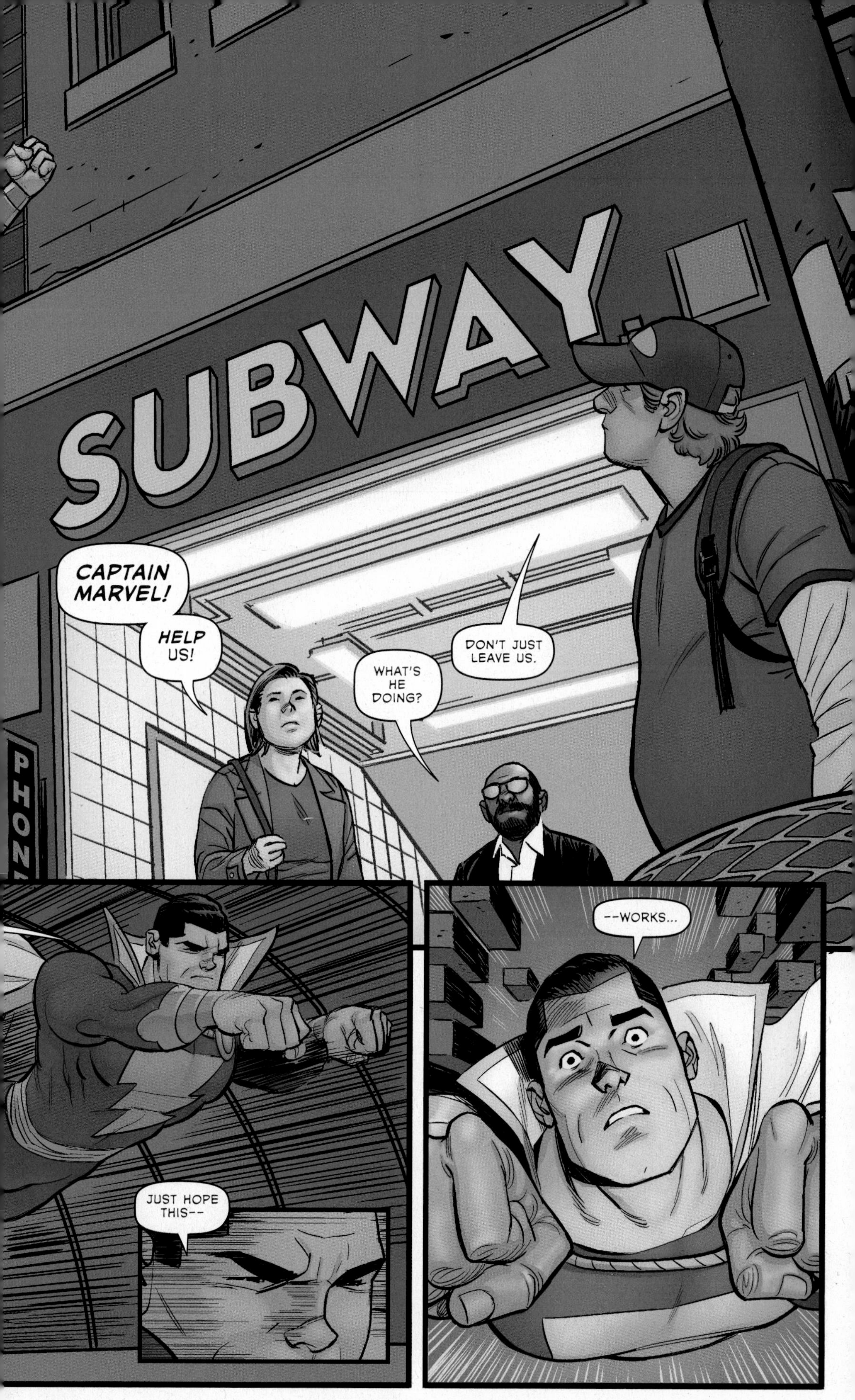
SUBWAY
CAPTAIN MARVEL!
HELP US!
WHAT'S HE DOING?
DON'T JUST LEAVE US.
PHON
JUST HOPE THIS--
--WORKS...

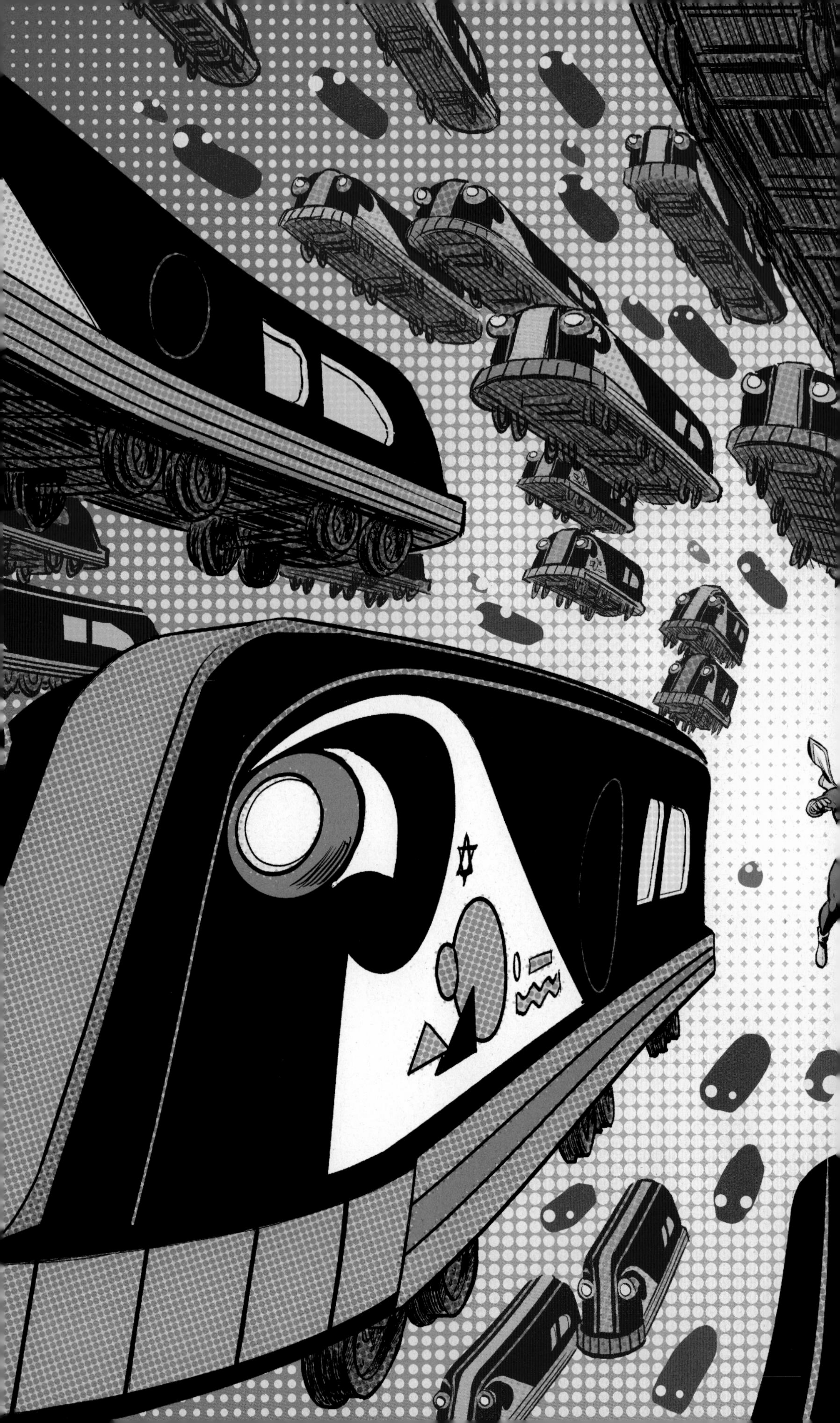

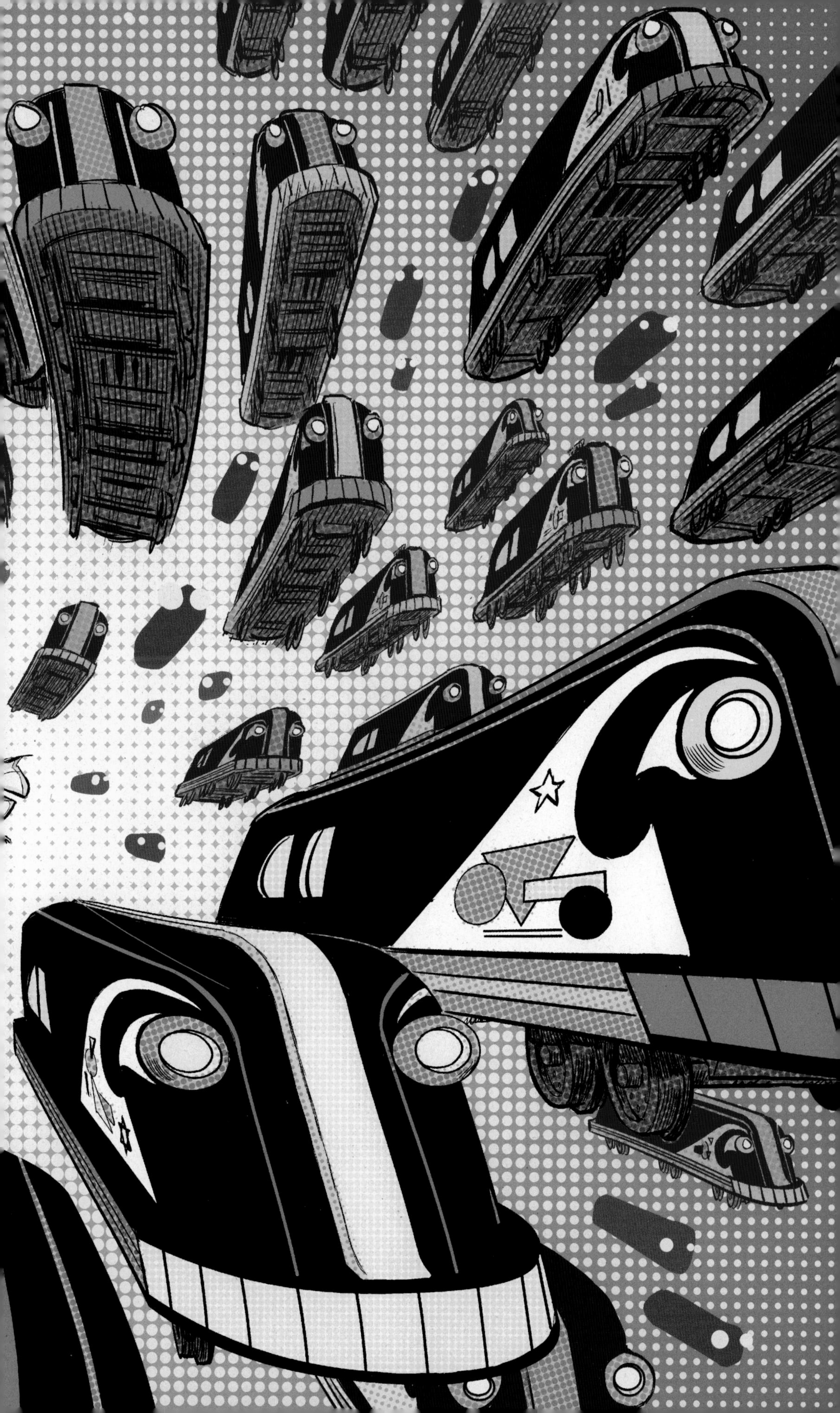

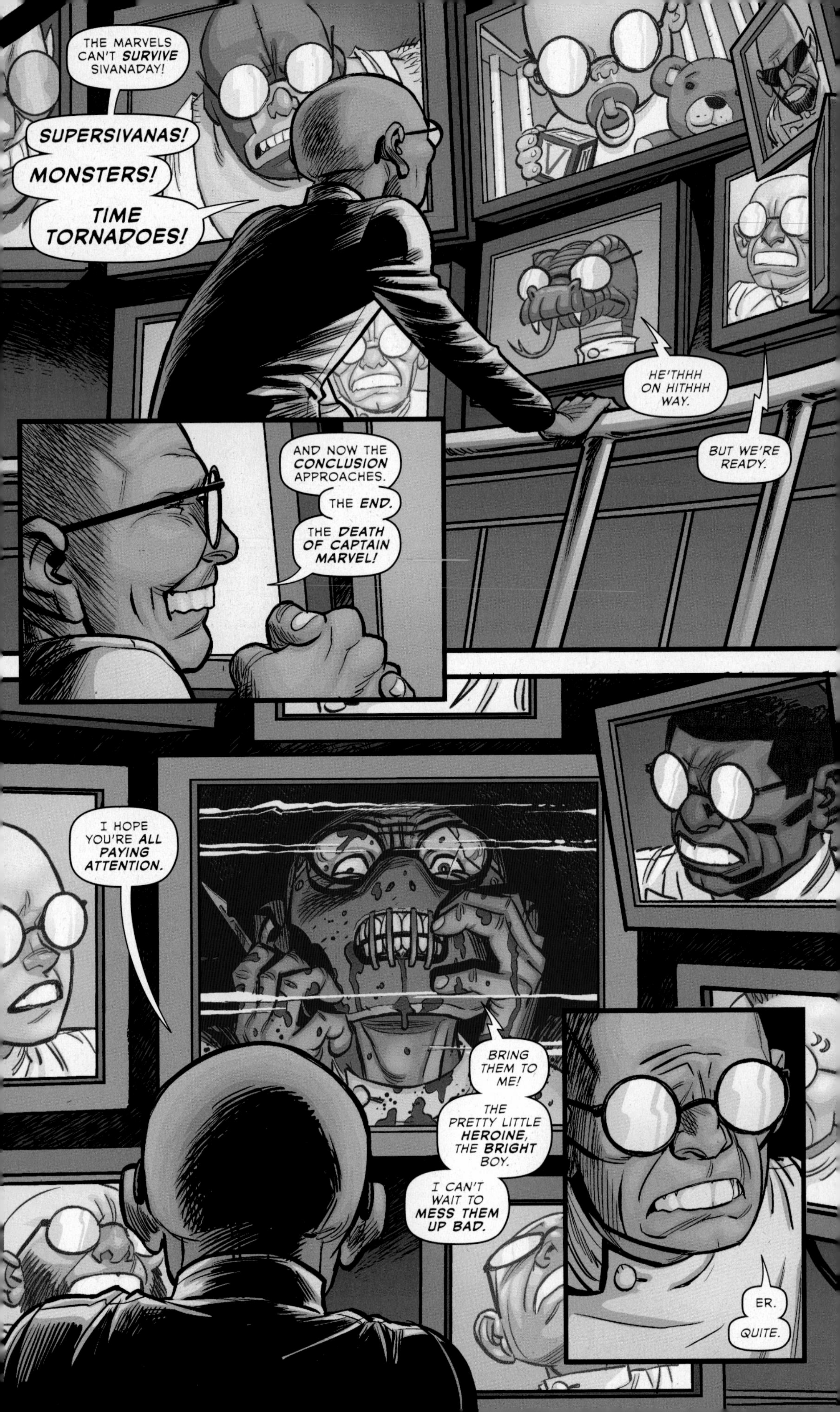
THE MARVELS CAN'T SURVIVE SIVANADAY!
SUPERSIVANAS!
MONSTERS!
TIME TORNADOES!
HE'THHH ON HITHHH WAY.
BUT WE'RE READY.
AND NOW THE CONCLUSION APPROACHES.
THE END.
THE DEATH OF CAPTAIN MARVEL!
I HOPE YOU'RE ALL PAYING ATTENTION.
BRING THEM TO ME!
THE PRETTY LITTLE HEROINE, THE BRIGHT BOY.
I CAN'T WAIT TO MESS THEM UP BAD.
ER.
QUITE.

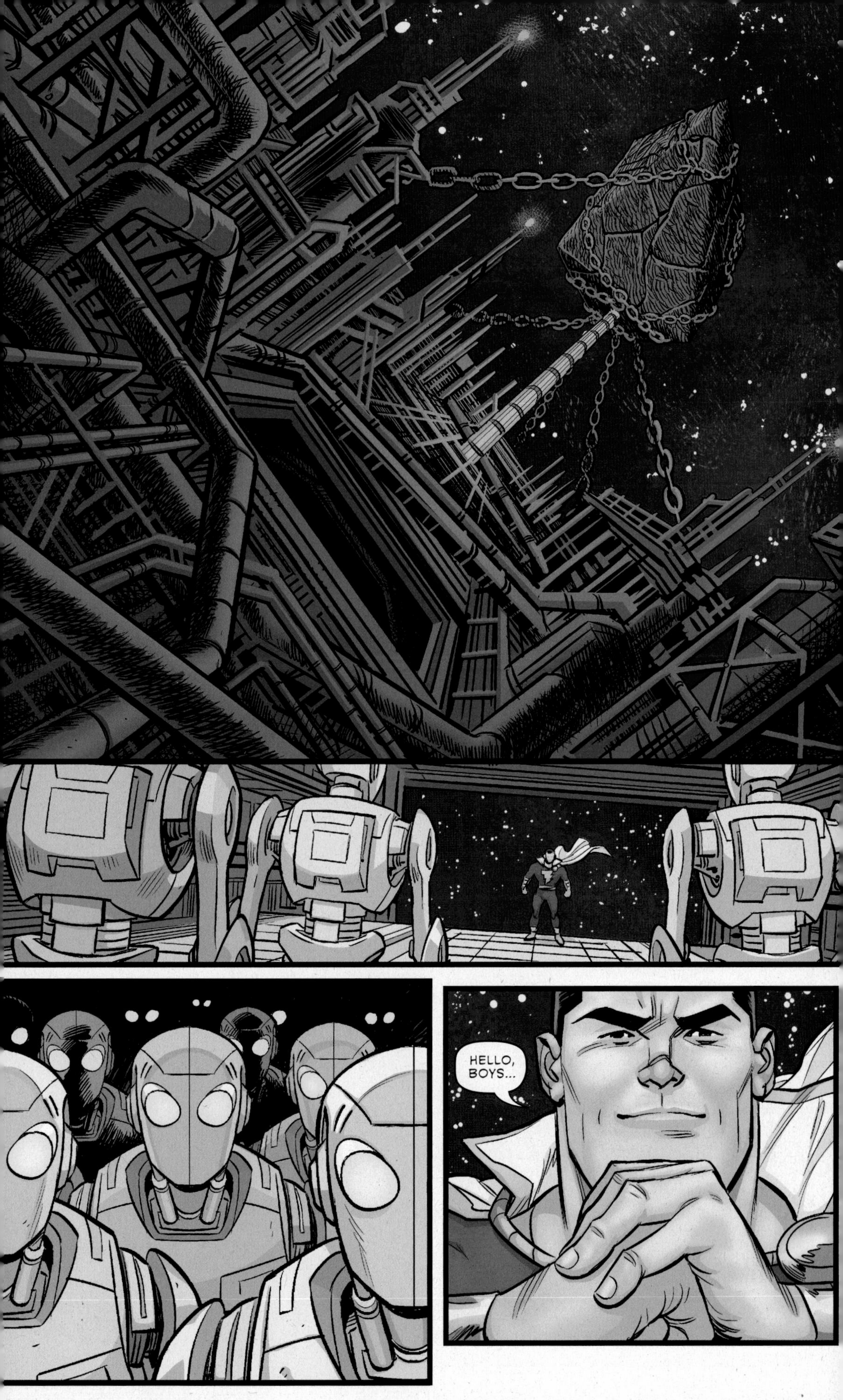
HELLO, BOYS...

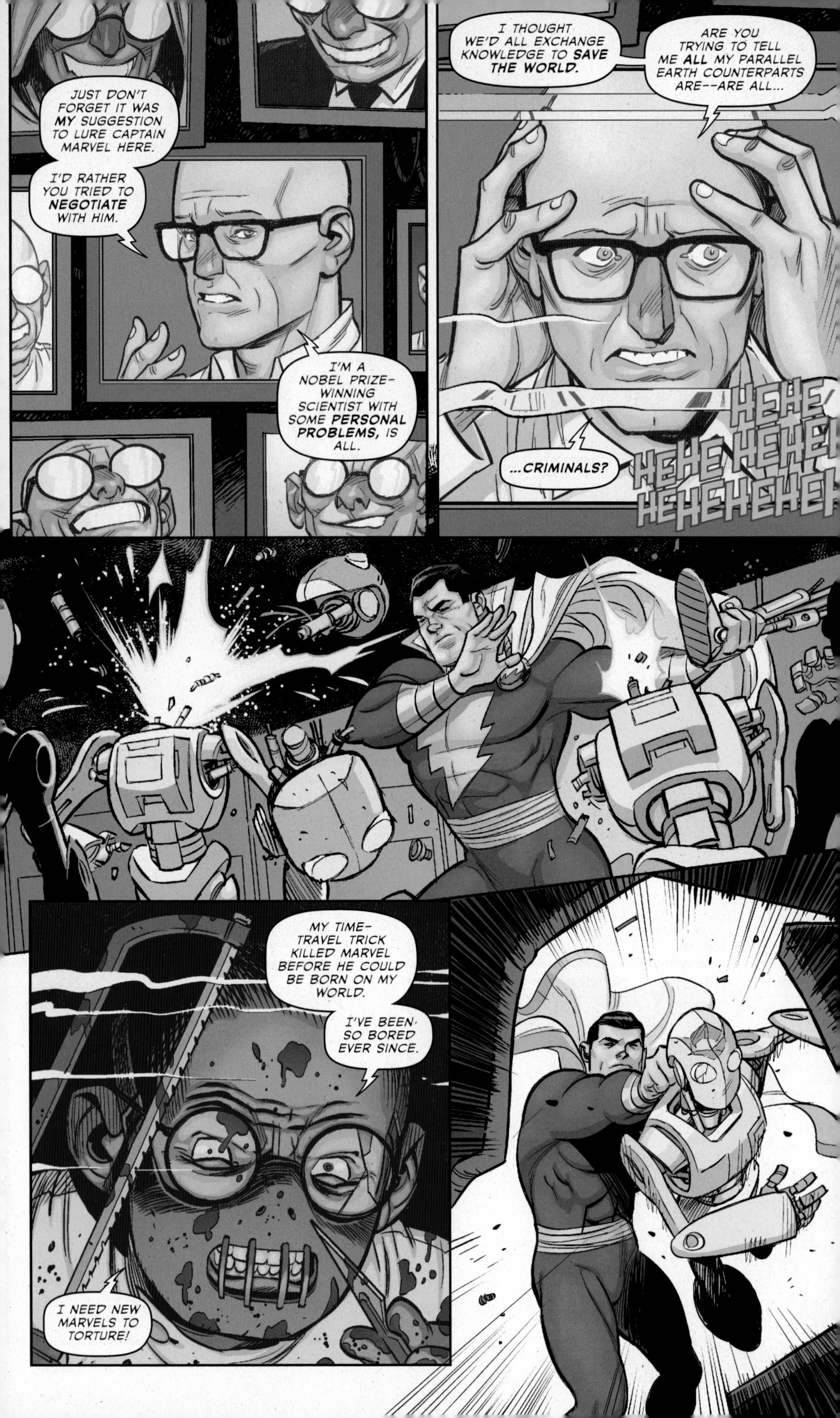
JUST DON'T FORGET IT WAS MY SUGGESTION TO LURE CAPTAIN MARVEL HERE.
I'D RATHER YOU TRIED TO NEGOTIATE WITH HIM.
I'M A NOBEL PRIZE-WINNING SCIENTIST WITH SOME PERSONAL PROBLEMS, IS ALL.
I THOUGHT WE'D ALL EXCHANGE KNOWLEDGE TO SAVE THE WORLD.
ARE YOU TRYING TO TELL ME ALL MY PARALLEL EARTH COUNTERPARTS ARE--ARE ALL...
...CRIMINALS?
HEHE HEHE HEHE HEHEHEHEHE
MY TIME-TRAVEL TRICK KILLED MARVEL BEFORE HE COULD BE BORN ON MY WORLD.
I'VE BEEN SO BORED EVER SINCE.
I NEED NEW MARVELS TO TORTURE!

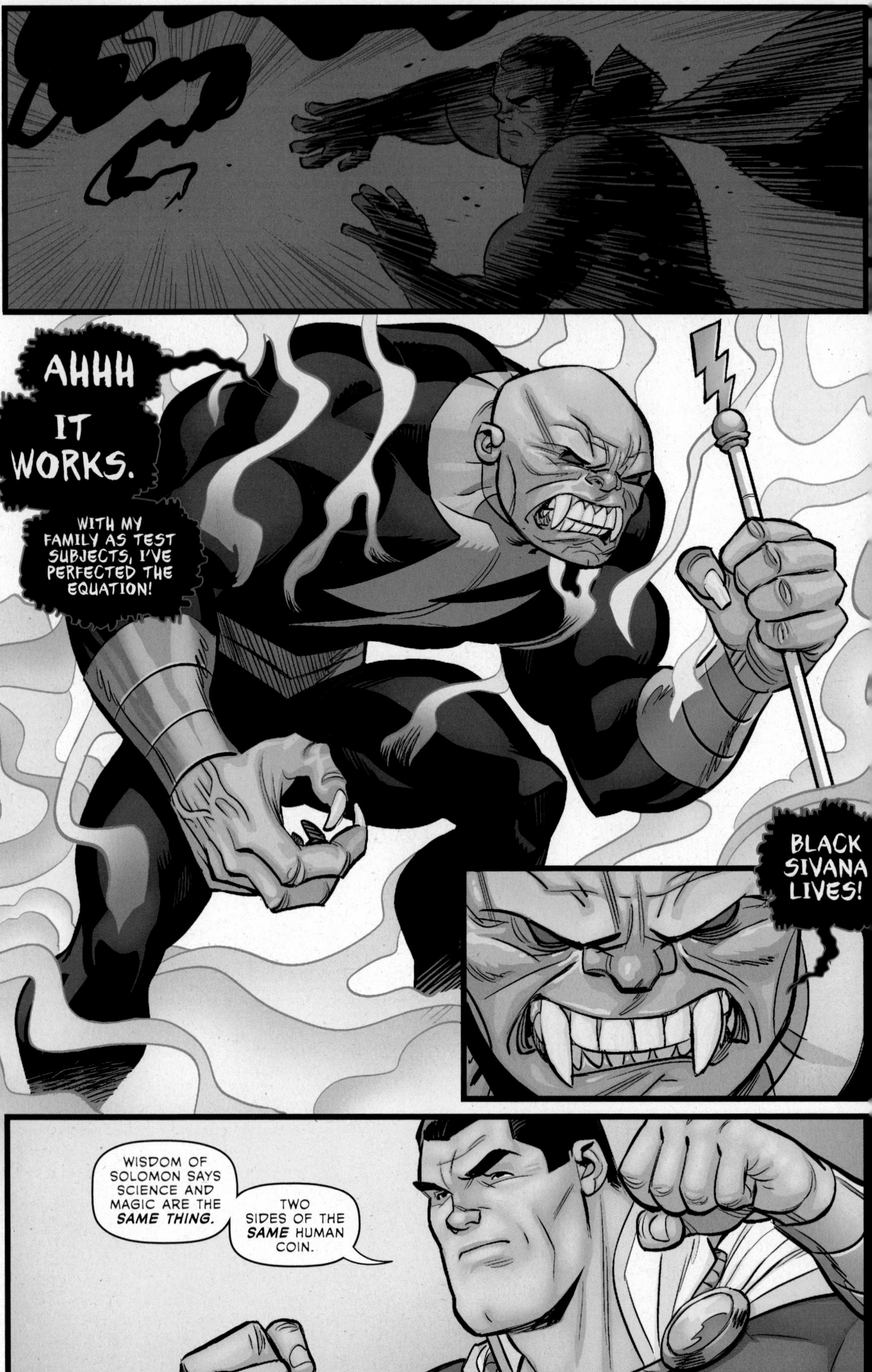
AHHH
IT WORKS.
WITH MY FAMILY AS TEST SUBJECTS, I'VE PERFECTED THE EQUATION!
BLACK SIVANA LIVES!
WISDOM OF SOLOMON SAYS SCIENCE AND MAGIC ARE THE *SAME THING.*
TWO SIDES OF THE *SAME* HUMAN COIN.

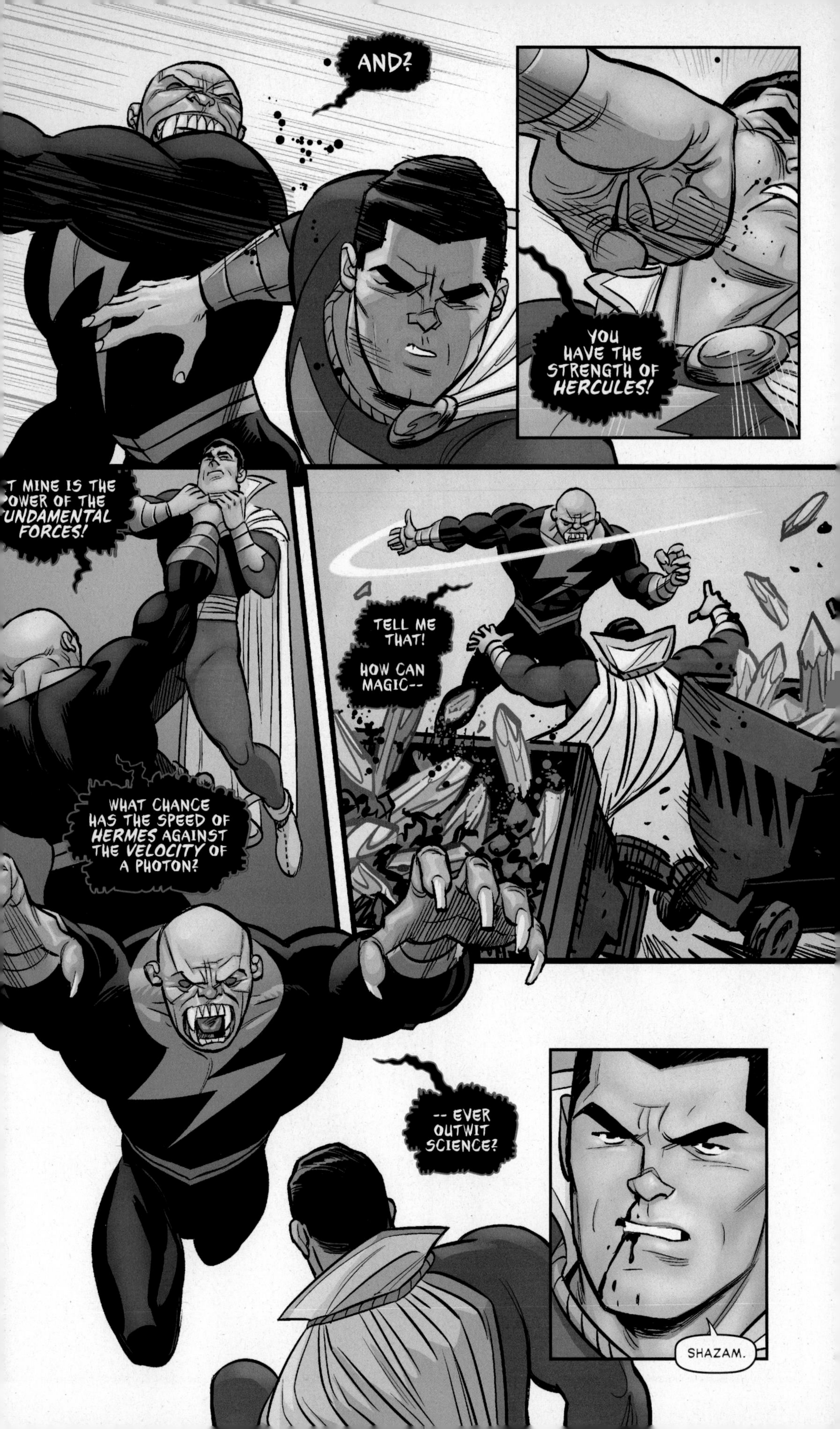
AND?
YOU HAVE THE STRENGTH OF HERCULES!
T MINE IS THE OWER OF THE UNDAMENTAL FORCES!
WHAT CHANCE HAS THE SPEED OF HERMES AGAINST THE VELOCITY OF A PHOTON?
TELL ME THAT!
HOW CAN MAGIC--
-- EVER OUTWIT SCIENCE?
SHAZAM.

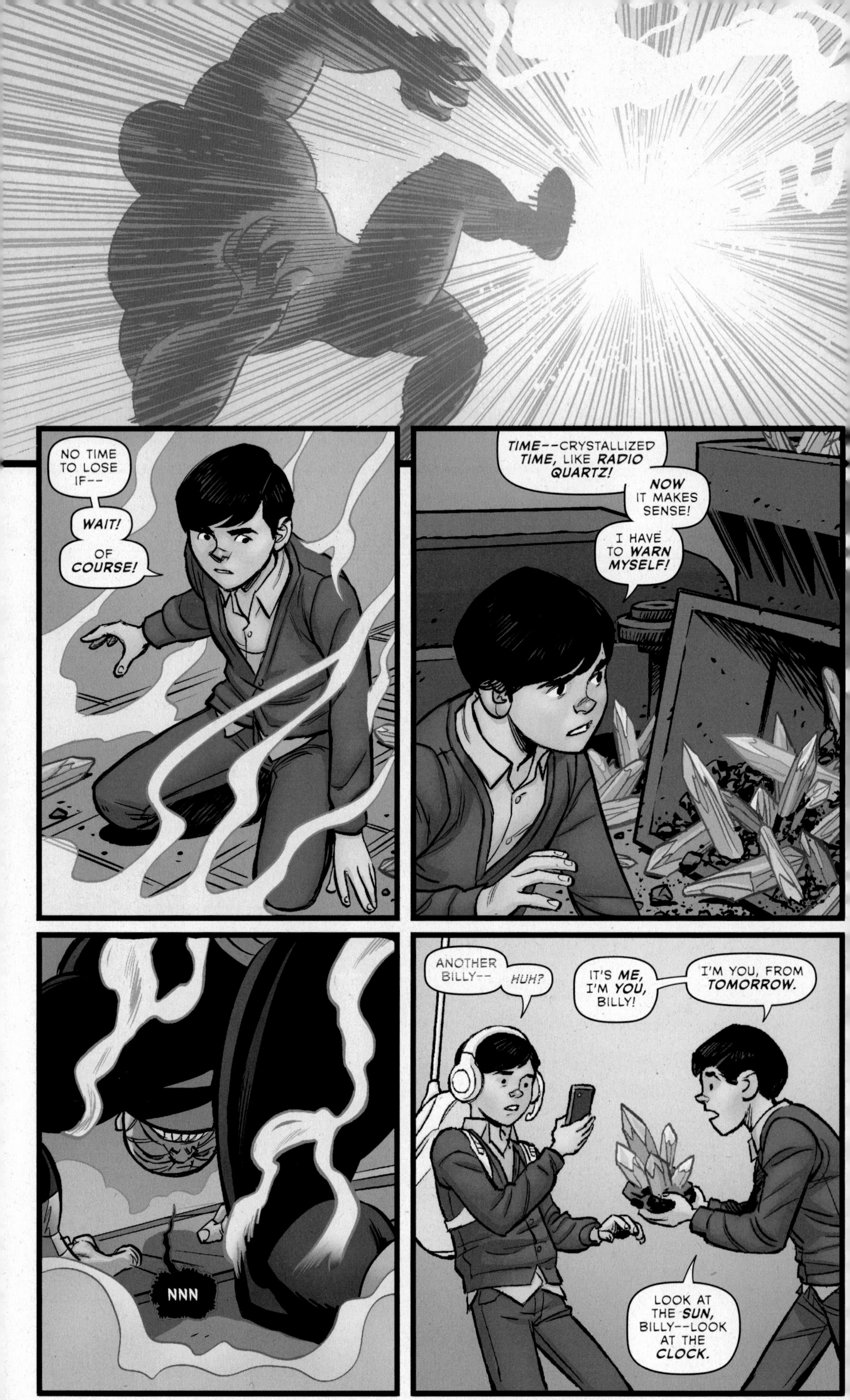
NO TIME TO LOSE IF--
WAIT!
OF COURSE!
TIME--CRYSTALLIZED TIME, LIKE RADIO QUARTZ!
NOW IT MAKES SENSE!
I HAVE TO WARN MYSELF!
NNN
ANOTHER BILLY--
HUH?
IT'S ME, I'M YOU, BILLY!
I'M YOU, FROM TOMORROW.
LOOK AT THE SUN, BILLY--LOOK AT THE CLOCK.

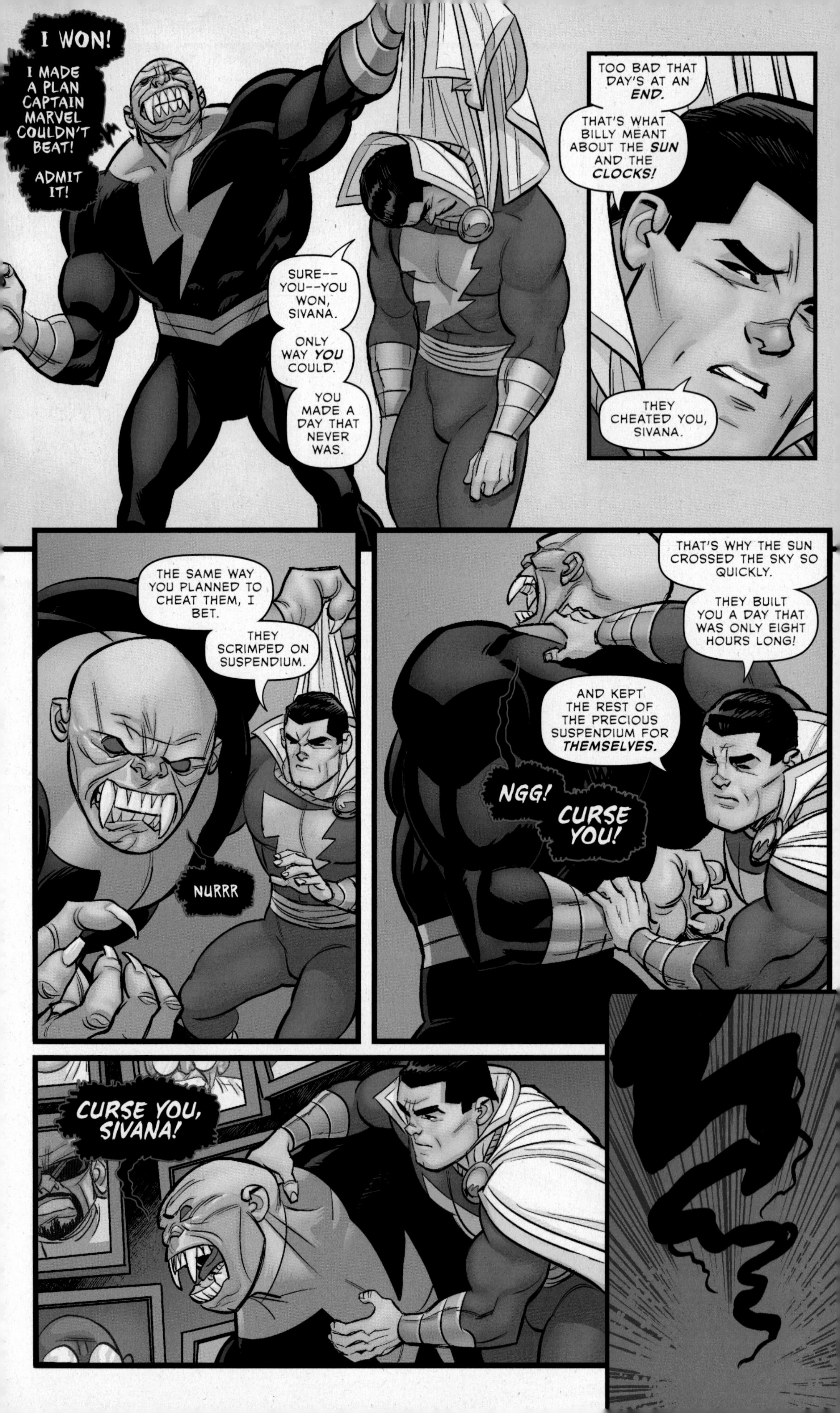
I WON!
I MADE A PLAN CAPTAIN MARVEL COULDN'T BEAT!
ADMIT IT!
SURE-- YOU--YOU WON, SIVANA.
ONLY WAY *YOU* COULD.
YOU MADE A DAY THAT NEVER WAS.
TOO BAD THAT DAY'S AT AN *END.*
THAT'S WHAT BILLY MEANT ABOUT THE *SUN* AND THE *CLOCKS!*
THEY CHEATED YOU, SIVANA.
THE SAME WAY YOU PLANNED TO CHEAT THEM, I BET.
THEY SCRIMPED ON SUSPENDIUM.
NURRR
THAT'S WHY THE SUN CROSSED THE SKY SO QUICKLY.
THEY BUILT YOU A DAY THAT WAS ONLY EIGHT HOURS LONG!
AND KEPT THE REST OF THE PRECIOUS SUSPENDIUM FOR *THEMSELVES.*
NGG!
CURSE YOU!
CURSE YOU, SIVANA!

SIVANA! SIVANA=$MEC2$! IT'S A SCIENTIFIC PROOF!

THAT WAS YESTERDAY, DOCTOR.

NEW DATA CAME TO LIGHT.

THERE WAS A SUDDEN PARADIGM SHIFT.

YOU GOT YOUR BIG CHANCE.

IN ALL TIME AND SPACE, THERE'S ONE DAY WHERE YOU WIN.

ON EVERY OTHER DAY, GENTLEMEN--

--YOU LOSE LIKE THE LAST TIME!

THIS ISN'T OVER.

NOW I'VE SEEN HER.

I WANT THAT GIRL.

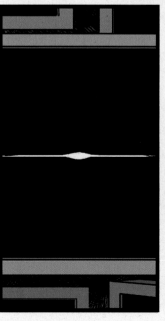

YOU NEVER FAIL ME, DO YOU, BOY?

I CHOSE MY CHAMPION WELL.

MEH!

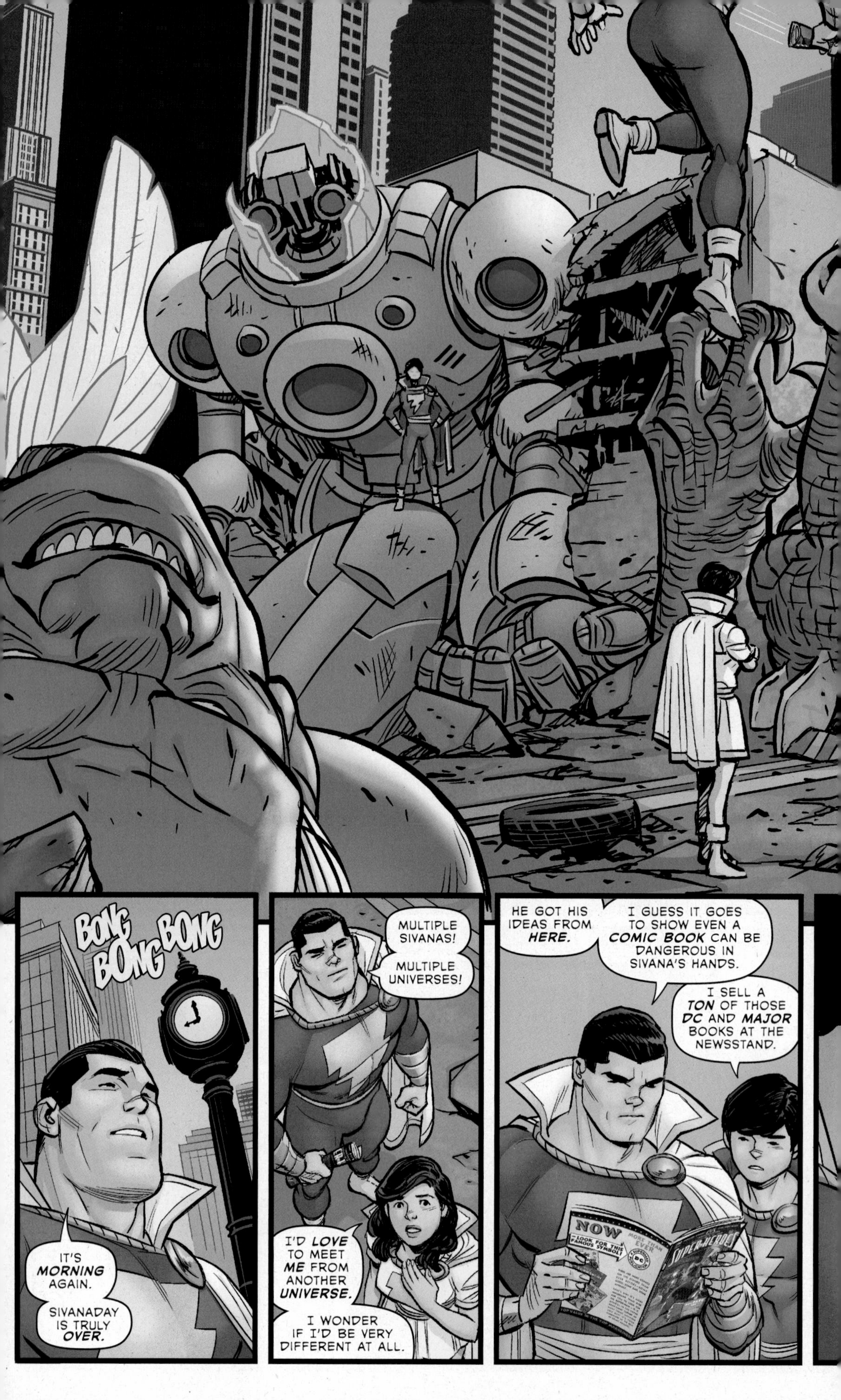

BONG BONG BONG
IT'S MORNING AGAIN.
SIVANADAY IS TRULY OVER.
MULTIPLE SIVANAS!
MULTIPLE UNIVERSES!
I'D LOVE TO MEET ME FROM ANOTHER UNIVERSE.
I WONDER IF I'D BE VERY DIFFERENT AT ALL.
HE GOT HIS IDEAS FROM HERE.
I GUESS IT GOES TO SHOW EVEN A COMIC BOOK CAN BE DANGEROUS IN SIVANA'S HANDS.
I SELL A TON OF THOSE DC AND MAJOR BOOKS AT THE NEWSSTAND.
NOW

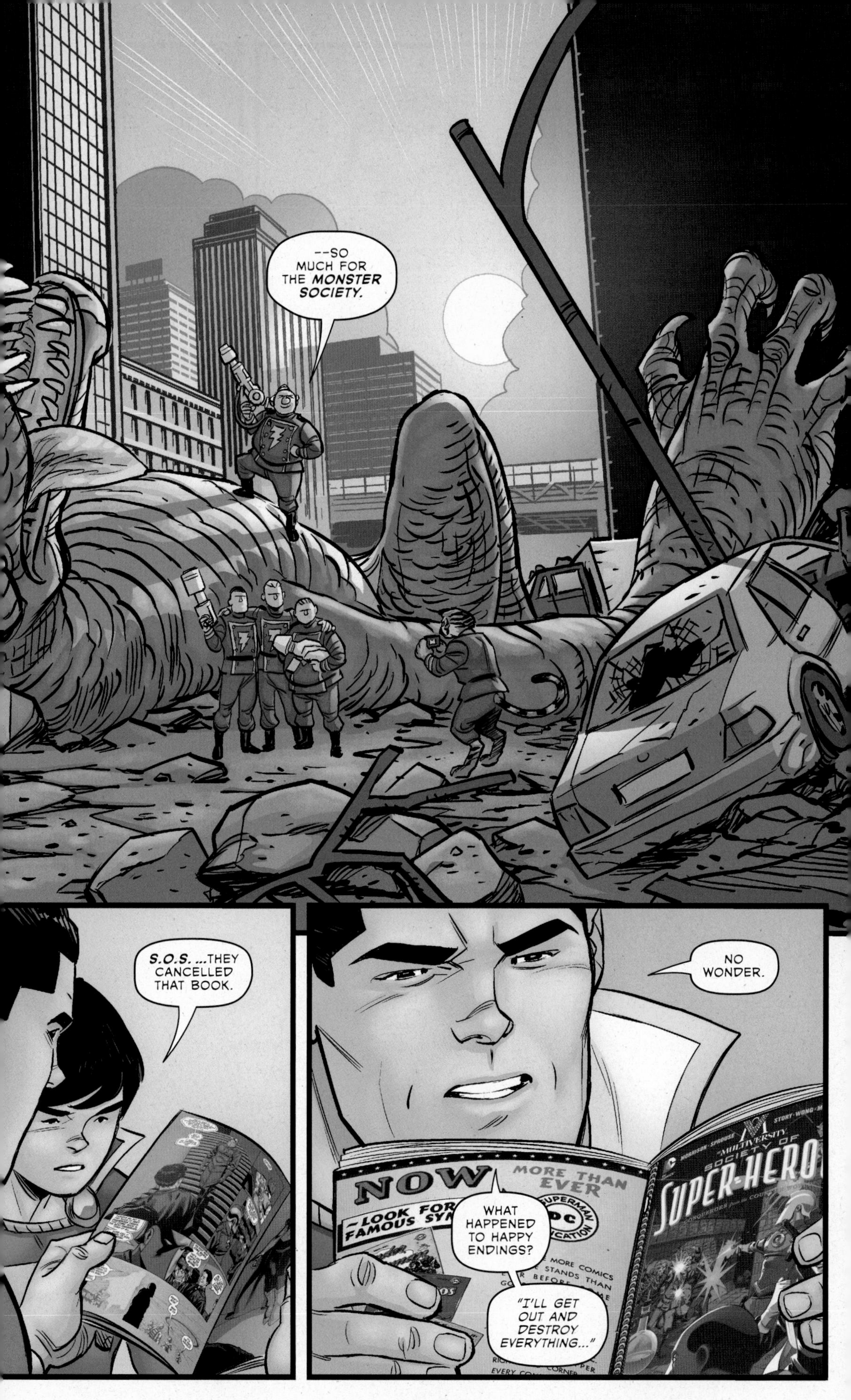
--SO MUCH FOR THE MONSTER SOCIETY.
S.O.S. ...THEY CANCELLED THAT BOOK.
NO WONDER.
WHAT HAPPENED TO HAPPY ENDINGS?
"I'LL GET OUT AND DESTROY EVERYTHING..."
NOW
MORE THAN EVER
SUPER-HEROES

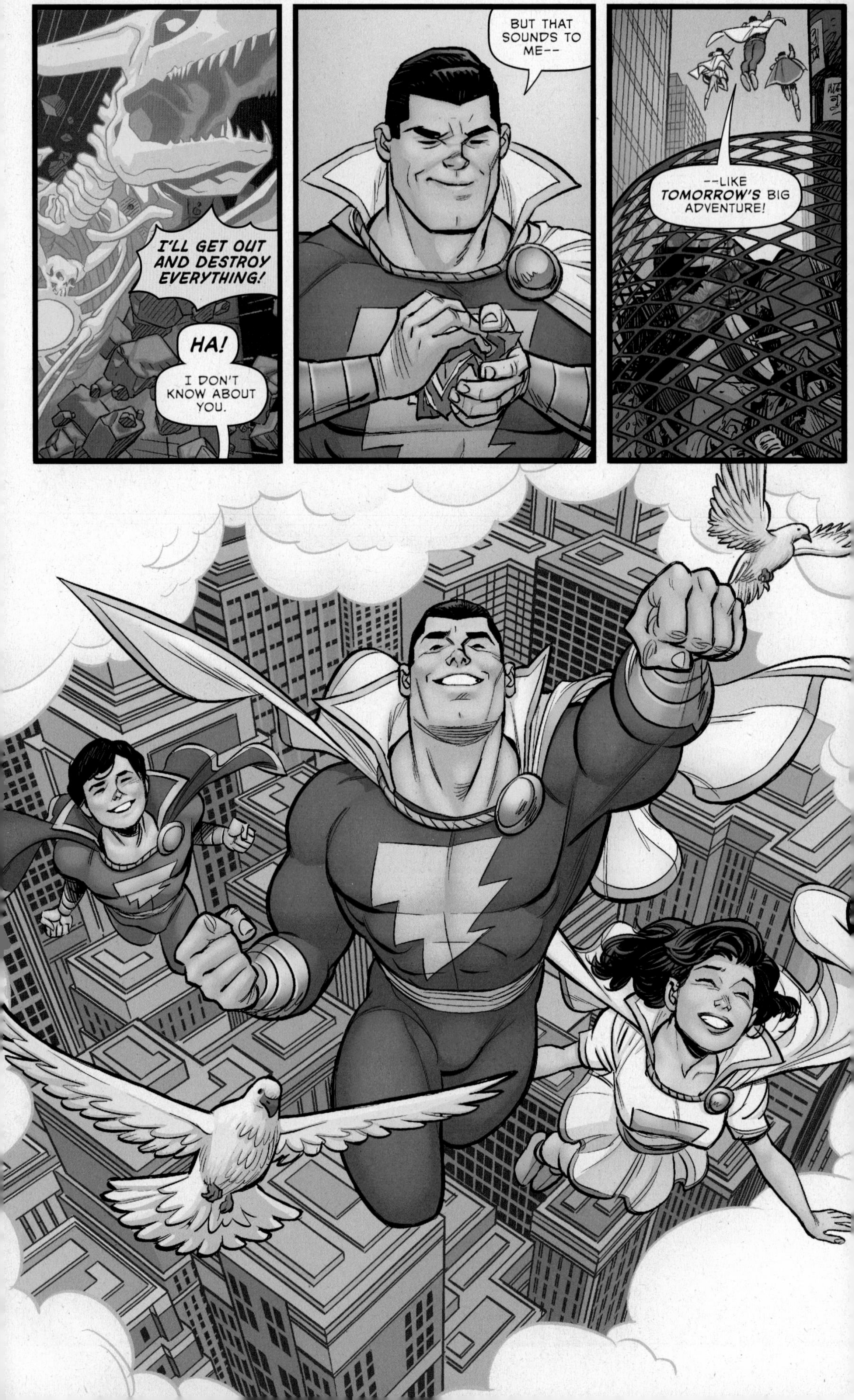
I'LL GET OUT AND DESTROY EVERYTHING!
HA!
I DON'T KNOW ABOUT YOU.
BUT THAT SOUNDS TO ME--
--LIKE TOMORROW'S BIG ADVENTURE!

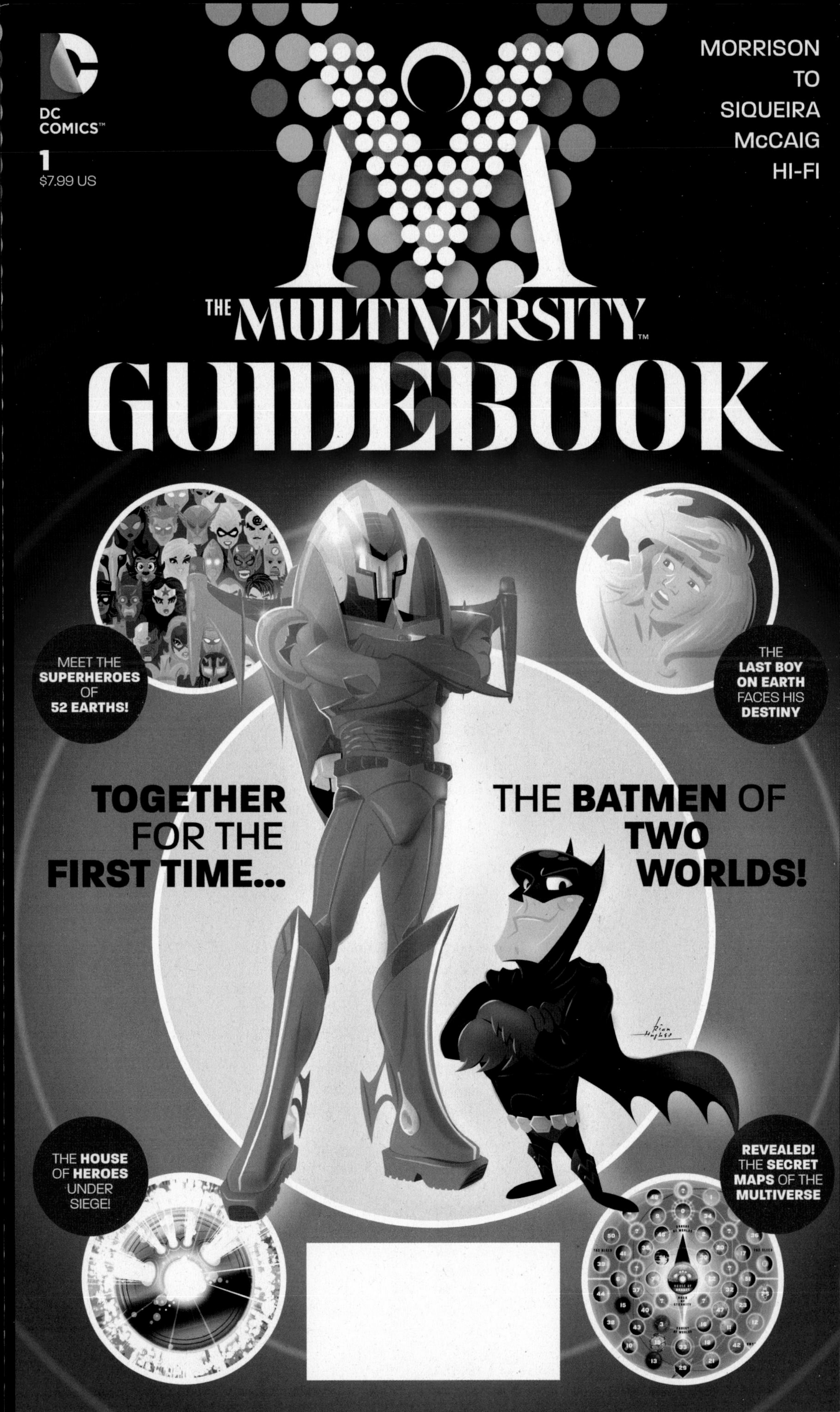
DC COMICS™
1
$7.99 US
MORRISON
TO
SIQUEIRA
McCAIG
HI-FI
THE MULTIVERSITY™
GUIDEBOOK
MEET THE SUPERHEROES OF 52 EARTHS!
THE LAST BOY ON EARTH FACES HIS DESTINY
TOGETHER FOR THE FIRST TIME...
THE BATMEN OF TWO WORLDS!
THE HOUSE OF HEROES UNDER SIEGE!
REVEALED! THE SECRET MAPS OF THE MULTIVERSE

CREDITS

Writer
GRANT MORRISON

BATMAN SECTION

Artist
MARCUS TO

Colorist
DAVE MCCAIG

KAMANDI SECTION

Layouts
SCOTT MCDANIEL

Finishes
PAULO SIQUEIRA

Colorist
HIFI

Letters
TODD KLEIN

THE MULTIVERSE ARTISTS

- Earth-**0**   Brett Booth and Norm Rapmund with Andrew Dalhouse
- Earth-**1**   Gary Frank with Nathan Fairbairn
- Earth-**2**   Nicola Scott and Trevor Scott with Pete Pantazis
- Earth-**3**   David Finch with Sonia Oback
- Earth-**4**   Juan Jose Ryp with Fairbairn
- Earth-**5**   Cameron Stewart with Fairbairn
- Earth-**6**   Marcus To with Tomeu Morey
- Earth-**7**   Joe Prado with Marcelo Maiolo
- Earth-**8**   Bryan Hitch with Alex Sinclair
- Earth-**9**   Dan Jurgens and Rapmund with Pantazis
- Earth-**10**   Mike Hawthorne with Fairbairn
- Earth-**11**   Emanuela Lupacchino with Tomeu Morey
- Earth-**12**   Jake Wyatt
- Earth-**13**   Jae Lee with June Chung
- Earth-**14**   ?
- Earth-**15**   Prado with Gabe Eltaeb
- Earth-**16**   Ben Oliver
- Earth-**17**   Kalman Andrasofszky with Fairbairn
- Earth-**18**   Andrew Robinson
- Earth-**19**   Giuseppe Camuncoli and Richard Friend with Fairbairn
- Earth-**20**   Chris Sprouse and Karl Story with Dave McCaig
- Earth-**21**   Darwyn Cooke
- Earth-**22**   Yildiray Cinar with Fairbairn
- Earth-**23**   Gene Ha
- Earth-**24**   ?
- Earth-**25**   ?
- Earth-**26**   Chris Burnham with Fairbairn
- Earth-**27**   ?
- Earth-**28**   ?
- Earth-**29**   Declan Shalvey with Jordie Bellaire
- Earth-**30**   Shalvey with Bellaire
- Earth-**31**   Cinar with McCaig
- Earth-**32**   Todd Nauck with Eltaeb
- Earth-**33**   Hitch with Sinclair
- Earth-**34**   Jeff Johnson with Fairbairn
- Earth-**35**   Camuncoli and Friend with Fairbairn
- Earth-**36**   Evan "Doc" Shaner with Fairbairn
- Earth-**37**   Jed Dougherty with Eltaeb
- Earth-**38**   by Jon Bogdanove with McCaig
- Earth-**39**   by To with McCaig
- Earth-**40**   Sprouse and Story with McCaig
- Earth-**41**   Hawthorne with Fairbairn
- Earth-**42**   To with McCaig
- Earth-**43**   Kelley Jones with McCaig
- Earth-**44**   Duncan Rouleau
- Earth-**45**   Andy MacDonald with McCaig
- Earth-**46**   ?
- Earth-**47**   Scott Hepburn with Fairbairn
- Earth-**48**   Camuncoli and Friend with Eltaeb
- Earth-**49**   ?
- Earth-**50**   Wyatt
- Earth-**51**   Paulo Siqueira with Eltaeb

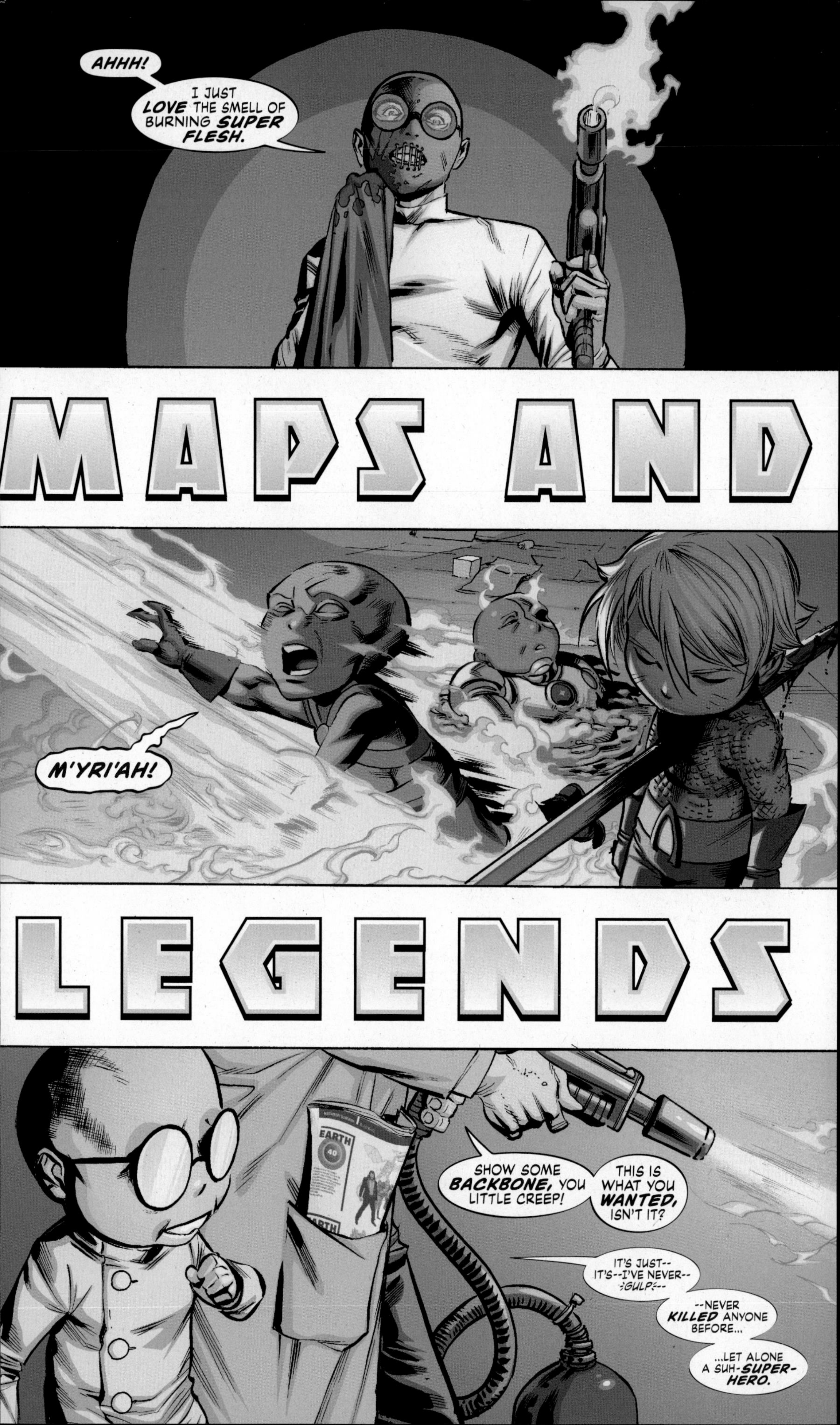
AHHH!
I JUST LOVE THE SMELL OF BURNING SUPER FLESH.
MAPS AND
M'YRI'AH!
LEGENDS
EARTH 40
SHOW SOME BACKBONE, YOU LITTLE CREEP!
THIS IS WHAT YOU WANTED, ISN'T IT?
IT'S JUST-- IT'S--I'VE NEVER-- *GULP*--
--NEVER KILLED ANYONE BEFORE...
...LET ALONE A SUH-SUPER-HERO.

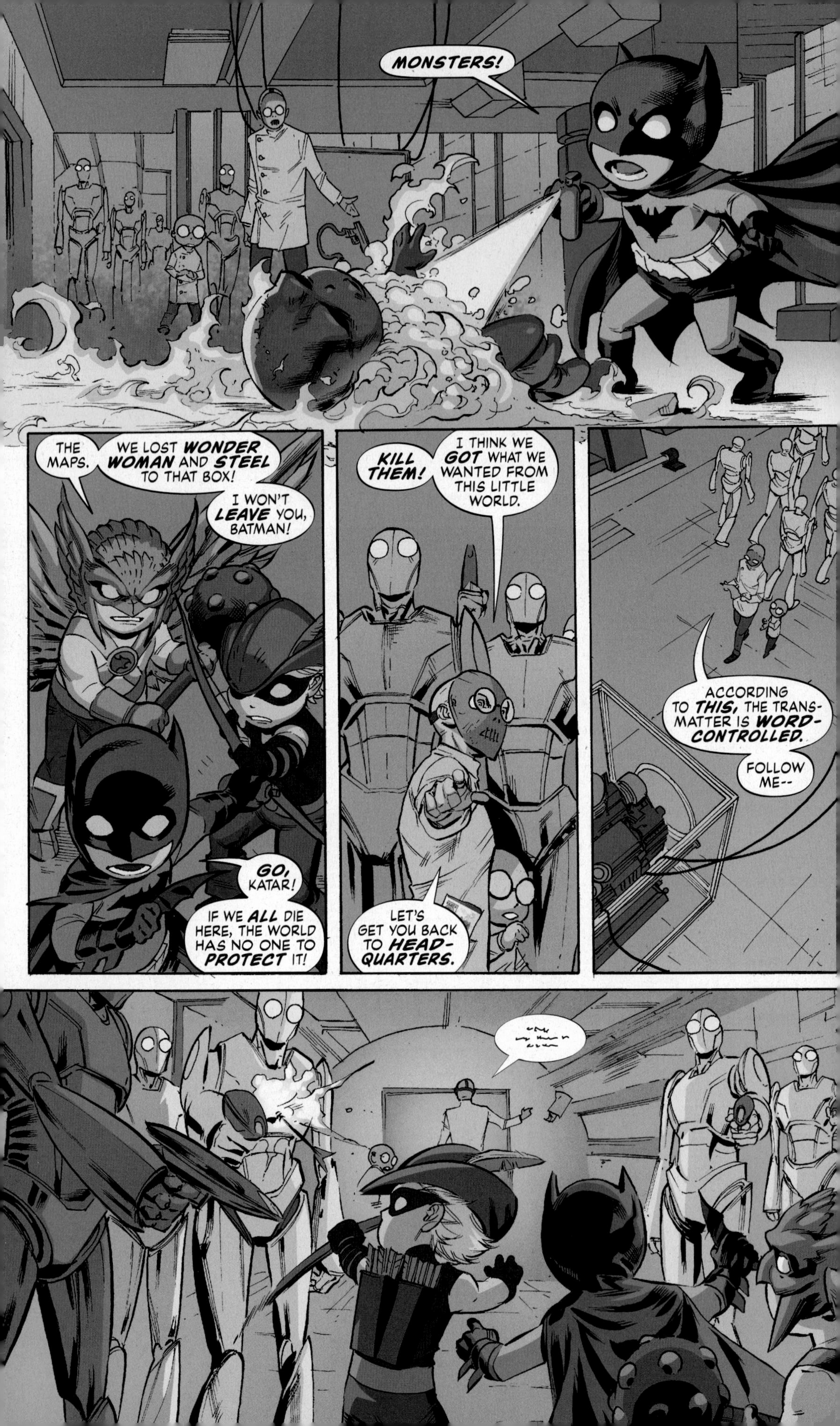
MONSTERS!
THE MAPS.
WE LOST WONDER WOMAN AND STEEL TO THAT BOX!
I WON'T LEAVE YOU, BATMAN!
GO, KATAR!
IF WE ALL DIE HERE, THE WORLD HAS NO ONE TO PROTECT IT!
KILL THEM!
I THINK WE GOT WHAT WE WANTED FROM THIS LITTLE WORLD.
LET'S GET YOU BACK TO HEAD-QUARTERS.
ACCORDING TO THIS, THE TRANS-MATTER IS WORD-CONTROLLED.
FOLLOW ME--

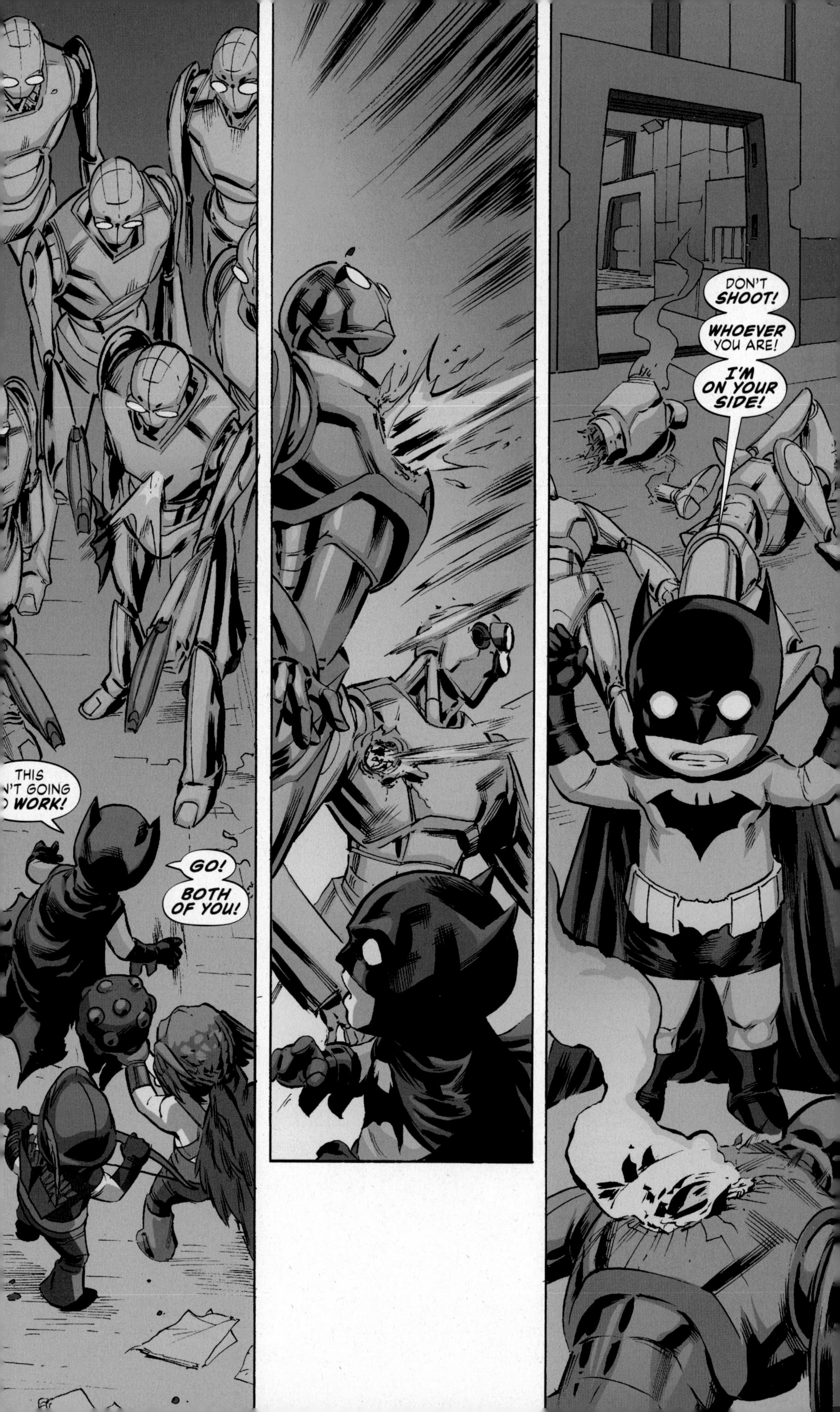
THIS N'T GOING O WORK!
GO! BOTH OF YOU!
DON'T SHOOT!
WHOEVER YOU ARE!
I'M ON YOUR SIDE!

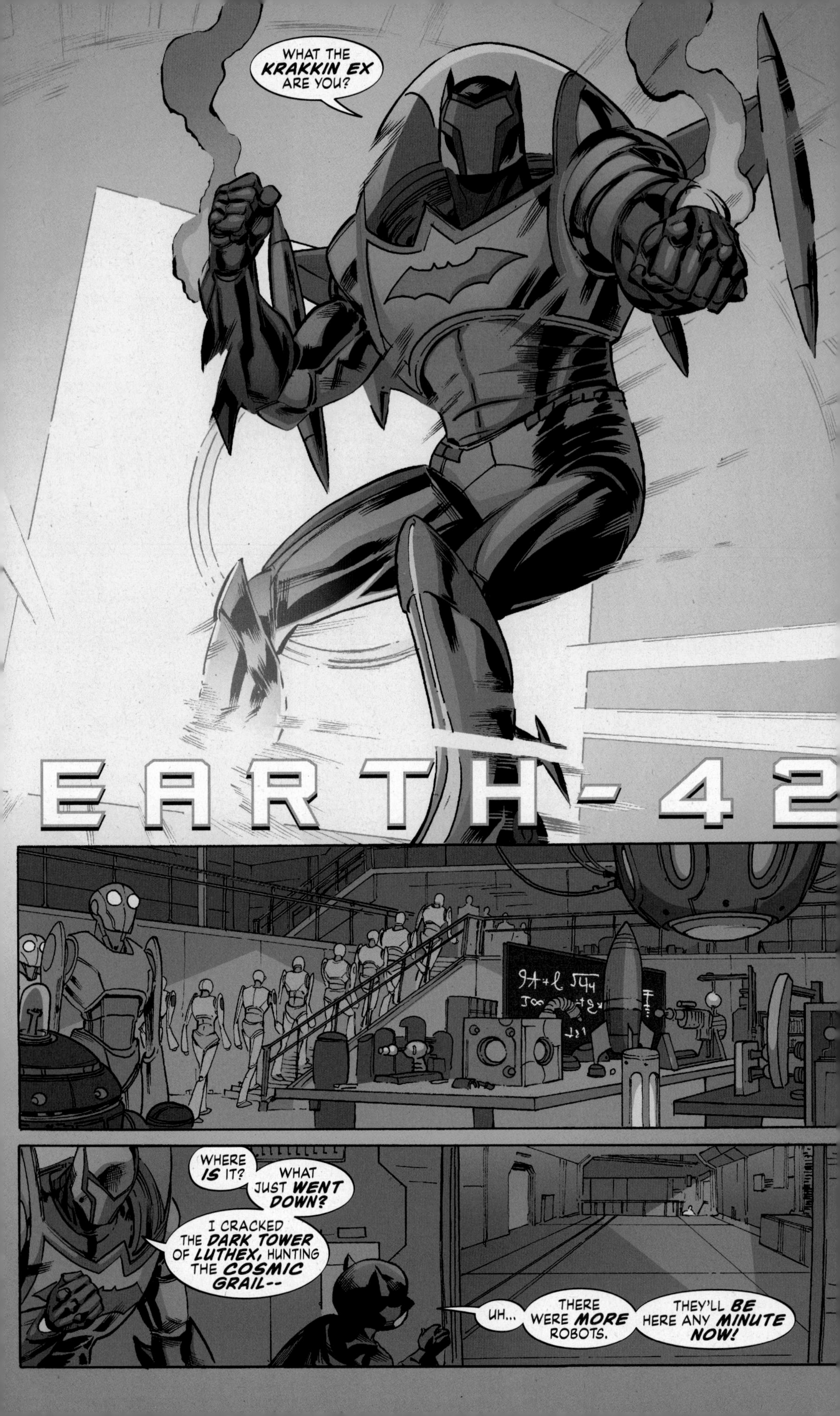
WHAT THE KRAKKIN EX ARE YOU?
EARTH-42
WHERE IS IT?
WHAT JUST WENT DOWN?
I CRACKED THE DARK TOWER OF LUTHEX, HUNTING THE COSMIC GRAIL--
UH...
THERE WERE MORE ROBOTS.
THEY'LL BE HERE ANY MINUTE NOW!

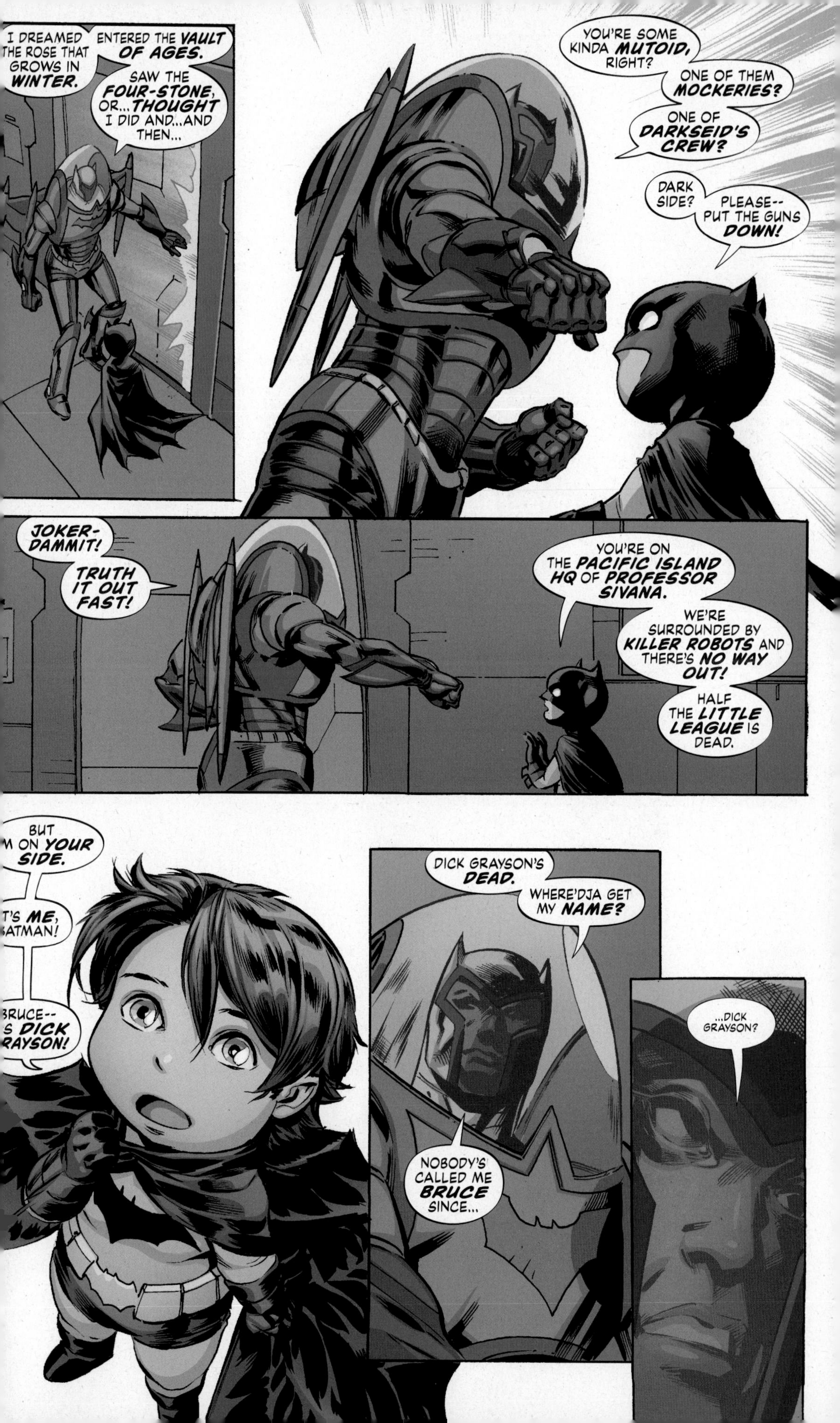

I DREAMED THE ROSE THAT GROWS IN WINTER.
ENTERED THE VAULT OF AGES.
SAW THE FOUR-STONE, OR...THOUGHT I DID AND...AND THEN...
YOU'RE SOME KINDA MUTOID, RIGHT?
ONE OF THEM MOCKERIES?
ONE OF DARKSEID'S CREW?
DARK SIDE?
PLEASE-- PUT THE GUNS DOWN!
JOKER-DAMMIT!
TRUTH IT OUT FAST!
YOU'RE ON THE PACIFIC ISLAND HQ OF PROFESSOR SIVANA.
WE'RE SURROUNDED BY KILLER ROBOTS AND THERE'S NO WAY OUT!
HALF THE LITTLE LEAGUE IS DEAD.
BUT
M ON YOUR SIDE.
T'S ME, ATMAN!
BRUCE--
S DICK RAYSON!
DICK GRAYSON'S DEAD.
WHERE'DJA GET MY NAME?
NOBODY'S CALLED ME BRUCE SINCE...
...DICK GRAYSON?

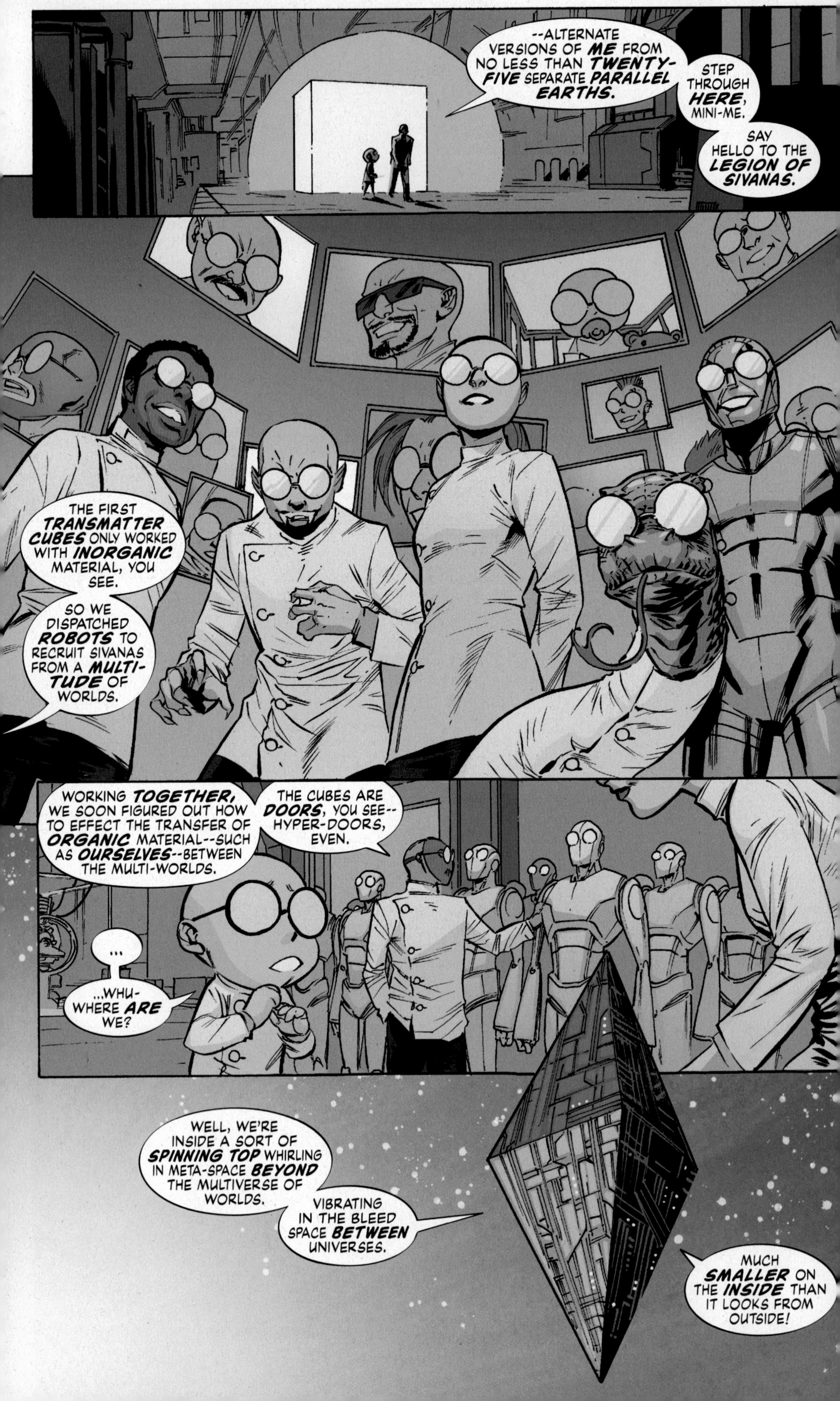
--ALTERNATE VERSIONS OF ME FROM NO LESS THAN TWENTY-FIVE SEPARATE PARALLEL EARTHS.
STEP THROUGH HERE, MINI-ME.
SAY HELLO TO THE LEGION OF SIVANAS.
THE FIRST TRANSMATTER CUBES ONLY WORKED WITH INORGANIC MATERIAL, YOU SEE.
SO WE DISPATCHED ROBOTS TO RECRUIT SIVANAS FROM A MULTI-TUDE OF WORLDS.
WORKING TOGETHER, WE SOON FIGURED OUT HOW TO EFFECT THE TRANSFER OF ORGANIC MATERIAL--SUCH AS OURSELVES--BETWEEN THE MULTI-WORLDS.
THE CUBES ARE DOORS, YOU SEE--HYPER-DOORS, EVEN.
...
...WHU-WHERE ARE WE?
WELL, WE'RE INSIDE A SORT OF SPINNING TOP WHIRLING IN META-SPACE BEYOND THE MULTIVERSE OF WORLDS.
VIBRATING IN THE BLEED SPACE BETWEEN UNIVERSES.
MUCH SMALLER ON THE INSIDE THAN IT LOOKS FROM OUTSIDE!

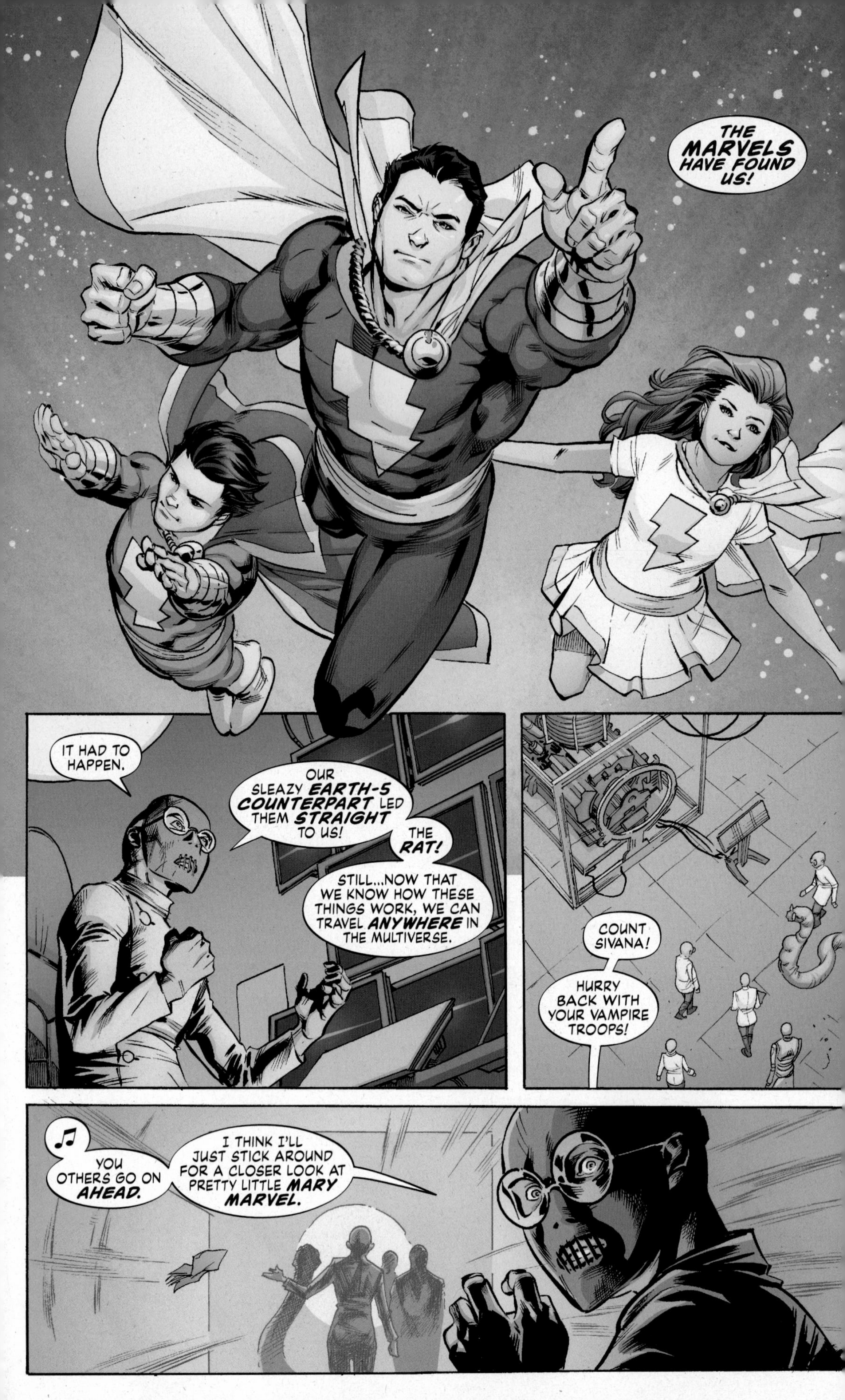
THE MARVELS HAVE FOUND US!
IT HAD TO HAPPEN.
OUR SLEAZY EARTH-5 COUNTERPART LED THEM STRAIGHT TO US!
THE RAT!
STILL...NOW THAT WE KNOW HOW THESE THINGS WORK, WE CAN TRAVEL ANYWHERE IN THE MULTIVERSE.
COUNT SIVANA!
HURRY BACK WITH YOUR VAMPIRE TROOPS!
♪
YOU OTHERS GO ON AHEAD.
I THINK I'LL JUST STICK AROUND FOR A CLOSER LOOK AT PRETTY LITTLE MARY MARVEL.

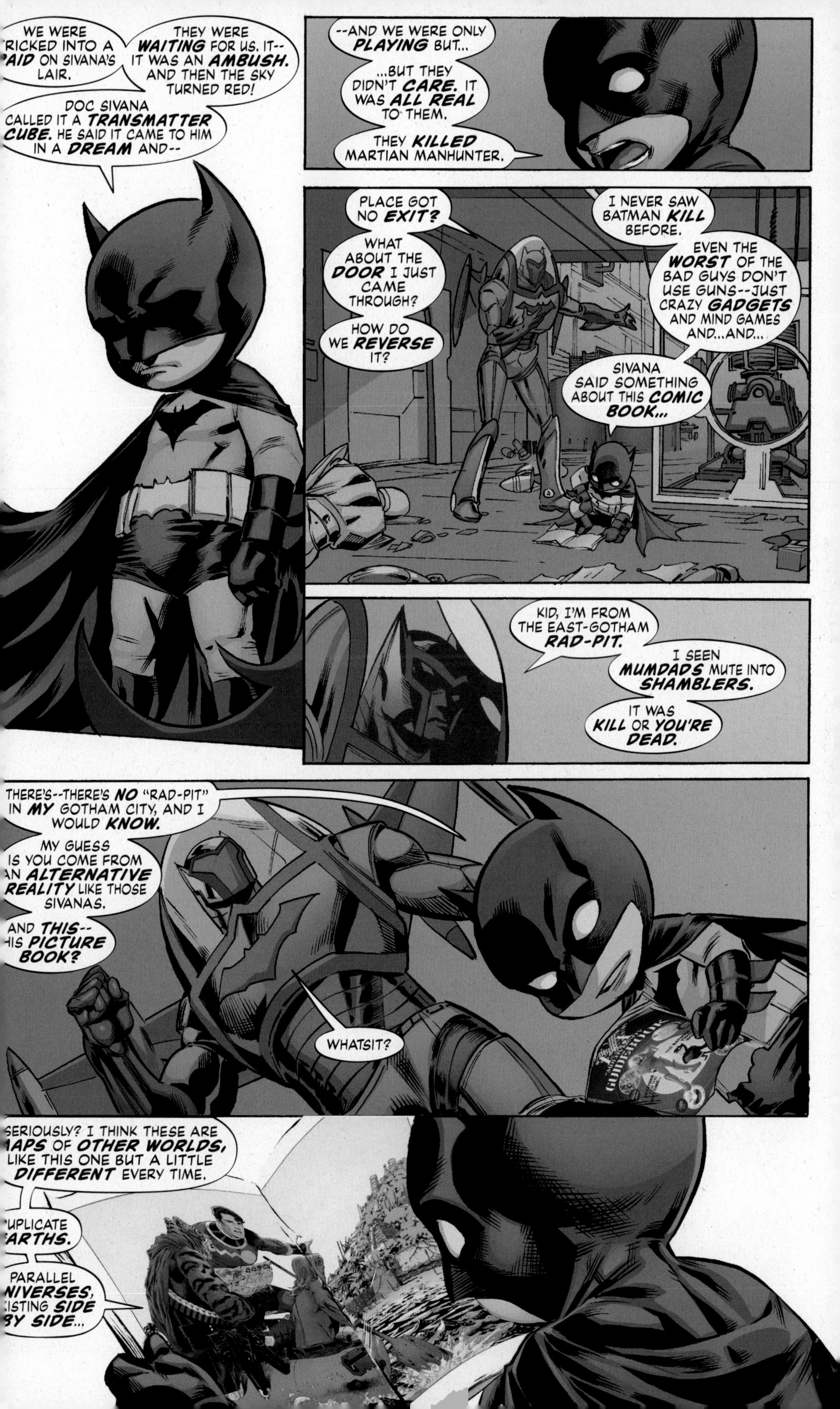

WE WERE
RICKED INTO A
AID ON SIVANA'S
LAIR.
THEY WERE WAITING FOR US. IT-- IT WAS AN AMBUSH. AND THEN THE SKY TURNED RED!
DOC SIVANA CALLED IT A TRANSMATTER CUBE. HE SAID IT CAME TO HIM IN A DREAM AND--
--AND WE WERE ONLY PLAYING BUT...
...BUT THEY DIDN'T CARE. IT WAS ALL REAL TO THEM.
THEY KILLED MARTIAN MANHUNTER.
PLACE GOT NO EXIT?
WHAT ABOUT THE DOOR I JUST CAME THROUGH?
HOW DO WE REVERSE IT?
I NEVER SAW BATMAN KILL BEFORE.
EVEN THE WORST OF THE BAD GUYS DON'T USE GUNS--JUST CRAZY GADGETS AND MIND GAMES AND...AND...
SIVANA SAID SOMETHING ABOUT THIS COMIC BOOK...
KID, I'M FROM THE EAST-GOTHAM RAD-PIT.
I SEEN MUMDADS MUTE INTO SHAMBLERS.
IT WAS KILL OR YOU'RE DEAD.
THERE'S--THERE'S NO "RAD-PIT" IN MY GOTHAM CITY, AND I WOULD KNOW.
MY GUESS IS YOU COME FROM
N ALTERNATIVE
REALITY LIKE THOSE SIVANAS.
AND THIS--
HIS PICTURE BOOK?
WHATSIT?
SERIOUSLY? I THINK THESE ARE
IAPS OF OTHER WORLDS,
LIKE THIS ONE BUT A LITTLE DIFFERENT EVERY TIME.
UPLICATE
ARTHS.
PARALLEL
NIVERSES,
ISTING SIDE
BY SIDE...

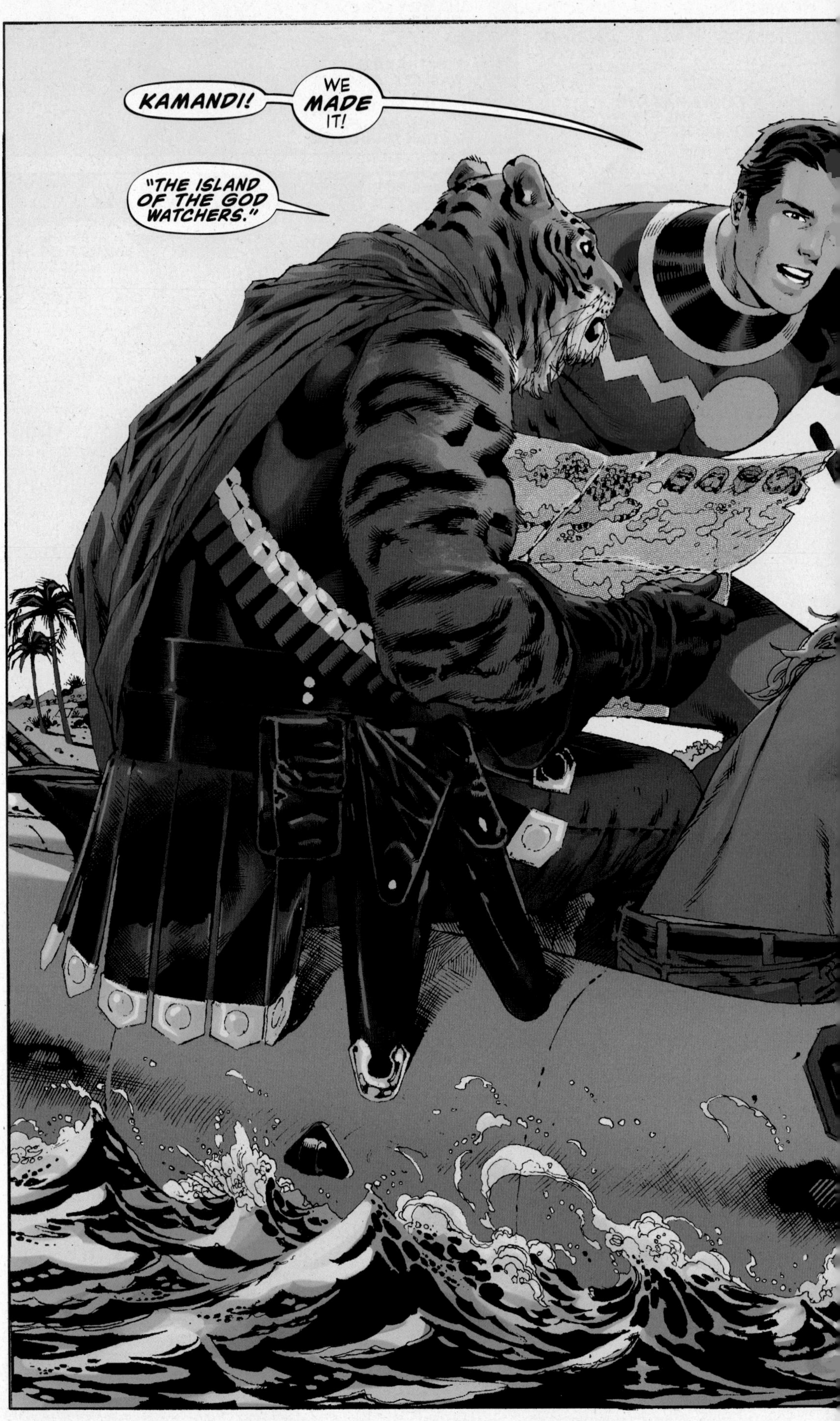
KAMANDI!
WE MADE IT!
"THE ISLAND OF THE GOD WATCHERS."

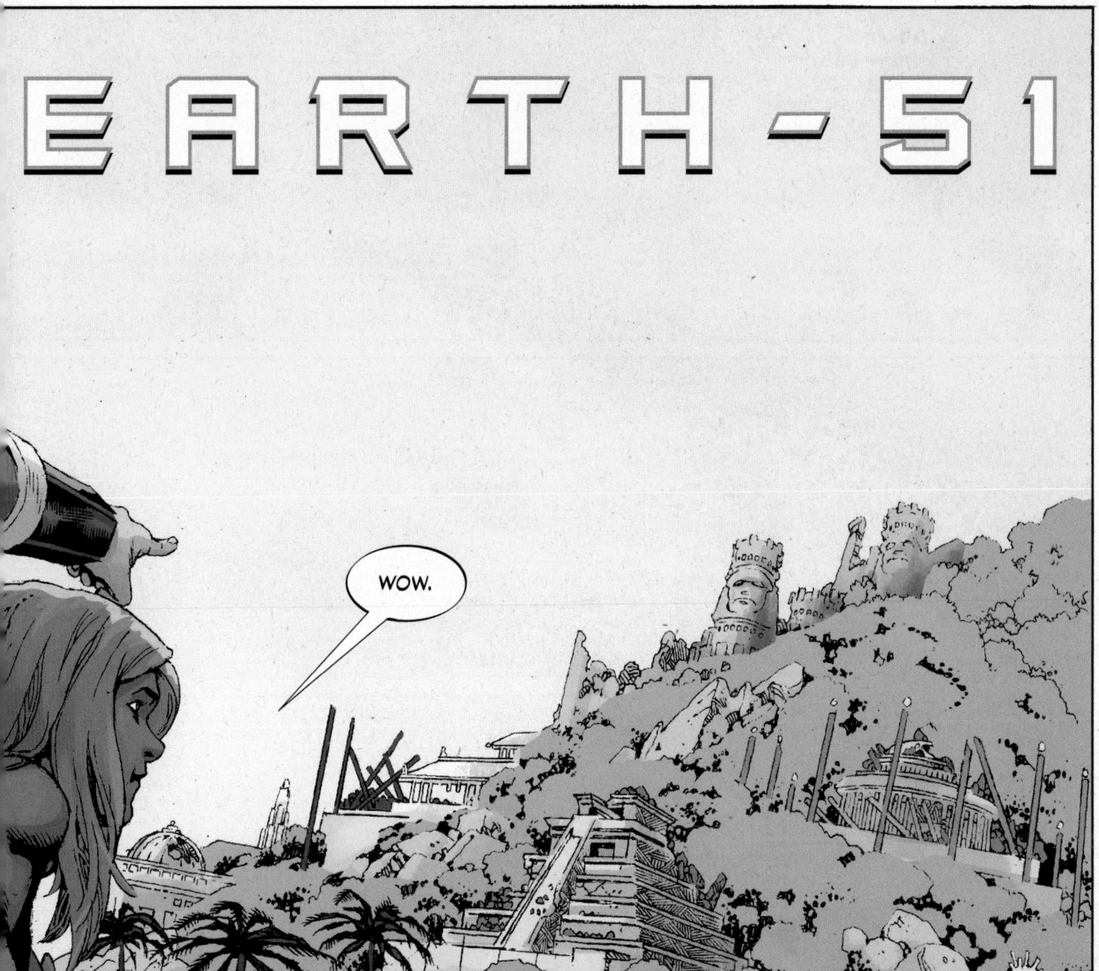
EARTH-51
WOW.

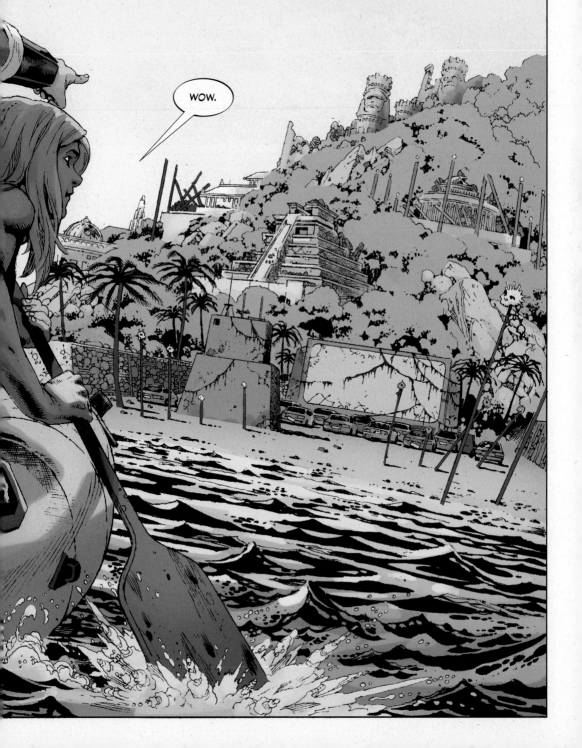

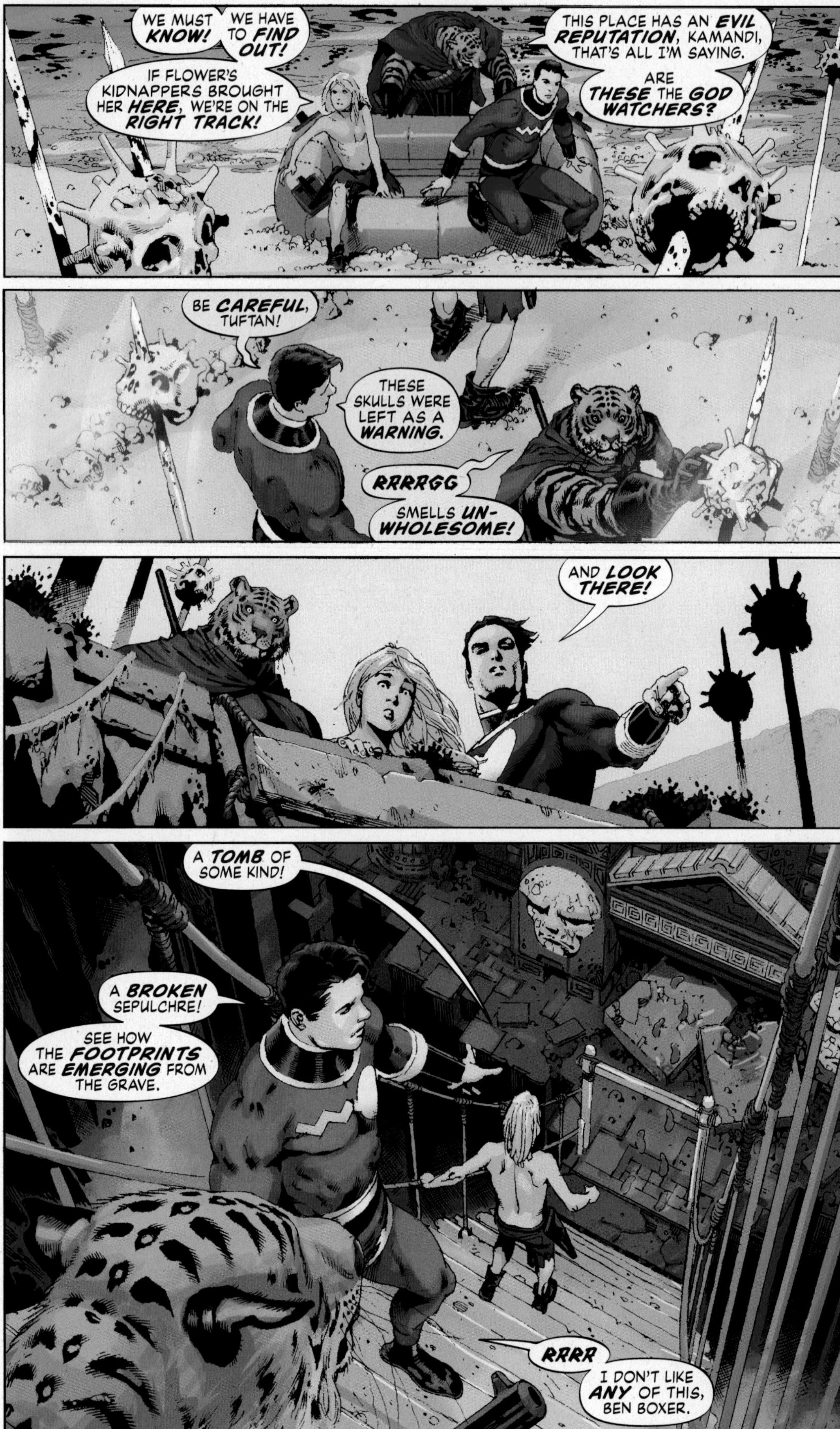
WE MUST KNOW!
WE HAVE TO FIND OUT!
IF FLOWER'S KIDNAPPERS BROUGHT HER HERE, WE'RE ON THE RIGHT TRACK!
THIS PLACE HAS AN EVIL REPUTATION, KAMANDI, THAT'S ALL I'M SAYING.
ARE THESE THE GOD WATCHERS?
BE CAREFUL, TUFTAN!
THESE SKULLS WERE LEFT AS A WARNING.
RRRRGG
SMELLS UN-WHOLESOME!
AND LOOK THERE!
A TOMB OF SOME KIND!
A BROKEN SEPULCHRE!
SEE HOW THE FOOTPRINTS ARE EMERGING FROM THE GRAVE.
RRRR
I DON'T LIKE ANY OF THIS, BEN BOXER.

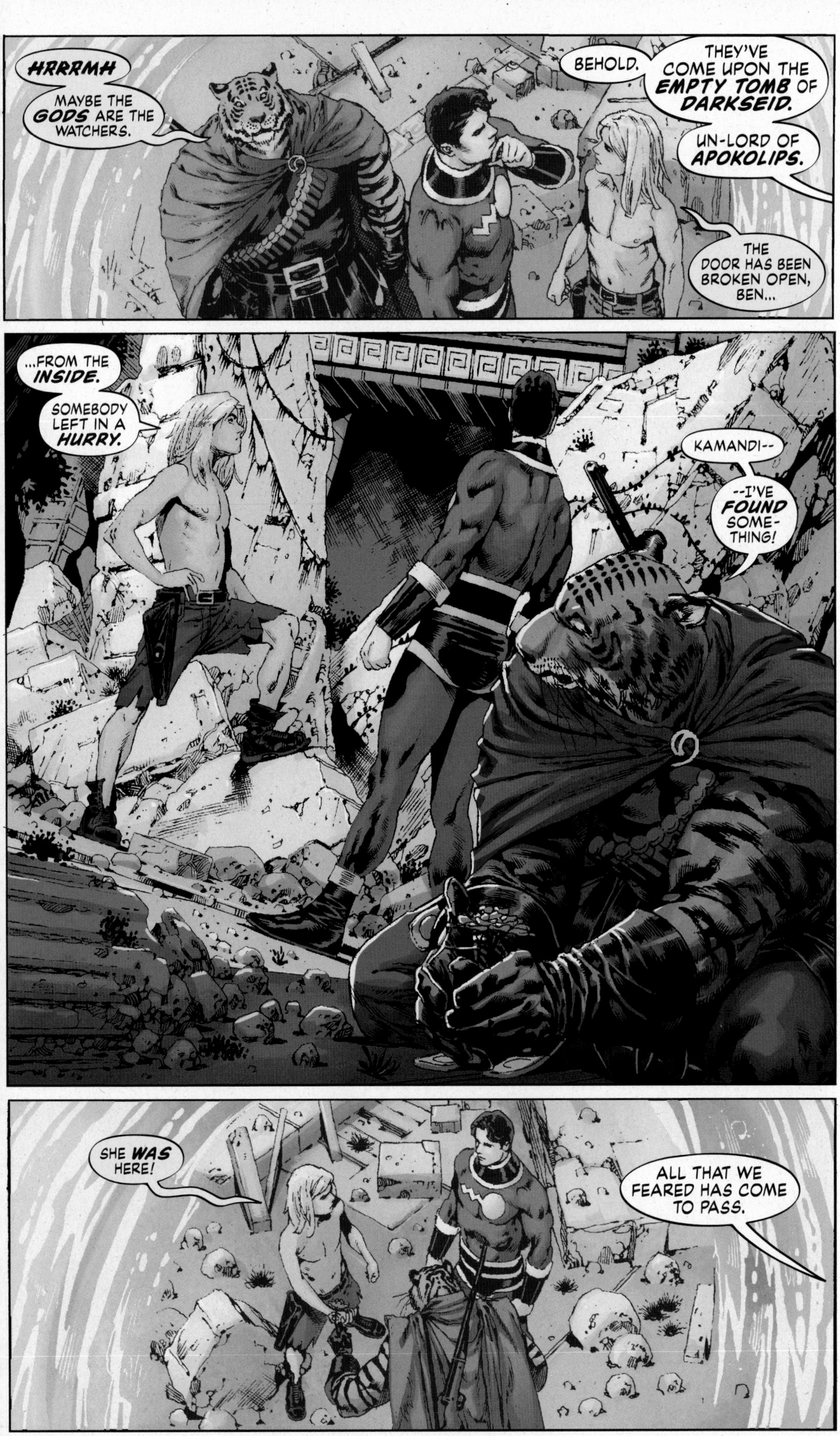

HRRRMH
MAYBE THE GODS ARE THE WATCHERS.
BEHOLD.
THEY'VE COME UPON THE EMPTY TOMB OF DARKSEID.
UN-LORD OF APOKOLIPS.
THE DOOR HAS BEEN BROKEN OPEN, BEN...
...FROM THE INSIDE.
SOMEBODY LEFT IN A HURRY.
KAMANDI--
--I'VE FOUND SOME-THING!
SHE WAS HERE!
ALL THAT WE FEARED HAS COME TO PASS.

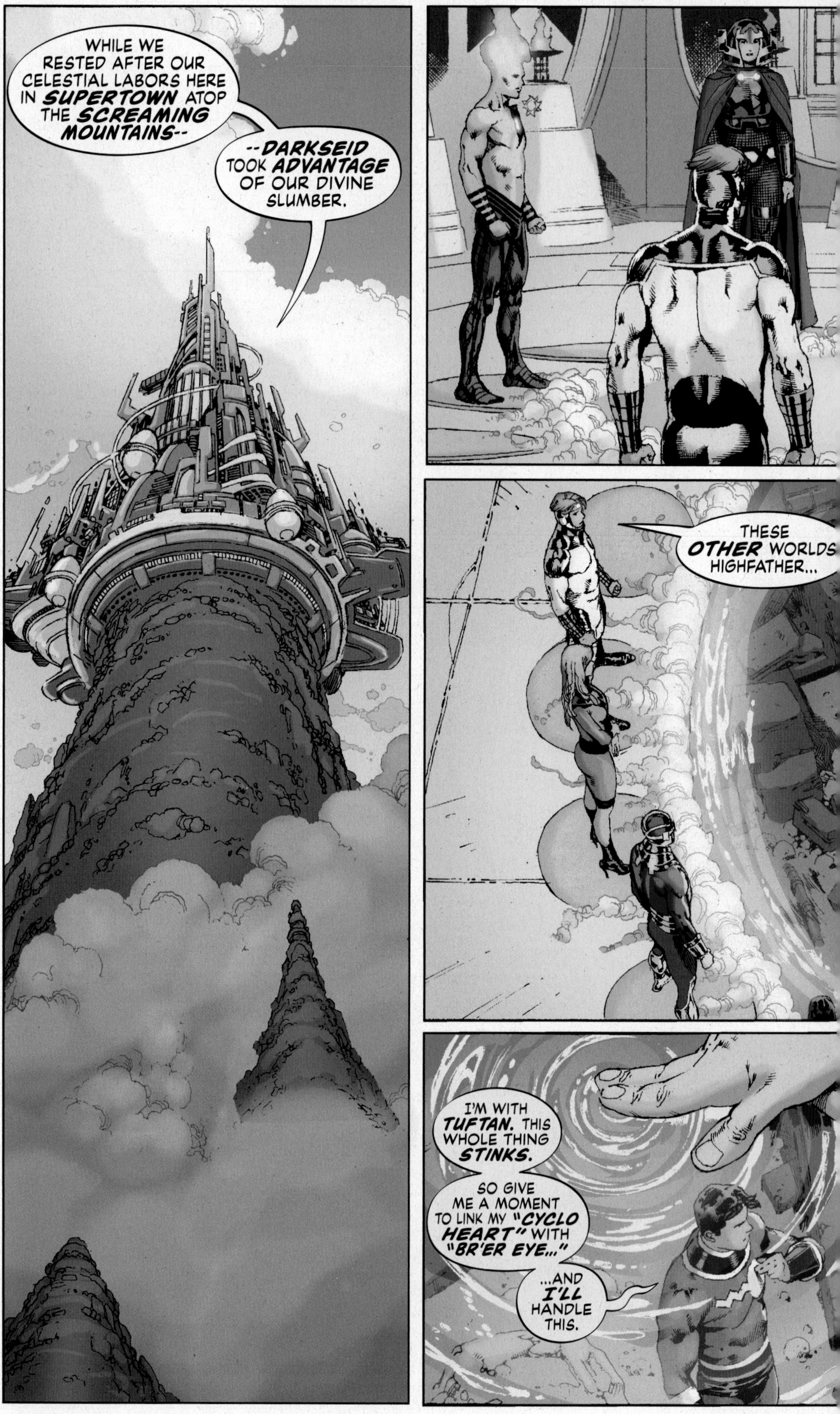
WHILE WE RESTED AFTER OUR CELESTIAL LABORS HERE IN SUPERTOWN ATOP THE SCREAMING MOUNTAINS--
--DARKSEID TOOK ADVANTAGE OF OUR DIVINE SLUMBER.
THESE OTHER WORLDS HIGHFATHER...
I'M WITH TUFTAN. THIS WHOLE THING STINKS.
SO GIVE ME A MOMENT TO LINK MY "CYCLO HEART" WITH "BR'ER EYE..."
...AND I'LL HANDLE THIS.

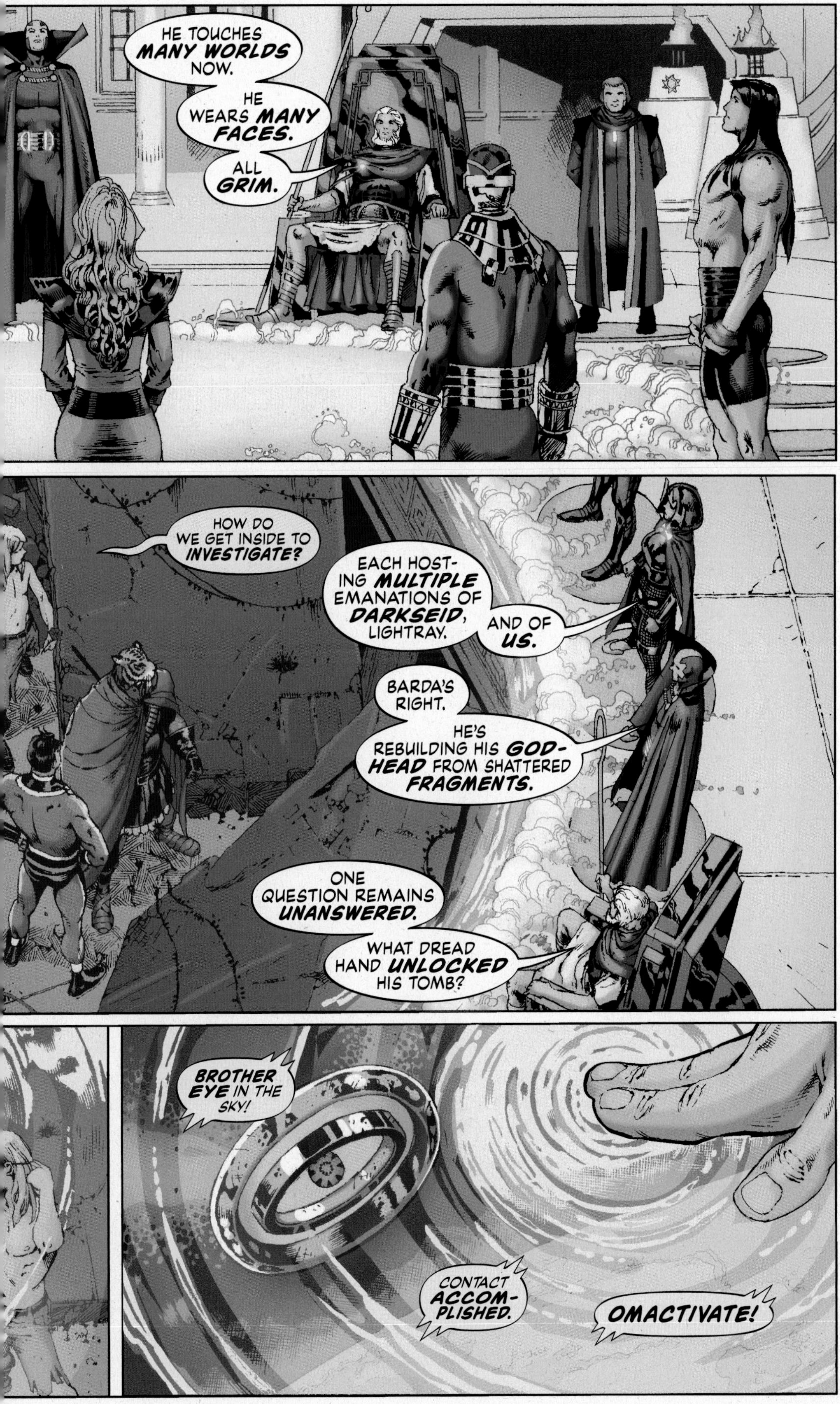
HE TOUCHES MANY WORLDS NOW.
HE WEARS MANY FACES.
ALL GRIM.
HOW DO WE GET INSIDE TO INVESTIGATE?
EACH HOSTING MULTIPLE EMANATIONS OF DARKSEID, LIGHTRAY.
AND OF US.
BARDA'S RIGHT.
HE'S REBUILDING HIS GODHEAD FROM SHATTERED FRAGMENTS.
ONE QUESTION REMAINS UNANSWERED.
WHAT DREAD HAND UNLOCKED HIS TOMB?
BROTHER EYE IN THE SKY!
CONTACT ACCOMPLISHED.
OMACTIVATE!

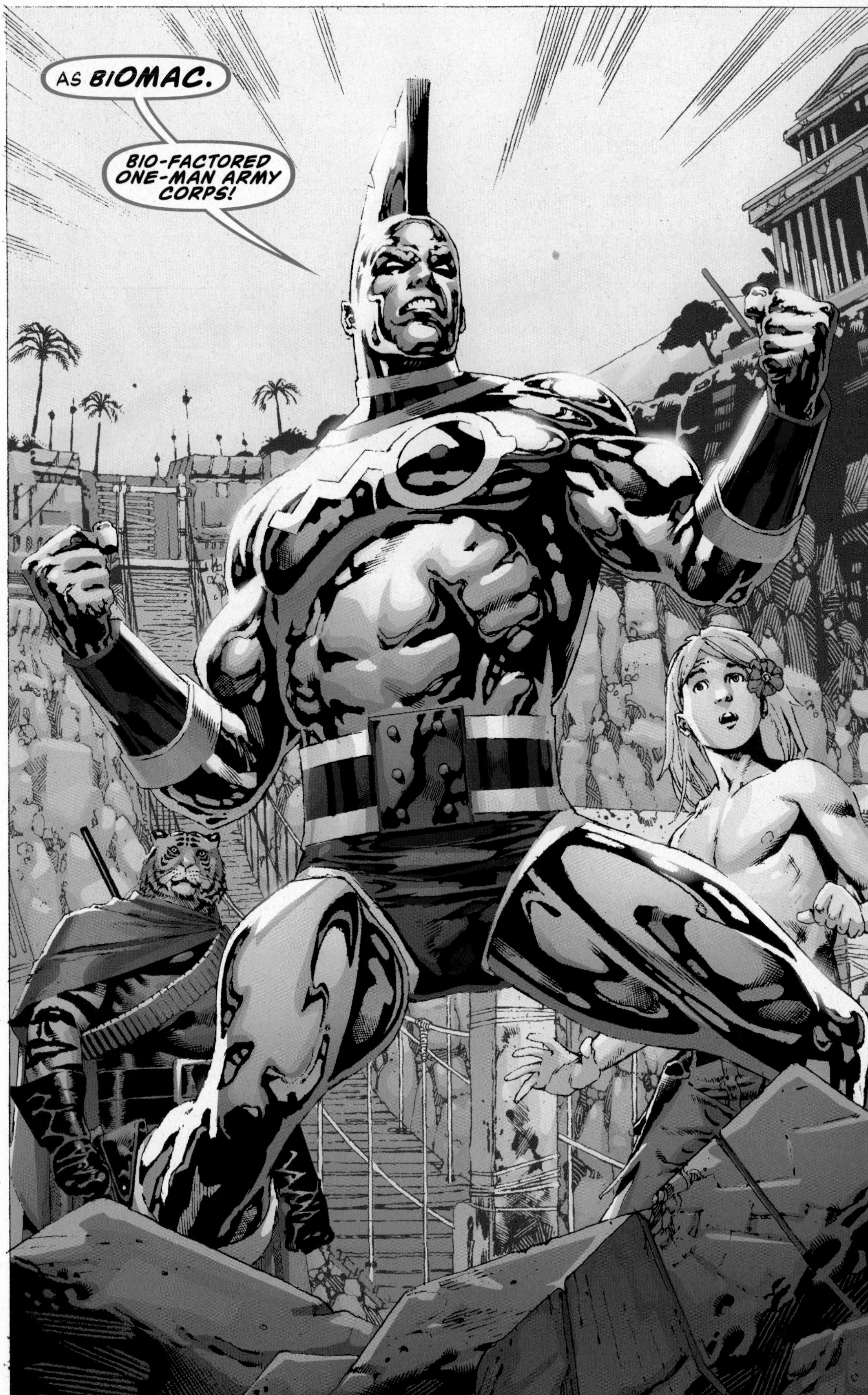
AS BIOMAC.
BIO-FACTORED ONE-MAN ARMY CORPS!

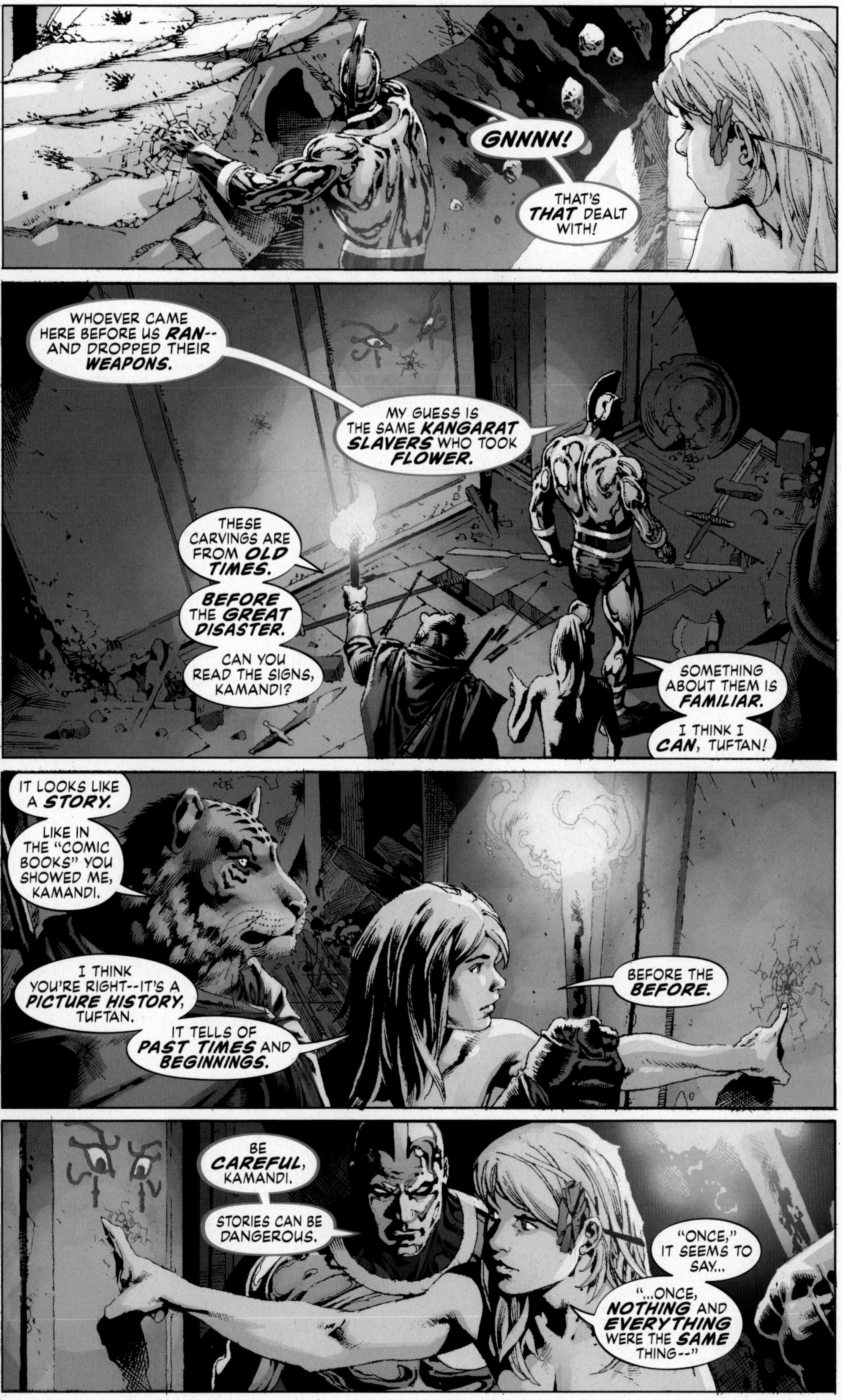
GNNNN!
THAT'S THAT DEALT WITH!
WHOEVER CAME HERE BEFORE US RAN-- AND DROPPED THEIR WEAPONS.
MY GUESS IS THE SAME KANGARAT SLAVERS WHO TOOK FLOWER.
THESE CARVINGS ARE FROM OLD TIMES.
BEFORE THE GREAT DISASTER.
CAN YOU READ THE SIGNS, KAMANDI?
SOMETHING ABOUT THEM IS FAMILIAR.
I THINK I CAN, TUFTAN!
IT LOOKS LIKE A STORY.
LIKE IN THE "COMIC BOOKS" YOU SHOWED ME, KAMANDI.
I THINK YOU'RE RIGHT--IT'S A PICTURE HISTORY, TUFTAN.
IT TELLS OF PAST TIMES AND BEGINNINGS.
BEFORE THE BEFORE.
BE CAREFUL, KAMANDI.
STORIES CAN BE DANGEROUS.
"ONCE," IT SEEMS TO SAY...
"...ONCE, NOTHING AND EVERYTHING WERE THE SAME THING--"

And Then!

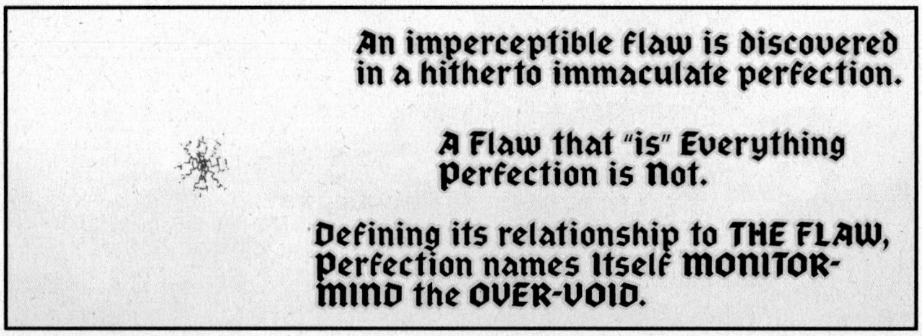
An imperceptible flaw is discovered in a hitherto immaculate perfection.
A Flaw that "is" Everything Perfection is Not.
Defining its relationship to THE FLAW, Perfection names Itself MONITOR-MIND the OVER-VOID.

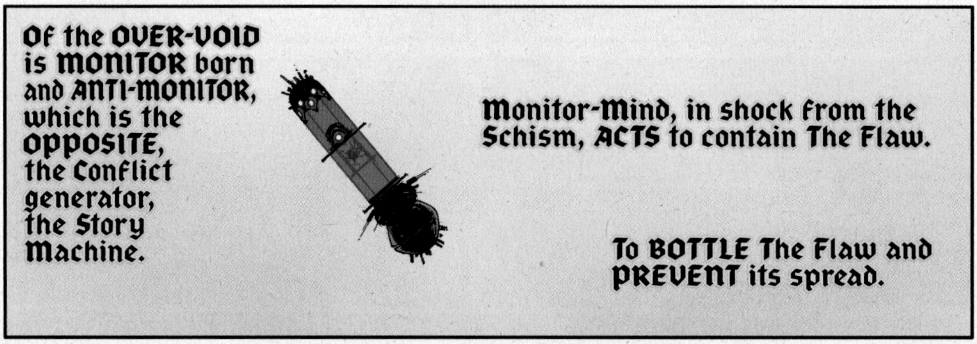
Of the OVER-VOID is MONITOR born and ANTI-MONITOR, which is the OPPOSITE, the Conflict generator, the Story Machine.
Monitor-Mind, in shock from the Schism, ACTS to contain The Flaw.
To BOTTLE The Flaw and PREVENT its spread.

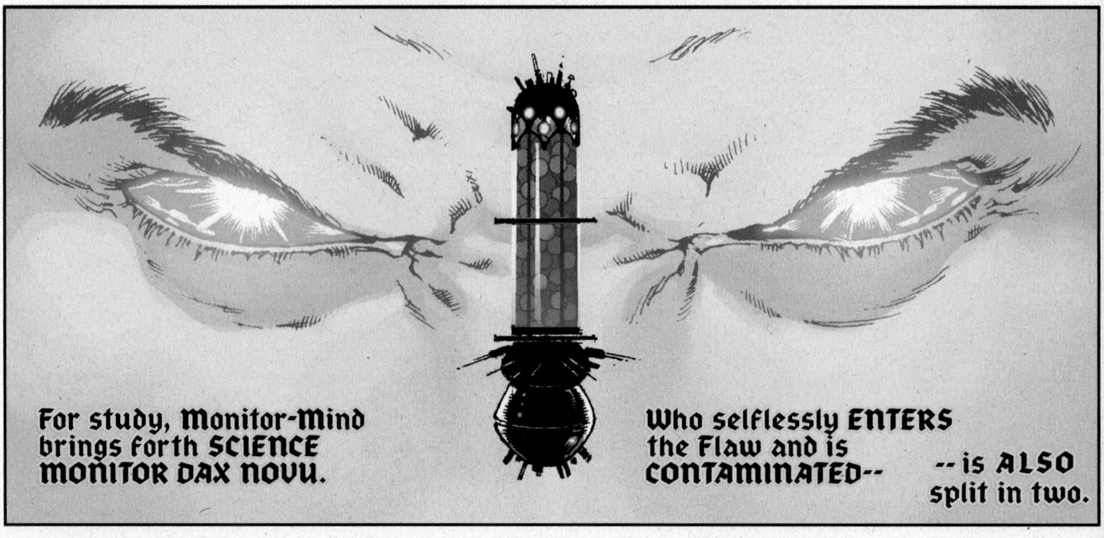
For study, Monitor-Mind brings forth SCIENCE MONITOR DAX NOVU.
Who selflessly ENTERS the Flaw and is CONTAMINATED--
--is ALSO split in two.

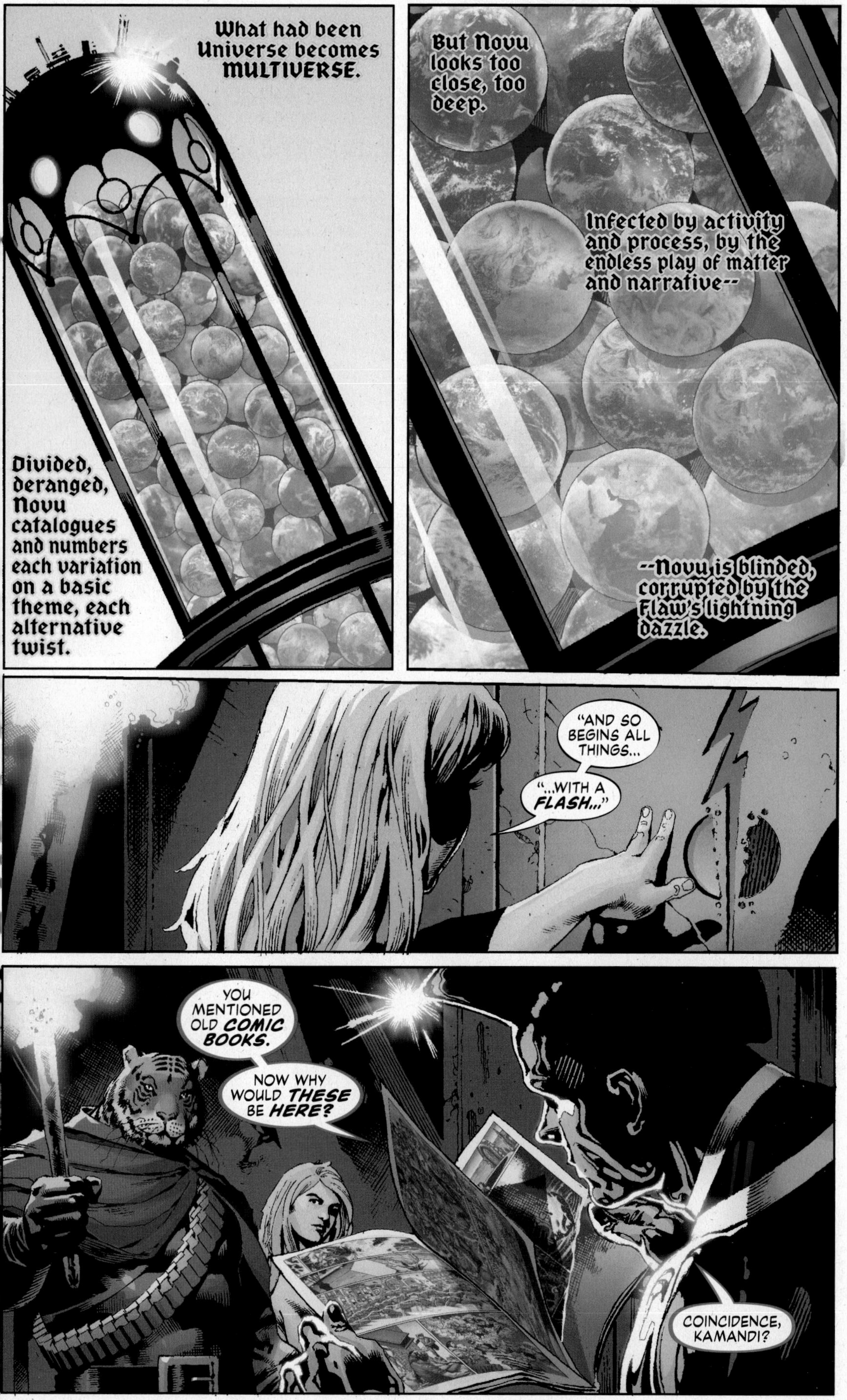
What had been Universe becomes MULTIVERSE.
Divided, deranged, Novu catalogues and numbers each variation on a basic theme, each alternative twist.
But Novu looks too close, too deep.
Infected by activity and process, by the endless play of matter and narrative--
--Novu is blinded, corrupted by the Flaw's lightning dazzle.
"AND SO BEGINS ALL THINGS...
"...WITH A FLASH..."
YOU MENTIONED OLD COMIC BOOKS.
NOW WHY WOULD THESE BE HERE?
COINCIDENCE, KAMANDI?

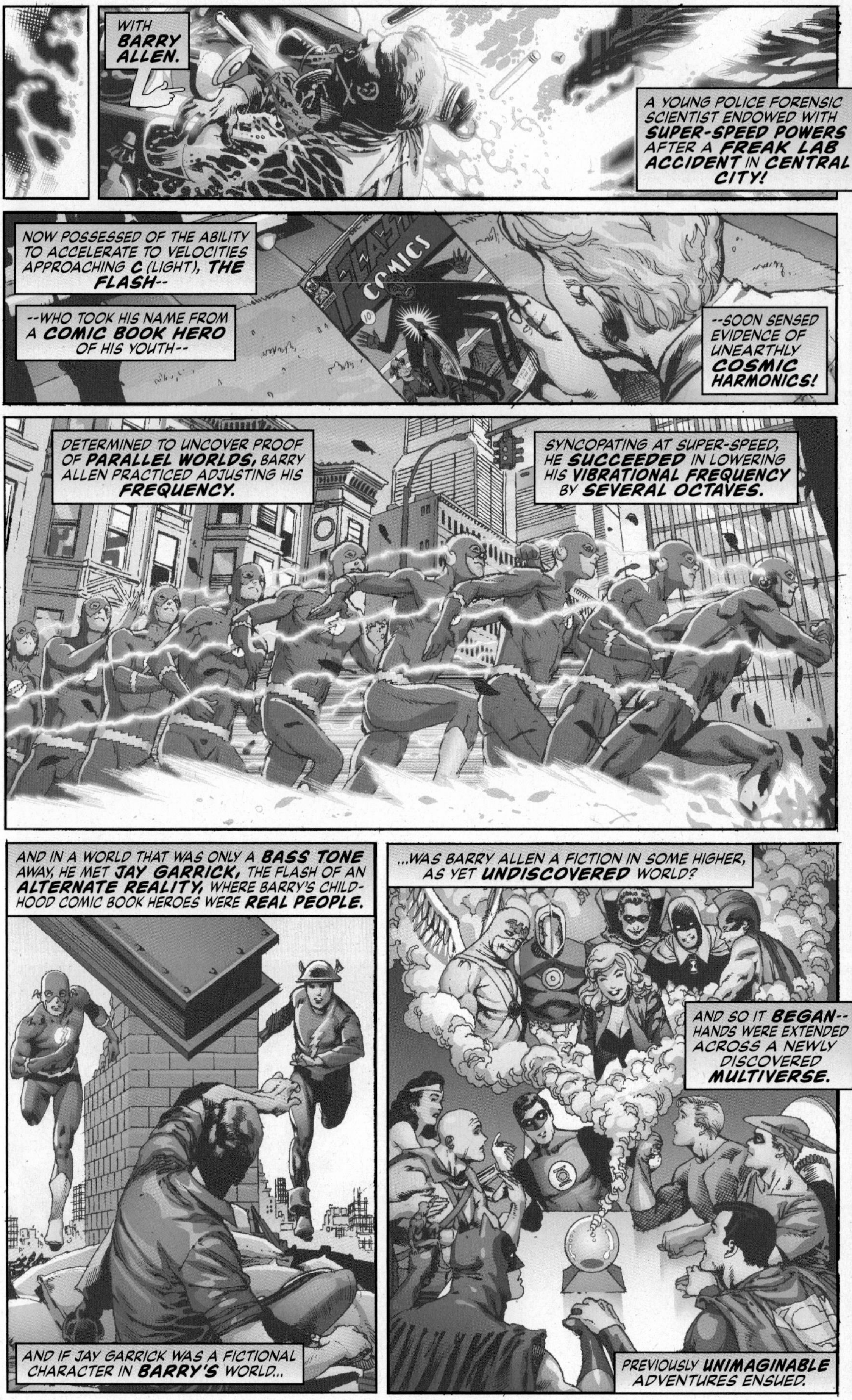
WITH BARRY ALLEN.
A YOUNG POLICE FORENSIC SCIENTIST ENDOWED WITH SUPER-SPEED POWERS AFTER A FREAK LAB ACCIDENT IN CENTRAL CITY!
NOW POSSESSED OF THE ABILITY TO ACCELERATE TO VELOCITIES APPROACHING C (LIGHT), THE FLASH--
--WHO TOOK HIS NAME FROM A COMIC BOOK HERO OF HIS YOUTH--
--SOON SENSED EVIDENCE OF UNEARTHLY COSMIC HARMONICS!
DETERMINED TO UNCOVER PROOF OF PARALLEL WORLDS, BARRY ALLEN PRACTICED ADJUSTING HIS FREQUENCY.
SYNCOPATING AT SUPER-SPEED, HE SUCCEEDED IN LOWERING HIS VIBRATIONAL FREQUENCY BY SEVERAL OCTAVES.
AND IN A WORLD THAT WAS ONLY A BASS TONE AWAY, HE MET JAY GARRICK, THE FLASH OF AN ALTERNATE REALITY, WHERE BARRY'S CHILDHOOD COMIC BOOK HEROES WERE REAL PEOPLE.
AND IF JAY GARRICK WAS A FICTIONAL CHARACTER IN BARRY'S WORLD...
...WAS BARRY ALLEN A FICTION IN SOME HIGHER, AS YET UNDISCOVERED WORLD?
AND SO IT BEGAN--HANDS WERE EXTENDED ACROSS A NEWLY DISCOVERED MULTIVERSE.
PREVIOUSLY UNIMAGINABLE ADVENTURES ENSUED.

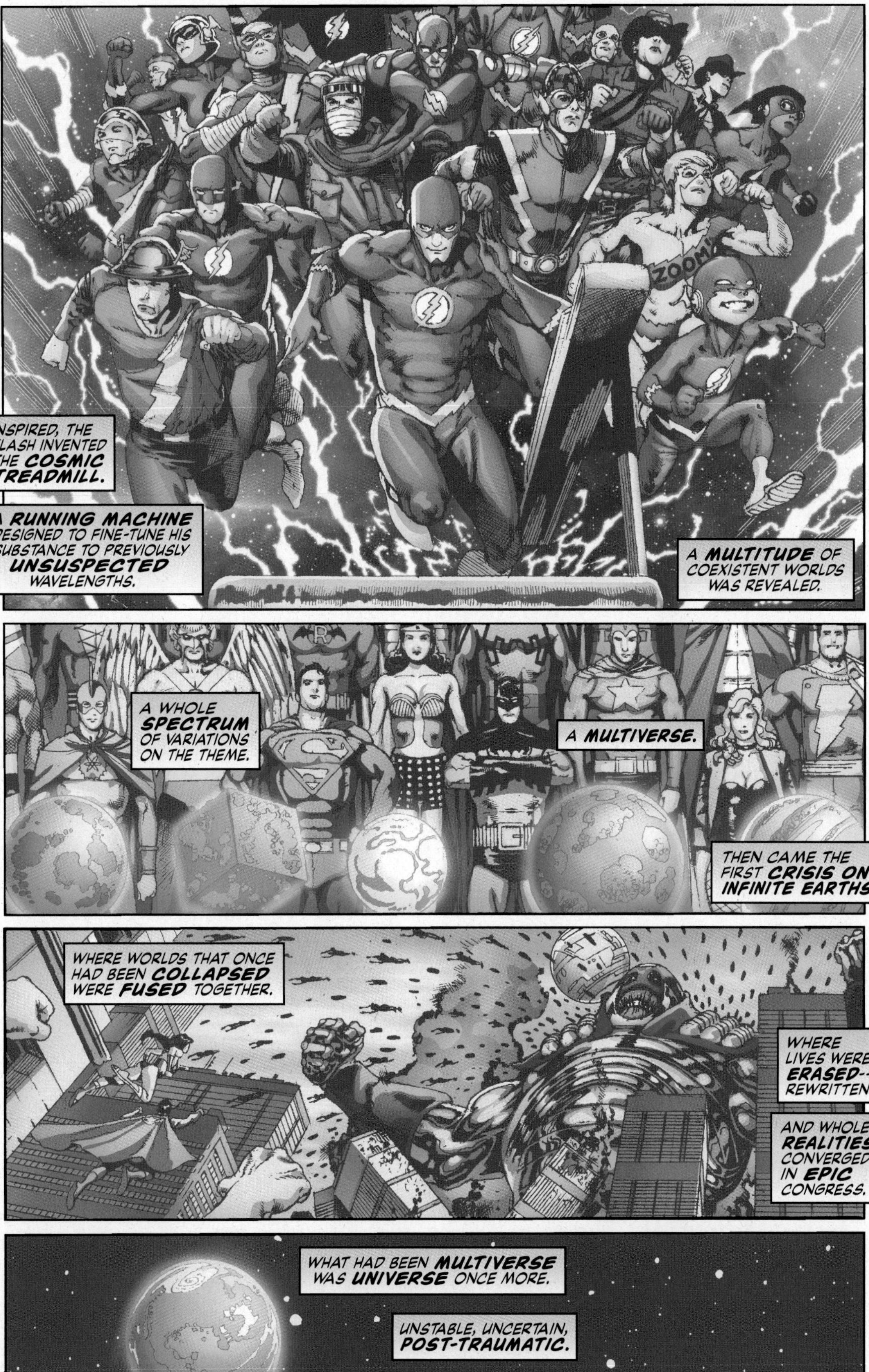
INSPIRED, THE FLASH INVENTED THE COSMIC TREADMILL.
A RUNNING MACHINE DESIGNED TO FINE-TUNE HIS SUBSTANCE TO PREVIOUSLY UNSUSPECTED WAVELENGTHS.
A MULTITUDE OF COEXISTENT WORLDS WAS REVEALED.
ZOOM
A WHOLE SPECTRUM OF VARIATIONS ON THE THEME.
A MULTIVERSE.
THEN CAME THE FIRST CRISIS ON INFINITE EARTHS.
WHERE WORLDS THAT ONCE HAD BEEN COLLAPSED WERE FUSED TOGETHER.
WHERE LIVES WERE ERASED--REWRITTEN.
AND WHOLE REALITIES CONVERGED IN EPIC CONGRESS.
WHAT HAD BEEN MULTIVERSE WAS UNIVERSE ONCE MORE.
UNSTABLE, UNCERTAIN, POST-TRAUMATIC.
AND ALL THE WHILE, FORCES BEYOND IMAGINATION WERE AT WORK.

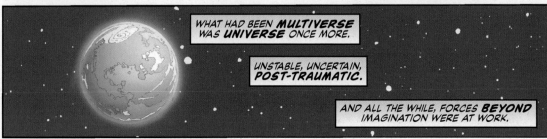

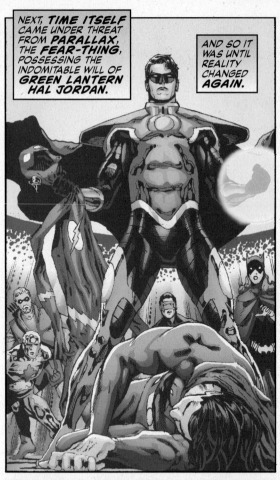

NEXT, **TIME ITSELF** CAME UNDER THREAT FROM **PARALLAX**, THE **FEAR-THING**, POSSESSING THE INDOMITABLE WILL OF **GREEN LANTERN HAL JORDAN.**

AND SO IT WAS UNTIL REALITY CHANGED **AGAIN.**

AND CHANGED **AGAIN.**

WHAT ONCE HAD BEEN WAS RENDERED **UNREMEMBERED.**

RE-FORGOTTEN.

ONCE MORE, A **MULTIVERSE** ERUPTED FROM THE FRAGILE, UNSTABLE UNIVERSE.

NEW SHOOTS, FRESH FRACTAL BRANCHES WORMED THEIR WAY THROUGH **HYPERTIME** AND **52 NEW UNIVERSES** WERE BORN.

AN ORDERED **ORRERY OF WORLDS.**

WHICH WERE ERASED AND RENEWED, AS CONTINUITIES **ROSE** AND **FELL** IN WAVES AND TROUGHS.

NO ONE KNEW.

NO ONE REMEMBERED.

ONLY THE **MONITORS** KEPT A RECORD OF IT ALL, WRITTEN INTO THE **FICTIONS** OF **EARTH-33.**

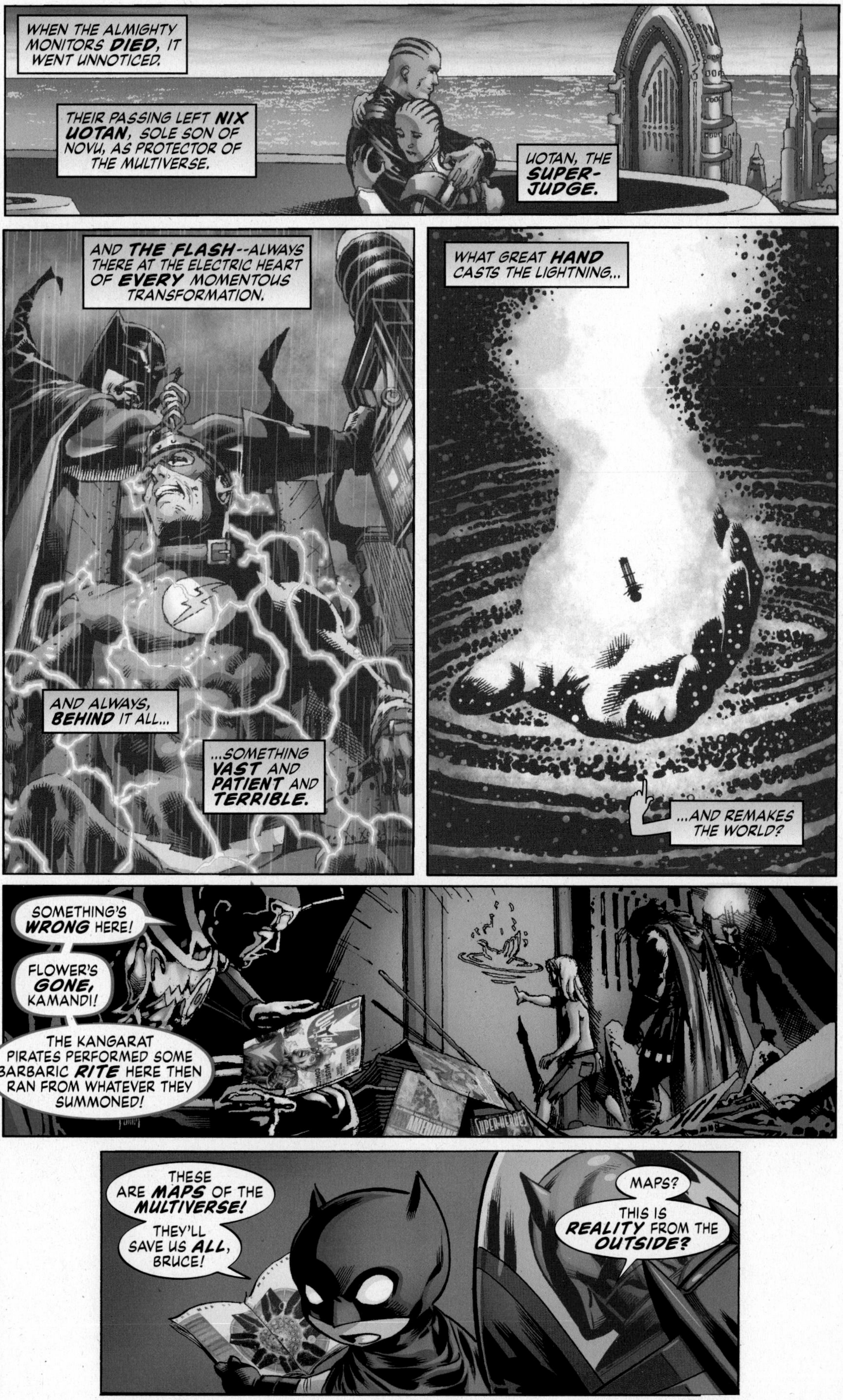

WHEN THE ALMIGHTY MONITORS DIED, IT WENT UNNOTICED.
THEIR PASSING LEFT NIX UOTAN, SOLE SON OF NOVU, AS PROTECTOR OF THE MULTIVERSE.
UOTAN, THE SUPER-JUDGE.
AND THE FLASH--ALWAYS THERE AT THE ELECTRIC HEART OF EVERY MOMENTOUS TRANSFORMATION.
AND ALWAYS, BEHIND IT ALL...
...SOMETHING VAST AND PATIENT AND TERRIBLE.
WHAT GREAT HAND CASTS THE LIGHTNING...
...AND REMAKES THE WORLD?
SOMETHING'S WRONG HERE!
FLOWER'S GONE, KAMANDI!
THE KANGARAT PIRATES PERFORMED SOME BARBARIC RITE HERE THEN RAN FROM WHATEVER THEY SUMMONED!
THESE ARE MAPS OF THE MULTIVERSE!
THEY'LL SAVE US ALL, BRUCE!
MAPS?
THIS IS REALITY FROM THE OUTSIDE?

THE MAP OF T

THE MULTIVERSAL VIBRATIONAL REALMS

SOURCE WALL

Here is the Limit even to Thought. Beyond lies only Monitor-mind, The Source and the Unknowable.

MONITOR SPHERE

Dwelling place of the mighty Monitor race – once countless in number, the 52 Monitors that remained after the CRISIS event were each tasked with the preservation and study of a separate universe.

LIMBO

Home of the Lost and Forgotten of the Orrery, Limbo is the furthest edge of the manifest DC universe. This is where matter and memory break down.

SPHERE OF THE GODS

From the heights of the Skyland Pantheons to the prison depths of the Underworld, this is the great realm of Archetypal Powers and Intelligences inhabited by Gods and New Gods, Demons, Angels and the Endless.

DREAM

On the borderlands is the magical realm of Morpheus the Dream-King, incorporating the Halls of The Endless, the Courts of Faerie and the Twelve Houses of Gemworld. Home to Oberon, Titania, Amethyst, Santa Claus and the Easter Bunny.

HEAVEN

The Silver City. The Word of the Voice. Home of the Spectre, Zauriel and the Guardian Angel Hosts of the Pax Dei – The Bull Host, The Eagle Host, The Lion Host and the Host of Adam.

NEW GENESIS

Sunlit lordly New Genesis is the proud home of the New Gods and the young Forever People. The floating city of Supertown is the dwelling place of Highfather, Orion, Lightray, Avia, Big Barda, Scott Free and others.

SKYLAND

Home of the Shining Ones, the Old Gods of Thunder and Lightning, Love and War and Death. Here is Asgard, Olympus, and the Throne of Zeus. The Pantheons of Celts, Mayans, the Divine Bureaucracies of China, and the Gods of Oceania, Mesopotamia and Egypt, the Loa and the Elohim are all gathered here, each with a peak of its own.

NIGHTMARE

The creepy-crawly Shadow Side of Morpheus's domain. Here is the Goblin Market where nothing is real. The Land of Nightshades. Home to the Bogeyman and the Corinthian, haunt of Witches, Yeth Hounds and Bad Dreams.

HELL

Known to some as Sheol, or Jigoku, the burning iron Place of Torment is home to Neron, Belial, Trigon, Azazel, Abnegazar, Rath, Ghast and the Demon Etrigan – high on a list of a legion of fiends. Here are the Djinns and the Fallen Angels, and the Haters of Humanity, waiting...

APOKOLIPS

The fiery planetasm ruled with the iron fist of the ultimate tyrant, Darkseid of the New Gods, and his cruel acolytes – Desaad the Torture God, Granny Goodness, Glorious Godfrey, Kalibak and many, many others.

UNDERWORLD

Here is Hades, Annwn, the realm of Pluto and the Throne of Erishkagal, the Land of No Return. Known also as The Phantom Zone, this gloomy prison of shades and formless shadows plays host to the criminals of the planet Krypton – General Zod, Ursa the She-Devil, Xadu the Phantom King and many others.

WONDERWORLD

Orbiting Creation itself at unimaginable velocities, Wonderworld is the "Worldquarters" of the long-lost Theocracy, a team of stupendous primal superheroes.

SPEED FORCE WALL

The Speed Force Wall is otherwise known to the denizens of the Orrery as the Speed of Light. It is only a limit to matter.

THE FREQUENCIES OF KWYZZ

Radio universe, home to KRAKKL the Defender.

ORRERY OF WORLDS

52 'brane universes vibrating in the same space, all at different frequencies, within the all-enclosing Bulk, otherwise known as Bleedspace. Four Bleed Siphons have been drilled in from the Monitor Sphere to the Orrery, to permit harvest of the miracle Ultramenstruum fluid.

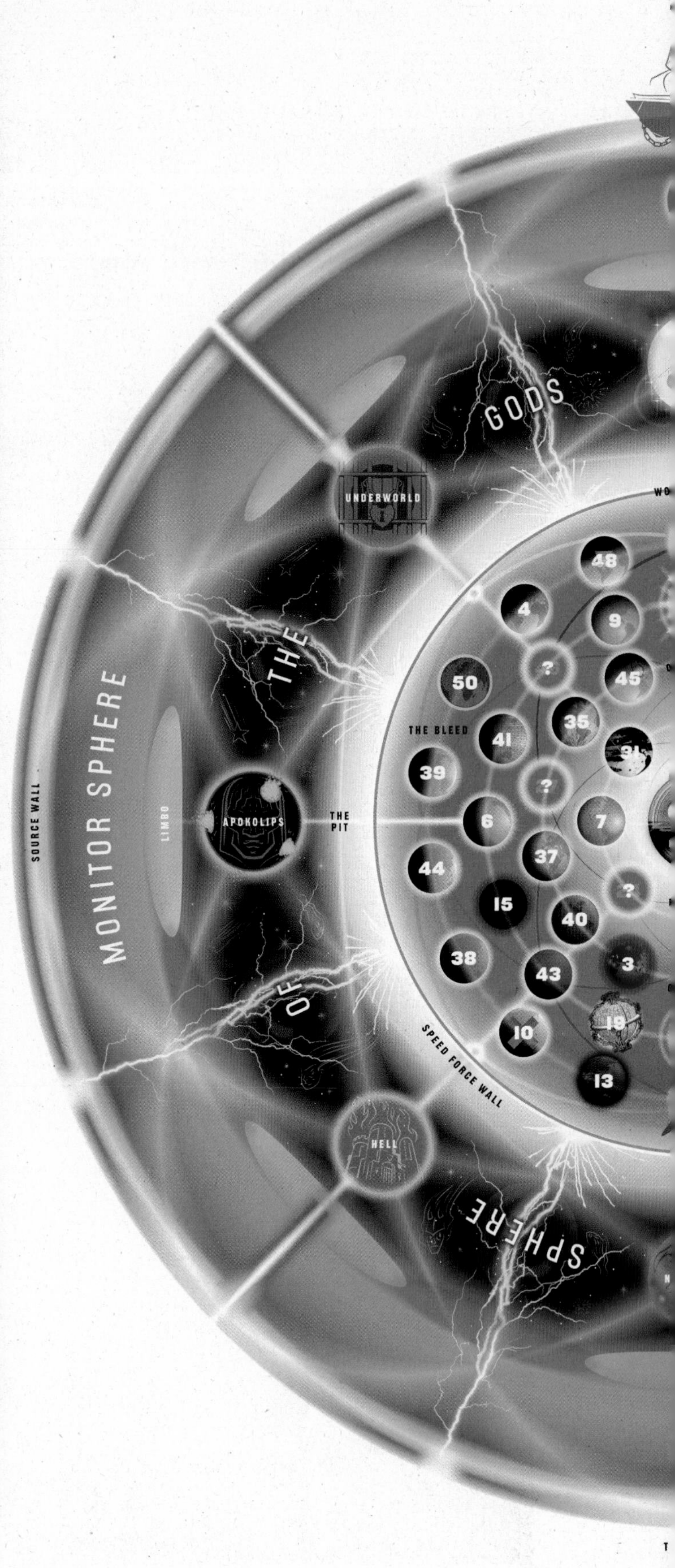

SOURCE WALL
MONITOR SPHERE
LIMBO
GODS
THE
OF
SPHERE
UNDERWORLD
APOKOLIPS
THE PIT
HELL
THE BLEED
SPEED FORCE WALL
48
4
9
?
45
50
35
41
39
?
6
7
44
37
?
15
40
38
3
43
10
19
13

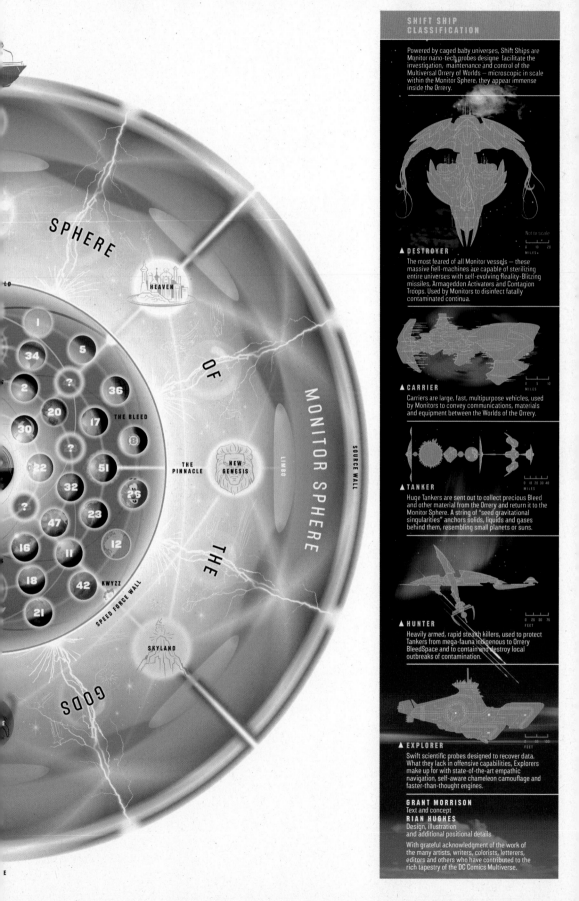

E MULTIVERSE

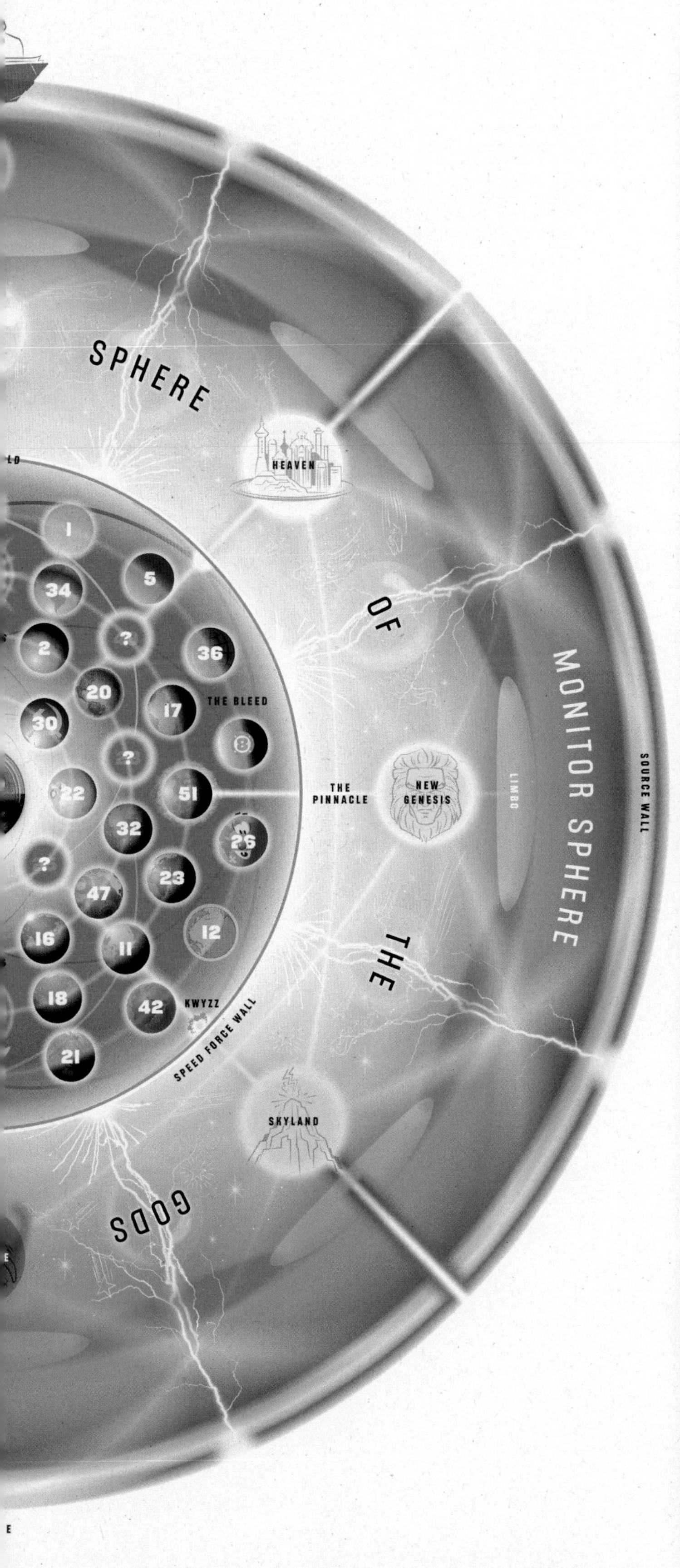

SPHERE OF THE GODS
HEAVEN
NEW GENESIS
SKYLAND
THE PINNACLE
THE BLEED
LIMBO
MONITOR SPHERE
SOURCE WALL
KWYZZ
SPEED FORCE WALL
1
5
34
?
2
36
20
17
30
8
?
22
51
32
26
?
23
47
12
16
11
18
42
21

SHIFT SHIP CLASSIFICATION

Powered by caged baby universes, Shift Ships are Monitor nano-tech probes designe facilitate the investigation, maintenance and control of the Multiversal Orrery of Worlds – microscopic in scale within the Monitor Sphere, they appear immense inside the Orrery.

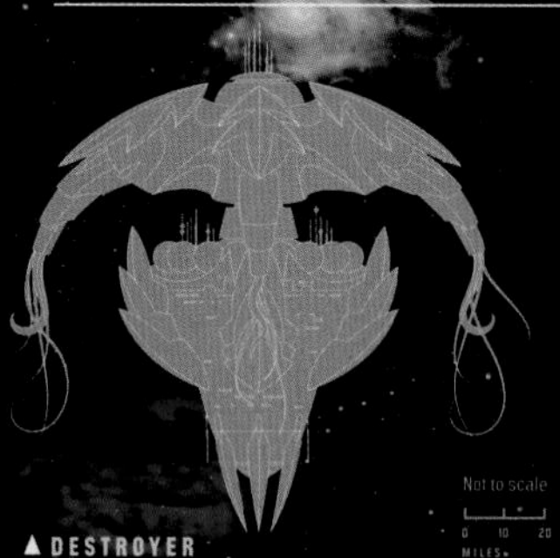

Not to scale
0 10 20
MILES

▲ DESTROYER

The most feared of all Monitor vessels – these massive hell-machines are capable of sterilizing entire universes with self-evolving Reality-Blitzing missiles, Armageddon Activators and Contagion Troops. Used by Monitors to disinfect fatally contaminated continua.

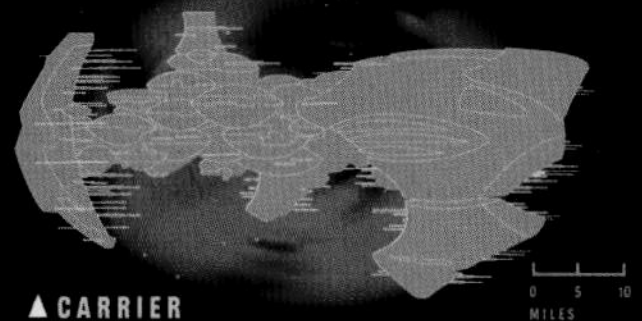

0 5 10
MILES

▲ CARRIER

Carriers are large, fast, multipurpose vehicles, used by Monitors to convey communications, materials and equipment between the Worlds of the Orrery.

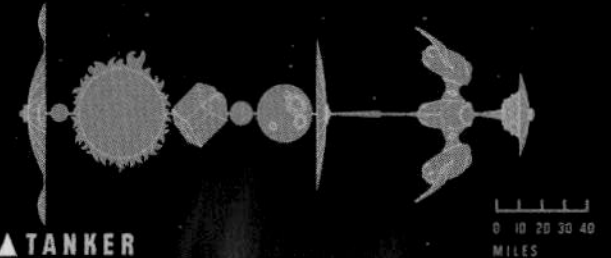

0 10 20 30 40
MILES

▲ TANKER

Huge Tankers are sent out to collect precious Bleed and other material from the Orrery and return it to the Monitor Sphere. A string of "seed gravitational singularities" anchors solids, liquids and gases behind them, resembling small planets or suns.

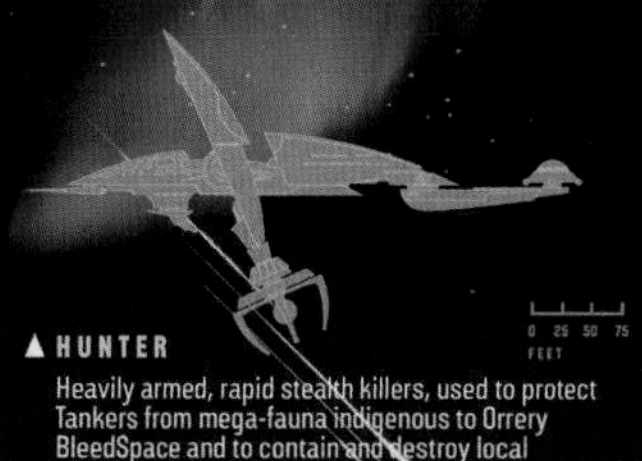

0 25 50 75
FEET

▲ HUNTER

Heavily armed, rapid stealth killers, used to protect Tankers from mega-fauna indigenous to Orrery BleedSpace and to contain and destroy local outbreaks of contamination.

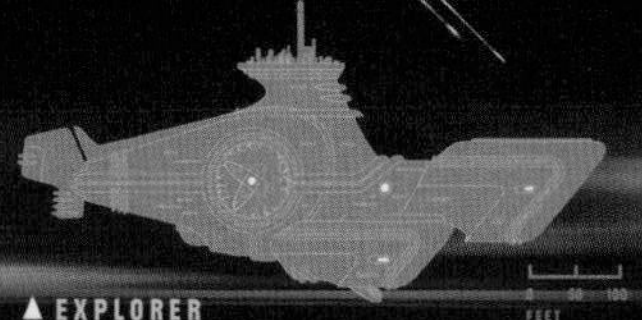

FEET

▲ EXPLORER

Swift scientific probes designed to recover data. What they lack in offensive capabilities, Explorers make up for with state-of-the-art empathic navigation, self-aware chameleon camouflage and faster-than-thought engines.

GRANT MORRISON
Text and concept

RIAN HUGHES
Design, illustration
and additional positional details

With grateful acknowledgment of the work of the many artists, writers, colorists, letterers, editors and others who have contributed to the rich tapestry of the DC Comics Multiverse.

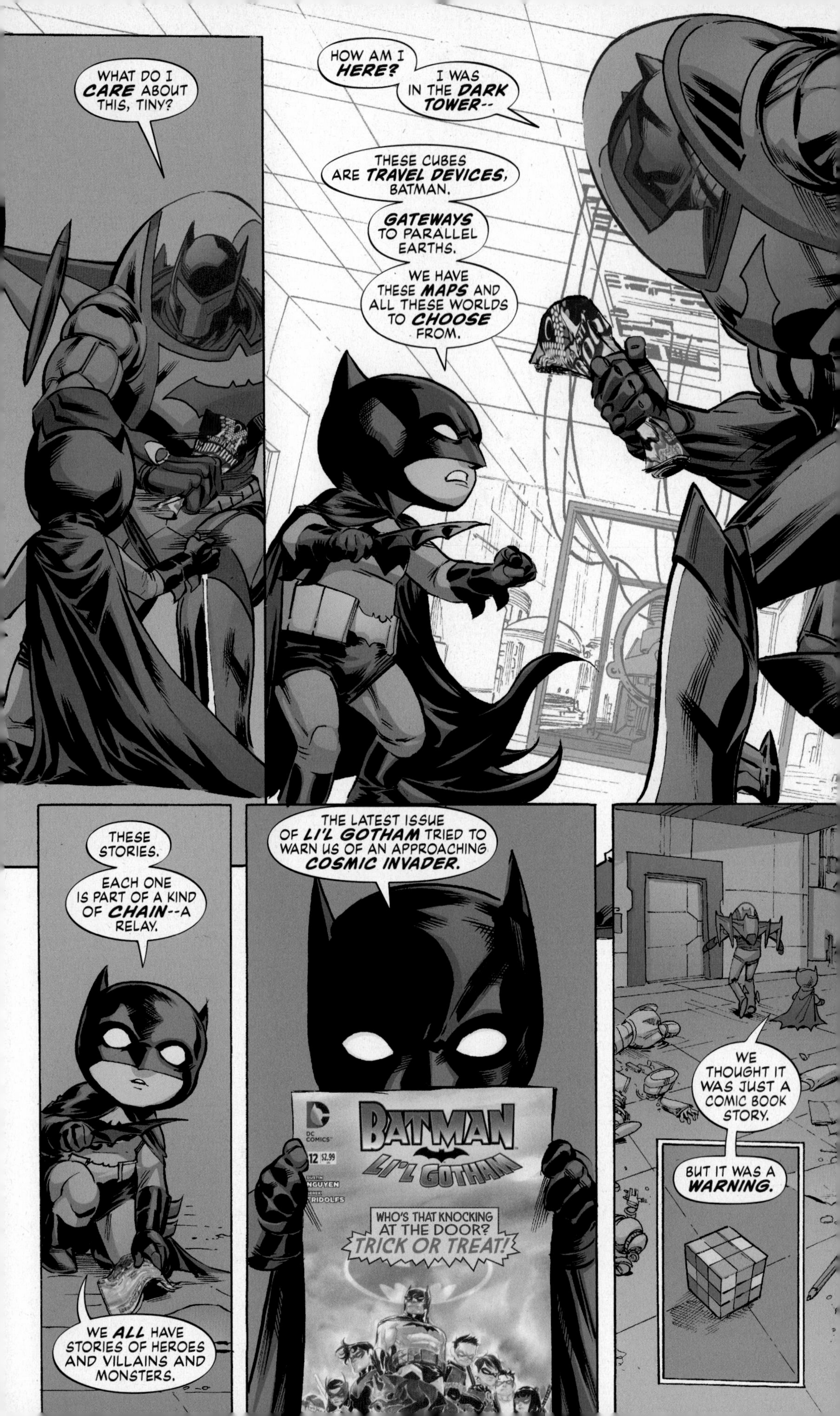
WHAT DO I CARE ABOUT THIS, TINY?
HOW AM I HERE?
I WAS IN THE DARK TOWER--
THESE CUBES ARE TRAVEL DEVICES, BATMAN.
GATEWAYS TO PARALLEL EARTHS.
WE HAVE THESE MAPS AND ALL THESE WORLDS TO CHOOSE FROM.
THESE STORIES.
EACH ONE IS PART OF A KIND OF CHAIN--A RELAY.
WE ALL HAVE STORIES OF HEROES AND VILLAINS AND MONSTERS.
THE LATEST ISSUE OF LI'L GOTHAM TRIED TO WARN US OF AN APPROACHING COSMIC INVADER.
BATMAN
LI'L GOTHAM
DC COMICS
12 $2.99
NGUYEN
FRIDOLFS
WHO'S THAT KNOCKING AT THE DOOR?
TRICK OR TREAT!
WE THOUGHT IT WAS JUST A COMIC BOOK STORY.
BUT IT WAS A WARNING.

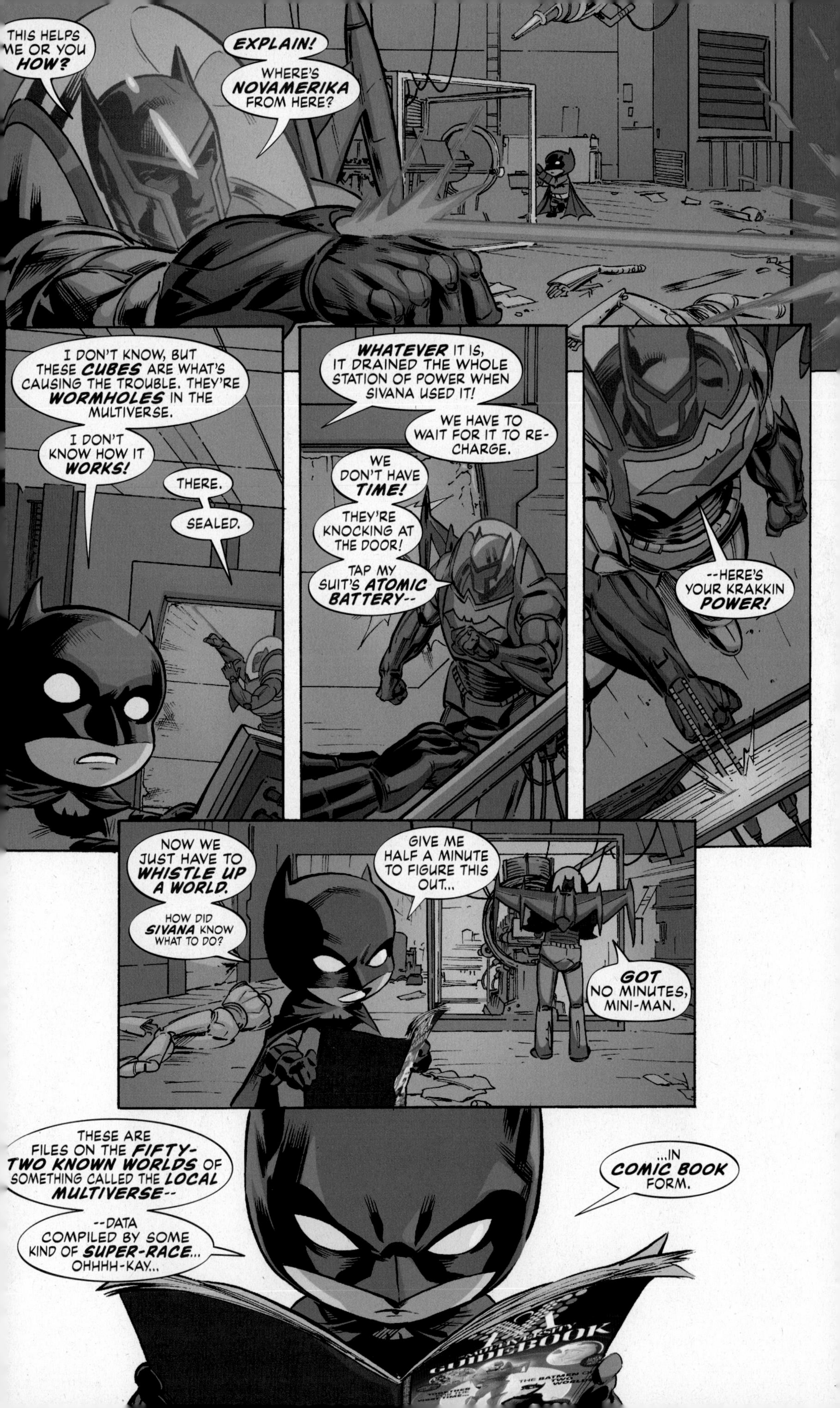

THIS HELPS ME OR YOU HOW?
EXPLAIN! WHERE'S NOVAMERIKA FROM HERE?
I DON'T KNOW, BUT THESE CUBES ARE WHAT'S CAUSING THE TROUBLE. THEY'RE WORMHOLES IN THE MULTIVERSE.
I DON'T KNOW HOW IT WORKS!
THERE.
SEALED.
WHATEVER IT IS, IT DRAINED THE WHOLE STATION OF POWER WHEN SIVANA USED IT!
WE HAVE TO WAIT FOR IT TO RE-CHARGE.
WE DON'T HAVE TIME!
THEY'RE KNOCKING AT THE DOOR!
TAP MY SUIT'S ATOMIC BATTERY--
--HERE'S YOUR KRAKKIN POWER!
NOW WE JUST HAVE TO WHISTLE UP A WORLD.
HOW DID SIVANA KNOW WHAT TO DO?
GIVE ME HALF A MINUTE TO FIGURE THIS OUT...
GOT NO MINUTES, MINI-MAN.
THESE ARE FILES ON THE FIFTY-TWO KNOWN WORLDS OF SOMETHING CALLED THE LOCAL MULTIVERSE--
--DATA COMPILED BY SOME KIND OF SUPER-RACE... OHHHH-KAY...
...IN COMIC BOOK FORM.
GUIDEBOOK

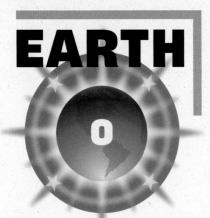

EARTH 0

Earth-0, also known as NEW EARTH, is the foundation stone of the Multiversal structure. It has survived several attacks, surgeries and reconstructions on the way to its current form. On Earth-0, the greatest young superheroes of the age are at the peak and pinnacle of their powers and achievements.

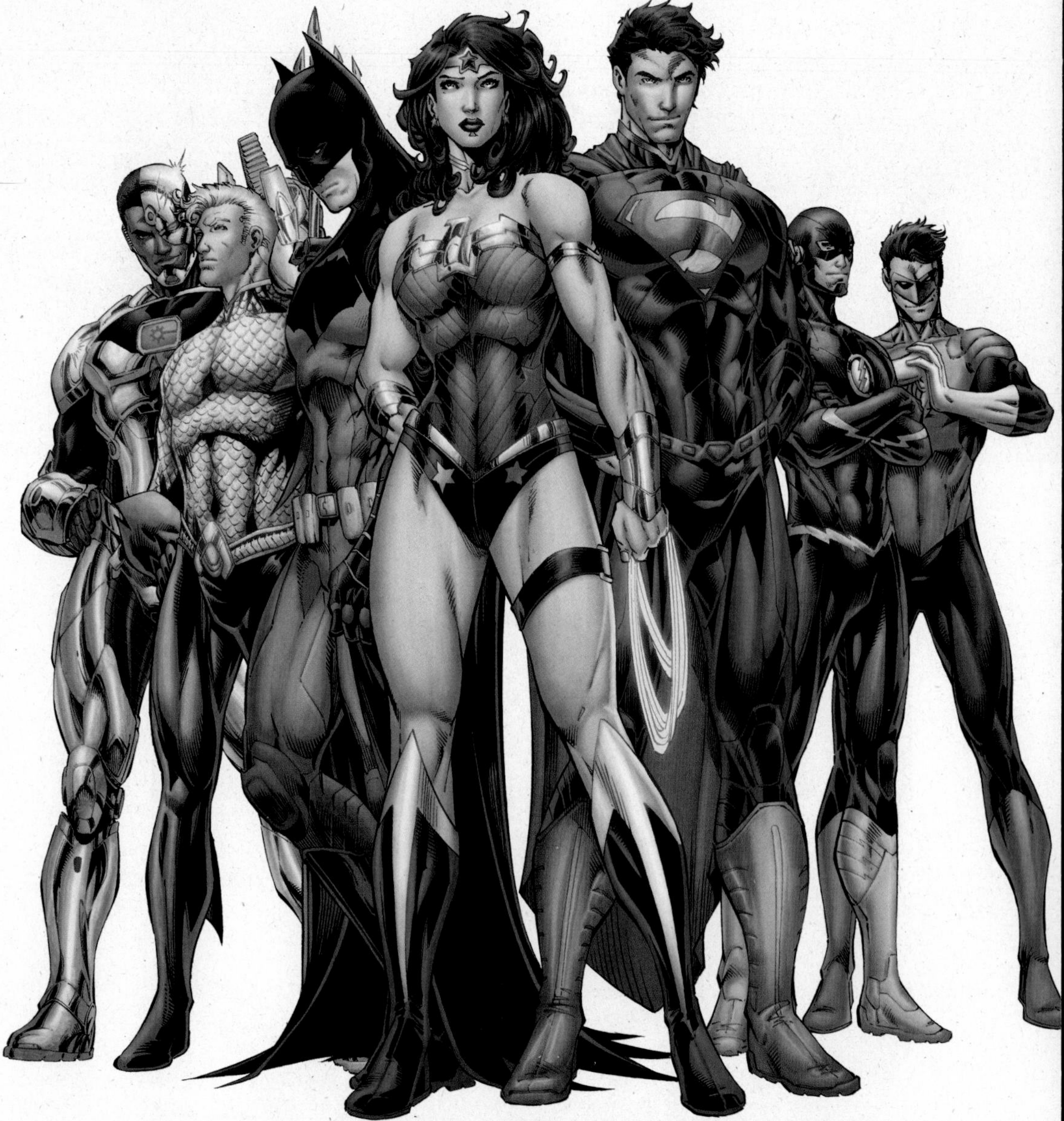

EARTH I

This freshly created Universe is still cooling and as yet unformed. Earth-I's known superbeings — SUPERMAN, BATMAN, WONDER WOMAN and the TEEN TITANS — are at the beginning of their careers. Time and space are still pliable, and nothing here is certain.

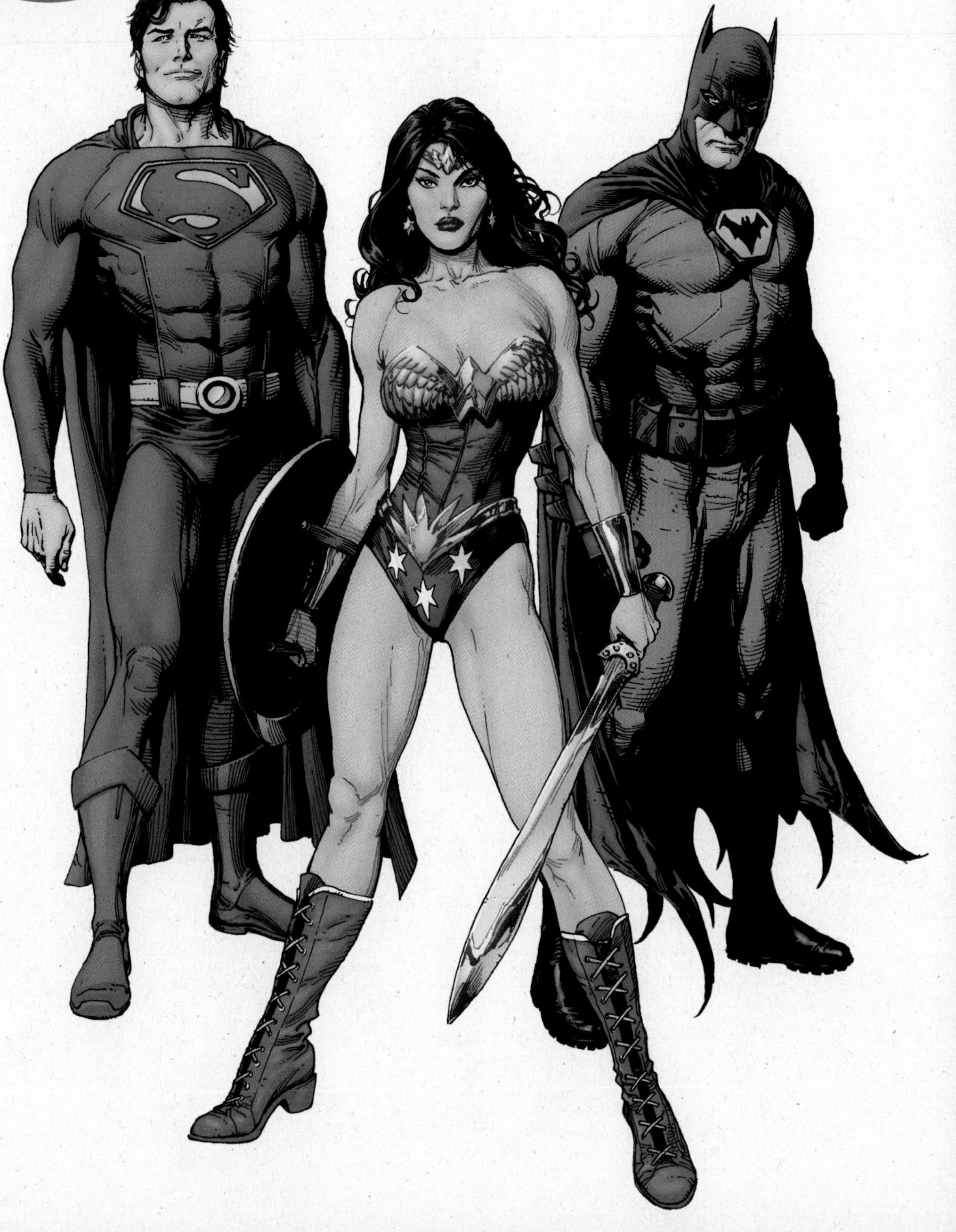

EARTH

2

Following the deaths of Superman, Batman and Wonder Woman in the War with the Great and Terrible Darkseid, a new generation of superheroes has emerged to continue the fight against immortal evil. This world includes a new BATMAN and SUPERMAN, RED TORNADO, DOCTOR FATE, FLASH, GREEN LANTERN, HAWKGIRL, HUNTRESS and POWER GIRL.

EARTH

3

This world is home to the villainous, despotic CRIME SYNDICATE OF AMERICA, including their leader, the tyrant ULTRAMAN, and his cohorts OWLMAN, SUPERWOMAN, JOHNNY QUICK, POWER RING, DEATHSTORM and ATOMICA — the world's greatest super-criminals in this universe, where Good and Evil are reversed.

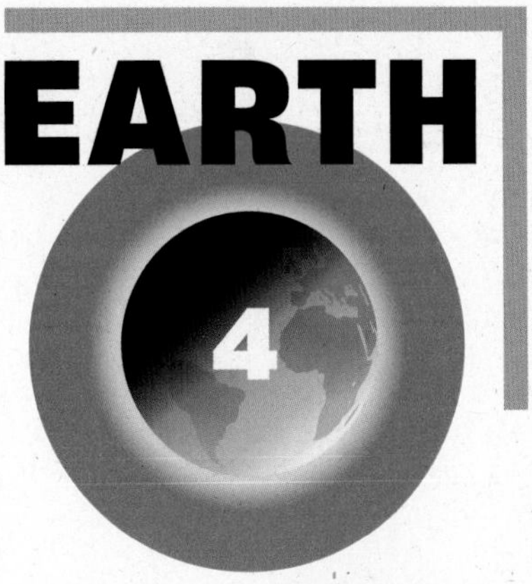
EARTH
4

Earth-4's only superhuman being is CAPTAIN ALLEN ADAM, endowed with "quantum senses" following close-quarters interactions with an unstable neo-element known as U-235.

The PAX AMERICANA is a group of specialized, uniformed, peacekeeping operatives including PEACEMAKER, BLUE BEETLE and NIGHTSHADE. THE QUESTION of this world is a rogue crimebuster.

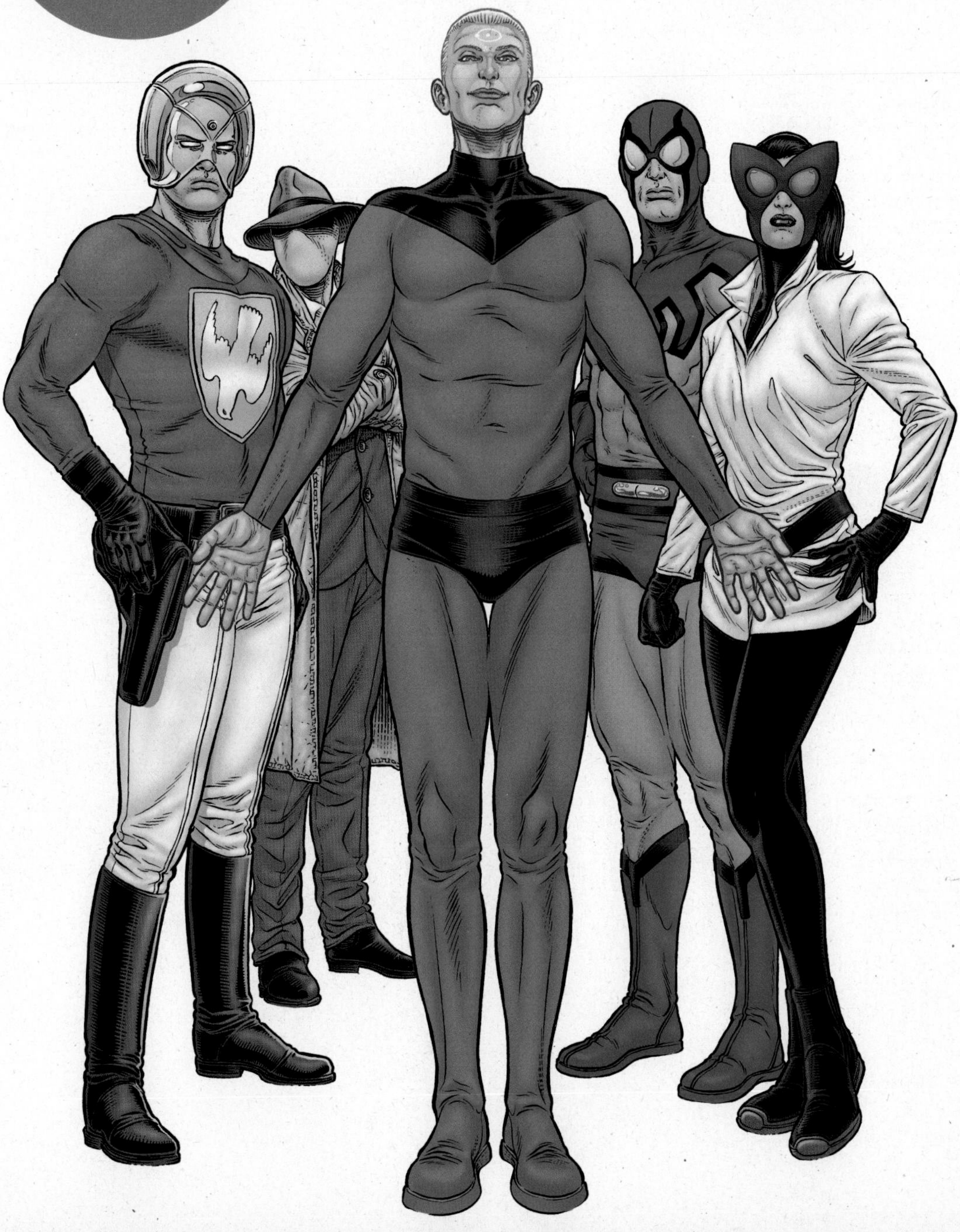

EARTH 5

Known throughout the Multiverse as "Thunderworld," this universe is the home of the Marvel Family paragons, their friends and their foes.

CAPTAIN MARVEL, CAPTAIN MARVEL JR., MARY MARVEL and the LIEUTENANT MARVELS fight an eternal battle to protect their world from monsters, aliens and the machinations of the power-mad genius DOCTOR SIVANA.

EARTH

The happening home of AQUAMAN, SANDMAN, BATMAN, GREEN LANTERN and other familiar names, given new and unfamiliar stories! On this world, SUPERMAN is a castaway cosmic cop from the planet Krypton. WONDER WOMAN wields the senses-sundering celestial staff of Manco Capac, the Inca Sun God, while the glistening GREEN LANTERN channels the peerless power of the wondrous World Tree Yggdrasil against the villainous REVEREND DARKK!

EARTH

On this world, the history of Earth-8 was recreated with subtle differences. In spite of its innovations and the protection of heroes like CRUSADER, GOLEM, "DOC" FUTURE, WALKÜRE, DEVILFIST and MICROBOT, Earth-7 was targeted and destroyed by the rapacious demons of the Gentry as part of their first incursion into the Multiverse. The sole survivor of Earth-7 is THUNDERER, an incarnate storm god.

EARTH 8

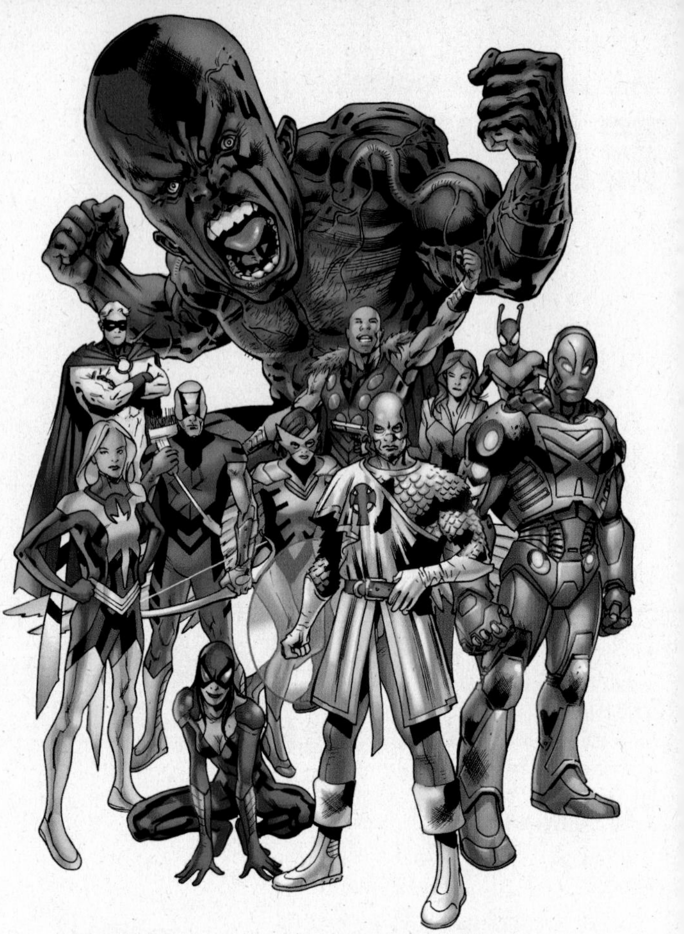

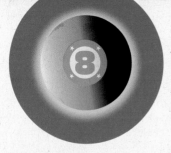

On this world, great power comes with great responsibility, and heroes often pay a high price for their dedication to justice. Earth-8 is home to the battlin' BUG, STUNTMASTER, bestial BIG BABY, HYPERIUS and MAJOR MAX.

Prominent hero teams include THE FUTURE FAMILY the 'Neo-human' G-('GENO-') MEN and THE RETALIATORS including DEADEYE, LADYBUG, KITE, WUNDAJIN, AMERICAN CRUSADER, RED DRAGON and MACHINEHEAD.

EARTH 9

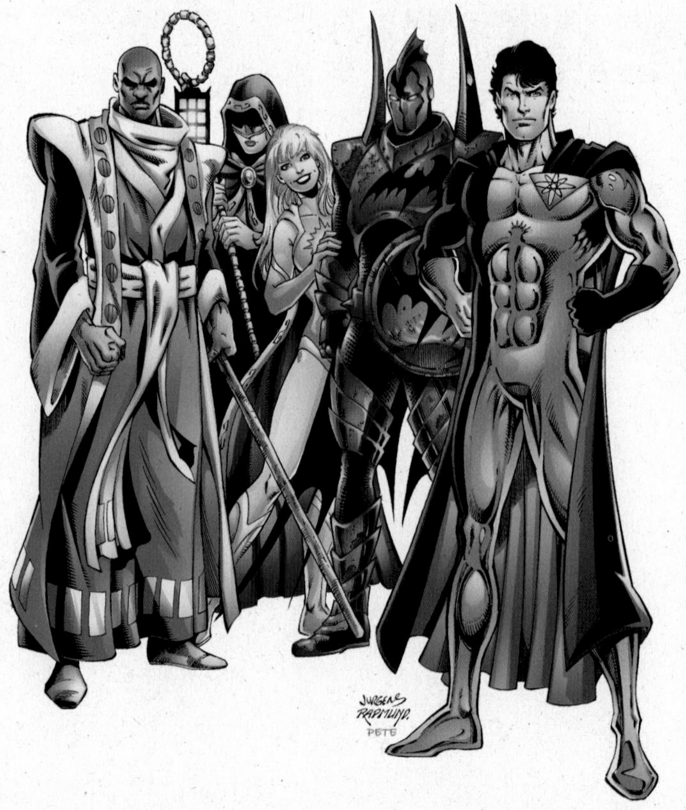
JURGENS

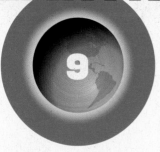

Here, SUPERMAN is a human being of vast intellect and mental power, while the ATOM takes his place as Earth's foremost superhero. Here, the light-powered FLASH is the first baby born in space. Here, GREEN LANTERN can resurrect the dead. Here, JOKER is an anarchist prankster on the side of freedom, and BATMAN is a time-lost armored spirit seeking justice throughout eternity.

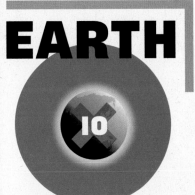

EARTH 10

Also designated EARTH-X, history was altered here when the rocket carrying the infant super-being Kal-L of Krypton landed in Nazi-occupied Czechoslovakia in 1938. Eighty years after assuring a German victory in World War II, the troubled OVERMAN leads LEATHERWING, BRÜNHILDE, BLITZEN, and UNDERWATERMAN — as the NEW REICHSMEN — in their war against UNCLE SAM and his terrorist FREEDOM FIGHTERS — THE RAY, BLACK CONDOR, THE HUMAN BOMB, PHANTOM LADY, DOLL MAN and DOLL WOMAN.

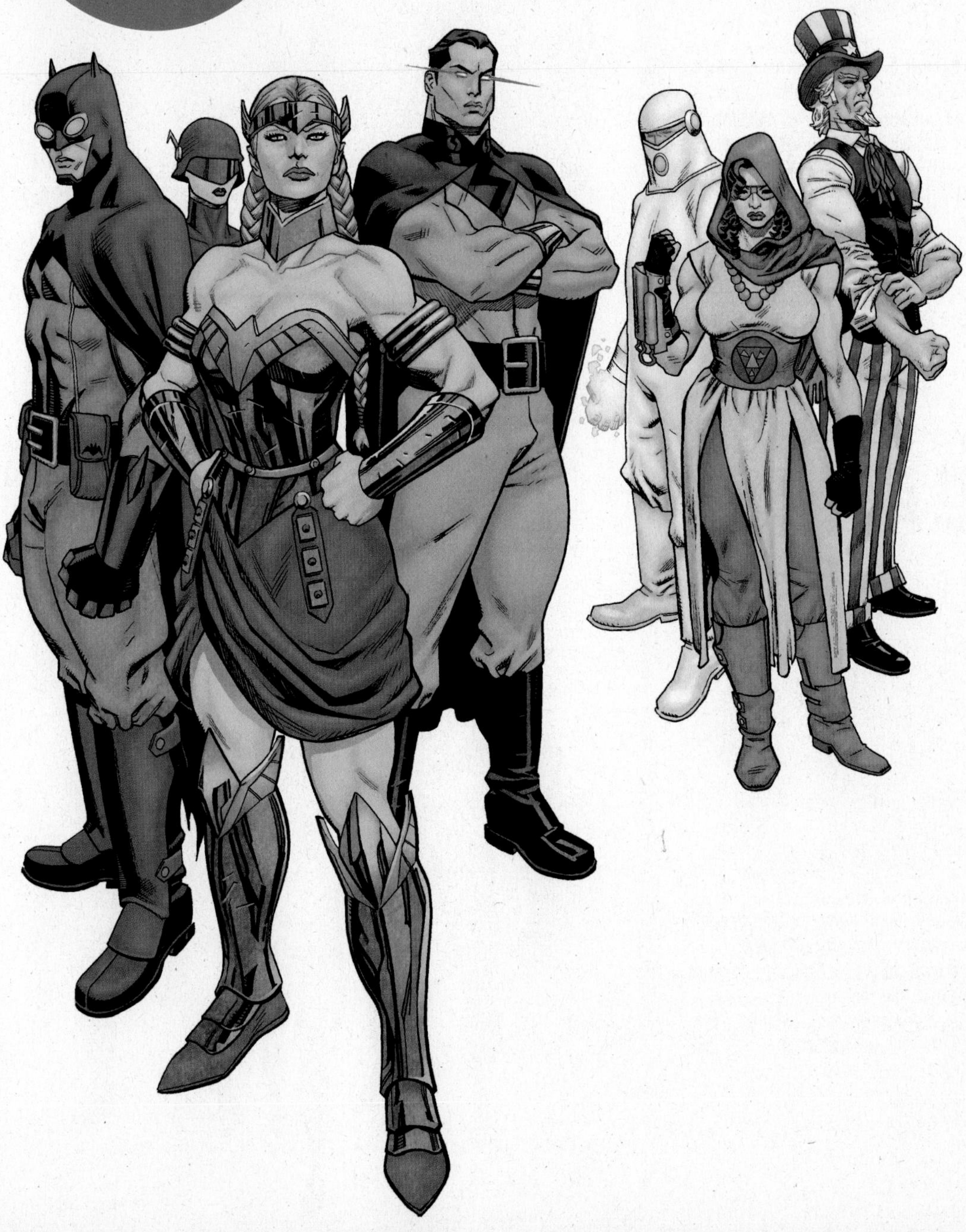

EARTH

II

On Earth-II, the Amazons of Themyscira imposed their law on the whole world and changed it forever, with new technology and philosophies, inspiring generations of women to take the lead in creating the future.

This world's JUSTICE GUILD comprises WONDEROUS MAN, AQUAWOMAN, BATWOMAN, SUPERWOMAN, JESSE QUICK, STAR SAPPHIRE, POWER MAN and ZATARA!

EARTH

12

With a timeline running slightly in advance of Earth-0, this is the near-future world of Batman's successor Terry McGinnis and his JUSTICE LEAGUE BEYOND allies, GREEN LANTERN, SUPERMAN, WARHAWK, AQUAGIRL, BIG BARDA, MICRON and others. Together they face the threats of an untamed future reality!

EARTH 13

On this world of permanent magical twilight, every day has 13 hours and each year has 13 months. Here, Etrigan the Demon, rocketed to Earth from the doomed planet Kamelot, fights evil in Merlin's name as SUPERDEMON!

Fellow members of the LEAGUE OF SHADOWS include HELLBLAZER, ANNATAZ, WITCHBOY, SWAMP-MAN, FATE, RAGMAN, DEADMAN and ENCHANTRESS.

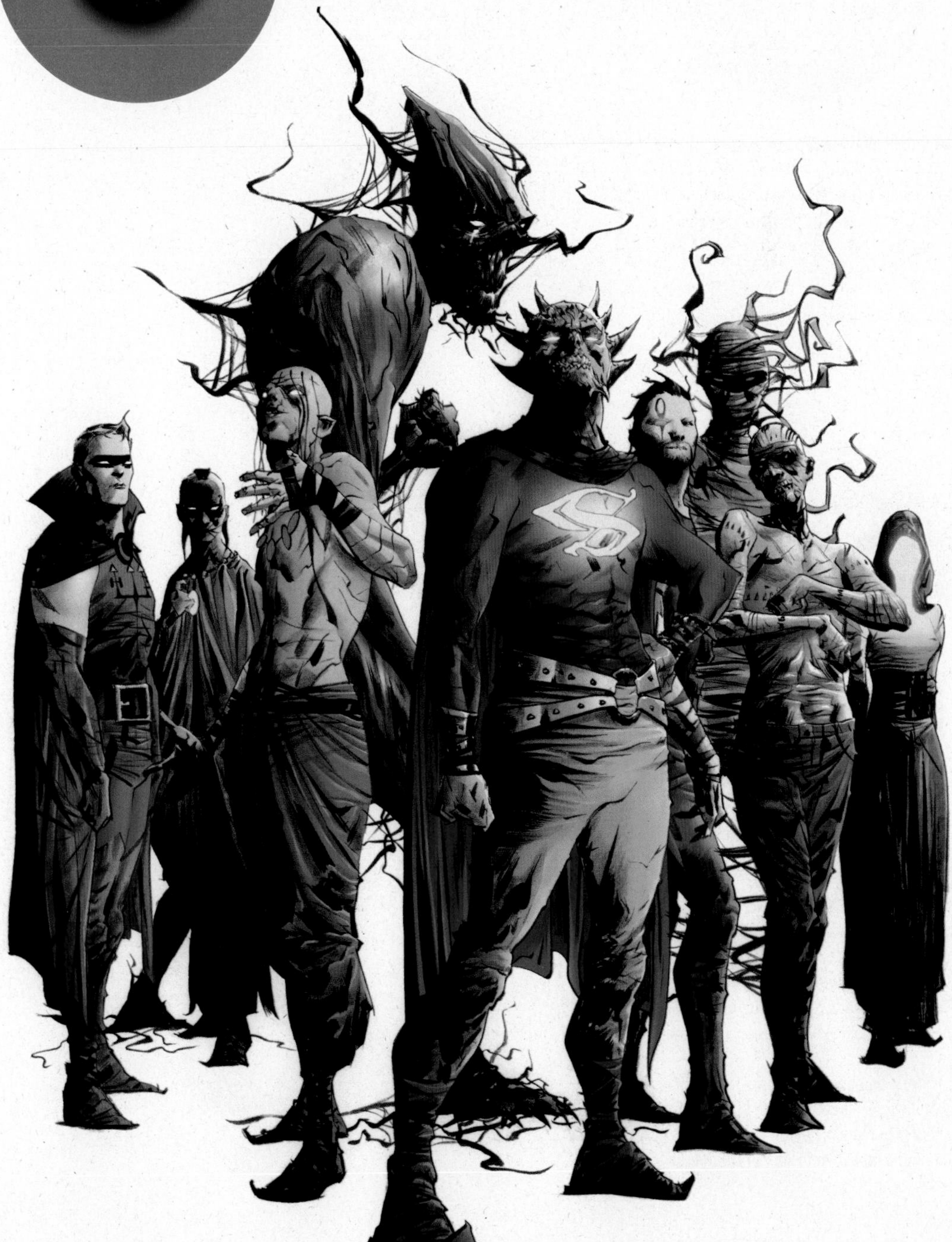

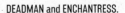

EARTH ?

Number I of 7 UNKNOWN WORLDS.

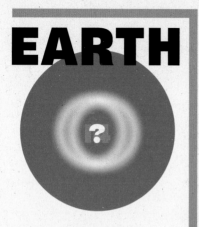

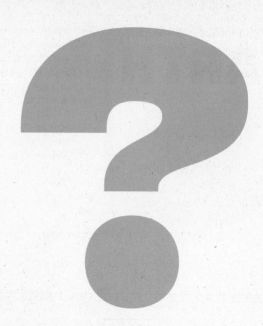

Created by an Inner Chamber of 7 Monitor Magi for a mysterious purpose yet to be revealed.

EARTH 15

The so-called Perfect Universe was destroyed during a rampage by the deranged and so-called SUPERBOY-PRIME of Earth-33, during which billions of fictional lives were lost and the delicate structure of spacetime itself was irreparably damaged.

A solitary, immensely powerful fragment of this universe — known as the COSMIC GRAIL — is said to remain, hidden somewhere among the many worlds of the Multiverse.

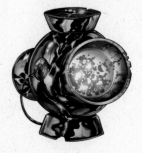

EARTH 16

Earth-Me — home of THE JUST — a world where peace, prosperity and boredom reign supreme. Here the Super-Sons of BATMAN and SUPERMAN are joined by others of a pampered second generation of superheroes, like SISTER MIRACLE, ARROWETTE, MEGAMORPHO and OFFSPRING.

While the older heroes of the JUSTICE LEAGUE indulge in nostalgic battle reenactments, the young live meaningless, self-absorbed lives.

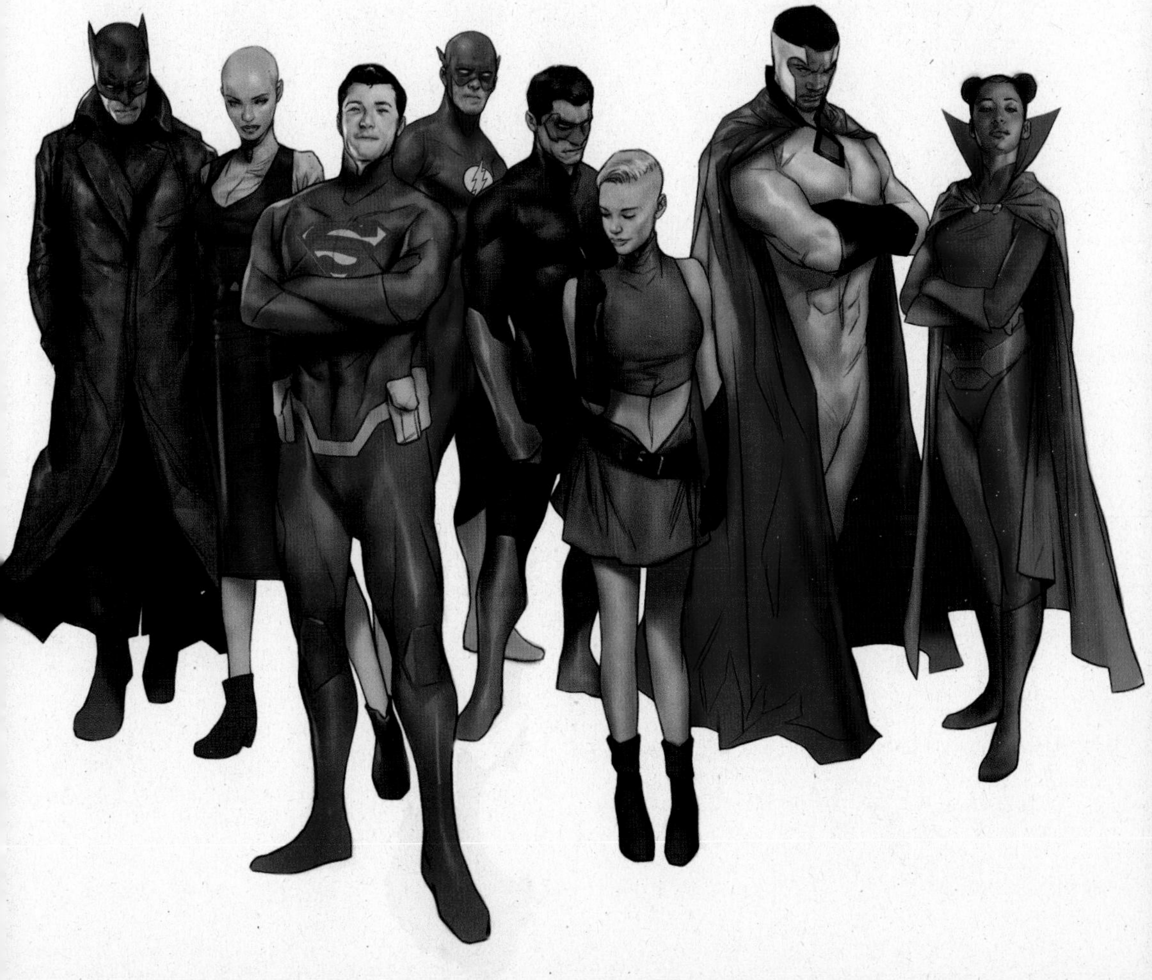

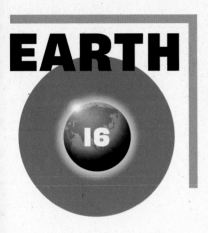

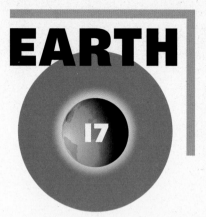

EARTH 17

CAPTAIN ADAM STRANGE leads his ATOMIC KNIGHTS OF JUSTICE on a desperate, last-chance quest to preserve the remnants of humanity 50 years after a nuclear war in 1963. Facing monstrous mutations, mad science, and human heartbreak on the way to rebuilding the ruined world of 21st century Novamerika, they seek the COSMIC GRAIL — the only weapon that will defend against the coming threat of DARKSEID the Destroyer.

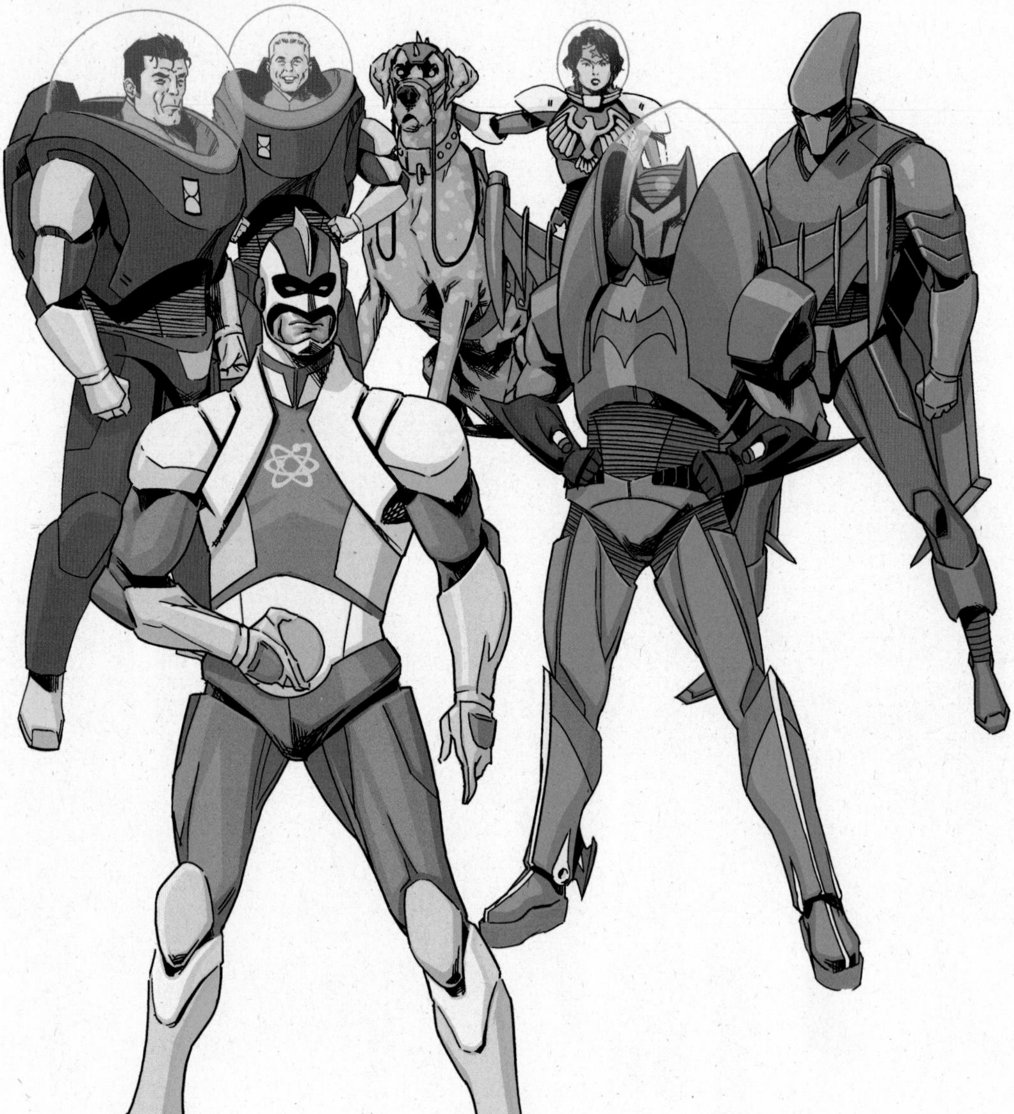

EARTH 18

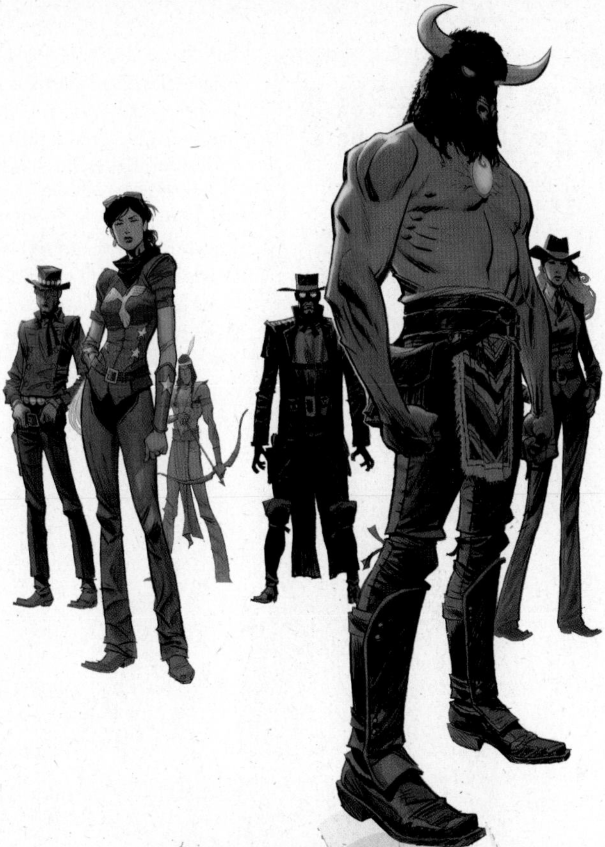

Led by Saganowana, the SUPERCHIEF, the JUSTICE RIDERS are BAT-LASH, MADAME .44, STRONGBOW, EL DIABLO, CINNAMON, THE TRIGGER TWINS, FIREHAIR, TOMAHAWKMAN, JOHNNY THUNDER, and POW-WOW SMITH.

They are sworn to protect a frontier world where the meddling Time Trapper froze technology and culture in the late 19th century. Here, human ingenuity has used the available resources of the 19th century to create everything humans take for granted in the 21st century, including a telegraph internet and air travel.

EARTH 19

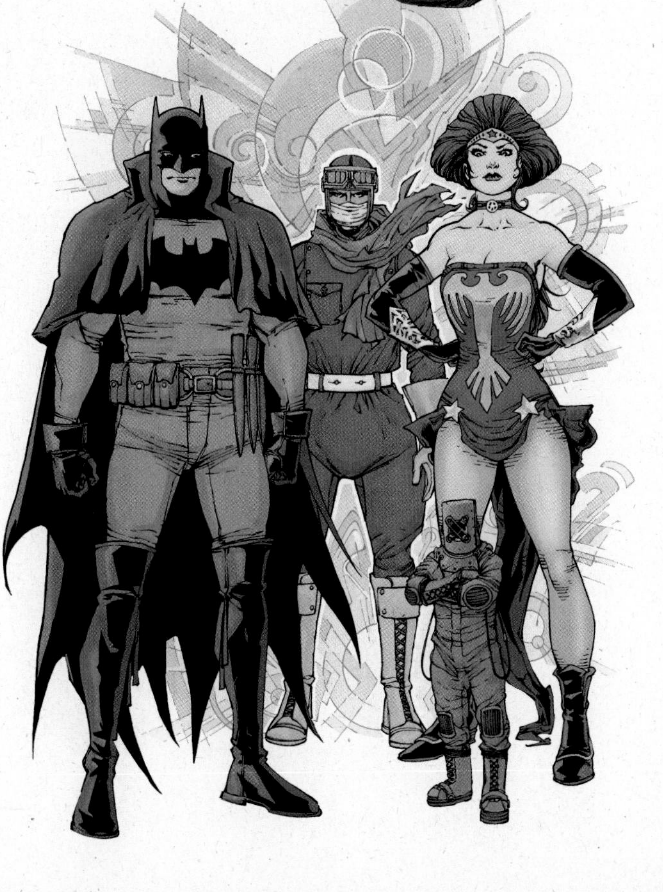

Queen Victoria is dead. King Edward rules a 20th-century empire of new electric technology in a rapidly changing social landscape. Into this Modernist ferment, this world of new ideas and new futures, the super-humans have arrived! BAT MAN! ACCELERATED MAN! THE WONDER WOMAN! THE SHRINKING MAN and others face unexpected challenges as history takes a twisted turn!

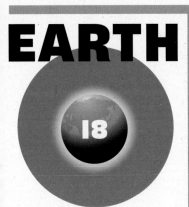

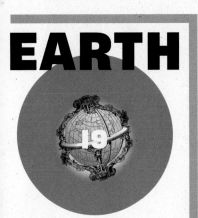

EARTH 20

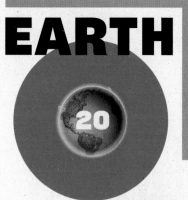

Home of the SOCIETY OF SUPER-HEROES, a team of adventurers and science champions assembled by DOC FATE to include GREEN LANTERN, THE MIGHTY ATOM, IMMORTAL MAN, LADY BLACKHAWK and the BLACKHAWKS.

Earth-20 occupies a binary universe, which tunes itself to occupy the same space as Earth-40 once every 100,000 years, with catastrophic consequences. See also EARTH-40.

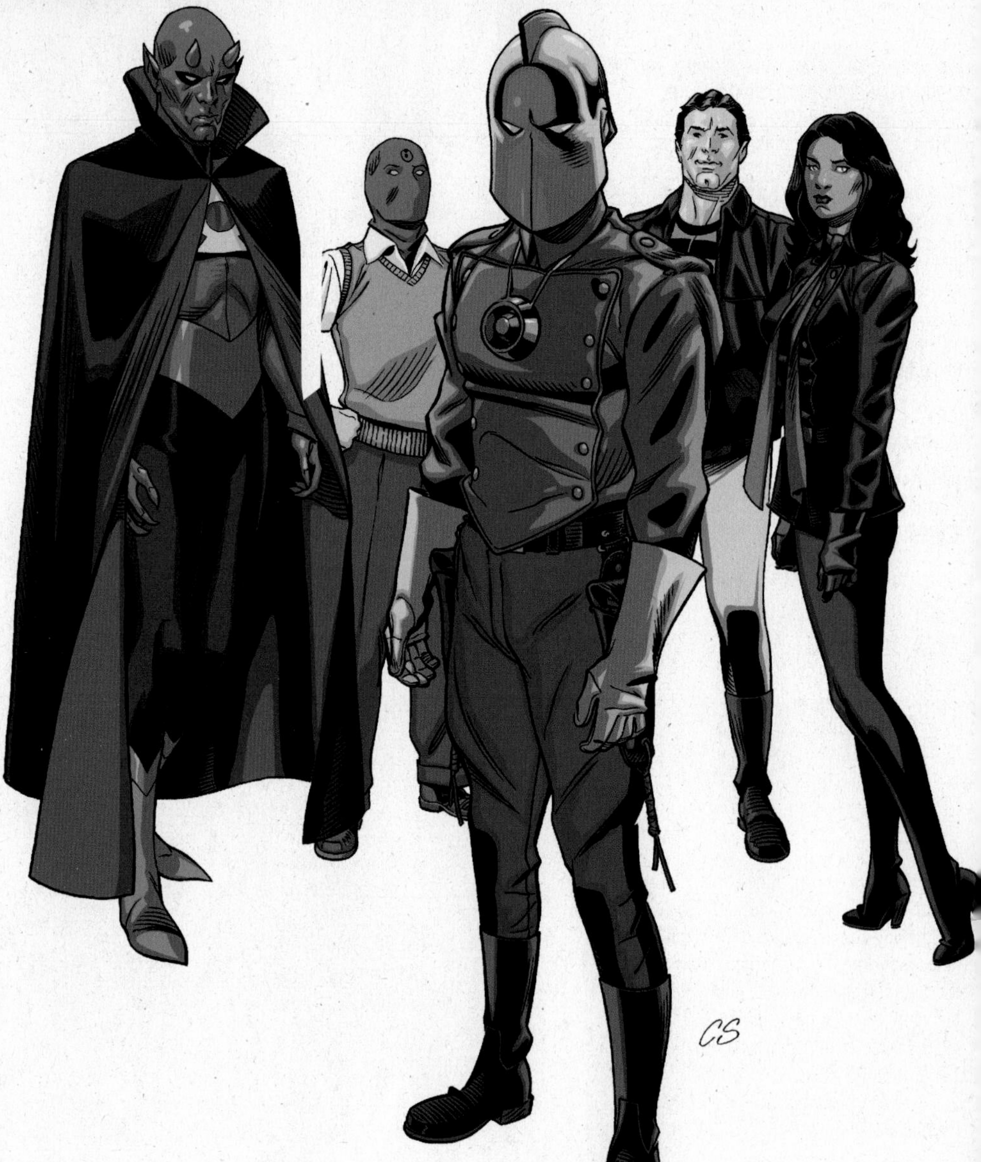
CS

EARTH 21

Here, a never-assassinated President John F. Kennedy stands forever poised to lead a newly superhuman, turned-on nation to the stars, while the indomitable young science heroes and pioneers of the JUSTICE LEAGUE OF AMERICA fight to protect their ideals against threats from this world — and others.

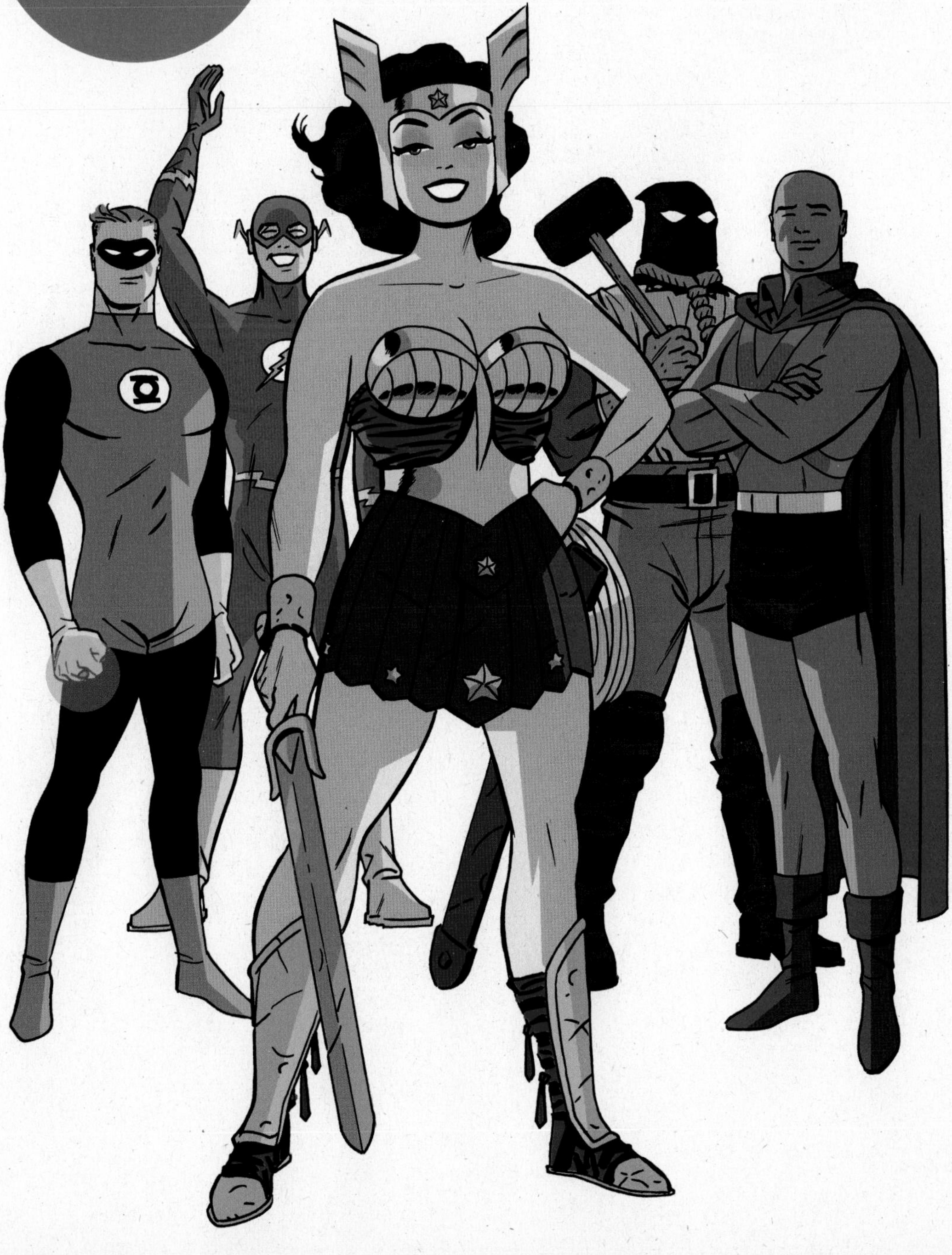

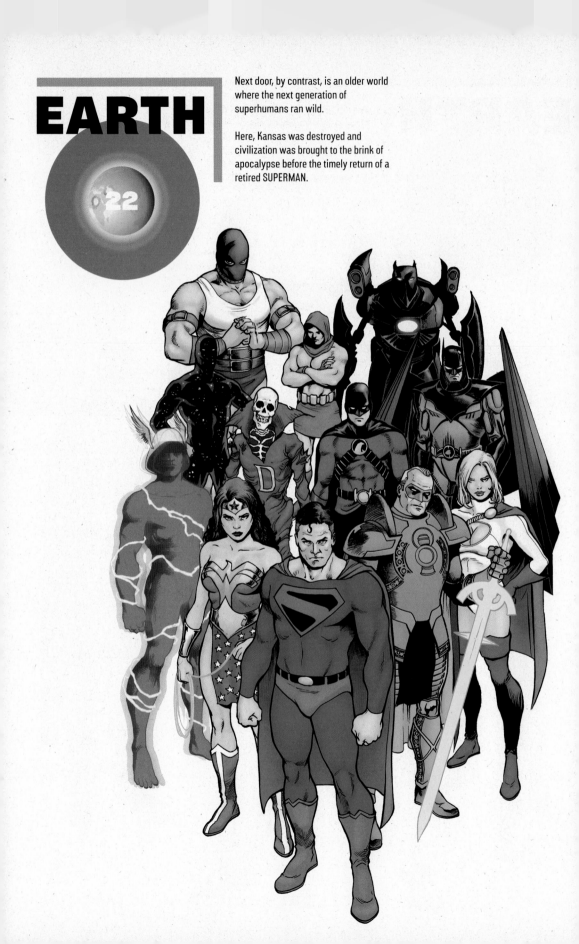

EARTH
22

Next door, by contrast, is an older world where the next generation of superhumans ran wild.

Here, Kansas was destroyed and civilization was brought to the brink of apocalypse before the timely return of a retired SUPERMAN.

EARTH 23

The arrival on Earth of KAL-L of KRYPTON – this world's SUPERMAN – was the catalyst for a generation of superheroes including NUBIA the WONDER WOMAN, GREEN LANTERN, VIXEN, STEEL, MISTER MIRACLE, BLACK LIGHTNING and AMAZING MAN.

In his alter ego of Calvin Ellis, Superman is President of the United States of America.

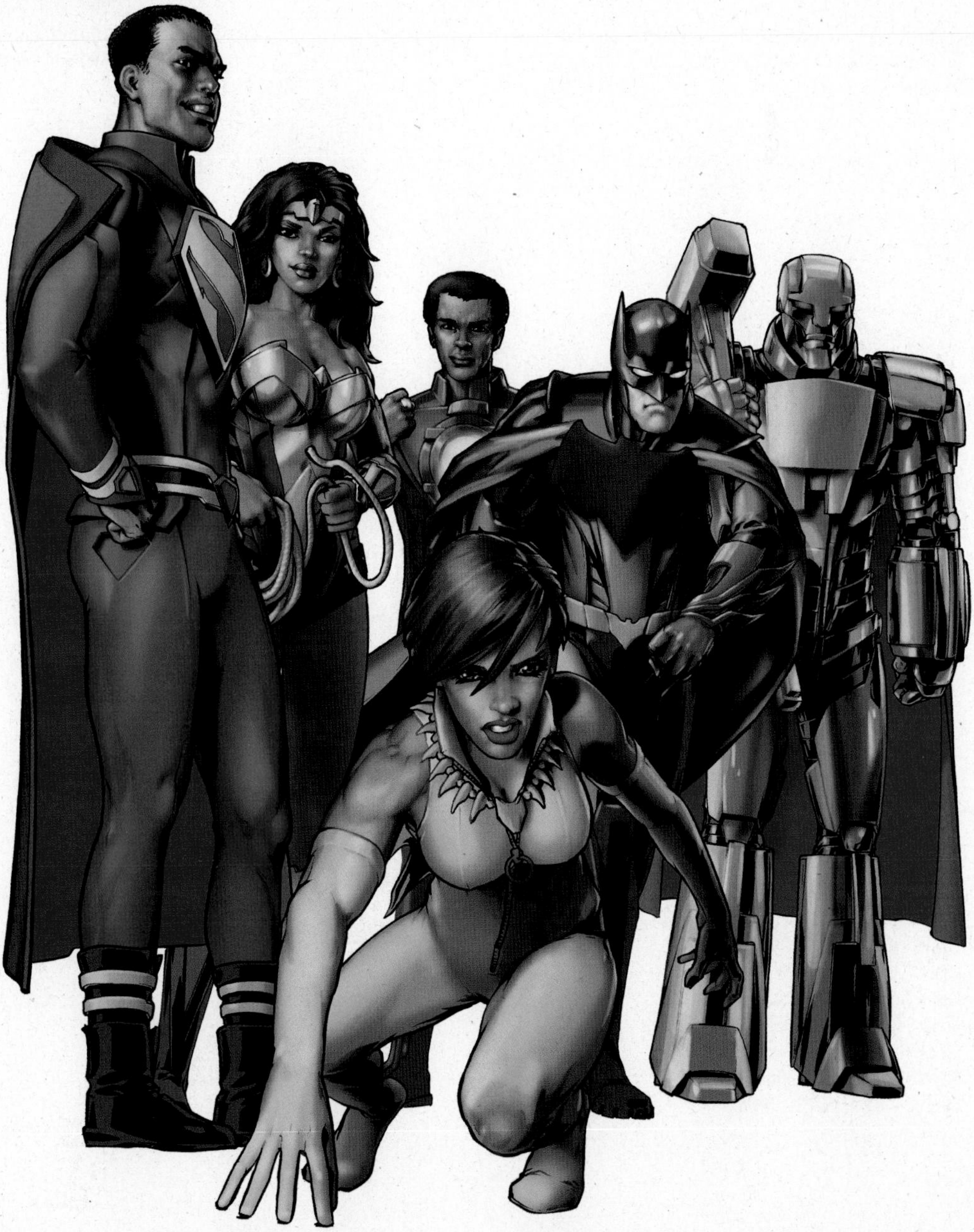

EARTH

Number 2 of 7 UNKNOWN WORLDS. Created by an Inner Chamber of 7 Monitor Magi for a mysterious purpose.

EARTH

Number 3 of 7 UNKNOWN WORLDS. Created by an Inner Chamber of 7 Monitor Magi for a mysterious purpose.

EARTH

Earth-26 was briefly destroyed, but the so-called CARTOON PHYSICS governing this world permits the inhabitants of Earth-26 to survive almost any known physical assault. In his superheroic guise as CAPTAIN CARROT, comic book writer/artist Rodney Rabbit leads FASTBACK, AMERICAN EAGLE, RUBBERDUCK, YANKEE POODLE, PIG-IRON, ALLEY-KAT-ABRA and LITTLE CHEESE — a.k.a. the ZOO CREW.

EARTH

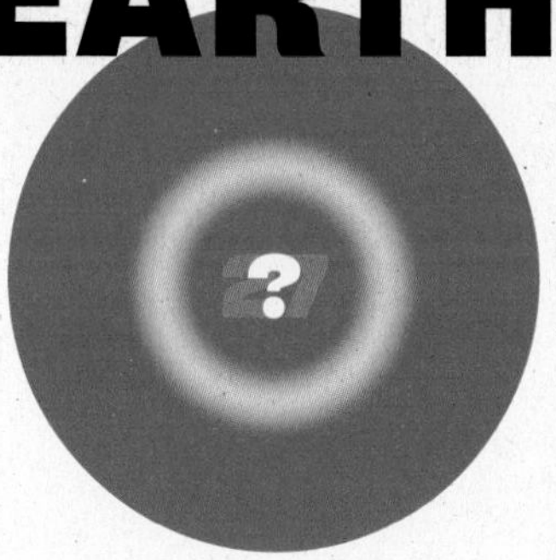
?

Number 4 of 7 UNKNOWN WORLDS. Created an Inner Chamber of 7 Monitor Magi for a mysterious purpose.

EARTH

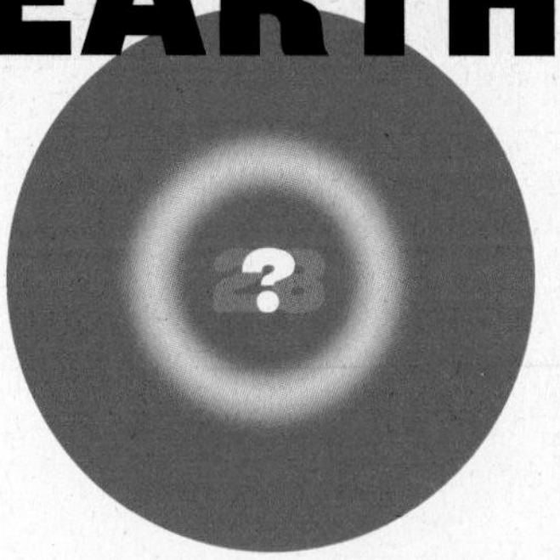
?

Number 5 of 7 UNKNOWN WORLDS. Created by an Inner Chamber of 7 Monitor Magi for a mysterious purpose.

EARTH

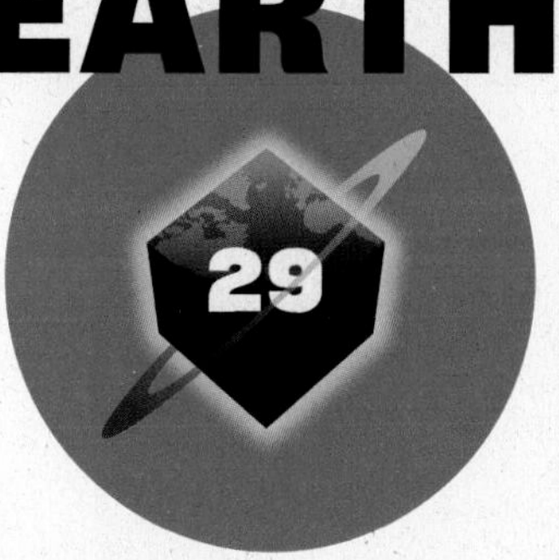
29

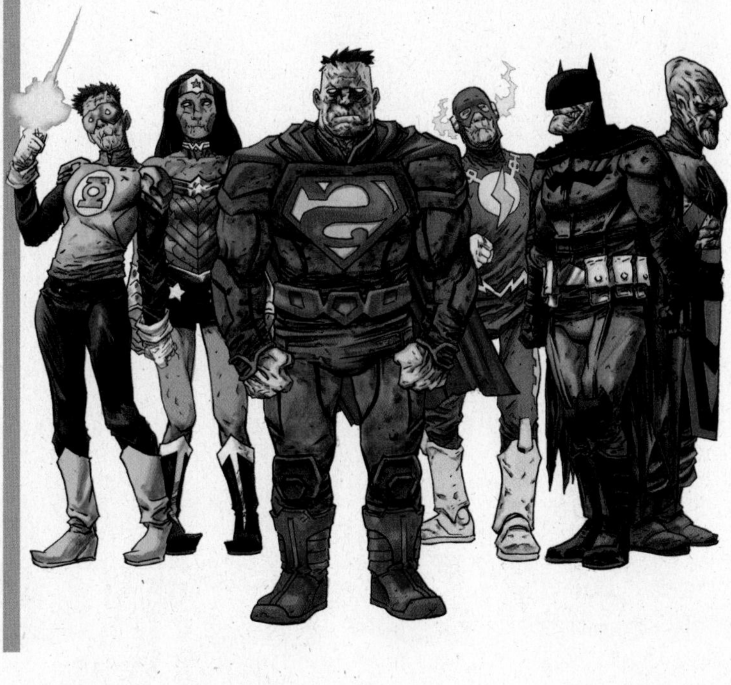

The square planet Htrae dominates Bizarroverse, a broken continuum with damaged laws of physics.BIZARRO-SUPERMAN leads his UNJUSTICE LEAGUE OF UNAMERICA on pointless, inexplicable and utterly futile adventures.

The Bizarroverse is crowded with nearby planets including Nnar, home of ADAM FAMILIAR; the overpopulated Sram, birthplace of the green SRAMIAN SNITCH; Raganaht, home planet of the flightless BIZARRO MANHAWK; Ao of the DISMISSERS OF THE UNIVERSE; etc, etc.

EARTH 30

World of the Soviet Superman, where Kal-L's rocket crash-landed on a Russian collective farm, resulting in a Communist Superman.

On Earth-30, BATMAN was a terrorist freedom fighter. GREEN LANTERN and BIZARRO were American super-weapons. Following the apparent death of Superman, this world prospered under the guidance of the LUTHOR FAMILY.

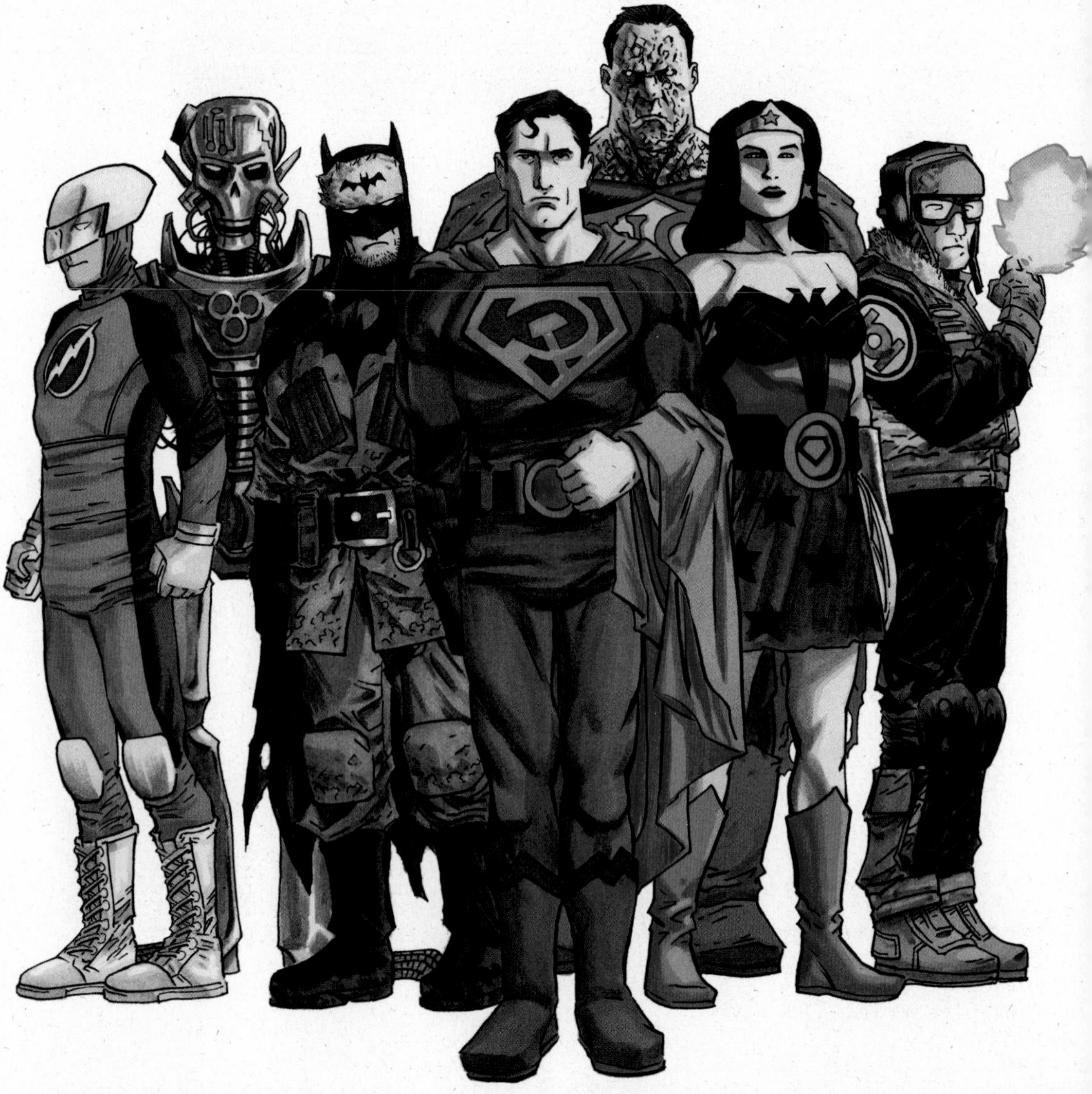

EARTH 31

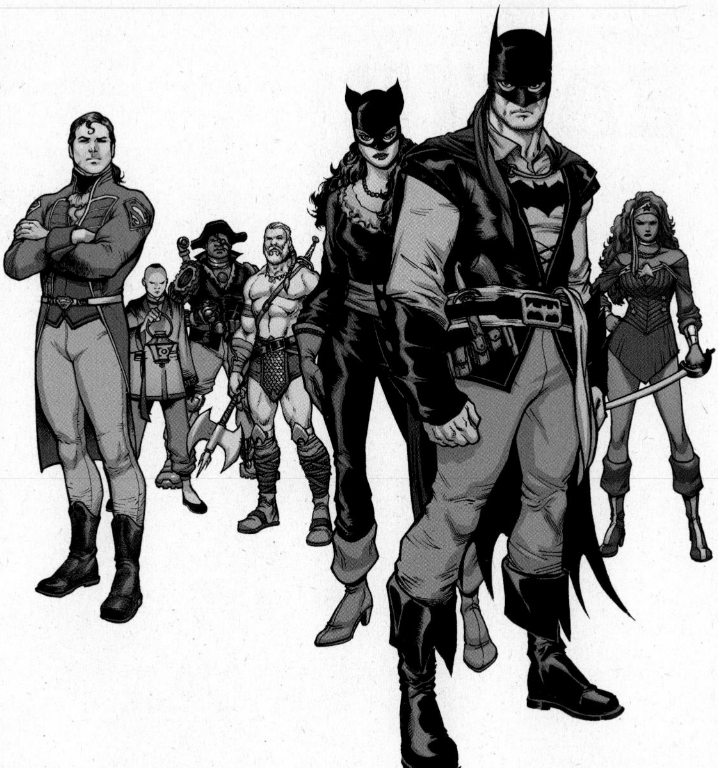

Global warming, mega-tsunamis and tectonic shifts have created a post-apocalyptic drowned world.
CAPTAIN LEATHERWING and the crew of the Flying Fox — including ROBIN REDBLADE — fight to preserve the safety of the Seven Seas.

EARTH 32

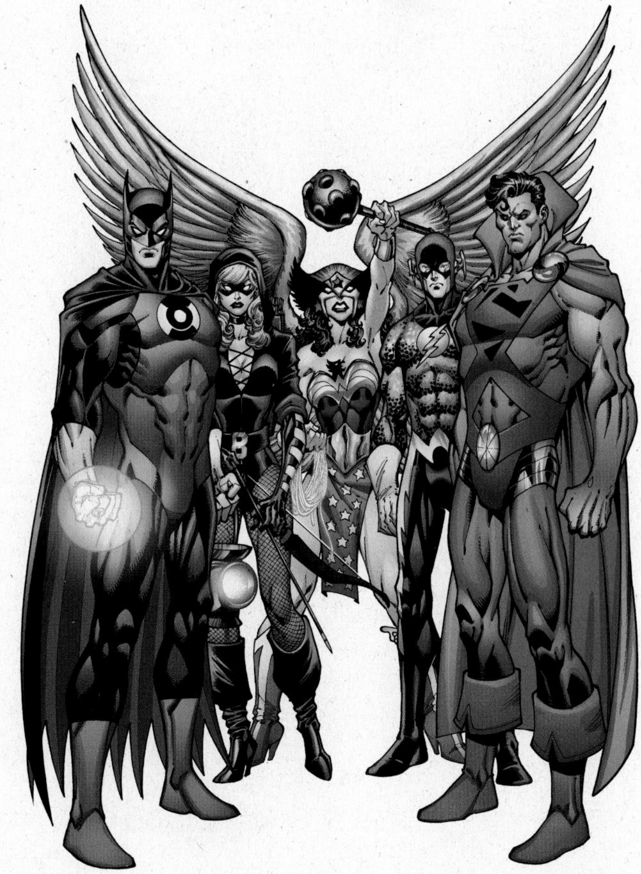

Here, Bruce Wayne is Earth's Green Lantern and fights evil as BAT-LANTERN, alongside BLACK ARROW, WONDERHAWK, AQUAFLASH, SUPER-MARTIAN, and other members of the JUSTICE TITANS.

EARTH 33

Known also as Earth-Prime, this mysterious world without superheroes exerts a powerful and unknown influence on the progress and development of the entire Multiverse.

Earth-Prime's only known superhuman inhabitant is known as ULTRA COMICS. That's him there...

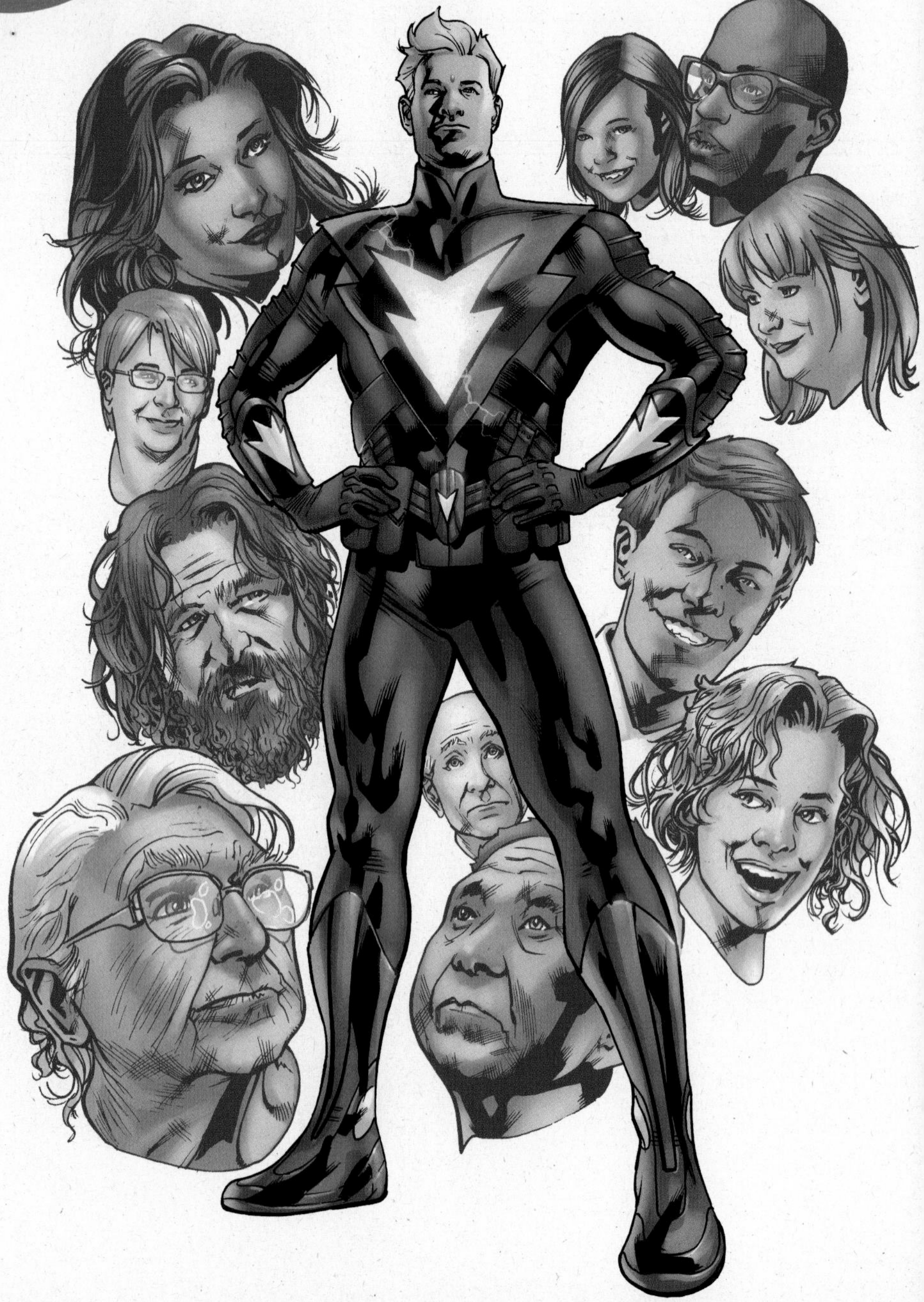

EARTH

34

One of numerous superheroes based in the city of COSMOVILLE, SAVIOR was the last survivor of the ancient super-civilization of MU. Sent into the future to escape a doomed past, he inaugurated the LIGHT BRIGADE along with HERCULINA, RADMAN, GOODFELLOW, FORMULA-I, GHOSTMAN, MASTER MOTLEY, CUTIE, THE STINGRAY and many others.

EARTH

35

SUPREMO is the greatest hero of Earth-35, an awesome "pseudoverse" or artificial universe constructed by Monitor "ideominers" operating from harvesting stations in Earth-35 "concept space." Supremo is a proud member of the SUPER-AMERICANS, alongside heroes including STARCOP, MERCURY-MAN, MISS X, MORPHIN' MAN, MAJESTY — QUEEN OF VENUS, OLYMPIAN and THE OWL.

EARTH 36

The homeworld of JUSTICE 9, where the alien OPTIMAN fought bravely alongside such heroes as FLASHLIGHT, CYBERION, WAR-WOMAN, MER-MAN, BLACKBIRD, BOWBOY, IRON KNIGHT, RED RACER and more. Optiman was apparently killed by the Earth-45 monster SUPERDOOMSDAY.

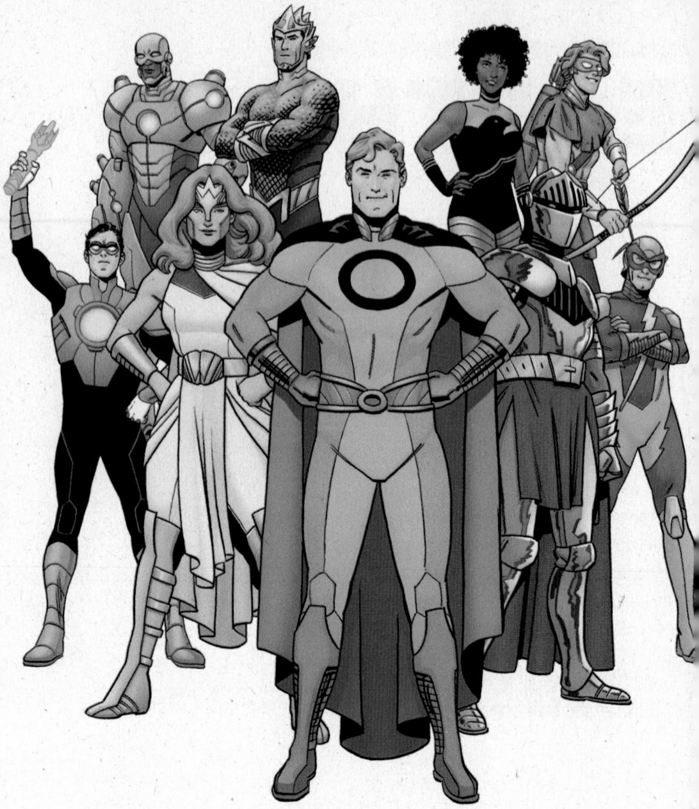

EARTH 37

A world of lawless heroes and cynical champions. On Earth-37 technology accelerated through the '60s, '70s and '80s. The beat cellars of the '50s gave way to the underground Mars base colonies of the '80s and the Europa bases of the '90s and then to the interstellar world of TOMMY TOMORROW, MANHUNTER 2015 and the SPACE RANGERS.

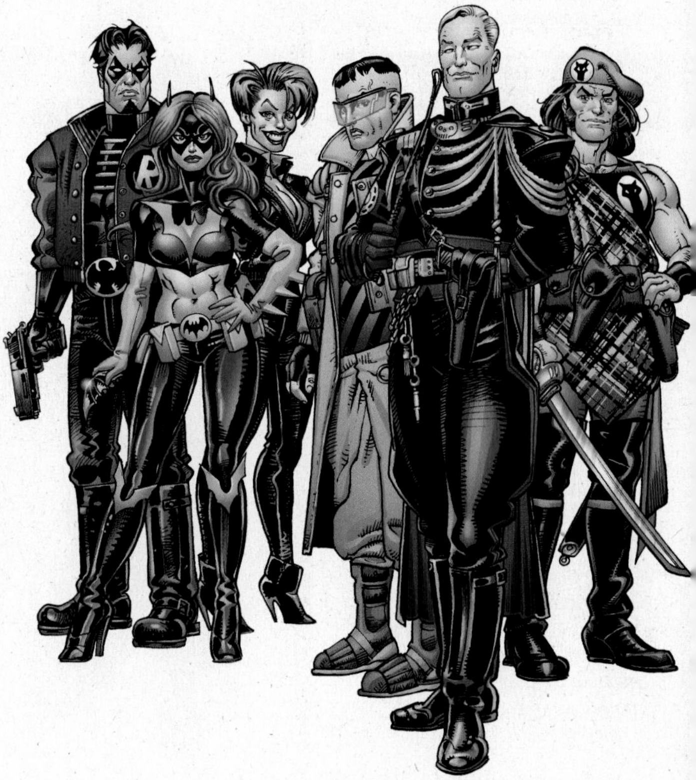

EARTH

38

Here, Superman and Batman first appeared in the 1930s, aging normally as their children inherited a world of wonder and tragedy, where heroes and heroines alike carry the heroic baton into an unknown future.

EARTH

39

Home of the AGENTS OF W.O.N.D.E.R., an organization of United Nations super-spies — CYCLOTRON, DOCTOR NEMO, CORVUS, ACCELERATOR and PSI-MAN — each equipped with an item of miracle technology designed by visionary boy genius Happy DaVinci — the Cyclo-Harness, the Accelerator Circuit, the Ghost Chamber, the LightWing and the Cypher Suit. Repeated use of this technology might be addictive and ruinous.

EARTH

40

A "binary universe" resonating in "catastrophic harmony" with Earth-20, of which it is the evil reflex. Colliding every 100,000 years with its counterpart, Earth-40 is home to the SOCIETY OF SUPER-CRIMINALS including DOC FAUST, VANDAL SAVAGE, LADY SHIVA, BLOCKBUSTER, and PARALLAX the FEAR-THING. See also EARTH-20.

EARTH

41

A dark and violent world. Home of the "necro floral" avenger SPORE, gruff DINO-COP, NIMROD SQUAD, NIGHTCRACKER, THE SCORPION and SEPULCHRE.

EARTH

42

The tiny inhabitants of Earth-42 knew nothing of mortality, evil or violence until the death of their Superman at the hands of the Earth-45 thought-monster, SUPERDOOMSDAY — but their world hides a great and terrible secret.

EARTH 43

A world of darkness and fear where super-vampires rule the night as the BLOOD LEAGUE.

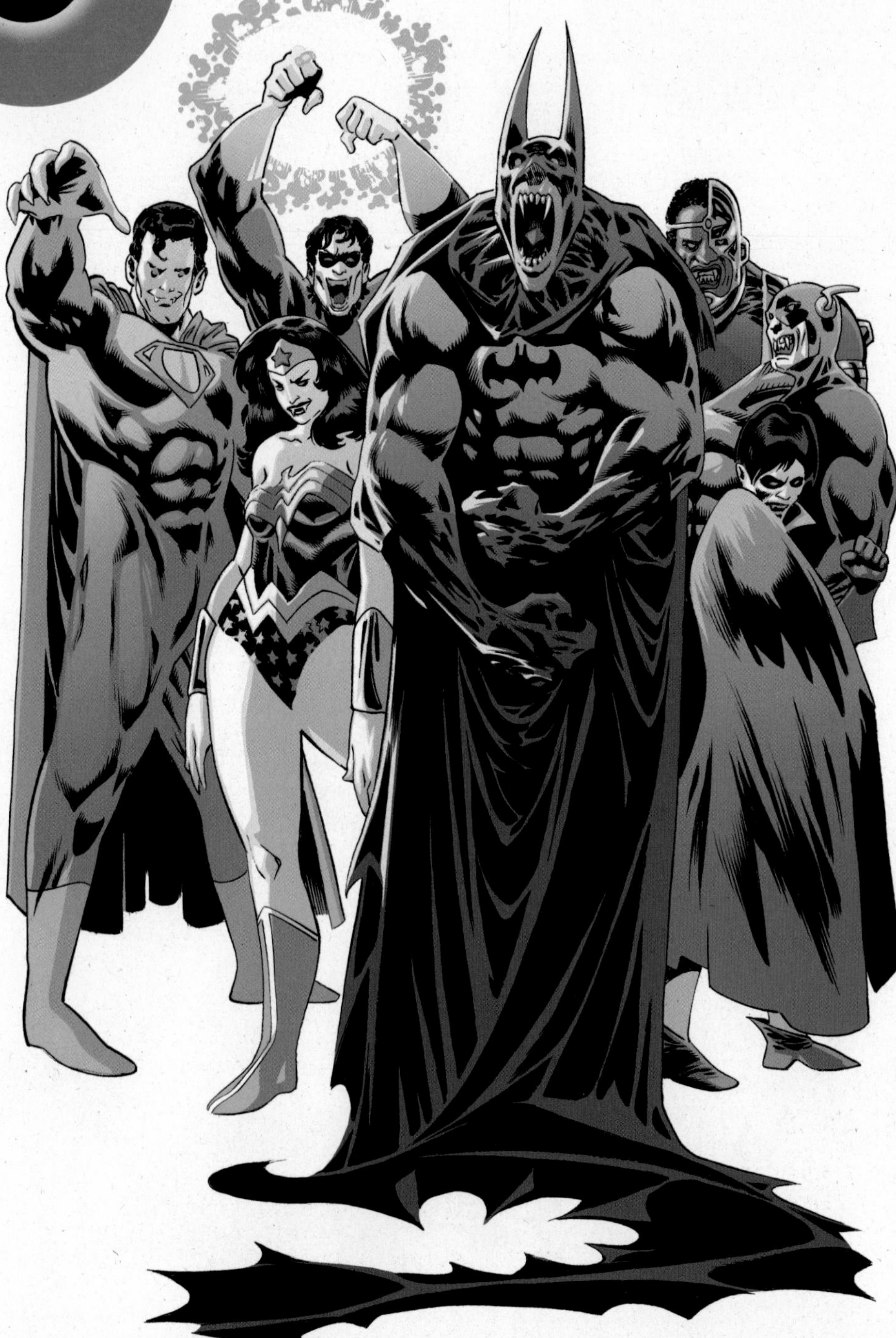

EARTH 44

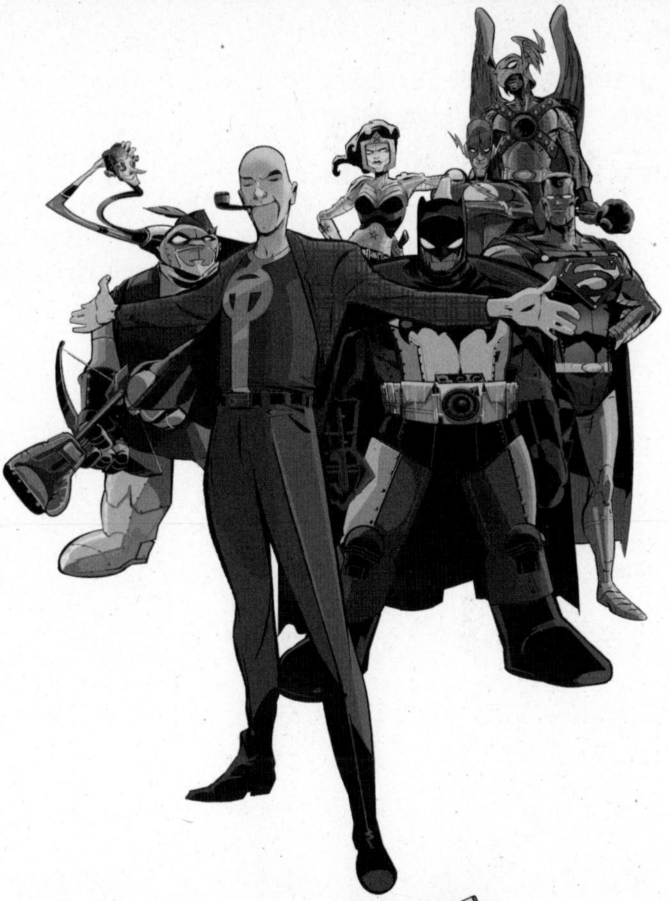

The home of world-changing superhero A.I.s designed and built by the brilliant, bipolar Doctor Will Tornado. "There were no super-heroes — there was no one to save the world — so I built them," says DOC TORNADO of his creations.

THE METAL LEAGUE comprises GOLD SUPER-MAN, IRON BATMAN, PLATINUM WONDER WOMAN, MERCURY FLASH, Nth METAL HAWKMAN, TIN ELONGATED MAN, and LEAD GREEN ARROW.

EARTH 45™

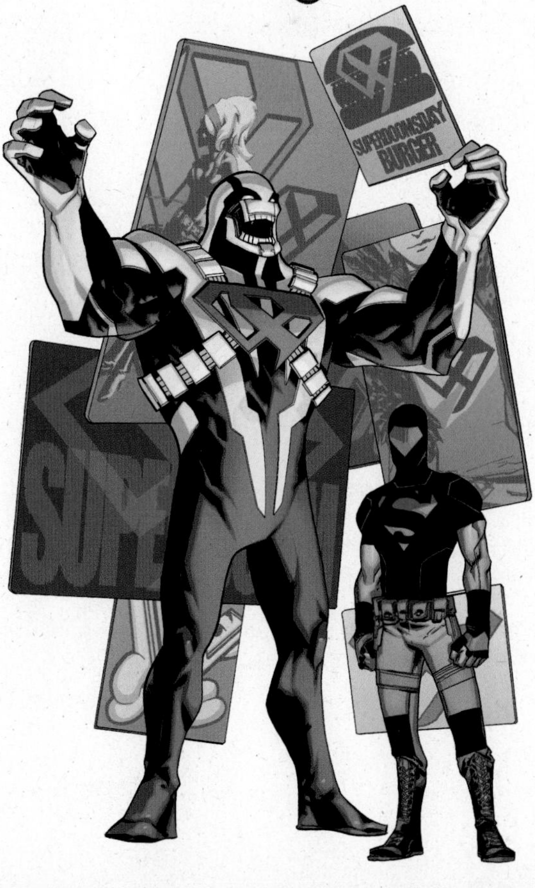
SUPERDOOMSDAY
BURGER
SUPE

On this world there were no superhuman beings until "SUPERMAN™" was created by CLARK KENT, LOIS LANE and JIMMY OLSEN using incredible new thought-powered technology. Co-opted by the business mavens of OVERCORP, Superman was redesigned as a monstrous, troubled anti-hero and came to be known as SUPERDOOMSDAY when his rampage through the worlds of the Multiverse resulted in the deaths of Superman of Earth-42 and Optiman of Earth-36 before his defeat at the hands of President Superman of Earth-23 and the Superman of Earth-0.

EARTH

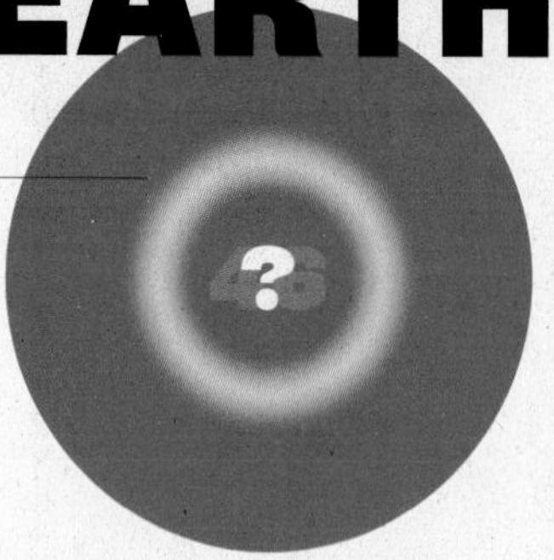

?

Number 6 of 7 UNKNOWN WORLDS. The second most mysterious of 7 UNKNOWN EARTHS.

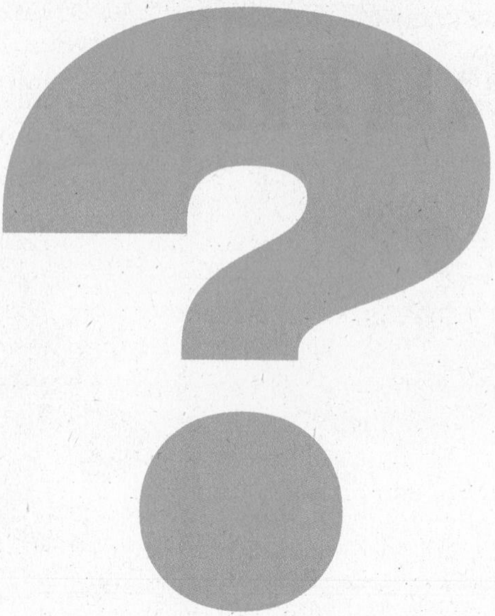

EARTH

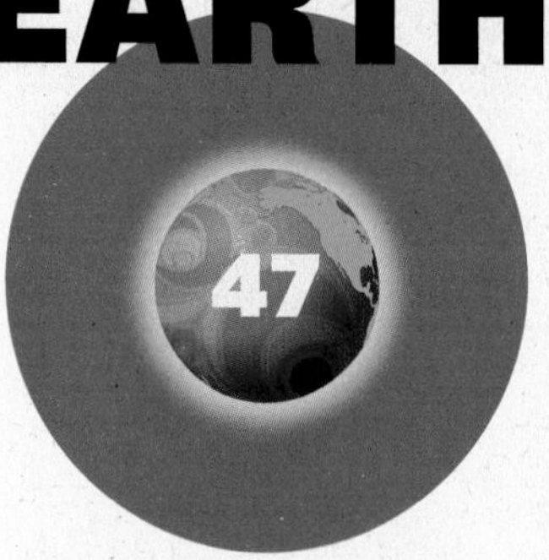

47

Home of the psychedelic champions of the LOVE SYNDICATE of DREAMWORLD led by SUNSHINE SUPERMAN, and including THE SHOOTING STAR, SPEED FREAK, MAGIC LANTERN, and BROTHER POWER, THE GEEK.

The Love Syndicate is financed by the immortal teenaged President PREZ RICKARD. All is groovy.

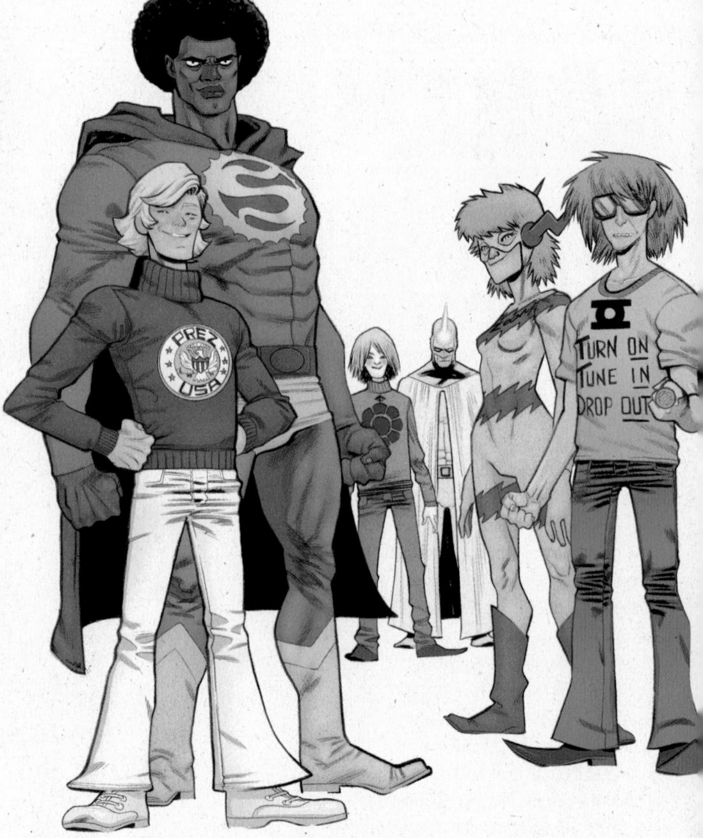

PREZ
USA
TURN ON
TUNE IN
DROP OUT

EARTH 48

The Earth of the FORERUNNERS — a race of super beings bred to be harvested as ultimate protectors of the Multiverse itself. Rapid evolution has resulted in super-trees, super-dogs, mice, and bacteria; super-weapons, super-food, super-TV shows. Every story is a crossover epic, every event an EVENT.

Sometimes known as Warworld, Earth-48 has been converted by benevolent aliens into a factory, designed to produce a race of Fifth World warriors to fight in the eternal war against Lord Darkseid. The Royal Family of Warworld includes LADY QUARK, LIANA, BROTHER EYES, ANTARCTIC MONKEY, DANGER DOG, LORD VOLT, KID VICIOUS and billions more.

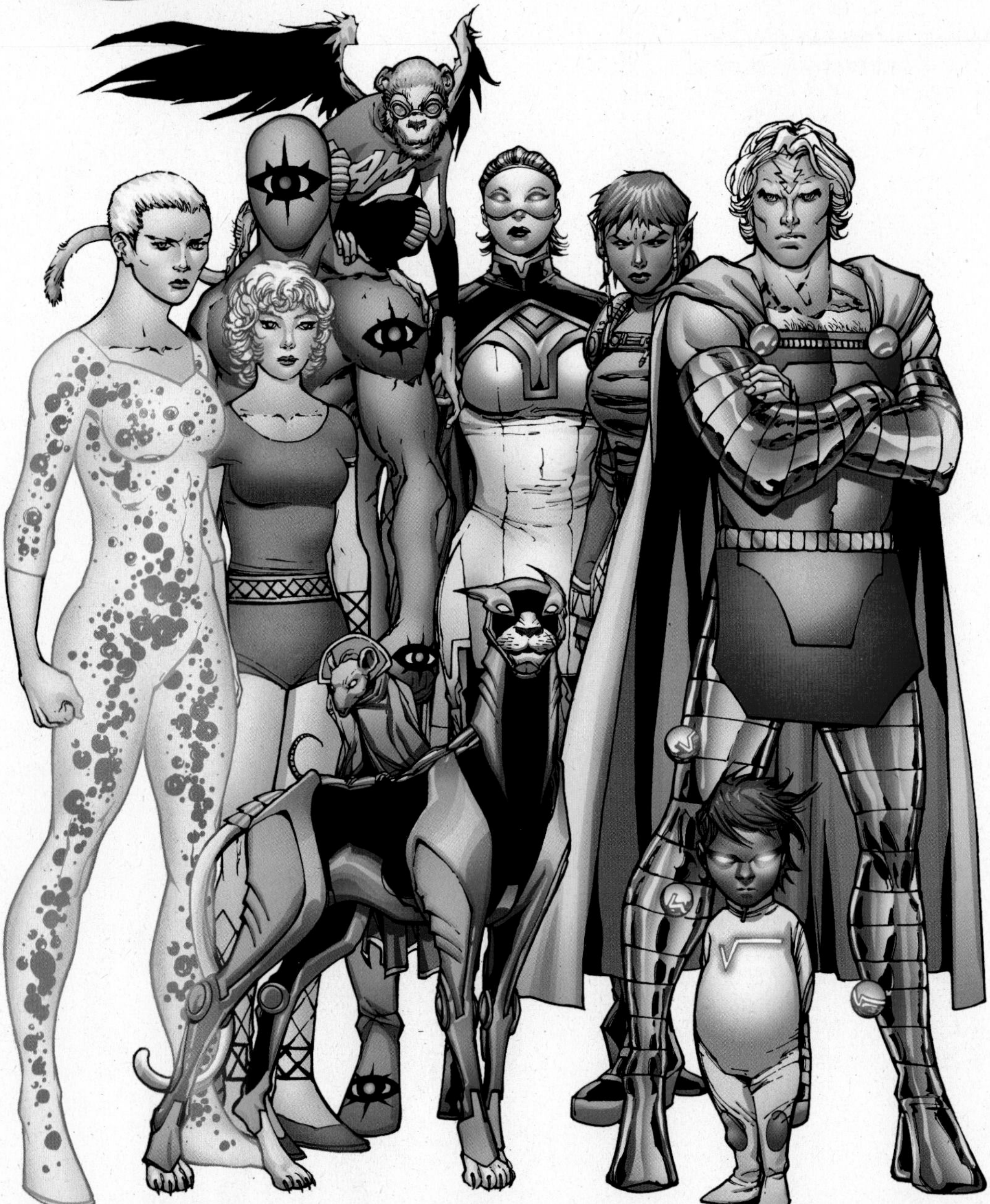

EARTH

Number 7 of 7 UNKNOWN WORLDS. The most mysterious of 7 UNKNOWN EARTHS.

EARTH

50

When PRESIDENT LEX LUTHOR murdered the FLASH, the SUPERMAN of this world took it upon himself to punish Luthor by death and instituted a global police state patrolled and maintained by the tyrannical, super-powered JUSTICE LORDS.

EARTH 51

On a fragile Earth ravaged by an unknown "Great Disaster," men act like beasts and beasts act like men!
Here, KAMANDI, the Last Boy on Earth, and his allies PRINCE TUFTAN of the Tiger-Men and BEN BOXER, a.k.a. biOMAC, have embarked on a mind-bending rescue mission to the ends of the earth, while vast, powerful and manipulative New Gods look on.

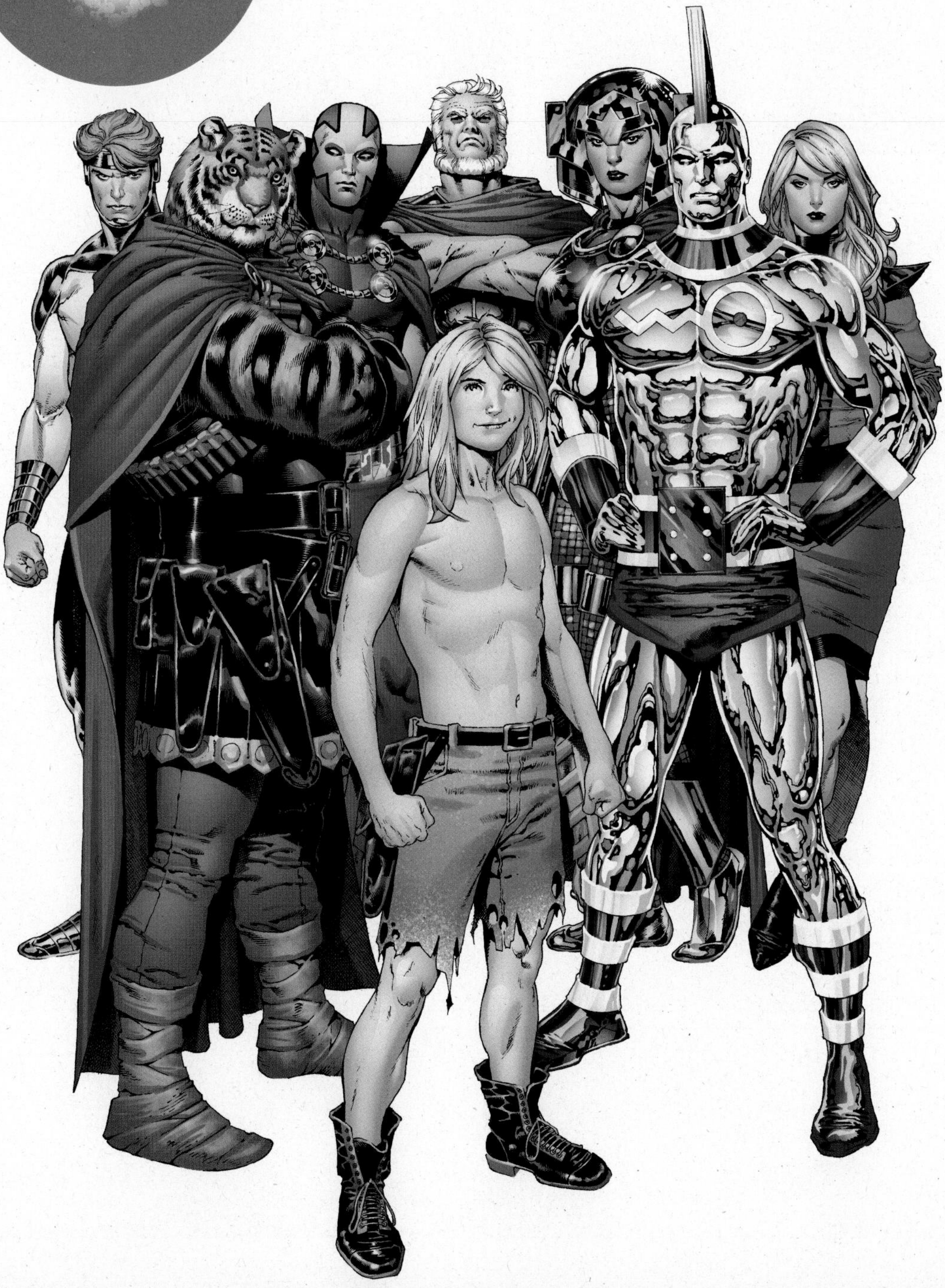

OUR WORLD IS ONLY *ONE* OF *MANY*?

SOMEWHERE, RIGHT NOW, ON AN ISLAND LIKE *THIS ONE*, PEOPLE LIKE *US* ARE--

THE GROUND! IT'S *SHAKING*!

BR'ER EYE WARNS OF *SEISMIC OVER-LOAD*!

WE SHOULDN'T HAVE COME HERE!

I FOU

BUT WE HAD TO *SEE*!

WE HAD TO *KNOW*!

THE *FLOWER*!

WHAT HAPPENED TO THE FLOWER?

IT'S ALL I *HAD* OF HER...

TAKE THESE WEAPONS AND *LEAVE*!

THESE ARE MYSTERIES FOR *ANOTHER* DAY!

LET'S GET OUT OF HERE!

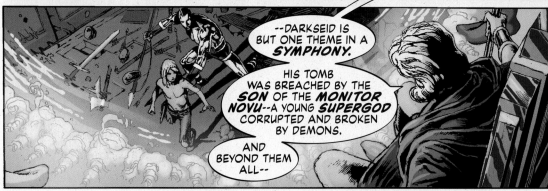

THE WALLS OF *ALL* THE WORLDS ARE SHAKING NOW--

--DARKSEID IS BUT ONE THEME IN A *SYMPHONY*.

HIS TOMB WAS BREACHED BY THE *SON OF THE MONITOR NOVU*--A YOUNG *SUPERGOD* CORRUPTED AND BROKEN BY DEMONS.

AND BEYOND THEM ALL--

--THAT *DREAD AND EMPTY HAND*!

WHOSE NAME *NONE* DARE VOICE.

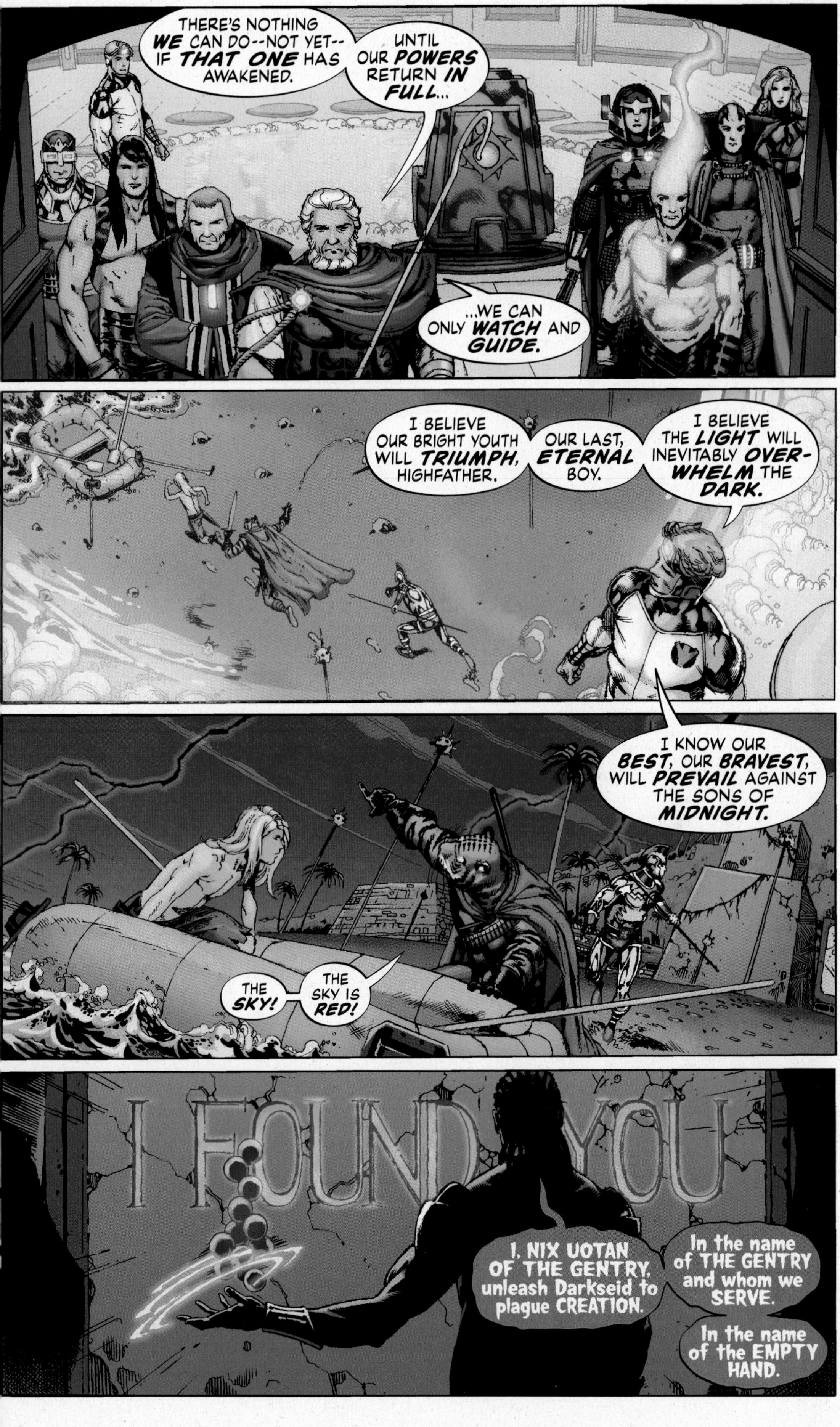

THERE'S NOTHING WE CAN DO--NOT YET--IF THAT ONE HAS AWAKENED.
UNTIL OUR POWERS RETURN IN FULL...
...WE CAN ONLY WATCH AND GUIDE.
I BELIEVE OUR BRIGHT YOUTH WILL TRIUMPH, HIGHFATHER.
OUR LAST, ETERNAL BOY.
I BELIEVE THE LIGHT WILL INEVITABLY OVER-WHELM THE DARK.
I KNOW OUR BEST, OUR BRAVEST, WILL PREVAIL AGAINST THE SONS OF MIDNIGHT.
THE SKY!
THE SKY IS RED!
I FOUND YOU
I, NIX UOTAN OF THE GENTRY, unleash Darkseid to plague CREATION.
In the name of THE GENTRY and whom we SERVE.
In the name of the EMPTY HAND.

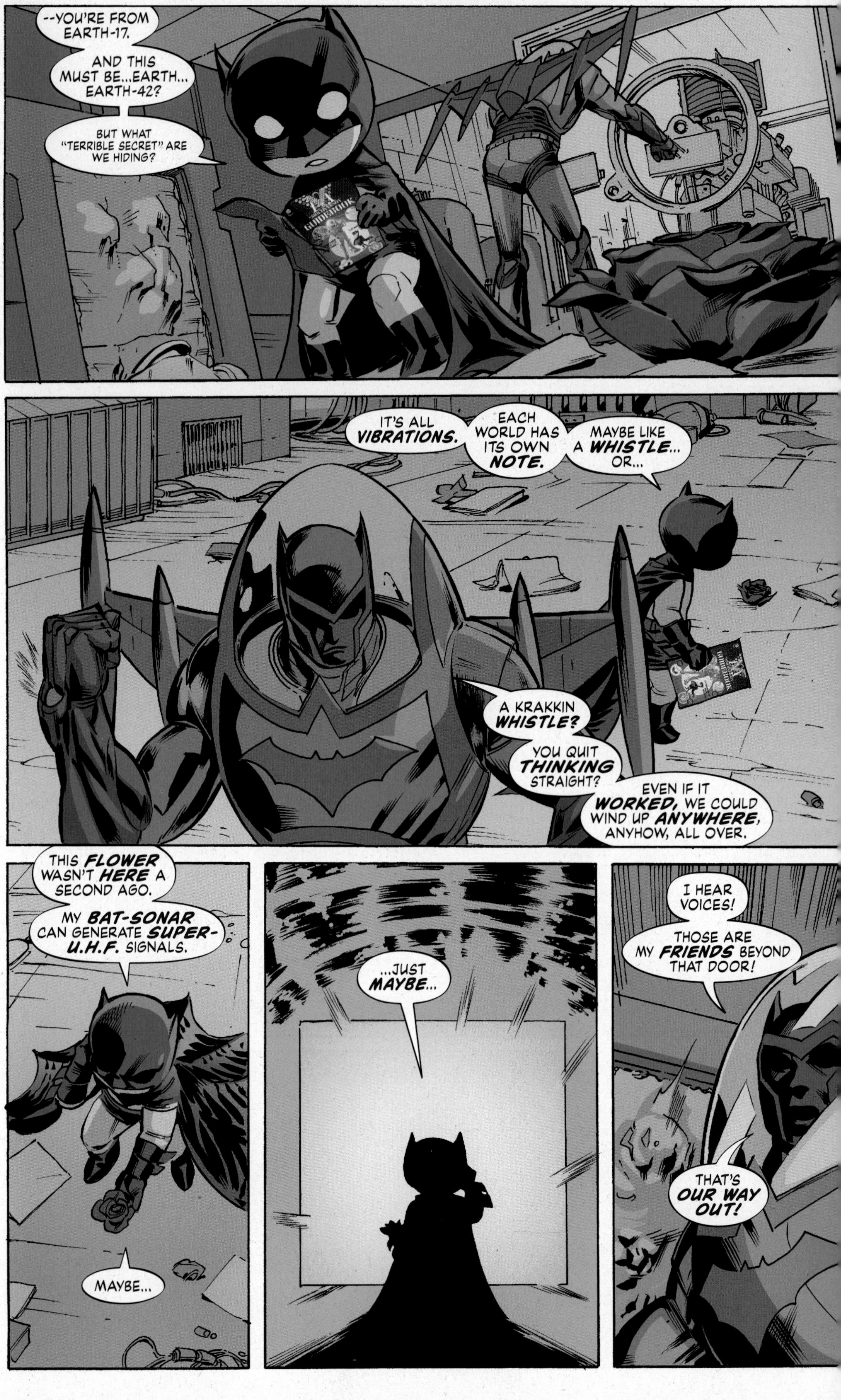

--YOU'RE FROM EARTH-17.
AND THIS MUST BE...EARTH... EARTH-42?
BUT WHAT "TERRIBLE SECRET" ARE WE HIDING?
IT'S ALL VIBRATIONS.
EACH WORLD HAS ITS OWN NOTE.
MAYBE LIKE A WHISTLE... OR...
A KRAKKIN WHISTLE?
YOU QUIT THINKING STRAIGHT?
EVEN IF IT WORKED, WE COULD WIND UP ANYWHERE, ANYHOW, ALL OVER.
THIS FLOWER WASN'T HERE A SECOND AGO.
MY BAT-SONAR CAN GENERATE SUPER-U.H.F. SIGNALS.
MAYBE...
...JUST MAYBE...
I HEAR VOICES!
THOSE ARE MY FRIENDS BEYOND THAT DOOR!
THAT'S OUR WAY OUT!

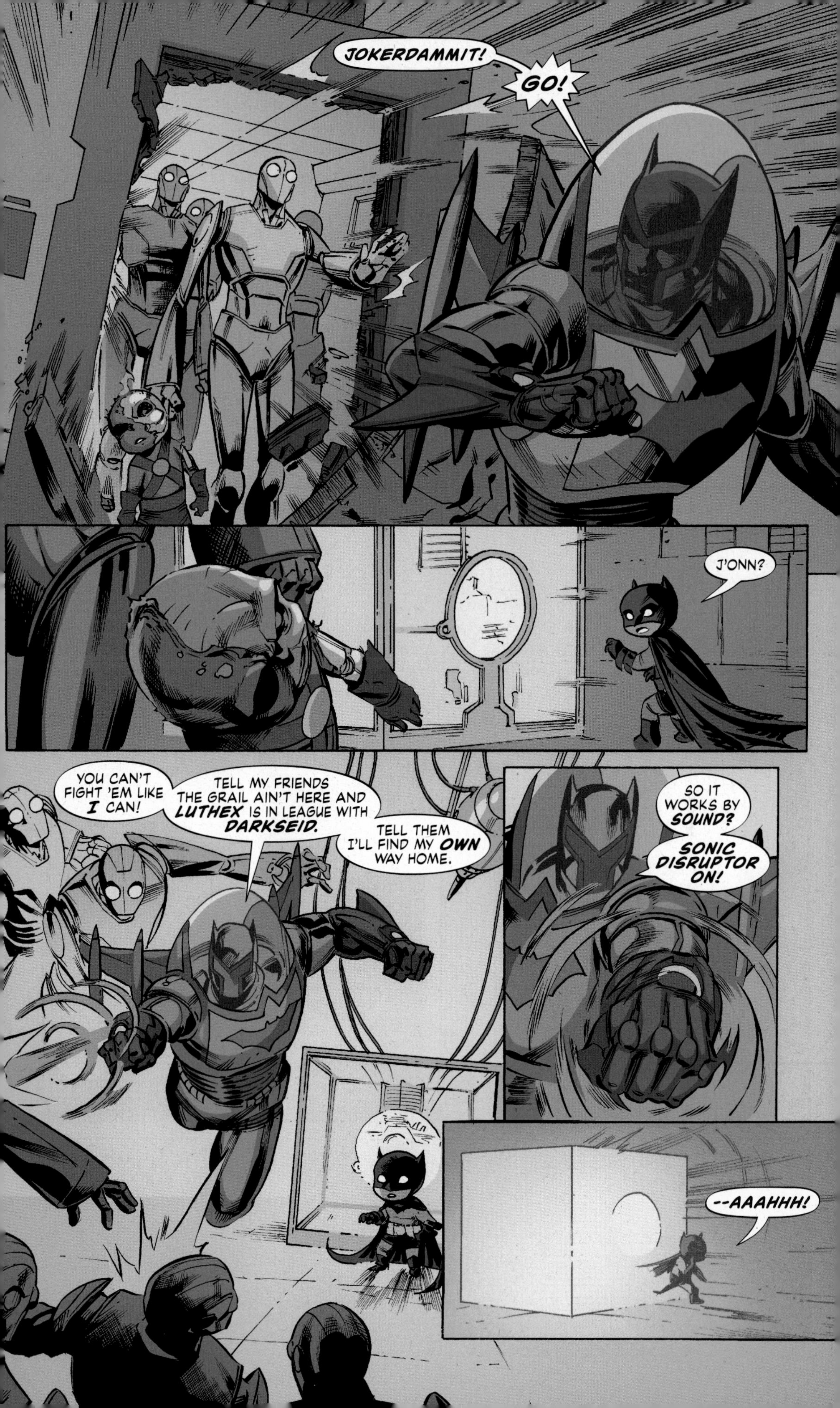
JOKERDAMMIT!
GO!
J'ONN?
YOU CAN'T FIGHT 'EM LIKE I CAN!
TELL MY FRIENDS THE GRAIL AIN'T HERE AND LUTHEX IS IN LEAGUE WITH DARKSEID.
TELL THEM I'LL FIND MY OWN WAY HOME.
SO IT WORKS BY SOUND?
SONIC DISRUPTOR ON!
--AAAHHH!

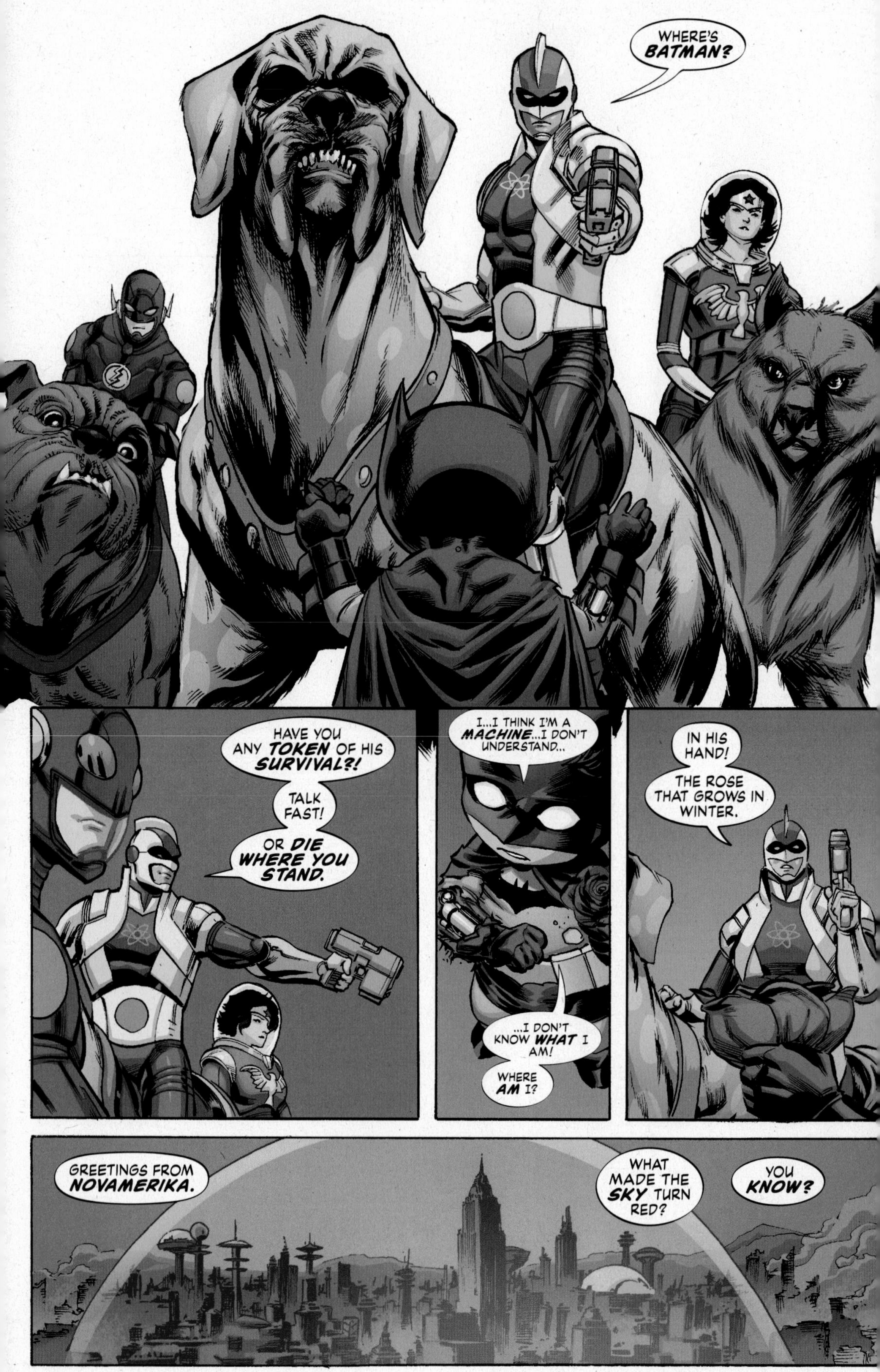
WHERE'S BATMAN?
HAVE YOU ANY TOKEN OF HIS SURVIVAL?!
TALK FAST!
OR DIE WHERE YOU STAND.
I...I THINK I'M A MACHINE...I DON'T UNDERSTAND...
...I DON'T KNOW WHAT I AM!
WHERE AM I?
IN HIS HAND!
THE ROSE THAT GROWS IN WINTER.
GREETINGS FROM NOVAMERIKA.
WHAT MADE THE SKY TURN RED?
YOU KNOW?

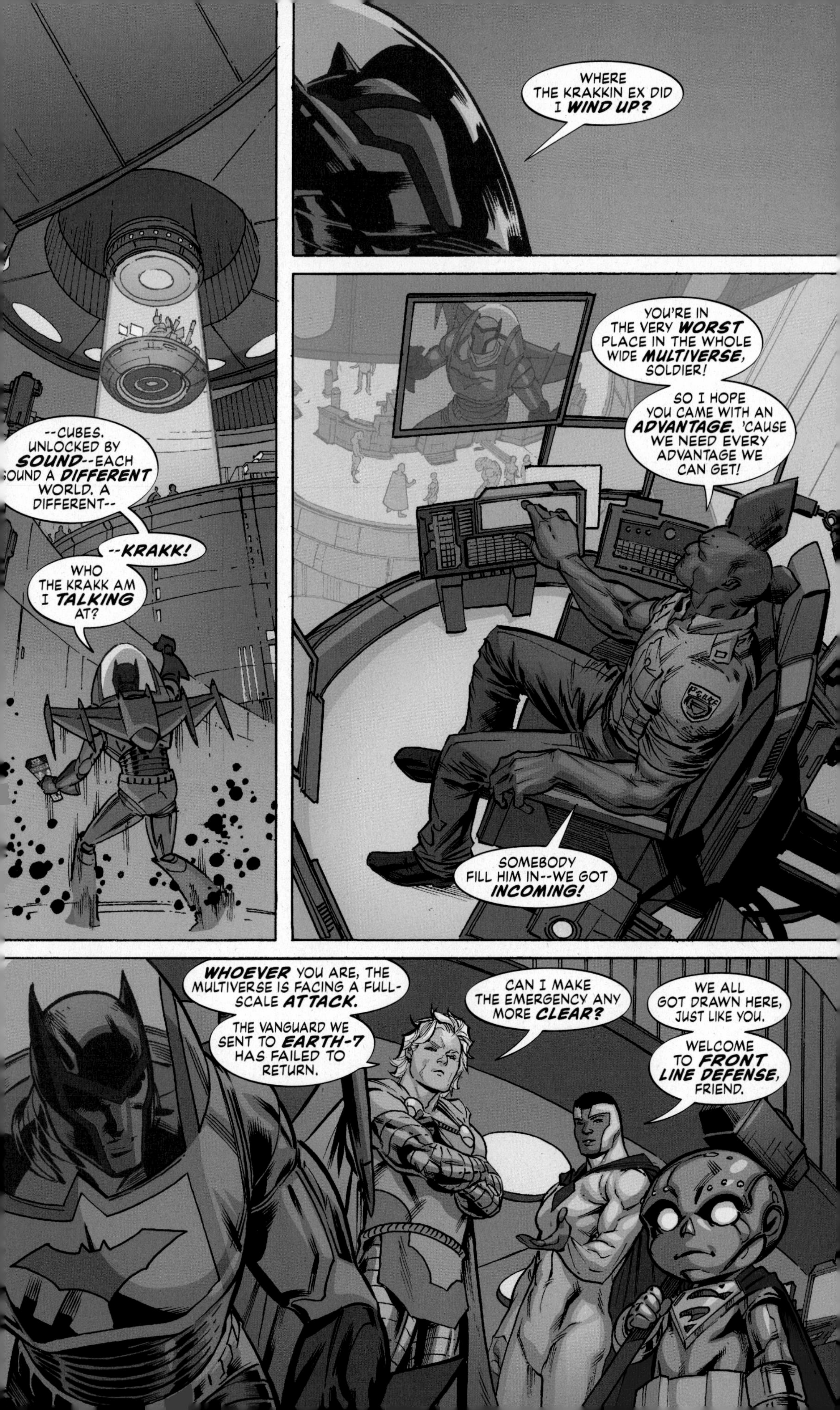
--CUBES. UNLOCKED BY SOUND--EACH SOUND A DIFFERENT WORLD. A DIFFERENT--
--KRAKK!
WHO THE KRAKK AM I TALKING AT?
WHERE THE KRAKKIN EX DID I WIND UP?
YOU'RE IN THE VERY WORST PLACE IN THE WHOLE WIDE MULTIVERSE, SOLDIER!
SO I HOPE YOU CAME WITH AN ADVANTAGE. 'CAUSE WE NEED EVERY ADVANTAGE WE CAN GET!
SOMEBODY FILL HIM IN--WE GOT INCOMING!
WHOEVER YOU ARE, THE MULTIVERSE IS FACING A FULL-SCALE ATTACK.
THE VANGUARD WE SENT TO EARTH-7 HAS FAILED TO RETURN.
CAN I MAKE THE EMERGENCY ANY MORE CLEAR?
WE ALL GOT DRAWN HERE, JUST LIKE YOU.
WELCOME TO FRONT LINE DEFENSE, FRIEND.

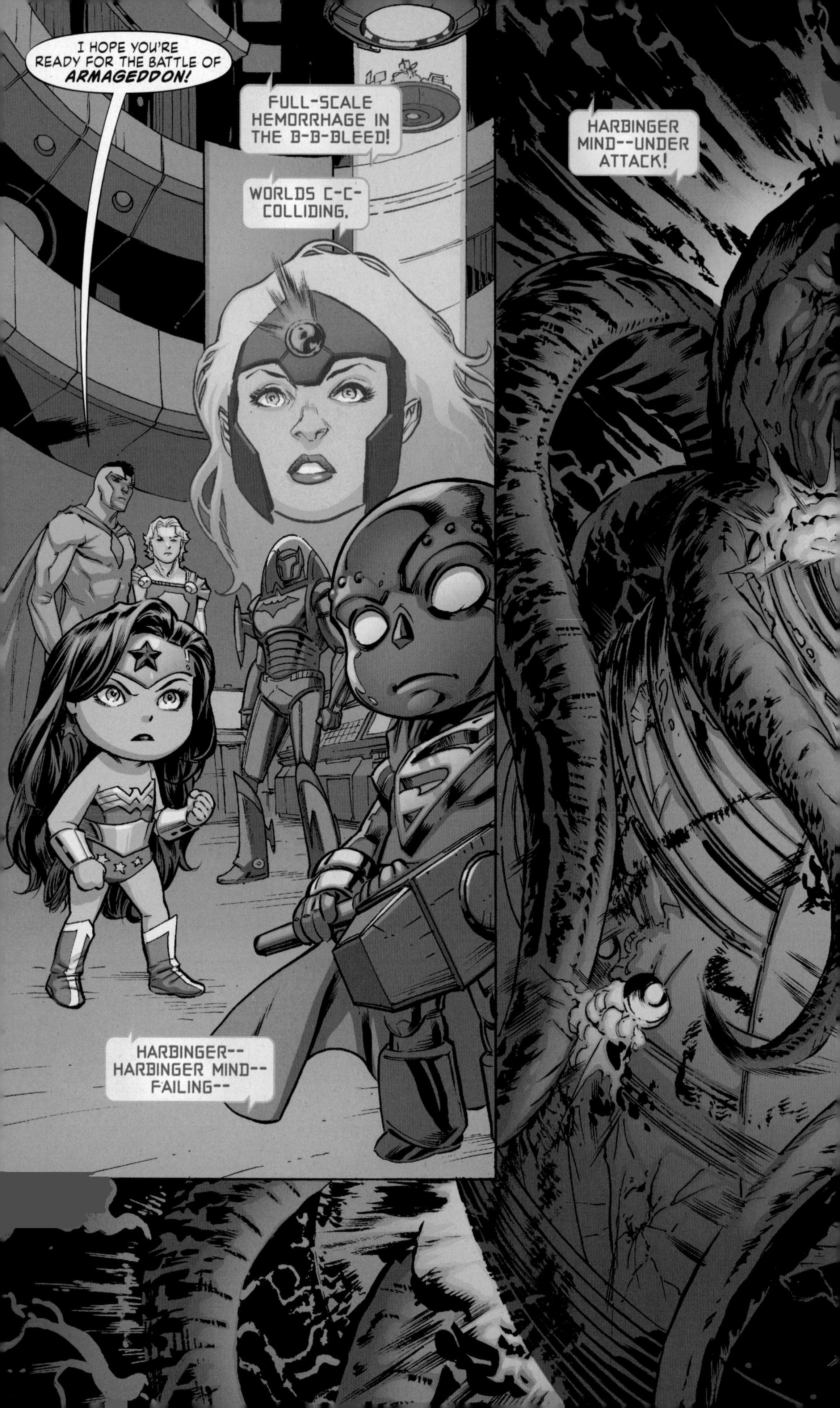

I HOPE YOU'RE READY FOR THE BATTLE OF ARMAGEDDON!
FULL-SCALE HEMORRHAGE IN THE B-B-BLEED!
WORLDS C-C-COLLIDING.
HARBINGER--HARBINGER MIND--FAILING--
HARBINGER MIND--UNDER ATTACK!

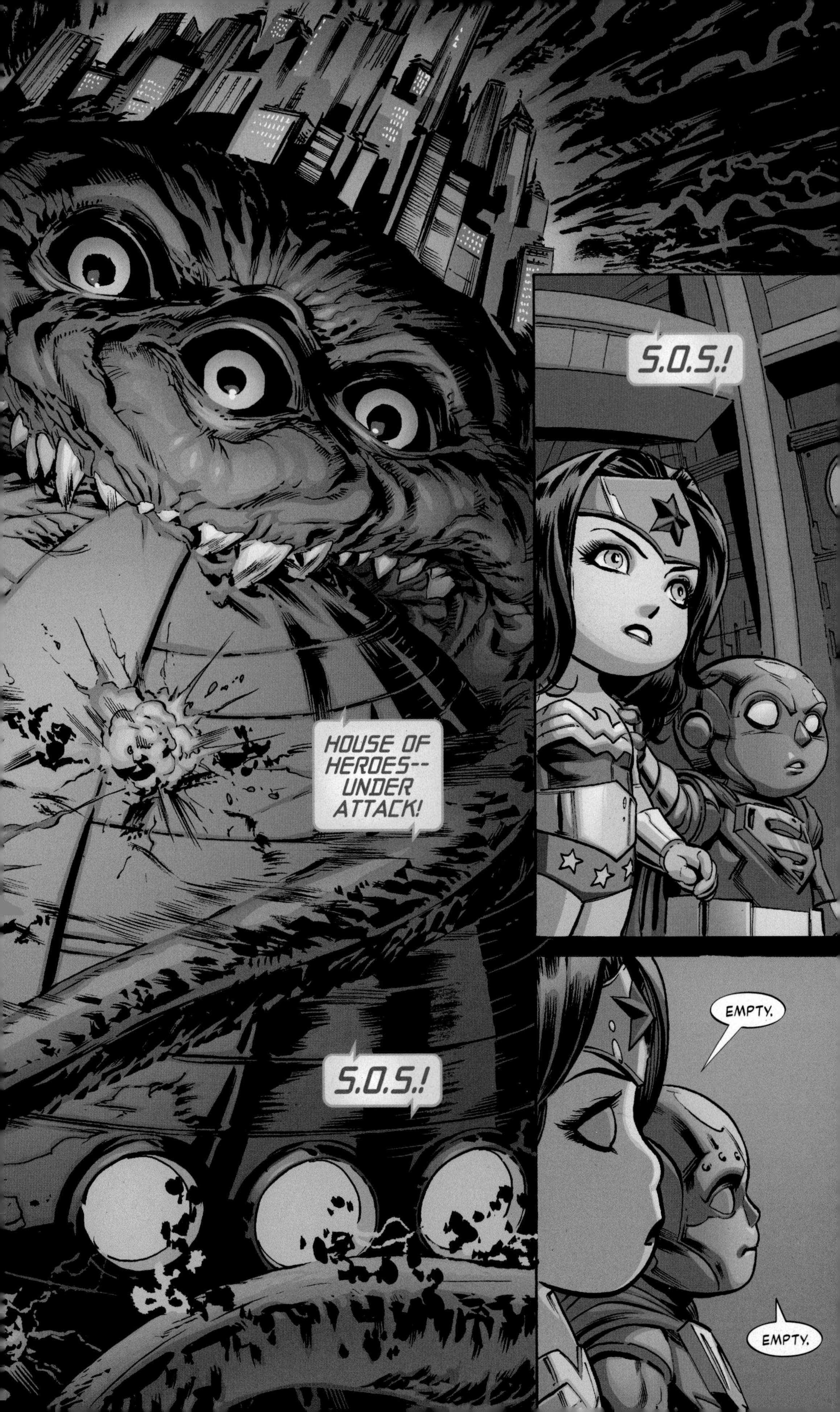
HOUSE OF HEROES--UNDER ATTACK!
S.O.S.!
S.O.S.!
EMPTY.
EMPTY.

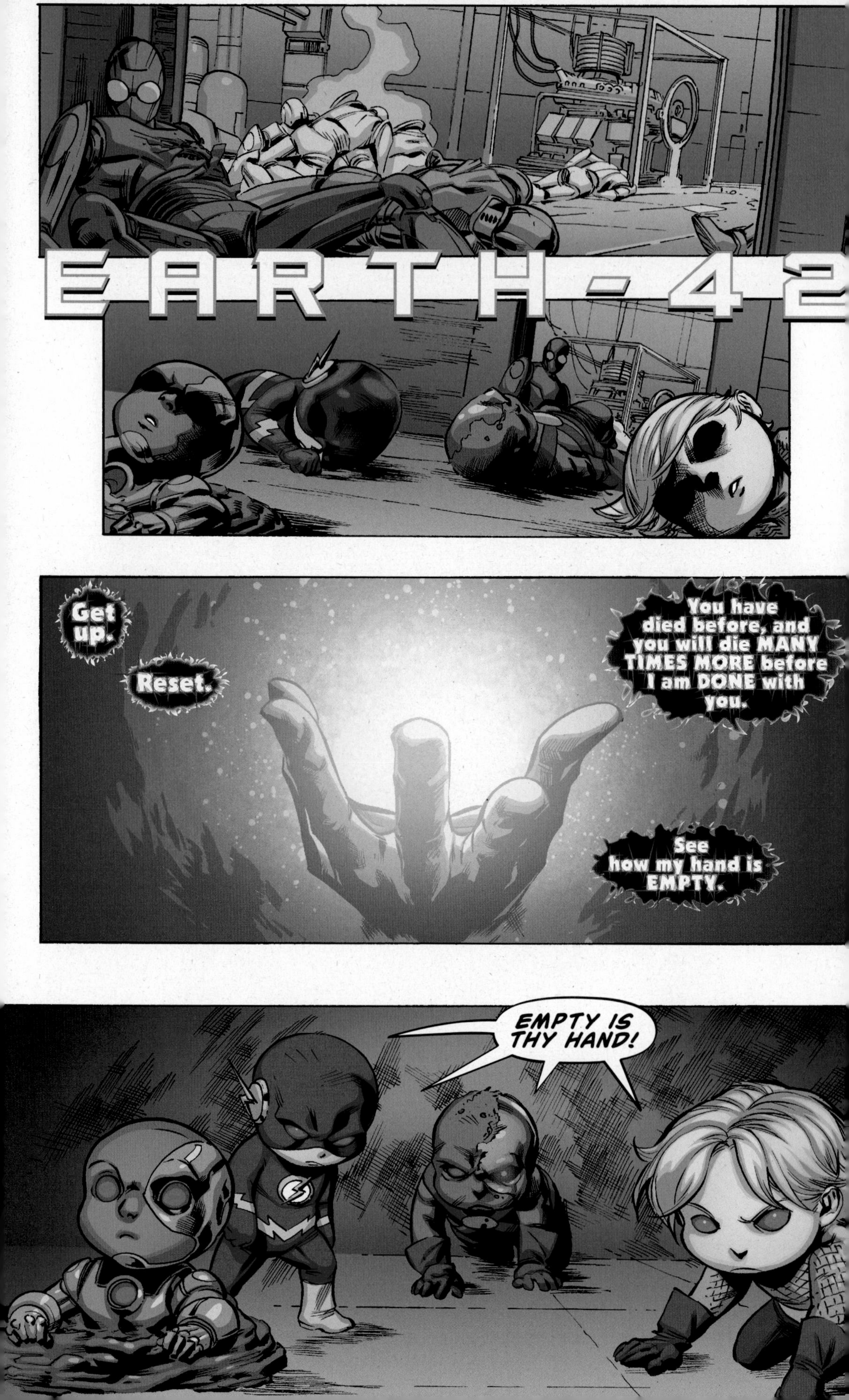
EARTH-42
Get up.
Reset.
You have died before, and you will die MANY TIMES MORE before I am DONE with you.
See how my hand is EMPTY.
EMPTY IS THY HAND!

DC COMICS™

1

$4.99 US

THE MULTIVERSITY™

MORRISON
LEE
WILLIAMS
SINCLAIR

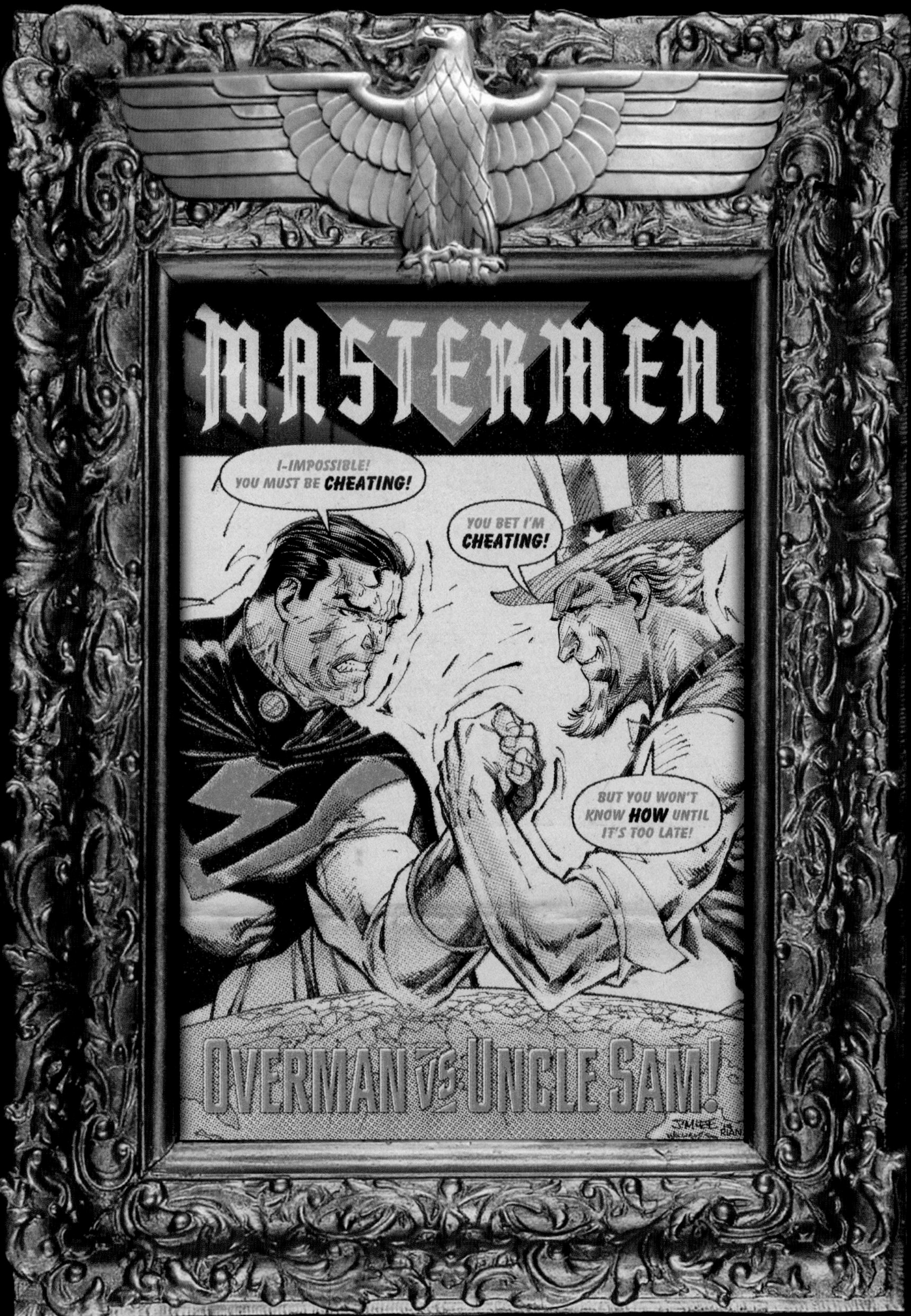
MASTERMEN
I-IMPOSSIBLE! YOU MUST BE CHEATING!
YOU BET I'M CHEATING!
BUT YOU WON'T KNOW HOW UNTIL IT'S TOO LATE!
OVERMAN VS UNCLE SAM!

DC COMICS™

1
$4.99 US

THE MULTIVERSITY™

MORRISO
LE
WILLIAM
SINCLAI

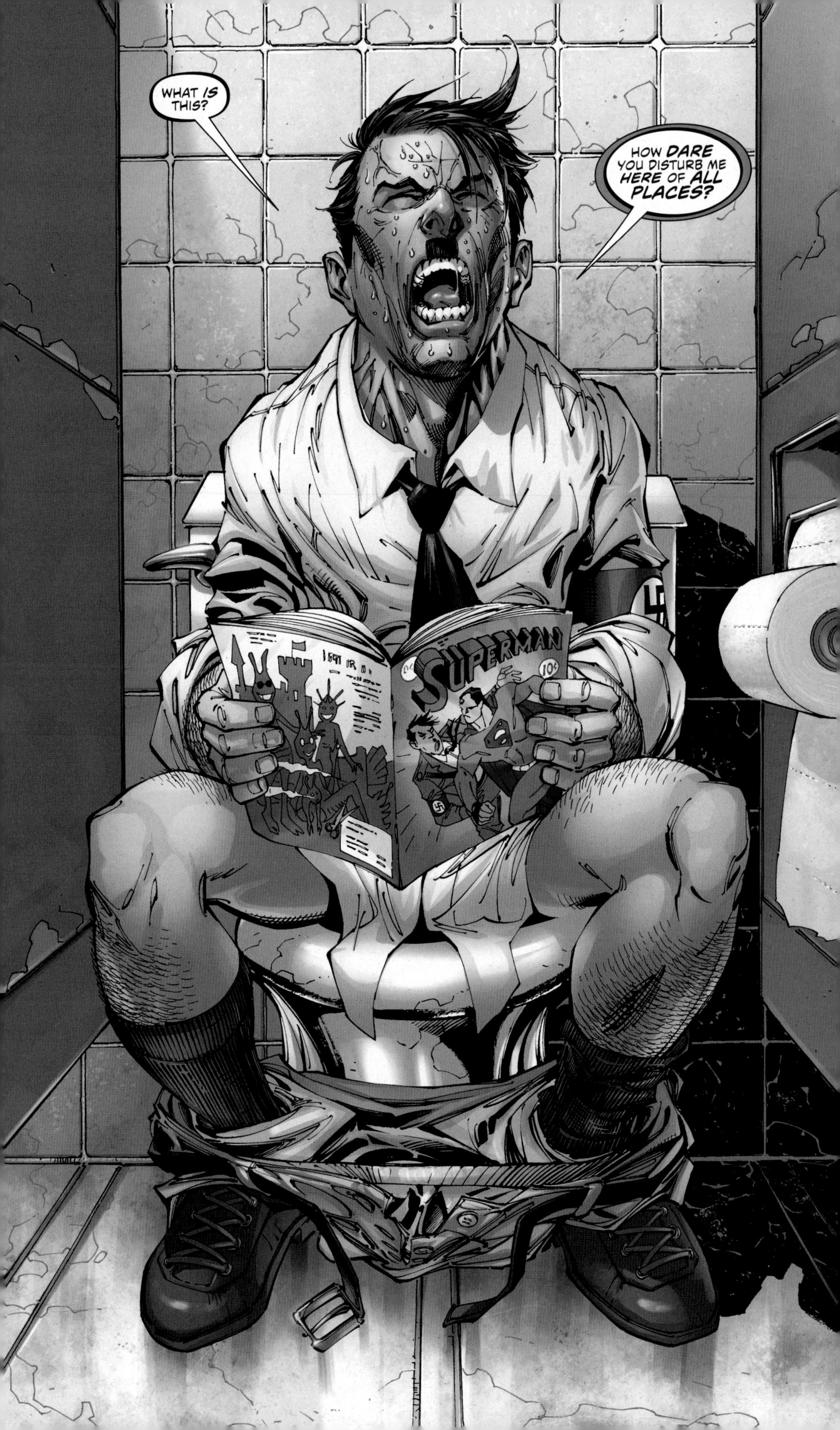
WHAT IS THIS?
HOW DARE YOU DISTURB ME HERE OF ALL PLACES?
SUPERMAN
10¢

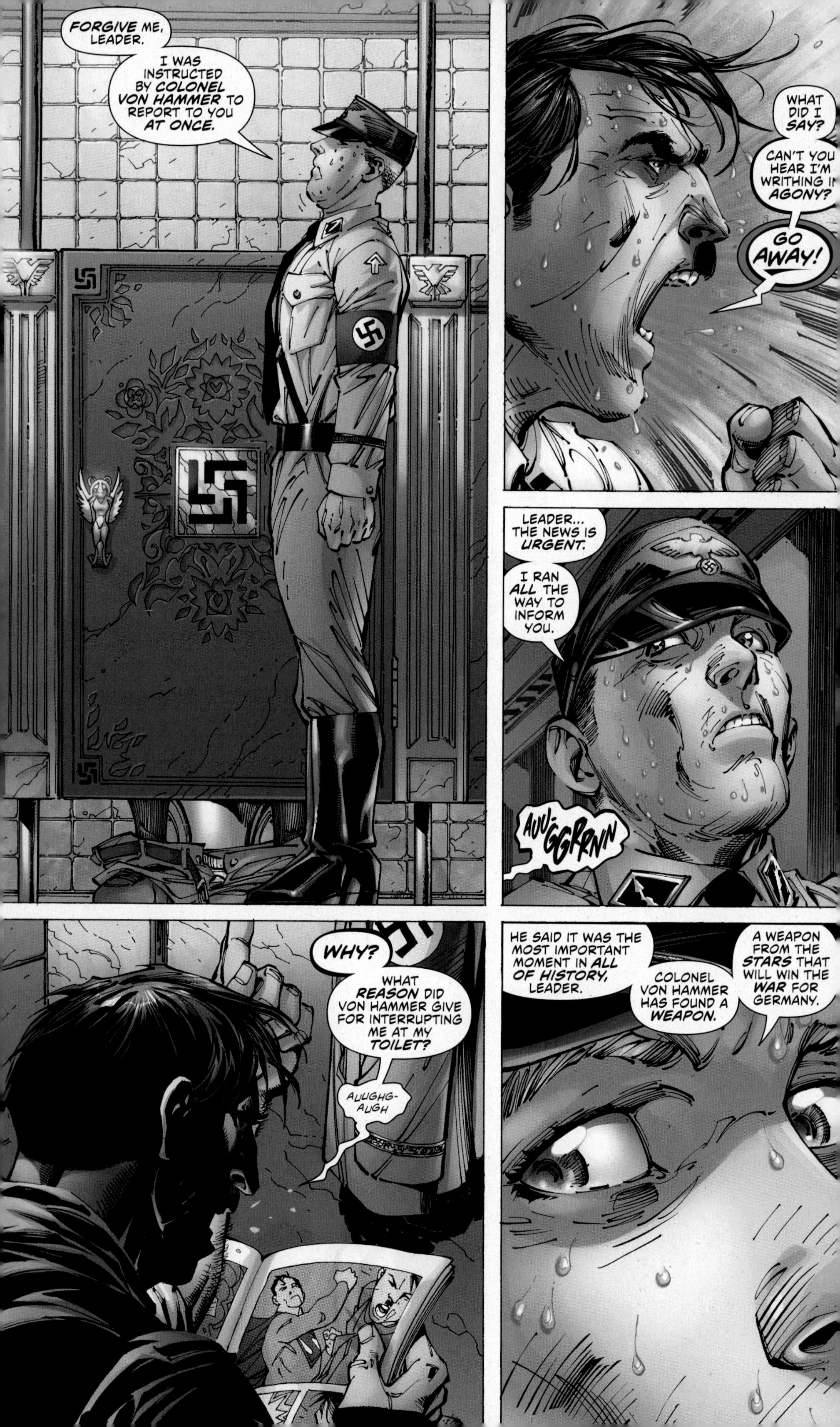
FORGIVE ME, LEADER.
I WAS INSTRUCTED BY COLONEL VON HAMMER TO REPORT TO YOU AT ONCE.
WHAT DID I SAY?
CAN'T YOU HEAR I'M WRITHING IN AGONY?
GO AWAY!
LEADER... THE NEWS IS URGENT.
I RAN ALL THE WAY TO INFORM YOU.
AUU-GGRRNN
WHY?
WHAT REASON DID VON HAMMER GIVE FOR INTERRUPTING ME AT MY TOILET?
AUUGHG-AUGH
HE SAID IT WAS THE MOST IMPORTANT MOMENT IN ALL OF HISTORY, LEADER.
COLONEL VON HAMMER HAS FOUND A WEAPON.
A WEAPON FROM THE STARS THAT WILL WIN THE WAR FOR GERMANY.

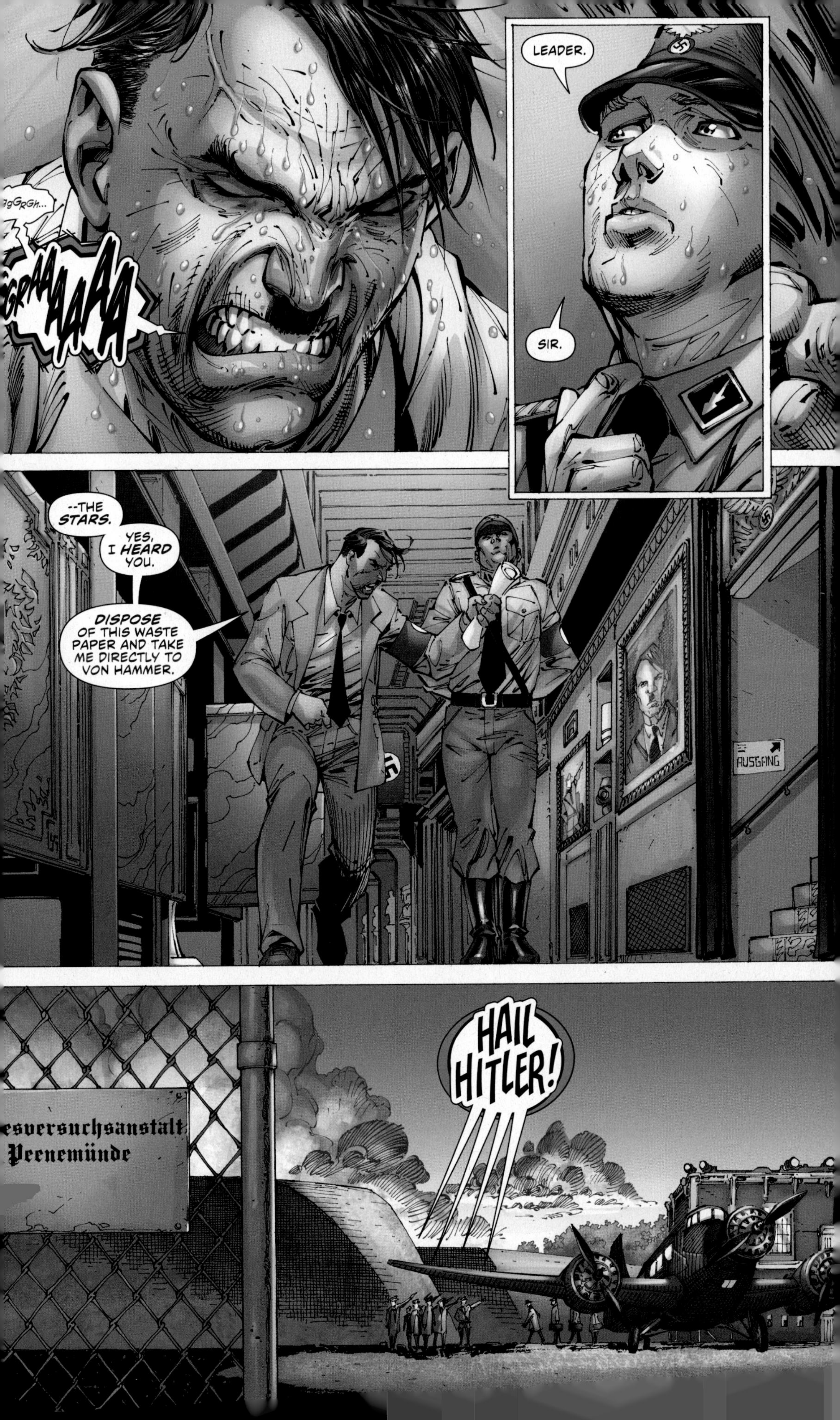

GGGRGH...
GRAAAAAAAA
LEADER.
SIR.
--THE STARS.
YES, I HEARD YOU.
DISPOSE OF THIS WASTE PAPER AND TAKE ME DIRECTLY TO VON HAMMER.
AUSGANG
esversuchsanstalt Peenemünde
HAIL HITLER!

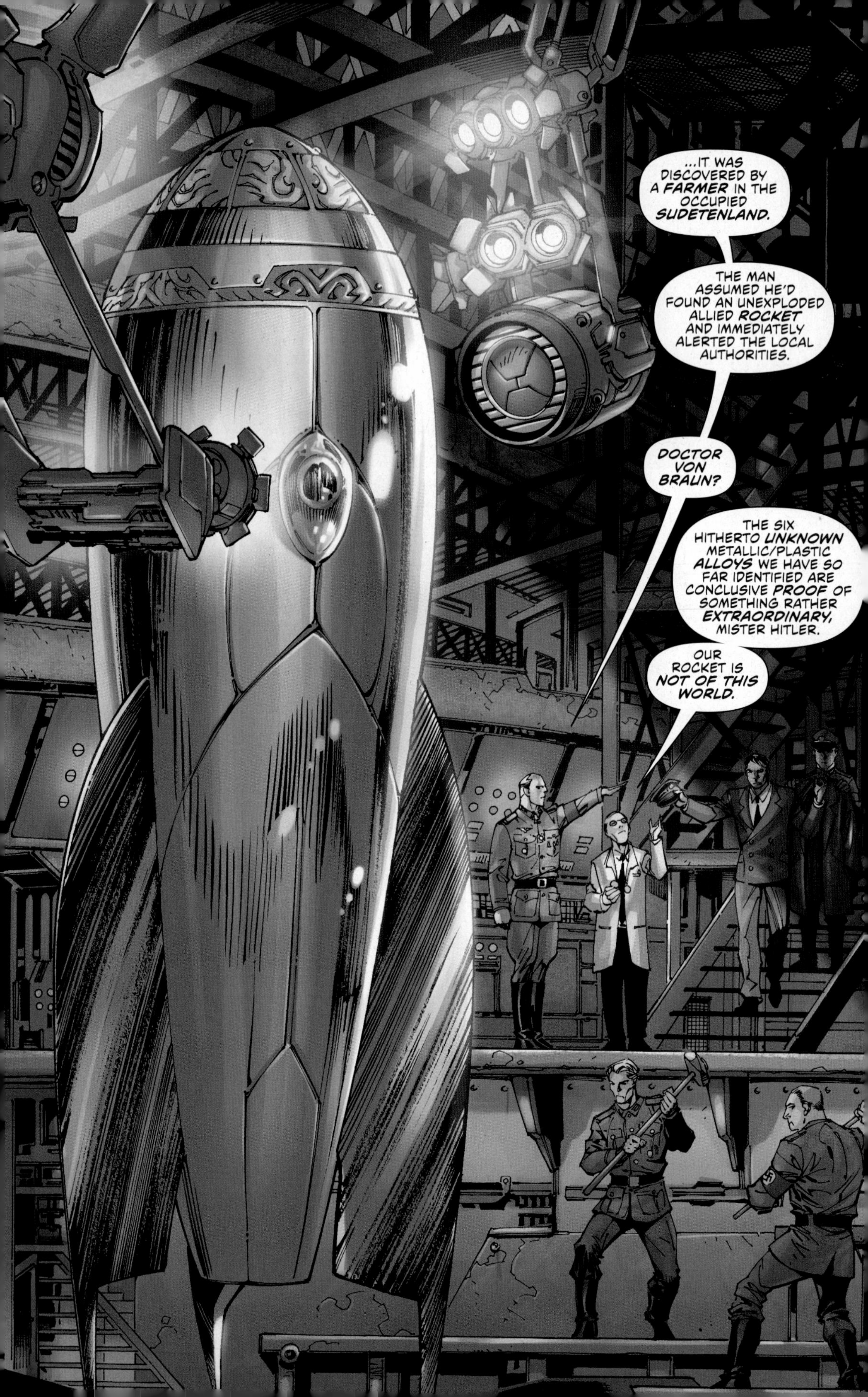
...IT WAS DISCOVERED BY A FARMER IN THE OCCUPIED SUDETENLAND.
THE MAN ASSUMED HE'D FOUND AN UNEXPLODED ALLIED ROCKET AND IMMEDIATELY ALERTED THE LOCAL AUTHORITIES.
DOCTOR VON BRAUN?
THE SIX HITHERTO UNKNOWN METALLIC/PLASTIC ALLOYS WE HAVE SO FAR IDENTIFIED ARE CONCLUSIVE PROOF OF SOMETHING RATHER EXTRAORDINARY, MISTER HITLER.
OUR ROCKET IS NOT OF THIS WORLD.

AS YOU CAN *SEE*, LEADER, THE EXTERIOR SHELL OF THE SPACECRAFT IS *UNDENTED*.

COMPLETELY *UNDAMAGED* BY OUR BLOWS.

AND HIS...

...THIS IS THE *LEAST* OF IT.

SPACE-CRAFT, YOU SAY.

FROM ANOTHER WORLD?

THEN WHAT OF THE *PILOT?*

IF THERE *WAS* A PILOT...

...HE MUST HAVE BEEN VERY *SMALL*, DOCTOR VON BRAUN.

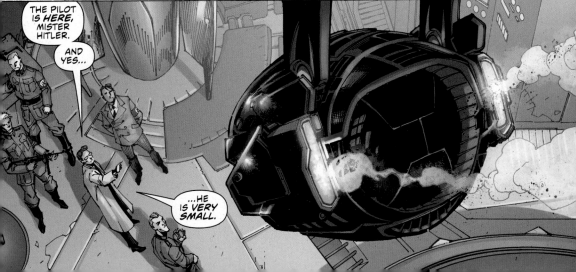

THE PILOT IS *HERE*, MISTER HITLER.

AND YES...

...HE IS *VERY* SMALL.

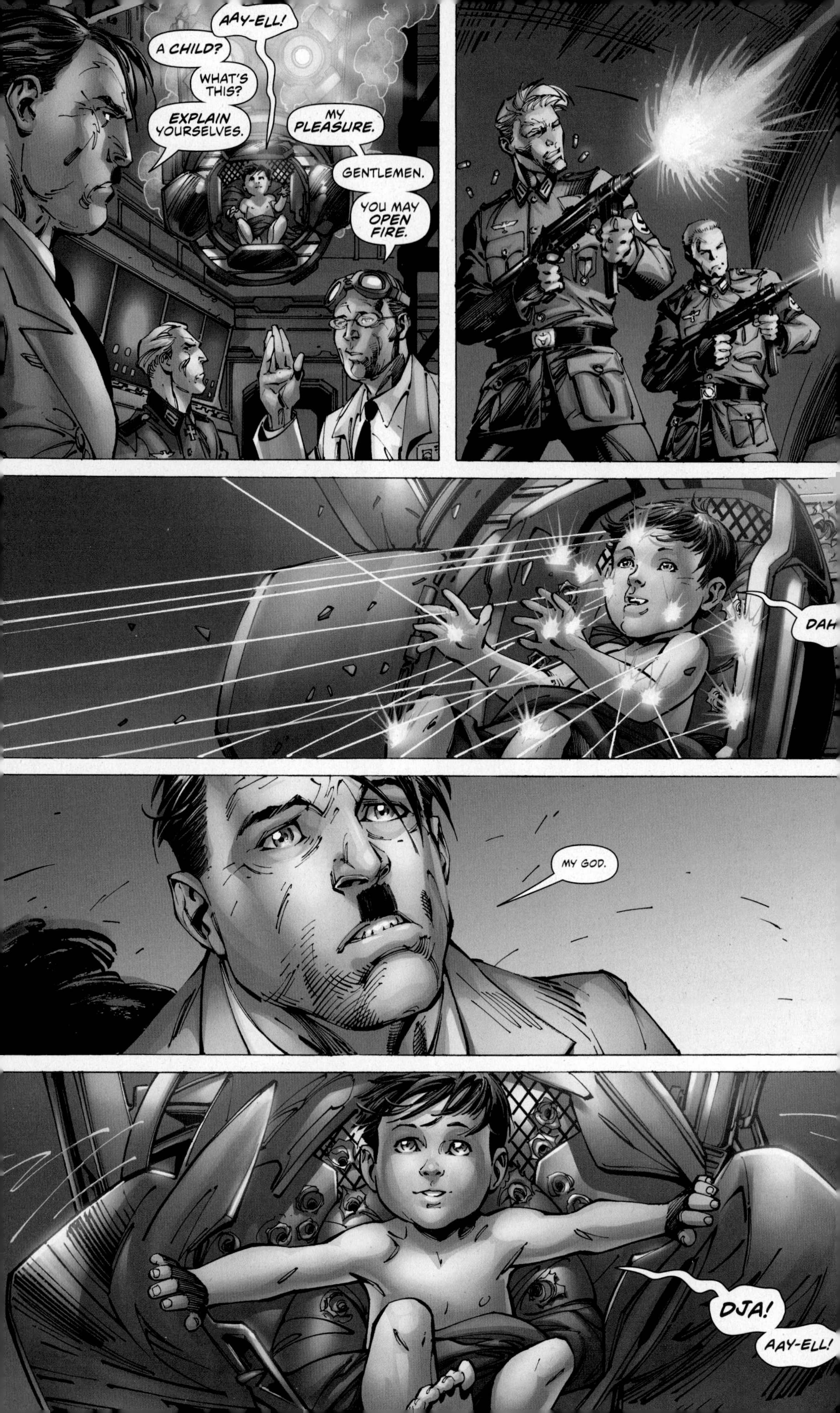
A CHILD?
WHAT'S THIS?
EXPLAIN YOURSELVES.
AAY-ELL!
MY PLEASURE.
GENTLEMEN.
YOU MAY OPEN FIRE.
DAH
MY GOD.
DJA!
AAY-ELL!

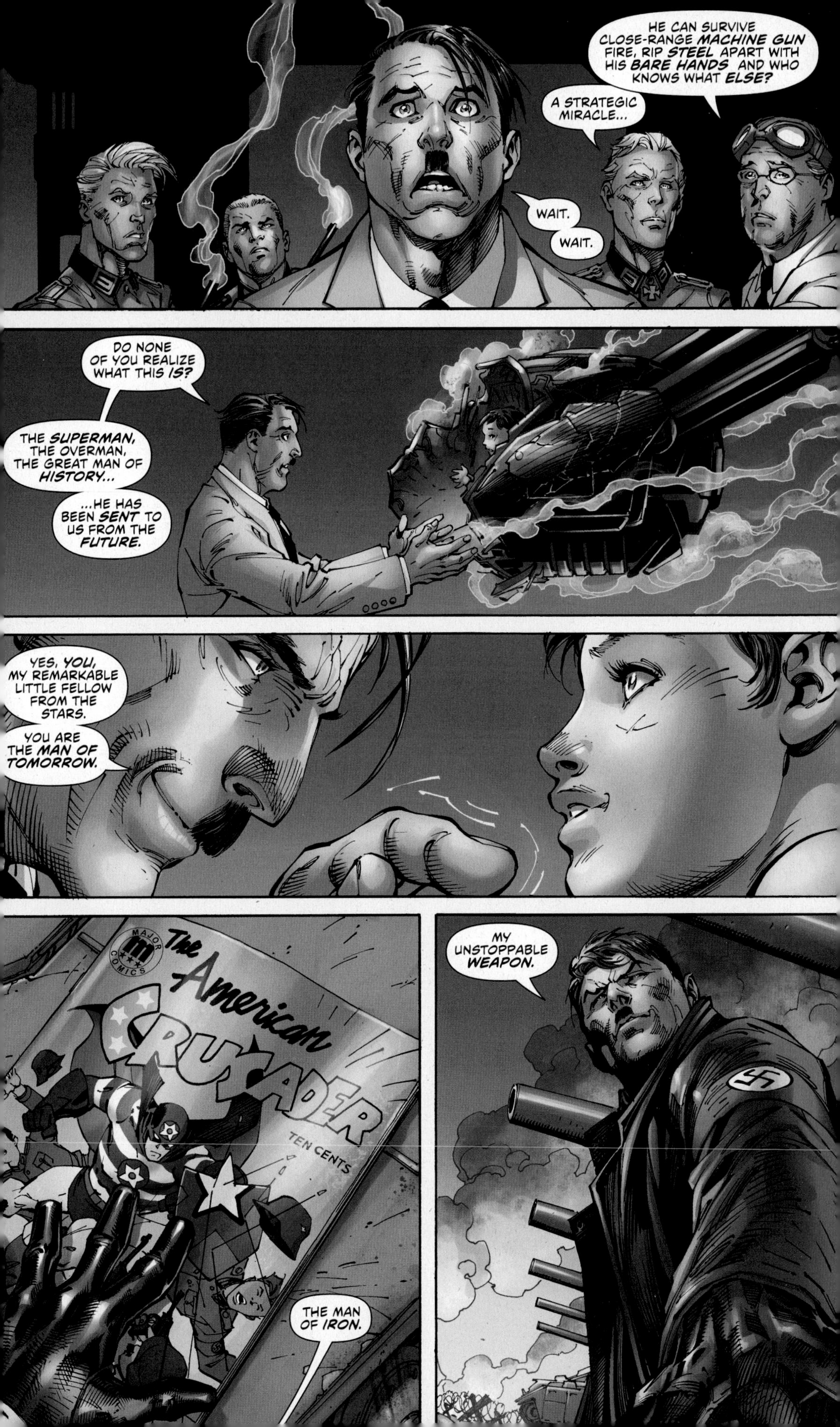
HE CAN SURVIVE CLOSE-RANGE MACHINE GUN FIRE, RIP STEEL APART WITH HIS BARE HANDS AND WHO KNOWS WHAT ELSE?
A STRATEGIC MIRACLE...
WAIT.
WAIT.
DO NONE OF YOU REALIZE WHAT THIS IS?
THE SUPERMAN, THE OVERMAN, THE GREAT MAN OF HISTORY...
...HE HAS BEEN SENT TO US FROM THE FUTURE.
YES, YOU, MY REMARKABLE LITTLE FELLOW FROM THE STARS.
YOU ARE THE MAN OF TOMORROW.
MAJOR COMICS
The American CRUSADER
TEN CENTS
THE MAN OF IRON.
MY UNSTOPPABLE WEAPON.

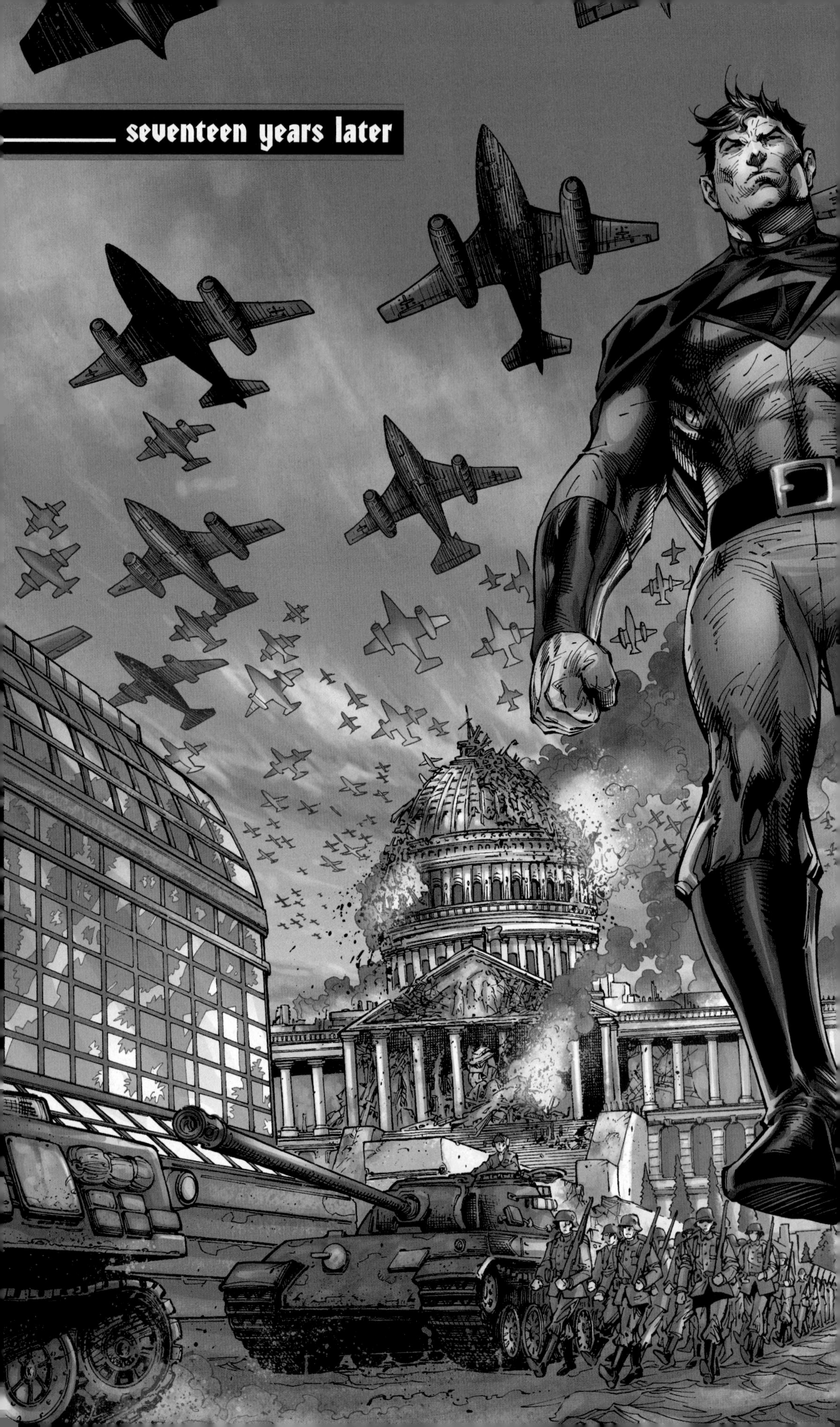
seventeen years later

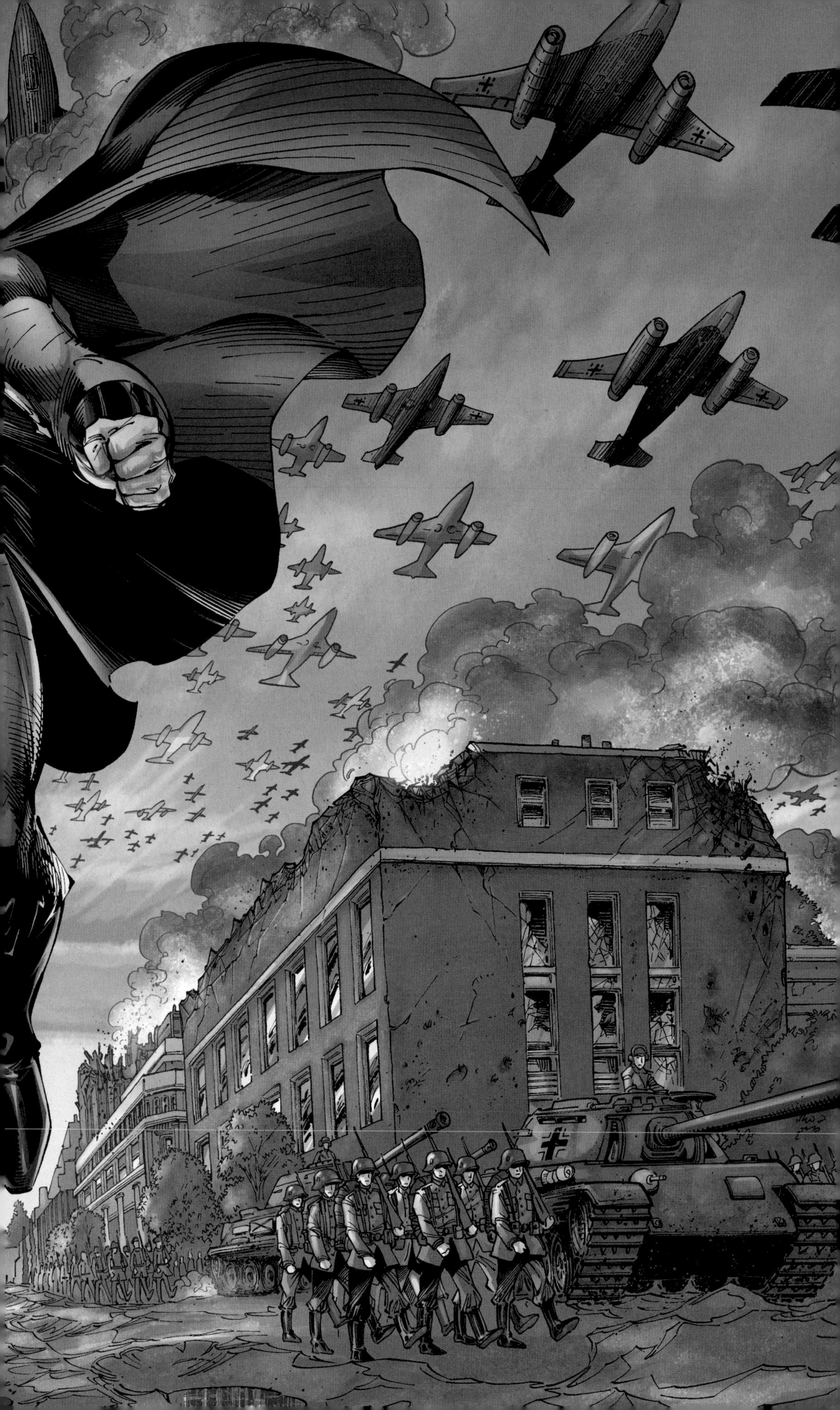

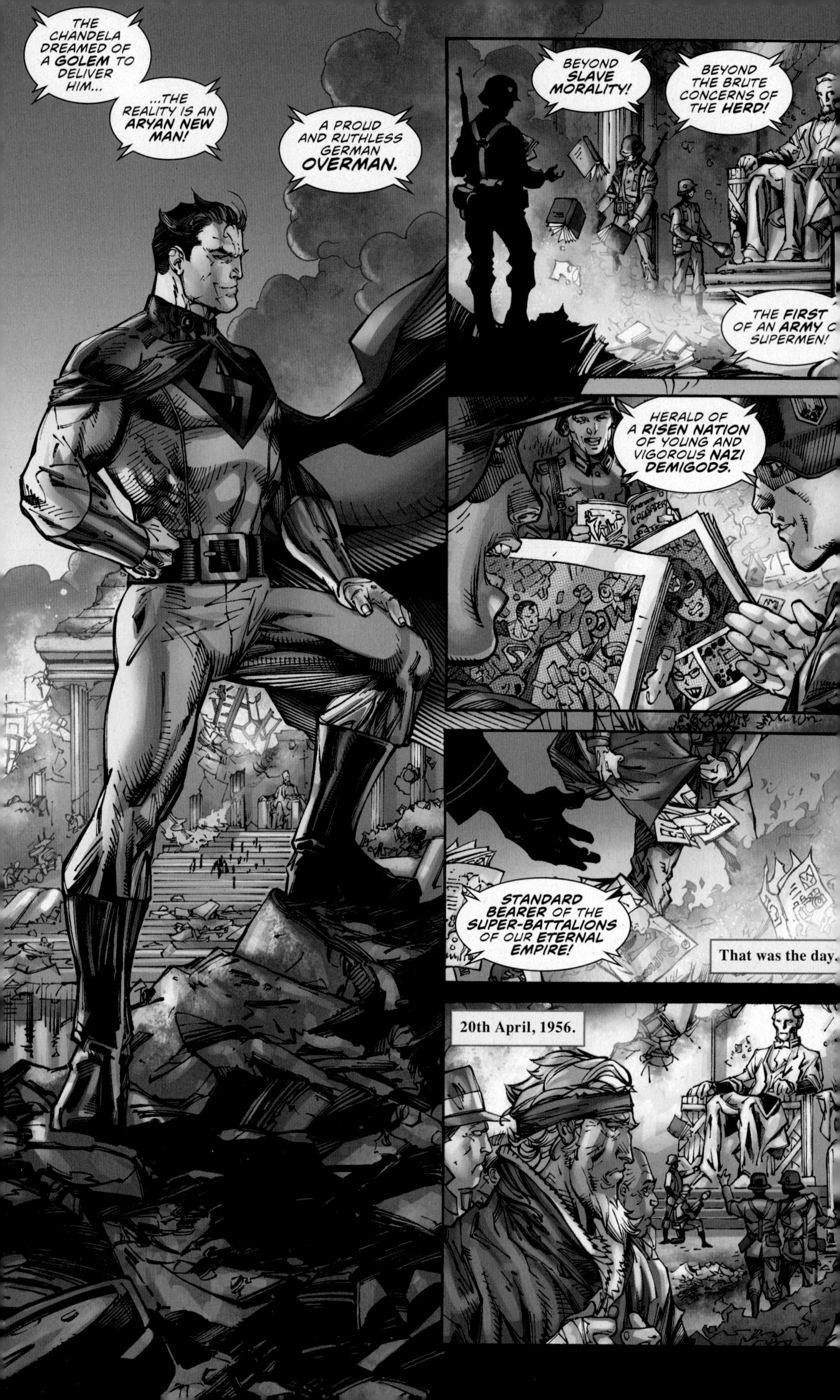
THE CHANDELA DREAMED OF A GOLEM TO DELIVER HIM...
...THE REALITY IS AN ARYAN NEW MAN!
A PROUD AND RUTHLESS GERMAN OVERMAN.
BEYOND SLAVE MORALITY!
BEYOND THE BRUTE CONCERNS OF THE HERD!
THE FIRST OF AN ARMY O SUPERMEN!
HERALD OF A RISEN NATION OF YOUNG AND VIGOROUS NAZI DEMIGODS.
STANDARD BEARER OF THE SUPER-BATTALIONS OF OUR ETERNAL EMPIRE!
That was the day.
20th April, 1956.

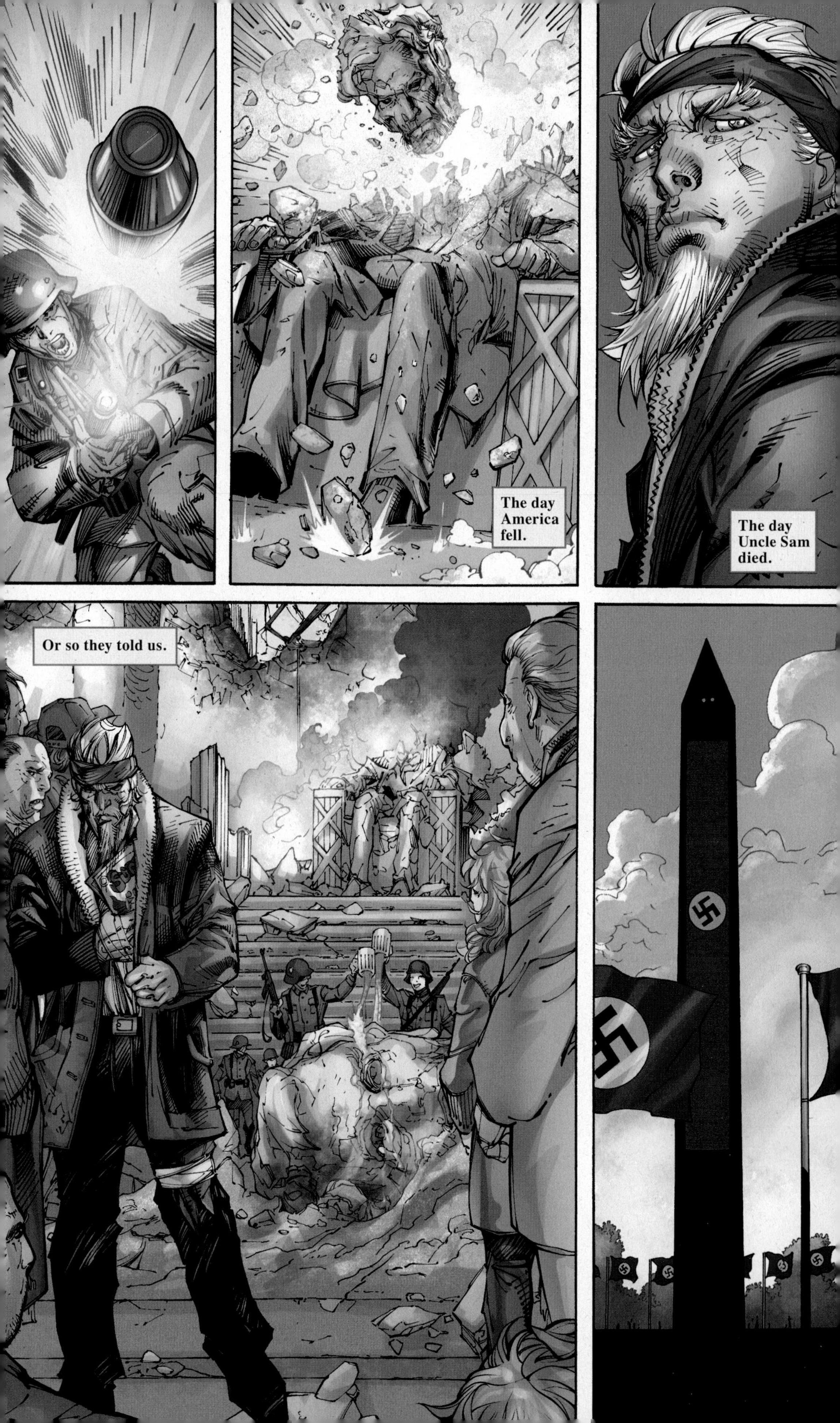
The day America fell.
The day Uncle Sam died.
Or so they told us.

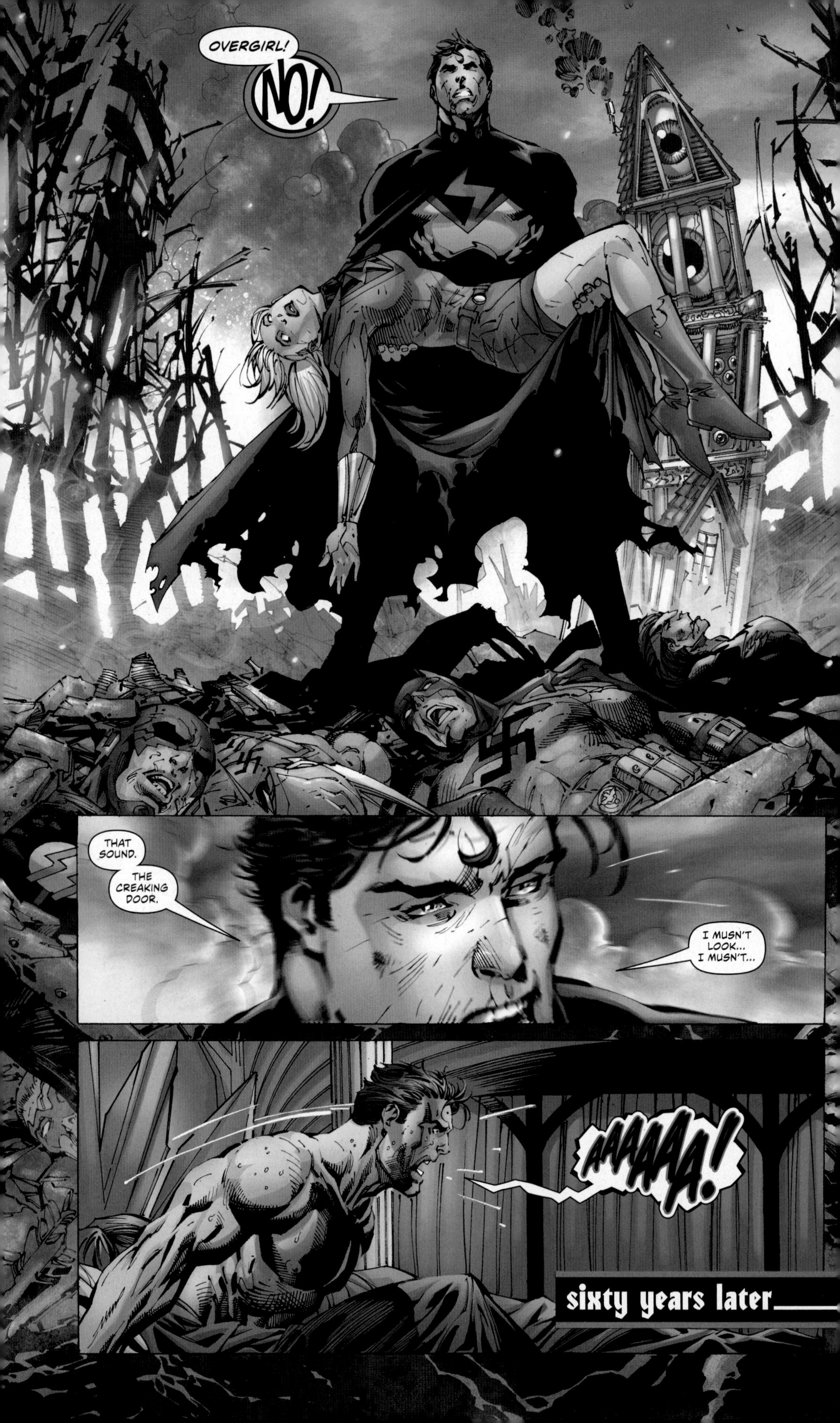
OVERGIRL!
NO!
THAT SOUND. THE CREAKING DOOR.
I MUSN'T LOOK... I MUSN'T...
AAAAAAA!
sixty years later

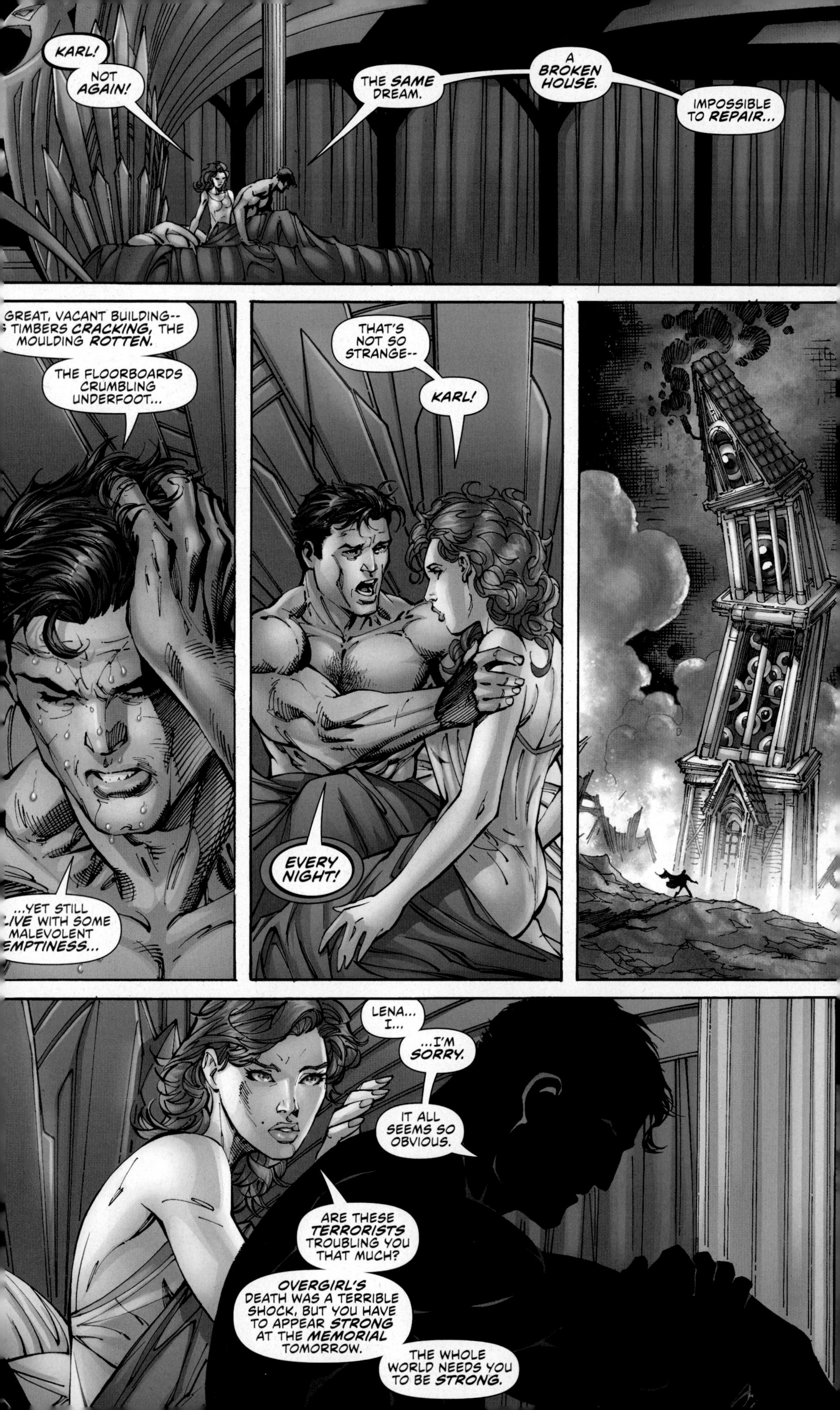
KARL!
NOT AGAIN!
THE SAME DREAM.
A BROKEN HOUSE.
IMPOSSIBLE TO REPAIR...
GREAT, VACANT BUILDING-- TIMBERS CRACKING, THE MOULDING ROTTEN.
THE FLOORBOARDS CRUMBLING UNDERFOOT...
...YET STILL LIVE WITH SOME MALEVOLENT EMPTINESS...
THAT'S NOT SO STRANGE--
KARL!
EVERY NIGHT!
LENA... I...
...I'M SORRY.
IT ALL SEEMS SO OBVIOUS.
ARE THESE TERRORISTS TROUBLING YOU THAT MUCH?
OVERGIRL'S DEATH WAS A TERRIBLE SHOCK, BUT YOU HAVE TO APPEAR STRONG AT THE MEMORIAL TOMORROW.
THE WHOLE WORLD NEEDS YOU TO BE STRONG.

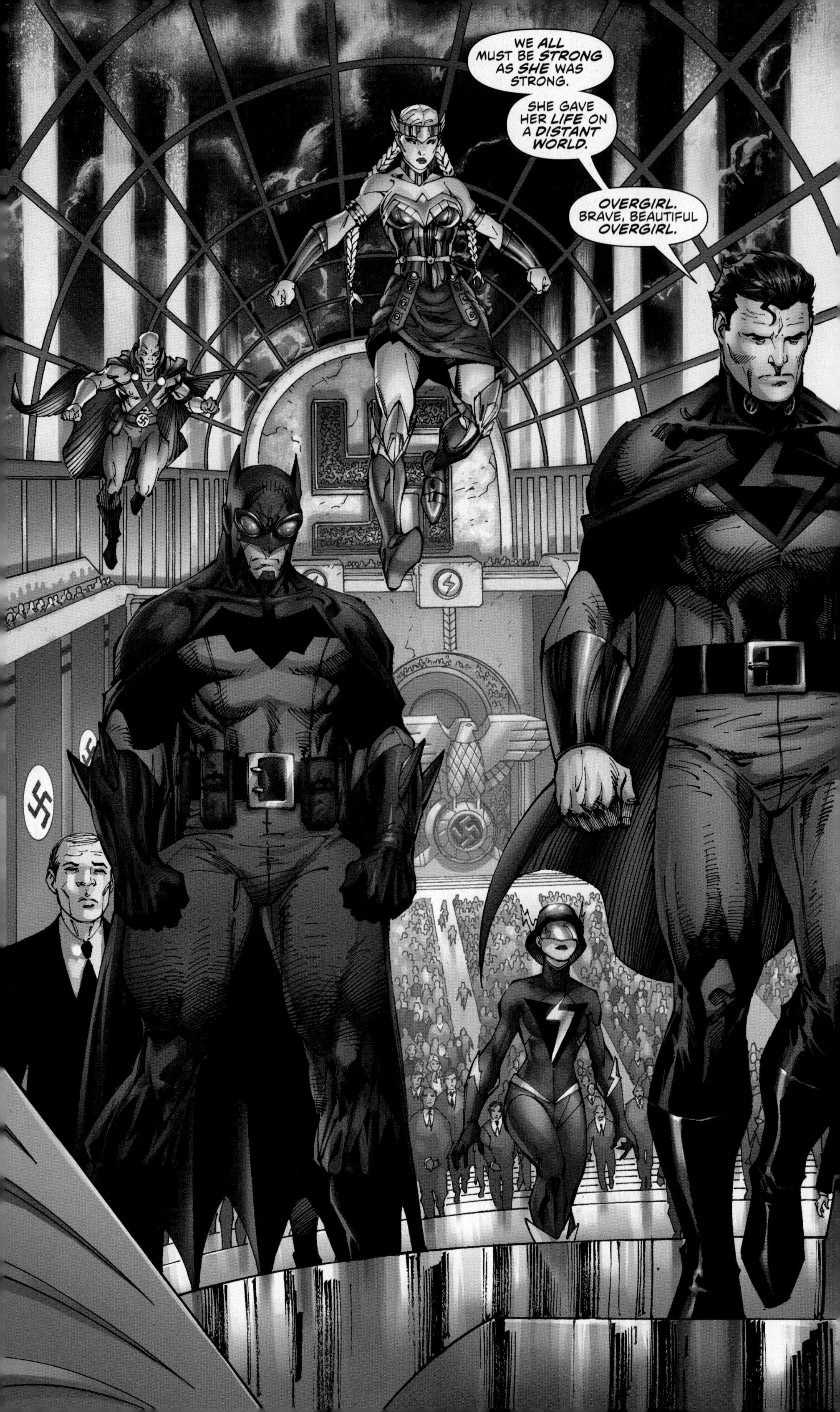
WE ALL MUST BE STRONG AS SHE WAS STRONG.
SHE GAVE HER LIFE ON A DISTANT WORLD.
OVERGIRL. BRAVE, BEAUTIFUL OVERGIRL.

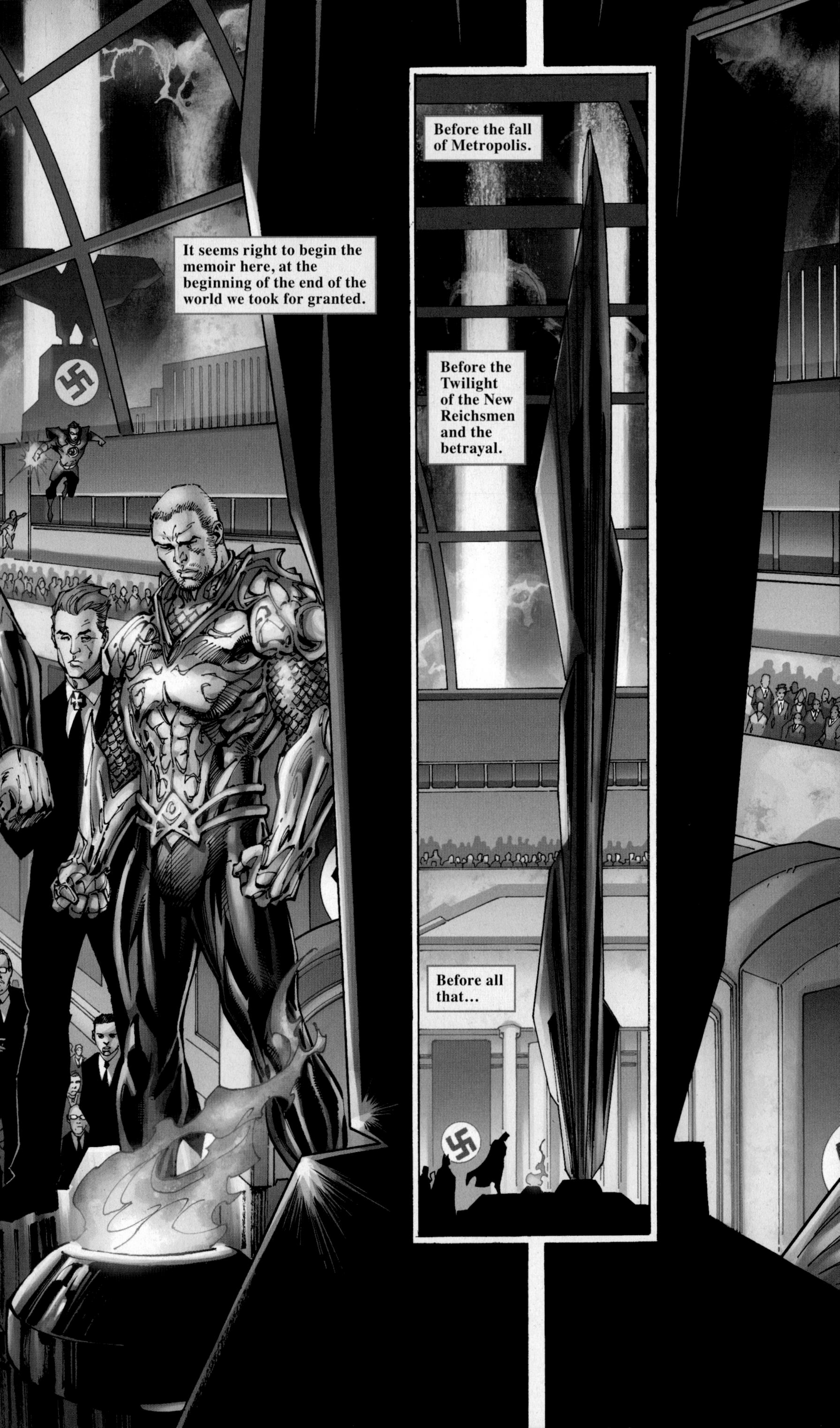
It seems right to begin the memoir here, at the beginning of the end of the world we took for granted.
Before the fall of Metropolis.
Before the Twilight of the New Reichsmen and the betrayal.
Before all that...

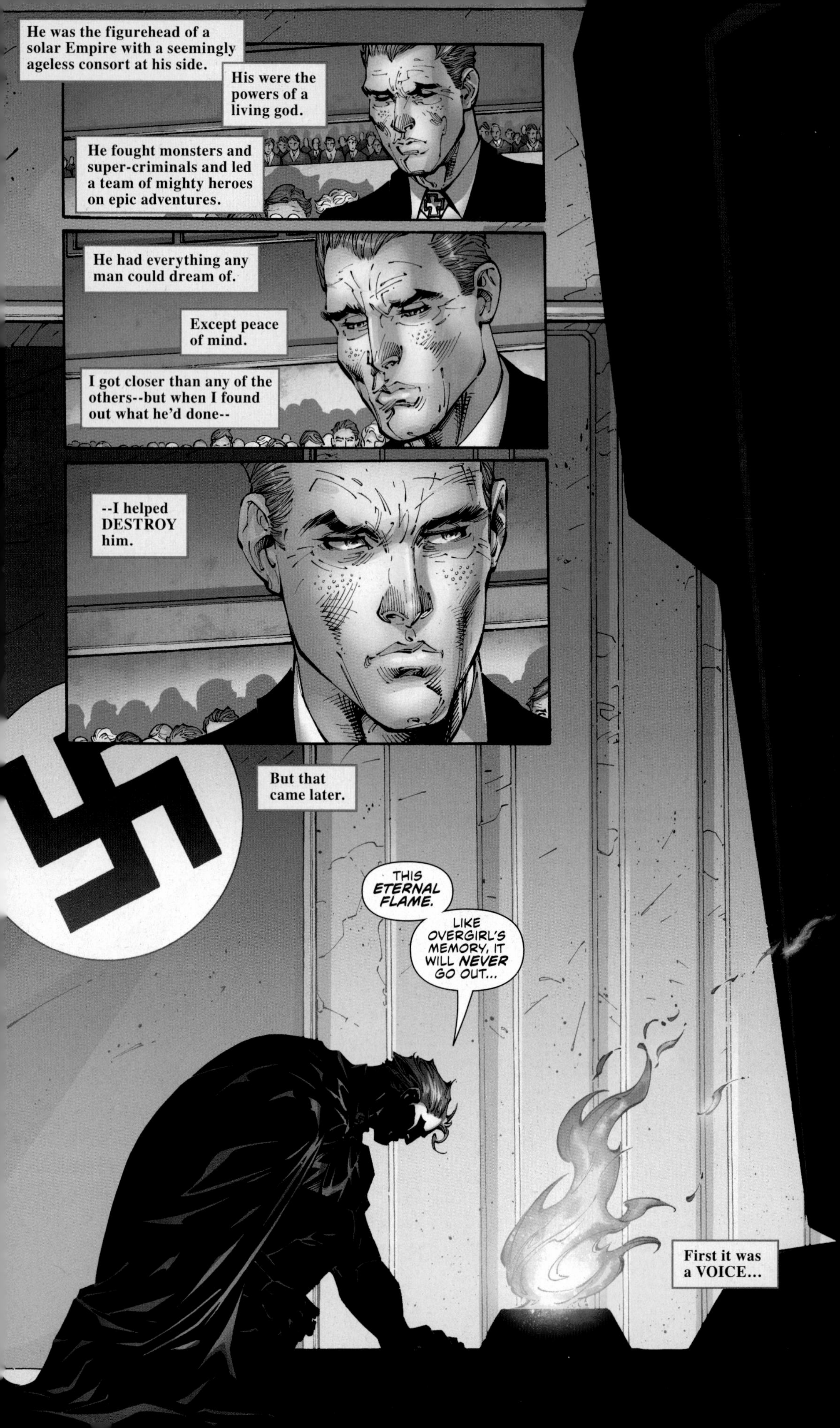
He was the figurehead of a solar Empire with a seemingly ageless consort at his side.
His were the powers of a living god.
He fought monsters and super-criminals and led a team of mighty heroes on epic adventures.
He had everything any man could dream of.
Except peace of mind.
I got closer than any of the others--but when I found out what he'd done--
--I helped DESTROY him.
But that came later.
THIS ETERNAL FLAME.
LIKE OVERGIRL'S MEMORY, IT WILL NEVER GO OUT...
First it was a VOICE...

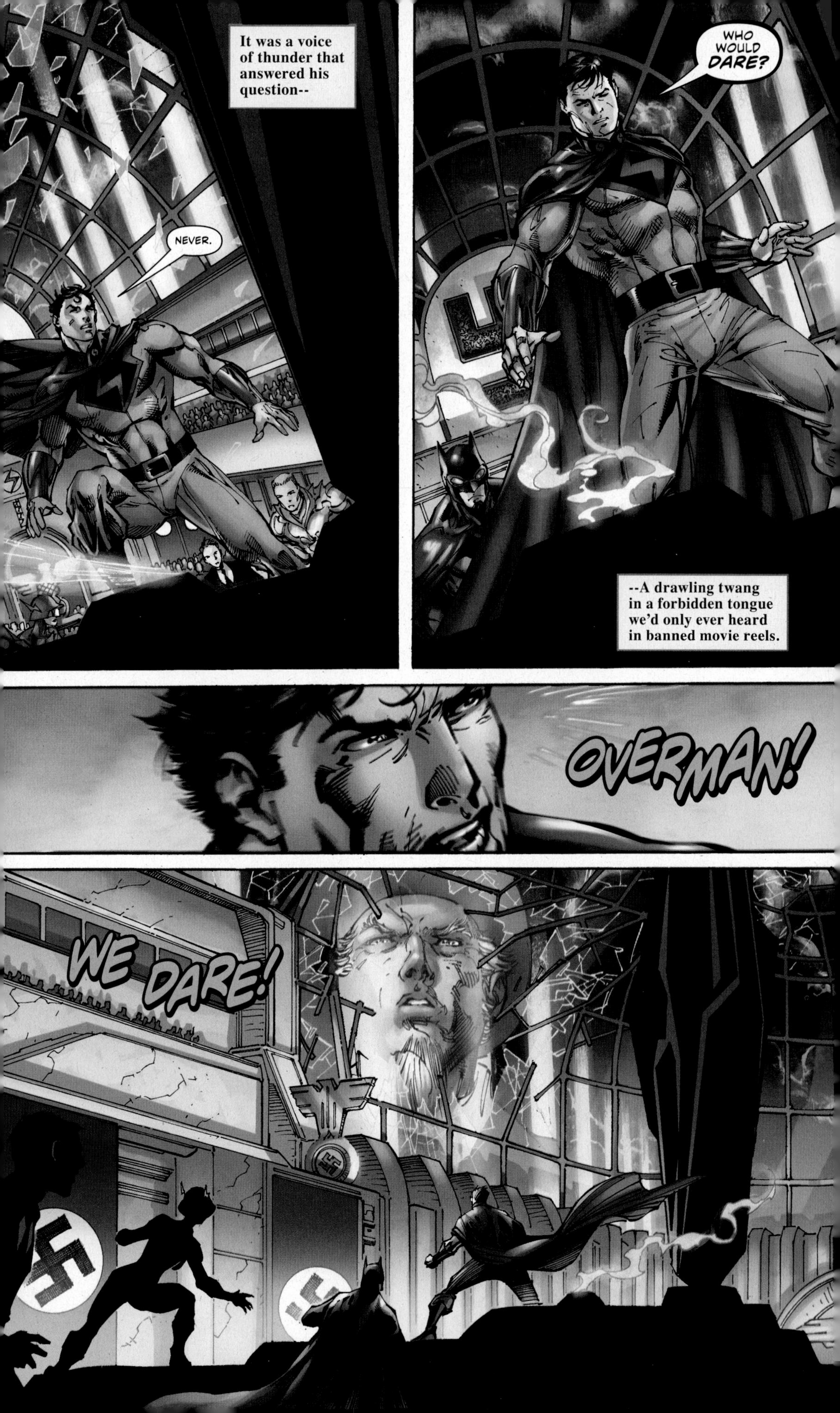

It was a voice of thunder that answered his question--
NEVER.
WHO WOULD DARE?
--A drawling twang in a forbidden tongue we'd only ever heard in banned movie reels.
OVERMAN!
WE DARE!

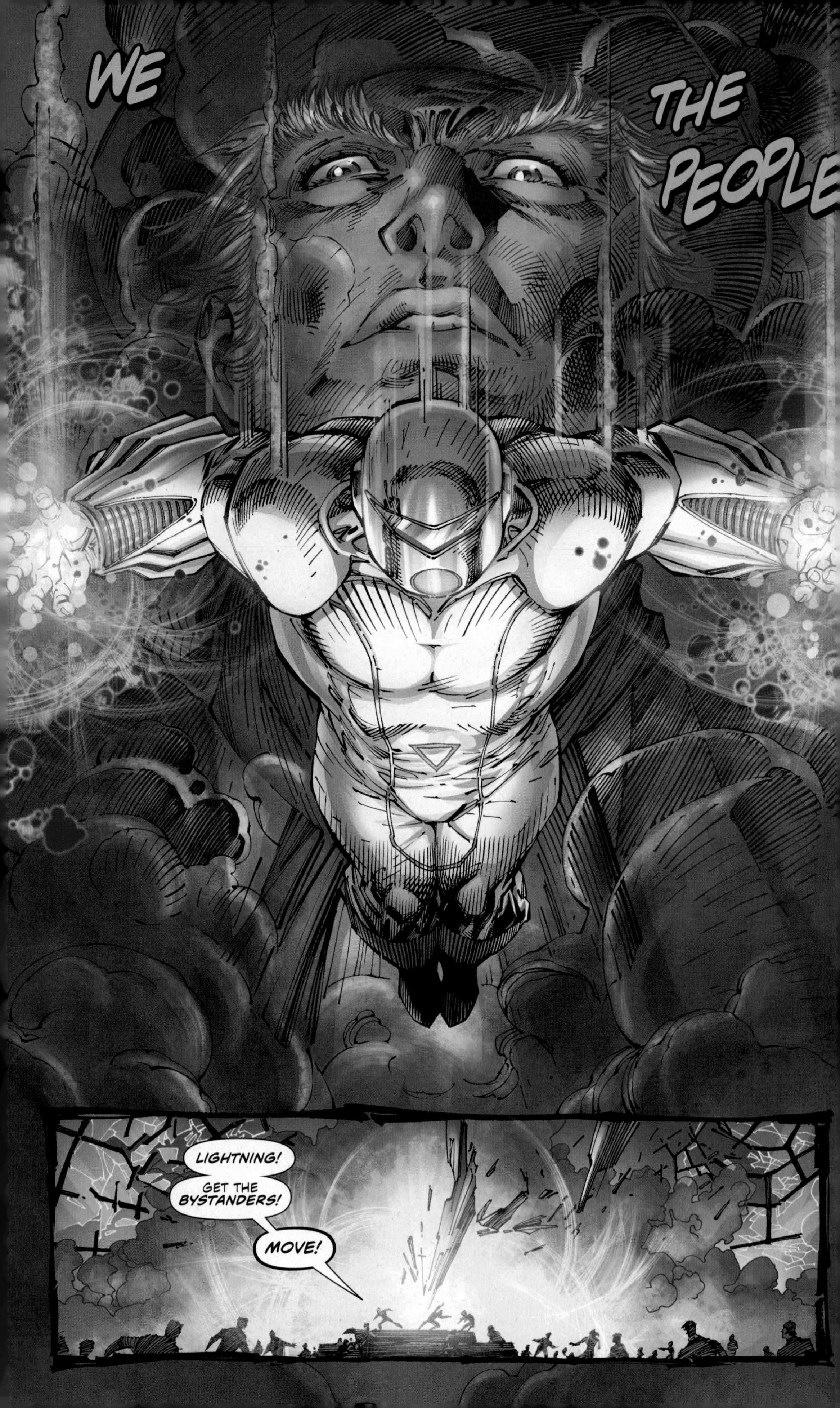
WE
THE
PEOPLE
LIGHTNING!
GET THE BYSTANDERS!
MOVE!

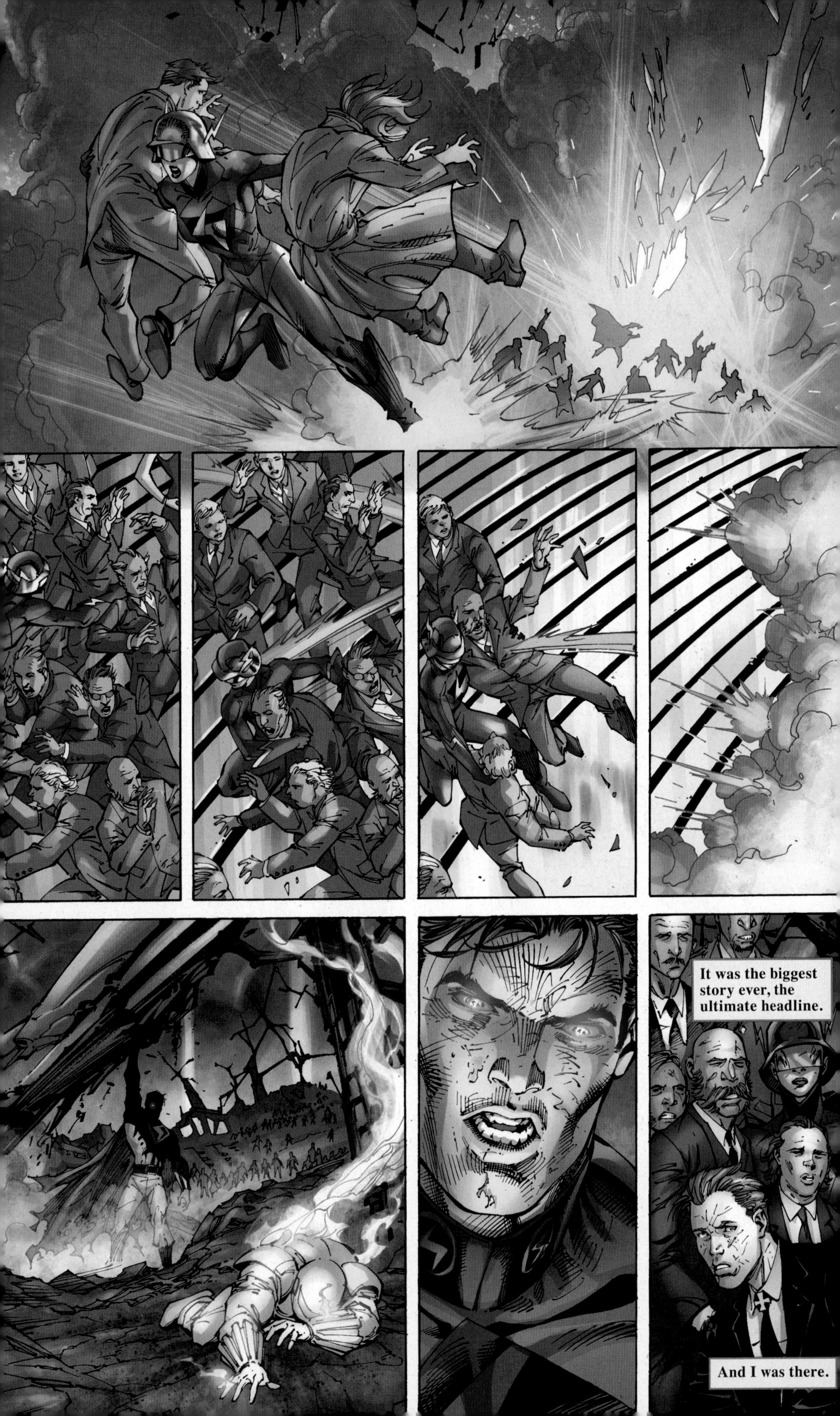
It was the biggest story ever, the ultimate headline.
And I was there.

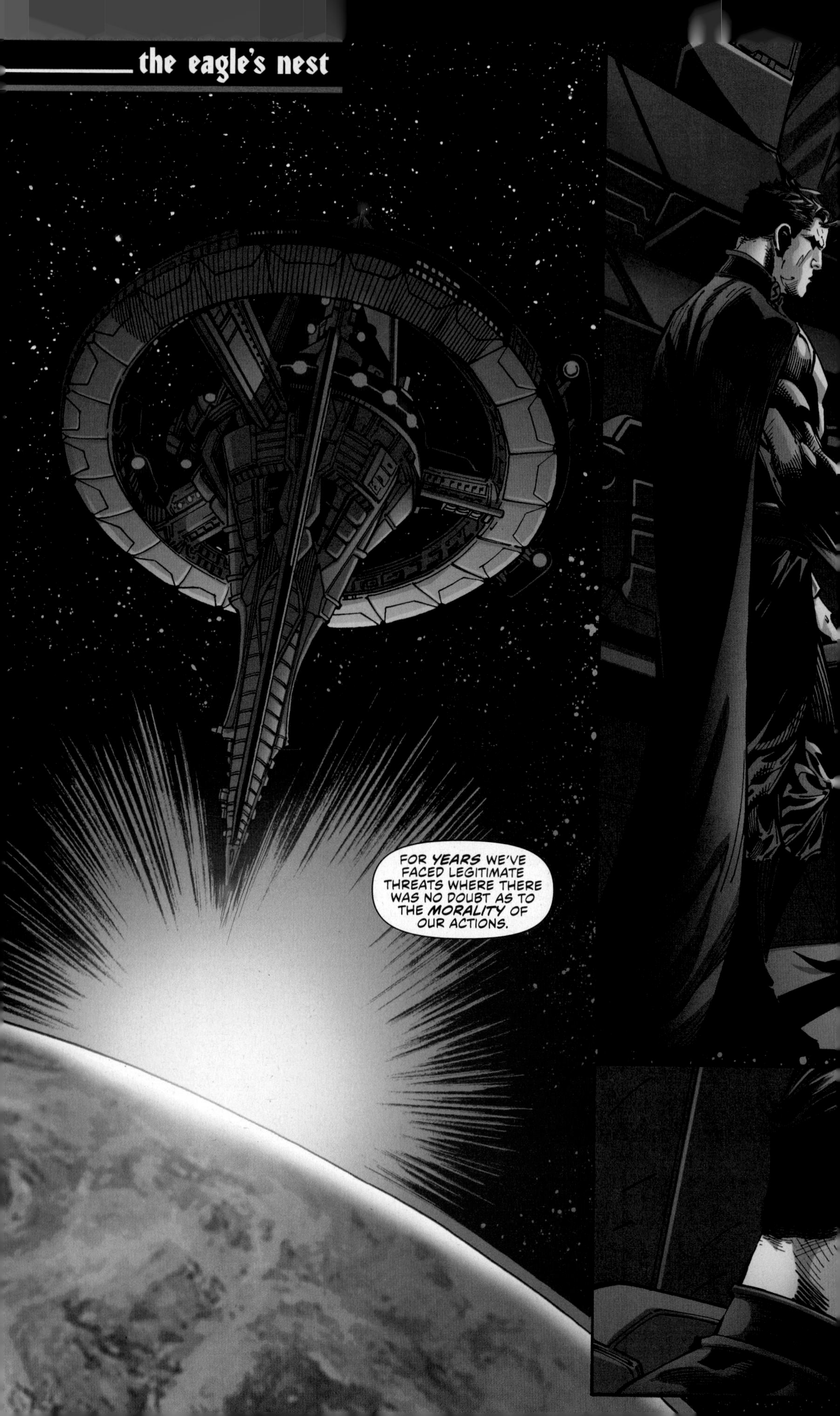
the eagle's nest
FOR YEARS WE'VE FACED LEGITIMATE THREATS WHERE THERE WAS NO DOUBT AS TO THE MORALITY OF OUR ACTIONS.

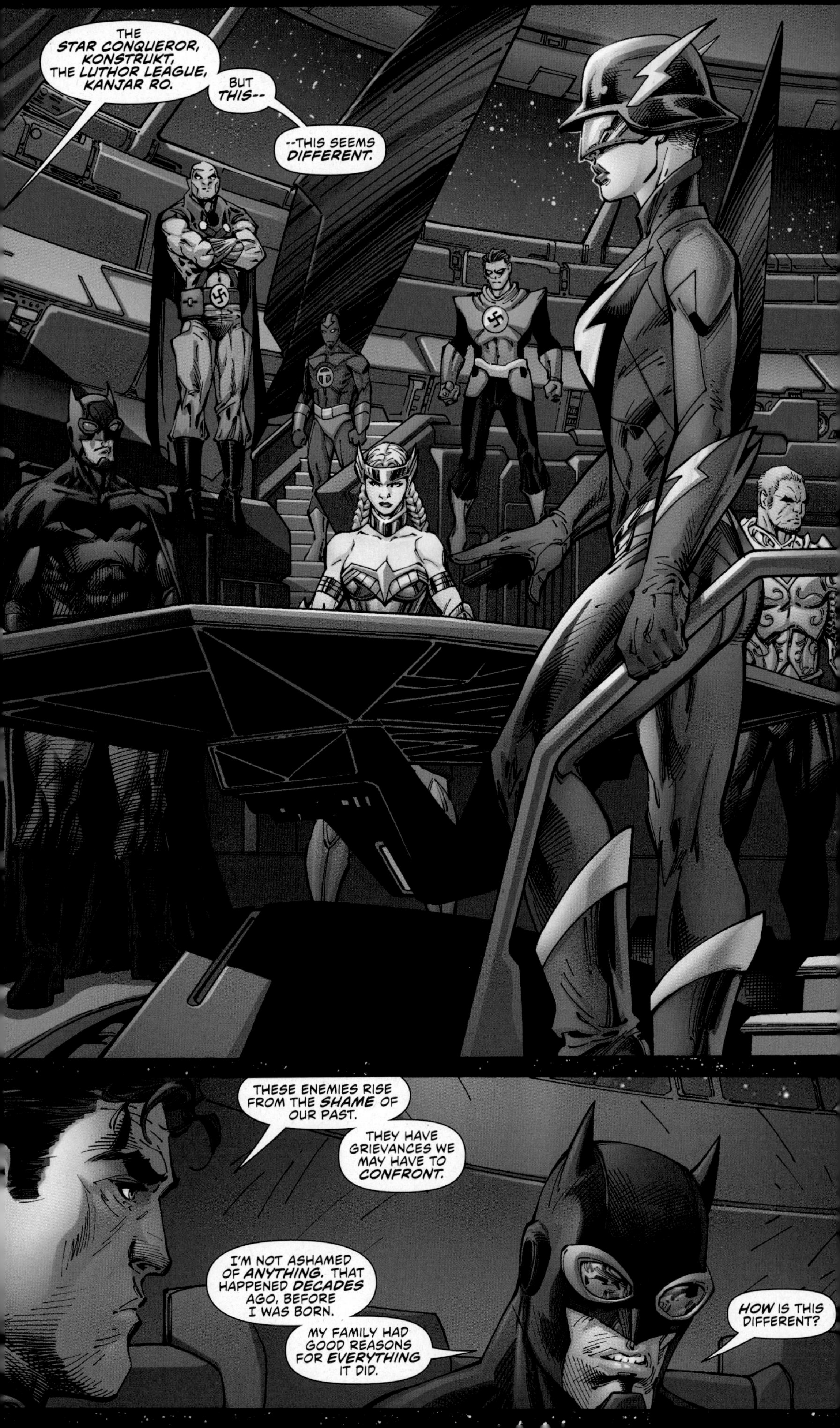

THE STAR CONQUEROR, KONSTRUKT, THE LUTHOR LEAGUE, KANJAR RO.
BUT THIS--
--THIS SEEMS DIFFERENT.
THESE ENEMIES RISE FROM THE SHAME OF OUR PAST.
THEY HAVE GRIEVANCES WE MAY HAVE TO CONFRONT.
I'M NOT ASHAMED OF ANYTHING. THAT HAPPENED DECADES AGO, BEFORE I WAS BORN.
MY FAMILY HAD GOOD REASONS FOR EVERYTHING IT DID.
HOW IS THIS DIFFERENT?

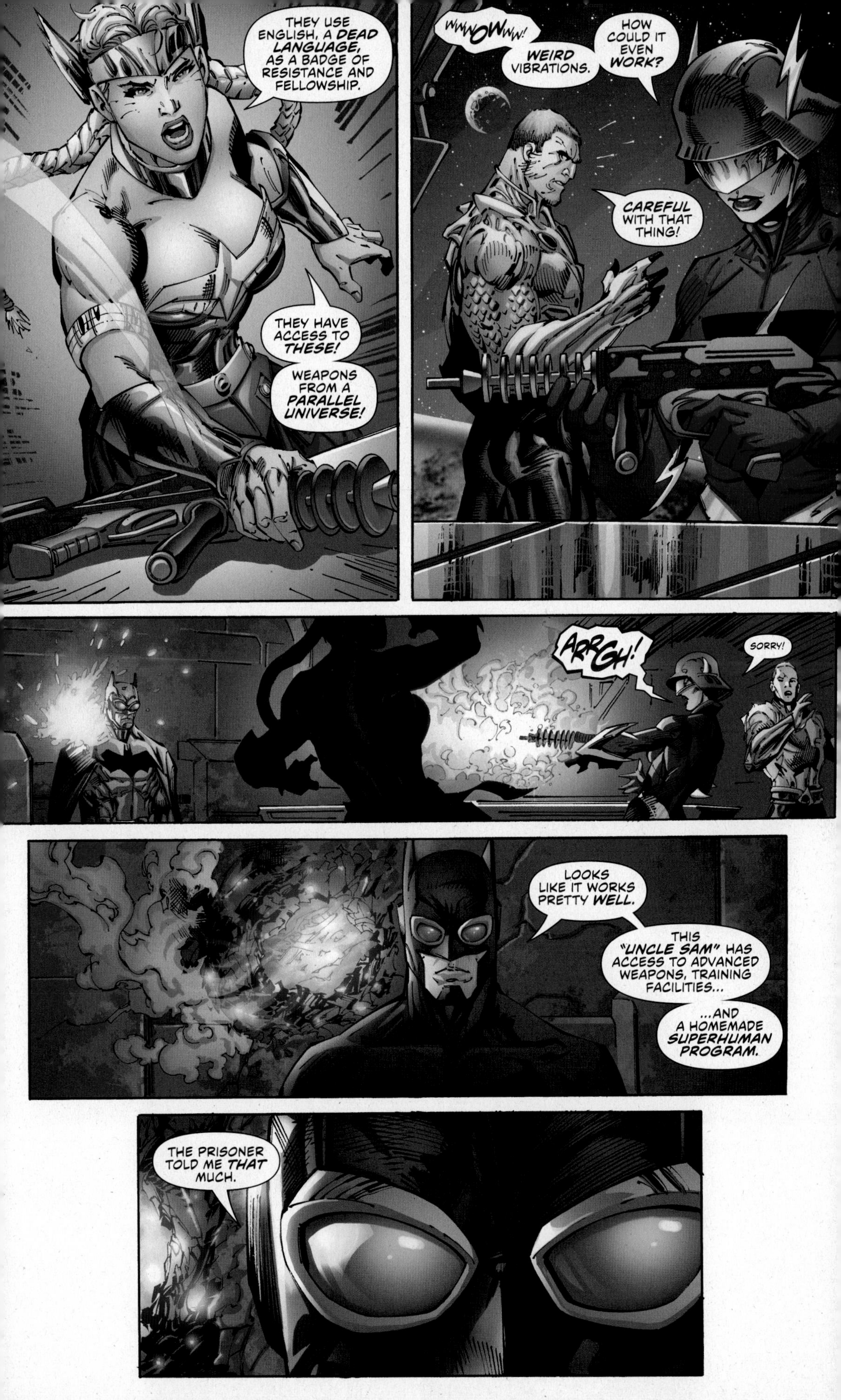
THEY USE ENGLISH, A DEAD LANGUAGE, AS A BADGE OF RESISTANCE AND FELLOWSHIP.
THEY HAVE ACCESS TO THESE!
WEAPONS FROM A PARALLEL UNIVERSE!
WWWOWWW!
WEIRD VIBRATIONS.
HOW COULD IT EVEN WORK?
CAREFUL WITH THAT THING!
ARRGH!
SORRY!
LOOKS LIKE IT WORKS PRETTY WELL.
THIS "UNCLE SAM" HAS ACCESS TO ADVANCED WEAPONS, TRAINING FACILITIES...
...AND A HOMEMADE SUPERHUMAN PROGRAM.
THE PRISONER TOLD ME THAT MUCH.

...AND THEN LEATHERWING BEAT HIM *SENSELESS* AGAIN.

I'M *UNCOMFORTABLE*, YES.

LEATHERWING, UNDERWATERMAN, THE MARTIAN.

THEY'RE *WORRIED* ABOUT YOU.

YOU THINK THAT'S NOT *OBVIOUS*?

I WAS *SURE* BEFORE... SURE WE COULD SOMEHOW OUTRACE OUR *PAST*.

THAT MOUNTAIN OF *DEAD*... BUT SOMETIMES I JUST THINK...

...WHAT IF WE *DESERVE* THIS?

THAT'S *RIDICULOUS* AND YOU KNOW IT.

IF YOU CAN'T *LEAD* US...

...I WON'T PLAY *NURSEMAID* TO A WOUNDED MAN OF IRON.

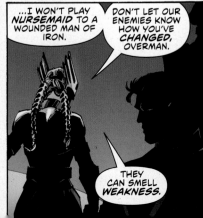

DON'T LET OUR ENEMIES KNOW HOW YOU'VE *CHANGED*, OVERMAN.

THEY CAN SMELL *WEAKNESS*.

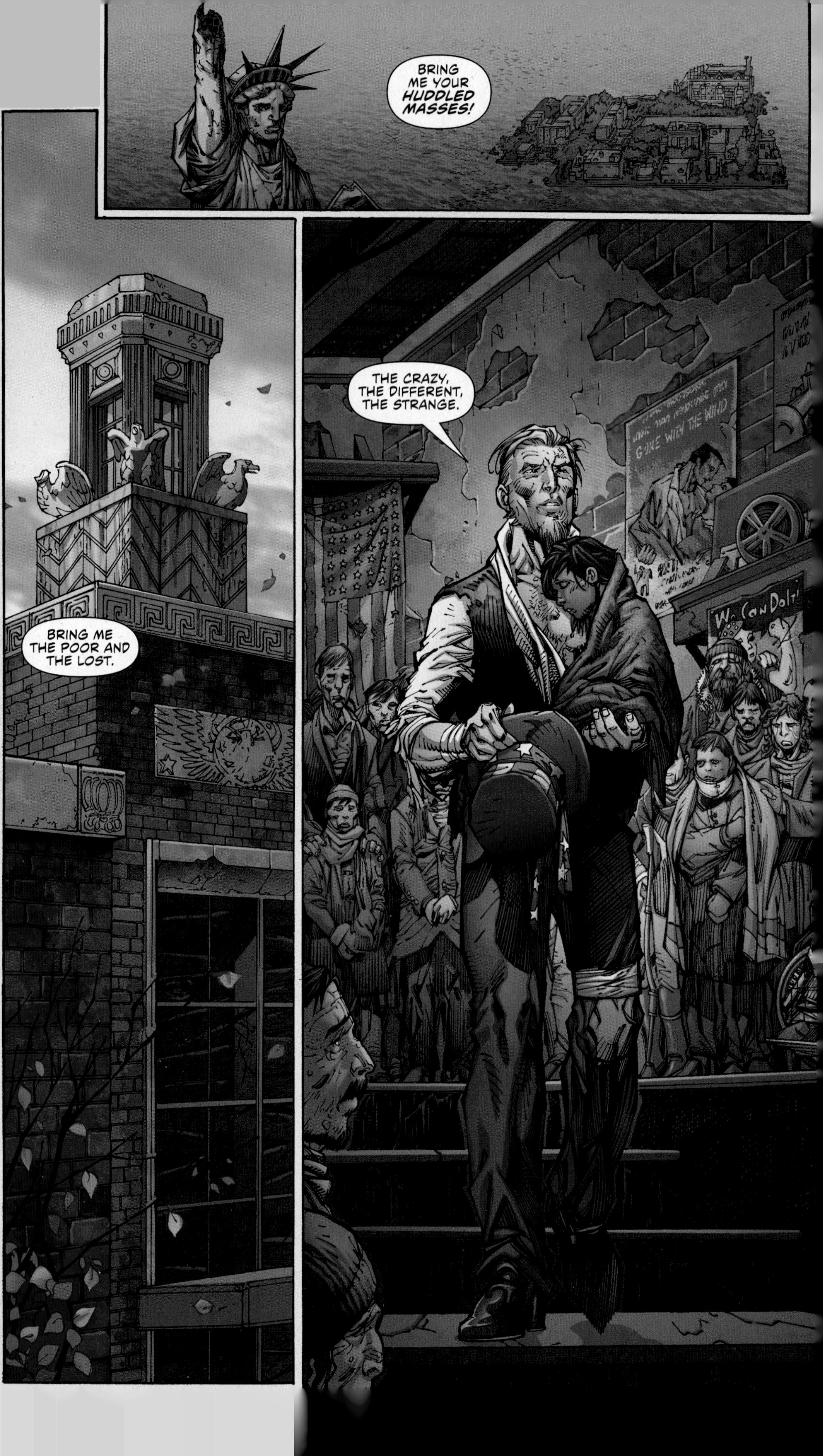
BRING ME YOUR HUDDLED MASSES!
BRING ME THE POOR AND THE LOST.
THE CRAZY, THE DIFFERENT, THE STRANGE.
GONE WITH THE WIND
WE CAN DO IT!

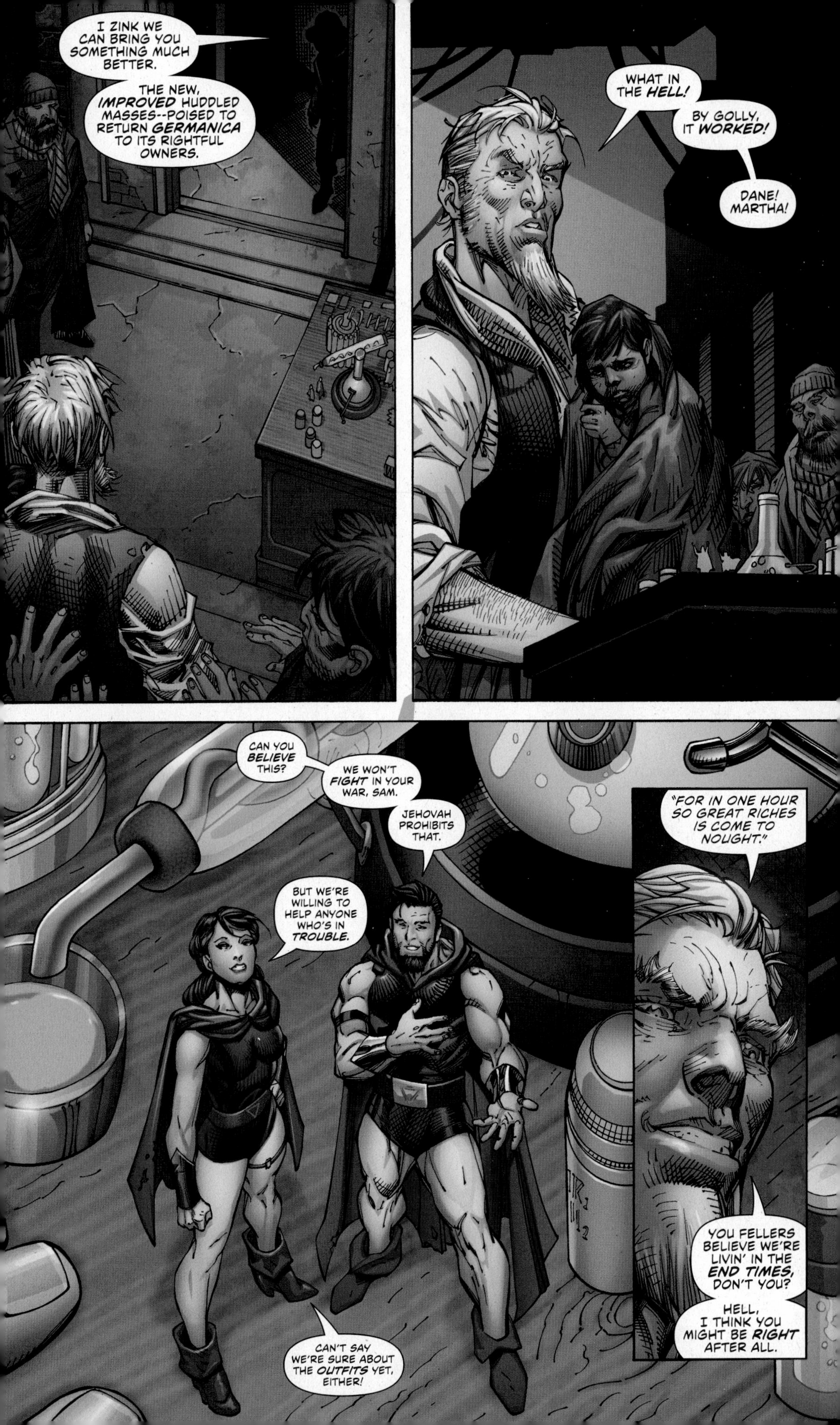
I ZINK WE CAN BRING YOU SOMETHING MUCH BETTER.
THE NEW, IMPROVED HUDDLED MASSES--POISED TO RETURN GERMANICA TO ITS RIGHTFUL OWNERS.
WHAT IN THE HELL!
BY GOLLY, IT WORKED!
DANE! MARTHA!
CAN YOU BELIEVE THIS?
WE WON'T FIGHT IN YOUR WAR, SAM.
JEHOVAH PROHIBITS THAT.
BUT WE'RE WILLING TO HELP ANYONE WHO'S IN TROUBLE.
CAN'T SAY WE'RE SURE ABOUT THE OUTFITS YET, EITHER!
"FOR IN ONE HOUR SO GREAT RICHES IS COME TO NOUGHT."
YOU FELLERS BELIEVE WE'RE LIVIN' IN THE END TIMES, DON'T YOU?
HELL, I THINK YOU MIGHT BE RIGHT AFTER ALL.

ZO...YOU HAVE SEEN VOT VE CAN DO UNT ZUR *TROJAN HORSE* IS NOW IN PLACE.

NOW SEE ZUR *REST*.

SIVANA *PARALLEL WORLD TECHNOLOGY* VILL MAKE YOU UNBEATABLE FOR A REASONABLE PRICE.

YOU'VE BEEN *MIGHTY KIND* TO THE CAUSE, MISTER.

BUT WHY SHOULD WE TRUST A *RATZI* LIKE YOU?

WHATEVER *YOU* GET OUT OF THIS, I'M BETTING IT AIN'T TOO *WHOLESOME*.

HE HE HE HE

PLEASE... NOT "MISTER," IT IS "DOKTOR."

HERR DOKTOR *SIVANA*, UNT ENGLISH IS NOT MY FIRST LANGUAGE.

VE HAVE SELECTED REPRESENTATIVES OF ZUR PRECIOUS FEW WHO *SURVIVED* ZUR *NAZI PURGES* OF ZUR '50s AND '60s.

JEWS, JEHOVAH'S VITNESSES, ROMANI, NEGROES... ZUR *USUAL* SUSPECTS...

...UNT VE HAVE ENDOWED ZEM MIT *SUPERPOWERS* ZUR *EQUAL* OF YOUR ENEMY.

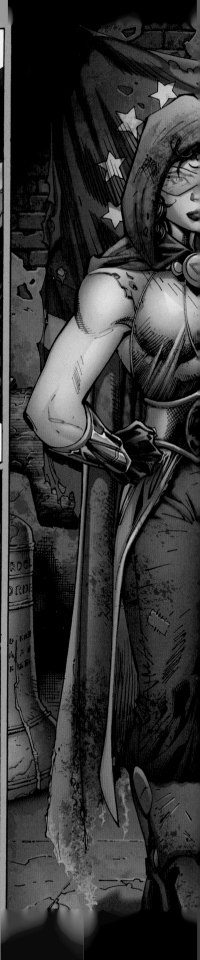

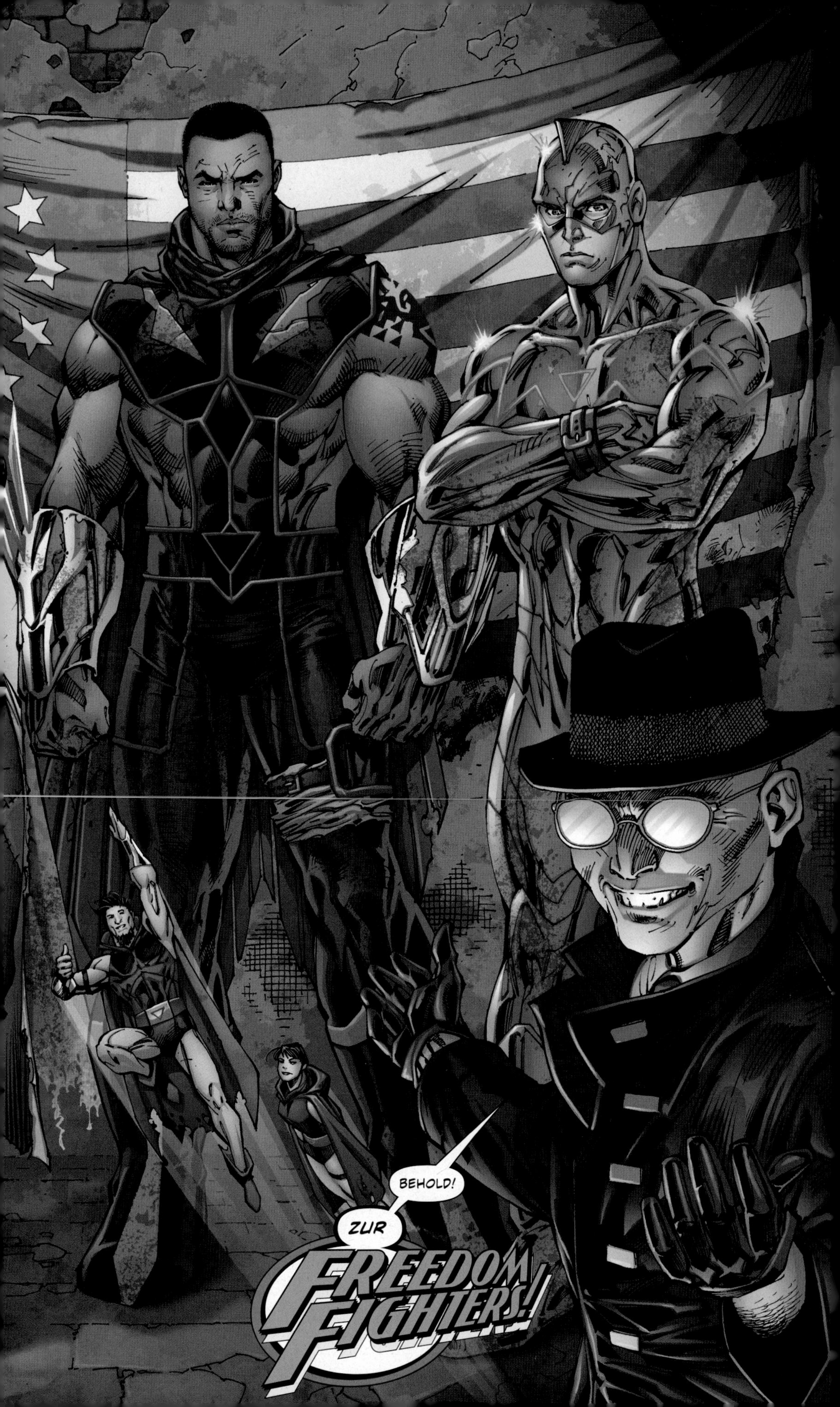
BEHOLD!
ZUR
FREEDOM FIGHTERS!

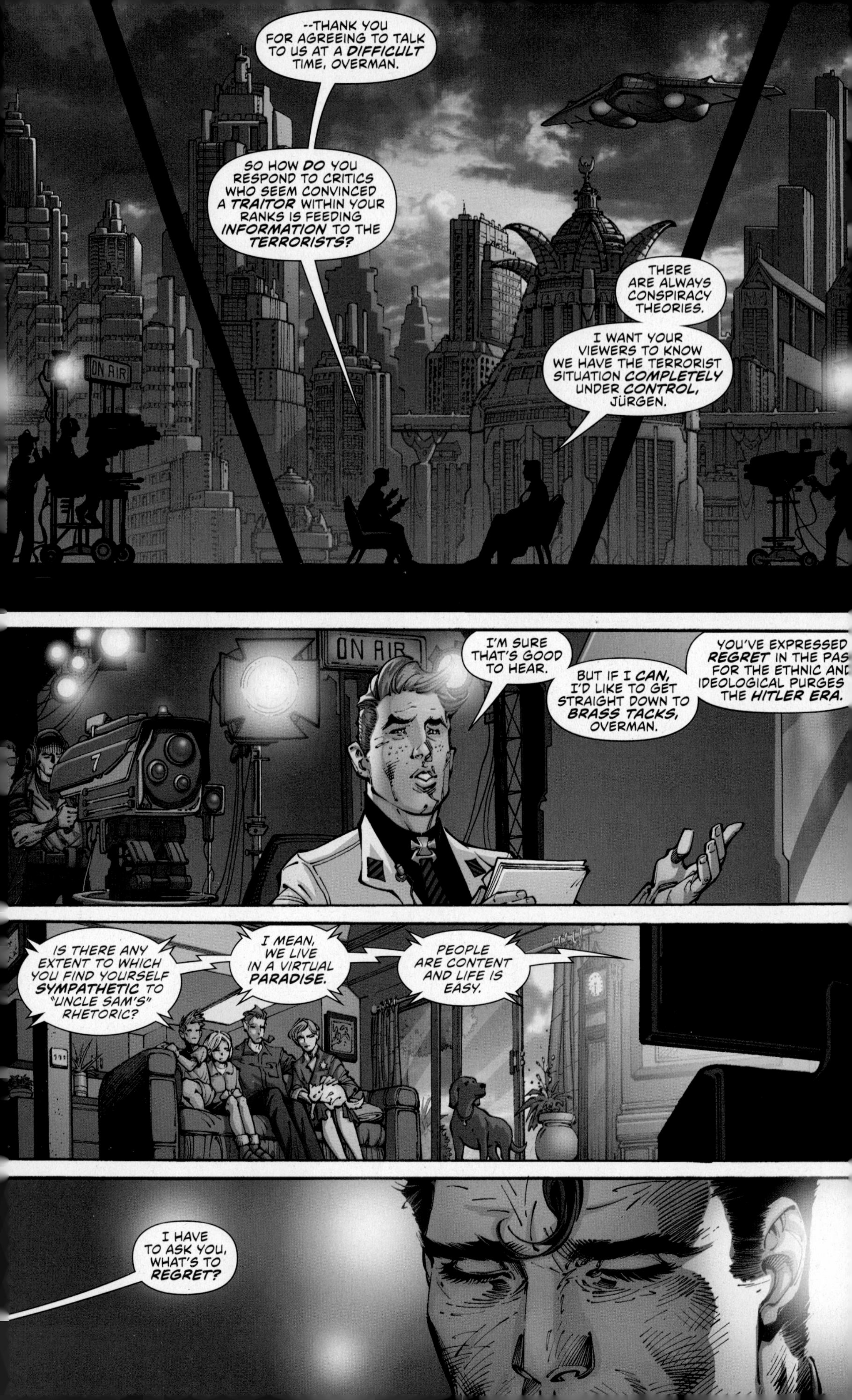
--THANK YOU FOR AGREEING TO TALK TO US AT A DIFFICULT TIME, OVERMAN.
SO HOW DO YOU RESPOND TO CRITICS WHO SEEM CONVINCED A TRAITOR WITHIN YOUR RANKS IS FEEDING INFORMATION TO THE TERRORISTS?
THERE ARE ALWAYS CONSPIRACY THEORIES.
I WANT YOUR VIEWERS TO KNOW WE HAVE THE TERRORIST SITUATION COMPLETELY UNDER CONTROL, JÜRGEN.
ON AIR
ON AIR
I'M SURE THAT'S GOOD TO HEAR.
BUT IF I CAN, I'D LIKE TO GET STRAIGHT DOWN TO BRASS TACKS, OVERMAN.
YOU'VE EXPRESSED REGRET IN THE PAS FOR THE ETHNIC AND IDEOLOGICAL PURGES THE HITLER ERA.
IS THERE ANY EXTENT TO WHICH YOU FIND YOURSELF SYMPATHETIC TO "UNCLE SAM'S" RHETORIC?
I MEAN, WE LIVE IN A VIRTUAL PARADISE.
PEOPLE ARE CONTENT AND LIFE IS EASY.
I HAVE TO ASK YOU, WHAT'S TO REGRET?

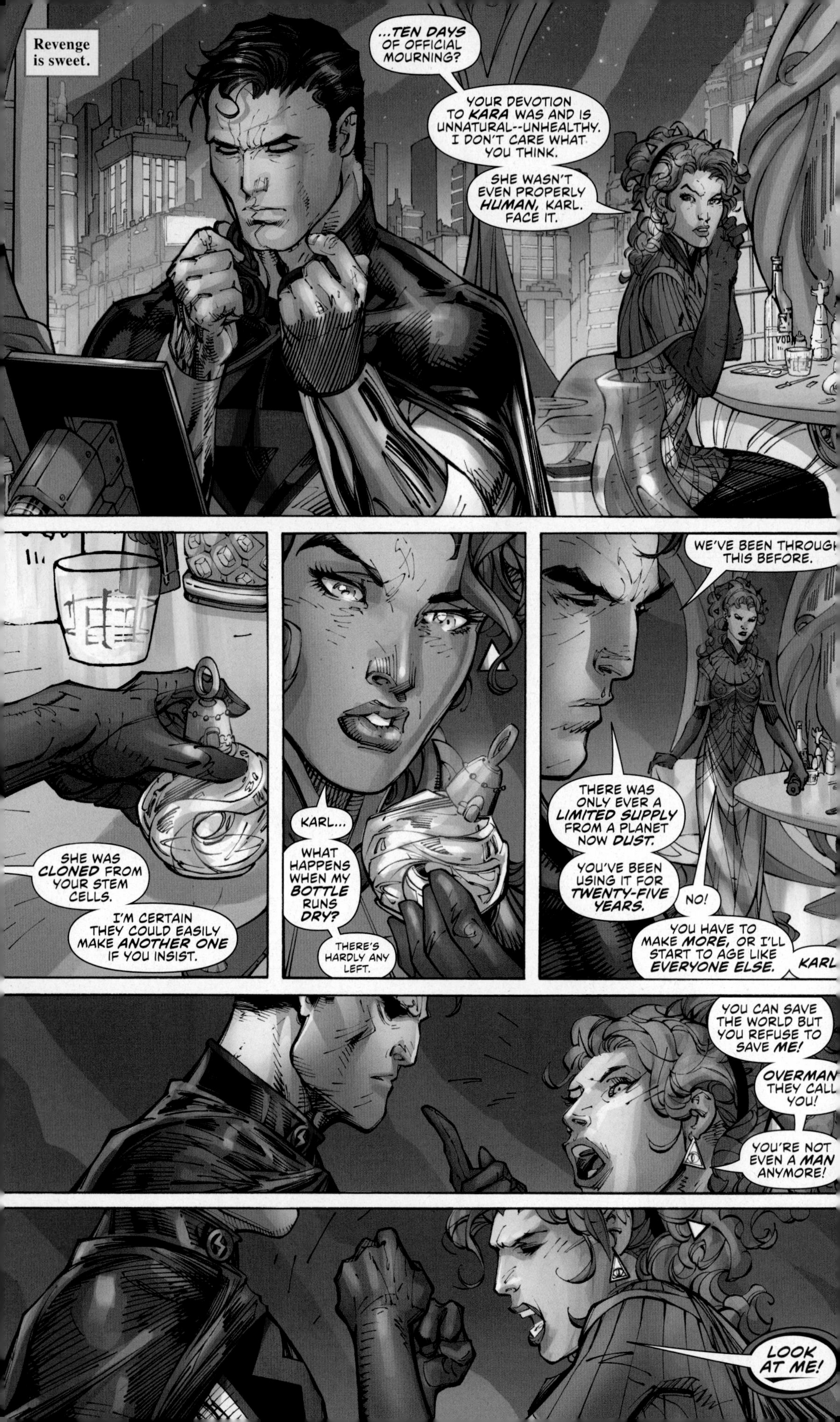

Revenge is sweet.
...TEN DAYS OF OFFICIAL MOURNING?
YOUR DEVOTION TO KARA WAS AND IS UNNATURAL--UNHEALTHY. I DON'T CARE WHAT YOU THINK.
SHE WASN'T EVEN PROPERLY HUMAN, KARL. FACE IT.
SHE WAS CLONED FROM YOUR STEM CELLS.
I'M CERTAIN THEY COULD EASILY MAKE ANOTHER ONE IF YOU INSIST.
KARL...
WHAT HAPPENS WHEN MY BOTTLE RUNS DRY?
THERE'S HARDLY ANY LEFT.
WE'VE BEEN THROUGH THIS BEFORE.
THERE WAS ONLY EVER A LIMITED SUPPLY FROM A PLANET NOW DUST.
YOU'VE BEEN USING IT FOR TWENTY-FIVE YEARS.
NO!
YOU HAVE TO MAKE MORE, OR I'LL START TO AGE LIKE EVERYONE ELSE.
KARL
YOU CAN SAVE THE WORLD BUT YOU REFUSE TO SAVE ME!
OVERMAN THEY CALL YOU!
YOU'RE NOT EVEN A MAN ANYMORE!
LOOK AT ME!

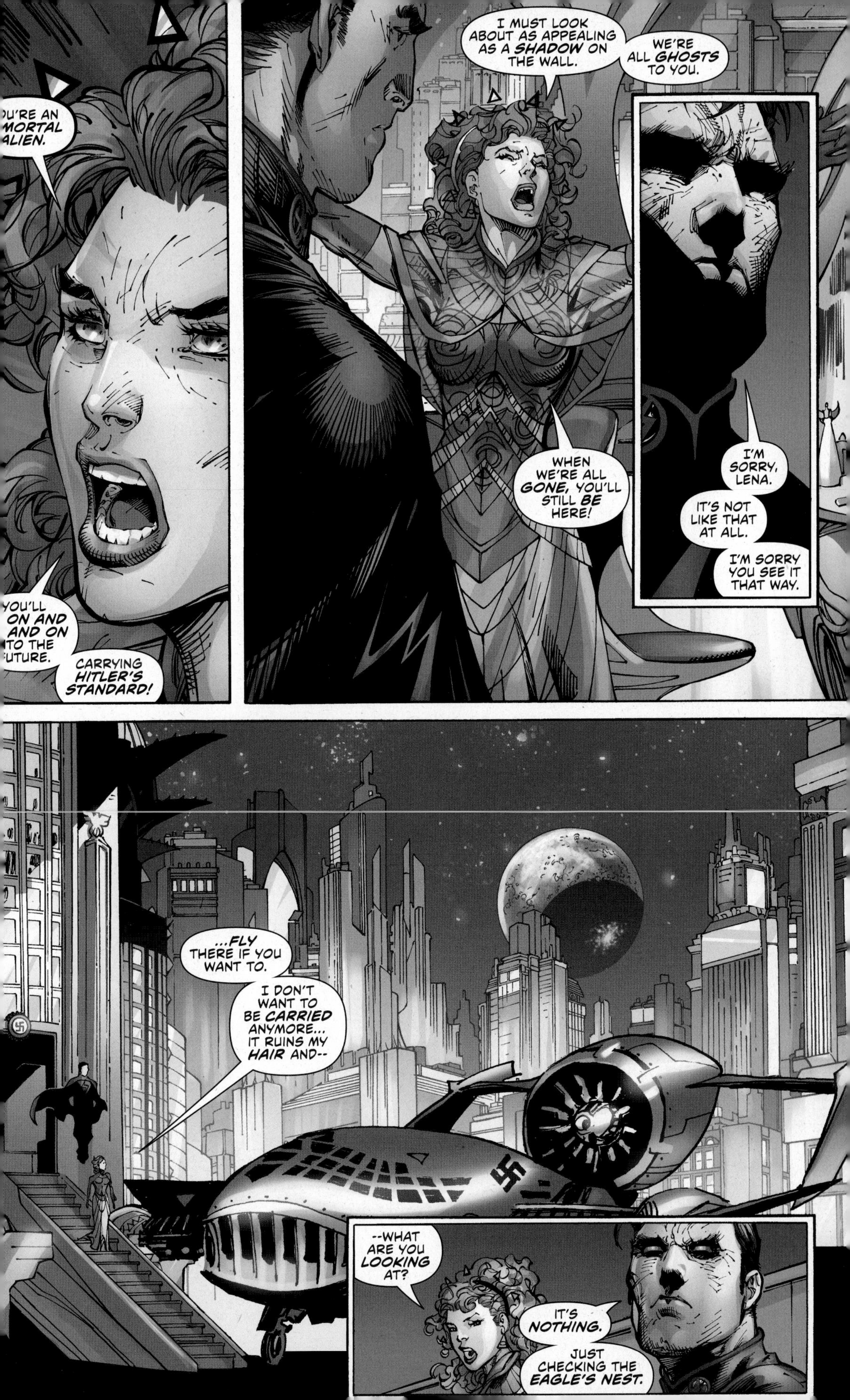

OU'RE AN MORTAL ALIEN.
YOU'LL ON AND AND ON TO THE FUTURE.
CARRYING HITLER'S STANDARD!
I MUST LOOK ABOUT AS APPEALING AS A SHADOW ON THE WALL.
WE'RE ALL GHOSTS TO YOU.
WHEN WE'RE ALL GONE, YOU'LL STILL BE HERE!
I'M SORRY, LENA.
IT'S NOT LIKE THAT AT ALL.
I'M SORRY YOU SEE IT THAT WAY.
...FLY THERE IF YOU WANT TO.
I DON'T WANT TO BE CARRIED ANYMORE... IT RUINS MY HAIR AND--
--WHAT ARE YOU LOOKING AT?
IT'S NOTHING.
JUST CHECKING THE EAGLE'S NEST.

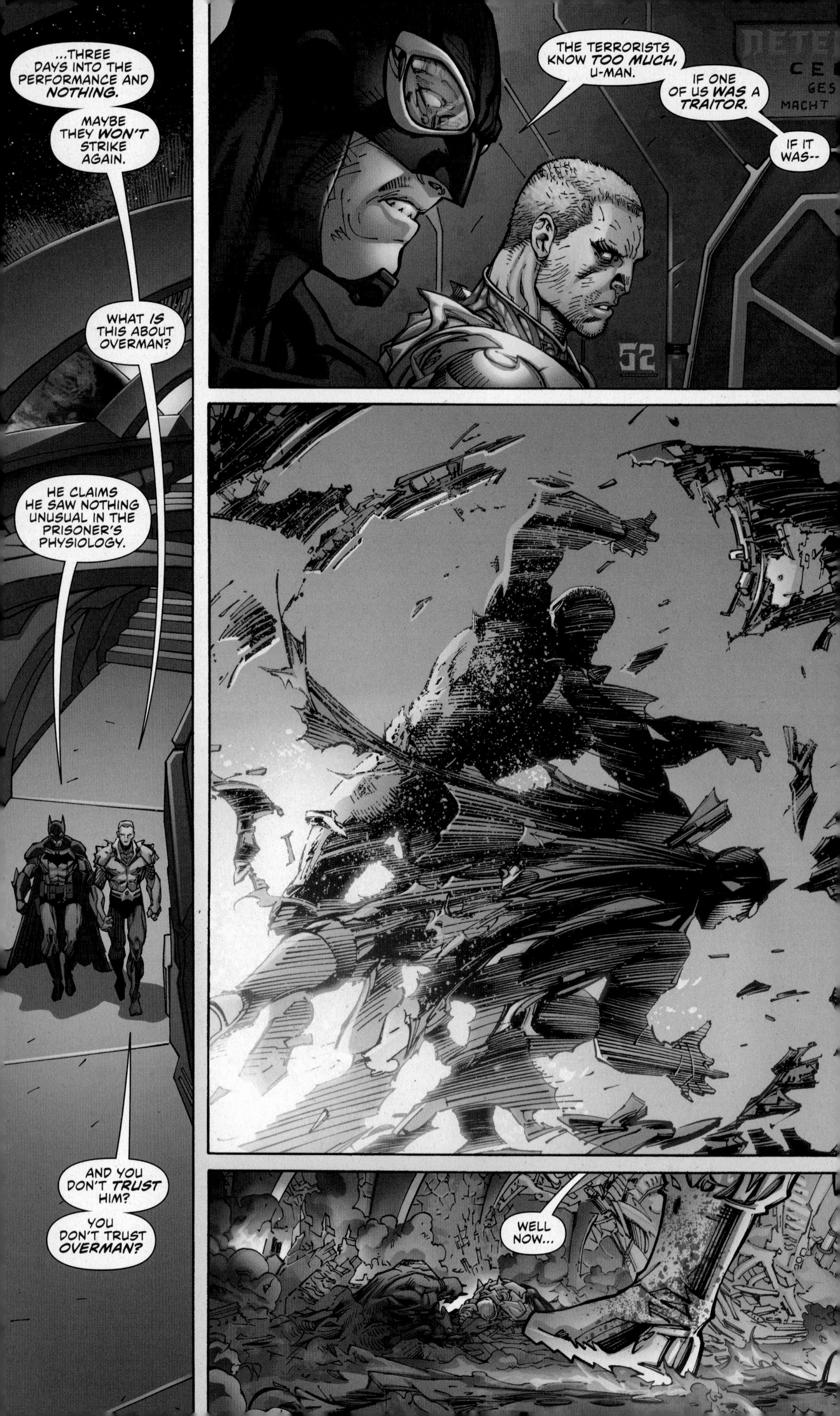

...THREE DAYS INTO THE PERFORMANCE AND *NOTHING.*
MAYBE THEY *WON'T* STRIKE AGAIN.
THE TERRORISTS KNOW *TOO MUCH,* U-MAN.
IF ONE OF US *WAS* A *TRAITOR.*
IF IT WAS--
WHAT *IS* THIS ABOUT OVERMAN?
HE CLAIMS HE SAW NOTHING UNUSUAL IN THE PRISONER'S PHYSIOLOGY.
AND YOU DON'T *TRUST* HIM?
YOU DON'T TRUST *OVERMAN?*
WELL NOW...

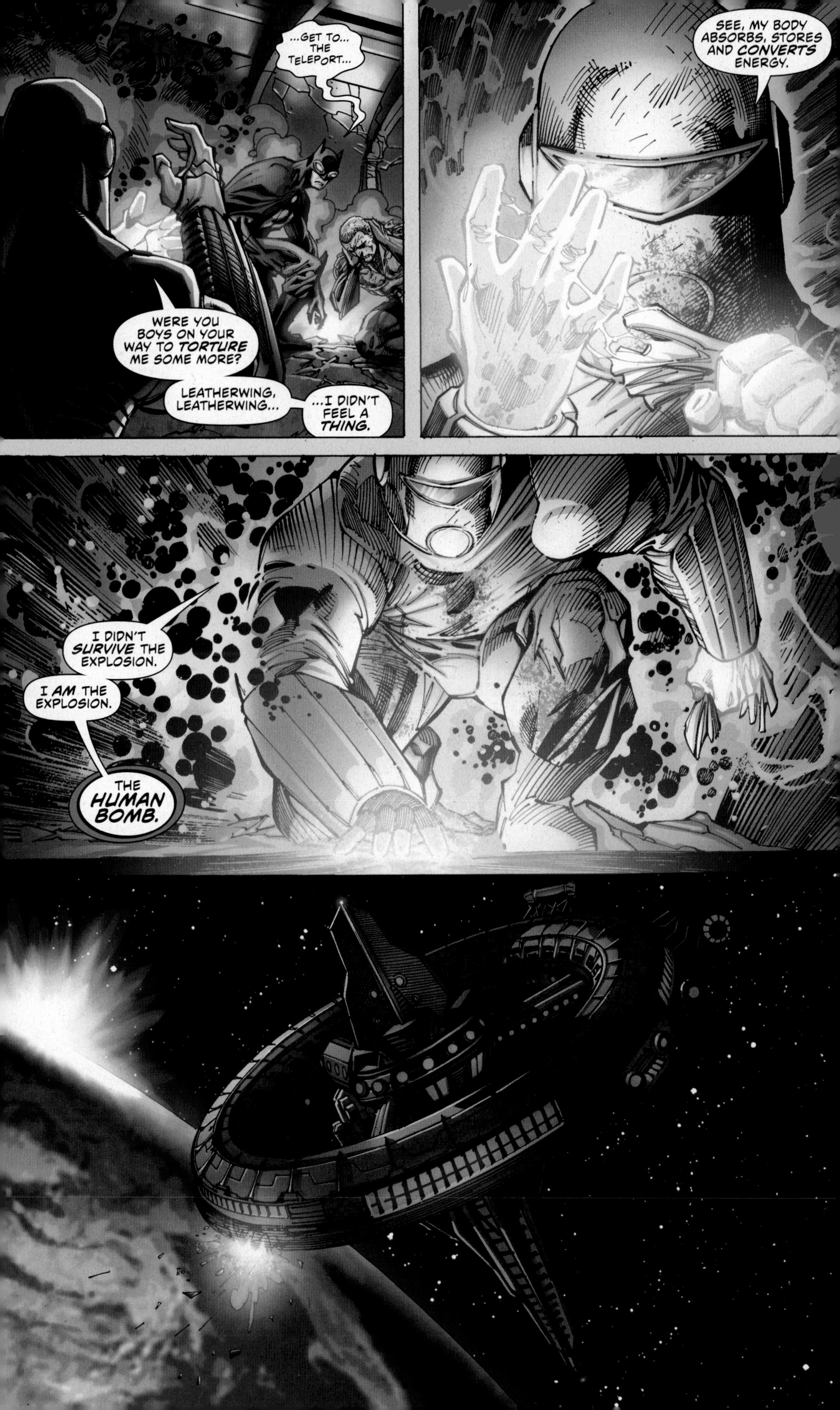

...GET TO... THE TELEPORT...
WERE YOU BOYS ON YOUR WAY TO TORTURE ME SOME MORE?
LEATHERWING, LEATHERWING...
...I DIDN'T FEEL A THING.
SEE, MY BODY ABSORBS, STORES AND CONVERTS ENERGY.
I DIDN'T SURVIVE THE EXPLOSION.
I AM THE EXPLOSION.
THE HUMAN BOMB.

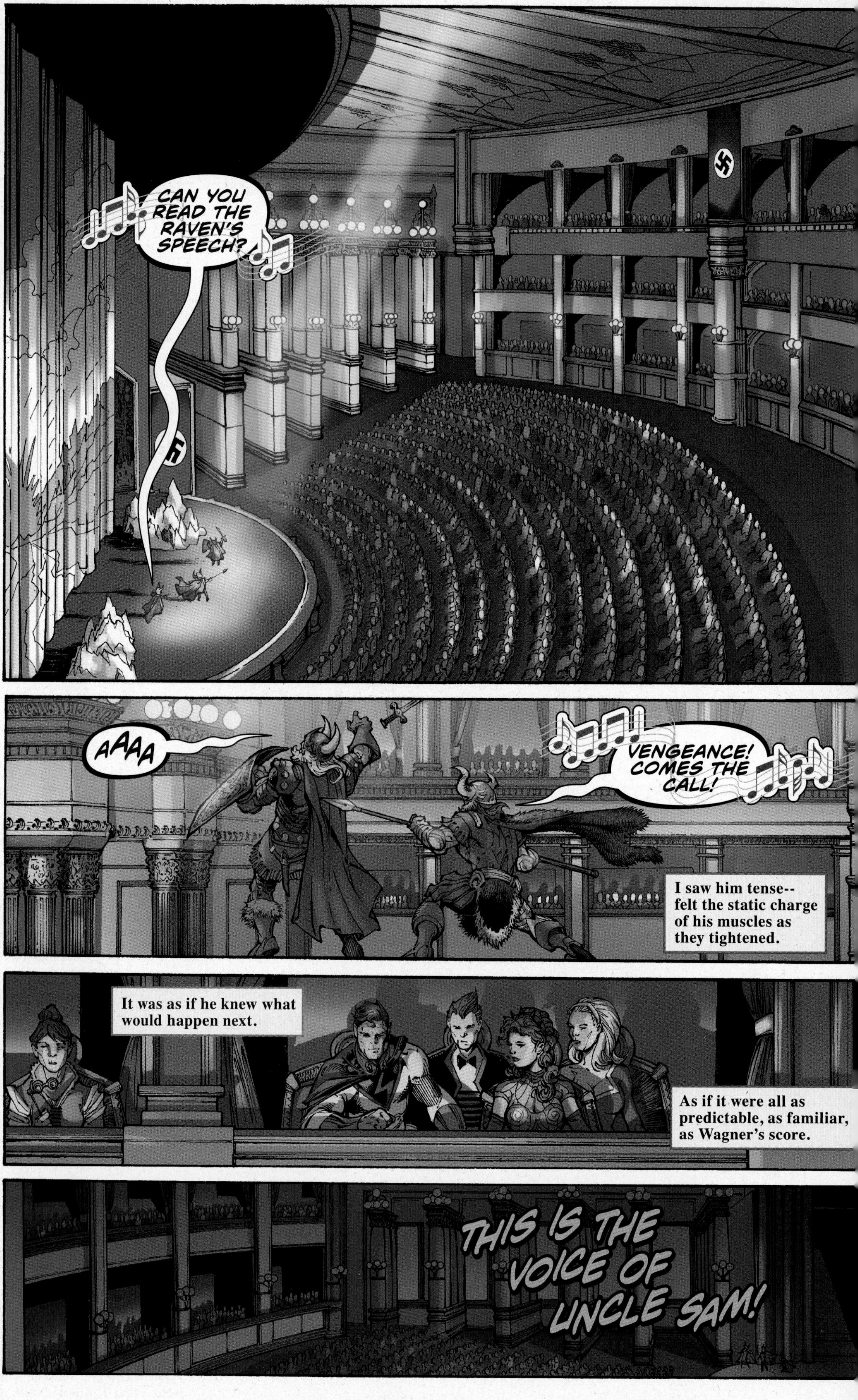
CAN YOU READ THE RAVEN'S SPEECH?
AAAA
VENGEANCE! COMES THE CALL!
I saw him tense--felt the static charge of his muscles as they tightened.
It was as if he knew what would happen next.
As if it were all as predictable, as familiar, as Wagner's score.
THIS IS THE VOICE OF UNCLE SAM!

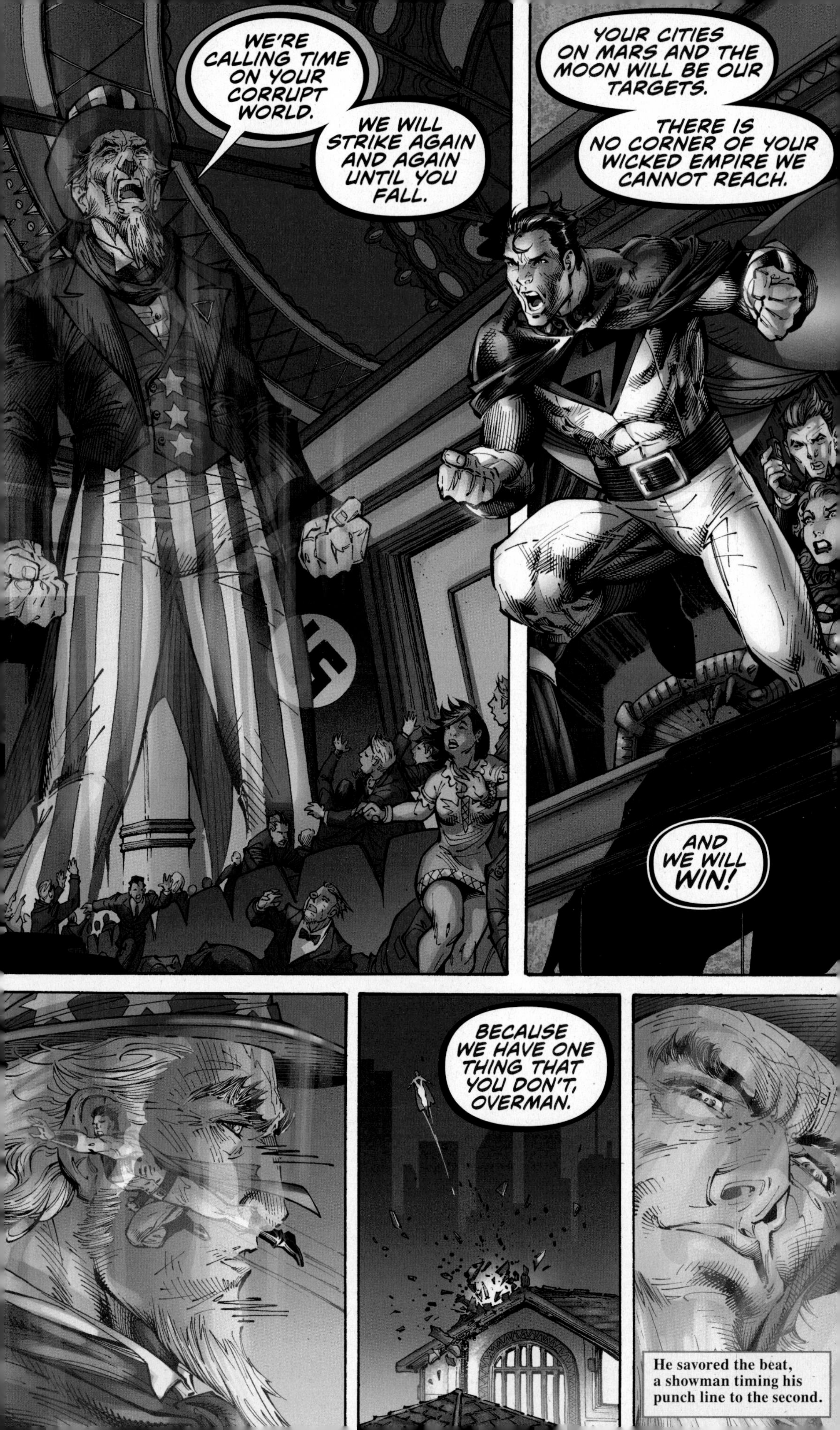
WE'RE CALLING TIME ON YOUR CORRUPT WORLD.
WE WILL STRIKE AGAIN AND AGAIN UNTIL YOU FALL.
YOUR CITIES ON MARS AND THE MOON WILL BE OUR TARGETS.
THERE IS NO CORNER OF YOUR WICKED EMPIRE WE CANNOT REACH.
AND WE WILL WIN!
BECAUSE WE HAVE ONE THING THAT YOU DON'T, OVERMAN.
He savored the beat, a showman timing his punch line to the second.

SOMETHING TO BELIEVE IN!

NINETY-EIGHT YEARS old, his strength failing under the massive weight of the Eagle's Nest as it hit the atmosphere.

His resolve failing.

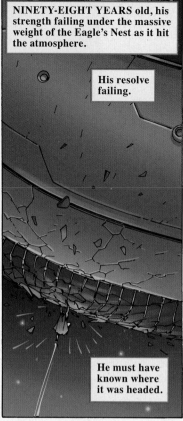

He must have known where it was headed.

WE WANT YOU!

TO PAY FOR YOUR CRIMES.

HEADS UP, RATZIS.

SAM SAYS YOU CAN RAM YOUR SIEGFRIED WHERE THE SUN DON'T SHINE.

He must have known where it would fall.

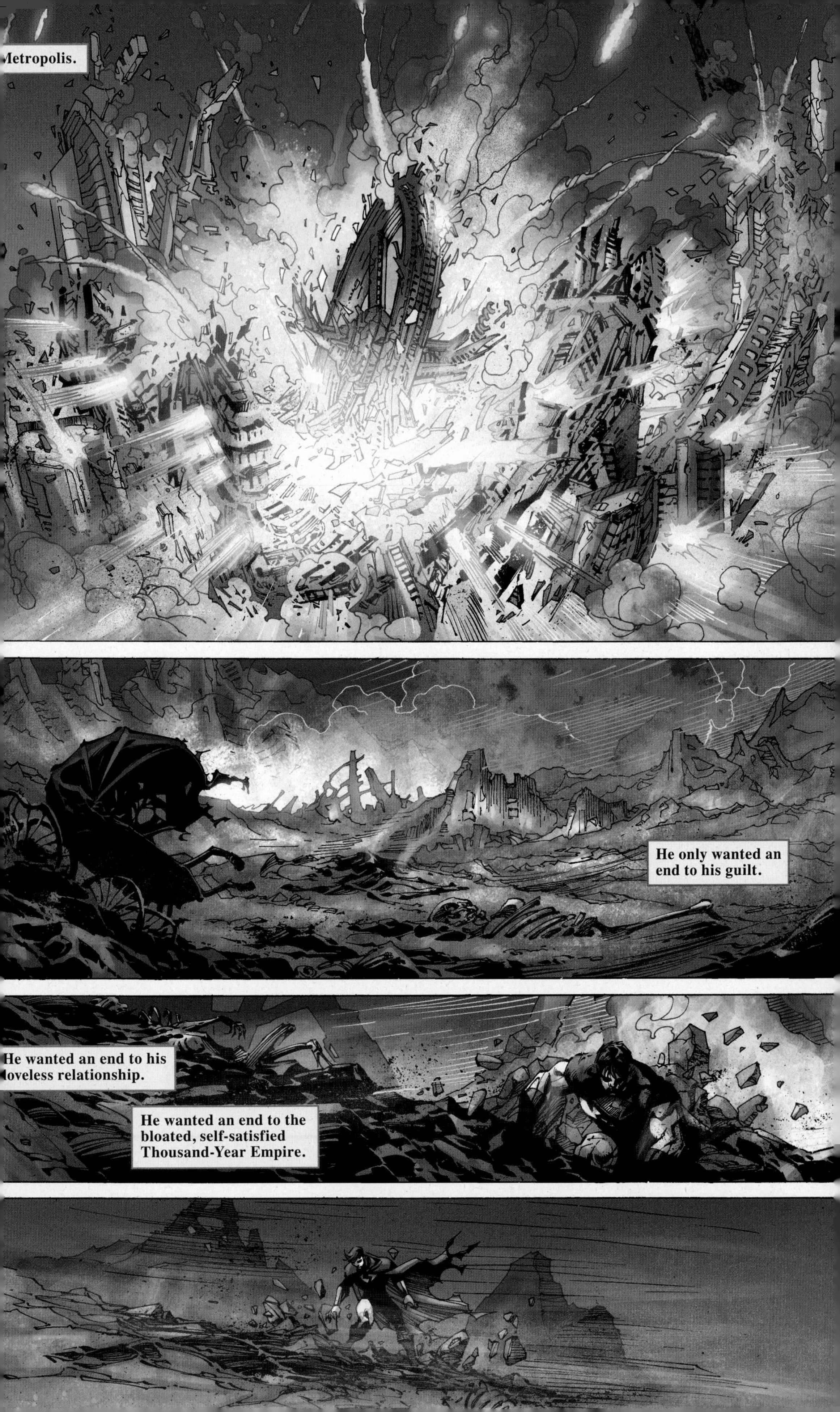
Metropolis.
He only wanted an end to his guilt.
He wanted an end to his loveless relationship.
He wanted an end to the bloated, self-satisfied Thousand-Year Empire.

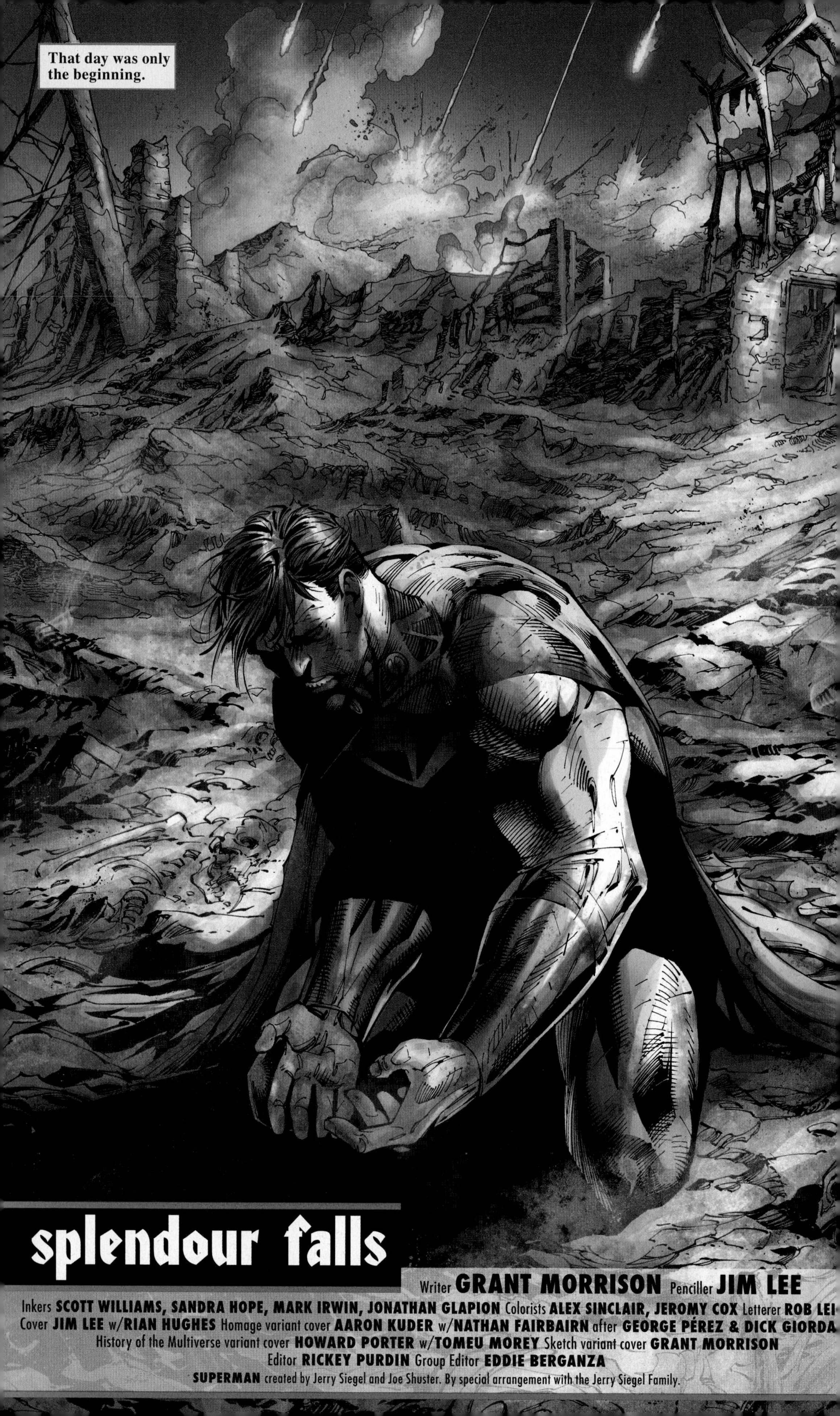
That day was only the beginning.
splendour falls
Writer GRANT MORRISON Penciller JIM LEE
Inkers SCOTT WILLIAMS, SANDRA HOPE, MARK IRWIN, JONATHAN GLAPION Colorists ALEX SINCLAIR, JEROMY COX Letterer ROB LEI
Cover JIM LEE w/RIAN HUGHES Homage variant cover AARON KUDER w/NATHAN FAIRBAIRN after GEORGE PÉREZ & DICK GIORDA
History of the Multiverse variant cover HOWARD PORTER w/TOMEU MOREY Sketch variant cover GRANT MORRISON
Editor RICKEY PURDIN Group Editor EDDIE BERGANZA
SUPERMAN created by Jerry Siegel and Joe Shuster. By special arrangement with the Jerry Siegel Family.

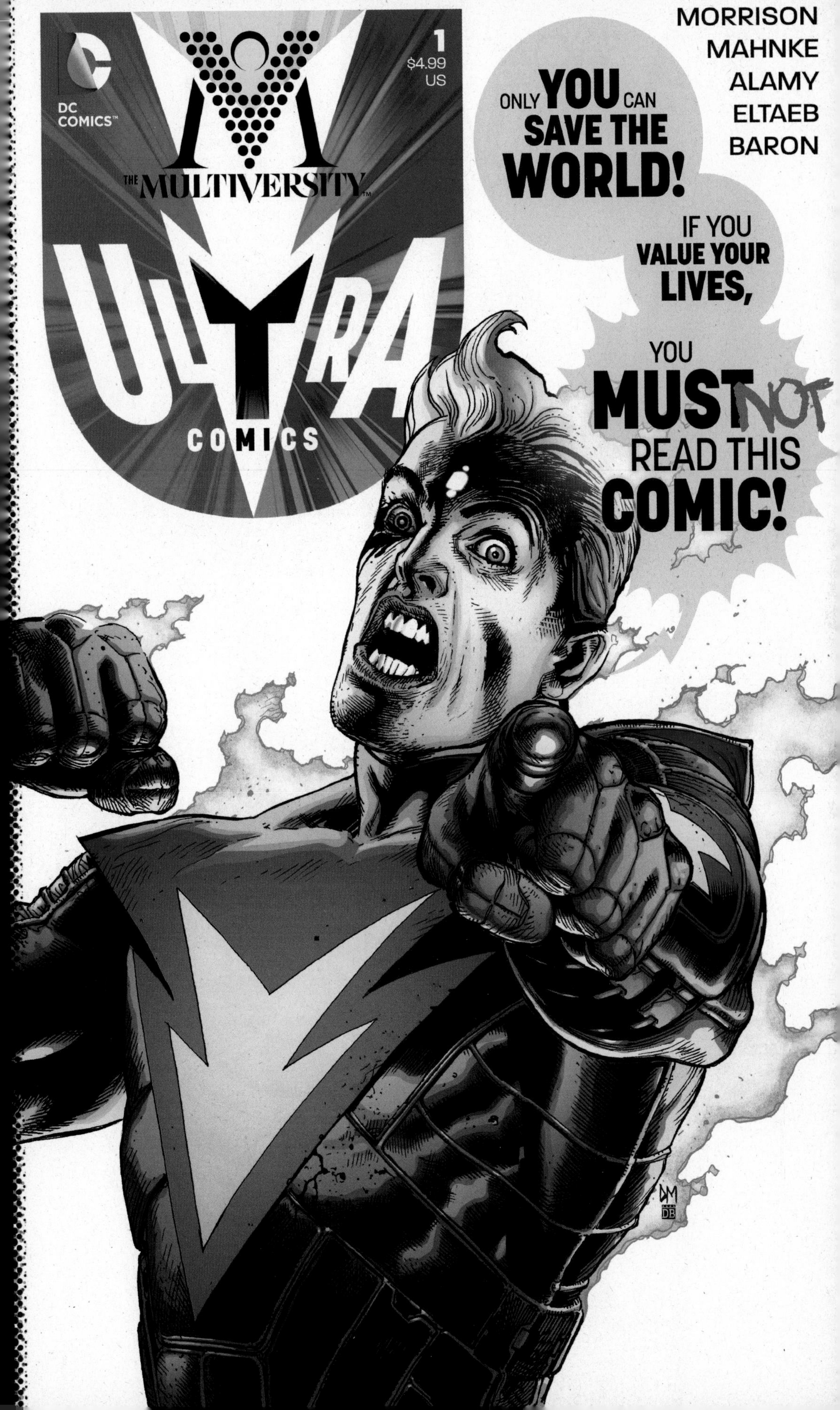
DC COMICS
1 $4.99 US
THE MULTIVERSITY
ULTRA COMICS
MORRISON
MAHNKE
ALAMY
ELTAEB
BARON
ONLY YOU CAN SAVE THE WORLD!
IF YOU VALUE YOUR LIVES,
YOU MUST NOT READ THIS COMIC!

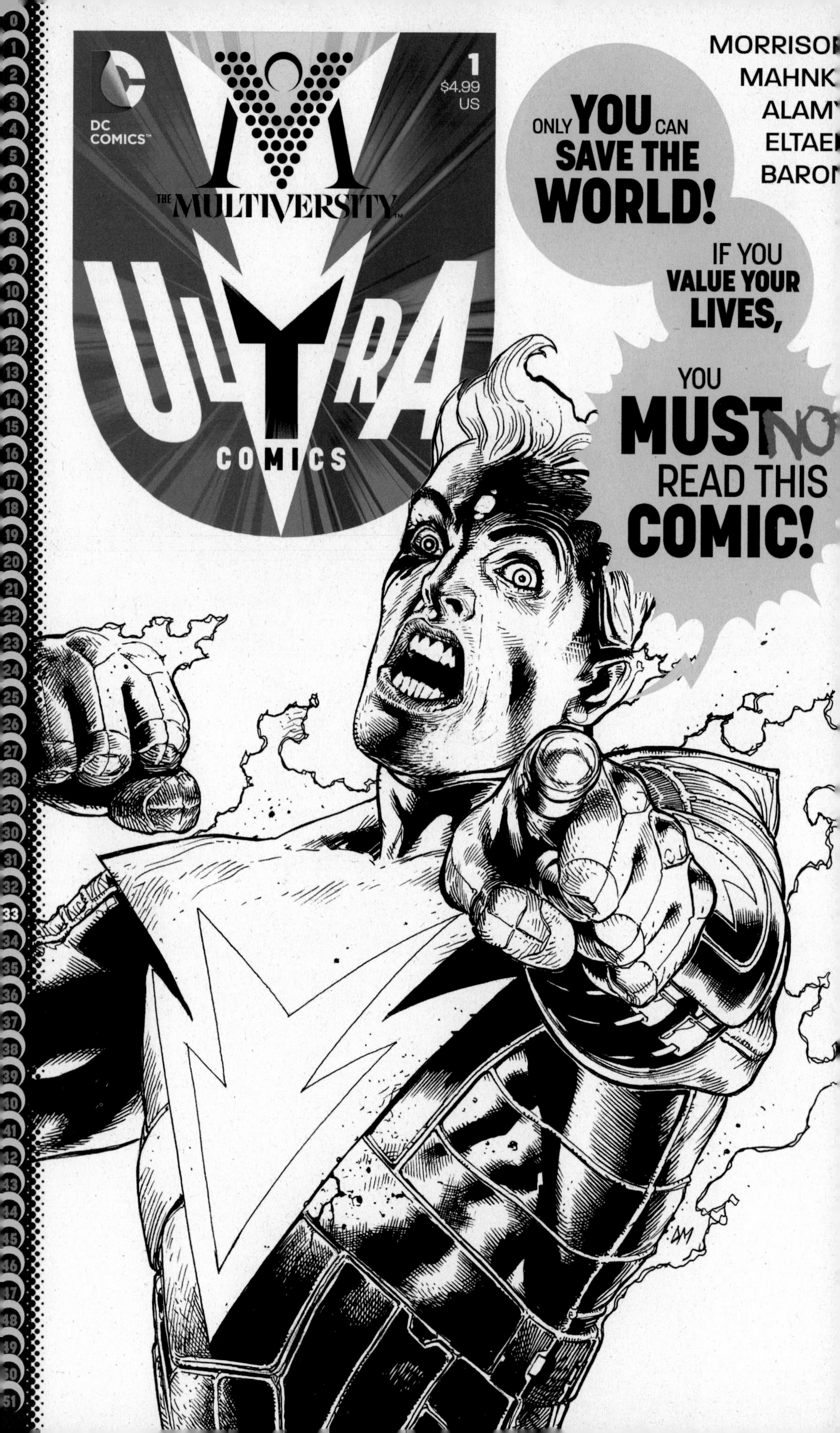
DC COMICS
1
$4.99
US
THE MULTIVERSITY
ULTRA COMICS
MORRISO
MAHNK
ALAMY
ELTAE
BARO
ONLY YOU CAN SAVE THE WORLD!
IF YOU VALUE YOUR LIVES,
YOU MUST NO READ THIS COMIC!

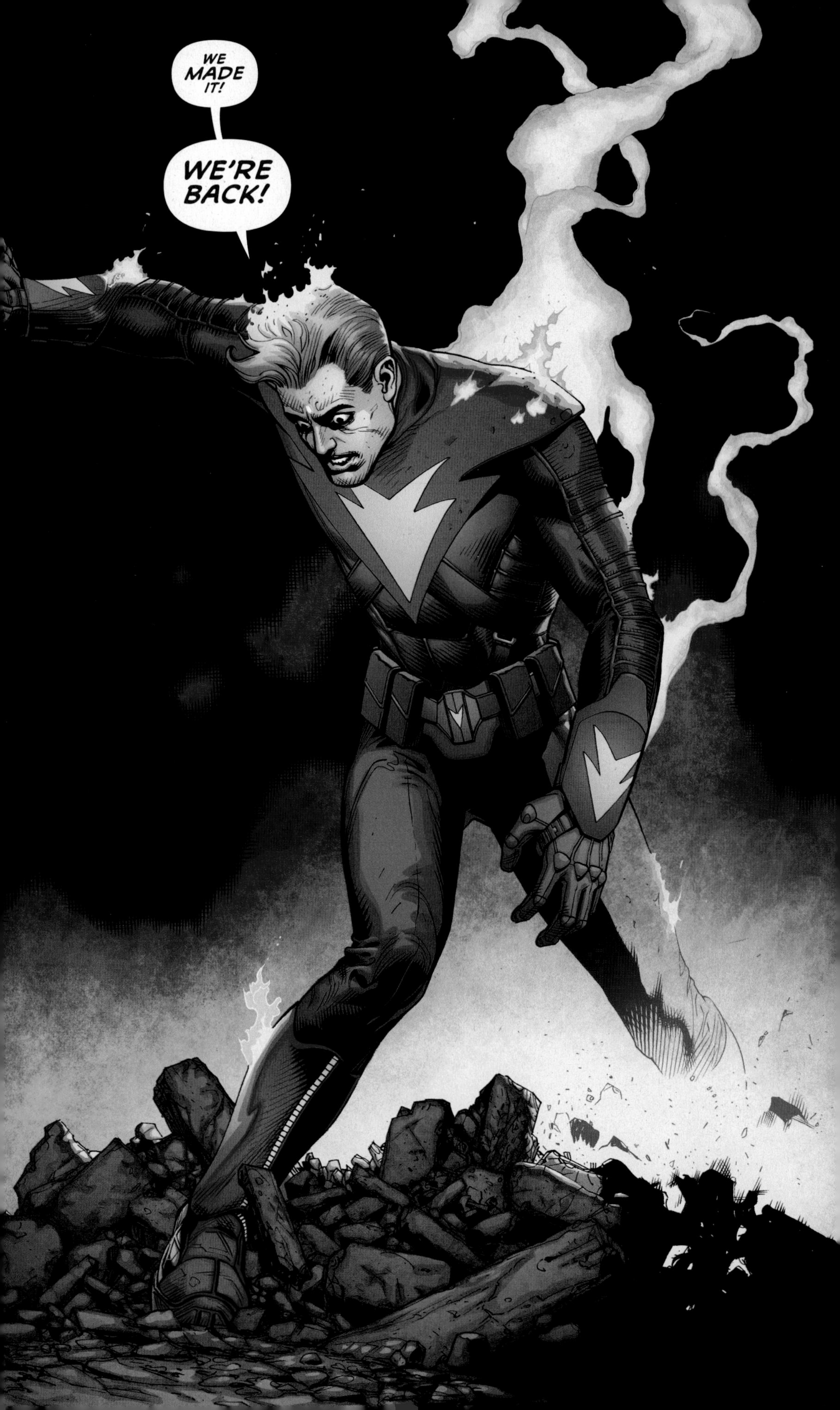
WE MADE IT!
WE'RE BACK!

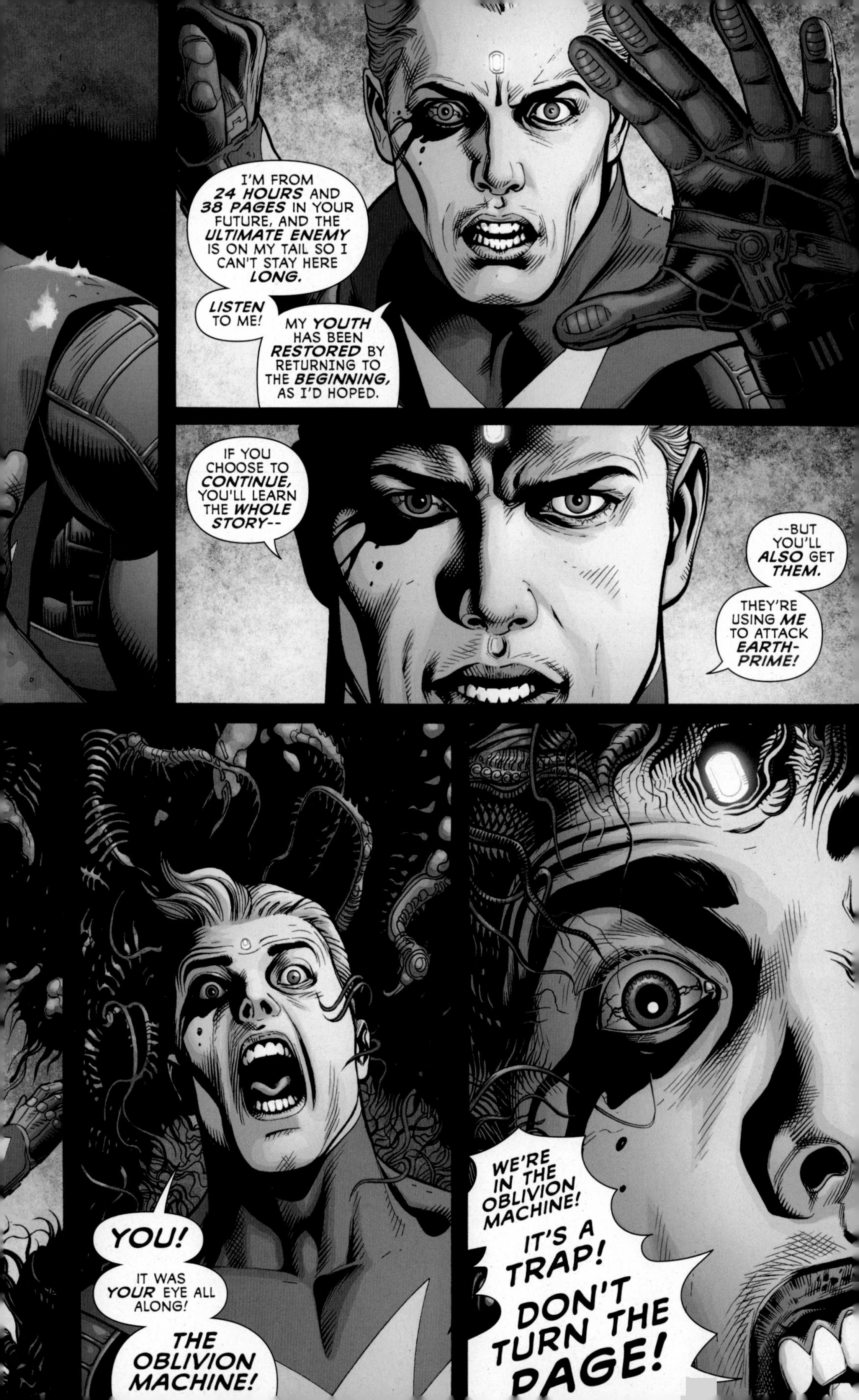

I'M FROM 24 HOURS AND 38 PAGES IN YOUR FUTURE, AND THE ULTIMATE ENEMY IS ON MY TAIL SO I CAN'T STAY HERE LONG.
LISTEN TO ME!
MY YOUTH HAS BEEN RESTORED BY RETURNING TO THE BEGINNING, AS I'D HOPED.
IF YOU CHOOSE TO CONTINUE, YOU'LL LEARN THE WHOLE STORY--
--BUT YOU'LL ALSO GET THEM.
THEY'RE USING ME TO ATTACK EARTH-PRIME!
YOU!
IT WAS YOUR EYE ALL ALONG!
THE OBLIVION MACHINE!
WE'RE IN THE OBLIVION MACHINE!
IT'S A TRAP!
DON'T TURN THE PAGE!

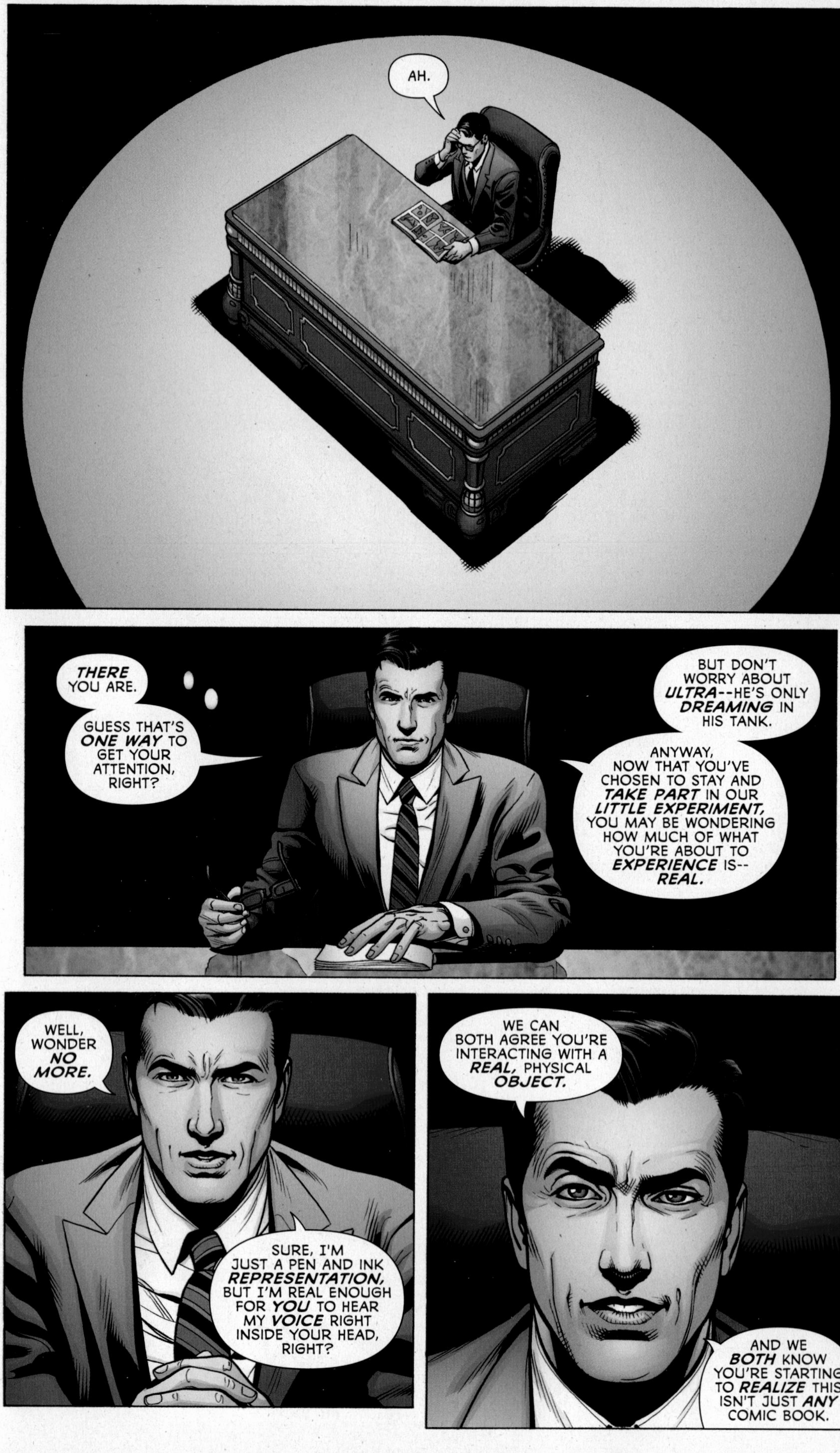
AH.
THERE YOU ARE.
GUESS THAT'S ONE WAY TO GET YOUR ATTENTION, RIGHT?
BUT DON'T WORRY ABOUT ULTRA--HE'S ONLY DREAMING IN HIS TANK.
ANYWAY, NOW THAT YOU'VE CHOSEN TO STAY AND TAKE PART IN OUR LITTLE EXPERIMENT, YOU MAY BE WONDERING HOW MUCH OF WHAT YOU'RE ABOUT TO EXPERIENCE IS-- REAL.
WELL, WONDER NO MORE.
SURE, I'M JUST A PEN AND INK REPRESENTATION, BUT I'M REAL ENOUGH FOR YOU TO HEAR MY VOICE RIGHT INSIDE YOUR HEAD, RIGHT?
WE CAN BOTH AGREE YOU'RE INTERACTING WITH A REAL, PHYSICAL OBJECT.
AND WE BOTH KNOW YOU'RE STARTING TO REALIZE THIS ISN'T JUST ANY COMIC BOOK.

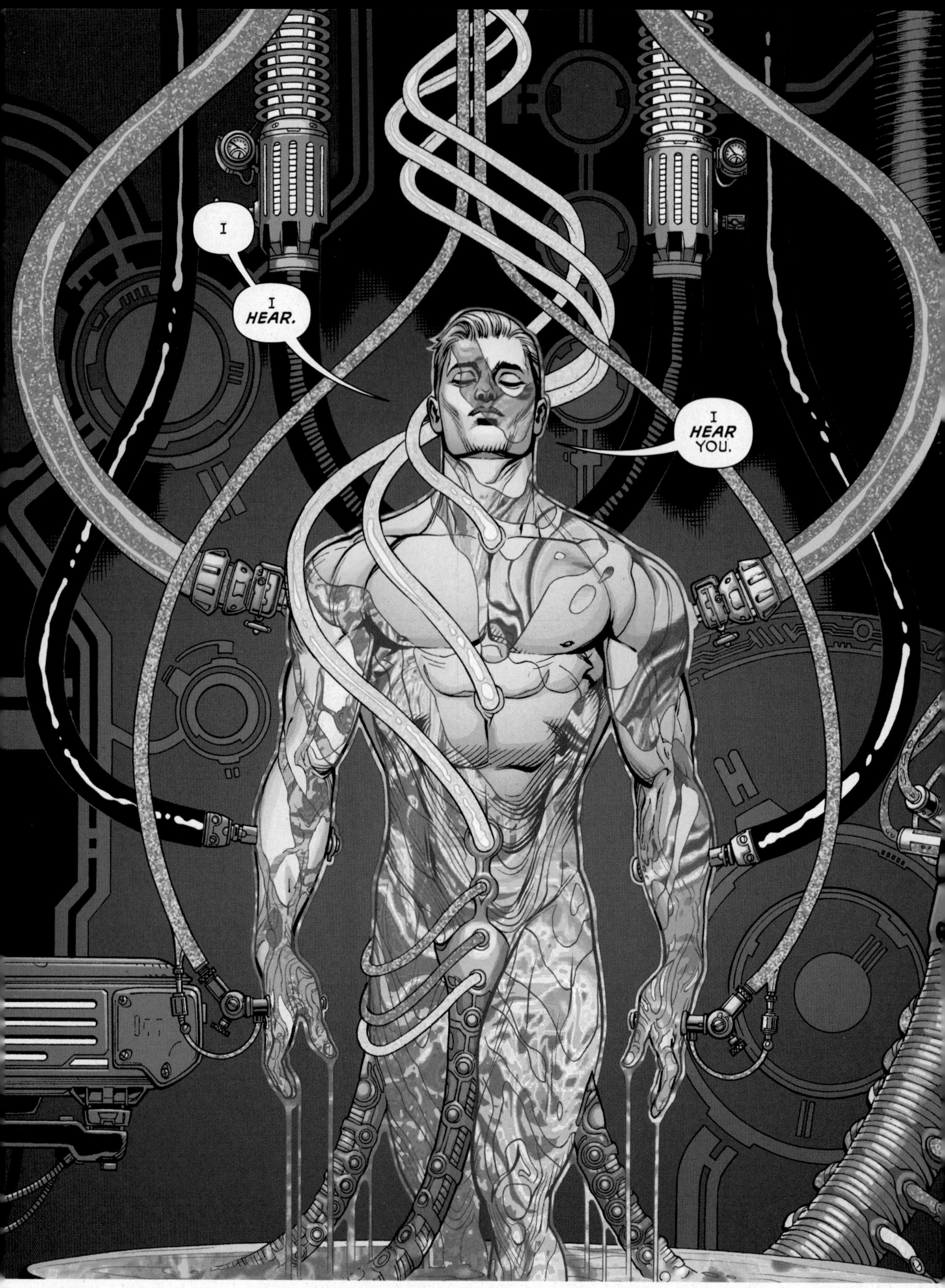
I
I HEAR.
I HEAR YOU.

ULTRA COMICS LIVES

MEMETICALLY ENGINEERED BY
GRANT MORRISON: WRITER DOUG MAHNKE: PENCILLER
CHRISTIAN ALAMY, MARK IRWIN, KEITH CHAMPAGNE, JAIME MENDOZA: INKERS
GABE ELTAEB, DAVID BARON: COLORISTS STEVE WANDS: LETTERER MAHNKE W/BARON: COVER
DUNCAN ROULEAU AFTER MIKE SEKOWSKY & MURPHY ANDERSON: HOMAGE VARIANT COVER
YANICK PAQUETTE W/ NATHAN FAIRBAIRN: HISTORY OF THE MULTIVERSE VARIANT COVER
MORRISON: SKETCH VARIANT COVER
RICKEY PURDIN: EDITOR EDDIE BERGANZA: GROUP EDITOR

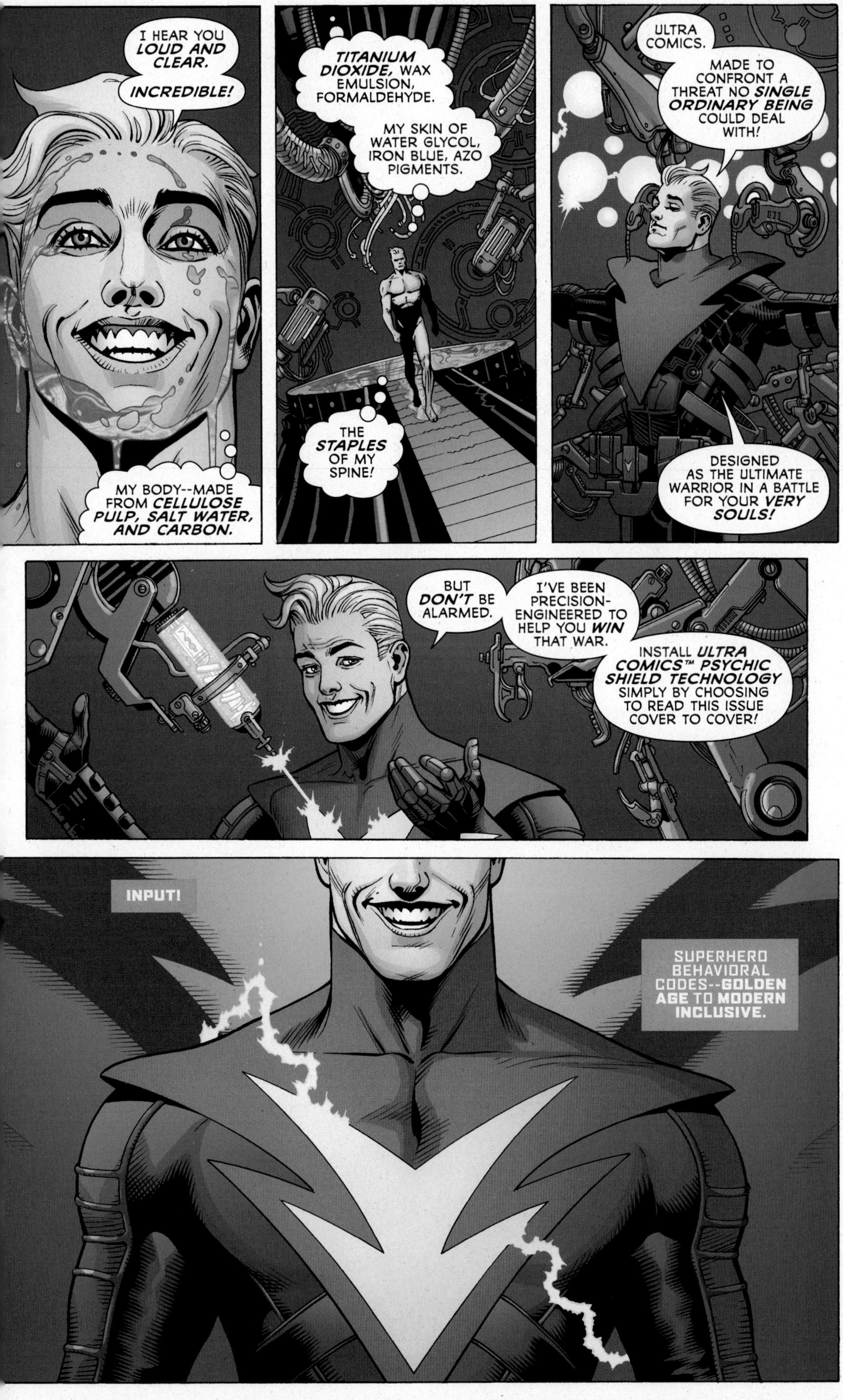

I HEAR YOU LOUD AND CLEAR.
INCREDIBLE!
MY BODY--MADE FROM CELLULOSE PULP, SALT WATER, AND CARBON.
TITANIUM DIOXIDE, WAX EMULSION, FORMALDEHYDE.
MY SKIN OF WATER GLYCOL, IRON BLUE, AZO PIGMENTS.
THE STAPLES OF MY SPINE!
ULTRA COMICS.
MADE TO CONFRONT A THREAT NO SINGLE ORDINARY BEING COULD DEAL WITH!
DESIGNED AS THE ULTIMATE WARRIOR IN A BATTLE FOR YOUR VERY SOULS!
BUT DON'T BE ALARMED.
I'VE BEEN PRECISION-ENGINEERED TO HELP YOU WIN THAT WAR.
INSTALL ULTRA COMICS™ PSYCHIC SHIELD TECHNOLOGY SIMPLY BY CHOOSING TO READ THIS ISSUE COVER TO COVER!
INPUT!
SUPERHERO BEHAVIORAL CODES--GOLDEN AGE TO MODERN INCLUSIVE.

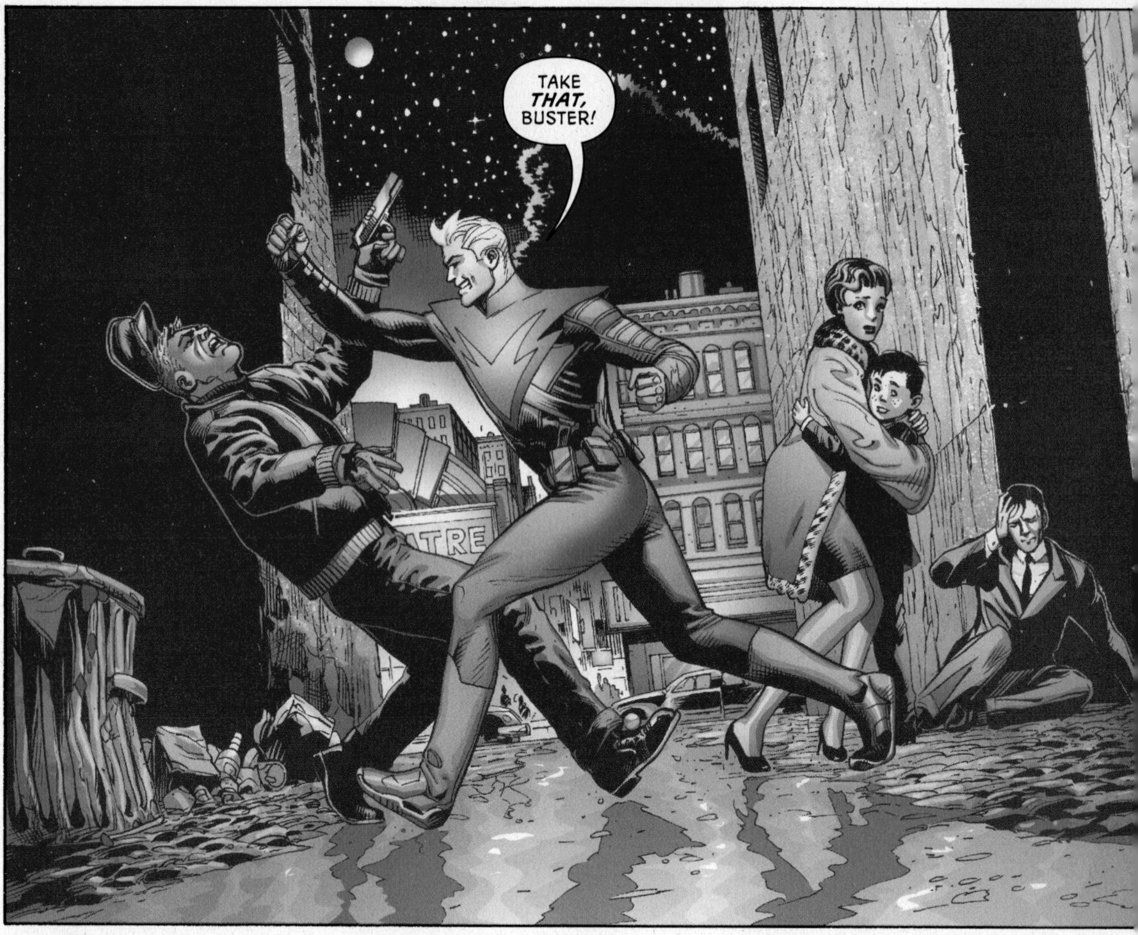
TAKE *THAT,* BUSTER!
TRE

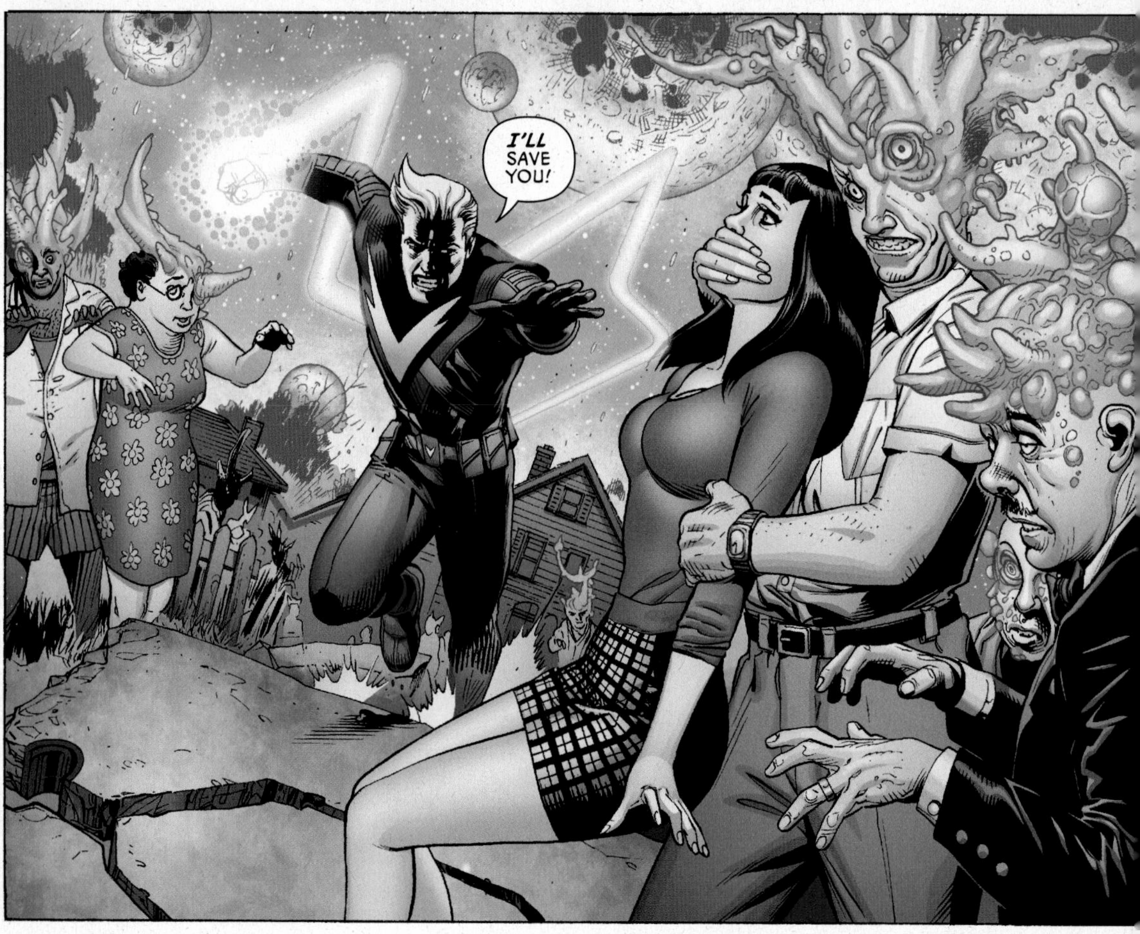
I'LL SAVE YOU!

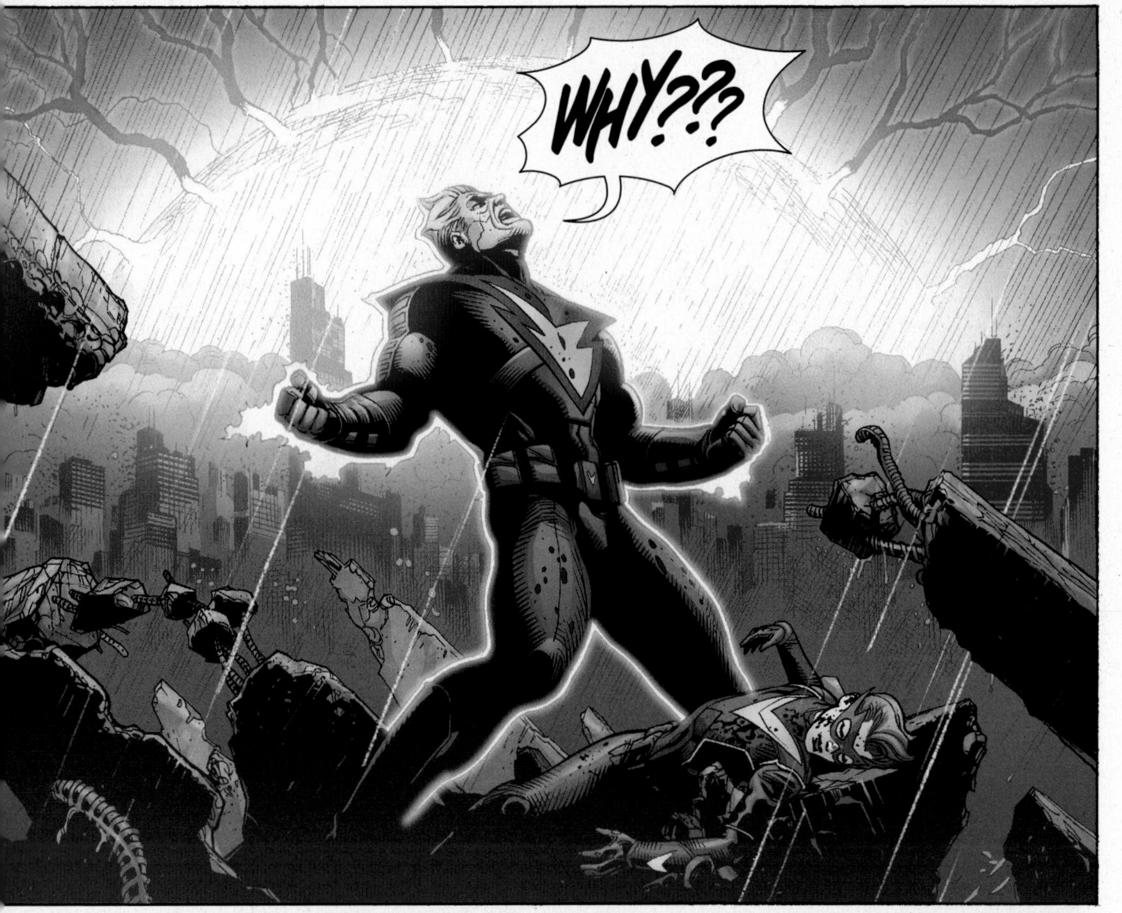
WHY???

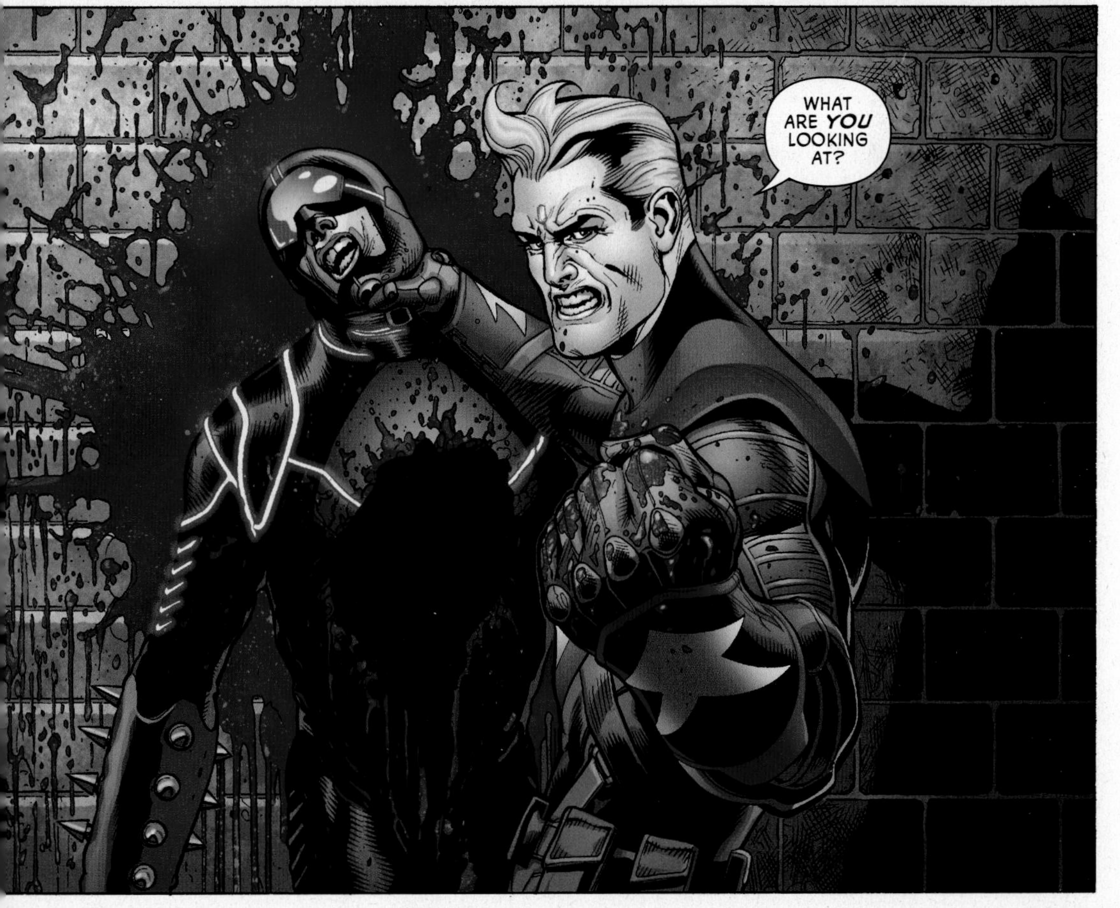
WHAT ARE YOU LOOKING AT?

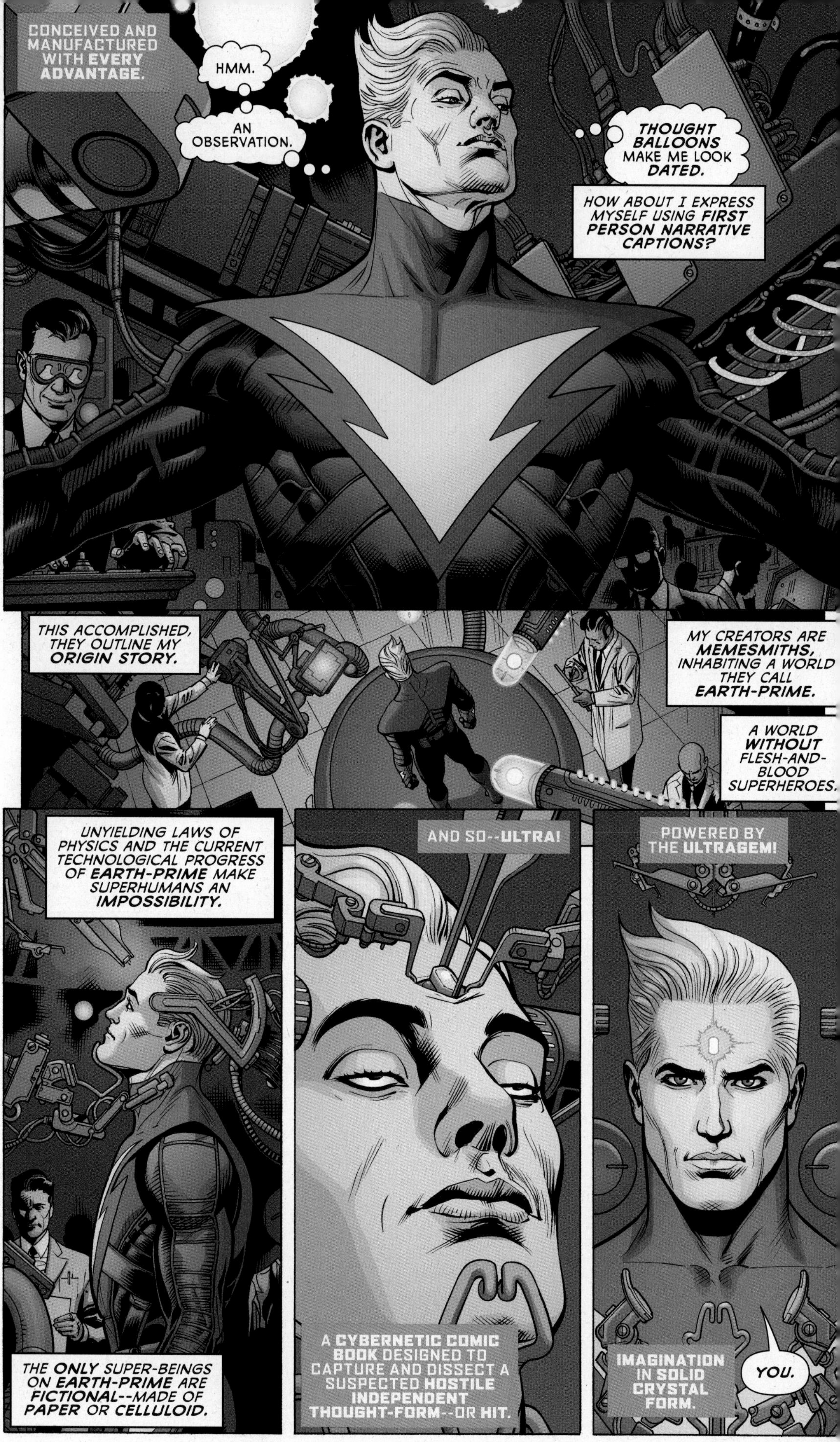

CONCEIVED AND MANUFACTURED WITH EVERY ADVANTAGE.
HMM.
AN OBSERVATION.
THOUGHT BALLOONS MAKE ME LOOK DATED.
HOW ABOUT I EXPRESS MYSELF USING FIRST PERSON NARRATIVE CAPTIONS?
THIS ACCOMPLISHED, THEY OUTLINE MY ORIGIN STORY.
MY CREATORS ARE MEMESMITHS, INHABITING A WORLD THEY CALL EARTH-PRIME.
A WORLD WITHOUT FLESH-AND-BLOOD SUPERHEROES.
UNYIELDING LAWS OF PHYSICS AND THE CURRENT TECHNOLOGICAL PROGRESS OF EARTH-PRIME MAKE SUPERHUMANS AN IMPOSSIBILITY.
THE ONLY SUPER-BEINGS ON EARTH-PRIME ARE FICTIONAL--MADE OF PAPER OR CELLULOID.
AND SO--ULTRA!
A CYBERNETIC COMIC BOOK DESIGNED TO CAPTURE AND DISSECT A SUSPECTED HOSTILE INDEPENDENT THOUGHT-FORM--OR HIT.
POWERED BY THE ULTRAGEM!
IMAGINATION IN SOLID CRYSTAL FORM.
YOU.

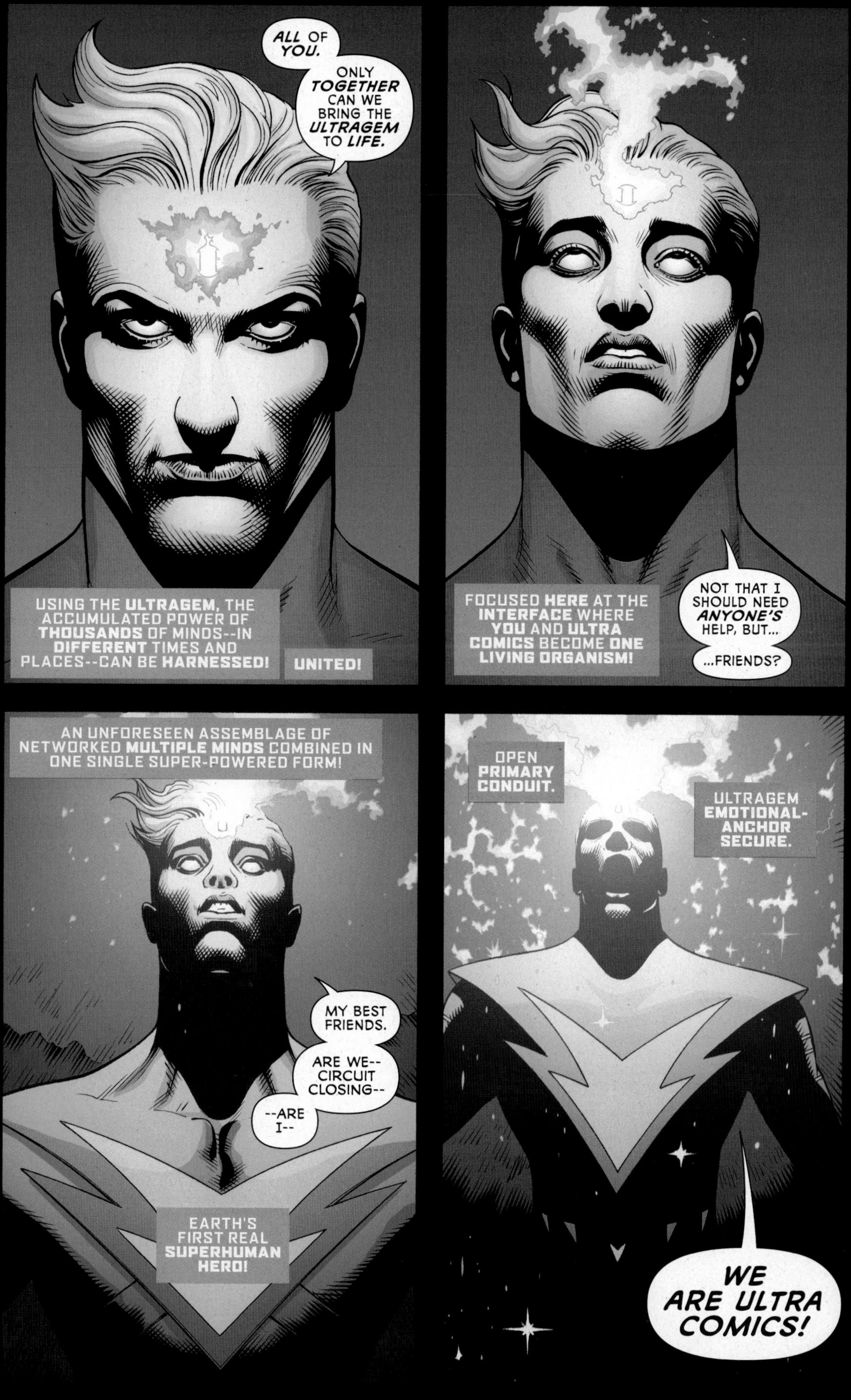
ALL OF YOU.
ONLY TOGETHER CAN WE BRING THE ULTRAGEM TO LIFE.
USING THE ULTRAGEM, THE ACCUMULATED POWER OF THOUSANDS OF MINDS--IN DIFFERENT TIMES AND PLACES--CAN BE HARNESSED!
UNITED!
FOCUSED HERE AT THE INTERFACE WHERE YOU AND ULTRA COMICS BECOME ONE LIVING ORGANISM!
NOT THAT I SHOULD NEED ANYONE'S HELP, BUT...
...FRIENDS?
AN UNFORESEEN ASSEMBLAGE OF NETWORKED MULTIPLE MINDS COMBINED IN ONE SINGLE SUPER-POWERED FORM!
MY BEST FRIENDS.
ARE WE--CIRCUIT CLOSING--
--ARE I--
EARTH'S FIRST REAL SUPERHUMAN HERO!
OPEN PRIMARY CONDUIT.
ULTRAGEM EMOTIONAL-ANCHOR SECURE.
WE ARE ULTRA COMICS!

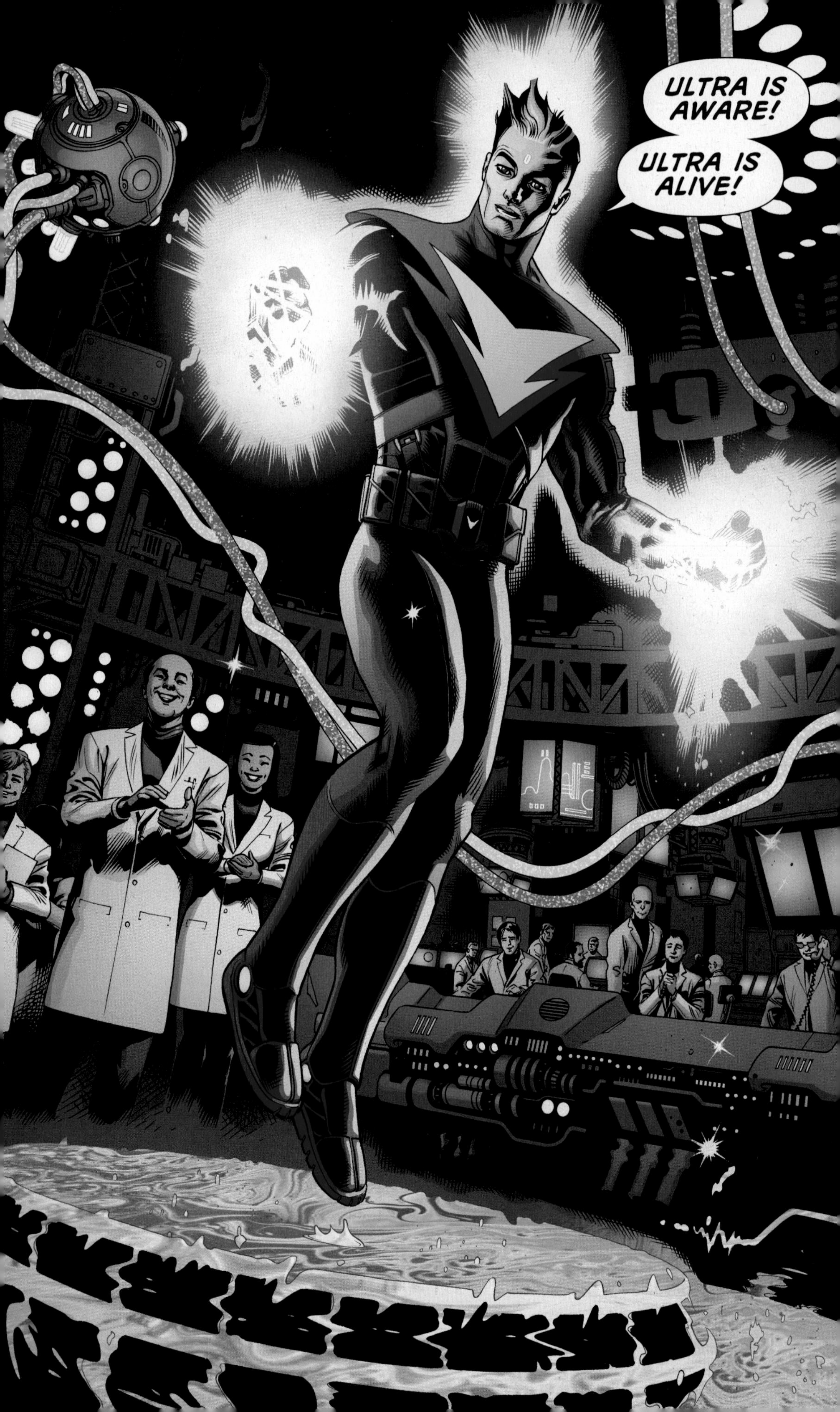
ULTRA IS AWARE!
ULTRA IS ALIVE!

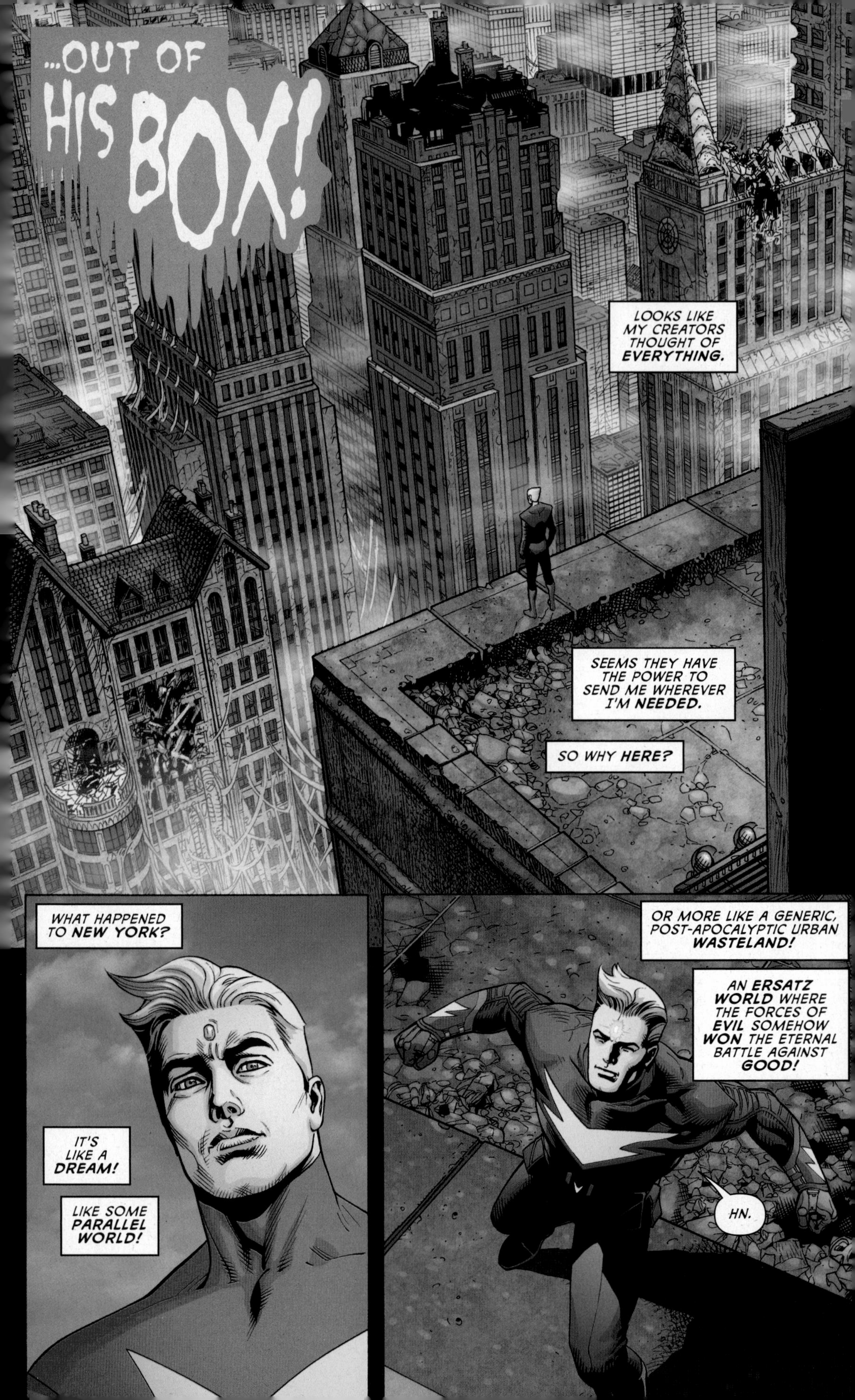

...OUT OF HIS BOX!
LOOKS LIKE MY CREATORS THOUGHT OF EVERYTHING.
SEEMS THEY HAVE THE POWER TO SEND ME WHEREVER I'M NEEDED.
SO WHY HERE?
WHAT HAPPENED TO NEW YORK?
IT'S LIKE A DREAM!
LIKE SOME PARALLEL WORLD!
OR MORE LIKE A GENERIC, POST-APOCALYPTIC URBAN WASTELAND!
AN ERSATZ WORLD WHERE THE FORCES OF EVIL SOMEHOW WON THE ETERNAL BATTLE AGAINST GOOD!
HN.

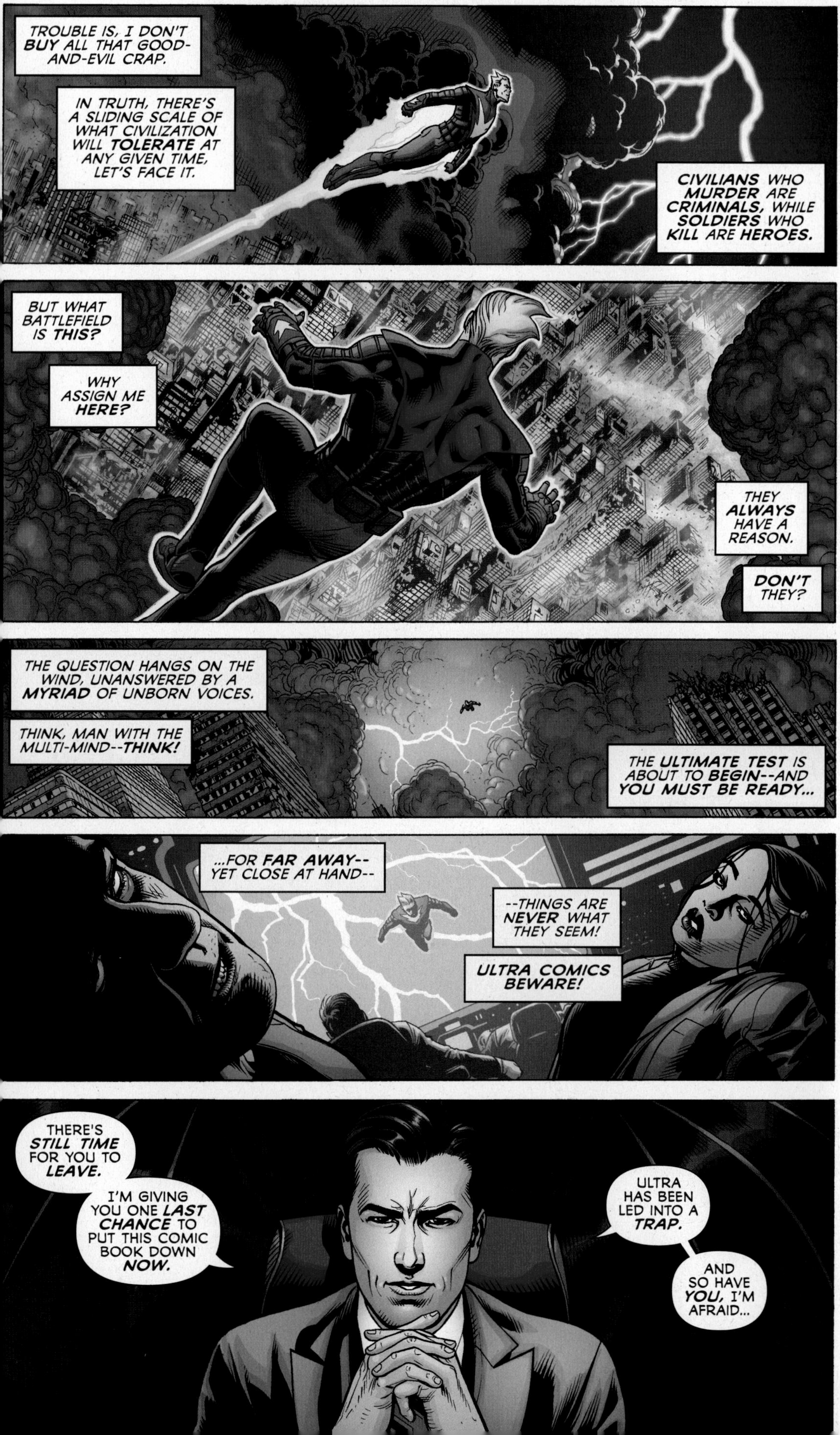
TROUBLE IS, I DON'T BUY ALL THAT GOOD-AND-EVIL CRAP.
IN TRUTH, THERE'S A SLIDING SCALE OF WHAT CIVILIZATION WILL TOLERATE AT ANY GIVEN TIME, LET'S FACE IT.
CIVILIANS WHO MURDER ARE CRIMINALS, WHILE SOLDIERS WHO KILL ARE HEROES.
BUT WHAT BATTLEFIELD IS THIS?
WHY ASSIGN ME HERE?
THEY ALWAYS HAVE A REASON.
DON'T THEY?
THE QUESTION HANGS ON THE WIND, UNANSWERED BY A MYRIAD OF UNBORN VOICES.
THINK, MAN WITH THE MULTI-MIND--THINK!
THE ULTIMATE TEST IS ABOUT TO BEGIN--AND YOU MUST BE READY...
...FOR FAR AWAY-- YET CLOSE AT HAND--
--THINGS ARE NEVER WHAT THEY SEEM!
ULTRA COMICS BEWARE!
THERE'S STILL TIME FOR YOU TO LEAVE.
I'M GIVING YOU ONE LAST CHANCE TO PUT THIS COMIC BOOK DOWN NOW.
ULTRA HAS BEEN LED INTO A TRAP.
AND SO HAVE YOU, I'M AFRAID...

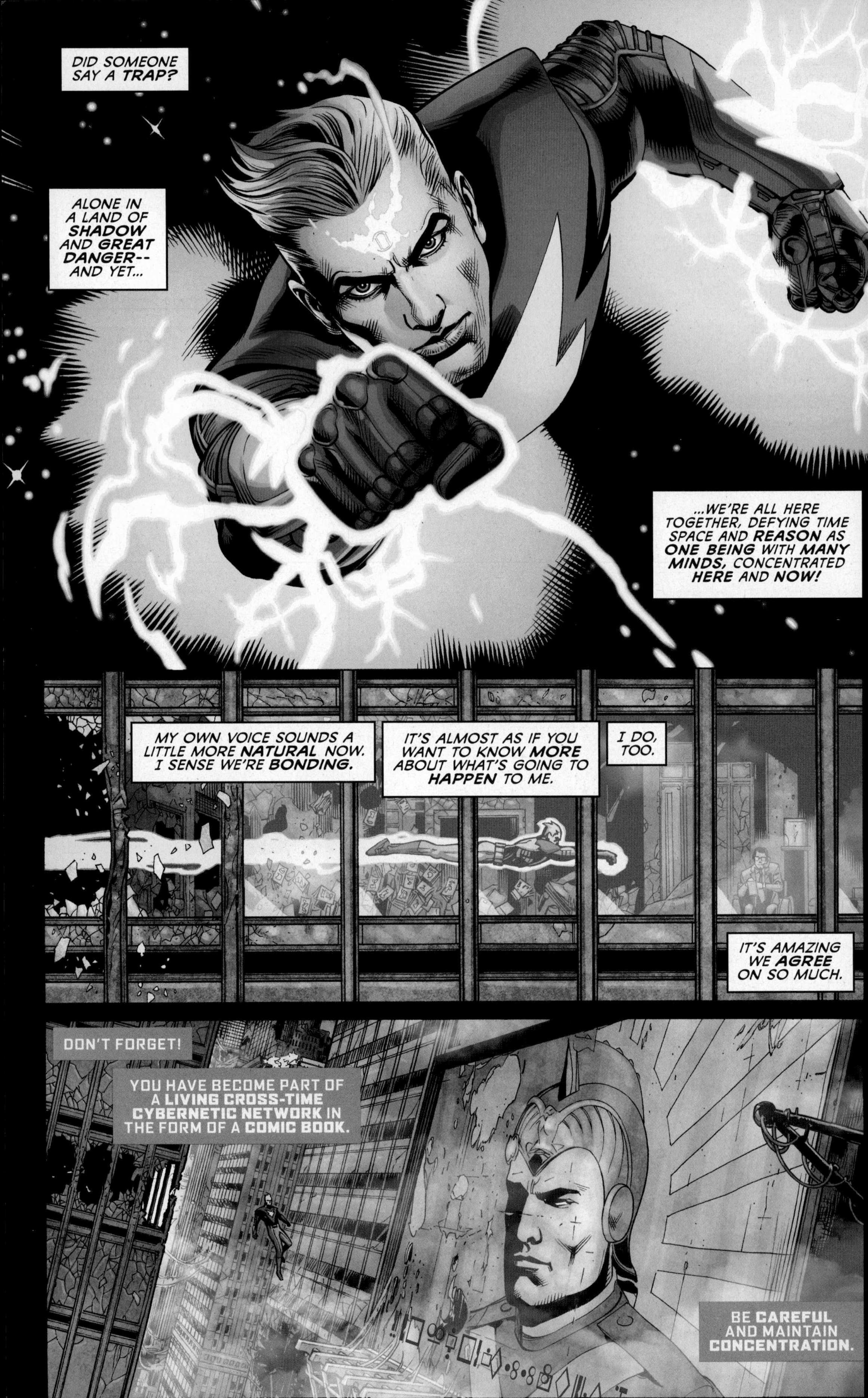

DID SOMEONE SAY A TRAP?
ALONE IN A LAND OF SHADOW AND GREAT DANGER-- AND YET...
...WE'RE ALL HERE TOGETHER, DEFYING TIME SPACE AND REASON AS ONE BEING WITH MANY MINDS, CONCENTRATED HERE AND NOW!
MY OWN VOICE SOUNDS A LITTLE MORE NATURAL NOW. I SENSE WE'RE BONDING.
IT'S ALMOST AS IF YOU WANT TO KNOW MORE ABOUT WHAT'S GOING TO HAPPEN TO ME.
I DO, TOO.
IT'S AMAZING WE AGREE ON SO MUCH.
DON'T FORGET!
YOU HAVE BECOME PART OF A LIVING CROSS-TIME CYBERNETIC NETWORK IN THE FORM OF A COMIC BOOK.
BE CAREFUL AND MAINTAIN CONCENTRATION.

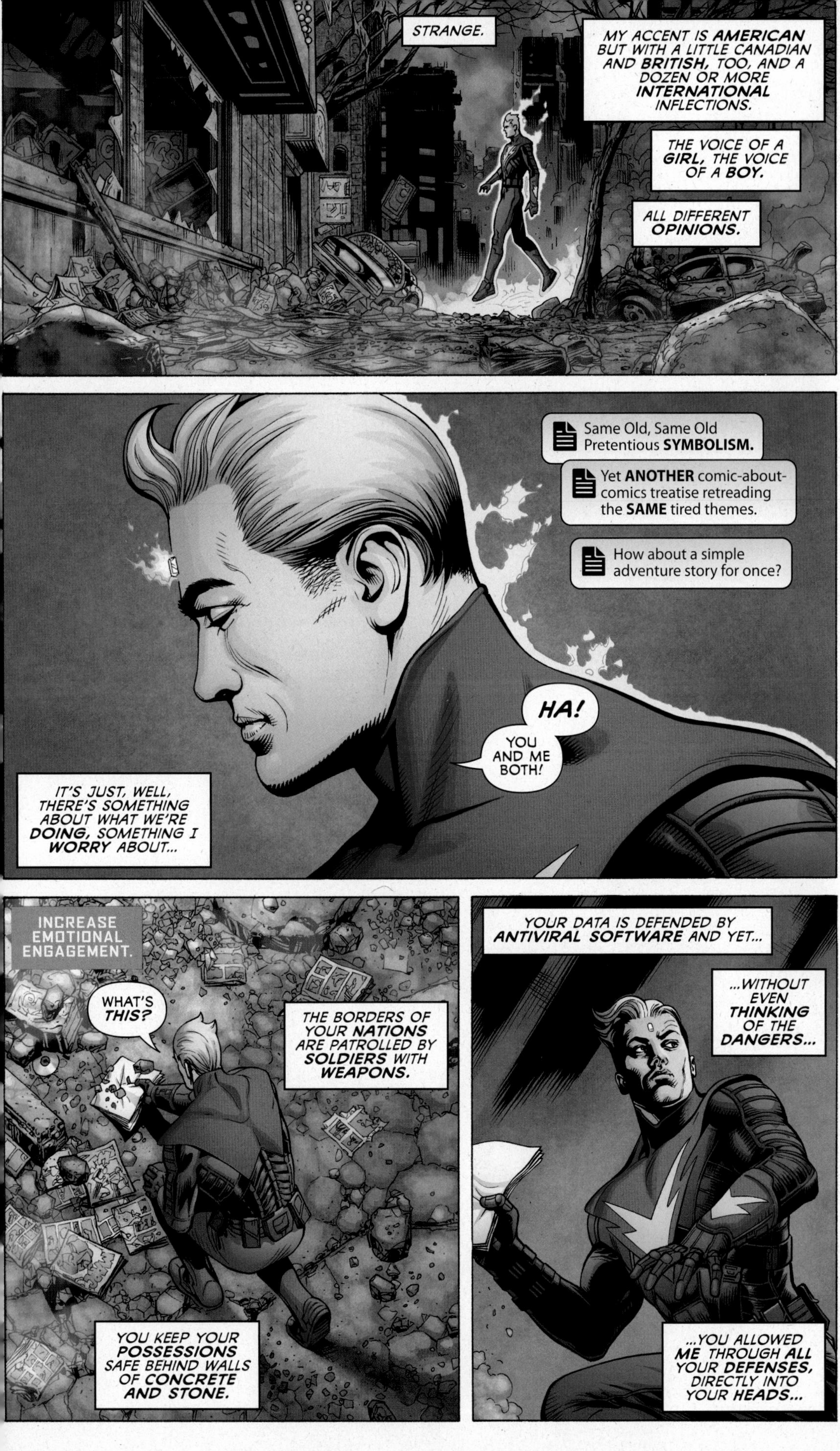
STRANGE.
MY ACCENT IS AMERICAN BUT WITH A LITTLE CANADIAN AND BRITISH, TOO, AND A DOZEN OR MORE INTERNATIONAL INFLECTIONS.
THE VOICE OF A GIRL, THE VOICE OF A BOY.
ALL DIFFERENT OPINIONS.
Same Old, Same Old Pretentious SYMBOLISM.
Yet ANOTHER comic-about-comics treatise retreading the SAME tired themes.
How about a simple adventure story for once?
HA!
YOU AND ME BOTH!
IT'S JUST, WELL, THERE'S SOMETHING ABOUT WHAT WE'RE DOING, SOMETHING I WORRY ABOUT...
INCREASE EMOTIONAL ENGAGEMENT.
WHAT'S THIS?
THE BORDERS OF YOUR NATIONS ARE PATROLLED BY SOLDIERS WITH WEAPONS.
YOU KEEP YOUR POSSESSIONS SAFE BEHIND WALLS OF CONCRETE AND STONE.
YOUR DATA IS DEFENDED BY ANTIVIRAL SOFTWARE AND YET...
...WITHOUT EVEN THINKING OF THE DANGERS...
...YOU ALLOWED ME THROUGH ALL YOUR DEFENSES, DIRECTLY INTO YOUR HEADS...

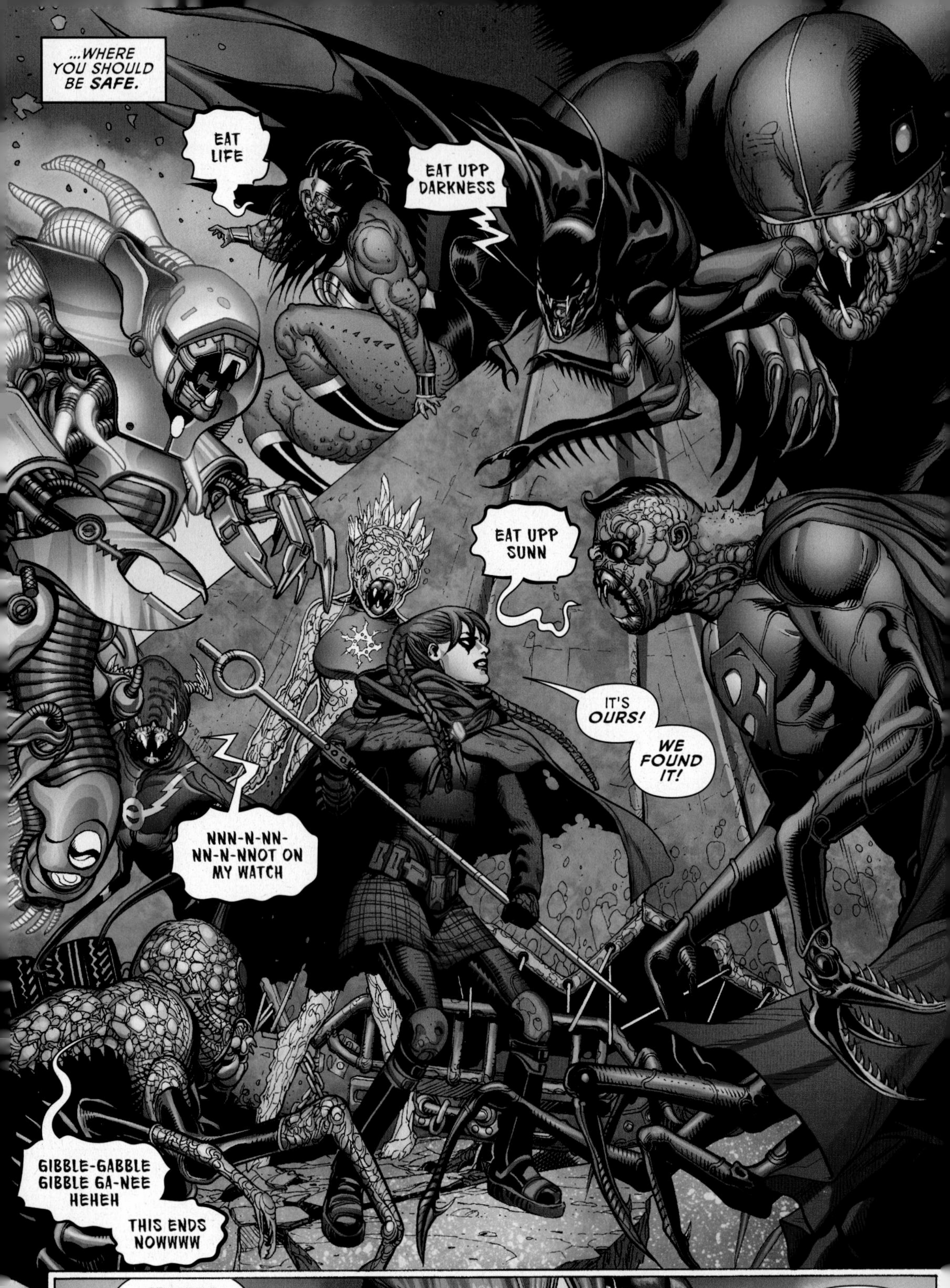
...WHERE YOU SHOULD BE SAFE.
EAT LIFE
EAT UPP DARKNESS
EAT UPP SUNN
IT'S OURS!
WE FOUND IT!
NNN-N-NN-NN-N-NNOT ON MY WATCH
GIBBLE-GABBLE GIBBLE GA-NEE HEHEH
THIS ENDS NOWWWW

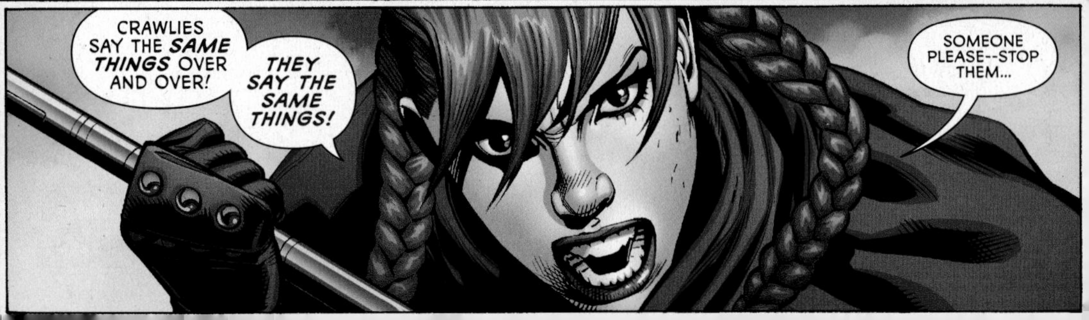
CRAWLIES SAY THE SAME THINGS OVER AND OVER!
THEY SAY THE SAME THINGS!
SOMEONE PLEASE--STOP THEM...

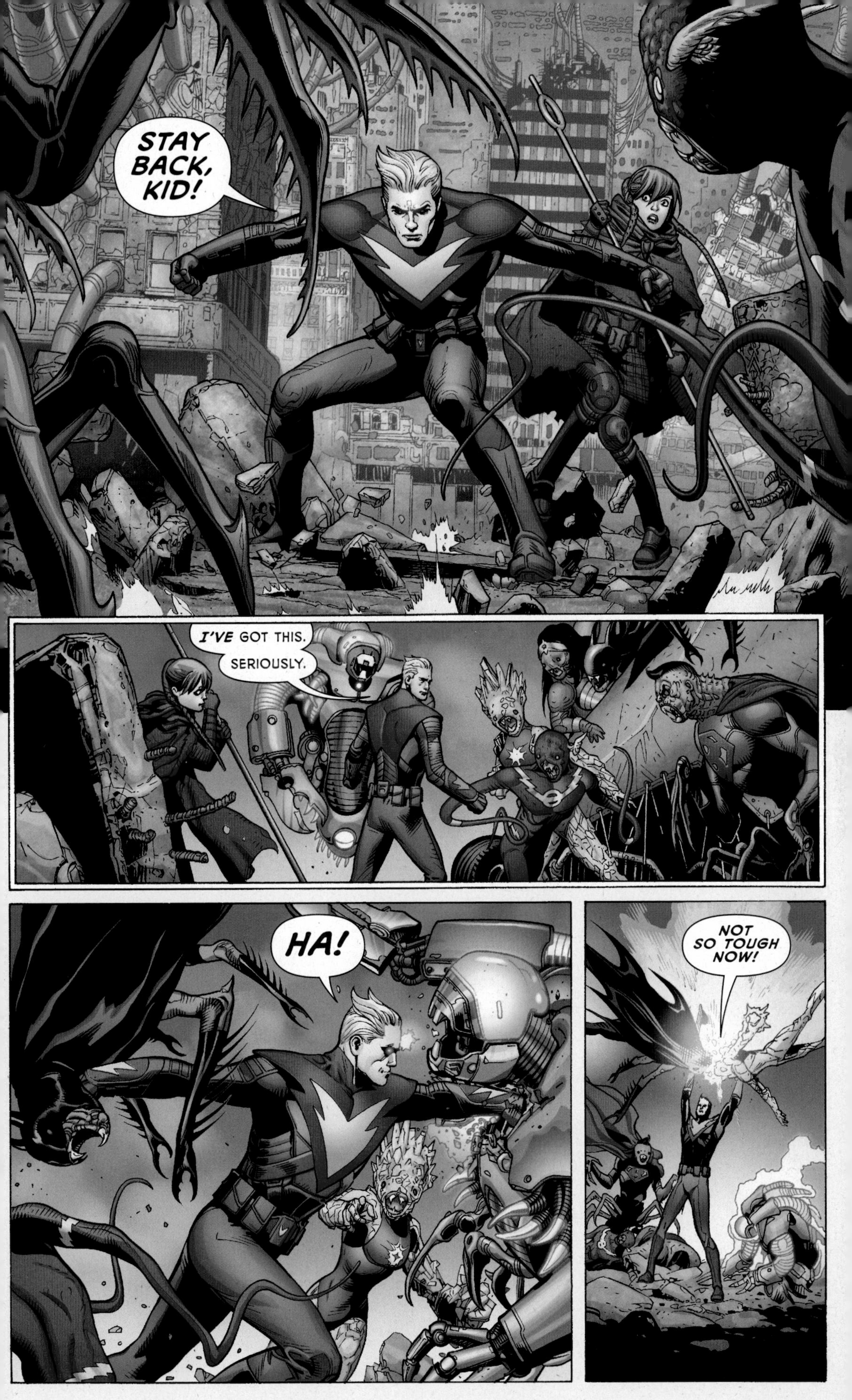
STAY BACK, KID!
I'VE GOT THIS.
SERIOUSLY.
HA!
NOT SO TOUGH NOW!

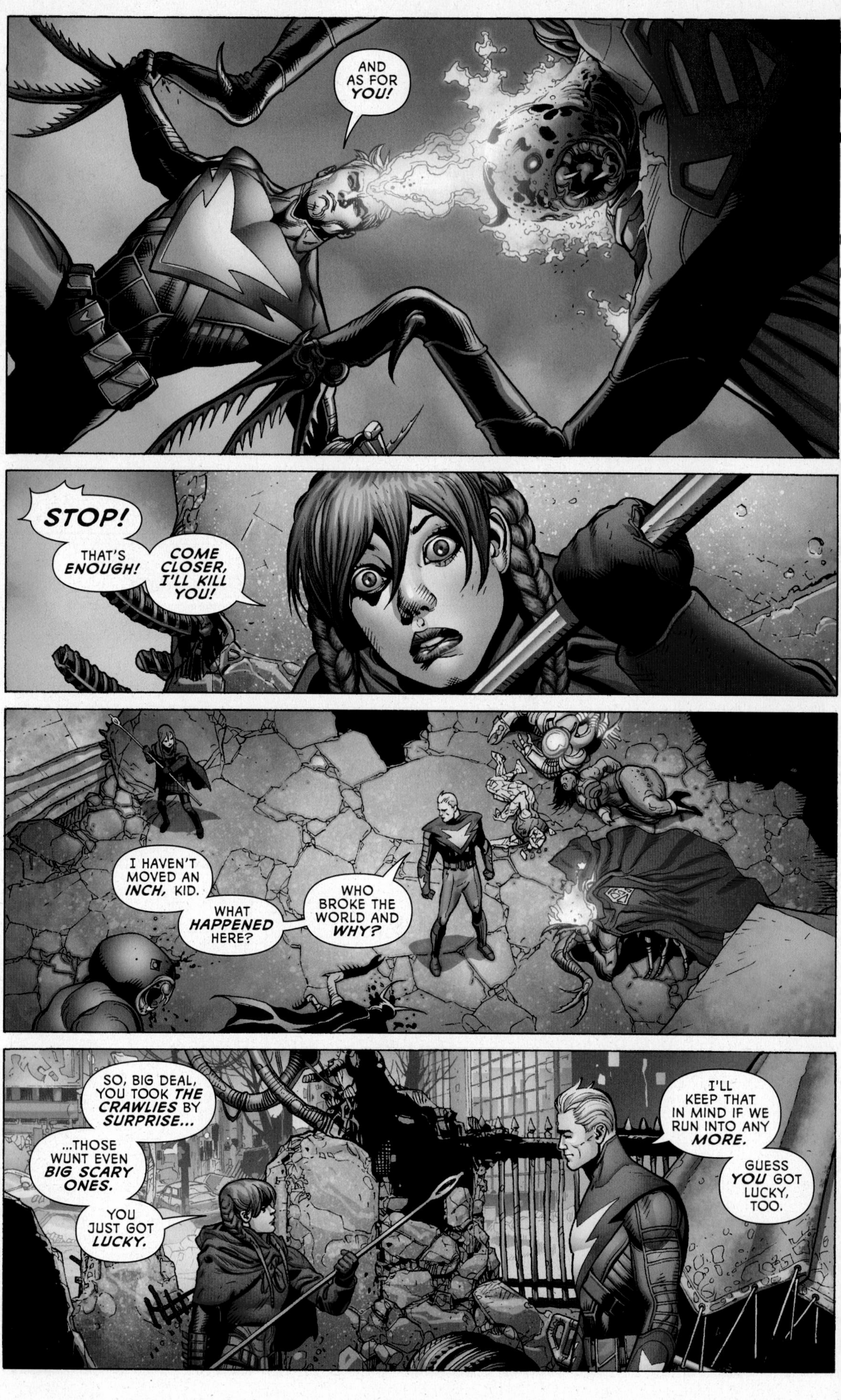

AND AS FOR *YOU!*
STOP!
THAT'S *ENOUGH!*
COME CLOSER, I'LL KILL YOU!
I HAVEN'T MOVED AN *INCH,* KID.
WHAT *HAPPENED* HERE?
WHO BROKE THE WORLD AND *WHY?*
SO, BIG DEAL, YOU TOOK *THE CRAWLIES* BY *SURPRISE...*
...THOSE WUNT EVEN *BIG SCARY ONES.*
YOU JUST GOT *LUCKY.*
I'LL KEEP THAT IN MIND IF WE RUN INTO ANY *MORE.*
GUESS *YOU* GOT LUCKY, TOO.

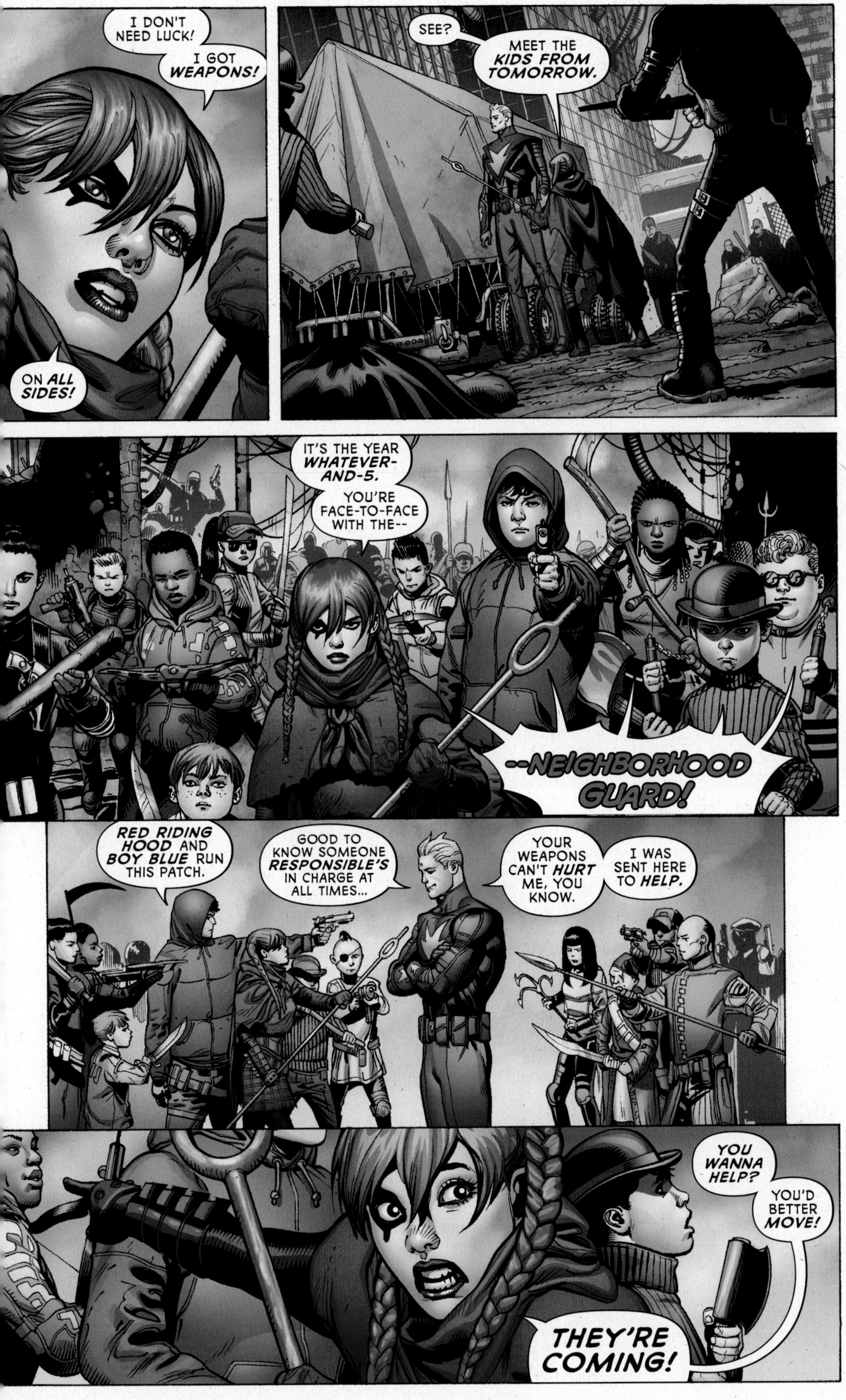
I DON'T NEED LUCK!
I GOT *WEAPONS!*
ON *ALL SIDES!*
SEE?
MEET THE *KIDS FROM TOMORROW.*
IT'S THE YEAR *WHATEVER-AND-5.*
YOU'RE FACE-TO-FACE WITH THE--
--NEIGHBORHOOD GUARD!
RED RIDING HOOD AND *BOY BLUE* RUN THIS PATCH.
GOOD TO KNOW SOMEONE *RESPONSIBLE'S* IN CHARGE AT ALL TIMES...
YOUR WEAPONS CAN'T *HURT* ME, YOU KNOW.
I WAS SENT HERE TO *HELP.*
YOU WANNA HELP?
YOU'D BETTER *MOVE!*
THEY'RE COMING!

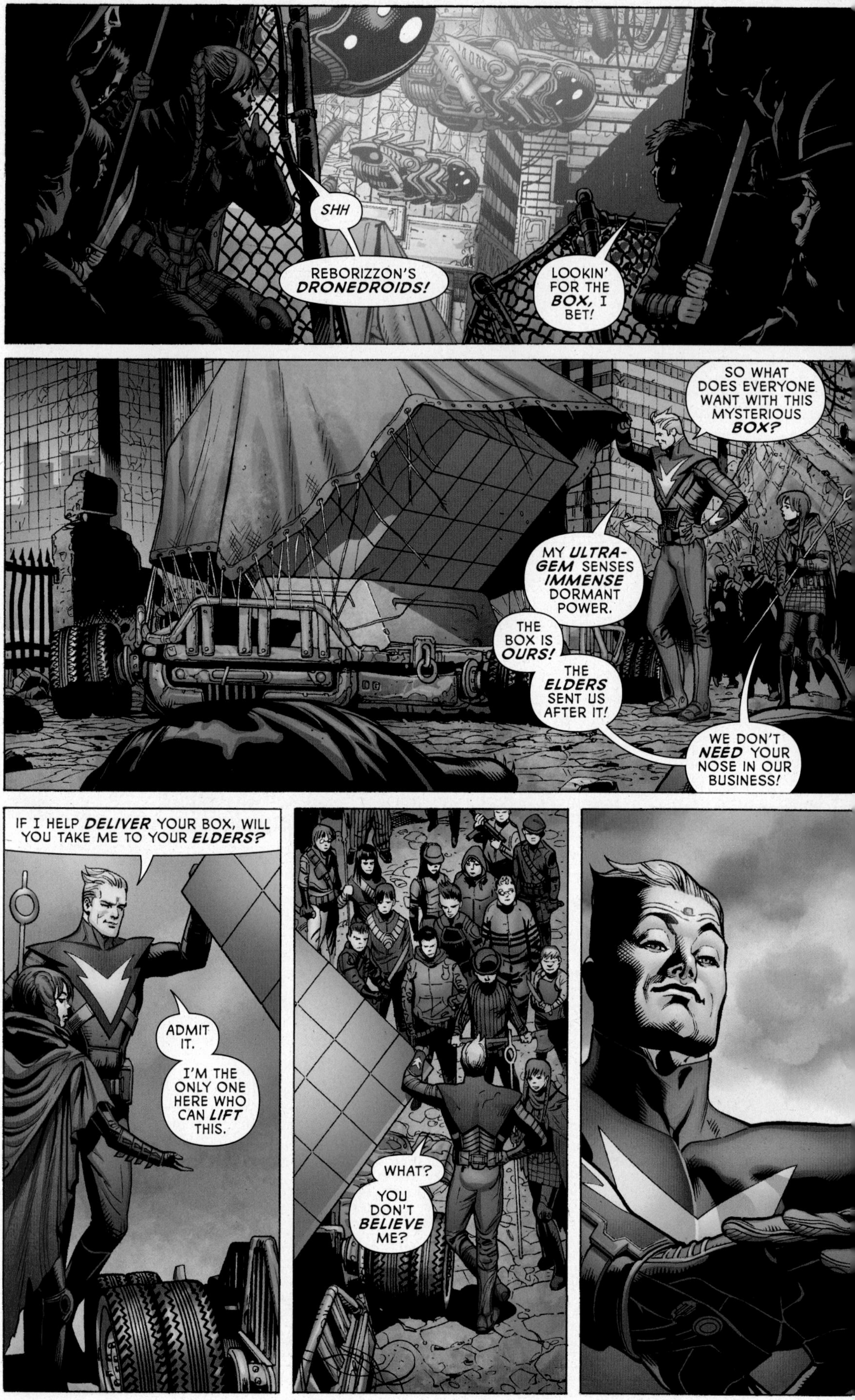
SHH
REBORIZZON'S DRONEDROIDS!
LOOKIN' FOR THE BOX, I BET!
SO WHAT DOES EVERYONE WANT WITH THIS MYSTERIOUS BOX?
MY ULTRA-GEM SENSES IMMENSE DORMANT POWER.
THE BOX IS OURS!
THE ELDERS SENT US AFTER IT!
WE DON'T NEED YOUR NOSE IN OUR BUSINESS!
IF I HELP DELIVER YOUR BOX, WILL YOU TAKE ME TO YOUR ELDERS?
ADMIT IT.
I'M THE ONLY ONE HERE WHO CAN LIFT THIS.
WHAT?
YOU DON'T BELIEVE ME?

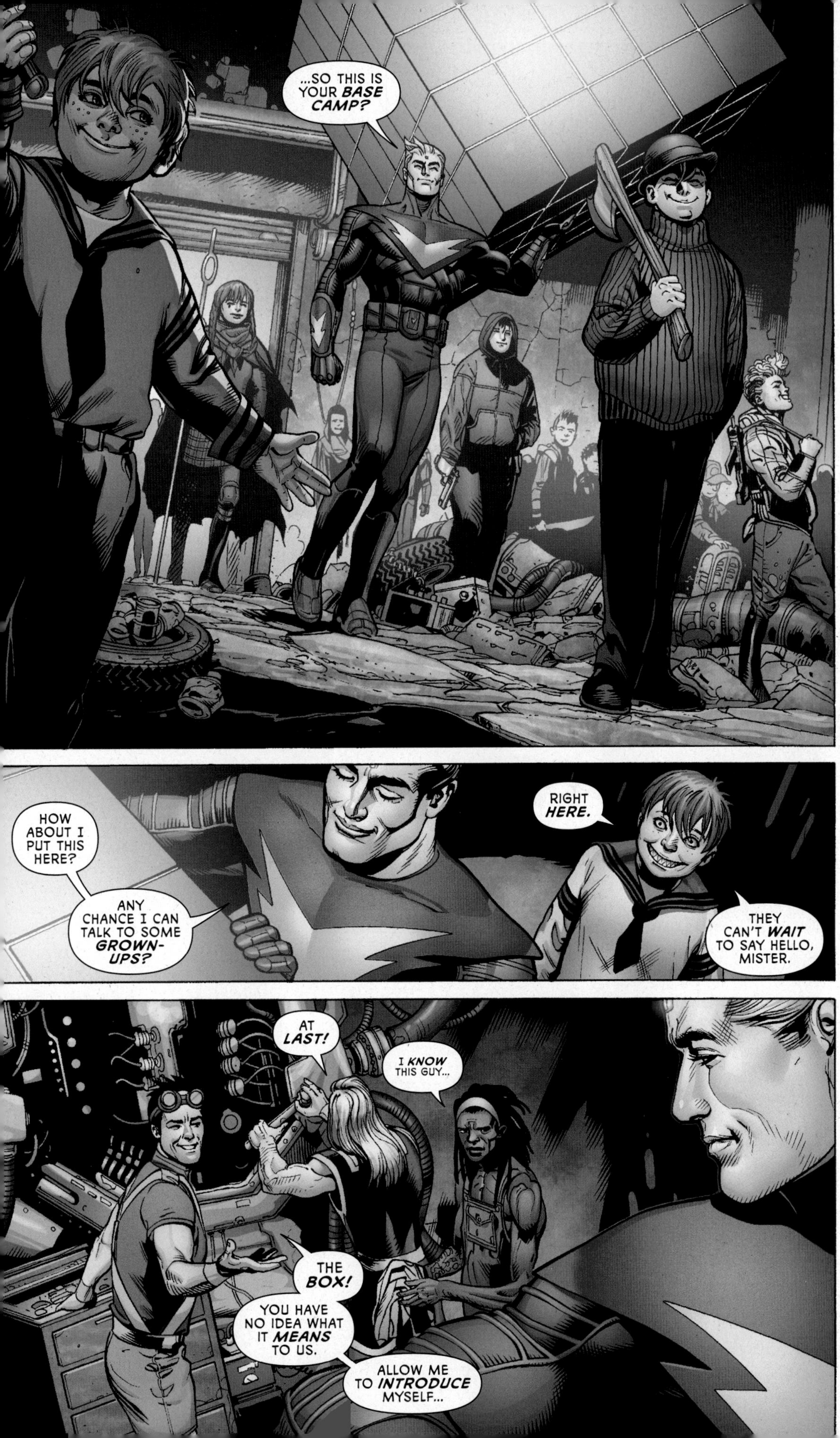
...SO THIS IS YOUR BASE CAMP?
HOW ABOUT I PUT THIS HERE?
ANY CHANCE I CAN TALK TO SOME GROWN-UPS?
RIGHT HERE.
THEY CAN'T WAIT TO SAY HELLO, MISTER.
AT LAST!
I KNOW THIS GUY...
THE BOX!
YOU HAVE NO IDEA WHAT IT MEANS TO US.
ALLOW ME TO INTRODUCE MYSELF...

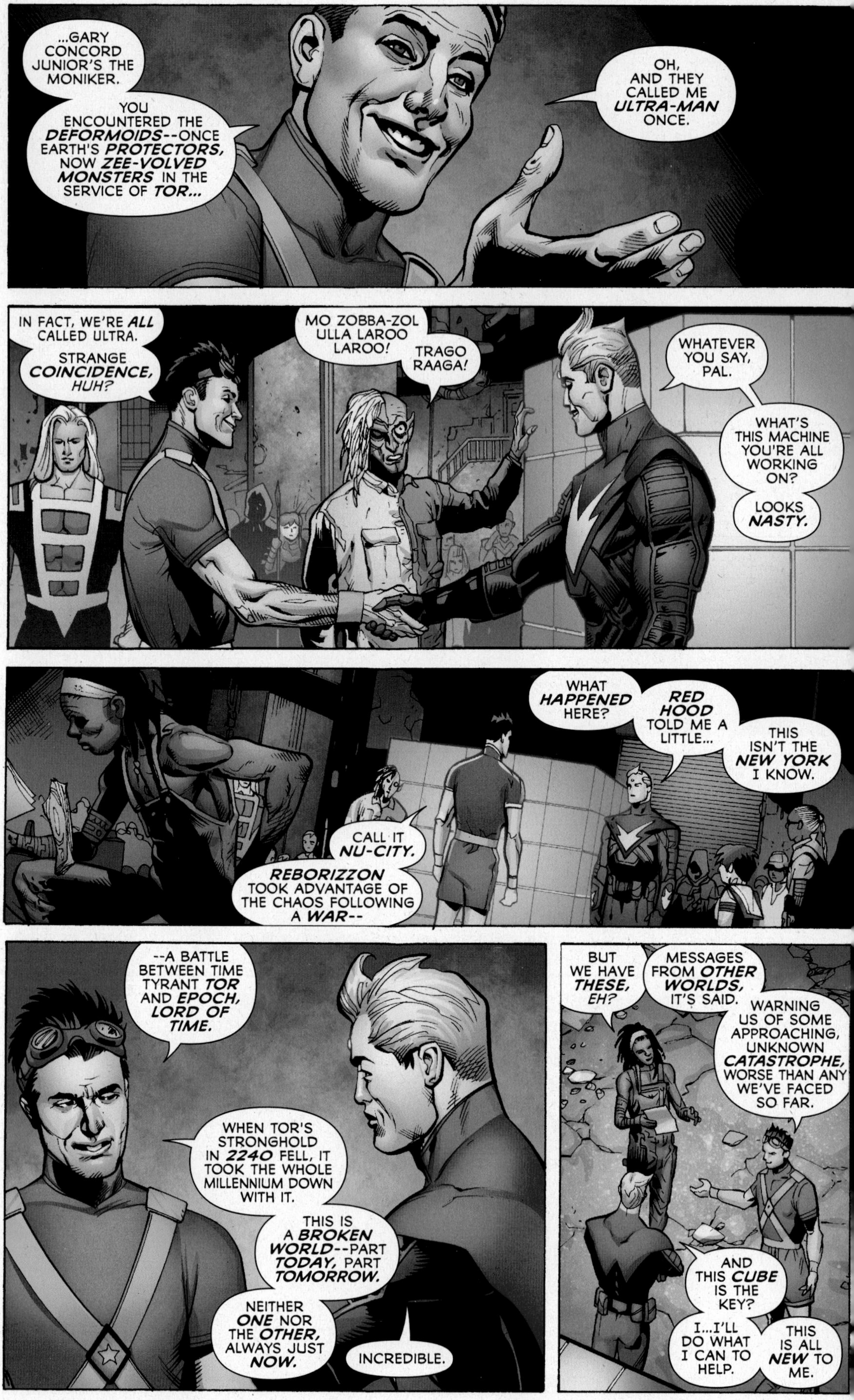
...GARY CONCORD JUNIOR'S THE MONIKER.
YOU ENCOUNTERED THE DEFORMOIDS--ONCE EARTH'S PROTECTORS, NOW ZEE-VOLVED MONSTERS IN THE SERVICE OF TOR...
OH, AND THEY CALLED ME ULTRA-MAN ONCE.
IN FACT, WE'RE ALL CALLED ULTRA.
STRANGE COINCIDENCE, HUH?
MO ZOBBA-ZOL ULLA LAROO LAROO!
TRAGO RAAGA!
WHATEVER YOU SAY, PAL.
WHAT'S THIS MACHINE YOU'RE ALL WORKING ON?
LOOKS NASTY.
WHAT HAPPENED HERE?
RED HOOD TOLD ME A LITTLE...
THIS ISN'T THE NEW YORK I KNOW.
CALL IT NU-CITY.
REBORIZZON TOOK ADVANTAGE OF THE CHAOS FOLLOWING A WAR--
--A BATTLE BETWEEN TIME TYRANT TOR AND EPOCH, LORD OF TIME.
WHEN TOR'S STRONGHOLD IN 2240 FELL, IT TOOK THE WHOLE MILLENNIUM DOWN WITH IT.
THIS IS A BROKEN WORLD--PART TODAY, PART TOMORROW.
NEITHER ONE NOR THE OTHER, ALWAYS JUST NOW.
INCREDIBLE.
BUT WE HAVE THESE, EH?
MESSAGES FROM OTHER WORLDS, IT'S SAID.
WARNING US OF SOME APPROACHING, UNKNOWN CATASTROPHE, WORSE THAN ANY WE'VE FACED SO FAR.
AND THIS CUBE IS THE KEY?
I...I'LL DO WHAT I CAN TO HELP.
THIS IS ALL NEW TO ME.

EACH *IS A WARNING*-- A CHAIN--AN *S.O.S.!*

AND *THIS!* THIS IS HOW I KNEW *YOU!*

THAT'S HOW MY *BODY* MIGHT LOOK FROM *OUTSIDE,* SURE.

BUT *I'M* NOT MISSING MOST OF *MY* CONTENT, AND I--

SAVE THE WORLD!

IF YOU VALUE YOUR LIVES, YOU *MUST* READ THIS COMIC!

ULTRA COMICS

HOW IS THIS A *BODY?*

HOW CAN THIS BE *YOU?*

EXPLAIN YOURSELF!

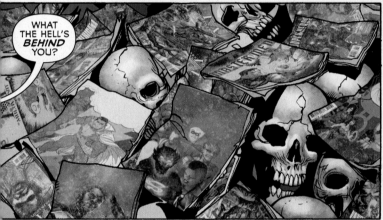

WHAT THE HELL'S *BEHIND* YOU?

SKULLS?

WAIT A MINUTE!

NOW I UNDERSTAND.

YOU'RE-- *SUPER-CANNIBALS!*

THE *DEFORMOIDS* KEPT THE ULTRABOX *SAFE*--NOT EVEN THE *ULTRA-KING* COULD *GET* TO IT UNTIL *YOU* CAME ALONG!

YOU ASKED WHAT WE WERE *BUILDING?*

ACE ARN, OUR SPACEMAN FROM THE FAR-FLUNG *FUTURE,* CAN EXPLAIN BETTER THAN ME--

ULTRA! BEHIND YOU!

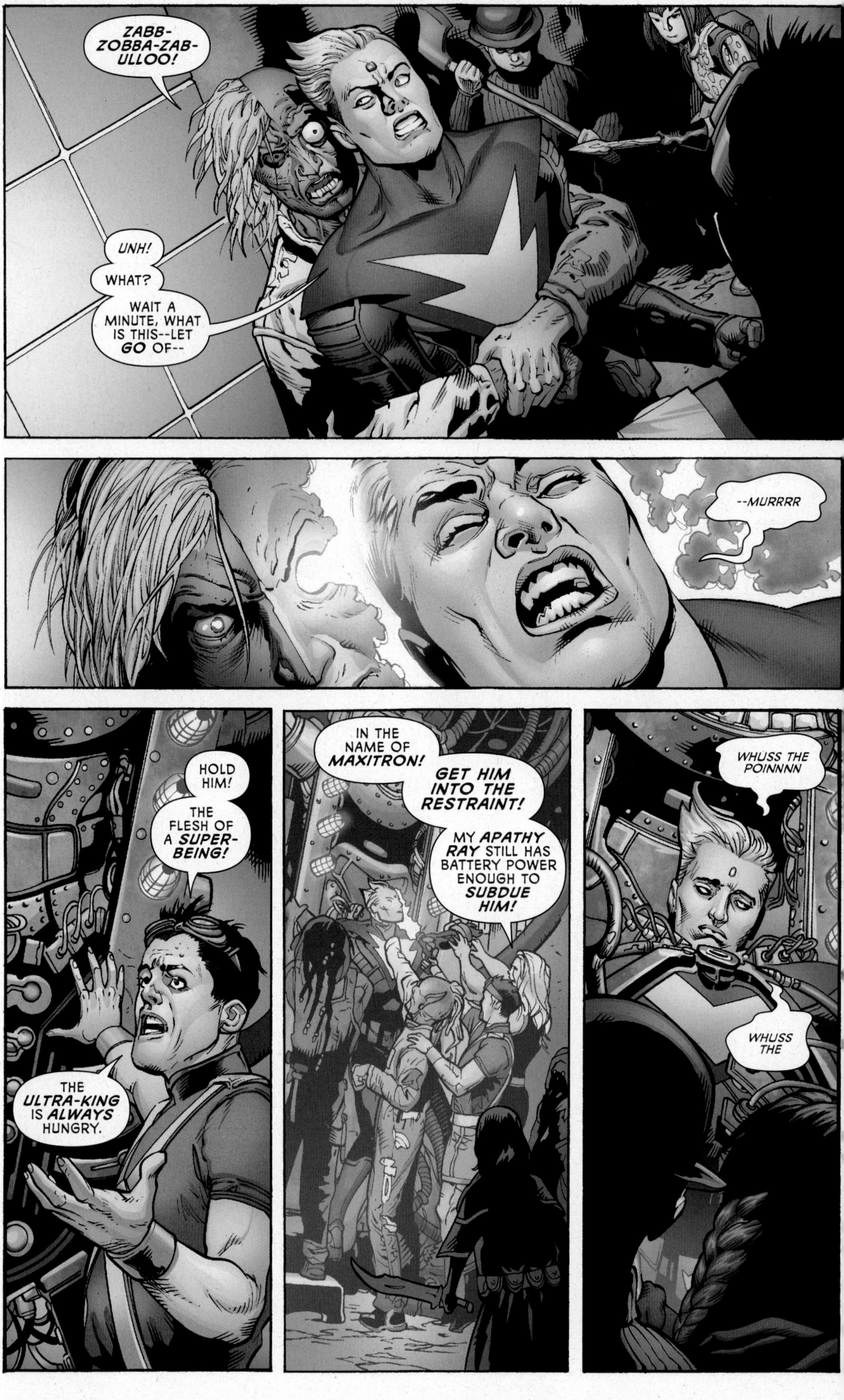
ZABB-ZOBBA-ZAB-ULLOO!
UNH!
WHAT?
WAIT A MINUTE, WHAT IS THIS--LET GO OF--
--MURRRR
HOLD HIM!
THE FLESH OF A SUPER-BEING!
THE ULTRA-KING IS ALWAYS HUNGRY.
IN THE NAME OF MAXITRON!
GET HIM INTO THE RESTRAINT!
MY APATHY RAY STILL HAS BATTERY POWER ENOUGH TO SUBDUE HIM!
WHUSS THE POINNNN
WHUSS THE

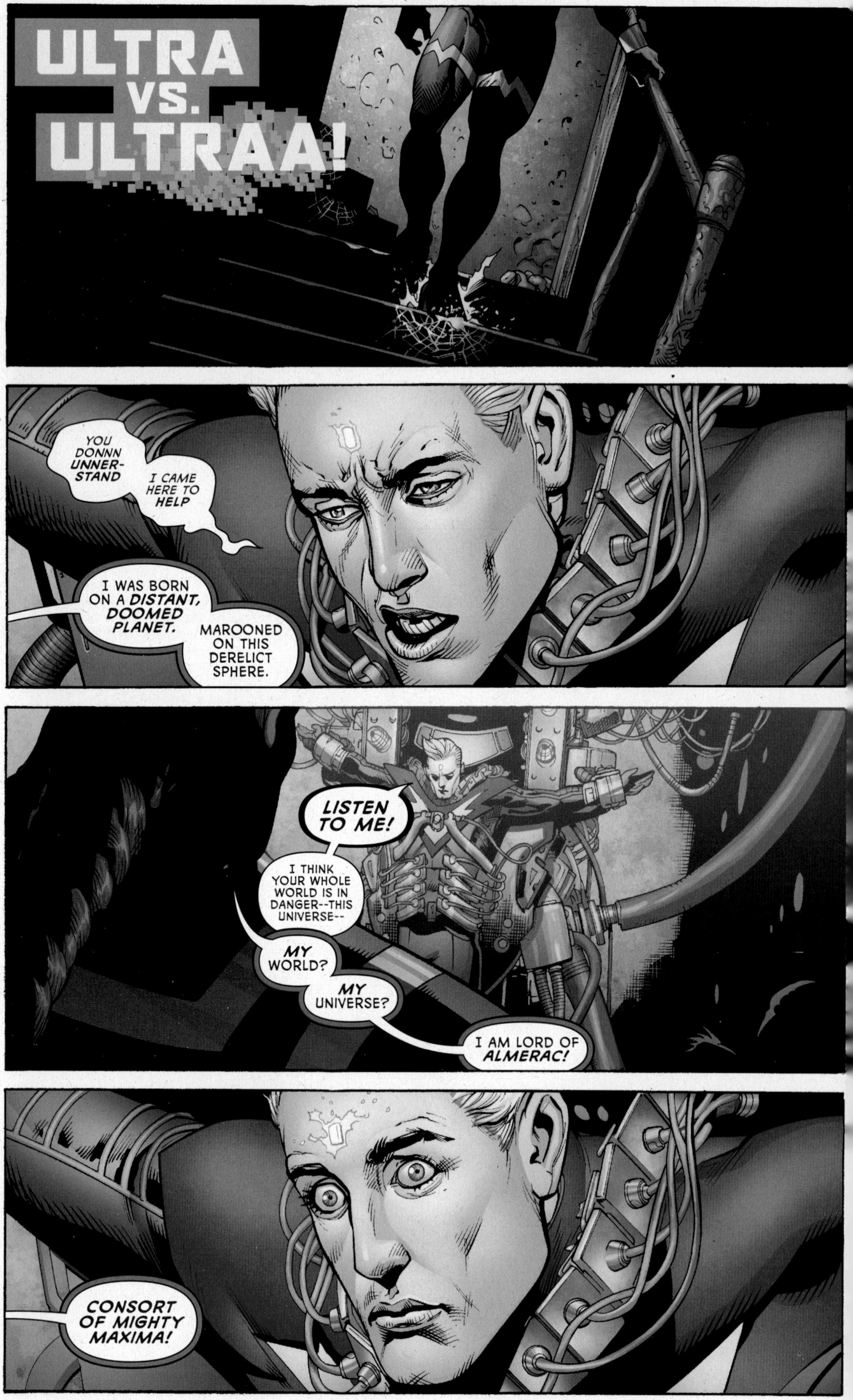
ULTRA VS. ULTRAA!
YOU DONNN UNNER-STAND
I CAME HERE TO HELP
I WAS BORN ON A DISTANT, DOOMED PLANET.
MAROONED ON THIS DERELICT SPHERE.
LISTEN TO ME!
I THINK YOUR WHOLE WORLD IS IN DANGER--THIS UNIVERSE--
MY WORLD?
MY UNIVERSE?
I AM LORD OF ALMERAC!
CONSORT OF MIGHTY MAXIMA!

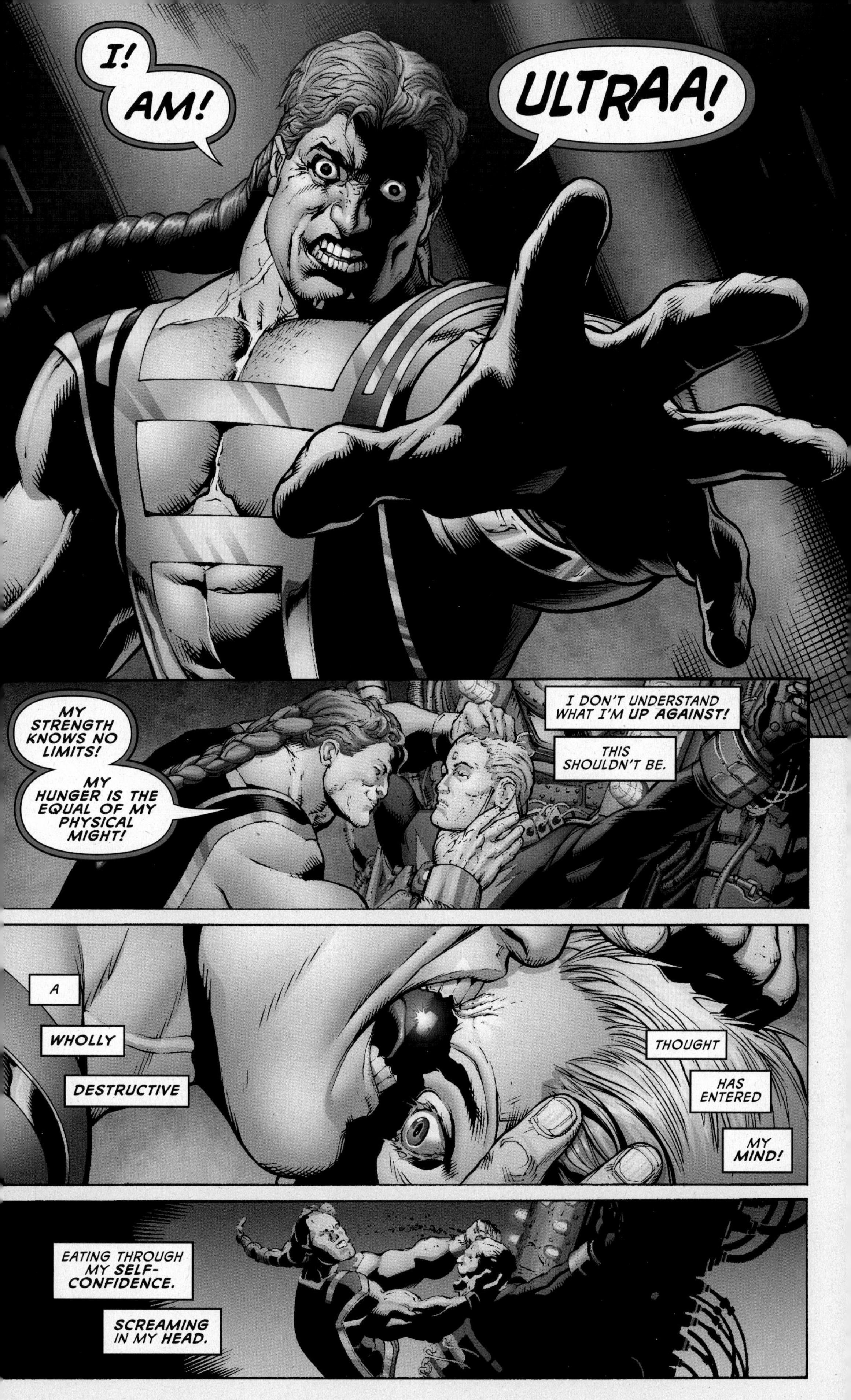
I!
AM!
ULTRAA!
MY STRENGTH KNOWS NO LIMITS!
MY HUNGER IS THE EQUAL OF MY PHYSICAL MIGHT!
I DON'T UNDERSTAND WHAT I'M UP AGAINST!
THIS SHOULDN'T BE.
A
WHOLLY
DESTRUCTIVE
THOUGHT
HAS ENTERED
MY MIND!
EATING THROUGH MY SELF-CONFIDENCE.
SCREAMING IN MY HEAD.

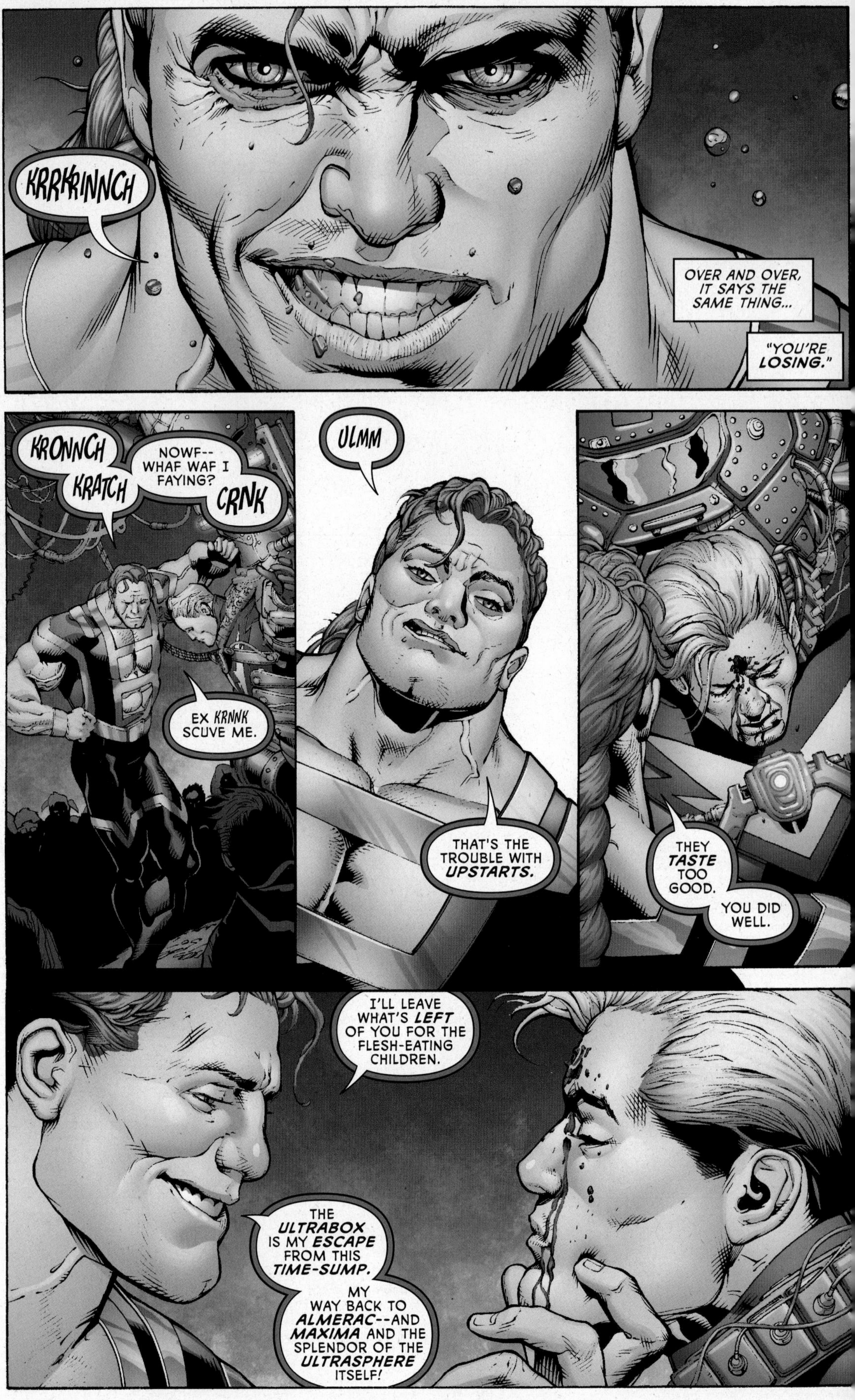
KRRKRINNCH
OVER AND OVER, IT SAYS THE SAME THING...
"YOU'RE LOSING."
KRONNCH
KRATCH
NOWF-- WHAF WAF I FAYING?
CRNK
EX KRNNK SCUVE ME.
ULMM
THAT'S THE TROUBLE WITH UPSTARTS.
THEY TASTE TOO GOOD.
YOU DID WELL.
I'LL LEAVE WHAT'S LEFT OF YOU FOR THE FLESH-EATING CHILDREN.
THE ULTRABOX IS MY ESCAPE FROM THIS TIME-SUMP.
MY WAY BACK TO ALMERAC--AND MAXIMA AND THE SPLENDOR OF THE ULTRASPHERE ITSELF!

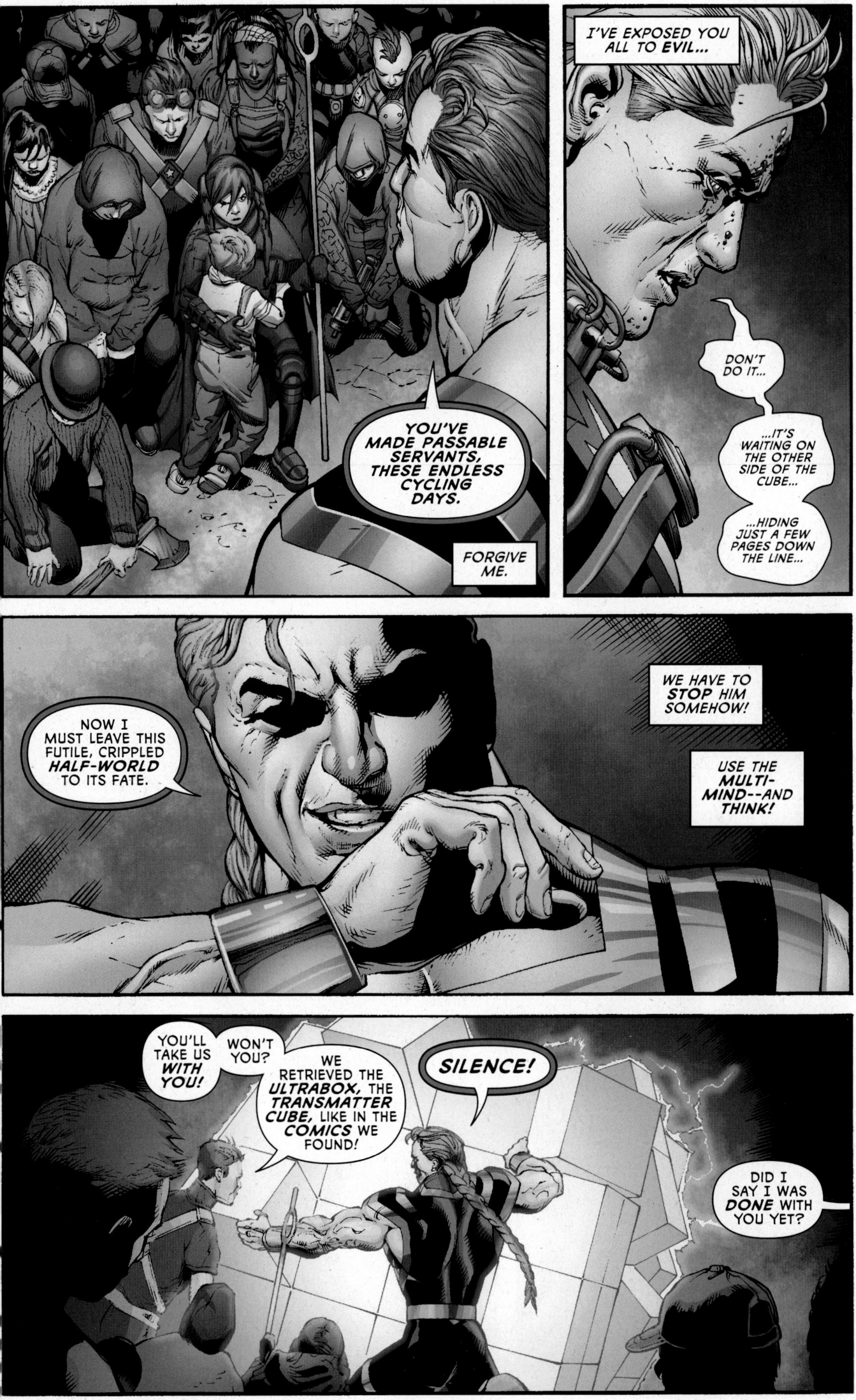
YOU'VE MADE PASSABLE SERVANTS, THESE ENDLESS CYCLING DAYS.
FORGIVE ME.
I'VE EXPOSED YOU ALL TO EVIL...
DON'T DO IT...
...IT'S WAITING ON THE OTHER SIDE OF THE CUBE...
...HIDING JUST A FEW PAGES DOWN THE LINE...
NOW I MUST LEAVE THIS FUTILE, CRIPPLED HALF-WORLD TO ITS FATE.
WE HAVE TO STOP HIM SOMEHOW!
USE THE MULTI-MIND--AND THINK!
YOU'LL TAKE US WITH YOU!
WON'T YOU?
WE RETRIEVED THE ULTRABOX, THE TRANSMATTER CUBE, LIKE IN THE COMICS WE FOUND!
SILENCE!
DID I SAY I WAS DONE WITH YOU YET?

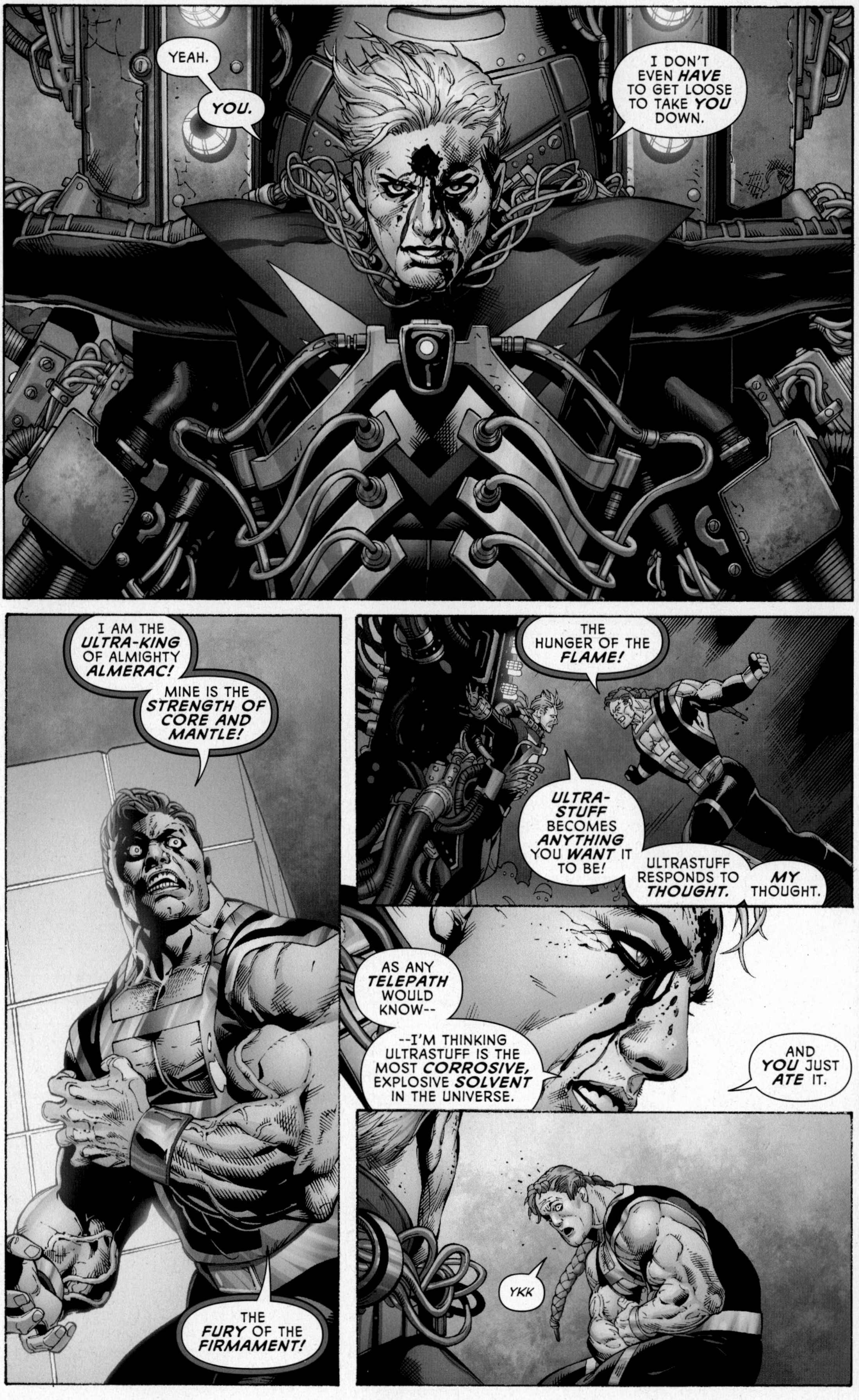
YEAH.
YOU.
I DON'T EVEN HAVE TO GET LOOSE TO TAKE YOU DOWN.
I AM THE ULTRA-KING OF ALMIGHTY ALMERAC!
MINE IS THE STRENGTH OF CORE AND MANTLE!
THE FURY OF THE FIRMAMENT!
THE HUNGER OF THE FLAME!
ULTRA-STUFF BECOMES ANYTHING YOU WANT IT TO BE!
ULTRASTUFF RESPONDS TO THOUGHT.
MY THOUGHT.
AS ANY TELEPATH WOULD KNOW--
--I'M THINKING ULTRASTUFF IS THE MOST CORROSIVE, EXPLOSIVE SOLVENT IN THE UNIVERSE.
AND YOU JUST ATE IT.
YKK

GET ME *OUT* OF THIS!

I'VE MADE A TERRIBLE *MISTAKE*--IT'S A *TRAP*.

THE *WHOLE THING* WAS BUILT TO *LURE* A HOSTILE ALIEN--A *HIT*.

AURRR-HOCKK

HEAR THAT KNOCKING?

YOU LET ME INTO YOUR *HEADS*--INTO YOUR SECRET, PERSONAL *PRIVATE SPACE*--AND THAT'S *EXACTLY* WHAT THEY *WANTED*.

DON'T *ANSWER* THE DOOR.

REX ULTRAA WAS ALL WE HAD TO *PROTECT* US--

--FROM *THE THING IN THE BOX!*

SEE?

THIS IS ONLY SILLY COMM-IX--MAKES NO SENSE--

THE THING IN THE BOX!

ONLY PRETEND!

GO ON-- READ ON!

WHAT HARM CAN COME TO YU?

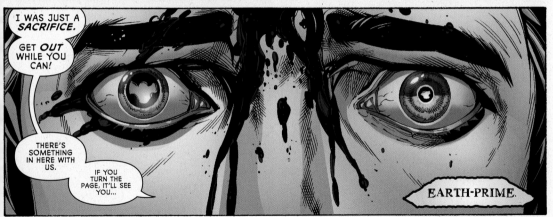

I WAS JUST A *SACRIFICE*.

GET *OUT* WHILE YOU CAN!

THERE'S SOMETHING IN HERE WITH US.

IF YOU TURN THE PAGE, IT'LL SEE YOU...

EARTH-PRIME.

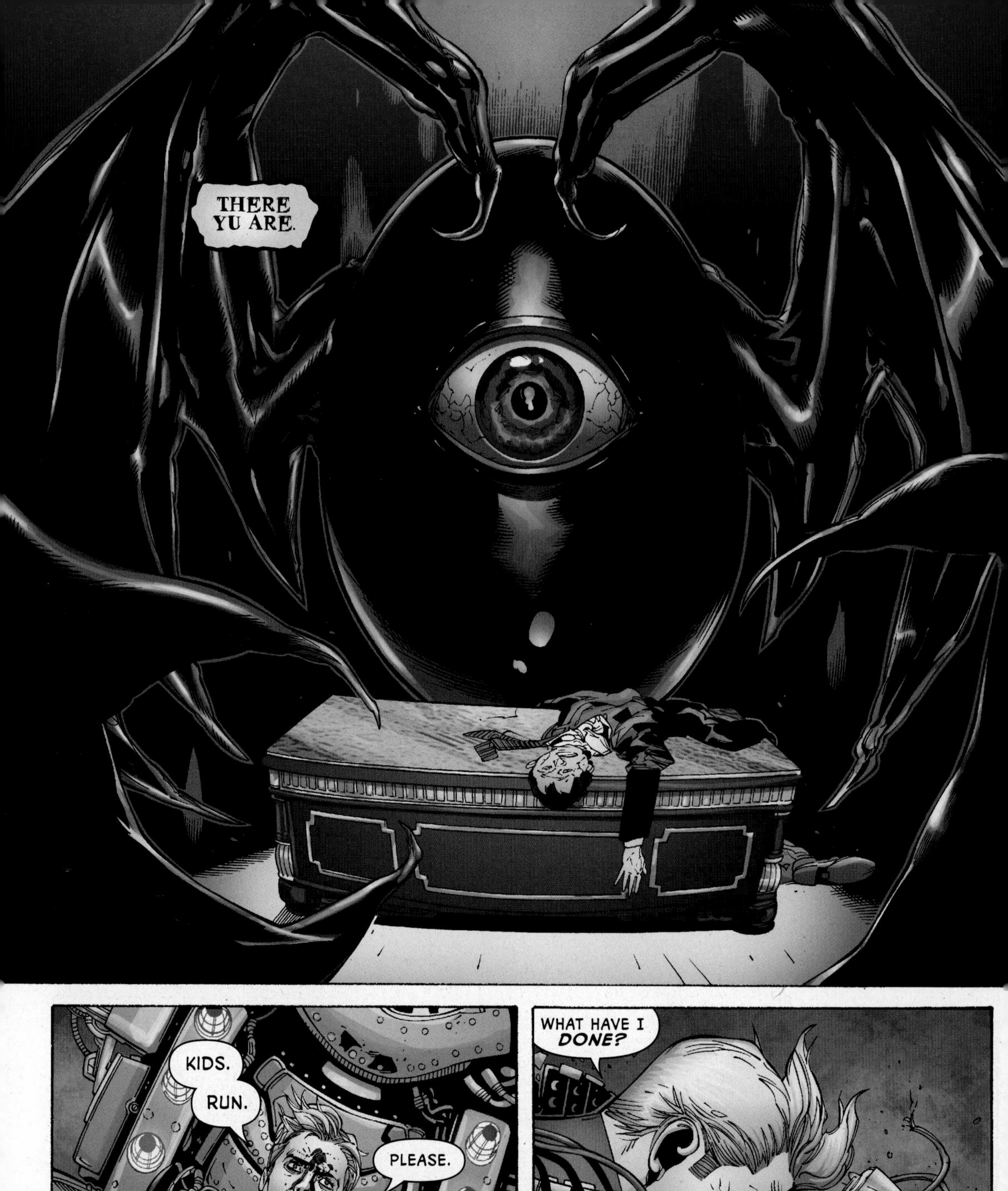
THERE YU ARE.

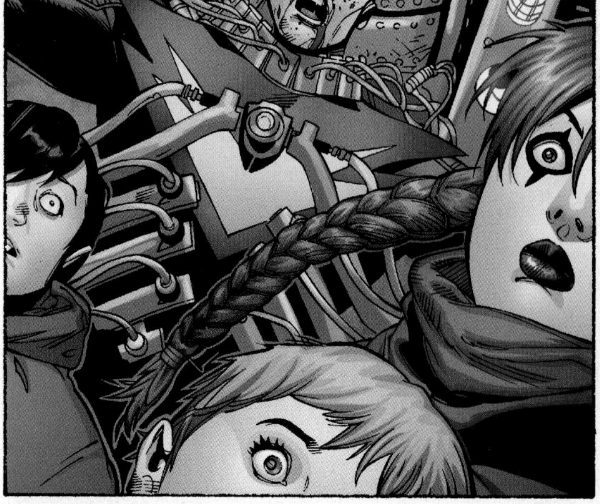
KIDS.
RUN.
PLEASE.

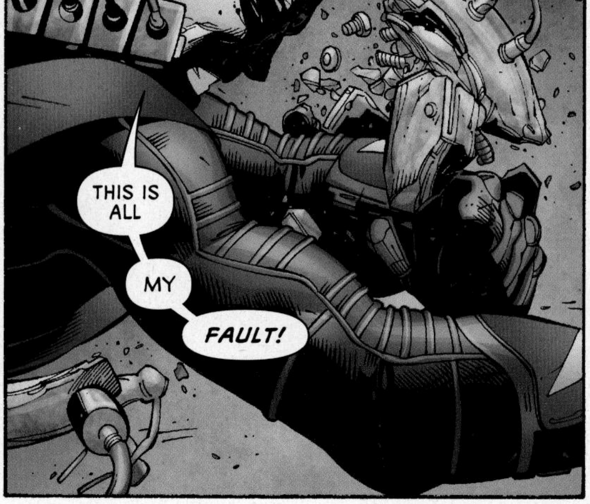
WHAT HAVE I *DONE?*
THIS IS ALL
MY
FAULT!

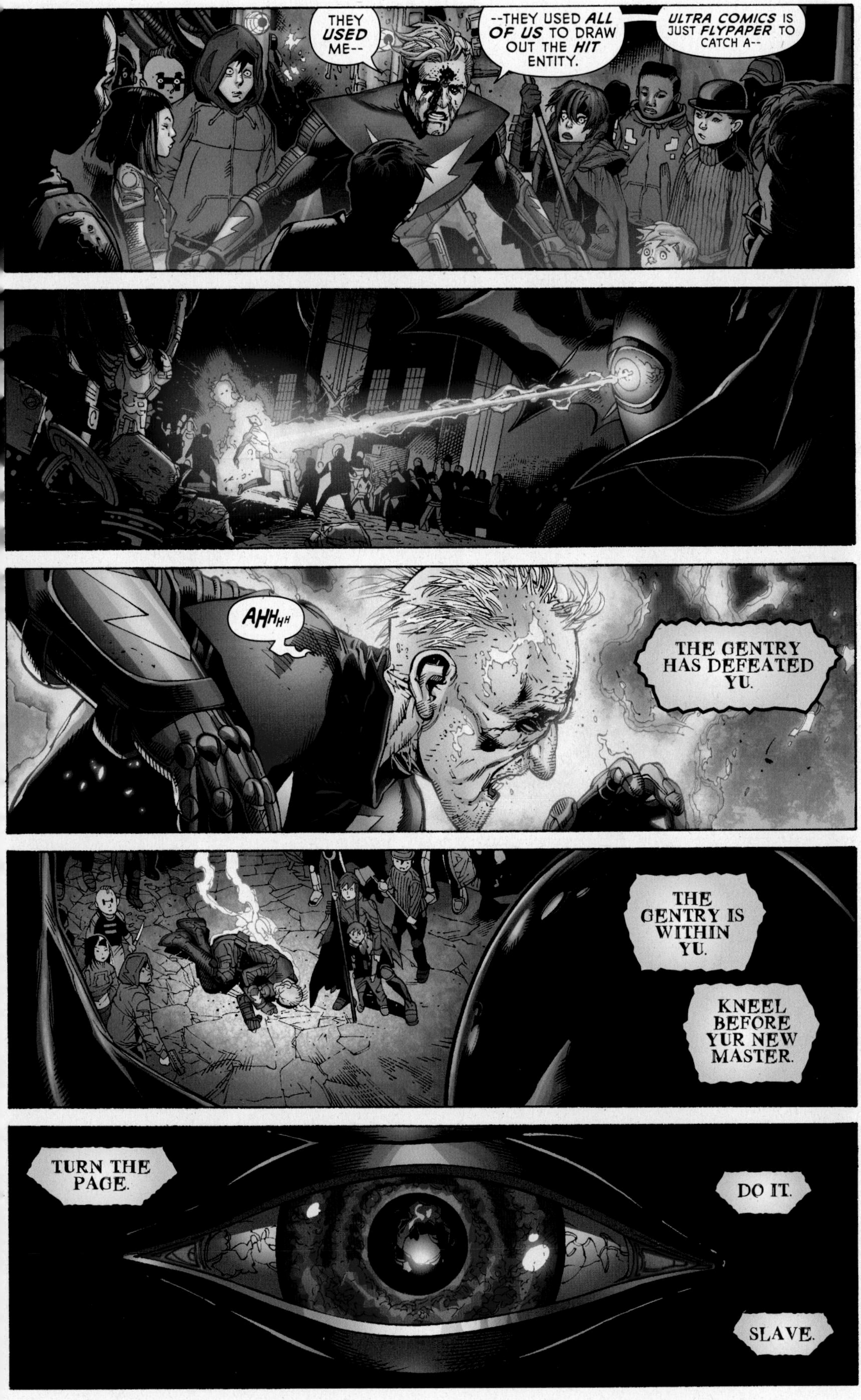
THEY USED ME--
--THEY USED ALL OF US TO DRAW OUT THE HIT ENTITY.
ULTRA COMICS IS JUST FLYPAPER TO CATCH A--
AHHHH
THE GENTRY HAS DEFEATED YU.
THE GENTRY IS WITHIN YU.
KNEEL BEFORE YUR NEW MASTER.
TURN THE PAGE.
DO IT.
SLAVE.

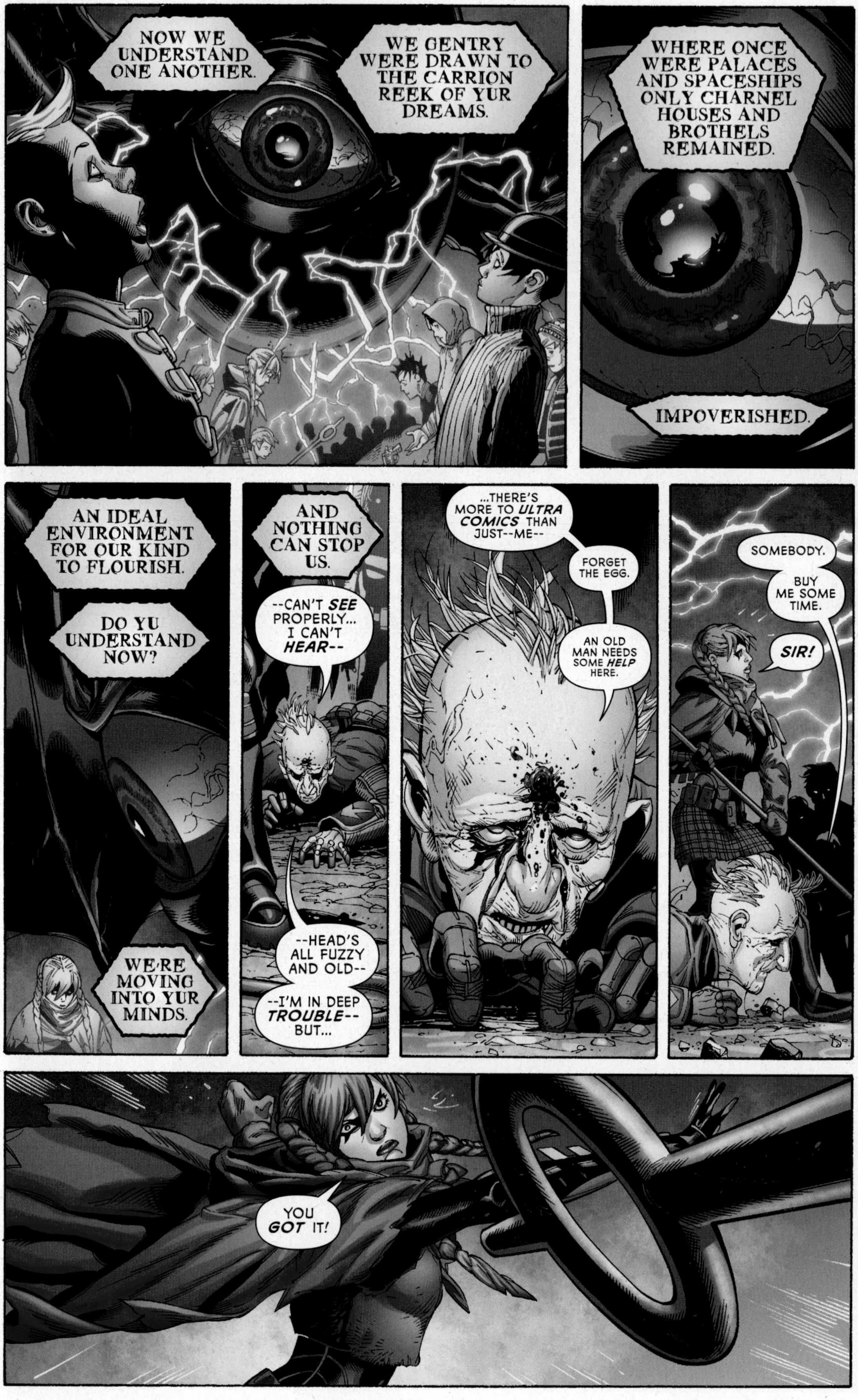
NOW WE UNDERSTAND ONE ANOTHER.
WE GENTRY WERE DRAWN TO THE CARRION REEK OF YUR DREAMS.
WHERE ONCE WERE PALACES AND SPACESHIPS ONLY CHARNEL HOUSES AND BROTHELS REMAINED.
IMPOVERISHED.
AN IDEAL ENVIRONMENT FOR OUR KIND TO FLOURISH.
DO YU UNDERSTAND NOW?
WE'RE MOVING INTO YUR MINDS.
AND NOTHING CAN STOP US.
--CAN'T SEE PROPERLY... I CAN'T HEAR--
--HEAD'S ALL FUZZY AND OLD--
--I'M IN DEEP TROUBLE-- BUT...
...THERE'S MORE TO ULTRA COMICS THAN JUST--ME--
FORGET THE EGG.
AN OLD MAN NEEDS SOME HELP HERE.
SOMEBODY.
BUY ME SOME TIME.
SIR!
YOU GOT IT!

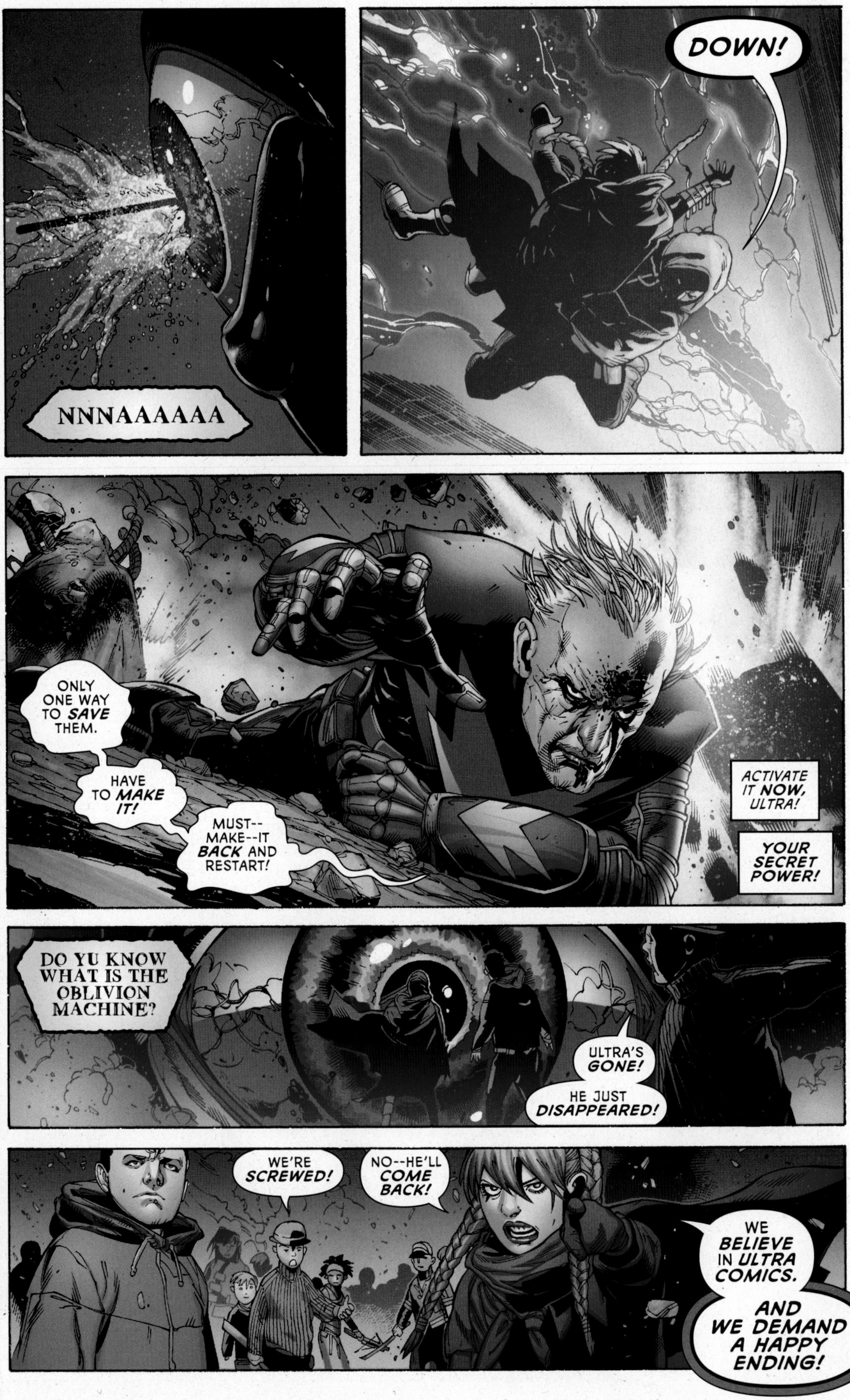
NNNAAAAAA
DOWN!
ONLY ONE WAY TO SAVE THEM.
HAVE TO MAKE IT!
MUST-- MAKE--IT BACK AND RESTART!
ACTIVATE IT NOW, ULTRA!
YOUR SECRET POWER!
DO YU KNOW WHAT IS THE OBLIVION MACHINE?
ULTRA'S GONE!
HE JUST DISAPPEARED!
WE'RE SCREWED!
NO--HE'LL COME BACK!
WE BELIEVE IN ULTRA COMICS.
AND WE DEMAND A HAPPY ENDING!

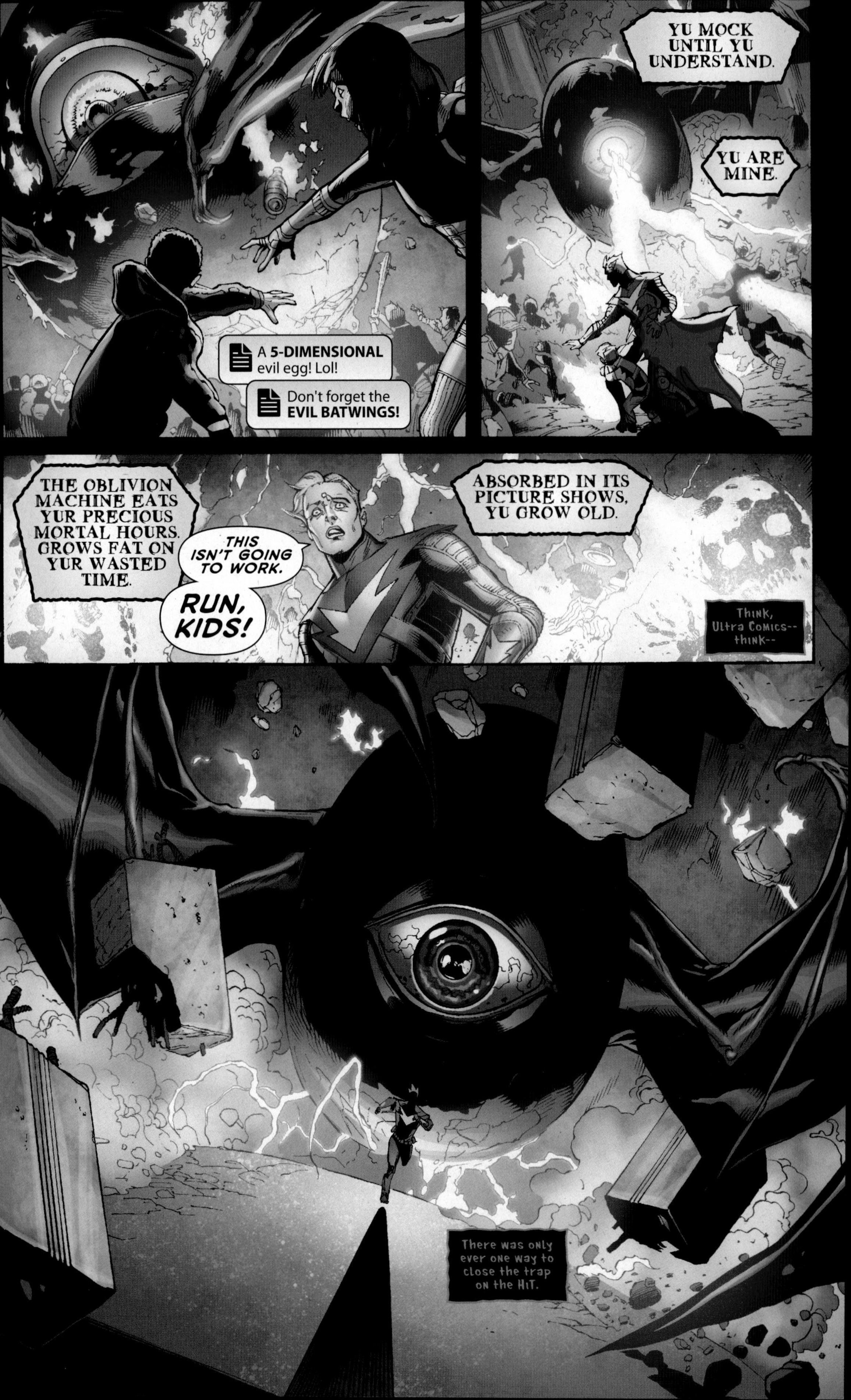
A 5-DIMENSIONAL evil egg! Lol!
Don't forget the EVIL BATWINGS!
YU MOCK UNTIL YU UNDERSTAND.
YU ARE MINE.
THE OBLIVION MACHINE EATS YUR PRECIOUS MORTAL HOURS. GROWS FAT ON YUR WASTED TIME.
THIS ISN'T GOING TO WORK.
RUN, KIDS!
ABSORBED IN ITS PICTURE SHOWS, YU GROW OLD.
Think, Ultra Comics-- think--
There was only ever one way to close the trap on the HiT.

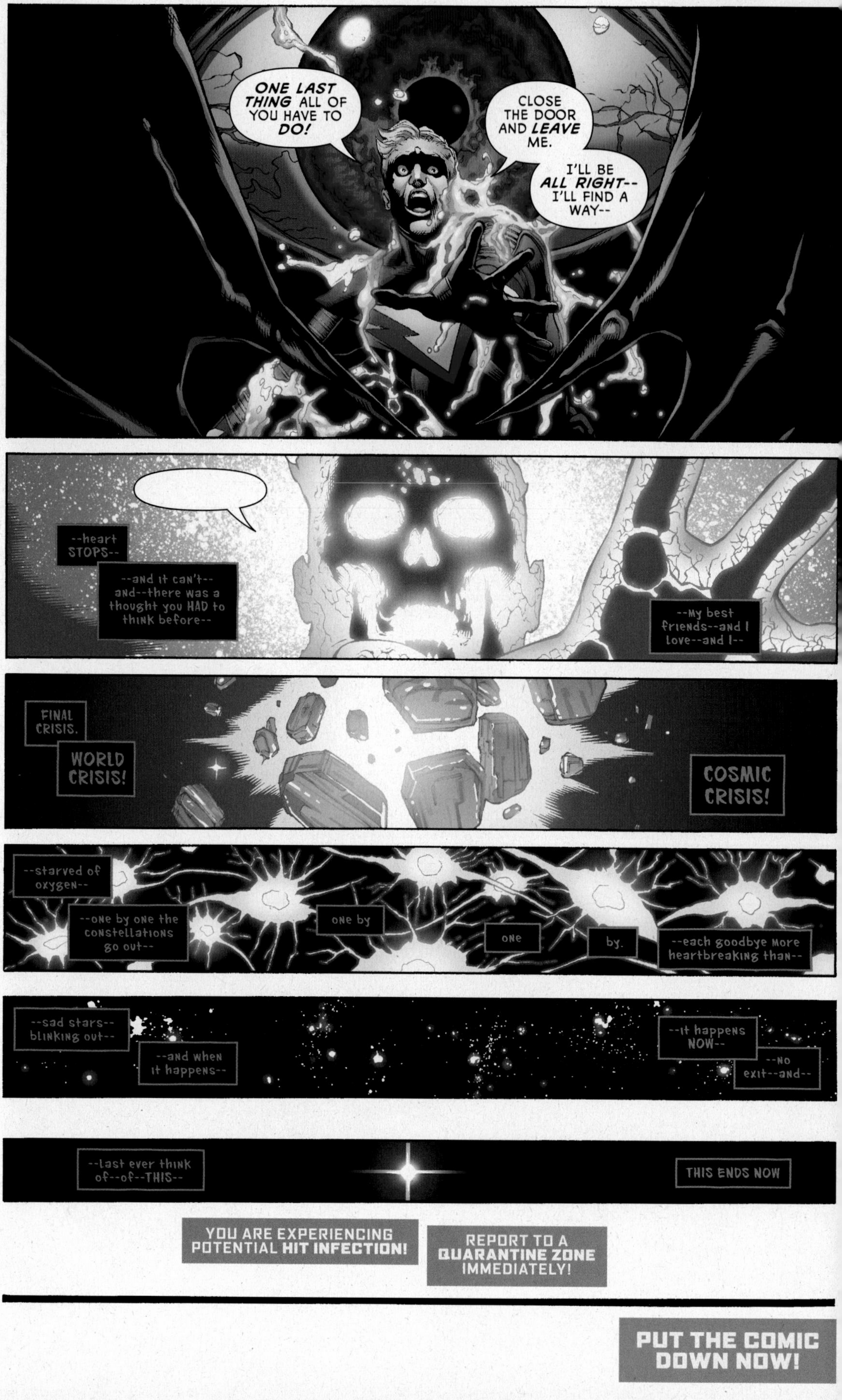

ONE LAST THING ALL OF YOU HAVE TO DO!
CLOSE THE DOOR AND LEAVE ME.
I'LL BE ALL RIGHT-- I'LL FIND A WAY--
--heart STOPS--
--and it can't--and--there was a thought you HAD to think before--
--my best friends--and I love--and I--
FINAL CRISIS.
WORLD CRISIS!
COSMIC CRISIS!
--starved of oxygen--
--one by one the constellations go out--
one by
one
by.
--each goodbye more heartbreaking than--
--sad stars--blinking out--
--and when it happens--
--it happens NOW--
--no exit--and--
--last ever think of--of--THIS--
THIS ENDS NOW
YOU ARE EXPERIENCING POTENTIAL HIT INFECTION!
REPORT TO A QUARANTINE ZONE IMMEDIATELY!
PUT THE COMIC DOWN NOW!

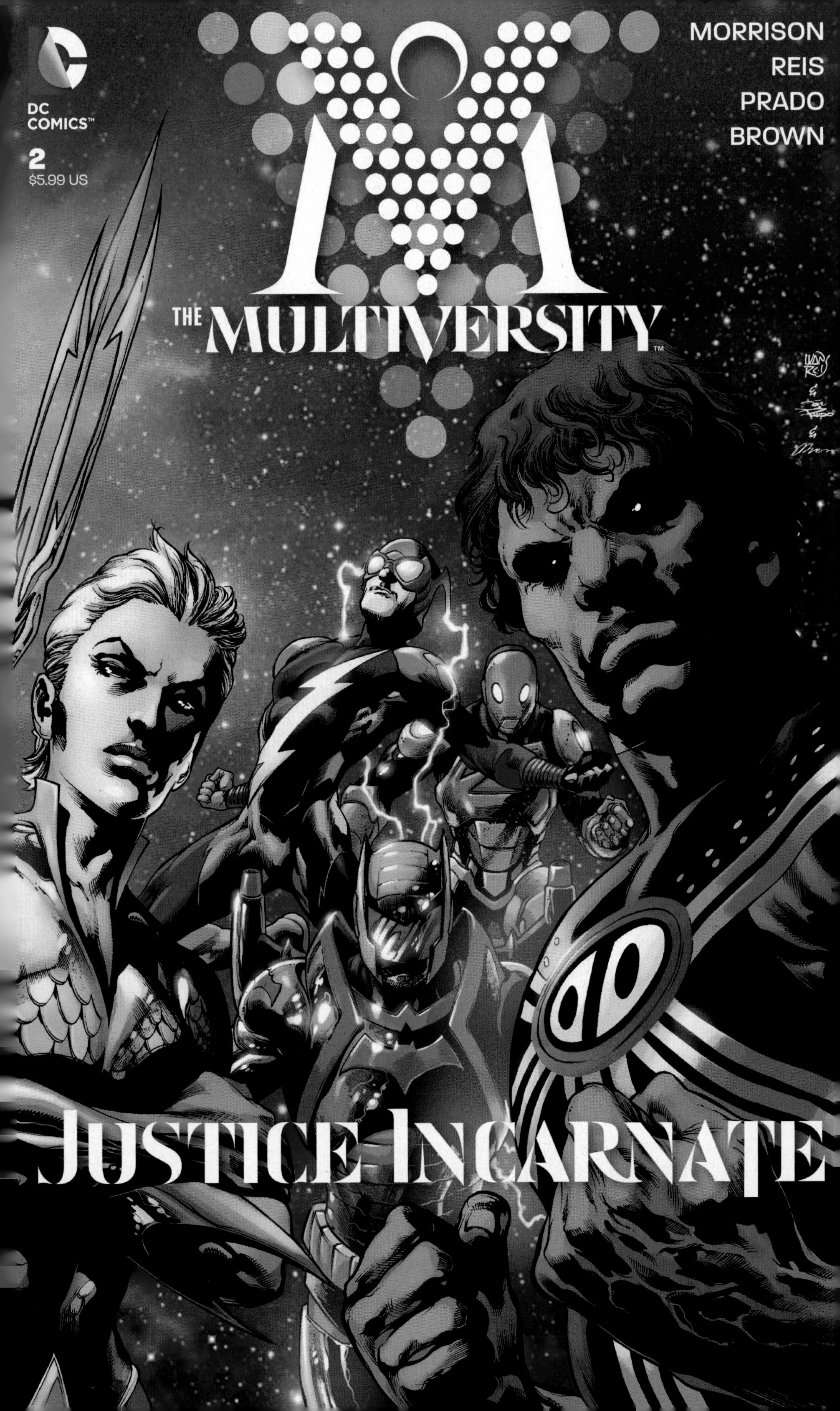
DC
COMICS™
2
$5.99 US
MORRISON
REIS
PRADO
BROWN
THE MULTIVERSITY™
JUSTICE INCARNATE

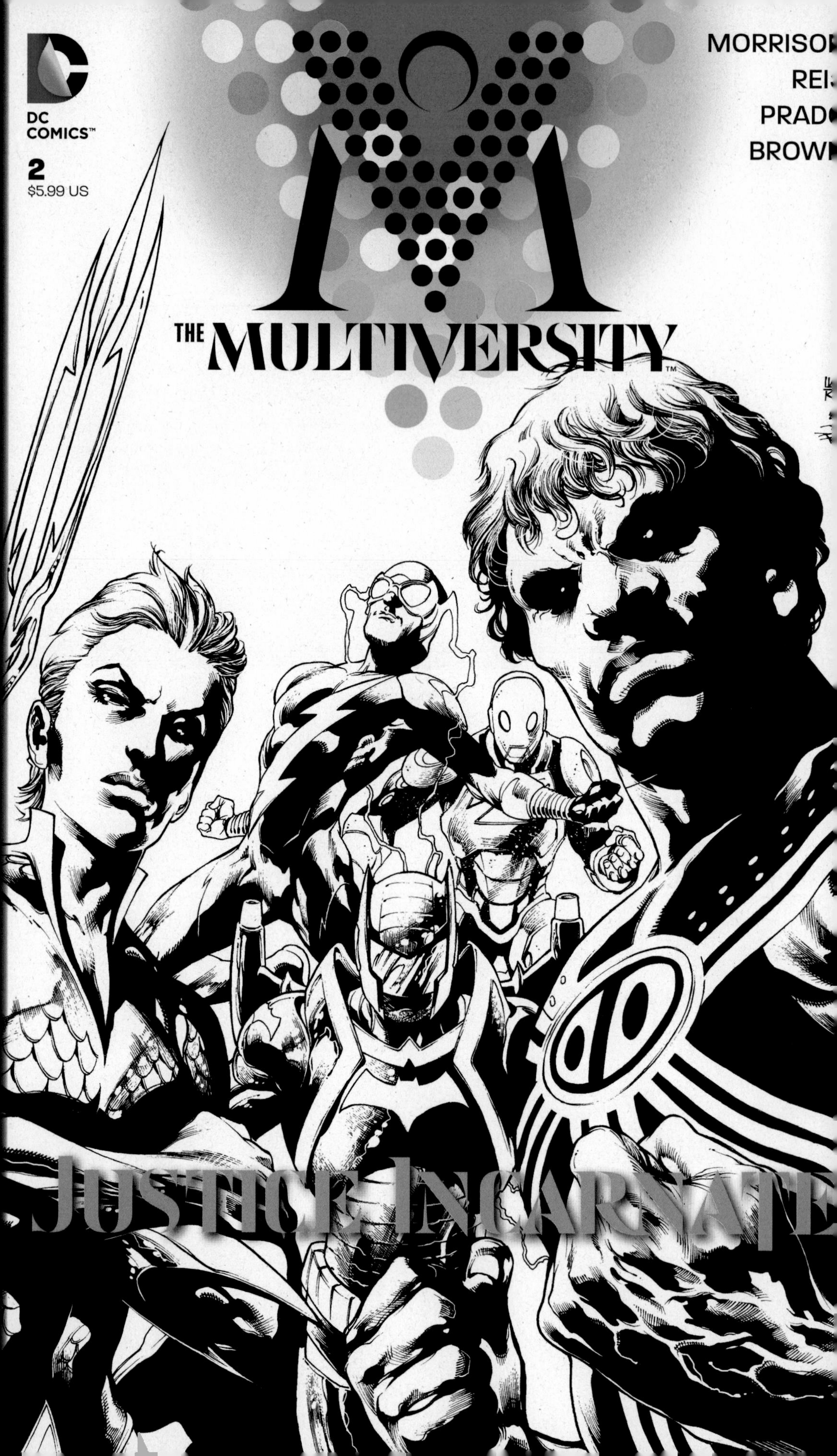
DC COMICS™
2
$5.99 US
MORRISO
REI
PRAD
BROW
THE MULTIVERSITY™
JUSTICE INCARNATE

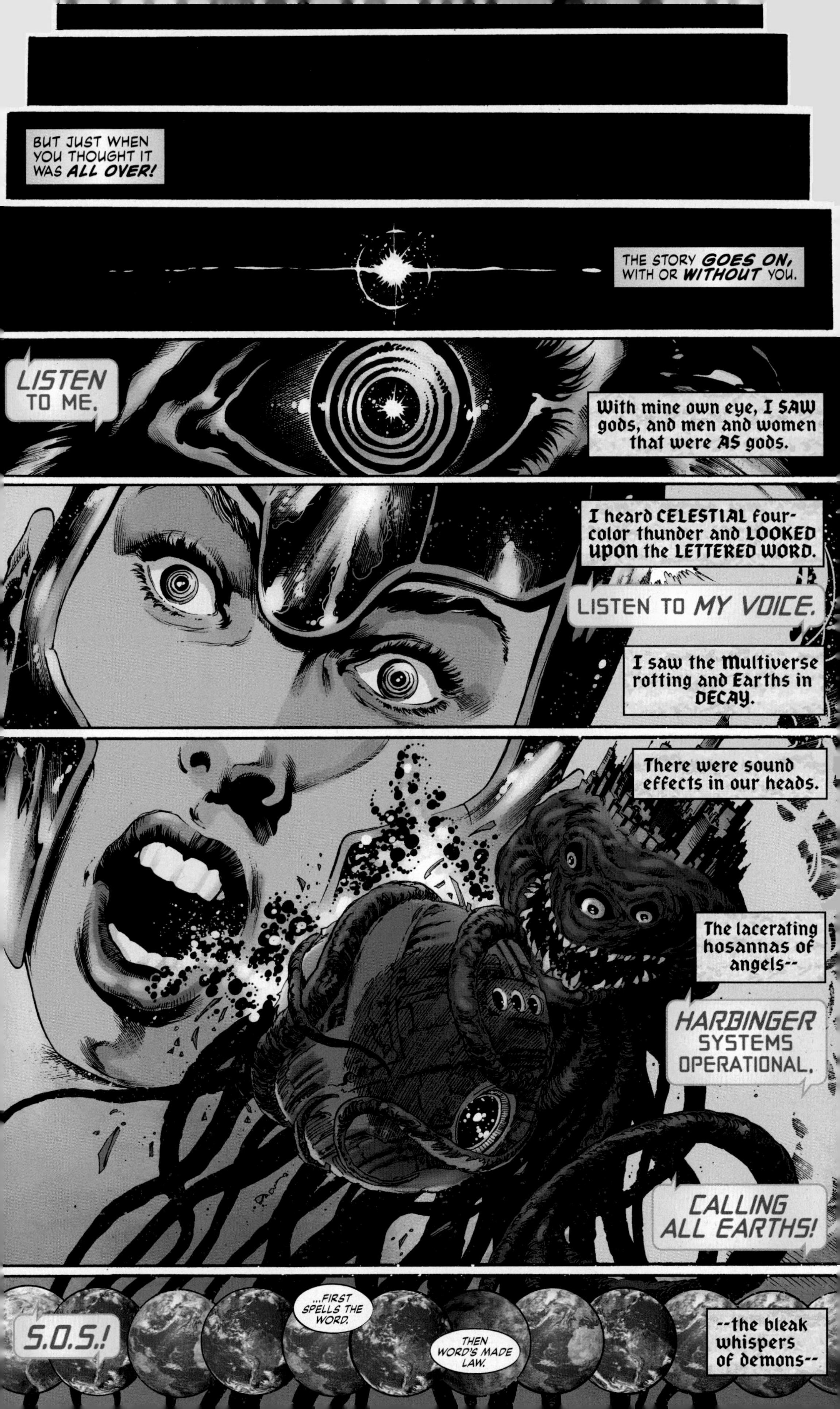

BUT JUST WHEN YOU THOUGHT IT WAS ALL OVER!
THE STORY GOES ON, WITH OR WITHOUT YOU.
LISTEN TO ME.
With mine own eye, I SAW gods, and men and women that were AS gods.
I heard CELESTIAL four-color thunder and LOOKED upon the LETTERED WORD.
LISTEN TO MY VOICE.
I saw the Multiverse rotting and Earths in DECAY.
There were sound effects in our heads.
The lacerating hosannas of angels--
HARBINGER SYSTEMS OPERATIONAL.
CALLING ALL EARTHS!
S.O.S.!
...FIRST SPELLS THE WORD.
THEN WORD'S MADE LAW.
--the bleak whispers of demons--

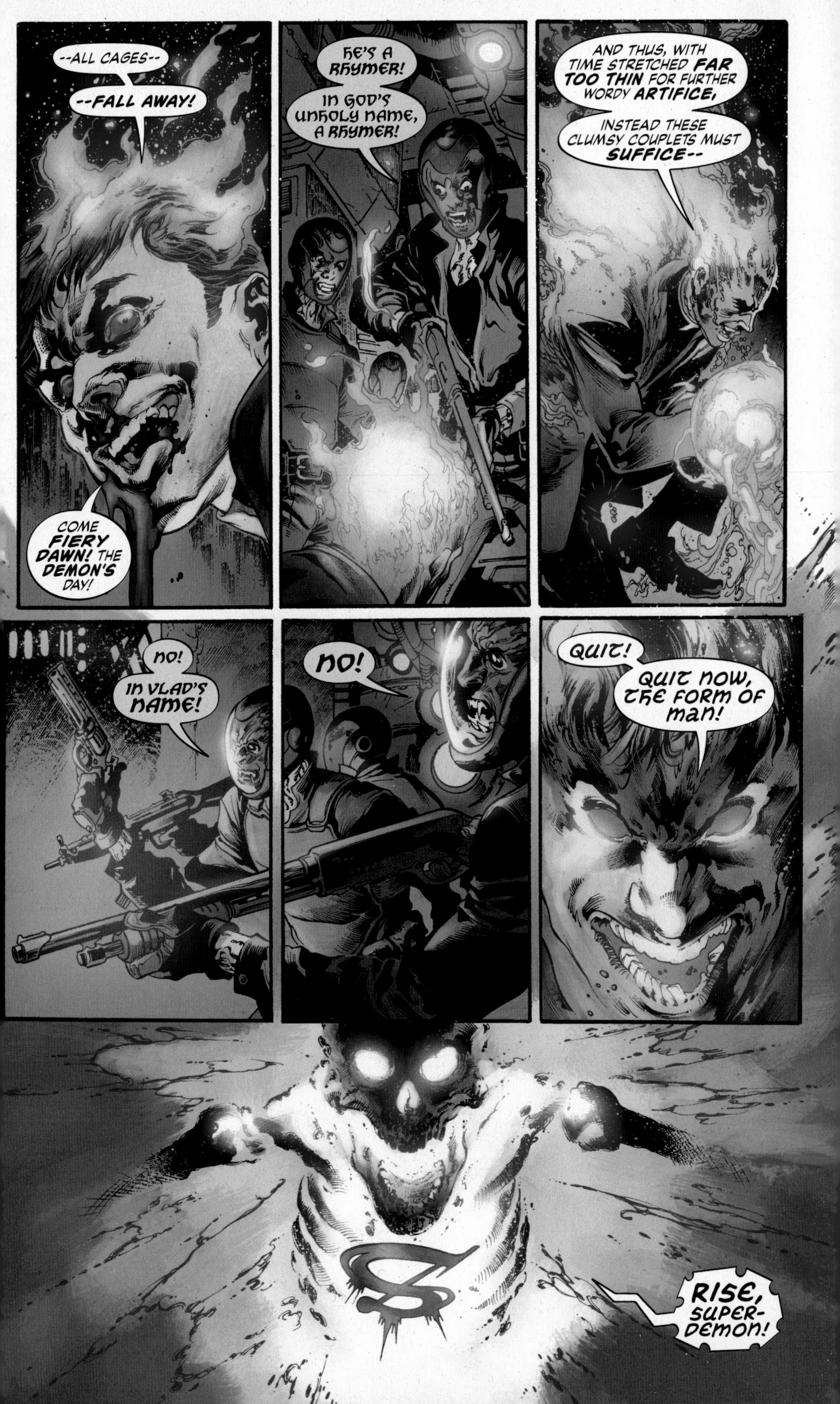
--ALL CAGES--
--FALL AWAY!
COME FIERY DAWN! THE DEMON'S DAY!
HE'S A RHYMER!
IN GOD'S UNHOLY NAME, A RHYMER!
AND THUS, WITH TIME STRETCHED FAR TOO THIN FOR FURTHER WORDY ARTIFICE,
INSTEAD THESE CLUMSY COUPLETS MUST SUFFICE--
NO! IN VLAD'S NAME!
NO!
QUIT!
QUIT NOW, THE FORM OF MAN!
RISE, SUPER-DEMON!

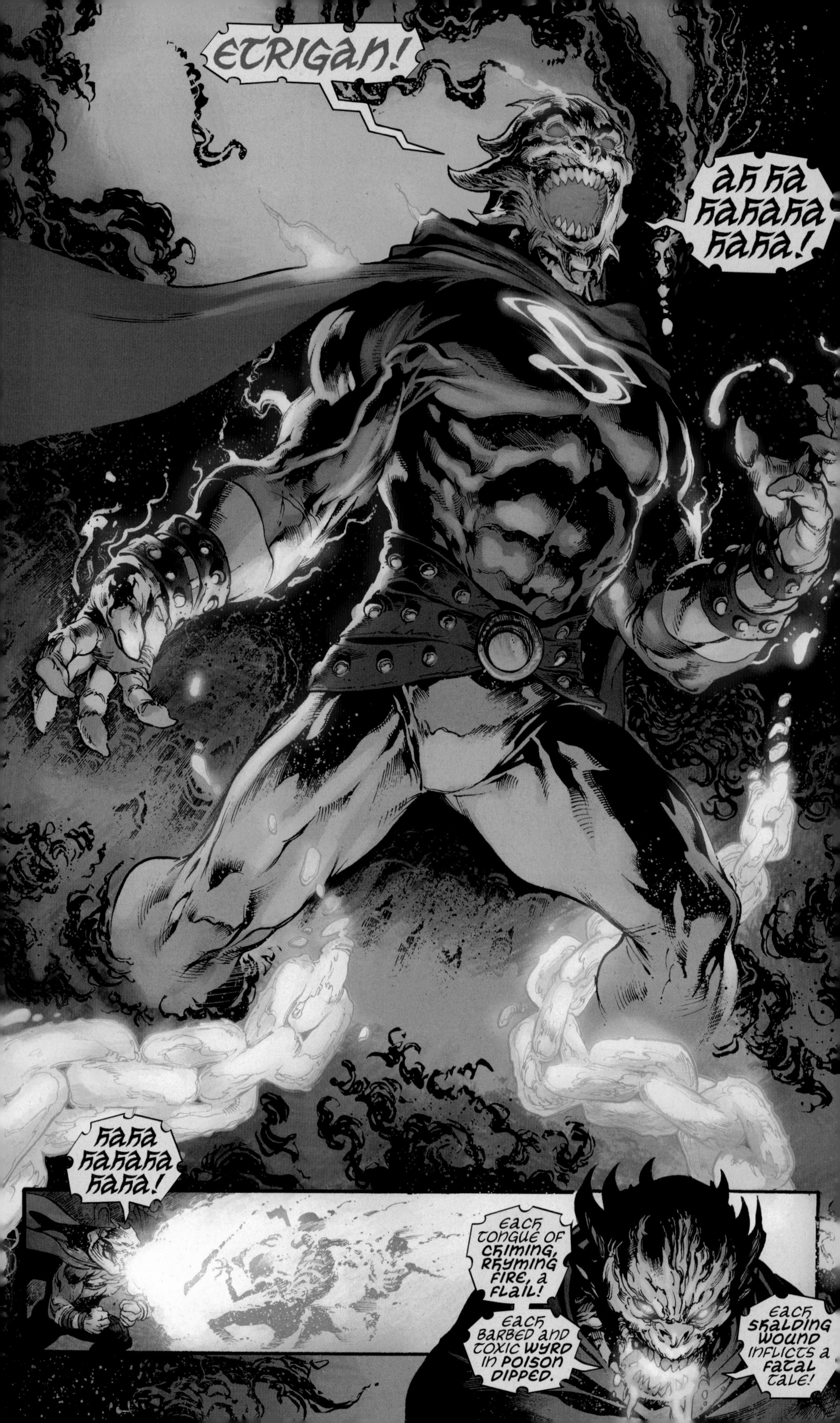

ETRIGAN!
AH HA HAHAHA HAHA!
HAHA HAHAHA HAHA!
EACH TONGUE OF CHIMING, RHYMING FIRE, A FLAIL!
EACH BARBED AND TOXIC WYRD IN POISON DIPPED.
EACH SKALDING WOUND INFLICTS A FATAL TALE!

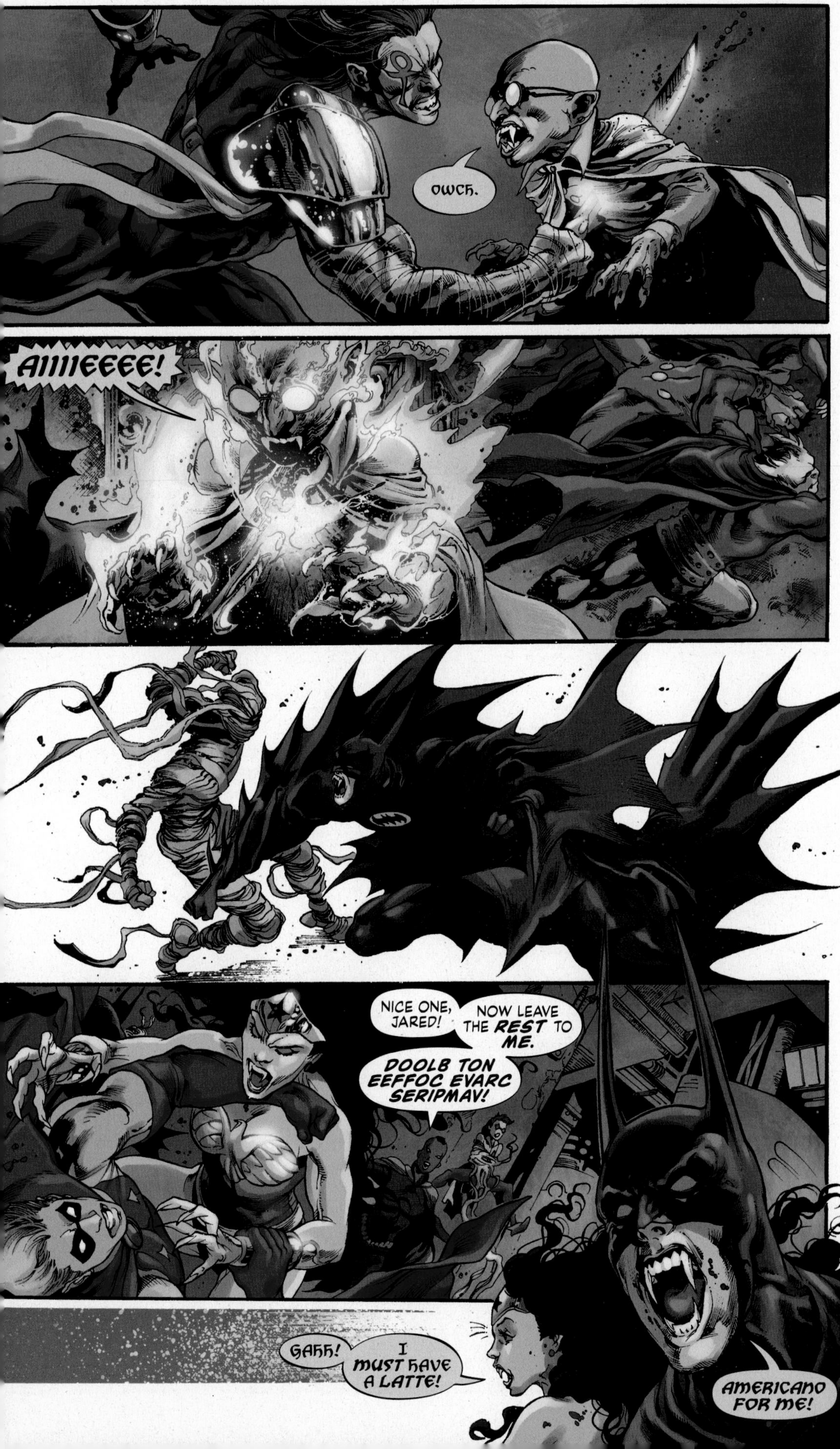
OWCH.
AIIIIEEEE!
NICE ONE, JARED!
NOW LEAVE THE REST TO ME.
DOOLB TON EEFFOC EVARC SERIPMAV!
GAHH!
I MUST HAVE A LATTE!
AMERICANO FOR ME!

:FF:
ONE LESS **IDIOT.**
NOW--

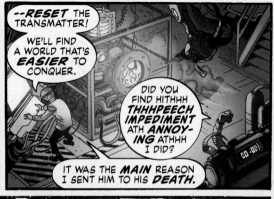

--**RESET** THE TRANSMATTER!
WE'LL FIND A WORLD THAT'S **EASIER** TO CONQUER.
DID YOU FIND HITHHH **THHHPEECH** IMPEDIMENT ATH **ANNOY-ING** ATHHH I DID?
IT WAS THE **MAIN** REASON I SENT HIM TO HIS **DEATH.**

WHAT THE **HELL'S** WRONG WITH YOUR **BREATH?**
THAT **SMELL!**
I--:URRP:

NOW IT'S **YOUR TURN!**
THE CUBE'S LOCATED A WORLD WHERE **YOU'LL** FIT RIGHT IN.

A HOT, DRY DESERT--
YOU THINK I'D TRUTHHHT A **THHHIVANA?!**
WE GO THHROUGH **TOGETHER**--

--OR NOT AT **ALL.**
HMMM.

AT LEATHHHT IT'THHHH NITHHHE AND **WARM!**

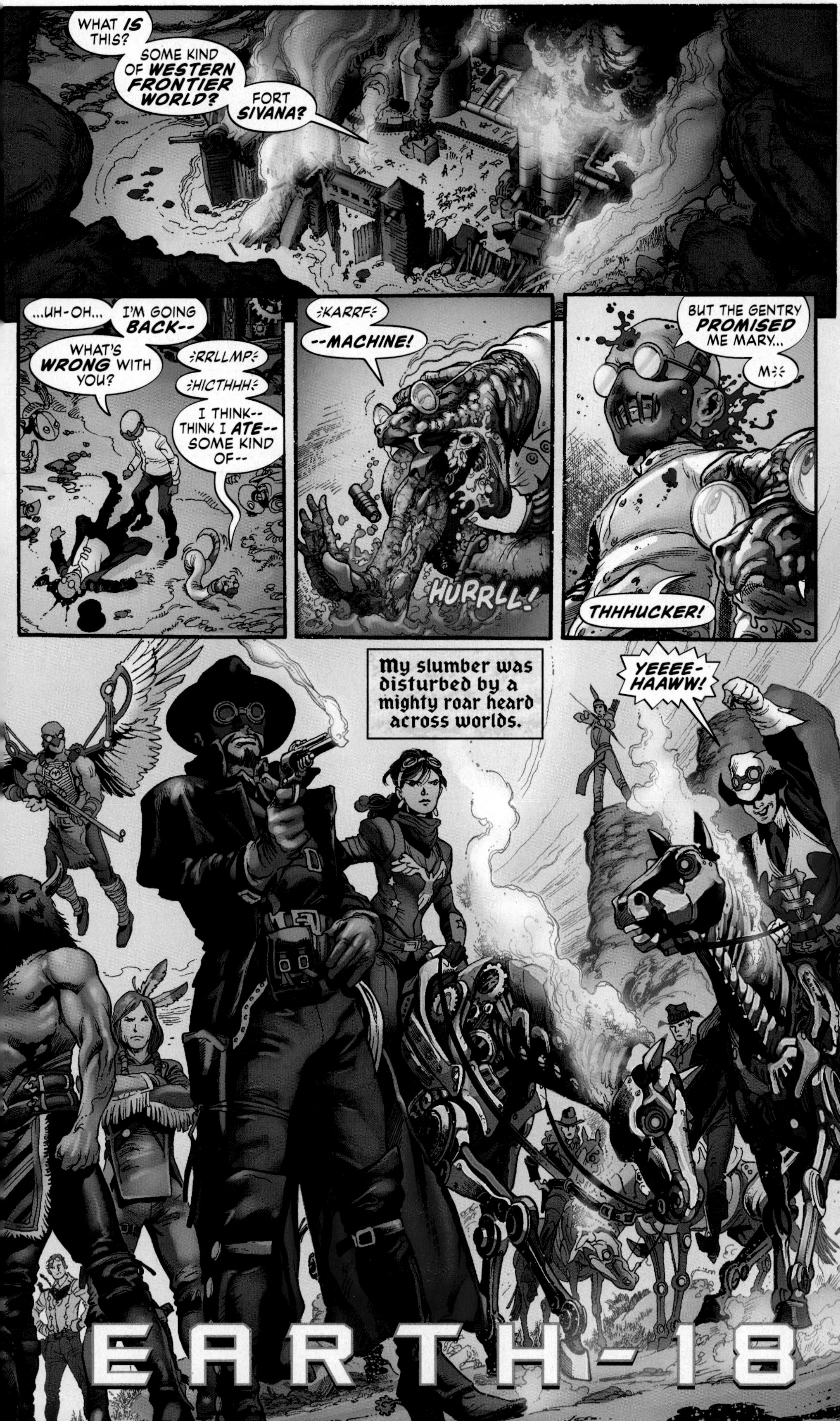
WHAT IS THIS?
SOME KIND OF WESTERN FRONTIER WORLD?
FORT SIVANA?
...UH-OH...
I'M GOING BACK--
WHAT'S WRONG WITH YOU?
RRLLMP
HICTHHH
I THINK-- THINK I ATE-- SOME KIND OF--
KARRF
--MACHINE!
HURRLL!
BUT THE GENTRY PROMISED ME MARY...
M
THHHUCKER!
My slumber was disturbed by a mighty roar heard across worlds.
YEEEE-HAAWW!
EARTH-18

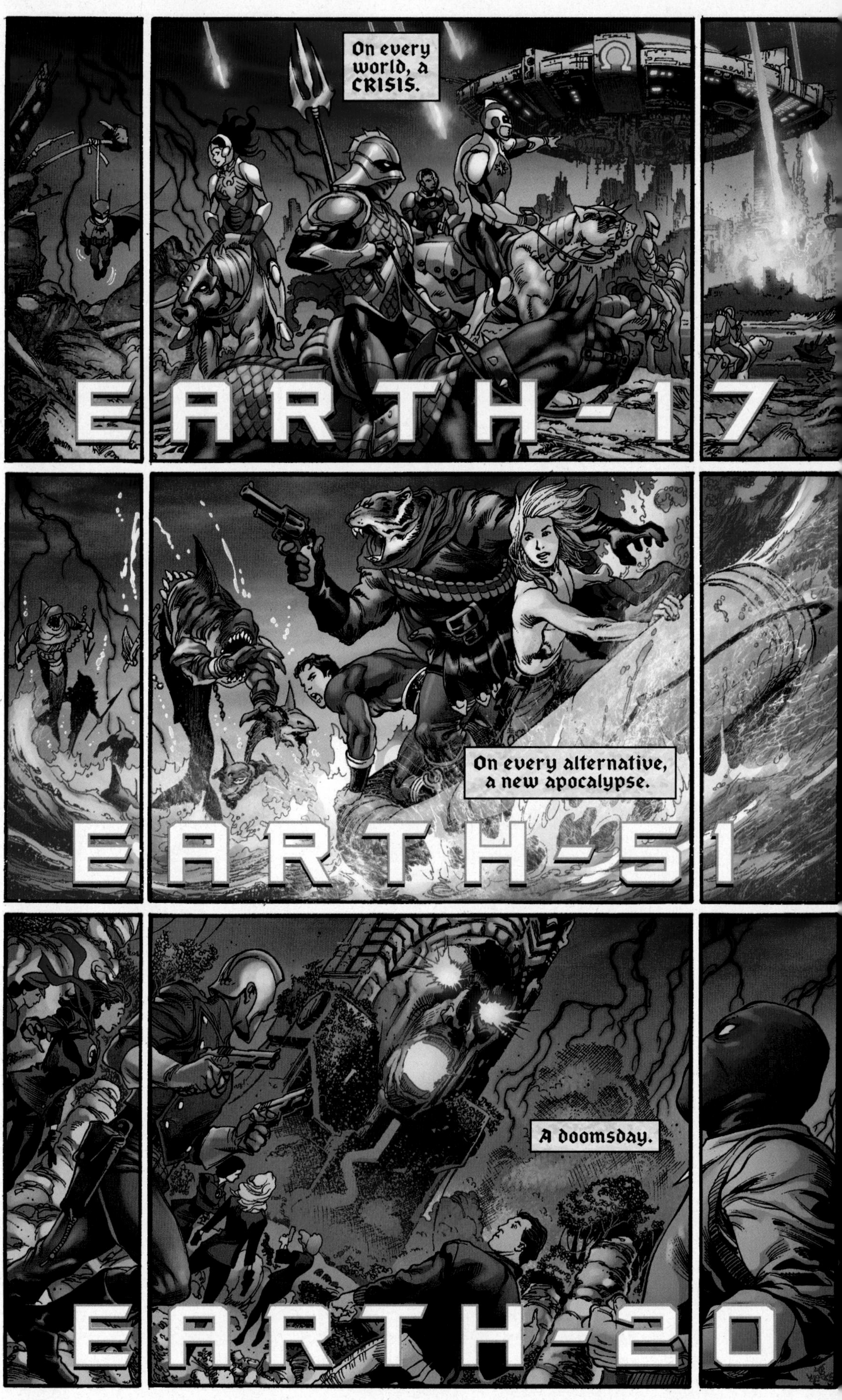
On every world, a CRISIS.
EARTH-17
On every alternative, a new apocalypse.
EARTH-51
A doomsday.
EARTH-20

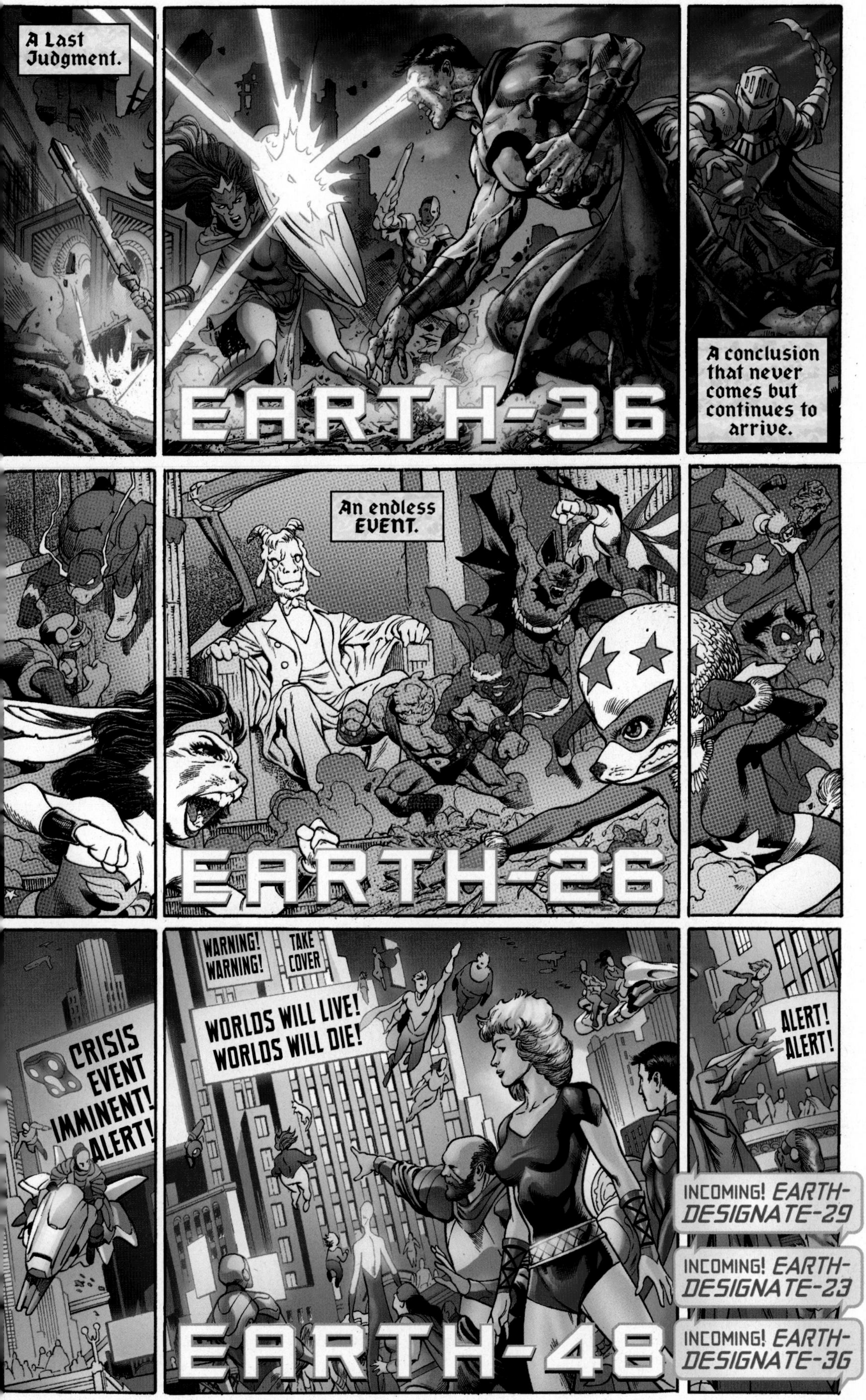
A Last Judgment.
EARTH-36
A conclusion that never comes but continues to arrive.
An endless EVENT.
EARTH-26
CRISIS EVENT IMMINENT! ALERT!
WARNING! WARNING!
TAKE COVER
WORLDS WILL LIVE! WORLDS WILL DIE!
ALERT! ALERT!
INCOMING! EARTH-DESIGNATE-29
INCOMING! EARTH-DESIGNATE-23
EARTH-48
INCOMING! EARTH-DESIGNATE-36

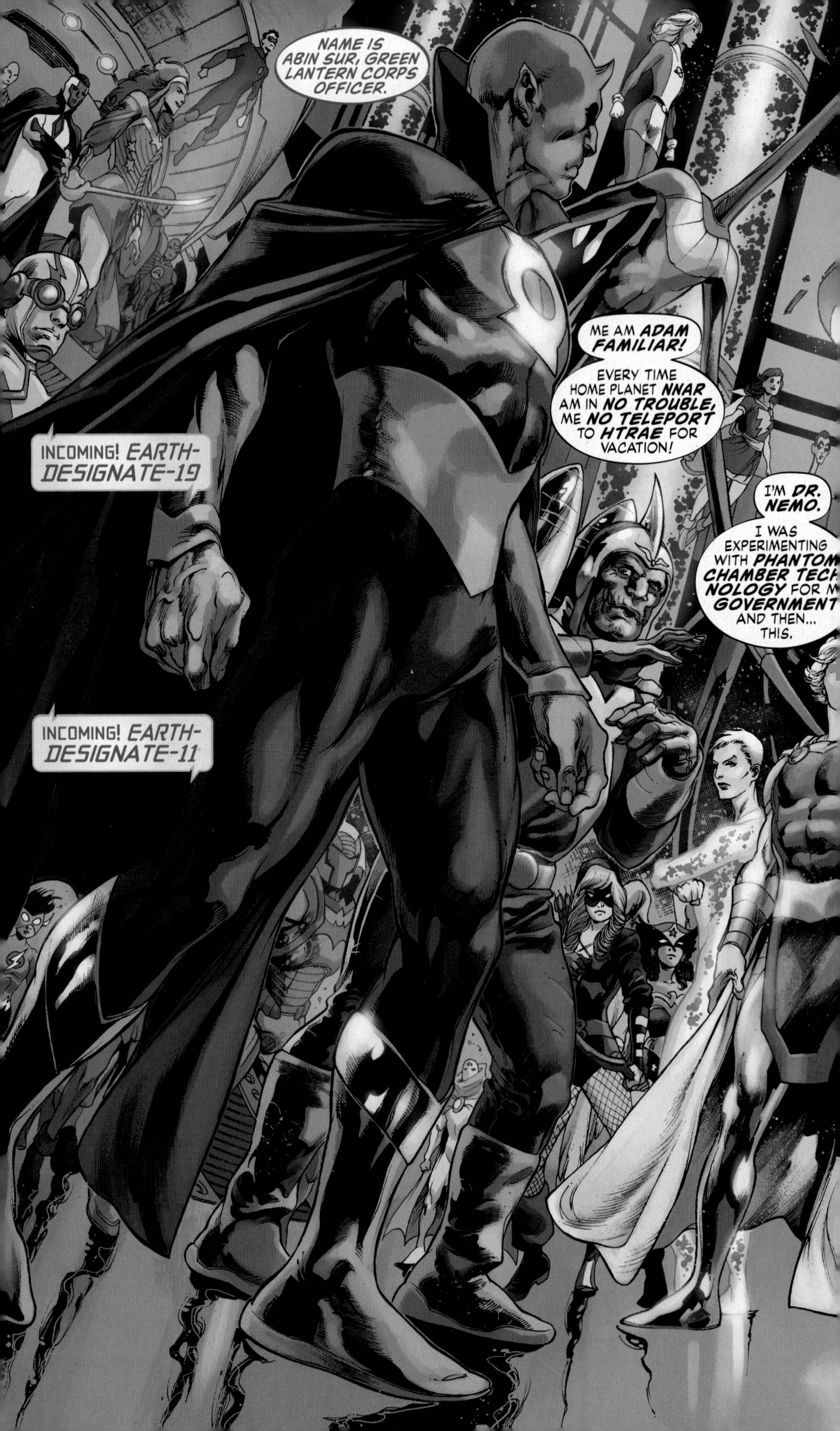
NAME IS ABIN SUR, GREEN LANTERN CORPS OFFICER.
INCOMING! EARTH-DESIGNATE-19
ME AM ADAM FAMILIAR!
EVERY TIME HOME PLANET NNAR AM IN NO TROUBLE, ME NO TELEPORT TO HTRAE FOR VACATION!
I'M DR. NEMO.
I WAS EXPERIMENTING WITH PHANTOM CHAMBER TECH-NOLOGY FOR M GOVERNMENT AND THEN... THIS.
INCOMING! EARTH-DESIGNATE-11

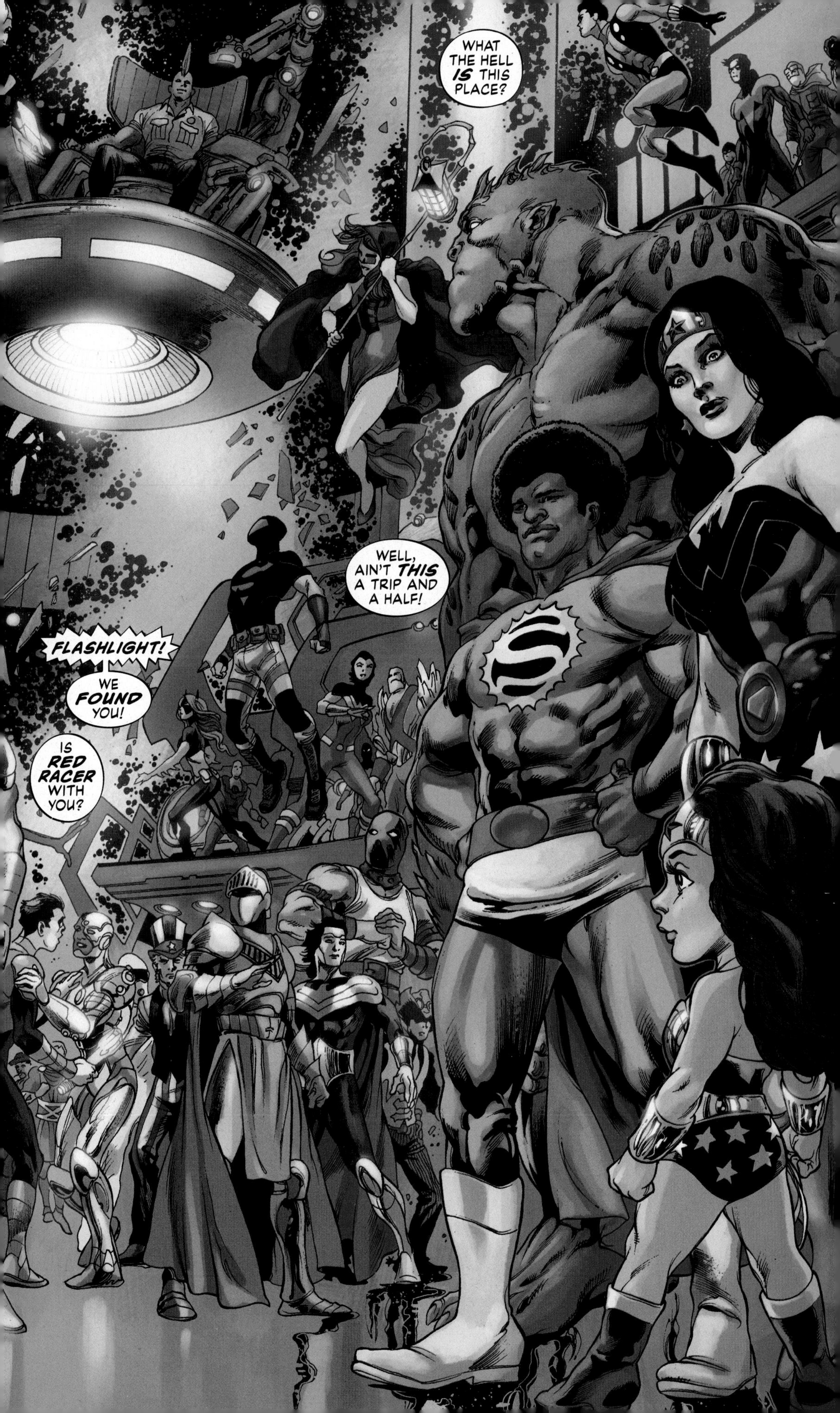
WHAT THE HELL *IS* THIS PLACE?
WELL, AIN'T *THIS* A TRIP AND A HALF!
FLASHLIGHT!
WE *FOUND* YOU!
IS *RED RACER* WITH YOU?

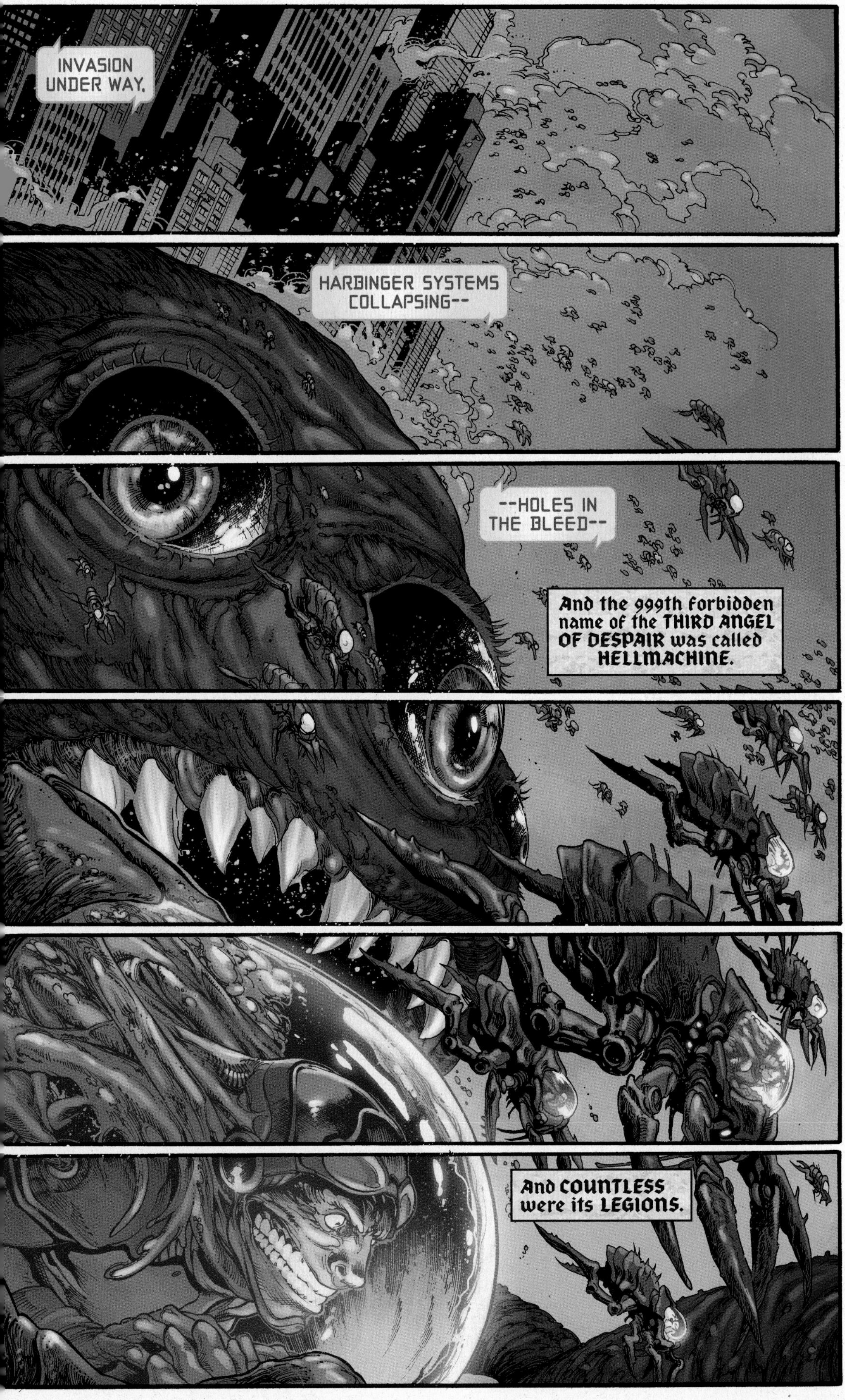
INVASION UNDER WAY.
HARBINGER SYSTEMS COLLAPSING--
--HOLES IN THE BLEED--
And the 999th forbidden name of the THIRD ANGEL OF DESPAIR was called HELLMACHINE.
And COUNTLESS were its LEGIONS.

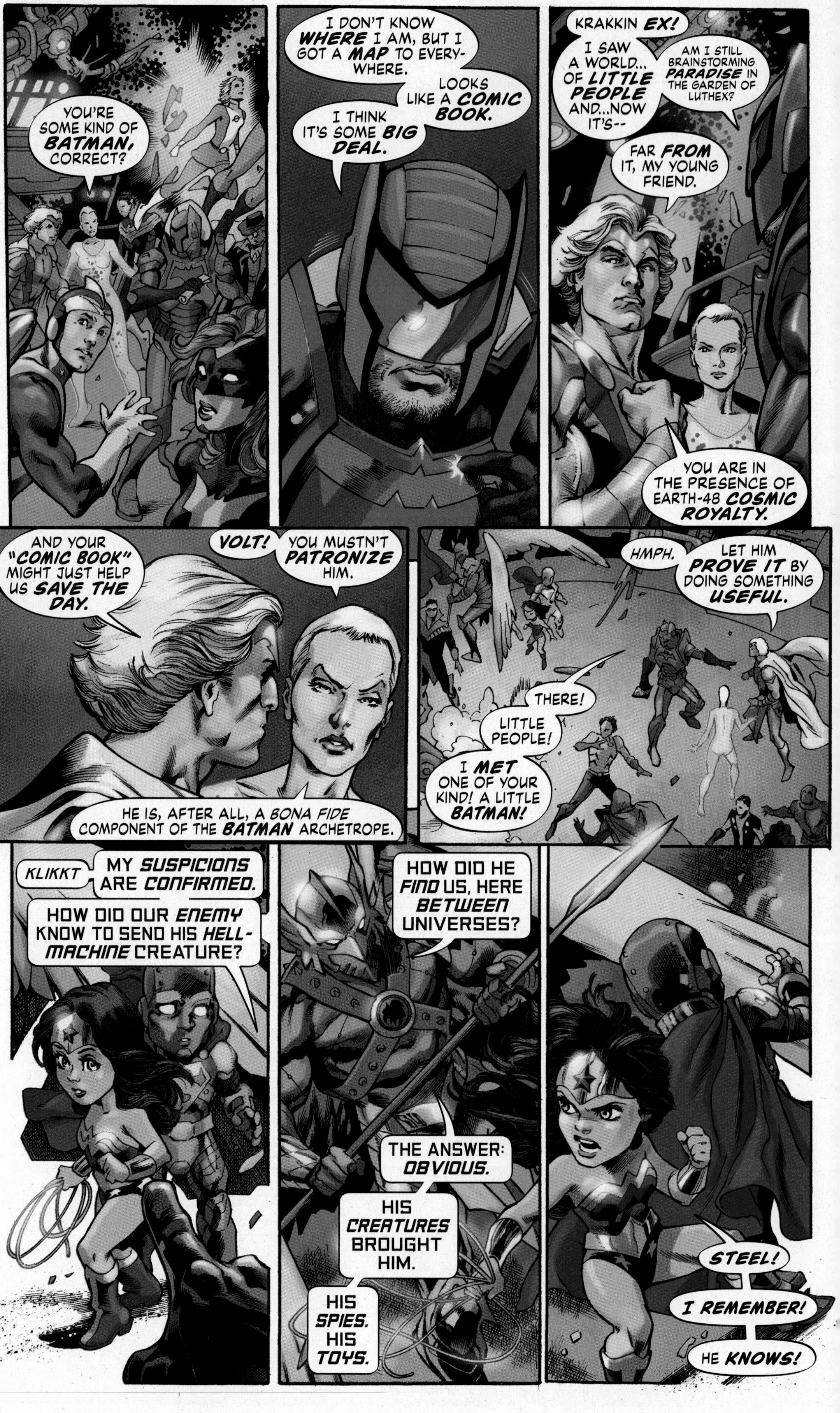
YOU'RE SOME KIND OF BATMAN, CORRECT?
I DON'T KNOW WHERE I AM, BUT I GOT A MAP TO EVERY-WHERE.
LOOKS LIKE A COMIC BOOK.
I THINK IT'S SOME BIG DEAL.
KRAKKIN EX!
I SAW A WORLD... OF LITTLE PEOPLE AND...NOW IT'S--
AM I STILL BRAINSTORMING PARADISE IN THE GARDEN OF LUTHEX?
FAR FROM IT, MY YOUNG FRIEND.
YOU ARE IN THE PRESENCE OF EARTH-48 COSMIC ROYALTY.
AND YOUR "COMIC BOOK" MIGHT JUST HELP US SAVE THE DAY.
VOLT!
YOU MUSTN'T PATRONIZE HIM.
HE IS, AFTER ALL, A BONA FIDE COMPONENT OF THE BATMAN ARCHETROPE.
HMPH.
LET HIM PROVE IT BY DOING SOMETHING USEFUL.
THERE!
LITTLE PEOPLE!
I MET ONE OF YOUR KIND! A LITTLE BATMAN!
KLIKKT
MY SUSPICIONS ARE CONFIRMED.
HOW DID OUR ENEMY KNOW TO SEND HIS HELL-MACHINE CREATURE?
HOW DID HE FIND US, HERE BETWEEN UNIVERSES?
THE ANSWER: OBVIOUS.
HIS CREATURES BROUGHT HIM.
HIS SPIES. HIS TOYS.
STEEL!
I REMEMBER!
HE KNOWS!

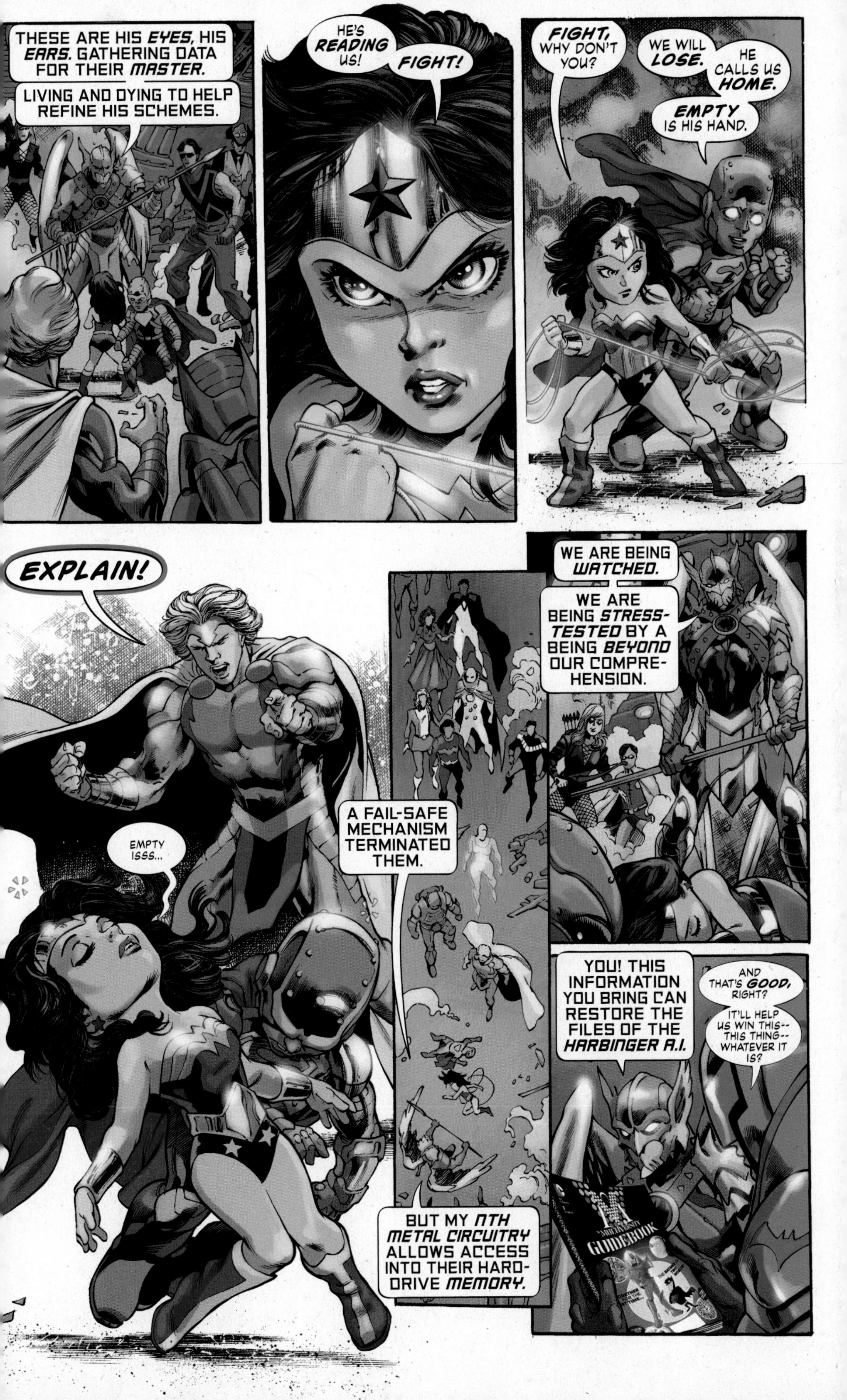
THESE ARE HIS *EYES*, HIS *EARS*. GATHERING DATA FOR THEIR *MASTER*.
LIVING AND DYING TO HELP REFINE HIS SCHEMES.
HE'S *READING* US!
FIGHT!
FIGHT, WHY DON'T YOU?
WE WILL *LOSE*.
HE CALLS US *HOME*.
EMPTY IS HIS HAND.
EXPLAIN!
EMPTY ISSS...
WE ARE BEING *WATCHED*.
WE ARE BEING *STRESS-TESTED* BY A BEING *BEYOND* OUR COMPRE-HENSION.
A FAIL-SAFE MECHANISM TERMINATED THEM.
BUT MY *NTH METAL CIRCUITRY* ALLOWS ACCESS INTO THEIR HARD-DRIVE *MEMORY*.
YOU! THIS INFORMATION YOU BRING CAN RESTORE THE FILES OF THE *HARBINGER A.I.*
AND THAT'S *GOOD,* RIGHT?
IT'LL HELP US WIN THIS-- THIS THING-- WHATEVER IT IS?
GUIDEBOOK

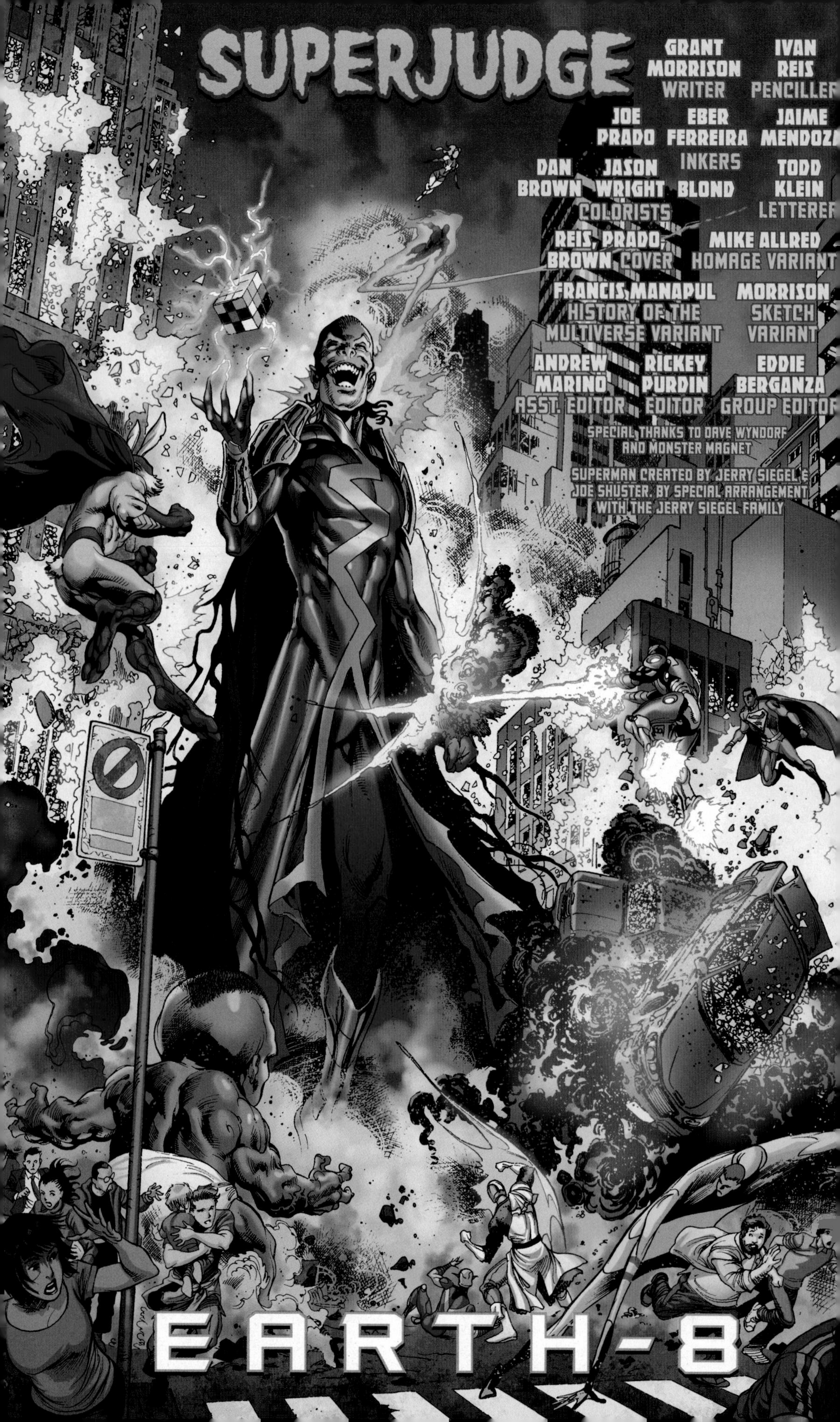

SUPERJUDGE
GRANT MORRISON WRITER
IVAN REIS PENCILLER
JOE PRADO EBER FERREIRA JAIME MENDOZA INKERS
DAN BROWN JASON WRIGHT BLOND COLORISTS
TODD KLEIN LETTERER
REIS, PRADO, BROWN COVER
MIKE ALLRED HOMAGE VARIANT
FRANCIS MANAPUL HISTORY OF THE MULTIVERSE VARIANT
MORRISON SKETCH VARIANT
ANDREW MARINO ASST. EDITOR
RICKEY PURDIN EDITOR
EDDIE BERGANZA GROUP EDITOR
SPECIAL THANKS TO DAVE WYNDORF AND MONSTER MAGNET
SUPERMAN CREATED BY JERRY SIEGEL & JOE SHUSTER. BY SPECIAL ARRANGEMENT WITH THE JERRY SIEGEL FAMILY
EARTH-8

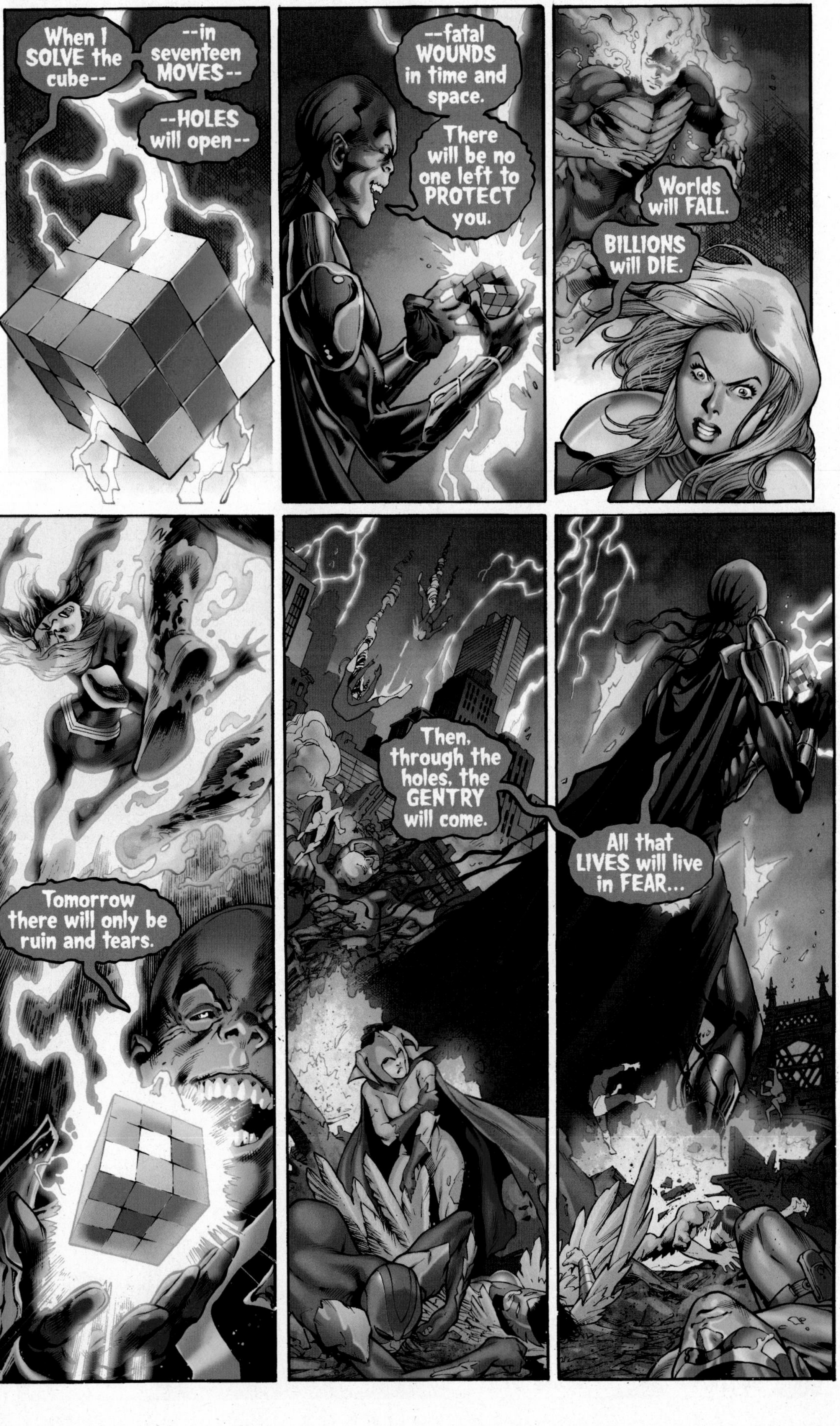
When I SOLVE the cube--
--in seventeen MOVES--
--HOLES will open--
--fatal WOUNDS in time and space.
There will be no one left to PROTECT you.
Worlds will FALL.
BILLIONS will DIE.
Tomorrow there will only be ruin and tears.
Then, through the holes, the GENTRY will come.
All that LIVES will live in FEAR...

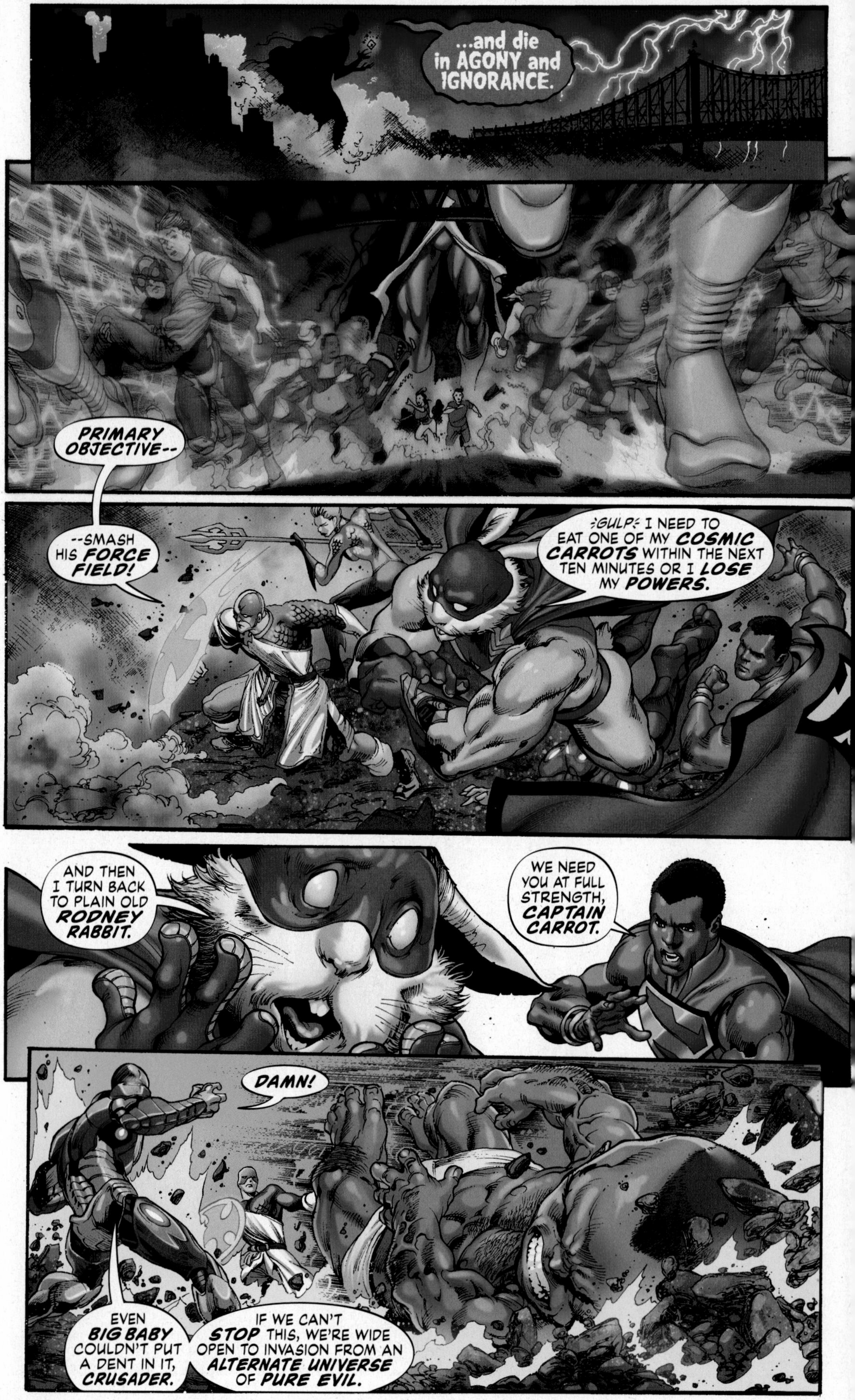
...and die in AGONY and IGNORANCE.
PRIMARY OBJECTIVE--
--SMASH HIS FORCE FIELD!
GULP I NEED TO EAT ONE OF MY COSMIC CARROTS WITHIN THE NEXT TEN MINUTES OR I LOSE MY POWERS.
AND THEN I TURN BACK TO PLAIN OLD RODNEY RABBIT.
WE NEED YOU AT FULL STRENGTH, CAPTAIN CARROT.
DAMN!
EVEN BIG BABY COULDN'T PUT A DENT IN IT, CRUSADER.
IF WE CAN'T STOP THIS, WE'RE WIDE OPEN TO INVASION FROM AN ALTERNATE UNIVERSE OF PURE EVIL.

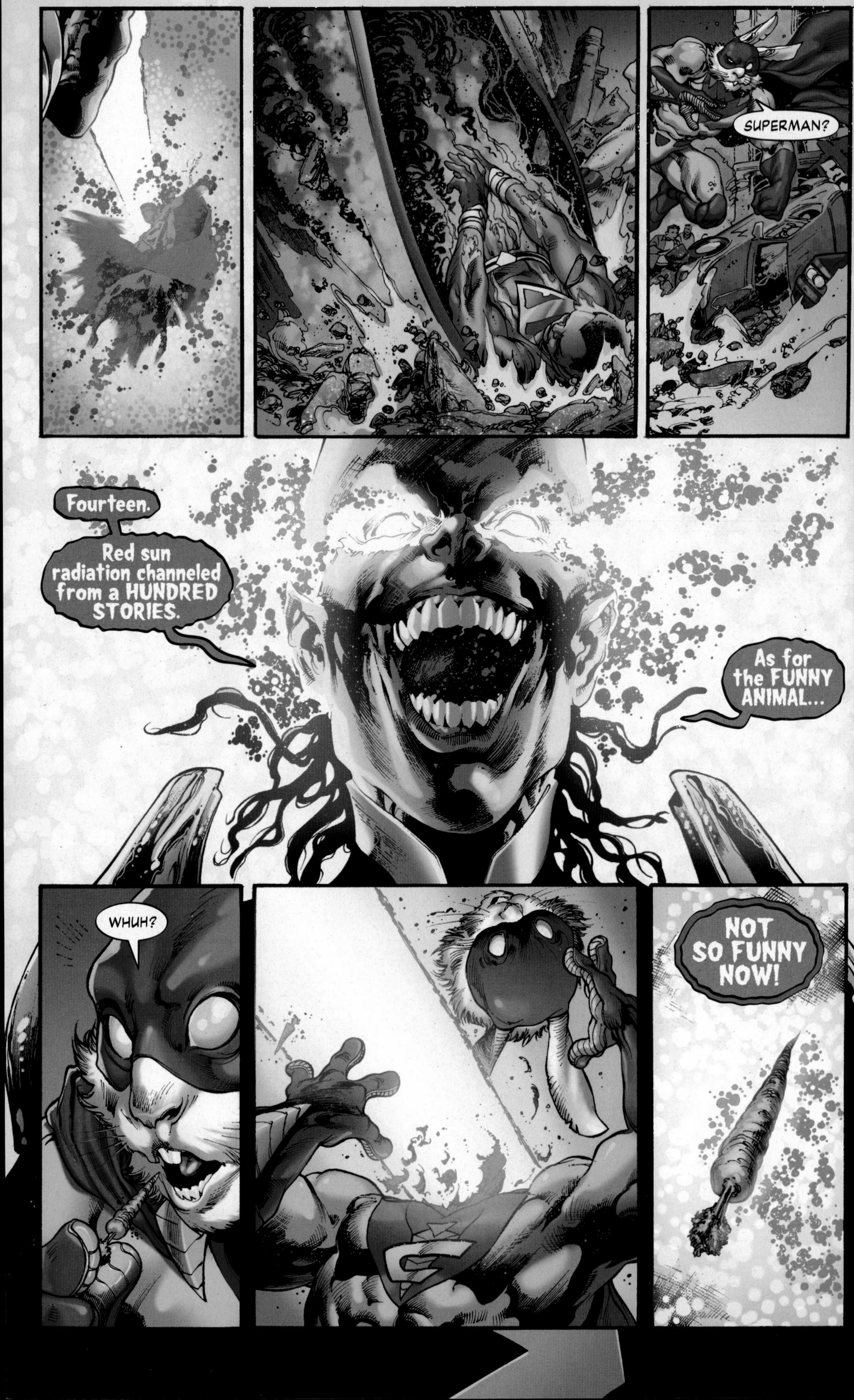
SUPERMAN?
Fourteen.
Red sun radiation channeled from a HUNDRED STORIES.
As for the FUNNY ANIMAL...
WHUH?
NOT SO FUNNY NOW!

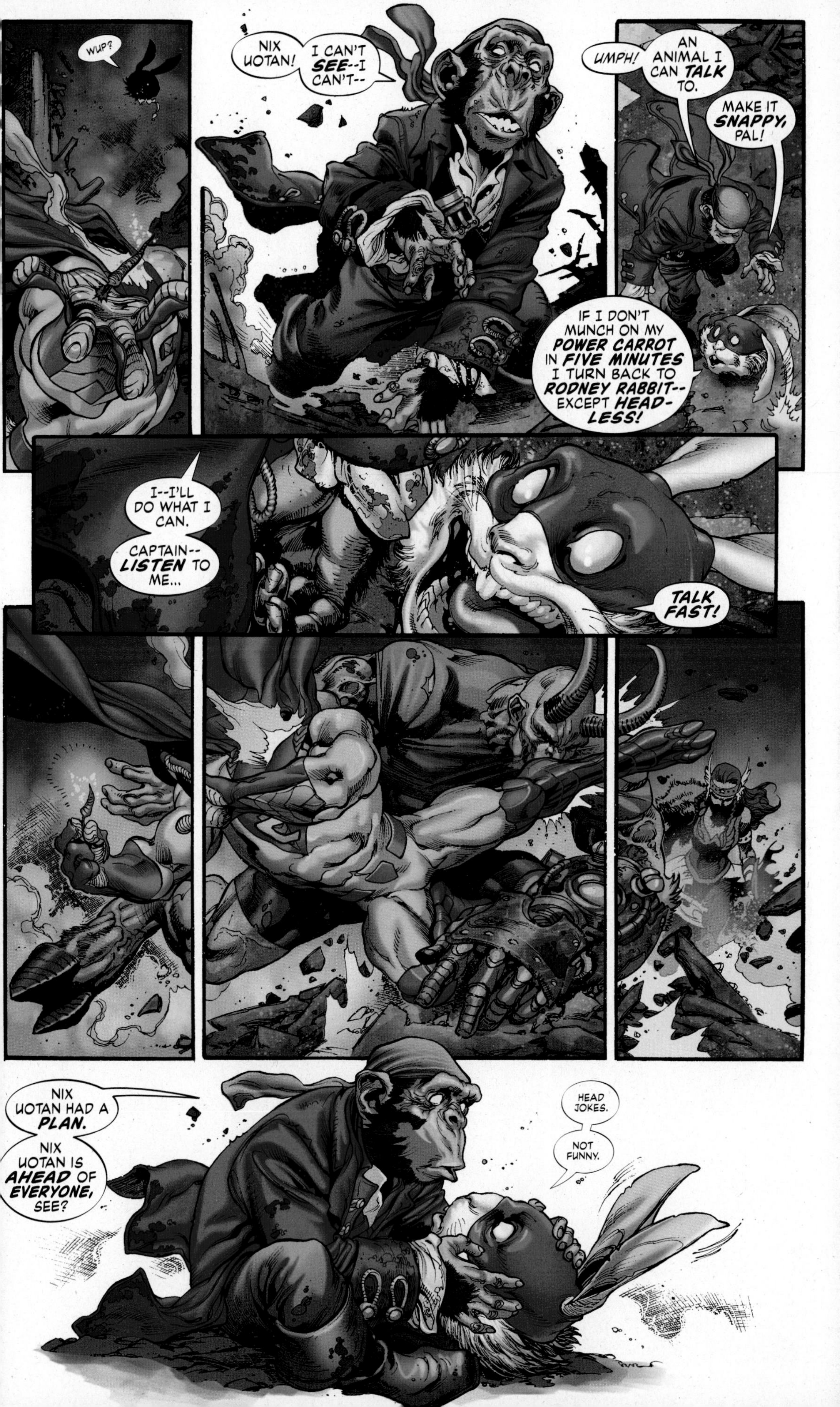
WUP?
NIX UOTAN!
I CAN'T SEE--I CAN'T--
UMPH!
AN ANIMAL I CAN TALK TO.
MAKE IT SNAPPY, PAL!
IF I DON'T MUNCH ON MY POWER CARROT IN FIVE MINUTES I TURN BACK TO RODNEY RABBIT-- EXCEPT HEAD-LESS!
I--I'LL DO WHAT I CAN.
CAPTAIN-- LISTEN TO ME...
TALK FAST!
NIX UOTAN HAD A PLAN.
NIX UOTAN IS AHEAD OF EVERYONE, SEE?
HEAD JOKES.
NOT FUNNY.

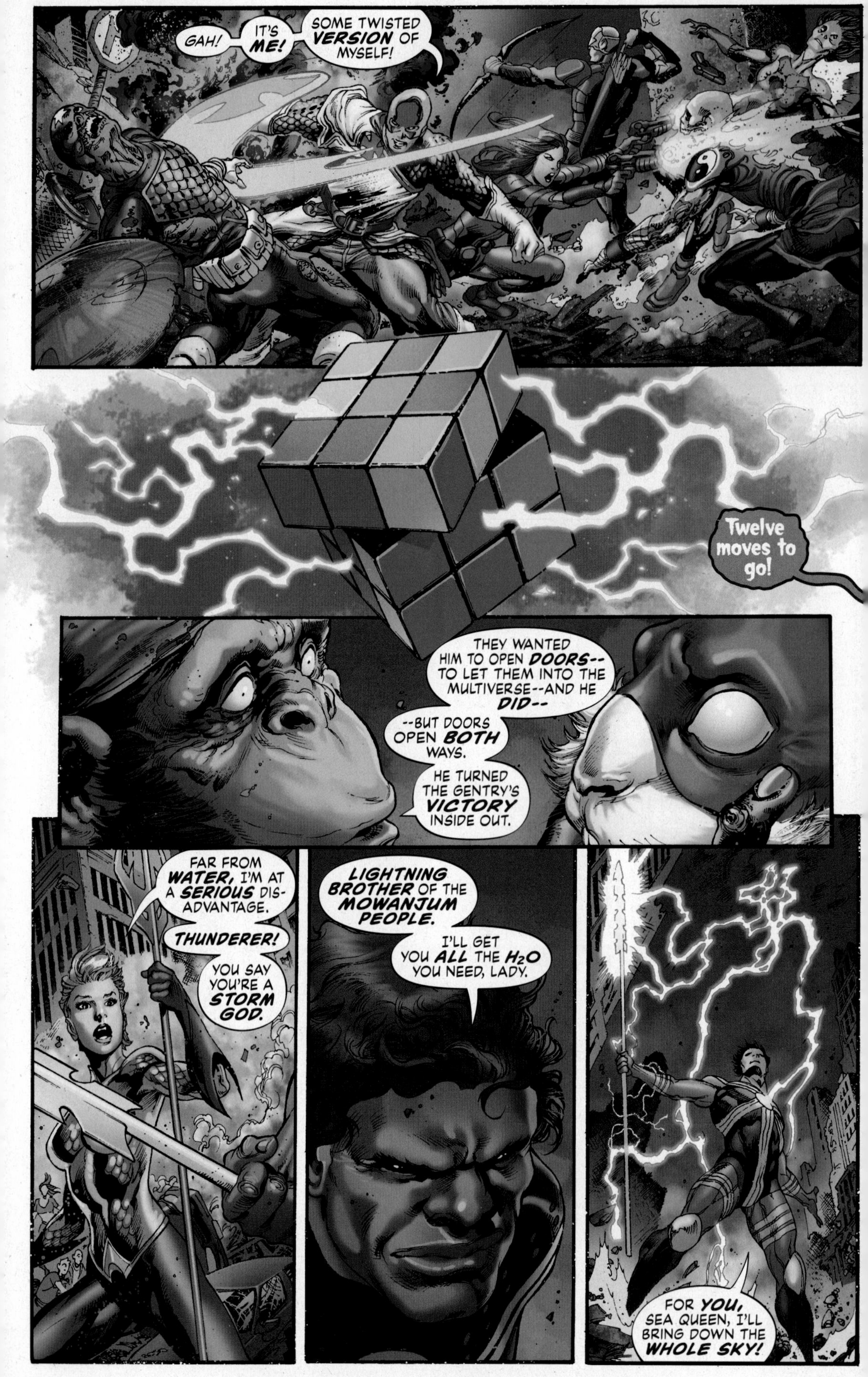
GAH!
IT'S ME!
SOME TWISTED VERSION OF MYSELF!
Twelve moves to go!
THEY WANTED HIM TO OPEN DOORS--TO LET THEM INTO THE MULTIVERSE--AND HE DID--
--BUT DOORS OPEN BOTH WAYS.
HE TURNED THE GENTRY'S VICTORY INSIDE OUT.
FAR FROM WATER, I'M AT A SERIOUS DIS-ADVANTAGE.
THUNDERER!
YOU SAY YOU'RE A STORM GOD.
LIGHTNING BROTHER OF THE MOWANJUM PEOPLE.
I'LL GET YOU ALL THE H2O YOU NEED, LADY.
FOR YOU, SEA QUEEN, I'LL BRING DOWN THE WHOLE SKY!

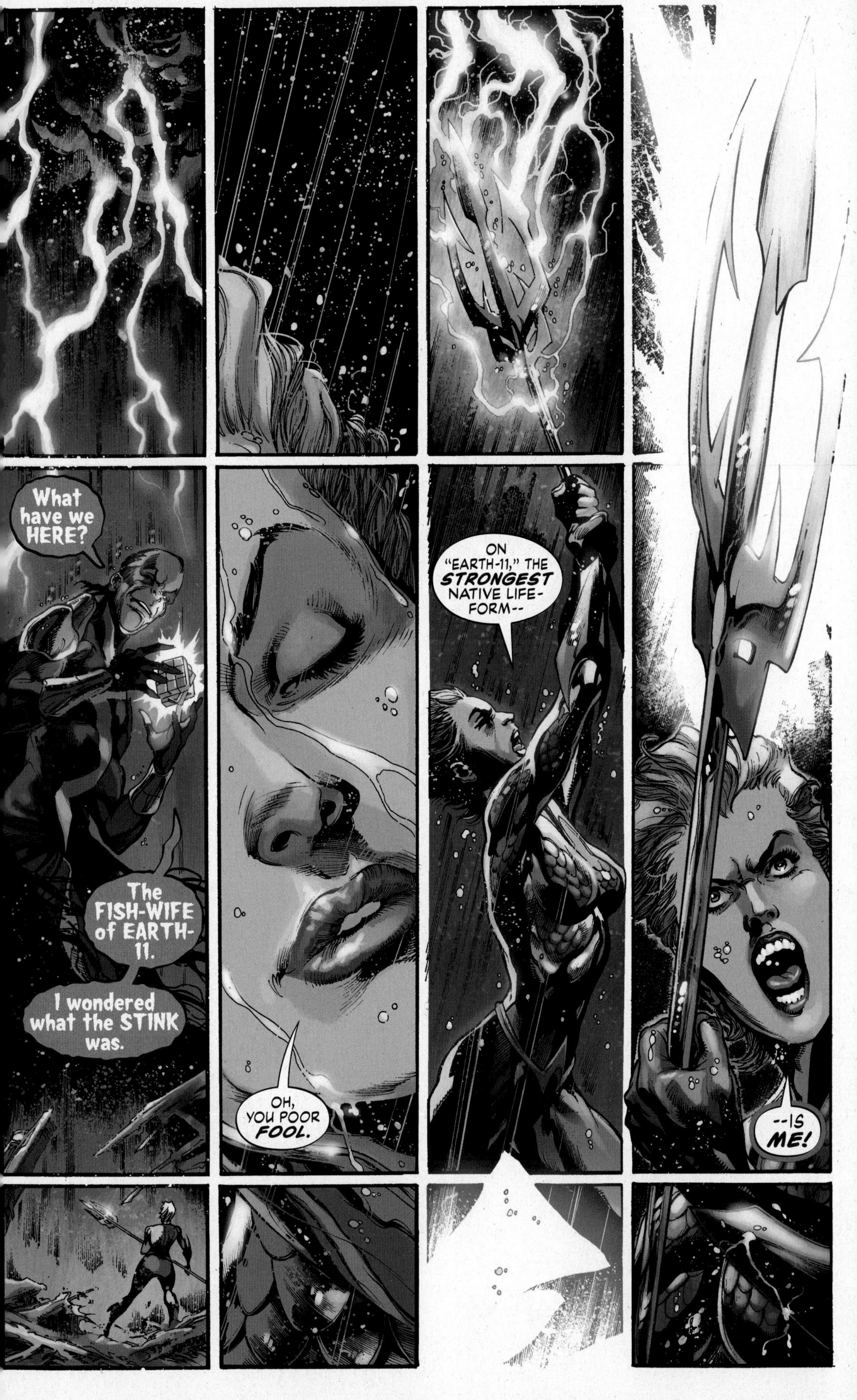
What have we HERE?
The FISH-WIFE of EARTH-11.
I wondered what the STINK was.
OH, YOU POOR FOOL.
ON "EARTH-11," THE STRONGEST NATIVE LIFE-FORM--
--IS ME!

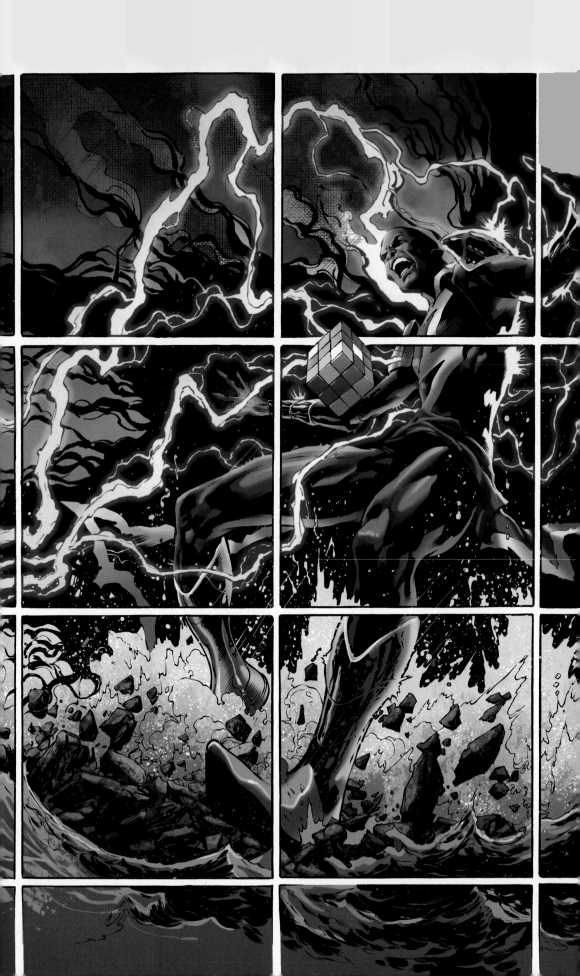

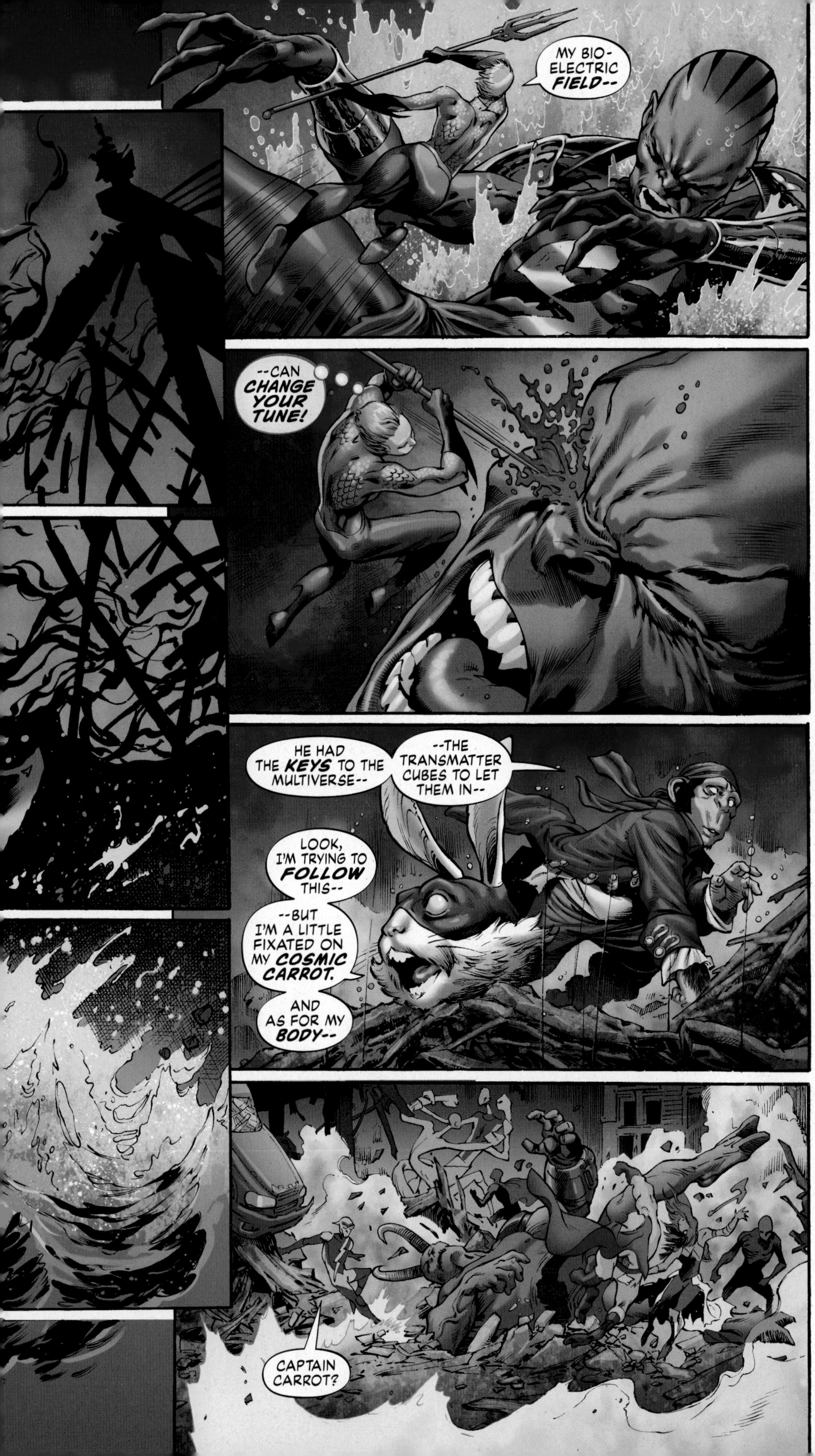
MY BIO-ELECTRIC FIELD--
--CAN CHANGE YOUR TUNE!
HE HAD THE KEYS TO THE MULTIVERSE--
--THE TRANSMATTER CUBES TO LET THEM IN--
LOOK, I'M TRYING TO FOLLOW THIS--
--BUT I'M A LITTLE FIXATED ON MY COSMIC CARROT.
AND AS FOR MY BODY--
CAPTAIN CARROT?

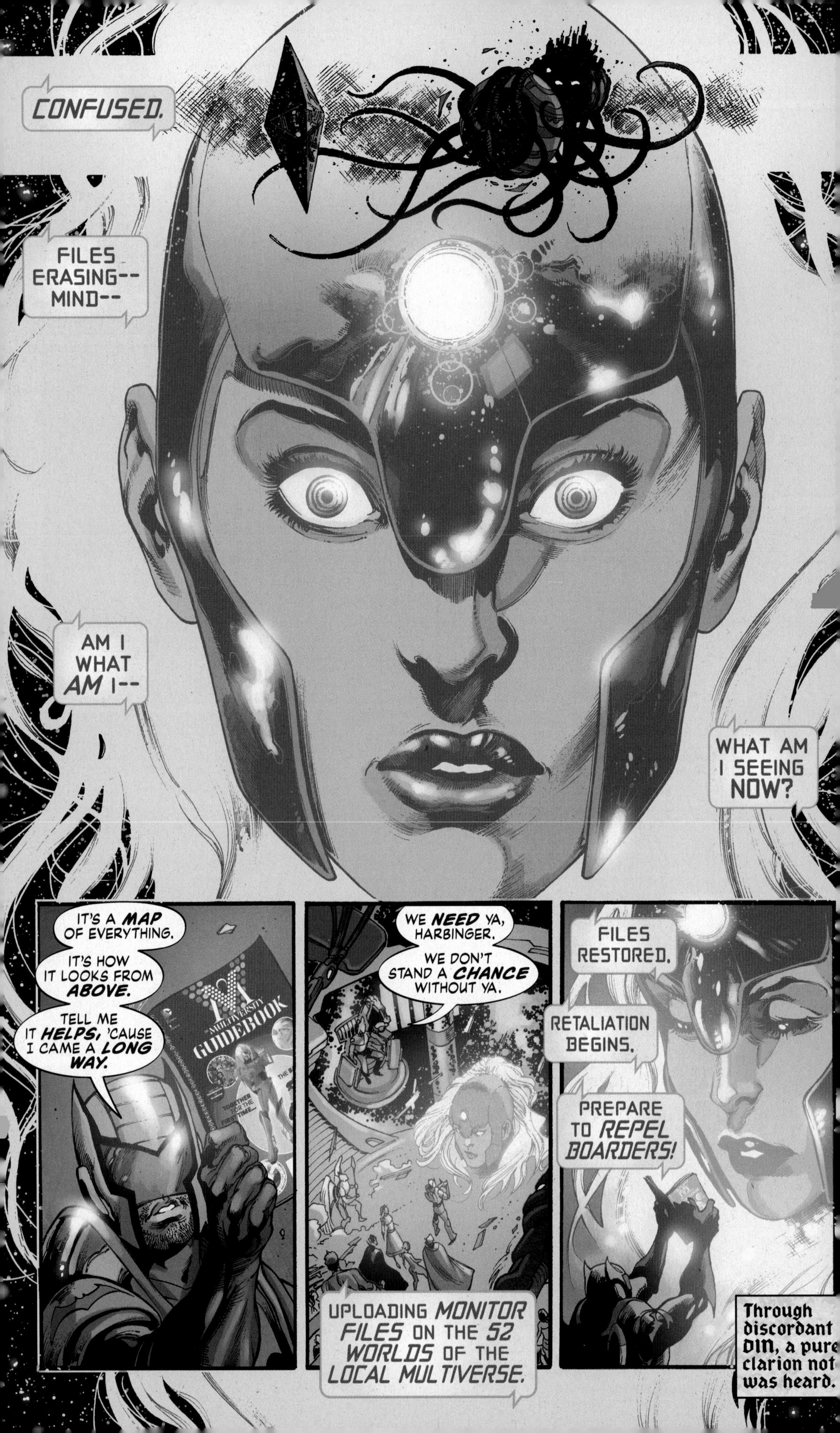
CONFUSED.
FILES ERASING-- MIND--
AM I WHAT AM I--
WHAT AM I SEEING NOW?
IT'S A MAP OF EVERYTHING.
IT'S HOW IT LOOKS FROM ABOVE.
TELL ME IT HELPS, 'CAUSE I CAME A LONG WAY.
MULTIVERSITY GUIDEBOOK
TOGETHER FOR THE FIRST TIME...
WE NEED YA, HARBINGER.
WE DON'T STAND A CHANCE WITHOUT YA.
UPLOADING MONITOR FILES ON THE 52 WORLDS OF THE LOCAL MULTIVERSE.
FILES RESTORED.
RETALIATION BEGINS.
PREPARE TO REPEL BOARDERS!
Through discordant DIN, a pure clarion not was heard.

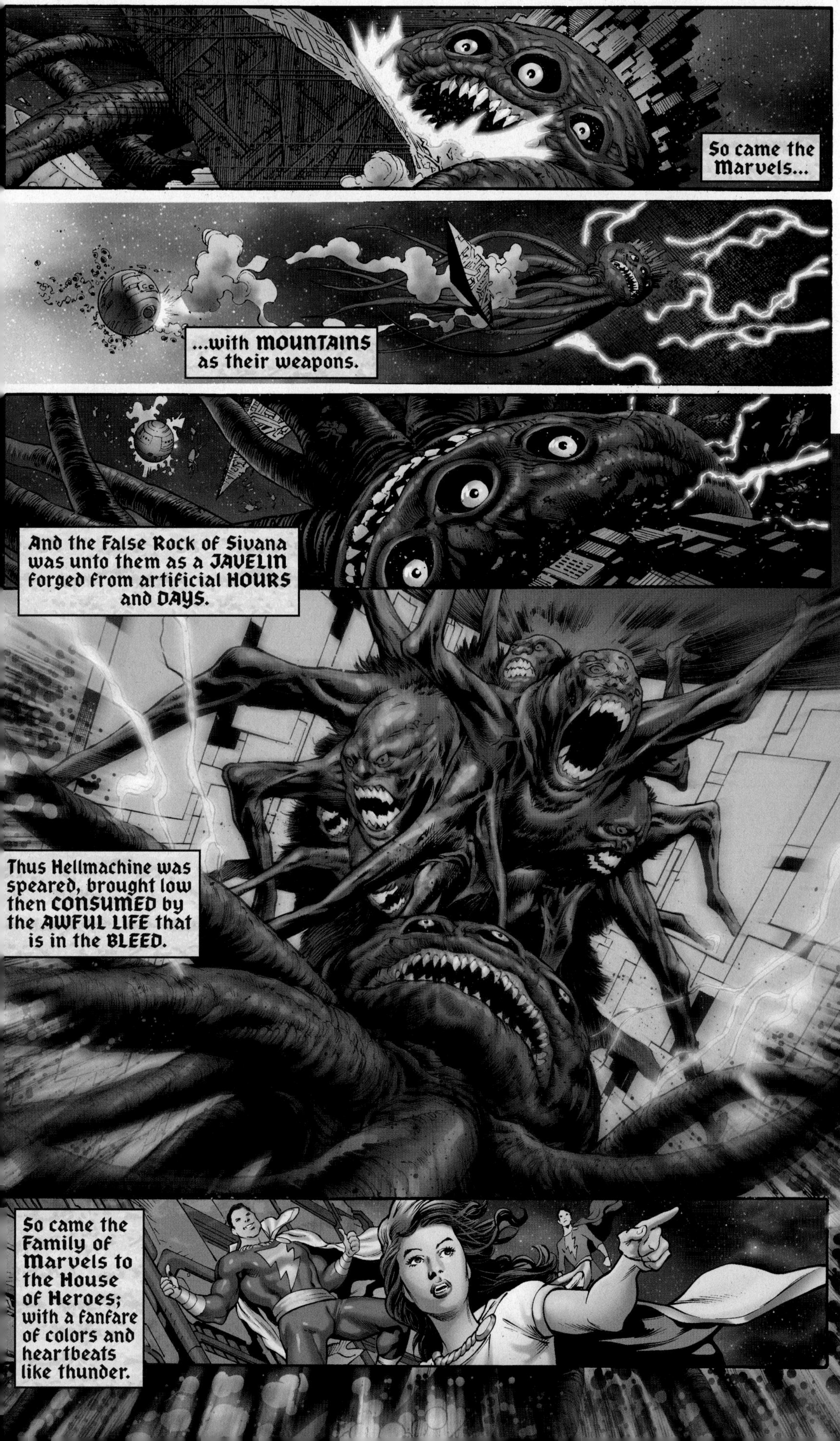
So came the Marvels...
...with MOUNTAINS as their weapons.
And the False Rock of Sivana was unto them as a JAVELIN forged from artificial HOURS and DAYS.
Thus Hellmachine was speared, brought low then CONSUMED by the AWFUL LIFE that is in the BLEED.
So came the Family of Marvels to the House of Heroes; with a fanfare of colors and heartbeats like thunder.

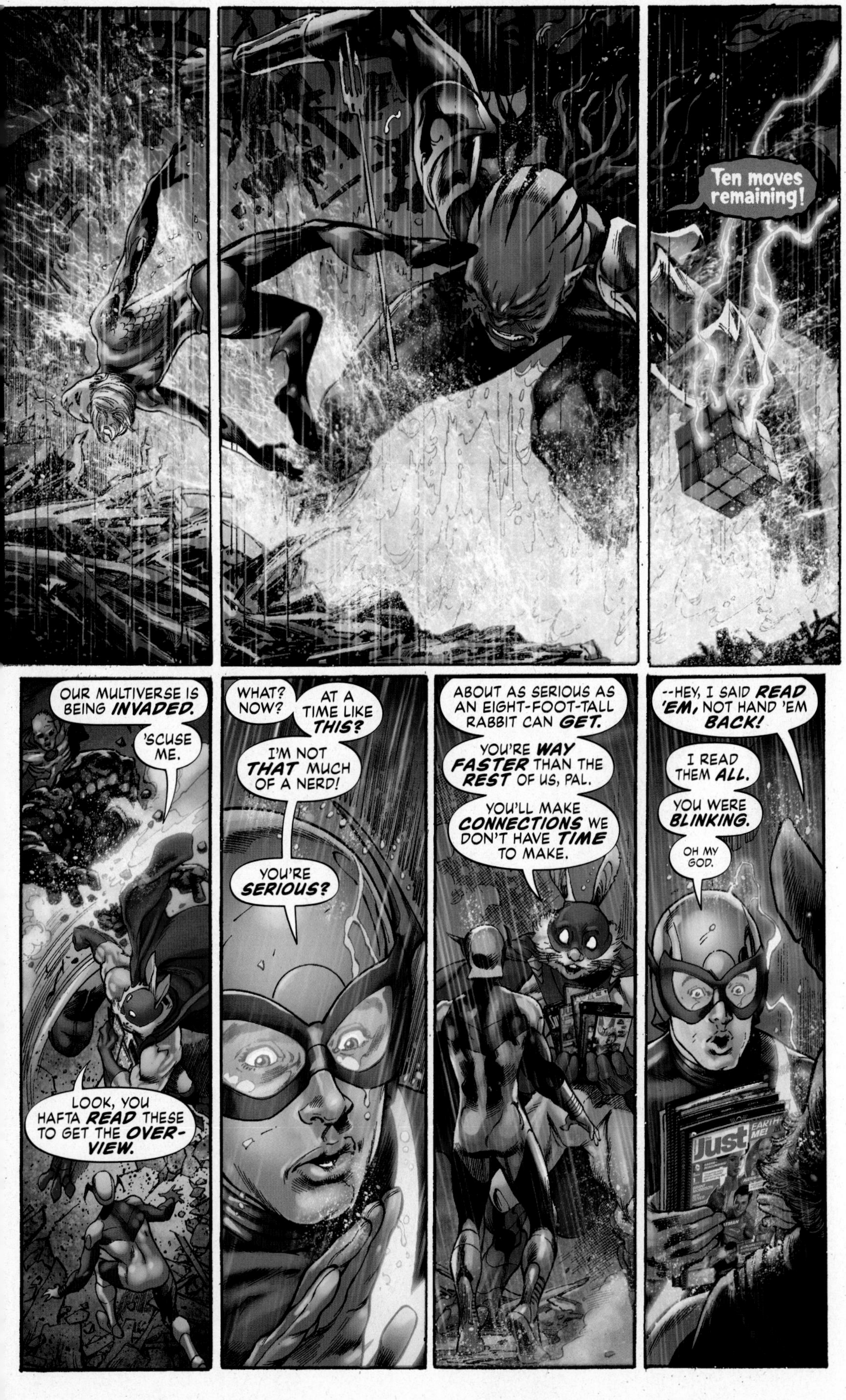

Ten moves remaining!
OUR MULTIVERSE IS BEING INVADED.
'SCUSE ME.
LOOK, YOU HAFTA READ THESE TO GET THE OVER-VIEW.
WHAT? NOW?
AT A TIME LIKE THIS?
I'M NOT THAT MUCH OF A NERD!
YOU'RE SERIOUS?
ABOUT AS SERIOUS AS AN EIGHT-FOOT-TALL RABBIT CAN GET.
YOU'RE WAY FASTER THAN THE REST OF US, PAL.
YOU'LL MAKE CONNECTIONS WE DON'T HAVE TIME TO MAKE.
--HEY, I SAID READ 'EM, NOT HAND 'EM BACK!
I READ THEM ALL.
YOU WERE BLINKING.
OH MY GOD.

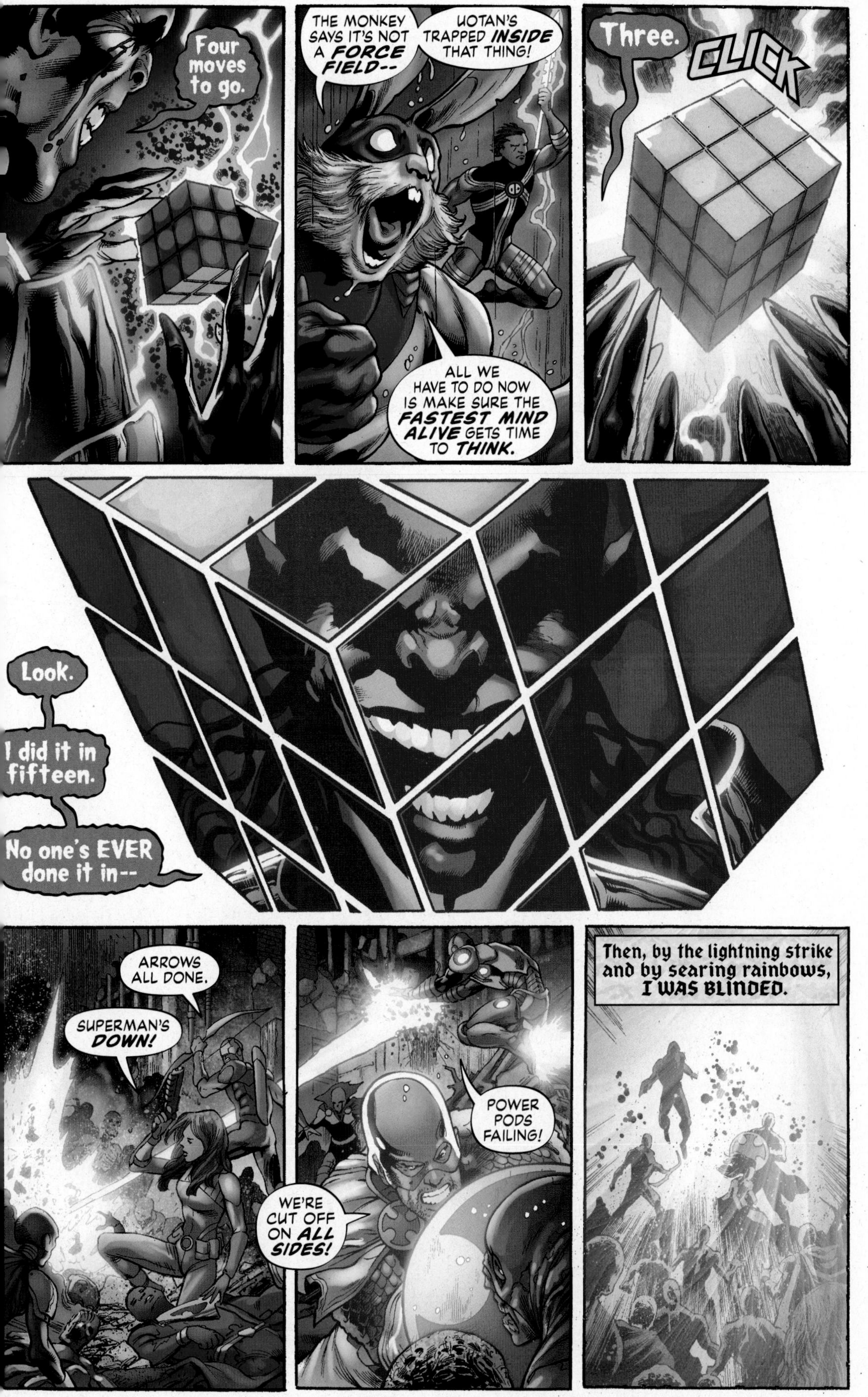

Four moves to go.
THE MONKEY SAYS IT'S NOT A *FORCE FIELD--*
UOTAN'S TRAPPED *INSIDE* THAT THING!
ALL WE HAVE TO DO NOW IS MAKE SURE THE *FASTEST MIND ALIVE* GETS TIME TO *THINK.*
Three.
CLICK
Look.
I did it in fifteen.
No one's EVER done it in--
ARROWS ALL DONE.
SUPERMAN'S *DOWN!*
POWER PODS FAILING!
WE'RE CUT OFF ON *ALL SIDES!*
Then, by the lightning strike and by searing rainbows, I WAS BLINDED.

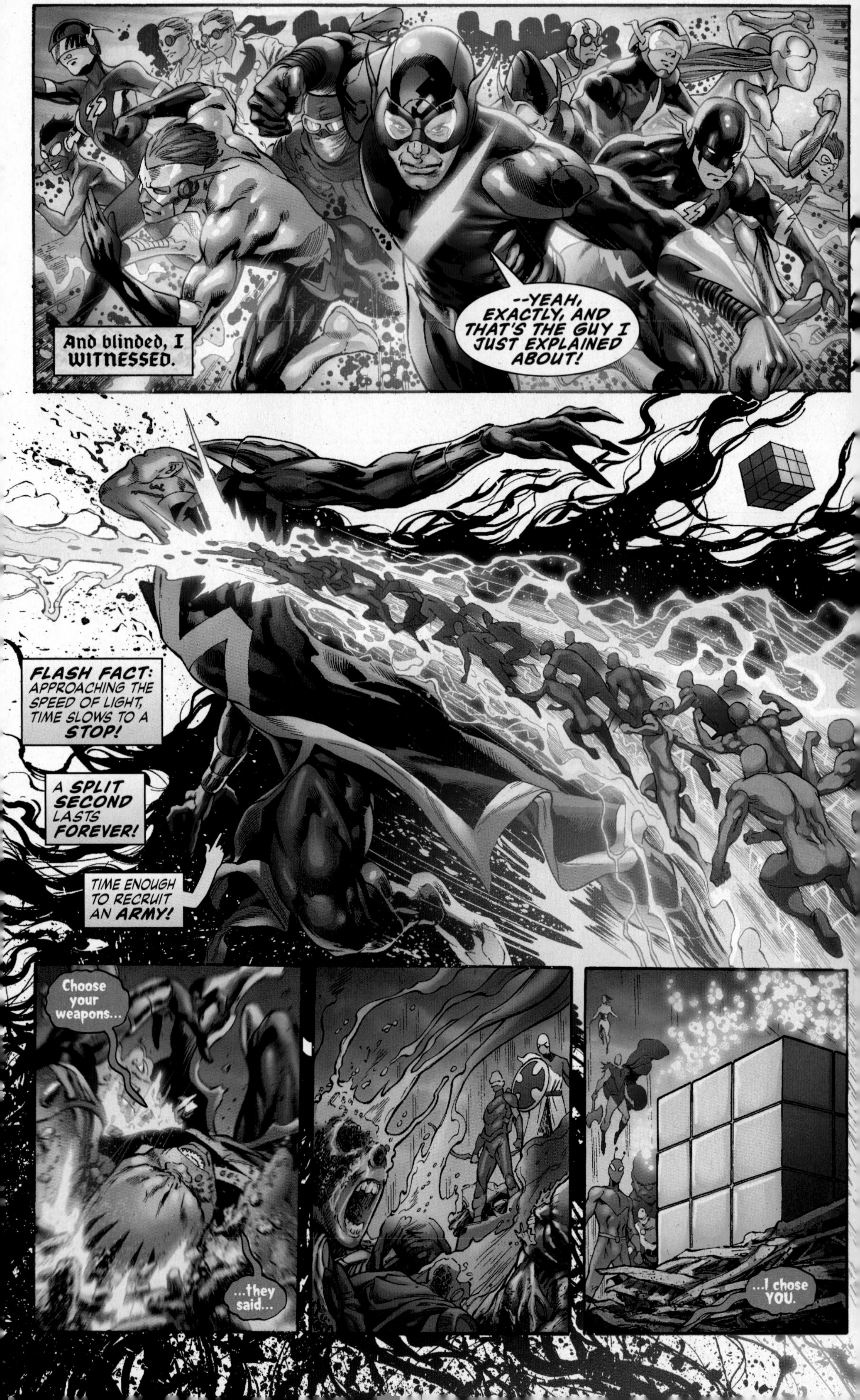
And blinded, I WITNESSED.
--YEAH, EXACTLY, AND THAT'S THE GUY I JUST EXPLAINED ABOUT!
FLASH FACT: APPROACHING THE SPEED OF LIGHT, TIME SLOWS TO A STOP!
A SPLIT SECOND LASTS FOREVER!
TIME ENOUGH TO RECRUIT AN ARMY!
Choose your weapons...
...they said...
...I chose YOU.

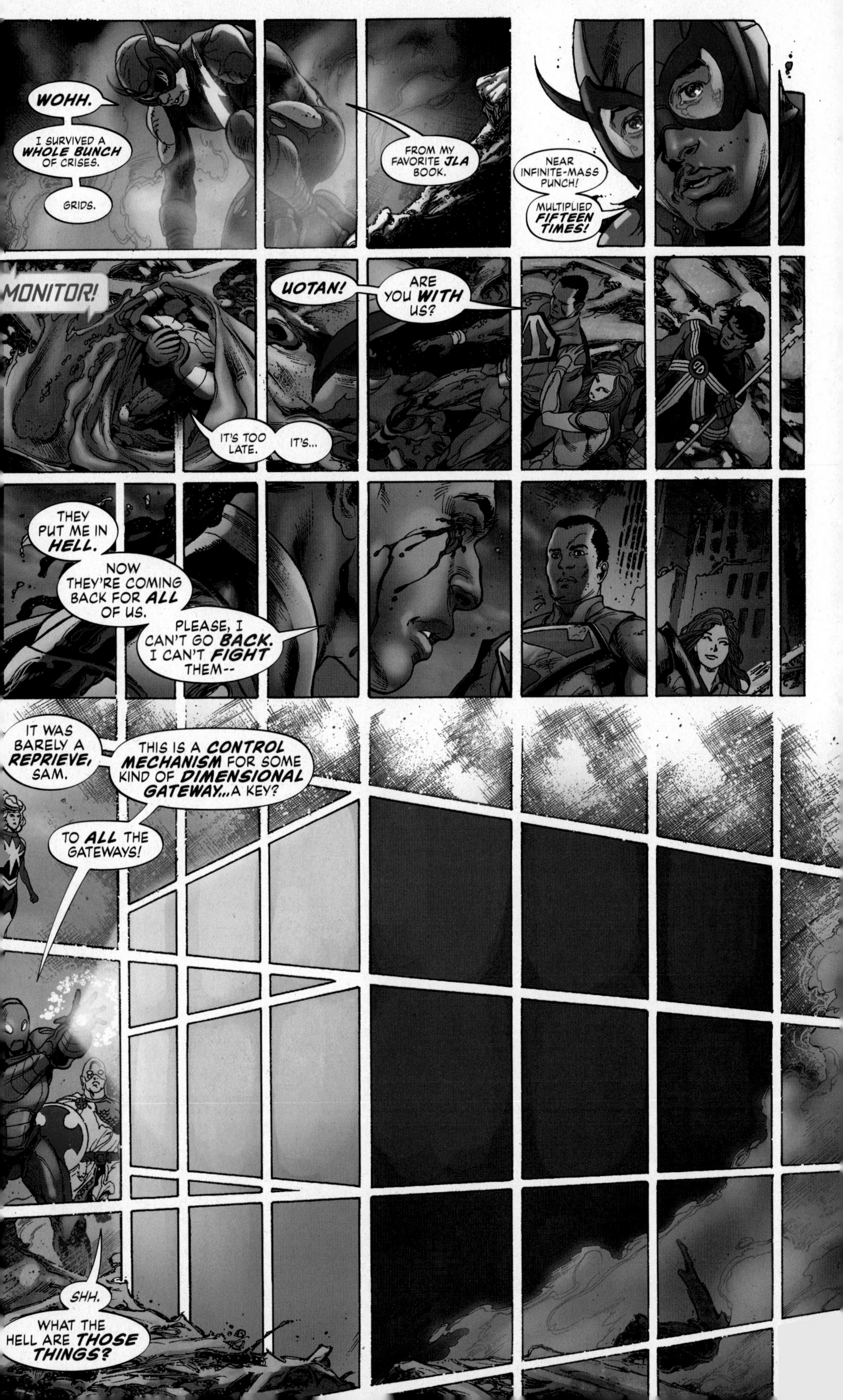
WOHH.
I SURVIVED A WHOLE BUNCH OF CRISES.
GRIDS.
FROM MY FAVORITE JLA BOOK.
NEAR INFINITE-MASS PUNCH!
MULTIPLIED FIFTEEN TIMES!
MONITOR!
UOTAN!
ARE YOU WITH US?
IT'S TOO LATE.
IT'S...
THEY PUT ME IN HELL.
NOW THEY'RE COMING BACK FOR ALL OF US.
PLEASE, I CAN'T GO BACK. I CAN'T FIGHT THEM--
IT WAS BARELY A REPRIEVE, SAM.
THIS IS A CONTROL MECHANISM FOR SOME KIND OF DIMENSIONAL GATEWAY...A KEY?
TO ALL THE GATEWAYS!
SHH.
WHAT THE HELL ARE THOSE THINGS?

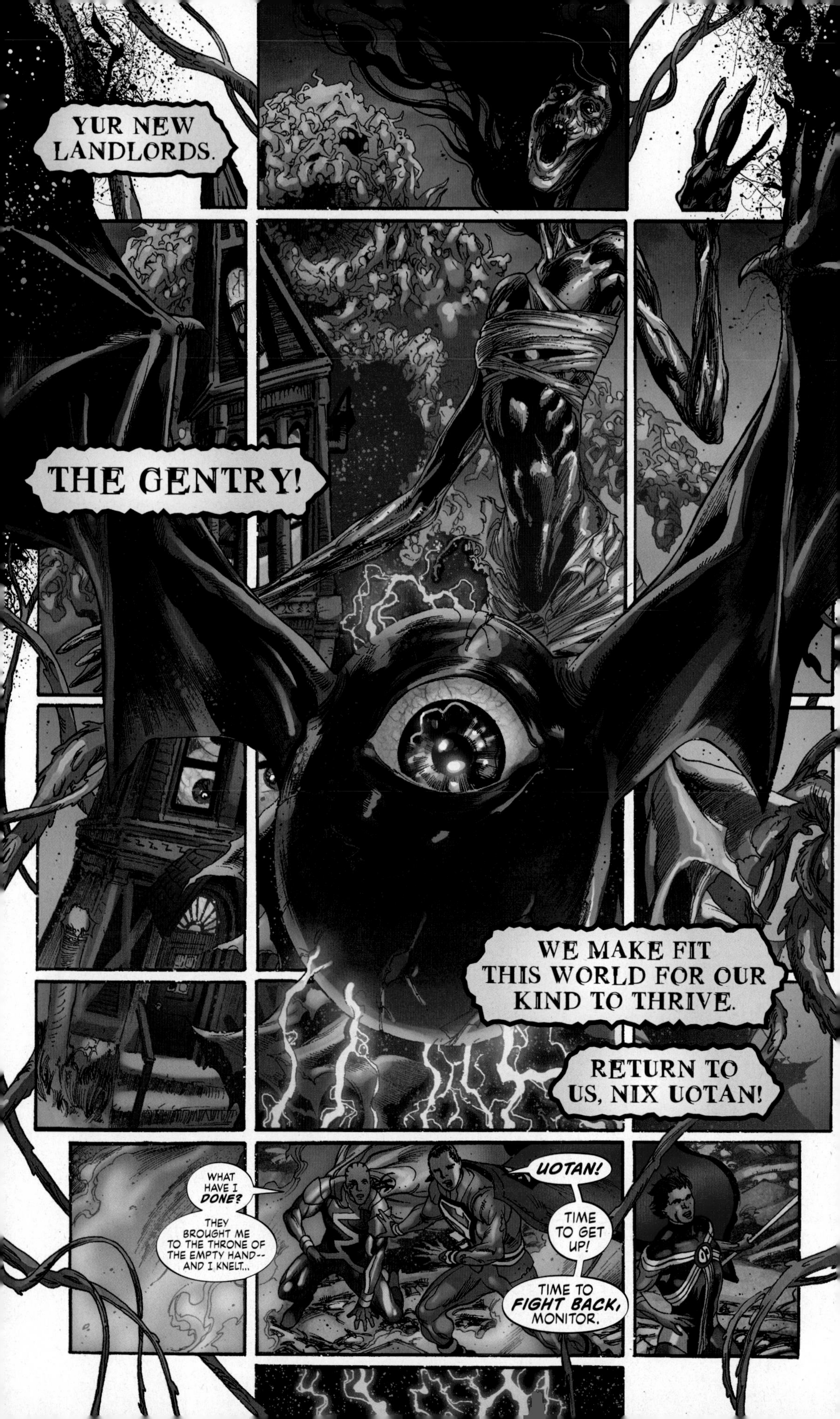
YUR NEW LANDLORDS.
THE GENTRY!
WE MAKE FIT THIS WORLD FOR OUR KIND TO THRIVE.
RETURN TO US, NIX UOTAN!
WHAT HAVE I DONE?
THEY BROUGHT ME TO THE THRONE OF THE EMPTY HAND-- AND I KNELT...
UOTAN!
TIME TO GET UP!
TIME TO FIGHT BACK, MONITOR.

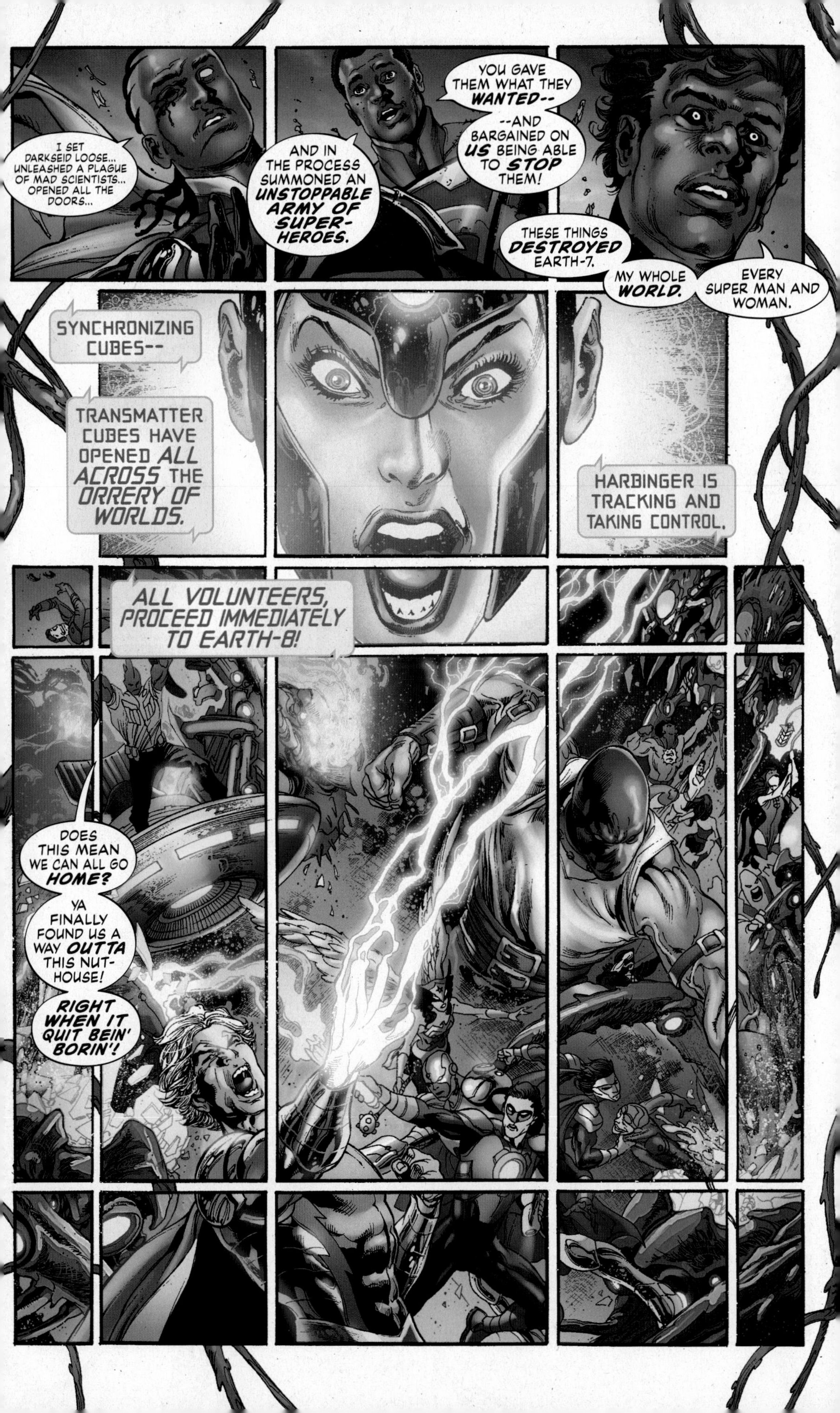
I SET DARKSEID LOOSE... UNLEASHED A PLAGUE OF MAD SCIENTISTS... OPENED ALL THE DOORS...
AND IN THE PROCESS SUMMONED AN UNSTOPPABLE ARMY OF SUPER-HEROES.
YOU GAVE THEM WHAT THEY WANTED--
--AND BARGAINED ON US BEING ABLE TO STOP THEM!
THESE THINGS DESTROYED EARTH-7.
MY WHOLE WORLD.
EVERY SUPER MAN AND WOMAN.
SYNCHRONIZING CUBES--
TRANSMATTER CUBES HAVE OPENED ALL ACROSS THE ORRERY OF WORLDS.
HARBINGER IS TRACKING AND TAKING CONTROL.
ALL VOLUNTEERS, PROCEED IMMEDIATELY TO EARTH-8!
DOES THIS MEAN WE CAN ALL GO HOME?
YA FINALLY FOUND US A WAY OUTTA THIS NUT-HOUSE!
RIGHT WHEN IT QUIT BEIN' BORIN'!

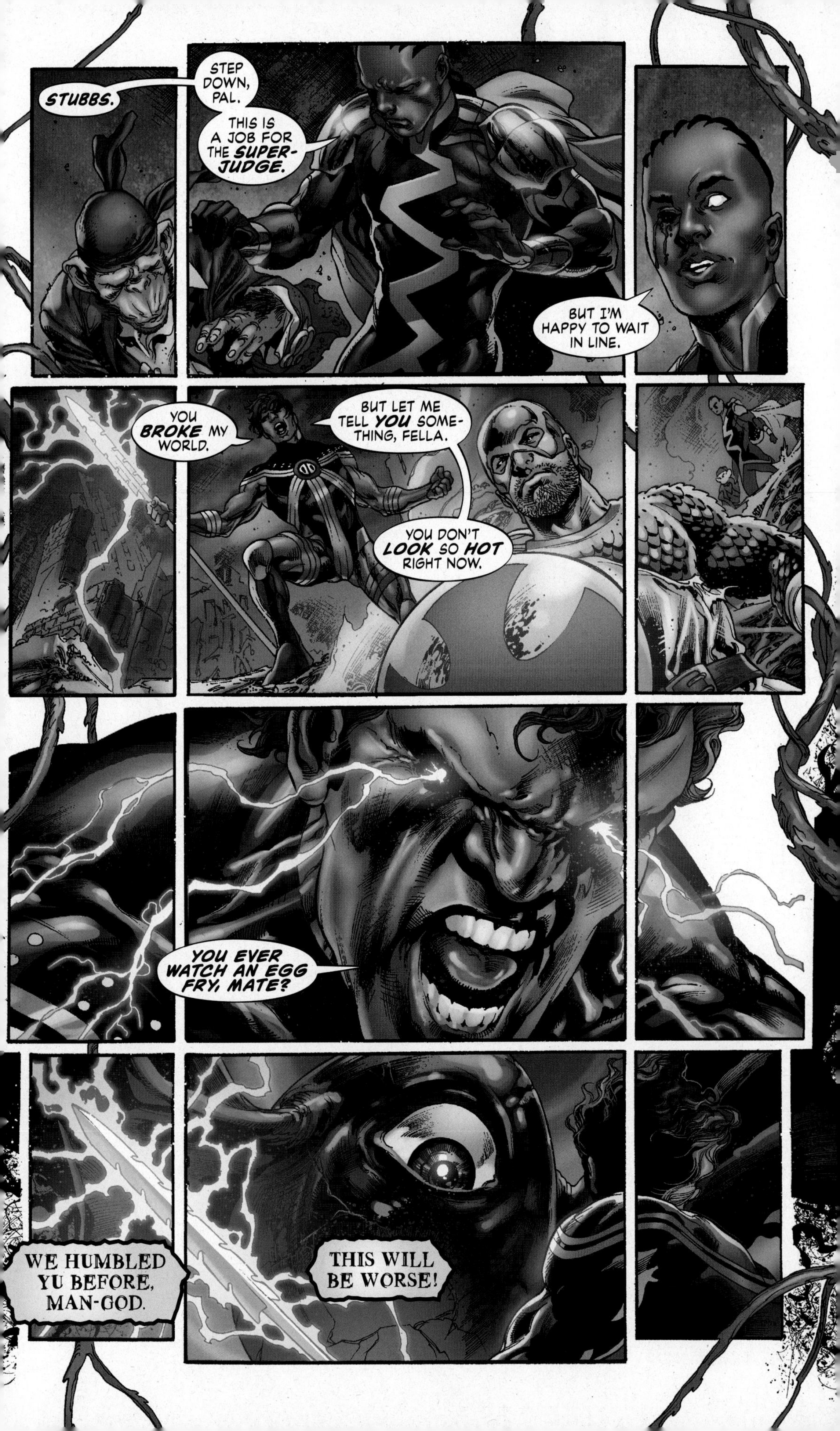

STUBBS.
STEP DOWN, PAL.
THIS IS A JOB FOR THE SUPER-JUDGE.
BUT I'M HAPPY TO WAIT IN LINE.
YOU BROKE MY WORLD.
BUT LET ME TELL YOU SOME-THING, FELLA.
YOU DON'T LOOK SO HOT RIGHT NOW.
YOU EVER WATCH AN EGG FRY, MATE?
WE HUMBLED YU BEFORE, MAN-GOD.
THIS WILL BE WORSE!

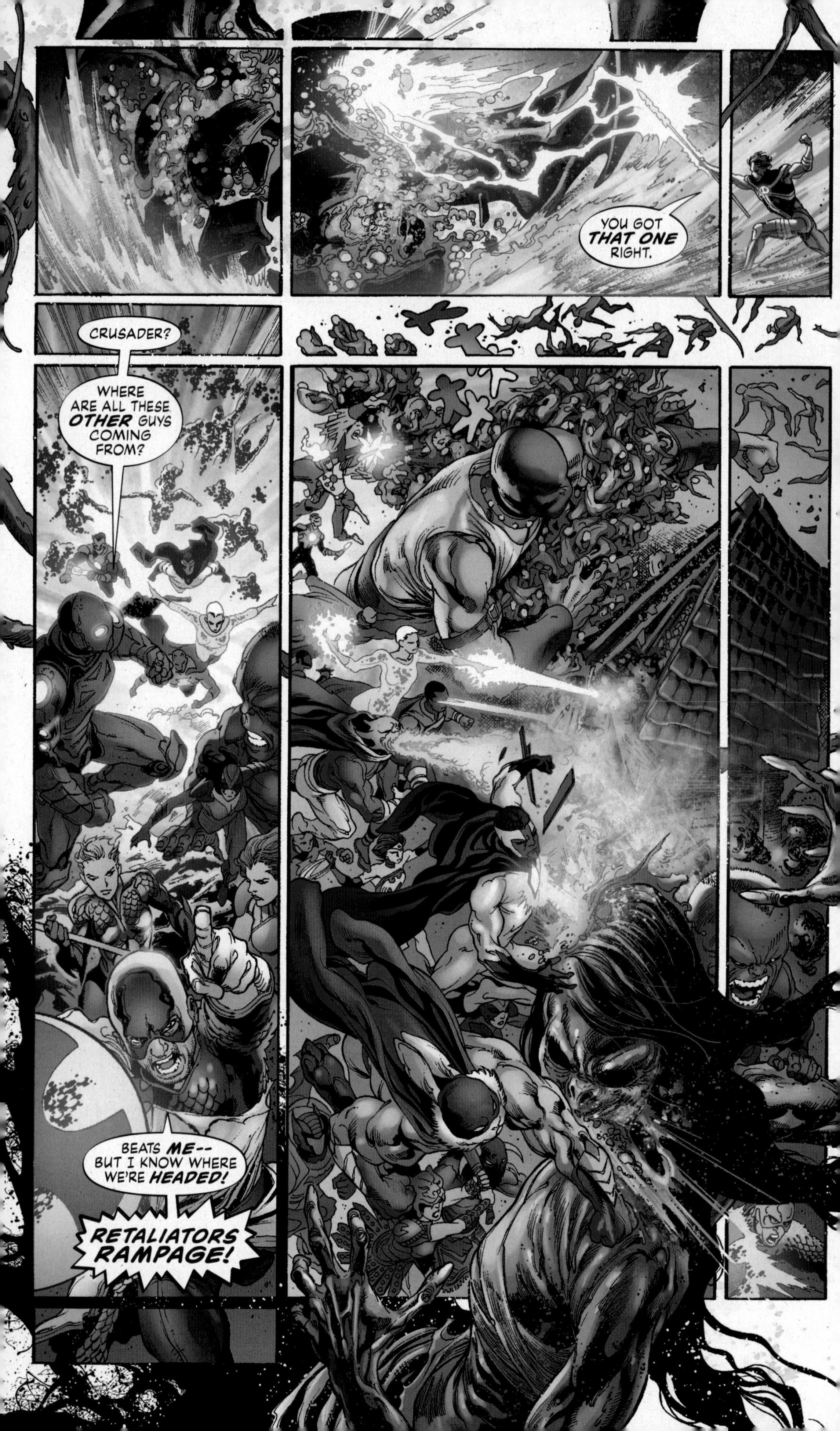
YOU GOT *THAT ONE* RIGHT.
CRUSADER?
WHERE ARE ALL THESE *OTHER* GUYS COMING FROM?
BEATS *ME*-- BUT I KNOW WHERE WE'RE *HEADED!*
RETALIATORS RAMPAGE!

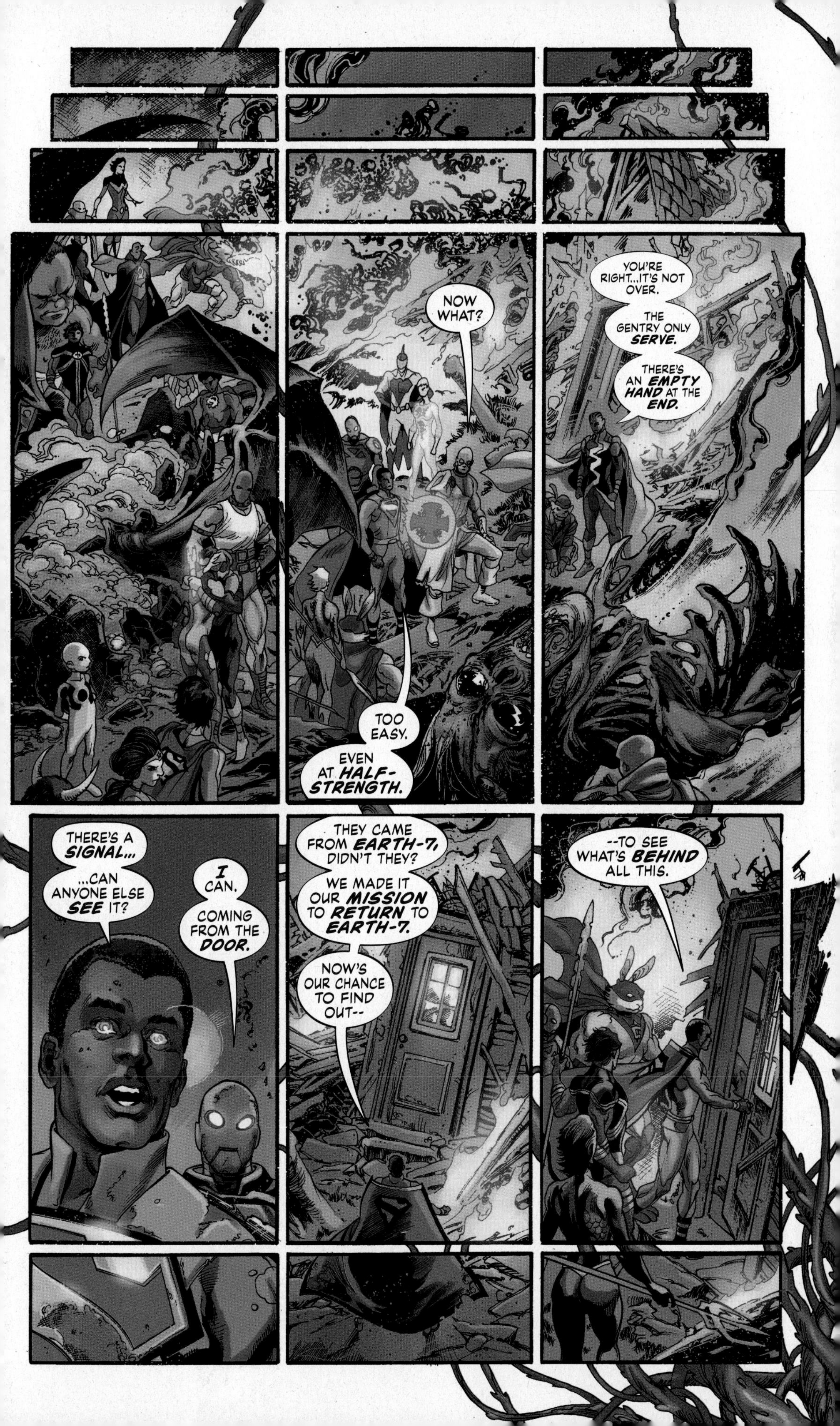
NOW WHAT?
TOO EASY.
EVEN AT HALF-STRENGTH.
YOU'RE RIGHT...IT'S NOT OVER.
THE GENTRY ONLY SERVE.
THERE'S AN EMPTY HAND AT THE END.
THERE'S A SIGNAL...
...CAN ANYONE ELSE SEE IT?
I CAN.
COMING FROM THE DOOR.
THEY CAME FROM EARTH-7, DIDN'T THEY?
WE MADE IT OUR MISSION TO RETURN TO EARTH-7.
NOW'S OUR CHANCE TO FIND OUT--
--TO SEE WHAT'S BEHIND ALL THIS.

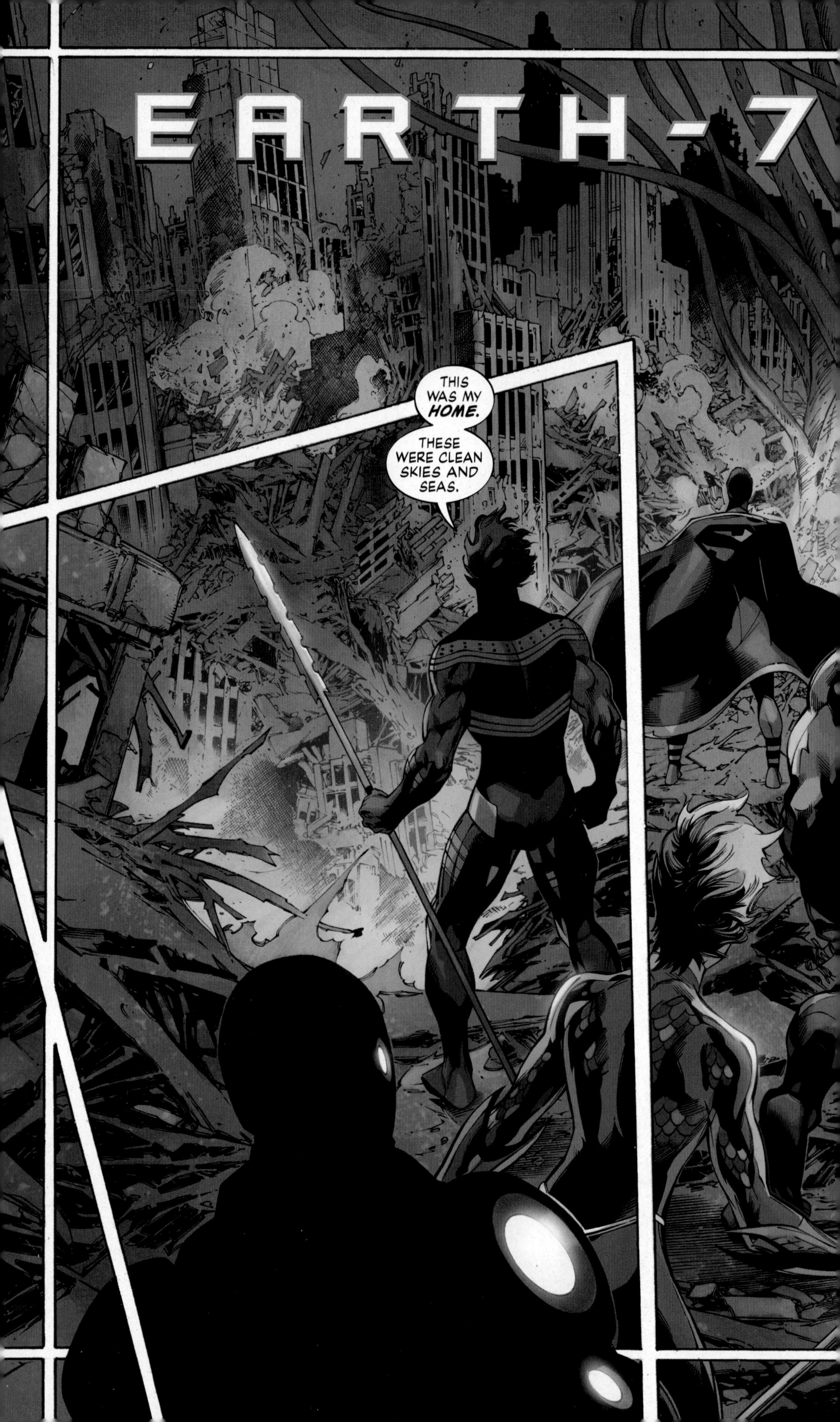
EARTH-7
THIS WAS MY HOME.
THESE WERE CLEAN SKIES AND SEAS.

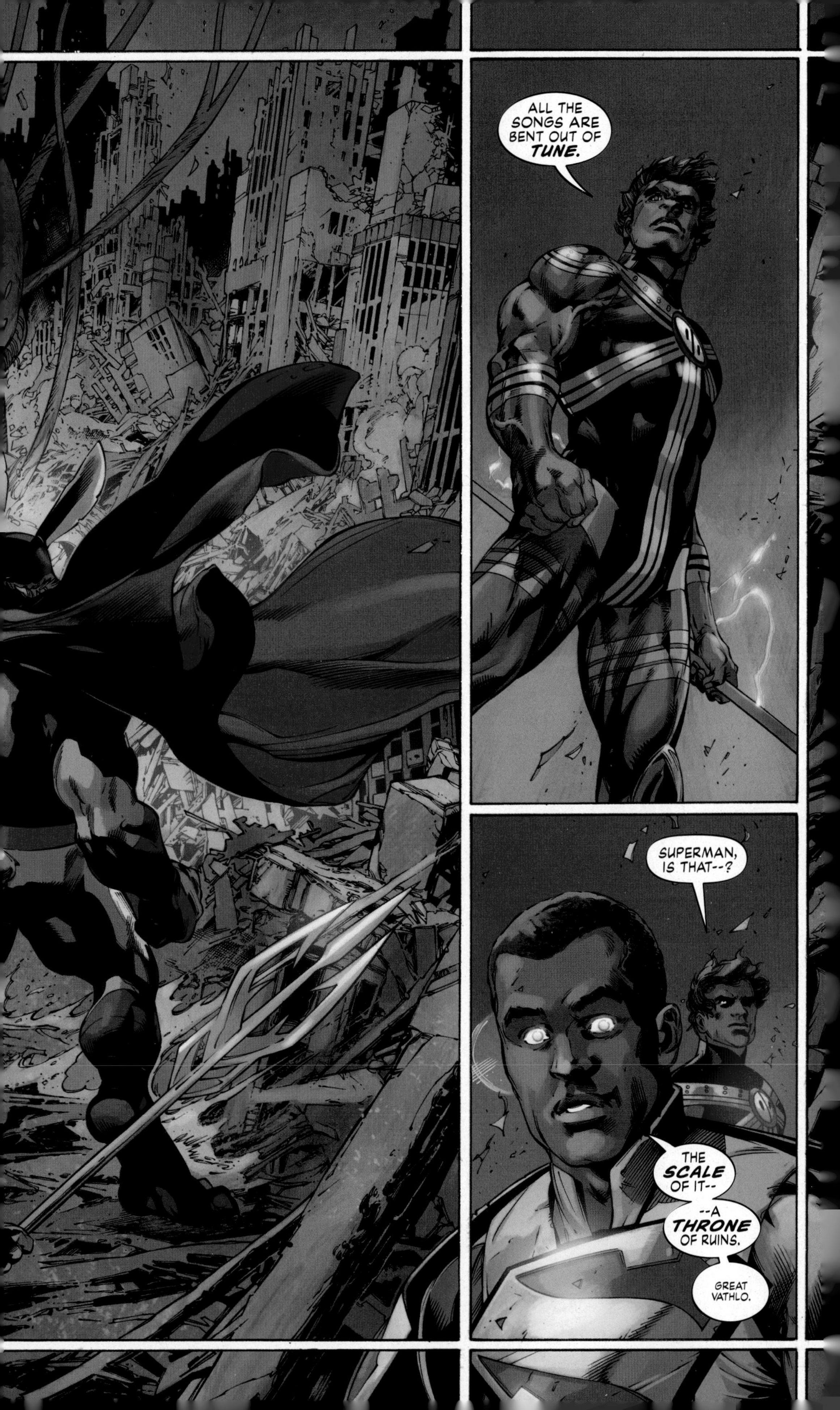

ALL THE SONGS ARE BENT OUT OF TUNE.
SUPERMAN, IS THAT--?
THE SCALE OF IT--
--A THRONE OF RUINS.
GREAT VATHLO.

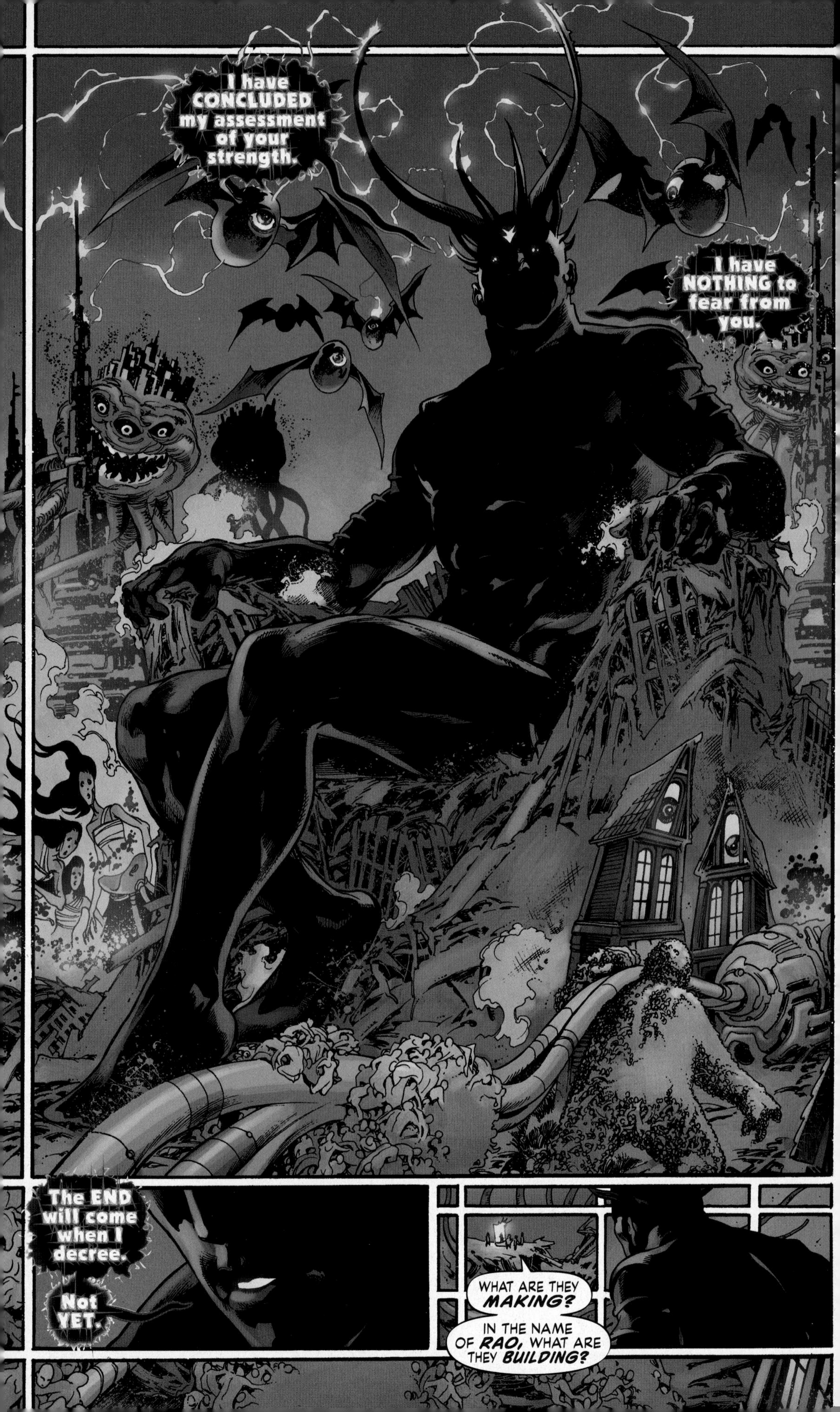
I have CONCLUDED my assessment of your strength.
I have NOTHING to fear from you.
The END will come when I decree.
Not YET.
WHAT ARE THEY MAKING?
IN THE NAME OF RAO, WHAT ARE THEY BUILDING?

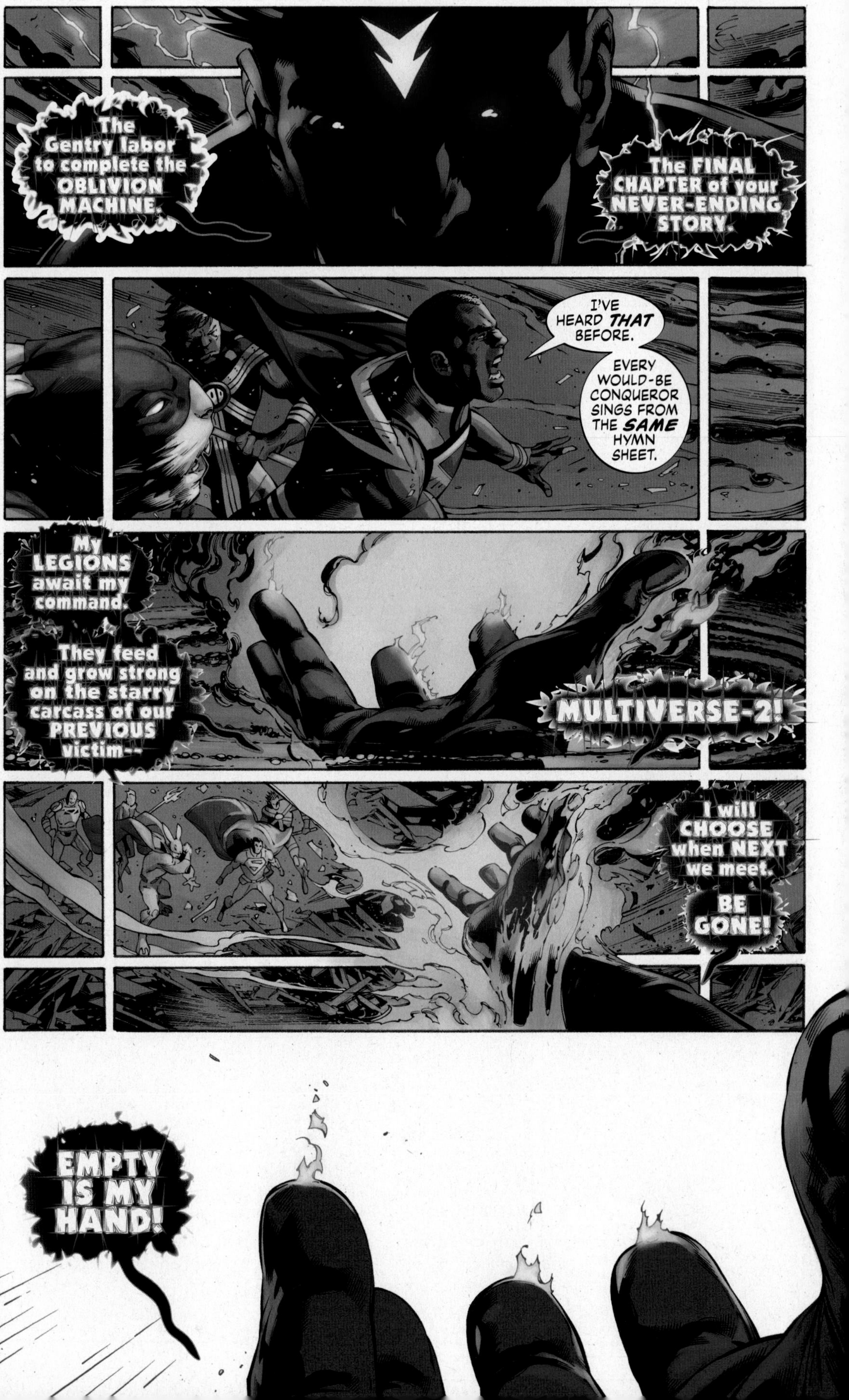
The Gentry labor to complete the OBLIVION MACHINE.
The FINAL CHAPTER of your NEVER-ENDING STORY.
I'VE HEARD THAT BEFORE.
EVERY WOULD-BE CONQUEROR SINGS FROM THE SAME HYMN SHEET.
My LEGIONS await my command.
They feed and grow strong on the starry carcass of our PREVIOUS victim--
MULTIVERSE-2!
I will CHOOSE when NEXT we meet.
BE GONE!
EMPTY IS MY HAND!

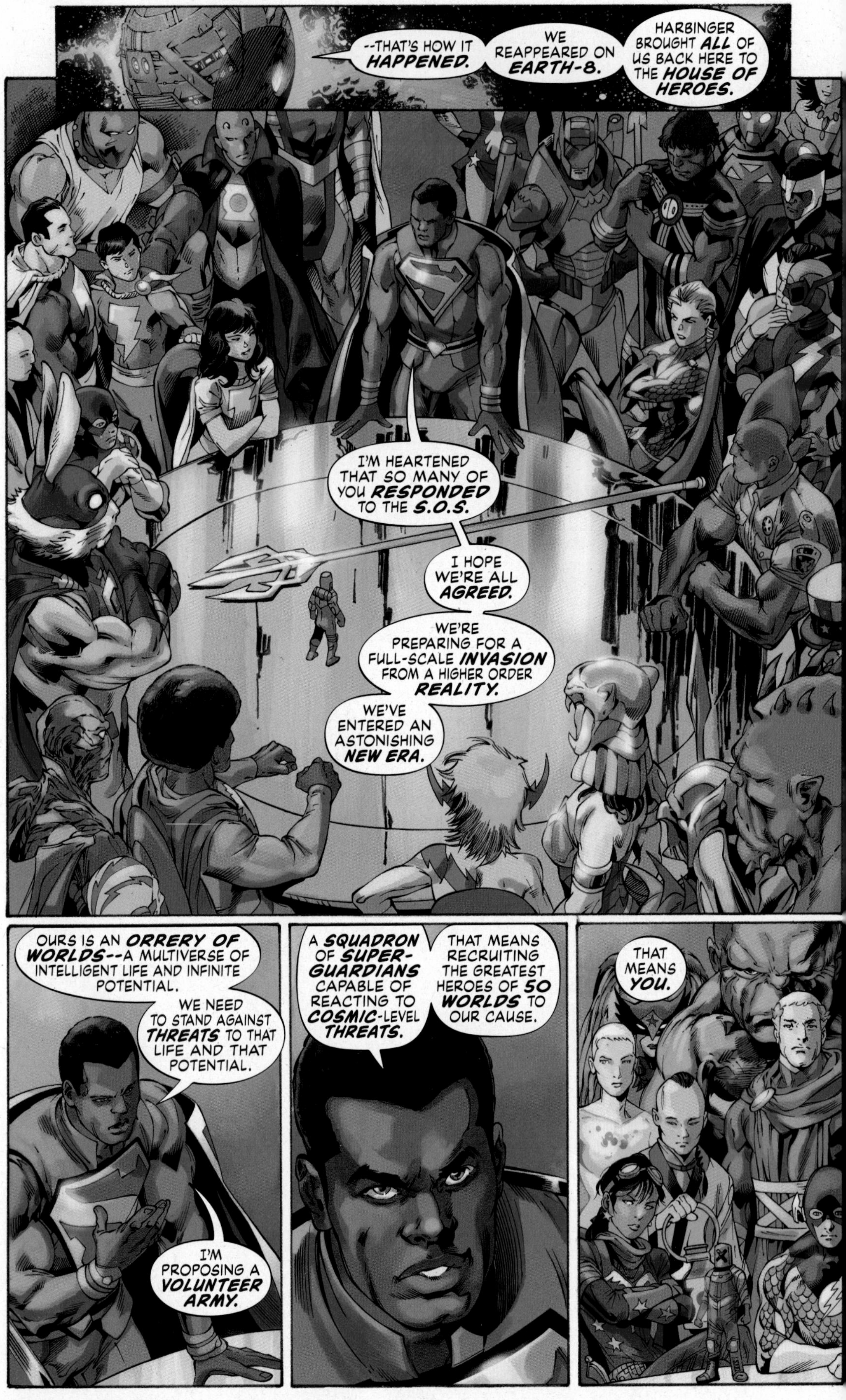

--THAT'S HOW IT HAPPENED.
WE REAPPEARED ON EARTH-8.
HARBINGER BROUGHT ALL OF US BACK HERE TO THE HOUSE OF HEROES.
I'M HEARTENED THAT SO MANY OF YOU RESPONDED TO THE S.O.S.
I HOPE WE'RE ALL AGREED.
WE'RE PREPARING FOR A FULL-SCALE INVASION FROM A HIGHER ORDER REALITY.
WE'VE ENTERED AN ASTONISHING NEW ERA.
OURS IS AN ORRERY OF WORLDS--A MULTIVERSE OF INTELLIGENT LIFE AND INFINITE POTENTIAL.
WE NEED TO STAND AGAINST THREATS TO THAT LIFE AND THAT POTENTIAL.
I'M PROPOSING A VOLUNTEER ARMY.
A SQUADRON OF SUPER-GUARDIANS CAPABLE OF REACTING TO COSMIC-LEVEL THREATS.
THAT MEANS RECRUITING THE GREATEST HEROES OF 50 WORLDS TO OUR CAUSE.
THAT MEANS YOU.

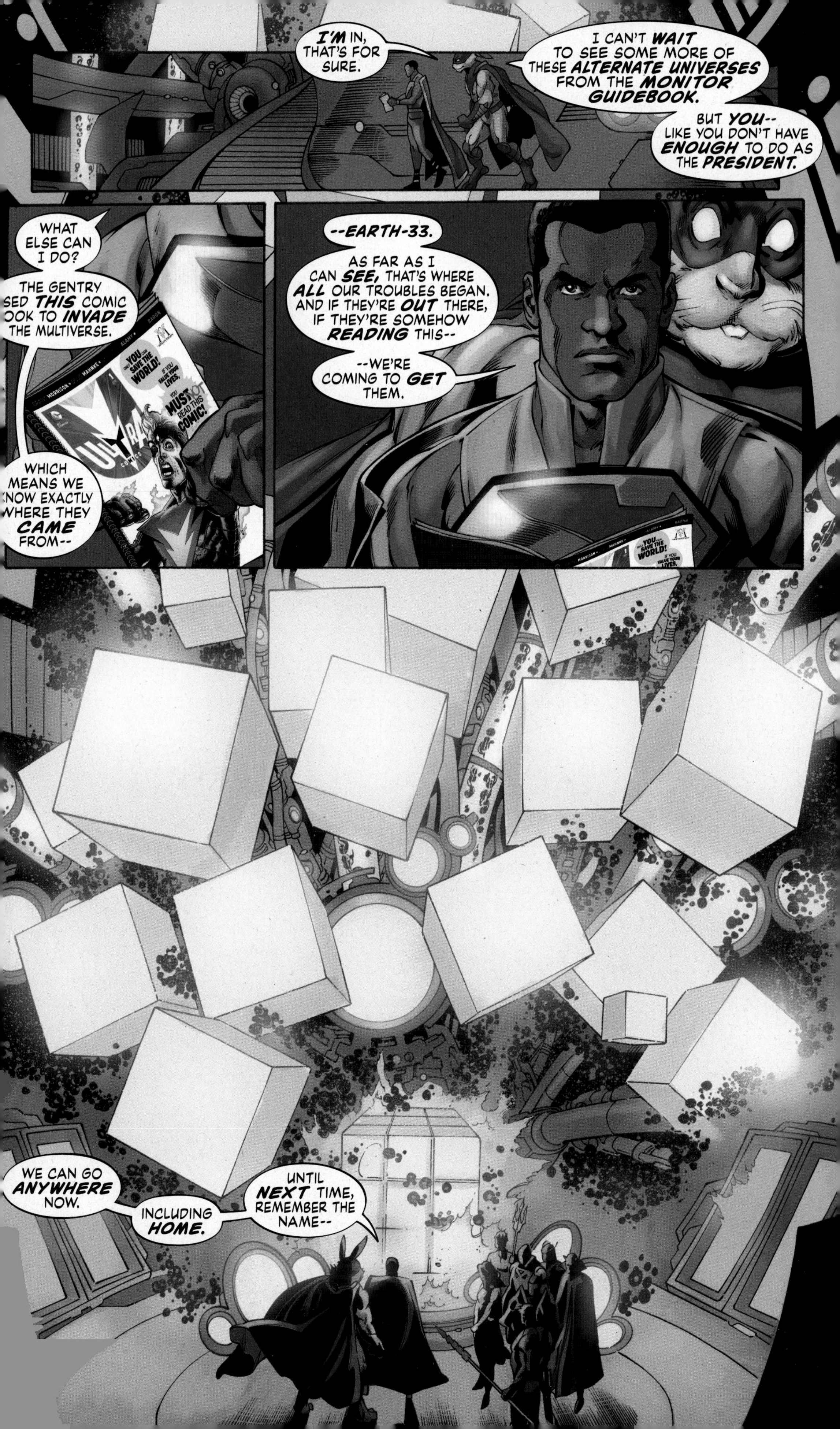
I'M IN, THAT'S FOR SURE.
I CAN'T WAIT TO SEE SOME MORE OF THESE ALTERNATE UNIVERSES FROM THE MONITOR GUIDEBOOK.
BUT YOU-- LIKE YOU DON'T HAVE ENOUGH TO DO AS THE PRESIDENT.
WHAT ELSE CAN I DO?
THE GENTRY SED THIS COMIC OOK TO INVADE THE MULTIVERSE.
WHICH MEANS WE NOW EXACTLY HERE THEY CAME FROM--
--EARTH-33.
AS FAR AS I CAN SEE, THAT'S WHERE ALL OUR TROUBLES BEGAN. AND IF THEY'RE OUT THERE, IF THEY'RE SOMEHOW READING THIS--
--WE'RE COMING TO GET THEM.
WE CAN GO ANYWHERE NOW.
INCLUDING HOME.
UNTIL NEXT TIME, REMEMBER THE NAME--

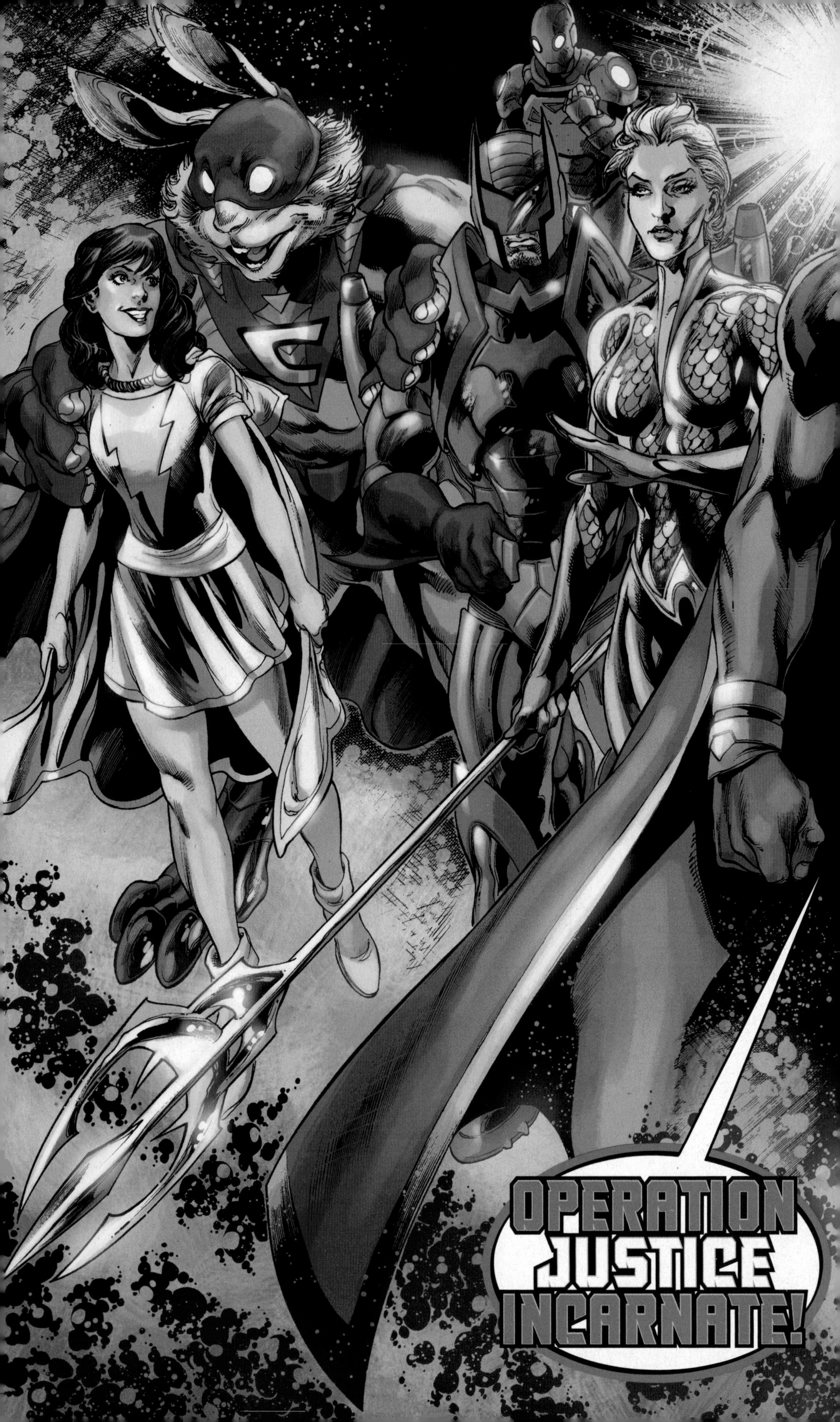
OPERATION JUSTICE INCARNATE!

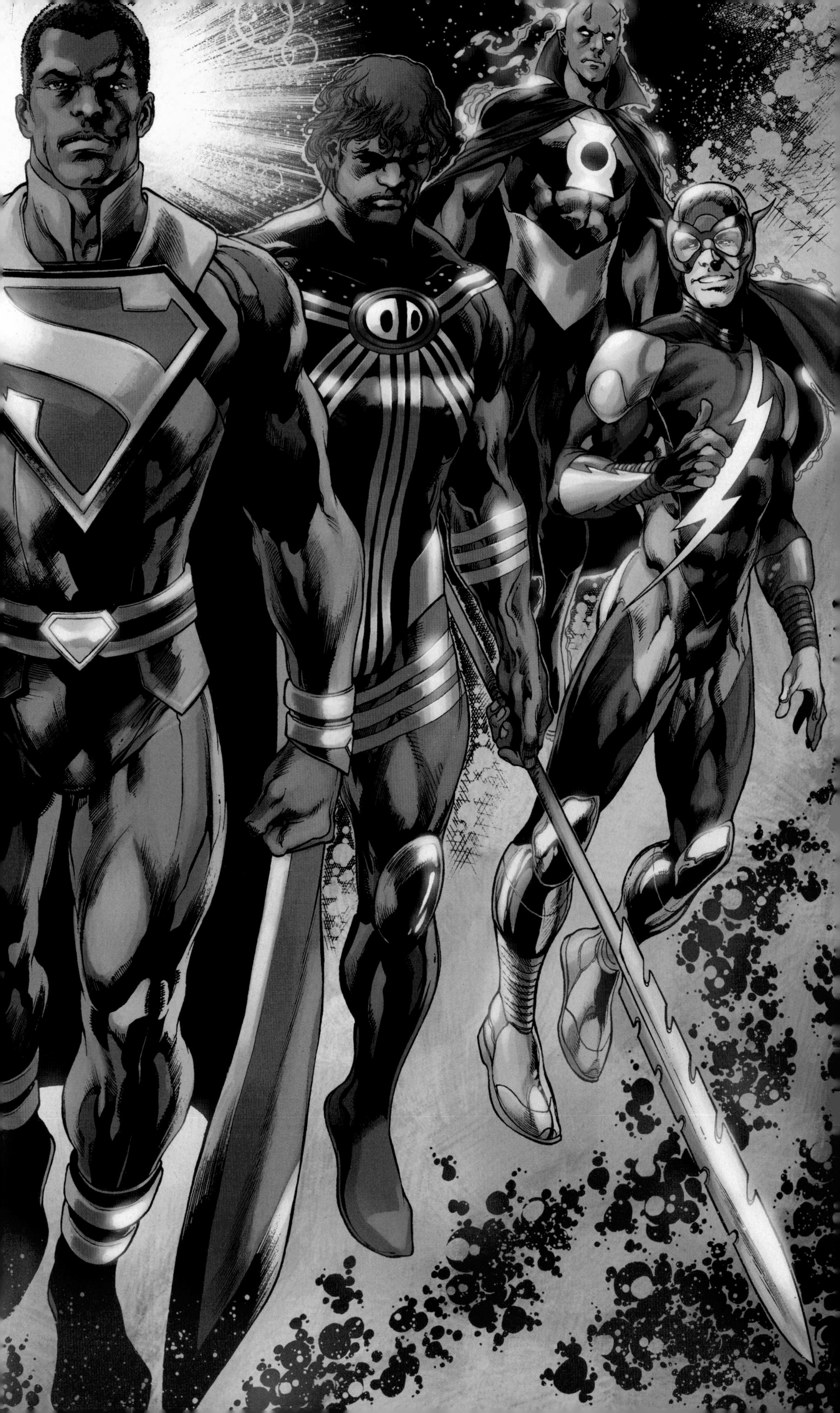

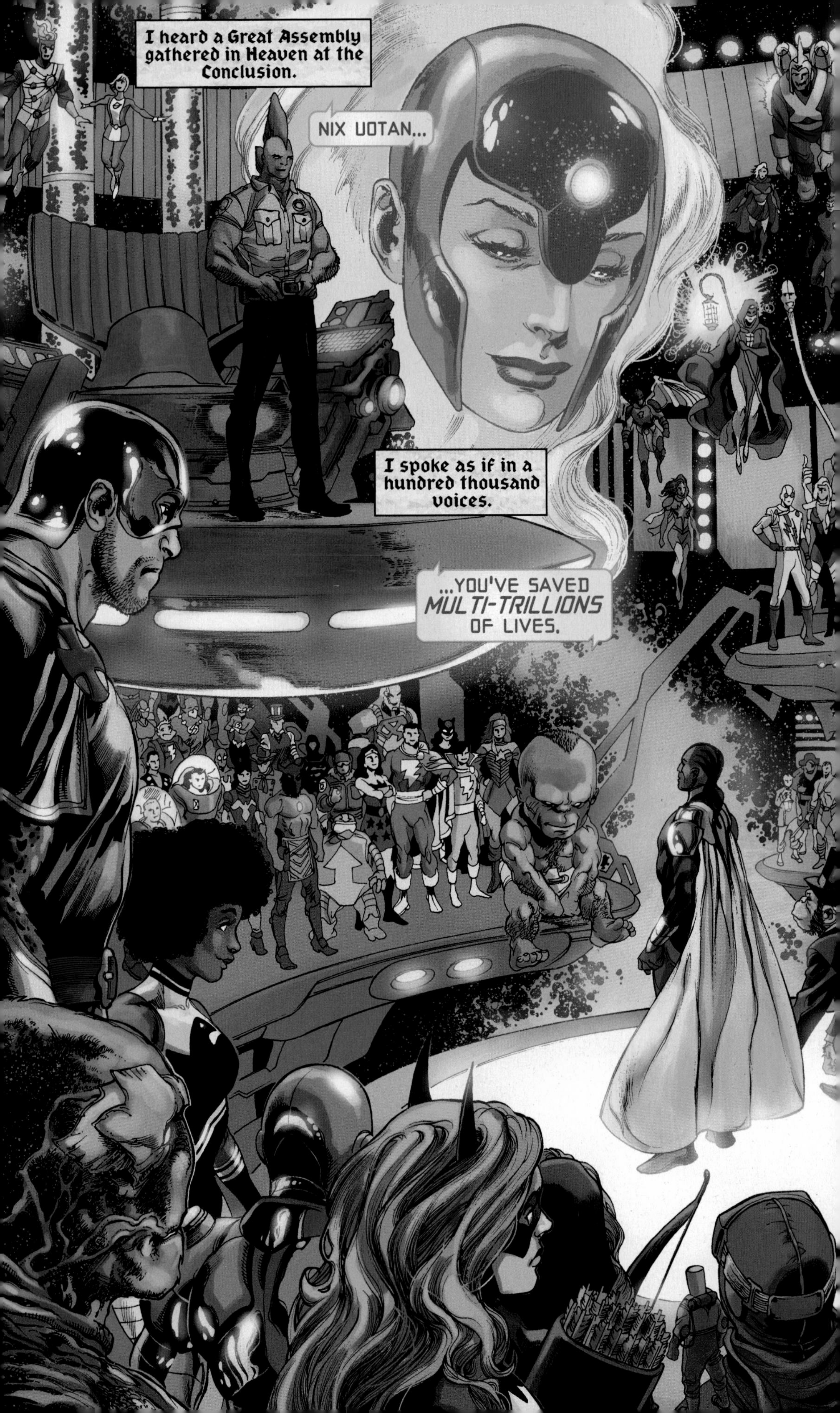
I heard a Great Assembly gathered in Heaven at the Conclusion.
NIX UOTAN...
I spoke as if in a hundred thousand voices.
...YOU'VE SAVED MULTI-TRILLIONS OF LIVES.

WHEREVER LIFE CAN TAKE ROOT. WHEREVER LIFE CAN FLOURISH.

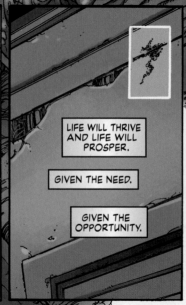

LIFE WILL THRIVE AND LIFE WILL PROSPER.

GIVEN THE NEED.

GIVEN THE OPPORTUNITY.

BE CAREFUL WHAT YOU LET INTO YOUR *HEAD.*

WHO *IS* THAT KNOCKING ON YOUR DOOR?

And then it was CONTINUED thereafter.

Unto all Eternity.

OW.

NO MORE *BYZANTINE* IMPLAUSIBLE EXCUSES.

YOU *OWE* ME--!

UH, SURE.

SURE, I OWE YOU.

AND *GUESS WHAT?*

COUNT 'EM.

EIGHT HUNDRED BUCKS.

EARTH-0

SOCIETY
SUPER-HEROES
PAX
AMERICANA
PAXAMERICANA

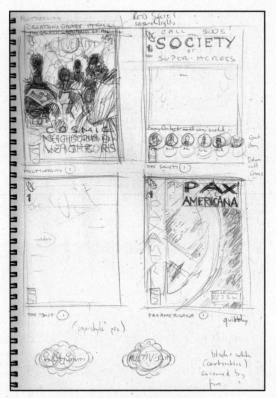

Cover sketches by Grant Morrison.

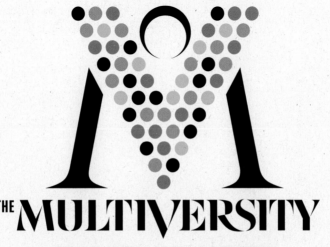

STRANGE ATTRACTORS

THE MULTIVERSITY

VARIANT COVERS OF THE MULTIVERSITY

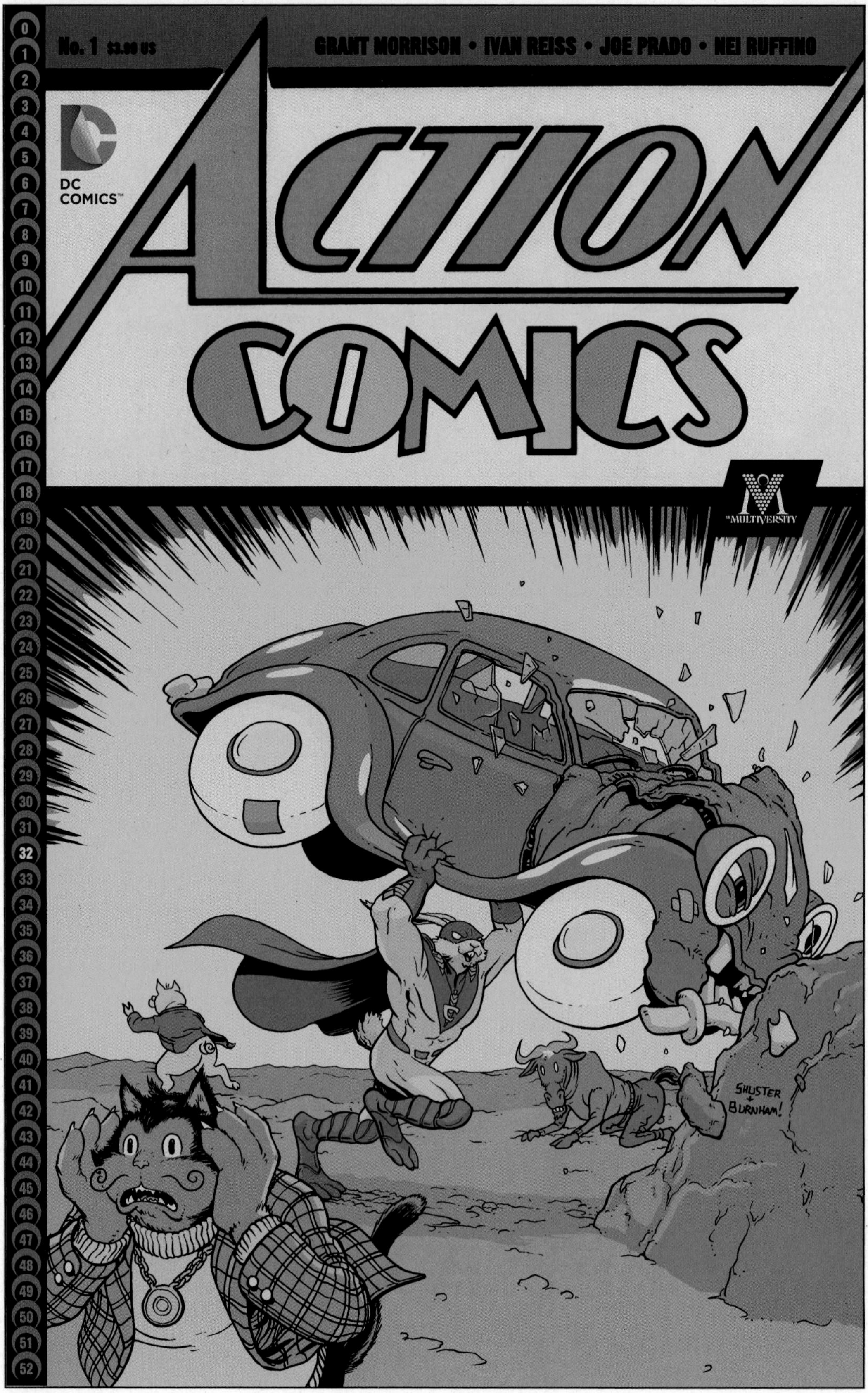
No. 1 $3.99 US
GRANT MORRISON • IVAN REISS • JOE PRADO • NEI RUFFINO
DC COMICS
ACTION COMICS
THE MULTIVERSITY
SHUSTER + BURNHAM!

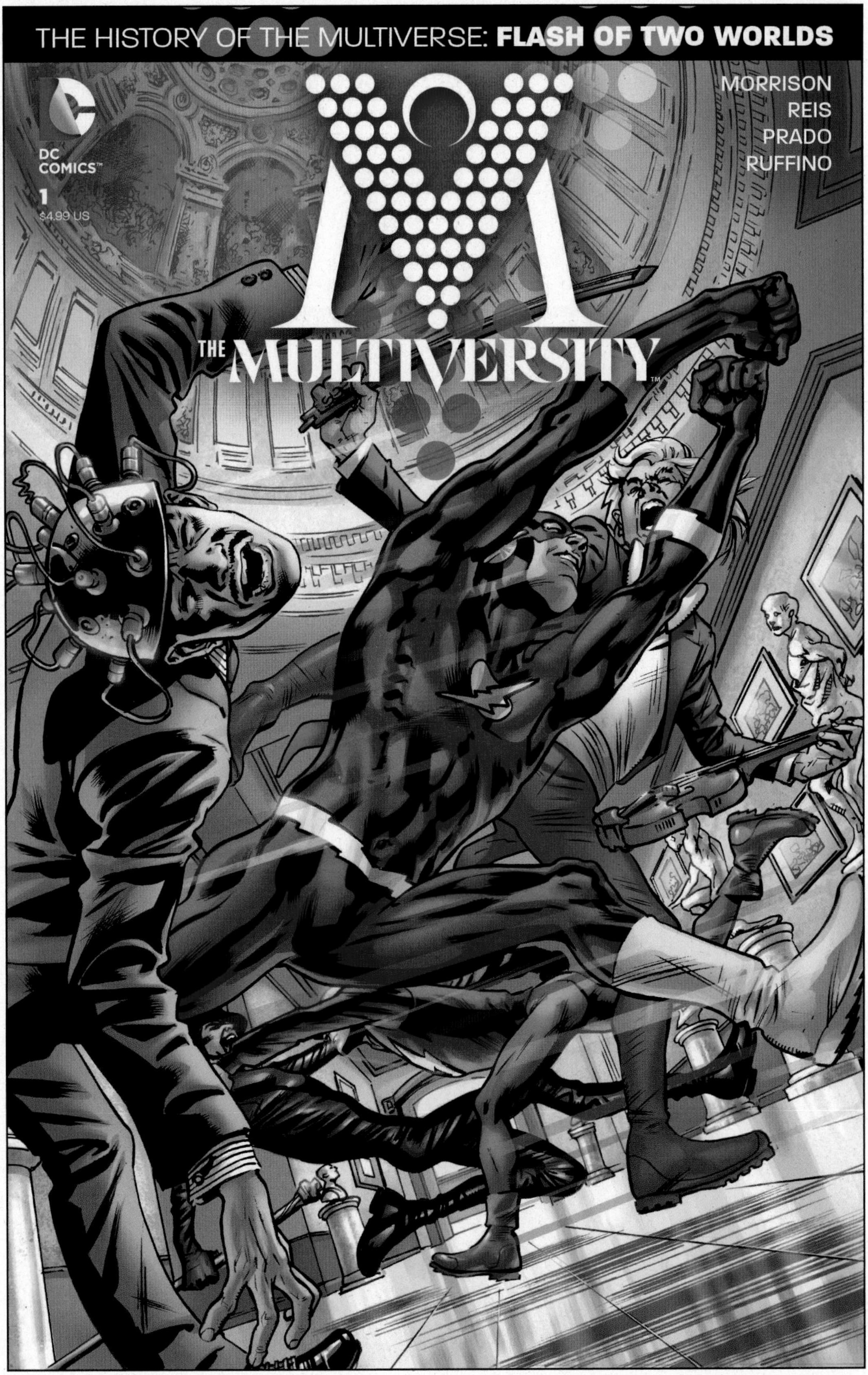
THE HISTORY OF THE MULTIVERSE: FLASH OF TWO WORLDS
DC COMICS™
1
$4.99 US
MORRISON
REIS
PRADO
RUFFINO
THE MULTIVERSITY™

Variant cover art for THE MULTIVERSITY #1 by Grant Morrison.

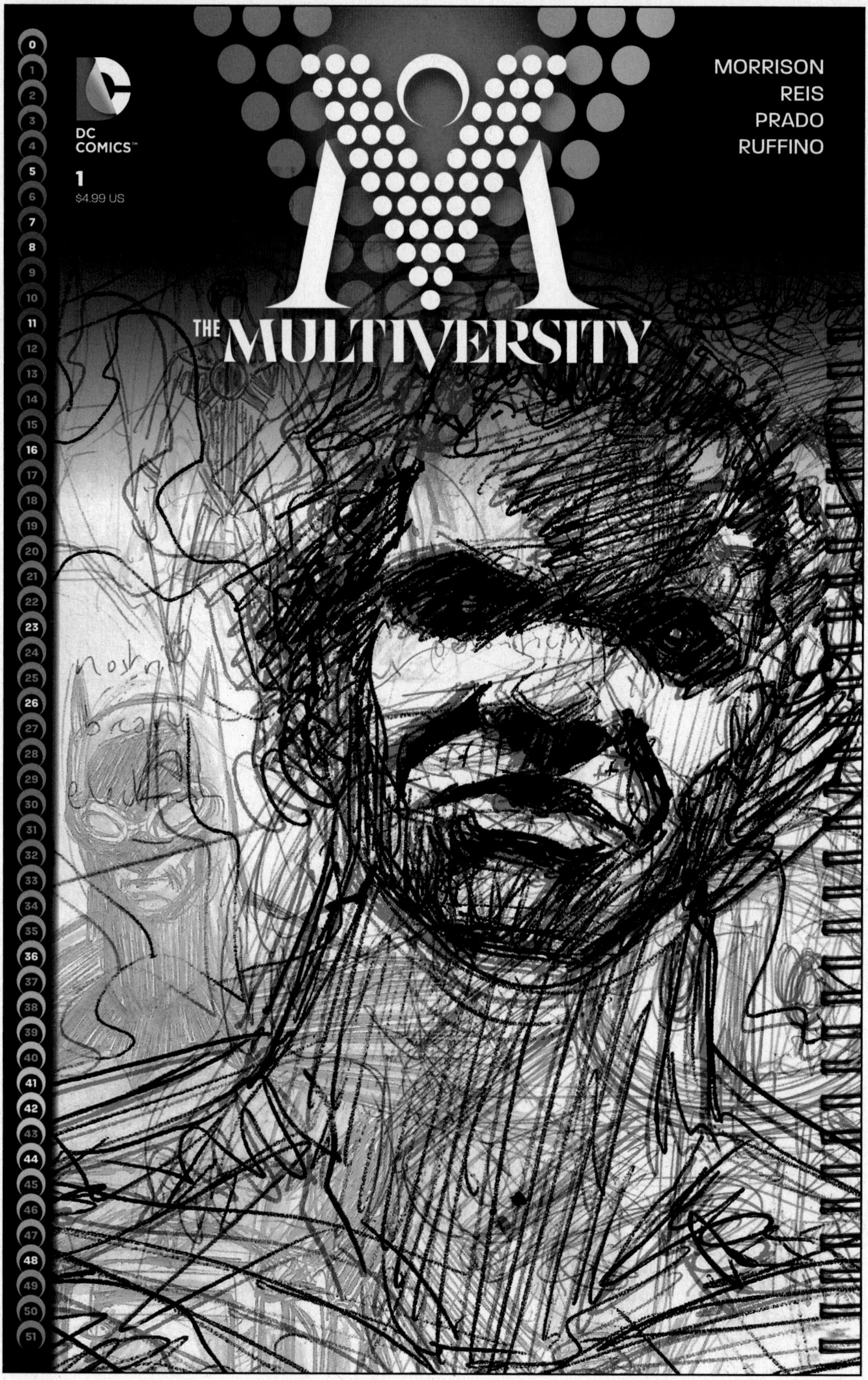
DC COMICS™
1
$4.99 US
MORRISON
REIS
PRADO
RUFFINO
THE MULTIVERSITY

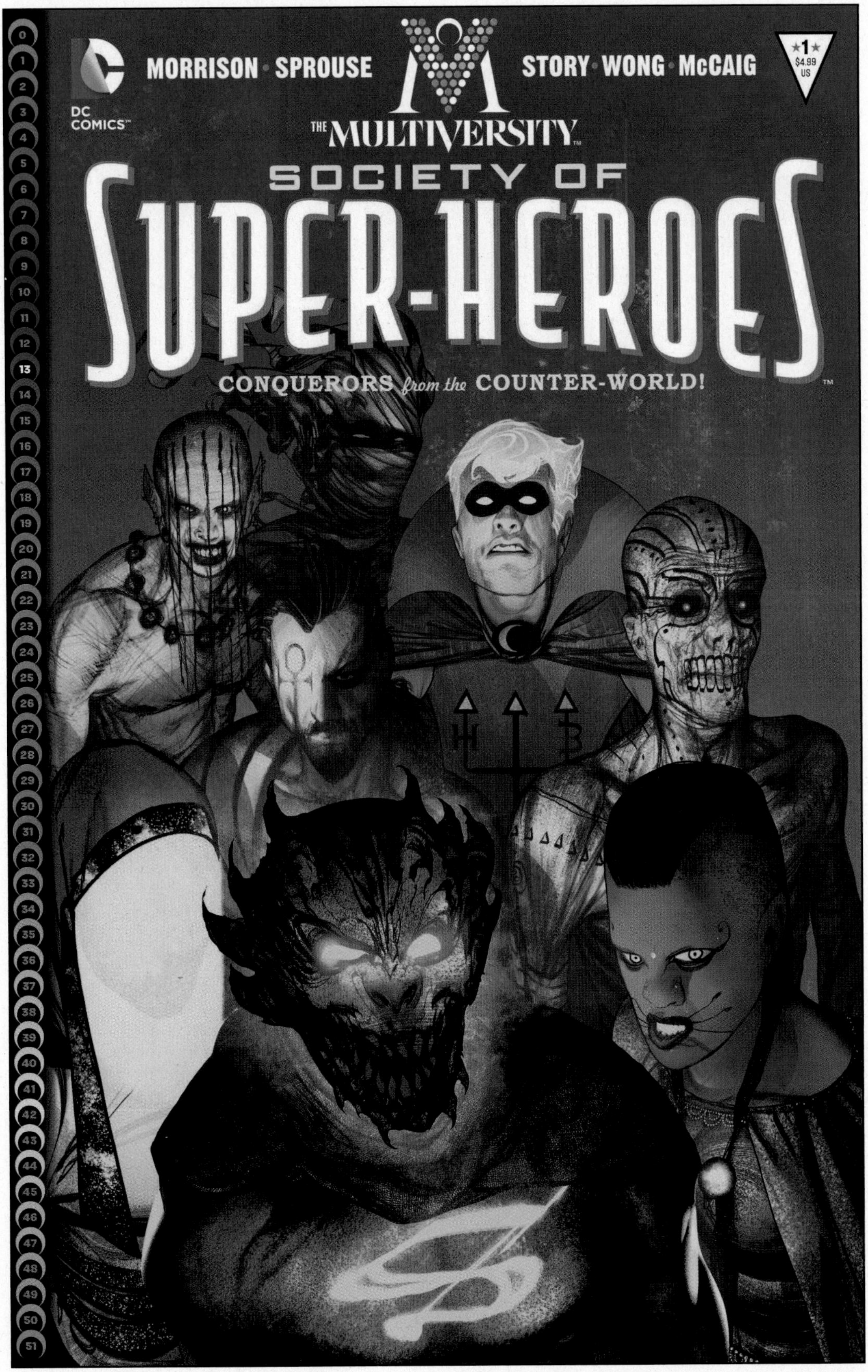
DC COMICS
MORRISON · SPROUSE
STORY · WONG · McCAIG
★1★ $4.99 US
THE MULTIVERSITY
SOCIETY OF
SUPER-HEROES
CONQUERORS from the COUNTER-WORLD!

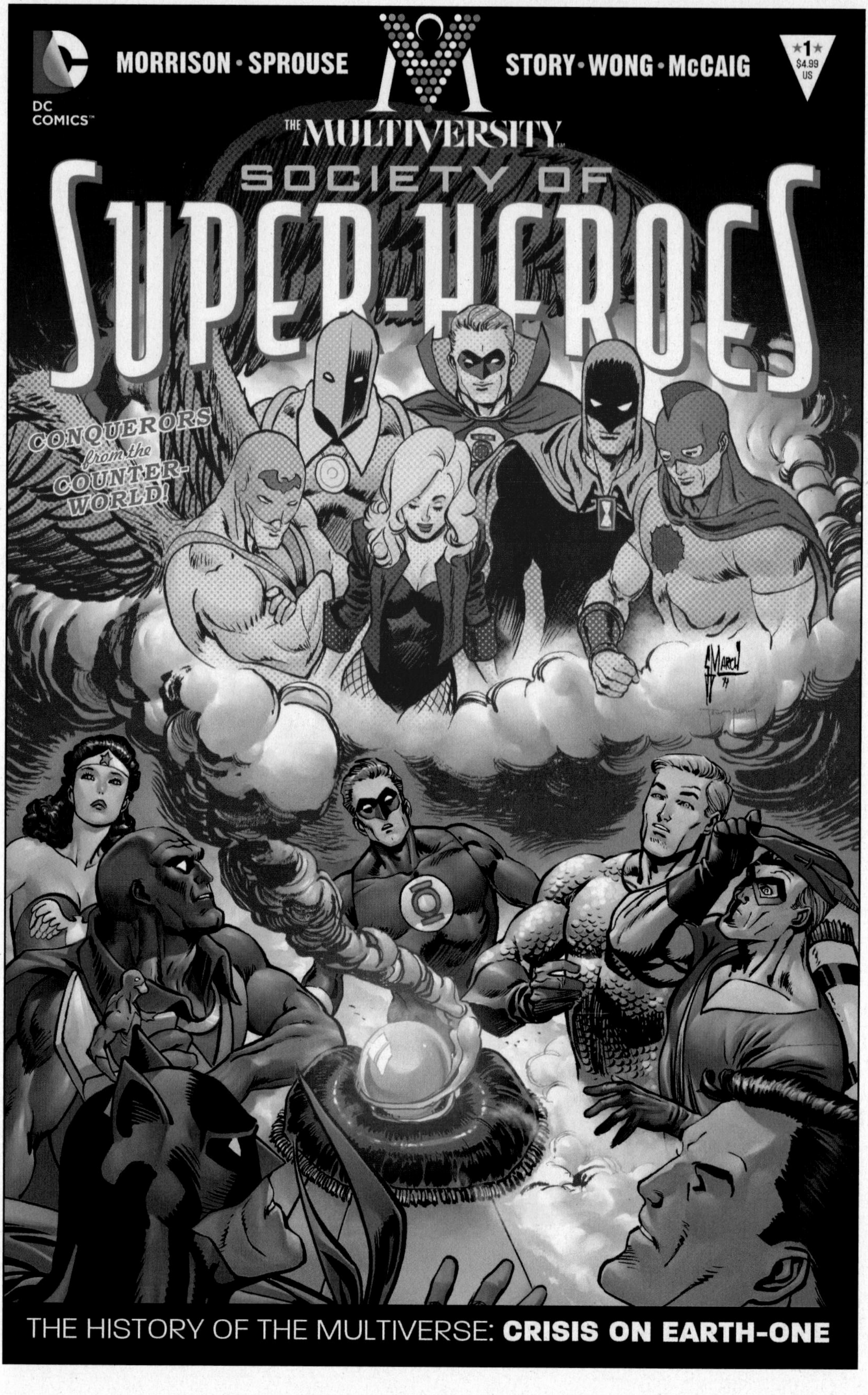
DC COMICS
MORRISON · SPROUSE
STORY · WONG · McCAIG
★1★ $4.99 US
THE MULTIVERSITY
SOCIETY OF
SUPER-HEROES
CONQUERORS from the COUNTER-WORLD!
THE HISTORY OF THE MULTIVERSE: CRISIS ON EARTH-ONE

Variant cover art for THE MULTIVERSITY: SOCIETY OF SUPER-HEROES #1 by Grant Morrison.

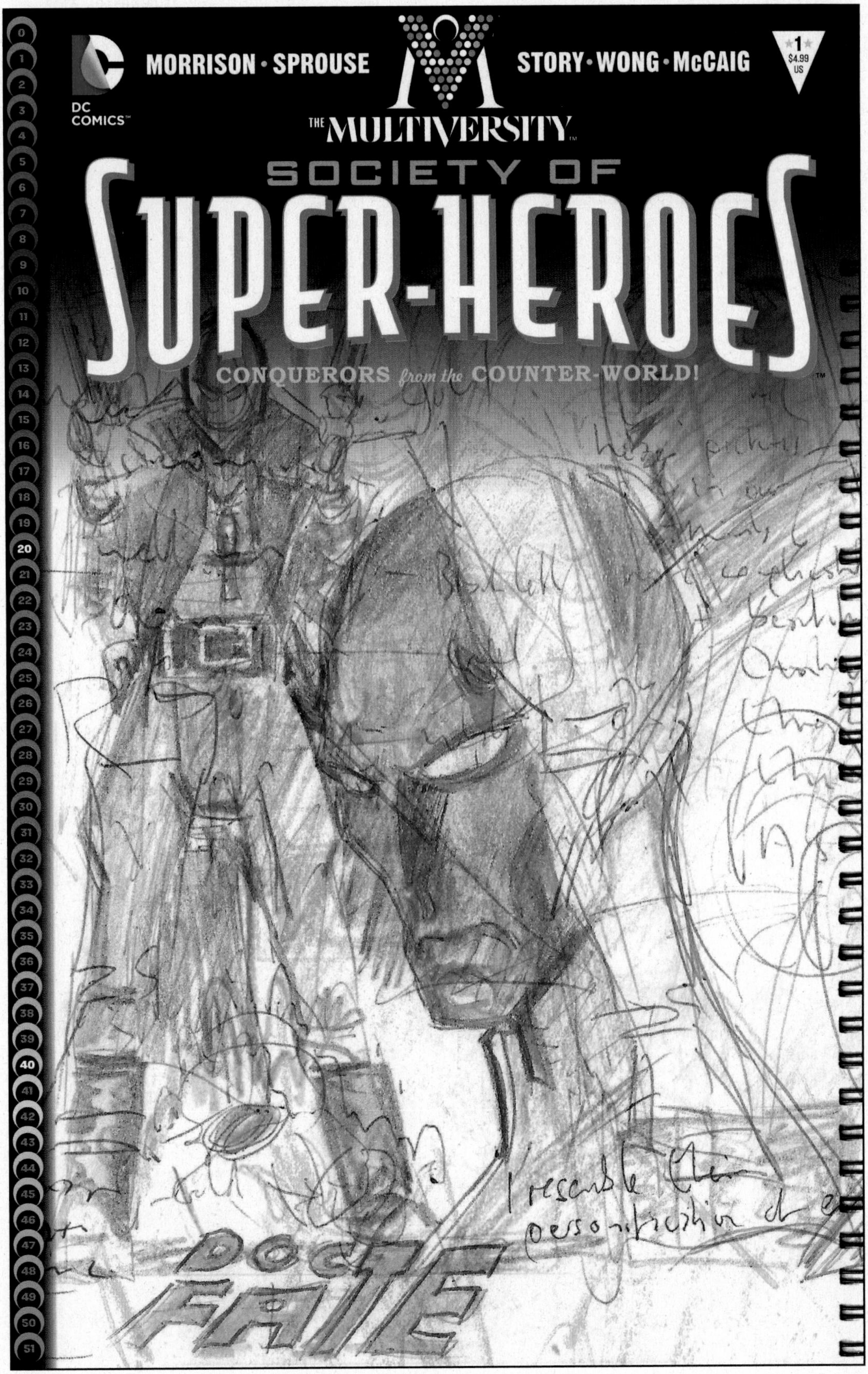
MORRISON · SPROUSE
STORY · WONG · McCAIG
DC COMICS
1 $4.99 US
THE MULTIVERSITY
SOCIETY OF
SUPER-HEROES
CONQUERORS from the COUNTER-WORLD!
DOC FATE

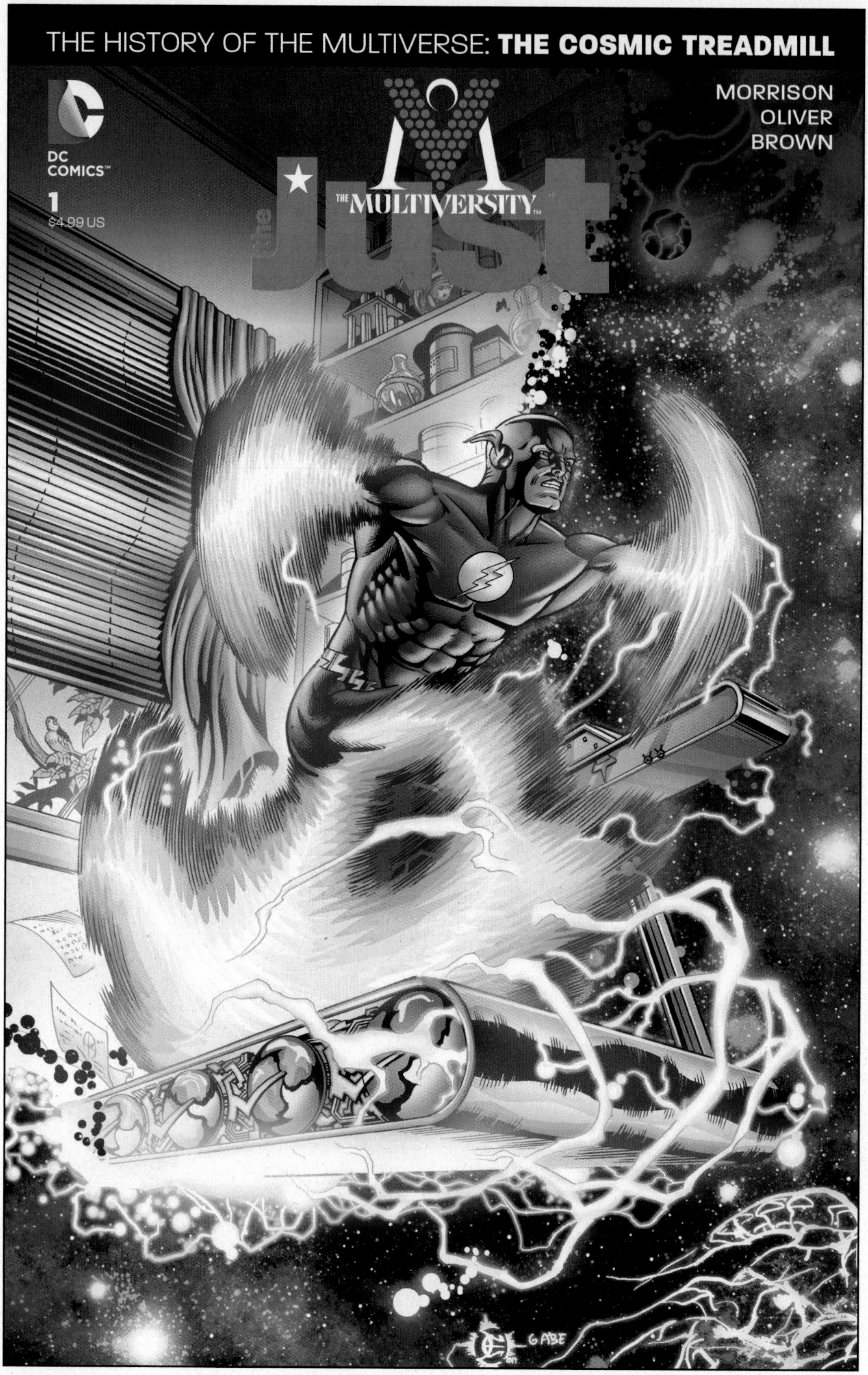
THE HISTORY OF THE MULTIVERSE: THE COSMIC TREADMILL
DC COMICS
1
$4.99 US
THE MULTIVERSITY
the Just
MORRISON
OLIVER
BROWN
GABE

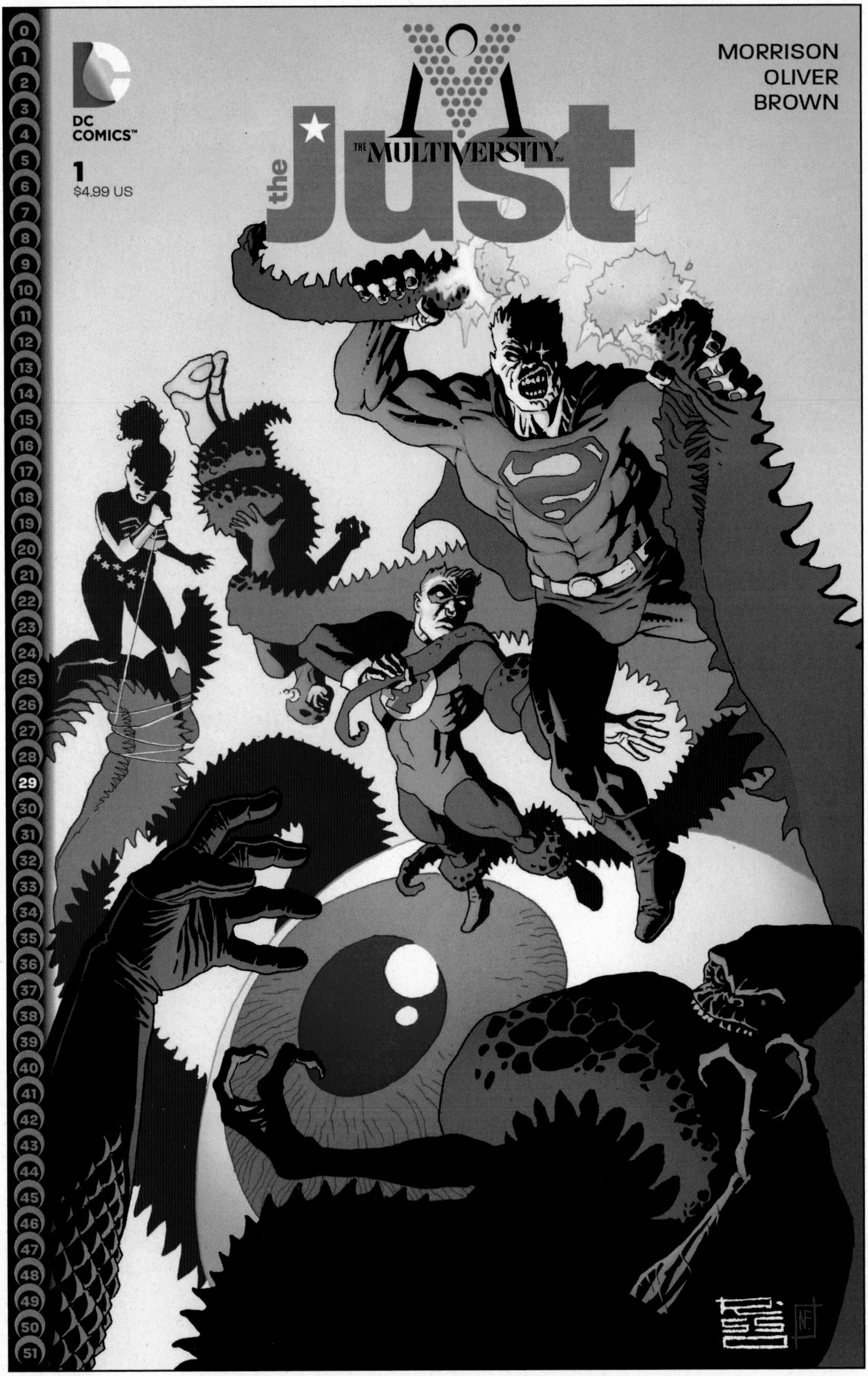

DC COMICS™
1
$4.99 US
MORRISON
OLIVER
BROWN
THE MULTIVERSITY™
the Just
0 1 2 3 4 5 6 7 8 9 10 11 12 13 14 15 16 17 18 19 20 21 22 23 24 25 26 27 28 29 30 31 32 33 34 35 36 37 38 39 40 41 42 43 44 45 46 47 48 49 50 51

Variant cover art for THE MULTIVERSITY: THE JUST #1 by Grant Morrison.

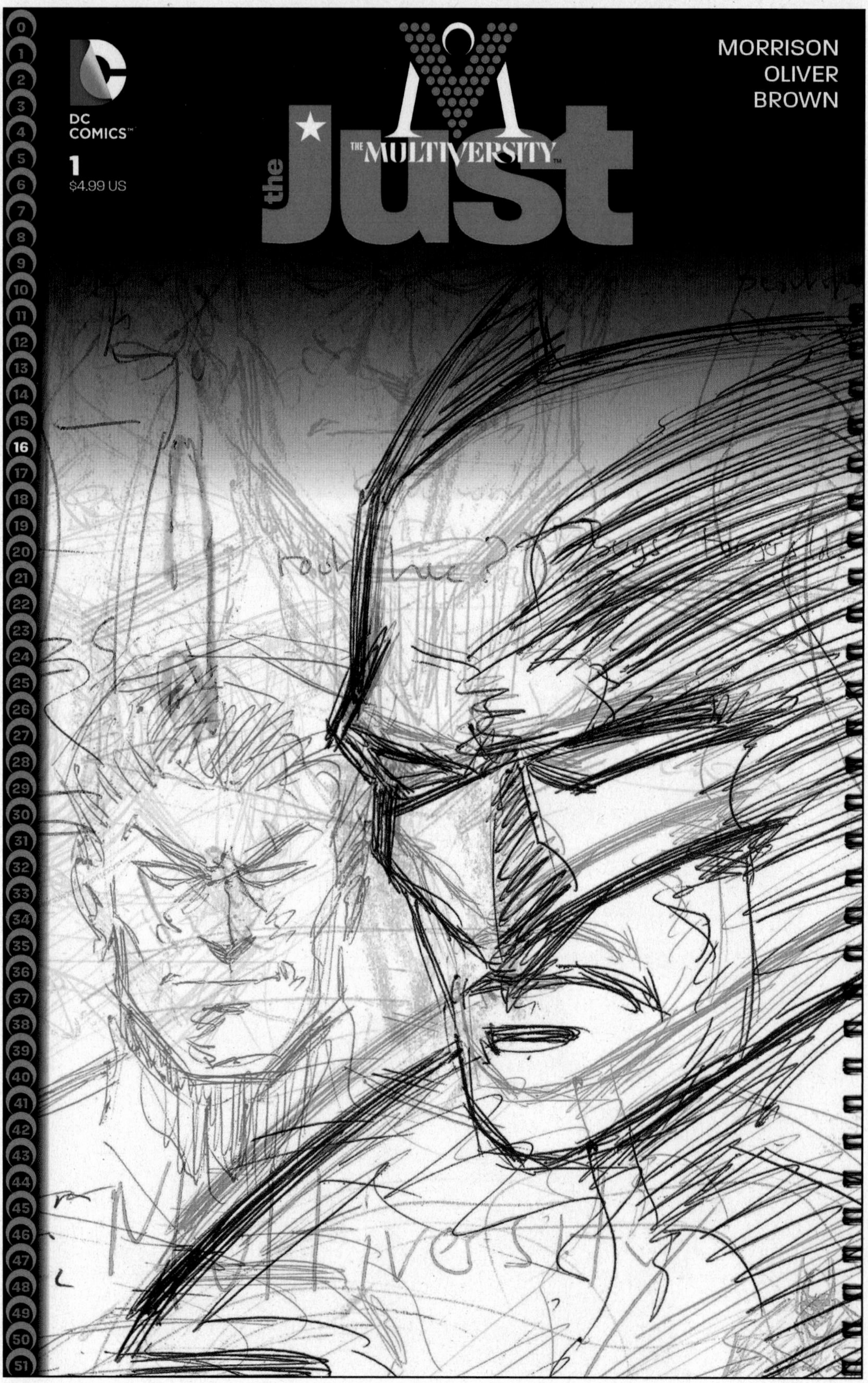
DC COMICS™
1
$4.99 US
THE MULTIVERSITY™
the Just
MORRISON
OLIVER
BROWN

Variant cover art for THE MULTIVERSITY: PAX AMERICANA #1 by Jae Lee (color by June Chung).

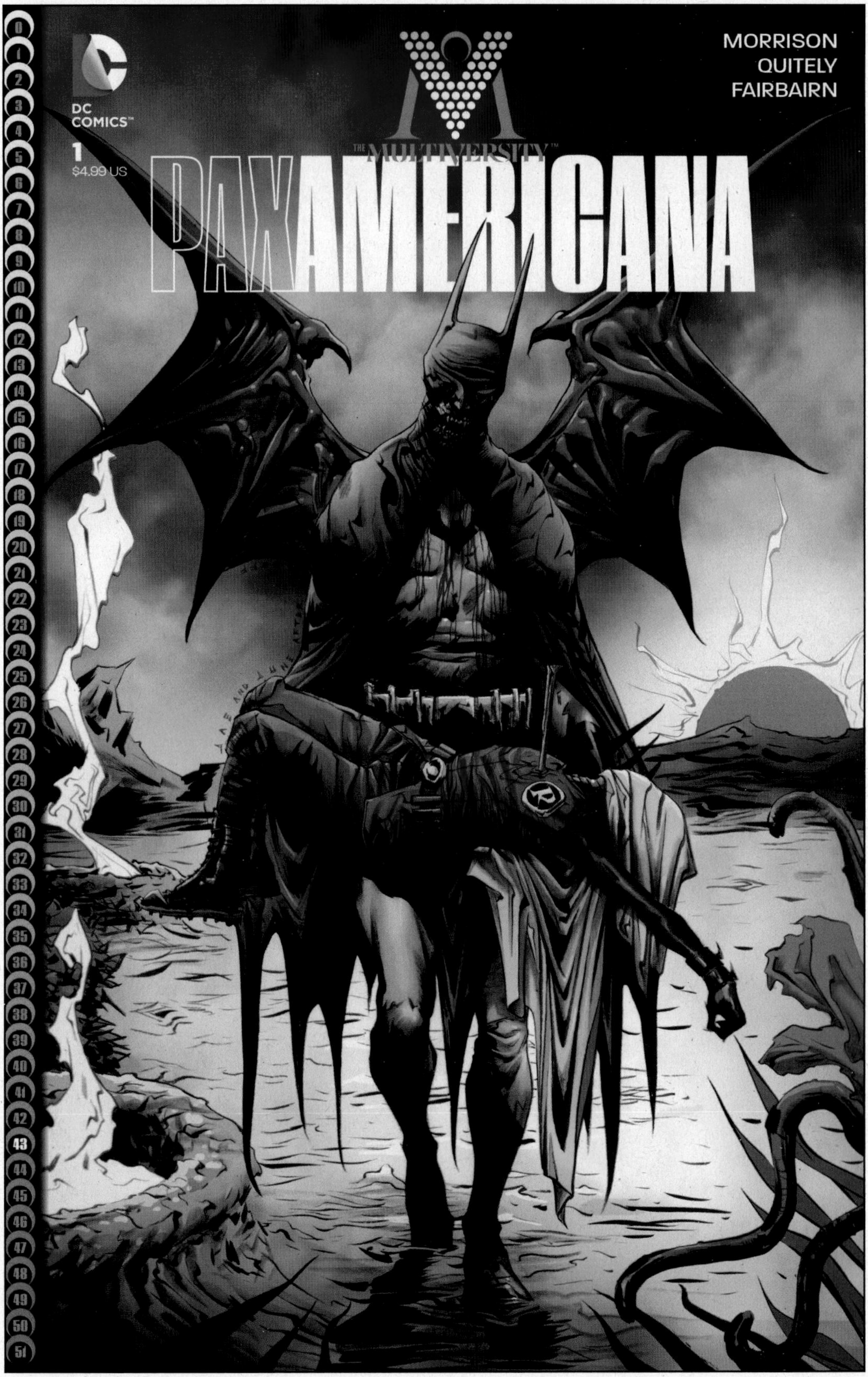
DC COMICS™
1
$4.99 US
MORRISON
QUITELY
FAIRBAIRN
THE MULTIVERSITY™
PAX AMERICANA

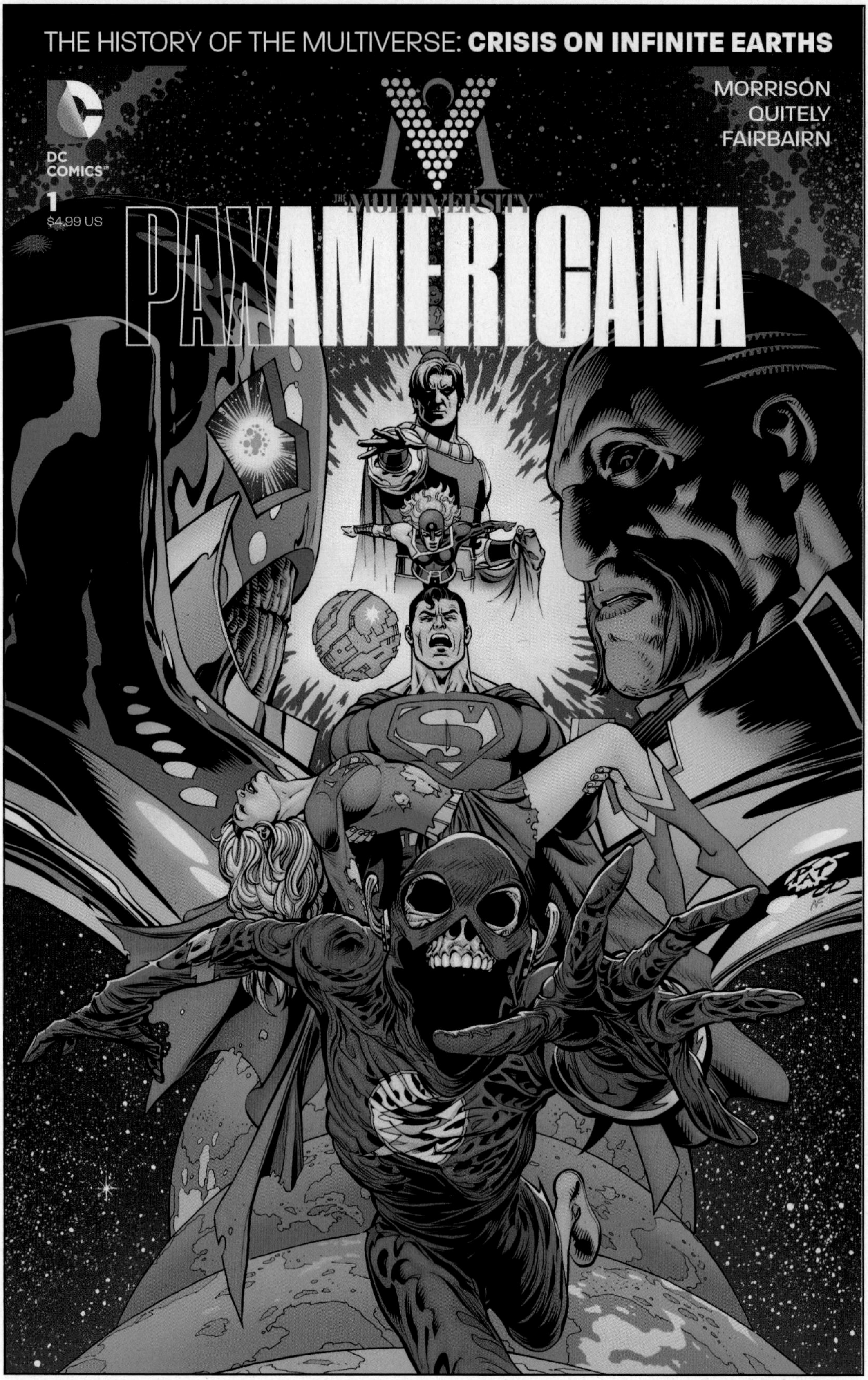
THE HISTORY OF THE MULTIVERSE: CRISIS ON INFINITE EARTHS
DC COMICS
1
$4.99 US
MORRISON
QUITELY
FAIRBAIRN
THE MULTIVERSITY
PAX AMERICANA

Variant cover art for THE MULTIVERSITY: PAX AMERICANA #1 by Michael Cho.

437

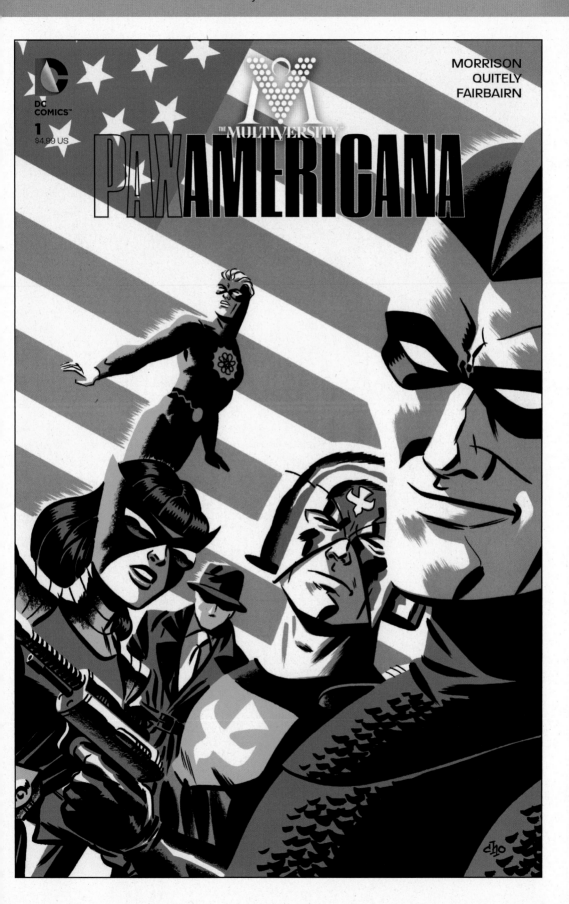

Variant cover art for THE MULTIVERSITY: PAX AMERICANA #1 by Grant Morrison.

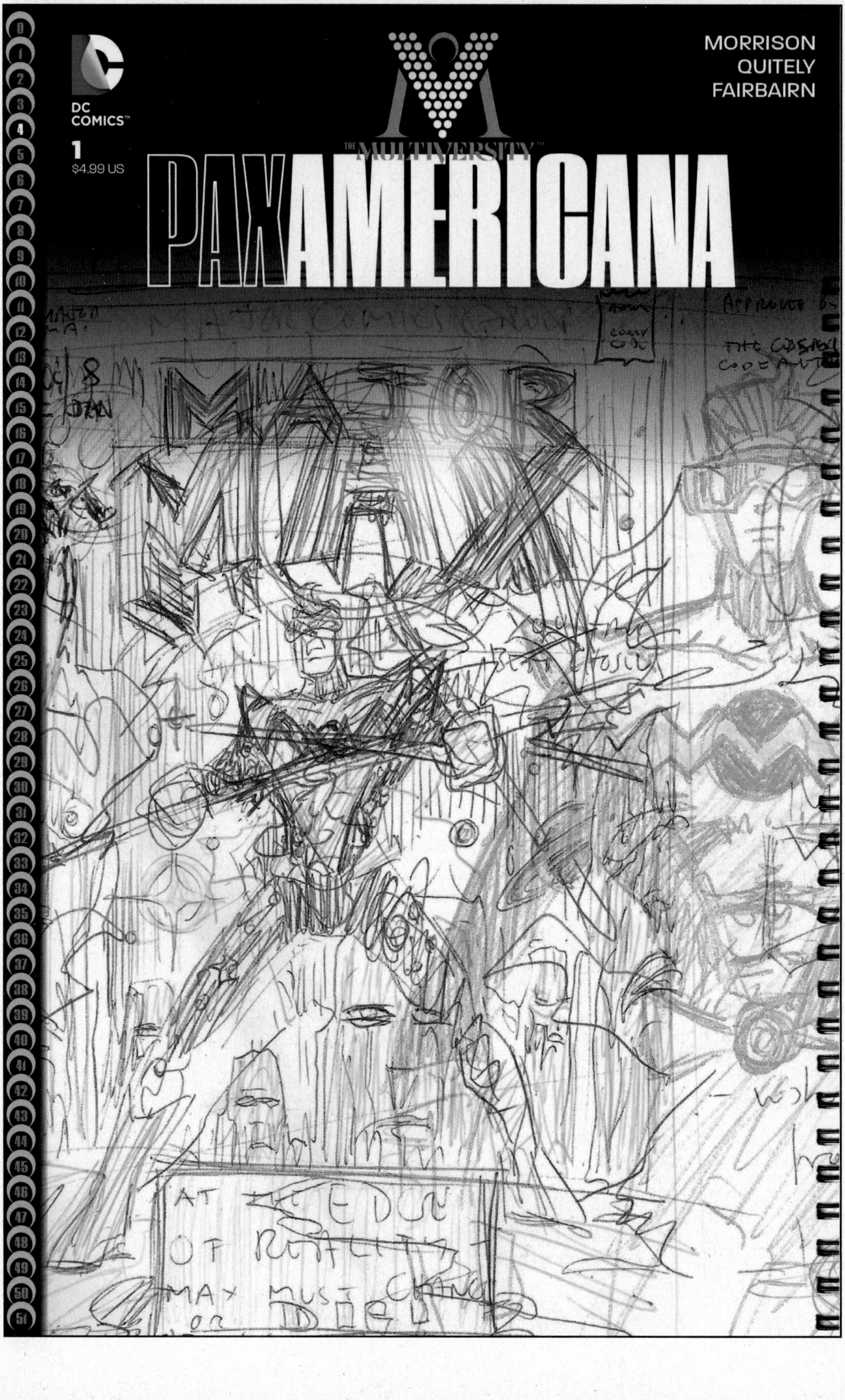
DC COMICS
1
$4.99 US
THE MULTIVERSITY
PAX AMERICANA
MORRISON
QUITELY
FAIRBAIRN
MAJOR
MAX

Variant cover art for THE MULTIVERSITY: THUNDERWORLD ADVENTURES #1 by Cliff Chiang.

439

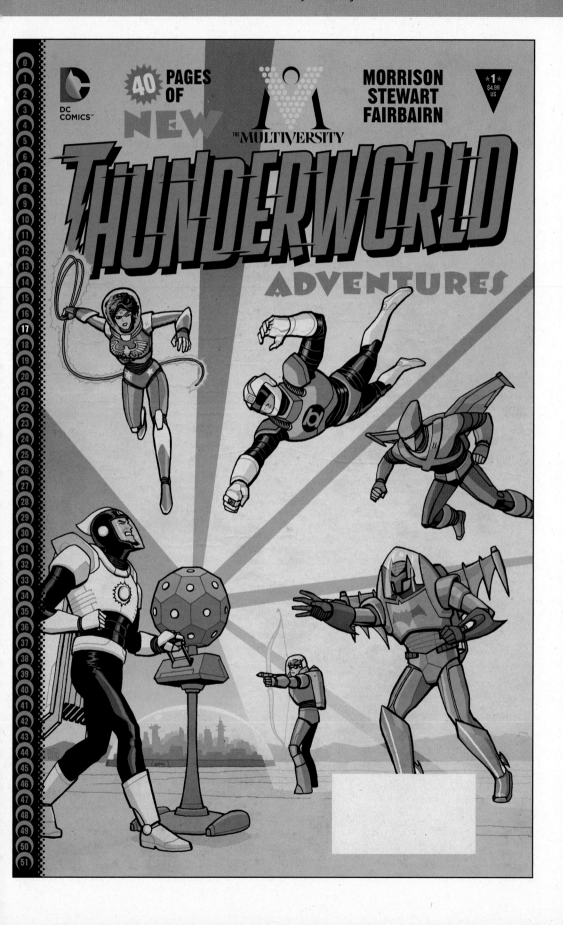

Variant cover art for THE MULTIVERSITY: THUNDERWORLD ADVENTURES #1 by Cully Hamner.

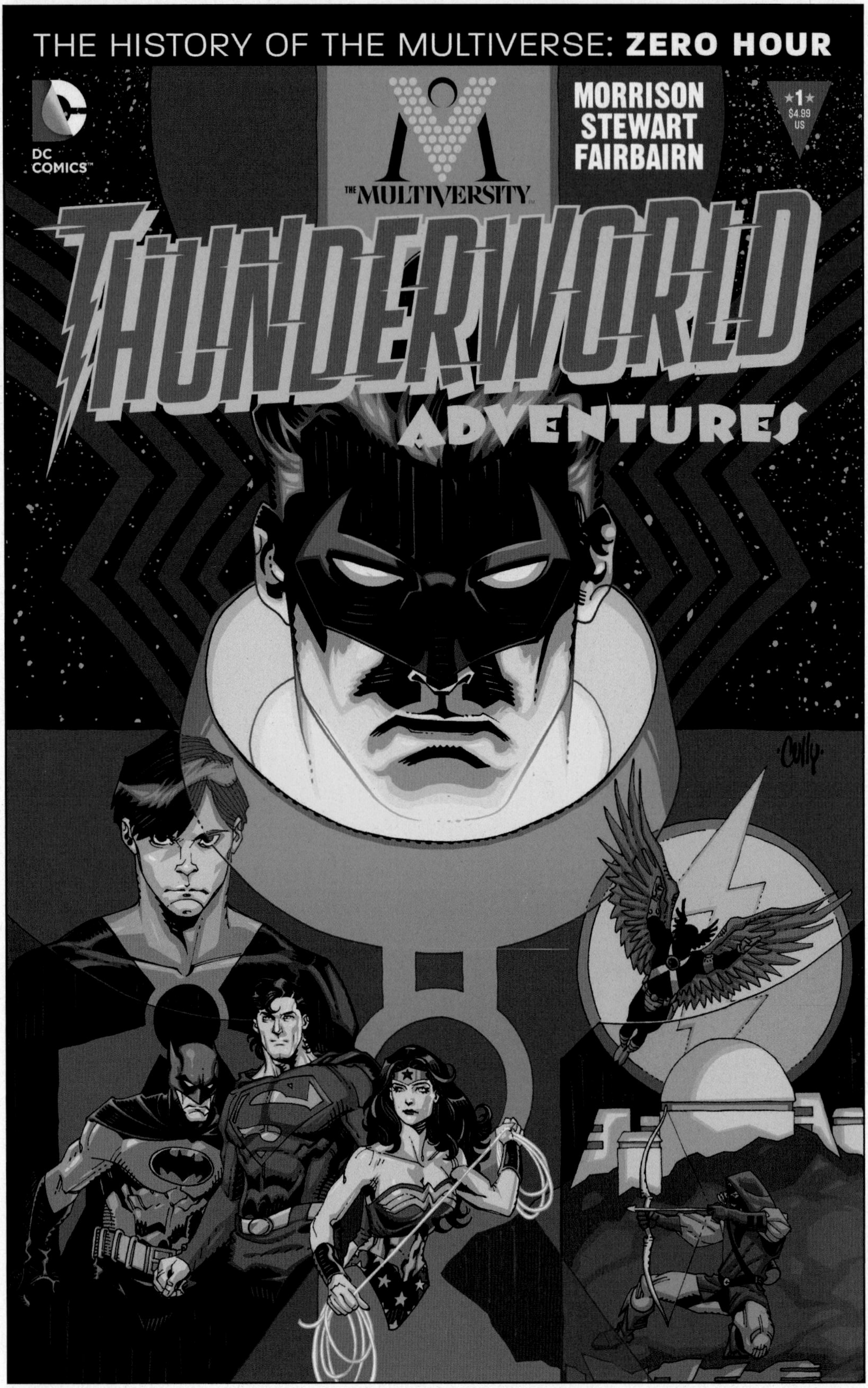
THE HISTORY OF THE MULTIVERSE: ZERO HOUR
DC COMICS
THE MULTIVERSITY
MORRISON
STEWART
FAIRBAIRN
★1★
$4.99
US
THUNDERWORLD
ADVENTURES
CULLY

Variant cover art for THE MULTIVERSITY: THUNDERWORLD ADVENTURES #1 by Grant Morrison.

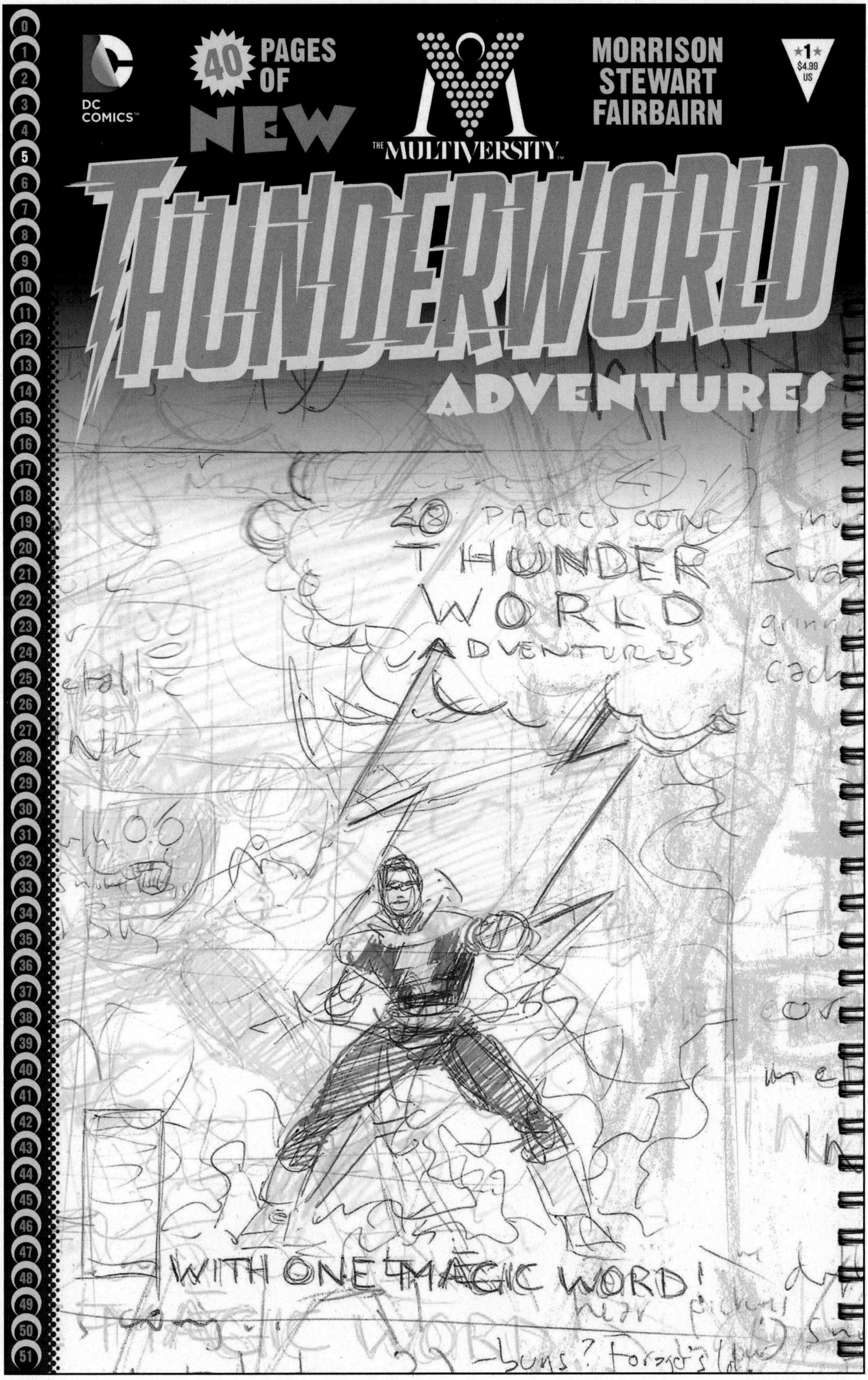
DC COMICS
40 PAGES OF NEW
THE MULTIVERSITY
MORRISON
STEWART
FAIRBAIRN
★1★ $4.99 US
THUNDERWORLD
ADVENTURES
THUNDER
WORLD
ADVENTURES
WITH ONE MAGIC WORD!

Variant cover art for THE MULTIVERSITY GUIDEBOOK #1 by Tom Fowler.

442

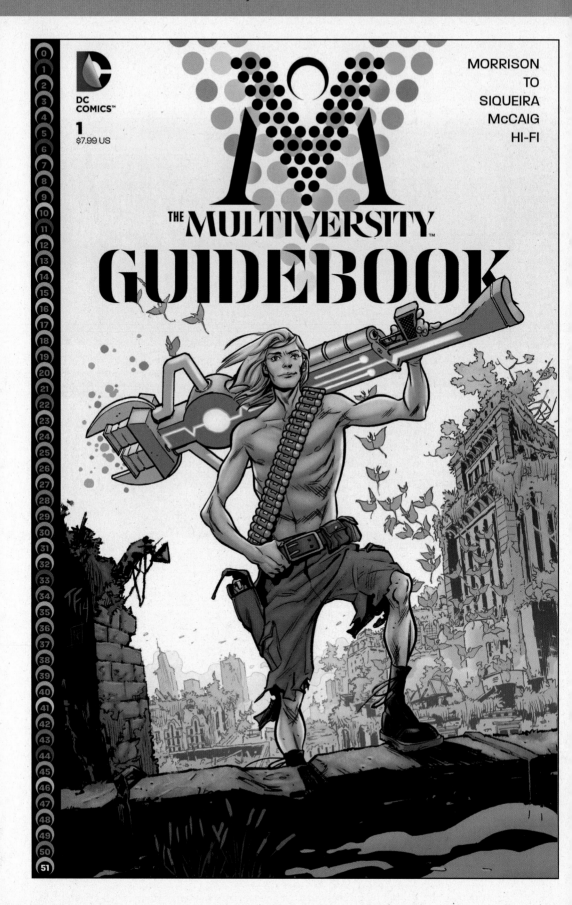

Variant cover art for THE MULTIVERSITY GUIDEBOOK #1 by Phil Jimenez (color by Dave McCaig).

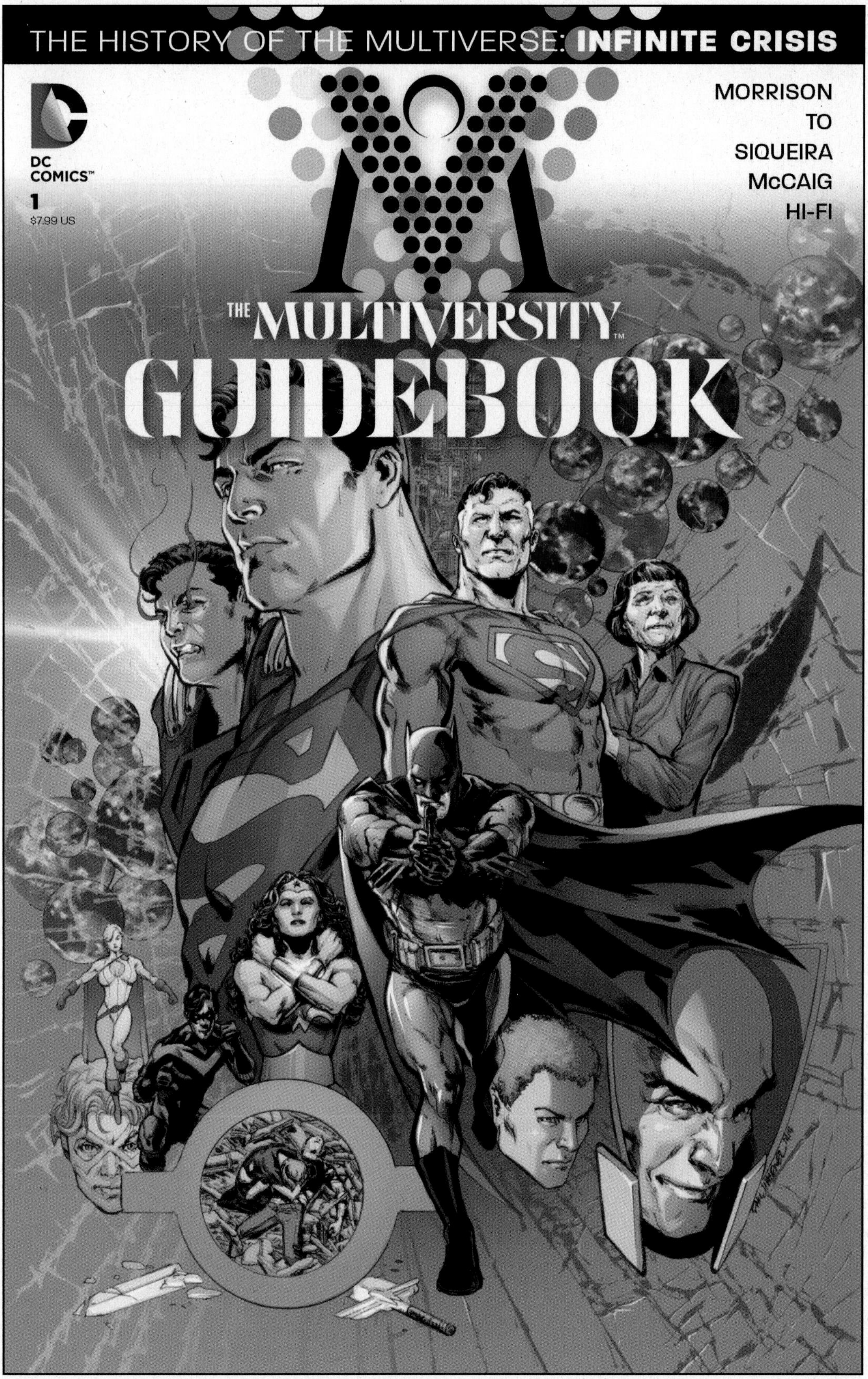
THE HISTORY OF THE MULTIVERSE: INFINITE CRISIS
DC COMICS
1
$7.99 US
MORRISON
TO
SIQUEIRA
McCAIG
HI-FI
THE MULTIVERSITY GUIDEBOOK

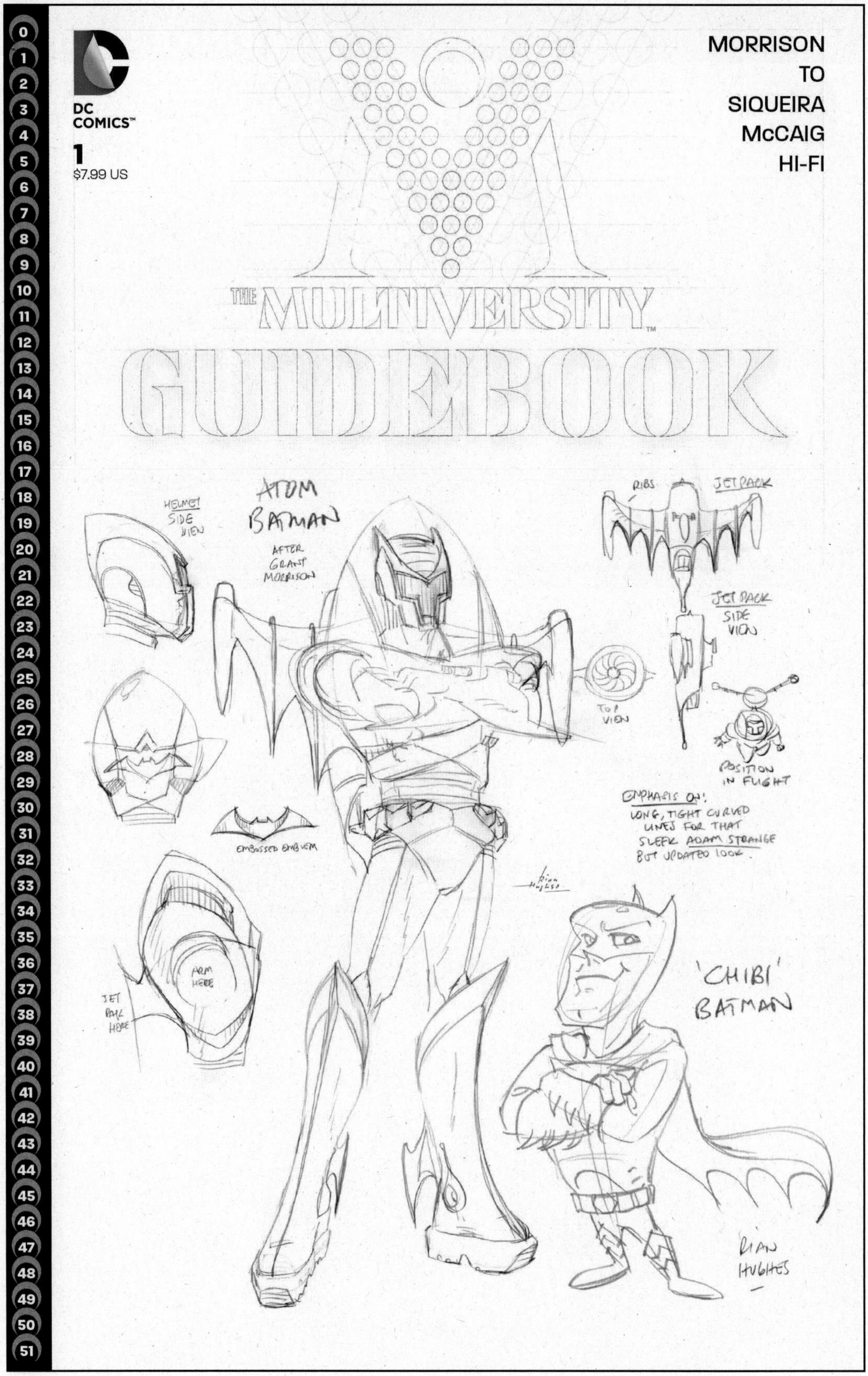
DC COMICS™
1
$7.99 US
MORRISON
TO
SIQUEIRA
McCAIG
HI-FI
THE MULTIVERSITY™
GUIDEBOOK
ATOM BATMAN
AFTER GRANT MORRISON
HELMET SIDE VIEW
RIBS
JET PACK
JET PACK SIDE VIEW
TOP VIEW
POSITION IN FLIGHT
EMBOSSED EMBLEM
EMPHASIS ON: LONG, TIGHT CURVED LINES FOR THAT SLEEK ADAM STRANGE BUT UPDATED LOOK.
ARM HERE
JET PACK HERE
'CHIBI' BATMAN
RIAN HUGHES

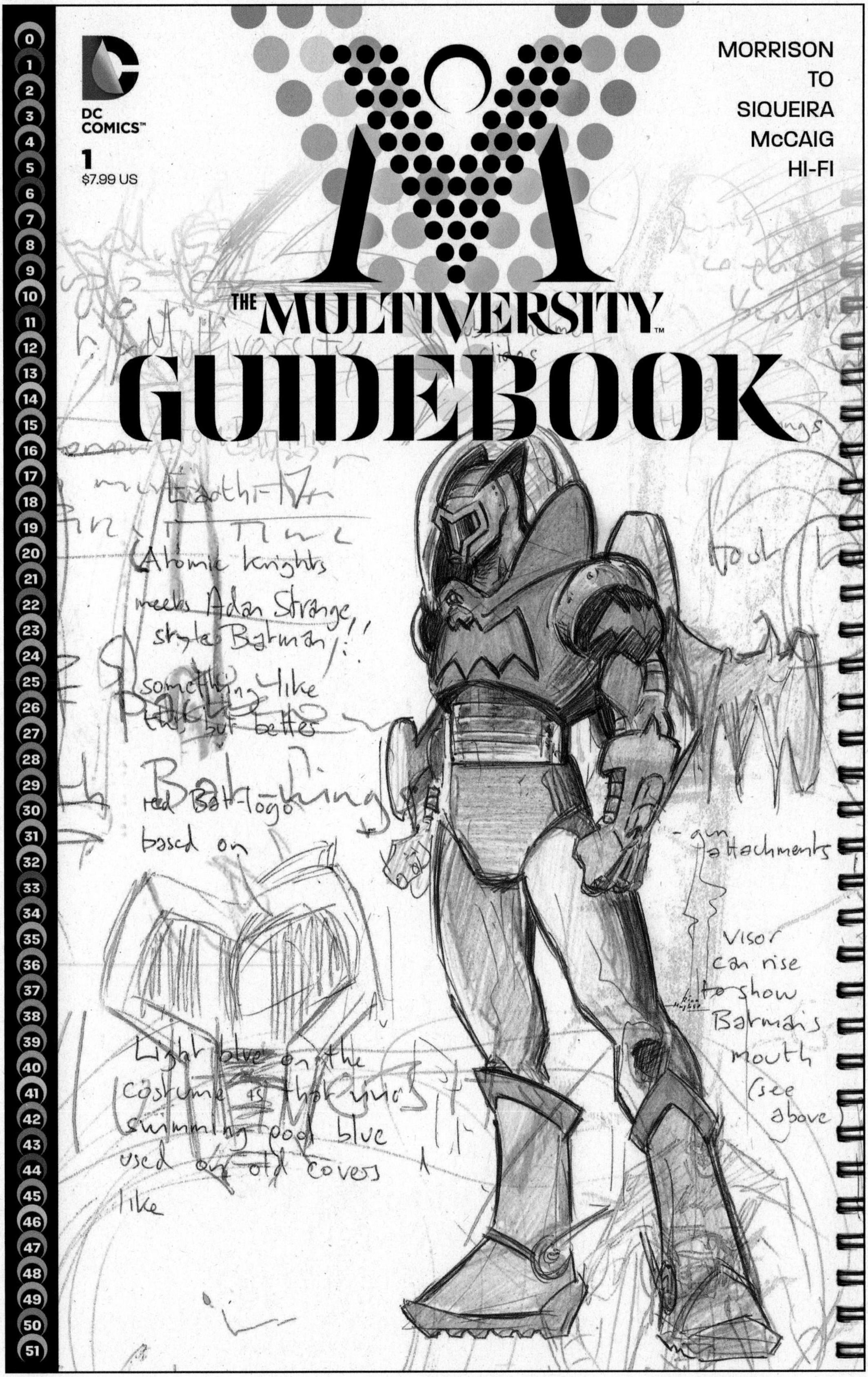
DC COMICS
1
$7.99 US
MORRISON
TO
SIQUEIRA
McCAIG
HI-FI
M
THE MULTIVERSITY
GUIDEBOOK
Earth-17
Atomic Knights
meets Adam Strange
style Batman!!
something like
this but better
Bat-thing
red Bat-logo
based on
Light blue on the
costume is that nice
swimming pool blue
used on old covers I
like
- gun
attachments
Visor
can rise
to show
Batman's
mouth
(see
above)

Variant cover art for THE MULTIVERSITY: MASTERMEN #1 by Aaron Kuder (color by Nathan Fairbairn).

446

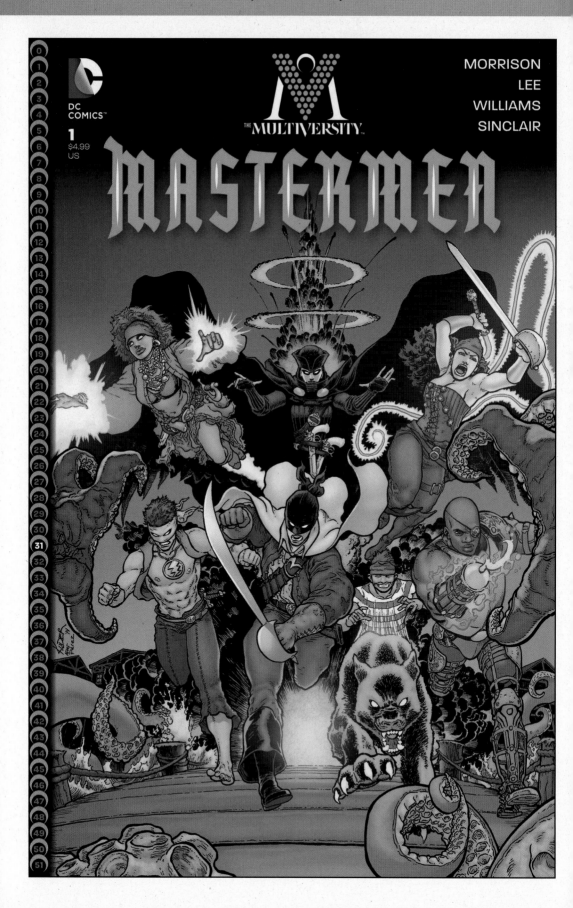

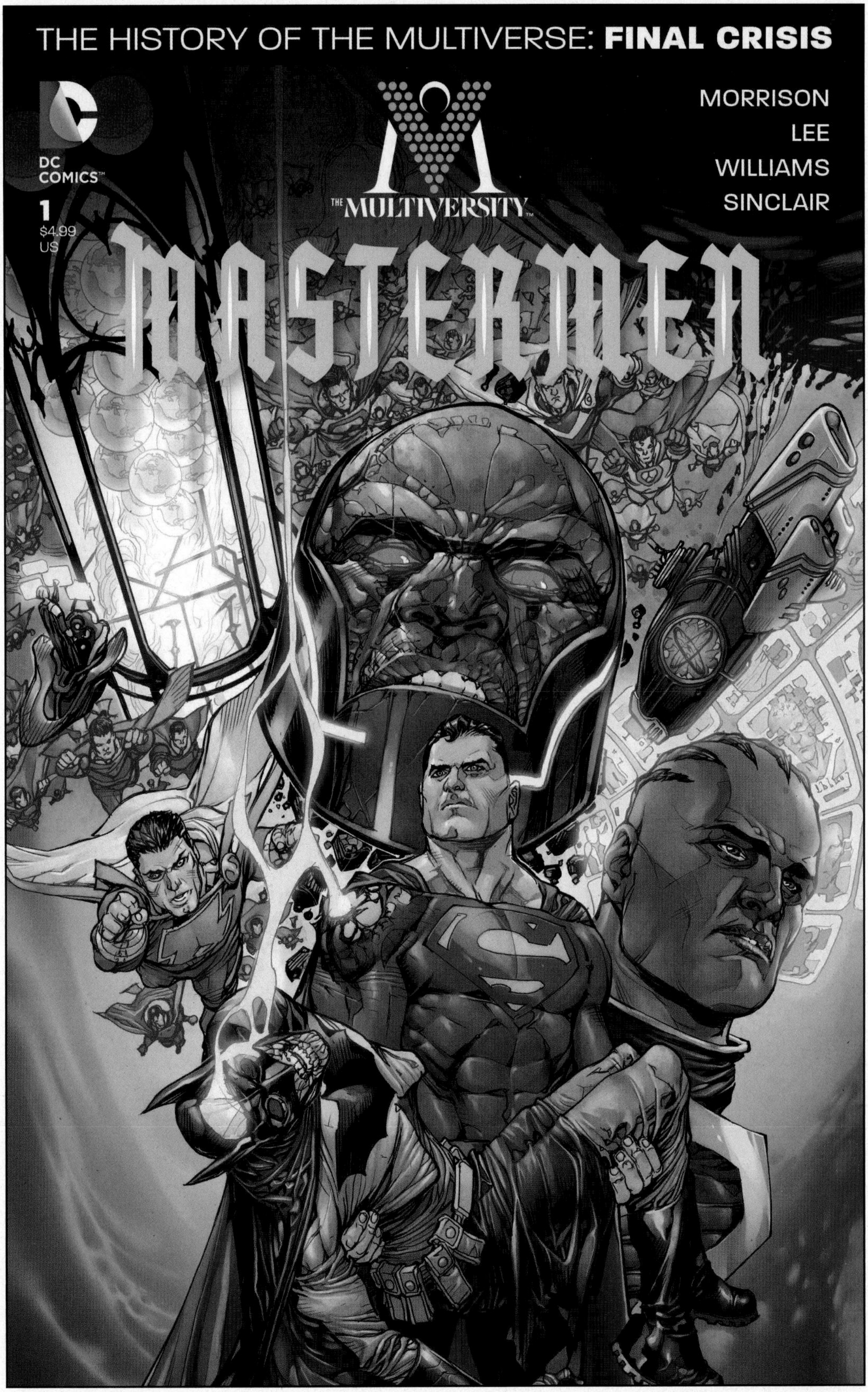
THE HISTORY OF THE MULTIVERSE: FINAL CRISIS
DC COMICS
1
$4.99
US
THE MULTIVERSITY
MORRISON
LEE
WILLIAMS
SINCLAIR
MASTERMEN

Variant cover art for THE MULTIVERSITY: MASTERMEN #1 by Grant Morrison.

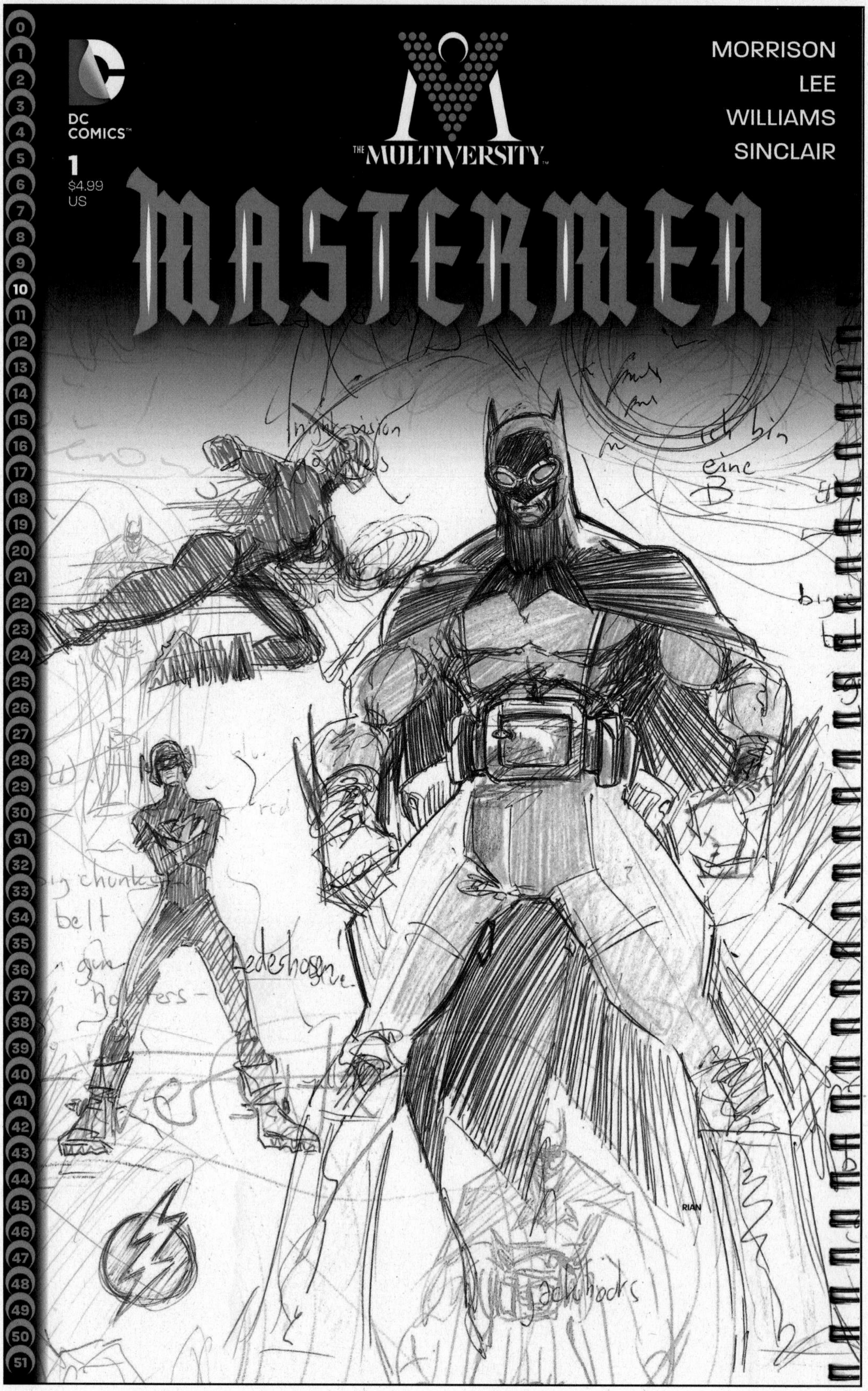
DC COMICS
1
$4.99
US
THE MULTIVERSITY
MASTERMEN
MORRISON
LEE
WILLIAMS
SINCLAIR
RIAN

Variant cover art for THE MULTIVERSITY: ULTRA COMICS #1 by Duncan Rouleau.

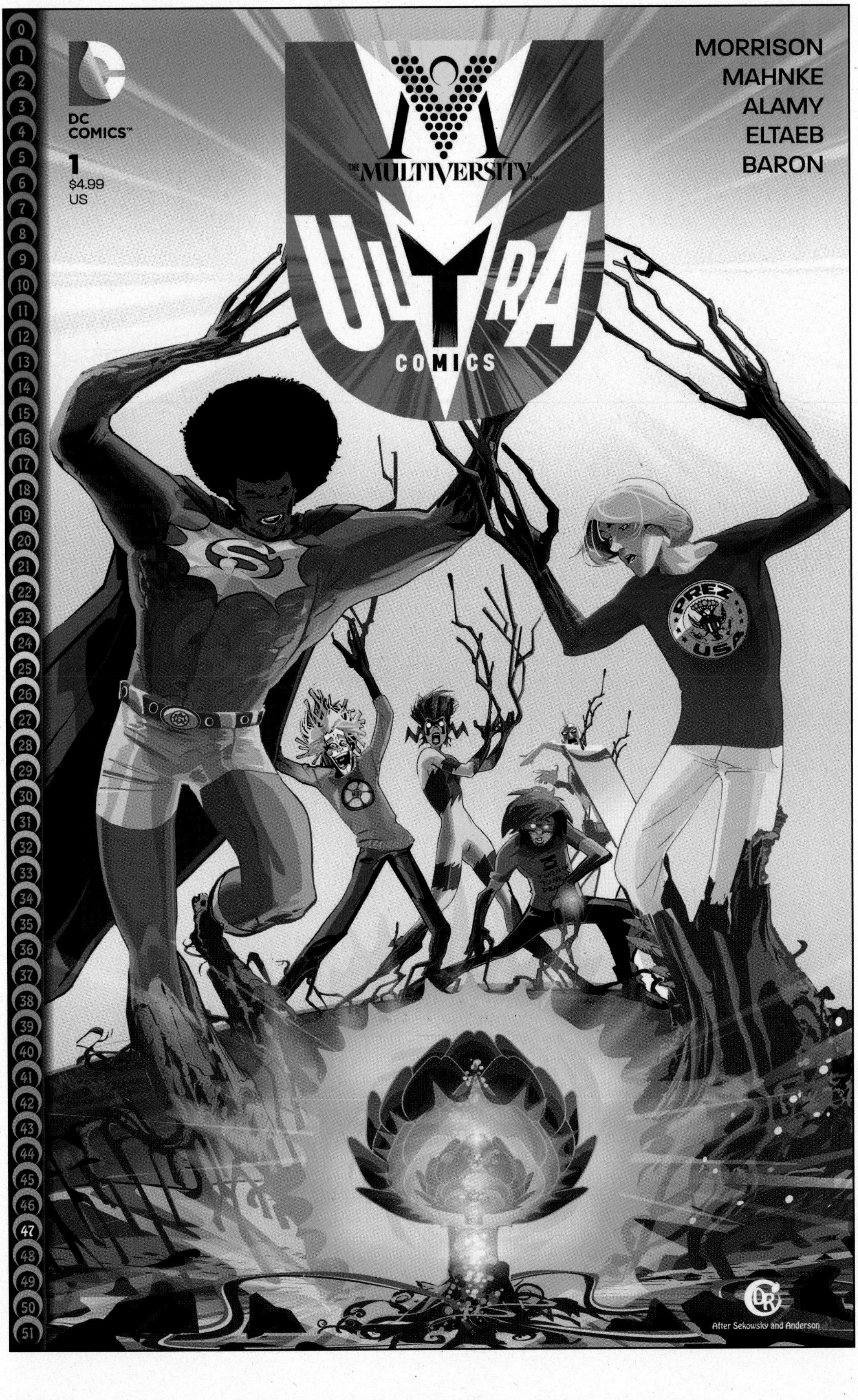
DC COMICS™
1
$4.99
US
THE MULTIVERSITY™
ULTRA
COMICS
MORRISON
MAHNKE
ALAMY
ELTAEB
BARON
0 1 2 3 4 5 6 7 8 9 10 11 12 13 14 15 16 17 18 19 20 21 22 23 24 25 26 27 28 29 30 31 32 33 34 35 36 37 38 39 40 41 42 43 44 45 46 47 48 49 50 51
PREZ
USA
After Sekowsky and Anderson

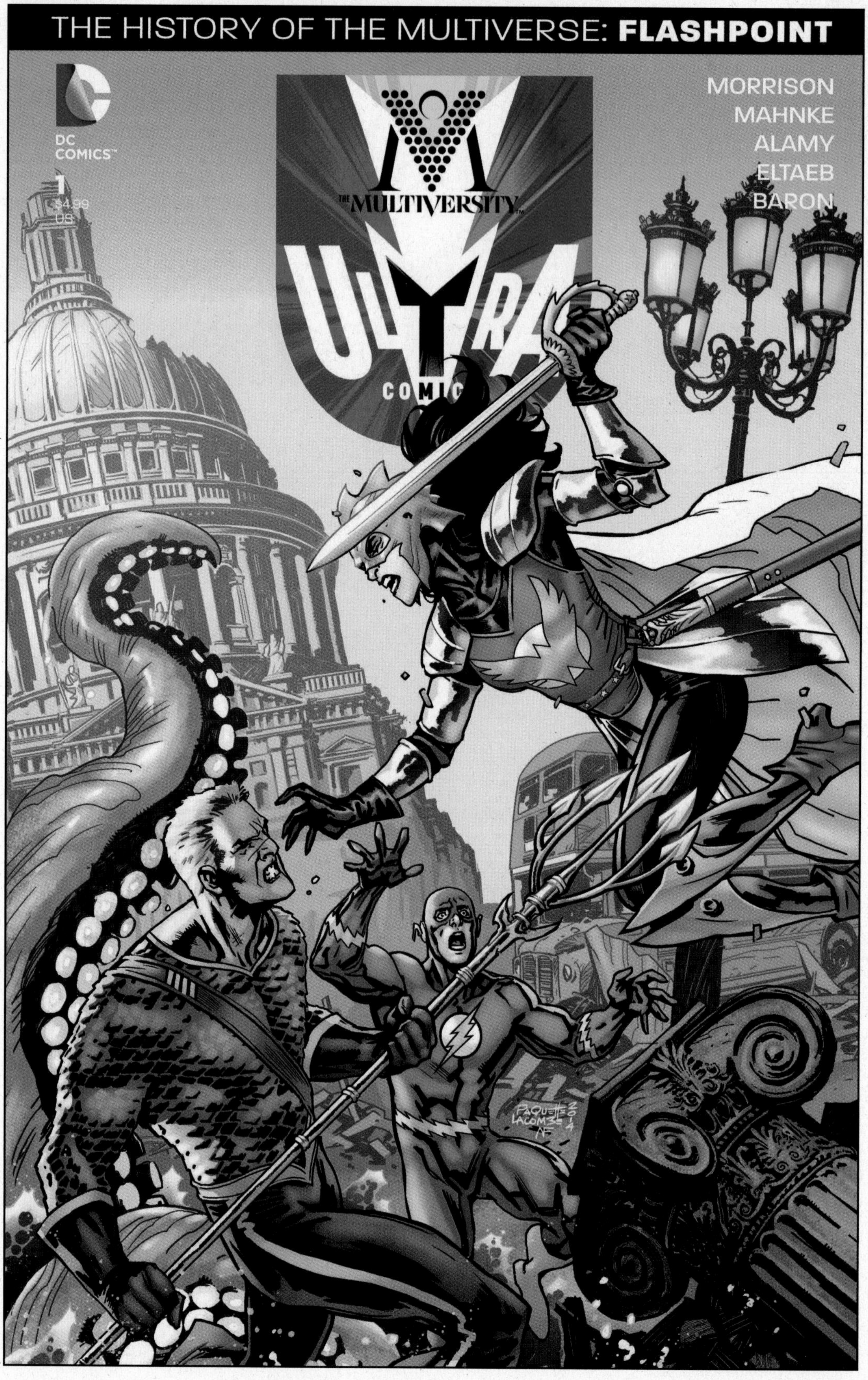
THE HISTORY OF THE MULTIVERSE: FLASHPOINT
DC COMICS
1
$4.99 US
THE MULTIVERSITY
ULTRA
COMICS
MORRISON
MAHNKE
ALAMY
ELTAEB
BARON
PAQUETTE LACOMBE 2014 NF

Variant cover art for THE MULTIVERSITY: ULTRA COMICS #1 by Grant Morrison.

451

Variant cover art for THE MULTIVERSITY #2 by Michael Allred (color by Laura Allred).

452

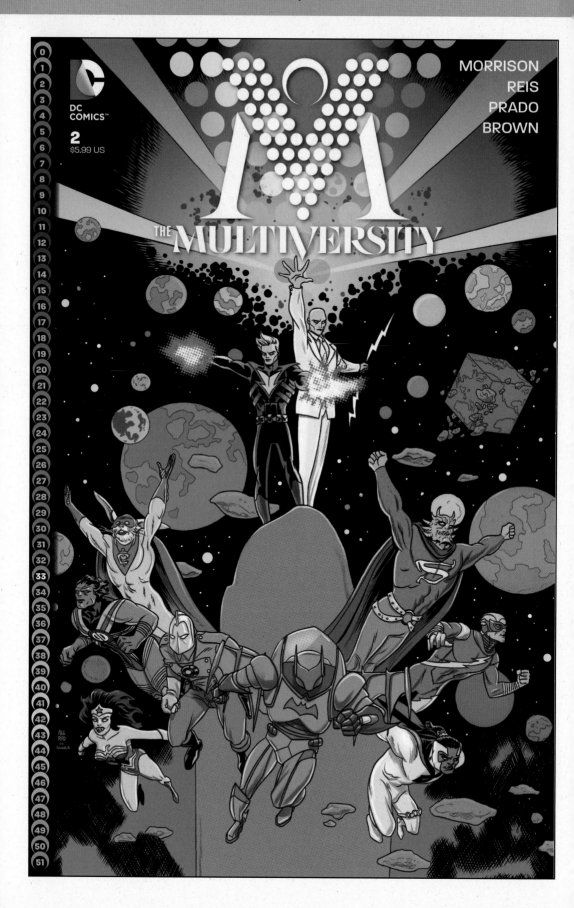

Variant cover art for THE MULTIVERSITY #2 by Francis Manapul.

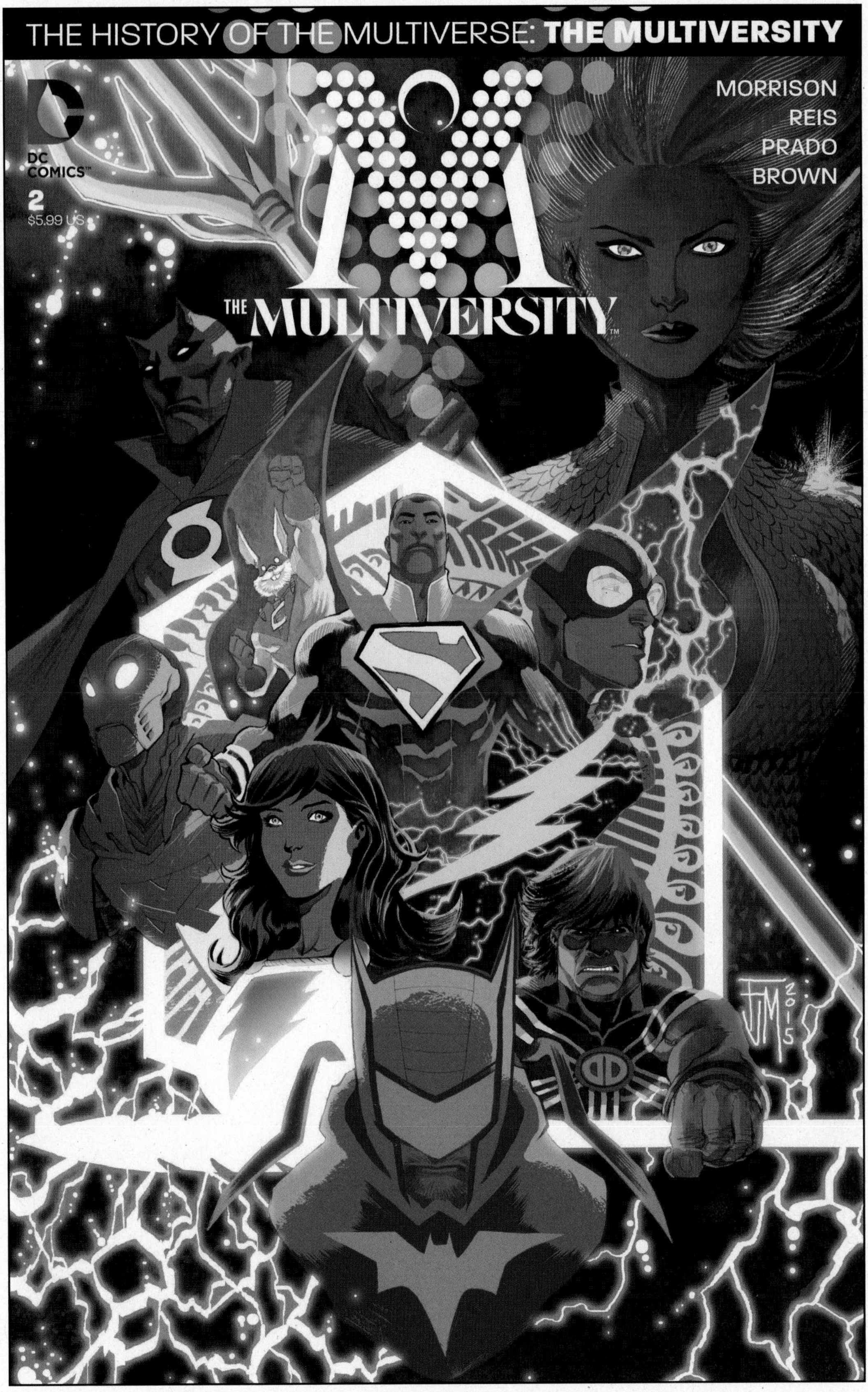
THE HISTORY OF THE MULTIVERSE: THE MULTIVERSITY
DC COMICS
2
$5.99 US
MORRISON
REIS
PRADO
BROWN
THE MULTIVERSITY
FJM 2015

Variant cover art for THE MULTIVERSITY #2 by Grant Morrison.

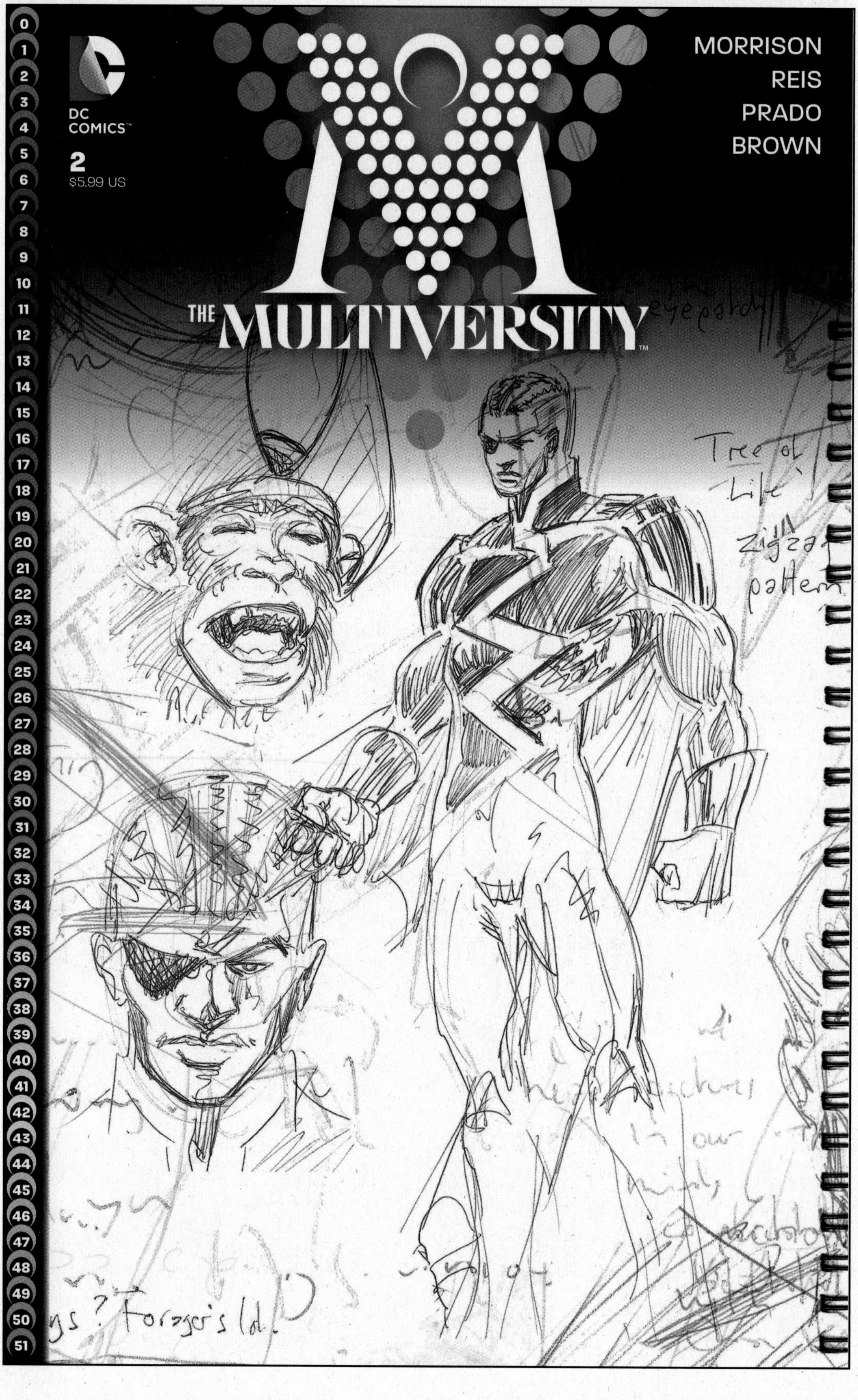
DC COMICS
2
$5.99 US
MORRISON
REIS
PRADO
BROWN
THE MULTIVERSITY
Tree of Life

VICTORY COMICS
The STINGRAY
SPIRE COMICS (TOWER)
CYCLOTRON

Cover sketches by Grant Morrison.

ASSEMBLY LANGUAGE

THE MULTIVERSITY

WEAVING THE TRANSMATTER WEB

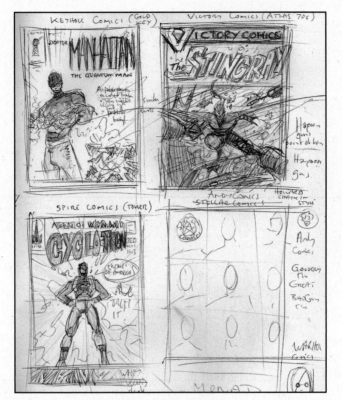

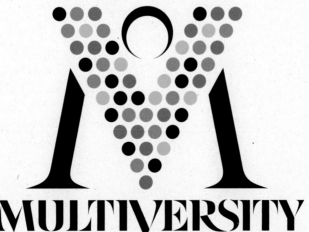

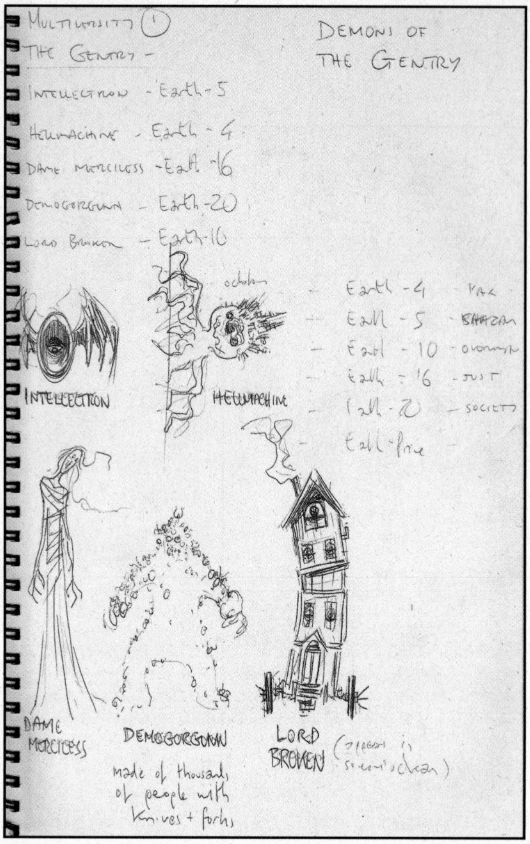
DEMONS OF
THE GENTRY
THE GENTRY -
INTELLECTRON - Earth-5
HELLMACHINE - Earth-4
DAME MERCILESS - Earth-16
DEMOGORGUNN - Earth-20
Earth-4
Earth-5
Earth-10
Earth-16
Earth-20
INTELLECTRON
HELLMACHINE
DAME MERCILESS
DEMOGORGUNN
made of thousands of people with knives + forks
LORD BROKEN

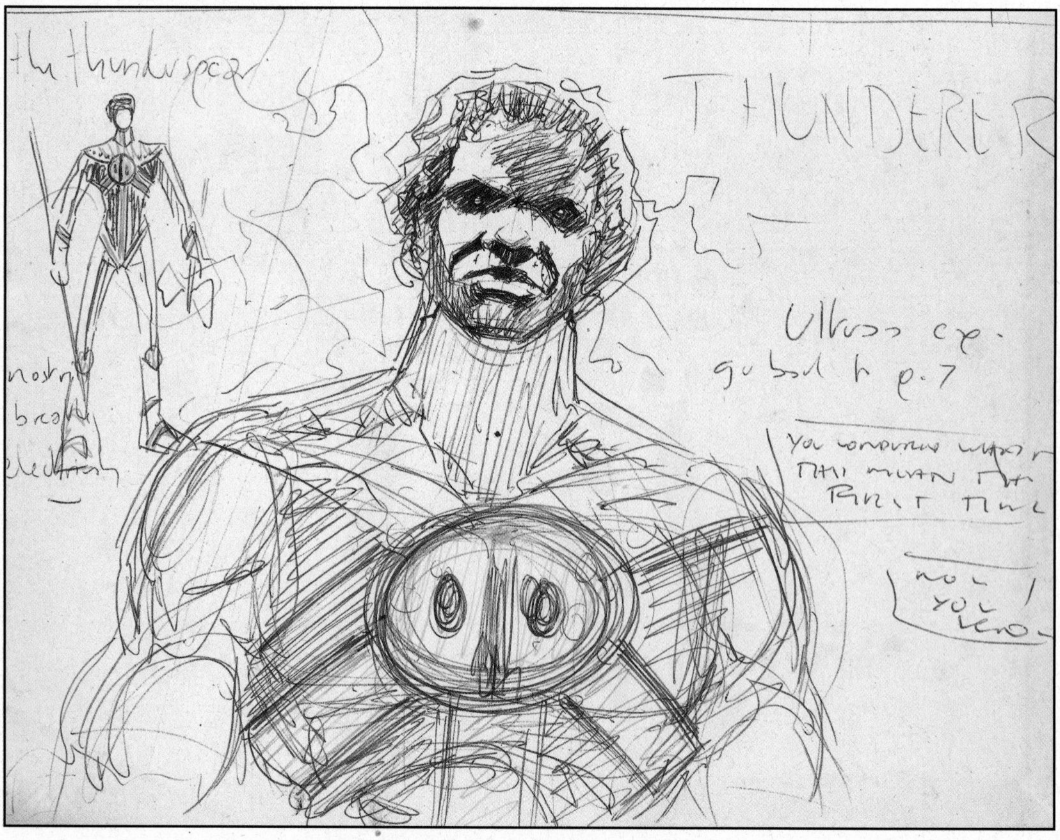
THUNDERER

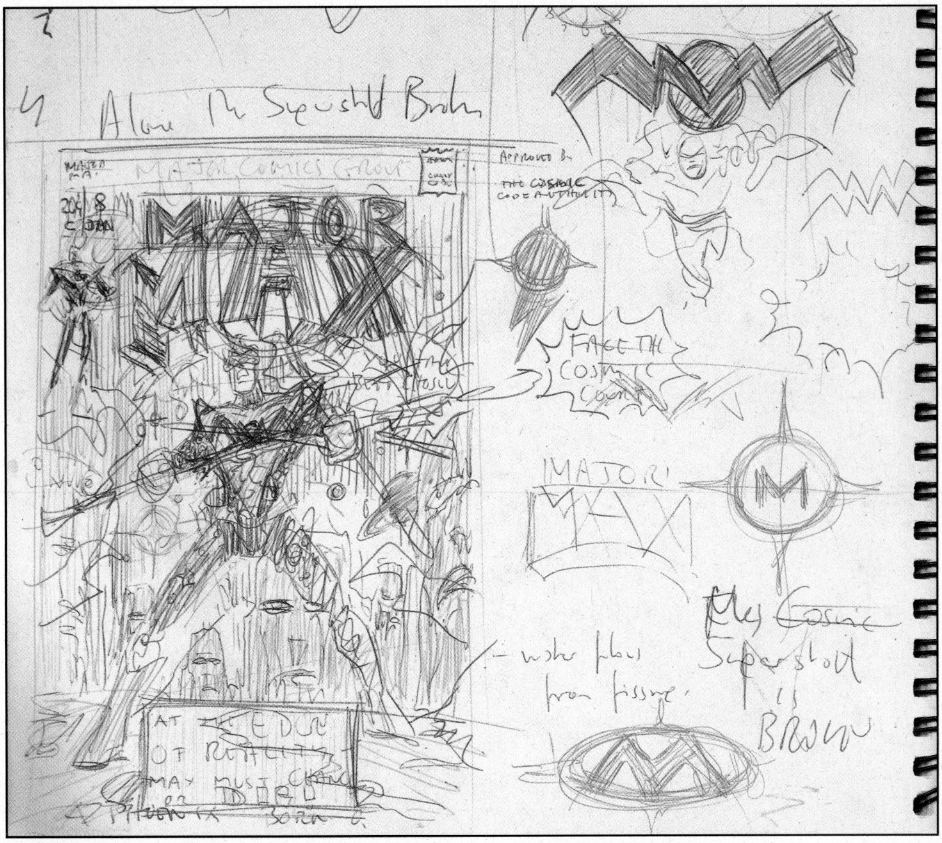
MAJOR MAX
MAJOR MAX

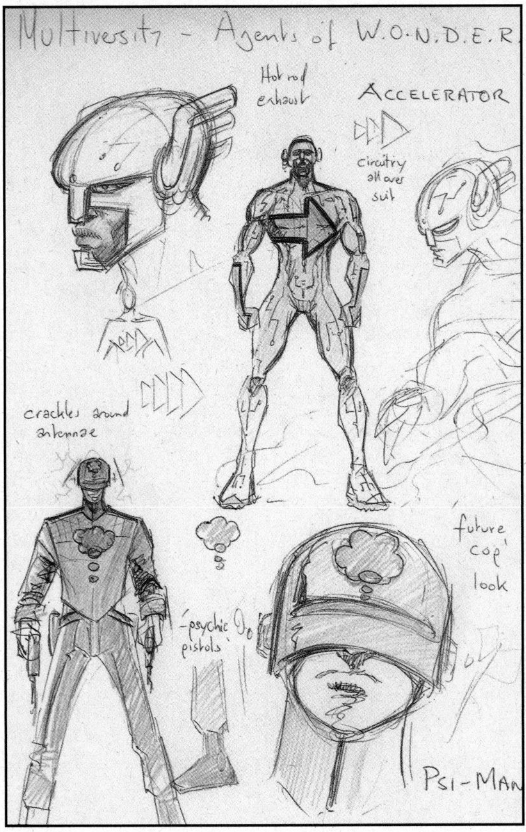
Multiversity - Agents of W.O.N.D.E.R.
Hot rod exhaust
ACCELERATOR
circuitry all over suit
crackles around antennae
future cop look
psychic pistols
PSI-MAN

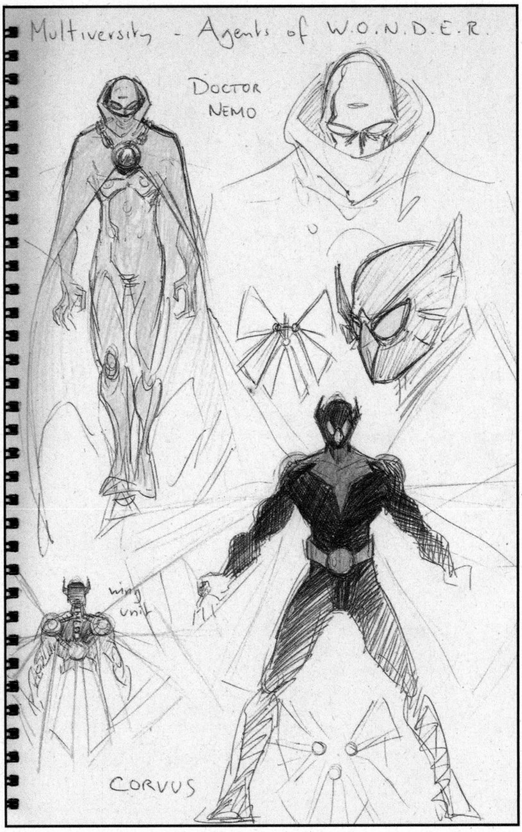
Multiversity - Agents of W.O.N.D.E.R.
DOCTOR NEMO
wing unit
CORVUS

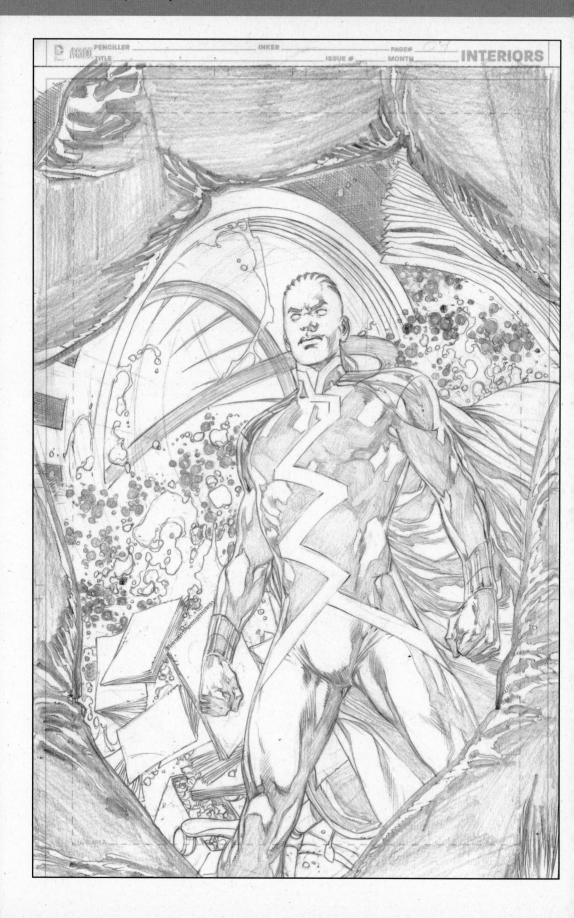

PENCILLER
TITLE
INKER
ISSUE #
PAGE#
MONTH
INTERIORS

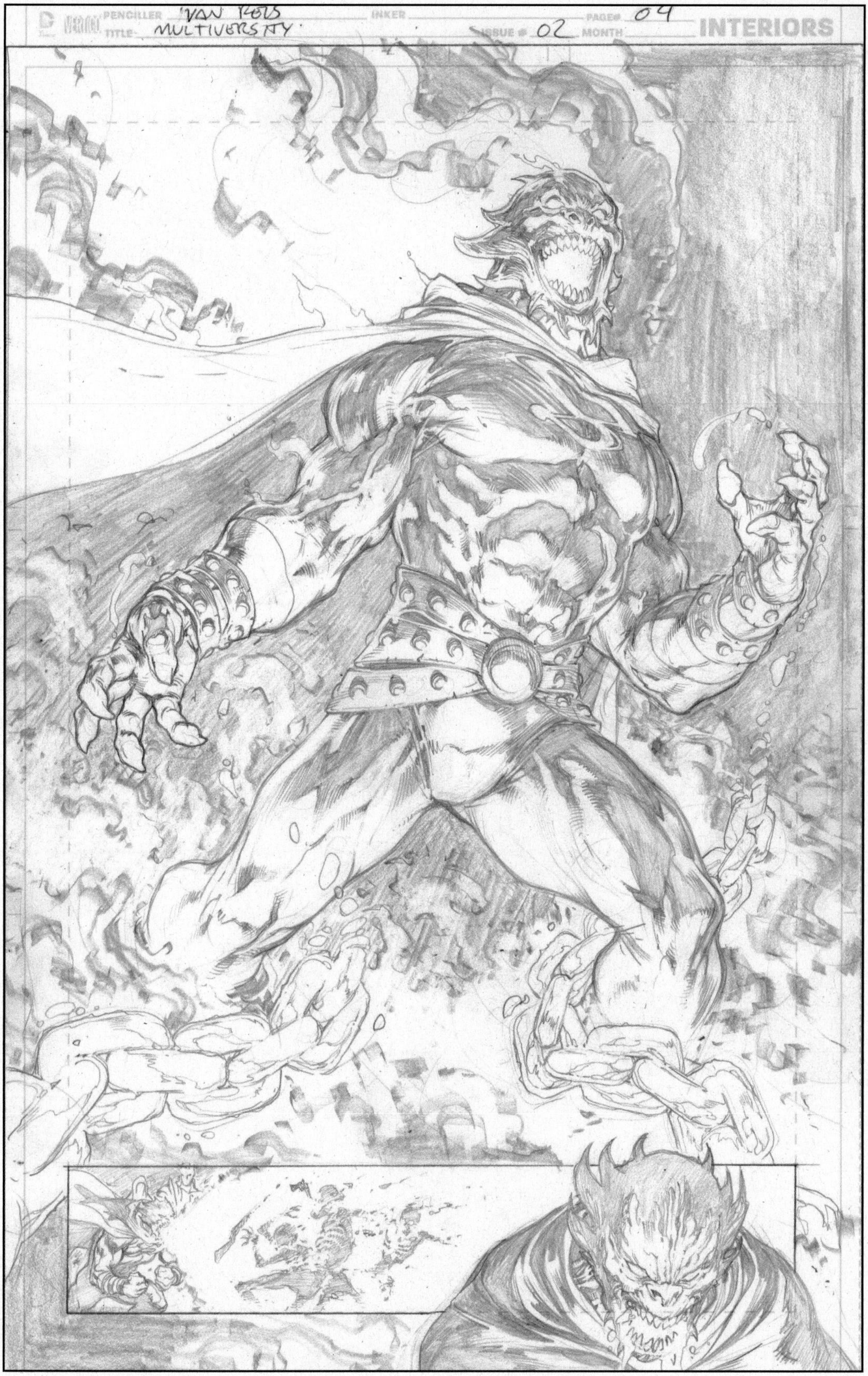
PENCILLER IVAN REIS
INKER
PAGE# 04
TITLE MULTIVERSITY
ISSUE # 02
MONTH
INTERIORS

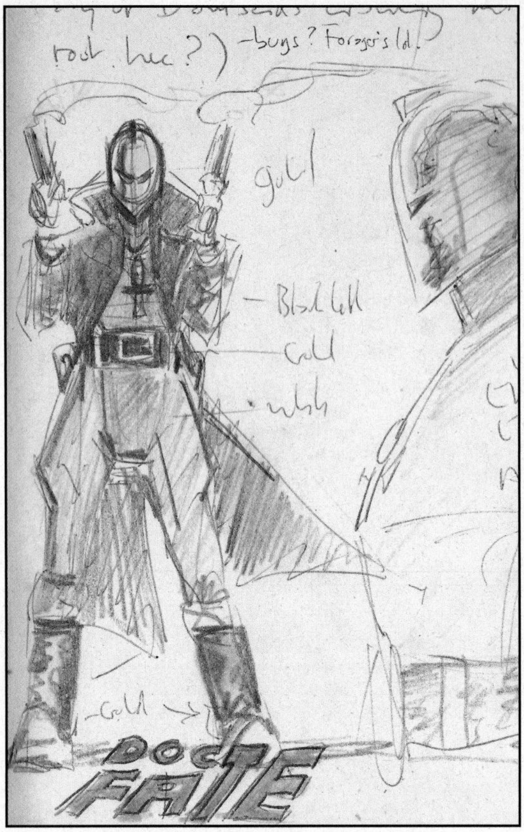
DOC FATE

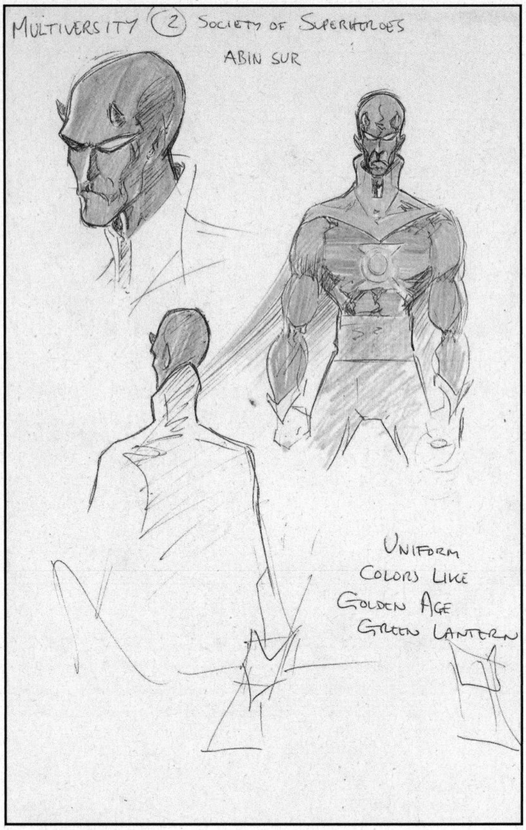
MULTIVERSITY (2) SOCIETY OF SUPERHEROES
ABIN SUR
UNIFORM COLORS LIKE GOLDEN AGE GREEN LANTERN

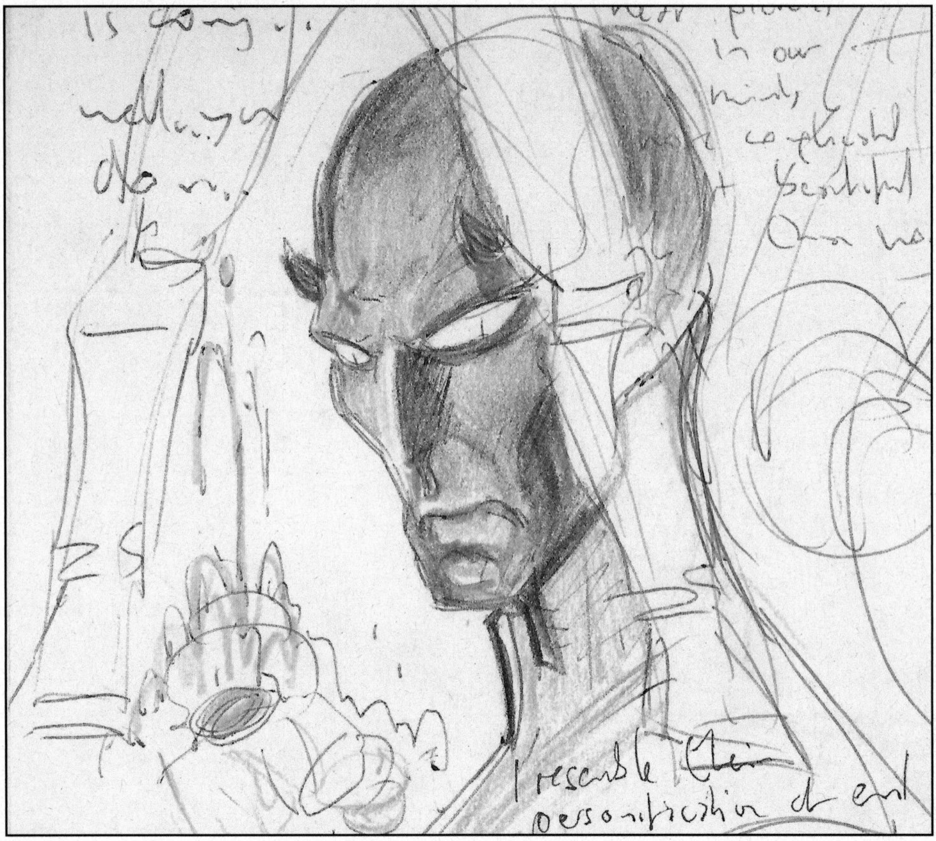

Final character designs by Chris Sprouse.

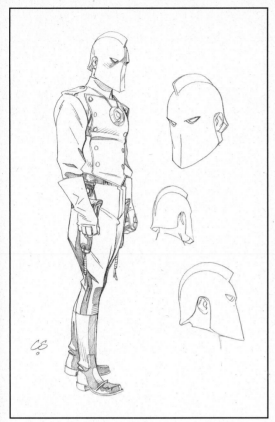

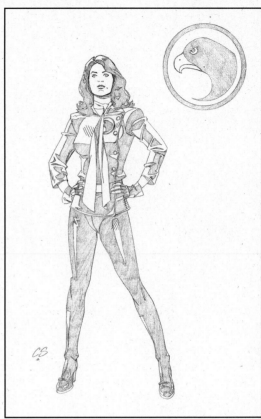

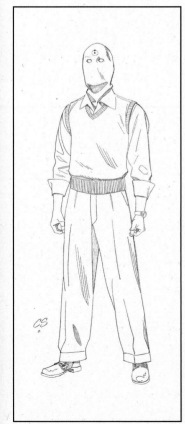

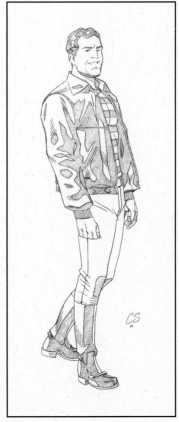

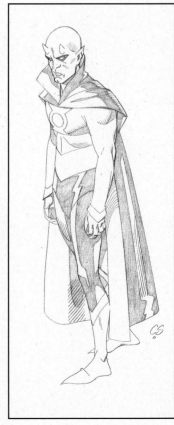

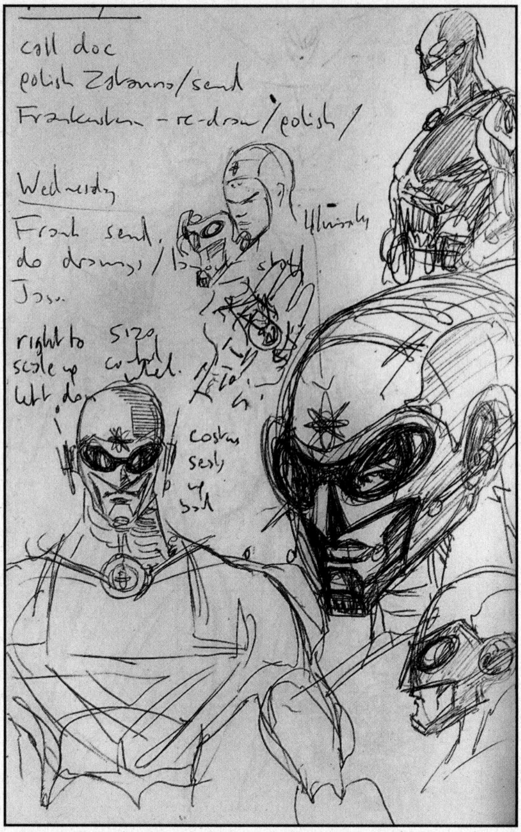
call doc
Wednesday

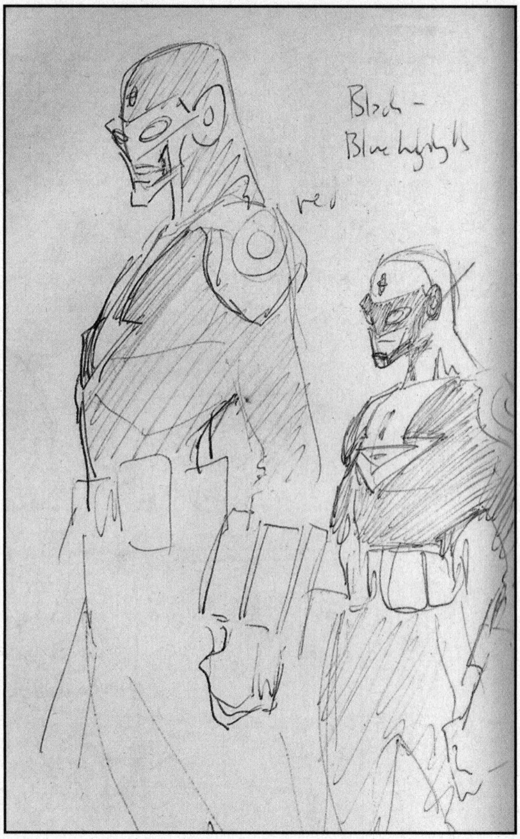
red

Final character designs by Ben Oliver.

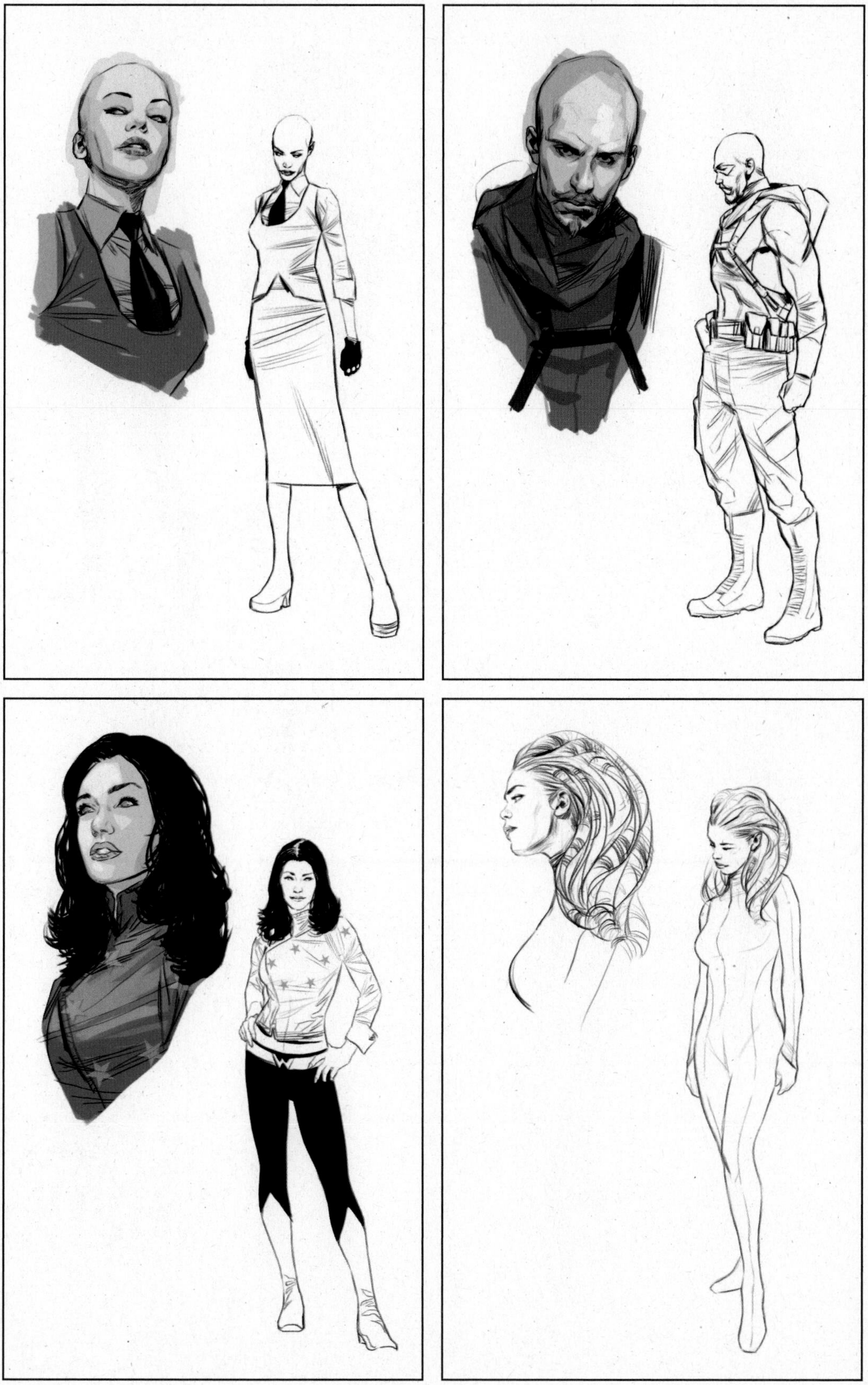

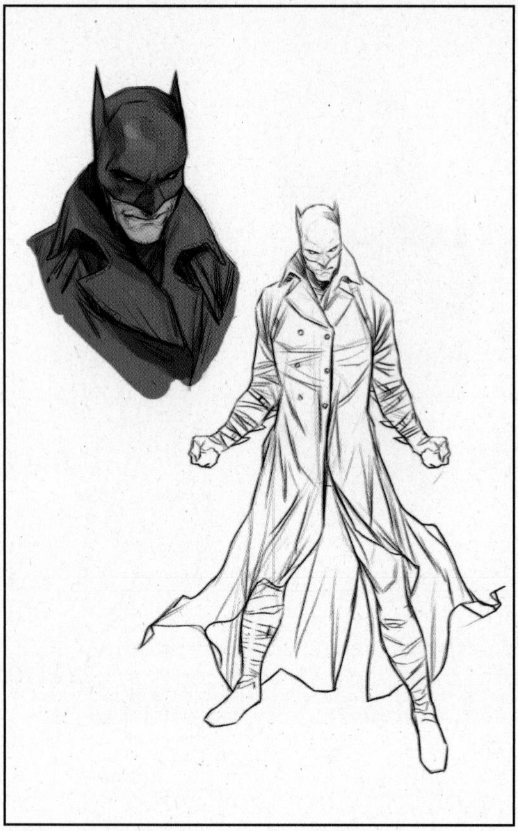

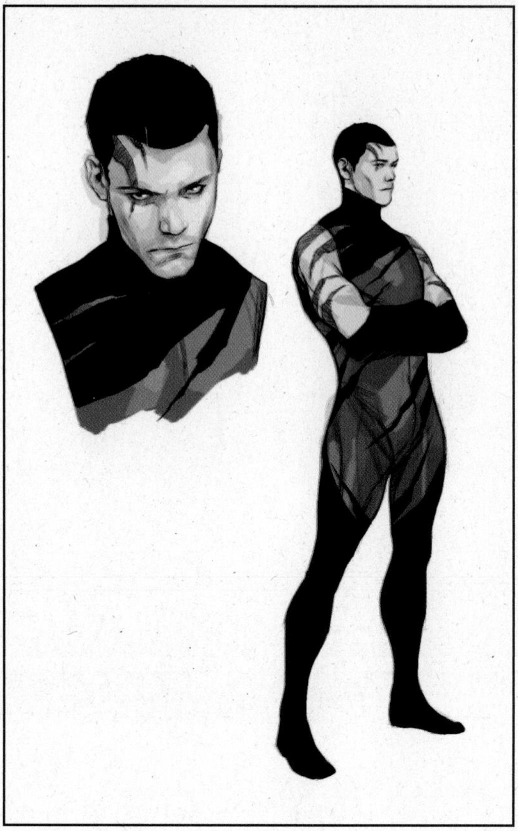

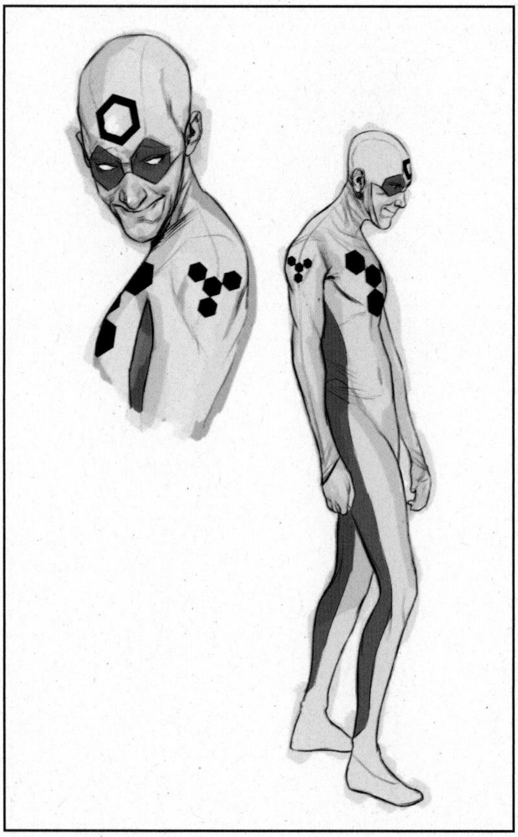

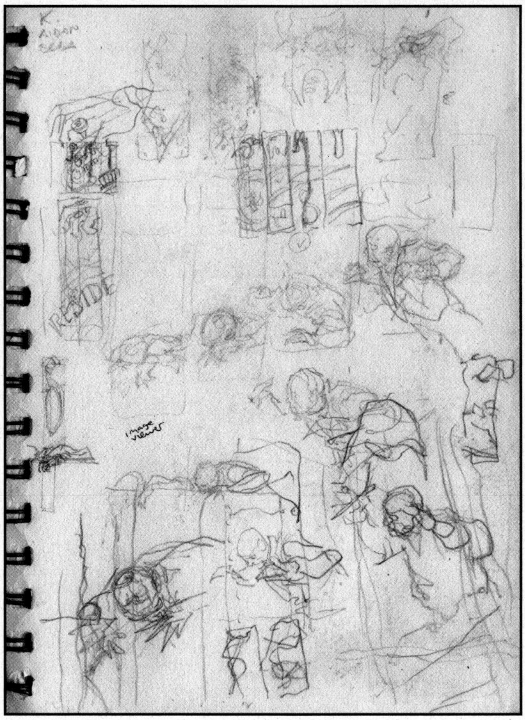

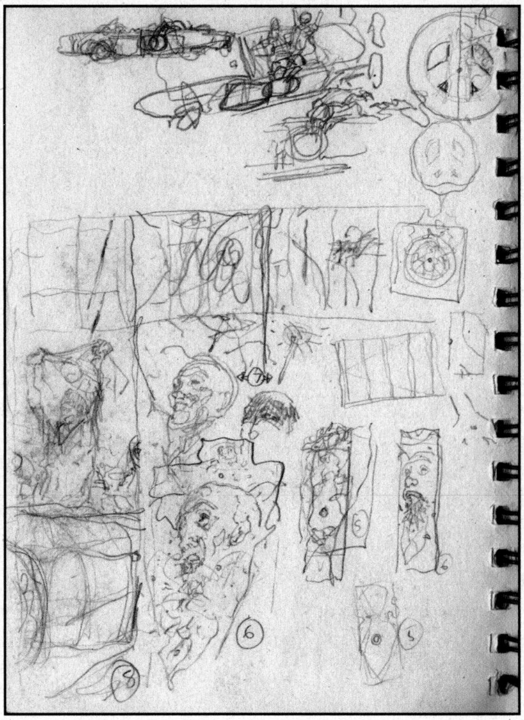

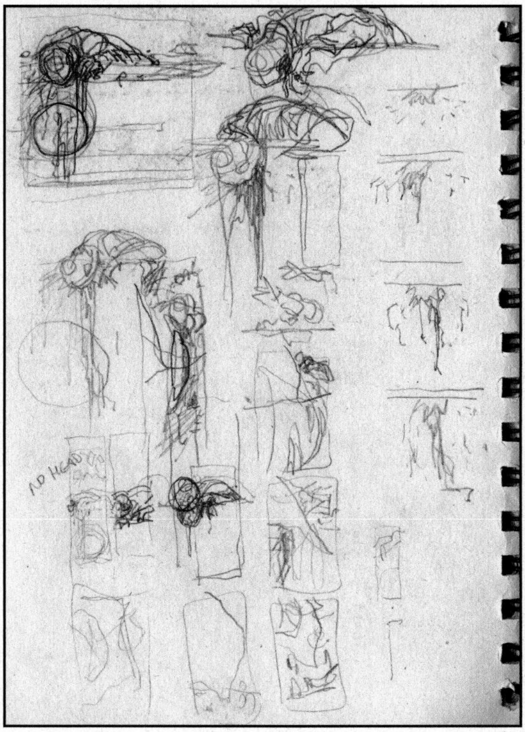

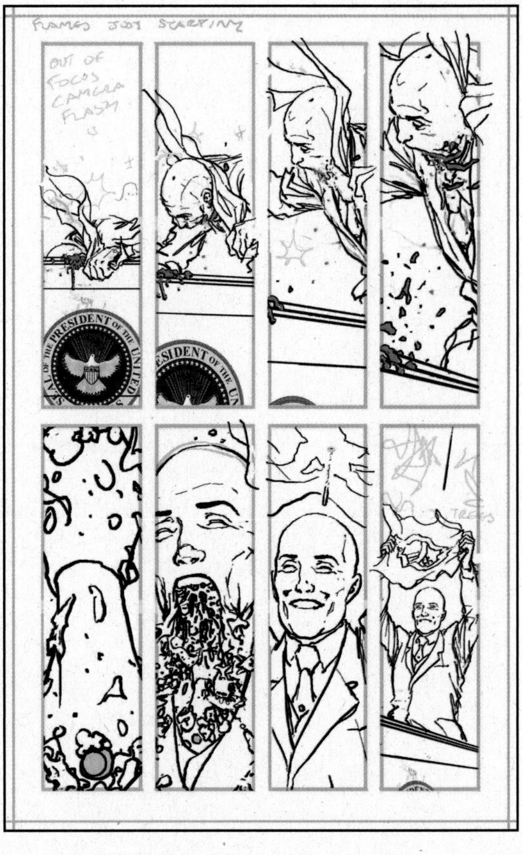
FLAMES JUST STARTING
OUT OF FOCUS CAMERA FLASH

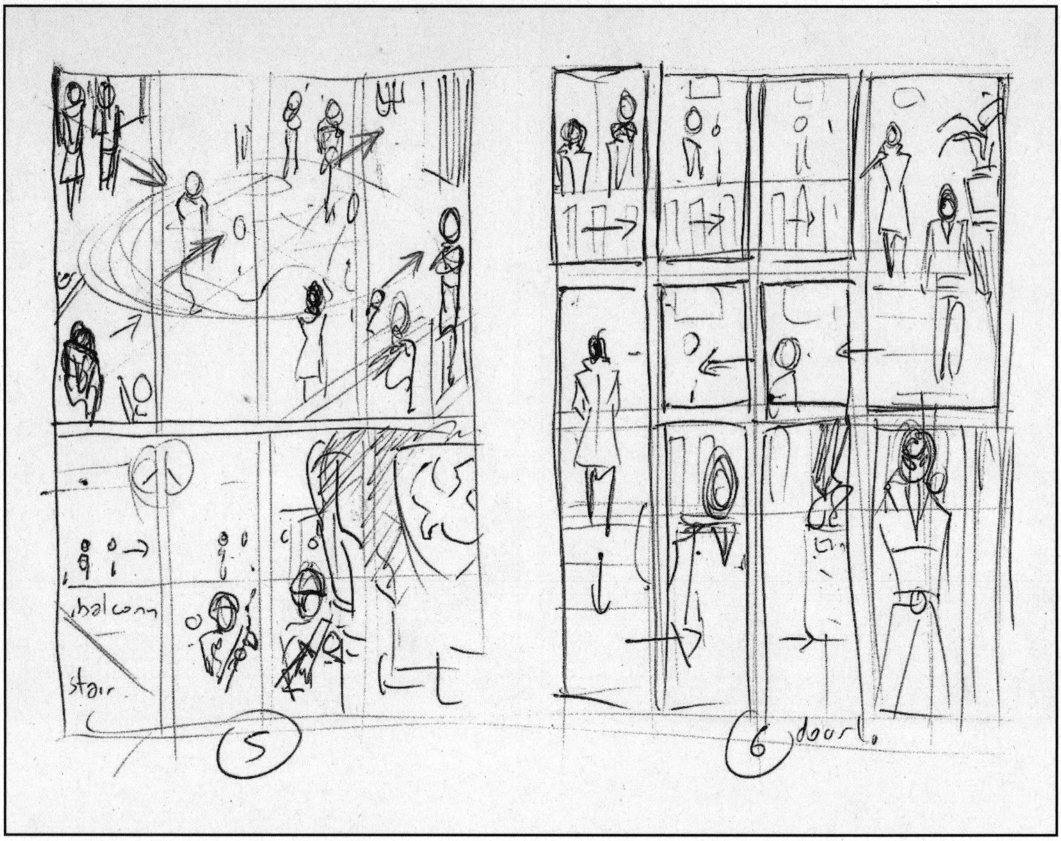
stair
5
6
door

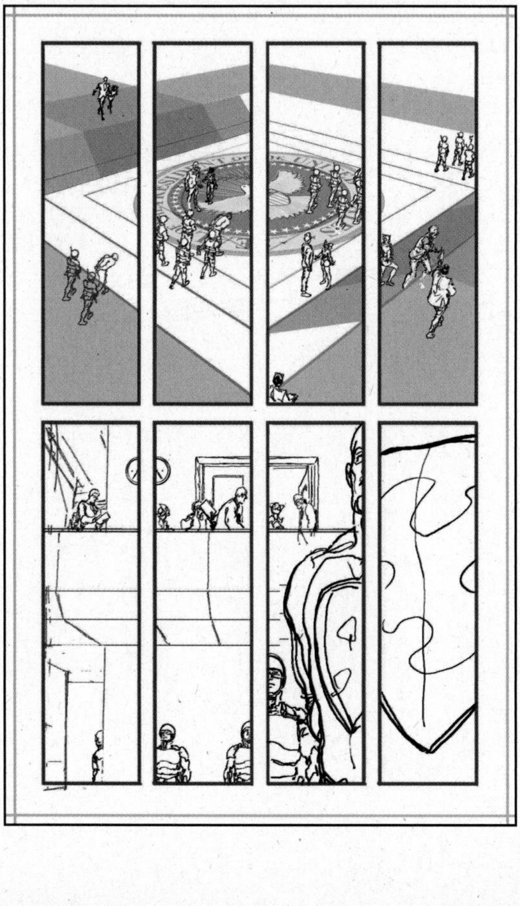

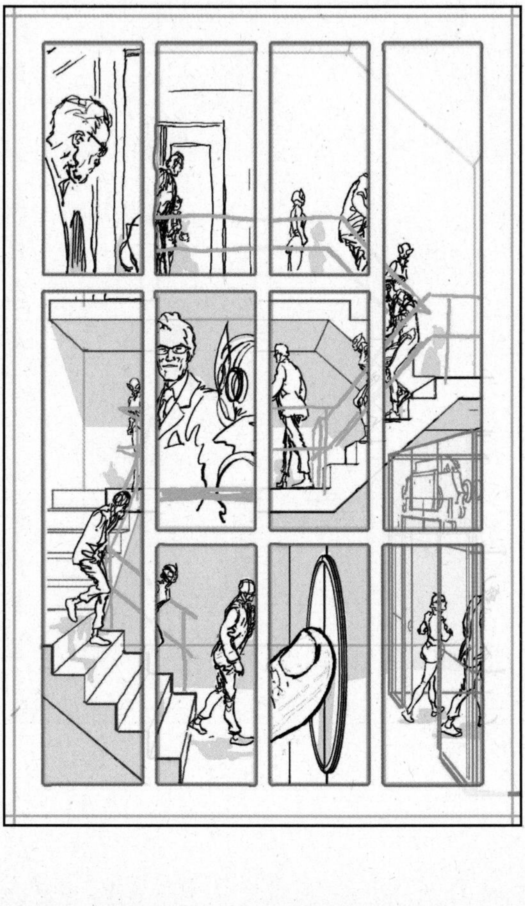

Breakdown for page 28 by Grant Morrison.

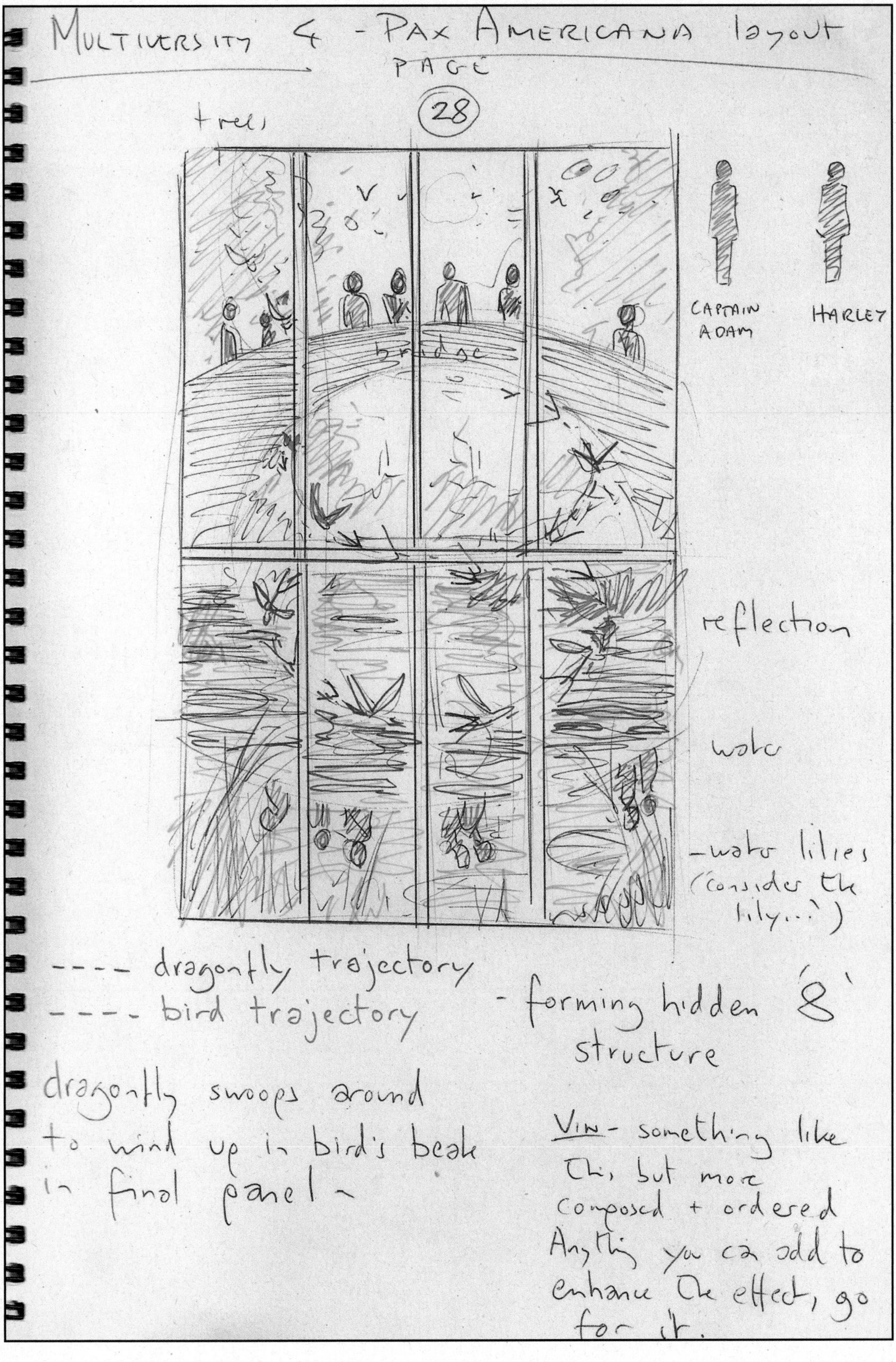
MULTIVERSITY 4 - PAX AMERICANA layout
PAGE
28
trees
bridge
CAPTAIN ADAM
HARLEY
reflection
water
- water lilies
(consider the lily...')
---- dragonfly trajectory
---- bird trajectory
- forming hidden '8' structure
dragonfly swoops around to wind up in bird's beak in final panel -
VIN - something like this but more composed + ordered
Anything you can add to enhance the effect, go for it.

THUNDERWORLD ADVENTURES Cover sketch by Grant Morrison.

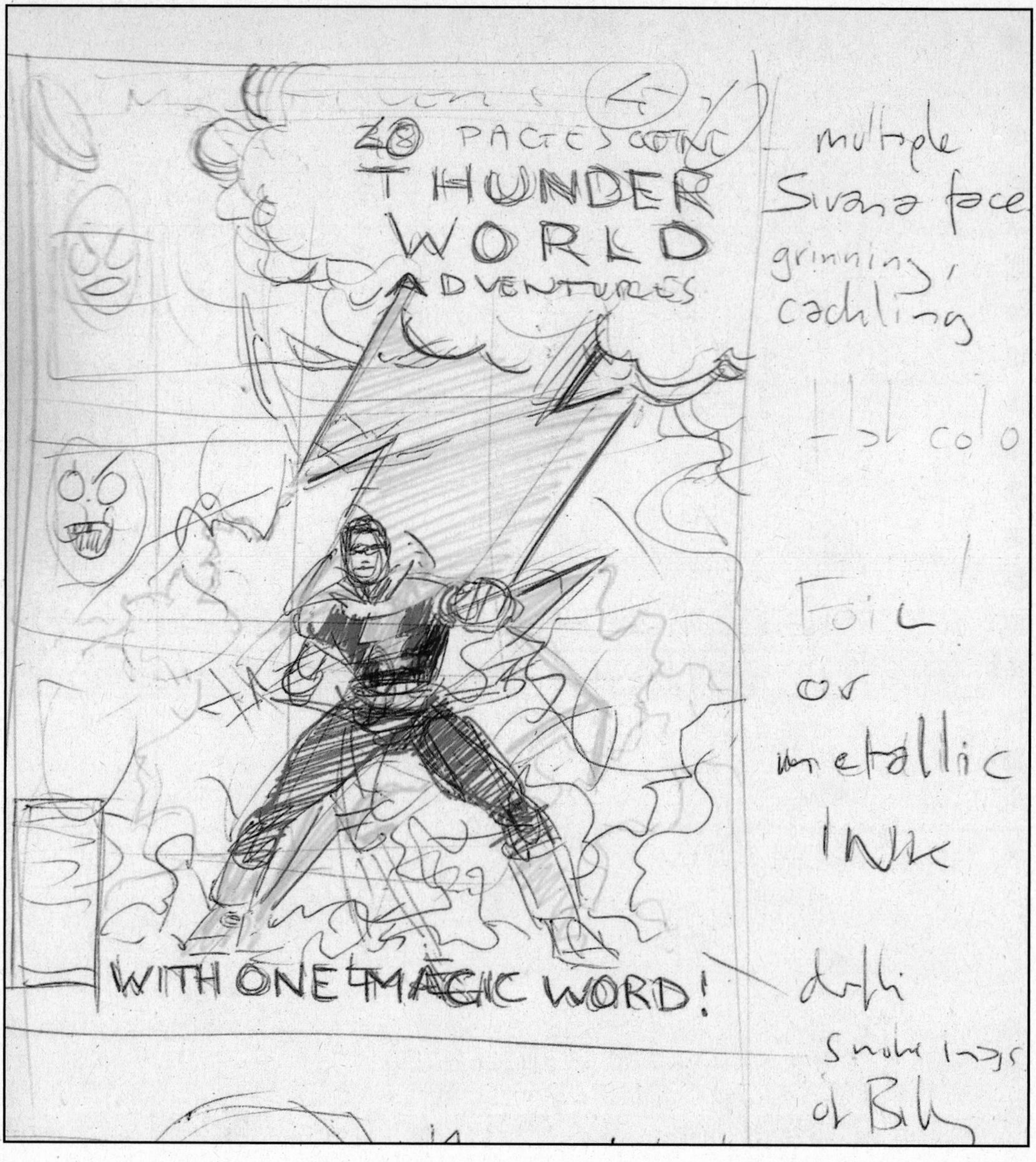
THUNDER WORLD ADVENTURES
WITH ONE MAGIC WORD!
multiple Sivana face grinning, cackling
Foil or metallic Ink

Conceptual art and character designs by Cameron Stewart.

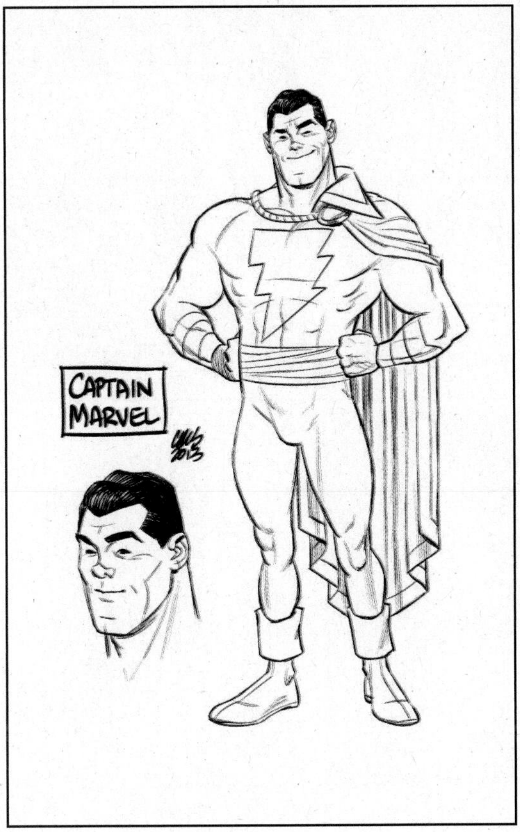
CAPTAIN MARVEL

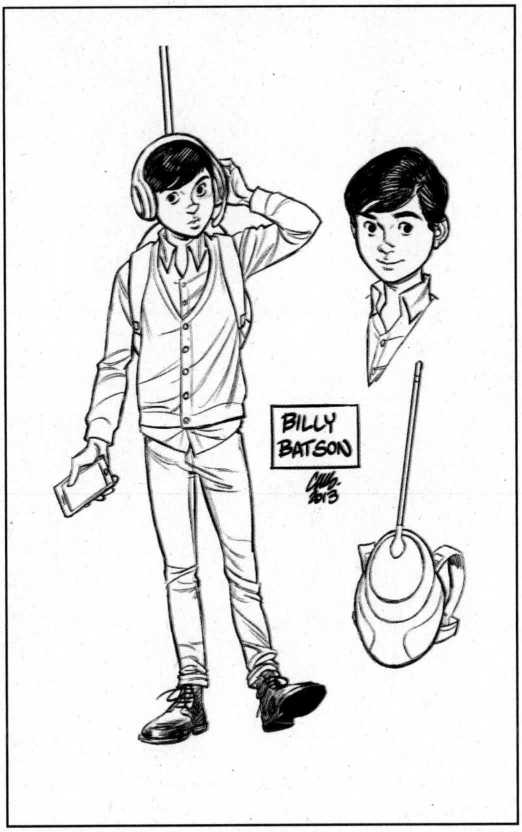
BILLY BATSON

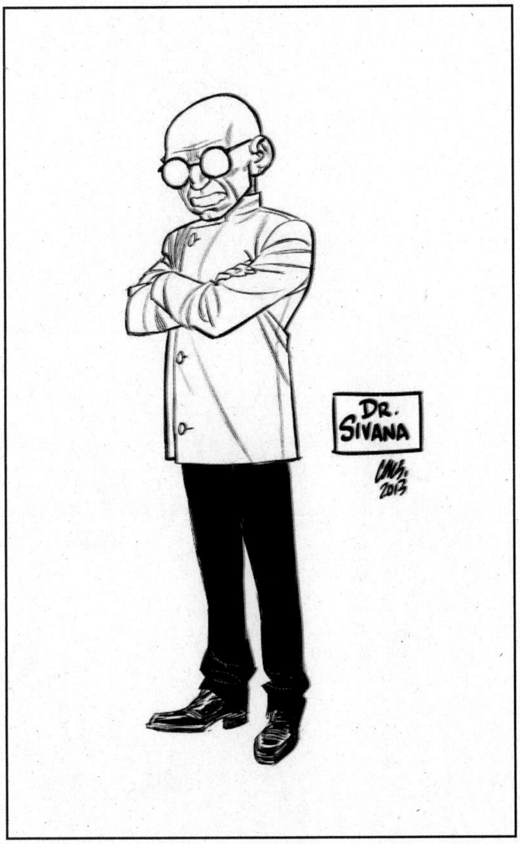
DR. SIVANA

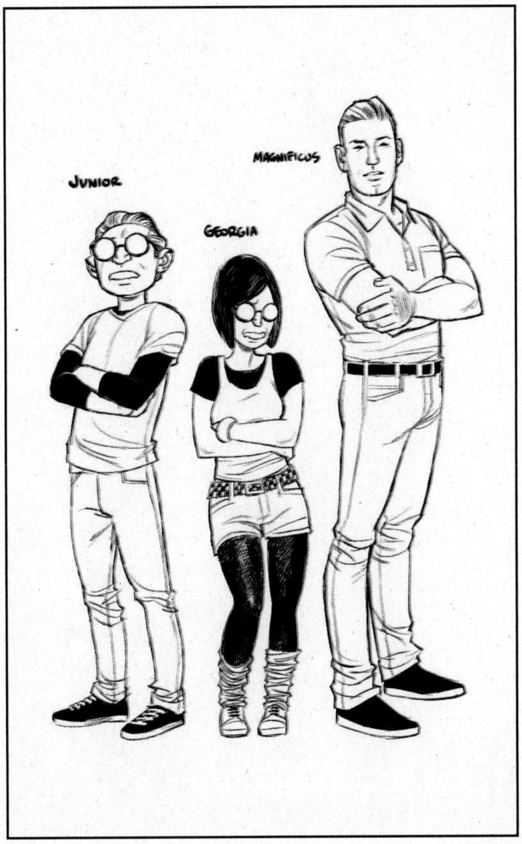
MAGNIFICUS
JUNIOR
GEORGIA

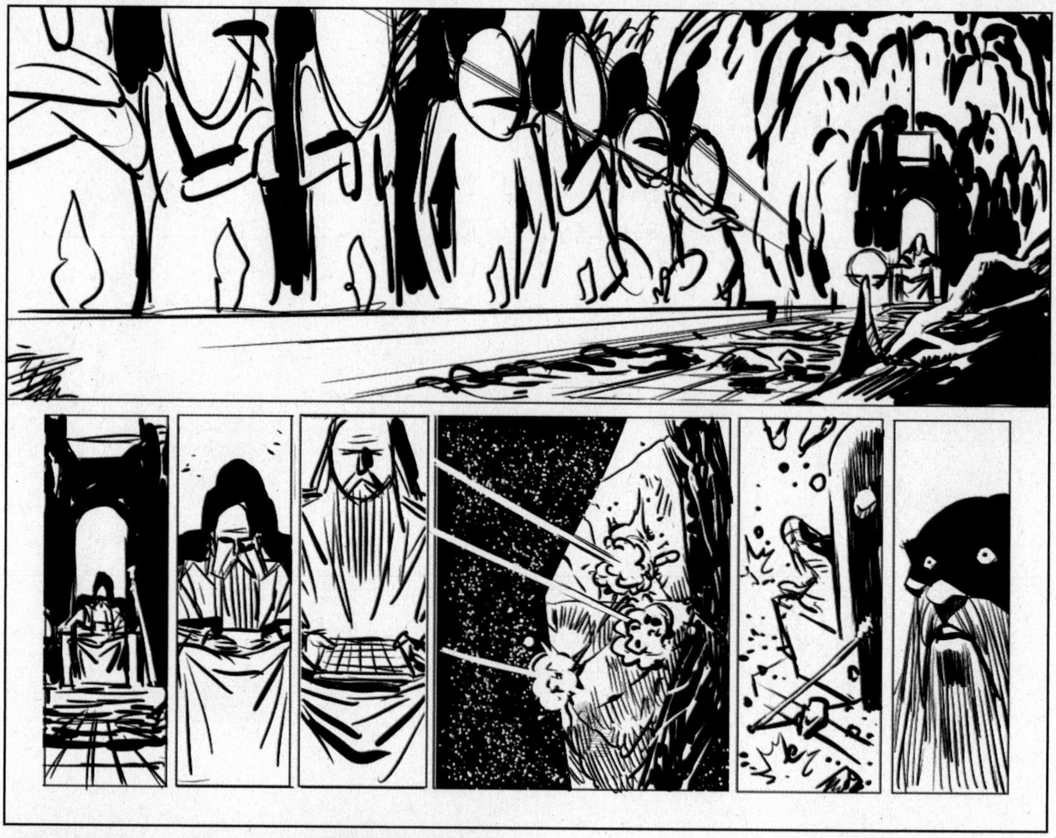

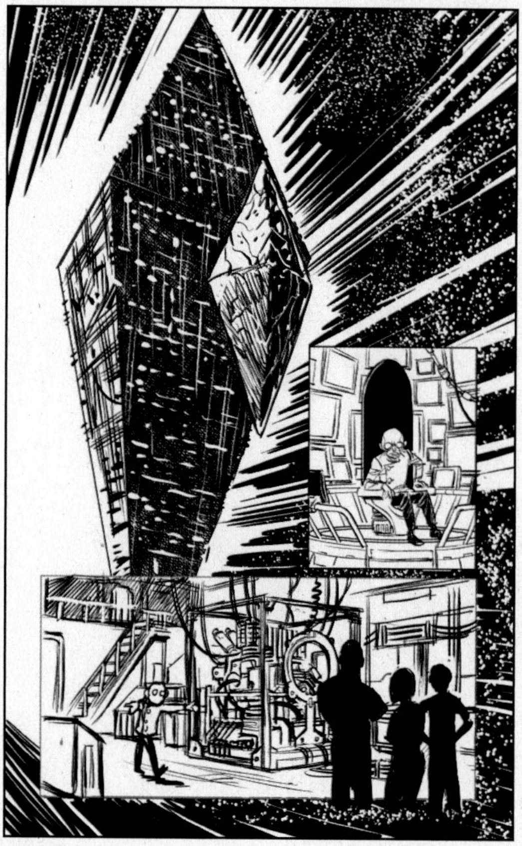

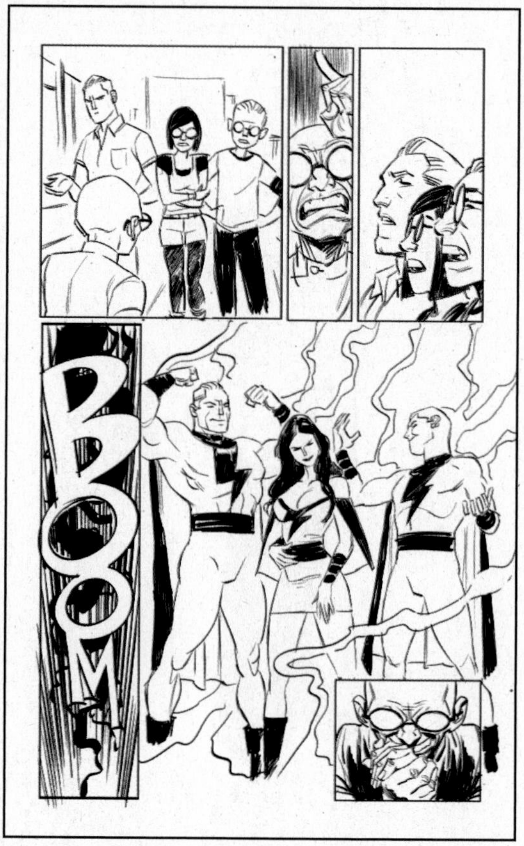
BOOM

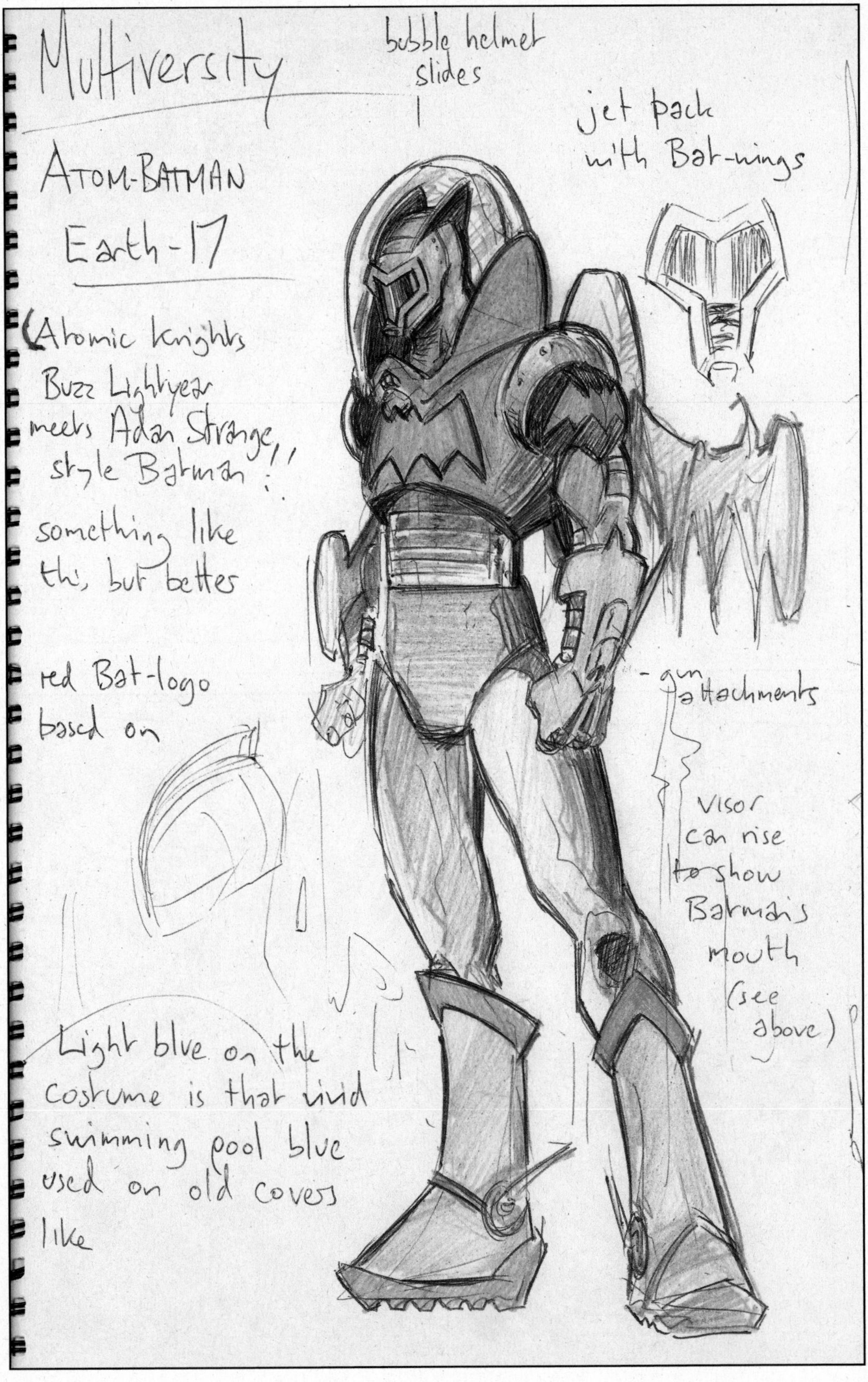
Multiversity
bubble helmet slides
jet pack with Bat-wings
ATOM-BATMAN
Earth-17
(Atomic Knights
Buzz Lightyear
meets Adam Strange,
style Batman!!
something like
this, but better
red Bat-logo
based on
-gun attachments
visor can rise to show Batman's mouth (see above)
Light blue on the
costume is that vivid
swimming pool blue
used on old covers
like

Breakdowns and layouts for pages 1-4 by Marcus To.

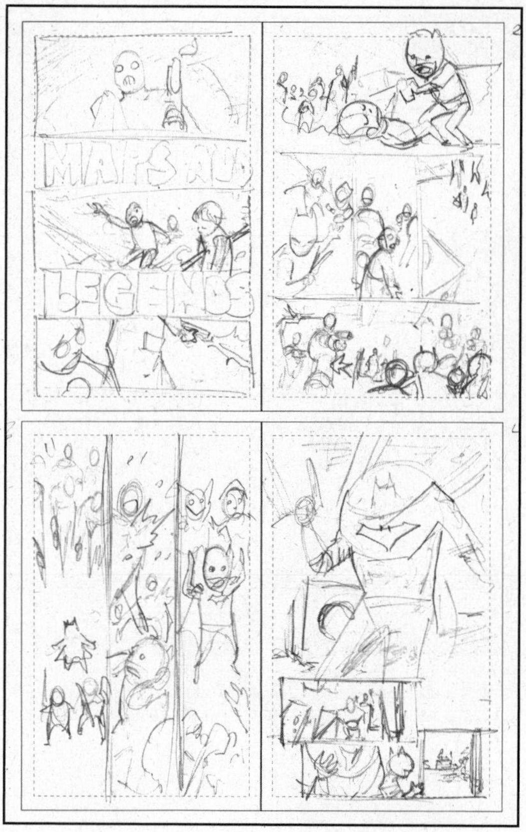
LEGENDS

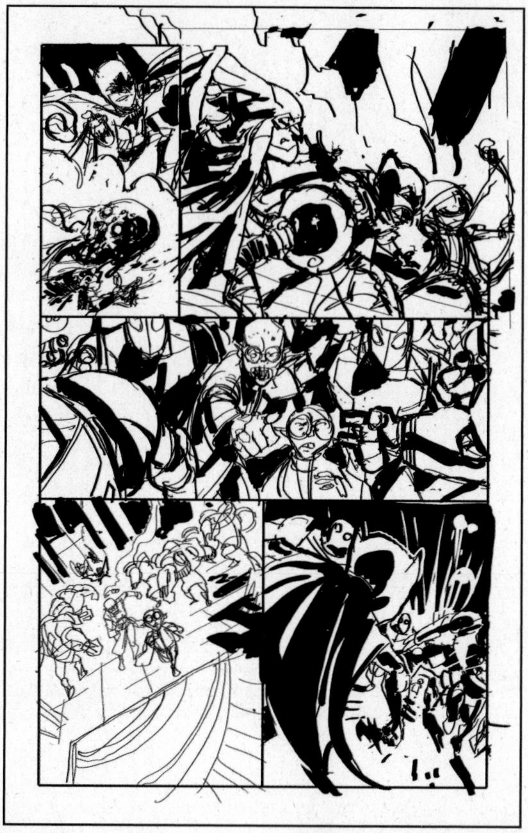

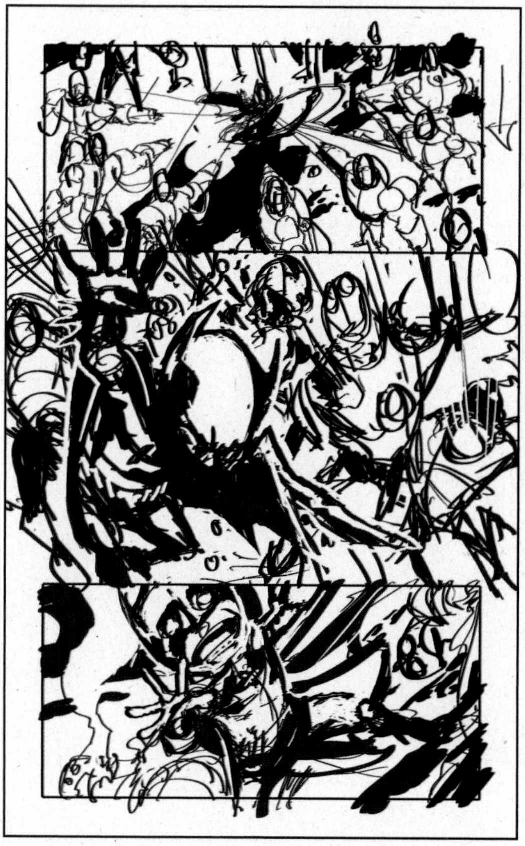

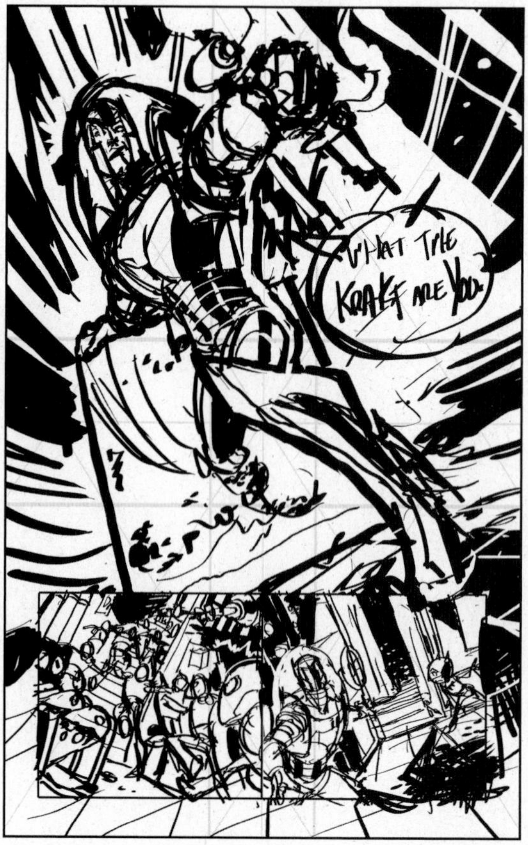

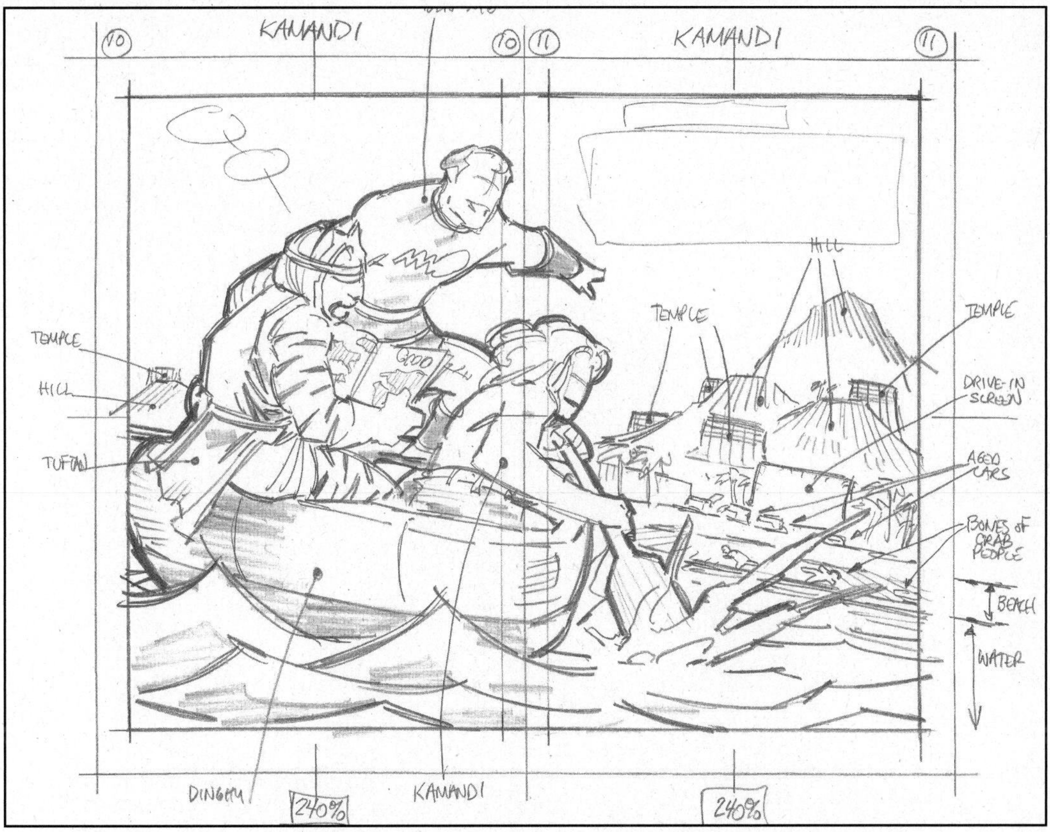
10
KAMANDI
10
11
KAMANDI
11
TEMPLE
HILL
TUFTAN
GOOD
HILL
TEMPLE
TEMPLE
DRIVE-IN SCREEN
AGED CARS
BONES OF CRAB PEOPLE
BEACH
WATER
DINGHY
240%
KAMANDI
240%

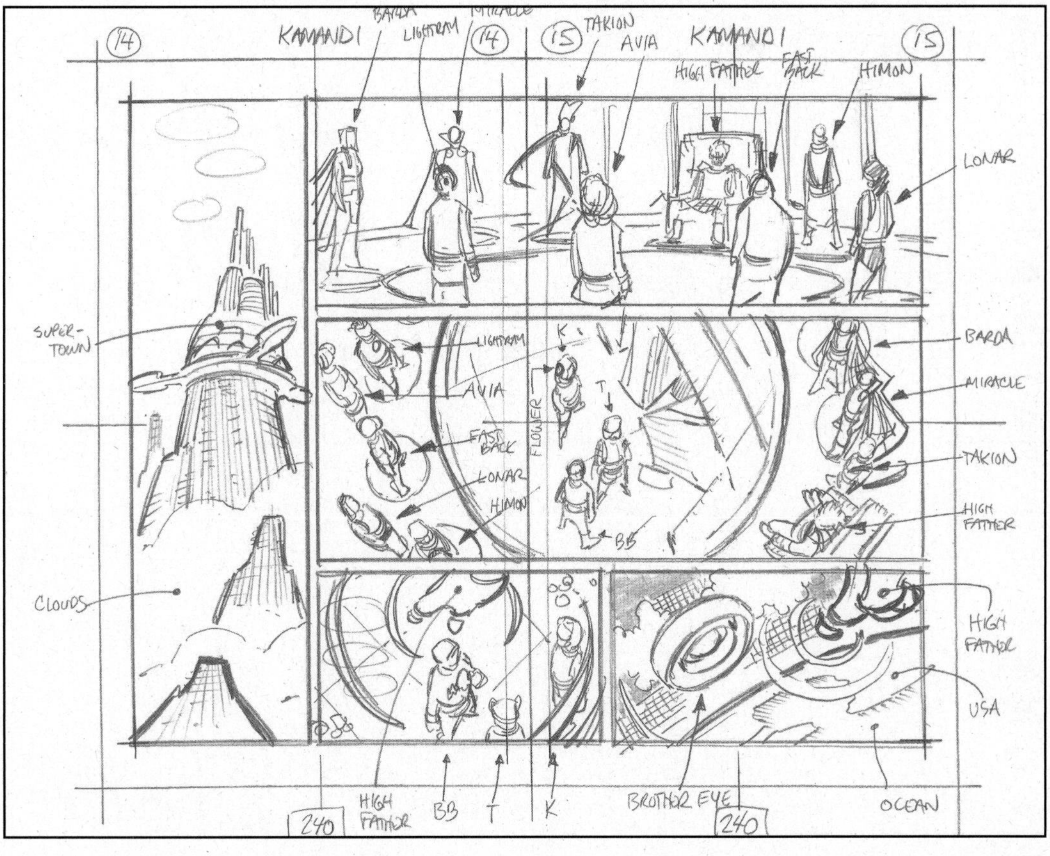
14
KAMANDI
BARDA
LIGHTRAY
MIRACLE
14
15
TAKION
AVIA
KAMANDI
HIGH FATHER
FAST BACK
HIMON
15
LONAR
SUPER-TOWN
LIGHTRAY
AVIA
FAST BACK
LONAR
HIMON
FLOWER
K
T
BB
BARDA
MIRACLE
TAKION
HIGH FATHER
CLOUDS
HIGH FATHER
USA
240
HIGH FATHER
BB
T
K
BROTHER EYE
240
OCEAN

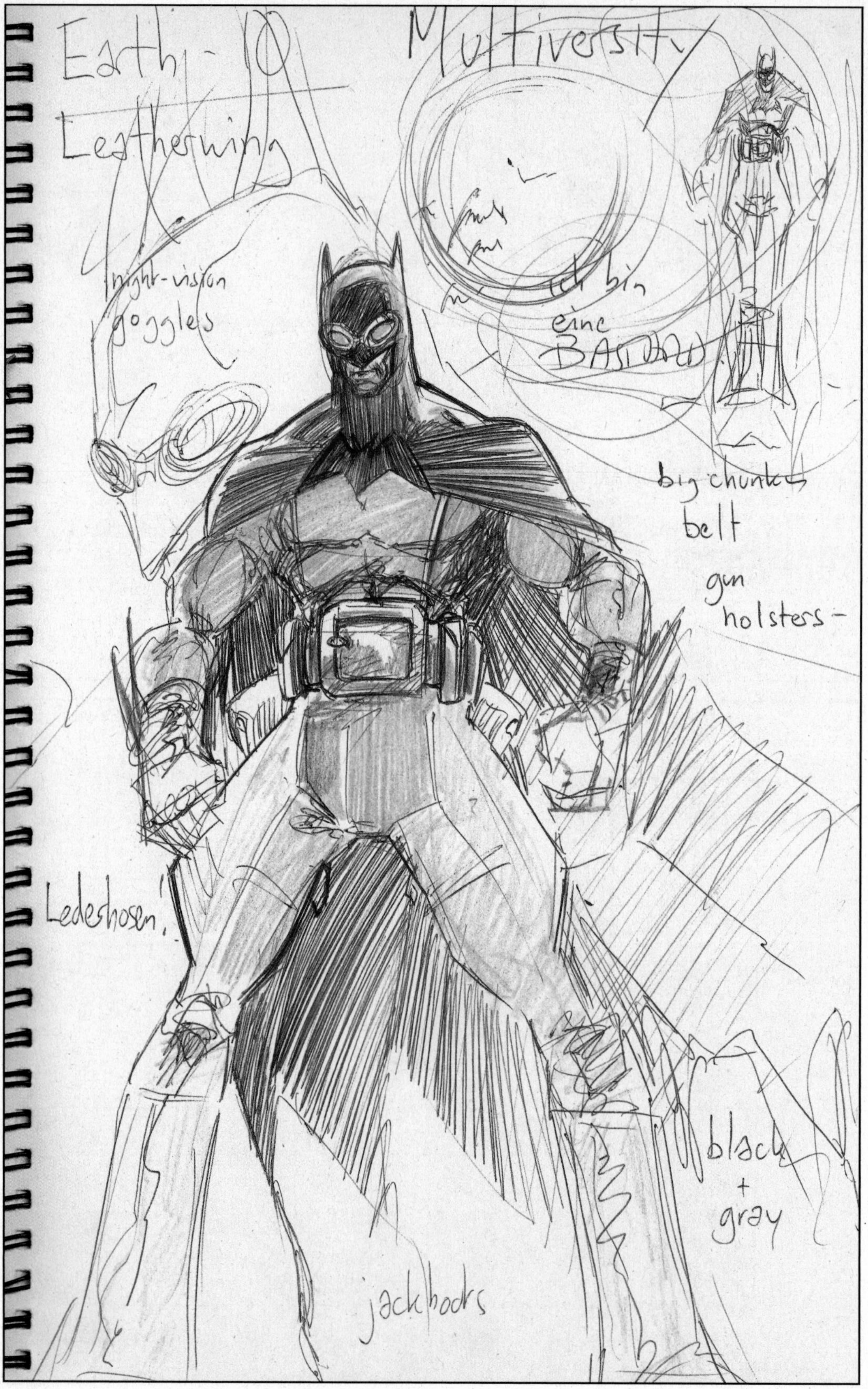
Earth-10
Multiversity
Leatherwing
night-vision goggles
ich bin eine
big chunky belt
gun holsters-
Lederhosen!
black + gray
jackboots

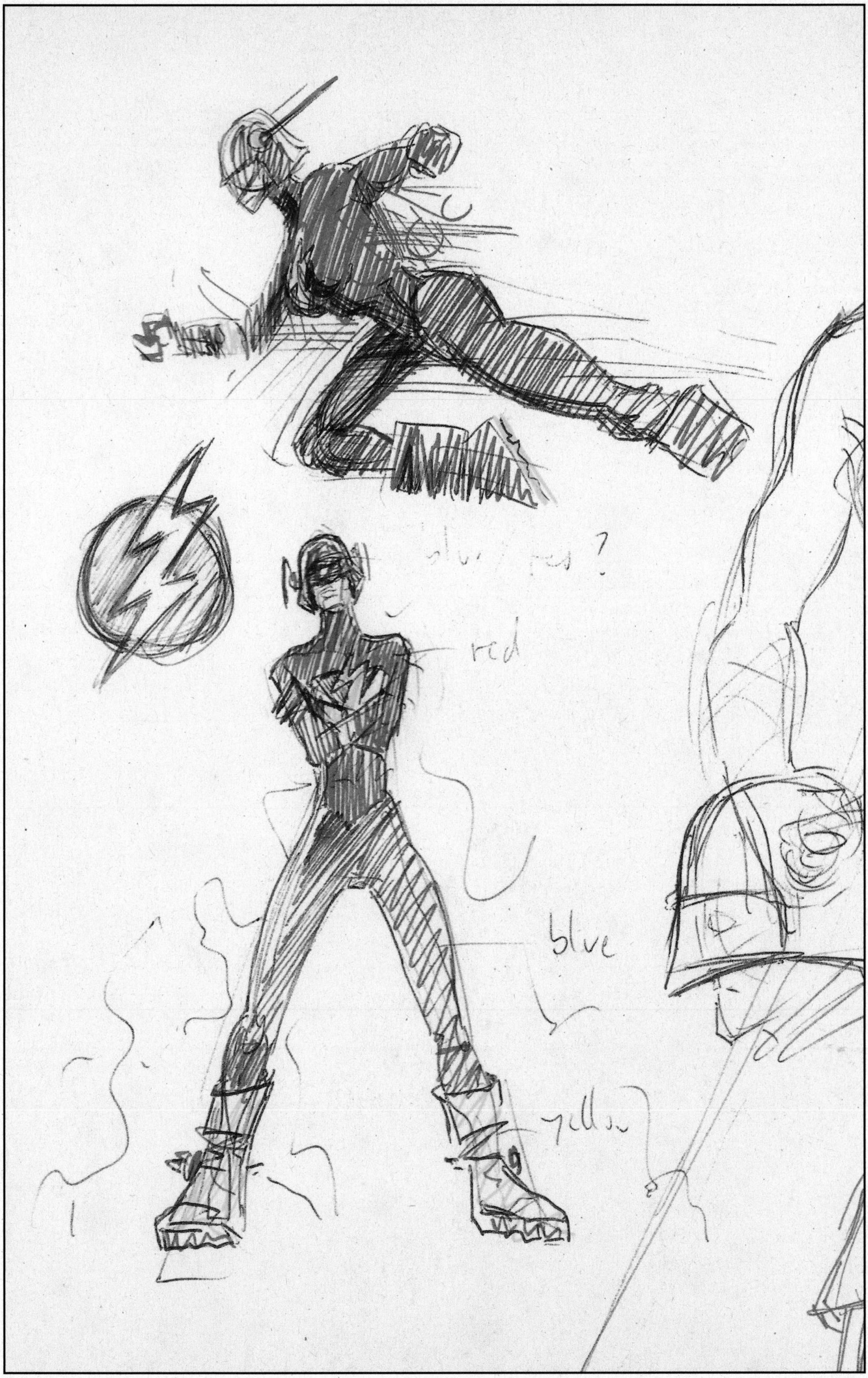
red
blue
yellow

Initial layout for pages 8-9 by Jim Lee.

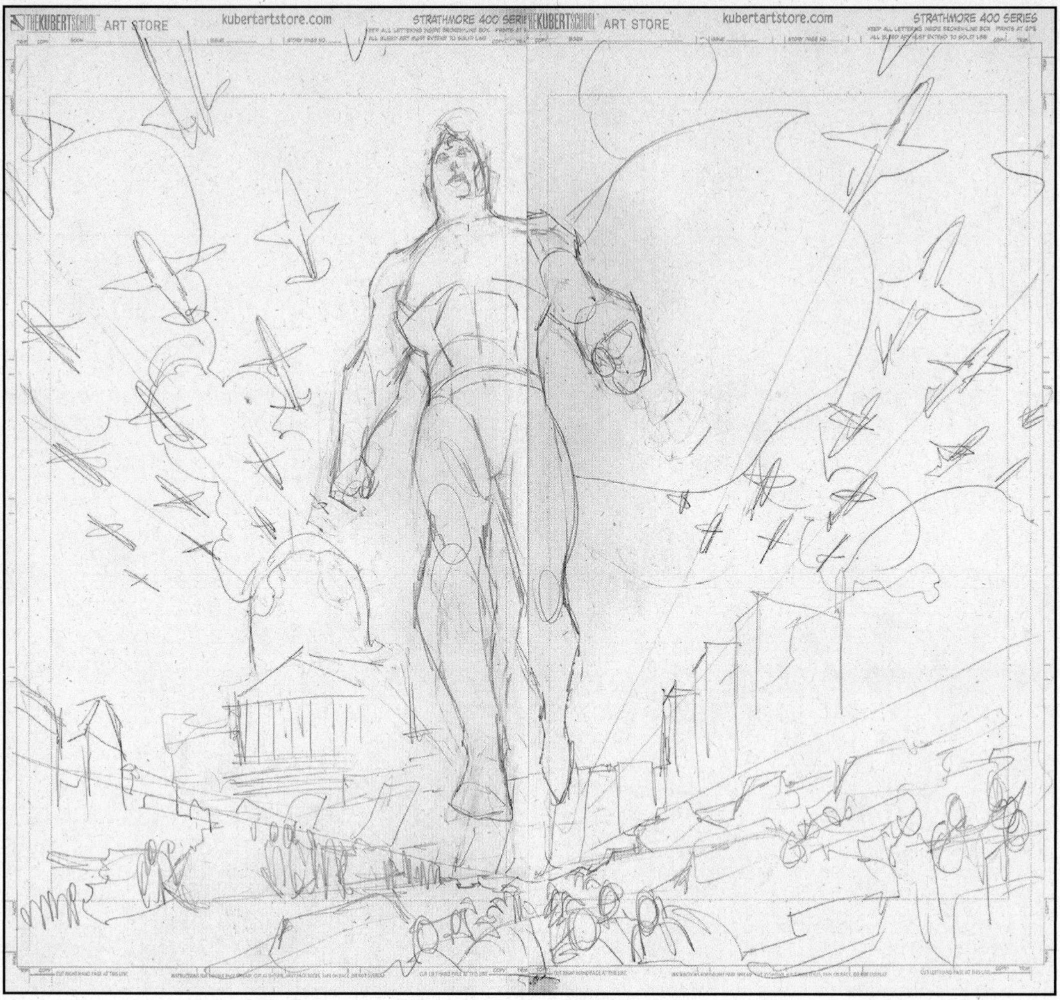
THE KUBERT SCHOOL ART STORE
kubertartstore.com
STRATHMORE 400 SERIES
THE KUBERT SCHOOL ART STORE
kubertartstore.com
STRATHMORE 400 SERIES

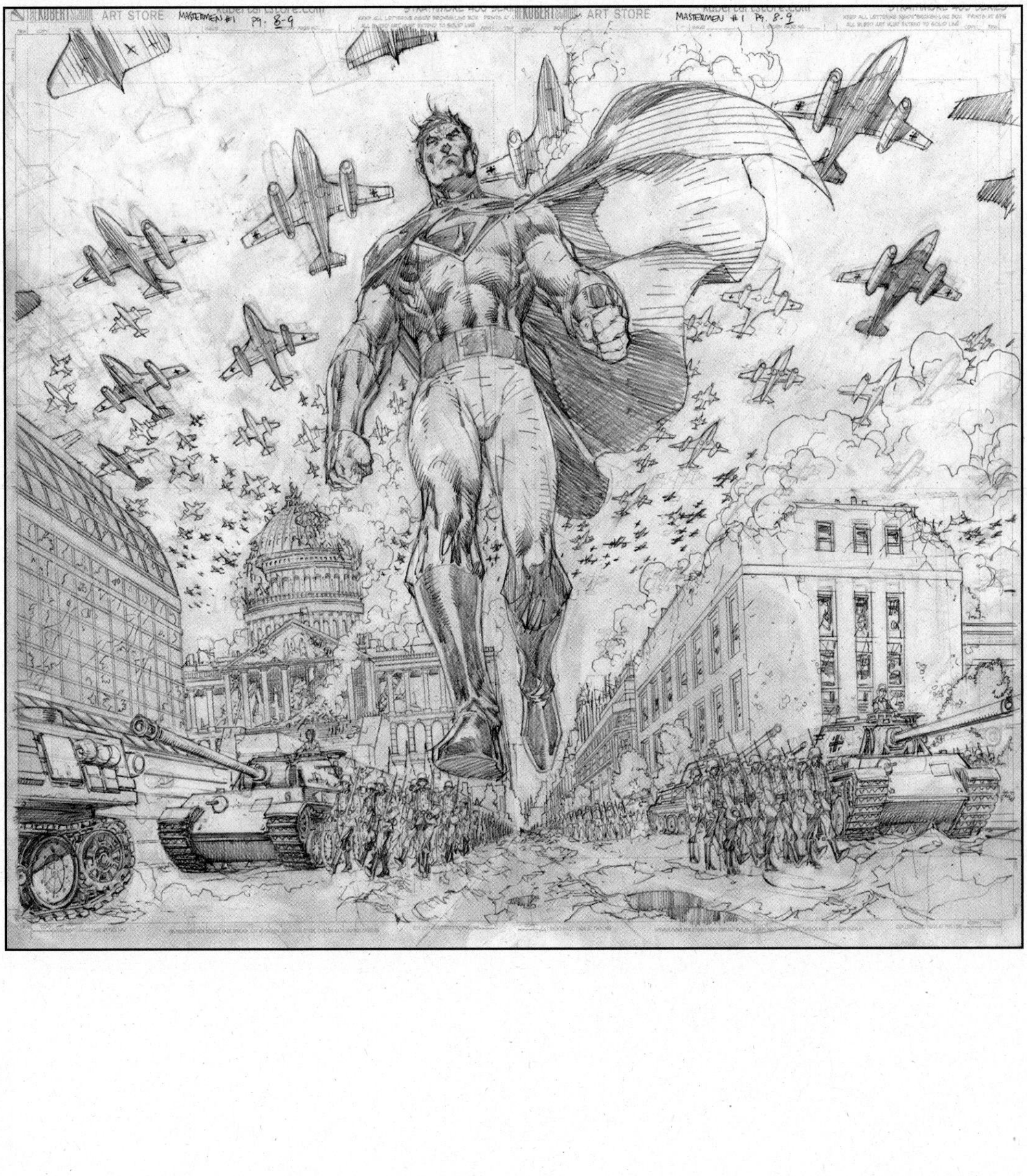
MASTERMEN #1 Pg. 8-9

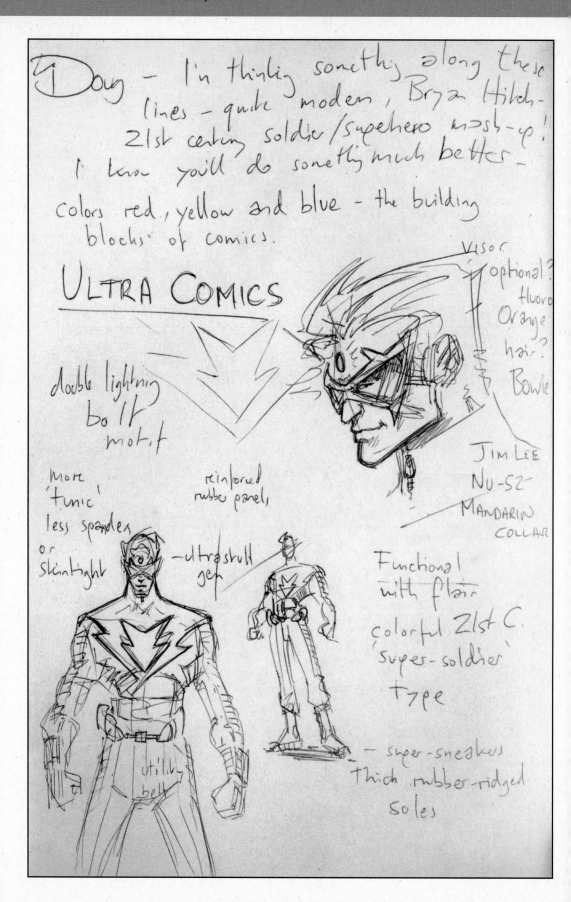

Doug — I'm thinking something along these lines — quite modern, Bryan Hitch — 21st century soldier/superhero mash-up! I know you'll do something much better — colors red, yellow and blue — the building blocks of comics.

ULTRA COMICS

double lightning bolt motif

Visor optional? fluoro Orange hair? Bowie

JIM LEE NU-52 MANDARIN COLLAR

More 'tunic' less spandex or skintight

reinforced rubber panels

—ultraskull gem

Functional with flair colorful 21st C. 'super-soldier' type

utility belt

— super-sneakers thick rubber-ridged soles

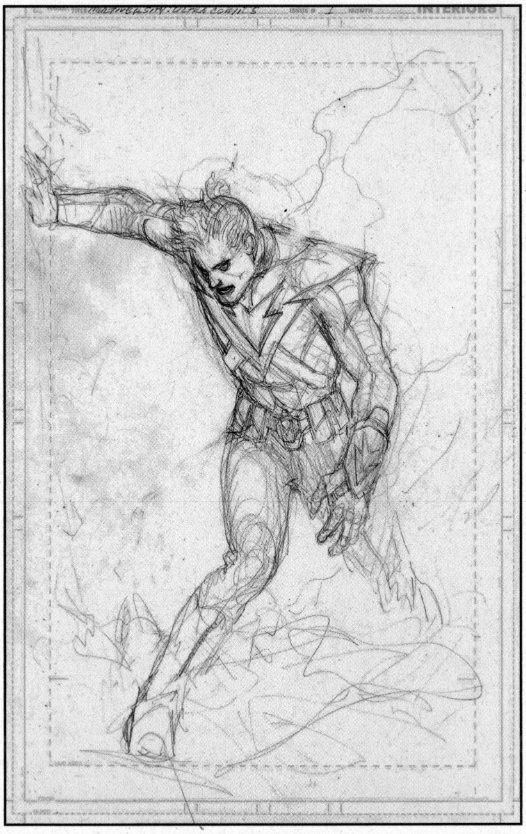
INTERIORS

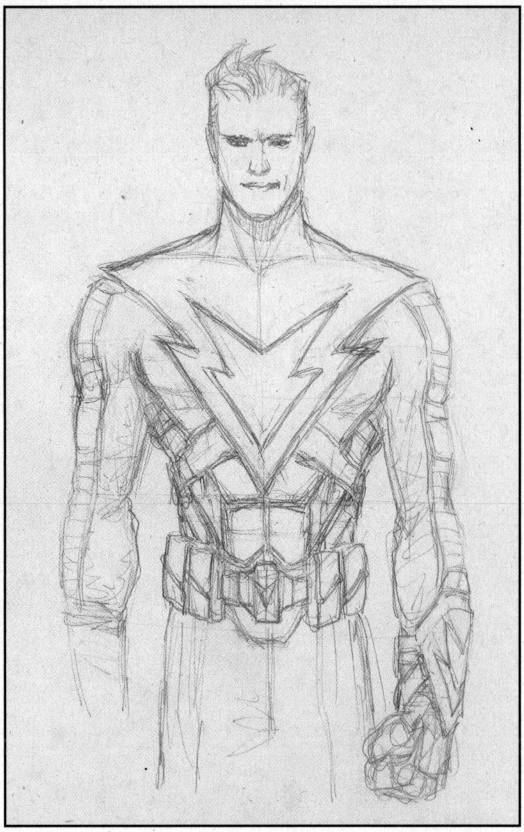

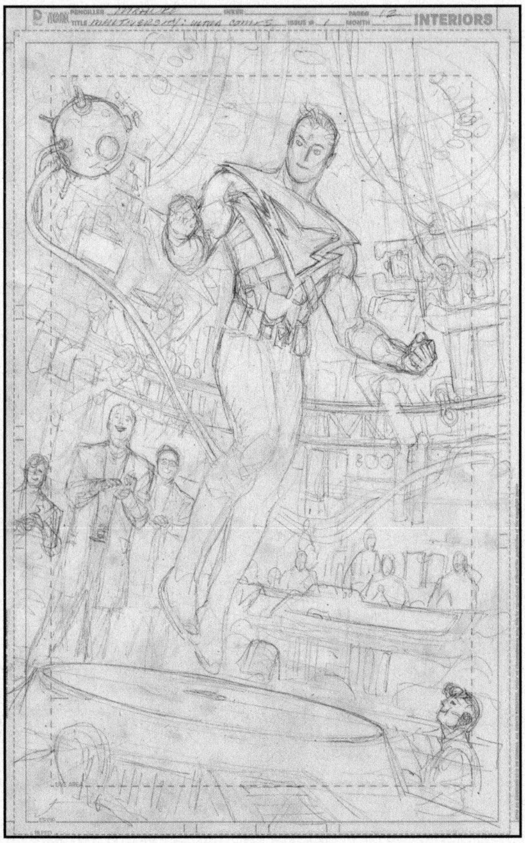
INTERIORS

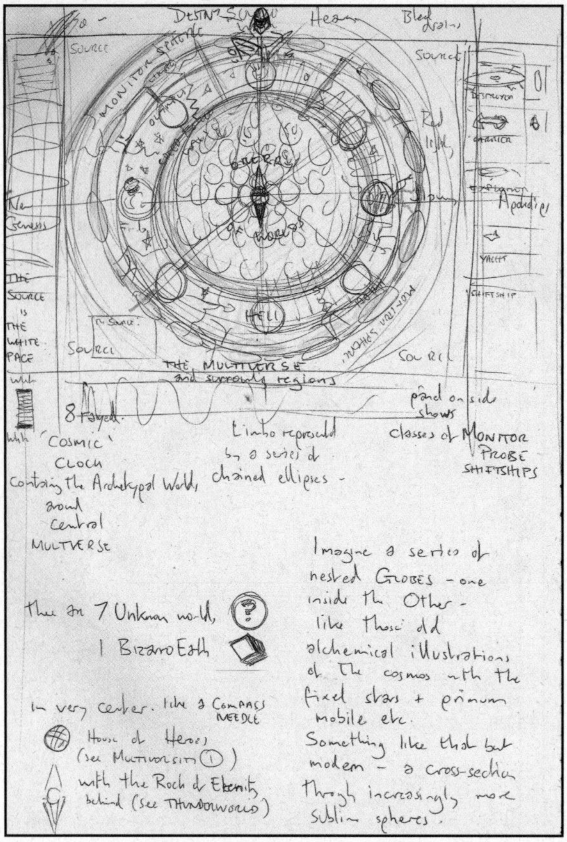
Source
Heaven
Bleed
Red light
New Genesis
Apokolips
Hell
The Source is the white space
The Multiverse and surrounding regions
8 fold
with 'Cosmic' Clock
Containing the Archetypal World around central Multiverse
Limbo represented by a series of chained ellipses -
panel on side shows classes of Monitor Probe Shiftships
Imagine a series of nested Globes - one inside the other - like those old alchemical illustrations of the cosmos with the fixed stars + primum mobile etc.
Something like that but modern - a cross-section through increasingly more sublime spheres.
There are 7 Unknown worlds
1 Bizarro Earth
In very center, like a compass needle
House of Heroes (see Multiversity 1)
with the Rock of Eternity behind (see Thunderworld)

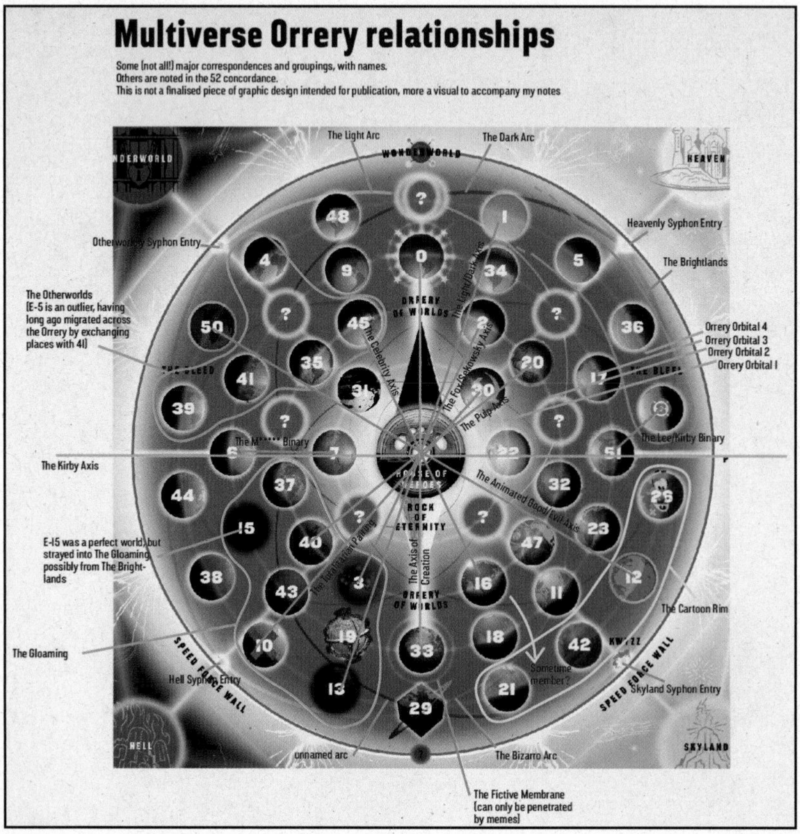
Multiverse Orrery relationships
Some (not all!) major correspondences and groupings, with names.
Others are noted in the 52 concordance.
This is not a finalised piece of graphic design intended for publication, more a visual to accompany my notes
The Light Arc
The Dark Arc
Wonderworld
Heaven
Heavenly Syphon Entry
The Brightlands
Otherworldly Syphon Entry
The Otherworlds (E-5 is an outlier, having long ago migrated across the Orrery by exchanging places with 41)
Orrery Orbital 4
Orrery Orbital 3
Orrery Orbital 2
Orrery Orbital 1
Orrery of Worlds
The Celebrity Axis
The Light/Dark Axis
The Fox/Gelkowsky Axis
The Pulp Axis
The Lee/Kirby Binary
The Kirby Axis
The Animated Good/Evil Axis
House of Heroes
Rock of Eternity
The Axis of Creation
E-15 was a perfect world, but strayed into The Gloaming possibly from The Bright-lands
The Cartoon Rim
The Gloaming
Speed Force Wall
Hell Syphon Entry
Sometime member?
Skyland Syphon Entry
Hell
Skyland
unnamed arc
The Bizarro Arc
The Fictive Membrane (can only be penetrated by memes)